10th Workshop on Statistical Machine Translation 2015

Held at EMNLP 2015

Lisbon, Portugal
17 – 18 September 2015

ISBN: 978-1-5108-1188-1

Printed from e-media with permission by:

Curran Associates, Inc.
57 Morehouse Lane
Red Hook, NY 12571

Some format issues inherent in the e-media version may also appear in this print version.

Printed by Curran Associates, Inc. (2015)

For permission requests, please contact the Association for Computational Linguistics at the address below.

Association for Computational Linguistics
209 N. Eighth Street
Stroudsburg, Pennsylvania 18360

Phone: 1-570-476-8006
Fax: 1-570-476-0860

acl@aclweb.org

Additional copies of this publication are available from:

Curran Associates, Inc.
57 Morehouse Lane
Red Hook, NY 12571 USA
Phone: 845-758-0400
Fax: 845-758-2634
Email: curran@proceedings.com
Web: www.proceedings.com

EMNLP 2015

Tenth Workshop on Statistical Machine Translation

Proceedings of the Workshop

17-18 September 2015
Lisbon, Portugal

Preface

The EMNLP 2015 Workshop on Statistical Machine Translation (WMT 2015) took place on Thursday and Friday, September 17-18, 2015 in Lisbon, Portugal, immediately preceding the Conference on Empirical Methods in Natural Language Processing (EMNLP).

This was the tenth time this workshop has been held. The first time it was held at HLT-NAACL 2006 in New York City, USA. In the following years the Workshop on Statistical Machine Translation was held at ACL 2007 in Prague, Czech Republic, ACL 2008, Columbus, Ohio, USA, EACL 2009 in Athens, Greece, ACL 2010 in Uppsala, Sweden, EMNLP 2011 in Edinburgh, Scotland, NAACL 2012 in Montreal, Canada, ACL 2013 in Sofia, Bulgaria, and ACL 2014 in Baltimore, Maryland, USA.

The focus of our workshop was to use parallel corpora for machine translation. Recent experimentation has shown that the performance of SMT systems varies greatly with the source language. In this workshop we encouraged researchers to investigate ways to improve the performance of SMT systems for diverse languages, including morphologically more complex languages, languages with partial free word order, and low-resource languages.

Prior to the workshop, in addition to soliciting relevant papers for review and possible presentation, we conducted five shared tasks: a general translation task, an automatic post-editing task, a quality estimation task, a metrics task, and a tuning task. The automatic post-editing task was introduced this year as a pilot to examine the capabilities of automatic methods for correcting errors produced by machine translation systems. This year's tuning task is a follow up of the WMT 2011 invitation-only tunable metrics task to assess a system's ability to optimize the parameters of a given hierarchical MT system. The results of all shared tasks were announced at the workshop, and these proceedings also include an overview paper for the shared tasks that summarizes the results, as well as provides information about the data used and any procedures that were followed in conducting or scoring the task. In addition, there are short papers from each participating team that describe their underlying system in greater detail.

Like in previous years, we have received a far larger number of submission than we could accept for presentation. This year we have received 28 full paper submissions and 47 shared task submissions. In total WMT 2015 featured 11 full paper oral presentations and 46 shared task poster presentations.

The invited talk was given by Jacob Devlin (Microsoft Research), entitled "A Practical Guide to Real-Time Neural Translation".

We would like to thank the members of the Program Committee for their timely reviews. We also would like to thank the participants of the shared task and all the other volunteers who helped with the evaluations.

Ondřej Bojar, Rajan Chatterjee, Christian Federmann, Barry Haddow, Chris Hokamp, Matthias Huck, Varvara Logacheva, Pavel Pecina, Philipp Koehn, Christof Monz, Matteo Negri, Matt Post, Carolina Scarton, Lucia Specia, and Marco Turchi.

Co-Organizers

Organizers:

Ondřej Bojar (Charles University in Prague)
Rajan Chatterjee (FBK)
Christian Federmann (MSR)
Barry Haddow (University of Edinburgh)
Chris Hokamp (Dublin City University)
Matthias Huck (University of Edinburgh)
Varvara Logacheva (University of Sheffield)
Pavel Pecina (Charles University in Prague)
Philipp Koehn (University of Edinburgh / Johns Hopkins University)
Christof Monz (University of Amsterdam)
Matteo Negri (FBK)
Matt Post (Johns Hopkins University)
Carolina Scarton (University of Sheffield)
Lucia Specia (University of Sheffield)
Marco Turchi (FBK)

Program Committee:

Alexandre Allauzen (Universite Paris-Sud / LIMSI-CNRS)
Tim Anderson (Air Force Research Laboratory)
Eleftherios Avramidis (German Research Center for Artificial Intelligence (DFKI)
Amittai Axelrod (University of Maryland)
Loic Barrault (LIUM, University of Le Mans)
Fernando Batista (INESC-ID, ISCTE-IUL)
Daniel Beck (University of Sheffield)
Jose Miguel Benedi (Universitat Politecnica de Valencia)
Nicola Bertoldi (FBK)
Arianna Bisazza (University of Amsterdam)
Graeme Blackwood (IBM Research)
Fabienne Braune (University of Stuttgart)
Chris Brockett (Microsoft Research)
Christian Buck (University of Edinburgh)
Hailong Cao (Harbin Institute of Technology)
Michael Carl (Copenhagen Business School)
Marine Carpuat (University of Maryland)
Francisco Casacuberta (Universitat Politecnica de Valencia)
Daniel Cer (Google)
Mauro Cettolo (FBK)
Rajen Chatterjee (Fondazione Bruno Kessler)
Boxing Chen (NRC)

Colin Cherry (NRC)
David Chiang (University of Notre Dame)
Kyunghyun Cho (New York University)
Vishal Chowdhary (Microsoft)
Steve DeNeefe (SDL Language Weaver)
Michael Denkowski (Carnegie Mellon University)
Jacob Devlin (Microsoft Research)
Markus Dreyer (SDL Language Weaver)
Kevin Duh (Nara Institute of Science and Technology)
Nadir Durrani (QCRI)
Marc Dymetman (Xerox Research Centre Europe)
Marcello Federico (FBK)
Minwei Feng (IBM Watson Group)
Yang Feng (Baidu)
Andrew Finch (NICT)
Jose A. R. Fonollosa (Universitat Politecnica de Catalunya)
Mikel Forcada (Universitat d'Alacant)
George Foster (NRC)
Alexander Fraser (Ludwig-Maximilians-Universität München)
Markus Freitag (RWTH Aachen University)
Ekaterina Garmash (University of Amsterdam)
Ulrich Germann (University of Edinburgh)
Kevin Gimpel (Toyota Technological Institute at Chicago)
Jesus Gonzalez-Rubio (Universitat Politecnica de Valencia)
Francisco Guzman (Qatar Computing Research Institute)
Nizar Habash (New York University Abu Dhabi)
Jan Hajic (Charles University in Prague)
Greg Hanneman (Carnegie Mellon University)
Eva Hasler (University of Edinburgh)
Yifan He (New York University)
Kenneth Heafield (University of Edinburgh)
John Henderson (MITRE)
Teresa Herrmann (Karlsruhe Institute of Technology)
Felix Hieber (Amazon Research)
Stephane Huet (Universite d'Avignon)
Young-Sook Hwang (SKPlanet)
Gonzalo Iglesias (University of Cambridge)
Abe Ittycheriah (IBM)
Laura Jehl (Heidelberg University)
Maxim Khalilov (BMMT)
Roland Kuhn (National Research Council of Canada)
Shankar Kumar (Google)
David Langlois (LORIA, Universite de Lorraine)

Gennadi Lembersky (NICE Systems)
Lemao Liu (NICT)
Qun Liu (Dublin City University)
Zhanyi Liu (Baidu)
Wolfgang Macherey (Google)
Saab Mansour (RWTH Aachen University)
Yuval Marton (Microsoft)
Arne Mauser (Google, Inc)
Wolfgang Menzel (Hamburg University)
Abhijit Mishra (Indian Institute of Technology Bombay)
Dragos Munteanu (SDL Language Technologies)
Maria Nadejde (University of Edinburgh)
Preslav Nakov (Qatar Computing Research Institute, HBKU)
Graham Neubig (Nara Institute of Science and Technology)
Jan Niehues (Karlsruhe Institute of Technology)
Kemal Oflazer (Carnegie Mellon University - Qatar)
Daniel Ortiz-Martinez (Technical University of Valencia)
Santanu Pal (Saarland University)
Stephan Peitz (RWTH Aachen University)
Sergio Penkale (Lingo24)
Daniele Pighin (Google Inc)
Maja Popovic (Humboldt University of Berlin)
Stefan Riezler (Heidelberg University)
Johann Roturier (Symantec)
Raphael Rubino (Prompsit Language Engineering)
Alexander M. Rush (MIT)
Hassan Sawaf (eBay Inc.)
Jean Senellart (SYSTRAN)
Rico Sennrich (University of Edinburgh)
Wade Shen (MIT)
Patrick Simianer (Heidelberg University)
Linfeng Song (University of Rochester)
Sara Stymne (Uppsala University)
Katsuhito Sudoh (NTT Communication Science Laboratories / Kyoto University)
Felipe Sanchez-Martinez (Universitat d'Alacant)
Jörg Tiedemann (Uppsala University)
Christoph Tillmann (IBM Research)
Antonio Toral (Dublin City Unversity)
Yulia Tsvetkov (Carnegie Mellon University)
Marco Turchi (Fondazione Bruno Kessler)
Ferhan Ture (BBN Technologies)
Masao Utiyama (NICT)
Ashish Vaswani (University of Southern California Information Sciences Institute)

David Vilar (Nuance)
Martin Volk (University of Zurich)
Aurelien Waite (University of Cambridge)
Taro Watanabe (NICT)
Marion Weller (Universität Stuttgart)
Philip Williams (University of Edinburgh)
Shuly Wintner (University of Haifa)
Hua Wu (Baidu)
Joern Wuebker (RWTH Aachen University)
Peng Xu (Google Inc.)
Wenduan Xu (Cambridge University)
Francois Yvon (LIMSI/CNRS)
Feifei Zhai (The City University of New York)
Joy Ying Zhang (Carnegie Mellon University)
Tiejun Zhao (Harbin Institute of Technology)
Yinggong Zhao (State Key Laboratory for Novel Software Technology at Nanjing University)

Invited Speaker:

Jacob Devlin (Microsoft Research)

Table of Contents

Conference Program

Thursday, September 17, 2015

09:00–09:05 ***Opening Remarks***

09:05–09:50 **Session 1: Shared Tasks**

09:05–09:50 *Findings of the 2015 Workshop on Statistical Machine Translation*
Ondřej Bojar, Rajen Chatterjee, Christian Federmann, Barry Haddow, Matthias Huck, Chris Hokamp, Philipp Koehn, Varvara Logacheva, Christof Monz, Matteo Negri, Matt Post, Carolina Scarton, Lucia Specia and Marco Turchi

09:50–10:30 **Session 2: Data Selection**

09:50–10:10 *Statistical Machine Translation with Automatic Identification of Translationese*
Naama Twitto, Noam Ordan and Shuly Wintner

10:10–10:30 *Data Selection With Fewer Words*
Amittai Axelrod, Philip Resnik, Xiaodong He and Mari Ostendorf

10:30–11:00 ***Coffee Break***

11:00–12:30 **Session 3: Poster Session**

11:00–12:30 *Shared Task: Translation*
Poster Presenters

DFKI's experimental hybrid MT system for WMT 2015
Eleftherios Avramidis, Maja Popović and Aljoscha Burchardt

ParFDA for Fast Deployment of Accurate Statistical Machine Translation Systems, Benchmarks, and Statistics
Ergun Bicici, Qun Liu and Andy Way

CUNI in WMT15: Chimera Strikes Again
Ondřej Bojar and Aleš Tamchyna

CimS - The CIS and IMS Joint Submission to WMT 2015 addressing morphological and syntactic differences in English to German SMT
Fabienne Cap, Marion Weller, Anita Ramm and Alexander Fraser

Thursday, September 17, 2015 (continued)

Thursday, September 17, 2015 (continued)

Morphological Segmentation and OPUS for Finnish-English Machine Translation
Jörg Tiedemann, Filip Ginter and Jenna Kanerva

Abu-MaTran at WMT 2015 Translation Task: Morphological Segmentation and Web Crawling
Raphael Rubino, Tommi Pirinen, Miquel Esplà-Gomis, Nikola Ljubešić, Sergio Ortiz Rojas, Vassilis Papavassiliou, Prokopis Prokopidis and Antonio Toral

The University of Illinois submission to the WMT 2015 Shared Translation Task
Lane Schwartz, Bill Bryce, Chase Geigle, Sean Massung, Yisi Liu, Haoruo Peng, Vignesh Raja, Subhro Roy and Shyam Upadhyay

Edinburgh's Syntax-Based Systems at WMT 2015
Philip Williams, Rico Sennrich, Maria Nadejde, Matthias Huck and Philipp Koehn

11:00–12:30 *Shared Task: Automatic Post-Editing*
Poster Presenters

The FBK Participation in the WMT15 Automatic Post-editing Shared Task
Rajen Chatterjee, Marco Turchi and Matteo Negri

USAAR-SAPE: An English–Spanish Statistical Automatic Post-Editing System
Santanu Pal, Mihaela Vela, Sudip Kumar Naskar and Josef van Genabith

Why Predicting Post-Edition is so Hard? Failure Analysis of LIMSI Submission to the APE Shared Task
Guillaume Wisniewski, Nicolas Pécheux and François Yvon

12:30–14:00 ***Lunch***

Thursday, September 17, 2015 (continued)

14:00–15:30 Session 4: Invited Talk

14:00–15:30 *A Practical Guide to Real-Time Neural Translation*
Jacob Devlin

15:30–16:00 ***Coffee Break***

16:00–17:00 Session 5: Syntax-Based Translation and Rescoring

16:00–16:20 *Hierarchical Machine Translation With Discontinuous Phrases*
Miriam Kaeshammer

16:20–16:40 *Discontinuous Statistical Machine Translation with Target-Side Dependency Syntax*
Nina Seemann and Andreas Maletti

16:40–17:00 *ListNet-based MT Rescoring*
Jan Niehues, Quoc-Khanh DO, Alexandre Allauzen and Alex Waibel

Friday, September 18, 2015

09:00–09:50 Session 6: Shared Tasks

09:00–09:20 *Overview of the Quality Estimation Task*
Multiple Speakers

Results of the WMT15 Metrics Shared Task
Miloš Stanojević, Amir Kamran, Philipp Koehn and Ondřej Bojar

Results of the WMT15 Tuning Shared Task
Miloš Stanojević, Amir Kamran and Ondřej Bojar

Friday, September 18, 2015 (continued)

09:50–10:30 Session 7: Translation Modeling

09:50–10:10 *Extended Translation Models in Phrase-based Decoding*
Andreas Guta, Joern Wuebker, Miguel Graca, Yunsu Kim and Hermann Ney

10:10–10:30 *Investigations on Phrase-based Decoding with Recurrent Neural Network Language and Translation Models*
Tamer Alkhouli, Felix Rietig and Hermann Ney

10:30–11:00 *Coffee Break*

11:00–12:30 Session 8: Poster Session

11:00–12:30 *Shared Task: Quality Estimation*
Poster Presenters

Referential Translation Machines for Predicting Translation Quality and Related Statistics
Ergun Bicici, Qun Liu and Andy Way

UAlacant word-level machine translation quality estimation system at WMT 2015
Miquel Esplà-Gomis, Felipe Sánchez-Martínez and Mikel Forcada

QUality Estimation from ScraTCH (QUETCH): Deep Learning for Word-level Translation Quality Estimation
Julia Kreutzer, Shigehiko Schamoni and Stefan Riezler

LORIA System for the WMT15 Quality Estimation Shared Task
David Langlois

Data enhancement and selection strategies for the word-level Quality Estimation
Varvara Logacheva, Chris Hokamp and Lucia Specia

USHEF and USAAR-USHEF participation in the WMT15 QE shared task
Carolina Scarton, Liling Tan and Lucia Specia

SHEF-NN: Translation Quality Estimation with Neural Networks
Kashif Shah, Varvara Logacheva, Gustavo Paetzold, Frédéric Blain, Daniel Beck, Fethi Bougares and Lucia Specia

Friday, September 18, 2015 (continued)

	Strategy-Based Technology for Estimating MT Quality Liugang Shang, Dongfeng Cai and Duo Ji
	UGENT-LT3 SCATE System for Machine Translation Quality Estimation Arda Tezcan, Veronique Hoste, Bart Desmet and Lieve Macken
11:00–12:30	*Shared Task: Metrics* Poster Presenters
	Multi-level Evaluation for Machine Translation Boxing Chen, Hongyu Guo and Roland Kuhn
	VERTa: a Linguistically-motivated Metric at the WMT15 Metrics Task Elisabet Comelles and Jordi Atserias
	UPF-Cobalt Submission to WMT15 Metrics Task Marina Fomicheva, Núria Bel, Irịa da Cunha and Anton Malinovskiy
	Machine Translation Evaluation using Recurrent Neural Networks Rohit Gupta, Constantin Orasan and Josef van Genabith
	Alignment-based sense selection in METEOR and the RATATOUILLE recipe Benjamin Marie and Marianna Apidianaki
	chrF: character n-gram F-score for automatic MT evaluation Maja Popović
	BEER 1.1: ILLC UvA submission to metrics and tuning task Miloš Stanojević and Khalil Sima'an
	Predicting Machine Translation Adequacy with Document Embeddings Mihaela Vela and Liling Tan
	LeBLEU: N-gram-based Translation Evaluation Score for Morphologically Complex Languages Sami Virpioja and Stig-Arne Grönroos
	CASICT-DCU Participation in WMT2015 Metrics Task Hui Yu, Qingsong Ma, Xiaofeng Wu and Qun Liu

Friday, September 18, 2015 (continued)

11:00–12:30 *Shared Task: Tuning*
Poster Presenters

Drem: The AFRL Submission to the WMT15 Tuning Task
Grant Erdmann and Jeremy Gwinnup

MT Tuning on RED: A Dependency-Based Evaluation Metric
Liangyou Li, Hui Yu and Qun Liu

Improving evaluation and optimization of MT systems against MEANT
Chi-kiu Lo, Philipp Dowling and Dekai Wu

12:30–14:00 ***Lunch***

14:00–15:20 **Session 9: Evaluation and System Combination**

An Investigation of Machine Translation Evaluation Metrics in Cross-lingual Question Answering
Kyoshiro Sugiyama, Masahiro Mizukami, Graham Neubig, Koichiro Yoshino, Sakriani Sakti, Tomoki Toda and Satoshi Nakamura

Dependency Analysis of Scrambled References for Better Evaluation of Japanese Translation
Hideki Isozaki and Natsume Kouchi

How do Humans Evaluate Machine Translation
Francisco Guzmán, Ahmed Abdelali, Irina Temnikova, Hassan Sajjad and Stephan Vogel

Local System Voting Feature for Machine Translation System Combination
Markus Freitag, Jan-Thorsten Peter, Stephan Peitz, Minwei Feng and Hermann Ney

15:20–16:00 ***Coffee Break***

Friday, September 18, 2015 (continued)

16:00–17:00	**Session 10: Closing**
16:00–17:00	*Open Discussion* Multiple Speakers

*** Formatting Issue - Best Available Paper/Graphic ***

Findings of the 2015 Workshop on Statistical Machine Translation

Ondřej Bojar Charles Univ. in Prague
Rajen Chatterjee FBK
Christian Federmann Microsoft Research
Barry Haddow Univ. of Edinburgh
Matthias Huck Univ. of Edinburgh
Chris Hokamp Dublin City Univ.
Philipp Koehn JHU / Edinburgh
Varvara Logacheva Univ. of Sheffield
Christof Monz Univ. of Amsterdam
Matteo Negri FBK
Matt Post Johns Hopkins Univ.
Carolina Scarton Univ. of Sheffield
Lucia Specia Univ. of Sheffield
Marco Turchi FBK

Abstract

This paper presents the results of the WMT15 shared tasks, which included a standard news translation task, a metrics task, a tuning task, a task for run-time estimation of machine translation quality, and an automatic post-editing task. This year, 68 machine translation systems from 24 institutions were submitted to the ten translation directions in the standard translation task. An additional 7 anonymized systems were included, and were then evaluated both automatically and manually. The quality estimation task had three subtasks, with a total of 10 teams, submitting 34 entries. The pilot automatic post-editing task had a total of 4 teams, submitting 7 entries.

1 Introduction

We present the results of the shared tasks of the Workshop on Statistical Machine Translation (WMT) held at EMNLP 2015. This workshop builds on eight previous WMT workshops (Koehn and Monz, 2006; Callison-Burch et al., 2007, 2008, 2009, 2010, 2011, 2012; Bojar et al., 2013, 2014). This year we conducted five official tasks: a translation task, a quality estimation task, a metrics task, a tuning task[1], and a automatic post-editing task.

In the translation task (§2), participants were asked to translate a shared test set, optionally restricting themselves to the provided training data. We held ten translation tasks this year, between English and each of Czech, French, German, Finnish, and Russian. The Finnish translation tasks were new this year, providing a lesser resourced data condition on a challenging language pair. The system outputs for each task were evaluated both automatically and manually.

The human evaluation (§3) involves asking human judges to rank sentences output by anonymized systems. We obtained large numbers of rankings from researchers who contributed evaluations proportional to the number of tasks they entered. We made data collection more efficient and used TrueSkill as ranking method.

The quality estimation task (§4) this year included three subtasks: sentence-level prediction of post-editing effort scores, word-level prediction of good/bad labels, and document-level prediction of Meteor scores. Datasets were released with English→Spanish news translations for sentence and word level, English↔German news translations for document level.

The first round of the automatic post-editing task (§5) examined automatic methods for correcting errors produced by an unknown machine translation system. Participants were provided with training triples containing source, target and human post-editions, and were asked to return automatic post-editions for unseen (source, target) pairs. This year we focused on correcting English→Spanish news translations.

The primary objectives of WMT are to evaluate the state of the art in machine translation, to disseminate common test sets and public training data with published performance numbers, and to refine evaluation and estimation methodologies for machine translation. As before, all of the data, translations, and collected human judgments are publicly available.[2] We hope these datasets serve as a valuable resource for research into statistical

[1]The metrics and tuning tasks are reported in separate papers (Stanojević et al., 2015a,b).

[2]`http://statmt.org/wmt15/results.html`

machine translation and automatic evaluation or prediction of translation quality.

2 Overview of the Translation Task

The recurring task of the workshop examines translation between English and other languages. As in the previous years, the other languages include German, French, Czech and Russian.

Finnish replaced Hindi as the special language this year. Finnish is a lesser resourced language compared to the other languages and has challenging morphological properties. Finnish represents also a different language family that we had not tackled since we included Hungarian in 2008 and 2009 (Callison-Burch et al., 2008, 2009).

We created a test set for each language pair by translating newspaper articles and provided training data, except for French, where the test set was drawn from user-generated comments on the news articles.

2.1 Test data

The test data for this year's task was selected from online sources, as before. We took about 1500 English sentences and translated them into the other 5 languages, and then additional 1500 sentences from each of the other languages and translated them into English. This gave us test sets of about 3000 sentences for our English-X language pairs, which have been either written originally written in English and translated into X, or vice versa.

For the French-English discussion forum test set, we collected 38 discussion threads each from the Guardian for English and from Le Monde for French. See Figure 1 for an example.

The composition of the test documents is shown in Table 1.

The stories were translated by the professional translation agency Capita, funded by the EU Framework Programme 7 project MosesCore, and by Yandex, a Russian search engine company.[3] All of the translations were done directly, and not via an intermediate language.

2.2 Training data

As in past years we provided parallel corpora to train translation models, monolingual corpora to train language models, and development sets to tune system parameters. Some training corpora were identical from last year (Europarl[4], United Nations, French-English 10^9 corpus, CzEng, Common Crawl, Russian-English parallel data provided by Yandex, Russian-English Wikipedia Headlines provided by CMU), some were updated (News Commentary, monolingual data), and new corpora was added (Finnish Europarl), Finnish-English Wikipedia Headline corpus).

Some statistics about the training materials are given in Figure 2.

2.3 Submitted systems

We received 68 submissions from 24 institutions. The participating institutions and their entry names are listed in Table 2; each system did not necessarily appear in all translation tasks. We also included 1 commercial off-the-shelf MT system and 6 online statistical MT systems, which we anonymized.

For presentation of the results, systems are treated as either *constrained* or *unconstrained*, depending on whether their models were trained only on the provided data. Since we do not know how they were built, these online and commercial systems are treated as unconstrained during the automatic and human evaluations.

3 Human Evaluation

Following what we had done for previous workshops, we again conduct a human evaluation campaign to assess translation quality and determine the final ranking of candidate systems. This section describes how we prepared the evaluation data, collected human assessments, and computed the final results.

This year's evaluation campaign differed from last year in several ways:

- In previous years each ranking task compared five different candidate systems which were selected without any pruning or redundancy cleanup. This had resulted in a noticeable amount of near-identical ranking candidates in WMT14, making the evaluation process unnecessarily tedious as annotators ran into a fair amount of ranking tasks containing very similar segments which are hard to inspect. For WMT15, we perform redundancy cleanup as an initial preprocessing step and

[3] `http://www.yandex.com/`

[4] As of Fall 2011, the proceedings of the European Parliament are no longer translated into all official languages.

***** Formatting Issue - Best Available Paper/Graphic *****

This is perfectly illustrated by the UKIP numbties banning people with HIV.
You mean Nigel Farage saying the NHS should not be used to pay for people coming to the UK as health tourists, and saying yes when the interviewer specifically asked if, with the aforementioned in mind, people with HIV were included in not being welcome.
You raise a straw man and then knock it down with thinly veiled homophobia.
Every time I or my family need to use the NHS we have to queue up behind bigots with a sense of entitlement and chronic hypochondria.
I think the straw man is yours.
Health tourism as defined by the right wing loonies is virtually none existent.
I think it's called democracy.
So no one would be affected by UKIP's policies against health tourism so no problem.
Only in UKIP La La Land could Carswell be described as revolutionary.
Quoting the bollox The Daily Muck spew out is not evidence.
Ah, shoot the messenger.
The Mail didn't write the report, it merely commented on it.
Whoever controls most of the media in this country should undead be shot for spouting populist propaganda as fact.
I don't think you know what a straw man is.
You also don't know anything about my personal circumstances or identity so I would be very careful about trying to eradicate a debate with accusations of homophobia.
Farage's comment came as quite a shock, but only because it is so rarely addressed.
He did not express any homophobic beliefs whatsoever.
You will just have to find a way of getting over it.
I'm not entirely sure what you're trying to say, but my guess is that you dislike the media reporting things you disagree with.
It is so rarely addressed because unlike Fararge and his Thatcherite loony disciples who think aids and floods are a signal from the divine and not a reflection on their own ignorance in understanding the complexities of humanity as something to celebrate,then no.

Figure 1: Example news discussion thread used in the French–English translation task.

Language	Sources (Number of Documents)
Czech	aktuálně.cz (4), blesk.cz (1), blisty.cz (1), ctk.cz (1), deník.cz (1), e15.cz (1), iDNES.cz (19), ihned.cz (3), lidovky.cz (6), Novinky.cz (2), tyden.cz (1).
English	ABC News (4), BBC (6), CBS News (1), Daily Mail (1), Euronews (1), Financial Times (1), Fox News (2), Globe and Mail (1), Independent (1), Los Angeles Times (1), News.com Australia (9), Novinite (2), Reuters (2), Sydney Morning Herald (1), stv.tv (1), Telegraph (8), The Local (1), The Nation (1), UPI (1), Washington Post (3).
German	Abendzeitung Nürnberg (1), Aachener Nachrichten (1), Der Standard (2), Deutsche Welle (1), Frankfurter Neue Presse (1), Frankfurter Rundschau (1), Generalanzeiger Bonn (2), Göttinger Tageblatt (1), Haller Kreisblatt (1), Hellweger Anzeiger (1), Junge Welt (1), Kreisanzeiger (1), Mainpost (1), Merkur (3), Mittelbayerische Nachrichten (2), Morgenpost (1), Mitteldeutsche Zeitung (1), Neue Presse Coburg (1), Nürtinger Zeitung (1), OE24 (1), Kölnische Rundschau (1), Tagesspiegel (1), Volksfreund (1), Volksstimme (1), Wiener Zeitung (1), Westfälische Nachrichten (2).
Finnish	Aamulehti (2), Etelä-Saimaa (1), Etelä-Suomen Sanomat (3), Helsingin Sanomat (13), Ilkka (7), Ilta-Sanomat (18), Kaleva (4), Karjalainen (2), Kouvolan Sanomat (1), Lapin Kansa (3), Maaseudun Tulevaisuus (1).
Russian	168.ru (1), aif (6), altapress.ru (1), argumenti.ru (8), BBC Russian (1), dp.ru (2), gazeta.ru (4), interfax (2), Kommersant (12), lenta.ru (8), lgng (3), mk (5), novinite.ru (1), rbc.ru (1), rg.ru (2), rusplit.ru (1), Sport Express (6), vesti.ru (10).

Table 1: Composition of the test set. For more details see the XML test files. The `docid` tag gives the source and the date for each document in the test set, and the `origlang` tag indicates the original source language.

***** Formatting Issue - Best Available Paper/Graphic *****

Europarl Parallel Corpus

	French ↔ English		German ↔ English		Czech ↔ English		Finnish ↔ English	
Sentences	2,007,723		1,920,209		646,605		1,926,114	
Words	60,125,563	55,642,101	50,486,398	53,008,851	14,946,399	17,376,433	37,814,266	52,723,296
Distinct words	140,915	118,404	381,583	115,966	172,461	63,039	693,963	115,896

News Commentary Parallel Corpus

	French ↔ English		German ↔ English		Czech ↔ English		Russian ↔ English	
Sentences	200,239		216,190		152,763		174,253	
Words	6,270,748	5,161,906	5,513,985	5,499,625	3,435,458	3,759,874	4,394,974	4,625,898
Distinct words	75,462	71,767	157,682	74,341	142,943	58,817	172,021	67,402

Common Crawl Parallel Corpus

	French ↔ English		German ↔ English		Czech ↔ English		Russian ↔ English	
Sentences	3,244,152		2,399,123		161,838		878,386	
Words	91,328,790	81,096,306	54,575,405	58,870,638	3,529,783	3,927,378	21,018,793	21,535,122
Distinct words	889,291	859,017	1,640,835	823,480	210,170	128,212	764,203	432,062

United Nations Parallel Corpus

	French ↔ English	
Sentences	12,886,831	
Words	411,916,781	360,341,450
Distinct words	565,553	666,077

Yandex 1M Parallel Corpus

	Russian ↔ English	
Sentences	1,000,000	
Words	24,121,459	26,107,293
Distinct words	701,809	387,646

10^9 Word Parallel Corpus

	French ↔ English	
Sentences	22,520,400	
Words	811,203,407	668,412,817
Distinct words	2,738,882	2,861,836

CzEng Parallel Corpus

	Czech ↔ English	
Sentences	14,833,358	
Words	200,658,857	228,040,794
Distinct words	1,389,803	920,824

Wiki Headlines Parallel Corpus

	Russian ↔ English		Finnish ↔ English	
Sentences	514,859		153,728	
Words	1,191,474	1,230,644	269,429	354,362
Distinct words	282,989	251,328	127,576	96,732

Europarl Language Model Data

	English	French	German	Czech	Finnish
Sentence	2,218,201	2,190,579	2,176,537	668,595	2,120,739
Words	59,848,044	63,439,791	53,534,167	14,946,399	39,511,068
Distinct words	123,059	145,496	394,781	172,461	711,868

News Language Model Data

	English	French	German	Czech	Russian	Finnish
Sentence	118,337,431	42,110,011	135,693,607	45,149,206	45,835,812	1,378,582
Words	2,744,428,620	1,025,132,098	2,427,581,519	745,645,366	823,284,188	16,501,511
Distinct words	4,895,080	2,352,451	13,727,336	3,513,784	3,885,756	925,201

Test Set

	French ↔ English		German ↔ English		Czech ↔ English		Russian ↔ English		Finnish ↔ English	
Sentences	1500		2169		2656		2818		1370	
Words	29,858	27,173	44,081	46,828	46,005	54,055	55,655	65,744	19,840	27,811
Distinct words	5,798	5,148	9,710	7,483	13,013	7,757	15,795	8,695	8,553	5,279

Figure 2: Statistics for the training and test sets used in the translation task. The number of words and the number of distinct words (case-insensitive) is based on the provided tokenizer.

***** Formatting Issue - Best Available Paper/Graphic *****

ID	Institution
AALTO	Aalto University (Grönroos et al., 2015)
ABUMATRAN	Abu-MaTran (Rubino et al., 2015)
AFRL-MIT-*	Air Force Research Laboratory / MIT Lincoln Lab (Gwinnup et al., 2015)
CHALMERS	Chalmers University of Technology (Kolachina and Ranta, 2015)
CIMS	University of Stuttgart and Munich (Cap et al., 2015)
CMU	Carnegie Mellon University
CU-CHIMERA	Charles University (Bojar and Tamchyna, 2015)
CU-TECTO	Charles University (Dušek et al., 2015)
DFKI	Deutsches Forschungszentrum für Künstliche Intelligenz (Avramidis et al., 2015)
ILLINOIS	University of Illinois (Schwartz et al., 2015)
IMS	University of Stuttgart (Quernheim, 2015)
KIT	Karsruhe Institut of Technology (Cho et al., 2015)
KIT-LIMSI	Karsruhe Institut of Technology / LIMSI (Ha et al., 2015)
LIMSI	LIMSI (Marie et al., 2015)
MACAU	University of Macau
MONTREAL	University of Montreal (Jean et al., 2015)
PROMT	ProMT
RWTH	RWTH Aachen (Peter et al., 2015)
SHEFF*	University of Sheffield (Steele et al., 2015)
UDS-SANT	University of Saarland (Pal et al., 2015a)
UEDIN-JHU	University of Edinburgh / Johns Hopkins University (Haddow et al., 2015)
UEDIN-SYNTAX	University of Edinburgh (Williams et al., 2015)
USAAR-GACHA	University of Saarland, Liling Tan
UU	Uppsala University (Tiedemann et al., 2015)
COMMERCIAL-1	Commercial machine translation system
ONLINE-[A,B,C,E,F,G]	Six online statistical machine translation systems

Table 2: Participants in the shared translation task. Not all teams participated in all language pairs. The translations from the commercial and online systems were not submitted by their respective companies but were obtained by us, and are therefore anonymized in a fashion consistent with previous years of the workshop.

create *multi-system translations*. As a consequence, we get ranking tasks with varying numbers of candidate systems. To avoid overloading the annotators we still allow a maximum of five candidates per ranking task. If we have more multi-system translations, we choose randomly.

A brief example should illustrate this more clearly: say we have the following two candidate systems:

```
sysA="This, is 'Magic'"
sysX="this is  magic"
```

After lowercasing, removal of punctuation and whitespace normalization, which are our criteria for identifying *near-identical* outputs, both would be collapsed into a single multi-system:

```
sysA+sysX="This, is 'Magic'"
```

The first representative of a group of near-identical outputs is used as a proxy representing all candidates in the group throughout the evaluation.

While there is a good chance that users would have used some of the stripped information, e.g., case to differentiate between the two systems relative to each other, the collapsed system's comparison result against the other candidates should be a good approximation of how human annotators would have ranked them individually. We get a near 2x increase in the number of pairwise comparisons, so the general approach seems helpful.

- After dropping external, crowd-sourced translation assessment in WMT14 we ended up with approximately seventy-five percent less raw comparison data. Still, we were able to compute good confidence intervals on the clusters based on our improved ranking approach.

  This year, due to the aforementioned cleanup, annotators spent their time more efficiently, resulting in an increased number of final ranking results. We collected a total of 542,732 individual "A > B" judgments this year, nearly double the amount of data compared to WMT14.

- Last year we compared three different models of producing the final system rankings: Expected Wins (used in WMT13), Hopkins and May (HM) and TrueSkill (TS). Overall, we found the TrueSkill method to work best which is why we decided to use it as our only approach in WMT15.

We keep using clusters in our final system rankings, providing a *partial ordering* (clustering) of all evaluated candidate systems. Semantics remain unchanged to previous years: systems in the same cluster could not be meaningfully distinguished and hence are considered to be of equal quality.

3.1 Evaluation campaign overview

WMT15 featured the largest evaluation campaign to date. Similar to last year, we decided to collect *researcher-based judgments* only. A total of 137 individual annotator accounts have been actively involved. Users came from 24 different research groups and contributed judgments on 9,669 HITs.

Overall, these correspond to 29,007 individual ranking tasks (plus some more from incomplete HITs), each of which would have spawned exactly 10 individual "A > B" judgments last year, so we expected at least >290,070 binary data points. Due to our redundancy cleanup, we are able to get a lot more, namely 542,732. We report our inter/intra-annotator agreement scores based on the actual work done (*otherwise, we'd artificially boost scores based on inferred rankings*) and use the full set of data to compute clusters (*where the inferred rankings contribute meaningful data*).

Human annotation effort was exceptional and we are grateful to all participating individuals and teams. We believe that human rankings provide the best decision basis for machine translation evaluation and it is great to see contributions on this large a scale. In total, our human annotators spent 32 days and 20 hours working in Appraise.

The average annotation time per HIT amounts to 4 minutes 53 seconds. Several annotators passed the mark of 100 HITs annotated, some worked for more than 24 hours. We don't take this enormous amount of effort for granted and will make sure to improve the evaluation platform and overall process for upcoming workshops.

3.2 Data collection

The system ranking is produced from a large set of pairwise judgments on the translation quality of

*** Formatting Issue - Best Available Paper/Graphic ***

candidate systems. Annotations are collected in an evaluation campaign that enlists participants in the shared task to help. Each team is asked to contribute one hundred "Human Intelligence Tasks" (HITs) per primary system submitted.

Each HIT consists of three so-called *ranking tasks*. In a ranking task, an annotator is presented with a source segment, a human reference translation, and the outputs of *up to five anonymized candidate systems*, randomly selected from the set of participating systems, and displayed in random order. This year, we perform redundancy cleanup as an initial preprocessing step and create *multi-system translations*. As a consequence, we get ranking tasks with varying numbers of candidate outputs.

There are two main benefits to this approach:

- Annotators are more efficient as they don't have to deal with near-identical translations which are notoriously hard to differentiate; and
- Potentially, we get higher quality annotations as near-identical systems will be assigned the same "A > B" ranks, improving consistency.

As in previous years, the evaluation campaign is conducted using Appraise[5] (Federmann, 2012), an open-source tool built using Python's Django framework. At the top of each HIT, the following instructions are provided:

> *You are shown a source sentence followed by several candidate translations. Your task is to rank the translations from best to worst (ties are allowed).*

Annotators can decide to skip a ranking task but are instructed to do this only as a last resort, e.g., if the translation candidates shown on screen are clearly misformatted or contain data issues (wrong language or similar problems). Only a small number of ranking tasks has been skipped in WMT15. A screenshot of the Appraise ranking interface is shown in Figure 3.

Annotators are asked to rank the outputs from 1 (best) to 5 (worst), with ties permitted. Note that a *lower* rank is better. The joint rankings provided by a ranking task are then reduced to the fully expanded set of *pairwise rankings* produced by considering all $\binom{n}{2} \leq 10$ combinations of all $n \leq 5$ outputs in the respective ranking task.

[5]https://github.com/cfedermann/Appraise

For example, consider the following annotation provided among outputs A, B, F, H, and J:

	1	2	3	4	5
F				•	
A				•	
B		•			
J					•
H			•		

As the number of outputs n depends on the number of corresponding *multi-system translations* in the original data, we get varying numbers of resulting binary judgments. Assuming that outputs A and F from above are actually *near-identical*, the annotator this year would see a shorter ranking task:

	1	2	3	4	5
AF				•	
B		•			
J					•
H			•		

Note that AF is a *multi-system translation* covering two candidate systems.

Both examples would be reduced to the following set of pairwise judgments:

$$A > B, A = F, A > H, A < J$$
$$B < F, B < H, B < J$$
$$F > H, F < J$$
$$H < J$$

Here, $A > B$ should be read is "A is ranked higher than (worse than) B". Note that by this procedure, the absolute value of ranks and the magnitude of their differences are discarded. Our WMT15 approach including redundancy cleanup allows to obtain these judgments at a lower cognitive cost for the annotators. This partially explains why we were able to collect more results this year.

For WMT13, nearly a million pairwise annotations were collected from both researchers and paid workers on Amazon's Mechanical Turk, in a roughly 1:2 ratio. Last year, we collected data from researchers only, an ability that was enabled by the use of TrueSkill for producing the partial ranking for each task (§3.4). This year, based on our redundancy cleanup we were able to nearly double the amount of annotations, collecting 542,732. See Table 3 for more details.

3.3 Annotator agreement

Each year we calculate annotator agreement scores for the human evaluation as a measure of

***** Formatting Issue - Best Available Paper/Graphic *****

Figure 3: Screenshot of the Appraise interface used in the human evaluation campaign. The annotator is presented with a source segment, a reference translation, and up to five outputs from competing systems (anonymized and displayed in random order), and is asked to rank these according to their translation quality, with ties allowed.

the reliability of the rankings. We measured pairwise agreement among annotators using Cohen's kappa coefficient (κ) (Cohen, 1960). If $P(A)$ be the proportion of times that the annotators agree, and $P(E)$ is the proportion of time that they would agree by chance, then Cohen's kappa is:

$$\kappa = \frac{P(A) - P(E)}{1 - P(E)}$$

Note that κ is basically a normalized version of $P(A)$, one which takes into account how meaningful it is for annotators to agree with each other by incorporating $P(E)$. The values for κ range from 0 to 1, with zero indicating no agreement and 1 perfect agreement.

We calculate $P(A)$ by examining all pairs of outputs[6] which had been judged by two or more judges, and calculating the proportion of time that they agreed that $A < B$, $A = B$, or $A > B$. In other words, $P(A)$ is the empirical, observed rate at which annotators agree, in the context of pairwise comparisons.

As for $P(E)$, it captures the probability that two annotators would agree randomly. Therefore:

$$P(E) = P(\text{A<B})^2 + P(\text{A=B})^2 + P(\text{A>B})^2$$

Note that each of the three probabilities in $P(E)$'s definition are squared to reflect the fact that we are considering the chance that *two* annotators would agree by chance. Each of these probabilities is computed empirically, by observing how often annotators actually rank two systems as being tied.

Table 4 shows final κ values for inter-annotator agreement for WMT11–WMT15 while Table 5 details intra-annotator agreement scores, including the division of researchers (WMT13$_r$) and MTurk (WMT13$_m$) data. The exact interpretation of the kappa coefficient is difficult, but according to Landis and Koch (1977), 0–0.2 is *slight*, 0.2–0.4 is *fair*, 0.4–0.6 is *moderate*, 0.6–0.8 is *substantial*, and 0.8–1.0 is *almost perfect*.

[6] regardless if they correspond to an individual system or to a set of systems ("multi-system") producing nearly identical translations

*** Formatting Issue - Best Available Paper/Graphic ***

Language Pair	Systems	Rankings	Average
Czech→English	17	85,877	5,051.6
English→Czech	16	136,869	8,554.3
German→English	14	40,535	2,895.4
English→German	17	55,123	3,242.5
French→English	8	29,770	3,721.3
English→French	8	34,512	4,314.0
Russian→English	14	46,193	3,299.5
English→Russian	11	49,582	4,507.5
Finnish→English	15	31,577	2,105.1
English→Finnish	11	32,694	2,972.2
Totals WMT15	131	542,732	4,143.0
WMT14	110	328,830	2,989.3
WMT13	148	942,840	6,370.5
WMT12	103	101,969	999.6
WMT11	133	63,045	474.0

Table 3: Amount of data collected in the WMT15 manual evaluation campagin. The final four rows report summary information from previous editions of the workshop. Note how many rankings we get for Czech language pairs. These include systems from the tuning shared task. Finnish, as a new language, sees a shortage of rankings for Finnnish→English Interest in French seems to have lowered this year with only seven systems. Overall, we see a nice increase in pairwise rankings, especially considering that we have dropped crowd-source annotation and are instead relying on researchers' judgments exclusively.

The inter-annotator agreement rates improve for most language pairs. On average, these are the best scores we have ever observed in one of our evaluation campaigns, including in WMT11, where results were inflated due to inclusion of the reference in the agreement rates. The results for intra-annotator agreement are more mixed: some improve greatly (Czech and German) while others degrade (French, Russian). Our special language, Finnish, also achieves very respectable scores. On average, again, we see the best intra-annotator agreement scores since WMT11.

It should be noted that the improvement is not caused by the "ties forced by our redundancy cleanup". If two systems A and F produced near-identical outputs, they are collapsed to one multi-system output AF and treated jointly in our agreement calculations, i.e. only in comparison with other outputs. It is only the final TrueSkill scores that include the tie $A = F$.

3.4 Producing the human ranking

The collected pairwise rankings are used to produce the official human ranking of the systems. For WMT14, we introduced a competition among multiple methods of producing this human ranking, selecting the method based on which could best predict the annotations in a portion of the collected pairwise judgments. The results of this competition were that (a) the competing metrics produced almost identical rankings across all tasks but that (b) one method, TrueSkill, had less variance across randomized runs, allowing us to make more confident cluster predictions. In light of these findings, this year, we produced the human ranking for each task using TrueSkill in the following fashion, following procedures adopted for WMT12: We produce 1,000 bootstrap-resampled runs over all of the available data. We then compute a *rank range* for each system by collecting the absolute rank of each system in each fold, throwing out the top and bottom 2.5%, and then clustering systems into equivalence classes containing systems with overlapping ranges, yielding a partial ordering over systems at the 95% confidence level.

The full list of the official human rankings for each task can be found in Table 6, which also reports all system scores, rank ranges, and clusters for all language pairs and all systems. The official interpretation of these results is that systems in the same cluster are considered tied. Given the large number of judgments that we collected, it was possible to group on average about two systems in a cluster, even though the systems in the middle are typically in larger clusters.

In Figure 4 and 5, we plotted the human evaluation result against everybody's favorite metric BLEU (some of the outlier online systems are

*** Formatting Issue - Best Available Paper/Graphic ***

Language Pair	WMT11	WMT12	WMT13	WMT13$_r$	WMT13$_m$	WMT14	WMT15
Czech→English	0.400	0.311	0.244	0.342	0.279	0.305	0.458
English→Czech	0.460	0.359	0.168	0.408	0.075	0.360	0.438
German→English	0.324	0.385	0.299	0.443	0.324	0.368	0.423
English→German	0.378	0.356	0.267	0.457	0.239	0.427	0.423
French→English	0.402	0.272	0.275	0.405	0.321	0.357	0.343
English→French	0.406	0.296	0.231	0.434	0.237	0.302	0.317
Russian→English	—	—	0.278	0.315	0.324	0.324	0.372
English→Russian	—	—	0.243	0.416	0.207	0.418	0.336
Finnish→English	—	—	—	—	—	—	0.388
English→Finnish	—	—	—	—	—	—	0.549
Mean	0.395	0.330	0.260	0.403	0.251	0.367	0.405

Table 4: κ scores measuring inter-annotator agreement for WMT15. See Table 5 for corresponding intra-annotator agreement scores. WMT13$_r$ and WMT$_m$ refer to researchers' judgments and crowd-sourced judgments obtained using Mechanical Turk, respectively. WMT14 and WMT15 results are based on researchers' judgments only (hence, comparable to WMT13$_r$).

Language Pair	WMT11	WMT12	WMT13	WMT13$_r$	WMT13$_m$	WMT14	WMT15
Czech→English	0.597	0.454	0.479	0.483	0.478	0.382	0.694
English→Czech	0.601	0.390	0.290	0.547	0.242	0.448	0.584
German→English	0.576	0.392	0.535	0.643	0.515	0.344	0.801
English→German	0.528	0.433	0.498	0.649	0.452	0.576	0.676
French→English	0.673	0.360	0.578	0.585	0.565	0.629	0.510
English→French	0.524	0.414	0.495	0.630	0.486	0.507	0.426
Russian→English	—	—	0.450	0.363	0.477	0.629	0.506
English→Russian	—	—	0.513	0.582	0.500	0.570	0.492
Finnish→English	—	—	—	—	—	—	0.562
English→Finnish	—	—	—	—	—	—	0.697
Mean	0.583	0.407	0.479	0.560	0.464	0.522	0.595

Table 5: κ scores measuring intra-annotator agreement, i.e., self-consistency of judges, across for the past few years of the human evaluation campaign. Scores are much higher for WMT15 which makes sense as we enforce annotation consistency through our initial preprocessing which joins *near-identical translation candidates* into multi-system entries. It seems that the focus on actual differences in our annotation tasks as well as the possibility of having "easier" ranking scenarios for $n < 5$ candidate systems results in a higher annotator agreement, both for inter- and intra-annotator agreement scores.

not included to make the graphs viewable). The plots cleary suggest that a fair comparison of systems of different kinds cannot rely on automatic scores. Rule-based systems receive a much lower BLEU score than statistical systems (see for instance English–German, e.g., PROMT-RULE). The same is true to a lesser degree for statistical syntax-based systems (see English–German, UEDIN-SYNTAX) and online systems that were not tuned to the shared task (see Czech–English, CU-TECTO vs. the cluster of tuning task systems TT-*).

4 Quality Estimation Task

The fourth edition of the WMT shared task on quality estimation (QE) of machine translation (MT) builds on the previous editions of the task (Callison-Burch et al., 2012; Bojar et al., 2013, 2014), with tasks including both sentence and word-level estimation, using new training and test datasets, and an additional task: document-level prediction.

The goals of this year's shared task were:

- Advance work on sentence- and word-level quality estimation by providing larger datasets.
- Investigate the effectiveness of quality labels, features and learning methods for document-level prediction.
- Explore differences between sentence-level and document-level prediction.
- Analyse the effect of training data sizes and quality for sentence and word-level predic-

***** Formatting Issue - Best Available Paper/Graphic *****

Czech–English

#	score	range	system
1	0.619	1	ONLINE-B
2	0.574	2	UEDIN-JHU
3	0.532	3-4	UEDIN-SYNTAX
	0.518	3-4	MONTREAL
4	0.436	5	ONLINE-A
5	-0.125	6	CU-TECTO
6	-0.182	7-9	TT-BLEU-MIRA-D
	-0.189	7-10	TT-ILLC-UVA
	-0.196	7-11	TT-BLEU-MERT
	-0.210	8-11	TT-AFRL
	-0.220	9-11	TT-USAAR-TUNA
7	-0.263	12-13	TT-DCU
	-0.297	13-15	TT-METEOR-CMU
	-0.320	13-15	TT-BLEU-MIRA-SP
	-0.320	13-15	TT-HKUST-MEANT
	-0.358	15-16	ILLINOIS

German–English

#	score	range	system
1	0.567	1	ONLINE-B
2	0.319	2-3	UEDIN-JHU
	0.298	2-4	ONLINE-A
	0.258	3-5	UEDIN-SYNTAX
	0.228	4-5	KIT
3	0.141	6-7	RWTH
	0.095	6-7	MONTREAL
4	-0.172	8-10	ILLINOIS
	-0.177	8-10	DFKI
	-0.221	9-10	ONLINE-C
5	-0.304	11	ONLINE-F
6	-0.489	12-13	MACAU
	-0.544	12-13	ONLINE-E

English–German

#	score	range	system
1	0.359	1-2	UEDIN-SYNTAX
	0.334	1-2	MONTREAL
2	0.260	3-4	PROMT-RULE
	0.235	3-4	ONLINE-A
3	0.148	5	ONLINE-B
4	0.086	6	KIT-LIMSI
5	0.036	7-9	UEDIN-JHU
	0.003	7-11	ONLINE-F
	-0.001	7-11	ONLINE-C
	-0.018	8-11	KIT
	-0.035	9-11	CIMS
6	-0.133	12-13	DFKI
	-0.137	12-13	ONLINE-E
7	-0.235	14	UDS-SANT
8	-0.400	15	ILLINOIS
9	-0.501	16	IMS

English–Czech

#	score	range	system
1	0.686	1	CU-CHIMERA
2	0.515	2-3	ONLINE-B
	0.503	2-3	UEDIN-JHU
3	0.467	4	MONTREAL
4	0.426	5	ONLINE-A
5	0.261	6	UEDIN-SYNTAX
6	0.209	7	CU-TECTO
7	0.114	8	COMMERCIAL1
8	-0.342	9-11	TT-DCU
	-0.342	9-11	TT-AFRL
	-0.346	9-11	TT-BLEU-MIRA-D
9	-0.373	12	TT-USAAR-TUNA
10	-0.406	13	TT-BLEU-MERT
11	-0.563	14	TT-METEOR-CMU
12	-0.808	15	TT-BLEU-MIRA-SP

French–English

#	score	range	system
1	0.498	1-2	ONLINE-B
	0.446	1-3	LIMSI-CNRS
	0.415	1-3	UEDIN-JHU
2	0.275	4-5	MACAU
	0.223	4-5	ONLINE-A
3	-0.423	6	ONLINE-F
4	-1.434	7	ONLINE-E

Finnish–English

#	score	range	system
1	0.675	1	ONLINE-B
2	0.280	2-4	PROMT-SMT
	0.246	2-5	ONLINE-A
	0.236	2-5	UU
	0.182	4-7	UEDIN-JHU
	0.160	5-7	ABUMATRAN-COMB
	0.144	5-8	UEDIN-SYNTAX
	0.081	7-8	ILLINOIS
3	-0.081	9	ABUMATRAN-HFS
4	-0.177	10	MONTREAL
5	-0.275	11	ABUMATRAN
6	-0.438	12-13	LIMSI
	-0.513	13-14	SHEFFIELD
	-0.520	13-14	SHEFF-STEM

English–French

#	score	range	system
1	0.540	1	LIMSI-CNRS
2	0.304	2-3	ONLINE-A
	0.258	2-4	UEDIN-JHU
	0.215	3-4	ONLINE-B
3	-0.001	5	CIMS
4	-0.338	6	ONLINE-F
5	-0.977	7	ONLINE-E

Russian–English

#	score	range	system
1	0.494	1	ONLINE-G
2	0.311	2	ONLINE-B
3	0.129	3-6	PROMT-RULE
	0.116	3-6	AFRL-MIT-PB
	0.113	3-6	AFRL-MIT-FAC
	0.104	3-7	ONLINE-A
	0.051	6-8	AFRL-MIT-H
	0.010	7-10	LIMSI-NCODE
	-0.021	8-10	UEDIN-SYNTAX
	-0.031	8-10	UEDIN-JHU
4	-0.218	11	USAAR-GACHA
5	-0.278	12	USAAR-GACHA
6	-0.781	13	ONLINE-F

English–Russian

#	score	range	system
1	1.015	1	PROMT-RULE
2	0.521	2	ONLINE-G
3	0.217	3	ONLINE-B
4	0.122	4-5	LIMSI-NCODE
	0.075	4-5	ONLINE-A
5	0.014	6	UEDIN-JHU
6	-0.138	7	UEDIN-SYNTAX
7	-0.276	8	USAAR-GACHA
8	-0.333	9	USAAR-GACHA
9	-1.218	10	ONLINE-F

English–Finnish

#	score	range	system
1	1.069	1	ONLINE-B
2	0.548	2	ONLINE-A
3	0.210	3	UU
4	0.042	4	ABUMATRAN-COMB
5	-0.059	5	ABUMATRAN-COMB
6	-0.143	6-7	AALTO
	-0.184	6-8	UEDIN-SYNTAX
	-0.212	6-8	ABUMATRAN
7	-0.342	9	CMU
8	-0.929	10	CHALMERS

Table 6: Official results for the WMT15 translation task. Systems are ordered by their inferred system means, though systems within a cluster are considered tied. Lines between systems indicate clusters according to bootstrap resampling at p-level $p \leq .05$. Systems with grey background indicate use of resources that fall outside the constraints provided for the shared task.

***** Formatting Issue - Best Available Paper/Graphic *****

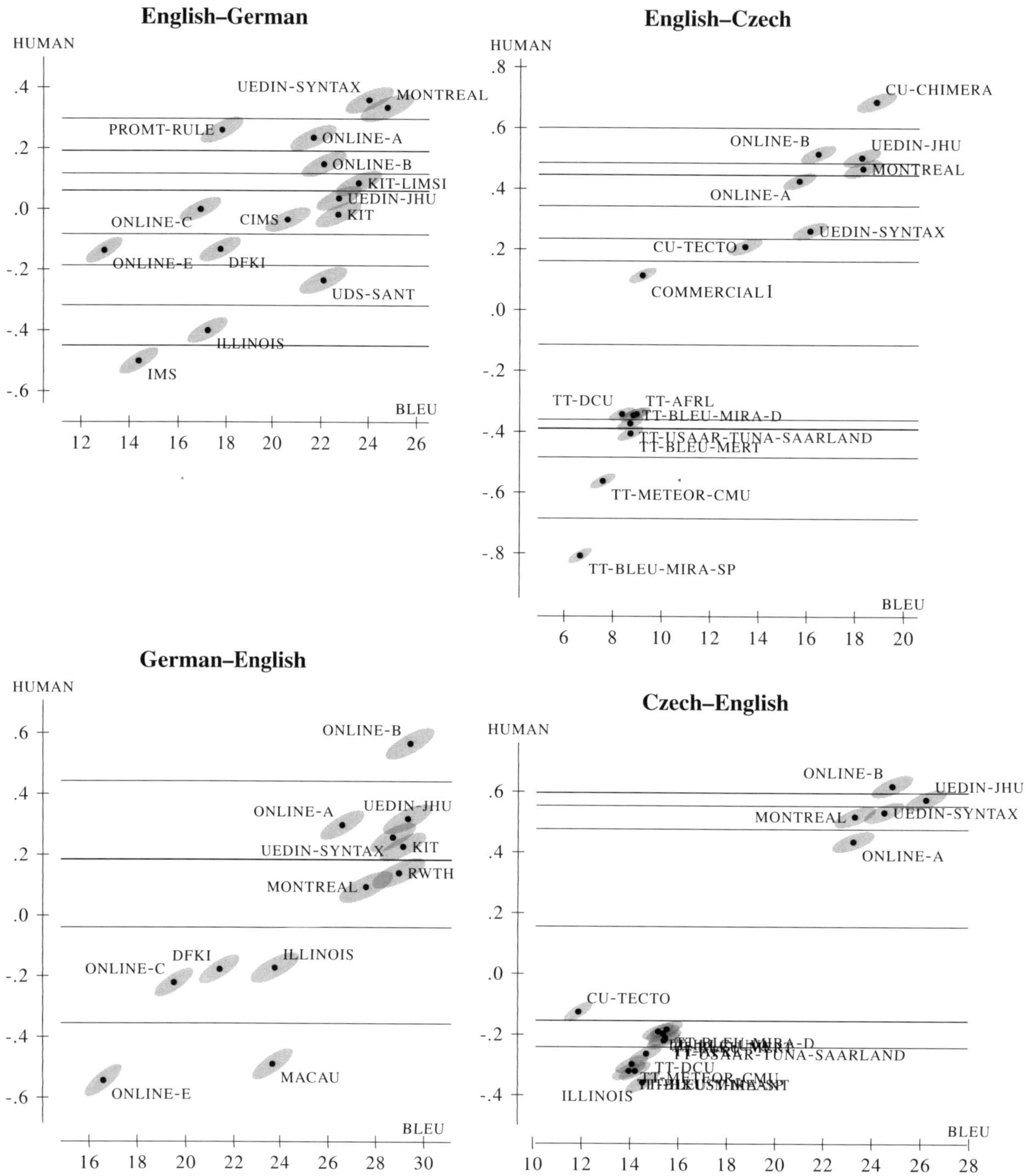

Figure 4: Human evaluation scores versus BLEU scores for the German–English and Czech–English language pairs illustrate the need for human evaluation when comparing systems of different kind. Confidence intervals are indicated by the shaded ellipses. Rule-based systems and to a lesser degree syntax-based statistical systems receive a lower BLEU score than their human score would indicate. The big cluster in the Czech-English plot are tuning task submissions.

*** Formatting Issue - Best Available Paper/Graphic ***

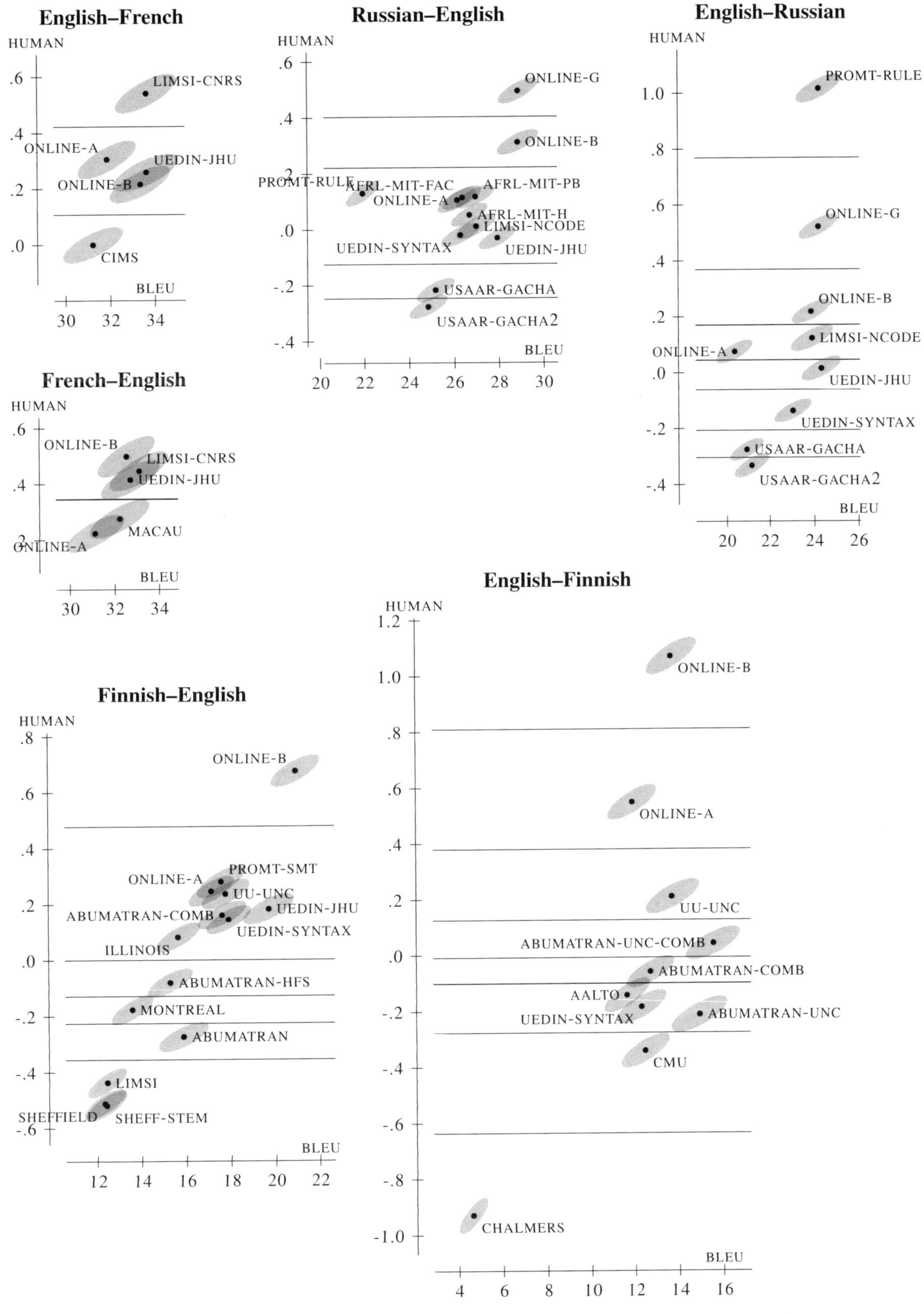

Figure 5: Human evaluation versus BLEU scores for the French–English, Russian–English, and Finnish-English language pairs.

tion, particularly the use of annotations obtained from crowdsourced post-editing.

Three tasks were proposed: Task 1 at sentence level (Section 4.3), Task 2 at word level (Section 4.4), and Task 3 at document level (Section 4.5). Tasks 1 and 2 provide the same dataset with English-Spanish translations generated by the statistical machine translation (SMT) system, while Task 3 provides two different datasets, for two language pairs: English-German (EN-DE) and German-English (DE-EN) translations taken from all participating systems in WMT13 (Bojar et al., 2013). These datasets were annotated with different labels for quality: for Tasks 1 and 2, the labels were automatically derived from the post-editing of the machine translation output, while for Task 3, scores were computed based on reference translations using Meteor (Banerjee and Lavie, 2005). Any external resource, including additional quality estimation training data, could be used by participants (no distinction between *open* and *close* tracks was made). As presented in Section 4.1, participants were also provided with a baseline set of features for each task, and a software package to extract these and other quality estimation features and perform model learning, with suggested methods for all levels of prediction. Participants, described in Section 4.2, could submit up to two systems for each task.

Data used to build MT systems or internal system information (such as model scores or n-best lists) were not made available this year as multiple MT systems were used to produce the datasets, especially for Task 3, including online and rule-based systems. Therefore, as a general rule, participants could only use black-box features.

4.1 Baseline systems

Sentence-level baseline system: For Task 1, QUEST[7] (Specia et al., 2013) was used to extract 17 MT system-independent features from the source and translation (target) files and parallel corpora:

- Number of tokens in the source and target sentences.
- Average source token length.
- Average number of occurrences of the target word within the target sentence.
- Number of punctuation marks in source and target sentences.
- Language model (LM) probability of source and target sentences based on models for the WMT News Commentary corpus.
- Average number of translations per source word in the sentence as given by IBM Model 1 extracted from the WMT News Commentary parallel corpus, and thresholded such that $P(t|s) > 0.2$/$P(t|s) > 0.01$.
- Percentage of unigrams, bigrams and trigrams in frequency quartiles 1 (lower frequency words) and 4 (higher frequency words) in the source language extracted from the WMT News Commentary corpus.
- Percentage of unigrams in the source sentence seen in the source side of the WMT News Commentary corpus.

These features were used to train a Support Vector Regression (SVR) algorithm using a Radial Basis Function (RBF) kernel within the SCIKIT-LEARN toolkit.[8] The γ, ϵ and C parameters were optimised via grid search with 5-fold cross validation on the training set. We note that although the system is referred to as "baseline", it is in fact a strong system. It has proved robust across a range of language pairs, MT systems, and text domains for predicting various forms of post-editing effort (Callison-Burch et al., 2012; Bojar et al., 2013, 2014).

Word-level baseline system: For Task 2, the baseline features were extracted with the MARMOT tool[9]. For the baseline system we used a number of features that have been found the most informative in previous research on word-level quality estimation. Our baseline set of features is loosely based on the one described in (Luong et al., 2014). It contains the following 25 features:

- Word count in the source and target sentences, source and target token count ratio. Although these features are sentence-level (i.e. their values will be the same for all words in a sentence), but the length of a sentence might influence the probability of a word being incorrect.

[7] https://github.com/lspecia/quest

[8] http://scikit-learn.org/

[9] https://github.com/qe-team/marmot

*** Formatting Issue - Best Available Paper/Graphic ***

- Target token, its left and right contexts of one word.

- Source token aligned to the target token, its left and right contexts of one word. The alignments were produced with the `force_align.py` script, which is part of **cdec** (Dyer et al., 2010). It allows to align new parallel data with a pre-trained alignment model built with the cdec word aligner (**fast_align**). The alignment model was trained on the Europarl corpus (Koehn, 2005).

- Boolean dictionary features: whether target token is a stopword, a punctuation mark, a proper noun, a number.

- Target language model features:
  - The order of the highest order n-gram which starts or ends with the target token.
  - Backoff behaviour of the n-grams (t_{i-2}, t_{i-1}, t_i), (t_{i-1}, t_i, t_{i+1}), (t_i, t_{i+1}, t_{i+2}), where t_i is the target token (the backoff behaviour is computed as described in (Raybaud et al., 2011)).

- The order of the highest order n-gram which starts or ends with the source token.

- Boolean pseudo-reference feature: 1 if the token is contained in a pseudo-reference, 0 otherwise. The pseudo-reference used for this feature is the automatic translation generated by an English-Spanish phrase-based SMT system trained on the Europarl corpus with standard settings.[10]

- The part-of-speech tags of the target and source tokens.

- The number of senses of the target and source tokens in WordNet.

We model the task as a sequence prediction problem and train our baseline system using the Linear-Chain Conditional Random Fields (CRF) algorithm with the CRF++ tool.[11]

Document-level baseline system: For Task 3, the baseline features for sentence-level prediction were used. These are aggregated by summing or averaging their values for the entire document. Features that were summed: number of tokens in the source and target sentences and number of punctuation marks in source and target sentences. All other features were averaged. The implementation for document-level feature extraction is available in QuEst++ (Specia et al., 2015).[12]

These features were then used to train a SVR algorithm with RBF kernel using the SCIKIT-LEARN toolkit. The γ, ϵ and C parameters were optimised via grid search with 5-fold cross validation on the training set.

4.2 Participants

Table 7 lists all participating teams submitting systems to any of the tasks. Each team was allowed up to two submissions for each task and language pair. In the descriptions below, participation in specific tasks is denoted by a task identifier.

DCU-SHEFF (Task 2): The system uses the baseline set of features provided for the task. Two pre-processing data manipulation techniques were used: data selection and data bootstrapping. Data selection filters out sentences which have the smallest proportion of erroneous tokens and are assumed to be the least useful for the task. Data bootstrapping enhances the training data with incomplete training sentences (e.g. the first k words of a sentence of the length N, where $k < N$). This technique creates additional data instances and boosts the importance of errors occurring in the training data. The combination of these techniques doubled the F_1 score for the "BAD" class, as compared to a models trained on the entire dataset given for the task. The labelling was performed with a CRF model trained using the CRF++ tool, as in the baseline system.

HDCL (Task 2): HDCL's submissions are based on a deep neural network that learns continuous feature representations from scratch, i.e. from bilingual contexts. The network was pre-trained by initialising the word lookup-table with distributed word representations,

[10] `http://www.statmt.org/moses/?n=Moses.Baseline`

[11] `http://taku910.github.io/crfpp/`

[12] `https://github.com/ghpaetzold/questplusplus`

*** Formatting Issue - Best Available Paper/Graphic ***

ID	Participating team
DCU-SHEFF	Dublin City University, Ireland and University of Sheffield, UK (Logacheva et al., 2015)
HDCL	Heidelberg University, Germany (Kreutzer et al., 2015)
LORIA	Lorraine Laboratory of Research in Computer Science and its Applications, France (Langlois, 2015)
RTM-DCU	Dublin City University, Ireland (Bicici et al., 2015)
SAU-KERC	Shenyang Aerospace University, China (Shang et al., 2015)
SHEFF-NN	University of Sheffield Team 1, UK (Shah et al., 2015)
UAlacant	Alicant University, Spain (Esplà-Gomis et al., 2015a)
UGENT	Ghent University, Belgium (Tezcan et al., 2015)
USAAR-USHEF	University of Sheffield, UK and Saarland University, Germany (Scarton et al., 2015a)
USHEF	University of Sheffield, UK (Scarton et al., 2015a)
HIDDEN	Undisclosed

Table 7: Participants in the WMT15 quality estimation shared task.

and fine-tuned for the quality estimation classification task by back-propagating word-level prediction errors using stochastic gradient descent. In addition to the continuous space deep model, a shallow linear classifier was trained on the provided baseline features and their quadratic expansion. One of the submitted systems (QUETCH) relies on the deep model only, the other (QUETCHPLUS) is a linear combination of the QUETCH system score, the linear classifier score, and binary and binned baseline features. The system combination yielded significant improvements, showing that the deep and shallow models each contributes complementary information to the combination.

LORIA (Task 1): The LORIA system for Task 1 is based on a standard machine learning approach where source-target sentences are described by numerical vectors and SVR is used to learn a regression model between these vectors and quality scores. Feature vectors used the 17 baseline features, two Latent Semantic Indexing (LSI) features and 31 features based on pseudo-references. The LSI approach considers source-target pairs as documents, and projects the TF-IDF words-documents matrix into a reduced numerical space. This leads to a measure of similarity between a source and a target sentence, which was used as a feature. Two of these features were used based on two matrices, one from the Europarl corpus and one from the official training data. Pseudo-references were produced by three online systems. These features measure the intersection between n-gram sets of the target sentence and of the pseudo-references. Three sets of features were extracted from each online system, and a fourth feature was extracted measuring the inter-agreement among the three online systems and the target system.

RTM-DCU (Tasks 1, 2, 3): RTM-DCU systems are based on referential translation machines (RTM) (Biçici, 2013; Biçici and Way, 2014). RTMs propose a language independent approach and avoid the need to access any task- or domain-specific information or resource. The submissions used features that indicate the closeness between instances to the available training data, the difficulty of translating them, and the presence of acts of translation for data transformation. SVR was used for document and sentence-level prediction tasks, also in combination with feature selection or partial least squares, and global linear models with dynamic learning were used for the word-level prediction task.

SAU (Task 2): The SAU submissions used a CRF model to predict the binary labels for Task 2. They rely on 12 basic features and 85 combination features. The ratio between OK and BAD labels was found to be 4:1 in the training set. Two strategies were proposed to solve this problem of label ratio imbalance. The first strategy is to replace "OK" labels with sub-labels to balance label distribution, where the sub-labels are OK_B, OK_I, OK_E, OK (depending on the position of the token in the sentence). The second strategy is to reconstruct the training set to include more "BAD" words.

SHEFF-NN (Tasks 1, 2): SHEFF-NN submissions were based on (i) a Continuous Space Language Model (CSLM) to extract additional features for Task 1 (SHEF-GP and SHEF-SVM), (ii) a Continuous Bag-of-Words (CBOW) model to produce word embeddings as features for Task 2 (SHEF-W2V), and (iii) a combination of features produced by QUEST++ and a feature produced with word embedding models (SHEF-QuEst++). SVR and Gaussian Processes were used to learn prediction models for Task 1, and a CRF algorithm for binary tagging models in Task 2 (Pystruct Linear-chain CRF trained with a structured SVM for system SHEF-W2V, and CRFSuite Adaptive Regularisation of Weight Vector (AROW) and Passive Aggressive (PA) algorithms for system SHEF-QuEst++). Interesting findings for Task 1 were that (i) CSLM features always bring improvements whenever added to either baseline or complete feature sets and (ii) CSLM features alone perform better than the baseline features. For Task 2, the results obtained by SHEF-W2V are promising: although it uses only features learned in unsupervised fashion (CBOW word embeddings), it was able to outperform the baseline as well as many other systems. Further, combining the source-to-target cosine similarity feature with the ones produced by QUEST++ led to improvements in the F_1 of "BAD" labels.

UAlacant (Task 2): The submissions of the Universitat d'Alacant team were obtained by applying the approach in (Esplà-Gomis et al., 2015b), which uses any source of bilingual information available as a black-box in order to spot sub-segment correspondences between a sentence S in the source language and a given translation hypothesis T in the target language. These sub-segment correspondences are used to extract a collection of features that is then used by a multilayer perceptron to determine the word-level predicted score. Three sources of bilingual information available online were used: two online machine translation systems, Apertium[13] and Google Translate; and the bilingual concordancer Reverso Context.[14] Two submissions were made for Task 2: one using only the 70 features described in (Esplà-Gomis et al., 2015b), and one combining them with the baseline features provided by the task organisers.

UGENT (Tasks 1, 2): The submissions for the word-level task used 55 new features in combination with the baseline feature set to train binary classifiers. The new features try to capture either accuracy (meaning transfer from source to target sentence) using word and phrase alignments, or fluency (well-formedness of target sentence) using language models trained on word surface forms and on part-of-speech tags. Based on the combined feature set, SCATE-MBL uses a memory-based learning (MBL) algorithm for binary classification. SCATE-HYBRID uses the same feature set and forms a classifier ensemble using CRFs in combination with the MBL system for predicting word-level quality. For the sentence-level task, SCATE-SVM-single uses a single feature to train SVR models, which is based on the percentage of words that are labelled as "BAD" by the word-level quality estimation system SCATE-HYBRID. SCATE-SVM adds 16 new features to this single feature and the baseline feature set to train SVR models using an RBF kernel. Additional language resources are used to extract the new features for both tasks.

USAAR-USHEF (Task 3): The systems submitted for both EN-DE and DE-EN (called BFF) were built by using a exhaustive search for feature selection over the official baseline features. In order to select the best features, a Bayesian Ridge classifier was trained for each feature combination and the classifiers were evaluated in terms of Mean Average Error (MAE): the classifier with the smallest

[13] `http://www.apertium.org`

[14] `http://context.reverso.net/translation/`

MAE was considered the best. For EN-DE, the selected features were: average source token length, percentage of unigrams and of trigrams in fourth quartile of frequency in a corpus of the source language. For DE-EN, the best features were: number of occurrences of the target word within the target hypothesis, percentage of unigrams and of trigrams in first quartile of frequency in a corpus of the source language. This provide an indication of which features of the baseline set contribute for document-level quality estimation.

USHEF (Task 3): The system submitted for the EN-DE document-level task was built by using the 17 official baseline features, plus discourse features (repetition of words, lemmas and nouns and ratio of repetitions – as implemented in QuEst++. For DE-EN, a combination of the 17 baseline features, the discourse repetition features and discourse-aware features extracted from syntactic and discourse parsers was used. The new discourse features are: number of pronouns, number of connectives, number of satellite and nucleus relations in the RST (Rhetorical Structure Theory) tree for the document and number of EDU (Elementary Discourse Units) breaks in the text. A backward feature selection approach, based on the feature rank of SCIKIT-LEARN's Random Forest implementation, was also applied. For both languages pairs, the same algorithm as that of the baseline system was used: the SCIKIT-LEARN implementation of SVR with RBF kernel and hyper-parameters optimised via grid-search.

HIDDEN (Task 3): This submission, whose creators preferred to remain anonymous, estimates the quality of a given document by explicitly identifying potential translation errors in it. Translation error detection is implemented as a combination of human expert knowledge and different language processing tools, including named entity recognition, part-of-speech tagging and word alignments. In particular, the system looks for patterns of errors defined by human experts, taking into account the actual words and the additional linguistic information. With this approach, a wide variety of errors can be detected: from simple misspellings and typos to complex lack of agreement (in genre, number and tense), or lexical inconsistencies. Each error category is assigned an "importance", again according to human knowledge, and the amount of error in the document is computed as the weighted sum of the identified errors. Finally, the documents are sorted according to this figure to generate the final submission to the ranking variant of Task 3.

4.3 Task 1: Predicting sentence-level quality

This task consists in scoring (and ranking) translation sentences according to the percentage of their words that need to be fixed. It is similar to Task 1.2 in WMT14. HTER (Snover et al., 2006b) is used as quality score, i.e. the minimum edit distance between the machine translation and its manually post-edited version in [0,1].

As in previous years, two variants of the results could be submitted:

- **Scoring**: An absolute HTER score for each sentence translation, to be interpreted as an error metric: lower scores mean better translations.
- **Ranking**: A ranking of sentence translations for all source sentences from best to worst. For this variant, it does not matter how the ranking is produced (from HTER predictions or by other means). The reference ranking is defined based on the true HTER scores.

Data The data is the same as that used for the WMT15 Automatic Post-editing task,[15] as kindly provided by Unbabel.[16] Source segments are tokenized English sentences from the news domain with at least four tokens. Target segments are tokenized Spanish translations produced by an online SMT system. The human post-editions are a manual revision of the target, collected using Unbabel's crowd post-editing platform. HTER labels were computed using the TERCOM tool[17] with default settings (tokenised, case insensitive, exact matching only), but with scores capped to 1.

As training and development data, we provided English-Spanish datasets with $11,271$ and $1,000$ source sentences, their machine translations, post-editions and HTER scores, respectively. As test data, we provided an additional

[15] http://www.statmt.org/wmt15/ape-task.html

[16] https://unbabel.com/

[17] http://www.cs.umd.edu/~snover/tercom/

set of 1,817 English-Spanish source-translations pairs produced by the same MT system used for the training data.

Evaluation Evaluation was performed against the true HTER label and/or ranking, using the same metrics as in previous years:

- Scoring: Mean Average Error (MAE) (primary metric, official score for ranking submissions), Root Mean Squared Error (RMSE).
- Ranking: DeltaAvg (primary metric) and Spearman's ρ rank correlation.

Additionally, we included Pearson's r correlation against the true HTER label, as suggested by Graham (2015).

Statistical significance on MAE and DeltaAvg was computed using a pairwise bootstrap resampling (1K times) approach with 95% confidence intervals. [18] For Pearson's r correlation, we measured significance using the Williams test, as also suggested in (Graham, 2015).

Results Table 8 summarises the results for the ranking variant of Task 1. They are sorted from best to worst using the DeltaAvg metric scores as primary key and the Spearman's ρ rank correlation scores as secondary key.

The results for the scoring variant are presented in Table 9, sorted from best to worst by using the MAE metric scores as primary key and the RMSE metric scores as secondary key.

Pearson's r coefficients for all systems against HTER is given in Table 10. As discussed in (Graham, 2015), the results according to this metric can rank participating systems differently. In particular, we note the SHEF/GP submission, are which is deemed significantly worse than the baseline system according to MAE, but substantially better than the baseline according to Pearson's correlation. Graham (2015) argues that the use of MAE as evaluation score for quality estimation tasks is inadequate, as MAE is very sensitive to variance. This means that a system that outputs predictions with high variance is more likely to have high MAE score, even if the distribution follows that of the true labels. Interestingly, according to Pearson's correlation, the systems are ranked exactly in the same way as according to our DeltaAvg metric. The only difference is that the 4th place is now considered significantly different from the three winning submissions. She also argues that the significance tests used with MAE, based on randomised resampling, assume that the data is independent, which is not the case. Therefore, we apply the suggested Williams significance test for this metric.

4.4 Task 2: Predicting word-level quality

The goal of this task is to evaluate the extent to which we can detect word-level errors in MT output. Often, the overall quality of a translated segment is significantly harmed by specific errors in a small proportion of words. Various classes of errors can be found in translations, but for this task we consider all error types together, aiming at making a binary distinction between 'GOOD' and 'BAD' tokens. The decision to bucket all error types together was made because of the lack of sufficient training data that could allow consideration of more fine-grained error tags.

Data This year's word-level task uses the same dataset as Task 1, for a single language pair: English-Spanish. Each instance of the training, development and test sets consists of the following elements:

- Source sentence (English).
- Automatic translation (Spanish).
- Manual post-edition of the automatic translation.
- Word-level binary ("OK"/"BAD") labelling of the automatic translation.

The binary labels for the datasets were acquired automatically with the TERCOM tool (Snover et al., 2006b).[19] This tool computes the edit distance between machine-translated sentence and its reference (in this case, its post-edited version). It identifies four types of errors: *substitution* of a word with another word, *deletion* of a word (word was omitted by the translation system), *insertion* of a word (a redundant word was added by the translation system), and word or sequence of words *shift* (word order error). Every word in the machine-translated sentence is tagged with one of these error types or not tagged if it matches a word from the reference.

[18] http://www.quest.dcs.shef.ac.uk/wmt15_files/bootstrap-significance.pl

[19] http://www.cs.umd.edu/~snover/tercom/

*** Formatting Issue - Best Available Paper/Graphic ***

System ID	**DeltaAvg** ↑	Spearman's ρ ↑
English-Spanish		
• LORIA/17+LSI+MT+FILTRE	6.51	0.36
• LORIA/17+LSI+MT	6.34	0.37
• RTM-DCU/RTM-FS+PLS-SVR	6.34	0.37
• RTM-DCU/RTM-FS-SVR	6.09	0.35
UGENT-LT3/SCATE-SVM	6.02	0.34
UGENT-LT3/SCATE-SVM-single	5.12	0.30
SHEF/SVM	5.05	0.28
SHEF/GP	3.07	0.28
Baseline SVM	2.16	0.13

Table 8: Official results for the ranking variant of the WMT15 quality estimation Task 1. The winning submissions are indicated by a •. These are the top-scoring submission and those that are not significantly worse according to pairwise bootstrap resampling (1K times) with 95% confidence intervals. The systems in the gray area are not different from the baseline system at a statistically significant level according to the same test.

System ID	**MAE** ↓	RMSE ↓
English-Spanish		
• RTM-DCU/RTM-FS+PLS-SVR	13.25	17.48
• LORIA/17+LSI+MT+FILTRE	13.34	17.35
• RTM-DCU/RTM-FS-SVR	13.35	17.68
• LORIA/17+LSI+MT	13.42	17.45
• UGENT-LT3/SCATE-SVM	13.71	17.45
UGENT-LT3/SCATE-SVM-single	13.76	17.79
SHEF/SVM	13.83	18.01
Baseline SVM	14.82	19.13
SHEF/GP	15.16	18.97

Table 9: Official results for the scoring variant of the WMT15 quality estimation Task 1. The winning submissions are indicated by a •. These are the top-scoring submission and those that are not significantly worse according to bootstrap resampling (1K times) with 95% confidence intervals. The systems in the gray area are not different from the baseline system at a statistically significant level according to the same test.

System ID	**Pearson's** r ↑
• LORIA/17+LSI+MT+FILTRE	0.39
• LORIA/17+LSI+MT	0.39
• RTM-DCU/RTM-FS+PLS-SVR	0.38
RTM-DCU/RTM-FS-SVR	0.38
UGENT-LT3/SCATE-SVM	0.37
UGENT-LT3/SCATE-SVM-single	0.32
SHEF/SVM	0.29
SHEF/GP	0.19
Baseline SVM	0.14

Table 10: Alternative results for the scoring variant of the WMT15 quality estimation Task 1. The winning submissions are indicated by a •. These are the top-scoring submission and those that are not significantly worse according to Williams test with 95% confidence intervals. The systems in the gray area are not different from the baseline system at a statistically significant level according to the same test.

All the untagged (correct) words were tagged with "OK", while the words tagged with substitution and insertion errors were assigned the tag "BAD". The deletion errors are not associated with any word in the automatic translation, so we could not consider them. We also disabled the shift errors by running TERCOM with the option '-d 0'. The reason for that is the fact that searching for shifts introduces significant noise in the annotation. The system cannot discriminate between cases where a word was really shifted and where a word (especially common words such as prepositions, articles and pronouns) was deleted in one part of the sentence and then independently inserted in another part of this sentence, i.e. to correct an unrelated error. The statistics of the datasets are outlined in Table 11.

	Sentences	Words	% of "BAD" words
Training	11,271	257,548	19.14
Dev	1,000	23,207	19.18
Test	1,817	40,899	18.87

Table 11: Datasets for Task 2.

Evaluation Submissions were evaluated in terms of classification performance against the original labels. The main evaluation metric is the average F_1 for the "BAD" class. Statistical significance on F_1 for the "BAD" class was computed using approximate randomization tests.[20]

Results The results for Task 2 are summarised in Table 12. The results are ordered by F_1 score for the error (BAD) class.

Using the F_1 score for the word-level estimation task has a number of drawbacks. First of all, we cannot use it as the single metric to evaluate the system's quality. The F_1 score of the class "BAD" becomes an inadequate metric when one is also interested in the tagging of correct words. In fact, a naive baseline which tags all words with the class "BAD" would yield 31.75 F_1 score for the "BAD" class in the test set of this task, which is close to some of the submissions and by far exceeds the baseline, although this tagging is uninformative.

We could instead use the weighted F_1 score, which would lead to a single F_1 figure where every class is given a weight according to its frequency in the test set. However, we believe the weighted F_1 score does not reflect the real quality of the systems either. Since there are many more instances of the "GOOD" class than there are of the "BAD" class, the performance on the "BAD" class does not contribute much weight to the overall score, and changes in accuracy of error prediction on this less frequent class can go unnoticed. The weighted F_1 score for the strategy which tags all words as "GOOD" would be 72.66, which is higher than the score of many submissions. However, similar to the case of tagging all words as "BAD", this strategy is uninformative. In an attempt to find more intuitive ways of evaluating word-level tasks, we introduce a new metric called *sequence correlation*. It gives higher importance to the instances of the "BAD" class and is robust against uninformative tagging.

The basis of the sequence correlation metric is the number of matching labels in the reference and the hypothesis, analogously to a precision metric. However, it has some additional features that are aimed at making it more reliable. We consider the tagging of each sentence separately as a sequence of tags. We divide each sequence into sub-sequences tagged by the same tag, for example, the sequence "OK BAD OK OK OK" will be represented as a list of 3 sub-sequences: ["OK", "BAD", "OK OK OK"]. Each subsequence has also the information on its position in the original sentence. The sub-sequences of the reference and the hypothesis are then intersected, and the number of matching tags in the corresponding sub-sequences is computed so that every sub-sequence can be used only once. Let us consider the following example:

```
Reference:   OK  BAD  OK  OK  OK
Hypothesis:  OK  OK   OK  OK  OK
```

Here, the reference has three sub-sequences, as in the previous example, and the hypothesis consists of only one sub-sequence which coincides with the hypothesis itself, because all the words were tagged with the "OK" label. The precision score for this sentence will be 0.8, as 4 of 5 labels match in this example. However, we notice that the hypothesis sub-sequence covers two matching sub-sequences of the reference: word 1 and words 3–5. According to our metric, the hypothesis sub-sequence can be used for the intersection only once, giving either 1 of 5 or 3 of 5 matching words. We choose the highest value and get the score of 0.6. Thus, the intersection procedure downweighs the uninformative hypotheses where all words are tagged with one tag.

In order to compute the sequence correlation we need to get the set of spans for each label in both the prediction and the reference, and then intersect them. A set of spans of each tag t in the string $\mathbf{w}$ is computed as follows:

[20] http://www.nlpado.de/~sebastian/software/sigf.shtml

*** Formatting Issue - Best Available Paper/Graphic ***

System ID	weighted F_1 All	F_1 **Bad** ↑	F_1 GOOD
English-Spanish			
• UAlacant/OnLine-SBI-Baseline	71.47	43.12	78.07
• HDCL/QUETCHPLUS	72.56	43.05	79.42
UAlacant/OnLine-SBI	69.54	41.51	76.06
SAU/KERC-CRF	77.44	39.11	86.36
SAU/KERC-SLG-CRF	77.4	38.91	86.35
SHEF2/W2V-BI-2000	65.37	38.43	71.63
SHEF2/W2V-BI-2000-SIM	65.27	38.40	71.52
SHEF1/QuEst++-AROW	62.07	38.36	67.58
UGENT/SCATE-HYBRID	74.28	36.72	83.02
DCU-SHEFF/BASE-NGRAM-2000	67.33	36.60	74.49
HDCL/QUETCH	75.26	35.27	84.56
DCU-SHEFF/BASE-NGRAM-5000	75.09	34.53	84.53
SHEF1/QuEst++-PA	26.25	34.30	24.38
UGENT/SCATE-MBL	74.17	30.56	84.32
RTM-DCU/s5-RTM-GLMd	76.00	23.91	88.12
RTM-DCU/s4-RTM-GLMd	75.88	22.69	88.26
Baseline	75.31	16.78	88.93

Table 12: Official results for the WMT15 quality estimation Task 2. The winning submissions are indicated by a •. These are the top-scoring submission and those that are not significantly worse according to approximate randomization tests with 95% confidence intervals. Submissions whose results are statistically different from others according to the same test are grouped by a horizontal line.

$$S_t(\mathbf{w}) = \{\mathbf{w}_{[b:e]}\},\ \forall i\ s.t.\ b \leqslant i \leqslant e : w_i = t$$

where $\mathbf{w}_{[b:e]}$ is a substring $w_b, w_{b+1}, ..., w_{e-1}, w_e$. Then the intersection of spans for all labels is:

$$Int(\mathbf{y}, \hat{\mathbf{y}}) = \sum_{t \in \{0;1\}} \lambda_t \sum_{s_\mathbf{y} \in S_t(\mathbf{y})} \sum_{s_{\hat{\mathbf{y}}} \in S_t(\hat{\mathbf{y}})} |s_\mathbf{y} \cap s_{\hat{\mathbf{y}}}|$$

Here λ_t is the weight of a tag t in the overall result. It is inversely proportional the number of instances of this tag in the reference:

$$\lambda_t = \frac{|\mathbf{y}|}{c_t(\hat{\mathbf{y}})}$$

where $c_t(\hat{\mathbf{y}})$ is the number of words labelled with the label t in the prediction. Thus we give the equal importance to all tags.

The sum of matching spans is also weighted by the ratio of the number of spans in the hypothesis and the reference. This is done to downweigh the system tagging if the number of its spans differs from the number of spans provided in the gold standard. This ratio is computed as follows:

$$r(\mathbf{y}, \hat{\mathbf{y}}) = \min(\frac{|\mathbf{y}|}{|\hat{\mathbf{y}}|}; \frac{|\hat{\mathbf{y}}|}{|\mathbf{y}|})$$

This ratio is 1 if the number of spans is equal for the hypothesis and the reference, and less than 1 otherwise.

The final score for a sentence is produced as follows:

$$SeqCor(\mathbf{y}, \hat{\mathbf{y}}) = \frac{r(\mathbf{y}, \hat{\mathbf{y}}) \cdot Int(\mathbf{y}, \hat{\mathbf{y}})}{|\mathbf{y}|} \quad (1)$$

Then the overall sequence correlation for the whole dataset is the average of sentence scores.

Table 13 shows the results of the evaluation according to the sequence correlation metric. The results for the two metrics are quite different: one of the highest scoring submissions according to the F_1-BAD score is only the third under the sequence correlation metric, and vice versa: the submissions with the highest sequence correlation feature in 3rd place according to F_1-BAD score. However, the system rankings produced by two metrics are correlated — their Spearman's correlation coefficient between them is 0.65.

*** Formatting Issue - Best Available Paper/Graphic ***

System ID	Sequence Correlation
English-Spanish	
• SAU/KERC-CRF	34.22
• SAU/KERC-SLG-CRF	34.09
• UAlacant/OnLine-SBI-Baseline	33.84
UAlacant/OnLine-SBI	32.81
HDCL/QUETCH	32.13
HDCL/QUETCHPLUS	31.38
DCU-SHEFF/BASE-NGRAM-5000	31.23
UGENT/SCATE-HYBRID	30.15
DCU-SHEFF/BASE-NGRAM-2000	29.94
UGENT/SCATE-MBL	28.43
SHEF2/W2V-BI-2000	27.65
SHEF2/W2V-BI-2000-SIM	27.61
SHEF1/QuEst++-AROW	27.36
RTM-DCU/s5-RTM-GLMd	25.92
SHEF1/QuEst++-PA	25.49
RTM-DCU/s4-RTM-GLMd	24.95
Baseline	0.2044

Table 13: Alternative results for the WMT15 quality estimation Task 2 according to the sequence correlation metric. The winning submissions are indicated by a •. These are the top-scoring submission and those that are not significantly worse according to approximate randomization tests with 95% confidence intervals. Submissions whose results are statistically different from others according to the same test are grouped by a horizontal line.

The sequence correlation metric gives preference to systems that use sequence labelling (modelling dependencies between the assigned tags). We consider this a desirable feature, as we are generally not interested in maximising the prediction accuracy for individual words, but in maximising the accuracy for word-level labelling in the context of the whole sentence. However, using the TER alignment to tag errors cannot capture "phrase-level errors", and each token is considered independently when the dataset is built. This is a fundamental issue with the current definition of the word-level quality estimation that we intend to address in future work.

Our intuition is that the sequence correlation metric should be closer to human perception of word-level QE than F_1 scores. The goal of word-level QE is to identify incorrect segments of a sentence — and the sequence correlation metric evaluates how good the segmentation of the sentence is into correct and incorrect phrases. A system can get very high F_1 score by (almost) randomly assigning a correct tag to a word, and giving very little information on correct and incorrect areas in the text. That was illustrated by the WMT14 word-level QE task results, where the baseline strategy that assigned tag "BAD" to all words had significantly higher F_1 score than any of the submissions. fundamental problem with the current task. I added a sentence about it at the end of the paragraph before this one.

4.5 Task 3: Predicting document-level quality

Predicting the quality of units larger than sentences can be useful in many scenarios. For example, consider a user searching for information about a product on the web. The user can only find reviews in German but he/she does not speak the language, so he/she uses an MT system to translate the reviews into English. In this case, predictions on the quality of individual sentences in a translated review are not as informative as predictions on the quality of the entire review.

With the goal of exploring quality estimation beyond sentence level, this year we proposed a document-level task for the first time. Due to the lack of large datasets with machine translated documents (by various MT systems), we consider short paragraphs as *documents*. The task consisted in scoring and ranking paragraphs according to their predicted quality.

Data The paragraphs were extracted from the WMT13 translation task test data (Bojar et al., 2013), using submissions from all participating MT systems. Source paragraphs were randomly chosen using the paragraph markup in the SGML files. For each source paragraph, a translation was taken from a different MT system such as to select approximately the same number of instances from each MT system. We considered EN-DE and DE-EN as language pairs, extracting $1,215$ paragraphs for each language pair. 800 paragraphs were used for training and 415 for test.

Since no human annotation exists for the quality of entire paragraphs (or documents), Meteor against reference translations was used as quality label for this task. Meteor was calculated using its implementation within the Asyia toolkit, with the following settings: exact match, tokenised and case insensitive (Giménez and Màrquez, 2010).

Evaluation The evaluation of the paragraph-level task was the same as that for the sentence-level task. MAE and RMSE are reported as evaluation metrics for the scoring task, with MAE as official metric for systems ranking. For the ranking task, DeltaAvg and Spearman's ρ correlation are reported, with DeltaAvg as official metric for systems ranking. To evaluate the significance of the results, bootstrap resampling (1K times) with 95% confidence intervals was used. Pearson's r correlation scores with the Williams significance test are also reported.

Results Table 14 summarises the results of the ranking variant of Task 3.[21] They are sorted from best to worst using the DeltaAvg metric scores as primary key and the Spearman's ρ rank correlation scores as secondary key. RTM-DCU submissions achieved the best scores: RTM-SVR was the winner for EN-DE, and RTM-FS-SVR for DE-EN. For EN-DE, the HIDDEN system did not show significant difference against the baseline. For DE-EN, USHEF/QUEST-DISC-BO, USAAR-USHEF/BFF and HIDDEN were not significantly different from the baseline.

The results of the scoring variant are given in Table 15, sorted from best to worst by using the MAE metric scores as primary key and the RMSE metric scores as secondary key. Again the RTM-DCU submissions scored the best for both language pairs. All systems were significantly better than the baseline. However, the difference between the baseline system and all submissions was much lower in the scoring evaluation than in the ranking evaluation.

Following the suggestion in (Graham, 2015), Table 16 shows an alternative ranking of systems considering Pearson's r correlation results. The alternative ranking differs from the official ranking in terms of MAE: for EN-DE, RTM-DCU/RTM-FS-SVR is no longer in the winning group, while for DE-EN, USHEF/QUEST-DISC-BO and USAAR-USHEF/BFF did not show statistically significant difference against the baseline. However, as with Task 1 these results are the same as the official ones in terms of DeltaAvg.

4.6 Discussion

In what follows, we discuss the main findings of this year's shared task based on the goals we had previously identified for it.

Advances in sentence- and word-level QE

For sentence-level prediction, we used similar data and quality labels as in previous editions of the task: English-Spanish, news text domain and HTER labels to indicate post-editing effort. The main differences this year were: (i) the much larger size of the dataset, (ii) the way post-editing was performed – by a large number of crowd-sourced translators, and (iii) the MT systems used – an online statistical system. We will discuss items (i) and (ii) later in this section. Regarding (iii), the main implication of using an online system was that one could not have access to many of the resources commonly used to extract features, such as the SMT training data and lexical tables. As a consequence, surrogate resources were used for certain features, including many of the baseline ones, which made them less effective. To avoid relying on such resources, novel features were explored, for example those based on deep neural network architectures (word embeddings and continuous space language models by SHEFF-NN) and those based on pseudo-references (n-gram overlap and agreement features by LORIA).

While it is not possible to compare results directly with those published in previous years, for sentence level we can observe the following with respect to the corresponding task in WMT14 (Task 1.2):

[21] Results for MAE, RMSE and DeltaAvg are multiplied by 100 to improve readability.

*** Formatting Issue - Best Available Paper/Graphic ***

System ID	**DeltaAvg** ↑	Spearman's ρ ↑
English-German		
• RTM-DCU/RTM-SVR	7.62	−0.62
RTM-DCU/RTM-FS-SVR	6.45	−0.67
USHEF/QUEST-DISC-REP	4.55	0.32
USAAR-USHEF/BFF	3.98	0.27
Baseline SVM	1.60	0.14
HIDDEN	1.04	0.05
German-English		
• RTM-DCU/RTM-FS-SVR	4.93	−0.64
RTM-DCU/RTM-FS+PLS-SVR	4.23	−0.55
USHEF/QUEST-DISC-BO	1.55	0.19
Baseline SVM	0.59	0.05
USAAR-USHEF/BFF	0.40	0.12
HIDDEN	0.12	−0.03

Table 14: Official results for the ranking variant of the WMT15 quality estimation Task 3. The winning submissions are indicated by a •. These are the top-scoring submission and those that are not significantly worse according to bootstrap resampling (1K times) with 95% confidence intervals. The systems in the gray area are not different from the baseline system at a statistically significant level according to the same test.

System ID	**MAE** ↓	RMSE ↓
English-German		
• RTM-DCU/RTM-FS-SVR	7.28	11.96
• RTM-DCU/RTM-SVR	7.5	11.35
USAAR-USHEF/BFF	9.37	13.53
USHEF/QUEST-DISC-REP	9.55	13.46
Baseline SVM	10.05	14.25
German-English		
• RTM-DCU/RTM-FS-SVR	4.94	8.74
RTM-DCU/RTM-FS+PLS-SVR	5.78	10.70
USHEF/QUEST-DISC-BO	6.54	10.10
USAAR-USHEF/BFF	6.56	10.12
Baseline SVM	7.35	11.40

Table 15: Official results for the scoring variant of the WMT15 quality estimation Task 3. The winning submissions are indicated by a •. These are the top-scoring submission and those that are not significantly worse according to bootstrap resampling (1K times) with 95% confidence intervals. The systems in the gray area are not different from the baseline system at a statistically significant level according to the same test.

- In terms of scoring, according to the primary metric – MAE, in WMT15 all systems except one were significantly better than the baseline. In both WMT14 and WMT15 only one system was significantly worse than the baseline. However, in WMT14 four others (out of nine) performed no different than the baseline. This year, no system tied with the baseline: the remaining seven systems were significantly better than the baseline. One could say systems are consistently better this year. It is worth mentioning that the baseline remains the same, but as previously noted, the resources used to extract baseline features are likely to be less useful this year given the mismatch between the data used to produce them and the data used to build the online SMT system.

- In terms of ranking, in WMT14 one system was significantly worse than the baseline, and the four remaining systems were significantly better. This year, all eight submissions are significantly better than the baseline. This can once more be seen as progress from last year's results. These results as well as the general ranking of systems were also found following Pearson's correlation as metric, as

*** Formatting Issue - Best Available Paper/Graphic ***

System ID	Pearson's r ↑
English-German	
• RTM-DCU/RTM-SVR	0.59
RTM-DCU/RTM-FS-SVR	0.53
USHEF/QUEST-DISC-REP	0.30
USAAR-USHEF/BFF	0.29
Baseline SVM	0.12
German-English	
• RTM-DCU/RTM-FS-SVR	0.52
RTM-DCU/RTM-FS+PLS-SVR	0.39
USHEF/QUEST-DISC-BO	0.10
USAAR-USHEF/BFF	0.08
Baseline SVM	0.06

Table 16: Alternative results for the scoring variant of the WMT15 quality estimation Task 3. The winning submissions are indicated by a •. These are the top-scoring submission and those that are not significantly worse according to the Williams test with 95% confidence intervals. The systems in the gray area are not different from the baseline system at a statistically significant level according to the same test.

suggested by Graham (2015).

For the word level task, a comparison with the WMT14 corresponding task is difficult to perform, as in WMT14 we did not have a meaningful baseline. The baseline used then for binary classification was to tag all words with the label "BAD". This baseline outperformed all the submissions in terms of F_1 for the "BAD" class, but it cannot be considered an appropriate baseline strategy (see Section 4.4). This year the submissions were compared against the output of a real baseline system and the set of baseline features was made available to participants. Although the baseline system itself performed worse than all the submitted systems, some other systems benefited from adding baseline features to their feature sets (UAlacant, UGENT, HDCL).

Considering the feature sets and methods used, the number of participants in the WMT14 word-level task was too small to draw reliable conclusion: four systems for English–Spanish and one system for all other three language pairs. The larger number of submissions this year is already a positive result: 16 submissions from eight teams. Inspecting the systems submitted this and last year, we can speculate about the most promising techniques. Last year's winning system used a neural network trained on pseudo-reference features (namely, features extracted from n-best lists) (Camargo de Souza et al., 2014). This year's winning systems are also based on pseudo-reference features (UAlacant) and deep neural network architectures (HDCL). Luong et al. (2013) had previously reported that pseudo-reference features improve the accuracy of word-level predictions. The two most recent editions of this shared task seem to indicate that the state of the art in word-level quality estimation relies upon such features, as well as the ability to model the relationship between the source and target languages using large datasets.

Effectiveness of quality labels, features and learning methods for document-level QE

The task of paragraph-level prediction received fewer submissions than the other two tasks: four submissions for the scoring variant and five for the ranking variant, for both language pairs. This is understandable as it was the first time the task was run. Additionally, paragraph-level QE is still fairly new as a task. However, we were able to draw some conclusions and learn valuable lessons for future research in the area.

By and large, most features are similar to those used for sentence-level prediction. Discourse-aware features showed only marginal improvements relative to the baseline system (USHEF systems for EN-DE and DE-EN). One possible reason for that is the way the training and test data sets were created, including paragraphs with only one sentence. Therefore, discourse features could not be fully explored as they aim to model relationships and dependencies across sentences, as well as within sentences. In future, data will be selected more carefully in order to consider only paragraphs or documents with more sentences.

*** Formatting Issue - Best Available Paper/Graphic ***

	EN-DE		DE-EN	
	AVG	STDEV	AVG	STDEV
Meteor (↑)	0.35	0.14	0.26	0.09

Table 17: Average metric scores for automatic metrics in the corpus for Task 3.

Systems applying feature selection techniques, such as USAAR-USHEF/BFF, did not obtain major improvements over the baseline. However, they provided interesting insights by finding a minimum set of baseline features that can be used to build models with the same performance as the entire baseline feature set. These are models with only three features selected as the best combination by exhaustive search.

The winning submissions for both language pairs and variants – RTM-DCU – explored features based on the source and target side information. These include distributional similarity, closeness of test instances to the training data, and indicators for translation quality. External data was used to select "interpretants", which contain data close to both training and test sets to provide context for similarity judgements.

In terms of quality labels, one problem observed in previous work on document-level QE (Scarton et al., 2015b) is the low variation of scores (in this case, Meteor) across instances of the dataset. Since the data collected for this task included translations from many different MT systems, this was not the case. Table 17 shows the average and standard deviation (STDEV) values for the datasets (both training and test set together). Although the variation is substantial, the average value of the training set is a good predictor. In other words, if we consider the average of the training set scores as the prediction value for all data points in the test set, we obtain results as good as the baseline system. For our datasets, the MAE figure for EN-DE is 10, and for DE-EN 7 – the same as the baseline system. We can only speculate that automatically assigned quality labels based on reference translations such as Meteor are not adequate for this task. Other automatic metrics tend to behave similarly to Meteor for document-level (Scarton et al., 2015b). Therefore, finding an adequate quality label for document-level QE remains an open issue. Having humans directly assign quality labels is much more complex than in the sentence and word level cases. Annotation of entire documents, or even paragraphs, becomes a harder, more subjective and much more costly task. For future editions of this task, we intend to collect datasets with human-targeted document-level labels obtained indirectly, e.g. through post-editing.

No submission focused on exploring learning algorithms specifically targeted at document-level prediction.

Differences between sentence-level and document-level QE

The differences between sentence and document-level prediction have not been explored to a great extent. Apart from the discourse-aware features by USHEF, the baseline and other features explored by participating teams for document level prediction were simple aggregations of sentence level feature values.

Also, none of the submitted systems use sentence-level predictions as features for paragraph-level QE. Although this technique is possible in principle, its effectiveness has not yet been proved. (Specia et al., 2015) report promising results when using word-level prediction for sentence-level QE, but inclusive results when using sentence-level prediction for document-level QE. They considered BLEU, TER and Meteor as quality labels, all leading to similar findings. Once more the use of inadequate quality labels for document-level prediction could have been the reason.

No submission evaluated different machine learning algorithms for this task. The same algorithms as those used for sentence-level prediction were applied by all participating teams.

Effect of training data sizes and quality for sentence and word-level QE

As it was previously mentioned, the post-editions used for this year's sentence and word-level tasks were obtained through a crowdsourcing platform where translators volunteered to post-edit machine translations. As such, one can expect that not all post-editions will reach the highest standards of professional translation. Manual inspection of a small sample of the data, however, showed that the post-editions were high quality, although stylistic differences are evident in some cases. This is likely due to the fact that different editors, with different styles and levels of expertise, worked on different segments. Another factor that may have influenced the quality of the post-editions is the fact that segments were fixed out of context. For word level, in particular, a potential issue is the fact that the labelling of the words was done completely automatically, using a tool for alignment based on minimum edit distance (TER).

On the positive side, this dataset is much larger dataset than any we have used before for prediction at any level: nearly 12K segments for training/development, as opposed to maximum 2K in previous years. For sentence-level prediction we did not expect massive gains from larger datasets, as it has been shown that small amounts of data can be as effective or even more effective than the entire collection, if selected in a clever way (Beck et al., 2013a,b). However, it is well known that data sparsity is an issue for word-level prediction, so we expected a large dataset to improve results considerably for this task.

Unfortunately, having access to a large number of samples did not seem to bring much improvement for word-level predictions accuracy. The main reason for that was the fact that the number of erroneous words in the training data was too small, as compared to the number of correct words: 50% of the sentences had zero incorrect words (15% of the sentences) or fewer than 15% incorrect words (35% of the sentences). Participants used various data manipulation strategies to improve results: filtering of the training data, as in DCU-SHEFF systems, alternative labelling of the data which discriminates between "OK" label in the beginning, middle, and end of a good segment, and insertion of additional incorrect words, as in SAU-KERC submissions. Additionally, most participants in the word-level task leveraged additional data in some way, which points to the need for even larger but more varied post-edited datasets in order to make significant progress in this task.

5 Automatic Post-editing Task

This year WMT hosted for the first time a shared task on automatic post-editing (APE) for machine translation. The task requires to automatically correct the errors present in a machine translated text. As pointed out in Parton et al. (2012) and Chatterjee et al. (2015b), from the application point of view, APE components would make it possible to:

- Improve MT output by exploiting information unavailable to the decoder, or by performing deeper text analysis that is too expensive at the decoding stage;
- Cope with systematic errors of an MT system whose decoding process is not accessible;
- Provide professional translators with improved MT output quality to reduce (human) post-editing effort;
- Adapt the output of a general-purpose MT system to the lexicon/style requested in a specific application domain.

The first pilot round of the APE task focused on the challenges posed by the "black-box" scenario in which the MT system is unknown and cannot be modified. In this scenario, APE methods have to operate at the downstream level (that is *after* MT decoding), by applying either rule-based techniques or statistical approaches that exploit knowledge acquired from human post-editions provided as training material. The objectives of this pilot were to: *i)* define a sound evaluation framework for the task, *ii)* identify and understand the most critical aspects in terms of data acquisition and system evaluation, *iii)* make an inventory of current approaches and evaluate the state of the art and *iv)* provide a milestone for future studies on the problem.

5.1 Task description

Participants were provided with training and development data consisting of (*source*, *target*, *human post-edition*) triplets, and were asked to return automatic post-editions for a test set of unseen (*source*, *target*) pairs.

Data

Training, development and test data were created by randomly sampling from a collection of English-Spanish (*source*, *target*, *human post-edition*) triplets drawn from the news domain.[22] Instances were sampled after applying a series of data cleaning steps aimed at removing duplicates and those triplets in which any of the elements (source, target, post-edition) was either too long or too short compared to the others, or included tags or special problematic symbols. The main reason for random sampling was to induce some homogeneity across the three datasets and, in turn,

[22] The original triplets were provided by Unbabel (https://unbabel.com/).

to increase the chances that correction patterns learned from the training set can be applied also to the test set. The downside of losing information yielded by text coherence (an aspect that some APE systems might take into consideration) has hence been accepted in exchange for a higher error repetitiveness across the three datasets. Table 18 provides some basic statistics about the data.

The training and development sets respectively consist of $11,272$ and $1,000$ instances. In each instance:

- The source (SRC) is a tokenized English sentence having a length of at least 4 tokens. This constraint on the source length was posed in order to increase the chances to work with grammatically correct full sentences instead of phrases or short keyword lists;
- The target (TGT) is a tokenized Spanish translation of the source, produced by an unknown MT system;
- The human post-edition (PE) is a manually-revised version of the target. PEs were collected by means of a crowdsourcing platform developed by the data provider.

Test data ($1,817$ instances) consists of (*source*, *target*) pairs having similar characteristics of those in the training set. Human post-editions of the test target instances were left apart to measure system performance.

The data creation procedure adopted, as well as the origin and the domain of the texts pose specific challenges to the participating systems. As discussed in Section 5.4, the results of this pilot task can be partially explained in light of such challenges. This dataset, however, has three major advantages that made it suitable for the first APE pilot: *i)* it is relatively large (hence suitable to apply statistical methods), *ii)* it was not previously published (hence usable for a fair evaluation), *iii)* it is freely available (hence easy to distribute and use for evaluation purposes).

Evaluation metric

System performance is evaluated by computing the distance between *automatic* and *human* post-editions of the machine-translated sentences present in the test set (*i.e.* for each of the *1,817* target test sentences). This distance is measured in terms of Translation Error Rate (TER) (Snover et al., 2006a), an evaluation metric commonly used in MT-related tasks (*e.g.* in quality estimation) to measure the minimum edit distance between an automatic translation and a reference translation.[23] Systems are ranked based on the average TER calculated on the test set by using the TERcom[24] software: lower average TER scores correspond to higher ranks. Each run is evaluated in two modes, namely: *i)* case insensitive and *ii)* case sensitive. Evaluation scripts to compute TER scores in both modalities have been made available to participants through the APE task web page.[25]

Baseline

The official baseline is calculated by averaging the distances computed between the raw MT output and the human post-edits. In practice, the baseline APE system is a system that leaves all the test targets unmodified.[26] Baseline results computed for both evaluation modalities (case sensitive/insensitive) are reported in Tables 20 and 21.

Monolingual translation as another term of comparison. To get further insights about the progress with respect to previous APE methods, participants' results are also analysed with respect to another term of comparison: a re-implementation of the state-of-the-art approach firstly proposed by Simard et al. (2007).[27] For this purpose, a phrase-based SMT system based on Moses (Koehn et al., 2007) is used. Translation and reordering models were estimated following the Moses protocol with default setup using MGIZA++ (Gao and Vogel, 2008) for word alignment. For language modeling we used the

[23] Edit distance is calculated as the number of edits (word insertions, deletions, substitutions, and shifts) divided by the number of words in the reference. Lower TER values indicate better MT quality.

[24] `http://www.cs.umd.edu/~snover/tercom/`

[25] `http://www.statmt.org/wmt15/ape-task.html`

[26] In this case, since edit distance is computed between each machine-translated sentence and its human-revised version, the actual evaluation metric is the human-targeted TER (HTER). For the sake of clarity, since TER and HTER compute edit distance in the same way (the only difference is in the origin of correct sentence used for comparison), henceforth we will use TER to refer to both metrics.

[27] This is done based on the description provided in Simard et al. (2007). Our re-implementation, however, is not meant to officially represent such approach. Discrepancies with the actual method are indeed possible due to our misinterpretation or to wrong guesses about details that are missing in the paper.

*** Formatting Issue - Best Available Paper/Graphic ***

	Tokens			Types			Lemmas		
	SRC	TGT	PE	SRC	TGT	PE	SRC	TGT	PE
Train (11,272)	238,335	257,643	257,879	23,608	25,121	27,101	13,701	7,624	7,689
Dev (1,000)	21,617	23,213	23,098	5,482	5,760	5,966	3,765	2,810	2,819
Test (1,817)	38,244	40,925	40,903	7,990	8,498	8,816	5,307	3,778	3,814

Table 18: Data statistics.

KenLM toolkit (Heafield, 2011) for standard n-gram modeling with an n-gram length of 5. Finally, the APE system was tuned on the development set, optimizing TER with Minimum Error Rate Training (Och, 2003). The results of this additional term of comparison, computed for both evaluation modalities (case sensitive/insensitive), are also reported in Tables 20 and 21.

For each submitted run, the statistical significance of performance differences with respect to the baseline and the re-implementation of Simard et al. (2007) is calculated with the bootstrap test (Koehn, 2004).

5.2 Participants

Four teams participated in the APE pilot task by submitting a total of seven runs. Participants are listed in Table 19; a short description of their systems is provided in the following.

Abu-MaTran. The Abu-MaTran team submitted the output of two statistical post-editing (SPE) systems, both relying on the MOSES phrase-based statistical machine translation toolkit (Koehn et al., 2007) and on sentence level classifiers. The first element of the pipeline, the SPE system, is trained on the automatic translation of the News Commentary v8 corpus from English to Spanish aligned with its reference. This translation is obtained with an out-of-the-box phrase-based SMT system trained on Europarl v7. Both translation and post-editing systems use a 5-gram Spanish LM with modified Kneser-Ney smoothed trained on News Crawl 2011 and 2012 with KenLM (Heafield, 2011). For the second element of the pipeline, a binary classifier to select the best translation between the given MT output or its automatic post-edition is used. Two different approaches are investigated: a 180-hand-crafted-based regression model trained with a Support Vector Machine (SVM) with a radial basis function kernel to estimate the sentence-level HTER score, and a Recurrent Neural Network (RNN) classifier using context word embeddings as input and classifying each word of a sentence as *good* or *bad*. An automatic translation to be post-edited is first decoded by our SPE system, then fed into one of the classifiers identified as SVM180feat and RNN. The HTER estimator selects the translation with the lower score while the binary word-level classifier selects the translation with the fewer amount of *bad* tags. The official evaluation of the shared task show an advantage of the RNN approach compared to SVM.

FBK. The two runs submitted by FBK (Chatterjee et al., 2015a) are based on combining the statistical phrase-based post-editing approach proposed by Simard et al. (2007) and its most significant variant proposed by Béchara et al. (2011). The APE systems are built-in an incremental manner. At each stage of the APE pipeline, the best configuration of a component is decided and then used in the next stage. The APE pipeline begins with the selection of the best language model from several language models trained on different types and quantities of data. The next stage addresses the possible data sparsity issues raised by the relatively small size of the training data. Indeed, an analysis of the original phrase table obtained from the training set revealed that a large part of its entries is composed of instances that occur only once in the training. This has the obvious effect of collecting potentially unreliable "translation" (or, in the case of APE, *correction*) rules. The problem is exacerbated by the "context-aware" approach proposed by Béchara et al. (2011), which builds the phrase table by joining source and target tokens thus breaking down the co-occurrence counts into smaller numbers. To cope with this problem, a novel feature (*neg-impact*) is designed to prune the phrase table by measuring the usefulness of each translation. The higher is the value of the *neg-impact* feature, the less useful is the translation option. After pruning, the final stage of the APE pipeline tries to raise the capability of the decoder to select the correct translation rule by the introduction of new task specific features integrated in

*** Formatting Issue - Best Available Paper/Graphic ***

ID	Participating team
Abu-MaTran	Abu-MaTran Project (Prompsit)
FBK	Fondazione Bruno Kessler, Italy (Chatterjee et al., 2015a)
LIMSI	Laboratoire d'Informatique pour la Mécanique et les Sciences de l'Ingénieur, France (Wisniewski et al., 2015)
USAAR-SAPE	Saarland University, Germany & Jadavpur University, India (Pal et al., 2015b)

Table 19: Participants in the WMT15 Automatic Post-editing pilot task.

the model. These features measure the similarity and the reliability of the translation options and help to improve the precision of the resulting APE system.

LIMSI. For the first edition of the APE shared task LIMSI submitted two systems (Wisniewski et al., 2015). The first one is based on the approach of Simard et al. (2007) and considers the APE task as a monolingual translation between a translation hypothesis and its post-edition. This straightforward approach does not succeed in improving translation quality. The second submitted system implements a series of sieves, each applying a simple post-editing rule. The definition of these rules is based on an analysis of the most frequent error corrections and aims at: *i*) predicting word case; *ii*) predicting exclamation and interrogation marks; and *iii*) predicting verbal endings. Experiments with this approach show that this system also hurts translation quality. An in-depth analysis revealed that this negative result is mainly explained by two reasons: *i*) most of the post-edition operations are nearly unique, which makes very difficult to generalize from a small amount of data; and *ii*) even when they are not, the high variability of post-editing, already pointed out by Wisniewski et al. (2013), results in predicting legitimate corrections that have not been made by the annotators, therefore preventing from improving over the baseline.

USAAR-SAPE. The USAAR-SAPE system (Pal et al., 2015b) is designed with three basic components: corpus preprocessing, hybrid word alignment and a state-of-the-art phrase-based SMT system integrated with the hybrid word alignment. The preprocessing of the training corpus is carried out by stemming the Spanish MT output and the PE data using Freeling (Padr and Stanilovsky, 2012). The hybrid word alignment method combines different kinds of word alignment: GIZA++ word alignment with the grow-diag-final-and (GDFA) heuristic (Koehn, 2010), SymGiza++ (Junczys-Dowmunt and Szal, 2011), the Berkeley aligner (Liang et al., 2006), and the edit distance-based aligners (Snover et al., 2006a; Lavie and Agarwal, 2007). These different word alignment tables (Pal et al., 2013) are combined by a mathematical union method. For the phrase-based SMT system various maximum phrase lengths for the translation model and n–gram settings for the language model are used. The best results in terms of BLEU (Papineni et al., 2002) score are achieved by a maximum phrase length of 7 for the translation model and a 5-gram language model.

5.3 Results

The official results achieved by the participating systems are reported in Tables 20 and 21. The seven runs submitted are sorted based on the average TER they achieve on test data. Table 20 shows the results computed in case sensitive mode, while Table 21 provides scores computed in the case insensitive mode.

Both rankings reveal an unexpected outcome: none of the submitted runs was able to beat the baselines (*i.e.* average TER scores of 22.91 and 22.22 respectively for case sensitive and case insensitive modes). All differences with respect to such baselines, moreover, are statistically significant. In practice, this means that what the systems learned from the available data was not reliable enough to yield valid corrections of the test instances. A deeper discussion about the possible causes of this unexpected outcome is provided in Section 5.4.

Unsurprisingly, for all participants the case insensitive evaluation results are slightly better than the case sensitive ones. Although the two rankings are not identical, none of the systems was particularly penalized by the case sensitive evaluation. Indeed, individual differences in the two modes are always close to the same value ($\sim$ 0.7 TER difference) measured for the two baselines.

*** Formatting Issue - Best Available Paper/Graphic ***

ID	Avg. TER
Baseline	22.913
FBK Primary	23.228
LIMSI Primary	23.331
USAAR-SAPE	23.426
LIMSI Contrastive	23.573
Abu-MaTran Primary	23.639
FBK Contrastive	23.649
(Simard et al., 2007)	23.839
Abu-MaTran Contrastive	24.715

Table 20: Official results for the WMT15 Automatic Post-editing task – average TER (↓) case sensitive.

ID	Avg. TER
Baseline	22.221
LIMSI Primary	22.544
FBK Primary	22.551
USAAR-SAPE	22.710
Abu-MaTran Primary	22.769
LIMSI Contrastive	22.861
FBK Contrastive	22.949
(Simard et al., 2007)	23.130
Abu-MaTran Contrastive	23.705

Table 21: Official results for the WMT15 Automatic Post-editing task – average TER (↓) case insensitive.

In light of this, and considering the importance of case sensitive evaluation in some language settings (*e.g.* having German as target), future rounds of the task will likely prioritize this more strict evaluation mode.

Overall, the close results achieved by participants reflect the fact that, despite some small variations, all systems share the same underlying statistical approach of Simard et al. (2007). As anticipated in Section 5.1, in order to get a rough idea about the extent of the improvements over such state-of-the-art method, we replicated it and considered its results as another term of comparison in addition to the baselines. As shown in Tables 20 and 21, the performance results achieved by our implementation of Simard et al. (2007) are 23.839 and 23.130 in terms of TER for the respective case sensitive and insensitive evaluations. Compared to these scores, most of the submitted runs achieve better performance, with positive average TER differences that are always statistically significant. We interpret this as a good sign: despite the difficulty of the task, the novelties introduced by each system allowed to make significant steps forward with respect to a prior reference technique.

5.4 Discussion

To better understand the results and gain useful insights about this pilot evaluation round, we perform two types of analysis. The first one is focused on the **data**, and aims to understand the possible reasons of the difficulty of the task. In particular, by analysing the challenges posed by the *origin* and the *domain* of the text material used, we try to find indications for future rounds of the APE task. The second type of analysis focuses on the **systems** and their behaviour. Although they share the same underlying approach and achieve similar results, we aim to check if interesting differences can be captured by a more fine grained analysis that goes beyond rough TER measurements.

Data analysis

In this section we investigate the possible relation between participants' results and the nature of the data used in this pilot task (*e.g.* quantity, sparsity, domain and origin) . For this purpose, we take advantage of a new dataset – the Autodesk Post-Editing Data corpus[28] – which has been publicly released after the organisation of the APE pilot task. Although it was not usable for this first round, its characteristics make it particularly suitable for our analysis purposes. In particular: *i)* Autodesk data predominantly covers the domain of `software user manuals` (that is, a restricted domain compared to a general one like `news`), and *ii)* post-edits come from professional translators (that is, at least in principle, a more reliable source of corrections compared to crowdsourced workforce). To guarantee a fair comparison, English-Spanish (*source, target, human post-edition*) triplets drawn from the Autodesk corpus are split in training, development and test sets under the constraint that the total number of target words and the TER in each set should be similar to the APE task splits. In this setting, performance differences between systems trained on the two datasets will only depend on the different nature of the data (*e.g.* domain). Statistics of the training sets are reported in Table 22 (those concerning the

[28]The corpus (`https://autodesk.app.box.com/Autodesk-PostEditing`) consists of parallel English source-MT/TM target segments post-edited into several languages (Chinese, Czech, French, German, Hungarian, Italian, Japanese, Korean, Polish, Brazilian Portuguese, Russian, *Spanish*) with between 30K to 410K segments per language.

*** Formatting Issue - Best Available Paper/Graphic ***

		APE Task	Autodesk
Tokens	SRC	238,335	220,671
	TGT	257,643	257.380
	PE	257,879	260,324
Types	SRC	23,608	11,858
	TGT	25,121	11,721
	PE	27,101	12,399
Lemmas	SRC	13,701	5,092
	TGT	7,624	3,186
	PE	7,689	3,334
RR	SRC	2.905	6.346
	TGT	3.312	8.390
	PE	3.085	8.482

Table 22: WMT APe Task and Autodesk training data statistics.

APE task data are the same of Table 18).

The impact of data sparsity. A key issue in most evaluation settings is the representativeness of the training data with respect to the test set used. In the case of the statistical approach at the core of all the APE task submissions, this issue is even more relevant given the limited amount of training data available. In the APE scenario, data representativeness relates to the fact that the correction patterns learned from the training set can be applied also to the test set (as mentioned in Section 5.1, in the data creation phase random sampling from an original data collection was applied for this purpose). From this point of view, dealing with restricted domains such as `software user manuals` should be easier than working with `news` data. Indeed, restricted domains are more likely to feature smaller vocabularies, be more repetitive (or, in other terms, less sparse) and, in turn, determine a higher applicability of the learned error correction patterns.

To check the relation between task difficulty and data repetitiveness, we compared different monolingual indicators (*i.e.* number of types and lemmas, and repetition rate[29] – RR) computed on the APE and the Autodesk source, target and post-edited sentences. Although both the datasets have the same amount of target tokens, Table 22 shows that the APE training set has nearly double of types and lemmas compared to the Autodesk data, which indicates the presence of less repeated information. A similar conclusion can be drawn by observing that the Autodesk dataset has a repetition rate that is more than twice the value computed for the APE task data.

This monolingual analysis does not provide any information about the level of repetitiveness of the correction patterns made by the post-editors, because it does not link the target and the post-edited sentences. To investigate this aspect, two instances of the re-implemented approach of Simard et al. (2007) introduced in Section 5.1 are respectively trained on the APE and the Autodesk training sets. We consider the distribution of the frequency of the translation options in the phrase table as a good indicator of the level of repetitiveness of the corrections in the data. For instance, a large number of translation options that appear just one or only few times in the data indicates a higher level of sparseness. As expected due to the limited size of the training set, the vast majority of the translation options in both phrase tables are singletons as shown in Table 23. Nevertheless, the Autodesk phrase table is more compact (731k versus 1,066k) and contains 10% fewer singletons than the APE task phrase table. This confirms that the APE task data is more sparse and suggests that it might be easier to learn more applicable correction patterns from the Autodesk domain-specific data.

To verify this last statement, the two APE systems are evaluated on their own test sets. As previously shown, the system trained on the APE task data is not able to improve over the performance achieved by a system that leaves all the test targets unmodified (see Table 20). On the contrary, starting from a baseline of 23.57, the system trained on the Autodesk data is able to reduce the TER by 3.55 points (20.02). Interestingly, the Autodesk APE system is able to correctly fix the target sentences and improve the TER by 1.43 points even with only 25% of the training data. These results confirm our intuitions about the usefulness of repetitive data and show that, at least in restricted-domain scenarios, automatic post-editing can be successfully used as an aid to improve the output of an MT system.

Professional vs. Crowdsourced post-editions Differently from the Autodesk data, for which the post-editions are created by professional translators, the APE task data contains crowdsourced MT corrections collected from unknown (likely non-

[29] Repetition rate measures the repetitiveness inside a text by looking at the rate of non-singleton n-gram types (n=1. . .4) and combining them using the geometric mean. Larger value means more repetitions in the text. For more details see Cettolo et al. (2014)

*** Formatting Issue - Best Available Paper/Graphic ***

Phrase Pair Count	Percentage of Phrase Pairs APE 2015 Training	Autodesk
1	95.2%	84.6%
2	2.5%	8.8%
3	0.7%	2.7%
4	0.3%	1.2%
5	0.2%	0.6%
6	0.15%	0.4%
7	0.10%	0.3%
8	0.07%	0.2%
9	0.06%	0.2%
10	0.04%	0.1%
> 10	0.3%	0.9%
Total Entries	1,066,344	703,944

Table 23: Phrase pair count distribution in two phrase tables built using the APE 2015 training and the Autodesk dataset.

expert) translators. One risk, given the high variability of valid MT corrections, is that the crowdsourced workforce follows post-editing attitudes and criteria that differ from those of professional translators. Professionals tend to: *i)* maximize productivity by doing only the necessary and sufficient corrections to improve translation quality, and *ii)* follow consistent translation criteria, especially for domain terminology. Such a tendency will likely result in coherent and minimally post-edited data from which learning and drawing statistics is easier. This is not guaranteed by crowdsourced workers which do not have specific time or consistency constraints. This suggests that non-professional post-editions and the correction patterns learned from them will feature less coherence, higher noise and higher sparsity.

To assess the potential impact of these issues on data representativeness (and, in turn, on the task difficulty), we analyse a subset of the APE test instances (221 triples randomly sampled) in which target sentences were post-edited by professional translators. The analysis focuses on TER scores computed between:

1. The target sentences and their crowdsourced post-editions (avg. TER = 26.02);

2. The target sentences and their professional post-editions (avg. TER = 23.85);

3. The crowdsourced post-editions and the professional ones, using the latter as references (avg. TER = 29.18).

The measured values indicate an attitude of non-professionals to correct *more often* and *differently* from the professional translators. Interestingly, and similar to the findings of Potet et al. (2012), crowdsourced post-editions feature a distance from the professional ones that is even higher than the distance between the original target sentences and the experts' corrections (29.18 vs. 23.85). If we consider the output of professional translators as a gold standard (made of coherent and minimally post-edited data), these figures suggest a higher difficulty in handling crowdsourced corrections.

Further insights can be drawn from the analysis of the word level corrections produced by the two translator profiles. To this aim, word insertions, deletions, substitutions and phrase shifts are extracted using the TERcom software similar to Blain et al. (2012) and Wisniewski et al. (2013). For each error type, the ratio between the number of edit operations and the total number of occurred errors operations performed is computed. This quantity provides us with a measure of the level of repetitiveness of the errors, with 100% indicating that all the error patterns are unique, and small values indicating that most of the errors are repeated. Our results show that non-experts have generally larger ratio values than the professional translators (insertion +6%, substitution +4%, deletion +4%). This seems to support our hypothesis that, independently from their quality, post-editions collected from non-experts are less coherent than those derived from professionals. It is unlikely that different crowdsourced workers will apply the same corrections in the same contexts. If this hypothesis holds, the difficulty of this APE pilot task could be partially ascribed to this unavoidable intrinsic property of crowdsourced data. This aspect, however, should be further investigated to draw definite conclusions.

System/performance analysis

The TER results presented in Tables 20 and 21 evidence small differences between participants, but they do not shed light on the real behaviour of the systems. To this aim, in this section the submitted runs are analysed by taking into consideration the changes made by each system to the test instances (case sensitive evaluation mode). In particular, Table 24 provides the number of modified, improved and deteriorated sentences, together with the percentage of edit operations performed (insertions,

*** Formatting Issue - Best Available Paper/Graphic ***

ID	Modified Sentences	Improved Sentences	Deteriorated Sentences	Edit operations Ins	Del	Sub	Shifts
FBK Primary	276	64	147	17.8	17.8	55.9	8.5
LIMSI Primary	339	75	217	19.4	16.8	55.2	8.6
USAAR-SAPE	422	53	229	17.6	17.4	56.7	8.4
LIMSI Contrastive	454	61	260	17.4	19.0	55.3	8.3
Abu-MaTran Primary	275	8	200	17.7	17.2	56.8	8.2
FBK Contrastive	422	52	254	18.4	17.0	56.2	8.4
Abu-MaTran Contrastive	602	14	451	17.8	16.4	57.7	8.0
(Simard et al., 2007)	488	55	298	18.3	17.0	56.4	8.3

Table 24: Number of test sentences modified, improved and deteriorated by each submitted run, together with the corresponding percentage of insertions, deletions, substitutions and shifts (case sensitive).

deletions, substitutions, shifts). Looking at these numbers, the following conclusions can be drawn. Although it varies considerably between the submitted runs, the number of modified sentences is quite small. Moreover, a general trend can be observed: the best systems are the most conservative ones. This situation likely reflects the aforementioned data sparsity and coherence issues. A small fraction of the correction patterns found in the training set seems to be applicable also to the test set, and the risk of performing corrections that are either wrong, redundant, or different from those in the reference post-editions is rather high.

From the system point of view, the context in which a learned correction pattern will be applied is crucial. For instance, the same word substitution (*e.g.* "*house*" → "*home*") is not applicable in all contexts. While sometimes it will be necessary (Example 1: "*The house team won the match*"), in some contexts it is optional (Example 2: "*I was in my house*") or wrong (Example 3: "*He worked for a brokerage house*"). Unfortunately, the unnecessary word replacement in Example 2 (human post-editors would likely leave it untouched) would increase the TER of the sentence exactly as in the clearly wrong replacement in Example 3.

From the evaluation point of view, not penalising such correct but unnecessary corrections is also crucial. Similar to MT, where a source sentence can have many valid translations, in the APE task a target sentence can have many valid post-editions. Indeed, nothing prevents that in our evaluation some correct post-editions are considered as "deteriorated" sentences simply because they differ from the human post-editions used as references. As in MT, this well known variability problem might penalise good systems, thus calling for alternative evaluation criteria (*e.g.* based on multiple references or sensitive to paraphrase matches). Interestingly, for all the systems the number of modified sentences is higher than the sum of the improved and the deteriorated ones. Such difference is represented by modified sentences for which the corrections do not yield TER variations. This grey area makes the evaluation problem related to variability even more evident.

The analysis of the edit operations performed by each system is not particularly informative. Similar to the overall performance results, also the proportion of correction types they perform reflects the adoption of the same underlying statistical approach. The distribution of the four types of edit operations is almost identical, with a predominance lexical substitutions (55.7%-57.7%) and rather few phrasal shifts (8.0%-8.6%).

5.5 Lessons learned and outlook

The objectives of this pilot APE task were to: *i)* define a sound evaluation framework for future rounds, *ii)* identify and understand the most critical aspects in terms of data acquisition and system evaluation, *iii)* make an inventory of current approaches, evaluate the state of the art and *iv)* provide a milestone for future studies on the problem. With respect to the first point, improving the evaluation is possible, but no major issues emerged or requested radical changes in future evaluation rounds. For instance, using multiple references or a metric sensitive to paraphrase matches to cope with variability in the post-editing would certainly help.

Concerning the most critical aspects of the evaluation, our analysis highlighted the strong dependence of system results on data repetitiveness/representativeness. This calls into question the actual usability of text material coming from general domains like news and, probably, of post-editions collected from crowdsourced workers (this aspect, however, should be further investigated to draw definite conclusions). Nevertheless, it's worth noting that collecting a large, unpublished, public, domain-specific and professional-quality dataset is a hardly achievable goal that will always require compromise solutions.

Regarding the approaches proposed, this first experience was a conservative but, at the same time, promising first step. Although participants performed the task sharing the same statistical approach to APE, the slight variants they explored allowed them to outperform the widely used monolingual translation technique. Moreover, results' analysis also suggests a possible limitation of this state-of-the-art approach: by always performing all the applicable correction patterns, it runs the risk of deteriorating the input translations that it was supposed to improve. This limitation, common to all the participating systems, is a clue of a major difference between the APE task and the MT framework. In MT the system must always process the entire source sentence by translating all of its words into the target language. In the APE scenario, instead, the system has another option for each word: keeping it untouched. A reasonable (and this year unbeaten) baseline is in fact a system that applies this conservative strategy for all the words. By raising this and other issues as promising research directions, attracting researchers' attention to a challenging application-oriented task, and establishing a sound evaluation framework to measure future advancements, this pilot has substantially achieved its goals, paving the way for future rounds of the APE evaluation exercise.

Acknowledgments

This work was supported in parts by the MosesCore, QT21, EXPERT and CRACKER projects funded by the European Commission (7th Framework Programme and H2020).

We would also like to thank Unbabel for providing the data used in the QE Tasks 1 and 2, and in the APE task.

References

Avramidis, E., Popović, M., and Burchardt, A. (2015). DFKI's experimental hybrid MT system for WMT 2015. In *Proceedings of the Tenth Workshop on Statistical Machine Translation*, pages 66–73, Lisboa, Portugal. Association for Computational Linguistics.

Banerjee, S. and Lavie, A. (2005). METEOR: An Automatic Metric for MT Evaluation with Improved Correlation with Human Judgments. In *Proceedings of the ACL 2005 Workshop on Intrinsic and Extrinsic Evaluation Measures for MT and/or Summarization.*

Béchara, H., Ma, Y., and van Genabith, J. (2011). Statistical Post-Editing for a Statistical MT System. In *Proceedings of the 13th Machine Translation Summit*, pages 308–315, Xiamen, China.

Beck, D., Shah, K., Cohn, T., and Specia, L. (2013a). SHEF-Lite: When less is more for translation quality estimation. In *Proceedings of the Eighth Workshop on Statistical Machine Translation*, pages 335–340, Sofia, Bulgaria. Association for Computational Linguistics.

Beck, D., Specia, L., and Cohn, T. (2013b). Reducing annotation effort for quality estimation via active learning. In *51st Annual Meeting of the Association for Computational Linguistics: Short Papers*, ACL, pages 543–548, Sofia, Bulgaria.

Biçici, E. (2013). Referential translation machines for quality estimation. In *Proceedings of the Eighth Workshop on Statistical Machine Translation*, Sofia, Bulgaria.

Biçici, E. and Way, A. (2014). Referential Translation Machines for Predicting Translation Quality. In *Ninth Workshop on Statistical Machine Translation*, pages 313–321, Baltimore, Maryland, USA.

Bicici, E., Liu, Q., and Way, A. (2015). Referential Translation Machines for Predicting Translation Quality and Related Statistics. In *Proceedings of the Tenth Workshop on Statistical Machine Translation*, pages 304–308, Lisboa, Portugal. Association for Computational Linguistics.

Blain, F., Schwenk, H., and Senellart, J. (2012). Incremental adaptation using translation information and post-editing analysis. In *International Workshop on Spoken Language Translation (IWSLT)*, pages 234–241, Hong-Kong (China).

Bojar, O., Buck, C., Callison-Burch, C., Federmann, C., Haddow, B., Koehn, P., Monz, C., Post, M., Soricut, R., and Specia, L. (2013).

Findings of the 2013 Workshop on Statistical Machine Translation. In *Proceedings of the Eighth Workshop on Statistical Machine Translation*, pages 1–42, Sofia, Bulgaria. Association for Computational Linguistics.

Bojar, O., Buck, C., Federmann, C., Haddow, B., Koehn, P., Leveling, J., Monz, C., Pecina, P., Post, M., Saint-Amand, H., Soricut, R., Specia, L., and Tamchyna, A. (2014). Findings of the 2014 workshop on statistical machine translation. In *Proceedings of the Ninth Workshop on Statistical Machine Translation*, pages 12–58, Baltimore, Maryland, USA. Association for Computational Linguistics.

Bojar, O. and Tamchyna, A. (2015). CUNI in WMT15: Chimera Strikes Again. In *Proceedings of the Tenth Workshop on Statistical Machine Translation*, pages 79–83, Lisboa, Portugal. Association for Computational Linguistics.

Callison-Burch, C., Fordyce, C., Koehn, P., Monz, C., and Schroeder, J. (2007). (Meta-) evaluation of machine translation. In *Proceedings of the Second Workshop on Statistical Machine Translation (WMT07)*, Prague, Czech Republic.

Callison-Burch, C., Fordyce, C., Koehn, P., Monz, C., and Schroeder, J. (2008). Further meta-evaluation of machine translation. In *Proceedings of the Third Workshop on Statistical Machine Translation (WMT08)*, Colmbus, Ohio.

Callison-Burch, C., Koehn, P., Monz, C., Peterson, K., Przybocki, M., and Zaidan, O. F. (2010). Findings of the 2010 joint workshop on statistical machine translation and metrics for machine translation. In *Proceedings of the Fourth Workshop on Statistical Machine Translation (WMT10)*, Uppsala, Sweden.

Callison-Burch, C., Koehn, P., Monz, C., Post, M., Soricut, R., and Specia, L. (2012). Findings of the 2012 workshop on statistical machine translation. In *Proceedings of the Seventh Workshop on Statistical Machine Translation*, pages 10–51, Montréal, Canada. Association for Computational Linguistics.

Callison-Burch, C., Koehn, P., Monz, C., and Schroeder, J. (2009). Findings of the 2009 workshop on statistical machine translation. In *Proceedings of the Fourth Workshop on Statistical Machine Translation (WMT09)*, Athens, Greece.

Callison-Burch, C., Koehn, P., Monz, C., and Zaidan, O. (2011). Findings of the 2011 workshop on statistical machine translation. In *Proceedings of the Sixth Workshop on Statistical Machine Translation*, pages 22–64, Edinburgh, Scotland.

Camargo de Souza, J. G., González-Rubio, J., Buck, C., Turchi, M., and Negri, M. (2014). Fbk-upv-uedin participation in the wmt14 quality estimation shared-task. In *Proceedings of the Ninth Workshop on Statistical Machine Translation*, pages 322–328, Baltimore, Maryland, USA. Association for Computational Linguistics.

Cap, F., Weller, M., Ramm, A., and Fraser, A. (2015). CimS - The CIS and IMS Joint Submission to WMT 2015 addressing morphological and syntactic differences in English to German SMT. In *Proceedings of the Tenth Workshop on Statistical Machine Translation*, pages 84–91, Lisboa, Portugal. Association for Computational Linguistics.

Cettolo, M., Bertoldi, N., and Federico, M. (2014). The Repetition Rate of Text as a Predictor of the Effectiveness of Machine Translation Adaptation. In *Proceedings of the 11th Biennial Conference of the Association for Machine Translation in the Americas (AMTA 2014)*, pages 166–179, Vancouver, BC, Canada.

Chatterjee, R., Turchi, M., and Negri, M. (2015a). The FBK Participation in the WMT15 Automatic Post-editing Shared Task. In *Proceedings of the Tenth Workshop on Statistical Machine Translation*, pages 210–215, Lisboa, Portugal. Association for Computational Linguistics.

Chatterjee, R., Weller, M., Negri, M., and Turchi, M. (2015b). Exploring the Planet of the APEs: a Comparative Study of State-of-the-art Methods for MT Automatic Post-Editing. In *Proceedings of the 53rd Annual Meeting of the Association for Computational Linguistics)*, Beijing, China.

Cho, E., Ha, T.-L., Niehues, J., Herrmann, T., Mediani, M., Zhang, Y., and Waibel, A. (2015). The Karlsruhe Institute of Technology Translation Systems for the WMT 2015. In *Proceedings of the Tenth Workshop on Statistical Machine Translation*, pages 92–97, Lisboa, Portugal. Association for Computational Linguistics.

Cohen, J. (1960). A coefficient of agreement for

nominal scales. *Educational and Psychological Measurment*, 20(1):37–46.

Dušek, O., Gomes, L., Novák, M., Popel, M., and Rosa, R. (2015). New Language Pairs in TectoMT. In *Proceedings of the Tenth Workshop on Statistical Machine Translation*, pages 98–104, Lisboa, Portugal. Association for Computational Linguistics.

Dyer, C., Lopez, A., Ganitkevitch, J., Weese, J., Ture, F., Blunsom, P., Setiawan, H., Eidelman, V., and Resnik, P. (2010). cdec: A decoder, alignment, and learning framework for finite-state and context-free translation models. In *Proceedings of the Association for Computational Linguistics (ACL)*.

Esplà-Gomis, M., Sánchez-Martínez, F., and Forcada, M. (2015a). UAlacant word-level machine translation quality estimation system at WMT 2015. In *Proceedings of the Tenth Workshop on Statistical Machine Translation*, pages 309–315, Lisboa, Portugal. Association for Computational Linguistics.

Esplà-Gomis, M., Sánchez-Martnez, F., and Forcada, M. L. (2015b). Using on-line available sources of bilingual information for word-level machine translation quality estimation. In *18th Annual Conference of the European Associtation for Machine Translation*, page 1926, Antalya, Turkey.

Federmann, C. (2012). Appraise: An Open-Source Toolkit for Manual Evaluation of Machine Translation Output. *The Prague Bulletin of Mathematical Linguistics (PBML)*, 98:25–35.

Gao, Q. and Vogel, S. (2008). Parallel Implementations of Word Alignment Tool. In *Proceedings of the ACL 2008 Software Engineering, Testing, and Quality Assurance Workshop*, pages 49–57, Columbus, Ohio.

Giménez, J. and Màrquez, L. (2010). Asiya: An Open Toolkit for Automatic Machine Translation (Meta-)Evaluation. *The Prague Bulletin of Mathematical Linguistics*, 94:77–86.

Graham, Y. (2015). Improving Evaluation of Machine Translation Quality Estimation. In *53rd Annual Meeting of the Association for Computational Linguistics and Seventh International Joint Conference on Natural Language Processing of the Asian Federation of Natural Language Processing*, pages 1804–1813, Beijing, China.

Grönroos, S.-A., Virpioja, S., and Kurimo, M. (2015). Tuning Phrase-Based Segmented Translation for a Morphologically Complex Target Language. In *Proceedings of the Tenth Workshop on Statistical Machine Translation*, pages 105–111, Lisboa, Portugal. Association for Computational Linguistics.

Gwinnup, J., Anderson, T., Erdmann, G., Young, K., May, C., Kazi, M., Salesky, E., and Thompson, B. (2015). The AFRL-MITLL WMT15 System: Theres More than One Way to Decode It! In *Proceedings of the Tenth Workshop on Statistical Machine Translation*, pages 112–119, Lisboa, Portugal. Association for Computational Linguistics.

Ha, T.-L., Do, Q.-K., Cho, E., Niehues, J., Allauzen, A., Yvon, F., and Waibel, A. (2015). The KIT-LIMSI Translation System for WMT 2015. In *Proceedings of the Tenth Workshop on Statistical Machine Translation*, pages 120–125, Lisboa, Portugal. Association for Computational Linguistics.

Haddow, B., Huck, M., Birch, A., Bogoychev, N., and Koehn, P. (2015). The Edinburgh/JHU Phrase-based Machine Translation Systems for WMT 2015. In *Proceedings of the Tenth Workshop on Statistical Machine Translation*, pages 126–133, Lisboa, Portugal. Association for Computational Linguistics.

Heafield, K. (2011). KenLM: faster and smaller language model queries. In *Proceedings of the Sixth Workshop on Statistical Machine Translation*, pages 187–197, Edinburgh, United Kingdom. Association for Computational Linguistics.

Jean, S., Firat, O., Cho, K., Memisevic, R., and Bengio, Y. (2015). Montreal Neural Machine Translation Systems for WMT15. In *Proceedings of the Tenth Workshop on Statistical Machine Translation*, pages 134–140, Lisboa, Portugal. Association for Computational Linguistics.

Junczys-Dowmunt, M. and Szal, A. (2011). SyMGiza++: Symmetrized Word Alignment Models for Statistical Machine Translation. In *SIIS*, volume 7053 of *Lecture Notes in Computer Science*, pages 379–390. Springer.

*** Formatting Issue - Best Available Paper/Graphic ***

Koehn, P. (2004). Statistical Significance Tests for Machine Translation Evaluation. In Lin, D. and Wu, D., editors, *Proceedings of EMNLP 2004*, pages 388–395, Barcelona, Spain.

Koehn, P. (2005). Europarl: A Parallel Corpus for Statistical Machine Translation. In *MT Summit X*.

Koehn, P. (2010). *Statistical Machine Translation*. Cambridge University Press, New York, NY, USA, 1st edition.

Koehn, P., Hoang, H., Birch, A., Callison-Burch, C., Federico, M., Bertoldi, N., Cowan, B., Shen, W., Moran, C., Zens, R., Dyer, C., Bojar, O., Constantin, A., and Herbst, E. (2007). Moses: Open source toolkit for statistical machine translation. In *ACL 2007 Demonstrations*, Prague, Czech Republic.

Koehn, P. and Monz, C. (2006). Manual and automatic evaluation of machine translation between European languages. In *Proceedings of NAACL 2006 Workshop on Statistical Machine Translation*, New York, New York.

Kolachina, P. and Ranta, A. (2015). GF Wide-coverage English-Finnish MT system for WMT 2015. In *Proceedings of the Tenth Workshop on Statistical Machine Translation*, pages 141–144, Lisboa, Portugal. Association for Computational Linguistics.

Kreutzer, J., Schamoni, S., and Riezler, S. (2015). QUality Estimation from ScraTCH (QUETCH): Deep Learning for Word-level Translation Quality Estimation. In *Proceedings of the Tenth Workshop on Statistical Machine Translation*, pages 316–322, Lisboa, Portugal. Association for Computational Linguistics.

Landis, J. R. and Koch, G. G. (1977). The measurement of observer agreement for categorical data. *Biometrics*, 33:159–174.

Langlois, D. (2015). LORIA System for the WMT15 Quality Estimation Shared Task. In *Proceedings of the Tenth Workshop on Statistical Machine Translation*, pages 323–329, Lisboa, Portugal. Association for Computational Linguistics.

Lavie, A. and Agarwal, A. (2007). Meteor: An Automatic Metric for MT Evaluation with High Levels of Correlation with Human Judgments. In *Proceedings of the Second Workshop on Statistical Machine Translation*, StatMT '07, pages 228–231.

Liang, P., Taskar, B., and Klein, D. (2006). Alignment by Agreement. In *HLTNAACL*, New York.

Logacheva, V., Hokamp, C., and Specia, L. (2015). Data enhancement and selection strategies for the word-level Quality Estimation. In *Proceedings of the Tenth Workshop on Statistical Machine Translation*, pages 330–335, Lisboa, Portugal. Association for Computational Linguistics.

Luong, N. Q., Besacier, L., and Lecouteux, B. (2014). LIG System for Word Level QE task at WMT14. In *Ninth Workshop on Statistical Machine Translation*, pages 335–341, Baltimore, Maryland, USA. Association for Computational Linguistics.

Luong, N. Q., Lecouteux, B., and Besacier, L. (2013). LIG system for WMT13 QE task: Investigating the usefulness of features in word confidence estimation for MT. In *Proceedings of the Eighth Workshop on Statistical Machine Translation*, pages 384–389, Sofia, Bulgaria. Association for Computational Linguistics.

Marie, B., Allauzen, A., Burlot, F., Do, Q.-K., Ive, J., knyazeva, e., Labeau, M., Lavergne, T., Löser, K., Pécheux, N., and Yvon, F. (2015). LIMSI@WMT'15 : Translation Task. In *Proceedings of the Tenth Workshop on Statistical Machine Translation*, pages 145–151, Lisboa, Portugal. Association for Computational Linguistics.

Och, F. J. (2003). Minimum Error Rate Training in Statistical Machine Translation. In *ACL03*, pages 160–167, Sapporo, Japan.

Padr, L. and Stanilovsky, E. (2012). Freeling 3.0: Towards wider multilinguality. In *Proceedings of the Eight International Conference on Language Resources and Evaluation (LREC'12)*, Istanbul, Turkey.

Pal, S., Naskar, S., and Bandyopadhyay, S. (2013). A Hybrid Word Alignment Model for Phrase-Based Statistical Machine Translation. In *Proceedings of the Second Workshop on Hybrid Approaches to Translation*, pages 94–101, Sofia, Bulgaria.

Pal, S., Naskar, S., and van Genabith, J. (2015a). UdS-Sant: English–German Hybrid Machine Translation System. In *Proceedings of the Tenth*

*** Formatting Issue - Best Available Paper/Graphic ***

Workshop on Statistical Machine Translation, pages 152–157, Lisboa, Portugal. Association for Computational Linguistics.

Pal, S., Vela, M., Naskar, S. K., and van Genabith, J. (2015b). USAAR-SAPE: An English–Spanish Statistical Automatic Post-Editing System. In *Proceedings of the Tenth Workshop on Statistical Machine Translation*, pages 216–221, Lisboa, Portugal. Association for Computational Linguistics.

Papineni, K., Roukos, S., Ward, T., and Zhu, W.-J. (2002). BLEU: a method for automatic evaluation of machine translation. In *Proceedings of the 40th Annual Meeting on Association for Computational Linguistics*, ACL '02, pages 311–318, Morristown, NJ, USA.

Parton, K., Habash, N., McKeown, K., Iglesias, G., and de Gispert, A. (2012). Can Automatic Post-Editing Make MT More Meaningful? In *Proceedings of the 16th Conference of the European Association for Machine Translation (EAMT)*, pages 111–118, Trento, Italy.

Peter, J.-T., Toutounchi, F., Wuebker, J., and Ney, H. (2015). The RWTH Aachen German-English Machine Translation System for WMT 2015. In *Proceedings of the Tenth Workshop on Statistical Machine Translation*, pages 158–163, Lisboa, Portugal. Association for Computational Linguistics.

Potet, M., Esperana-Rodier, E., Besacier, L., and Blanchon, H. (2012). Collection of a large database of french-english smt output corrections. In *LREC*, pages 4043–4048. European Language Resources Association (ELRA).

Quernheim, D. (2015). Exact Decoding with Multi Bottom-Up Tree Transducers. In *Proceedings of the Tenth Workshop on Statistical Machine Translation*, pages 164–171, Lisboa, Portugal. Association for Computational Linguistics.

Raybaud, S., Langlois, D., and Smali, K. (2011). this sentence is wrong. detecting errors in machine-translated sentences. *Machine Translation*, 25(1):1–34.

Rubino, R., Pirinen, T., Esplà-Gomis, M., Ljubešić, N., Ortiz Rojas, S., Papavassiliou, V., Prokopidis, P., and Toral, A. (2015). Abu-MaTran at WMT 2015 Translation Task: Morphological Segmentation and Web Crawling. In *Proceedings of the Tenth Workshop on Statistical Machine Translation*, pages 184–191, Lisboa, Portugal. Association for Computational Linguistics.

Scarton, C., Tan, L., and Specia, L. (2015a). USHEF and USAAR-USHEF participation in the WMT15 QE shared task. In *Proceedings of the Tenth Workshop on Statistical Machine Translation*, pages 336–341, Lisboa, Portugal. Association for Computational Linguistics.

Scarton, C., Zampieri, M., Vela, M., van Genabith, J., and Specia, L. (2015b). Searching for Context: a Study on Document-Level Labels for Translation Quality Estimation. In *The 18th Annual Conference of the European Association for Machine Translation*, pages 121–128, Antalya, Turkey.

Schwartz, L., Bryce, B., Geigle, C., Massung, S., Liu, Y., Peng, H., Raja, V., Roy, S., and Upadhyay, S. (2015). The University of Illinois submission to the WMT 2015 Shared Translation Task. In *Proceedings of the Tenth Workshop on Statistical Machine Translation*, pages 192–198, Lisboa, Portugal. Association for Computational Linguistics.

Shah, K., Logacheva, V., Paetzold, G., Blain, F., Beck, D., Bougares, F., and Specia, L. (2015). SHEF-NN: Translation Quality Estimation with Neural Networks. In *Proceedings of the Tenth Workshop on Statistical Machine Translation*, pages 342–347, Lisboa, Portugal. Association for Computational Linguistics.

Shang, L., Cai, D., and Ji, D. (2015). Strategy-Based Technology for Estimating MT Quality. In *Proceedings of the Tenth Workshop on Statistical Machine Translation*, pages 348–352, Lisboa, Portugal. Association for Computational Linguistics.

Simard, M., Goutte, C., and Isabelle, P. (2007). Statistical Phrase-Based Post-Editing. In *Proceedings of the Annual Conference of the North American Chapter of the Association for Computational Linguistics (NAACL HLT)*, pages 508–515, Rochester, New York.

Snover, M., Dorr, B., Schwartz, R., Micciulla, L., and Makhoul, J. (2006a). A Study of Translation Edit Rate with Targeted Human Annotation. In *Proceedings of Association for Machine Translation in the Americas*, pages 223–231, Cambridge, Massachusetts, USA.

Snover, M., Dorr, B., Schwartz, R., Micciulla, L., and Makhoul, J. (2006b). A study of translation edit rate with targeted human annotation. In *Proceedings of the 7th Biennial Conference of the Association for Machine Translation in the Americas (AMTA-2006)*, Cambridge, Massachusetts.

Specia, L., Paetzold, G., and Scarton, C. (2015). Multi-level Translation Quality Prediction with QuEst++. In *53rd Annual Meeting of the Association for Computational Linguistics and Seventh International Joint Conference on Natural Language Processing of the Asian Federation of Natural Language Processing: System Demonstrations*, pages 115–120, Beijing, China.

Specia, L., Shah, K., de Souza, J. G., and Cohn, T. (2013). QuEst - A translation quality estimation framework. In *51st Annual Meeting of the Association for Computational Linguistics: System Demonstrations*, ACL-2013, pages 79–84, Sofia, Bulgaria.

Stanojević, M., Kamran, A., and Bojar, O. (2015a). Results of the WMT15 Tuning Shared Task. In *Proceedings of the Tenth Workshop on Statistical Machine Translation*, pages 274–281, Lisboa, Portugal. Association for Computational Linguistics.

Stanojević, M., Kamran, A., Koehn, P., and Bojar, O. (2015b). Results of the WMT15 Metrics Shared Task. In *Proceedings of the Tenth Workshop on Statistical Machine Translation*, pages 256–273, Lisboa, Portugal. Association for Computational Linguistics.

Steele, D., Sim Smith, K., and Specia, L. (2015). Sheffield Systems for the Finnish-English WMT Translation Task. In *Proceedings of the Tenth Workshop on Statistical Machine Translation*, pages 172–176, Lisboa, Portugal. Association for Computational Linguistics.

Tezcan, A., Hoste, V., Desmet, B., and Macken, L. (2015). UGENT-LT3 SCATE System for Machine Translation Quality Estimation. In *Proceedings of the Tenth Workshop on Statistical Machine Translation*, pages 353–360, Lisboa, Portugal. Association for Computational Linguistics.

Tiedemann, J., Ginter, F., and Kanerva, J. (2015). Morphological Segmentation and OPUS for Finnish-English Machine Translation. In *Proceedings of the Tenth Workshop on Statistical Machine Translation*, pages 177–183, Lisboa, Portugal. Association for Computational Linguistics.

Williams, P., Sennrich, R., Nadejde, M., Huck, M., and Koehn, P. (2015). Edinburgh's Syntax-Based Systems at WMT 2015. In *Proceedings of the Tenth Workshop on Statistical Machine Translation*, pages 199–209, Lisboa, Portugal. Association for Computational Linguistics.

Wisniewski, G., Pécheux, N., and Yvon, F. (2015). Why Predicting Post-Edition is so Hard? Failure Analysis of LIMSI Submission to the APE Shared Task. In *Proceedings of the Tenth Workshop on Statistical Machine Translation*, pages 222–227, Lisboa, Portugal. Association for Computational Linguistics.

Wisniewski, G., Singh, A. K., Segal, N., and Yvon, F. (2013). Design and Analysis of a Large Corpus of Post-edited Translations: Quality Estimation, Failure Analysis and the Variability of Post-edition. *Machine Translation Summit*, 14:117–124.

*** Formatting Issue - Best Available Paper/Graphic ***

	ONLINE-B	UEDIN-JHU	UEDIN-SYNTAX	MONTREAL	ONLINE-A	CU-TECTO	TT-BLEU-MIRA-D	TT-ILLC-UVA	TT-BLEU-MERT	TT-AFRL	TT-USAAR-TUNA	TT-DCU	TT-METEOR-CMU	TT-BLEU-MIRA-SP	TT-HKUST-MEANT	ILLINOIS
ONLINE-B	–	.46†	**.52**	.46†	.39‡	.25‡	.21‡	.21‡	.21‡	.21‡	.20‡	.20‡	.19‡	.17‡	.16‡	.17‡
UEDIN-JHU	**.54**†	–	.48	.47⋆	.44‡	.26‡	.21‡	.22‡	.20‡	.21‡	.20‡	.19‡	.19‡	.19‡	.19‡	.19‡
UEDIN-SYNTAX	.48	**.52**	–	**.51**	.46⋆	.28‡	.21‡	.22‡	.22‡	.21‡	.21‡	.19‡	.18‡	.20‡	.19‡	.17‡
MONTREAL	**.54**†	**.53**⋆	.49	–	.45†	.28‡	.24‡	.25‡	.24‡	.24‡	.25‡	.24‡	.21‡	.20‡	.20‡	.23‡
ONLINE-A	**.61**‡	**.56**‡	**.54**⋆	**.55**†	–	.29‡	.24‡	.26‡	.25‡	.25‡	.24‡	.23‡	.22‡	.23‡	.23‡	.22‡
CU-TECTO	**.75**‡	**.74**‡	**.72**‡	**.72**‡	**.71**‡	–	.48	.47	.47	.46†	.48	.44‡	.43‡	.43‡	.43‡	.41‡
TT-BLEU-MIRA-D	**.79**‡	**.79**‡	**.79**‡	**.76**‡	**.76**‡	**.52**	–	**.51**	.41†	.43⋆	.38†	.43†	.41‡	.39‡	.39‡	.43‡
TT-ILLC-UVA	**.79**‡	**.78**‡	**.78**‡	**.75**‡	**.74**‡	**.53**	.49	–	.48	.47	.45	.41‡	.45⋆	.42‡	.40‡	.42‡
TT-BLEU-MERT	**.79**‡	**.80**‡	**.78**‡	**.76**‡	**.75**‡	**.53**	**.59**†	**.52**	–	**.51**	.48	.44†	.45†	.41‡	.40‡	.41‡
TT-AFRL	**.79**‡	**.79**‡	**.79**‡	**.76**‡	**.75**‡	**.54**†	**.57**⋆	**.53**	.49	–	.49	.45⋆	.43†	.42‡	.42‡	.41‡
TT-USAAR-TUNA	**.80**‡	**.80**‡	**.79**‡	**.75**‡	**.76**‡	**.52**	**.62**†	**.55**	**.52**	**.51**	–	.45⋆	.45†	.41‡	.41‡	.42‡
TT-DCU	**.80**‡	**.81**‡	**.81**‡	**.76**‡	**.77**‡	**.56**‡	**.57**†	**.59**‡	**.56**†	**.55**⋆	**.55**⋆	–	.47	.45†	.44†	.45†
TT-METEOR-CMU	**.81**‡	**.81**‡	**.82**‡	**.79**‡	**.78**‡	**.57**‡	**.59**‡	**.55**⋆	**.55**†	**.57**†	**.55**†	**.53**	–	.48	.49	.48
TT-BLEU-MIRA-SP	**.83**‡	**.81**‡	**.80**‡	**.80**‡	**.77**‡	**.57**‡	**.61**‡	**.58**‡	**.59**‡	**.58**‡	**.59**‡	**.55**†	**.52**	–	**.53**	.50
TT-HKUST-MEANT	**.84**‡	**.81**‡	**.81**‡	**.80**‡	**.77**‡	**.57**‡	**.61**‡	**.60**‡	**.60**‡	**.58**‡	**.59**‡	**.56**†	**.51**	.47	–	.48
ILLINOIS	**.82**‡	**.81**‡	**.83**‡	**.77**‡	**.78**‡	**.59**‡	**.57**‡	**.58**‡	**.59**‡	**.59**‡	**.58**‡	**.55**†	**.52**	.50	**.52**	–
score	.61	.57	.53	.51	.43	-.12	-.18	-.18	-.19	-.21	-.22	-.26	-.29	-.32	-.32	-.35
rank	1	2	3-4	3-4	5	6	7-9	7-10	7-11	8-11	9-11	12-13	13-15	13-15	13-15	15-16

Table 25: Head to head comparison, ignoring ties, for Czech-English systems

A Pairwise System Comparisons by Human Judges

Tables 25–34 show pairwise comparisons between systems for each language pair. The numbers in each of the tables' cells indicate the percentage of times that the system in that column was judged to be better than the system in that row, ignoring ties. Bolding indicates the winner of the two systems.

Because there were so many systems and data conditions the significance of each pairwise comparison needs to be quantified. We applied the Sign Test to measure which comparisons indicate genuine differences (rather than differences that are attributable to chance). In the following tables $\star$ indicates statistical significance at $p \leq 0.10$, † indicates statistical significance at $p \leq 0.05$, and ‡ indicates statistical significance at $p \leq 0.01$, according to the Sign Test.

Each table contains final rows showing how likely a system would win when paired against a randomly selected system (the expected win ratio score) and the rank range according bootstrap resampling ($p \leq 0.05$). Gray lines separate clusters based on non-overlapping rank ranges.

*** Formatting Issue - Best Available Paper/Graphic ***

	CU-CHIMERA	ONLINE-B	UEDIN-JHU	MONTREAL	ONLINE-A	UEDIN-SYNTAX	CU-TECTO	COMMERCIAL1	TT-DCU	TT-AFRL	TT-BLEU-MIRA-D	TT-USAAR-TUNA	TT-BLEU-MERT	TT-METEOR-CMU	TT-BLEU-MIRA-SP
CU-CHIMERA	–	.42‡	.43‡	.44‡	.38‡	.33‡	.29‡	.27‡	.15‡	.15‡	.15‡	.14‡	.14‡	.11‡	.10‡
ONLINE-B	**.58**‡	–	.50	.50	.44‡	.40‡	.37‡	.32‡	.16‡	.17‡	.17‡	.17‡	.16‡	.13‡	.08‡
UEDIN-JHU	**.57**‡	.50	–	**.51**	.44‡	.39‡	.41‡	.35‡	.18‡	.18‡	.18‡	.18‡	.16‡	.13‡	.10‡
MONTREAL	**.56**‡	.50	.49	–	.46†	.43‡	.39‡	.36‡	.22‡	.21‡	.21‡	.21‡	.19‡	.19‡	.16‡
ONLINE-A	**.62**‡	**.56**‡	**.56**‡	**.54**†	–	.43‡	.40‡	.36‡	.20‡	.19‡	.20‡	.18‡	.17‡	.15‡	.12‡
UEDIN-SYNTAX	**.67**‡	**.60**‡	**.61**‡	**.57**‡	**.57**‡	–	.48	.43‡	.25‡	.25‡	.26‡	.25‡	.23‡	.23‡	.17‡
CU-TECTO	**.71**‡	**.62**‡	**.59**‡	**.61**‡	**.60**‡	**.52**	–	.44‡	.29‡	.30‡	.28‡	.28‡	.28‡	.23‡	.17‡
COMMERCIAL1	**.73**‡	**.68**‡	**.65**‡	**.64**‡	**.64**‡	**.57**‡	**.56**‡	–	.29‡	.28‡	.28‡	.27‡	.27‡	.22‡	.18‡
TT-DCU	**.85**‡	**.84**‡	**.82**‡	**.78**‡	**.80**‡	**.75**‡	**.71**‡	**.71**‡	–	**.52**	.48	.45†	.40‡	.36‡	.27‡
TT-AFRL	**.85**‡	**.83**‡	**.82**‡	**.79**‡	**.81**‡	**.75**‡	**.70**‡	**.72**‡	.48	–	.49	.46⋆	.37‡	.33‡	.29‡
TT-BLEU-MIRA-D	**.85**‡	**.83**‡	**.82**‡	**.79**‡	**.80**‡	**.74**‡	**.72**‡	**.72**‡	**.52**	**.51**	–	.39‡	.36‡	.36‡	.27‡
TT-USAAR-TUNA	**.86**‡	**.83**‡	**.82**‡	**.79**‡	**.82**‡	**.75**‡	**.72**‡	**.73**‡	**.55**†	**.54**⋆	**.61**‡	–	.36‡	.37‡	.28‡
TT-BLEU-MERT	**.86**‡	**.84**‡	**.84**‡	**.81**‡	**.83**‡	**.77**‡	**.72**‡	**.73**‡	**.60**‡	**.63**‡	**.64**‡	**.64**‡	–	.39‡	.28‡
TT-METEOR-CMU	**.89**‡	**.87**‡	**.87**‡	**.81**‡	**.85**‡	**.77**‡	**.77**‡	**.78**‡	**.64**‡	**.67**‡	**.64**‡	**.63**‡	**.61**‡	–	.32‡
TT-BLEU-MIRA-SP	**.90**‡	**.92**‡	**.90**‡	**.84**‡	**.88**‡	**.83**‡	**.83**‡	**.82**‡	**.73**‡	**.71**‡	**.73**‡	**.72**‡	**.72**‡	**.68**‡	–
score	.68	.51	.50	.46	.42	.26	.20	.11	-.34	-.34	-.34	-.37	-.40	-.56	-.80
rank	1	2-3	2-3	4	5	6	7	8	9-11	9-11	9-11	12	13	14	15

Table 26: Head to head comparison, ignoring ties, for English-Czech systems

	ONLINE-B	UEDIN-JHU	ONLINE-A	UEDIN-SYNTAX	KIT	RWTH	MONTREAL	ILLINOIS	DFKI	ONLINE-C	ONLINE-F	MACAU	ONLINE-E
ONLINE-B	–	.41‡	.43‡	.39‡	.39‡	.33‡	.38‡	.25‡	.26‡	.27‡	.26‡	.19‡	.22‡
UEDIN-JHU	**.59**‡	–	**.51**	.46⋆	.45†	.43†	.44†	.31‡	.33‡	.36‡	.30‡	.28‡	.27‡
ONLINE-A	**.57**‡	.49	–	**.52**	**.53**	.48	.44‡	.36‡	.32‡	.31‡	.28‡	.29‡	.26‡
UEDIN-SYNTAX	**.61**‡	**.54**⋆	.48	–	.49	.48	.45†	.23‡	.33‡	.34‡	.35‡	.27‡	.26‡
KIT	**.61**‡	**.55**†	.47	**.51**	–	.47	.46⋆	.35‡	.38‡	.36‡	.35‡	.26‡	.32‡
RWTH	**.67**‡	**.57**†	**.52**	**.52**	**.53**	–	.46⋆	.38‡	.39‡	.40‡	.36‡	.31‡	.35‡
MONTREAL	**.62**‡	**.56**†	**.56**‡	**.55**†	**.54**⋆	**.54**⋆	–	.42‡	.43‡	.41‡	.35‡	.32‡	.34‡
ILLINOIS	**.75**‡	**.69**‡	**.64**‡	**.77**‡	**.65**‡	**.62**‡	**.58**‡	–	.48	.49	.48	.38‡	.42‡
DFKI	**.74**‡	**.67**‡	**.68**‡	**.67**‡	**.62**‡	**.61**‡	**.57**‡	**.52**	–	.43†	.46⋆	.39‡	.37‡
ONLINE-C	**.73**‡	**.64**‡	**.69**‡	**.66**‡	**.64**‡	**.60**‡	**.59**‡	**.51**	**.57**†	–	.46⋆	.42‡	.39‡
ONLINE-F	**.74**‡	**.70**‡	**.72**‡	**.65**‡	**.65**‡	**.64**‡	**.64**‡	**.52**	**.54**⋆	**.54**⋆	–	.44‡	.40‡
MACAU	**.81**‡	**.72**‡	**.71**‡	**.73**‡	**.74**‡	**.69**‡	**.68**‡	**.62**‡	**.61**‡	**.58**‡	**.56**‡	–	.50
ONLINE-E	**.78**‡	**.73**‡	**.74**‡	**.74**‡	**.68**‡	**.65**‡	**.66**‡	**.58**‡	**.63**‡	**.61**‡	**.60**‡	.50	–
score	.56	.31	.29	.25	.22	.14	.09	-.17	-.17	-.22	-.30	-.48	-.54
rank	1	2-3	2-4	3-5	4-5	6-7	6-7	8-10	8-10	9-10	11	12-13	12-13

Table 27: Head to head comparison, ignoring ties, for German-English systems

	UEDIN-SYNTAX	MONTREAL	PROMT-RULE	ONLINE-A	ONLINE-B	KIT-LIMSI	UEDIN-JHU	ONLINE-F	ONLINE-C	KIT	CIMS	DFKI	ONLINE-E	UDS-SANT	ILLINOIS	IMS
UEDIN-SYNTAX	–	**.52**	.47	.48	.42‡	.36‡	.36‡	.33‡	.37‡	.32‡	.29‡	.32‡	.31‡	.33‡	.19‡	.21‡
MONTREAL	.48	–	.47	.44†	.41‡	.35‡	.35‡	.42‡	.37‡	.35‡	.33‡	.33‡	.37‡	.35‡	.24‡	.27‡
PROMT-RULE	**.53**	**.53**	–	.46★	.45†	.46★	.40‡	.35‡	.42‡	.41‡	.37‡	.36‡	.33‡	.37‡	.29‡	.24‡
ONLINE-A	**.52**	**.56**†	**.54**★	–	.40‡	.43†	.37‡	.42‡	.39‡	.39‡	.41‡	.36‡	.36‡	.33‡	.27‡	.28‡
ONLINE-B	**.58**‡	**.59**‡	**.55**†	**.60**‡	–	.45†	.45†	.45†	.44†	.39‡	.42‡	.37‡	.41‡	.35‡	.29‡	.32‡
KIT-LIMSI	**.64**‡	**.65**‡	**.54**★	**.57**†	**.55**†	–	**.52**	.49	.44†	.40‡	.47	.38‡	.39‡	.37‡	.29‡	.30‡
UEDIN-JHU	**.64**‡	**.65**‡	**.60**‡	**.63**‡	**.55**†	.48	–	.47	**.51**	.46★	.43†	.45★	.44†	.41‡	.34‡	.30‡
ONLINE-F	**.67**‡	**.58**‡	**.65**‡	**.58**‡	**.55**†	**.51**	**.53**	–	.50	.46★	.49	.44†	.46★	.39‡	.36‡	.36‡
ONLINE-C	**.63**‡	**.63**‡	**.58**‡	**.61**‡	**.56**†	**.56**†	.49	.50	–	**.52**	.48	.45	.40‡	.42‡	.36‡	.35‡
KIT	**.68**‡	**.65**‡	**.59**‡	**.61**‡	**.61**‡	**.60**‡	**.54**★	**.54**★	.48	–	**.51**	.43‡	.47	.37‡	.35‡	.33‡
CIMS	**.71**‡	**.67**‡	**.62**‡	**.59**‡	**.58**‡	**.53**	**.57**†	**.51**	**.52**	.49	–	.47	.45†	.44†	.23‡	.34‡
DFKI	**.68**‡	**.67**‡	**.64**‡	**.64**‡	**.63**‡	**.62**‡	**.55**★	**.56**†	**.55**	**.57**‡	**.53**	–	.50	.44†	.41‡	.36‡
ONLINE-E	**.69**‡	**.63**‡	**.67**‡	**.64**‡	**.59**‡	**.61**‡	**.56**†	**.54**★	**.60**‡	**.53**	**.55**†	.50	–	.45†	.42‡	.38‡
UDS-SANT	**.67**‡	**.65**‡	**.63**‡	**.67**‡	**.65**‡	**.63**‡	**.59**‡	**.61**‡	**.58**‡	**.63**‡	**.56**†	**.56**†	**.55**†	–	.45†	.41‡
ILLINOIS	**.81**‡	**.76**‡	**.71**‡	**.73**‡	**.71**‡	**.71**‡	**.66**‡	**.64**‡	**.64**‡	**.65**‡	**.77**‡	**.59**‡	**.58**‡	**.55**†	–	.48
IMS	**.79**‡	**.73**‡	**.76**‡	**.72**‡	**.68**‡	**.70**‡	**.70**‡	**.64**‡	**.65**‡	**.67**‡	**.66**‡	**.64**‡	**.62**‡	**.59**‡	**.52**	–
score	.35	.33	.26	.23	.14	.08	.03	.00	-.00	-.01	-.03	-.13	-.13	-.23	-.40	-.50
rank	1-2	1-2	3-4	3-4	5	6	7-9	7-11	7-11	8-11	9-11	12-13	12-13	14	15	16

Table 28: Head to head comparison, ignoring ties, for English-German systems

	ONLINE-B	LIMSI-CNRS	UEDIN-JHU	MACAU	ONLINE-A	ONLINE-F	ONLINE-E
ONLINE-B	–	.50	.49	.47†	.44‡	.35‡	.22‡
LIMSI-CNRS	.50	–	.49	.46‡	.45‡	.37‡	.25‡
UEDIN-JHU	**.51**	**.51**	–	.47†	.46†	.35‡	.26‡
MACAU	**.53**†	**.54**‡	**.53**†	–	.48	.39‡	.28‡
ONLINE-A	**.56**‡	**.55**‡	**.54**†	**.52**	–	.38‡	.26‡
ONLINE-F	**.65**‡	**.63**‡	**.65**‡	**.61**‡	**.62**‡	–	.37‡
ONLINE-E	**.78**‡	**.75**‡	**.74**‡	**.72**‡	**.74**‡	**.63**‡	–
score	.49	.44	.41	.27	.22	-.42	-1.43
rank	1-2	1-3	1-3	4-5	4-5	6	7

Table 29: Head to head comparison, ignoring ties, for French-English systems

	LIMSI-CNRS	ONLINE-A	UEDIN-JHU	ONLINE-B	CIMS	ONLINE-F	ONLINE-E
LIMSI-CNRS	–	.45‡	.44‡	.45‡	.38‡	.36‡	.28‡
ONLINE-A	**.55**‡	–	.49	.48★	.45‡	.37‡	.32‡
UEDIN-JHU	**.56**‡	**.51**	–	.48★	.44‡	.41‡	.31‡
ONLINE-B	**.55**‡	**.52**★	**.52**★	–	.46‡	.40‡	.31‡
CIMS	**.62**‡	**.55**‡	**.56**‡	**.54**‡	–	.45‡	.36‡
ONLINE-F	**.64**‡	**.63**‡	**.59**‡	**.60**‡	**.55**‡	–	.41‡
ONLINE-E	**.72**‡	**.68**‡	**.69**‡	**.69**‡	**.64**‡	**.59**‡	–
score	.54	.30	.25	.21	-.00	-.33	-.97
rank	1	2-3	2-4	3-4	5	6	7

Table 30: Head to head comparison, ignoring ties, for English-French systems

*** Formatting Issue - Best Available Paper/Graphic ***

	ONLINE-B	PROMT-SMT	ONLINE-A	UU-UNC	UEDIN-JHU	ABUMATRAN-COMB	UEDIN-SYNTAX	ILLINOIS	ABUMATRAN-HFS	MONTREAL	ABUMATRAN	LIMSI	SHEFFIELD	SHEFF-STEM
ONLINE-B	–	.36‡	.32‡	.35‡	.29‡	.35‡	.35‡	.29‡	.29‡	.31‡	.17‡	.18‡	.15‡	.15‡
PROMT-SMT	**.64**‡	–	.49	.49	.48	.46	.44†	.43†	.36‡	.34‡	.25‡	.28‡	.25‡	.24‡
ONLINE-A	**.68**‡	**.51**	–	.50	.46	.42‡	.47	.45⋆	.38‡	.40‡	.32‡	.30‡	.25‡	.25‡
UU-UNC	**.65**‡	**.51**	.50	–	.50	.45⋆	.47	.47	.37‡	.34‡	.35‡	.26‡	.26‡	.26‡
UEDIN-JHU	**.71**‡	**.52**	**.54**	.50	–	.49	.50	.47	.42‡	.38‡	.33‡	.31‡	.24‡	.24‡
ABUMATRAN-COMB	**.65**‡	**.54**	**.58**‡	**.55**⋆	**.51**	–	.49	.46	.33‡	.38‡	.23‡	.33‡	.24‡	.24‡
UEDIN-SYNTAX	**.65**‡	**.56**†	**.53**	**.53**	.50	**.51**	–	.44†	.41‡	.42‡	.36‡	.29‡	.30‡	.30‡
ILLINOIS	**.71**‡	**.57**†	**.55**⋆	**.53**	**.53**	**.54**	**.56**†	–	.45⋆	.41‡	.37‡	.33‡	.28‡	.27‡
ABUMATRAN-HFS	**.71**‡	**.64**‡	**.62**‡	**.63**‡	**.58**‡	**.67**‡	**.59**‡	**.55**⋆	–	.42‡	.43†	.38‡	.38‡	.37‡
MONTREAL	**.69**‡	**.66**‡	**.60**‡	**.66**‡	**.62**‡	**.62**‡	**.58**‡	**.59**‡	**.58**‡	–	.48	.43†	.39‡	.39‡
ABUMATRAN	**.83**‡	**.75**‡	**.68**‡	**.65**‡	**.67**‡	**.77**‡	**.64**‡	**.63**‡	**.57**†	**.52**	–	.46	.41‡	.41‡
LIMSI	**.82**‡	**.72**‡	**.70**‡	**.74**‡	**.69**‡	**.67**‡	**.71**‡	**.67**‡	**.62**‡	**.57**†	**.54**	–	**.52**	**.52**
SHEFFIELD	**.85**‡	**.75**‡	**.75**‡	**.74**‡	**.76**‡	**.76**‡	**.70**‡	**.72**‡	**.62**‡	**.61**‡	**.59**‡	.48	–	.00
SHEFF-STEM	**.85**‡	**.76**‡	**.75**‡	**.74**‡	**.76**‡	**.76**‡	**.70**‡	**.73**‡	**.63**‡	**.61**‡	**.59**‡	.48	**1.00**	–
score	.67	.28	.24	.23	.18	.16	.14	.08	-.08	-.17	-.27	-.43	-.51	-.52
rank	1	2-4	2-5	2-5	4-7	5-7	5-8	7-8	9	10	11	12-13	13-14	13-14

Table 31: Head to head comparison, ignoring ties, for Finnish-English systems

	ONLINE-B	ONLINE-A	UU-UNC	ABUMATRAN-UNC-COM	ABUMATRAN-COMB	AALTO	UEDIN-SYNTAX	ABUMATRAN-UNC	CMU	CHALMERS
ONLINE-B	–	.40‡	.31‡	.28‡	.24‡	.26‡	.25‡	.25‡	.23‡	.18‡
ONLINE-A	**.60**‡	–	.40‡	.41‡	.36‡	.33‡	.36‡	.34‡	.29‡	.26‡
UU-UNC	**.69**‡	**.60**‡	–	.47⋆	.43‡	.41‡	.37‡	.41‡	.36‡	.27‡
ABUMATRAN-UNC-COM	**.72**‡	**.59**‡	**.53**⋆	–	.45†	.46†	.45‡	.40‡	.41‡	.32‡
ABUMATRAN-COMB	**.76**‡	**.64**‡	**.57**‡	**.55**†	–	.45†	.46†	.47	.42‡	.34‡
AALTO	**.74**‡	**.67**‡	**.59**‡	**.54**†	**.55**†	–	.47	.47⋆	.46†	.33‡
UEDIN-SYNTAX	**.75**‡	**.64**‡	**.63**‡	**.55**‡	**.54**†	**.53**	–	.49	.44‡	.34‡
ABUMATRAN-UNC	**.75**‡	**.66**‡	**.59**‡	**.60**‡	**.53**	**.53**⋆	**.51**	–	.50	.39‡
CMU	**.77**‡	**.71**‡	**.64**‡	**.59**‡	**.58**‡	**.54**†	**.56**‡	.50	–	.40‡
CHALMERS	**.82**‡	**.74**‡	**.73**‡	**.68**‡	**.66**‡	**.67**‡	**.66**‡	**.61**‡	**.60**‡	–
score	1.06	.54	.21	.04	-.05	-.14	-.18	-.21	-.34	-.92
rank	1	2	3	4	5	6-7	6-8	6-8	9	10

Table 32: Head to head comparison, ignoring ties, for English-Finnish systems

*** Formatting Issue - Best Available Paper/Graphic ***

	ONLINE-G	ONLINE-B	PROMT-RULE	AFRL-MIT-PB	AFRL-MIT-FAC	ONLINE-A	AFRL-MIT-H	LIMSI-NCODE	UEDIN-SYNTAX	UEDIN-JHU	USAAR-GACHA	USAAR-GACHA	ONLINE-F
ONLINE-G	–	.40‡	.39‡	.35‡	.38‡	.38‡	.34‡	.32‡	.36‡	.33‡	.25‡	.24‡	.21‡
ONLINE-B	**.60**‡	–	.41‡	.44†	.42‡	.43†	.40‡	.38‡	.37‡	.35‡	.29‡	.31‡	.22‡
PROMT-RULE	**.61**‡	**.59**‡	–	.46⋆	.47	**.51**	.47	.47	.46†	.48	.40‡	.41‡	.24‡
AFRL-MIT-PB	**.65**‡	**.56**†	**.54**⋆	–	.49	**.53**	.46	.48	.44†	.44†	.33‡	.33‡	.29‡
AFRL-MIT-FAC	**.62**‡	**.58**‡	**.53**	**.51**	–	.50	.48	.45†	.45†	.46⋆	.34‡	.28‡	.29‡
ONLINE-A	**.62**‡	**.57**†	.49	.47	.50	–	.44†	.49	.48	.44†	.36‡	.36‡	.29‡
AFRL-MIT-H	**.66**‡	**.60**‡	**.53**	**.54**	**.52**	**.56**†	–	.50	.47	.46⋆	.40‡	.34‡	.30‡
LIMSI-NCODE	**.68**‡	**.62**‡	**.53**	**.52**	**.55**†	**.51**	.50	–	.48	.49	.43†	.39‡	.33‡
UEDIN-SYNTAX	**.64**‡	**.63**‡	**.54**†	**.56**†	**.55**†	**.52**	**.53**	**.52**	–	.48	.40‡	.40‡	.34‡
UEDIN-JHU	**.67**‡	**.65**‡	**.52**	**.56**†	**.54**⋆	**.56**†	**.54**⋆	**.51**	**.52**	–	.36‡	.38‡	.33‡
USAAR-GACHA	**.75**‡	**.71**‡	**.60**‡	**.67**‡	**.66**‡	**.64**‡	**.60**‡	**.57**†	**.60**‡	**.64**‡	–	.44⋆	.38‡
USAAR-GACHA	**.76**‡	**.69**‡	**.59**‡	**.67**‡	**.72**‡	**.64**‡	**.66**‡	**.61**‡	**.60**‡	**.62**‡	**.56**⋆	–	.40‡
ONLINE-F	**.79**‡	**.78**‡	**.76**‡	**.71**‡	**.71**‡	**.71**‡	**.70**‡	**.67**‡	**.66**‡	**.67**‡	**.62**‡	**.60**‡	–
score	.49	.31	.12	.11	.11	.10	.05	.01	-.02	-.03	-.21	-.27	-.78
rank	1	2	3-6	3-6	3-6	3-7	6-8	7-10	8-10	8-10	11	12	13

Table 33: Head to head comparison, ignoring ties, for Russian-English systems

	PROMT-RULE	ONLINE-G	ONLINE-B	LIMSI-NCODE	ONLINE-A	UEDIN-JHU	UEDIN-SYNTAX	USAAR-GACHA	USAAR-GACHA	ONLINE-F
PROMT-RULE	–	.39‡	.29‡	.27‡	.28‡	.26‡	.21‡	.21‡	.21‡	.07‡
ONLINE-G	**.61**‡	–	.40‡	.38‡	.33‡	.36‡	.30‡	.25‡	.24‡	.12‡
ONLINE-B	**.71**‡	**.60**‡	–	.49	.44‡	.44‡	.37‡	.33‡	.32‡	.19‡
LIMSI-NCODE	**.73**‡	**.62**‡	**.51**	–	.49	.46†	.38‡	.36‡	.34‡	.22‡
ONLINE-A	**.72**‡	**.67**‡	**.56**‡	**.51**	–	.47⋆	.43‡	.40‡	.36‡	.18‡
UEDIN-JHU	**.74**‡	**.64**‡	**.56**‡	**.54**†	**.53**⋆	–	.46†	.40‡	.36‡	.25‡
UEDIN-SYNTAX	**.79**‡	**.70**‡	**.63**‡	**.62**‡	**.57**‡	**.54**†	–	.45†	.39‡	.25‡
USAAR-GACHA	**.79**‡	**.75**‡	**.67**‡	**.64**‡	**.60**‡	**.60**‡	**.55**†	–	.46	.29‡
USAAR-GACHA	**.79**‡	**.76**‡	**.68**‡	**.66**‡	**.64**‡	**.64**‡	**.61**‡	**.54**	–	.28‡
ONLINE-F	**.93**‡	**.88**‡	**.81**‡	**.78**‡	**.82**‡	**.75**‡	**.75**‡	**.71**‡	**.72**‡	–
score	1.01	.52	.21	.12	.07	.01	-.13	-.27	-.33	-1.21
rank	1	2	3	4-5	4-5	6	7	8	9	10

Table 34: Head to head comparison, ignoring ties, for English-Russian systems

Statistical Machine Translation with Automatic Identification of Translationese

Naama Twitto-Shmuel
Dept. of Computer Science
University of Haifa
Israel
naama.twitto@gmail.com

Noam Ordan
Cluster of Excellence, MMCI
Universität des Saarlandes
Germany
noam.ordan@gmail.com

Shuly Wintner
Dept. of Computer Science
University of Haifa
Israel
shuly@cs.haifa.ac.il

Abstract

Translated texts (in any language) are so markedly different from original ones that text classification techniques can be used to tease them apart. Previous work has shown that awareness to these differences can significantly improve statistical machine translation. These results, however, required meta-information on the ontological status of texts (original or translated) which is typically unavailable. In this work we show that the predictions of translationese classifiers are as good as meta-information. First, when a monolingual corpus in the target language is given, to be used for constructing a language model, predicting the translated portions of the corpus, and using only them for the language model, is as good as using the entire corpus. Second, identifying the portions of a parallel corpus that are translated in the direction of the translation task, and using only them for the translation model, is as good as using the entire corpus. We present results from several language pairs and various data sets, indicating that these results are robust and general.

1 Introduction

Research in Translation Studies suggests that translated texts are considerably different from original texts, constituting a sublanguage known as *Translationese* (Gellerstam, 1986). Awareness to translationese can significantly improve statistical machine translation (SMT). Kurokawa et al. (2009) showed that French-to-English SMT systems whose translation models were constructed from human translations from French to English yielded better translation quality than ones created from translations in the other direction. These results were corroborated by Lembersky et al. (2012a, 2013), who showed that translation models can be adapted to translationese, thereby improving the quality of SMT even further. Awareness to translationese also benefits the *language* models used in SMT: Lembersky et al. (2011, 2012b) showed that language models complied from translated texts better fit the reference sets in term of perplexity, and SMT systems constructed from such language models perform much better than those constructed from original texts.

To benefit from these results, however, one has to know whether the texts used for training SMT systems are original or translated, and previous work indeed used such meta-information. Unfortunately, annotation reflecting the status of texts, or the direction of translation, is typically unavailable. The research question we investigate in this work is whether the predictions of translationese classifiers can replace manual annotation. In a variety of evaluation scenarios, we demonstrate that this is indeed the case. When a monolingual corpus in the target language is given for constructing a language model for SMT, we show that automatically identifying the translated portions of the corpus, and using only them for the language model, is as good as using the entire corpus. Similarly, when a parallel corpus is given, we show that automatically identifying the portions of the corpus that are translated in the direction of the translation task, and using only them for training the translation model, is again as good as using the entire corpus. We present results from several language pairs and various data sets, indicating that the approach we advocate is general and robust.

The main contribution of this work is a general approach that, provided labeled data for training classifiers, can be applied to *any* corpus before it is used for constructing SMT systems, resulting in systems that are as good as (or better than) those that use the entire corpus, but that rely on significantly smaller language and translation models.

We briefly review related work in Section 2. Section 3 describes our methodology and experimental setup. Section 4 details the experiments and their results. We conclude with an analysis of the results and suggestions for future research.

2 Related work

Until recently, SMT systems were agnostic to the ontological status of a text (as original vs. translated). Several recent works, however, underscore the relevance of translationese for SMT. Kurokawa et al. (2009) were the first to show that translationese matters for SMT. They defined two translation tasks, English-to-French and French-to-English, and used a parallel corpus in which the translation direction of each text was indicated. They showed that for the English-to-French task, translation models compiled from English-translated-to-French texts were better than translation models compiled from texts translated in the reverse direction; and the same holds for the reverse translation task. These results were corroborated by Lembersky et al. (2012a, 2013), who further demonstrated that translation models can be adapted to translationese, thereby improving the quality of SMT even further.

Lembersky et al. (2011, 2012b) focused on the *language* model (LM). They built several SMT systems for several pairs of languages. For each language pair they built two systems, one in which the LM was compiled from original English text, and another in which the LM was compiled from text translated to English from each of the languages. They showed that LMs complied from translated texts better fit the reference set in term of perplexity. Moreover, SMT systems that were constructed from translationese-based LMs perform much better than those constructed from original LMs. In fact, an original corpus must be as much as ten times larger in order to yield the same translation quality as a translated corpus.

To benefit from these results, one has to know whether the texts used for training SMT systems are original or translated; such meta-information is typically unavailable. Due to the unique properties of translationese, however, this information can be determined automatically using text-classification techniques. Several works address this task, using various feature sets, and reporting excellent accuracy (Baroni and Bernardini, 2006; van Halteren, 2008; Ilisei et al., 2010; Eetemadi and Toutanova, 2014). Some of these works, however, only conduct in-domain evaluation; much evidence suggests that out-of-domain accuracy is much lower (Koppel and Ordan, 2011; Islam and Hoenen, 2013; Avner et al., Forthcoming).

A thorough investigation was conducted by Volansky et al. (2015), who focused on the features of translationese (in English) from a translation theory perspective. They defined several classifiers based on various linguistically-informed features, implementing several hypotheses of Translation Studies. We adopt some of their best-performing classifiers in this work.[1]

3 Experimental setup

The experiments we describe in Section 4 consist of three parts: 1. Training classifiers to tease apart original from translated texts. 2. Constructing SMT systems with language models compiled from the predicted translations, comparing them with similar SMT systems whose language models consist of the entire monolingual corpora. 3. Constructing SMT systems with translation models compiled from bitexts that are predicted as translated in the same direction as the direction of the SMT task, comparing them with similar SMT systems whose translation models consist of the entire parallel corpora. In this section we describe the language resources and tools required for performing these experiments.

3.1 Tools

Our first task is text classification; to ensure that the length of each text does not influence the classification, we partition the training corpus in most experiments into chunks of approximately 2000 tokens (ending on a sentence boundary). We henceforth use *chunk units* to define the size of a sub-corpus. Our major experiments involve 2,500 chunks (of approximately 2,000 tokens each, hence 5M tokens). To detect sentence

[1] Volansky et al. (2015) only identified English translationese; we extend the experimentation also to French and adapt their classifiers accordingly.

boundaries, we use the UIUC CCG tool.[2]

We use MOSES (Koehn et al., 2007) for tokenization and case normalization. Part-of-speech (POS) tagging is done with *OpenNLP*[3] for English and the *Stanford* tagger[4] for French. For classification we use *Weka* (Hall et al., 2009) with the *SMO* algorithm, a support-vector machine with a linear kernel, in its default configuration.

To construct language models and measure perplexity, we use *SRILM* (Stolcke, 2002) with interpolated modified Kneser-Ney discounting (Chen and Goodman, 1996) and with a fixed vocabulary. We limit language models to a fixed vocabulary and map out-of-vocabulary (OOV) tokens to a unique symbol to overcome sparsity and better control the OOV rates among various corpora.

We train and build the SMT systems using MOSES. For evaluation we use MultEval (Clark et al., 2011), which takes machine translation hypotheses from several runs of an optimizer and provides three popular metric scores, BLEU (Papineni et al., 2002), METEOR (Denkowski and Lavie, 2011), and TER (Snover et al., 2006)), as well as standard deviations and p-values.

3.2 Corpora

To construct SMT systems we need both monolingual corpora (for the language model) and bilingual ones (for the translation model). The main corpora we use are Europarl (Koehn, 2005) and the Canadian Hansard. Europarl is a multilingual corpus recording the proceedings of the European Parliament. Some portions of the corpus are annotated with the original language of the utterances, and we use the method of Lembersky et al. (2012a) to identify the source language of other segments. The Hansard is a parallel corpus consisting of transcriptions of the Canadian parliament in English and (Canadian) French from 2001-2009. We use a version that is annotated with the original language of each parallel sentence.[5] We also use the News Commentary corpus (Callison-Burch et al., 2007), a French-English corpus in the domain of politics, economics and science. The direction of translation of this corpus is not annotated.[6]

3.2.1 Language model experiments

Our main experiments focus on French translated to English (FR→EN), and we define a classifier that can identify English translationese. However, to further establish the robustness of our approach, we also experiment with German translated to English (DE→EN) and with English translated to French (EN→FR). We also conduct cross-corpus experiments in which we train translationese classifier on one corpus (Europarl) and test its contribution to SMT on another (Hansard, News). These experiments are crucial for evaluating the robustness of our approach, in light of the findings that translationese classification is much less accurate outside the training domain.

From the Europarl corpus we use several portions, collected over the years 1996 to 1999 and 2001 to 2009. In all experiments, the split of the monolingual corpora to translated vs. original texts is balanced (in terms of chunks). The parallel corpora are divided to two sections according to the direction of the translation (when it is known). For example, for the French-to-English translation task, we divide the Europarl corpus to a French-original section (FR→EN) and an English-original section. We also use portions of Europarl to define reference sets for evaluating the perplexity of LMs. For this task we only use translated texts.

For constructing translation models we use parallel corpora. For the FR→EN and EN→FR tasks we use original French text, aligned with its translation to English (FR→EN). For the DE→EN translation task we use original German text, aligned with its translation to English (DE→EN). The parallel portions we use are disjoint from those used for the language model and are evenly balanced between the original text and the aligned translated text. From Europarl we use portions from the period of January to September 2000.

To tune and evaluate SMT systems we use reference sets that are extracted from a parallel, aligned corpus. These include 1000 sentence pairs for tuning and 1000 (different) sentence pairs for evaluation. The sentences are randomly extracted from another portion of the Europarl corpus, collected over the period of October to December 2000, and another portion of Hansard. All tuning and references sets are disjoint from the training materials.

3.2.2 Translation model experiments

In this set of experiments we focus again on FR→EN systems, but also experiment with

[2] `http://cogcomp.cs.illinois.edu/page/tools_view/2`, accessed 11.10.2013.

[3] `http://opennlp.apache.org`, 24.08.2012.

[4] `http://nlp.stanford.edu/software/tagger.shtml`, accessed 08.02.2013.

[5] We are grateful to Cyril Goutte, George Foster and Pierre Isabelle for providing us with this version of the corpus.

[6] The precise data sets we used will be made available.

DE→EN and EN→FR. We conduct in-domain experiments using the Europarl corpus, and a cross-corpus experiment in which we train on one corpus and test on another. From the Europarl corpus we use several portions, collected over the years 1996 to 1999 and 2001 to 2009.

To construct language models for the in-domain experiments we use Europarl portions from the period of January to September 2000 (this is the English/French side of the training data used for building the translation model in the language model experiments). For cross-corpus experiments we use the LM built from translated texts that we use in the Hansard language model experiments. For tuning and evaluation we use the same sets used in the language model experiments.

4 Experiments and results

4.1 Language models experiments

We build several SMT systems that use the same translation model, but differ in their language models. This involves three tasks detailed below.

4.1.1 Classification of translationese

The first task is to train a classifier to detect translationese. This has been done before, and we adapt some of the classifiers of Volansky et al. (2015). Specifically, our classifier is based on *Contextual function words*: we use counts of (contiguous) trigrams $\langle w_1, w_2, w_3 \rangle$, where each element w_i is either a word or its part of speech (POS), at least two of the elements are function words, and at most one is a POS tag. An example feature is the triple ⟨*in,the,Noun*⟩. This feature set combines lexical and shallow syntactic information in a way that was proven useful for identifying translationese. We also add counts of punctuation marks, another feature that was shown accurate.[7] We evaluate the accuracy of this classifier intrinsically, using ten-fold cross-validation.

Then, we use the prediction of the classifier to determine whether test texts are original or translated. The classifier thus defines a partition of the training corpus to (predicted) originals vs. translations. Based on the classifier's prediction, we build language models from the sub-corpus determined as translated. We then evaluate the fitness of this sub-corpus to the reference set, in terms of perplexity. Specifically, we train 1-, 2-, 3-, and 4-gram LMs for this sub-corpus and measure their perplexity on the reference set. This provides an extrinsic evaluation for the quality of the classifier.

The results are reported in Table 1. Replicating the results of Volansky et al. (2015), we demonstrate that the classifier is indeed excellent. Not surprisingly, good classification yields good language models. The rightmost columns of Table 1 list the perplexity of language models trained on the sub-corpus that was predicted as translated, when applied to the reference set. For comparison, we provide in Table 1 also the perplexity of language models compiled from the entire training set; from the *actual* (as opposed to predicted) translated texts; and from the actual *original* texts. Clearly, and consistently with the results of Lembersky et al. (2012b), the original texts yield the worst language models (highest perplexity), whereas the actual translated texts yield an upper bound (lowest perplexity). Still, due to the high accuracy of the classifier, its perplexity is very similar to this upper bound. The model that is built from all texts, both original and translated, is twice as large as the corpus used for the other models, hence the lower perplexity rates.

To further establish the robustness of these results, we repeat the experiments with other corpora, this time consisting of German translated to English (DE→EN), and also English translated to French (EN→FR). We only report results for the 4-gram LMs (Table 2). The accuracies of the classifiers are high, comparable to the case of FR→EN. Moreover, the perplexities of the induced language models are very close to the upper bound obtained by taking actual translated texts.

4.1.2 Language models compiled from predicted translationese

We established the fact that translated texts can be identified with high accuracy, and that language models compiled from predicted translations fit the reference sets well. Next, we construct SMT systems with these language models. Our hypothesis is that language models compiled from (predicted) translationese will perform as well as (or even better than) language models compiled from the entire corpus. We evaluate this hypothesis in several scenarios: when the corpus used for the language model is the same corpus used for training the classifiers; or a different one, but of the same type; or from a completely different domain.

We begin with a French-to-English translation task. We use the same (4-gram) language models

[7] The code for feature generation will be released.

Data set	Chunks	Acc. (%)	Perplexity 1-gram	2-gram	3-gram	4-gram
Predicted translations	1245	98.96	463.51	94.81	71.60	68.76
Translated texts	1255		463.58	94.59	71.24	68.37
Original texts	1258		500.56	115.48	91.14	88.31
All texts	2513		473.00	93.34	67.84	64.47

Table 1: Classification of translationese, and fitness to the reference set of FR→EN language models compiled from texts predicted as translated

	DE→EN			EN→FR		
Data set	Chunks	Acc. (%)	Ppl	Chunks	Acc. (%)	Ppl
Predicted translations	1,146	99.08	62.23	1,410	98.47	47.92
Translated texts	1,153		62.07	1,413		47.89
Original texts	1,153		76.68	1,411		59.75
All	2,306		57.48	2,824		44.49

Table 2: Accuracy of the classification, and fitness of language models compiled from texts predicted as translated to the reference set, DE→EN and EN→FR

described in Section 4.1.1, constructed from the predictions of the classifier. We also fix a single translation model, compiled from the parallel portion of the training corpus (Section 3.2). We then train a French-to-English SMT system with the (predicted) LM. As a baseline, we build an SMT system that uses the entire training corpus for its language model; we refer to this system as *All*. As an upper bound (for a system that uses only a portion of the corpus), we build a system that uses the (actual) translated texts for its LM. We also report results on a system that uses only original texts for its LM. All systems are tuned on the same tuning set of 1000 parallel sentences, and are tested on the same reference set of 1000 parallel sentences.

We evaluate the quality of each of the SMT systems using MultEval (Section 3.1). The results are presented in Table 3, reporting the BLEU, METEOR (MET), and TER evaluation measures, as well as the p-value defining the statistical significance with which the system is different from the baseline (with respect to the BLEU score only).

Replicating some of the results of Lembersky et al. (2011, 2012b), we find that using only translated texts for the language model is not inferior to using the entire corpus (although the size of the latter is double the size of the former). In terms of BLEU scores, both yield the same score, 29.1. Similarly, as reported by Lembersky et al. (2011, 2012b), using only original texts is markedly worse, with a BLEU score of 27.8. The main novelty of our current results, however, is the observation that the language model that only uses *predicted*, rather than actual translated texts, performs just as well.[8]

For completeness, we repeat the same experiments with two more language pairs: German to English and English to French. The setup is identical, and we report the same evaluation metrics. The results are presented in Table 4. The emerging pattern is identical to that of French to English.

The results of all the experiments confirm our hypothesis; SMT systems built from *predicted* translationese language models perform as well as SMT systems built from (actual) translated language models, and similarly to (twice as large) mixed language models.

4.1.3 Cross-corpus experiments

The experiments discussed above all use the same type of corpus both for training the translationese classifiers and for training the SMT systems (the actual portions differ, but all are taken from the same corpus). In a typical translation scenario, a monolingual corpus is available for constructing a language model, but the status of its texts (original or translated) is unknown, and has to be predicted by a classifier that was trained on a potentially dif-

[8]In Table 3 and henceforth we highlight in boldface entries that correspond to classifiers whose performance is better than, or not significantly worse than, the performance of the *All* classifier, which is considered the baseline against which all other systems are compared.

Data set	BLEU↑	MET↑	TER↓	p
Predicted translations	**28.9**	**33.2**	**53.8**	0.16
Translated texts	**29.1**	**33.3**	**53.6**	0.58
Original texts	27.8	32.9	54.7	0.00
All	**29.1**	**33.3**	**53.8**	

Table 3: Evaluation of the FR→EN SMT system built from LMs compiled from predicted translationese

	DE→EN				EN→FR			
Data set	BLEU↑	MET↑	TER↓	p	BLEU↑	MET↑	TER↓	p
Predicted translations	**21.9**	**28.6**	**63.8**	0.87	**26.3**	47.8	**58.3**	0.47
Translated texts	**21.8**	**28.6**	**63.9**	0.37	26.1	47.7	**58.5**	0.03
Original texts	21.0	28.4	64.6	0.00	25.1	47.0	59.5	0.00
All	**21.9**	**28.6**	**63.7**		**26.3**	**48.0**	**58.7**	

Table 4: Evaluation of the DE→EN and EN→FR SMT systems built from LMs compiled from predicted translationese

ferent domain. The question we investigate here, then, is whether a classifier trained on texts in one domain is useful for predicting translationese in a different domain.

As a first experiment, we use an (English) translationese classifier that is trained on the Europarl training data, but use the Hansard training data for constructing the SMT system. In this experiment, we do not use the meta-information of the Hansard corpus, but instead use the predictions of the classifier. Based on these predictions, we define a partition of the Hansard training corpus to (predicted) originals vs. translations and use the text chunks that were classified as translated to build 4-grams language models.

Again, as in the in-domain experiment, we construct a single, fixed translation model from the parallel portion of the (Hansard) corpus. We then train a French-to-English SMT system with the (predicted) LM. As a baseline, we build an SMT system that uses the entire Hansard training corpus for its language model (*All*). As an upper bound, we build a system that uses the (real) translated texts for its LM. We also report results on a system that uses only original texts for its LM. All systems are tuned and tested on the same tuning and evaluation reference set.

The results (Table 5) are consistent with the findings of the in-domain experiments. Although the classifier only performs at 78% accuracy, its predictions are sufficient for defining a language model whose BLEU score (37.8) is statistically indistinguishable with the score (38.0) of LMs based on real translations or the entire corpus.

We repeat the cross-corpus experiments with the News Commentary corpus, a French-English parallel corpus for which the direction of translation is not annotated; we only use its English side. Presumably, most of the texts in this corpus consist of original English, but we hypothesize that the classifier may be able to select chunks with translationese-like features and consequently provide a better SMT system. Additionally, as the News Commentary corpus is a collection of editorials, we partition the corpus into (not necessarily equal-length) articles, rather than to 2000-token chunks, to maintain the coherence of chunks.

The results (Table 6) reveal the same pattern: the predicted-translationese system yields a BLEU score of 27.0, statistically insignificant difference compared with the *All* system that uses the entire corpus (27.2). This is obtained with much smaller corpora, only 1,470 chunks (58% of the entire corpus of 2,527 chunks).

4.2 Translation model experiments

We now move to experiments that address the translation model. We build SMT systems that use a fixed language model but differ in their translation model training data. For all systems we use fixed tuning and evaluation sets.

4.2.1 Translation models compiled from predicted translationese

We first train a classifier to detect the direction of the translation (FR→EN vs. EN→FR). We classify the English side of the parallel corpus; for the

Data set	Chunks	Acc. (%)	BLEU↑	MET↑	TER↓	p
Predicted translations	1,321	78.22	**37.8**	**37.7**	**45.9**	0.11
Translated texts	2001		**38.0**	**37.8**	**45.7**	0.86
Original texts	2001		37.5	37.6	46.1	0.00
All	4002		**38.0**	**37.7**	**45.8**	

Table 5: Cross-corpus evaluation: Hansard-based SMT system, Europarl-based classification

Data set	Chunks	BLEU↑	MET↑	TER↓	p
Predicted translations	1,470	27.0	**33.0**	**55.2**	0.02
All	2,527	**27.2**	**33.0**	**55.2**	

Table 6: Cross-corpus evaluation: News Commentary corpus

FR→EN and DE→EN tasks, chunks predicted as *translated* are assumed to be translated in the right direction ($S \rightarrow T$). For the EN→FR task, chunks predicted as *original* are assumed to be translated in the right direction. Then, we use the prediction of the classifier to construct translation models: we only use the chunks predicted as translated in the right direction. For each partition, we match the English with the aligned French (or German) sentences, thereby defining the SMT training data.

We hypothesize that translation models built from such training data are better for SMT. To explore this hypothesis we fix a single language model (Section 3.2), and train an SMT system with the (predicted) partitions and their aligned sentences. As a baseline, we build an SMT system, *All*, that uses the entire training corpus for its translation model. As an upper bound, we build a system that uses for its translation model the portion of the parallel corpus that was indeed translated in the right direction ($S \rightarrow T$). We also report results on a system that uses only the portion of the parallel corpus that was translated in the opposite direction ($T \rightarrow S$) for its translation model. All systems are tuned on the same tuning set and are tested on the same reference set.

The results are presented in Table 7. They are consistent with previous works that showed that SMT systems trained on $S \rightarrow T$ parallel texts outperformed systems trained on $T \rightarrow S$ texts (Kurokawa et al., 2009; Lembersky et al., 2012a, 2013). Indeed, the best-performing systems use either (actual) $S \rightarrow T$ texts (BLEU score of 31.3), or the entire corpus (31.3); the worst system uses (actual) $T \rightarrow S$ texts (28.4). What we add to previous results is the corroboration of the hypothesis that a predicted-translationese system performs just as well as the actual ones.

As in the language model experiments, we repeat the same experiments with two more translation tasks: German to English and English to French. The setup is identical, and we report the same evaluation metrics. The emerging pattern (Table 7) confirms our hypothesis: SMT systems built from *predicted* $S \rightarrow T$ systems perform as well as SMT systems built from the entire corpus.

4.2.2 Cross-corpus experiments

The above results are not very surprising given the high accuracy of the translationese classifier. The question we investigate in this section is whether a classifier trained on texts in one domain is useful for predicting translationese in a different domain.

We train an (English) translationese classifier on the Europarl training data, but use the Hansard corpus for the translation model. We apply the classifier to the English side of the Hansard corpus, and based on its predictions, define a partition of the Hansard training corpus to use for the translation model. As in the in-domain experiment, we construct a single, fixed language model from a portion of the (Hansard) corpus. We then train a French-to-English SMT system with the (predicted) translation model, comparing it to systems that use the entire Hansard training corpus, the (actual) $S \rightarrow T$ texts and the actual $T \rightarrow S$ texts.

Table 8 reports the results. The best-performing systems use either actual $S \rightarrow T$ texts or the entire corpus (BLEU score of 37.3). The classifier performs worse, at 36.3, but still much better than the system that is based on $T \rightarrow S$ texts. This should be attributed to the very small number of chunks predicted by the classifier as $S \rightarrow T$.

Task	Data set	Chunks	Acc. (%)	BLEU↑	MET↑	TER↓	p
FR→EN	Predicted $S \rightarrow T$	1,678	98.93	**31.1**	**34.7**	**52.1**	0.13
	$S \rightarrow T$	1,690		**31.3**	**34.8**	**51.7**	0.94
	$T \rightarrow S$	1,689		28.4	33.3	54.4	0.00
	All	3,379		**31.3**	**34.7**	**51.9**	
DE→EN	Predicted $S \rightarrow T$	1,607	99.44	23.7	30.3	61.6	0.00
	$S \rightarrow T$	1,613		**24.0**	30.4	**61.3**	0.05
	$T \rightarrow S$	1,612		21.7	29.0	63.9	0.00
	All	3,225		**24.2**	**30.5**	**61.1**	
EN→FR	Predicted $S \rightarrow T$	1,678	98.93	**29.4**	**50.7**	**55.3**	0.11
	$S \rightarrow T$	1,689		**29.3**	**50.8**	**56.1**	0.18
	$T \rightarrow S$	1,690		26.7	48.2	58.2	0.00
	All	3,379		**29.1**	**50.6**	**56.0**	

Table 7: Accuracy of the classification and evaluation of SMT systems built from translation models compiled from predicted translationese

Data set	Chunks	Acc. (%)	BLEU↑	MET↑	TER↓	p
Predicted $S \rightarrow T$	1,840	79.36	36.3	36.9	46.6	0.00
$S \rightarrow T$	3,000		**37.3**	**37.3**	**46.2**	0.94
$T \rightarrow S$	3,000		34.1	35.8	48.9	0.00
All	6,000		**37.3**	**37.4**	**46.0**	

Table 8: Cross-corpus evaluation: Hansard-based SMT system, Europarl-based classification

5 Conclusion

Two fundamental insights, motivated by research in Translation Studies, drive our work:

1. *Direction matters.* When constructing translation models from parallel texts it is important to identify which side of the bitext is the source and which is the target. Translation from the source of the SMT task to its target is always better than the reverse option. In fact, direction itself was utilized as features for classification of translationese by selecting alignment patterns from O to T and vice versa (Eetemadi and Toutanova, 2014, 2015).
2. *Translationese matters.* When constructing language models, translated texts (especially from the source language, but not only) are preferable to texts written originally in the target language of the task at hand.

Our main hypothesis was that these benefits to SMT still hold when meta-information on the status of the texts is unavailable, and has to be predicted, especially in light of the deterioration in the accuracy of translationese classifiers in the face of out-of-domain texts. We trained classifiers to identify translationese, and then used their predictions to construct language- and translation-models for SMT, demonstrating that attention to translationese can yield state-of-the-art translation quality with only a fraction of the corpora. We find that one can generally rely on classifiers that identify at least half of the data as translated for both the language model and the translation model.

In future work we would like to improve our classifiers such that smaller chunks of text suffice for accurate identification of translationese. We also believe that combining various feature sets is a key to improving the accuracy, and especially the robustness, of translationese classifiers. In this work we combined two complementary feature sets; more work should be done in this direction. In particular, there is ample evidence that features should be sensitive to language *family*, as translations from similar languages look more similar than translations from unrelated languages (Pym and Chrupała, 2005; Koppel and Ordan, 2011). To further improve the generality and domain-independence, we currently experiment with *unsupervised* classification of translationese, with very encouraging preliminary results (Rabinovich and Wintner, 2015).

Finally, we mainly experimented with English and French in this work, but we are confident that many language pairs can benefit from the methodology we propose.

Acknowledgments

This research was supported by a grant from the Israeli Ministry of Science and Technology. The second author was supported by Cluster of Excellence MMCI at Saarland University. We are grateful to Gennadi Lembersky for his continuous help.

References

Ehud Alexander Avner, Noam Ordan, and Shuly Wintner. Identifying translationese at the word and sub-word level. *Digital Scholarship in the Humanities*, Forthcoming. doi: http://dx.doi.org/10.1093/llc/fqu047. URL `http://dx.doi.org/10.1093/llc/fqu047`.

Marco Baroni and Silvia Bernardini. A new approach to the study of Translationese: Machine-learning the difference between original and translated text. *Literary and Linguistic Computing*, 21(3): 259–274, September 2006. URL `http://llc.oxfordjournals.org/cgi/content/short/21/3/259?rss=1`.

Chris Callison-Burch, Cameron Fordyce, Philipp Koehn, Christof Monz, and Josh Schroeder. (Meta-) evaluation of machine translation. In *Proceedings of the Second Workshop on Statistical Machine Translation*, pages 136–158, Prague, Czech Republic, June 2007. Association for Computational Linguistics. URL `http://www.aclweb.org/anthology/W/W07/W07-0718`.

Stanley F. Chen and Joshua Goodman. An empirical study of smoothing techniques for language modeling. In *Proceedings of the 34th Annual Meeting on Association for Computational Linguistics*, ACL '96, pages 310–318, Stroudsburg, PA, USA, 1996. Association for Computational Linguistics. doi: 10.3115/981863.981904. URL `http://dx.doi.org/10.3115/981863.981904`.

Jonathan H. Clark, Chris Dyer, Alon Lavie, and Noah A. Smith. Better hypothesis testing for statistical machine translation: Controlling for optimizer instability. In *Proceedings of the 49th Annual Meeting of the Association for Computational Linguistics: Human Language Technologies*, pages 176–181, Portland, Oregon, USA, June 2011. Association for Computational Linguistics. URL `http://www.aclweb.org/anthology/P11-2031`.

Michael Denkowski and Alon Lavie. Meteor 1.3: Automatic metric for reliable optimization and evaluation of machine translation systems. In *Proceedings of the Sixth Workshop on Statistical Machine Translation*, pages 85–91. Association for Computational Linguistics, July 2011. URL `http://www.aclweb.org/anthology/W11-2107`.

Sauleh Eetemadi and Kristina Toutanova. Asymmetric features of human generated translation. In *Proceedings of the 2014 Conference on Empirical Methods in Natural Language Processing (EMNLP)*, pages 159–164. Association for Computational Linguistics, October 2014. URL `http://www.aclweb.org/anthology/D14-1018`.

Sauleh Eetemadi and Kristina Toutanova. Detecting translation direction: A cross-domain study. In *NAACL Student Research Workshop*. ACL – Association for Computational Linguistics, June 2015. URL `http://research.microsoft.com/apps/pubs/default.aspx?id=249114`.

Martin Gellerstam. Translationese in Swedish novels translated from English. In Lars Wollin and Hans Lindquist, editors, *Translation Studies in Scandinavia*, pages 88–95. CWK Gleerup, Lund, 1986.

Mark Hall, Eibe Frank, Geoffrey Holmes, Bernhard Pfahringer, Peter Reutemann, and Ian H. Witten. The WEKA data mining software: an update. *SIGKDD Explorations*, 11(1):10–18, 2009. ISSN 1931-0145. doi: 10.1145/1656274.1656278. URL `http://dx.doi.org/10.1145/1656274.1656278`.

Iustina Ilisei, Diana Inkpen, Gloria Corpas Pastor, and Ruslan Mitkov. Identification of translationese: A machine learning approach. In Alexander F. Gelbukh, editor, *Proceedings of CICLing-2010: 11th International Conference on Computational Linguistics and Intelligent Text Processing*, volume 6008 of *Lecture Notes in Computer Science*, pages 503–511. Springer, 2010. ISBN 978-3-642-12115-9. URL `http://dx.doi.org/10.1007/978-3-642-12116-6`.

Zahurul Islam and Armin Hoenen. Source and translation classification using most frequent words. In *Proceedings of the Sixth International Joint Conference on Natural Language Processing*, pages 1299–1305, Nagoya, Japan, October 2013. Asian Federation of Natural Language Processing. URL http://www.aclweb.org/anthology/I13-1185.

Philipp Koehn. Europarl: A parallel corpus for statistical machine translation. In *Proceedings of the tenth Machine Translation Summit*, pages 79–86. AAMT, 2005. URL http://mt-archive.info/MTS-2005-Koehn.pdf.

Philipp Koehn, Hieu Hoang, Alexandra Birch, Chris Callison-Burch, Marcello Federico, Nicola Bertoldi, Brooke Cowan, Wade Shen, Christine Moran, Richard Zens, Chris Dyer, Ondrej Bojar, Alexandra Constantin, and Evan Herbst. Moses: Open source toolkit for statistical machine translation. In *Proceedings of the 45th Annual Meeting of the Association for Computational Linguistics Companion Volume Proceedings of the Demo and Poster Sessions*, pages 177–180, Prague, Czech Republic, June 2007. Association for Computational Linguistics. URL http://www.aclweb.org/anthology/P07-2045.

Moshe Koppel and Noam Ordan. Translationese and its dialects. In *Proceedings of the 49th Annual Meeting of the Association for Computational Linguistics: Human Language Technologies*, pages 1318–1326, Portland, Oregon, USA, June 2011. Association for Computational Linguistics. URL http://www.aclweb.org/anthology/P11-1132.

David Kurokawa, Cyril Goutte, and Pierre Isabelle. Automatic detection of translated text and its impact on machine translation. In *Proceedings of MT-Summit XII*, pages 81–88, 2009.

Gennadi Lembersky, Noam Ordan, and Shuly Wintner. Language models for machine translation: Original vs. translated texts. In *Proceedings of the 2011 Conference on Empirical Methods in Natural Language Processing*, pages 363–374, Edinburgh, Scotland, UK, July 2011. Association for Computational Linguistics. URL http://www.aclweb.org/anthology/D11-1034.

Gennadi Lembersky, Noam Ordan, and Shuly Wintner. Adapting translation models to translationese improves SMT. In *Proceedings of the 13th Conference of the European Chapter of the Association for Computational Linguistics*, pages 255–265, Avignon, France, April 2012a. Association for Computational Linguistics. URL http://www.aclweb.org/anthology/E12-1026.

Gennadi Lembersky, Noam Ordan, and Shuly Wintner. Language models for machine translation: Original vs. translated texts. *Computational Linguistics*, 38(4):799–825, December 2012b. URL http://dx.doi.org/10.1162/COLI_a_00111.

Gennadi Lembersky, Noam Ordan, and Shuly Wintner. Improving statistical machine translation by adapting translation models to translationese. *Computational Linguistics*, 39(4):999–1023, December 2013. URL http://dx.doi.org/10.1162/COLI_a_00159.

Kishore Papineni, Salim Roukos, Todd Ward, and Wei-Jing Zhu. BLEU: a method for automatic evaluation of machine translation. In *ACL '02: Proceedings of the 40th Annual Meeting on Association for Computational Linguistics*, pages 311–318, Morristown, NJ, USA, 2002. Association for Computational Linguistics. doi: http://dx.doi.org/10.3115/1073083.1073135.

Anthony Pym and Grzegorz Chrupała. The quantitative analysis of translation flows in the age of an international language. In Albert Branchadell and Lovell M. West, editors, *Less Translated Languages*, pages 27–38. John Benjamins, Amsterdam, 2005.

Ella Rabinovich and Shuly Wintner. Unsupervised identification of translationese. *Transactions of the Association for Computational Linguistics*, 3:419–432, 2015. ISSN 2307-387X. URL https://tacl2013.cs.columbia.edu/ojs/index.php/tacl/article/view/618.

Matthew Snover, Bonnie Dorr, Richard Schwartz, Linnea Micciulla, and John Makhoul. A study of translation edit rate with targeted human annotation. In *Proceedings of Association for Machine Translation in the Americas*, pages 223–231, 2006. URL http://www.cs.umd.edu/~snover/tercom/.

Andreas Stolcke. SRILM—an extensible language modeling toolkit. In *Proced-*

ings of International Conference on Spoken Language Processing, pages 901–904, 2002. URL `citeseer.ist.psu.edu/stolcke02srilm.html`.

Hans van Halteren. Source language markers in EUROPARL translations. In Donia Scott and Hans Uszkoreit, editors, *COLING 2008, 22nd International Conference on Computational Linguistics, Proceedings of the Conference, 18-22 August 2008, Manchester, UK*, pages 937–944, 2008. ISBN 978-1-905593-44-6. URL `http://www.aclweb.org/anthology/C08-1118`.

Vered Volansky, Noam Ordan, and Shuly Wintner. On the features of translationese. *Digital Scholarship in the Humanities*, 30(1):98–118, April 2015.

Data Selection With Fewer Words

Amittai Axelrod
University of Maryland
amittai@umd.edu

Philip Resnik
University of Maryland
resnik@umd.edu

Xiaodong He
Microsoft Research
xiaohe@microsoft.com

Mari Ostendorf
University of Washington
ostendo@uw.edu

Abstract

We present a method that improves data selection by combining a hybrid word/part-of-speech representation for corpora, with the idea of distinguishing between rare and frequent events. We validate our approach using data selection for machine translation, and show that it maintains or improves BLEU and TER translation scores while substantially improving vocabulary coverage and reducing data selection model size. Paradoxically, the coverage improvement is achieved by abstracting away over 97% of the total training corpus vocabulary using simple part-of-speech tags during the data selection process.

1 Introduction

Data selection uses a small set of domain-relevant data to select additional training items from a much larger, out-of-domain dataset. Its goal is to filter Big Data down to Good Data: finding the best, most relevant data to use to train a model for a particular task.

The prevalent data selection method, cross-entropy difference (Moore and Lewis, 2010), can produce domain-specific systems that are usually as good as or better than systems using all available training data (Axelrod et al., 2011). The size of these domain-specific systems scales roughly linearly with the amount of selected data: a system trained on the most domain-relevant 10% of the full out-of-domain dataset will be only one tenth of the size of a system trained using all the available data. This can be a large win in settings where training time matters, and also where compactness of the final system matters, e.g. running speech recognition or translation on mobile devices.

While data selection thus eliminates the need to train systems on the entire pool of available data, the data selection process itself does not scale well (it still requires a language model built on the entire pool) and, more significantly, it comes at a cost: training on selected subsets leads to reductions in vocabulary coverage compared to training on the full out-of-domain data pool. This coverage is important, because most NLP systems face the problem of handling words that were not seen in training the system, i.e. out-of-vocabulary (OOV) words. In automatic speech recognition (ASR), for example, OOV words pose a substantial problem, since the system will hallucinate a phonetically similar word in its vocabulary when an OOV word is encountered. In machine translation (MT), our focal application in this paper, OOVs can sometimes be transliterated, but often they are ignored or passed through without translation, and gaps in vocabulary coverage can have a significant effect on MT performance (Daumé III and Jagarlamudi, 2011; Irvine and Callison-burch, 2013).

We introduce a method that preserves the data selection benefit of reducing translation system size. Our method performs as well or better than the standard cross-entropy difference method, as measured by downstream MT results. To this we add the benefits of substantially improved lexical coverage, as well as lower memory requirements for the data selection model itself.

This improvement stems from constructing a hybrid representation of the text that abstracts away words that are infrequent in either of the in-domain and general corpora. They are replaced with their part-of-speech (POS) tags, permitting their n-gram statistics to be robustly aggregated: intuitively, if a domain-relevant sentence includes a rare word in some non-rare context (e.g. "An earthquake in Port-au-Prince"), then another sentence with the same context but a *different* rare word is probably also just as relevant (e.g. "An earthquake in Kodari"). While this method requires pre-processing the corpora to POS tag the data, the idea should generalize to automatically-derived word classes.

We present results using data selection to train domain-relevant SMT systems, yielding favorable performance compared against the standard approaches of Moore and Lewis (2010) and Axelrod et al. (2011). Paradoxically, this is achieved by a selection process in which the specific lexical items for infrequent words – up to 97% of the total vocabulary – are replaced with POS tags.

2 Related Work

Data selection is a widely-used variant of domain adaptation that requires quantifying the relevance to the domain of the sentences in a pooled corpus of additional data. The pool is sorted by relevance score, the highest ranked portion is kept, and the rest discarded.This process – also known as "rank-and-select" in language modeling (Sethy et al., 2009) – identifies the subset of the data pool that is most like the in-domain corpus and keeps it for translation system training, in lieu of using the entire data pool. The resulting translation systems are more compact and cheaper to train and run than the full-corpus system. The catch, of course, is that any large data pool can be expected to contain sentences that are at best irrelevant to the domain, and at worst detrimental: the goals of fidelity (matching in-domain data as closely as possible) and broad coverage are often at odds (Gascó et al., 2012). As a result, much work has focused on fidelity. Mirkin and Besacier (2014) survey the difficulties of increasing coverage while minimizing impact on model performance.

We build on the standard approach for data selection in language modeling, which uses *cross-entropy difference* as the similarity metric (Moore and Lewis, 2010). The Moore-Lewis procedure first trains an in-domain language model (LM) on the in-domain data, and another LM on the full pool of general data. It assigns to each full-pool sentence s a *cross-entropy difference score*,

$$H_{LM_{IN}}(s) - H_{LM_{POOL}}(s), \qquad (1)$$

where $H_m(s)$ is the per-word cross entropy of s according to language model m. Lower scores for cross-entropy difference indicate more relevant sentences, i.e. those that are most like the target domain and unlike the full pool average. In bilingual settings, the *bilingual Moore-Lewis* criterion, introduced by Axelrod et al. (2011), combines the cross-entropy difference scores from each side of the corpus; i.e. for sentence pair $\langle s_1, s_2 \rangle$:

$$\begin{aligned}&(H_{LM_{IN_1}}(s_1) - H_{LM_{POOL_1}}(s_1))\\ &+(H_{LM_{IN_2}}(s_2) - H_{LM_{POOL_2}}(s_2)) \qquad (2)\end{aligned}$$

After sorting on the relevant criterion, the top-n sentences (or sentence pairs) are added to the in-domain data to create the new, combined training set. Typically a range of values for n is considered, selecting the n that performs best on held-out in-domain data.

While shown to be effective, however, word-based scores may not capture all facets of relevance. The strategy of a *hybrid* word/POS representation was first explored by Bulyko et al. (2003), who used class-dependent weights for mixing multi-source language models. The classes were a combination of the 100 most frequent words and POS tags. Bisazza and Federico (2012) target in-domain coverage by using a hybrid word/POS representation to train an additional LM for decoding in an MT pipeline. Toral (2013) uses a hybrid word/class representation for data selection for language modeling; he replaces all named entities with their type (e.g. 'person', 'organization'), and experiments with also lemmatizing the remaining words.

3 Our Approach: Abstracting Away Words in the Long Tail

Our approach is motivated by the observation that domain mismatches can have a strong register component, and this comprises both lexical and syntactic differences. We are inspired, as well, by work in stylometry, observing that attempts to quantify differences between text datasets try to learn too much from the long tail (Koppel et al., 2003): most words occur very rarely, meaning that empirical statistics for them are probably overestimating their seen contexts and underestimating unseen ones.

We therefore adopt a hybrid word/POS representation strategy, but, crucially, we focus not on restricting attention to *frequent* words, but on avoiding the undue effects of *infrequent* words. The proposal can be realized straightforwardly: after part-of-speech tagging the in-domain and pool corpora, we identify all words that appear infrequently in either one of the two corpora, and replace each of their word tokens with its POS tag.

Relevance computation, sentence ranking and subset selection then proceed as usual according to the Moore-Lewis or bilingual Moore-Lewis criterion.

As an example, consider again the phrases *"an earthquake in Port-au-Prince"* and *"an earthquake in Kodari"*, and suppose that the words *an*, *in*, and *earthquake* are above-threshold in frequency. Our hybrid word/POS representation for both sentences would be the same: *"an earthquake in NNP"*.

Our approach differs from the standard data selection method most significantly in its handling of rare words in frequent contexts. Consider a domain-specific n-gram context c that appears with a rare word w. For example, in a hypothetical news domain, let c = *"an earthquake in"*, made up of common words, and let w = *Port-au-Prince*. Suppose that the in-domain corpus contains the phrase *"an earthquake in Port-au-Prince"* eight times. The word w does not appear any other times in the in-domain corpus, and the word w' = *Kodari* never appears at all.

Now suppose the out-of-domain pool corpus contains a sentence with *"an earthquake in Kodari"*. The standard Moore-Lewis method considers *Kodari* to be an unknown word, and so only credits that pool sentence with matching the elements of c. In contrast, our method replaces both rare words w and w' with their POS tag, *NNP*, so that the pool sentence contains *"an earthquake in NNP"*. Our method thus credits c from the in-domain corpus, like Moore-Lewis, but we *also* credit the sentence with matching the 4-gram *"an earthquake in NNP"*, which appears eight times in the in-domain corpus. Despite not appearing in the pool corpus, the rare word w from the in-domain corpus now provides us information about the relevance of pool sentences containing a syntactically similar rare word w' that shares the same context c.

4 Experimentation

We evaluate our data selection approach in a realistic small-in-domain-corpus setting, in two ways. First, as an intrinsic evaluation, we look at vocabulary coverage of the selected data relative to the in-domain training set, i.e. how many words from the in-domain corpus are out-of-vocabulary for selected data, since models trained on those data would not not be able to handle those words. Second, as an extrinsic evaluation, we use statistical machine translation as a downstream task.

4.1 Evaluation Framework

We define our in-domain corpus as the TED talk translations in the WIT^3 TED Chinese-English corpus (Cettolo et al., 2012), a good example of a subdomain with little available training data. We used the IWSLT *dev2010* and *test2010* sets (also from WIT^3) for tuning and evaluation. The larger pool from which we selected data was constructed from an aggregation of 47 LDC Chinese-English parallel datasets.[1] Table 1 contains the corpus statistics for the task and pool bilingual corpora.

Corpus	Sentences	Vocab (En)	Vocab (Zh)
TED (task)	145,901	49,323	64,616
LDC (pool)	6,025,295	458,570	714,628

Table 1: Chinese-English Parallel Data.

We used the KenLM toolkit (Heafield, 2011) to build all language models used in this work (i.e., both for data selection and for the MT systems used for extrinsic evaluation). In all cases the models were 4-gram LMs. We used the Stanford part-of-speech tagger (Toutanova et al., 2003) when constructing our hybrid representations, to generate the POS tags for each of the English and Chinese sides of the corpora.[2]

We consider three ways of applying data selection using the standard (fully lexicalized) corpus representation and our hybrid representation. The first two use the monolingual Moore-Lewis method (Equation 1) to respectively compute relevance scores using the English (output) side and the Chinese (input) side of the parallel corpora. The third uses bilingual Moore-Lewis (Equation 2) to compute the bilingual score over both sides.

Each of these three variants produces a version of the full pool in which the sentences are ranked by relevance score, from lowest score

[1] Specifically: LDC2000T47 LDC2002T01 LDC2003E07 LDC2003T17 LDC2004E12 LDC2004T07 LDC2005T06 LDC2006T04 LDC2007E101 LDC2007T09 LDC2007T23 LDC2008E40 LDC2008E56 LDC2008T06 LDC2008T08 LDC2008T18 LDC2009E16 LDC2009E95 LDC2009T02 LDC2009T06 LDC2009T15 LDC2010T03 LDC2010T10 LDC2010T11 LDC2010T12 LDC2010T14 LDC2010T17 LDC2010T21 LDC2012T16 LDC2012T20 LDC2012T24 LDC2013E119 LDC2013E125 LDC2013E132 LDC2013E83 LDC2013T03 LDC2013T05 LDC2013T07 LDC2013T11 LDC2013T16 LDC2014E08 LDC2014E111 LDC2014E50 LDC2014E69 LDC2014E99 LDC2014T04 LDC2014T11.

[2] The Stanford NLP tools use the Penn tagsets, which comprise 43 tags for English and 35 for Chinese.

	English	Chinese
TED vocab	49,323	64,616
LDC vocab	458,570	714,628
Joint vocab	470,154	729,283
LDC minus singletons	243,882	373,381
Baseline selection vocab	257,744	388,927

Table 2: Chinese and English vocabulary for the baseline selection process.

	English	Chinese
Joint vocab	470,154	729,283
Vocab with count ≥ 10	10,036	11,440
POS tags	42	35
Hybrid vocab	10,078	11,475

Table 3: Chinese and English vocabulary for the proposed selection process.

(most domain-like) to highest score (least domain-like). For each of those ranked pools, we consider increasingly larger subsets of the data: the best n = 50K, the best n = 100K, and so on. The largest subset we consider consists of the best n = 4M sentence pairs out of the 6M available.

4.1.1 Cross-Entropy Difference Baseline

In addition to comparing against a system trained on all the data, we compare against systems trained on data selected via the standard cross-entropy difference method. The joint vocabulary for the TED and LDC data is shown in Table 2. However, when training the language models used for the baseline selection process, we first pruned the singletons from the LDC vocabulary. This step is not necessary, but provides a slightly stronger baseline. The rationale is that ignoring LDC singletons avoids reserving too much probability mass for rare words outside of the domain of interest. Unlike the experimental systems below, pruning the lexicon simply ignores the words in the corpus and does not replace them with anything. This process removed 47% of the LDC vocabulary in each language. We then merged the remaining words from LDC with the complete TED lexicon. This produced a final vocabulary of 257,744 (En) and 388,927 (Zh) words for the baseline cross-entropy difference selection process, as shown in Table 2.

4.1.2 Hybrid Representation Systems

As our infrequent-word threshold (selected ahead of our experimentation), we retained words with a count of 10 or more in each corpus, and replaced all other words with their POS tags to create the hybrid corpus representation. The minimum count requirement reduced the vocabulary to 10,036 English words and 11,440 Chinese words, as shown in Table 3. All other words were replaced, thus a minimum count of 10 in each corpus eliminates over 97% of the vocabulary in each language. We previously found that setting the threshold to 10 is slightly better than a minimum count of 20 (Axelrod, 2014), and varying the threshold further is a topic for future work; see Section 5.

4.2 Results

4.2.1 Intrinsic Evaluation

As noted, each of the bilingual Moore-Lewis method and our hybrid word/POS variation produces a version of the additional training pool in which sentences are ranked by relevance. We then select increasingly larger slices of the data from 50k to 4M, as described in Section 4.1, and report results. As shown in Figures 1 and 2, the hybrid-selected models show consistently improved vocabulary coverage when compared head-to-head with models trained on data selected via a Moore-Lewis method, across all subsets. The only exception is when examining the vocabulary coverage in one language while selecting data based on the other one (*e.g.* selecting data using the English half but measuring the TED vocabulary coverage in Chinese), where our method provides only negligible improvement. Overall, the in-domain (TED) vocabulary coverage is up to 10% better with our proposed method, and the general-data (LDC) vocabulary coverage is up to 20% better.

Table 4 illustrates what this looks like in more detail for a single slice containing the top 2M sentence pairs. The table shows how many more vocabulary items are covered by the 2M sentence slice selected using our hybrid representation (the *Hyb* columns) than are covered by the best 2M sentences selected using the standard lexical representation (the *Std* columns).

Our method shows this improved vocabulary coverage regardless of whether one compares the vocabulary coverage of the methods on the English side (the first three rows) or the Chinese side (the second three rows) of the corpora. Furthermore, the results also hold regardless of which of the three ways of performing cross-entropy-

		TED Coverage		LDC Coverage	
Lang	Method	Std	Hyb	Std	Hyb
	Mono-en	67%	72%	42%	52%
En	Mono-Zh	70%	71%	48%	54%
	Bilingual	68%	72%	42%	52%
	Mono-En	70%	71%	38%	46%
Zh	Mono-Zh	69%	73%	43%	62%
	Bilingual	69%	73%	37%	54%

Table 4: Vocabulary coverage comparison between standard and hybrid-based data selection, for data-selected samples of 2M sentences.

based data selection one uses. The three ways are: monolingual Moore-Lewis for the English and Chinese sides of the parallel corpus (*Mono-En* and *Mono-Zh*, respectively), as well as bilingual Moore-Lewis (*Bilingual*).

When selecting 2M sentences, Table 4 shows that the hybrid representation provides up to an extra 4-5% in-domain vocabulary coverage in either language. Furthermore, the hybrid-based methods obtain up to 10% more general-domain vocabulary coverage for English, and up to 19% more Chinese general-domain vocabulary coverage. All improvements are absolute percentage increases.

Figure 2 shows that our hybrid method's pool vocabulary coverage increases more rapidly than the baseline. The standard approach shows vocabulary coverage increasing more or less linearly with the amount of selection data. By contrast, our proposed method appears to asymptotically approach full in-domain vocabulary coverage, particularly for Chinese. Similarly, Figure 1 shows that our hybrid method also increases more rapidly to asymptotically approach full in-domain vocabulary coverage as well.

4.2.2 Extrinsic Evaluation

Improved vocabulary coverage is a positive result, but we are also interested in downstream application performance. Accordingly, we trained SMT systems using cdec (Dyer et al., 2010) on subsets of selected data. All SMT systems were tuned using MIRA (Chiang et al., 2008) on the dev2010 data from IWSLT (Federico et al., 2011), and then evaluated on the test2010 IWSLT test set using both BLEU (Papineni et al., 2002) and TER (Snover et al., 2006). To isolate the impact of the data selection method, we present results just using the selected data, without the combining with the in-domain data into a multi-model system. Note that the hybrid word/POS representations were only used to compute the cross-entropy difference scores for determining sentences' relevance; the MT systems themselves are trained using the sentences containing the original words.

Figure 3 shows our MT results using both BLEU and TER. The horizontal line is a static baseline that uses all the available training data without data selection. The dashed grey line is from systems trained on data selected via the standard Moore-Lewis cross-entropy-difference method, and the black line is from systems trained on data selected with our hybrid approach. To account for variability in MT tuning, each of the curves in Figure 3 is the average of three tuning/decoding runs.

In terms of system accuracy, our results confirm prior work on data selection, demonstrating that in comparison to training using all available data, comparable or even better MT performance can be obtained using only a fraction of the out-of-domain data available.

Table 5 shows SMT results for the same subset size of 2M sentences used for the coverage results in Table 4. Systems trained on data selected using the hybrid representation are up to +0.5 BLEU better, regardless of whether the selection process is monolingual or bilingual. Indeed, at least for BLEU, it appears that our hybrid method may tend to converge to comparable performance more quickly, a possibility worthy of future experimentation.

The TER results are mixed for this data selection subset size. The MT evaluation scores are low in absolute terms, due to only using the general-domain data, yet are still not inconsistent with prior research done using this dataset (Federico et al., 2011). Fluctuations in the performance curves are also consistent with prior work, as IWSLT scores are very jittery. We averaged results over three tuning runs, for stability. Despite that, Figure 3 shows how high-variance TER scores are on this task.

4.2.3 Selection Model Size

The resulting translation system sizes conform with prior work: selecting smaller subsets yields smaller downstream MT systems. For example, an MT system trained on 1M selected sentences is ~2.3GB in size, a factor of 5 smaller than the 11.3GB baseline MT system trained on all 6M sentences. In addition, we observe a healthy re-

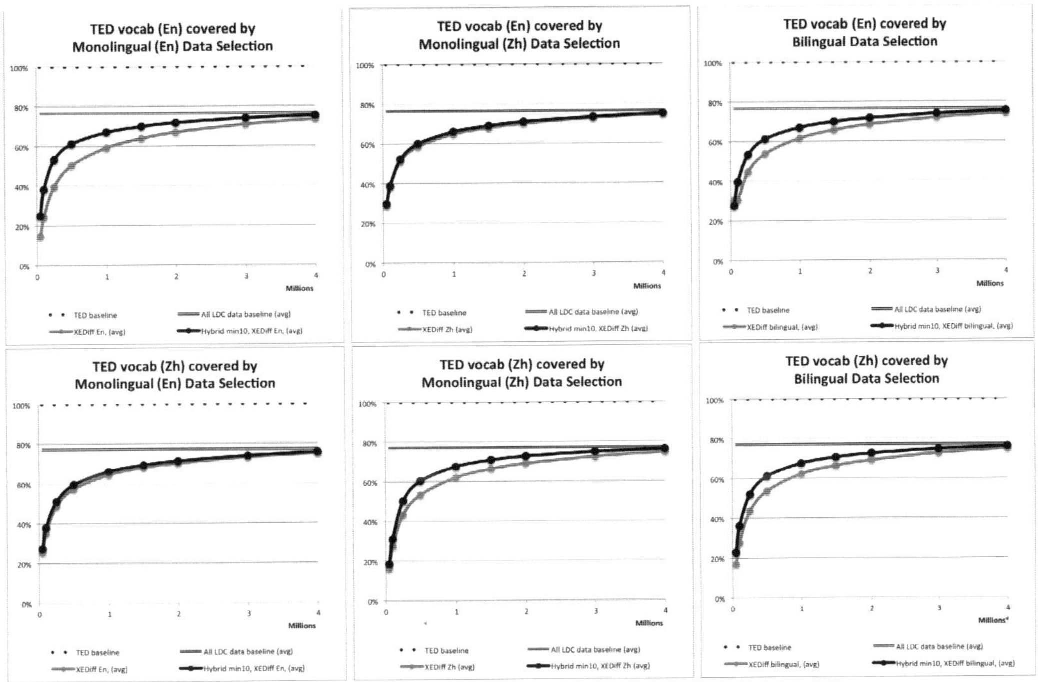

Figure 1: Percentage of TED vocabulary covered vs. number of selected sentences by method.

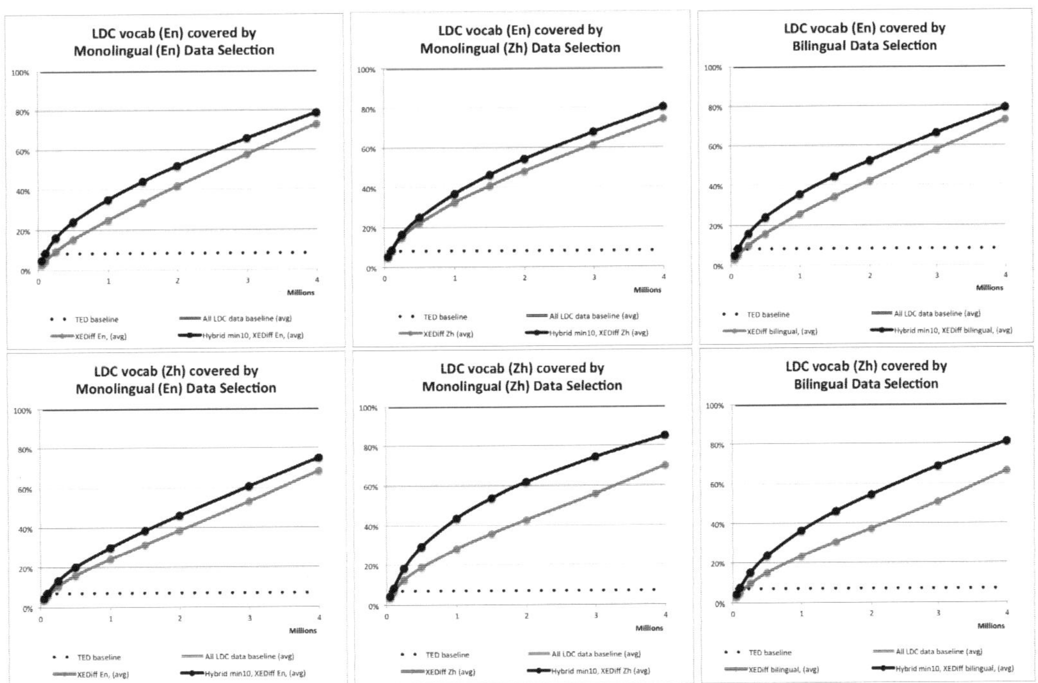

Figure 2: Percentage of LDC vocabulary covered vs. number of selected sentences by method.

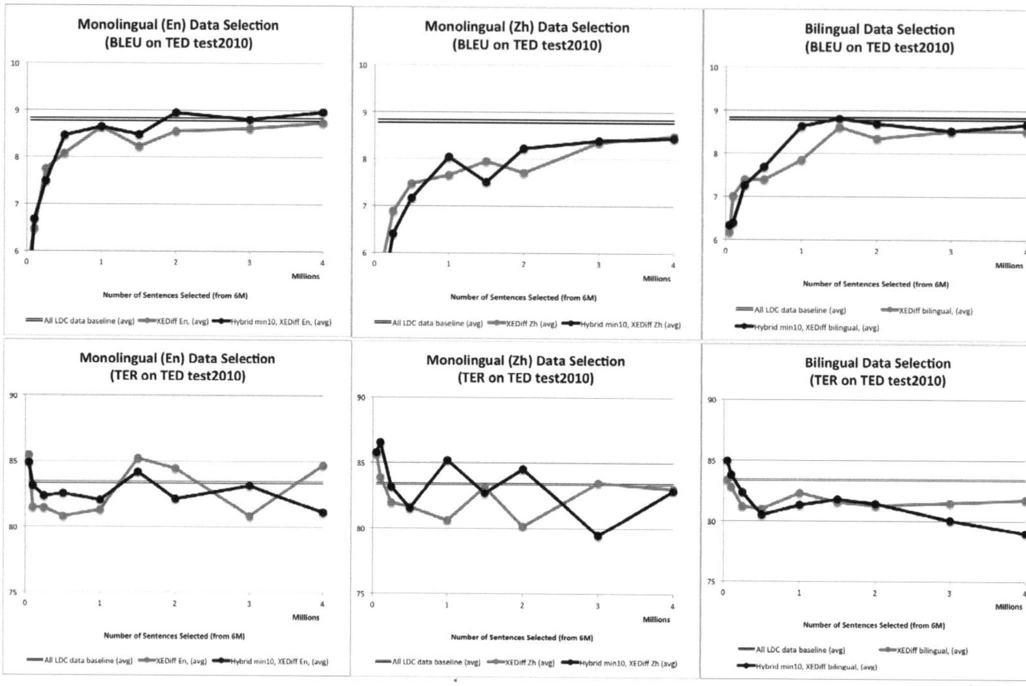

Figure 3: SMT system scores on the TED Zh-En test2010 set vs. number of selected sentences by method.

Metric	Method	Std	Hyb
	Mono-en	8.55	8.95
BLEU	Mono-Zh	7.70	8.22
	Bilingual	8.34	8.68
	Mono-En	84.44	82.15
TER	Mono-Zh	80.16	84.51
	Bilingual	81.27	81.44

Table 5: SMT system score comparison between standard and hybrid-based data selection, for data-selected samples of 2M sentences.

duction in the memory requirements for the data selection process, which requires training a language model on the entire data pool. The binarized language model built using the standard data selection baseline on the full corpus of 6M sentences requires about 2GB, whereas the equivalent all-data LM for our approach is 25% smaller.[3] This means that for any given amount of available memory, the hybrid method can scale up data selection to a larger out-of-domain sentence pool. As a rough example, an 8GB desktop machine can be used to train an LM on 32M sentences using the hybrid representation rather than 24M using the standard text; for a large-memory 128GB machine, our method would allow us to increase the size of the corpus used to train the full-data LM from a maximum of 384M sentences to more than half a billion sentences.

[3]Our back-of-the-envelope estimates ignore the in-domain LM, which is tiny in comparison.

5 Conclusions

We have presented a new method for data selection that retains the existing advantages of the state-of-the-art approach, while improving vocabulary coverage and also improving the ability to scale up to larger out-of-domain datasets. Our motivation is in the practical application of NLP technology, which often requires working with constrained resources and in specific domains with limited training data. The proposal is conceptually simple, uses widely available tools, and is easily applied. A drawback of the proposed approach is that it requires an additional pre-processing step of tagging all of the training data. For languages for which a POS tagger is not available, we expect that data-driven word classes would be a good substitute. In future work we plan to explore hybrid representations further, e.g. abstracting away from infrequent lexical items via distributional clustering or morphological analysis, rather than using part-of-speech information.

Acknowledgments

We gratefully thank the anonymous reviewers and Timo Baumann for their detailed feedback.

References

Axelrod, A. (2014). *Data Selection for Statistical Machine Translation*. PhD thesis, University of Washington.

Axelrod, A., He, X., and Gao, J. (2011). Domain Adaptation Via Pseudo In-Domain Data Selection. *EMNLP (Empirical Methods in Natural Language Processing)*.

Bisazza, A. and Federico, M. (2012). Cutting the Long Tail : Hybrid Language Models for Translation Style Adaptation. *EACL (European Association for Computational Linguistics)*, pages 439–448.

Bulyko, I., Ostendorf, M., and Stolcke, A. (2003). Getting More Mileage From Web Text Sources For Conversational Speech Language Modeling Using Class-Dependent Mixtures. *NAACL (North American Association for Computational Linguistics)*.

Cettolo, M., Girardi, C., and Federico, M. (2012). WIT^3 : Web Inventory of Transcribed and Translated Talks. *EAMT (European Association for Machine Translation)*.

Chiang, D., Marton, Y., and Resnik, P. (2008). Online large-margin training of syntactic and structural translation features. *EMNLP (Empirical Methods in Natural Language Processing)*.

Daumé III, H. and Jagarlamudi, J. (2011). Domain Adaptation for Machine Translation by Mining Unseen Words University of Maryland. *ACL (Association for Computational Linguistics)*.

Dyer, C., Lopez, A., Ganitkevitch, J., Weese, J., Ture, F., Blumson, P., Setiawan, H., Eidelman, V., and Resnik, P. (2010). cdec: A Decoder, Alignment, and Learning Framework for Finite-State and Context-Free Translation Models. *ACL (Association for Computational Linguistics) Interactive Poster and Demonstration Sessions*, (July):7–12.

Federico, M., Bentivogli, L., Paul, M., and Stüker, S. (2011). Overview of the IWSLT 2011 Evaluation Campaign. *IWSLT (International Workshop on Spoken Language Translation)*.

Gascó, G., Rocha, M.-A., Sanchis-Trilles, G., Andrés-Ferrer, J., and Casacuberta, F. (2012). Does More Data Always Yield Better Translations? *EACL (European Association for Computational Linguistics)*.

Heafield, K. (2011). KenLM : Faster and Smaller Language Model Queries. *WMT (Workshop on Statistical Machine Translation)*.

Irvine, A. and Callison-burch, C. (2013). Combining Bilingual and Comparable Corpora for Low Resource Machine Translation. *WMT (Workshop on Statistical Machine Translation)*.

Koppel, M., Akiva, N., and Dagan, I. (2003). A Corpus-Independent Feature Set for Style-Based Text Categorization. *IJCAI Workshop on Computational Approaches to Style Analysis and Synthesis*.

Mirkin, S. and Besacier, L. (2014). Data Selection for Compact Adapted SMT Models. *AMTA (Association for Machine Translation in the Americas)*.

Moore, R. C. and Lewis, W. D. (2010). Intelligent Selection of Language Model Training Data. *ACL (Association for Computational Linguistics)*.

Papineni, K., Roukos, S., Ward, T., and Zhu, W.-j. (2002). BLEU: a method for automatic evaluation of machine translation. *ACL (Association for Computational Linguistics)*.

Sethy, A., Georgiou, P. G., Ramabhadran, B., and Narayanan, S. S. (2009). An iterative relative entropy minimization based data selection approach for n-gram model adaptation. *IEEE Transactions on Audio, Speech, and Language Processing*, 17(1):13–23.

Snover, M., Dorr, B., Schwartz, R., Micciulla, L., and Makhoul, J. (2006). A Study of Translation Edit Rate with Targeted Human Annotation. *AMTA (Association for Machine Translation in the Americas)*, (August):223–231.

Toral, A. (2013). Hybrid Selection of Language Model Training Data Using Linguistic Information and Perplexity. *Workshop on Hybrid Approaches to Translation*, pages 8–12.

Toutanova, K., Klein, D., Manning, C. D., and Singer, Y. (2003). Feature-Rich Part-of-Speech Tagging with a Cyclic Dependency Network. *NAACL (North American Association for Computational Linguistics)*.

DFKI's experimental hybrid MT system for WMT 2015

Eleftherios Avramidis, Maja Popović* and Aljoscha Burchardt
German Research Center for Artificial intelligence (DFKI)
Language Technology Lab
firstname.lastname@dfki.de
* Humboldt University of Berlin
maja.popovic@hu-berlin.de

Abstract

DFKI participated in the shared translation task of WMT 2015 with the German-English language pair in each translation direction. The submissions were generated using an experimental hybrid system based on three systems: a statistical Moses system, a commercial rule-based system, and a serial coupling of the two where the output of the rule-based system is further translated by Moses trained on parallel text consisting of the rule-based output and the original target language. The outputs of three systems are combined using two methods: (a) an empirical selection mechanism based on grammatical features (primary submission) and (b) IBM1 models based on POS 4-grams (contrastive submission).

1 Introduction

The system architecture we will describe has been developed within the QTLEAP project.[1] The goal of the project is to explore different combinations of shallow and deep processing for improving MT quality. The system presented in this paper is the first of a series of MT system prototypes developed in the project. Figure 1 shows the overall architecture that includes:

- A statistical Moses system,
- the commercial transfer-based system Lucy,
- their serial combination ("LucyMoses"), and
- an informed selection mechanism ("ranker").

The components of this hybrid system will be detailed in the sections below.

[1] http://qtleap.eu/

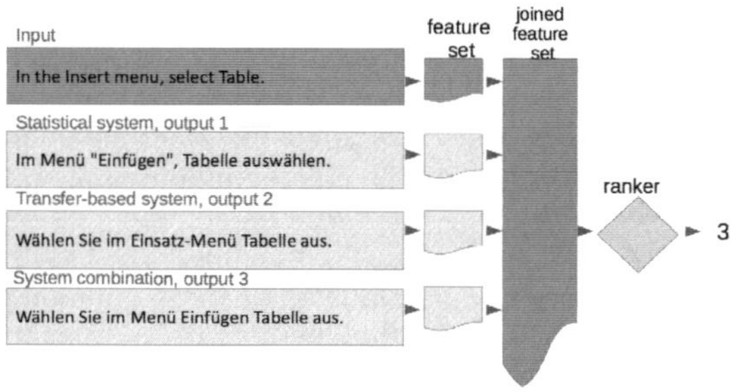

l: Architecture of System Combination.

ıslation systems

istical machine translation system was a vanilla phrase-based system built with Koehn et al., 2007) trained on the cor- oparl ver. 7, News Commentary ver. 9 al., 2014), Commoncrawl (Smith et al., d MultiUN (Eisele and Chen, 2010). Lan- odels of order 5 have been built and inter- with SRILM (Stolcke, 2002) and KenLM l, 2011). For German to English, we also nted with the method of pre-ordering e side based on the target-side grammar and Ney, 2006). As a tuning set we used *-test 2013.*

ısfer-based Lucy system (Alonso and , 2003) includes the results of long lin- fforts over the last decades and that has d in previous projects including EURO- , EUROMATRIX+ and QTLAUNCHPAD, evant hybrid systems have been submit- MT (Chen et al., 2007; Federmann et ; Hunsicker et al., 2012). The transfer- proach has shown good results that com- ı pure statistical systems, whereas it fo- translating according to linguistic structures. Its functionality is based on hand-written linguistic rules and there are no major empirical components. Translations are processed on three phases:

- the **analysis phase**, where the source-language text is parsed and a tree of the source language is constructed
- the **transfer phase**, where the analysis tree is used for the transfer phase, where canonical forms and categories of the source are transferred into similar representations of the target language
- the **generation phase**, where the target sentence is formed out of the transfered representations by employing inflection and agreement rules.

LucyMoses

As an alternative way of automatic post-editing of the transfer-based system, a serial transfer+SMT system combination is used, as described in (Simard et al., 2007). For building it, the first stage is translation of the source language part of the training corpus by the transfer-based system. In the second stage, an SMT system is trained using the transfer-based translation output as a source language and the target language part as a target language. Later, the test set is first translated by the transfer-based system, and the obtained translation is translated by the SMT system. In previous experiments, however, the method on its own could not outperform Moses trained on a large parallel corpus. The example in Figure 1 (taken from the QTLEAP corpus used in the project) nicely illustrates how the serial coupling operates. While the SMT output used the right terminology ("Menü Einfügen" – "insert menu"), the instruction is not formulated in a very polite manner. In contrast, the output of the transfer-based system is formulated politely, yet mistranslating the menu type. The serial system combination produces a perfect translation. In this particular case, the machine translation is even better than the human reference ("Wählen Sie im Einfügen Menü die Tabelle aus.") as the latter is introducing a determiner for "table", which is not justified by the source.

2.1 Sentence level selection

We present two methods for performing sentence level selection, one with pairwise classifier and one based on POS 4-gram IBM1 models.

2.1.1 Empirical machine learning classifier (primary submission)

The machine learning (ML) selection mechanism is based on encouraging results of previous projects including EUROMATRIX+ (Federmann and Hunsicker, 2011), META-NET (Federmann, 2012), QTLAUNCHPAD (Avramidis, 2013; Shah et al., 2013). It has been extended to include several features that can only be generated on a sentence level and would otherwise blatantly increase the complexity of the transfer or decoding algorithm. In the architecture at hand, automatic syntactic and dependency analysis is employed on a sentence level, in order to choose the sentence that fulfills the basic quality aspects of the translation: (a) assert the fluency of the generated sentence, by analyzing the quality of its syntax (b) ensure its adequacy, by comparing the structures of the source with the structures of the generated sentence.

All produced features are used to build a machine-learned ranking mechanism (ranker) against training preference labels. Preference labels are part of the training data and rank different system outputs for a given source sentence based on the translation quality. Preference labels are generated either by automatic reference-based metrics, or derived from human preferences. The ranker was a result of experimenting with various combinations of feature sets and machine learning algorithms and choosing the one that performs best on the development corpus.

The implementation of the selection mechanism is based on the "Qualitative" toolkit that was presented at the MT Marathon, as an open-source contribution by QTLEAP (Avramidis et al., 2014).

Feature sets We experimented with feature sets that performed well in previous experiments. In particular:

- Basic syntax-based feature set: unknown words, count of tokens, count of alternative parse trees, count of verb phrases, PCFG parse log likelihood. The parsing was performed with the Berkeley Parser (Petrov and Klein, 2007) and features were extracted from both source and target. This feature set has performed well as a metric in WMT-11 metrics task (Avramidis et al., 2011).
- Basic feature set + 17 QuEst baseline features: this feature set combines the basic syntax-based feature set described above

with the baseline feature set of the QuEst toolkit (Specia et al., 2013) as per WMT-13 (Bojar et al., 2013). This feature set combination got the best result in WMT-13 quality estimation task (Avramidis and Popović, 2013). The 17 features set includes shallow features such as the number of tokens, LM probabilities, number of occurences of the target work within the target probability, average numbers of translations per source word in the sentence, percentages of unigrams, bigrams and trigrams in quartiles 1 and 4 of frequency of source words in a source language corpus and the count of punctuation marks.

Machine Learning As explained above, the core of the selection mechanism is a ranker which reproduces ranking by aggregating pairwise decisions by a binary classifier (Avramidis, 2013). Such a classifier is trained on binary comparisons in order to select the best out of two different MT outputs given one source sentence at a time. As a training material, we used the evaluation dataset of the WMT shared tasks (years 2008-2014), where each source sentence was translated by many systems and their outputs were consequently ranked by human annotators. These preference labels provided the binary pairwise comparisons for training the classifiers. Additionally to the human labels, we also experimented on training the classifiers against automatically generated preference labels, after ranking the outputs with METEOR (Banerjee and Lavie, 2005). In each translation direction, we chose the label type (human vs. METEOR) which maximizes if possible all automatic scores on our development set, including document-level BLEU.

We exhaustively tested all suggested feature sets with many machine learning methods, including Support Vector Machines (with both RBF and linear kernel), Logistic Regression, Extra/Decision Trees, k-neighbors, Gaussian Naive Bayes, Linear and Quadratic Discriminant Analysis, Random Forest and Adaboost ensemble over Decision Trees. The binary classifiers were wrapped into rankers using the *soft pairwise recomposition* (Avramidis, 2013) to avoid ties between the systems. When ties occurred, the system selected based on a predefined system priority (Lucy, Moses, LucyMoses). The predefined priority was defined manually based on preliminary observations in order to prioritize the transfer-based system, due to its tension to achieve better grammaticality. Further analysis on this aspect may be required.

Best combination The optimal systems are using:

1. the *Basic feature set + 17 QuEst baseline features* for German$rightarrow$English, trained with Suppor Vector Machines (Basak et al., 2007) against human ranking labels.

2. the *basic syntax-based feature set* for English→German, trained with Support Vector Machines against METEOR scores. METEOR was chosen since for this language pair, the empirical mechanism trained on human judgments had very low performance in term of correlation with humans.

2.1.2 POS 4-gram IBM1 models (contrastive submission)

Using the IBM1 scores (Brown et al., 1993) for automatic evaluation of MT outputs without reference translations has been proposed in Popović et al. (2011), and the best variant in terms of correlation with human ranking was the target-from-source direction based on POS 4-grams. Therefore, we investigated this variant for our sentence selection, and we submitted the obtained translation outputs as contrastive.

The IBM1 scores are defined in the following way:

$$\text{IBM1} = \frac{1}{(S+1)^H} \prod_{i=1}^{H} \sum_{j=0}^{S} p(h_i|s_j) \qquad (1)$$

where s_j are the POS 4-grams of the source language sentence, S is the POS 4-gram length of this sentence, h_i are the POS 4-grams of the target language translation output (hypothesis), and H is the POS 4-gram length of this hypothesis.

A parallel bilingual corpus for the desired language pair and a tool for training the IBM1 model are required in order to obtain IBM1 probabilities $p(h_i|s_j)$. For the POS n-gram scores, appropriate POS taggers for each of the languages are necessary. The POS tags cannot be only basic but must have all details (e.g. verb tenses, cases, number, gender, etc.).

The bilingual IBM1 probabilities used in our experiments are learnt from the German-English part of the WMT 2010 News Commentary bilingual corpora. Both German and English POS tags were produced using TreeTagger (Schmid, 1994).

3 Experimental results

Table 1 presents BLEU scores (Papineni et al., 2002), word F-scores and POS F-scores (Popović, 2011) for all individual systems and system combinations for both translation directions. The following interesting tendencies can be observed:

- German→English:
  - Moses and LucyMoses are comparable on the word level (BLEU and WORDF)
  - LucyMoses is best on the syntactic (POS) level
  - LucyMoses achieves better scores than both its components
  - using all three systems with a selection mechanism is the best option
- English→German:
  - Lucy is comparable with Moses on the word level and better on syntactic level
  - LucyMoses improves all scores
  - LucyMoses+Moses (LM+M) is the best combination for word level scores
  - Lucy+LucyMoses (L+LM) is comparable with the combination of all three systems (L+LM+M) for the syntactic oriented POSF score

We submitted the combination of all three systems for both selection mechanisms and for both translation directions. It should be noted that the ML classifier is used for the project's first official prototype, whereas the IBM1 classifier has been investigated only recently in the framework of the project – therefore the primary submission for the shared task is the ML classifier although it yielded lower automatic scores than the IBM1 classifier.

In order to estimate the limits of the classifiers for the given three MT systems, upper bound scores are presented in the last two rows, when selecting criteria were the WORDF and POSF scores themselves. It can be seen that there is a room for improvement for both selection methods. Further investigation, tuning and extension of the selection mechanisms will provide more insights and has potential for future improvements of the selection itself as well as of the MT systems.

Preliminary results concerning analysis of differences between the systems and behaviour of classifiers are shown in the following section.

3.1 Analysis of the results

First step towards better understanding of the selection mechanisms is to investigate the contribution of each of the individual systems in the final translation output. The results are presented in Table 2 in the form of percentage of sentences selected from each system. It is notable that:

- the ML classifier mostly favors the transfer-based output;
- for the English→German translation, the same holds for the IBM1 classifier; for the other translation direction, Lucy is selected very rarely – for less than 2% sentences;
- upper bound selection yields a more or less uniform distribution, however WORDF is clearly biased towards LucyMoses and POSF towards Lucy.

First indication is that the deep features of the ML classifier are active and therefore this classifier has a bias towards the transfer-based output. Furthermore, system contributions of upper bound selection methods indicate that the transfer-based outputs are more grammatical and thus favored by the syntax-oriented POSF score, whereas the LucyMoses system, which can be seen as a lexical reparation of a grammatical output, is favored by the lexical WORDF score. Nevertheless, these first hypotheses need to be confirmed by further studies that are planned.

Table 3 shows examples of differences between the selection methods as well as between the three individual MT systems. The sentences are taken from the WMT-15 test set. First column denotes the selection method which choose the particular translation output. Sentence 1 illustrates the differences between two classifiers as well as between two F-scores; POSF score and ML classifier opt for the transfer-based translation, whereas IBM1 choses Moses and WORDF score prefers LucyMoses. Sentences 2-4 show the discrepance between the ML classifier and the automatic scores; the IBM1 score selection differs from the upper bound selections only for the sentence 4. Such sentences are the most probable reason for lower overall MLC performance in terms of automatic scores. The last sentence shows an example where both classifiers agree, but they disagree with both F-scores.

(a) De→En

German→English			BLEU	WORDF	POSF
individual systems		Lucy (L)	20.8	25.9	42.6
		Moses (M)	23.2	28.2	42.7
		LucyMoses (LM)	23.2	27.9	44.2
selection mechanism	ML classifier	L+LM+M	22.6	27.4	43.6
	POS 4-gram IBM1	L+M	23.2	28.2	42.8
		L+LM	23.2	27.9	44.2
		LM+M	23.7	28.6	44.5
		L+LM+M	23.7	28.6	44.5
upper bounds	max(WORDF)	L+LM+M	**26.9**	**30.8**	46.8
	max(POSF)	L+LM+M	25.6	30.7	**48.6**

(b) En→De

English→German			BLEU	WORDF	POSF
individual systems		Lucy (L)	17.3	22.9	44.5
		Moses (M)	17.1	23.1	41.9
		LucyMoses (LM)	18.9	24.4	45.3
selection mechanism	ML classifier	L+LM+M	18.1	23.7	44.4
	POS 4-gram IBM1	L+M	18.2	23.6	44.7
		L+LM	18.6	24.0	45.7
		LM+M	19.1	24.4	45.1
		L+LM+M	18.9	24.1	45.4
upper bounds	max(WORDF)	L+LM+M	**22.4**	**26.6**	47.1
	max(POSF)	L+LM+M	21.0	26.1	**49.4**

Table 1: Translation results [%] for the German-English language pair.

(a) De→En

German→English		Lucy	Moses	LucyMoses
ML classifier		42.1	36.6	21.3
POS 4-gram IBM1	L+M	2.8	97.2	/
	L+LM	2.5	/	97.5
	LM+M	/	42.4	57.6
	L+LM+M	1.7	56.0	42.3
WORDF	L+LM+M	29.3	31.8	38.9
POSF	L+LM+M	34.5	33.7	31.8

(b) En→De

English→German		Lucy	Moses	LucyMoses
ML classifier		44.0	8.0	48.0
POS 4-gram IBM1	L+M	56.5	43.5	/
	L+LM	63.3	/	36.7
	LM+M	/	45.5	54.5
	L+LM+M	41.5	22.1	36.3
WORDF	L+LM+M	34.2	29.4	36.3
POSF	L+LM+M	42.3	27.1	30.5

Table 2: Percentage of selected sentences from each individual system.

The table also illustrates advantages of the serial LucyMoses system – this system produces the best translation output for all presented sentences except for sentence 3.

4 Summary and outlook

We described a hybrid MT system based on three different individual systems where the final translation output is produced by a sentence level selection mechanism, with the possibility to include deep linguistic and grammatical features. Preliminary analysis suggests that various improvements are possible, starting from improvements on the transfer-based system (handling of lexical items such as terminology, MWEs, OOVs and robustness of parsing), the serial combination (e.g., improved disambiguation), up to more detailed analysis and testing and improvement of the selection mechanism (e.g., integrating more "deep" information from external parsing).

Acknowledgments

This paper has received funding from the European Union's Seventh Framework Programme for research, technological development and demonstration under grant agreement no 610516 (QTLeap: Quality Translation by Deep Language Engineering Approaches). We are grateful to the anonymous reviewers for their valuable feedback.

References

Juan A. Alonso and Gregor Thurmair. 2003. The comprendium translator system. In *Proceedings of the Ninth Machine Translation Summit*, New Orleans, LA, September.

Eleftherios Avramidis and Maja Popović. 2013. Machine learning methods for comparative and time-oriented Quality Estimation of Machine Translation output. In *Proceedings of the Eighth Workshop on Statistical Machine Translation*, pages 329–336, Sofia, Bulgaria, August. Association for Computational Linguistics.

Eleftherios Avramidis, Maja Popović, David Vilar, and Aljoscha Burchardt. 2011. Evaluate with Confidence Estimation : Machine ranking of translation outputs using grammatical features. In *Proceedings of the Sixth Workshop on Statistical Machine Translation*, pages 65–70, Edinburgh, Scotland, July. Association for Computational Linguistics.

Eleftherios Avramidis, Lukas Poustka, and Sven Schmeier. 2014. Qualitative: Open source python tool for quality estimation over multiple machine translation outputs. *The Prague Bulletin of Mathematical Linguistics*, 102(1):5–16.

Eleftherios Avramidis. 2013. Sentence-level ranking with quality estimation. *Machine Translation (MT)*, 28(Special issue on Quality Estimation):1–20.

Satanjeev Banerjee and Alon Lavie. 2005. METEOR: An Automatic Metric for MT Evaluation with Improved Correlation with Human Judgements. In *Proceedings of the ACL 05 Workshop on Intrinsic and Extrinsic Evaluation Measures for MT and/or Summarization*, pages 65–72, Ann Arbor, MI, June.

Debasish Basak, Srimanta Pal, and Dipak Chandra Patranabis. 2007. Support vector regression. *Neural Information Processing-Letters and Reviews*, 11(10):203–224.

Ondřej Bojar, Christian Buck, Chris Callison-Burch, Christian Federmann, Barry Haddow, Philipp Koehn, Christof Monz, Matt Post, Radu Soricut, and Lucia Specia. 2013. Findings of the 2013 Workshop on Statistical Machine Translation. In *8th Workshop on Statistical Machine Translation*, Sofia, Bulgaria, August. Association for Computational Linguistics.

Ondřej Bojar, Christian Buck, Christian Federmann, Barry Haddow, Philipp Koehn, Johannes Leveling, Christof Monz, Pavel Pecina, Matt Post, Herve Saint-Amand, Radu Soricut, Lucia Specia, and Aleš Tamchyna. 2014. Findings of the 2014 Workshop on Statistical Machine Translation. In *Proceedings of the Ninth Workshop on Statistical Machine Translation*, pages 12–58, Baltimore, Maryland, USA, June. Association for Computational Linguistics.

Peter F. Brown, Stephen A. Della Pietra, Vincent J. Della Pietra, and Robert L. Mercer. 1993. The mathematics of statistical machine translation: Parameter estimation. *Computational Linguistics*, 19(2):263–311, June.

Yu Chen, Andreas Eisele, Christian Federmann, Eva Hasler, Michael Jellinghaus, and Silke Theison. 2007. Multi-Engine Machine Translation with an Open-Source (SMT) Decoder. In *Proceedings of the Second Workshop on Statistical Machine Translation.*, pages 193–196. Association for Computational Linguistics.

Andreas Eisele and Yu Chen. 2010. MultiUN: A Multilingual Corpus from United Nation Documents. In Daniel Tapias, Mike Rosner, Stelios Piperidis, Jan Odjik, Joseph Mariani, Bente Maegaard, Khalid Choukri, and Nicoletta Calzolari (Conference Chair), editors, *Proceedings of the Seventh conference on International Language Resources and Evaluation. International Conference on Language Resources and Evaluation (LREC-2010), May 19-21, La Valletta, Malta*, pages 2868–2872. European Language Resources Association (ELRA).

1)	src:	Die Geschichte erinnert sich, und das sollten wir auch tun.
	ref:	History remembers, as should we.
POSF, MLC	Lucy:	The history remembers, and we should also do that.
IBM1	Moses:	Remembers the history, and we should do this.
WORDF	LucyMoses:	History remembers, and we should do the same.
2)	src:	Eine neue Runde indirekter Gespräche wird voraussichtlich noch in diesem Monat in Ägypten beginnen .
	ref:	A new round of indirect talks is expected to begin later this month in Egypt.
MLC	Lucy:	A new round of indirect conversations will probably still begin in this month in Egypt.
	Moses:	A new round of indirect talks is likely to begin in this month in Egypt.
WORDF, POSF, IBM1	LucyMoses:	A new round of indirect talks is likely to begin this month in Egypt.
3)	src:	Ich denke schon.
	ref:	I think so.
	Lucy:	I already think.
WORDF, POSF, IBM1	Moses:	I think so.
MLC	LucyMoses:	I have already think.
4)	src:	Über mehrere Jahre hatte niemand in dem Haus gelebt.
	ref:	No one had lived in the house for several years.
WORDF, POSF	Lucy:	Over several years nobody had lived in the house.
IBM1	Moses:	No one had over several years lived in the House.
MLC	LucyMoses:	For several years, no one had lived in the House.
5)	src:	Mach es nicht schlecht, wenn du nicht weißt, wovon du redest.
	ref:	Don't slag it off if you don't know what you're talking about.
	Lucy:	Do not make it bad if you do not know which you talk about.
MLC, IBM1	Moses:	Do it not bad, if you do not know what they are.
WORDF, POSF	LucyMoses:	Do not make it bad if you do not know what they are talking about.

Table 3: Examples of differences between the selection results and between the three individual systems.

Christian Federmann and Sabine Hunsicker. 2011. Stochastic Parse Tree Selection for an Existing RBMT System. In *Proceedings of the Sixth Workshop on Statistical Machine Translation*, pages 351–357, Edinburgh, Scotland, July. Association for Computational Linguistics.

Christian Federmann, Andreas Eisele, Hans Uszkoreit, Yu Chen, Sabine Hunsicker, and Jia Xu. 2010. Further Experiments with Shallow Hybrid MT Systems. In Chris Callison-Burch, Philipp Koehn, Christof Monz, Kay Peterson, and Omar Zaidan, editors, *Proceedings of the Joint Fifth Workshop on Statistical Machine Translation and MetricsMATR. Workshop on Statistical Machine Translation (WMT-10), located at ACL 2010, July 15-16, Uppsala, Sweden*, pages 77–81, 209 N. Eighth Street Stroudsburg, PA 18360 USA. Association for Computational Linguistics (ACL), ACL.

Christian Federmann. 2012. Can Machine Learning Algorithms Improve Phrase Selection in Hybrid Machine Translation? In *Proceedings of the 13th Conference of the European Chapter of the Association for Computational Linguistics. Joint Workshop on Exploiting Synergies between Information Retrieval and Machine Translation (ESIRMT) and Hybrid Approaches to Machine Translation*, pages 113–118, Avignon, France, April. European Chapter of the Association for Computational Linguistics (EACL).

Kenneth Heafield. 2011. KenLM : Faster and Smaller Language Model Queries. In *Proceedings of the Sixth Workshop on Statistical Machine Translation*, number 2009, pages 187–197, Edinburgh, Scotland, July. Association for Computational Linguistics.

Sabine Hunsicker, Chen Yu, and Christian Federmann. 2012. Machine Learning for Hybrid Machine Translation. In *Proceedings of the Seventh Workshop on Statistical Machine Translation*, pages 312–316, Montréal, Canada, June. Association for Computational Linguistics.

Philipp Koehn, Hieu Hoang, Alexandra Birch, Chris Callison-Burch, Marcello Federico, Nicola Bertoldi, Brooke Cowan, Wade Shen, Christine Moran, Chris Zens, Richard a nd Dyer, Ondřej Bojar, Alexandra Constantin, and Evan Herbst. 2007. Moses: open source toolkit for statistical machine translation. In *Proceedings of the 45th Annual Meeting of the ACL on Interactive Poster and Demonstration Sessions*, ACL '07, pages 177–180, Stroudsburg, PA, USA. Association for Computational Linguistics.

Kishore Papineni, Salim Roukos, Todd Ward, and Wei-Jing Zhu. 2002. BLEU: a Method for Automatic Evaluation of Machine Translation. In *Proceedings of the 40th Annual Meeting of the Association for Computational Linguistics (ACL 02)*, pages 311–318, Philadelphia, PA, July.

Slav Petrov and Dan Klein. 2007. Improved inference for unlexicalized parsing. In *Proceedings of the 2007 Annual Conference of the North American Chapter of the Association for Computational Linguistics*, Rochester, New York. Association for Computational Linguistics.

Maja Popović and Hermann Ney. 2006. POS-based Word Reorderings for Statistical Machine Translation. In *Proceedings of the 5th International Conference on Language Resources and Evaluation (LREC 06)*, pages 1278–1283, Genoa, Italy, May.

Maja Popović, David Vilar Torres, Eleftherios Avramidis, and Aljoscha Burchardt. 2011. Evaluation without references: IBM1 scores as evaluation metrics. In *Proceedings of the Sixth Workshop on Statistical Machine Translation (WMT 2011)*, pages 99–103, Edinburgh, Scotland, July.

Maja Popović. 2011. Morphemes and POS tags for n-gram based evaluation metrics. In *Proceedings of the Sixth Workshop on Statistical Machine Translation (WMT 2011)*, pages 104–107, Edinburgh, Scotland, July.

Helmut Schmid. 1994. Probabilistic part-of-speech tagging using decision trees. In *Proceedings of the international conference on new methods in language processing*, volume 12, pages 44–49. Citeseer.

Kashif Shah, Eleftherios Avramidis, Ergun Biçici, and Lucia Specia. 2013. QuEst: Design, Implementation and Extensions of a Framework for Machine Translation Quality Estimation. *The Prague Bulletin of Mathematical Linguistics (PBML)*, 100:19–30.

Michel Simard, Cyril Goutte, and Pierre Isabelle. 2007. Statistical phrase-based post-editing. In *Proceedings of The North American Chapter of the Association for Computational Linguistics Conference (NAACL-07)*, pages 508–515, Rochester, NY, April.

Jason R Smith, Herve Saint-Amand, Magdalena Plamada, Philipp Koehn, Chris Callison-Burch, and Adam Lopez. 2013. Dirt Cheap Web-Scale Parallel Text from the Common Crawl. In *Proceedings of the 51st Annual Meeting of the Association for Computational Linguistics (Volume 1: Long Papers)*, pages 1374–1383, Sofia, Bulgaria, August. Association for Computational Linguistics.

Lucia Specia, Kashif Shah, José Guilherme Camargo de Souza, and Trevor Cohn. 2013. QuEst - A translation quality estimation framework. In *Proceedings of the 51st Annual Meeting of the Association for Computational Linguistics: System Demonstrations*, pages 79–84, Sofia, Bulgaria, August. Association for Computational Linguistics.

Andreas Stolcke. 2002. Srilm — an Extensible Language Modeling Toolkit. In *System*, volume 2, pages 901–904. ISCA, September.

ParFDA for Fast Deployment of Accurate Statistical Machine Translation Systems, Benchmarks, and Statistics

Ergun Biçici
ADAPT Research Center
School of Computing
Dublin City University, Ireland
ergun.bicici@computing.dcu.ie

Qun Liu
ADAPT Research Center
School of Computing
Dublin City University, Ireland
qliu@computing.dcu.ie

Andy Way
ADAPT Research Center
School of Computing
Dublin City University, Ireland
away@computing.dcu.ie

Abstract

We build parallel FDA5 (ParFDA) Moses statistical machine translation (SMT) systems for all language pairs in the workshop on statistical machine translation (Bojar et al., 2015) (WMT15) translation task and obtain results close to the top with an average of 3.176 BLEU points difference using significantly less resources for building SMT systems. ParFDA is a parallel implementation of feature decay algorithms (FDA) developed for fast deployment of accurate SMT systems (Biçici, 2013; Biçici et al., 2014; Biçici and Yuret, 2015). ParFDA Moses SMT system we built is able to obtain the top TER performance in French to English translation. We make the data for building ParFDA Moses SMT systems for WMT15 available: https://github.com/bicici/ParFDAWMT15.

1 Parallel FDA5 (ParFDA)

Statistical machine translation performance is influenced by the data: if you already have the translations for the source being translated in your training set or even portions of it, then the translation task becomes easier. If some token does not appear in your language model (LM), then it becomes harder for the SMT engine to find its correct position in the translation. The importance of ParFDA increases with the proliferation of training material available for building SMT systems. Table 1 presents the statistics of the available training and LM corpora for the constrained (C) systems in WMT15 (Bojar et al., 2015) as well as the statistics of the ParFDA selected training and LM data.

ParFDA (Biçici, 2013; Biçici et al., 2014) runs separate FDA5 (Biçici and Yuret, 2015) models on randomized subsets of the training data and combines the selections afterwards. FDA5 is available at http://github.com/bicici/FDA. We run ParFDA SMT experiments using Moses (Koehn et al., 2007) in all language pairs in WMT15 (Bojar et al., 2015) and obtain SMT performance close to the top constrained Moses systems. ParFDA allows rapid prototyping of SMT systems for a given target domain or task.

We use ParFDA for selecting parallel training data and LM data for building SMT systems. We select the LM training data with ParFDA based on the following observation (Biçici, 2013):

> No word not appearing in the training set can appear in the translation.

Thus we are only interested in correctly ordering the words appearing in the training corpus and collecting the sentences that contain them for building the LM. At the same time, a compact and more relevant LM corpus is also useful for modeling longer range dependencies with higher order n-gram models. We use 3-grams for selecting training data and 2-grams for LM corpus selection.

2 Results

We run ParFDA SMT experiments for all language pairs in both directions in the WMT15 translation task (Bojar et al., 2015), which include English-Czech (en-cs), English-German (en-de), English-Finnish (en-fi), English-French (en-fr), and English-Russian (en-ru). We truecase all of the corpora, set the maximum sentence length to 126, use 150-best lists during tuning, set the LM order to a value in $[7, 10]$ for all language pairs, and train the LM using SRILM (Stolcke, 2002) with `-unk` option. For GIZA++ (Och and Ney, 2003), max-fertility is set to 10, with the number of iterations set to 7,3,5,5,7 for IBM models 1,2,3,4, and the HMM model, and 70 word

$S \rightarrow T$	Data	Training Data					LM Data	
		#word S (M)	#word T (M)	#sent (K)	SCOV	TCOV	#word (M)	TCOV
en-cs	C	253.8	224.1	16083	0.832	0.716	841.2	0.862
en-cs	ParFDA	49.0	42.1	1206	0.828	0.648	447.2	0.834
cs-en	C	224.1	253.8	16083	0.716	0.832	5178.5	0.96
cs-en	ParFDA	42.0	46.3	1206	0.71	0.786	1034.2	0.934
en-de	C	116.3	109.8	4525	0.814	0.72	2380.6	0.899
en-de	ParFDA	37.6	33.1	904	0.814	0.681	513.1	0.854
de-en	C	109.8	116.3	4525	0.72	0.814	5111.2	0.951
de-en	ParFDA	33.3	33.1	904	0.72	0.775	969.1	0.923
en-fi	C	52.8	37.9	2072	0.684	0.419	52.7	0.559
en-fi	ParFDA	37.2	26.4	1035	0.684	0.41	79.1	0.559
fi-en	C	37.9	52.8	2072	0.419	0.684	5054.2	0.951
fi-en	ParFDA	25.1	34.5	1035	0.419	0.669	985.9	0.921
en-fr	C	1096.9	1288.5	40353	0.887	0.905	2989.4	0.956
en-fr	ParFDA	58.8	63.2	1261	0.882	0.857	797.1	0.937
fr-en	C	1288.5	1096.9	40353	0.905	0.887	5961.6	0.962
fr-en	ParFDA	72.4	60.1	1261	0.901	0.836	865.3	0.933
en-ru	C	51.3	48.0	2563	0.814	0.683	848.7	0.881
en-ru	ParFDA	37.2	33.1	1281	0.814	0.672	434.8	0.857
ru-en	C	48.0	51.3	2563	0.683	0.814	5047.8	0.958
ru-en	ParFDA	33.8	36.0	1281	0.683	0.803	996.3	0.933

Table 1: Data statistics for the available training and LM corpora in the constrained (C) setting compared with the ParFDA selected training and LM data. #words is in millions (M) and #sents in thousands (K).

classes are learned over 3 iterations with the mkcls tool during training. The development set contains up to 5000 sentences randomly sampled from previous years' development sets (2010-2014) and remaining come from the development set for WMT15.

2.1 Statistics

The statistics for the ParFDA selected training data and the available training data for the constrained translation task are given in Table 1. For en and fr, we have access to the LDC Gigaword corpora (Parker et al., 2011; Graff et al., 2011), from which we extract only the story type news. The size of the LM corpora includes both the LDC and the monolingual LM corpora provided by WMT15. Table 1 shows the significant size differences between the constrained dataset (C) and the ParFDA selected data and also present the source and target coverage (SCOV and TCOV) in terms of the 2-grams of the test set. The quality of the training corpus can be measured by TCOV, which is found to correlate well with the BLEU performance achievable (Biçici, 2011).

The space and time required for building the ParFDA Moses SMT systems are quantified in Table 2 where size is in MB and time in minutes. PT stands for the phrase table. We used Moses version 3.0, from `www.statmt.org/moses`. Building a ParFDA Moses SMT system can take about half a day.

2.2 Translation Results

ParFDA Moses SMT results for each translation direction together with the LM order used and the top constrained submissions to WMT15 are given in Table 3 [1], where BLEUc is cased BLEU. ParFDA significantly reduces the time required for training, development, and deployment of an SMT system for a given translation task. The average difference to the top constrained submission in WMT15 is 3.176 BLEU points whereas the difference was 3.49 BLEU points in WMT14 (Biçici et al., 2014). Performance improvement over last year's results is likely due to using higher order n-grams for data selection. ParFDA Moses SMT system is able to obtain the top TER performance in fr-en.

[1] We use the results from matrix.statmt.org.

$S \rightarrow T$	Time (Min)							Space (MB)		
	ParFDA			Moses			Overall	Moses		
	Train	LM	Total	Train	Tune	Total		PT	LM	ALL
en-cs	10	73	83	999	1085	2154	2237	3914	4826	41930
cs-en	11	524	535	965	413	1445	1980	3789	6586	39661
en-de	9	146	155	852	359	1279	1434	3333	4867	36638
de-en	6	232	238	797	421	1285	1523	3065	6233	34316
en-fi	7	0	7	591	569	1212	1219	2605	18746	24948
fi-en	5	308	313	543	164	744	1057	2278	6115	22933
en-fr	22	233	255	2313	331	2730	2985	5628	7359	76970
fr-en	26	330	356	2810	851	3749	4105	6173	6731	86442
en-ru	11	463	474	704	643	1429	1903	4081	4719	43479
ru-en	42	341	383	704	361	1140	1523	4039	6463	40948

Table 2: The space and time required for building the ParFDA Moses SMT systems. The sizes are in MB and time in minutes. PT stands for the phrase table. ALL does not contain the size of the LM.

BLEUc	$S \rightarrow en$					$en \rightarrow T$				
	cs-en	de-en	fi-en	fr-en	ru-en	en-cs	en-de	en-fi	en-fr	en-ru
ParFDA	0.204	0.2441	0.1541	0.3263	0.2598	0.148	0.1761	0.1135	0.3195	0.22
TopC	0.262	0.293	0.179	0.331	0.279	0.184	0.249	0.127	0.336	0.243
diff	0.058	0.0489	0.0249	0.0047	0.0192	0.036	0.0729	0.0135	0.0165	0.023
LM order	8	8	8	8	8	8	8	10	8	8

Table 3: BLEUc for ParFDA results, for the top constrained result in WMT15 (TopWMTC, from `matrix.statmt.org`), their difference, and the ParFDA LM order used are presented. Average difference is 3.176 BLEU points

2.3 LM Data Quality

A LM selected for a given translation task allows us to train higher order language models, model longer range dependencies better, and achieve lower perplexity as shown in Table 4. We compare the perplexity of the ParFDA selected LM with a LM trained on the ParFDA selected training data and a LM trained using all of the available training corpora. We build LM using SRILM with interpolated Kneser-Ney discounting (`-kndiscount -interpolate`). We also use `-unk` option to build open-vocabulary LM. We are able to achieve significant reductions in the number of OOV tokens and the perplexity, reaching up to 78% reduction in the number of OOV tokens and up to 63% reduction in the perplexity. ParFDA can achieve larger reductions in perplexity than the 27% that can be achieved using a morphological analyzer and disambiguator for Turkish (Yuret and Biçici, 2009) and can decrease the OOV rate at a similar rate. Table 4 also presents the average log probability of tokens and the log probability of token `<unk>`. The increase in the ratio between them in the last column shows that OOV in ParFDA LM are not just less but also less likely at the same time.

3 Conclusion

We use ParFDA for solving computational scalability problems caused by the abundance of training data for SMT models and LMs and still achieve SMT performance that is on par with the top performing SMT systems. ParFDA raises the bar of expectations from SMT with highly accurate translations and lower the bar to entry for SMT into new domains and tasks by allowing fast deployment of SMT systems. ParFDA enables a shift from general purpose SMT systems towards task adaptive SMT solutions. We make the data for building ParFDA Moses SMT systems for WMT15 available: `https://github.com/bicici/ParFDAWMT15`.

Acknowledgments

This work is supported in part by SFI as part of the ADAPT research center

		OOV Rate				perplexity				avg log probability			<unk> log probability			<unk>/avg
$S \rightarrow T$	order	C train	FDA5 train	FDA5 LM	%red	C train	FDA5 train	FDA5 LM	%red	C train	FDA5 train	FDA5 LM	C train	FDA5 train	FDA5 LM	%inc
en-cs	3	.038	.055	.014	.64	763	694	444	.42	-2.91	-2.89	-2.66	-4.94	-5.58	-5.69	.26
	4					716	668	403	.44	-2.89	-2.87	-2.62				.27
	5					703	662	396	.44	-2.88	-2.87	-2.61				.27
	8					699	660	394	.44	-2.88	-2.86	-2.61				.27
cs-en	3	.035	.046	.014	.62	281	255	196	.3	-2.46	-2.42	-2.3	-4.84	-5.33	-5.83	.29
	4					260	243	157	.39	-2.43	-2.4	-2.2				.33
	5					251	237	150	.4	-2.41	-2.39	-2.18				.33
	8					247	236	148	.4	-2.41	-2.39	-2.18				.33
en-de	3	.092	.107	.034	.63	425	383	303	.29	-2.68	-2.64	-2.5	-5.69	-5.92	-5.52	.04
	4					414	377	268	.35	-2.67	-2.64	-2.45				.06
	5					412	376	262	.37	-2.67	-2.64	-2.44				.06
	8					412	376	261	.37	-2.67	-2.64	-2.43				.06
de-en	3	.05	.06	.025	.5	289	265	205	.29	-2.48	-2.45	-2.32	-5.69	-5.85	-5.81	.09
	4					277	258	164	.41	-2.46	-2.44	-2.22				.13
	5					275	257	156	.43	-2.46	-2.43	-2.2				.14
	8					275	257	154	.44	-2.46	-2.43	-2.2				.14
en-fi	3	.203	.213	.128	.37	1413	1290	1347	.05	-3.44	-3.42	-3.31	-4.17	-5.45	-4.2	.05
	4					1403	1285	1323	.06	-3.44	-3.41	-3.3				.05
	5					1401	1284	1320	.06	-3.44	-3.41	-3.3				.05
	8					1400	1284	1319	.06	-3.44	-3.41	-3.3				.05
fi-en	3	.087	.107	.019	**.78**	505	465	228	.55	-2.75	-2.72	-2.37	-4.34	-5.86	-5.91	.58
	4					485	449	188	.61	-2.73	-2.71	-2.28				.63
	5					482	447	179	**.63**	-2.73	-2.71	-2.26				.64
	8					481	446	177	**.63**	-2.73	-2.71	-2.26				.65
en-fr	3	.019	.031	.01	.49	196	146	155	.21	-2.3	-2.18	-2.19	-5.28	-5.56	-5.36	.07
	4					173	137	125	.27	-2.25	-2.15	-2.1				.08
	5					167	136	119	.29	-2.23	-2.15	-2.08				.09
	8					165	136	117	.29	-2.23	-2.15	-2.07				.09
fr-en	3	.022	.031	.01	.52	290	217	220	.24	-2.47	-2.35	-2.35	-5.28	-5.44	-5.31	.06
	4					266	208	187	.3	-2.44	-2.33	-2.28				.08
	5					260	207	181	.3	-2.43	-2.33	-2.26				.08
	8					258	207	180	.3	-2.42	-2.33	-2.26				.08
en-ru	3	.049	.054	.014	.71	547	515	313	.43	-2.77	-2.75	-2.51	-3.57	-4.87	-5.45	.69
	4					537	507	273	.49	-2.77	-2.75	-2.44				.73
	5					536	507	264	.51	-2.77	-2.74	-2.43				**.74**
	8					535	507	259	.52	-2.77	-2.74	-2.42				**.74**
ru-en	3	.041	.046	.017	.58	225	214	188	.16	-2.37	-2.35	-2.28	-3.65	-4.9	-5.79	.65
	4					216	207	148	.31	-2.35	-2.33	-2.18				.71
	5					215	206	140	.35	-2.35	-2.33	-2.15				.73
	8					215	206	138	.36	-2.34	-2.33	-2.15				.73

Table 4: Perplexity comparison of the LM built from the training corpus (train), ParFDA selected training data (FDA5 train), and the ParFDA selected LM data (FDA5 LM). %red is proportion of reduction.

(www.adaptcentre.ie, 07/CE/I1142) at Dublin City University and in part by SFI for the project "Monolingual and Bilingual Text Quality Judgments with Translation Performance Prediction" (computing.dcu.ie/~ebicici/Projects/TIDA_RTM.html, 13/TIDA/I2740). We also thank the SFI/HEA Irish Centre for High-End Computing (ICHEC, www.ichec.ie) for the provision of computational facilities and support.

References

Ergun Biçici and Deniz Yuret. 2015. Optimizing instance selection for statistical machine translation with feature decay algorithms. *IEEE/ACM Transactions On Audio, Speech, and Language Processing (TASLP)*, 23:339–350.

Ergun Biçici, Qun Liu, and Andy Way. 2014. Parallel FDA5 for fast deployment of accurate statistical machine translation systems. In *Proc. of the Ninth Workshop on Statistical Machine Translation*, pages 59–65, Baltimore, USA, June.

Ergun Biçici. 2011. *The Regression Model of Machine Translation*. Ph.D. thesis, Koç University. Supervisor: Deniz Yuret.

Ergun Biçici. 2013. Feature decay algorithms for fast deployment of accurate statistical machine translation systems. In *Proc. of the Eighth Workshop on Statistical Machine Translation*, Sofia, Bulgaria, August.

Ondrej Bojar, Rajan Chatterjee, Christian Federmann,

Barry Haddow, Chris Hokamp, Matthias Huck, Pavel Pecina, Philipp Koehn, Christof Monz, Matteo Negri, Matt Post, Carolina Scarton, Lucia Specia, and Marco Turchi. 2015. Findings of the 2015 workshop on statistical machine translation. In *Proc. of the Tenth Workshop on Statistical Machine Translation*, Lisbon, Portugal, September.

David Graff, ngelo Mendona, and Denise DiPersio. 2011. French Gigaword third edition, Linguistic Data Consortium.

Philipp Koehn, Hieu Hoang, Alexandra Birch, Chris Callison-Burch, Marcello Federico, Nicola Bertoldi, Brooke Cowan, Wade Shen, Christine Moran, Richard Zens, Chris Dyer, Ondrej Bojar, Alexandra Constantin, and Evan Herbst. 2007. Moses: Open source toolkit for statistical machine translation. In *Proceedings of the 45th Annual Meeting of the Association for Computational Linguistics Companion Volume Proceedings of the Demo and Poster Sessions*, pages 177–180. Association for Computational Linguistics.

Franz Josef Och and Hermann Ney. 2003. A systematic comparison of various statistical alignment models. *Computational Linguistics*, 29(1):19–51.

Robert Parker, David Graff, Junbo Kong, Ke Chen, and Kazuaki Maeda. 2011. English Gigaword fifth edition, Linguistic Data Consortium.

Andreas Stolcke. 2002. SRILM - an extensible language modeling toolkit. In *Proc. Intl. Conf. on Spoken Language Processing*, pages 901–904.

Deniz Yuret and Ergun Biçici. 2009. Modeling morphologically rich languages using split words and unstructured dependencies. In *Proc. of the ACL-IJCNLP 2009 Conference Short Papers*, pages 345–348, Suntec, Singapore, August.

CUNI in WMT15: Chimera Strikes Again

Ondřej Bojar and **Aleš Tamchyna**
Charles University in Prague, Faculty of Mathematics and Physics
Institute of Formal and Applied Linguistics
Malostranské náměstí 25, Prague, Czech Republic
surname@ufal.mff.cuni.cz

Abstract

This paper describes our WMT15 system submission for the translation task, a hybrid system for English-to-Czech translation. We repeat the successful setup from the previous two years.

1 Introduction

CHIMERA (Bojar et al., 2013; Tamchyna et al., 2014) is our English-to-Czech MT system designed as a combination of three very different components:

- TectoMT (Popel and Žabokrtský, 2010), a deep-syntactic transfer-based system,
- Moses (Koehn et al., 2007), where we use a factored phrase-based setup with large language models,
- Depfix (Rosa et al., 2012), an automatic post-editing system, aimed at correcting mainly errors in morphological agreement but successful also in semantic corrections, esp. recovery of lost negation.

The overall setup as well as the details on each of the components have been described in the past. We nevertheless briefly review it here, to make the paper self-contained.

This year, our submission mainly differed in the additional data we were able to collect. We thus evaluate how much do the additional data help in contrast with an identical setup using WMT15 training data only.[1] For the manual evaluation in WMT15, we submitted the non-constrained system, and even the "constrained" setup might not qualify as such, since it is a system combination and both TectoMT and Depfix rely on handcrafted rules to some extent.

In the following, we provide various details of the setup. We leave Depfix aside, since we simply applied it as a post-processing step and the relevant analysis of its rules was published previously (Bojar et al., 2013).

2 Chimera in WMT15

2.1 Factored Setup

We use our established setup, translating from English word form in one translation step to the Czech word form and morphological tag. This allows us to use language models over morphological tags, see §2.5 below.

Our word forms are in truecase, i.e. the words at sentence beginnings are lowercased, unless they are names. We rely on Czech and English lemmatizers[2] to select the true case.

Otherwise, our setup is fairly standard. We do not use any models of reordering, relying on basic distortion penalty.

2.2 Our System Combination

The first two components of CHIMERA, TectoMT (which appears in WMT evaluations as CU-TECTOMT) and Moses are independent MT systems on their own. CHIMERA combines them in a way remotely similar to standard system combination techniques (Matusov et al., 2008) and adds the third component, Depfix, for automatic correction of some grammar and semantic errors. For clarity, we will use the abbreviation CH0 to refer to the basic Moses setup without CU-TECTOMT. CH1 refers to the first stage, where CU-TECTOMT has been added, and CH2 is the complete combination.

To obtain the output of CH1 from CH0 and CU-TECTOMT, we could have used some of the standard system combination tools, e.g. Barrault

[1] http://www.statmt.org/wmt15/translation-task.html

[2] http://ufal.mff.cuni.cz/morphodita

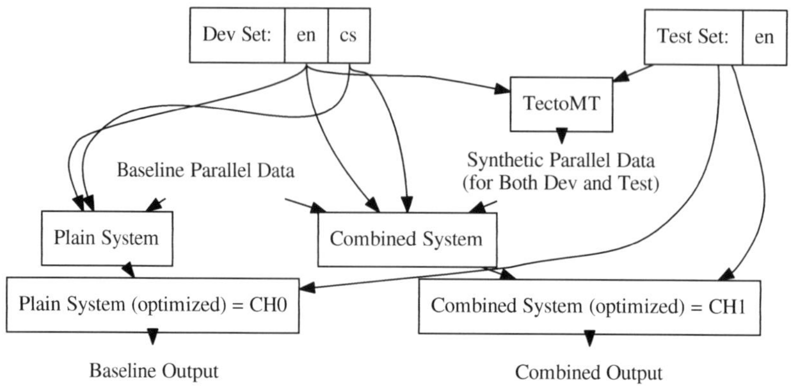

Figure 1: "Poor man's" system combination: adding CU-TECTOMT outputs to CH0 in a separate phrase table, optimizing the combination with standard MERT and translating the test set.

(2010) or Heafield and Lavie (2010). Instead, we simply use Moses to do the job.

Figure 1 provides a graphical summary of the technique. To obtain the combined system CH1, we add one additional phrase table to the primary phrase-based system CH0. This new phrase table is "synthetic", its source side comes from the input text and the target side comes from the output of CU-TECTOMT. The process to construct this phrase table is straightforward: we translate the source side of the development sets *and* the test set with CU-TECTOMT and treat it as a standard parallel corpus. We align it with GIZA++, using lemmas instead of word forms, but aligning only this relatively small corpus, not the main parallel training data. After symmetrization (grow-diag-final-and), we extract phrases without any smoothing. Moses is set up to use simultaneously the two phrase tables, the CH0 one and the new from CU-TECTOMT, in two alternative decoding paths.

The main and only trick is to include the development set(s) and the test set in this phrase table. Covering the development set ensures that MERT will correctly assess the relative importance of the two tables. And covering the test set is essential in the main run.

We dub the approach "poor man's" system combination, but we have recently found that this approach has surprising benefits over the standard approaches. It allows the combined system CH1 to react to (usually longer) phrases coming from CU-TECTOMT and use words and phrases from the standard CH0 phrase table that were not previously selected to CH0 single-best output but make the sentence overall more fluent. See Tamchyna and Bojar (2015) for a detailed analysis.

This year, we translated the source side of all WMT news test sets from the years 2007 till 2015 with CU-TECTOMT, contributing to the phrase table. The MERT is tuned only on WMT newstest 2013. We used newstest2014 to decide which exact configuration to submit and the final results of WMT are obviously based on newstest2015.

2.3 Parallel Data and Phrase Tables

Table 1 summarizes the parallel data used in our experiments. We use the CzEng 1.0 corpus and Europarl in both the constrained and unconstrained setting.

Our full system additionally uses OpenSubtitles datasets from OPUS.[3] We downloaded all three corpora (2011, 2012, 2013) and ran context-aware de-duplication on the whole dataset. (A sentence is removed only if it was already seen in the context of one preceding and one following sentence. The same sentence can thus appear in the corpus many times, if its context was different.)

For DGT Acquis, we do not rely on OPUS. Instead, we downloaded the corpus from the official website, aligned the sentences using HunAlign (Varga et al., 2005) and de-duplicated them.

We also use the small translation memories from ECDC[4] and EAC.[5]

[3] http://opus.lingfil.uu.se/

[4] https://ec.europa.eu/jrc/en/language-technologies/ecdc-translation-memory

[5] https://ec.europa.eu/jrc/en/language-technologies/eac-translation-memory

Source	# sents	# en tokens	# cs tokens	Constrained?
CzEng 1.0	14.83M	235.19M	206.05M	✓
Europarl	0.65M	17.62M	15.00M	✓
OpenSubtitles	33.25M	291.38M	237.61M	-
DGT Acquis	3.82M	93.44M	84.81M	-
EAC-TM	3351	24330	23106	-
ECDC-TM	2499	4092	41591	-

Table 1: Summary of parallel data used in our constrained and full setup.

			Full				Constrained		
	# sents	# tokens	long	big	morph	longmorph	long	morph	longmorph
Czech Press	305.41M	4852.59M	-	✓	-	-	-	-	-
CWC articles	38.42M	627.97M	-	✓	-	-	-	-	-
CzEng news	0.20M	4.22M	-	✓	✓	✓	-	✓	✓
RSS	4.81M	73.68M	✓	✓	✓	✓	-	-	-
WMT mono	44.08M	738.88M	✓	✓	✓	✓	✓	✓	✓

Table 2: Monolingual data sources and LMs.

2.4 Monolingual Data

Table 2 summarizes the monolingual data that we use in the full and in the constrained setup. Czech Press is a very large collection of news texts acquired in 2012. From CzEng 1.0, we use only the news section. CWC stands for Czech Web Corpus collected at our department from various web sites; here, we restrict it to articles (as opposed to discussion fora). RSS are our own collected news from six Czech web news sites and WMT are the standard monolingual data collected by WMT organizers in the years 2007–2014. Only CzEng and WMT data are allowed in the constrained runs.

Note that several of the resources are likely to overlap, e.g. our RSS collection probably follows the same sources as WMT data and Czech Web Corpus is also likely to be gathered from similar websites.

Except CWC, all the LM texts are strictly from the news domain. In other words, while we use as much and as diverse parallel texts as possible, we keep our LM in domain. We believe that at our current order of data size, preserving the domain is more important than using more monolingual data.

2.5 Language Models

As detailed in Table 2, we build several separate language models from the data. The constrained setup uses three LMs and the full setup uses four:

Long is a 7-gram model based on our truecased word forms. While the remaining LMs are trained directly with KenLM (Heafield, 2011), this 7-gram LMs is interpolated with SRILM from separate (KenLM) ARPA files estimated from each of the years separately. The lambdas for the interpolation are set to optimize the perplexity on WMT newstest2012. This approach allows us to use the relatively high order of the model and probably serves also as a kind of smoothing, distributing more probability mass to n-grams that are important across several years.

Big is a 4-gram LM based on our truecased word forms. It uses all our data, and as such, it cannot be included in the constrained setup. The motivation for using both "big" and "long" models is to cover long sequences as well as to have as precise statistics for shorter sequences as possible. We would not be able to train a 7-gram model using all our data.

Morph is a 10-gram LM based on Czech morphological tags. There are around 4000 distinct morphological tags, so we can afford training such a high order of the LM.

LongMorph is a 15-gram variation of "morph". We were hoping that given again some more training data this year, the morphological tags would be dense enough to capture sentence patterns within 15-grams. As it turns out, standard n-gram modelling techniques were not able to reach this goal.

Table 3 lists the BLEU scores (newstest2014) for all sensible (non-constrained) combinations of the LMs in CH0. We see that the LMs indeed have some complementary effect. The absolute differences in BLEU scores are rather small (and most of them are probably not statistically significant), but arguably using "big", "long" and one of the morphological LMs is the most beneficial setup.

LMs	BLEU
long	21.32
long morph longmorph	22.00
big	22.00
long morph	22.01
long longmorph	22.14
big morph	22.21
big long	22.26
big morph longmorph	22.28
big longmorph	22.29
big long morph	22.48
big long longmorph	22.69
all	22.59

Table 3: Complementary effect of adding TectoMT and language models.

3 Results

Table 4 shows (tokenized) BLEU scores on the WMT14 test set, comparing CH0 (i.e. plain factored phrase-based Moses setup) and CH1 (i.e. the combination with CU-TECTOMT), in the constrained and full-data runs. The BLEU scores are case-sensitive. The scores indicate that adding CU-TECTOMT is more important than the additional training data. With more data, the benefit of CU-TECTOMT slightly decreases, but still remains rather high, 1.65 BLEU points absolute.

In Table 5, we list scores of different variants of CHIMERA and competing MT systems for WMT15. Our system ranked first according to both automatic and manual evaluation. Some of the gains are due to large training data (other academic submissions were constrained systems). On the other hand, we also outperform Google Translate which likely uses all data available.

	Constrained	Full	Delta
CH0	21.28	22.59	1.31
CH1	23.37	24.24	0.87
Delta	2.09	1.65	-

Table 4: BLEU scores on WMT newstest2014 of the first two components of Chimera.

System	BLEU	TER	Manual
CH2	**18.8**	**0.715**	**0.686**
CH1	18.7	0.717	–
JHU-SMT	18.2	0.725	0.503
CH0	17.6	0.730	–
GOOGLE TRANSLATE	16.4	0.750	0.515
CU-TECTOMT	13.4	0.763	0.209

Table 5: Automatic scores and results of manual ranking in WMT 2015 (preliminary results). BLEU (cased) and TER from `matrix.statmt.org`. The top other system JHU-SMT and GOOGLE TRANSLATE are reported for reference.

4 Conclusion

We briefly described our submission to the WMT15 translation shared task. Our setup is fairly standard with the exception of our language model suite and the system combination with a transfer-based system. We showed that we benefit both from the large training data and from the system combination. Our submission ranked first according to both automatic and manual evaluation.

Acknowledgements

This research was supported by the grants H2020-ICT-2014-1-644402 (HimL), H2020-ICT-2014-1-644753 (KConnect), and SVV 260 224. This work has been using language resources developed, stored and distributed by the LINDAT/CLARIN project of the Ministry of Education, Youth and Sports of the Czech Republic (project LM2010013).

References

Loic Barrault. 2010. MANY, Open Source Machine Translation System Combination. In *Prague Bulletin of Mathematical Linguistics - Special Issue on Open Source Machine Translation Tools*, number 93 in Prague Bulletin of Mathematical Linguistics. Charles University, January.

Ondřej Bojar, Rudolf Rosa, and Aleš Tamchyna. 2013.

Chimera – Three Heads for English-to-Czech Translation. In *Proceedings of the Eighth Workshop on Statistical Machine Translation*, pages 92–98, Sofia, Bulgaria, August. Association for Computational Linguistics.

Kenneth Heafield and Alon Lavie. 2010. Combining Machine Translation Output with Open Source, The Carnegie Mellon Multi-Engine Machine Translation Scheme. In *Prague Bulletin of Mathematical Linguistics - Special Issue on Open Source Machine Translation Tools*, number 93 in Prague Bulletin of Mathematical Linguistics. Charles University, January.

Kenneth Heafield. 2011. Kenlm: Faster and smaller language model queries. In *Proceedings of the Sixth Workshop on Statistical Machine Translation*, Edinburgh, UK, July. Association for Computational Linguistics.

Philipp Koehn, Hieu Hoang, Alexandra Birch, Chris Callison-Burch, Marcello Federico, Nicola Bertoldi, Brooke Cowan, Wade Shen, Christine Moran, Richard Zens, Chris Dyer, Ondřej Bojar, Alexandra Constantin, and Evan Herbst. 2007. Moses: Open Source Toolkit for Statistical Machine Translation. In *ACL 2007, Proceedings of the 45th Annual Meeting of the Association for Computational Linguistics Companion Volume Proceedings of the Demo and Poster Sessions*, pages 177–180, Prague, Czech Republic, June. Association for Computational Linguistics.

Evgeny Matusov, Gregor Leusch, Rafael E. Banchs, Nicola Bertoldi, Daniel Dechelotte, Marcello Federico, Muntsin Kolss, Young-Suk Lee, Jose B. Marino, Matthias Paulik, Salim Roukos, Holger Schwenk, and Hermann Ney. 2008. System Combination for Machine Translation of Spoken and Written Language. *IEEE Transactions on Audio, Speech and Language Processing*, 16(7):1222–1237, September.

Martin Popel and Zdeněk Žabokrtský. 2010. TectoMT: Modular NLP framework. In Hrafn Loftsson, Eirikur Rögnvaldsson, and Sigrun Helgadottir, editors, *Lecture Notes in Artificial Intelligence, Proceedings of the 7th International Conference on Advances in Natural Language Processing (IceTAL 2010)*, volume 6233 of *Lecture Notes in Computer Science*, pages 293–304, Berlin / Heidelberg. Iceland Centre for Language Technology (ICLT), Springer.

Rudolf Rosa, David Mareček, and Ondřej Dušek. 2012. DEPFIX: A System for Automatic Correction of Czech MT Outputs. In *Proceedings of the Seventh Workshop on Statistical Machine Translation*, pages 362–368, Montréal, Canada, June. Association for Computational Linguistics.

Aleš Tamchyna and Ondřej Bojar. 2015. What a Transfer-Based System Brings to the Combination with PBMT. In *Proc. of ACL Workshop HyTra*, Peking, China, July. Association for Computational Linguistics. in print.

Aleš Tamchyna, Martin Popel, Rudolf Rosa, and Ondřej Bojar. 2014. CUNI in WMT14: Chimera still awaits bellerophon. In *Proceedings of the Ninth Workshop on Statistical Machine Translation*, pages 195–200, Baltimore, MD, USA. Association for Computational Linguistics.

Dániel Varga, László Németh, Péter Halácsy, András Kornai, Viktor Trón, and Viktor Nagy. 2005. Parallel corpora for medium density languages. In *Proceedings of the Recent Advances in Natural Language Processing RANLP 2005*, pages 590–596, Borovets, Bulgaria.

CimS - The CIS and IMS Joint Submission to WMT 2015 addressing morphological and syntactic differences in English to German SMT

Fabienne Cap[1], **Marion Weller**[1,2], **Anita Ramm**[1] **and Alexander Fraser**[1]
[1] CIS, Ludwig-Maximilian University of Munich – (cap|ramm|fraser)@cis.uni-muenchen.de
[2] IMS, University of Stuttgart – wellermn@ims.uni-stuttgart.de

Abstract

We present the CimS submissions to the WMT 2015 Shared Task for the translation direction English to German. Similar to our previous submissions, all of our systems are aware of the complex nominal morphology of German. In this paper, we combine source-side reordering and target-side compound processing with basic morphological processing in order to obtain improved translation results. We also report on morphological processing for English to French.

1 Introduction

This paper presents our submissions to the WMT shared task 2015. We use customised solutions to address morphological challenges in the English to German translation direction. Our goal is to make German and English as similar as possible in order to obtain better word alignments and hence an improved translation quality. We base our work on three main components, which we have carefully investigated separately in the past.

(i) Nominal Inflection We use context-based prediction of German inflectional endings. This improves fluency and enables the creation of morphological forms which have not occurred in the training data.

(ii) Source-side Reordering We reorder the English source text in order to make it more similar to the German word order. This improves word alignment and thus translation quality. It also makes the reordering task in decoding easier.

(iii) Compound Processing We split German compounds into simple words for training. In decoding, we translate only simple words, some of which are re-combined into compounds afterwards in post-processing. This allows us to create compounds which have not occurred in the training data.

This year, our main focus is on combining nominal inflection prediction and source-side reordering. We investigated both of these components separately in the past and expect an additive positive effect on translation quality when combined. We then added compound processing, which we already have investigated in combination with nominal inflection before, but not together with source-side reordering. Here, we also expect the combination to outperform the single components in terms of translation quality.

2 Methodology

The underlying idea of all of our systems is to improve translation quality by making the source and target languages more similar than they usually are. We address three common problems in English to German SMT: morphological richness in terms of inflectional variants, productive compounding and different word orders. In Figure 1, we illustrate the latter two of these problems using an example sentence which contains both a German compound (*"Mehrheitsvotum"* = "majority vote") and different word orders.

The methods we use to solve all three of these problems are implemented as pre- and post-processing steps. For nominal inflection and compound handling, the German data is transformed into an underspecified representation prior to training. After translation we transform the underspecified output into fluent German by merging some adjacent words into compounds and generating suitable inflectional endings. As for the differing word orders of German and English, only one pre-processing step is required, reordering the English source sentences into German word order.

In this section, we describe the different steps in more detail.

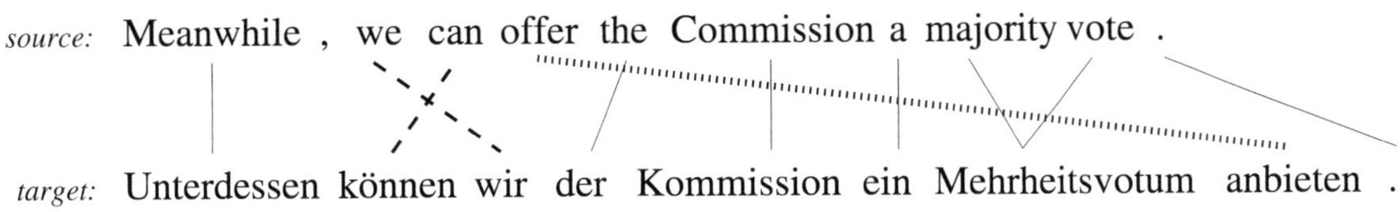

Figure 1: Illustration of structural differences between English and German. Dashed and dotted lines indicate a different word order, while the bold lines indicates a potentially problematic 1:n alignment due to a compound. Such structural differences may lead to erroneous word alignments.

stemmed SMT output with feature markup	morph. features	generated forms	gloss
auf[APPR-auf-**Dat**]	–	auf	*on*
die<+ART><Def>[ARTdef]	Fem.Dat.Sg.St	der	*the*
Tag<NN>Ordnung<+NN><**Fem**><**Sg**>[NN]	Fem.Dat.Sg.Wk	Tagesordnung	*agenda*
stehen[VVFIN]	–	stehen	*are*
die<+ART><Def>[ARTdef]	Masc.Nom.Pl.St	die	*the*
Plan<+NN><**Masc**><**Pl**>[NN]	Masc.Nom.Pl.Wk	Pläne	*plans*
für[APPR-für-**Acc**]	–	für	*for*
eine<+ART><Indef>[ARTindef]	Fem.Acc.Sg.St	eine	*a*
groß<+ADJ><Comp>[ADJA]	Fem.Acc.Sg.St	größere	*bigger*
nuklear<+ADJ><Pos>[ADJA]	Fem.Acc.Sg.St	nukleare	*nuclear*
Zusammenarbeit<+NN><**Fem**><**Sg**>[NN]	Fem.Acc.Sg.Wk	Zusammenarbeit	*co-operation*

Table 1: Overview of the morphology-aware SMT system for the input sentence "... *on the agenda are plans for greater nuclear co-operation*".

2.1 Morphology-aware SMT

In order to build an SMT system which is aware of German nominal inflection, the German data is reduced to a lemmatised representation, which contains translation-relevant morphological features (stem-markup, cf. first column in Table 1). This stem-markup consists of *number* and *gender* annotated at nouns: *gender* is considered as part of the lemma of a noun. The annotation of *number* onto target-side nouns aims at preserving the number of the source phrase during translation, as we expect nouns to be translated with their appropriate number value. This markup is only applied to nouns, i.e. the head of NPs or PPs, because the grammatical features of adjectives and determiners are dependent on the translation context in which they appear. For nominal inflection, the morphological features *number, gender, case and strong/weak inflection* need to be modelled. For each of the four morphological features, we use a linear chain CRF (Lafferty et al. (2001)) trained on stems/lemmas and the respective feature, using the Wapiti toolkit (Lavergne et al., 2010). During feature prediction, the features that are set by the stem-markup (*number, gender* on nouns) are propagated over the rest of the linguistic phrase. In contrast, *grammatical case* depends on the role of the NP in the sentence (e.g. subject or direct/indirect object) and is therefore determined entirely from the surrounding context in the sentence. The value for *strong/weak inflection* depends on the combination of the other features, cf. second column in Table 1. Based on the lemma and the predicted features, inflected forms are then generated using the rule-based morphological analyser SMOR (Schmid et al., 2004), cf. third column in Table 1.

Even though this basic nominal inflection does not handle compounds, it is able to model simple word formation processes: portmanteau prepositions (prepostion+determiner, e.g. *zum=zu+dem* "to the") are split in pre-processing and re-merged in the post-processing step, following a simple set of rules (e.g. merging only in singular, never in plural for a limited set of prepositions).

2.2 Reordering

The different word order of clauses in English and German may often lead to misaligned verbal elements. While German verbs often occur in clause-final position, English verbs mostly appear in rigid SVO order. We parsed the English section of the parallel data with (Charniak and Johnson, 2005) using a model we trained on the standard Penn Treebank sections. The scripts we used for reordering the English input are similar to the ones we previously described in (Gojun and Fraser, 2012). Figure 2 illustrates how reordering

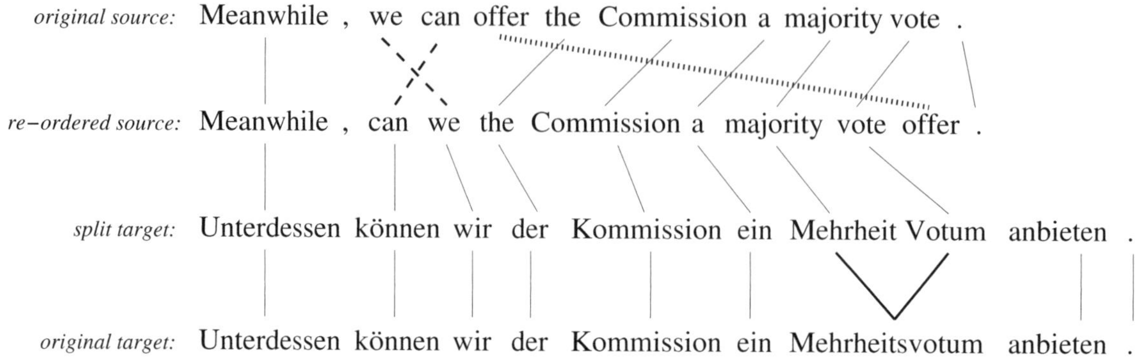

Figure 2: Illustration of how re-ordering the English input may help to reduce crossing and long-distance alignments and how target-side compound splitting may transform 1:n into 1:1 alignments.

the English input sentence can lead to less crossing and long-distance alignments.

2.3 Compound Processing

German allows for closed compounds where in English two or more words are required to express a certain content. This asymmetry can lead to alignment and thus translation errors. Moreover, German allows for **productive** compounding, i.e. new compounds can be generated from scratch and may not have occurred in the training data. Compound processing solves these two problems through splitting compounds for translation and, when translating into German, deciding whether to recombine words into compounds based on the context.

For compound splitting we use a rule-based morphological analyser where ambiguous analyses are disambiguated using corpus statistics. In general, we follow the method described in (Fritzinger and Fraser, 2010) for splitting: we disambiguate multiple analyses using context-sensitive POS and corpus-based word frequencies. The example given in Figure 2 shows how compound splitting can transform a 1:n alignment into a 1:1 alignment.

Note that for English to German translation, we always combine compound processing with nominal inflection prediction in order to maximise the generalisation over seen word parts in the training corpus. We thus translate from English into a split and underspecified version of German. Then, in a second step, compounds are merged using sequence prediction of good merge points (based on source language and target language features). Finally, words taking nominal inflection are re-inflected using the nominal inflection procedure. More details can be found in (Cap et al., 2014a).

3 Experimental Settings

For the WMT shared task, we combined the three components which we have described in the previous section. An overview of all systems we trained can be found in Table 2.

Data For all of our systems, we exclusively used data distributed for the WMT shared task 2015. We used all of the available monolingual data for German and all of the available parallel data for German and English.

UTF8 Cleaning Even though the submitted training data is provided in UTF-8 encoding, it contains a considerable number of characters that are not cleanly encoded into UTF8. We identified these characters and sequences thereof by reading all data bytewise and mapping it to the main UTF-8 encoding tables covering the Western European languages. All lines that contained one or more characters which did not fit these tables – either because they have been broken or because they belong to non-latin scripts like, e.g., Chinese or Arabic, were removed from the corpora as we expected those lines to lead to erroneous analyses in the subsequent preprocessing steps of our pipeline.

Length Constraints To ensure good alignment quality, we removed sentence pairs where one language is considerably longer than the other (pairs exceeding the ratio 1:9 words), as well as sentences containing many special characters (e.g. several dashes in row) indicating that the line in question is part of e.g. a table. Furthermore, we removed all sentences with a sentence length of more than 100 words. Table 3 gives an overview of the parallel data after cleaning and pre-processing.

Experiment	portmanteau merging	nominal inflection	source-side re-ordering	compound merging
Inflection^{Contrastive}	+	+		
Inflection_Reordering^{Primary}	+	+	+	
Inflection_Compounds	+	+		+
Inflection_Reordering_Compounds	+	+	+	+

Table 2: Names and components of our SMT systems; the submitted system are named *CIMS-primary* and *CIMS*.

	original	encoding	length or ratio	not parseable	cleaned
News	272,807	203	1,381	12,095	259,128
Europarl	1,920,209	24	17,637	3,855	1,898,693
CommonCrawl	2,399,123	17,508	7,489	26,623	2,347,503
parallel data	4,592,139	17,735	37,221	289,606	4,505,324

Table 3: Overview of the parallel data after cleaning and pre-processing.

English Variants The English source-side is mapped into British English in order to make the data as consistent as possible.

Linguistic Preprocessing The abstract representation for the nominal inflection requires the annotation of morphological features. After tokenization, we thus parsed all target-side data with BitPar (Schmid, 2004). To obtain the lemmas and suitable compound splittings, we applied SMOR (Schmid et al., 2004).

Language Model We trained 5-gram Language Models for each of the available German monolingual corpora and the German sections of the parallel data. For each corpus (the monolingual news corpora 07-14 and the parallel corpora europarl, commoncrawl and news), we built separate language models using the SRILM toolkit (Stolcke, 2002) with Kneser-Ney smoothing and then interpolated[1] them using weights optimized on development data (cf. tuning set 08-13). We then used KenLM (Heafield, 2011) for faster processing.

We performed this language model training for two different kinds of experiments: those **without** compound processing are trained on the underspecified (= lemmatised) representation, while those **with** compound processing are trained on a split underspecified representation.

Phrase-based Translation Model For word alignment, we use the multi-threaded GIZA++ toolkit (Och and Ney, 2003; Gao and Vogel, 2008). Our translation models were trained using Moses (Koehn et al., 2007), following the instructions for a baseline shared task system, using default settigs. All our systems are trained identically – what differs is the degree to which the underlying training data has been modified.

Tuning We tuned feature weights using batch-mira with 'safe–hope' (Cherry and Foster, 2012) until convergence (or up to 25 runs). We used the tuning data of all previous shared tasks from 2008 to 2013, which gave us 16,071 sentences for tuning. We tuned each experiment separately against an underspecified (i.e. lemmatised) version of the tuning reference optimising BLEU scores (Papineni et al., 2002). Note also that we integrated the CRF-based compound prediction and merging procedure for each experiment with compound processing into each tuning iteration and thus scored the output against a non-split lemmatised reference.

Testing After decoding, some post-processing is required in order to retransform the underspecified representation into fluent German text. Our post-processing consists of the following steps:

1) translate into (split) underspecified German
2) merge compounds
3) predict nominal inflection
4) merge portmanteaus

Finally, the output was recapitalised and detokenised using the shared task tools and all available German training data. We calculated BLEU scores using the NIST script version 11b.

[1]/mosesdecoder/scripts/ems/support/interpolate-lm.perl

Experiment	news2014	news2015
	$BLEU_{ci}$	$BLEU_{ci}$
submitted contrastive: Inflection	–	21.46
submitted primary: Inflection_Reordering	–	21.65
Raw	19.92	21.44
Raw_Portmanteau	19.83	21.54
Inflection	19.86	21.49
Inflection_Reordering	20.35	21.64
Inflection_Compounds	19.08	20.43
Inflection_Reordering_Compounds	19.65	21.19

Table 4: BLEU scores for all our systems. The upper part lists the submitted results (using a language model built on a subset of the available data), the lower part compares all our variants which have been computed after the deadline with a language model based on all available data for the constrained task.

4 Results

For evaluation, we used the 3,003 sentences of the 2014 shared task as well as the 2,169 sentences of this year's shared task. The results are given in Table 4. In the upper part of the table we present the results for the submitted systems, in the lower part we compare all variants of our systems. Note that we compare our systems against two baselines: *Raw* denotes a system built on all parallel and monolingual data available for the shared task, while *Raw_Portmanteau* denotes a system based on the same data, though restricted to parseable sentences, as we split portmanteaus based on POS tags.

It can be seen that dealing with nominal inflection alone does not considerably improve or decrease the BLEU scores of the two baselines. However, the combination of nominal inflection and source-side reordering has a positive effect on translation quality. When it comes to the combination of compound processing and nominal inflection, which we have successfully applied in the past (Cap et al., 2014a; Cap et al., 2014b), we do not see any improvement in terms of BLEU score for this combination here. This does not necessarily mean that the compound systems quality is worse, as previous manual evaluations have shown that BLEU scores do not adequately reflect all compound-related improvements in translation quality (Cap et al., 2014a). Finally the results given in Table 4 show that adding source-side reordering to the combination of compound processing and nominal inflection does improve the BLEU scores, even though they still remain lower than for nominal inflection and source-side reordering without compound processing. We have never combined all three components before, but despite the lower performance in terms of BLEU scores we will further pursue this combination in the future.

4.1 Comparison to Other Shared Task Submissions

In addition to automatic metrics, the shared task submissions are also manually evaluated. In this evaluation, our primary system (BLEU score of 21.65) was placed in a cluster with 4 other systems, of which at least two have BLEU scores of 23 and higher. Furthermore, our system was placed in a cluster ranked higher in the manual evaluation than a cluster containing a single system with a BLEU score of 22.6 (one BLEU point higher than our system). This shows clearly that BLEU underestimates the quality of our submission. Despite its comparatively low BLEU scores it is perceived to be of similar or better quality than systems with considerably higher BLEU scores when judged by human annotators. This supports our hypothesis that morphological modeling in combination with reordering improves translation quality and is consistent with human evaluations of morphological modeling we have carried out in the past, see, e.g., (Weller et al., 2013; Cap et al., 2014a).

5 Additional Experiments: English to French translation

In an additional set of experiments, we applied the nominal inflection system also to an English–French system.

Nominal Inflection for French The general pipeline is the same as for translation into German.

We used RFTagger for French (Schmid and Laws, 2008) for morphological tagging and a French version of SMOR to generate inflected forms. The stem-markup on the French data corresponds to that of the German markup (*number* and *gender* on nouns). In contrast to four morphological features for nominal inflection in German, only *number* and *gender* need to be modelled for French.

Data The EN–FR data set is much larger than that for EN–DE; after applying the same pre-processing steps, we obtained a parallel corpus of more than 36 million sentence pairs. For the language model, we used an additional 45.9 million lines (news07-14 and newsdiscuss corpus). The language model was interpolated over separate language models built on the different corpora using the development set to obtain optimal weights.

Results The results of the submitted systems are shown in the table below:

Raw		**Nominal Inflection**^{P}	
BLEU$_{ci}$	BLEU$_{cs}$	BLEU$_{ci}$	BLEU$_{cs}$
32.24	31.19	32.26	31.22

The nominal inflection system is our primary system. Due to the large amount of EN–FR parallel training data, we assume that here the BLEU score correctly shows that there is not much difference in performance between the two systems.

6 Previous Work

Nominal Inflection The approach we use for nominal inflection prediction which was first described by (Toutanova et al., 2008). The approach consists of two steps: i) translate into an underspecified representation of German (most words being lemmatised) and ii) after translation predict inflectional endings depending on the actual context of the word(s). While developed for Russian and Arabic morphology, we adapted the approach of Toutanova et al. (2008) to the needs of German in (Fraser et al., 2012). In (Weller et al., 2013), we extended this work to use subcategorisation information and source-side syntactic features in order to improve the accuracy of case prediction. Note that we did not use this extension of our pipeline in the present shared task.

Reordering Different word orders have already been addressed in previous approaches. For example, Collins et al. (2005) reordered German prior to translating into English, which lead to improved translations. In (Gojun and Fraser, 2012), we switched the translation direction and reordered the English input sentence before translating into German, which in turn resulted in improved translation quality.

Compound Processing In the past, there have been numerous attempts to address compound splitting for German to English. Almost every German to English SMT system nowadays incorporates some kind of compound processing, either using corpus-based word frequencies (Koehn and Knight, 2003), POS-contraints (Stymne et al., 2008), lattice-based approaches (Dyer, 2009) or language-independent segmentation (Macherey et al., 2011). In our work we have been using a rule-based morphological analyser combined with corpus statistics for compound splitting (Fritzinger and Fraser, 2010), a procedure which we have updated since that work. Details can be found in (Cap et al., 2014a).

For compound merging, we translate from English into split and lemmatized German. Then, in a second step, compounds are merged using a CRF-based approach based on (Stymne and Cancedda, 2011) and then re-inflected using the nominal inflection procedure as described above. More details of our compound merging approach can be found in (Cap et al., 2014a).

7 Conclusion and Future Work

In our submission to WMT 2015, we combined the three components nominal inflection, source-side reordering and compound processing. We expected a positive effect on translation quality above the performance of each of these components when applied in isolation.

While this effect was not evident in the obtained BLEU scores, the manual evaluation, in which our system was found to be of equal or better quality than systems achieving higher BLEU scores, makes it clear that in fact our approaches do improve translation quality.

Our current systems are built on the standard version of Moses with default settings; as part of future work we plan to investigate better strategies to exploit Moses' numerous methods for optimization.

Acknowledgments

This project has received funding from the European Union's Horizon 2020 research and innovation programme under grant agreement No 644402 (HimL) and the DFG grants *Distributional Approaches to Semantic Relatedness* and *Models of Morphosyntax for Statistical Machine Translation (Phase 2)*.

References

Fabienne Cap, Alexander Fraser, Marion Weller, and Aoife Cahill. 2014a. How to Produce Unseen Teddy Bears: Improved Morphological Processing of Compounds in SMT. In *Proceedings of the 14th Conference of the European Chapter of the Association for Computational Linguistics*.

Fabienne Cap, Marion Weller, Anita Ramm, and Alexander Fraser. 2014b. CimS - The CIS and IMS joing submission to WMT 2014 – Translating from English to German. In *Proceedings of the 9th Workshop on Statistical Machine Translation at ACL, System Papers*.

Eugene Charniak and Mark Johnson. 2005. Coarse-to-fine n-best parsing and MaxEnt discriminative reranking. In *Proceedings of the 43rd Annual Meeting on Association for Computational Linguistics (ACL)*.

Colin Cherry and George Foster. 2012. Batch Tuning Strategies for Statistical Machine Translation. In *Proceedings of the Human Language Technology Conference of the North American Chapter of the Association for Computational Linguistics (HLT-NAACL)*.

Michael Collins, Philipp Koehn, and Ivona Kučerová. 2005. Clause Restructuring for Statistical Machine Translation. In *Proceedings of 43rd Annual Meeting of the Association for Computational Linguistics (ACL)*.

Chris Dyer. 2009. Using a Maximum Entropy Model to Build Segmentation Lattices for MT. In *Proceedings of the North American Chapter of the Association for Computational Linguistics - Human Language Technologies (NAACL HLT)*.

Alexander Fraser, Marion Weller, Aoife Cahill, and Fabienne Cap. 2012. Modeling Inflection and Word Formation in SMT. In *Proceedings of the 13th Conference of the European Chapter of the Association for Computational Linguistics (EACL)*.

Fabienne Fritzinger and Alexander Fraser. 2010. How to Avoid Burning Ducks: Combining Linguistic Analysis and Corpus Statistics for German Compound Processing. In *Proceedings of the Fifth Workshop on Statistical Machine Translation*.

Qin Gao and Stephan Vogel. 2008. Parallel Implementations of Word Alignment Tool. In *Proceedings of the Workshop on Software Engineering, Testing, and Quality Assurance for Natural Language Processing*.

Anita Gojun and Alexander Fraser. 2012. Determining the Placement of German Verbs in English-to-German SMT. In *Proceedings of the 13th Conference of the European Chapter of the Association for Computational Linguistics (EACL)*.

Kenneth Heafield. 2011. KenLM: Faster and Smaller Language Model Queries. In *Proceedings of the Sixth Workshop on Statistical Machine Translation*.

Philipp Koehn and Kevin Knight. 2003. Empirical Methods for Compound Splitting. In *Proceedings of the 10th Conference of the European Chapter of the Association for Computational Linguistics (EACL)*.

Philipp Koehn, Hieu Hoang, Alexandra Birch, Chris Callison-Burch, Marcello Federico, Nicola Bertoldi, Brooke Cowan, Wade Shen, Christine Moran, Richard Zens, Chris Dyer, Ondrej Bojar, Alexandra Constantin, and Evan Herbst. 2007. Moses: Open Source Toolkit for Statistical Machine Translation. In *Proceedings of the Association for Computational Linguistics, Demonstration Session*.

John Lafferty, Andrew McCallum, and Fernando Pereira. 2001. Conditional Random Fields: Probabilistic Models for Segmenting and Labeling Sequence Data. In *ICML'01: Proceedings of the 18th International Conference on Machine Learning*.

Thomas Lavergne, Olivier Cappé, and François Yvon. 2010. Practical Very Large Scale CRFs. In *Proceedings the 48th Annual Meeting of the Association for Computational Linguistics (ACL)*.

Klaus Macherey, Andrew M. Dai, David Talbot, Ashok C. Popat, and Franz Och. 2011. Language-independent Compound Splitting with Morphological Operations. In *Proceedings of the 49th annual meeting of the Association for Computational Linguistics (ACL)*.

Franz Josef Och and Hermann Ney. 2003. A Systematic Comparison of Various Statistical Alignment Models. *Computational Linguistics*, 29(1):19–51.

Kishore Papineni, Salim Roukos, Todd Ward, and Wei-Jing Zhu. 2002. Bleu: A Method for Automatic Evaluation of Machine Translation. In *Proceedings of the 40th Annual Meeting of the Association for Computational Linguistics (ACL)*.

Helmut Schmid and Florian Laws. 2008. Estimation of Conditional Probabilities with Decision Trees and an Application to Fine-grained POS Tagging. In *Proceedings of the 22nd International Conference on Computational Linguistics (COLING)*.

Helmut Schmid, Arne Fitschen, and Ulrich Heid. 2004. SMOR: a German Computational Morphology Covering Derivation, Composition, and Inflection. In *Proceedings of the 4th International Conference on Language Resources and Evaluation (LREC)*.

Helmut Schmid. 2004. Efficient Parsing of Highly Ambiguous Context-Free Grammars with Bit Vectors. In *Proceedings of The 20th International Conference on Computational Linguistics (COLING)*.

Andreas Stolcke. 2002. SRILM – an Extensible Language Modelling Toolkit. In *ICSLN'02: Proceedings of the international conference on spoken language processing*.

Sara Stymne and Nicola Cancedda. 2011. Productive Generation of Compound Words in Statistical Machine Translation. In *Proceedings of the 6th Workshop on Statistical Machine Translation and Metrics MATR of the Conference on Empirical Methods in Natural Language Processing*.

Sara Stymne, Maria Holmqvist, and Lars Ahrenberg. 2008. Effects of Morphological Analysis in Translation between German and English. In *Proceedings of the 3rd Workshop on Statistical Machine Translation*.

Kristina Toutanova, Hisami Suzuki, and Achim Ruopp. 2008. Applying Morphology Generation Models to Machine Translation. In *Proceedings of the 46th Annual Meeting of the Association for Computational Linguistics: Human Language Technologies*.

Marion Weller, Alexander Fraser, and Sabine Schulte im Walde. 2013. Using Subcategorization Knowledge to Improve Case Prediction for Translation to German. In *Proceedings of the 51st Annual Meeting of the Association for Computational Linguistics (ACL)*.

The Karlsruhe Institute of Technology Translation Systems for the WMT 2015

Eunah Cho, Thanh-Le Ha, Jan Niehues, Teresa Herrmann, Mohammed Mediani, Yuqi Zhang and Alex Waibel
Institute for Anthropomatics and Robotics
KIT - Karlsruhe Institute of Technology
firstname.lastname@kit.edu

Abstract

In this paper, the KIT systems submitted to the Shared Translation Task are presented. We participated in two translation directions: from German to English and from English to German. Both translations are generated using phrase-based translation systems.

The performance of the systems was boosted by using language models built based on different tokens such as word, part-of-speech, and automacally generated word clusters. The difference in word order between German and English is addressed by part-of-speech and syntactic tree-based reordering models. In addition to a discriminative word lexicon, we used hypothesis rescoring using the ListNet algorithm after generating the translation with the phrase-based system. We evaluated the rescoring using only the baseline features as well as using additional computational complex features.

1 Introduction

We describe the KIT systems submitted to the Shared Translation Task of the EMNLP 2015 Tenth Workshop on Statistical Machine Translation. They are phrase-based English→German and German→English systems.

In order to clean a large amount of noisy web-crawled data, we applied a filtering technique using an SVM classifier. Language models are built based on different tokens, such as word, part-of-speech, and automacally generated word clusters. Final systems also include bilingual language models, part-of-speech and syntactic tree-based reordering models as well as a lexicalized reordering model. For language modeling, a data selection strategy is also applied. A discriminative word lexicon using source context information is used for both translation directions. In this evaluation campaign we also show that rescoring using the ListNet algorithm improves the translation performance for both directions.

This paper is organized as follows. In Section 2, we describe the data we used for training the systems. A detailed description of the systems is given in Section 3. Section 4 shows experimental setups and results along with an analysis. Finally, Section 5 concludes this paper.

2 Data

For training data, we use the European Parliament (EPPS), News Commentary (NC) and Common Crawl parallel corpora for both translation directions. For training the language models, we utilize the monolingual target side of the parallel corpora. The News Shuffle data is also used for language modeling. For German→English, we use the Gigaword corpus in addition.

The systems are optimized on the newstest2013 set and tested on the newstest2014 set.

3 System Description

A preprocessing step is applied to the raw data before the actual training. It includes removing excessively long sentences. Sentences with a length mismatch are also filtered out based on a threshold, and special symbols, dates and numbers are normalized. The preprocessing includes smart-casing of the first letter of every sentence. For German→English translation, we apply compound splitting (Koehn and Knight, 2003) on the source side, in order to handle the out-of-vocabulary (OOV) issue of German compound words.

The web-crawled Common Crawl corpus often contains sentence pairs which are not matching. In order to remove such noisy parts of the corpus, we use an SVM classifier for both translation tasks as described in Mediani et al. (2011).

Language models (LM) are built using the SRILM toolkit (Stolcke, 2002) with modified Kneser-Ney smoothing and scored in the decoding process with KenLM (Heafield, 2011). The in-house phrase-based translation system (Vogel, 2003) is used for generating translations. For optimization, we use minimum error rate training (MERT) (Och, 2003; Venugopal et al., 2005). For German→English, the GIZA++ Toolkit (Och and Ney, 2003) is used to generate the word alignment of the parallel corpora. Discriminative word alignment (DWA), as described in Niehues and Vogel (2008), is used for the English→German direction.

We build the phrase tables (PT) using the Moses toolkit (Koehn et al., 2007).

3.1 Word Reordering Models

Reordering rules encode how the words in the source sentence are to be ordered according to the target word order. They are learned automatically based on part-of-speech (POS) as well as syntactic parse tree constituents. In order to learn the rules, we use POS tags (Schmid, 1994) of the source side and the word alignment information. The rules cover short range reorderings (Rottmann and Vogel, 2007) as well as long range reorderings (Niehues and Kolss, 2009).

The differences in word order between German and English can be better addressed by using a tree-based reordering model as shown in Herrmann et al. (2013). The tree-based reordering rules are learned from a word alignment and syntactic parse trees (Rafferty and Manning, 2008; Klein and Manning, 2003) from the source side of the training corpus. The rules encode the information on how to reorder constituents in the syntactic tree of the source sentence.

Before translation, the POS-based and tree-based reordering rules are applied to the each sentence. The variants of differently reordered sentences, including the original order of the sentence, are encoded in a word lattice. The word lattice is then used as an input to the decoder.

Lattice phrase extraction (LPE) (Niehues et al., 2010) is applied on the training corpus, in order to get phrase pairs that match the reordered sentences. In this scheme, we use the reordered sentences to extract the phrases from, instead of the original sentences.

The lexicalized reordering (Koehn et al., 2005) encodes reordering probabilities for each phrase pair. By using the lexicalized reordering model, the reordering orientation of each phrase pair at the phrase boundaries can be determined during decoding. The probability for the respective orientation with respect to the original position of the words is included as an additional score in the log-linear model of the translation system.

3.2 Language Models

In addition to word-based language models, we use different types of non-word language models for each of the systems.

The bilingual language model (Niehues et al., 2011) is designed to increase the bilingual context between source and target words beyond phrase boundaries. Target words and all their aligned source words form bilingual tokens on which a LM is trained. The tokens are then ordered according to the target language word order.

For the English→German system, we use language models based on fine-grained POS tags (Schmid and Laws, 2008). In addition, we use language models based on word classes learned by clustering the words of the corpus using the MKCLS algorithm (Och, 1999). Using such language models, we can generalize better and therefore alleviate the sparsity problem for surface words. In order to build these language models, we replace each word token of the target language corpus by its corresponding POS tag or cluster ID. The n-gram language models are then built on this new corpus consisting of either POS tags or cluster IDs. During decoding, these language models are used as additional models in the log-linear combination.

For the German→English system, the data selection language model is trained on data automatically selected using cross-entropy differences between development sets from previous WMT workshops and the English side of all data, including the filtered crawled data (Moore and Lewis, 2010). We selected the top 10M sentences to train this language model. For building all non-word language models used in this work smoothing is applied.

3.3 Discriminative Word Lexicon

First introduced by Mauser et al. (2009), a discriminative word lexicon (DWL) models the probability of a target word appearing in the translation given the words of the source sentence. For every target word, a maximum entropy model is trained to determine whether this target word should be in the translated sentence or not using one feature per source word.

Two simplifications of this model are used to improve the translation quality while maintaining the time efficiency as shown in Mediani et al. (2011). First, the score for every phrase pair is calculated before translation. Then we restrict the negative training examples to words that occur within matching phrase pairs.

In this evaluation, the DWL is further extended with n-gram source context features proposed by Niehues and Waibel (2013). In this paper, this model will be referred to as source-context DWL. The source sentence is represented as a bag-of-n-grams, instead of a bag-of-words. By doing so it is possible to include information about source word order in the model. We used one feature per n-gram up to the order of three and applied count filtering for bigrams and trigrams.

In addition to this DWL, we integrated a DWL in the reverse direction in rescoring. We will refer to this model as source DWL. This model predicts the target word for a given source word as described in detail in (Herrmann, 2015).

In a first step, we identify the 20 most frequent translations of each word. Then we build a multi-class classifier to predict the correct translation. For the classifier, we used a binary maximum-entropy classifier[1] trained using the one-against-all approach.

As features for the classifier, we used the previous and following three words. Each word is represented by a continuous vector of 100 dimensions as described in (Mikolov et al., 2013).

Using the predictions, we calculated four additional features. The first two features are the absolute and relative number of words, where the translation predicted by the classifier and the translation in the hypothesis is the same. The third feature is the sum of the word to word translation probabilities predicted by the classifier that occur in the hypothesis. Given the translation used in the hypothesis, we determine their rank in the ranking by the classifier and use the sum of these ranks as the last feature.

[1]http://hal3.name/megam/

3.4 ListNet-based Rescoring

In order to facilitate more complex models like neural network translation models, we rescored the n-best lists. In our experiments we generated 300 best lists for the development and test data respectively. We used the same data to train the rescoring that we have used for optimizing the translation system.

We trained the weights for the log-linear combination used during rescoring using the ListNet algorithm (Cao et al., 2007; Niehues et al., 2015). This technique defines a probability distribution on the permutations of the list based on the scores of the log-linear model and one based on a reference metric. In our experiments we used the BLEU+1 score introduced by Liang et al. (2006). Then we use the cross entropy between both distributions as the loss function for our training.

Using this loss function, we can compute the gradient and use stochastic gradient descent. We used batch updates with ten samples and tuned the learning rate on the development data.

The range of the scores of the different models may greatly differ and many of these values are negative numbers with high absolute value since they are computed as the logarithm of relatively small probabilities. Therefore, we rescale all scores observed on the development data to the range of $[-1, 1]$ prior to rescoring.

3.5 RBM Translation Model

In rescoring, we used an restricted Boltzmann machine (RBM)-based translation model inspired by the work of Devlin et al. (2014).

The model is based on the RBM-based language model introduced in Niehues and Waibel (2012). The RBM models the joint probability of eight target words and a set of attached source words. The set of attached source words is calculated as follows: We first use the source word aligned to the last target word in the 8-gram. If this does not exist, we take the source word aligned to the nearest target word. The set of source words consists then of this source word, its previous five source words and its following five source words.

We create this set of 8 target and 11 source words for every target 8-gram in the parallel corpus and train the model using unigram sampling as described in Niehues et al. (2014). In rescoring, we then calculate the free energy of the RBM given the 8-gram and its source set as input. The sum of all free energies in the sentence is used as an additional feature for rescoring.

4 Results

In this section, we present a summary of our experiments in the evaluation campaign. Individual components that lead to improvements in the translation performance are described step by step.

The scores are reported in case-sensitive BLEU (Papineni et al., 2002).

4.1 English-German

Table 1 shows the results of our system for English→German translation task.

The baseline system consists of a phrase table derived from DWA, the word-based language models built from different parts of the corpus and POS-based long-range reordering rules. Reordering rules, however, are extracted from the POS-tagged EPPS and NC only, and encoded as word lattices.

The parallel data used to build the word alignments and the PT are EPPS, NC and the filtered Crawl data. Similarly, the data used to train the language models includes the monolingual versions of EPPS, NC and the filtered Crawl data. The BLEU scores of the baseline system over the development and test sets are 19.70 and 19.38, respectively.

The system gains 0.2 points on the development set and 0.13 on the test set in BLEU when adding non-word language models, such as a 4-gram bilingual language model, which is based on bilingual word tokens, two 5-gram POS-based language models and a 4-gram cluster language model. The bilingual language model is trained on the Crawl corpus and the other models are trained on the monolingual parts of all corpora. In case of the cluster language model, MKCLS is used to group of words into 1,000 clusters as mentioned in Section 3.2.

A further improvement can be observed when we apply tree-based and lexicalized reorderings. The improvement is considerable on the development set, gaining 0.6 BLEU points, but the system performs similar on the test set.

Adding source-context DWL helps to improve the score, especially on the test set, with the difference of 0.67 BLEU points compared to the above-mentioned system.

Finally, we use the new ListNet-based rescoring described in Section 3.4 for the log-linear combination of features. By doing so, we improve the translation performance by another 0.8 BLEU points on the test set. This system was submitted to WMT 2015 and used for the translation of the official test set.

System	Dev	Test
Baseline	19.70	19.38
+ Non-word LMs	19.90	19.51
+ Tree + Lex. Reorderings	20.50	19.52
+ Source–context DWL	20.58	20.19
+ ListNet rescoring	19.95	**20.98**

Table 1: Experiments for English→German

4.2 German-English

Table 2 shows the development steps of the German→English translation system.

The baseline system uses EPPS, NC, and filtered web-crawled data for training the translation model. The phrase table is built using GIZA++ word alignment and lattice phrase extraction.

Altogether four language models are used in the baseline system. As described in Section 3.2, we build a cluster language model using the MKCLS algorithm. Words from EPPS, NC, and the filtered crawl data are clustered into $1,000$ different classes. It also includes a language model trained on 10M of selected data from the monolingual corpora. All language models are 4-gram.

The word lattices are generated using short and long-range reordering rules, as well as tree-based reordering rules. A lexicalized reordering model is also included in the baseline system.

The baseline system uses a DWL with source context.

Using the ListNet-based rescoring increased the score on the test set by 0.1 BLEU point. Translation predictions based on source DWL improve the system performance by 0.3 BLEU points. Finally, adding an RBM-based translation model gave another small improvement. This system was used to generate the translation submitted to the evaluation.

5 Conclusion

In this paper, we have described the systems developed for our participation in the Shared Translation Task of the EMNLP 2015 evaluation for

System	Dev	Test
Baseline	28.38	27.77
+ ListNet rescoring	28.00	27.87
+ Source DWL	27.89	28.18
+ RBMTM	27.94	**28.28**

Table 2: Experiments for German→English

English→German and German→English translation. Both translations were generated using a phrase-based translation system which was extended by additional models such as bilingual and cluster-based language models. Discriminative word lexica with source context proved beneficial.

For English→German translation, adding source-context information to guide word choice and using a new method to rescore the translation candidates brought the most improvements.

Rescoring based on ListNet and using source DWL as well as applying an RBM-based translation model helped improve the system performance for German→English translation.

Acknowledgments

The project leading to this application has received funding from the European Union's Horizon 2020 research and innovation programme under grant agreement n° 645452.

References

Zhe Cao, Tao Qin, Tie-Yan Liu, Ming-Feng Tsai, and Hang Li. 2007. Learning to rank: from pairwise approach to listwise approach. In *Proceedings of the 24th international conference on Machine learning*, pages 129–136, New York, NY, USA. Acm.

Jacob Devlin, Rabih Zbib, Zhongqiang Huang, Thomas Lamar, Richard Schwartz, and John Makhoul. 2014. Fast and robust neural network joint models for statistical machine translation. In *Proceedings of the 52st Annual Meeting of the Association for Computational Linguistics (ACL 2014)*, volume 1, pages 1370–1380, Baltimore, Maryland, USA.

Kenneth Heafield. 2011. KenLM: Faster and Smaller Language Model Queries. In *Proceedings of the Sixth Workshop on Statistical Machine Translation*, Edinburgh, Scotland, United Kingdom.

Teresa Herrmann, Jan Niehues, and Alex Waibel. 2013. Combining Word Reordering Methods on different Linguistic Abstraction Levels for Statistical Machine Translation. In *Proceedings of the Seventh Workshop on Syntax, Semantics and Structure in Statistical Translation*, Altanta, Georgia, USA.

Teresa Herrmann. 2015. Linguistic structure in statistical machine translation.

Dan Klein and Christopher D. Manning. 2003. Accurate Unlexicalized Parsing. In *Proceedings of the 41st Annual Meeting on Association for Computational Linguistics (ACL 2003)*, Sapporo, Japan.

Philipp Koehn and Kevin Knight. 2003. Empirical Methods for Compound Splitting. In *Proceedings of the Eleventh Conference of the European Chapter of the Association for Computational Linguistics (EACL 2003)*, Budapest, Hungary.

Philipp Koehn, Amittai Axelrod, Alexandra B. Mayne, Chris Callison-Burch, Miles Osborne, and David Talbot. 2005. Edinburgh System Description for the 2005 IWSLT Speech Translation Evaluation. In *Proceedings of the Second International Workshop on Spoken Language Translation (IWSLT 2005)*, Pittsburgh, PA, USA.

Philipp Koehn, Hieu Hoang, Alexandra Birch, Chris Callison-Burch, Marcello Federico, Nicola Bertoldi, Brooke Cowan, Wade Shen, Christine Moran, Richard Zens, Chris Dyer, Ondrej Bojar, Alexandra Constantin, and Evan Herbst. 2007. Moses: Open Source Toolkit for Statistical Machine Translation. In *Proceedings of the 45th Annual Meeting of the Association for Computational Linguistics (ACL 2007), Demonstration Session*, Prague, Czech Republic.

Percy Liang, Alexandre Bouchard-Côté, Dan Klein, and Ben Taskar. 2006. An end-to-end discriminative approach to machine translation. In *Proceedings of the 44th Annual Meeting of the Association for Computational Linguistics (ACL 2006)*, pages 761–768, Sydney, Australia.

Arne Mauser, Saša Hasan, and Hermann Ney. 2009. Extending Statistical Machine Translation with Discriminative and Trigger-based Lexicon Models. In *Proceedings of the 2009 Conference on Empirical Methods in Natural Language Processing (EMNLP)*, Suntec, Singapore.

Mohammed Mediani, Eunah Cho, Jan Niehues, Teresa Herrmann, and Alex Waibel. 2011. The KIT English-French Translation systems for IWSLT 2011. In *Proceedings of the Eight International Workshop on Spoken Language Translation (IWSLT 2011)*, San Francisco, CA, USA.

Tomas Mikolov, Kai Chen, Greg Corrado, and Jeffery Dean. 2013. Efficient Estimation of Word Representations in Vector Space. In *Workshop at ICLR*, Scottsdale, AZ, USA.

Robert C. Moore and William Lewis. 2010. Intelligent Selection of Language Model Training Data. In *Proceedings of the ACL 2010 Conference Short Papers*, Uppsala, Sweden.

Jan Niehues and Muntsin Kolss. 2009. A POS-Based Model for Long-Range Reorderings in SMT. In *Proceedings of the Fourth Workshop on Statistical Machine Translation (WMT 2009)*, Athens, Greece.

Jan Niehues and Stephan Vogel. 2008. Discriminative Word Alignment via Alignment Matrix Modeling. In *Proceedings of the Third Workshop on Statistical Machine Translation (WMT 2008)*, Columbus, OH, USA.

Jan Niehues and Alex Waibel. 2012. Continuous Space Language Models using Restricted Boltzmann Machines. In *Proceedings of the Ninth International Workshop on Spoken Language Translation (IWSLT 2012)*, Hong Kong, HK.

Jan Niehues and Alex Waibel. 2013. An MT Error-Driven Discriminative Word Lexicon using Sentence Structure Features. In *Proceedings of the Eighth Workshop on Statistical Machine Translation*, Sofia, Bulgaria.

Jan Niehues, Teresa Herrmann, Mohammed Mediani, and Alex Waibel. 2010. The Karlsruhe Institute of Technology Translation System for the ACL-WMT 2010. In *Proceedings of the Fifth Workshop on Statistical Machine Translation (WMT 2010)*, Uppsala, Sweden.

Jan Niehues, Teresa Herrmann, Stephan Vogel, and Alex Waibel. 2011. Wider Context by Using Bilingual Language Models in Machine Translation. In *Sixth Workshop on Statistical Machine Translation (WMT 2011)*, Edinburgh, Scotland, United Kingdom.

Jan Niehues, Alexander Allauzen, François Yvon, and Alex Waibel. 2014. Combining Techniques from Different NN-based Language Models for Machine Translation. In *Proceedings of the 11th Conference of the Association for Machine Translation in the Americas*, Vancouver, BC, Canada.

Jan Niehues, Quoc Khanh Do, Alexandre Allauzen, and Alex Waibel. 2015. ListNet-based MT Rescoring. In *Proceedings of the Tenth Workshop on Statistical Machine Translation (WMT 2015)*, Lisboa, Portugal.

Franz Josef Och and Hermann Ney. 2003. A Systematic Comparison of Various Statistical Alignment Models. *Computational Linguistics*, 29(1):19–51.

Franz Josef Och. 1999. An Efficient Method for Determining Bilingual Word Classes. In *Proceedings of the Ninth Conference of the European Chapter of the Association for Computational Linguistics (EACL 1999)*, Bergen, Norway.

Franz Josef Och. 2003. Minimum error rate training in statistical machine translation. In *Proceedings of the 41st Annual Meeting on Association for Computational Linguistics (ACL 2003)*.

Kishore Papineni, Salim Roukos, Todd Ward, and Wei-Jing Zhu. 2002. Bleu: a Method for Automatic Evaluation of Machine Translation. Technical Report RC22176 (W0109-022), IBM Research Division, T. J. Watson Research Center.

Anna N. Rafferty and Christopher D. Manning. 2008. Parsing Three German Treebanks: Lexicalized and Unlexicalized Baselines. In *Proceedings of the Workshop on Parsing German*, Columbus, OH, USA.

Kay Rottmann and Stephan Vogel. 2007. Word Reordering in Statistical Machine Translation with a POS-Based Distortion Model. In *Proceedings of the 11th International Conference on Theoretical and Methodological Issues in Machine Translation (TMI 2007)*, Skövde, Sweden.

Helmut Schmid and Florian Laws. 2008. Estimation of Conditional Probabilities with Decision Trees and an Application to Fine-Grained POS Tagging. In *International Conference on Computational Linguistics (COLING 2008)*, Manchester, Great Britain.

Helmut Schmid. 1994. Probabilistic Part-of-Speech Tagging Using Decision Trees. In *International Conference on New Methods in Language Processing*, Manchester, United Kingdom.

Andreas Stolcke. 2002. SRILM – An Extensible Language Modeling Toolkit. In *International Conference on Spoken Language Processing*, Denver, Colorado, USA.

Ashish Venugopal, Andreas Zollman, and Alex Waibel. 2005. Training and Evaluation Error Minimization Rules for Statistical Machine Translation. In *Proceedings of the ACL Workshop on Building and Using Parallel Texts*, Ann Arbor, Michigan, USA.

Stephan Vogel. 2003. SMT Decoder Dissected: Word Reordering. In *International Conference on Natural Language Processing and Knowledge Engineering*, Beijing, China.

New Language Pairs in TectoMT

Ondřej Dušek,* **Luís Gomes,‡** **Michal Novák,*** **Martin Popel,*** and **Rudolf Rosa***
*Charles University in Prague, Faculty of Mathematics and Physics,
Institute of Formal and Applied Linguistics
{odusek,mnovak,popel,rosa}@ufal.mff.cuni.cz
‡University of Lisbon, Faculty of Sciences, Department of Informatics
luis.gomes@di.fc.ul.pt

Abstract

The TectoMT tree-to-tree machine translation system has been updated this year to support easier retraining for more translation directions. We use multilingual standards for morphology and syntax annotation and language-independent base rules. We include a simple, non-parametric way of combining TectoMT's transfer model outputs.

We submitted translations by the English-to-Czech and Czech-to-English TectoMT pipelines to the WMT shared task. While the former offers a stable performance, the latter is completely new and will require more tuning and debugging.

1 Introduction

The TectoMT tree-to-tree machine translation (MT) system (Žabokrtský et al., 2008) has been competing in WMT translation tasks since 2008 and has seen a number of improvements. Until now, the only supported translation direction was English to Czech. This year, as a part of the QTLeap project,[1] we have enhanced TectoMT and its underlying natural language processing (NLP) framework, Treex (Popel and Žabokrtský, 2010), to support more language pairs. We simplified the training pipeline to be able to retrain the translation models faster, and we use abstracted language-independent rules with the help of Interset (Zeman, 2008) where possible.

Together with our partners on the QTLeap project, we have implemented translation systems for other language pairs (English to and from Dutch, Spanish, Basque, and Portuguese) which are not part of WMT shared Translation Task this year. However, we were also able to submit the results of a newly built Czech-English translation system in the shared task. The performance of the current version leaves a lot of room for improvement, but proves the potential of TectoMT for different language pairs.

The original TectoMT system for English-Czech translation has seen just small changes, e.g., adding specialized translation models for selected pronouns (Novák et al., 2013a; Novák et al., 2013b) and fine-tuning of a handful of rules. Therefore, its performance is virtually identical to that of the last year's version.

This paper is structured as follows: in Section 2, we introduce the TectoMT basic architecture. In Section 3, we describe the improvements to TectoMT that were added for an easier support of new language pairs. Section 4 then details the Czech-to-English TectoMT system submitted to WMT15. We discuss TectoMT's performance in the task and examine the most severe error sources in Section 5. Section 6 then concludes the paper.

2 The TectoMT Translation System

TectoMT (Žabokrtský et al., 2008) is a tree-to-tree MT system system consisting of an analysis-transfer-synthesis pipeline, with transfer on the level of deep syntax. It is based on the Prague Tectogrammatics theory (Sgall et al., 1986) and distinguishes two levels of syntactic description (see Figure 1):

- *Surface dependency syntax* (*a-layer*) – surface dependency trees containing all the tokens in the sentence.

- *Deep syntax* (*t-layer*) – dependency trees that contain only content words (nouns, main verbs, adjectives, adverbs) as nodes. Each node has a deep lemma (*t-lemma*), a semantic function label (*functor*), a morpho-syntactic form label (*formeme*), and various grammatical attributes (*grammatemes*), such as number, gender, tense, or modality.

[1] http://qtleap.eu

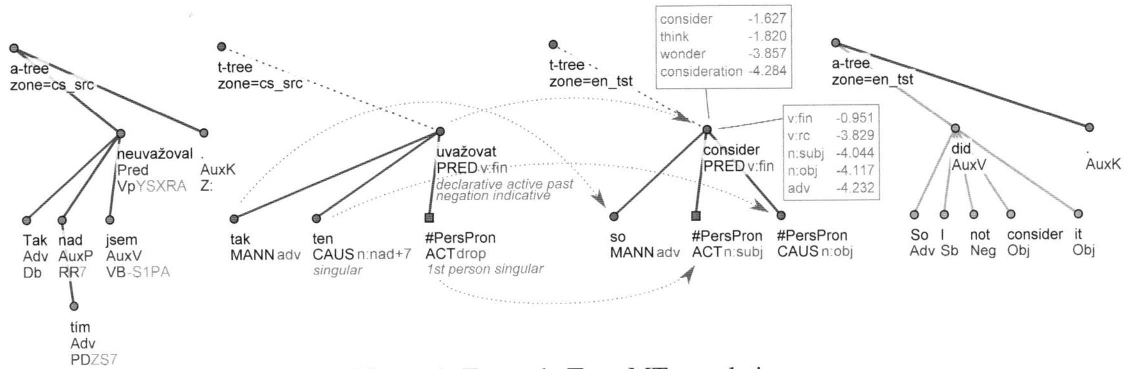

Figure 1: Example TectoMT translation.

From the left to the right: (1) source Czech sentence analyzed to surface dependencies (a-layer), (2) Czech sentence analyzed to deep syntax (t-layer), with t-lemmas (black), functors (capitals), formemes (purple), and grammatemes (teal), (3) translated English t-layer tree (with MaxEnt model logarithmic probabilities for t-lemmas and formemes shown in red for a selected node), (4) generated English surface dependency tree.

Formemes are not part of the t-layer according to the original theory; they have been added in TectoMT to work around the difficult task of functor assignment (semantic role labeling). Formemes are much simpler to obtain – they are assigned by rules based on the surface dependency trees (Dušek et al., 2012). Apart from a few specific cases, functors are not used in TectoMT, and formemes are used instead.

T-layer representations of the same sentence in different languages are closer to each other than the surface texts; in many cases, there is a 1:1 node correspondence among the t-layer trees. TectoMT's transfer exploits this by translating the tree isomorphically, i.e., node-by-node and assuming that the shape will not change in most cases (apart from a few exceptions handled by specific rules).

The translation is further factorized – t-lemmas, formemes, and grammatemes are translated using separate models. The t-lemma and formeme translation models are an interpolation of maximum entropy discriminative models (MaxEnt) of Mareček et al. (2010) and simple conditional probability models. The MaxEnt models are in fact an ensemble of models, one for each individual source t-lemma/formeme. The combined translation models provide several translation options for each node along with their estimated probability (see Section 1). The best options are then selected using a Hidden Markov Tree Model (HMTM) with a target-language tree model (Žabokrtský and Popel, 2009), which roughly corresponds to the target-language n-gram model in phrase-based MT. Grammateme transfer is rule-based; in most cases, grammatemes remain the same as in the source language.

3 Adding New Language Pairs

Using different languages in an MT system with deep transfer is mainly hindered by differences in the analysis and synthesis of the individual languages. To overcome these problems, we decided to use existing multilingual annotation standards (see Section 3.1) and to simplify and automate translation model training (see Section 3.2). In addition, we introduce an easier way of combining the results of the individual translation models than HMTM (in Section 3.3).

3.1 Annotation Standards for Language Independence

We decided to use Interset (Zeman, 2008) as the standard morphological representation since its features capture all important morphological phenomena in many different languages, including all languages required in the QTLeap project. The Interset Perl library includes conversions from many commonly used language-specific tagsets. To represent surface dependency syntax, we use the HamleDT 1.5 annotation style (Zeman et al., 2012; Zeman et al., 2014), which also supports many different languages and comes with tools for the conversion of various pre-existing treebanks. This allows us to use existing taggers and parsers without retraining them – analyzed sentences are simply converted to Interset+HamleDT annotation style.

Most TectoMT/Treex rules for the conversion from surface dependencies to deep syntax (t-layer) have been adapted to expect Interset morphological features and HamleDT-style dependencies, which improves their usability for different languages. Their implementation involves a common language-independent base class and language-specific derived classes.[2]

For t-layer representation, we stick to the TectoMT annotation style as used for Czech and English, which is originally based on PDT and Prague Czech-English Dependency Treebank annotation (Hajič et al., 2006; Hajič et al., 2012). However, we are aware that this annotation style has problems in other languages (e.g., grammatemes cannot express all required grammatical meaning), and that changing or extending it will probably be required.

3.2 Support for Training New Language Pairs

Other improvements to support adding new language pairs quickly are rather technical. We automated the translation model training in a set of makefiles. To train a new translation pair, one only needs to implement analysis and synthesis pipelines for both languages and edit a configuration file. Debugging and testing of the new analysis and synthesis pipelines is supported by monolingual "roundtrip" experiments: a development data set is first analyzed up to t-layer, then synthesized back to word forms. BLEU score measurements (Papineni et al., 2002) and a direct comparison of the results are then used to improve performance before the translation models are trained and other transfer blocks are implemented.[3]

3.3 Combining Transfer Models More Simply

The t-lemma and formeme translation models are independent of each other to simplify their decisions and reduce data sparsity. This often results in the best translation alternatives suggested by both models being incompatible with each other, which leads to disfluent outputs.

In English-to-Czech translation, an HMTM is used to select compatible t-lemma–formeme pairs (see Section 2). However, the HMTM needs to be trained on a large monolingual data set annotated on the t-layer. To simplify and speed up development of TectoMT translation for new language pairs, we have introduced a simpler method of selecting a compatible t-lemma–formeme pair which does not require any training. In this approach, t-lemma and formeme probabilities of congruous pairs[4] are combined by a non-parametric function into a single score that is then used to select the best translation option. Incongruous combinations are discarded.[5]

We evaluated five non-parametric functions combining the two translation models' outputs:

- *AM-P* – arithmetic mean of probabilities,
- *GM-P* – geometric mean of probabilities,[6]
- *HM-P* – harmonic mean of probabilities,
- *GM-Log-P* – geometric mean of logarithmic probabilities,[7]
- *HM-Log-P* – harmonic mean of logarithmic probabilities.[8]

We compared the functions against a baseline of just using the first option given by each of the models (regardless of compatibility). We used corpora of 1,000 sentences from the IT domain collected in the QTLeap project to evaluate all variants in English-to-Czech, English-to-Spanish, and English-to-Portuguese translation. For the English-to-Czech direction, we could also compare our combination functions to using an HMTM. The results are given in Tables 1, 2, and 3 for English to Czech, Spanish, and Portuguese, respectively.

We can see that the performance of the individual variants is very similar and that they bring an improvement over the baseline in almost all cases.

[2]Some Czech and English TectoMT blocks have not been converted to Interset yet; they use the Czech positional tagset from the Prague Dependency Treebank (PDT) of Hajič et al. (2006) and the Penn Treebank tagset (Santorini, 1990).

[3]The "roundtrip" experiments are not necessarily needed for the translation. We just consider them a best practice which helps to quickly reveal bugs that could deteriorate the translation, but remain unnoticed for a long time.

[4]The "congruency" of t-lemma and formeme is based on the syntactic part-of-speech encoded in the formeme and the Interset part-of-speech of the t-lemma. There are five simple rules, e.g., verbal t-lemmas are compatible only with formemes beginning with "v:".

[5]The non-parametric functions are weaker than the HMTM with the target-language tree model, which considers the context of the parent t-lemma and models the compatibility with real-valued probabilities.

[6]Maximizing GM-P gives the same result as maximizing the product of probabilities $P(\textit{t-lemma}) \cdot P(\textit{formeme})$, which is the theoretically sound approach.

[7]Logarithmic probabilities are negative and geometric mean of two negative numbers is positive, so we actually use *negative* GM-Log-P, so the best option has the highest score.

[8]*AM-Log-P*, the arithmetic mean of logarithmic probabilities, seems to be missing from the list above, but since maximizing over AM-Log-P gives the same results as maximizing over GM-P, we omit AM-Log-P from our experiments.

Function	NIST	BLEU
Baseline	6.7500	0.2785
HMTM	**6.8212**	**0.2876**
AM-P	6.7602	0.2811
GM-P	6.7690	0.2818
HM-P	**6.7713**	**0.2820**
GM-Log-P	6.7707	0.2817
HM-Log-P	6.7580	0.2810

Table 1: NIST and BLEU scores for non-parametric combining functions in English-to-Czech translation.

Function	NIST	BLEU
Baseline	5.2757	0.1670
AM-P	**5.4342**	0.1808
GM-P	5.4315	0.1806
HM-P	5.4306	0.1806
GM-Log-P	5.4314	**0.1809**
HM-Log-P	5.4336	0.1808

Table 2: NIST and BLEU scores for non-parametric combining functions in English-to-Spanish translation.

HMTM in the English-to-Czech translation performs better as expected.

4 Czech to English Translation

This section is a detailed description of the TectoMT Czech-to-English translation pipeline as used in the WMT translation task. The analysis part (Section 4.1) is not new and thus is described only briefly, we focus more on the simple transfer (Section 4.2) and the English synthesis (Section 4.3).

Function	NIST	BLEU
Baseline	5.1584	0.1677
AM-P	**5.2612**	**0.1719**
GM-P	5.2219	0.1711
HM-P	5.0613	0.1620
GM-Log-P	5.2452	0.1719
HM-Log-P	5.2583	0.1719

Table 3: NIST and BLEU scores for non-parametric combining functions in English-to-Portuguese translation.

4.1 Czech Analysis

The Czech analysis is a slightly improved version of the pipeline used to train previous versions of the English-to-Czech translation in TectoMT as well as to analyze the Czech part of the CzEng 1.0 parallel corpus (Bojar et al., 2012).

The first part, the surface syntactic analysis, consists of a rule-based sentence segmenter and tokenizer, followed by a part-of-speech tagger – we use MorphoDiTa (Straková et al., 2014) in the current version – and a dependency parser (McDonald et al., 2005; Novák and Žabokrtský, 2007).

The surface dependency trees are then converted into deep syntactic (t-layer) trees using a series of mostly rule-based modules that collapse auxiliary words and decide upon the t-lemma, formeme, and grammatemes. They also reconstruct pro-drop pronoun subjects based on verbal morphology.

4.2 Transfer

The Czech-to-English transfer is relatively basic and does not contain many components besides the translation models for t-lemmas and formemes (see Section 2). Due to limited time to train the system for the new translation direction, we used the non-parametric t-lemma–formeme combination functions as described in Section 3.3 instead of a Hidden Markov Tree Model (cf. Section 2). We chose the HM-P setting based on performance on the development set.[9]

The additional components are rule-based and are listed below:

- Overrides and additions to the translation models, tuned on the development set,
- Removing Czech gender from common nouns not referring to persons,
- Fixing translation of names based on a lexicon compiled from Wikipedia (in particular, reverting the Czech female surname ending *-ová* in non-Czech names),
- Removing subjects of verbs where the translation model chose an infinitival form,
- Removing double negatives (which are the rule in Czech but not in English),

[9]We used the WMT news-test2012 data to tune our system.

- Fixing grammatemes, in particular number and negation, for some translations, such as *těstoviny* (pl.) → *pasta* (sg.), or *nedbalý* (negative) → *sloppy* (positive).

4.3 English Synthesis

The English synthesis (surface realization) pipeline has been newly developed for TectoMT translation into English; it is mostly rule-based and is inspired by the Czech synthesis pipeline. Besides the Czech-to-English translation, it is used in other TectoMT systems translating into English within the QTLeap project and in the TGen natural language generator (Dušek and Jurčíček, 2015).

In the synthesis pipeline, a new surface dependency (a-layer) tree is created as a copy of the source t-layer tree, with lemmas copied from t-lemmas and dependency labels, word forms, and morphology left undecided. All further changes are performed on the surface dependency tree, consulting information from the t-layer tree. The pipeline consists of the following steps:

1. Morphological attributes are filled in based on grammatemes.
2. Subjects are marked (to support subject-predicate agreement).
3. Basic English word order for declarative sentences is enforced. This only contains very general rules, e.g., SVO-order or adjective-noun order, but preliminary tests with source-language ordering from several different languages indicated that it is sufficient in most cases.
4. Subject-predicate agreement in number and person is enforced – predicates have their number and person filled based on their subject(s).
5. Auxiliary words are added. These are based on the contents of formemes (prepositions, subordinating conjunction, infinitive particles, possessive markers) and t-lemmas (phrasal verb particles).
6. English articles are added based on a handful of rules from an older surface realizer by Ptáček (2008).
7. Auxiliary verbs are added, expressing the voice, tense, and modality. Auxiliaries are also added for questions and sentences with existential *there*.
8. Imperative subjects are removed, question subjects are moved after the auxiliary verb.
9. Negation particles are added for verbs as well as selected adjectives and adverbs.
10. Punctuation is added to the end of the sentence, into coordinations and appositions, after clause-initial phrases preceding the subject, and in selected phrases (based on formemes).
11. Words are inflected based on their lemma and morphological attributes. We use rules for personal pronouns, MorphoDiTa (Straková et al., 2014) English dictionary for unambiguous words, and Flect (Dušek and Jurčíček, 2013) for all remaining words requiring inflection.[10]
12. The indefinite article *a* is changed into *an* based on the following word.
13. Repeated coordinated prepositions and conjunctions are deleted.
14. The first word in the sentence is capitalized.

The output sentence is then obtained by just combining all the nodes in the resulting surface dependency tree.

5 WMT 2015 Translation Task Results

TectoMT reached a BLEU score of 13.9 for the English-to-Czech direction in the WMT 2015 Translation Task. This ranks it among the last systems, which is consistent with results from previous years. However, English-to-Czech TectoMT has also been used in the Chimera system combination, which ranks first in both automatic and human evaluation results. TectoMT plays a very important role in Chimera (Tamchyna and Bojar, 2015).

TectoMT's Czech-to-English translation reached a BLEU score of 12.8, and finished last

[10] Alternatively, an n-gram language model *could* be used to select the word forms. Flect uses just a short context of neighboring lemmas, but it generalizes also to unseen words (thanks to morphological features). Currently, no n-gram language model is used in the whole TectoMT system.

in the automatic evaluation; human evaluation scores indicate a second-to-last position.

We believe that the major cause for the lower scores does not lie in TectoMT's basic architecture, but that improvements to translation models are required, as well as better tuning and debugging of the whole pipeline for the Czech-to-English direction. We examined closely a sample of the translation output (in both directions) and identified the following error sources:

- Translation models will require more tuning and possibly more powerful features. The English-to-Czech model leaves many relatively common words untranslated, which suggests that pruning has been too strict.[11]
- The non-parametric t-lemma–formeme combination functions are not ideal; training an HMTM will be necessary to improve English-to-Czech performance.
- Word ordering rules need to be improved, and more different cases need to be covered. We consider using a statistical ranker for local node ordering.
- The rule-based article assignment in English synthesis is lacking; indefinite articles are assigned much more often than they should be. This will probably not be possible without using a statistical module.

There are also other, rather technical issues related to punctuation or tokenization that will require more debugging.

6 Conclusions and Future Work

We presented TectoMT, a tree-to-tree machine translation system with deep transfer, and its new features in this year's edition of the WMT shared task, the main one being opening the system to new language pairs. TectoMT in the English-to-Czech direction is stable and provides useful translations though its results are worse than that of other systems; it is also used in the Chimera system combination. The new Czech-to-English system requires more development but shows that it is possible to adapt TectoMT to a new translation direction in a very short amount of time.

In future, we plan to tune the current Czech-to-English setup, and to include further improvements. We intend to use Interset instead of grammatemes on the t-layer to support categories of grammatical meaning not present in grammatemes (see Section 3.1). We also consider switching the TectoMT annotation style to Universal Dependencies. To improve translation models, we are planning to use Vowpal Wabbit (Langford et al., 2007) and to include word embeddings from word2vec (Mikolov et al., 2013) as features. We are also investigating the possibilities of non-isomorphic transfer in TectoMT.

[11] Same as for the English-to-Czech direction, the MaxEnt model was trained only for (source) lemmas occurring at least 100 times in the training data and only with translations (target lemmas) occurring at least 5 times. For the simple conditional ("static") model, we used the same constants (by mistake).

Acknowledgments

This work has been supported by the 7th Framework Programme of the EU grant QTLeap (No. 610516), and SVV project 260 104 and GAUK grants 2058214 and 338915 of the Charles University in Prague. It is using language resources hosted by the LINDAT/CLARIN Research Infrastructure, Project No. LM2010013 of the Ministry of Education, Youth and Sports.

References

O. Bojar, Z. Žabokrtský, O. Dušek, P. Galuščáková, M. Majliš, D. Mareček, J. Maršík, M. Novák, M. Popel, and A. Tamchyna. 2012. The joy of parallelism with CzEng 1.0. In *LREC*, page 3921–3928, Istanbul.

O. Dušek and F. Jurčíček. 2013. Robust Multilingual Statistical Morphological Generation Models. In *51st Annual Meeting of the Association for Computational Linguistics Proceedings of the Student Research Workshop*, pages 158–164, Sofia. Association for Computational Linguistics.

O. Dušek and F. Jurčíček. 2015. Training a natural language generator from unaligned data. In *Proceedings of the 53rd Annual Meeting of the Association for Computational Linguistics and the 7th International Joint Conference on Natural Language Processing*, pages 451–461. Association for Computational Linguistics.

O. Dušek, Z. Žabokrtský, M. Popel, M. Majliš, M. Novák, and D. Mareček. 2012. Formemes in English-Czech deep syntactic MT. In *Proceedings of the Seventh Workshop on Statistical Machine Translation*, page 267–274.

J. Hajič, E. Hajičová, J. Panevová, P. Sgall, O. Bojar, S. Cinková, E. Fučíková, M. Mikulová, P. Pajas,

J. Popelka, J. Semecký, J. Šindlerová, J. Štěpánek, J. Toman, Z. Urešová, and Z. Žabokrtský. 2012. Announcing Prague Czech-English Dependency Treebank 2.0. In *Proceedings of LREC*, pages 3153–3160, Istanbul.

J. Hajič, J. Panevová, E. Hajičová, P. Sgall, P. Pajas, J. Štěpánek, J. Havelka, M. Mikulová, Z. Žabokrtský, M. Ševčíková Razímová, and Z. Urešová. 2006. *Prague Dependency Treebank 2.0*. Number LDC2006T01. LDC, Philadelphia, PA, USA.

J. Langford, L. Li, and A. Strehl. 2007. Vowpal Wabbit online learning project. `http://hunch.net/~vw/`.

D. Mareček, M. Popel, and Z. Žabokrtský. 2010. Maximum entropy translation model in dependency-based mt framework. In *Proceedings of the Joint Fifth Workshop on Statistical Machine Translation and MetricsMATR*, pages 201–206. Association for Computational Linguistics.

R. McDonald, F. Pereira, K. Ribarov, and J. Hajič. 2005. Non-projective dependency parsing using spanning tree algorithms. In *Proceedings of the conference on Human Language Technology and Empirical Methods in Natural Language Processing*, pages 523–530.

T. Mikolov, K. Chen, G. Corrado, and J. Dean. 2013. Efficient estimation of word representations in vector space. *arXiv preprint arXiv:1301.3781*.

M. Novák, A. Nedoluzhko, and Z. Žabokrtský. 2013a. Translation of "it" in a deep syntax framework. In *51st Annual Meeting of the Association for Computational Linguistics Proceedings of the Workshop on Discourse in Machine Translation*, pages 51–59, Sofija, Bulgaria. Bălgarska akademija na naukite, Omnipress, Inc.

M. Novák, Z. Žabokrtský, and A. Nedoluzhko. 2013b. Two case studies on translating pronouns in a deep syntax framework. In *Proceedings of the 6th International Joint Conference on Natural Language Processing*, pages 1037–1041, Nagoya, Japan. Asian Federation of Natural Language Processing.

V. Novák and Z. Žabokrtský. 2007. Feature engineering in maximum spanning tree dependency parser. In *Text, Speech and Dialogue*, pages 92–98. Springer.

K. Papineni, S. Roukos, T. Ward, and W.-J. Zhu. 2002. BLEU: a method for automatic evaluation of machine translation. In *Proceedings of the 40th annual meeting of the Association for Computational Linguistics*, page 311–318.

M. Popel and Z. Žabokrtský. 2010. TectoMT: modular NLP framework. *Advances in Natural Language Processing*, pages 293–304.

J. Ptáček. 2008. Two Tectogrammatical Realizers Side by Side: Case of English and Czech. In *Fourth International Workshop on Human-Computer Conversation*, Bellagio, Italy.

B. Santorini. 1990. Part-of-speech tagging guidelines for the Penn Treebank project (3rd revision). Technical Report No. MS-CIS-90-47, University of Pennsylvania Department of Computer and Information Science, Philadelphia, PA, USA.

P. Sgall, E. Hajičová, and J. Panevová. 1986. *The meaning of the sentence in its semantic and pragmatic aspects*. D. Reidel, Dordrecht.

J. Straková, M. Straka, and J. Hajič. 2014. Open-Source Tools for Morphology, Lemmatization, POS Tagging and Named Entity Recognition. In *Proceedings of 52nd Annual Meeting of the Association for Computational Linguistics: System Demonstrations*, pages 13–18. Association for Computational Linguistics.

A. Tamchyna and O. Bojar. 2015. What a transfer-based system brings to the combination with PBMT. In *Proceedings of the Fourth Workshop on Hybrid Approaches to Translation (HyTra)*, pages 11–20, Beijing, July. Association for Computational Linguistics.

Z. Žabokrtský and M. Popel. 2009. Hidden Markov Tree Model in Dependency-based Machine Translation. In *Proceedings of the ACL-IJCNLP 2009 Conference Short Papers*, pages 145–148, Singapore. Association for Computational Linguistics.

Z. Žabokrtský, J. Ptáček, and P. Pajas. 2008. TectoMT: highly modular MT system with tectogrammatics used as transfer layer. In *Proceedings of the Third Workshop on Statistical Machine Translation*, page 167–170. Association for Computational Linguistics.

D. Zeman, D. Mareček, M. Popel, L. Ramasamy, J. Štěpánek, Z. Žabokrtský, and J. Hajič. 2012. HamleDT: To parse or not to parse? In *Proceedings of the Eight International Conference on Language Resources and Evaluation (LREC'12)*, Istanbul, Turkey. European Language Resources Association (ELRA).

D. Zeman, O. Dušek, D. Mareček, M. Popel, L. Ramasamy, J. Štěpánek, Z. Žabokrtský, and J. Hajič. 2014. HamleDT: Harmonized multi-language dependency treebank. *Language Resources and Evaluation*, 48(4):601–637.

D. Zeman. 2008. Reusable Tagset Conversion Using Tagset Drivers. In *Proceedings of LREC*, pages 213–218.

Tuning Phrase-Based Segmented Translation for a Morphologically Complex Target Language

Stig-Arne Grönroos
Department of Signal Processing and Acoustics
Aalto University, Finland
stig-arne.gronroos@aalto.fi

Sami Virpioja
Department of Computer Science
Aalto University, Finland
sami.virpioja@aalto.fi

Mikko Kurimo
Department of Signal Processing and Acoustics
Aalto University, Finland
mikko.kurimo@aalto.fi

Abstract

This article describes the Aalto University entry to the English-to-Finnish shared translation task in WMT 2015. The system participates in the constrained condition, but in addition we impose some further constraints, using no language-specific resources beyond those provided in the task. We use a morphological segmenter, Morfessor FlatCat, but train and tune it in an unsupervised manner. The system could thus be used for another language pair with a morphologically complex target language, without needing modification or additional resources.

1 Introduction

In isolating languages, such as English, suitable smallest units of translation are easy to find using whitespace and punctuation characters as delimiters. This approach of using words as the smallest unit of translation is problematic for synthetic languages with rich inflection, derivation or compounding. Such languages have very large vocabularies, leading to sparse statistics and many out-of-vocabulary words.

A synthetic language uses fewer words than an isolating language to express the same sentence, by combining several grammatical markers into each word and using compound words. This difference in granularity is problematic in alignment, when a word in the isolating language properly aligns with only a part of a word in the synthetic language.

In order to balance the number of tokens between target and source, it is often possible to segment the morphologically richer side. Oversegmentation is detrimental, however, as longer windows of history need to be used, and useful phrases become more difficult to extract. It is therefore important to find a balance in the amount of segmentation. A linguistically accurate segmentation may be oversegmented for the task of translation, if some of the distinctions are either unmarked or marked in a similar way in the other language.

An increase in the number of tokens means that the distance spanned by dependencies becomes longer. Recurrent Neural Network (RNN) based language models have been shown to perform well for English (Mikolov et al., 2011). Their strength lies in being theoretically capable of modeling arbitrarily long dependencies.

Moreover, a huge vocabulary is particularly detrimental for neural language models due to their computationally heavy training and need to marginalize over the whole vocabulary during prediction. As morphological segmentation can reduce the vocabulary size considerably, using RNN language models seems even more suitable for this approach.

Our system is designed for translation in the direction from a morphologically less complex to a more complex language. The opposite direction – simplifying morphology – has received more attention, especially with English as the target language.

Of the target languages in this year's task, Finnish is the most difficult to translate into, shown by Koehn (2005) and reconfirmed by the evaluations of this shared task. Even though the use of supervised linguistic tools (such as taggers, parsers, or morphological analyzers) was allowed in the constrained condition, our method does not use them. It is therefore applicable to other morphologically complex target languages.

1.1 Related work

The idea of transforming morphology to improve statistical machine translation (SMT) is well established in the literature. An early example is Nießen and Ney (2004), who apply rule-based morphological analysis to enhance German→English translation.

In particular, many efforts have focused on increasing the symmetry between languages in order to improve alignment. Lee (2004) uses this idea for Arabic→English translation. In this translation direction, symmetry is increased through morphological simplification.

It has been shown that a linguistically correct segmentation does not coincide with the optimal segmentation for purposes of alignment, both using rule-based simplification of linguistic analysis (Habash and Sadat, 2006), and through the use of statistical methods (Chung and Gildea, 2009).

Using segmented translation with unsupervised statistical segmentation methods has yielded mixed results. Virpioja et al. (2007) used Morfessor Categories-MAP in translation between three Nordic languages, including Finnish, while Fishel and Kirik (2010) used Morfessor Categories-MAP in English↔Estonian translation. In these studies, segmentation has in many cases worsened BLEU compared to word-based translation. The main benefit of segmentation has been a decrease in the ratio of untranslated words.

Salameh et al. (2015) translate English→Arabic, and find that segmentation is most useful when the extracted phrases are morphologically productive, and that using a word-level language model reduces this productivity (albeit increasing the BLEU score).

The desegmentation process, and the effect of different strategies for marking the word-internal token boundaries, have mostly been examined in recombining split compound words. Stymne and Cancedda (2011) explore different marking strategies, including use of part-of-speech tags, in order to allow the translation system to produce compounds unseen in the training data.

2 System overview

An overview of the system is shown in Figure 1. The four main contributions of this work are indicated by numbered circles:

1. Use of unsupervised Morfessor FlatCat (Grönroos et al., 2014) for morphological segmentation,

2. Tuning the morphological segmentation directly to balance the number of translation tokens between source and target,

3. A new marking strategy for morph boundaries,

4. Rescoring n-best lists with RNNLM (Mikolov et al., 2010).

Our system extends an existing phrase-based SMT system to perform segmented translation, by adding pre-processing and post-processing steps, with no changes to the decoder. As translation system to be extended, we used the Moses release 3.0 (Koehn et al., 2007). We used GIZA++ alignment, and a 5-gram LM with modified-KN smoothing. Many Moses settings were left at their default values: phrase length 10, grow-diag-final-and alignment symmetrization, msd-bidirectional-fe reordering, and distortion limit 6.

The standard pre-processing steps not specified in Figure 1 consist of normalization of punctuation, tokenization, and statistical truecasing. All three of these were performed with the tools included in Moses.

In addition, the parallel data was cleaned and duplicate sentences were removed. Cleaning was performed after morphological segmentation, as the segmentation can increase the length in tokens of a sentence.

The post-processing steps are the reverse of the pre-processing steps: desegmentation, detruecasing, and detokenization. Rescoring of the n-best list was done before post-processing.

The feature weights were tuned using MERT (Och, 2003), with BLEU (Papineni et al., 2002) of the post-processed hypothesis

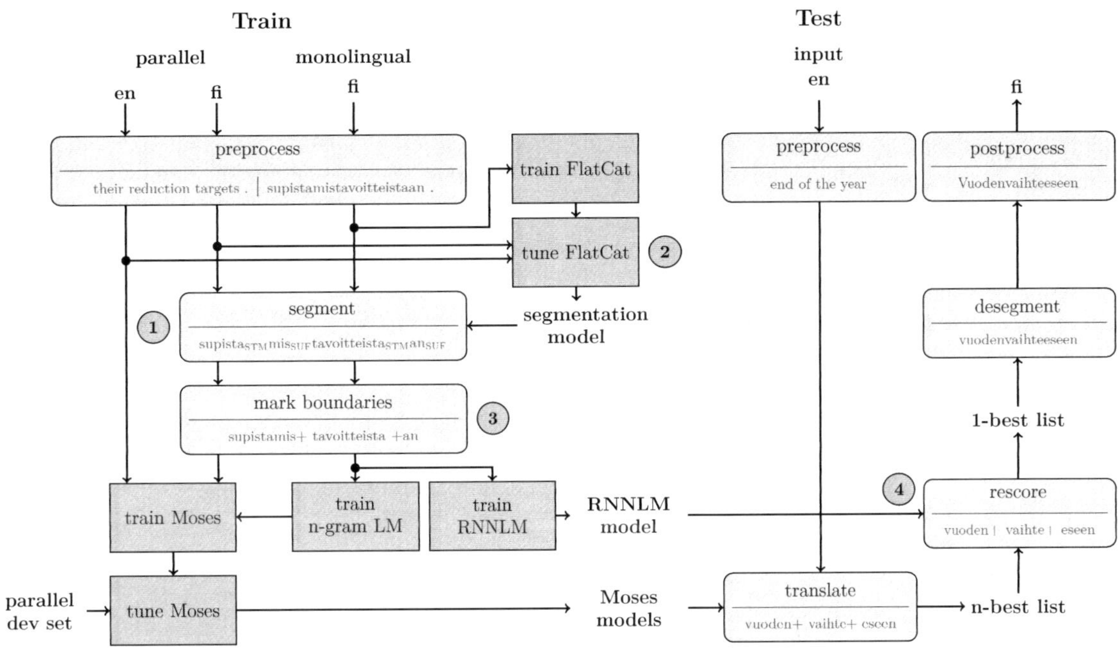

Figure 1: A pipeline overview of training and testing of the system. Main contributions are hilighted with numbers 1-4.

against a tuning set as the metric. 20 random restarts per MERT iteration were used, with iterations repeated until convergence.

A similar MERT procedure was also used for choosing the interpolation weights for rescoring, with 100 random restarts in a single iteration. A single-iteration approach was chosen, as there was no need to translate a new n-best list during the MERT for rescoring.

2.1 Morphological segmentation

For morphological segmentation, we use the latest Morfessor variant, FlatCat (Grönroos et al., 2014). Morfessor FlatCat is a probabilistic method for learning morphological segmentations, using a prior over morph lexicons inspired by the Minimum Description Length principle (Rissanen, 1989).

Morfessor FlatCat applies a Hidden Markov model for morphotactics. Compared to Morfessor Baseline, it provides morph category tags (stem, prefix, suffix) and has superior consistency especially in compound word splitting. In contrast to Categories-MAP (Creutz and Lagus, 2005), used for statistical machine translation e.g. by Clifton and Sarkar (2011), it supports semi-supervised learning and hyper-parameter tuning.

No annotated data was used in the training of Morfessor FlatCat, neither in training nor parameter tuning. Instead of aiming for a linguistic morphological segmentation, our goal was to balance the number of translation tokens between source and target languages.

In order to bring the number of tokens on the Finnish target side closer to the English source side, we segmented the Finnish text with an unsupervised Morfessor FlatCat model, tuned specifically to achieve this balance. The corpus weight hyper-parameter α was chosen by minimizing the sentence-level difference in token counts between the English and the segmented Finnish sides of the parallel corpus

$$\alpha = \arg\min_{\alpha} \sum_{(e,f)\in(E,F)} \Big|\#(e) - \#\big(M(f;\alpha)\big)\Big|, \tag{1}$$

where $\#$ gives the number of tokens in the sentence, and $M(f;\alpha)$ is the segmentation with a particular α.

Numbers and URLs occurring in the parallel corpus were passed through Morfessor unsegmented, but translated by Moses without any special handling.

2.2 Morph boundary marking strategy

In the desegmentation step, consecutive tokens are concatenated either with or without an intermediary space. Morph boundaries must be distinguished from word boundaries, so that the desegmentation step can reconstruct the words correctly. There are various ways to mark the boundaries, some of them shown in Table 1.

Strategy	Example
Surface form	supistamistavoitteistaan
Segmentation	$\text{supista}_{\text{STM}}\text{mis}_{\text{SUF}}\text{tavoitteista}_{\text{STM}}\text{an}_{\text{SUF}}$
Translation	of their reduction targets
right-only	supista +mis +tavoitteista +an
both-sides	supista+ +mis+ +tavoitteista+ +an
compound-sym	supista +mis +@+ tavoitteista +an
compound-left	supista +mis@ tavoitteista +an
advanced	supistamis+ tavoitteista +an

Table 1: Morph boundary marking strategies.

A common way is to attach a symbol to all morphs on the right (or left) side of the morph boundary. We call this strategy *right-only*.

Alternatively *both-sides* of the boundary can be marked. In this strategy, a decision must be made whether to be aggressive or conservative in joining morphs, if the translation system outputs an incorrect sequence where the markers do not match up on both sides. For these experiments we chose the conservative approach, removing the unmatched marker from a half-marked boundary, and treating it as a word boundary.

A downside of the *right-only* and *both-sides* strategies is that a stem is marked differently depending on whether it has a prefix attached or not, even if the surface form of the stem does not change.

The morph categories produced by FlatCat can be used for marking boundaries according to the structure of the word. We can mark affixes from the side that points towards the stem, leaving stems unmarked regardless of the presence of affixes. However, this would leave the boundaries between compound parts indistinguishable from word boundaries, making some additional marking necessary.

Marking affixes by category and compound boundaries with a special linking token is called the *compound-symbol* strategy. Instead marking the last morpheme in the compound modifiers (non-final compound parts), results in the *compound-left* strategy.

After initial unimpressive results with the compound marking strategies, we concluded that segmenting the compound modifiers does not lead to productive translation phrases, in contrast to boundaries between compound parts and boundaries separating inflective affixes. In response, we formulated the *advanced* marking strategy, which goes beyond boundary marking to modify the segmentation, by rejoining the morphs in the modifier parts of compounds.

The sequence of morph categories is used for grouping the morphs into compound parts. A word consists of one or more compound parts. Each compound part consists of exactly one stem, and any number of preceding prefixes and following suffixes.

$$\begin{aligned} \textsc{CompoundPart} &= \textsc{Pre}^{*}\ \textsc{Stm}\ \textsc{Suf}^{*} \\ \textsc{Word} &= \textsc{CompoundPart}^{+} \end{aligned} \tag{2}$$

For all compound parts except the last one, the affixes are rejoined to their stem. Morphs of length 5 or above were treated as stems, regardless of the category assigned to them by FlatCat.

Prefixes and compound modifiers are marked with a trailing '+', suffixes are marked with a leading '+', and the stems of the word-final compound parts are left unmarked.

2.3 Rescoring n-best lists

Segmentation of the word forms increases the distances spanned by dependencies that should be modeled by the language model. To compensate this, we apply a strong recurrent neural network language model (RNNLM) (Mikolov et al., 2010). The additional language model is used in a separate rescoring step, to speed up translation, and for ease of implementation.

The RNNLM model was trained on morphologically segmented data. Morphs occurring only once were removed from the vocabulary, and replaced with <UNK>. The parameters were set to 300 nodes in the hidden layer, 500 vocabulary classes, 2M direct connections of

Purpose	Monolingual data news2014 v2	Parallel data europarl v8	wikititles	newsdev2015	test2006
Training Morfessor	fi	fi	fi		
Training LMs	fi	fi	fi		
Training Moses		en – fi	en – fi		
Tuning Morfessor		en – fi			
Tuning RNNLM				fi	
Tuning Moses				en – fi	
Development testing					en – fi
Sentences	1378582	1926114	153728	1500	2000

Table 2: The data sets used for different purposes. "en–fi" signifies that parallel data was used, "fi" signifies monolingual data, or using only the Finnish side of parallel data.

order 4, backpropagation through 5 time steps, with blocksize 25.

At translation time, 1000-best lists of morph segmented hypotheses produced by Moses were scored using the RNNLM.

The Moses features were extended by including the RNNLM score as an additional feature. A new linear combination of the features was optimized with MERT, and used for the final hypothesis ranking. For the BLEU measurement in MERT the segmented hypothesis was post-processed (including desegmentation) and compared to an un-preprocessed reference.

3 Data

The data sets used in training and tuning are shown in Table 2. Both *europarl v8* and *wikititles* were used as parallel training data, but only europarl was used for tuning the hyperparameter α, as the titles do not follow a typical sentence structure.

The Finnish side of the parallel sets was used to extend the monolingual training data. The monolingual data were concatenated for LM training, instead of interpolating different n-gram models.

After cleaning, the combined parallel training data contained 2,004,450 sentences. The parallel set used for testing during development is *test2006*, a europarl subset of 2000 sentences sampled from three last months of 2000.[1]

[1] `http://matrix.statmt.org/test_sets/list`

Configuration	dev-test test2006 BLEU	test newstest2015 BLEU
advanced, $\alpha = 0.7$	**.147**	.112
+rescoring	**.147**	**.116**
advanced, $\alpha = 0.4$	.145	.112
both-sides	.141	.114
compound-left	.140	.113
compound-sym	.139	.111
right-only	.139	.111
(word)	.146	.100

Table 3: Results of evaluation.

4 Results

Table 3 shows cased BLEU scores on the in-domain development set and out-of-domain test set, for various configurations. The entry marked *word* is a baseline system without segmentation.

When evaluating on the in-domain development set, most configurations that use segmentation achieve worse BLEU compared to the word baseline. Only the best configurations, using the *advanced* strategy, are able to achieve slightly higher BLEU.

Switching domains to the test corpus leads to a larger difference, in favor of the segmenting methods. The choice of morph boundary marking strategy and the sentence-based tuning of the segmentation had a moderate effect on BLEU. The addition of rescoring did not improve BLEU on the in-domain dev-test corpus, but resulted in a slight improvement on the out-of-domain test corpus.

The proportion of word tokens that were segmented into at least two parts was 19.8%. The joining of compound modifiers did not have a large effect on the total number of tokens, causing a reduction from 49,524,520 to 49,475,291 (0.1%).

Using the sentence-level balancing, the optimal value for the corpus weight hyper-parameter α was 0.7. The change in the number of tokens caused by the joining of compound modifiers did not affect the optimum. Balancing the token count of the whole corpus yielded a much lower α of 0.4, leading to oversegmentation and lower BLEU.

The weight of the RNNLM in the final linear combination was 0.092, compared to 0.119 of the n-gram LM. This indicates that it is able to complement the n-gram model, but does not dominate it.

In the human evaluation of WMT15, the system with advanced morph boundary marking strategy and RNNLM rescoring was ranked in tied second place of five methods participating in the constrained condition.

5 Conclusions

To improve English-to-Finnish translation in a phrase-based machine translation system, we tuned an unsupervised morphological segmentation preprocessor to balance the token count between source and target languages. Appropriate choice of morph boundary marking strategy and amount of segmentation brought the BLEU score slightly above a word-based baseline, in contrast to some previous work with unsupervised segmentation (Virpioja et al., 2007; Fishel and Kirik, 2010).

To compensate for the need of longer contexts, we added a recurrent neural network language model as a rescoring step. It did not help for the in-domain development corpus, but improved results on the out-of-domain test corpus.

Possible directions for future work include Minimum Bayes Risk combination of translation hypotheses from systems trained with different segmentations and marking strategies (De Gispert et al., 2009), using morphology generation instead of segmented translation (Clifton and Sarkar, 2011), and improving the alignment directly in addition to balancing of token counts (Snyder and Barzilay, 2008).

Acknowledgments

This research has been supported by the Academy of Finland under the Finnish Centre of Excellence Program 2012–2017 (grant n°251170), and LASTU Programme (grants n°256887 and 259934). Computer resources within the Aalto University School of Science "Science-IT" project were used.

References

[Chung and Gildea2009] Tagyoung Chung and Daniel Gildea. 2009. Unsupervised tokenization for machine translation. In *Proceedings of the 2009 Conference on Empirical Methods in Natural Language Processing: Volume 2-Volume 2*, pages 718–726. Association for Computational Linguistics.

[Clifton and Sarkar2011] Ann Clifton and Anoop Sarkar. 2011. Combining morpheme-based machine translation with post-processing morpheme prediction. In *Proceedings of ACL-HLT*, pages 32–42. Association for Computational Linguistics.

[Creutz and Lagus2005] Mathias Creutz and Krista Lagus. 2005. Inducing the morphological lexicon of a natural language from unannotated text. In Timo Honkela, Ville Könönen, Matti Pöllä, and Olli Simula, editors, *Proceedings of AKRR'05*, pages 106–113, Espoo, Finland, June. Helsinki University of Technology, Laboratory of Computer and Information Science.

[De Gispert et al.2009] Adrià De Gispert, Sami Virpioja, Mikko Kurimo, and William Byrne. 2009. Minimum Bayes risk combination of translation hypotheses from alternative morphological decompositions. In *Proceedings of HLT-NAACL 2009: Short Papers*, pages 73–76. Association for Computational Linguistics.

[Fishel and Kirik2010] Mark Fishel and Harri Kirik. 2010. Linguistically motivated unsupervised segmentation for machine translation. In *LREC*.

[Grönroos et al.2014] Stig-Arne Grönroos, Sami Virpioja, Peter Smit, and Mikko Kurimo. 2014. Morfessor FlatCat: An HMM-based method for unsupervised and semi-supervised learning of morphology. In *Proceedings of COLING 2014, the 25th International Conference on Computational Linguistics*, pages 1177–1185. Association for Computational Linguistics.

[Habash and Sadat2006] Nizar Habash and Fatiha Sadat. 2006. Arabic preprocessing schemes for statistical machine translation. In *Proceedings of HLT-NAACL*. Association for Computational Linguistics.

[Koehn et al.2007] Philipp Koehn, Hieu Hoang, Alexandra Birch, Chris Callison-Burch, Marcello Federico, Nicola Bertoldi, Brooke Cowan, Wade Shen, Christine Moran, Richard Zens, et al. 2007. Moses: Open source toolkit for statistical machine translation. In *Proceedings of the 45th annual meeting of the ACL on interactive poster and demonstration sessions*, pages 177–180. Association for Computational Linguistics.

[Koehn2005] Philipp Koehn. 2005. Europarl: A parallel corpus for statistical machine translation. In *MT summit*, volume 5, pages 79–86.

[Lee2004] Young-Suk Lee. 2004. Morphological analysis for statistical machine translation. In *Proceedings of HLT-NAACL 2004: Short Papers*, pages 57–60. Association for Computational Linguistics.

[Mikolov et al.2010] Tomas Mikolov, Martin Karafiát, Lukas Burget, Jan Cernockỳ, and Sanjeev Khudanpur. 2010. Recurrent neural network based language model. In *INTERSPEECH 2010, 11th Annual Conference of the International Speech Communication Association, Makuhari, Chiba, Japan, September 26-30, 2010*, pages 1045–1048.

[Mikolov et al.2011] Tomas Mikolov, Anoop Deoras, Stefan Kombrink, Lukas Burget, and Jan Honza Cernocky. 2011. Empirical evaluation and combination of advanced language modeling techniques. In *Interspeech*. ISCA, August.

[Nießen and Ney2004] Sonja Nießen and Hermann Ney. 2004. Statistical machine translation with scarce resources using morpho-syntactic information. *Computational linguistics*, 30(2):181–204.

[Och2003] Franz Josef Och. 2003. Minimum error rate training in statistical machine translation. In *Proceedings of the 41st Annual Meeting on Association for Computational Linguistics-Volume 1*, pages 160–167. Association for Computational Linguistics.

[Papineni et al.2002] Kishore Papineni, Salim Roukos, Todd Ward, and Wei-Jing Zhu. 2002. BLEU: a method for automatic evaluation of machine translation. In *Proceedings of the 40th annual meeting on association for computational linguistics*, pages 311–318. Association for Computational Linguistics.

[Rissanen1989] Jorma Rissanen. 1989. *Stochastic Complexity in Statistical Inquiry*, volume 15. World Scientific Series in Computer Science, Singapore.

[Salameh et al.2015] Mohammad Salameh, Colin Cherry, and Grzegorz Kondrak. 2015. What matters most in morphologically segmented SMT models? *Syntax, Semantics and Structure in Statistical Translation*, page 65.

[Snyder and Barzilay2008] Benjamin Snyder and Regina Barzilay. 2008. Unsupervised multilingual learning for morphological segmentation. In *ACL*, pages 737–745.

[Stymne and Cancedda2011] Sara Stymne and Nicola Cancedda. 2011. Productive generation of compound words in statistical machine translation. In *Proceedings of the Sixth Workshop on Statistical Machine Translation*, pages 250–260. Association for Computational Linguistics.

[Virpioja et al.2007] Sami Virpioja, Jaakko J Väyrynen, Mathias Creutz, and Markus Sadeniemi. 2007. Morphology-aware statistical machine translation based on morphs induced in an unsupervised manner. *Machine Translation Summit XI*, 2007:491–498.

The AFRL-MITLL WMT15 System: There's More than One Way to Decode It!

Jeremy Gwinnup[†], **Timothy Anderson**, **Grant Erdmann**, **Katherine Young**[†], **Christina May**[†]
Air Force Research Laboratory
jeremy.gwinnup.ctr,timothy.anderson.20, grant.erdmann,katherine.young.1.ctr, christina.may.3.ctr@us.af.mil

Michaeel Kazi[‡], **Elizabeth Salesky**[‡], **Brian Thompson**[‡]
MIT Lincoln Laboratory
michaeel.kazi,elizabeth.salesky, brian.thompson@ll.mit.edu

Abstract

This paper describes the AFRL-MITLL statistical MT systems and the improvements that were developed during the WMT15 evaluation campaign. As part of these efforts we experimented with a number of extensions to the standard phrase-based model that improve performance on the Russian to English translation task creating three submission systems with different decoding strategies. Out of vocabulary words were addressed with named entity postprocessing.

1 Introduction

As part of the 2015 Workshop on Machine Translation (WMT15) shared translation task, the MITLL and AFRL human language technology teams participated in the Russian–English translation task. Our machine translation systems represent enhancements to both our systems from IWSLT2014 (Kazi et al., 2014) and WMT14 (Schwartz et al., 2014), the addition of hierarchical decoding systems (Hoang and Koehn, 2008), neural network joint models (Devlin et al., 2014) and the utilization of Drem (Erdmann and Gwinnup, 2015), a method of scaled derivative-free trust-region optimization, during the system tuning process.

2 System Description

We submitted systems for the Russian-to-English machine translation shared task. In all submitted systems, we used either phrase-based or hierarchical variants of the `moses` decoder (Koehn et al., 2007). As in previous years, our submitted systems used only the constrained data supplied when training.

2.1 Data Usage

In training our Russian–English systems we utilized the following corpora to train translation and language models: Yandex[1], Commoncrawl (Smith et al., 2013), LDC Gigaword English v5 (Parker et al., 2011) and News Commentary. The Wikipedia Headlines corpus[2] was reserved to train named entity recognizers.

2.2 Data Preprocessing

As with our WMT14 submission systems, preprocessing to address issues with the training data was required to ensure optimal system performance. Unicode characters in the private use, control character(C0, C1, zero-width, non-breaking, joiner, directionality and paragraph markers), and unallocated ranges were removed. Punctuation normalization and tokenization using Moses preprocessing scripts were then applied before lowercasing the data. The Commoncrawl corpus was further processed as in Schwartz et al. (2014) to exclude wrong-language text and to normalize mixed-alphabet spellings.

2.3 Factored Data Generation

We generated a class-factored version of the parallel Russian–English training data by using `mkcls` to produce 600 word classes for each side of the data. The factored data was then used to create a factored translation model and an in-domain class language model (Brown et al., 1993) for the English portion.

[†]This work is sponsored by the Air Force Research Laboratory under Air Force contract FA-8650-09-D-6939-029.
[‡]This work is sponsored by the Air Force Research Laboratory under Air Force contract FA-8721-05-C-0002.

[1]`https://translate.yandex.ru/corpus?lang=en`
[2]`http://statmt.org/wmt15/wiki-titles.tgz`

2.4 Phrase and Rule Table Training

Phrase tables and rule tables were trained on the preprocessed data using scripts provided with the `moses` distribution. Both rule tables and phrase tables utilized Good-Turing discounting (Gale, 1995). Hierarchical lexicalized reordering models (Galley and Manning, 2008) were also trained for use in the phrase-based systems.

An additional phrase table was trained on the lemmatized forms of the Russian training data. These lemmatized forms were generated by the `mystem`[3] tool.

2.5 Language Model Training

The English data sources listed in §2.1 were used to train a very large 6-gram language model (BigLM15). The English portion of the parallel data was processed into class form as outlined in §2.3 to generate an in-domain 600 class language model. `kenlm` (Heafield, 2011) was used to train these 6-gram models. These models were then binarized and stored on local solid-state disks for each machine in our cluster to improve load time and reduce fileserver traffic.

2.6 Operation Sequence Models

Using both the Russian and English data generated in §2.3, we trained order-5 Operation Sequence models (Durrani et al., 2011) for both the surface and class-factored forms of the data. These models improve translation quality by introducing information on the sequence of operations occuring at both the surface and class factor level. These models were then used in our factored phrase-based system.

2.7 Neural Network Joint Models

Neural network joint models (Devlin et al., 2014) are neural network based language models with a source window context. We trained these models on the alignments produced by `mgiza` (Gao and Vogel, 2008) over the parallel training data and then used them to rescore n-best lists. As in (Devlin et al., 2014), we trained four different models. The standard model is "source-to-target, left-to-right," (s2t, ltr) which evaluates $p(t_i|T, S)$ with target window $T = (t_{i-1}, t_{i-2}, \ldots, t_{i-n})$ and $S = (s_{k-m}, \ldots s_k, \ldots, s_{k+m})$, where s_k is word-aligned to t_i. The four permutations of this are defined by (a) whether to count upwards from i, instead of downwards (this is left-to-right vs right-to-left), and (b) whether to swap the sources and targets entirely (source-to-target vs target-to-source).

We experimented with NNJM decoding (via a simple feature function in Moses). We achieved some benefit (+0.48 BLEU) with this approach but rescoring a single NNJM source-to-target on 200-best lists produced better results in this case (+0.90 BLEU). This was on a single system tuned on `newstest2013`, tested on `newstest2014` (baseline 29.07 BLEU). In testing, 2-hidden layer rescoring models outperformed the 1-hidden layer decoding model.

The vocabulary for the NNJMs were created by using all words that appeared at least a certain number of times in the training data. We experimented with minimum counts of 20 and 25. Using 20, our vocabulary was approximately 80,000 Russian words and 40,000 English; with 25, it was 70,000 and 34,000, respectively. We compared rescoring with a single, standard model (s2t, l2r) to rescoring with all directions with results listed in Table 1.

	Baseline	1 NNJM		4 NNJMs	
		20	25	20	25
max	27.71	27.90	28.05	27.90	28.07
mean	27.48	27.61	27.81	27.67	27.60

Table 1: NNJM Rescoring on `newstest2015`, optimizing on `newstest2014`, case-insensitive BLEU.

2.8 Processing of Unknown Words

In our submission systems, we allowed words unknown to the decoder to be passed through to the translated output. We developed three post-processing techniques to address unknown words: named entity (NE) tagging and translation (§2.8.2), permissive NE translation (§2.8.3), and selective transliteration of the remaining OOV words (§2.8.4). The first two techniques rely on our in-house transliteration mining of NE pairs, which is described in §2.8.1.

We applied all three post-processing steps to the output of our factored phrase-based submission system; due to time constraints, only the last two steps were applied to the output of our phrase-based and hierarchical submission systems.

Score improvements in uncased BLEU are reported in Table 2. We see that application of

[3] `https://tech.yandex.ru/mystem`

permissive lookup and selective transliteration yielded an improvement of +0.48 BLEU versus a baseline system, while the application of named entity tagging and translation, permissive lookup and selective transliteration yielded a +0.57 BLEU gain.

2.8.1 Transliteration Mining

Both NE processing steps (§2.8.2 and §2.8.3) make use of a NE pairs list that we developed through transliteration mining of the Russian-English CommonCrawl. In transliteration mining (Kumaran et al., 2010; Zhang et al., 2012), we use transliteration as a tool to detect similar-sounding words in the parallel text that may correspond to names. Our process for detecting transliterated NE is generative and rule-based. We used `mystem` to tag NE in the Russian text, and then used capitalization and transliteration as clues to find matching NE in the parallel English sentences. English words were considered candidate matches if they were capitalized, but not sentence-initial; we excluded all-caps words, since acronyms often do not transliterate well. We also required the English candidate words to match the initial sound of the Russian NE.

We checked the initial sound match by transliterating the Russian words according to the textbook values of the Russian letters, and then checking for matches with the English spellings, allowing certain spelling variations. These variations include instances where Russian lacks an English sound, and substitutes a similar sound (e.g., English h written in Russian with the letters for x or g, and English w written with the Russian letters for v or u), as well as common English spelling alternations like n/kn, s/c, c/k, etc.

An iterative process of refining spelling alternations was applied by manual observation of known NE pairs that were not matched via existing rules; notably, this introduced spelling variations for words originating from a third language. For example, English j typically represents [dʒ] but may also indicate [h] in words of Spanish origin, so we need to allow the spelling alternation x/j . Similarly, the letters gi may represent [dʒ] in Italian names like *Giovanni*, so we need to allow transliterated Russian dzh to match English gi.

At this point in the transliteration mining process, we have derived a list of capitalized English words that have initial spellings potentially matching the initial sound of the Russian NE word. If the English sentence contains more than one such candidate, we select the word with the smallest edit distance from the Russian transliteration, using a length-normalized Levenshtein distance. For this calculation, any spelling variation counts as an edit distance change, so we penalize variations such as k for c.

For NE tagging and translation (§2.8.2), we return only the NE pairs with zero edit distance. For permissive NE translation, we allow some variation, as described in §2.8.3.

2.8.2 Named Entity Tagging and Translation

The named entity post-process uses Russian–English pairs in the combined names and titles lists from the Wikipedia Headlines corpus (the "Wiki pairs list") and the transliteration-mined list (§2.8.1) to replace unknown words with English equivalents. We began by stemming each list to remove Russian noun and adjective endings. To the Wiki pairs list, we added additional pairs yielded by replacing word-internal punctuation marks in existing Wiki pairs with spaces. We used `giza++` (Och and Ney, 2003) to align Russian–English phrases from the Wiki list. We then used these alignments to start a generated list of pairs with only one Russian word and one English word in a pair. Of the aligned pairs, we only included pairs that were aligned with one another three or more times. Only one-to-one alignments would count toward the three alignment rule. We also removed entries where the English word in the pair occurred in a list of stop-words as well as where the English word consisted of only digits. To the generated list, we also added pairs directly from the Wiki list with both single Russian words and single English words. Finally, we also added the highest quality pairs from the transliteration-mined list.

Upon encountering a single word without word-internal punctuation, the system first searches through the generated list, and returns a list of found guesses. If no items are found in the generated list, the Wiki list is then searched. If still no guesses are found, then the transliteration-mined list is searched. The same process occurs for a word containing word-internal punctuation, but after a failed iteration of the search process, the punctuation is replaced with a space and the Wiki lists are searched. Finally if that iteration fails, then the search process occurs on each individual word and a concatenation of English definitions is added to the guess list for every possible combination of guesses for each component word. An English language model is used to choose among the guesses.

2.8.3 Permissive Named Entity Translation

Permissive NE look-up is applied to translate OOV words that remain untranslated after NE tagging and translation (§2.8.2), or when the NE tagging and translation step is unavailable. In this second step, we expand the NE pairs list to include pairs with greater edit distance when they are validated by repeat occurrence.

While the NE tagging and translation step only uses transliteration-mined NE pairs which match exactly, the permissive step allows NE pairs that have some spelling variation. We apply two additional restrictions to ensure good quality matches, length disparity and instance ratio. We restrict the output to words which come from sentences that do not differ too much in length. A large length disparity suggests a sentence alignment error in the parallel text, which would make the NE match unreliable.

We also restrict the output to words which are fairly frequent among other matches for the same Russian words, calculating an instance ratio as the number of times we see this English word with this Russian word, divided by the total number of English matches we record for this Russian word. Rare instances may be mistakes or spelling variants that we would prefer to exclude. For example, we found the Russian name *Константин* matched with English *Constantine* 117 times, and matched with the spelling *Konstantine* only 1 time, so we do not want to collect *Константин/Konstantine* as a NE pair.

We keep the NE pairs if:

1. The length-normalized edit distance < 0.2
2. The length-normalized edit distance falls between 0.2 and 0.5, inclusive, and sentence length disparity < 2 and instance ratio > 0.01

With these restrictions, we derived 32,560 potential NE pairs.

Subsequently, an additional transliteration mining step was conducted, to collect NE pairs from any capitalized Russian words, not just the words tagged as NE by `mystem`. We excluded Russian acronyms, sentence-initial words, and personal pronouns (which are capitalized in some styles of Russian writing). Applying the previously described restrictions for edit distance, instance ratio, and sentence length disparity, we derived an additional 22,370 capitalized-word NE pairs. The combined `mystem` tagged and capitalized-word NE pairs lists were used in the permissive translation of OOV words, considering both the original form of the Russian OOV word and its stemmed form.

For the phrase-based and hierarchical systems, which were processed without the NE tagging and translation step, the wiki pairs list was added to the mined NE pairs list for permissive OOV translation.

2.8.4 Selective Transliteration of Remaining Out-of-Vocabulary Words

As a final post-processing step, we transliterate some of the remaining OOV words. We attempt to distinguish OOV NE from common words, dropping common words and transliterating names. We hypothesize that retaining transliterated forms of NE will improve readability, even if the output is not a direct match to the English reference.

We attempt to distinguish NE from common words on the basis of capitalization in the Russian source file. Capitalized words that do not begin a sentence are assumed to be NE, and are transliterated. For example, transliteration is the source of the name *Kostenok* in first example sentence shown in Figure 1. Lowercased words, and capitalized words that begin a sentence, are assumed to be common words and are dropped from the output.

3 Results

We submitted three systems for evaluation, each employing a different decoding strategy: traditional phrased-based, hierarchical, and factored phrased-based. Each system is described below. Automatically scored results reported in BLEU (Papineni et al., 2002) for our submission systems can be found in Table 3.

Finally, as part of WMT15, the results of our submission systems listed in Tables 3 were ranked by monolingual human judges against the machine translation output of other WMT15 participants. These judgements are reported in WMT (2015).

3.1 Phrased-Based

We used a standard phrase-based approach, using lowercased data. The lemma-based phrase table

System	Process Applied	baseline BLEU	postproc BLEU	Δ BLEU
phrase-based	PermLookup + SelTranslit	27.72	28.20	+0.48
hiero	PermLookup + SelTranslit	27.43	27.91	+0.48
pb-factored	NEProc + PermLookup+ SelTranslit	27.18	27.75	+0.57

Table 2: NE post-processing improvement measured in uncased BLEU

described in §2.4 was used as a backoff phrase table. We trained a hierarchical lexicalized reordering model, and used two separate class based (factored) language models; one using 600 classes on the in-domain target-side parallel data, and the other using the LDC Gigaword-English v5 NYT corpus. N-best lists from moses were rescored with 4-way NNJMs, and the system weights were tuned with PRO (Hopkins and May, 2011). Selective transliteration as described in §2.8.4 was then applied to the decoder output.

3.2 Hierarchical

New for this year, we trained a hierarchical system using the same parallel data as our phrase-based systems. The rule table was created as outlined in §2.4 and then filtered to only contain rules relating to the Russian content of the `newstest` test set for years 2012–2015. This filtering was performed in order to reduce the size of the rule table for both system memory requirements and expediency. The incremental-search algorithm (Heafield et al., 2013) and BigLM15 were used to decode the dev (`newstest2014`) and test (`newstest2015`) data. Drem was employed to tune feature weights, optimizing the sum of the expected sentence-level BLEU and expected sentence-level Meteor (Denkowski and Lavie, 2014) metrics. Finally, selective transliteration was employed as described in §2.8.4.

3.3 Factored Phrase-Based

For our last system, we used a factored phrase-based approach (Koehn and Hoang, 2007) where the surface form of the training data was augmented with word classes. These classes were generated on the parallel training data outlined in §2.4 using `mkcls` to group the words into 600 classes for both English and Russian portions of the parallel training corpus. A phrase table and hierarchical reordering model was then trained using the `moses` training process on both the surface form and the class factor. Order-5 operation sequence models were separately trained on the surface forms and the class factors. An order-6 class-factor LM (Shen et al., 2006) was also trained on the English portion of the parallel training data to supplement the use of BigLM15. NNJMs as outlined in §2.7 were used to rescore the n-best lists from the decode. Following this rescoring, Drem was employed to tune feature weights, optimizing expected corpus-level BLEU (Smith and Eisner, 2006). After optimization and decoding of the test set, remaining unknown words were processed as described in §2.8.2 and §2.8.4.

System	Cased BLEU	Uncased BLEU
phrase-based	27.0	28.2
hiero	26.7	27.9
pb-factored	26.4	27.8

Table 3: MT Submission Systems decoding `newstest2015`

4 Discussion

Our three submitted systems all scored similarly against the official test set. Manual examination of our systems' output shows that there are significant differences in sentence structure and content.

4.1 Comparing Submitted Systems for Similarity

We scored one system output against another (as reference) with `mteval13a.pl` in both directions as BLEU scores are not symmetric. Results are listed in Table 4. Interestingly, the factored phrase-based and hierarchical systems were more similar to each other than to the traditional phrase-based system. This suggests that the addition of class factors serves a similar function to the use of hierarchical decoding.

4.2 A Closer Analysis of Performance between Submission Systems

We now examine two sentences translated with each of our submission systems and compare them with the supplied reference translation and a literal

Test	Ref	BLEU
PB	Hiero	57.18
PBFac	Hiero	76.34
Hiero	PB	57.09
PBFac	PB	60.54
PB	PBFac	60.47
Hiero	PBFac	70.18

Table 4: Submission system similarity measured in uncased BLEU

translation. These comparisons are shown in Figure 1.

In the first sentence, the reference translation shows a reordering of the first clause to the end. The phrase-based system drops this clause. The pb-factored system has *informed* instead of *reported* which shifts the meaning; perhaps the translation was influenced by the fluent but different-meaning phrase *informed the Minister*. The hierarchical system follows the original order of the source sentence clauses; while missing *the*, it reads the best overall.

In the second sentence, *Учебный* "school" (adjective) is the probable source of *school*, *academic*, and *teach*. The phrase-based system handles this word best; the phrase-based factored system generates *academic* and *teach* but separates them; the hierarchical system generates *year to teach*. The hierarchical system does the best job with *no earlier than October*. The phrase-based factored system generates *no earlier* and *October* but reorders them (perhaps influenced by the common phrase, *in October*); and the phrase-based system creates *before October*, which reverses the meaning. The phrase-based system would have read best here, had it not neglected the negative particle.

5 Conclusion

In this paper, we present data preparation and processing techniques for our Russian–English submissions to the 2015 Workshop on Machine Translation (WMT15) shared translation task. Our submissions examine three different decoding strategies and the effectiveness of sophisticated handling of unknown words. While scoring similarly, each system produced markedly different output.

References

Peter Brown, Vincent Della Pietra, Stephen Della Pietra, and Robert Mercer. 1993. The mathematics of statistical machine translation: parameter estimation. *Computational Linguistics*, 19(2):263–311, June.

Michael Denkowski and Alon Lavie. 2014. Meteor universal: Language specific translation evaluation for any target language. In *Proceedings of the Ninth Workshop on Statistical Machine Translation*, pages 376–380, Baltimore, Maryland, USA, June. Association for Computational Linguistics.

Jacob Devlin, Rabih Zbib, Zhongqiang Huang, Thomas Lamar, Richard Schwartz, and John Makhoul. 2014. Fast and robust neural network joint models for statistical machine translation. In *Proceedings of the 52nd Annual Meeting of the Association for Computational Linguistics (Volume 1: Long Papers)*, Proceedings of the ACL, Long Papers, pages 1370–1380, Baltimore, MD, USA.

Nadir Durrani, Helmut Schmid, and Alexander Fraser. 2011. A joint sequence translation model with integrated reordering. In *Proceedings of the 49th Annual Meeting of the Association for Computational Linguistics (ACL '11)*, pages 1045–1054, Portland, Oregon, June.

Grant Erdmann and Jeremy Gwinnup. 2015. Drem: The AFRL submission to the WMT15 tuning task. In *Proceedings of the Tenth Workshop on Statistical Machine Translation (WMT'15)*, Lisbon, Portugal, September. To appear.

William A. Gale. 1995. Good-turing smoothing without tears. *Journal of Quantitative Linguistics*, 2.

Michel Galley and Christopher D. Manning. 2008. A simple and effective hierarchical phrase reordering model. In *Proceedings of the Conference on Empirical Methods in Natural Language Processing*, EMNLP '08, pages 848–856.

Qin Gao and Stephan Vogel. 2008. Parallel implementations of word alignment tool. In *Software Engineering, Testing and Quality Assurance for Natural Language Processing*, pages 49–57, Columbus, Ohio, June.

Kenneth Heafield, Philipp Koehn, and Alon Lavie. 2013. Grouping language model boundary words to speed k-best extraction from hypergraphs. In *Proceedings of the 2013 Conference of the North American Chapter of the Association for Computational Linguistics: Human Language Technologies*, pages 958–968, Atlanta, Georgia, USA, June.

Kenneth Heafield. 2011. KenLM: faster and smaller language model queries. In *Proceedings of the EMNLP 2011 Sixth Workshop on Statistical Machine*

Opinions, interpretations, conclusions and recommendations are those of the authors and are not necessarily endorsed by the United States Government. Cleared for public release on 11 Jun 2015. Originator reference number RH-15-114103. Case number 88ABW-2015-2973.

Example 1

source:	Об этом сообщил министр образования и науки самопровозглашенной республики Игорь Костенок
literal:	Of this reported minister education and science self-proclaimed republic, Igor Kostenok
reference:	The Minister of Education and Science for the self-proclaimed republic, Igor Kostenok, reported this.
phrase-based:	The Minister of Education and Science of the self-declared republic, Igor Kostenok.
pb-factored:	This was informed the Minister of Education and Science of the self-declared republic, Igor Kostenok.
hierarchical:	This was announced by Minister of Education and Science of the self-proclaimed republic Igor Kostenok.

Example 2

source:	Учебный год в ДНР начнется не раньше октября.
literal:	School year in DNR begins not before October.
reference:	The academic school year in the DPR will begin no earlier than October.
phrase-based:	The school year in DNR will begin before October.
pb-factored:	Academic year in October, teach will begin.
hierarchical:	School year to teach will begin no earlier than October.

Figure 1: Comparison of Submission System Translation Output

Translation, pages 187–197, Edinburgh, Scotland, United Kingdom, July.

Hieu Hoang and Philipp Koehn. 2008. Design of the moses decoder for statistical machine translation. In *Software Engineering, Testing, and Quality Assurance for Natural Language Processing*, SETQA-NLP '08, pages 58–65.

Mark Hopkins and Jonathan May. 2011. Tuning as ranking. In *Proceedings of the 2011 Conference on Empirical Methods in Natural Language Processing (EMNLP '11)*, pages 1352–1362, Edinburgh, Scotland, U.K.

Michaeel Kazi, Elizabeth Salesky, Brian Thompson, Jessica Ray, Michael Coury, Tim Shen, Wade Anderson, Grant Erdmann, Jeremy Gwinnup, Katherine Young, Brian Ore, and Michael Hutt. 2014. The MIT-LL/AFRL IWSLT-2014 MT system. In *Proceedings of the 11th International Workshop on Spoken Language Translation (IWSLT'14)*, pages 65–72, Lake Tahoe, California, December.

Philipp Koehn and Hieu Hoang. 2007. Factored translation models. In *Proceedings of the 2007 Joint Conference on Empirical Methods in Natural Language Processing and Computational Natural Language Learning (EMNLP-CoNLL)*, pages 868–876.

Philipp Koehn, Hieu Hoang, Alexandra Birch, Chris Callison-Burch, Marcello Federico, Nicola Bertoldi, Brooke Cowan, Wade Shen, Christine Moran, Richard Zens, Chris Dyer, Ondřej Bojar, Alexandra Constantin, and Evan Herbst. 2007. Moses: Open source toolkit for statistical machine translation. In *Proceedings of the 45th Annual Meeting of the ACL on Interactive Poster and Demonstration Sessions*, ACL '07, pages 177–180, Stroudsburg, PA, USA. Association for Computational Linguistics.

A Kumaran, Mitesh M. Khapra, and Haizhou Li. 2010. Whitepaper of news 2010 shared task on transliteration mining. In *Proceedings of the 2010 Named Entities Workshop*, pages 29–38, Uppsala, Sweden, July. Association for Computational Linguistics.

Franz Josef Och and Hermann Ney. 2003. A systematic comparison of various statistical alignment models. *Computational Linguistics*, 29(1):19–51, March.

Kishore Papineni, Salim Roukos, Todd Ward, and Wei-Jing Zhu. 2002. BLEU: A method for automatic evaluation of machine translation. In *Proceedings of the 40th Annual Meeting of the Association for Computational Linguistics (ACL '02)*, pages 311–318, Philadelphia, Pennsylvania, July.

Robert Parker, David Graff, Junbo Kong, Ke Chen, and Kazuaki Maeda. 2011. English Gigaword Fifth Edition LDC2011T07. *Philadelphia: Linguistic Data Consortium*.

Lane Schwartz, Timothy Anderson, Jeremy Gwinnup, and Katherine Young. 2014. Machine translation and monolingual postediting: The AFRL WMT-14 system. In *Proceedings of the Ninth Workshop on Statistical Machine Translation (WMT'14)*, pages 186–194, Baltimore, Maryland, USA, June.

Wade Shen, Richard Zens, Nicola Bertoldi, and Marcello Federico. 2006. The JHU workshop 2006 IWSLT system. In *Proc. of the International Workshop on Spoken Language Translation*, Kyoto, Japan, November.

David A. Smith and Jason Eisner. 2006. Minimum risk annealing for training log-linear models. In *Proceedings of the COLING/ACL 2006 Main Conference Poster Sessions*, pages 787 – 794, Sydney, Australia.

Jason R. Smith, Herve Saint-Amand, Magdalena Plamada, Philipp Koehn, Chris Callison-Burch, and Adam Lopez. 2013. Dirt cheap web-scale parallel text from the common crawl. In *Proceedings of the 51st Annual Meeting of the Association for Computational Linguistics (ACL '13)*, pages 1374–1383, Sofia, Bulgaria, August.

WMT. 2015. Findings of the 2015 Workshop on Statistical Machine Translation. In *Proceedings of the Tenth Workshop on Statistical Machine Translation (WMT '15)*, Lisbon, Portugal, September.

Min Zhang, Haizhou Li, A. Kumaran, and Ming Liu, 2012. *Proceedings of the 4th Named Entity Workshop (NEWS) 2012*, chapter Report of NEWS 2012 Machine Transliteration Shared Task, pages 10–20. Association for Computational Linguistics.

The KIT-LIMSI Translation System for WMT 2015

†Thanh-Le Ha, *Quoc-Khanh Do, †Eunah Cho, †Jan Niehues,
*Alexandre Allauzen, *François Yvon and †Alex Waibel
†Karlsruhe Institute of Technology, Karlsruhe, Germany
*LIMSI-CNRS, Orsay, France
†firstname.surname@kit.edu *firstname.surname@limsi.fr

Abstract

This paper presented the joined submission of KIT and LIMSI to the English to German translation task of WMT 2015. In this year submission, we integrated a neural network-based translation model into a phrase-based translation model by rescoring the n-best lists.

Since the computation complexity is one of the main issues for continuous space models, we compared two techniques to reduce the computation cost. We investigated models using a structured output layer as well as models trained with noise contrastive estimation. Furthermore, we evaluated a new method to obtain the best log-linear combination in the rescoring phase.

Using these techniques, we were able to improve the BLEU score of the baseline phrase-based system by 1.4 BLEU points.

1 Introduction

In this paper, we present the English→German joint translation system from KIT and LIMSI participating in the Shared Translation Task of the EMNLP 2015 - Tenth Workshop on Statistical Machine Translation (WMT2015). Our system is the combination of two different approaches. First, a strong phrase-based system from KIT is used to generate a k-best list of translated candidates. Second, an n-gram translation model from LIMSI, named *SOUL* (*Structured OUtput Layer*), helps to rescore the k-best list by utilizing features extracted from translated tuples. In this year participation, we also use a version of the neural network translation models (Le et al., 2012) trained using *NCE* algorithm (Gutmann and Hyvärinen, 2010) as counterpart to *SOUL* models. A ListNet-based rescoring method is then applied to integrate two abovementioned approaches.

Section 2 describes the KIT phrase-based translation system which is conducted over the phrase pairs. Section 3 describes the LIMSI *SOUL* and *NCE* translation models estimated on source-and-target n-gram tuples. We explain the rescoring approach in Section 4. Finally, Section 5 summarizes the experimental results of our joint system submitted to WMT2015.

2 KIT Phrase-based Translation System

The KIT translation system uses a phrase-based in-house decoder (Vogel, 2003) which finds the best combinations of features in a log-linear framework. The features consist of translation scores, distortion-based and lexicalized reordering scores as well as conventional and non-word language models. In addition, several reordering rules, including short-range, long-range and tree-based reorderings, are applied before decoding step as they are encoded as word lattices. The decoder then generates a list of the best candidates from the lattices. To optimize the factors of individual features on a development dataset, we use minimum error rate training (MERT) (Venugopal et al., 2005). We are going to describe those components in detail as follows.

2.1 Data and Preprocessing

The parallel data mainly used are the corpora extracted from Europarl Parliament (EPPS), News Commentary (NC) and the common part of web-crawled data (Common Crawl). The monolingual data are the monolingual part of those corpora.

A preprocessing step is applied to the raw data before the actual training. It includes removing excessively long and length-mismatched sentences pairs. Special symbols and nummeric data are normalized, and smartcasing is applied. Sentence pairs which contain textual elements in different languages to some extent, are also taken away. The data is further filtered by using an SVM classifier to remove noisy sentences which are not the actual translation from their counterparts.

2.2 Phrase-table Scores

We obtain the word alignments using the GIZA++ toolkit (Och and Ney, 2003) and Discriminative Word Alignment method (Niehues and Vogel, 2008) from the parallel EPPS, NC and Common Crawl. Then the Moses toolkit (Koehn et al., 2007) is used to build the phrase tables. Translation scores, which are used as features in our log-linear framework, are derived from those phrase tables. Additional scores, e.g. distortion information, word penalties and lexicalized reordering probabilities (Koehn et al., 2005), are also extracted from the phrase tables.

2.3 Discriminative Word Lexicon

The presence of words in the source sentence can be used to guide the choice of target words. (Mauser et al., 2009) build a maximum entropy classifier for every target words, taking the presence of source words as its features, in order to predict whether the word should appear in the target sentence or not. In KIT system, we use an extended version described in Niehues and Waibel (2013), which utilizes the presence of source n-grams rather than source words. The parallel data of EPPS and NC are used to train those classifiers.

2.4 Language Models

Besides word-based n-gram language models trained on all preprocessed monolingual data, the KIT system includes several non-word language models. A 4-gram bilingual language model (Niehues et al., 2011) trained on the parallel corpora is used to exploit wider bilingual contexts beyond phrase boundaries. 5-gram Part-of-Speech (POS) language models trained on the POS-tagged parts of all monolingual data incorporate some morphological information into the decision process. They also help to reduce the impact of the data sparsity problem, as cluster language models do. Our 4-gram cluster language model is trained on monolingual EPPS and NC as we use MKCLS algorithm (Och, 1999) to group the words into 1,000 classes and build the language model of the corresponding class IDs instead of the words.

All of the language models are trained using the SRILM toolkit (Stolcke, 2002); The word-based language model scores are estimated by KenLM toolkit (Heafield, 2011) while the non-word language models are estimated by SRILM.

2.5 Prereorderings

The short-range reordering (Rottmann and Vogel, 2007) and long-range reordering (Niehues and Kolss, 2009) rules are extracted from POS-tagged versions of parallel EPPS and NC. The POS tags of those corpora are produced using the TreeTagger (Schmid, 1994). The learnt rules are used to reorder source sentences based on the POS sequences of their target sentences and to build reordering lattices for the translation model. Additionally, a tree-based reordering model (Herrmann et al., 2013) trained on syntactic parse trees (Klein and Manning, 2003) is applied to the source side to better address the differences in word order between English and German.

3 Continuous Space Translation Models

Neural networks, working on top of conventional n-gram back-off language models (BOLMs), have been introduced in (Bengio et al., 2003; Schwenk, 2007) as a potential means to improve discrete language models. More recently, these techniques have been applied to statistical machine translation in order to estimate continuous-space translation models (CTMs) (Schwenk et al., 2007; Le et al., 2012; Devlin et al., 2014)

3.1 n-gram Translation Models

The n-gram-based approach in machine translation is a variant of the phrase-based approach (Koehn et al., 2003). Introduced in (Casacuberta and Vidal, 2004), and extended in (Mariño et al., 2006; Crego and Mariño, 2006), this approach is based on a specific factorization of the joint probability of parallel sentence pairs, where the source sentence has been reordered beforehand as illustrated in Figure 1.

Let $(\mathbf{s}, \mathbf{t})$ denote a sentence pair made of a source $\mathbf{s}$ and target $\mathbf{t}$ sides. This sentence pair is decomposed into a sequence of L bilingual units called *tuples* defining a joint segmentation. In this framework, tuples constitute the basic translation units: like phrase pairs, a matching between a source and target chunks. The joint probability of a *synchronized* and *segmented* sentence pair can be estimated using the n-gram assumption. During training, the segmentation is obtained as a

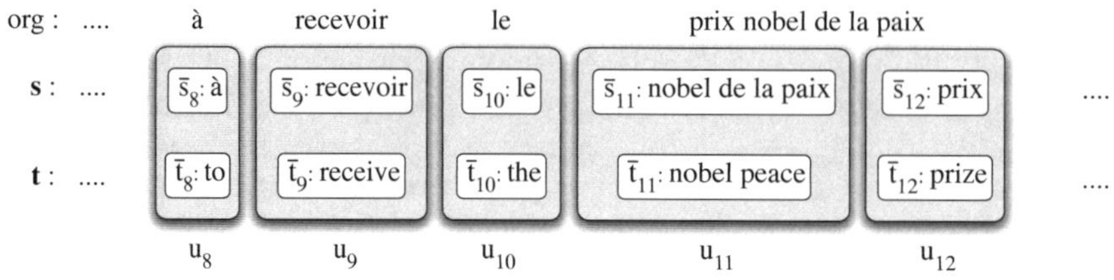

Figure 1: Extract of a French-English sentence pair segmented into bilingual units. The original (*org*) French sentence appears at the top of the figure, just above the reordered source $\mathbf{s}$ and the target $\mathbf{t}$. The pair $(\mathbf{s}, \mathbf{t})$ decomposes into a sequence of L bilingual units (*tuples*) $\mathrm{u}_1, ..., \mathrm{u}_L$. Each tuple u_i contains a source and a target phrase: $\overline{s}_i$ and $\overline{t}_i$.

by-product of source reordering, (see (Crego and Mariño, 2006) for details). During the inference step, the SMT decoder is assumed to output for each source sentence a set of hypotheses along with their derivations, which allow CTMs to score the generated sentence pairs.

Note that the n-gram translation model manipulates bilingual tuples. The underlying set of events is thus much bigger than for word-based models, whereas the training data (parallel corpora) are typically order of magnitude smaller than monolingual resources. As a consequence, data sparsity issues for this model are particularly severe. Effective workarounds consist in factorizing the conditional probabitily of tuples into terms involving smaller units: the resulting model thus splits bilingual phrases in two sequences of respectively source and target words, synchronised by the tuple segmentation. Such bilingual word-based n-gram models were initially described in (Le et al., 2012) and extended in (Devlin et al., 2014). We assume here the same decomposition.

3.2 Neural Architectures

In such models, the size of output vocabulary is a bottleneck when normalized distributions are needed (Bengio et al., 2003; Schwenk et al., 2007). Various workarounds have been proposed, relying for instance on a structured output layer using word-classes (Mnih and Hinton, 2008; Le et al., 2011). A different alternative, which however only delivers *quasi-normalized* scores, is to train the network using the *Noise Contrastive Estimation* or *NCE* for short (Gutmann and Hyvärinen, 2010; Mnih and Teh, 2012). This technique is readily applicable for CTMs. Therefore, *NCE* models deliver a positive score, by applying the exponential function to the output layer activities, instead of the more costly softmax function. We propose here to compare these both approaches, *SOUL* and *NCE* to estimate CTMs. The only difference relies on the output structure of the networks. In terms of computation cost, while the training using the two approaches takes quite similar amounts of time, the inference with *NCE* is slightly faster than the one with *SOUL* as it ignores the score normalization. While the CTMs under study in this paper were initially introduced within the framework of n-gram-based systems (Le et al., 2012), they could be used with any phrase-based system.

Initialization is an important issue when optimizing neural networks. For CTMs, a solution consists in pre-training monolingual n-gram models. Their parameters are then used to initialize bilingual models.

3.3 Integration CTMs

Given the computational cost of computing n-gram probabilities with neural network models, a solution is to resort to a two-pass approach as described in Section 4: the first pass uses a conventional system to produce a k-best list (the k most likely hypotheses); in the second pass, probabilities are computed by the CTMs for each hypothesis and added as new features. Since the phrase-based system described in Section 2 uses source reordering, the decoder was modified to generate k-best lists containing necessary word alignment information between the reordered source sentence and its associated translation. The goal is to recover the information that allows us to apply the n-gram decomposition of a sentence pair.

4 Rescoring

After generating translation probabilities using the neural network translation models, we need to combine them with the baseline scores of the phrase-based system in order to select better translations from the k-best lists. As it is done in the baseline decoder, we used a log-linear combination of all features. We trained the model using the ListNet algorithm (Niehues et al., 2015; Cao et al., 2007).

This technique defines a probability distribution on the permutations of the list based on the scores of the log-linear model and one based on a reference metric. Therefore, a sentence-based translation quality metric is necessary. In our experiments we used the BLEU+1 score introduced by Liang et al. (2006). Then the model was trained by minimizing the cross entropy between both distributions on the development data.

Using this loss function, we can compute the gradient with respect to the weight ω_k as follows:

$$\Delta\omega_k = \sum_{j=1}^{n^{(i)}} f_k(x_j^{(i)}) * \qquad (1)$$

$$\Big(\frac{\exp(f_\omega(x_j^{(i)}))}{\sum_{j'=1}^{n^{(i)}} \exp(f_\omega(x_{j'}^{(i)}))} - \frac{\exp(BLEU(x_j^{(i)}))}{\sum_{j'=1}^{n^i} \exp(BLEU(x_{j'}^{(i)})}\Big)$$

When using the ith sentence, we calculate the derivation by summing over all $n^{(i)}$ items of the k-best lists. The kth feature value $f_k(x_j^{(i)})$ is multiplied with the difference. This difference depends on $f_\omega(x_j^{(i)})$, the score of the log-linear model for the j hypothesis of the list and the BLEU score $BLEU(x_j^{(i)})$ assigned to this item. Using this derivation, we used stochastic gradient descent to train the model. We used batch updates with ten samples and tuned the learning rate on the development data. The training process ends after 100k batches and the final model is selected according to its performance on the development data.

The range of the scores of the different models may greatly differ and many of these values are negative numbers with high absolute value since they are computed as the logarithm of relatively small probabilities. Therefore, we rescale all scores observed on the development data to the range of $[-1, 1]$ prior to reranking.

5 Results

System	Dev	Test
Baseline	20.58	20.19
+ *ListNet* rescoring	19.95	20.98
+ *NCE*	21.00	21.51
+ *SOUL*	21.02	21.54
+ *NCE* + *SOUL*	**21.14**	**21.63**

Table 1: Results of English→German joint system

In this section we present the experimental results of the joint system we submitted for the English→German Shared Translation Task for WMT2015. The systems are tuned on *newtest2013* (Dev) and the BLEU scores we get when applying them over *newtest2014* (Test) are reported in Table 1.

KIT phrase-based system, labeled as the Baseline, reaches 20.58 and 20.19 BLEU points on Dev and Test sets, respectively. Using our new rescoring ListNet-based instead of traditional MERT yields upto 0.8 BLEU points. Adding features estimated from different neural architectures of CTMs gains a further 0.56 BLEU point improvement. More precisely, when CTMs scores are computed using neural networks trained with *NCE* output layer and added to the new k-best list for rescoring, we can observe that the BLEU score on the test set achieves 21.51. With similar procedures using *SOUL* output layer, the gain is slightly better, reaching 21.54. Finally, adding all of the scores derived from those two alternative output structures results to our submitted system with the BLEU of 21.63, which is 1.4 BLEU points different from the baseline system.

Expensive computational cost is an important issue while using CTMs estimated on large vocabularies (Section 3.2). Table 2 compares the training and inference speed for *SOUL* and *NCE* models. While the two kinds of models have a same speed in training, in inference the *NCE* models benefit from their un-normalized scoring. Both ap-

	training speed	inference speed
SOUL	1000 / s	15500 / s
NCE	1000 / s	19400 / s

Table 2: Speeds of the training and the inference corresponding to *SOUL* and *NCE* models, expressed in number of processed words per second.

proaches are plausible workarounds to overcome the computational difficulty by speeding up both the training and the inference, contrary to some propositions in the literature which only reduces the inference time (Devlin et al., 2014).

6 Conclusion

In the experiments we showed that a strong baseline phrase-based translation system, which already used several models during decoding, could be improved significantly by adding computational complex models in a rescoring step.

Firstly, in our experiments, the translation quality was improved by rescoring the n-best list of the baseline system. We could improve the BLEU score by 0.8 points without adding additional features. When adding CTMs features, additional gains of 0.6 BLEU points were achieved.

Secondly, we compared two approaches to limit the computation complexity of continuous space models. The *SOUL* and *NCE* models perform similarly; both improved the translation quality by 0.5 points. Small additional gains of 0.1 BLEU points were achieved by using both models together.

Acknowledgments

The project leading to this application has received funding from the European Union's Horizon 2020 research and innovation programme under grant agreement n° 645452.

References

Yoshua Bengio, Réjean Ducharme, Pascal Vincent, and Christian Janvin. 2003. A neural probabilistic language model. *Journal of Machine Learning Research*, 3:1137–1155.

Zhe Cao, Tao Qin, Tie-Yan Liu, Ming-Feng Tsai, and Hang Li. 2007. Learning to Rank: from Pairwise Approach to Listwise Approach. In *Proceedings of the 24th International Conference on Machine Learning (ICML 2007)*, pages 129–136. ACM.

Francesco Casacuberta and Enrique Vidal. 2004. Machine translation with inferred stochastic finite-state transducers. *Computational Linguistics*, 30(3):205–225.

Josep Maria Crego and José B Mariño. 2006. Improving statistical mt by coupling reordering and decoding. *Machine Translation*, 20(3):199–215.

Jacob Devlin, Rabih Zbib, Zhongqiang Huang, Thomas Lamar, Richard Schwartz, and John Makhoul. 2014. Fast and robust neural network joint models for statistical machine translation. In *Proceedings of the 52nd Annual Meeting of the Association for Computational Linguistics (Volume 1: Long Papers)*, pages 1370–1380, Baltimore, Maryland.

Michael Gutmann and Aapo Hyvärinen. 2010. Noise-contrastive estimation: A new estimation principle for unnormalized statistical models. In Yeh Whye Teh and Mike Titterington, editors, *Proceedings of th International Conference on Artificial Intelligence and Statistics (AISTATS)*, volume 9, pages 297–304.

Kenneth Heafield. 2011. KenLM: faster and smaller language model queries. In *Proceedings of the Sixth Workshop on Statistical Machine Translation*, pages 187–197, Edinburgh, Scotland, United Kingdom, July.

Teresa Herrmann, Jan Niehues, and Alex Waibel. 2013. Combining Word Reordering Methods on different Linguistic Abstraction Levels for Statistical Machine Translation. In *Proceedings of the Seventh Workshop on Syntax, Semantics and Structure in Statistical Translation*, Altanta, Georgia, USA, June. Association for Computational Linguistics.

Dan Klein and Christopher D. Manning. 2003. Accurate Unlexicalized Parsing. In *Proceedings of ACL 2003*.

Philipp Koehn, Franz Josef Och, and Daniel Marcu. 2003. Statistical Phrase-Based Translation. In *HLT/NAACL 2003*.

Philipp Koehn, Amittai Axelrod, Alexandra B. Mayne, Chris Callison-Burch, Miles Osborne, and David Talbot. 2005. Edinburgh System Description for the 2005 IWSLT Speech Translation Evaluation. In *Proceedings of the International Workshop on Spoken Language Translation (IWSLT)*, Pittsburgh, PA, USA.

Philipp Koehn, Hieu Hoang, Alexandra Birch, Chris Callison-Burch, Marcello Federico, Nicola Bertoldi, Brooke Cowan, Wade Shen, Christine Moran, Richard Zens, Chris Dyer, Ondrej Bojar, Alexandra Constantin, and Evan Herbst. 2007. Moses: Open Source Toolkit for Statistical Machine Translation. In *Proceedings of ACL 2007, Demonstration Session*, Prague, Czech Republic.

Hai-Son Le, Ilya Oparin, Alexandre Allauzen, Jean-Luc Gauvain, and François Yvon. 2011. Structured output layer neural network language model. In *Proceedings of ICASSP*, pages 5524–5527.

Hai-Son Le, Alexandre Allauzen, and François Yvon. 2012. Continuous space translation models with neural networks. In *Proceedings of the North American Chapter of the Association for Computational Linguistics: Human Language Technologies (NAACL-HLT)*, pages 39–48, Montréal, Canada, June. Association for Computational Linguistics.

Percy Liang, Alexandre Bouchard-Côté, Dan Klein, and Ben Taskar. 2006. An End-to-end Discriminative Approach to Machine Translation. In *Proceedings of the 21st International Conference on Computational Linguistics and the 44th annual meeting of the Association for Computational Linguistics*, pages 761–768. Association for Computational Linguistics.

José B. Mariño, Rafael E. Banchs, Josep M. Crego, Adrià de Gispert, Patrick Lambert, José A.R. Fonollosa, and Marta R. Costa-Jussà. 2006. N-gram-based machine translation. *Computational Linguistics*, 32(4):527–549.

Arne Mauser, Saša Hasan, and Hermann Ney. 2009. Extending Statistical Machine Translation with Discriminative and Trigger-based Lexicon Models. In *Proceedings of the 2009 Conference on Empirical Methods in Natural Language Processing: Volume 1*, EMNLP '09, Singapore.

Andriy Mnih and Geoffrey E Hinton. 2008. A scalable hierarchical distributed language model. In D. Koller, D. Schuurmans, Y. Bengio, and L. Bottou, editors, *Advances in Neural Information Processing Systems 21*, volume 21, pages 1081–1088.

Andriy Mnih and Yeh Whye Teh. 2012. A fast and simple algorithm for training neural probabilistic language models. In *Proceedings of the International Conference of Machine Learning (ICML)*.

Jan Niehues and Muntsin Kolss. 2009. A POS-Based Model for Long-Range Reorderings in SMT. In *Fourth Workshop on Statistical Machine Translation (WMT 2009)*, Athens, Greece.

Jan Niehues and Stephan Vogel. 2008. Discriminative Word Alignment via Alignment Matrix Modeling. In *Proceedings of Third ACL Workshop on Statistical Machine Translation*, Columbus, USA.

Jan Niehues and Alex Waibel. 2013. An MT Error-driven Discriminative Word Lexicon Using Sentence Structure Features. In *Proceedings of the Eighth Workshop on Statistical Machine Translation, Sofia, Bulgaria*, pages 512–520.

Jan Niehues, Teresa Herrmann, Stephan Vogel, and Alex Waibel. 2011. Wider Context by Using Bilingual Language Models in Machine Translation. In *Sixth Workshop on Statistical Machine Translation (WMT 2011)*, Edinburgh, UK.

Jan Niehues, Quoc Khanh Do, Alexandre Allauzen, and Alex Waibel. 2015. ListNet-based MT Rescoring. In *Proceedings of the Tenth Workshop on Statistical Machine Translation (WMT 2015)*, Lisboa, Portugal.

Franz Josef Och and Hermann Ney. 2003. A Systematic Comparison of Various Statistical Alignment Models. *Computational Linguistics*, 29(1):19–51.

Franz Josef Och. 1999. An Efficient Method for Determining Bilingual Word Classes. In *EACL'99*.

Kay Rottmann and Stephan Vogel. 2007. Word Reordering in Statistical Machine Translation with a POS-Based Distortion Model. In *Proceedings of the 11th International Conference on Theoretical and Methodological Issues in Machine Translation (TMI)*, Skövde, Sweden.

Helmut Schmid. 1994. Probabilistic Part-of-Speech Tagging Using Decision Trees. In *International Conference on New Methods in Language Processing*, Manchester, United Kingdom.

Holger Schwenk, Marta R. Costa-jussa, and Jose A. R. Fonollosa. 2007. Smooth bilingual n-gram translation. In *Proceedings of the Conference on Empirical Methods in Natural Language Processing (EMNLP)*, pages 430–438, Prague, Czech Republic.

Holger Schwenk. 2007. Continuous space language models. *Computer Speech and Language*, 21(3):492–518, July.

Andreas Stolcke. 2002. SRILM – An Extensible Language Modeling Toolkit. In *International Conference on Spoken Language Processing*, Denver, Colorado, USA.

Ashish Venugopal, Andreas Zollman, and Alex Waibel. 2005. Training and Evaluating Error Minimization Rules for Statistical Machine Translation. In *Workshop on Data-drive Machine Translation and Beyond (WPT-05)*, Ann Arbor, Michigan, USA.

Stephan Vogel. 2003. SMT Decoder Dissected: Word Reordering. In *International Conference on Natural Language Processing and Knowledge Engineering*, Beijing, China.

The Edinburgh/JHU Phrase-based Machine Translation Systems for WMT 2015

Barry Haddow[1], Matthias Huck[1], Alexandra Birch[1], Nikolay Bogoychev[1], Philipp Koehn[1,2]
[1]School of Informatics, University of Edinburgh
[2]Center for Speech and Language Processing, The Johns Hopkins University
a.birch@ed.ac.uk {nbogoych,bhaddow,mhuck}@inf.ed.ac.uk phi@jhu.edu

Abstract

This paper describes the submission of the University of Edinburgh and the Johns Hopkins University for the shared translation task of the EMNLP 2015 Tenth Workshop on Statistical Machine Translation (WMT 2015). We set up phrase-based statistical machine translation systems for all ten language pairs of this year's evaluation campaign, which are English paired with Czech, Finnish, French, German, and Russian in both translation directions.

Novel research directions we investigated include: neural network language models and bilingual neural network language models, a comprehensive use of word classes, and sparse lexicalized reordering features.

1 Introduction

The Edinburgh/JHU phrase-based translation systems for our participation in the WMT 2015 shared translation task[1] are based on the open source Moses toolkit (Koehn et al., 2007). We built upon Edinburgh's strong baselines from WMT submissions in previous years (Durrani et al., 2014a) as well as our recent research within the framework of other evaluation campaigns and projects such as IWSLT[2] and EU-BRIDGE[3] (Birch et al., 2014; Freitag et al., 2014a; Freitag et al., 2014b).

We first discuss novel features that we integrated into our systems for the 2015 Edinburgh/JHU submission. Next we give a general system overview with details on our training pipeline and decoder configuration. We finally present empirical results for the individual language pairs and translation directions.

[1]http://www.statmt.org/wmt15/
[2]http://workshop2014.iwslt.org
[3]http://www.eu-bridge.eu

2 Novel Methods

2.1 Neural Network LM with NPLM

For some language pairs (notably French↔English and Finnish↔English) we experimented with feed-forward neural network language models using the NPLM toolkit (Vaswani et al., 2013). This toolkit enables such language models to be trained efficiently on large datasets, and provides a querying API which is fast enough to be used during decoding. NPLM is fully integrated into Moses, including appropriate wrapper scripts for training the language models within the Moses experiment management system.

2.2 Bilingual Neural Network LM

We also experimented with our re-implementation of the "joint" model by Devlin et al. (2014). Referred to as *bilingual LM* in Moses, this was previously employed in the Edinburgh IWSLT system submissions, although with limited success (Birch et al., 2014).

The idea of the bilingual LM is quite straightforward. We define a language model where each target token is conditioned on the previous $(n-1)$ target tokens (as in a standard n-gram language model) as well as its aligned source token, and a window of m tokens on either side of the aligned source token. At training time, the aligned source token is found from the automatic alignment, and at test time the alignment is supplied by the decoder. The bilingual LM is trained using a feed-forward neural network and we use the NPLM toolkit for this.

Prior to submission we tested bilingual LMs on the French↔English tasks and on English→Russian task. For French↔English, we had resource issues[4] in training such large

[4]These can now be addressed using the -mmap option to create a binarized version of the corpus which is then memory-mapped.

models so we randomly subsampled 10% of the data for training. Since we did not observe gains in translation quality, the bilingual LM was not integrated into our primary system submissions. In post-submission experiments, we tried training bilingual LM on a 10% domain-specific portion of the training data selected using modified Moore-Lewis (Moore and Lewis, 2010; Axelrod et al., 2011), but only observed a small improvement in translation performance.

2.3 Comprehensive Use of Word Classes

In Edinburgh's submission from the previous year, we used automatically generated word classes in additional language models and in additional operation sequence models (Durrani et al., 2014b). This year, we pushed the use of word classes into the remaining feature functions: the reordering model and the sparse word features.

We generated Och clusters (Och, 1999) — a variant of Brown clusters — using `mkcls`. We have to choose a hyper parameter: the number of clusters. Our experiments and also prior work (Stewart et al., 2014) suggest that instead of committing to a single value, it is beneficial to use multiple numbers and use them in multiple feature functions concurrently. We used 50, 200, 600, and 2000 clusters, hence having 4 additional interpolated language models, 4 additional operation sequence models, 4 additional lexicalized reordering models, and 4 additional sets of sparse features.

The feature functions for word classes were trained exactly the same way as the corresponding feature functions for words. For instance, this means that the word class language model required training of individual models on the subcorpora, and then interpolation.

We carried out a study to assess the contribution of the use of such word class feature functions. Table 1 summarizes the results. Use of word classes in each of the models yields small gains, except for the reordering model, where there is no observable difference. The biggest gains were observed in the language model. Note that the English–German baseline already included additional feature functions based on POS and morphological tags, and basically no additional gains were observed due to the class based feature functions.

2.4 Sparse Lexicalized Reordering

We implemented sparse lexicalized reordering features (Cherry, 2013) in Moses and evaluated them in English↔German setups. The experiments were conducted on top of the standard hierarchical lexicalized reordering model (Galley and Manning, 2008). We applied features based on Och clusters with 200 classes on both source and target side. Active feature groups are *between*, *phrase*, and *stack*.

In addition to optimizing the feature weights directly with k-best MIRA (Cherry and Foster, 2012), we also examined maximum expected BLEU training of the sparse lexicalized reordering features via stochastic gradient descent (Auli et al., 2014).

3 System Overview

3.1 Preprocessing

The training data was preprocessed using scripts from the Moses toolkit. We first normalized the data using the `normalize-punctuation.perl` script, then performed tokenization (using the `-a` option), and then truecasing. We did not perform any corpus filtering other than the standard Moses method, which removes sentence pairs with extreme length ratios.

3.2 Word Alignment

For word alignment we used either `fast_align` (Dyer et al., 2013) or MGIZA++ (Gao and Vogel, 2008), followed by the standard `grow-diag-final-and` symmetrization heuristic. An empirical comparison of `fast_align` and MGIZA++ on the Finnish-English and English-Russian language pairs using the constrained data sets did not reveal any significant difference.

3.3 Language Model

We used all available monolingual data to train 5-gram language models with modified Kneser-Ney smoothing (Chen and Goodman, 1998). Typically, language models for each monolingual corpus were first trained using either KenLM (Heafield et al., 2013) or the SRILM toolkit (Stolcke, 2002) and then linearly interpolated using weights tuned to minimize perplexity on the development set.

3.4 Baseline Features

We follow the standard approach to SMT of scoring translation hypotheses using a weighted linear combination of features. The core features of our

	de-en	en-de	cs-en	en-cs	ru-en	en-ru	avg Δ
Baseline (no clusters)	28.0	20.5	29.1	21.2	31.8	29.1	-
Comprehensive setup	28.5 (+.5)	20.5 (±.0)	29.7 (+.6)	21.8 (+.6)	32.3 (+.5)	29.7 (+.6)	+.5
w/o sparse features	28.2 (–.3)	20.4 (–.1)	29.6 (–.1)	21.7 (–.1)	32.2 (–.1)	30.0 (+.3)	–.2
w/o language model	28.3 (–.2)	20.5 (±.0)	29.5 (–.2)	21.4 (–.4)	31.5 (–.8)	29.2 (–.6)	–.4
w/o reordering model	28.5 (±.0)	20.5 (±.0)	-	21.8 (±.0)	32.3 (±.0)	29.8 (+.1)	±.0
w/o operation sequence model	28.3 (–.2)	20.3 (–.1)	29.7 (±.0)	21.7 (–.1)	32.0 (–.3)	29.5 (–.2)	–.2

Table 1: Use of additional feature functions based on Och clusters (see Section 2.3). The last four lines refer to ablation studies where one of the sets of clustered feature functions is removed from the comprehensive setup. Note that the word-based feature functions are used in all cases. BLEU scores on `newstest2014` are reported.

model are a 5-gram LM score, phrase translation and lexical translation scores, word and phrase penalties, and a linear distortion score. The phrase translation probabilities are smoothed with Good-Turing smoothing (Foster et al., 2006). We used the hierarchical lexicalized reordering model (Galley and Manning, 2008) with 4 possible orientations (monotone, swap, discontinuous left and discontinuous right) in both left-to-right and right-to-left direction. We also used the operation sequence model (OSM) (Durrani et al., 2013) with 4 count based supportive features. We further employed domain indicator features (marking which training corpus each phrase pair was found in), binary phrase count indicator features, sparse phrase length features, and sparse source word deletion, target word insertion, and word translation features (limited to the top K words in each language, typically with $K = 50$).

3.5 Tuning

Since our feature set (generally around 500 to 1000 features) was too large for MERT, we used k-best batch MIRA for tuning (Cherry and Foster, 2012). To speed up tuning we applied threshold pruning to the phrase table, based on the direct translation model probability.

3.6 Decoding

In decoding we applied cube pruning (Huang and Chiang, 2007) with a stack size of 5000 (reduced to 1000 for tuning), Minimum Bayes Risk decoding (Kumar and Byrne, 2004), a maximum phrase length of 5, a distortion limit of 6, 100-best translation options and the no-reordering-over-punctuation heuristic (Koehn and Haddow, 2009).

4 Experimental Results

In this section we describe peculiarities of individual systems and present experimental results.

4.1 French↔English

Our submitted systems for the French-English language pair are quite similar for the two translation directions. We used all the constrained parallel data to build a phrase-based translation model and the language model was build from the target side of this data, the monolingual news data and the LDC GigaWord corpora. During system development we used the `newsdiscussdev2015` for tuning and development testing, using 2-fold cross validation. For tuning the submitted system, and the post-submission experiments, we tuned on the whole of `newsdiscussdev2015`, and report cased BLEU on `newsdiscusstest2015`.

Prior to submission we experimented with bilingual LM and an NPLM-based neural network language model (Sections 2.2 and 2.1) but did not obtain positive results. These were trained on a randomly selected 10% portion of the parallel training data. We also experimented with class-based language models (using Och clusters from `mkcls`), including the 50 class language model in the English→French submission but not in the French→English one, since it helped in our development setup in the former but not the latter.

In the post-submission experiments (Table 2), we show the comparison of the baseline system (as described in Section 3) with systems enhanced with bilingual LM, NPLM and class-based language models. For the class-based language models, we tested with 50 Och clusters, 200 Och clusters, and with both class-based LMs. For the bilingual LM, we created both "combined" (a 5-gram on the target and a 9-gram on the source) and "source" (1-gram on the target and 15-gram on

System	fr-en	en-fr
Baseline	33.0	33.5
Submitted	32.7	33.6
50 classes	32.8	33.8
200 classes	32.9	33.9
50+200 classes	32.9	33.7
BiLM combined	32.9	33.6
BiLM source & combined	33.2	33.5
NPLM	33.0	34.2

Table 2: Comparison of baseline with post-submission experiments on class-based language models, bilingual LM and NPLM. Note that for French→English the submitted system was the same as the baseline (retuned) whilst for English→French it was the same as the third line (retrained).

System	fi-en	en-fi
Baseline	19.6	13.4
Submitted	19.7	n/a
Without OPUS	17.0	11.5
50 classes	19.4	13.2
200 classes	19.8	13.3
50+200 classes	19.7	13.3
BiLM combined	19.1	13.5
BiLM source & combined	19.1	13.4
NPLM	20.0	13.8

Table 3: Comparison of baseline with post-submission experiments on class-based language models, bilingual LM and NPLM. Note that the submitted system for Finnish→English was the same as the baseline (but retuned).

source) models. The bilingual LMs are trained on 10% of the available parallel data, selected using modified Moore-Lewis data selection (Moore and Lewis, 2010; Axelrod et al., 2011). The NPLM is a 5-gram model trained on all available language model data.

We observe from Table 2 that the bilingual LM has a minimal effect on BLEU, only showing an increase for one language pair, one configuration, and the margin of improvement is probably within the margin of tuning variation. We do not have a good explanation for the lack of success with bilingual LM, in contrast to (Devlin et al., 2014), however we note that all reports of improvements with this type of model are for distantly related language pairs. We also did not observe any improvement with the class-based language models for French→English, although we did observe small gains from English→French. Building an NPLM model for all data gives a reasonable improvement (+0.7) for the French target, but not the English. In fact French→English was the only language pair where NPLM did not improve BLEU after building the LM on all data. It is possible that the limited morphology of English means that the improved generalisation of the NPLM is not as helpful, and also that the conventional n-gram LM is already strong for this language pair.

4.2 Finnish↔English

For the Finnish-English language pair we built systems using only the constrained data, and systems using all the OPUS (Tiedemann, 2012) parallel data. Our baselines include this extra data, but we also show results just using the constrained parallel data. We did not employ the morphological splitting as in Edinburgh's syntax-based system (Williams et al., 2015) and consequently the English→Finnish systems performed poorly in development and we did not submit a phrase-based system for this pair.

Our development setup was similar to French↔English; we used the `newsdev2015` for tuning and test during system development (in 2-fold cross-validation) then for the submission and subsequent experiments we used the whole of `newsdev2015` for tuning. Also in common with our work on French↔English, we performed several post-submission experiments to examine the effect of class-based language models, bilingual LM and NPLM. We show the results in Table 3. For training bilingual LM and NPLM models we encountered some numerical issues, probably due to the large vocabulary size in Finnish. These were partially addressed by employing *dropout* to prevent overfitting (Srivastava et al., 2014), enabling us to train the models for at least 2 epochs.

We note that, as with French↔English, our application of bilingual LM did not result in significant improvement. Finnish and English are quite distantly related, but we can speculate that using words as a representation for Finnish is not appropriate. The NPLM, however, offers modest (+0.4) improvements over the baseline in both directions.

4.3 Czech↔English

The development of the Czech↔English systems followed the ideas in Section 2.3, i.e., with a focus on word classes (50, 200, 600 classes) for all component models. We combined the test sets from 2008 to 2012 for tuning. No neural language model or bilingual language model was used.

4.4 Russian↔English

To Russian. For the English→Russian system, we used all the parallel data specified in the task. The Wiki Headlines data was appended onto the combined parallel corpus. For the monolingual corpora, we used all the constrained track corpora except for Newscrawl 2008-2010 which were overlooked as they were much smaller than other resources. We trained word classes with three different settings (50, 200, and 600 clusters) on both source and target languages. On applying clusters, we trained 6-gram language models on the target side. We used all four factors (words and clusters) in both source and target languages for the the translation model and the OSM, but we used only the word factor for the alignment and the reordering models. We performed transliteration (Durrani et al., 2014c) after decoding for all three experimental conditions. We used `newstest2012` for LM interpolation and batch MIRA model tuning. In Table 4, the only difference between the baseline system and the official submission is that the baseline has no cluster factors. The final model (BiLM source & combined & NPLM) is the same as the submitted system, apart from the fact that we applied two bilingual neural network models: one over the source and one over the source and target, and an NPLM language model over the target. This did not improve over the factored model and so was not submitted for the evaluation.

System	en-ru
Baseline	25.0
Submitted	25.2
BiLM source & combined & NPLM	25.1

Table 4: Experimental results (cased BLEU) for English→Russian averaged over `newstest2013` and `newstest2014`.

From Russian. The Russian→English system used the same settings as the Czech system, except for the addition of a factor over 2000 word classes and a smaller tuning set (just `newstest2012`).

4.5 German↔English

Our German-English training corpus comprises all permissible parallel data of the constrained track for this language pair. A concatenation of `newssyscomb2009` and `newstest2008-2012` served as tuning set.

From German. For translation from German, we applied syntactic pre-reordering (Collins et al., 2005) and compound splitting (Koehn and Knight, 2003) in a preprocessing step on the source side. A rich set of translation factors was exploited in addition to word surface forms: Och clusters (50 classes), morphological tags, part-of-speech tags, and word stems on the German side (Schmid, 2000), as well as Och clusters (50 classes), part-of-speech tags (Ratnaparkhi, 1996), and word stems (Porter, 1980) on the English side. The factors were utilized in the translation model and in OSMs. The lexicalized reordering model was trained on stems. Individual 7-gram Och cluster LMs were trained with KenLM's `--discount_fallback --prune '0 0 1'` parameters,[5] then interpolated with the SRILM toolkit and added to the log-linear model as a second LM feature. Our 5-gram word LM was trained on all English data at once, also with pruning of singleton n-grams of order 3 and higher. We included the English LDC Gigaword Fifth Edition. Sparse lexical features (source word deletion, target word insertion, word translation) were limited to the top $K = 200$ words for German→English.

To German. Translation factors for the English→German translation direction are word surface forms, Och clusters (50 classes), morphological tags, and part-of-speech tags. Morphological tags were employed on the target side only, all other factors on both source and target side. The lexicalized reordering model was trained on word surface forms. We added an interpolated 7-gram Och cluster LM and a 7-gram LM over morphological tags. LMs were trained in a similar way as the ones for translation from German. Sparse phrase length features and sparse lexical features were not used for English→German.

[5] `http://www.statmt.org/mtm14/uploads/Projects/KenLMFunWithLanguageModel_MTM2014p9.pdf`

System	de-en		en-de	
	2013	2014	2013	2014
Baseline	27.3	28.6	20.6	20.9
+ sparse LR (MIRA)	**27.2**	**28.8**	20.7	20.8
+ sparse LR (SGD)	27.2	28.5	**20.8**	**21.1**

Table 5: Experimental results for German→English and English→German. We report cased BLEU scores on the newstest2013 and newstest2014 sets. Primary submission results are highlighted in bold.

Sparse lexicalized reordering. We investigated sparse lexicalized reordering features (Section 2.4) on the German-English language pair in both translation directions. Two methods for learning the weights of the sparse lexicalized reordering feature set have been compared: (1.) direct tuning in MIRA along with all other features in the model combination (*sparse LR (MIRA)*), and (2.) separate optimization with stochastic gradient descent (SGD) with a maximum expected BLEU objective (*sparse LR (SGD)*). For the latter variant, we used the MT tuning set for training (13 573 sentence pairs) and otherwise followed the approach outlined by Auli et al. (2014). We tuned the baseline feature weights with MIRA before SGD training and ran two final MIRA iterations after it. SGD training was stopped after 80 epochs.

Empirical results for the German-English language pair are presented in Table 5. We observe minor gains of up to +0.2 points BLEU. The results are not consistent in the two translation directions: The MIRA-trained variant seems to perform better when translating from German, the SGD-trained variant when translating to German. However, in both cases the baseline score is almost identical to the best results with sparse lexicalized reordering features.

In future work we plan to adopt hypergraph MIRA, as well as larger training sets for maximum expected BLEU training. We also consider scaling the method to word surface forms in addition to Och clusters, and trying RPROP instead of SGD.

5 Conclusion

The Edinburgh/JHU team built phrase-based translation systems using the open source Moses toolkit for all language pairs of the WMT 2015 shared translation task. Our submitted system outputs ranked first according to cased BLEU on the newstest2015 evaluation set on six out of ten language pairs:[6] Czech→English, German→English, Finnish→English, Russian→English, English→French, and English→Russian.

Acknowledgements

This project has received funding from the European Union's Horizon 2020 research and innovation programme under grant agreements 645452 (QT21), 645487 (MMT), 644333 (TraMOOC) and 644402 (HimL).

References

Michael Auli, Michel Galley, and Jianfeng Gao. 2014. Large-scale Expected BLEU Training of Phrase-based Reordering Models. In *Proceedings of the 2014 Conference on Empirical Methods in Natural Language Processing (EMNLP)*, pages 1250–1260, Doha, Qatar, October.

Amittai Axelrod, Xiaodong He, and Jianfeng Gao. 2011. Domain Adaptation via Pseudo In-Domain Data Selection. In *Proceedings of the 2011 Conference on Empirical Methods in Natural Language Processing*, pages 355–362, Edinburgh, Scotland, UK.

Alexandra Birch, Matthias Huck, Nadir Durrani, Nikolay Bogoychev, and Philipp Koehn. 2014. Edinburgh SLT and MT System Description for the IWSLT 2014 Evaluation. In *Proc. of the International Workshop on Spoken Language Translation (IWSLT)*, pages 49–56, Lake Tahoe, CA, USA, December.

Stanley F. Chen and Joshua Goodman. 1998. An empirical study of smoothing techniques for language modeling. Technical report, Harvard University.

Colin Cherry and George Foster. 2012. Batch Tuning Strategies for Statistical Machine Translation. In *Proceedings of the 2012 Conference of the North American Chapter of the Association for Computational Linguistics: Human Language Technologies*, pages 427–436, Montréal, Canada, June.

Colin Cherry. 2013. Improved Reordering for Phrase-Based Translation using Sparse Features. In *Proceedings of the 2013 Conference of the North American Chapter of the Association for Computational Linguistics: Human Language Technologies*, pages 22–31, Atlanta, GA, USA, June.

Michael Collins, Philipp Koehn, and Ivona Kucerova. 2005. Clause Restructuring for Statistical Machine Translation. In *Proceedings of the 43rd Annual*

[6] http://matrix.statmt.org/?mode=all&test_set[id]=21

Meeting of the Association for Computational Linguistics (ACL'05), pages 531–540, Ann Arbor, MI, USA, June.

Jacob Devlin, Rabih Zbib, Zhongqiang Huang, Thomas Lamar, Richard Schwartz, and John Makhoul. 2014. Fast and Robust Neural Network Joint Models for Statistical Machine Translation. In *Proceedings of the 52nd Annual Meeting of the Association for Computational Linguistics (Volume 1: Long Papers)*, pages 1370–1380, Baltimore, MD, USA, June.

Nadir Durrani, Alexander Fraser, Helmut Schmid, Hieu Hoang, and Philipp Koehn. 2013. Can Markov Models Over Minimal Translation Units Help Phrase-Based SMT? In *Proceedings of the 51st Annual Meeting of the Association for Computational Linguistics (Volume 2: Short Papers)*, pages 399–405, Sofia, Bulgaria, August.

Nadir Durrani, Barry Haddow, Philipp Koehn, and Kenneth Heafield. 2014a. Edinburgh's Phrase-based Machine Translation Systems for WMT-14. In *Proceedings of the Ninth Workshop on Statistical Machine Translation*, pages 97–104, Baltimore, MD, USA, June.

Nadir Durrani, Philipp Koehn, Helmut Schmid, and Alexander Fraser. 2014b. Investigating the Usefulness of Generalized Word Representations in SMT. In *Proceedings of COLING 2014, the 25th International Conference on Computational Linguistics: Technical Papers*, pages 421–432, Dublin, Ireland, August.

Nadir Durrani, Hassan Sajjad, Hieu Hoang, and Philipp Koehn. 2014c. Integrating an unsupervised transliteration model into statistical machine translation. In *Proceedings of the 14th Conference of the European Chapter of the Association for Computational Linguistics, volume 2: Short Papers*, pages 148–153, Gothenburg, Sweden, April. Association for Computational Linguistics.

Chris Dyer, Victor Chahuneau, and Noah A. Smith. 2013. A Simple, Fast, and Effective Reparameterization of IBM Model 2. In *Proceedings of the 2013 Conference of the North American Chapter of the Association for Computational Linguistics: Human Language Technologies*, pages 644–648, Atlanta, GA, USA, June.

George Foster, Roland Kuhn, and Howard Johnson. 2006. Phrasetable Smoothing for Statistical Machine Translation. In *Proceedings of the Conference on Empirical Methods for Natural Language Processing (EMNLP)*, pages 53–61, Sydney, Australia, July.

Markus Freitag, Stephan Peitz, Joern Wuebker, Hermann Ney, Matthias Huck, Rico Sennrich, Nadir Durrani, Maria Nadejde, Philip Williams, Philipp Koehn, Teresa Herrmann, Eunah Cho, and Alex Waibel. 2014a. EU-BRIDGE MT: Combined Machine Translation. In *Proceedings of the Ninth Workshop on Statistical Machine Translation*, pages 105–113, Baltimore, MD, USA, June.

Markus Freitag, Joern Wuebker, Stephan Peitz, Hermann Ney, Matthias Huck, Alexandra Birch, Nadir Durrani, Philipp Koehn, Mohammed Mediani, Isabel Slawik, Jan Niehues, Eunah Cho, Alex Waibel, Nicola Bertoldi, Mauro Cettolo, and Marcello Federico. 2014b. Combined Spoken Language Translation. In *International Workshop on Spoken Language Translation*, pages 57–64, Lake Tahoe, CA, USA, December.

Michel Galley and Christopher D. Manning. 2008. A Simple and Effective Hierarchical Phrase Reordering Model. In *Proceedings of the 2008 Conference on Empirical Methods in Natural Language Processing*, pages 848–856, Honolulu, HI, USA.

Qin Gao and Stephan Vogel. 2008. Parallel implementations of word alignment tool. In *Software Engineering, Testing, and Quality Assurance for Natural Language Processing*, SETQA-NLP '08, pages 49–57, Stroudsburg, PA, USA.

Kenneth Heafield, Ivan Pouzyrevsky, Jonathan H. Clark, and Philipp Koehn. 2013. Scalable modified Kneser-Ney language model estimation. In *Proceedings of the 51st Annual Meeting of the Association for Computational Linguistics*, pages 690–696, Sofia, Bulgaria, August.

Liang Huang and David Chiang. 2007. Forest Rescoring: Faster Decoding with Integrated Language Models. In *Proceedings of the 45th Annual Meeting of the Association of Computational Linguistics*, pages 144–151, Prague, Czech Republic.

Philipp Koehn and Barry Haddow. 2009. Edinburgh's Submission to all Tracks of the WMT 2009 Shared Task with Reordering and Speed Improvements to Moses. In *Proceedings of the Fourth Workshop on Statistical Machine Translation*, pages 160–164, Athens, Greece.

Philipp Koehn and Kevin Knight. 2003. Empirical Methods for Compound Splitting. In *Proceedings of the 10th Conference of the European Chapter of the Association for Computational Linguistics (EACL)*, pages 187–194, Budapest, Hungary, April.

Philipp Koehn, Hieu Hoang, Alexandra Birch, Chris Callison-Burch, Marcello Federico, Nicola Bertoldi, Brooke Cowan, Wade Shen, Christine Moran, Richard Zens, Chris Dyer, Ondřej Bojar, Alexandra Constantin, and Evan Herbst. 2007. Moses: Open Source Toolkit for Statistical Machine Translation. In *Proceedings of the ACL 2007 Demo and Poster Sessions*, pages 177–180, Prague, Czech Republic, June.

Shankar Kumar and William Byrne. 2004. Minimum Bayes-Risk Decoding for Statistical Machine Translation. In *HLT-NAACL 2004: Main Proceedings*, pages 169–176, Boston, MA, USA.

Robert C. Moore and William Lewis. 2010. Intelligent Selection of Language Model Training Data. In *Proceedings of the ACL 2010 Conference Short Papers*, pages 220–224, Uppsala, Sweden.

Franz Josef Och. 1999. An Efficient Method for Determining Bilingual Word Classes. In *Proceedings of the 9th Conference of the European Chapter of the Association for Computational Linguistics (EACL)*, pages 71–76.

Martin Porter. 1980. An algorithm for suffix stripping. *Program: electronic library and information systems*, 14(3):130–137.

Adwait Ratnaparkhi. 1996. A Maximum Entropy Part-Of-Speech Tagger. In *Proceedings of the Conference on Empirical Methods in Natural Language Processing*, Philadelphia, PA, USA, May.

Helmut Schmid. 2000. LoPar: Design and Implementation. Bericht des Sonderforschungsbereiches “Sprachtheoretische Grundlagen für die Computerlinguistik” 149, Institute for Computational Linguistics, University of Stuttgart.

Nitish Srivastava, Geoffrey Hinton, Alex Krizhevsky, Ilya Sutskever, and Ruslan Salakhutdinov. 2014. Dropout: A Simple Way to Prevent Neural Networks from Overfitting. *Journal of Machine Learning Research*, 15:1929–1958.

Darlene Stewart, Roland Kuhn, Eric Joanis, and George Foster. 2014. Coarse split and lump bilingual language models for richer source information in SMT. In *Proceedings of the Eleventh Conference of the Association for Machine Translation in the Americas (AMTA)*, volume 1, pages 28–41.

Andreas Stolcke. 2002. SRILM – an Extensible Language Modeling Toolkit. In *Proc. of the Int. Conf. on Spoken Language Processing (ICSLP)*, volume 3, Denver, CO, USA, September.

Jörg Tiedemann. 2012. Parallel Data, Tools and Interfaces in OPUS. In *Proc. of the Int. Conf. on Language Resources and Evaluation (LREC)*, pages 2214–2218, Istanbul, Turkey, May.

Ashish Vaswani, Yinggong Zhao, Victoria Fossum, and David Chiang. 2013. Decoding with Large-Scale Neural Language Models Improves Translation. In *Proceedings of the 2013 Conference on Empirical Methods in Natural Language Processing*, pages 1387–1392, Seattle, WA, USA.

Philip Williams, Rico Sennrich, Maria Nadejde, Matthias Huck, and Philipp Koehn. 2015. Edinburgh's Syntax-Based Systems at WMT 2015. In *Proceedings of the EMNLP 2015 Tenth Workshop on Statistical Machine Translation*, Lisbon, Portugal, September.

Montreal Neural Machine Translation Systems for WMT'15

Sébastien Jean[⋆]
University of Montreal
jeasebas@iro.umontreal.ca

Orhan Firat[⋆]
Middle East Technical University, Turkey
orhan.firat@ceng.metu.edu.tr

Kyunghyun Cho
University of Montreal

Roland Memisevic
University of Montreal

Yoshua Bengio
University of Montreal
CIFAR Senior Fellow

firstname.lastname@umontreal.ca

Abstract

Neural machine translation (NMT) systems have recently achieved results comparable to the state of the art on a few translation tasks, including English→French and English→German. The main purpose of the Montreal Institute for Learning Algorithms (MILA) submission to WMT'15 is to evaluate this new approach on a greater variety of language pairs. Furthermore, the human evaluation campaign may help us and the research community to better understand the behaviour of our systems. We use the RNNsearch architecture, which adds an attention mechanism to the encoder-decoder. We also leverage some of the recent developments in NMT, including the use of large vocabularies, unknown word replacement and, to a limited degree, the inclusion of monolingual language models.

1 Introduction

Neural machine translation (NMT) is a recently proposed approach for machine translation that relies only on neural networks. The NMT system is trained end-to-end to maximize the conditional probability of a correct translation given a source sentence (Kalchbrenner and Blunsom, 2013; Cho et al., 2014; Sutskever et al., 2014; Bahdanau et al., 2015). Although NMT has only recently been introduced, its performance has been found to be comparable to the state-of-the-art statistical machine translation (SMT) systems on a number of translation tasks (Luong et al., 2015; Jean et al., 2015). The main purpose of our submission to WMT'15 is to test the NMT system on a greater variety of language pairs. As such, we trained systems on Czech↔English, German↔English and Finnish→English. Furthermore, the human evaluation campaign of WMT'15 will help us better understand the quality of NMT systems which have mainly been evaluated using the automatic evaluation metric such as BLEU (Papineni et al., 2002).

Most NMT systems are based on the *encoder-decoder* architecture (Cho et al., 2014; Sutskever et al., 2014; Kalchbrenner and Blunsom, 2013). The source sentence is first read by the encoder, which compresses it into a real-valued vector. From this vector representation the decoder may then generate a translation word-by-word. One limitation of this approach is that a source sentence of any length must be encoded into a fixed-length vector. To address this issue, our systems for WMT'15 use the *RNNsearch* architecture from (Bahdanau et al., 2015). In this case, the encoder assigns a context-dependent vector, or annotation, to every source word. The decoder then selectively combines the most relevant annotations to generate each target word.

NMT systems often use a limited vocabulary of approximately $30,000$ to $80,000$ target words, which leads them to generate many out-of-vocabulary tokens ($\langle$UNK$\rangle$). This may easily lead to the degraded quality of the translations. To sidestep this problem, we employ a variant of importance sampling to help increase the target vocabulary size (Jean et al., 2015). Even with a larger vocabulary, there will almost assuredly be words in the test set that were unseen during training. As such, we replace generated out-of-vocaulbary tokens with the corresponding source words with a technique similar to those proposed by (Luong et al., 2015).

Most NMT systems rely only on parallel data, ignoring the wealth of information found in large monolingual corpora. On Finnish→English, we combine our systems with a recurrent neural net-

⋆ equal contribution

work (RNN) language model by recently proposed *deep fusion* (Gülçehre et al., 2015). For the other language pairs, we tried reranking n-best lists with 5-gram language models (Chen and Goodman., 1998).

2 System Description

In this section, we describe the RNNsearch architecture as well as the additional techniques we used.

Mathematical Notations Capital letters are used for matrices, and lower-case letters for vectors and scalars. x and y are used for a word in source and target sentences, respectively. We boldface them into $\mathbf{x}$, $\mathbf{y}$ and $\hat{\mathbf{y}}$ to denote their continuous-space representation (word embeddings).

2.1 Bidirectional Encoder

To encode a source sentence $(x_1, \ldots, x_{T_x})$ of length T_x into a sequence of annotations, we use a bidirectional recurrent neural network (Schuster and Paliwal, 1997). The bidirectional recurrent neural network (BiRNN) consists of two recurrent neural networks (RNN) that read the sentence either forward (from left to right) or backward. These RNNs respectively compute the sequences of hidden states $(\overrightarrow{h}_1, \ldots, \overrightarrow{h}_{T_x})$ and $(\overleftarrow{h}_1, \ldots, \overleftarrow{h}_{T_x})$. These two sequences are concatenated at each time step to form the annotations $(h_1, \ldots, h_{T_x})$. Each annotation h_i summarizes the entire sentence, albeit with more emphasis on word x_i and the neighbouring words.

We built the BiRNN with gated recurrent units (GRU, (Cho et al., 2014)), although long short-term memory (LSTM) units could also be used (Hochreiter and Schmidhuber, 1997), as in (Sutskever et al., 2014). More precisely, for the forward RNN, the hidden state at the i-th word is computed as

$$\overrightarrow{h}_i = \begin{cases} (1 - \overrightarrow{z}_i) \odot \overrightarrow{h}_{i-1} + \overrightarrow{z}_i \odot \overrightarrow{\underline{h}}_i & \text{, if } i > 0 \\ 0 & \text{, if } i = 0 \end{cases}$$

where

$$\begin{aligned} \overrightarrow{\underline{h}}_i &= \tanh\left(\overrightarrow{W}\mathbf{x}_i + \overrightarrow{U}\left[\overrightarrow{r}_i \odot \overrightarrow{h}_{i-1}\right] + \overrightarrow{b}\right) \\ \overrightarrow{z}_i &= \sigma\left(\overrightarrow{W}_z\mathbf{x}_i + \overrightarrow{U}_z\overrightarrow{h}_{i-1}\right) \\ \overrightarrow{r}_i &= \sigma\left(\overrightarrow{W}_r\mathbf{x}_i + \overrightarrow{U}_r\overrightarrow{h}_{i-1}\right). \end{aligned}$$

To form the new hidden state, the network first computes a proposal $\overrightarrow{\underline{h}}_i$. This is then additively combined with the previous hidden state $\overrightarrow{h}_{i-1}$, and this combination is controlled by the update gate $\overrightarrow{z}_i$. Such gated units facilitate capturing long-term dependencies.

2.2 Attentive Decoder

After computing the initial hidden state $s_0 = \tanh\left(W_s\overleftarrow{h}_1\right) + b_s$, the *RNNsearch* decoder alternates between three steps: *Look*, *Generate* and *Update*.

During the *Look* phase, the network determines which parts of the source sentence are most relevant. Given the previous hidden state s_{i-1} of the decoder recurrent neural network (RNN), each annotation h_j is assigned a score e_{ij}:

$$e_{ij} = v_a^\top \tanh\left(W_a s_{i-1} + U_a h_j\right).$$

Although a more complex scoring function can potentially learn more non-trivial alignments, we observed that this single-hidden-layer function is enough for most of the language pairs we considered.

These scores e_{ij} are then normalized to sum to 1:

$$\alpha_{ij} = \frac{\exp\left(e_{ij}\right)}{\sum_{k=1}^{T_x}\exp\left(e_{ik}\right)}, \tag{1}$$

which we call alignment weights.

The context vector c_i is computed as a weighted sum of the annotations $(h_1, ..., h_{T_x})$ according to the alignment weights:

$$c_i = \sum_{j=1}^{T_x} \alpha_{ij} h_j.$$

This formulation allows the annotations with higher alignment weights to be more represented in the context vector c_i.

In the *Generate* phase, the decoder predicts the next target word. We first combine the previous hidden state s_{i-1}, the previous word y_{i-1} and the current context vector c_i into a vector $\tilde{t}_i$:

$$\tilde{t}_i = U_o s_{i-1} + V_o \mathbf{y}_{i-1} + C_o c_i + b_o.$$

We then transform $\tilde{t}_i$ into a hidden state m_i with an arbitrary feedforward network. In our submission, we apply the maxout non-linearity (Goodfellow et al., 2013) to $\tilde{t}_i$, followed by an affine transformation.

Phase	Output $\leftarrow$ Input
Look	$c_i \leftarrow s_{i-1}, (h_1, ..., h_{T_x})$
Generate	$y_i \leftarrow s_{i-1}, y_{i-1}, c_i$
Update	$s_i \leftarrow s_{i-1}, y_i, c_i$

Table 1: Summary of *RNNsearch* decoder phases

For a target vocabulary V, the probability of word y_i is then

$$p(y_i|s_{i-1}, y_{i-1}, c_i) = \frac{\exp\left(\hat{\mathbf{y}}_i^\top m_i + b_{y_i}\right)}{\sum_{y \in V} \exp\left(\hat{\mathbf{y}}^\top m_i + b_y\right)}. \tag{2}$$

Finally, in the *Update* phase, the decoder computes the next recurrent hidden state s_i from the context c_i, the generated word y_i and the previous hidden state s_{i-1}. As with the encoder we use gated recurrent units (GRU).

Table 1 summarizes this three-step procedure. We observed that it is important to have *Update* to follow *Generate*. Otherwise, the next step's *Look* would not be able to resolve the uncertainty embedded in the previous hidden state about the previously generated word.

2.3 Very Large Target Vocabulary Extension

Training an RNNsearch model with hundreds of thousands of target words easily becomes prohibitively time-consuming due to the normalization constant in the softmax output (see Eq. (2).) To address this problem, we use the approach presented in (Jean et al., 2015), which is based on importance sampling (Bengio and Sénécal, 2008). During training, we choose a smaller vocabulary size τ and divide the training set into partitions, each of which contains approximately τ unique target words. For each partition, we train the model as if only the unique words within it existed, leaving the embeddings of all the other words fixed.

At test time, the corresponding subset of target words for each source sentence is not known in advance, yet we still want to keep computational complexity manageable. To overcome this, we run an existing word alignment tool on the training corpus in advance to obtain word-based conditional probabilities (Brown et al., 1993). During decoding, we start with an initial target vocabulary containing the K most frequent words. Then, reading a few sentences at once, we arbitrarily replace some of these initial words by the K' most likely ones for each source word.[1]

No matter how large the target vocabulary is, there will almost always be those words, such as proper names or numbers, that will appear only in the development or test set, but not during training. To handle this difficulty, we replace unknown words in a manner similar to (Luong et al., 2015). More precisely, for every predicted out-of-vocabulary token ($\langle$UNK$\rangle$), we determine its most likely origin by choosing the source word with the largest alignment weight α_{ij} (see Eq. (1).) We may then replace $\langle$UNK$\rangle$ by either the most likely word according to a dictionary, or simply by the source word itself. Depending on the language pairs, we used different heuristics according to performance on the development set.

2.4 Integrating Language Models

Unlike some data-rich language pairs, most of the translation tasks do not have enough parallel text to train end-to-end machine translation systems. To overcome with this issue of low-resource language pairs, external monolingual corpora is exploited by using the method of *deep fusion* (Gülçehre et al., 2015).

In addition to the RNNsearch model, we train a separate language model (LM) with a large monolingual corpus. Then, the trained LM is plugged into the decoder of the trained RNNsearch with an additional controller network which modulates the contributions from the RNNsearch and LM. The controller network takes as input the hidden state of the LM, and optionally RNNsearch's hidden state, and outputs a scalar value in the range $[0, 1]$. This value is multiplied to the LM's hidden state, controlling the amount of information coming from the LM. The combined model, the RNNsearch, the LM and the controller network, is jointly tuned as the final translation model for a low-resource pair.

In our submission, we used recurrent neural network language model (RNNLM). More specifically, let s_i^{LM} be the hidden state of a pre-trained RNNLM and s_i^{TM} be that of a pre-trained RNNsearch at time i. The controller network is defined as

$$g_t = \sigma\left(V_g^\top s_t^{\text{LM}} + W_g^\top s_t^{\text{TM}} + b_g\right),$$

[1]This step differs very slightly from (Jean et al., 2015), where the sentence-specific words were added on top of the K common ones instead of replacing them.

where σ is a logistic sigmoid function, v_g, w_g and b_g are model parameters. The output of the controller network is multiplied to the LM's hidden state s_i^{LM}:

$$p_t^{\text{LM}} = s_t^{\text{LM}} \odot g_t.$$

The *Generate* phase in Sec. 2.2 is updated as,

$$\tilde{t}_i = U_o^{\text{TM}} s_{i-1}^{\text{TM}} + U_o^{\text{LM}} p_{t-1}^{\text{LM}} + V_o \mathbf{y}_{i-1} + C_o c_i + b_o.$$

This lets the decoder fully use the signal from the translation model, while the the signal from the LM is modulated by the controller output.

Among all the pairs of languages in WMT'15, Finnish↔English translation has the least amount of parallel text, having approximately $2M$ aligned sentences only. Thus, we use the *deep fusion* for the Fi-En in the official submission. However, we further experimented German→English, having the second least parallel text, and Czech→English, which has comparably larger data. We include the results from these two language pairs here for completeness.

3 Experimental Details

We now describe the settings of our experiments. Except for minor differences, all the settings were similar across all the considered language pairs.

3.1 Data

All the systems, except for the English→German (En→De) system, were built using all the data made available for WMT'15. The En→De system, which was showcased in (Jean et al., 2015), was built earlier than the others, using only the data from the last year's workshop (WMT'14.)

Each corpus was tokenized, but neither lowercased nor truecased. We avoided badly aligned sentence pairs by removing any source-target sentence pair with a large mismatch between their lengths. Furthermore, we removed sentences that were likely written in an incorrect language, either with a simple heuristic for En→De, or with a publicly available toolkit for the other language pairs (Shuyo, 2010). In order to limit the memory use during training, we only trained the systems with sentences of length up to 50 words only. Finally, for some but not all models, we reshuffled the data a few times and concatenated the different segments before training.

In the case of German (De) source, we performed compound splitting (Koehn and Knight, 2003), as implemented in the Moses toolkit (Koehn et al., 2007). For Finnish (Fi), we used Morfessor 2.0 for morpheme segmentation (Virpioja et al., 2013) by using the default parameters.

An Issue with Apostrophes In the training data, apostrophes appear in many forms, such as a straight vertical line (U+0027) or as a right single quotation mark (U+0019). The use of, for instance, the normalize-punctuation script[2] could have helped, but we did not use it in our experiments. Consequently, we encountered an issue of the tokenizer from the Moses toolkit not applying the same rule for both kinds of apostrophes. We fixed this issue in time for Czech→English (Cs→En), but all the other systems were affected to some degree, in particular, the system for De→En.

3.2 Settings

We used the RNNsearch models of size identical to those presented in (Bahdanau et al., 2015; Jean et al., 2015). More specifically, all the words in both target and source vocabularies were projected into a 620-dimensional vector space. Each recurrent neural network (RNN) had a 1000-dimensional hidden state. The models were trained with Adadelta (Zeiler, 2012), and the norm of the gradient at each update was rescaled (Pascanu et al., 2013). For the language pairs other than Cs→En and Fi→En, we held the word embeddings fixed near the end of training, as described in (Jean et al., 2015).

With the very large target vocabulary technique in Sec. 2.3, we used 500K source and target words for the En→De system, while 200K source and target words were used for the De→En and Cs↔En systems.[3] During training we set τ between 15K and 50K, depending on the hardware availability. As for decoding, we mostly used $K = 30,000$ and $K' = 10$.

Given the small sizes of the Fi→En corpora, we simply used a fixed vocabulary size of 40K tokens to avoid any adverse effect of including every unique target word in the vocabulary. The inclusion of every unique word would prevent the network from decoding out ⟨UNK⟩ at all, even if

[2] `http://www.statmt.org/wmt11/normalize-punctuation.perl`

[3] This choice was made mainly to cope with the limited storage availability.

Language pair	BLEU-c		BLEU-c ranking		Human ranking
	single	ensemble	constrained	unconstrained	
En→Cs	15.7	18.3	1/6	2/7	4/8
En→De	22.4	24.8	1/11	1/13	1-2/16
Cs→En	20.2	23.3	3/6	3/6	3-4/7
De→En	25.6	27.6	6/9	6/10	6-7/13
Fi→En	10.1	13.6	7/9	9/12	10/14

Table 2: Results on the official WMT'15 test sets for single models and primary ensemble submissions. All our own systems are constrained. When ranking by BLEU, we only count one system from each submitter. Human rankings include all primary and online systems, but exclude those used in the Cs↔En tuning task.

out-of-vocabulary words will assuredly appear in the test set.

For each language pair, we trained a total of four independent models that differed in parameter initialization and data shuffling, monitoring the training progress on either *newstest2012+2013*, *newstest2013* or *newsdevs2015*.[4] Translations were generated by beam search, with a beam width of 20, trying to find the sentence with the highest log-probability (single model), or highest average log-probability over all models (ensemble), divided by the sentence length (Boulanger-Lewandowski et al., 2013). This length normalization addresses the tendency of the recurrent neural network to output shorter sentences.

For Fi→En, we augmented models by *deep fusion* with an RNN-LM. The RNN-LM, which was built using the LSTM units, was trained on the English Gigaword corpus using the vocabulary comprising of the 42K most frequent words in the English side of the intersection of the parallel corpora of Fi→En, De→En and Cs→En. Importantly, we use the same RNN-LM for both Fi→En, Cs→En and De→En. In the experiments with deep fusion, we used the randomly selected $2/3$ of *newsdev2015* as a validation set and the rest as a held-out set. In the case of De→En, we used $newstest2013$ for validation and $newstest2014$ for test.

For all language pairs except Fi→En, we also simply built 5-gram language models, this time on all appropriate provided data, with the exception of the English Gigaword (Heafield, 2011). In our contrastive submissions only, we re-ranked our 20-best lists with the LM log-probabilities, once again divided by sentence length. The relative weight of the language model was manually chosen to maximize BLEU on the development set.

[4]For En→De, we created eight semi-independent models. See (Jean et al., 2015) for more details.

4 Results

Results for single systems and primary ensemble submissions are presented in Table 2.[5] When translating from English to another language, neural machine translation works particularly well, achieving the best BLEU-c scores among all the constrained systems. On the other hand, NMT is generally competitive even in the case of translating to English, but it not yet as good as well as the best SMT systems according to BLEU. If we rather rely on human judgement instead of automated metrics, the NMT systems still perform quite well over many language pairs, although they are in some instances surpassed by other statistical systems that have slightly lower BLEU scores.

In our contrastive submissions for Cs↔En and De↔En where we re-ranked 20-best lists with a 5-gram language model, BLEU scores went up modestly by 0.1 to 0.5 BLEU, but interestingly translation error rate (TER) always worsened. One possible drawback about the manner we integrated language models here is the lack of translation models in the reverse direction, meaning we do not implicitely leverage the Bayes' rule as most other translation systems do.

In our further experiments, which are not part of our WMT'15 submission, for single models we observed the improvements of approximately 1.0/0.5 BLEU points for *dev/test* in $\{$Cs,De$\}$→En tasks, when we employ *deep fusion* for incorporating language models.[6]

[5]Also available at `http://matrix.statmt.org/matrix/`

[6]Improvements are for single models only. See (Gülçehre et al., 2015) for more details.

5 Conclusion

We presented the MILA neural machine translation (NMT) systems for WMT'15, using the encoder–decoder model with the attention mechanism (Bahdanau et al., 2015) and the recent developments in NMT (Jean et al., 2015; Gülçehre et al., 2015). We observed that the NMT systems are now competitive against the conventional SMT systems, ranking first by BLEU among the constrained submission on both the En→Cs and En→De tasks. In the future, more analysis is needed on the influence of the source and target languages for neural machine translation. For instance, it would be interesting to better understand why performance relative to other approaches was somewhat weaker when translating into English, or how the amount of reordering influences the translation quality of neural MT systems.

Acknowledgments

The authors would like to thank the developers of Theano (Bergstra et al., 2010; Bastien et al., 2012). We thank Kelvin Xu, Bart van Mërrienboer, Dzmitry Bahdanau and Étienne Simon for their help. We also thank the two anonymous reviewers and everyone who contributed to the manual evaluation campaign. We acknowledge the support of the following agencies for research funding and computing support: NSERC, Calcul Québec, Compute Canada, the Canada Research Chairs, CIFAR, Samsung and TUBITAK.

References

Dzmitry Bahdanau, Kyunghyun Cho, and Yoshua Bengio. 2015. Neural machine translation by jointly learning to align and translate. In *ICLR'2015, arXiv:1409.0473*.

Frédéric Bastien, Pascal Lamblin, Razvan Pascanu, James Bergstra, Ian J. Goodfellow, Arnaud Bergeron, Nicolas Bouchard, and Yoshua Bengio. 2012. Theano: new features and speed improvements. Deep Learning and Unsupervised Feature Learning NIPS 2012 Workshop.

Yoshua Bengio and Jean-Sébastien Sénécal. 2008. Adaptive importance sampling to accelerate training of a neural probabilistic language model. *IEEE Trans. Neural Networks*, 19(4):713–722.

James Bergstra, Olivier Breuleux, Frédéric Bastien, Pascal Lamblin, Razvan Pascanu, Guillaume Desjardins, Joseph Turian, David Warde-Farley, and Yoshua Bengio. 2010. Theano: a CPU and GPU math expression compiler. In *Proceedings of the Python for Scientific Computing Conference (SciPy)*, June. Oral Presentation.

Nicolas Boulanger-Lewandowski, Yoshua Bengio, and Pascal Vincent. 2013. Audio chord recognition with recurrent neural networks. In *ISMIR*.

Peter F Brown, Vincent J Della Pietra, Stephen A Della Pietra, and Robert L Mercer. 1993. The mathematics of statistical machine translation: Parameter estimation. *Computational linguistics*, 19(2):263–311.

Stanley F. Chen and Joshua T. Goodman. 1998. An empirical study of smoothing techniques for language modeling. Technical Report TR-10-98, Computer Science Group, Harvard University.

Kyunghyun Cho, Bart van Merrienboer, Caglar Gulcehre, Fethi Bougares, Holger Schwenk, and Yoshua Bengio. 2014. Learning phrase representations using RNN encoder-decoder for statistical machine translation. In *Proceedings of the Empiricial Methods in Natural Language Processing (EMNLP 2014)*, October.

Ian Goodfellow, David Warde-Farley, Mehdi Mirza, Aaron Courville, and Yoshua Bengio. 2013. Maxout networks. In *Proceedings of The 30th International Conference on Machine Learning*, pages 1319–1327.

Çaglar Gülçehre, Orhan Firat, Kelvin Xu, Kyunghyun Cho, Loïc Barrault, Huei-Chi Lin, Fethi Bougares, Holger Schwenk, and Yoshua Bengio. 2015. On using monolingual corpora in neural machine translation. *CoRR*, abs/1503.03535.

Kenneth Heafield. 2011. KenLM: faster and smaller language model queries. In *Proceedings of the EMNLP 2011 Sixth Workshop on Statistical Machine Translation*, pages 187–197, Edinburgh, Scotland, United Kingdom, July.

S. Hochreiter and J. Schmidhuber. 1997. Long short-term memory. *Neural Computation*, 9(8):1735–1780.

Sébastien Jean, Kyunghyun Cho, Roland Memisevic, and Yoshua Bengio. 2015. On using very large target vocabulary for neural machine translation. In *Proceedings of ACL*.

Nal Kalchbrenner and Phil Blunsom. 2013. Recurrent continuous translation models. In *Proceedings of the ACL Conference on Empirical Methods in Natural Language Processing (EMNLP)*, pages 1700–1709. Association for Computational Linguistics.

Philipp Koehn and Kevin Knight. 2003. Empirical methods for compound splitting. In *Proceedings of the tenth conference on European chapter of the Association for Computational Linguistics-Volume 1*, pages 187–193. Association for Computational Linguistics.

Philipp Koehn, Hieu Hoang, Alexandra Birch, Chris Callison-Burch, Marcello Federico, Nicola Bertoldi, Brooke Cowan, Wade Shen, Christine Moran, Richard Zens, Chris Dyer, Ondřej Bojar, Alexandra Constantin, and Evan Herbst. 2007. Moses: Open source toolkit for statistical machine translation. In *Proceedings of the 45th Annual Meeting of the ACL on Interactive Poster and Demonstration Sessions*, ACL '07, pages 177–180, Stroudsburg, PA, USA. Association for Computational Linguistics.

Minh-Thang Luong, Ilya Sutskever, Quoc V. Le, Oriol Vinyals, and Wojciech Zaremba. 2015. Addressing the rare word problem in neural machine translation. In *Proceedings of ACL*.

Kishore Papineni, Salim Roukos, Todd Ward, and Wei-Jing Zhu. 2002. BLEU: A method for automatic evaluation of machine translation. In *Proceedings of the 40th Annual Meeting on Association for Computational Linguistics*, ACL '02, pages 311–318, Stroudsburg, PA, USA. Association for Computational Linguistics.

Razvan Pascanu, Tomas Mikolov, and Yoshua Bengio. 2013. On the difficulty of training recurrent neural networks.

Mike Schuster and Kuldip K Paliwal. 1997. Bidirectional recurrent neural networks. *Signal Processing, IEEE Transactions on*, 45(11):2673–2681.

Nakatani Shuyo. 2010. Language detection library for java.

Ilya Sutskever, Oriol Vinyals, and Quoc V. Le. 2014. Sequence to sequence learning with neural networks. In *NIPS'2014*.

Sami Virpioja, Peter Smit, Stig-Arne Grönroos, Mikko Kurimo, et al. 2013. Morfessor 2.0: Python implementation and extensions for morfessor baseline.

Matthew D Zeiler. 2012. ADADELTA: An adaptive learning rate method. *arXiv:*1212.5701 [cs.LG].

GF Wide-coverage English-Finnish MT system for WMT 2015

Prasanth Kolachina
Computing Science
Chalmers University of Technology
prasanth.kolachina@cse.gu.se

Aarne Ranta
Computing Science
Chalmers University of Technology
aarne.ranta@cse.gu.se

Abstract

This paper describes the GF Wide-coverage MT system submitted to WMT 2015 for translation from English to Finnish. Our system uses a interlingua based approach, in which the interlingua is a shared formal representation, that abstracts syntactic structures over multiple languages. Our final submission is a re-ranked system in which we combine this baseline MT system with a factored LM model.

1 Introduction

Interlingual translation is an old idea that has been suggested numerous times and refuted almost as many times. A typical criticism is that the very idea is utopistic: that one can never build an interlingua that faithfully represents meaning in all languages of the world. However, as the focus in machine translation has shifted from the perfect rendering of meaning to less modest goals, the idea of an interlingua can be reconsidered.

In the current paper, we describe our system submission to the WMT shared task in the English-Finnish track. Our system is an interlingua-based system, the interlingua based on an *abstract syntax* in the sense of Grammatical Framework (GF) (Ranta, 2011). GF has been previously shown to work for domain-specific MT outperforming state-of-art systems using semantic interlinguas (Ranta et al., 2011). Departing from this, the GF wide-coverage Translator is an attempt following the current mainstream in the field of MT: we are content with browsing quality in the output of the MT systems, while achieving the low cost of interlingual MT systems. As such, the shared *abstract syntax* is mapped to different "surface" languages representing an abstraction of the deep syntactic structure for each of the languages. The abstraction from word order, morphology and certain deep syntactic phenomena, allows the interlingua to cope with unrelated languages. At the same time, these systems are scalable beyond toy examples, into wide-coverage systems.

We submit this system as our baseline over the English Finnish language pair for the WMT shared task. In addition, we also submitted a "re-ranked" variant of the same system as our primary submission, using statistical language models to re-score the translations from the baseline. Automatic evaluation metrics have shown small improvements from re-ranking our baseline system [1].

The paper is organized as follows: we describe our baseline system in Section 2 and the re-ranked variant in Section 3. We present our experiments and relevant discussion in Section 4.

2 GF Wide-coverage Translator

The GF Translator pipeline has three main phases:

- **Parsing** converts the source sentence into a forest of *abstract syntax trees* (AST), i.e. interlingual representations.
- **Disambiguation** selects the most probable AST.
- **Linearization** converts the AST into a sentence in each of the target languages.

Disambiguation is for efficiency reasons integrated in the parser, which enumerates the results lazily in order of decreasing probability (Angelov and Ljunglöf, 2014). Our current system performs disambiguation by using tree probabilities estimated from the Penn Treebank, converted into GF abstract syntax (Angelov, 2011). Unlike most K-best parsers, there is no upper limit on how many

---

tp://matrix.statmt.

results can be obtained. Additionally, we use reversible mappings in our interlingua, thus reducing the work to define multilingual grammars for MT.

Translation is performed using the following components:

- A PGF grammar consisting of an abstract syntax (defining the ASTs) and, for each language, a concrete syntax that defines linearization and (by reversibility) parsing for the language.
- A probabilistic model for disambiguation
- The PGF interpreter, that consists of a generic parser and linearizer.

Since the PGF grammar forms a vital component of the MT system, we will now describe the wide-coverage grammar used in our system submission. All our submissions use this grammar as the "baseline". There is a large-scale single generic grammar based on the GF Resource Grammar Library (Ranta, 2009) that forms the central "backbone" of the wide-coverage grammar. As a whole, the grammar has the following components:

1. **RGL**, defining morphology and most of the syntax.
2. **Syntax extensions**, about 10% addition to RGL.
3. **Dictionary**, mapping abstract *word senses* to concrete words using open resources such as linked wordnets and wiktionaries (Virk et al., 2014); morphology mostly by the RGL's "smart paradigms" (Détrez and Ranta, 2012). Abstract dictionary entries are presented as English words split into distinct **senses**.
4. **Chunk grammar**, to make the translation robust for input that does not parse as complete sentences. It is inspired by Apertium(Forcada et al., 2011), which is a rule-based system operating only using chunks rather than deep syntactic analyses. In GF, it is derived from the RGL by enabling sub-sentential categories as start categories. The result can contain local agreement and reordering.
5. **Probabilities**, estimated from the Penn Treebank.

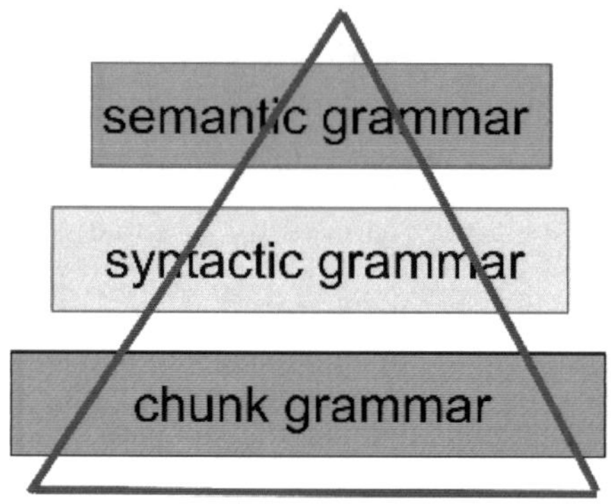

6. **CNL** using Semantic grammars, an optional part enabling domain adaptation via Embedded CNLs (Ranta, 2014). If something is parsable in the CNL, the CNL translation is given priority.

The GF Translator is not meant to be yet another browsing-quality system on the market. GF was originally designed for high-quality systems on specific domains. The novelty in our current system is that we can combine both coverage and quality in one and the same system. From the point of view of domain-specific applications, this means that the system does not just fail with out-of-grammar input as before, but offers robustness. From the open-domain point of view, the system offers a clear recipe for quality improvements by domain adaptation. In other words, the system we have built incorporates three levels of the Vauquois triangle in one and the same system: semantic, syntactic, and chunk-based translation, each of which and not just the highest level is based on its own part of the interlingua:

3 System Description

As mentioned in Section 1, our submission uses the GF Wide-coverage translator described in Section 2 as a baseline.
We are aware of one short-coming in the disambiguation model used in the baseline: the inference by the parser is carried out by context-free approximations. The context-free approximation is a reasonable approximation in the monolingual parsing scenario as shown by previous works in parsing literature. However, in the translation problem, the context-free assumption provides a poor approximation for inference. A simple example to illustrate this is the problem of sense selection by the parser. The choice of selecting a

particular word sense depends on both local contexts and entire sentential context. For e.g. the word “time” can refer to the sense that refers to temporality or the number of an attempt (as in *first time* or *hundredth time*). The choice of sense in this example can be made using surface context or *n-gram* information. Motivated primarily by this, we developed a re-ranked variant of the baseline system as described below.

Our re-ranked system re-estimates the scores of the K-best translations from the baseline using a linear mixture model. The mixture model uses the tree probability score obtained from the disambiguation model of the baseline system as the primary component. Each hypothesis in the K-best list is augmented using scores from n-gram language model (LM) that estimates the likelihood of the surface translations. Since our baseline system is an interlingua-based system, it is possible to integrate LM over multiple languages as different components in our mixture model. The resulting model selects the best translation by choosing the hypothesis with both the highest scoring abstract syntax tree and the best linearization of the abstract syntax tree.

4 Experiments

As part of the shared task contest, we carried out experiments with the wide-coverage translator and its re-ranked variant on the English-Finnish track. Table 1 shows the scores obtained by automatic evaluation for our system submissions.

On the *devel* set, the baseline system takes 27 minutes to carry out the translation pipeline i.e. the 1-best parsing of the English sentences combined with the 1-best linearization into Finnish. In comparison, the *test* set takes about 22 minutes for the pipeline. Of the 1500 sentences in the *devel* dataset, 600 sentences are parsed by the full RGL grammar, while the rest of the 900 sentences are parsed using the chunking grammar. We obtained similar statistics on the *test* dataset, where 560 sentences were parsed by the RGL and 810 sentences using the chunking grammar. This version of our translation pipeline is available online[2]. Manual evaluation and error analysis on a small sample from the *devel* dataset showed that the loss in MT quality from the chunking grammar was small, but significant. This is because the chunking grammar still allows for local agreement and reordering, while relaxing the RGL grammar. Nonetheless, we decided to use this version of the chunking grammar, without extending the RGL with new syntactic constructions. One reason for this decision was the speed up in the pipeline obtained by relaxing the full RGL grammar and adding the chunking grammar. It should be noted here that the quality of the MT system can be further improved by adding the full RGL at an additional computational cost. Evaluation experiments also showed that automatic evaluation metrics like BLEU substantially under-evaluate the perform of our system when used with a static translation as reference.

In the next round of experiments, we ran the parser and the linearizer in K-best modes, collecting the 50-best abstract syntax trees and the 30-best linearizations for each abstract syntax tree. Since the parsing and the linearization are carried out independent of one another, the 1500 hypothesis obtained from this run often contained identical translations. The overall number of distinct hypothesis in the K-best lists was typically found to be between 300 and 400. Collecting the K-best lists took about 93 minutes on the *devel* dataset and 80 minutes on the *test* dataset. We *re-order* these K-best lists using our reranking models, which consists of a re-scoring the hypothesis translations using a language model (LM) and estimating the mixed score for each hypothesis. The reordering combined with the re-scoring takes about 3-4 minutes on our lists of 1500-best hypotheses.

The LM for Finnish was trained on the Europarl corpus. Finnish sentences were morphologically analyzed and converted into a lemmatized corpus with morphological factors tagged along with the lemmas. We train a factored language model on this corpus, using the lemma and the part-of-speech and suffix as factors. In our current experiments, the hypothesis are re-scored using the Finnish language model alone, though in principle the re-scoring can be carried out using language models for multiple languages.

We train a ordinal regression model using the parse tree probability estimated using the GF disambiguation model and the factored LM score to re-order the K-best lists. A small set of 2500 sentences from the Europarl corpus were randomly taken and used as training samples for the regres-

[2] `http://cloud.grammaticalframework.org/wc.html`

System	BLEU	TER
Baseline	4.7	1.138
Reranked	4.8	1.135

Table 1: BLEU (11b) and TER scores obtained on the *newstest2015* dataset

sion model. The K-best lists in the training samples are ranked based on BLEU scores and TER scores.

Experiments with the *devel* dataset showed small improvements from using the LM to rescore the hypothesis. Comparatively, reranking resulted in even smaller improvements on the the *test* dataset. At this point, we carried out a analysis of the K-best lists on the *devel* set. We found that there was a very small variation in the K-best lists given the number of distinct hypothesis that were considered. Most of the variation was attributed to punctuation and orthography rather than *word senses* or *word order* as we initially expected.

Following this, we experimented with random sampling in the parse forests to evaluate the oracle quality of our translation system. The results of this study are pending error analysis and evaluation.

5 Conclusions

We described our system submission to the WMT shared task in the English-Finnish track in the current paper. Our system uses as interlingual-based approach, in which the interlingual is based on a shared representation of surface structures across languages. Our final submission is a hybrid system in which the K-best translations from the baseline system are re-ranked using a factored language model. We explain why our system results in a low-scoring baseline and discuss reasons why reranking provides minor improvements compared to previous approaches.

We plan to work on two extensions to the work described in this paper: first, we plan on increasing the variation in our K-best lists using sampling and incorporating heuristics into the parser. We hope that this will result in better improvements from re-ranking the K-best lists using a language model. Another extension we would like to experiment is the use of multiple language LMs to rescore the translations, this is uniquely possible only in our system since it allows for translation into multiple languages with little cost compared to other MT systems.

References

Krasimir Angelov and Peter Ljunglöf. 2014. Fast statistical parsing with parallel multiple context-free grammars. In *Proceedings of the 14th Conference of the European Chapter of the Association for Computational Linguistics*, pages 368–376, Gothenburg, Sweden, April. Association for Computational Linguistics.

Krasimir Angelov. 2011. *The Mechanics of the Grammatical Framework*. Ph.D. thesis, Chalmers University of Technology.

Grégoire Détrez and Aarne Ranta. 2012. Smart paradigms and the predictability and complexity of inflectional morphology. In *Proceedings of the 13th Conference of the European Chapter of the Association for Computational Linguistics*, pages 645–653, Avignon, France, April. Association for Computational Linguistics.

Mikel L Forcada, Mireia Ginestí-Rosell, Jacob Nordfalk, Jim ORegan, Sergio Ortiz-Rojas, Juan Antonio Pérez-Ortiz, Felipe Sánchez-Martínez, Gema Ramírez-Sánchez, and Francis M Tyers. 2011. Apertium: a free/open-source platform for rule-based machine translation. *Machine Translation*, 25(2):127–144.

Aarne Ranta, Ramona Enache, and Grgoire Dtrez. 2011. Controlled Language for Everyday Use: the MOLTO Phrasebook. *Proceeding of CNL 2010, Zurich*.

A. Ranta. 2009. The GF Resource Grammar Library. *Linguistics in Language Technology*, 2. `http://elanguage.net/journals/index.php/lilt/article/viewFile/214/158`.

Aarne Ranta. 2011. *Grammatical Framework: Programming with Multilingual Grammars*. CSLI Publications, Stanford. ISBN-10: 1-57586-626-9 (Paper), 1-57586-627-7 (Cloth).

Aarne Ranta. 2014. Embedded controlled languages. In *Controlled Natural Language - 4th International Workshop, CNL 2014, Galway, Ireland, August 20-22, 2014. Proceedings*.

Shafqat Mumtaz Virk, KVS Prasad, Aarne Ranta, and Krasimir Angelov. 2014. Developing an interlingual translation lexicon using wordnets and grammatical framework. *COLING 2014*, page 55.

LIMSI @ WMT'15 : Translation Task

Benjamin Marie[1,2,3], **Alexandre Allauzen**[1,2], **Franck Burlot**[1], **Quoc-Khanh Do**[1,2],
Julia Ive[1,2,4], **Elena Knyazeva**[1,2], **Matthieu Labeau**[1,2], **Thomas Lavergne**[1,2],
Kevin Löser[1,2], **Nicolas Pécheux**[1,2], **François Yvon**[1]
[1]LIMSI-CNRS, 91 403 Orsay, France
[2]Université Paris-Sud, 91 403 Orsay, France
[3]Lingua et Machina
[4]Centre Cochrane français
firstname.lastname@limsi.fr

Abstract

This paper describes LIMSI's submissions to the shared WMT'15 translation task. We report results for French-English, Russian-English in both directions, as well as for Finnish-into-English. Our submissions use NCODE and MOSES along with continuous space translation models in a post-processing step. The main novelties of this year's participation are the following: for Russian-English, we investigate a tailored normalization of Russian to translate into English, and a two-step process to translate first into simplified Russian, followed by a conversion into inflected Russian. For French-English, the challenge is domain adaptation, for which only monolingual corpora are available. Finally, for the Finnish-to-English task, we explore unsupervised morphological segmentation to reduce the sparsity of data induced by the rich morphology on the Finnish side.

1 Introduction

This paper documents LIMSI's participation to the machine translation shared task for three language pairs: French-English and Russian-English in both directions, as well as Finnish-into-English. Each of these tasks poses its own challenges.

For French-English, the task differs slightly from previous years as it considers user-generated news discusssions. While the domain remains the same, the texts that need to be translated are of a less formal type. To cope with the style shift, new monolingual corpora have been made available; they represent the only available in-domain resources to adapt statistical machine translation (SMT) systems.

For Russian-English, the main source of difficulty is the processing of Russian, a morphologically rich language with a much more complex inflectional system than English. To mitigate the effects of having too many Russian word forms, we explore ways to normalize Russian prior to translation into English, so as to reduce the number of forms by removing some "redundant" morphological information. When translating into Russian, we consider a two-step scenario. A conventional SMT system is first built to translate from English into a simplified version of Russian; a post-processing step then restores the correct inflection wherever needed.

Finally, for Finnish-into-English, we report preliminary experiments that explore unsupervised morphological segmentation techniques to reduce the sparsity issue induced by the rich morphology of Finnish.

2 Systems Overview

Our experiments use NCODE[1], an open source implementation of the n-gram approach, as well as MOSES, which implements a vanilla phrase-based approach.[2] For more details about these toolkits, the reader can refer to (Koehn et al., 2007) for MOSES and to (Crego et al., 2011) for NCODE.

2.1 Tokenization and word alignments

Tokenization for French and English text relies on in-house text processing tools (Déchelotte et al., 2008). All bilingual corpora provided by the organizers were used, except for the French-English tasks where the UN corpus was not considered.[3] We also used a heavily filtered version of the Common Crawl corpus, where we discard all sentences pairs that do not look like proper French/English parallel sentences. For all cor-

[1]http://ncode.limsi.fr

[2]http://www.statmt.org/moses/

[3]In fact, when used in combination with the Giga Fr-En corpus, no improvement could be observed (Koehn and Haddow, 2012).

pora, we finally removed all sentence pairs that did not match the default criteria of the MOSES script `clean-corpus-n.pl` or that contained more than 70 tokens.

Statistics regarding the parallel corpora used to train SMT systems are reported in Table 1 for the three language pairs under study. Word-level alignments are computed using `fast_align` (Dyer et al., 2013) with options "-d -o -v".

2.2 Language Models

The English language model (LM) was trained on all the available English monolingual data, plus the English side of the bilingual data for the Fr-En, Ru-En and Fi-En language pairs. For the French language model, we also used all the provided monolingual data and the French side of the bilingual En-Fr data. We removed all duplicate lines[4] and trained a 4-gram language model, pruning all singletons, with `lmplz` (Heafield et al., 2013).

2.3 SOUL

Neural networks, working on top of conventional n-gram back-off language models, have been introduced in (Bengio et al., 2003; Schwenk et al., 2006) as a potential means to improve conventional language models. As in our previous participations (Le et al., 2012b; Allauzen et al., 2013; Pécheux et al., 2014), we take advantage of the proposal of (Le et al., 2011). Using a specific neural network architecture, the *Structured OUtput Layer* (SOUL), it becomes possible to estimate n-gram models that use large output vocabulary, thereby making the training of large neural network language models feasible both for target language models and translation models (Le et al., 2012a). Moreover, the peculiar parameterization of continuous models allows us to consider longer dependencies than the one used by conventional n-gram models (e.g. $n = 10$ instead of $n = 4$).

3 Experiments for French-English

This year, the French-English translation task focuses on user-generated News discusssions, a less formal type of texts than the usual News articles of the previous WMT editions. Therefore, the main challenge for this task is domain adaptation, for which only monolingual data are distributed.

3.1 Development and test sets

Since this is the first time this translation task is considered, only a small development set of news-discusssions is available. In order to properly tune and test our systems, we performed a 3-fold cross-validation, splitting the 1,500 in-domain sentences in two parts. Each random split respects document boundary, and yields roughly 1,000 sentences for tuning and 500 sentences for testing. The source of the documents, the newspapers *Le Monde* and *The Guardian* are also known. This allows us to balance the proportion of documents from each source in the development and test sets. The BLEU scores for the French-English experiments are computed on the concatenation of each test set decoded using weights tuned on the corresponding 1,000 sentence tuning set.

3.2 Domain adaptation

The vast majority of bilingual data distributed for the translation task are News articles, meaning that they correspond to a more formal register than the News discussions. The only in-domain texts provided for this task are monolingual corpora. Nevertheless, these monolingual data have been used to adapt both the translation and language models. To adapt the bilingual data, we subsampled the concatenation of the noisy Common Crawl and Giga Fr-En corpus, which represent around 90% of all our bilingual data, using the so-called Modified Moore-Lewis (Axelrod et al., 2011) filtering method (`MML`). We kept all the Europarl and News-Commentary data. `MML` expects 4 LMs to score sentence pairs in the corpus we wish to filter: for the source and target languages, it requires a LM trained with in-domain data, along with an out-of-domain LM estimated on the data to filter.[5] The `MML` score of a sentence pair is the sum of the source and target's perplexity differences for both in-domain and out-of-domain LMs. Sentences pairs are ranked according to the `MML` score and the top N parallel sentences are used to learn the translation table used during decoding.

For LM adaptation, we used a log-linear combination of our large LM with a smaller one trained only on the monolingual in-domain corpus.[6]

[4]Experiments not reported in this paper showed no changes in BLEU score between keeping or removing duplicate lines, but removing duplicate lines conveniently reduced the size of the models due to singleton pruning.

[5]All language models for the `MML` scoring are 4-grams trained with `lmplz`.

[6]Corresponding respectively to 3.5 and 50 millions sen-

Corpus	Fr-En		Ru-En		Fi→En	
	Sentences	Tokens (Fr-En)	Sentences	Tokens (Ru-En)	Sentences	Tokens (Fi-En)
parallel data	24.3M	712.8M-597.7M	2.3M	45.7M-47.3M	2M	37.3M-51.7M
monolingual data		2.2B-2.7B		834.7M-2.7B		-2.7B

Table 1: Statistical description of the training corpora

3.3 Reranking

The N-best reranking steps uses the following feature sets to find a better hypothesis among the 1,000-best hypotheses of the decoder:

- **IBM1**: IBM1 features (Hildebrand and Vogel, 2008);
- **POSLM**: 6-gram Witten-Bell smoothed POS LM trained with SRILM on all the monolingual news-discussions corpus;
- **SOUL**: Five features, one monolingual target language model and 4 translation models, see section 2.3 for details;
- **TagRatio**: ratio of translation hypothesis by number of source tokens tagged as verb, noun or adjective;
- **WPP**: count-based word posterior probability (Ueffing and Ney, 2007);

POS tagging is performed using the `Stanford Tagger`[7]. The reranking system is trained using the `kb-mira` algorithm (Cherry and Foster, 2012) implemented in MOSES.

3.4 Experimental results

For all French-English experiments, we used MOSES and NCODE with the default options, including lexicalized reordering models. Tuning is performed using `kb-mira` with default options on 200-best hypotheses.

Table 2 reports experimental results for filtering the bilingual data using `MML` before or after learning the word alignment step. Results for filtering are always lower when the word alignments are learnt only on the filtered data. The baseline system, which uses all the bilingual data, yields better performance than all our filtered systems, even though keeping only 25% of the bi-sentences, gives almost similar results. However, since there is no clear gain in filtering, we kept all the data without any `MML` filtering for the following experiments. The additional LM learned only on the in-domain data gives a slight improvement, +0.18 BLEU, for Fr-En, and a larger improvement for En-Fr (+0.66 BLEU, see Table 3).

Configuration		Fr-En
baseline		29.33
before	10%	28.63
	25%	29.09
	50%	28.96
after	10%	29.14
	25%	29.31
	50%	29.11

Table 2: Results (BLEU) for keeping the top 10%, 25% or 50% of the bi-sentences scored with `MML`, before and after word alignment. The baseline system uses all the bilingual data.

Configuration	Fr-En	En-Fr
w/o additional LM	29.15	29.56
w/ additional LM	29.33	30.22

Table 3: Results (BLEU) with and without the additional in-domain language model.

Table 4 reports the comparison between NCODE and MOSES. MOSES outperforms NCODE on our in-house test set using the 3-fold cross-validation procedure. However, when tuning on the complete development set and testing on the official test set, we observed a different result where NCODE outperforms MOSES for Fr-En (+0.69 BLEU), while MOSES remains the best choice for En-Fr (+0.74 BLEU). These differences between the results obtained with our dev/test configuration and the official ones may be due to the lack of tuning data when performing the 3-fold cross-validation, leaving only 1,000 sentences for tuning. Nonetheless, further investigations will be helpful to better understand these discrepancies.

Regarding reranking, results in Table 5 show that SOUL is the most useful feature and significantly improves translation performance when reranking a 1,000-best list generated by the decoder: we observe an improvement of nearly +0.9 BLEU for both translation directions. These re-

tences for French and English.

[7] http://nlp.stanford.edu/software/tagger.shtml

System	in-house test		official test	
	Fr-En	En-Fr	Fr-En	En-Fr
MOSES	29.33	30.22	32.16	35.74
NCODE	28.66	30.17	32.85	35.00

Table 4: Results (BLEU) for NCODE and MOSES on respectively the in-house and official test set.

Feature sets	Fr-En	En-Fr
baseline	29.33	30.22
+ **IBM1**	29.24	30.25
+ **POSLM**	29.45	30.28
+ **SOUL**	30.20	31.15
+ **TagRatio**	29.33	30.30
+ **WPP**	29.40	30.20
`all`	30.45	31.25

Table 5: Reranking results (BLEU) using different feature sets individually and their combination. For the `all` configurations these features are introduced during a reranking step.

sults can be further improved by adding more features during the reranking phase, with a final gain of +1.12 and +1.03 BLEU, for respectively Fr-En and En-Fr.

Our primary submissions for Fr-En and En-Fr use MOSES to generate n-best list, with phrase and reordering tables learned from all our bilingual data; the reranking step includes all the features presented in section 3.3.

4 Russian-English

Russian is a morphologically rich language characterized notably by a much more complex inflection system than English. This observation was the starting point of our work and led us to explore ways to process Russian in order to make it closer to English.

4.1 Preprocessing Russian

Inflections in Russian encode much more information than in English. For instance, while English adjectives are invariable, their Russian counterparts surface as twelve distinct word forms, expressing variations in gender (3), number (2) and case (6). Such a diversity of forms creates data sparsity issues, since many word forms are not observed in training corpora. When translating from Russian, the number of unknown words is accordingly high, making it impossible to translate many forms, even when they exist in the training corpus with a different inflection mark. Conversely, when translating into Russian, the system may not be able to generate the correct word form in a given context. Finally note that training translation models for such a language pair causes each English word to be typically paired with a lot of translations of low probability, corresponding to morphological variants on the Russian side.

To address this issue, we decided to normalize Russian by replacing all case marks by the corresponding nominative inflection: this applies to nouns, adjectives and pronouns. For these word types, the case information is thus lost, but the gender and number marks are preserved.

4.2 Predicting Case Marks

When translating into Russian, the normalization scheme described above is not well suited because of its lossy reduction of Russian word forms. Its use therefore requires a post processing step which aims to recover the inflected forms from the output of the SMT system. Since normalization essentially removes the case information, this last step consists in predicting the right case for a given normalized word before generating the correctly inflected form.

For this purpose, we designed a cascade of Conditional Random Fields (CRFs) models. A first model predicts POS tags, which are then used by a second model to predict the gender and number information. A last model is then used to infer the case from this information. POS, gender and number prediction are used to disambiguate the normalized words, which is necessary to generate the correct word forms. All predictions were performed considering only the target side output, meaning that no information from the source was used. The first two models use standard features for POS tagging as described in (Lavergne et al., 2010). The last one (for case prediction) additionally contains features testing the presence of a verb or a preposition in the close vicinity of the word under consideration.

4.3 Experimental results

Standard NCODE and MOSES configurations with lexicalized reordering models were used for all the English-Russian and Russian-English experiments. Alignments in both directions were computed with normalized Russian. The models were tuned with `kb-mira` using 300-best lists.

The results reported in Table 6 show a similar trend for NCODE and MOSES in both translation directions. Note that MOSES outperforms NCODE (+0.72 BLEU) for Ru-En task. Using normalized Russian as the source language allows us to achieve a slight gain of +0.4 over the baseline for both systems. Moreover, the addition of SOUL models yields a further improvement of 1.1 BLEU score (see Table 7). The English-into-normalized-Russian task has been performed for the sake of comparison, to assess the gain we could expect if we were able to always predict the right case for the normalized Russian output. The comparison of BLEU scores between translating directly into Russian and producing an intermediate normalized Russian shows differences of 3.15 BLEU for NCODE and 3.44 BLEU for MOSES. These scores represent an upper-bound that unfortunately we were not able to reach with our post-processing scheme.

System	MOSES	NCODE
Baseline	26.85	26.02
+ Normalized Ru	27.27	26.44
+ SOUL		27.28

Table 6: Results (BLEU) for Russian-English with NCODE and MOSES on the official test.

System	MOSES	NCODE
Baseline	22.91	22.97
+ SOUL		24.08
En-Rx	26.35	26.12
En-Rx-Ru	19.99	19.88

Table 7: Results (BLEU) for English-Russian (Rx stands for normalized Russian) with NCODE and MOSES on the official test. The score for En-Rx was obtained over the normalized test.

4.4 Error Analysis

As Russian is a morphologically rich language, which has many features not observed in the English language, we conducted a simple error analysis to better understand the possible morphological mistakes made by our NCODE baseline. We used METEOR to automatically align the outputs with the original references at the word level, discarding multiple alignment links. About 56.3% of the words in the NCODE output have a counterpart in the human references, which is consistent with the BLEU unigram precision (53.3%). Among those, 85.4% are identical and 9.8% are different but share a common lemma. This last situation happens when our system fails to predict the correct form. The remaining 4.8% (different word forms with no common lemma), correspond either to synonyms or to METEOR alignment errors. Figure 1 also suggests that, within the 9.8% word form errors, most morphological errors are related to case prediction. Figure 1 displays detailed results split by POS. Results for MOSES or when rescoring NCODE outputs with SOUL are very similar.

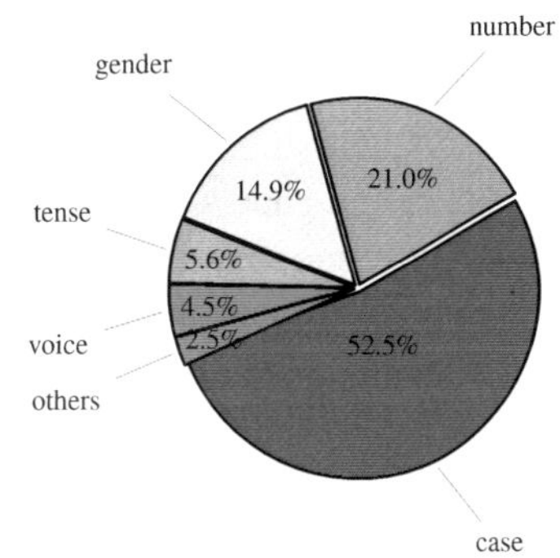

(a) Incorrectly predicted inflections

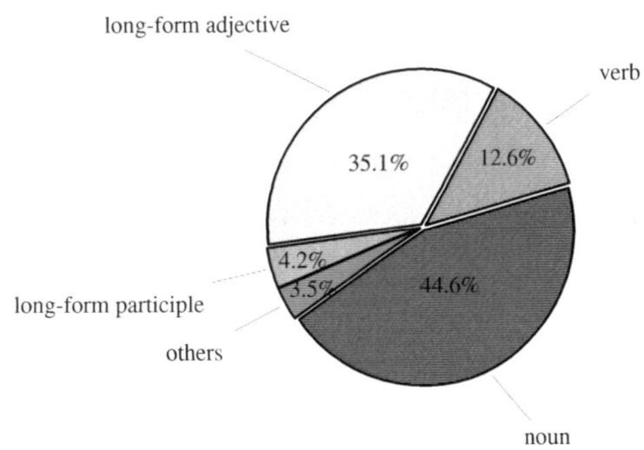

(b) Word form errors *wrt* POS

Figure 1: Distribution of mispredictions for NCODE outputs, according to the mispredicted inflection (a) and their POS (b).

5 Translating Finnish into English

This is our first attempt to translate from Finnish to English. The provided development set contains only 1,500 parallel sentences. Therefore all the results are computed using a two-fold cross validation. The baseline system is a conventional phrase-based system built with the MOSES toolkit. Experimental results are in Table 8. The first two

Configuration	dev.	test
Baseline	13.2	12.8
+ large LM	16.1	15.7
+ Morph. segmentation	16.2	15.9

Table 8: BLEU scores for the Finnish to English translation task, obtained with different configurations after a two-fold cross-validation.

lines give the BLEU scores obtained with a basic tokenization of the Finnish side. When the English LM is only estimated on the parallel data, the system achieves a BLEU score of 12.8, while using a LM estimated on all the available monolingual data yields a 1.8 BLEU point improvement.

Finnish is a synthetic language that employs extensive regular agglutination. This peculiarity implies a large variety of word forms and, again, severe sparsity issues. For instance, we observed on the available parallel training data 860K different Finnish forms for 37.3M running words and only 2M sentences. Among these forms, more than half are hapax. For comparison purposes, we observed in English 208K word forms for 51.7M running words. To address this issue, we have tried to reduce the number of forms in the Finnish part of the data. For that purpose, we use `Morfessor` [8] to perform an unsupervised morphological segmentation. The new Finnish corpus therefore contains 67K types for 77M running words. With this new version, we obtain only a slight improvement of 0.2 BLEU point. We assume that the Finnish data was over-segmented and that a better tradeoff can be found with an extensive tuning of `Morfessor`.

6 Discussion and Conclusion

This paper described LIMSI's submissions to the shared WMT'15 translation task. We reported results for French-English, Russian-English in both direction, as well as for Finnish-into-English. Our submissions used NCODE and MOSES along with continuous space translation models in a post-processing step. Most of our efforts for this years participation were dedicated to domain adaptation and more importantly to explore different strategies when translating from and into a morphologically rich language.

For French-English, we experimented adaptation using only monolingual data that represents the targeted text, *i.e* news-discussions. Our attempt to filter the available parallel corpora did not bring any gain, while the use of an additional language model estimated on news-discussions yielded slight improvement.

When translating from Russian into English, small improvements were observed with a tailored normalization of Russian. This normalization was designed to reduce the number of word forms and to make it closer to English. However, experiments in the other direction were disappointing. While the first step that translates from English to the normalized version of Russian showed positive results, the second step designed to recover Russian inflected forms failed. This failure may be related to the cascade of statistical models, working solely on the target side. However, the reasons need to be better understood with a more detailed study.

To translate from Finnish into English, we explored the use of unsupervised morphological segmentation. Our attempt to reduce the number of forms on the Finnish side did not significantly change the the BLEU score. This under-performance can be explained by an over-segmentation of the Finnish data, and maybe a better tradeoff can be found with a more adapted segmentation strategy.

We finally reiterate our past observations that continuous space translation models used in a post-processing step always yielded significant improvements across the board.

Acknowledgements

We would like to thank the anonymous reviewers for their helpful comments and suggestions. This work has been partly funded by the European Unions Horizon 2020 research and innovation programme under grant agreement No. 645452 (QT21).

[8] `https://github.com/aalto-speech/morfessor`

References

Alexandre Allauzen, Nicolas Pécheux, Quoc Khanh Do, Marco Dinarelli, Thomas Lavergne, Aurélien Max, Hai-son Le, and François Yvon. 2013. LIMSI @ WMT13. In *Proceedings of WMT*, Sofia, Bulgaria.

Amittai Axelrod, Xiaodong He, and Jianfeng Gao. 2011. Domain adaptation via pseudo in-domain data selection. In *Proceedings of EMNLP*, Edinburgh, Scotland.

Yoshua Bengio, Réjean Ducharme, Pascal Vincent, and Christian Jauvin. 2003. A neural probabilistic language model. *Journal of Machine Learning Research.*

Colin Cherry and George Foster. 2012. Batch tuning strategies for statistical machine translation. In *Proceedings of NAACL-HLT*, Montréal, Canada.

Josep M. Crego, François Yvon, and José B. Mariño. 2011. N-code: an open-source bilingual N-gram SMT toolkit. *Prague Bulletin of Mathematical Linguistics*, 96.

Daniel Déchelotte, Gilles Adda, Alexandre Allauzen, Olivier Galibert, Jean-Luc Gauvain, Hélène Maynard, and François Yvon. 2008. LIMSI's statistical translation systems for WMT'08. In *Proceedings of NAACL-HTL Statistical Machine Translation Workshop*, Columbus, Ohio.

Chris Dyer, Victor Chahuneau, and Noah A. Smith. 2013. A simple, fast, and effective reparameterization of ibm model 2. In *Proceedings of NAACL*, Atlanta, Georgia.

Kenneth Heafield, Ivan Pouzyrevsky, Jonathan H. Clark, and Philipp Koehn. 2013. Scalable modified Kneser-Ney language model estimation. In *Proceedings of ACL*, Sofia, Bulgaria.

Almut Silja Hildebrand and Stephan Vogel. 2008. Combination of machine translation systems via hypothesis selection from combined n-best lists. In *Proceedings of AMTA*, Honolulu, Hawa.

Philipp Koehn and Barry Haddow. 2012. Towards effective use of training data in statistical machine translation. In *Proceedings of WMT*, Montréal, Canada.

Philipp Koehn, Hieu Hoang, Alexandra Birch, Chris Callison-Burch, Marcello Federico, Nicola Bertoldi, Brooke Cowan, Wade Shen, Christine Moran, Richard Zens, Chris Dyer, Ondrej Bojar, Alexandra Constantin, and Evan Herbst. 2007. Moses: Open source toolkit for statistical machine translation. In *Proceedings of the ACL Demo*, Prague, Czech Republic.

Thomas Lavergne, Olivier Cappé, and François Yvon. 2010. Practical very large scale CRFs. In *Proceedings of ACL*, Uppsala, Sweden.

Hai-Son Le, Ilya Oparin, Alexandre Allauzen, Jean-Luc Gauvain, and François Yvon. 2011. Structured output layer neural network language model. In *Proceedings of ICASSP*, Prague, Czech Republic.

Hai-Son Le, Alexandre Allauzen, and François Yvon. 2012a. Continuous space translation models with neural networks. In *Proceedings of NAACL-HLT*, Montréal, Canada.

Hai-Son Le, Thomas Lavergne, Alexandre Allauzen, Marianna Apidianaki, Li Gong, Aurélien Max, Artem Sokolov, Guillaume Wisniewski, and François Yvon. 2012b. LIMSI @ WMT12. In *Proceedings of WMT*, Montréal, Canada.

Nicolas Pécheux, Li Gong, Quoc Khanh Do, Benjamin Marie, Yulia Ivanishcheva, Alexandre Allauzen, Thomas Lavergne, Jan Niehues, Aurélien Max, and François Yvon. 2014. LIMSI @ WMT14 Medical Translation Task. In *Proceedings of WMT*, Baltimore, Maryland.

Holger Schwenk, Daniel Déchelotte, and Jean-Luc Gauvain. 2006. Continuous space language models for statistical machine translation. In *Proceedings of the COLING/ACL*, Morristown, US.

Nicola Ueffing and Hermann Ney. 2007. Word-Level Confidence Estimation for Machine Translation. *Computational Linguistics*, 33.

UdS-Sant: English–German Hybrid Machine Translation System

Santanu Pal[1], **Sudip Kumar Naskar**[2], **Josef van Genabith**[1]
[1]Universität des Saarlandes, Saarbrücken, Germany
[2] Jadavpur University, Kolkata, India
`{santanu.pal, josef.vangenabith}@uni-saarland.de`
`sudip.naskar@cse.jdvu.ac.in`

Abstract

This paper describes the UdS-Sant English–German Hybrid Machine Translation (MT) system submitted to the Translation Task organized in the Workshop on Statistical Machine Translation (WMT) 2015. Our proposed hybrid system brings improvements over the baseline system by incorporating additional knowledge such as extracted bilingual named entities and bilingual phrase pairs induced from example-based methods. The reported final submission is the result of a hybrid system obtained from confusion network based system combination that combines the best performance of each individual system in a multi-engine pipeline.

1 Introduction

In this paper, we present Universität des Saarlandes (UdS) submission (named UdS-Sant) to WMT 2015 using a Hybrid MT framework. We participated in the generic translation shared task for the English-German (EN-DE) language pair.

Corpus-based MT (CBMT) has delivered progressively improved quality translations since its inception. There are two main approaches to corpus-based MT – Example Based Machine Translation (EBMT) (Carl and Way, 2003) and Statistical Machine Translation (SMT) (Brown et al., 1993; Koehn, 2010). Out of these two, in terms of large-scale evaluations, SMT is the most successful MT paradigm. However, each approach has its own advantages and disadvantages along with its own methods of applying and acquiring translation knowledge from the bilingual parallel training data. EBMT phrases tend to be more linguistically motivated compared to SMT phrases which essentially operate on n-grams. The knowledge extraction as well as representation process, in both EBMT and SMT, uses very different techniques in order to extract resources. Even though, SMT is the most popular MT paradigm, it sometimes fails to deliver sufficient quality in translation output for some languages, since each language has its own difficulties.

Multiword Expressions (MWEs) and Named Entities (NEs) offer challenges within a language. MWEs are defined as idiosyncratic interpretations that cross word boundaries (Sag et al., 2002). Named entities on the other hand often consist of more than one word, so that they can be considered as a specific type of MWEs such as noun compounds (Jackendoff, 1997). Traditional approaches to word alignment such as IBM Models (Brown et al., 1993) are unable to tackle NEs and MWEs properly due to their inability to handle many-to-many alignments. In another well-known word alignment approach, Hidden Markov Model (HMM: (Vogel et al., 1996)), the alignment probabilities depend on the alignment position of the previous word. It does not explicitly consider many-to-many alignment either.

We address this alignment problem indirectly. The objective of the present work is threefold. Firstly, we would like to determine how treatment of MWEs as a single unit affects the overall MT quality (Pal et al., 2010; Pal et al., 2011). Secondly, whether a prior automatic NE aligned parallel corpus as well as example based parallel phrases can bring about any further improvement on top of that. And finally, whether system combination can provide any additional advantage in terms of translation quality and performance.

The remainder of the paper is organised as follows. Section 2 details the components of our system, in particular named entity extraction, translation memory, and EBMT, followed by description of 3 types of Hybrid systems and the system combination module. In Section 3, we outline the complete experimental setup for the shared task and provide results and analysis on the performance on the test set in Section 4. Section 5 concludes the proposed research.

2 System Description

Our system is designed with three basic components: (i) preprocessing, (ii) hybrid systems and (iii) system combination.

2.1 Preprocessing

Data pre-processing plays a very crucial part in any data-driven approach. We carried out preprocessing in two steps:

- Cleaning and clustering sentences based on sentence length.
- Effective preprocessing of data in the form of explicit alignment of bilingual terminology (viz. NEs and MWEs).

The preprocessing has been shown (cf. Section 2.1.2) to improve the output quality of the baseline PB-SMT system (Pal et al., 2013; Tan and Pal, 2014).

2.1.1 Corpus cleaning

We utilized all the parallel training data provided by the WMT 2015 shared task organizers for English–German translation. The training data include Europarl, News Commentary and Common Crawl. The provided corpus is noisy and contains some non-German as well as non-English words and sentences. Therefore, we applied a Language Identifier (Shuyo, 2010) on both bilingual English–German parallel data and monolingual German corpora. We discarded those parallel sentences from the bilingual training data which were detected as belonging to some different language by the language identifier. The same method was also applied to the monolingual data.

Successively, the corpus cleaning process was carried out first by calculating the global mean ratio of the number of characters in a source sentence to that in a target sentence and then filtering out sentence pairs that exceed or fall below 20% of the global ratio (Tan and Pal, 2014). We sorted the entire parallel training corpus based on their sentence length.Tokenisation and punctuation normalisation were performed using Moses scripts. In the final step of cleaning, we filtered the parallel training data on maximum allowable sentence length of 100 and sentence length ratio of 1:2 (either direction). Approximately 36% sentences were removed from the total training data during the cleaning process.

2.1.2 Explicit Preprocessing of Terminologies

Two kinds of terminologies, viz. NEs and MWEs, were considered in the present work. Intuitively, MWEs should be both aligned in the parallel corpus and translated as a whole. However, state-of-the-art PB-SMT (or any other approaches to SMT) does not generally treat MWEs as special tokens. This is the motivation behind considering MWEs for special treatment in this work. By converting the MWEs into single tokens, we make sure that PB-SMT also treats them as a whole.

NE Alignment (NEA): For NE alignment, we first identify NEs on both sides of the parallel corpus using Stanford NER[1]. Next, we try to align the extracted source and target NEs. If both sides contain only one NE then the alignment is trivial, and we add such NE pairs to seed another parallel NE corpus that contains examples having only one token in both sides. Otherwise, we establish alignments between the source and target NEs using minimum edit distance method. For language pairs having different orthographies (e.g. English–Hindi) NE alignments can be established through transliteration (Pal et al., 2010). If both the source and target sides contain n number of NEs, and the alignments of $n-1$ NEs can be established through minimum edit distance method or by means of already existing alignments, then the nth alignment is trivial. The bilingual NE pairs extracted thus serve as additional training material and they improve the word alignment at the start of the MT pipeline.

MWE Identification: Translation correspondences between English MWEs and German MWEs are mainly many-to-one correspondences. Therefore, instead of extracting a bilingual MWE list between source and target, we identify the MWEs from the English training sentences and prepare an English MWE list. Once the MWEs are identified, they are converted into single tokens by replacing the spaces with underscores ("_") so that their alignments can be mapped to single tokens . Before decoding, MWEs in the source side of the testset are also single tokenized by looking up the extracted MWE list. In this experiment, we have followed Point-wise Mutual Infor-

[1] http://nlp.stanford.edu/software/CRF-NER.shtml

mation (PMI), Log-likelihood Ratio (LLR), Phi-coefficient and Co-occurrence measures for identification of MWEs on the English side. Finally, a system combination model has been developed which provides a normalized score for each of the extracted MWEs. A predefined cut-off score has been considered and the candidates having scores above the threshold value are considered as MWEs.

Example Based Phrase Extraction: We use EBMT techniques to extract additional phrase pairs from the training data to augment the SMT (baseline) phrase pairs in our experiments. We extract EBMT phrase pairs based on the work described in (Cicekli and Güvenir, 2001), a compiled approach of EBMT to automatically extract translation templates from sentence-aligned bilingual text. They observed the similarities and differences between two example pairs. Two types of translation templates, i.e. *generalized* and *atomic* templates, are extracted by applying this approach. A generalized translation template replaces similar or differing sequences with variables while an atomic translation template does not contain any variable. The atomic translation templates are used as additional phrase pairs for our Hybrid MT system. This particular approach has a cubic runtime complexity with respect to the number of sentences in the parallel corpus. It takes a significant amount of time to extract phrase pairs even from a small corpus. Therefore we used heuristics to reduce the time complexity. We divided the entire corpus into n clusters based on sentence length such that similar length sentences belong to the same cluster. We extract atomic translations from each of these clusters. For this task, we applied EBMT phrases as addition parallel training example to explicitly enhanced the word alignment model of the MT pipeline.

2.2 Hybrid System

The Hybrid approach is investigated by combining multiple knowledge sources such as NEA, EBMT Phrases and MWEs and followed different strategies. As mentioned earlier, we implemented several different systems, namely:

(1) Baseline **PB-SMT**,

(2) Baseline PB-SMT with NE alignment (**NEA**),

(3) NEA with EBMT phrase extraction (**NEA–EBMT**),

(4) NEA with EBMT phrase extraction and single-tokenised MWE (**NEA–EBMT–MWE**) and

(5) **LM–NEA–EBMT–MWE** hybrid system (see Section 2.2.1).

The baseline SMT system is trained on the cleaned English-German parallel corpus. The NEA system makes use of NE aligned parallel data as additional parallel examples. Similarly, EBMT phrase pairs as well as NE aligned data are also used as additional training example in the NEA–EBMT system. The NEA–EBMT–MWE system is very similar to the above mentioned the NEA–EBMT system, the only difference being that the identified source side English MWEs are converted into single tokens for NEA–EBMT–MWE. In order to achieve optimal performance from the component modules, we finally generated a composite translation output using confusion network-based system combination (cf. Section 2.3).

2.2.1 LM-NEA-EBMT-SMT hybrid system

In this system, we experiment with the above described models with varying size of monolingual data. We experimented with 4 folds of monolingual data to train the language Models (LM):

- LM_1: Only using the target side (i.e. German) of the parallel training data (L) for language modeling
- LM_2: L + double size of L in terms of number of sentences, collected from the cleaned monolingual corpus
- LM_3: L + triple size of L from the cleaned monolingual corpus
- LM_4: L + all the cleaned monolingual data

Therefore, finally there were 16 different systems (4 systems, i.e., Baseline, NEA, NEA–EBMT and NEA–EBMT–MWE, each with 4 LM settings) output available for system combination.

2.2.2 Post-processing

As a final step, we try to generate translations of out-of-vocabulary (OOV) words that remain untranslated in the output. These OOV words may include some NEs that are already there in the parallel NE list, however they might remain untranslated during decoding. Our system post processed the output by replacing each such OOV NE with the corresponding target language NE after looking up the extracted NE list from the parallel corpus (cf. Section 2.1.2).

2.3 System Combination

System Combination is a technique, which combines translation hypotheses (outputs) produced by multiple MT systems. We applied a system combination method on the outputs of the different MT system described earlier. We implement the Minimum Bayes Risk coupled with Confusion Network (MBR-CN) framework described in (Du et al., 2009). The MBR decoder (Kumar and Byrne, 2004) selects the single best hypothesis from amongst the multiple candidate translations by minimising BLEU (Papineni et al., 2002) loss. This single best hypothesis serves as the backbone (also referred to as skeleton) of the confusion network and determines the general word order of the confusion network. A confusion network (Matusov et al., 2006) is built from the backbone while the remaining hypotheses are aligned against the backbone using METEOR (Lavie and Agarwal, 2007) and the TER metric (Snover et al., 2006). The features used to score each arc in the confusion network are word posterior probability, target language model (3-gram, 4-gram), and length penalties. Minimum Error Rate Training (MERT) (Och, 2003) is applied to tune the CN weights (Pal et al., 2014).

3 Experiment Setup

3.1 Baseline Settings

The effectiveness of the present work is demonstrated by using the standard log-linear PB-SMT model as our baseline system. For building the baseline system, we used a maximum phrase length of 7 and a 5-gram language model. The other experimental settings were: SymGIZA++ aligner (Junczys-Dowmunt and Szał, 2012), which is a modified version of GIZA++ word alignment models by updating the symmetrizing models between chosen iterations of the original word alignment training algorithms and phrase-extraction (Koehn et al., 2003). The reordering model was trained on hier-mslr-bidirectional (i.e. using both forward and backward models) and conditioned on both source and target language. The reordering model was built by calculating the probabilities of the phrase pairs being associated with the given orientation such as monotone (m), swap (s) and discontinuous (d). The 5-gram target language model was trained using KENLM (Heafield, 2011). Parameter tuning was carried out using both k-best MIRA (Cherry and Foster, 2012) and Minimum Error Rate Training (MERT) (Och, 2003) on a held-out development set. After the parameters were tuned, decoding was carried out on the held out testset.

Note that all the systems described in Section 2 employ the same PB-SMT settings (apart from the feature weights which are obtained via MERT) as the Baseline system.

4 Results and Analysis

As described in Section 2.2.1, we developed 16 different systems. Instead of using all these 16 different systems, we apply only the 6 best performing systems for system combination. Performance is measured on the devset. Table 1 reports the final evaluation results obtained on the test dataset. The best 6 systems are as follows:

- System 1: NEA–EBMT (selective high frequency phrases) with baseline PB-SMT settings and LM_1.
- System 2: System 1 experimental settings + single tokenised source MWEs (i.e. **NEA–EBMT–MWE**, cf. Section 2.2).
- System 3: System 2 with MIRA-MERT coupled tuning.
- System 4: System 3 with LM_2.
- System 5: System 3 with LM_3.
- System 6: System 3 with LM_4.

System 6 provides the individual best system. System combination (System-7 in Table 1) of the 6 best performing individual systems brings considerable improvements over each of the individual component systems.

5 Conclusions and Future Work

A hybrid system (System 6) with NE alignment, EBMT phrases, single-tokenized source MWEs, and MIRA-MERT coupled tuning results in the best performing system. However, confusion

Systems	BLEU	BLEU(Cased)	TER
Baseline	16.7	16.2	89.6
System 1	18.1	17.5	88.2
System 2	18.1	17.6	87.8
System 3	19.0	18.4	85.3
System 4	20.0	19.5	84.1
System 5	20.3	19.7	83.8
System 6	20.7	20.2	83.5
System 7	**22.6**	**22.1**	**82.3**

Table 1: Results.

network-based system combination outperforms all the individual MT systems. The fact that the systems were tuned with BLEU scores may be one of the reasons behind the poor TER scores produced by the systems. In future, we will carry out in depth investigation of the impacts of MWEs within the current experimental settings. We will also analyze the usability and contribution of the novel EBMT phrases in the SMT decoder.

Acknowledgments

The research leading to these results has received funding from the EU FP7 Project EXPERT - the People Programme (Marie Curie Actions) (Grant No. 317471)

References

Peter F Brown, Vincent J Della Pietra, Stephen A Della Pietra, and Robert L Mercer. 1993. The Mathematics of Statistical Machine Translation: Parameter Estimation. *Computational linguistics*, 19(2):263–311.

Michael Carl and Andy Way. 2003. *Recent advances in example-based machine translation*, volume 21. Springer Science & Business Media.

Colin Cherry and George Foster. 2012. Batch Tuning Strategies for Statistical Machine Translation. In *Proceedings of the 2012 Conference of the North American Chapter of the Association for Computational Linguistics: Human Language Technologies*, pages 427–436.

Ilyas Cicekli and H Altay Güvenir. 2001. Learning Translation Templates From Bilingual Translation Examples. *Applied Intelligence*, 15(1):57–76.

Jinhua Du, Yifan He, Sergio Penkale, and Andy Way. 2009. MATREX: The DCU MT System for WMT 2009. In *Proceedings of the 4th Workshop on Statistical Machine Translation*, pages 95–99, March.

Kenneth Heafield. 2011. KenLM: Faster and Smaller Language Model Queries. In *Proceedings of the Sixth Workshop on Statistical Machine Translation*, pages 187–197.

Ray Jackendoff. 1997. *The architecture of the language faculty*. Number 28. MIT Press.

Marcin Junczys-Dowmunt and Arkadiusz Szał. 2012. SyMGiza++: Symmetrized Word Alignment Models for Statistical Machine Translation. In *Proceedings of the 2011 International Conference on Security and Intelligent Information Systems*, pages 379–390.

Philipp Koehn, Franz Josef Och, and Daniel Marcu. 2003. Statistical Phrase-based Translation. In *Proceedings of the 2003 Conference of the North American Chapter of the Association for Computational Linguistics on Human Language Technology*, pages 48–54.

Philipp Koehn. 2010. *Statistical Machine Translation*. Cambridge University Press, New York, NY, USA, 1st edition.

Shankar Kumar and William Byrne. 2004. Minimum Bayes Risk Decoding for Statistical Machine Translation. In *Proceedings of the North American Association for Computational Linguistics (NAACL)*, pages 169–176, March.

Alon Lavie and Abhaya Agarwal. 2007. METEOR: An Automatic Metric for MT Evaluation with High Levels of Correlation with Human Judgments. In *Proceedings of the Second Workshop on Statistical Machine Translation*, pages 228–231.

Evgeny Matusov, Nicola Ueffing, and Hermann Ney. 2006. Computing Consensus Translation from Multiple Machine Translation Systems Using Enhanced Hypotheses Alignment. In *Conference of the European Chapter of the Association for Computational Linguistics*, pages 33–40, Trento, Italy, April.

Franz Josef Och. 2003. Minimum Error Rate Training in Statistical Machine Translation. In *Proceedings of the 41st Annual Meeting on Association for Computational Linguistics - Volume 1*, pages 160–167.

Santanu Pal, Sudip Kumar Naskar, Pavel Pecina, Sivaji Bandyopadhyay, and Andy Way. 2010. Handling Named Entities and Compound Verbs in Phrase-Based Statistical Machine Translation. In *In Proceedings of the of Multiword Expression Workshop (MWE-2010)*. The 23rd International conference of computational linguistics (Coling 2010).

Santanu Pal, Tanmoy Chakraborty, and Sivaji Bandyopadhyay. 2011. Handling Multiword Expressions in Phrase-Based Statistical Machine Translation. *Machine Translation Summit XIII*, pages 215–224.

Santanu Pal, Sudip Kumar Naskar, and Sivaji Bandyopadhyay. 2013. MWE Alignment in Phrase Based Statistical Machine Translation. *The XIV Machine Translation Summit*, pages 61–68.

Santanu Pal, Ankit Srivastava, Sandipan Dandapat, Josef van Genabith, Qun Liu, and Andy Way. 2014. USAAR-DCU Hybrid Machine Translation System for ICON 2014. In *Proceedings of the 11th International Conference on Natural Language Processing*, Goa, India.

Kishore Papineni, Salim Roukos, Todd Ward, and Wei-Jing Zhu. 2002. BLEU: A Method for Automatic Evaluation of Machine Translation. In *Proceedings of the 40th Annual Meeting on Association for Computational Linguistics*, ACL '02, pages 311–318.

Ivan A Sag, Timothy Baldwin, Francis Bond, Ann Copestake, and Dan Flickinger. 2002. Multiword Expressions: A Pain in the Neck for NLP. In *Computational Linguistics and Intelligent Text Processing*, pages 1–15. Springer.

Nakatani Shuyo. 2010. Language Detection Library for Java.

Matthew Snover, Bonnie Dorr, Richard Schwartz, Linnea Micciulla, and John Makhoul. 2006. A study of Translation Edit Rate with Targeted Human Annotation. In *Proceedings of association for machine translation in the Americas*, pages 223–231.

Liling Tan and Santanu Pal. 2014. Manawi: Using Multi-word Expressions and Named Entities to Improve Machine Translation. In *Proceedings of Ninth Workshop on Statistical Machine Translation*.

Stephan Vogel, Hermann Ney, and Christoph Tillmann. 1996. HMM-based word alignment in statistical translation. In *Proceedings of the 16th conference on Computational linguistics-Volume 2*, pages 836–841. Association for Computational Linguistics.

The RWTH Aachen German-English Machine Translation System for WMT 2015

Jan-Thorsten Peter, Farzad Toutounchi, Joern Wuebker and Hermann Ney
Human Language Technology and Pattern Recognition Group
Computer Science Department
RWTH Aachen University
D-52056 Aachen, Germany
<surname>@cs.rwth-aachen.de

Abstract

This paper describes the statistical machine translation system developed at RWTH Aachen University for the German→English translation task of the *EMNLP 2015 Tenth Workshop on Statistical Machine Translation* (WMT 2015). A phrase-based machine translation system was applied and augmented with hierarchical phrase reordering and word class language models. Further, we ran discriminative maximum expected BLEU training for our system. In addition, we utilized multiple feed-forward neural network language and translation models and a recurrent neural network language model for reranking.

1 Introduction

For the WMT 2015 shared translation task[1], RWTH utilized a state-of-the-art phrase-based translation system. We participated in the German→English translation task. The system included a hierarchical reordering model, a word class (cluster) language model, and discriminative maximum expected BLEU training. Further, we reranked the nbest lists produced by our system with three feed-forward neural network models and a recurrent neural language model.

This paper is structured as follows: First, we briefly describe our preprocessing pipeline for the language pair German→English in Section 2, which is based on our 2014 pipeline. Next, morpho-syntactic analysis for preprocessing the data is described in Section 2.3. Different alignment methods are discussed in Section 3. In Section 4, we present a summary of all methods used in our submission. More details are given about the language models (Section 4.2), maximum expected BLEU training (Section 4.4), the hierarchical reordering model (Section 4.5), feed-forward neural network training (Section 4.6), and recurrent neural network language model (Section 4.7). Experimental results are discussed in Section 5. We conclude the paper in Section 6.

[1] http://www.statmt.org/wmt15/translation-task.html

2 Preprocessing

In this section we briefly describe our preprocessing pipeline, which is a modification of our WMT 2014 German→English preprocessing pipeline (Peitz et al., 2014).

2.1 Categorization

We worked on the categorization of the digits and written numbers for the translation task. All written numbers were categorized. As the training data and also the test sets contain several errors for numbers in the source as well as in the target part, we put effort into producing correct English numbers. In addition, ',' and '.' marks were inverted in most cases, as in German the former mark is the decimal mark and the latter is the thousand separator.

2.2 Remove Foreign Languages

The WMT German→English Common Crawl corpora contains bilingual sentence pairs with non-German source or non-English target sentences. By using an ASCII filtering, we removed all sentences with more than 5% non-ASCII characters from the Common Crawl corpus. Chinese, Arabic and Russian are among the languages which can be easily filtered by deleting the sentences containing too many non-ASCII words. Our experiments showed that the translation quality does not change by removing sentences with wrong languages. Nevertheless, this method reduced the training data size and also the vocabulary size without introducing any degradation in translation

Table 1: Comparison of a simple GIZA++ alignment vs. merging multiple alignments. Even though the multiple alignment approach did not improve the GIZA++ alignment for the baseline system, it improved translation quality in combination with a neural network joint model (NNJM). BLEU and TER are given in percentage.

	newstest2011		newstest2012		newstest2013		newstest2014	
	BLEU	TER	BLEU	TER	BLEU	TER	BLEU	TER
GIZA++	23.1	58.8	23.7	58.2	26.5	54.7	25.9	54.2
+ NNJM	23.3	58.4	24.0	57.7	26.6	54.3	26.2	53.7
Multiple alignment	23.0	58.9	23.8	58.2	26.6	54.6	25.9	54.2
+ NNJM	23.3	58.4	24.1	57.8	27.0	54.3	26.3	53.8

quality. Further, this method prevents us from generating words from these languages.

2.3 Compound Splitting and POS-based Word Reordering

We reduced the source vocabulary size for the German→English translation and split the German compound words with the frequency-based method described in Koehn and Knight (2003). To reduce translation complexity, we employed the long-range part-of-speech based reordering rules proposed by Popović and Ney (2006). In this regard, we did no further morphological analysis in our preprocessing pipeline.

3 Alignment

We experimented with creating multiple alignments and merging them via a majority vote. For the majority voting to work in a meaningful way we need obviously more than two different alignments. A larger number of alignments gives us more confidence that the alignment points are correct.

To create these different alignments, we used `fast_align` (Dyer et al., 2013) and two implementations of GIZA++ (Och and Ney, 2003). The alignment was trained in both source to target direction and target to source direction. To double the number of alignments, we trained each setup also with a reverse ordered source side and reversed it back after the alignment process finished (Freitag et al., 2013). Using a reversed source side usually creates a different alignment since the word order influences the results of `fast_align` and GIZA++. This gave us a total of 12 different alignments (three toolkits × two translation directions × two source side direction). These alignments were merged by keeping all alignment points generated by at least 5 of the methods.

We compared this setup with an alignment generated by GIZA++. The voting setup did not improve directly on the baseline system as shown in Table 1. However, in combination with a feed-forward neural network joint model (Section 4.6) the results on `newstest2013` improved by 0.4% BLEU after reranking. We stuck in the following experiments to the multiple alignments approach.

4 Translation System

In this evaluation, we used the open source machine translation toolkit *Jane*[2] (Vilar et al., 2012; Wuebker et al., 2012). This open-source toolkit was developed at the RWTH Aachen University and includes a phrase-based decoder used in all of our experiments.

4.1 Phrase-based System

Our phrase based decoder includes an implementation of the source cardinality synchronous search procedure described in Zens and Ney (2008). We used the standard set of models with phrase translation probabilities, lexical smoothing in both directions, word and phrase penalty, distance-based distortion model, a 4-gram target language model and enhanced low frequency feature (Chen et al., 2011). Additional models used in this evaluation were the hierarchical reordering model (*HRM*) (Galley and Manning, 2008) and a word class language model (*wcLM*) (Wuebker et al., 2013). The parameter weights were optimized with minimum error rate training (MERT) (Och, 2003). The op-

[2]`http://www.hltpr.rwth-aachen.de/jane/`

timization criterion was BLEU (Papineni et al., 2002).

4.2 Language Models

We used a 4-gram language model trained on the target side of the bilingual data, $\frac{1}{2}$ of the Shuffled News Crawl corpus, $\frac{1}{2}$ of the 10^9 French-English corpus and $\frac{1}{4}$ of the LDC Gigaword Fifth Edition corpus. The monolingual data selection was based on cross-entropy difference as described in Moore and Lewis (2010). For this language model, we trained separate language models using SRILM for each corpus, which were then interpolated. The interpolation weights are tuned by minimizing the perplexity of the interpolated model on the development data. In addition, a word class language model was utilized. We trained 200 classes on the target side of the bilingual training data (Brown et al., 1992; Och, 1999). We used the same data as the 4-gram language model for training a 7-gram wcLM. Furthermore, we also trained a single unpruned language model on the concatenation of all monolingual data using KenLM, which was used as an extra model in our final experiments. All language models used interpolated Kneser-Ney smoothing.

4.3 Evaluation

All setups were evaluated with *MultEval* (Clark et al., 2011). To evaluate our models, we used the average of three MERT optimization runs for case sensitive BLEU (Papineni et al., 2002) and case insensitive TER[3] (Snover et al., 2006).

4.4 Maximum Expected BLEU Training

In our baseline translation system the phrase tables were extracted from word alignments and the probabilities were estimated as relative frequencies, which is still the state-of-the-art for many standard SMT systems. For the WMT 2015 German→English task, we applied discriminative maximum expected BLEU training as described by Wuebker et al. (2015). The expected BLEU objective function is optimized with the resilient backpropagation algorithm (RPROP) (Riedmiller and Braun, 1993). Similar to He and Deng (2012), the objective function is computed on n-best lists (here: $n = 100$) generated by the translation decoder. To avoid over-fitting due to spurious

[3]TER is always evaluated in case insensitive form by MultEval.

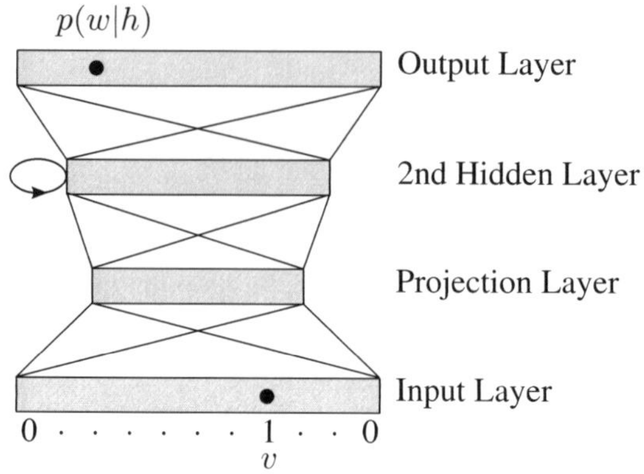

Figure 1: LM neural network

segmentations, we apply a leave-one-out heuristic (Wuebker et al., 2010) during the n-best list generation step. Using these n-best lists, we iteratively trained the phrasal and lexical feature sets, denoted as (a) and (b) in Wuebker et al. (2015). Each of the two feature types are condensed into a single model within the log-linear model combination. After every five iterations we ran MERT, and finally selected the iteration performing best on `newstest2013`. In this work, we used a subset of the training data to generate the n-best lists, namely the concatenation of `newstest2008` through `newstest2010` and the News-Commentary corpus.

4.5 Hierarchical Reordering Model

In Galley and Manning (2008), a hierarchical reordering model for phrase-based machine translation was introduced. The model scores *monotone*, *swap*, and *discontinuous* phrase orientations in the manner of the one presented by Tillmann (2004). The orientation classes are determined based on phrase *blocks*, which can subsume multiple phrase pairs and are computed with an SR-parser. The model has proven effective in previous evaluations. As the word order is more flexible in German compared to English, we expected that an additional reordering model could improve the translation quality.

4.6 Feed-Forward Neural Network Training

We used three feed-forward neural network (*FFNN*) models with a similar structure as the network models used by Devlin et al. (2014) and Le et al. (2012). All networks were trained with different input features:

- Translation Model (TM), the 5 source words around the alignment source word

Table 2: Results for the German→English translation task. The results are the average of three optimization runs. newstest2011 and newstest2012 were used as development data. The submission system used all models and the best optimization run on the development data. BLEU and TER are given in percentage.

	newstest2011		newstest2012		newstest2013		newstest2014	
	BLEU	TER	BLEU	TER	BLEU	TER	BLEU	TER
Baseline	23.0	58.9	23.8	58.2	26.6	54.6	25.9	54.2
+ max. exp. BLEU	23.1	58.6	24.0	57.8	26.8	54.4	26.2	53.9
+ updated LM	23.2	58.7	24.0	57.9	26.8	54.3	26.3	53.7
+ unpruned LM	23.2	59.0	24.1	58.1	26.9	54.6	26.6	54.0
+ 3 × FFNN	23.7	58.4	24.5	57.7	27.4	54.0	27.1	53.3
+ LSTM	23.8	58.4	24.7	57.4	27.5	53.8	27.1	53.2
Submission System	24.1	57.6	25.0	56.5	28.1	52.9	27.6	52.3

- Language Model (LM), the 7 last words on the target side
- Joint Model (JM), the 5 source words around the alignment source word and the 4 last words on the target side

The TM and LM were trained with two hidden layers (1000 and 500 nodes) while the JM contained three hidden layers with 2000 nodes each. The output layer was in all cases a softmax layer with a short list of 10000. All remaining words were clustered into 1000 classes and their class probabilities were predicted. The neural networks were applied to rerank 1000-best lists.

4.7 Recurrent Neural Network Language Model

In addition to the feed-forward neural network model we employed a recurrent neural network model. The recurrency was handled with the long short-term memory (*LSTM*) architecture (Hochreiter and Schmidhuber, 1997) and we used a class-factored output layer for increased efficiency as described in Sundermeyer et al. (2012). The topology of the network is illustrated in Figure 1. All neural network models were trained on the bilingual data with 2000 word classes. The language models were set up with 500 nodes in both the projection layer and the hidden LSTM layer. The recurrent network models were applied together with the feed-forward models to rerank 1000-best lists.

5 Setup

We trained the phrase-based system on all available bilingual training data. The preprocessed bilingual corpus contained around 4 million sentences. The preprocessed data contained a source vocabulary size of 814K and a target vocabulary size of 733K.

We used the target side of the bilingual data along with the monolingual corpora for training the language models. First, we started using our old language models from our WMT 2014 setup as baseline. Then we updated our system to the new language models trained according to Section 4.2. All results are reported as average of three optimization runs.

5.1 Experimental Results

The results of the phrase-based system are summarized in Table 2. It was tuned on the concatenation of newstest2011 and newstest2012.

The phrase-based baseline system, which included the hierarchical reordering model (Galley and Manning, 2008) and a word class language model (*wcLM*) (Wuebker et al., 2013), reached a performance of 25.9% BLEU on newstest2014. Maximum expected BLEU training selected on newstest2013 improved the results on newstest2014 by 0.3% BLEU absolute.

There was improvement of 0.1% in BLEU on newstest2014 by replacing the old language models from WMT 2014 with an updated general 4-gram LM and word class LM. Furthermore, adding an extra unpruned language model trained on the concatenation of the monolingual data improved the results on newstest2014 by 0.3% BLEU.

Adding three feed-forward neural network models yielded an improvement of 0.5% BLEU on `newstest2013` and `newstest2014`. Adding the LSTM language model improved the TER by an additional 0.1% on `newstest2014` and by 0.2% on `newstest2013`.

The submission system used all models and we chose the best optimization run on the development data. This optimization run by itself was 0.5% BLEU stronger on `newstest2014` compared to the average across three optimization runs which included this run.

6 Conclusion

For the participation in the WMT 2015 shared translation task, RWTH experimented with a phrase-based translation system. For this approach, we applied a hierarchical phrase reordering model and a word class language model. `fast_align` and two versions of GIZA++ were used for training word alignments, and a voting setup was implemented, which improved the results in combination with neural network models. We also employed discriminative maximum expected BLEU training. Additionally, we utilized feed-forward and recurrent neural networks models for our phrase-based system, which improved the performance. Furthermore, we adapted our preprocessing pipeline based on our WMT 2014 setup. Filtering the corpus for non-ASCII letters gave us lower vocabulary sizes for both source and target side without loss in performance.

Acknowledgments

This paper has received funding from the European Union's Horizon 2020 research and innovation programme under grant agreement n^{0} 645452 (QT21). We further thank the anonymous reviewers for their valuable comments.

References

Peter F. Brown, Vincent J. Della Pietra, P. V. deSouza deSouza, J. C. Lai, and Robert L. Mercer. 1992. Class-Based n-gram Models of Natural Language. *Computational Linguistics*, 18(4):467–479.

Boxing Chen, Roland Kuhn, George Foster, and Howard Johnson. 2011. Unpacking and transforming feature functions: New ways to smooth phrase tables. In *MT Summit XIII*, pages 269–275, Xiamen, China, September.

Jonathan H. Clark, Chris Dyer, Alon Lavie, and Noah A. Smith. 2011. Better hypothesis testing for statistical machine translation: Controlling for optimizer instability. In *Proceedings of the 49th Annual Meeting of the Association for Computational Linguistics: Human Language Technologies: Short Papers - Volume 2*, HLT '11, pages 176–181, Stroudsburg, PA, USA. Association for Computational Linguistics.

Jacob Devlin, Rabih Zbib, Zhongqiang Huang, Thomas Lamar, Richard Schwartz, and John Makhoul. 2014. Fast and robust neural network joint models for statistical machine translation. In *Proceedings of the 52nd Annual Meeting of the Association for Computational Linguistics (Volume 1: Long Papers)*, pages 1370–1380, Baltimore, Maryland, June. Association for Computational Linguistics.

Chris Dyer, Victor Chahuneau, and Noah A. Smith. 2013. A simple, fast, and effective reparametrization of ibm model 2. In *Proceedings of the NAACL 7th Workshop on Syntax, Semantics and Structure in Statistical Translation*, Atlanta, Georgia, USA, June.

Markus Freitag, Minwei Feng, Matthias Huck, Stephan Peitz, and Hermann Ney. 2013. Reverse word order models. In *Machine Translation Summit*, pages 159–166, Nice, France, September.

Michel Galley and Christopher D. Manning. 2008. A Simple and Effective Hierarchical Phrase Reordering Model. In *Proceedings of the 2008 Conference on Empirical Methods in Natural Language Processing*, pages 847–855, Honolulu, Hawaii, USA, October.

Xiaodong He and Li Deng. 2012. Maximum Expected BLEU Training of Phrase and Lexicon Translation Models. In *Proceedings of the 50th Annual Meeting of the Association for Computational Linguistics (ACL)*, pages 292–301, Jeju, Republic of Korea, Jul.

Sepp Hochreiter and Jürgen Schmidhuber. 1997. Long short-term memory. *Neural Computation*, 9(8):1735–1780.

Philipp Koehn and Kevin Knight. 2003. Empirical Methods for Compound Splitting. In *Proceedings of European Chapter of the ACL (EACL 2009)*, pages 187–194.

Hai-Son Le, Alexandre Allauzen, and François Yvon. 2012. Continuous space translation models with neural networks. pages 39–48, Montréal, Canada, June. Association for Computational Linguistics.

Robert C. Moore and William Lewis. 2010. Intelligent Selection of Language Model Training Data. In *ACL (Short Papers)*, pages 220–224, Uppsala, Sweden, July.

Franz Josef Och and Hermann Ney. 2003. A Systematic Comparison of Various Statistical Alignment Models. *Computational Linguistics*, 29(1):19–51, March.

Franz Josef Och. 1999. An Efficient Method for Determining Bilingual Word Classes. In *Proc. 9th Conf. of the Europ. Chapter of the Assoc. for Computational Linguistics*, pages 71–76, Bergen, Norway, June.

Franz Josef Och. 2003. Minimum Error Rate Training in Statistical Machine Translation. In *Proc. of the 41th Annual Meeting of the Association for Computational Linguistics (ACL)*, pages 160–167, Sapporo, Japan, July.

Kishore Papineni, Salim Roukos, Todd Ward, and Wei-Jing Zhu. 2002. Bleu: a Method for Automatic Evaluation of Machine Translation. In *Proceedings of the 41st Annual Meeting of the Association for Computational Linguistics*, pages 311–318, Philadelphia, Pennsylvania, USA, July.

Stephan Peitz, Joern Wuebker, Markus Freitag, and Hermann Ney. 2014. The RWTH Aachen German-English Machine Translation System for WMT 2014. In *Proceedings of the ACL 2014 Ninth Workshop on Statistical Machine Translation*, Baltimore, MD, USA, June.

Maja Popović and Hermann Ney. 2006. POS-based Word Reorderings for Statistical Machine Translation. In *International Conference on Language Resources and Evaluation*, pages 1278–1283, Genoa, Italy, May.

Martin Riedmiller and Heinrich Braun. 1993. A direct adaptive method for faster backpropagation learning: The rprop algorithm. In *IEEE International Conference on Neural Networks*, pages 586–591.

Matthew Snover, Bonnie Dorr, Richard Schwartz, Linnea Micciulla, and John Makhoul. 2006. A Study of Translation Edit Rate with Targeted Human Annotation. In *Proceedings of the 7th Conference of the Association for Machine Translation in the Americas*, pages 223–231, Cambridge, Massachusetts, USA, August.

Martin Sundermeyer, Ralf Schlüter, and Hermann Ney. 2012. Lstm neural networks for language modeling. In *Interspeech*, Portland, OR, USA, September.

Christoph Tillmann. 2004. A Unigram Orientation Model for Statistical Machine Translation. In *Proceedings of HLT-NAACL 2004: Short Papers*, HLT-NAACL-Short '04, pages 101–104, Boston, MA, USA.

David Vilar, Daniel Stein, Matthias Huck, and Hermann Ney. 2012. Jane: an advanced freely available hierarchical machine translation toolkit. *Machine Translation*, 26(3):197–216, September.

Joern Wuebker, Arne Mauser, and Hermann Ney. 2010. Training phrase translation models with leaving-one-out. In *Proceedings of the 48th Annual Meeting of the Assoc. for Computational Linguistics*, pages 475–484, Uppsala, Sweden, July.

Joern Wuebker, Matthias Huck, Stephan Peitz, Malte Nuhn, Markus Freitag, Jan-Thorsten Peter, Saab Mansour, and Hermann Ney. 2012. Jane 2: Open Source Phrase-based and Hierarchical Statistical Machine Translation. In *International Conference on Computational Linguistics*, pages 483–491, Mumbai, India, December.

Joern Wuebker, Stephan Peitz, Felix Rietig, and Hermann Ney. 2013. Improving statistical machine translation with word class models. In *Conference on Empirical Methods in Natural Language Processing*, pages 1377–1381, Seattle, USA, October.

Joern Wuebker, Sebastian Muehr, Patrick Lehnen, Stephan Peitz, and Hermann Ney. 2015. A comparison of update strategies for large-scale maximum expected bleu training. In *Conference of the North American Chapter of the Association for Computational Linguistics: Human Language Technologies*, pages 1516–1526, Denver, CO, USA, May.

Richard Zens and Hermann Ney. 2008. Improvements in Dynamic Programming Beam Search for Phrase-based Statistical Machine Translation. In *International Workshop on Spoken Language Translation*, pages 195–205, Honolulu, Hawaii, USA, October.

Exact Decoding with Multi Bottom-Up Tree Transducers*

Daniel Quernheim
Institut für Maschinelle Sprachverarbeitung
University of Stuttgart
daniel@ims.uni-stuttgart.de

Abstract

We present an experimental statistical tree-to-tree machine translation system based on the multi-bottom up tree transducer including rule extraction, tuning and decoding. Thanks to input parse forests and a "no pruning" strategy during decoding, the obtained translations are competitive. The drawbacks are a restricted coverage of 70% on test data, in part due to exact input parse tree matching, and a relatively high runtime. Advantages include easy redecoding with a different weight vector, since the full translation forests can be stored after the first decoding pass.

1 Introduction

In this contribution, we present an implementation of a translation model that is based on ℓ-XMBOT (the multi bottom-up tree transducer of Arnold and Dauchet (1982) and Lilin (1978)).[1] Intuitively, an MBOT is a synchronous tree sequence substitution grammar (STSSG, Zhang et al. (2008a); Zhang et al. (2008b); Sun et al. (2009)) that has discontiguities only on the target side (Maletti, 2011). From an algorithmic point of view, this makes the MBOT more appealing than STSSG as demonstrated by Maletti (2010). Formally, MBOT is expressive enough to express all sensible translations (Maletti, 2012)[2]. Figure 2 displays sample rules of the MBOT variant, called ℓ-XMBOT, that we use (in a graphical representation of the trees and the alignment). Recently, a shallow version of MBOT has been integrated into the popular Moses toolkit (Braune et al., 2013). Our implementation is exact in the sense that it does absolutely no pruning during decoding and thus preserves all translation candidates, while having no mechanism to handle unknown structures. (We added dummy rules that leave unseen lexical material untranslated.) The coverage is thus limited, but still considerably high. Source-side and target-side syntax restrict the search space so that decoding stays tractable. Only the language model scoring is implemented as a separate reranker. This has several advantages: (1) We can use input parse forests (Liu et al., 2009). (2) Not only is the output optimal with regard to the theoretical model, also the space of translation candidates can be efficiently stored as a weighted regular tree grammar. The best translations can then be extracted using the k-best algorithm by Huang and Chiang (2005). Rule weights can be changed without the need for explicit redecoding, the parameters of the log-linear model can be changed, and even new features can be added. These properties are especially helpful in tuning, where only the k-best algorithm has to be re-run in each iteration. A model in similar spirit has been described by Huang et al. (2006); however, it used target syntax only (using a top-down tree-to-string transducer backwards), and was restricted to sentences of length at most 25. We do not make such restrictions.

The theoretical aspects of ℓ-XMBOT and their use in our translation model are presented in Section 2. Based on this, we implemented a machine translation system that we are going to make available to the public. Section 4 presents the most important components of our ℓ-XMBOT implemen-

*This work was supported by Deutsche Forschungsgemeinschaft grant MA/4959/1–1.

[1]The system presented in this paper is variant of the system presented at last year's workshop (Quernheim and Cap, 2014), without morphological enhancements.

[2]A translation is sensible if it is of linear size increase and can be computed by some (potentially copying) top-down tree transducer.

tation, and Section 5 presents our submission to the WMT15 shared translation task.

2 Theoretical Model

In this section, we present the theoretical generative model that is used in our approach to syntax-based machine translation: the multi bottom-up tree transducer (Maletti, 2011). It is a variant of the linear and nondeleting extended multi bottom-up tree transducers without states. We omit the technical details and give graphical examples only to illustrate how the device works, but refer to the literature for the theoretical background. Roughly speaking, a local multi bottom-up tree transducer (ℓMBOT) has rules that replace one nonterminal symbol N on the source side by a tree, and a sequence of nonterminal symbols on the target side linked to N by one tree each. These trees again have linked nonterminals, thus allowing further rule applications.

Our ℓMBOT rules are obtained automatically from data like that in Figure 1. Thus, we (word) align the bilingual text and parse it in both the source and the target language. In this manner we obtain sentence pairs like the one shown in Figure 1. To these sentence pairs we apply the rule extraction method of Maletti (2011). The rules extracted from the sentence pair of Figure 1 are shown in Figure 2. Note the discontiguous alignment of *went* to *ist* and *gegangen*, resulting in discontiguous rules.

The application of those rules is illustrated in Figure 3 (a *pre-translation* is a pair consisting of a source tree and a sequence of target trees). While it shows a synchronous derivation, our main use case of ℓMBOT rules is *forward application* or *input restriction*, that is the calculation of all target trees that can be derived given a source tree. For a given synchronous derivation d, the source tree generated by d is $s(d)$, and the target tree is $t(d)$. The yield of a tree is the string obtained by concatenating its leaves.

The theoretical justification for decomposing the translation model into a source model and a target model is a theorem that states that every ℓMBOT can be replaced by a composition of a linear nondeleting extended top-down tree transducer (XTOP) and a linear homomorphic MBOT (Engelfriet et al., 2009). We implemented the first step of the composition as an XTOP that generates possible derivation trees. States in this device are linked nonterminals in the ℓMBOT rules, and it translates left-hand sides into rule identifiers. The second step is implemented as a homomorphic multi bottom-up tree transducer. While we construct the first step of the composition explicitly, we only use the second device to evaluate single trees.

Apart from ℓMBOT application to input trees, we can even apply ℓMBOT to *parse forests* and even *weighted regular tree grammars* (RTGs) (Fülöp and Vogler, 2009). RTGs offer an efficient representation of weighted forests, which are sets of trees such that each individual tree is equipped with a weight. This representation is even more efficient than packed forests (Mi et al., 2008) and moreover can represent an infinite number of weighted trees. The most important property that we utilize is that the output tree language is regular, so we can represent it by an RTG (cf. preservation of regularity (Maletti, 2011)). Indeed, every input tree can only be transformed into finitely many output trees by our model, so for a given finite input forest (which the output of the parser is) the computed output forest will also be finite and thus regular.

3 Translation Model

Given a source language sentence e and corresponding weighted parse forest $F(e)$, our translation model aims to find the best corresponding target language translation $\hat{g}$;[3] i.e.,

$$\hat{g} = \arg\max_g p(g|e) \ .$$

We estimate the probability $p(g|e)$ through a log-linear combination of component models with parameters λ_m scored on the derivations d such that the source tree $s(d)$ of d is in the parse forest of e and the yield of the target tree $t(d)$ reads g. With

$$D(e,g) = \{d \mid s(d) \in F(e) \text{ and } \text{yield}(t(d)) = g\},$$

we thus have: [4]

$$p(g|e) \propto \sum_{d \in D(e,g)} \prod_{m=1}^{11} h_m(d)^{\lambda_m}$$

Our model uses the following features $h_m(\cdot)$ for a derivation:

[3] Our main translation direction is English to German.

[4] While this is the clean theoretical formulation, we make two approximations to $D(e,g)$: (1) The parser we use returns a pruned parse forest. (2) We only sum over derivations with the same target sentence that actually appear in the k-best list.

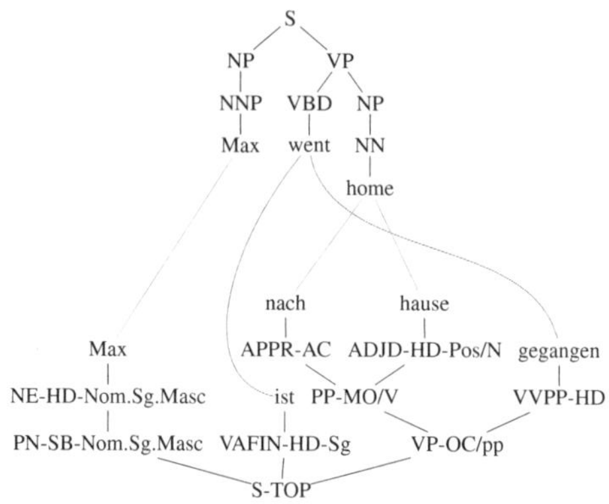

Figure 1: Aligned parsed sentences.

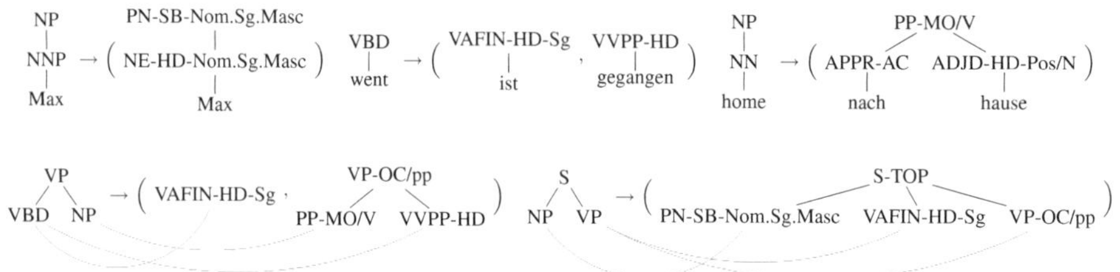

Figure 2: Extracted rules.

(1) Translation weight normalized by source root symbol
(2) Translation weight normalized by all root symbols
(3) Lexical translation weight source $\rightarrow$ target
(4) Lexical translation weight target $\rightarrow$ source
(5) Target side language model: $p(g)$
(6) Input parse tree probability assigned to $s(t)$ by the parser of e

The rule weights required for (1) are relative frequencies normalized over all extracted rules with the same root symbol on the left-hand side. In the same fashion the rule weights required for (2) are relative frequencies normalized over all rules with the same root symbols on both sides. The lexical weights for (3) and (4) are obtained by multiplying the word translations $w(g_i|e_j)$ [respectively, $w(e_j|g_i)$] of lexically aligned words (g_i, e_j) across (possibly discontiguous) target side sequences.[5] Whenever a source word e_j is aligned to multiple target words, we average over the word translations:[6]

$$h_3(d) = \prod_{\substack{\text{lexical item} \\ e \text{ occurs in } s(d)}} \text{average} \, \{w(g|e) \mid g \text{ aligned to } e\}$$

4 Implementation

Our implementation is very close to the theoretical model and consists of several independent components, most of which are implemented in Python. The system does not have any dependencies other than the need for parsers for the source and target language, a word alignment tool and optionally an implementation of some tuning algorithm.

Rule extraction From a parallel corpus of which both halves have been parsed and word aligned, multi bottom-up tree transducer rules are extracted according to the procedure laid out in (Maletti, 2011). In order to handle unknown words, we add dummy identity translation rules for lexical material that was not present in the training data.

[5] The lexical alignments are different from the links used to link nonterminals.

[6] If the word e_j has no alignment to a target word, then it is assumed to be aligned to a special NULL word and this alignment is scored.

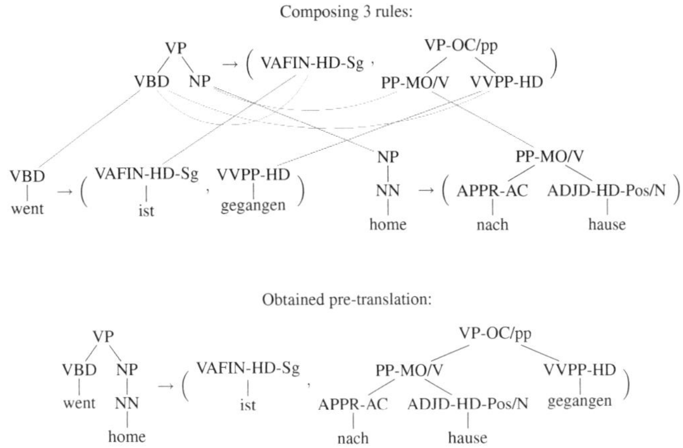

Figure 3: Synchronous rule application.

Translation model building Given a set of rules, translation weights (see above) are computed for each unique rule. The translation model is then converted into a source, a weight and a target model. The source model (an RTG represented in an efficient binary format) is used for decoding and maps input trees to trees over rule identifiers representing derivations. The weight model and the target model can be used to reconstruct the weight and the target realization of a given derivation.

Decoder For every input sentence, the decoder transforms a forest of parse trees to a forest of translation derivations by means of forward application. These derivations are trees over the set of rules (represented by rule identifiers). One of the most useful aspects of our model is the fact that decoding is completely independent of the weights, as no pruning is performed and all translation candidates are preserved in the translation forest. Thus, even after decoding, the weight model can be changed, augmented by new features, etc.; even the target model can be changed, e.g. to support parse tree output instead of string output. In all of our experiments, we used string output, but it is conceivable to use other realizations. For instance, a syntactic language model could be used for output tree scoring. Also, recasing is extremely easy when we have part-of-speech tags to base our decision on (proper names are typically uppercase, as are all nouns in German).

Another benefit of having a packed representation of all candidates is that we can easily check whether the reference translation is included in the candidate set ("force decoding"). The freedom to allow arbitrary target models that rewrite derivations is related to current work on interpreted regular tree grammars (Koller and Kuhlmann, 2011), where arbitrary algebras can be used to compute a realization of the output tree.

k-best extractor From the translation derivation RTGs, a k-best list of derivations can be extracted (Huang and Chiang, 2005) very efficiently. This is the only step that has to be repeated if the rule weights or the parameters of the log-linear model change. The derivations are then mapped to target language sentences (if several derivations realize the same target sentence, their weights are summed) and reranked according to a language model (as was done in Huang et al. (2006)). This is the only part of the pipeline where we deviate from the theoretical log-linear model, and this is where we might make search errors. In principle, one could integrate the language model by intersection with the translation model (as the stateful MBOT model is closed under intersection with finite automata), but this is (currently) not computationally feasible due to the size of models.

Tuning Minimum error rate training (Och, 2003) is implemented using Z-MERT[7] (Zaidan, 2009). A set of source sentences is (forest-)parsed and decoded; the translation forests are stored on disk. Then, in each iteration of Z-MERT, it suffices to extract k-best lists from the translation forests according to the current weight vector.

[7] http://cs.jhu.edu/~ozaidan/zmert/

5 WMT15 Experimental setup

We used the training data that was made available for the WMT15 shared translation task on English–German[8]. It consists of three parallel corpora (1.8M sentences of European parliament proceedings, 216K sentences of newswire text, and 2.3M sentences of web text after cleanup) and additional monolingual news data for language model training.

The English half of the parallel data was parsed using Egret[9] which is a re-implementation of the Berkeley parser (Petrov et al., 2006). For the German parse, we used the BitPar parser (Schmid, 2004; Schmid, 2006). The BitPar German grammar is highly detailed, which makes the syntactic information contained in the parses extremely useful. Part-of-speech tags and category label are augmented by case, number and gender information, as can be seen in the German parse tree in Figure 1. We only kept the best parse for each sentence during training.

We then trained a 5-gram language model on monolingual data using KenLM[10] (Heafield, 2011; Heafield et al., 2013). Word alignment was achieved using the `fast_align`[11] word aligner from `cdec` (Dyer et al., 2010). As usual, we discarded sentence pairs where one sentence was significantly longer than the other, as well as those that were too long or too short.

For tuning, we chose the WMT12 test set (3,003 sentences of newswire text), available as part of the development data for the WMT13 shared translation task. Since our system had limited coverage on this tuning set, we limited ourselves to the first a subset of sentences we could translate.

When translating the test set, our models used parse trees delivered by the Egret parser. After translation, recasing was done by examining the output syntax tree, using a simple heuristics looking for nouns and sentence boundaries as well as common abbreviations. Since coverage on the test set was also limited, we used a simple word-based fallback system whenever an untranslated state was encountered in a derivation tree.

[8] `http://www.statmt.org/wmt15/translation-task.html`

[9] `https://sites.google.com/site/zhangh1982/egret`

[10] `http://kheafield.com/code/kenlm/`

[11] `http://www.cdec-decoder.org/guide/fast_align.html`

BLEU	BLEU-cased	TER
15.3	14.4	.777

Table 1: BLEU and TER scores of our system.

6 Results

We report the overall translation quality, as listed on `http://matrix.statmt.org/`, measured using BLEU (Papineni et al., 2002) and TER (Snover et al., 2006), in Table 1.

Results are significantly worse compared to last year's system which used morphological enhancements such as compound splitting (Quernheim and Cap, 2014) and a phrase-based fallback system for sentences that the exact decoder could not handle. However, we should note that where the fallback system was not needed, we achieved a BLEU score of 16.7.

From a linguistic point of view, constructions that involve long-distance reordering and agreement are typically handled well. Figure 4 shows some example sentences from the WMT13 test set in comparison to a phrase-based baseline system.

On the other hand, our system frequently makes mistakes in lexical choice, and often uses rules that have been extracted from erroneous alignments. Sometimes, these mistakes cannot be alleviated by the language model due to data sparsity (no competing good candidate translation).

7 Conclusion and further work

We presented our submission to the WMT15 shared translation task based on a novel, promising "full syntax, no pruning" tree-to-tree approach to statistical machine translation, inspired by Huang et al. (2006). There are, however, still major drawbacks and open problems associated with our approach. Firstly, the coverage can still be significantly improved. In these experiments, our model was able to translate only 70% of the test sentences. To some extent, this number can be improved by providing more training data. Also, more rules can be extracted if we not only use the best parse for rule extraction, but multiple parse trees, or even switch to forest-based rule extraction (Mi and Huang, 2008). Finally, the size of the input parse forest plays a role. For instance, if we only supply the best parse to our model, translation will fail for approximately half of the input.

However, there are inherent coverage limits. Since our model is extremely strict, it will never

Verb missing:
(M) wir haben zwei spezialisten für ihre stellungnahme *gebeten* .
("we have two specialists for their statement asked .")
(P) wir haben zwei spezialisten für ihre stellungnahme .
("we have two specialists for their statement .")
(R) wir haben die meinung von zwei fachärzten *eingeholt* .
(S) We *asked* two specialists for their opinion.

Plural noun with singular verb:
(M) auch *das technische personal hat* mir sehr viel gebracht .
("also the technical staff has me much brought .")
(P) auch *die technischen mitarbeiter hat* mir sehr viel gebracht .
("also the technical co-workers has me much brought .")
(R) *das technische personal* hat mir ebenfalls viel gegeben .
(S) *The technical staff has* also brought me a lot.

No agreement between noun and adjective:
(M) in diesem sinne werden die maßnahmen zum teil *das amerikanische demokratische system* untergraben .
("in this sense will the measures to part (the american democratic system)$_{NEUT}$ *undermine .")*
(P) in diesem sinne werden die maßnahmen teilweise , *die amerikanischen demokratische system* untergraben .
("in this sense will the measures partially , the$_{FEM}$ *american democratic system*$_{NEUT}$ *undermine .")*
(R) in diesem sinne untergraben diese maßnahmen teilweise *das demokratische system der usa* .
(S) In this sense, the measures will partially undermine *the American democratic system*.

Long-distance reordering:
(M) er zögert nicht , zu antworten , dass er einen antrag von einer unbekannten person nie *akzeptieren würde* .
("he hesitates not , to reply , that he a request from an unknown person never accept would .")
(P) er zögert nicht , sagen , dass er niemals *akzeptieren würde* einen antrag von einer unbekannten person .
("he hesitates not , say , that he never accept would a request from an unknown person .")
(R) gefragt antwortet er , dass er nie eine einladung von einem unbekannten *annehmen würde* .
(S) He does not hesitate to reply that he *would* never *accept* a request from an unknown person.

Garbled output:
(M) wie ich versprochen habe , ist meine tätigkeit teilweise reduziert worden .
("as I promised have , has my activity partially reduced been .")
(P) wie ich ihnen zugesichert hatte , bestätigte , die meine aktivitäten wurden teilweise reduziert .
("as I you assured had , confirmed , the my activities were partially reduced .")
(R) wie versprochen , habe ich meine aktivitäten teilweise zurückgefahren .
(S) As I promised, my activities have been partially reduced.

Figure 4: Examples from the test set where our ℓMBOT system performed better, linguistically speaking; (M = ℓMBOT system; P = phrase-based baseline system; R = reference translation; S = source sentence). Rough interlinear glosses are provided.

be able to translate sentences whose parse trees contain structures it has never seen before, since it has to match at least one input parse tree exactly. While we implemented a simple solution to handle unknown words, the issue with unknown structures is not so easy to solve without breaking the otherwise theoretically sound approach. Possibly, glue rules can help.

The second drawback is runtime. We were able to translate about 20 sentences per hour on one processor. Distributing the translation task on different machines, we were able to translate the WMT15 test set (3k sentences) in roughly three days. Given that the trend goes towards parallel programming, and considering the fact that our decoder is written in the rather slow language Python, we are confident that this is not a major problem. We were able to run the whole pipeline of training, tuning and evaluation on the WMT15 shared task data in less than one week. We are currently investigating whether A* k-best algorithms (Pauls and Klein, 2009; Pauls et al., 2010) can help to guide the translation process while maintaining optimality.

Thirdly, currently the language model is not integrated, but implemented as a separate reranking component. We are aware that an integrated language model might improve translation quality (see e.g. Chiang (2007) where 3–4 BLEU points are gained by LM integration). Some research on this topic already exists, e.g. (Rush and Collins, 2011) who use dual decomposition, and (Aziz et al., 2013) who replace intersection with an upper bound which is easier to compute. It might also be feasible to intersect the language model (represented by a regular string grammar) lazily.

References

André Arnold and Max Dauchet. 1982. Morphismes et bimorphismes d'arbres. *Theoret. Comput. Sci.*, 20(1):33–93.

Wilker Aziz, Marc Dymetman, and Sriram Venkatapathy. 2013. Investigations in exact inference for hierarchical translation. In *Proc. 8th WMT*, pages 472–483.

Fabienne Braune, Nina Seemann, Daniel Quernheim, and Andreas Maletti. 2013. Shallow local multi-bottom-up tree transducers in statistical machine translation. In *Proc. 51th ACL*, pages 811–821.

David Chiang. 2007. Hierarchical phrase-based translation. *Computat. Linguist.*, 33(2):201–228.

Chris Dyer, Adam Lopez, Juri Ganitkevitch, Johnathan Weese, Ferhan Ture, Phil Blunsom, Hendra Setiawan, Vladimir Eidelman, and Philip Resnik. 2010. cdec: A decoder, alignment, and learning framework for finite-state and context-free translation models. In *Proc. 48th ACL*.

Joost Engelfriet, Eric Lilin, and Andreas Maletti. 2009. Extended multi bottom-up tree transducers: Composition and decomposition. *Acta Inf.*, 46(8):561–590, October.

Zoltán Fülöp and Heiko Vogler. 2009. Weighted tree automata and tree transducers. In Manfred Droste, Werner Kuich, and Heiko Vogler, editors, *Handbook of Weighted Automata*, EATCS Monographs on Theoret. Comput. Sci., chapter 9, pages 313–403. Springer.

Kenneth Heafield, Ivan Pouzyrevsky, Jonathan H. Clark, and Philipp Koehn. 2013. Scalable modified Kneser-Ney language model estimation. In *Proc. 51st ACL*.

Kenneth Heafield. 2011. KenLM: faster and smaller language model queries. In *Proc. 6th WMT*, pages 187–197.

Liang Huang and David Chiang. 2005. Better k-best parsing. In *Proc. IWPT*, pages 53–64.

Liang Huang, Kevin Knight, and Aravind Joshi. 2006. Statistical syntax-directed translation with extended domain of locality. In *Proc. 7th Conf. AMTA*, pages 66–73.

Alexander Koller and Marco Kuhlmann. 2011. A generalized view on parsing and translation. In *Proc. IWPT*, pages 2–13.

Eric Lilin. 1978. *Une généralisation des transducteurs d'états finis d'arbres: les S-transducteurs*. Thèse 3ème cycle, Université de Lille.

Yang Liu, Yajuan Lü, and Qun Liu. 2009. Improving tree-to-tree translation with packed forests. In *Proc. 47th ACL*, pages 558–566.

Andreas Maletti. 2010. Why synchronous tree substitution grammars? In *Proc. HLT-NAACL*, pages 876–884.

Andreas Maletti. 2011. How to train your multi bottom-up tree transducer. In *Proc. 49th ACL*, pages 825–834.

Andreas Maletti. 2012. Every sensible extended top-down tree transducer is a multi bottom-up tree transducer. In *Proc. HLT-NAACL*, pages 263–273.

Haitao Mi and Liang Huang. 2008. Forest-based translation rule extraction. In *Proc. EMNLP*, pages 206–214.

Haitao Mi, Liang Huang, and Qun Liu. 2008. Forest-based translation. In *Proc. 46th ACL*, pages 192–199. ACL.

Franz Josef Och. 2003. Minimum error rate training in statistical machine translation. In *Proc. 41st ACL*, pages 160–167.

Kishore Papineni, Salim Roukos, Todd Ward, and Wei jing Zhu. 2002. BLEU: a method for automatic evaluation of machine translation. In *Proc. 40th ACL*, pages 311–318.

Adam Pauls and Dan Klein. 2009. K-best A* parsing. In *Proc. 47th ACL*, pages 958–966.

Adam Pauls, Dan Klein, and Chris Quirk. 2010. Top-down k-best A* parsing. In *Proc. 48th ACL*, pages 200–204.

Slav Petrov, Leon Barrett, Romain Thibaux, and Dan Klein. 2006. Learning accurate, compact, and interpretable tree annotation. In *Proc. COLING-ACL*, pages 433–440.

Daniel Quernheim and Fabienne Cap. 2014. Large-scale exact decoding: The ims-ttt submission to wmt14. In *Proc. 9th WMT*, pages 163–170.

Alexander M. Rush and Michael Collins. 2011. Exact decoding of syntactic translation models through lagrangian relaxation. In *Proc. 49th ACL*, pages 72–82.

Helmut Schmid. 2004. Efficient parsing of highly ambiguous context-free grammars with bit vectors. In *Proc. 20th COLING*, pages 162–168.

Helmut Schmid. 2006. Trace prediction and recovery with unlexicalized PCFGs and slash features. In *Proc. 44th ACL*.

Matthew Snover, Bonnie Dorr, Richard Schwartz, Linnea Micciulla, and John Makhoul. 2006. A study of translation edit rate with targeted human annotation. In *Proc. AMTA*.

Jun Sun, Min Zhang, and Chew Lim Tan. 2009. A non-contiguous tree sequence alignment-based model for statistical machine translation. In *Proc. 47th ACL*, pages 914–922.

Omar F. Zaidan. 2009. Z-MERT: A fully configurable open source tool for minimum error rate training of machine translation systems. *The Prague Bulletin of Mathematical Linguistics*, 91:79–88.

Min Zhang, Hongfei Jiang, Aiti Aw, Haizhou Li, Chew Lim Tan, and Sheng Li. 2008a. A tree sequence alignment-based tree-to-tree translation model. In *Proc. 46th ACL*, pages 559–567.

Min Zhang, Hongfei Jiang, Haizhou Li, Aiti Aw, and Sheng Li. 2008b. Grammar comparison study for translational equivalence modeling and statistical machine translation. In *Proc. 22nd COLING*, pages 1097–1104.

Sheffield Systems for the Finnish-English WMT Translation Task

Karin Sim Smith **Lucia Specia** **David Steele**
Department of Computer Science
The University of Sheffield
Sheffield, UK
{kmsimsmith1, l.specia, dbsteele1}@sheffield.ac.uk

Abstract

This paper provides an overview of the Sheffield University submission to the WMT15 Translation Task for the Finnish-English language pair. The submitted translations were created from a system built using the CDEC decoder. Finnish is a morphologically rich language with elements such as nouns and verbs carrying a large number of inflectional types. Consequently, our improvements are based on morphology and include preprocessing steps to handle of morphological inflections inherent in the language, and which otherwise result in lexical sparsity and loss of information.

1 Introduction

This paper outlines The University of Sheffield's submission for the shared translation task, which is part of the 2015 Workshop on Machine Translation. We participated in the Finnish-English language pair task which used news-test-2015 data. 23 systems from 12 organisations took part in this task.

Finnish is an inflectional language containing a productive morphology. The morphological phenomena can lead to a great many inflectional forms. This complex productive morphology can be a barrier to machine translation, with many forms unseen at training. As such, our work was focussed on handling the morphological variation in Finnish with the aim of extracting and transferring as much information as possible - in terms of nominal forms and declensions.

For this paper we describe our baseline system in Section 3, followed by our improvements in Section 4 and potential gains in Section 5. We report our results in Section 6.

2 Related work

In terms of previous work in the translation of morphologically rich languages in MT, Finnish-English has previously featured as a language pair, in the 2005 shared task (Koehn and Monz, 2005).

Chahuneau et al. (2013) experimented specifically with models into morphologically rich languages, we opted to do from Finnish, as a morphologically rich language, into English. Their approach is, however, more systematic, deploying a morphological grammar.

Another approach, used by Ammar et al. (2013) is that of *synthetic translation options*, supplementing the phrase tables to compensate for the sparseness in translating from/to highly inflected languages.

Luong et al. (2010) also investigate morpheme-level extraction, but integrate this into the decoding process itself, instead of the pre-processing step we have. They also incorporate unsupervised morphological analysis and do not rely on language-specific tools, whereas we used a Finnish parser for our morphological analysis

3 Baseline system

For our decoder we used CDEC (Dyer et al., 2010), which essentially is used for rule extraction and decoding. CDEC uses synchronous context-free grammars (SCFGs) as the model for natural language syntax.

The initial tokenization and lower casing were performed using the 'tokenize-anything' and 'lowercase.pl' scripts respectively. They are both included as part of the CDEC suite of tools (similar to those provided with Moses). Fast-align was used to learn the word alignments.

To train the translation model we used the Europarl data set provided. We additionally investigated some of the newly available DCEP corpus (Hajlaoui et al., 2014). This is a resource containing multilingual output from the European Parliament beyond the plenary sessions of Europarl that has recently been made available for use. It contains the parliamentary reports (from the parliamentary committees of the European Parliament), oral and written questions, and press releases, and alignments can be derived for any language pairs in the language matrix. However, through experimentation we discovered issues with misalignments and determined better alignments when isolating the parliamentary reports from the questions and deriving them separately. We subsequently also isolated the press releases and aligned those as well. Although taken as a whole, the system seemed to actually cope with poor alignments - we subsequently experimented with the entire DCEP corpus (Hajlaoui et al., 2014) and achieved comparable results.

The grammar extraction is made up of SCFGs, which generate strings in two languages. The process ultimately builds an SCFG translation grammar (typically from a word-aligned parallel corpus) and in this case is a HIERO grammar . For the purposes of increased speed, per-sentence grammars (PSGs) were used in the translation. PSGs only contain rules that match a single sentence (filtered from larger grammars) and, despite the fact that rules are created for each individual sentence to be translated, they are quickly loadable.

For our Language Model we examined two different approaches. The basic approach purely used the given Europarl dataset, whilst the enhanced approach incorporated a partial selection of monolingual Newscrawl data (provided) taken from the Gigaword corpus in addition to the Europarl data. During experimentation we found that adding the extra Newscrawl data to the language model significantly improved the BLEU score (+0.5). However, due to time constraints we were unable to test this improvement alongside our stemming experiments (Section 4) so did not obtain a compound score (for stemming coupled with the additional monolingual data), which we believe could have been significantly better.

The final output translation initially only had the first letter in every sentence changed to uppercase. The translation was then converted into the SGML format using the 'wrap-xml.perl' script. Unfortunately, just simply converting the initial letter in each of the sentences led to a comparatively poor BLEU-cased score, which we decided had to be improved (see True-casing in section 4)

4 Improvements

4.1 Morphological stemming

Our main improvement to the system was based on the idea that there is a need to deal with the highly inflectional nature of Finnish, as the source language. The fact that Finnish is a morphologically rich language is problematic for machine translation systems. For example, it has 15 grammatical cases which results in a great many declensions of the nouns. This in turn leads to a great deal of lexical sparsity when estimating parameters for the translation model. Ultimately, there is a high incidence of out of vocabulary words, and valuable linguistic information is lost. While inflected forms may have occurred at training time, this means that the simple base form will not necessarily be resolved at decoding time. Even if base forms occurred in training, the inflectional form at decoding time will generally fail to match. The agglutinative nature of Finnish increases the problem further, as many nouns are compounded.

We therefore parsed our data using the Turku Finnish Dependency Parser (Haverinen et al., 2014) which is now available[1]. This parser works efficiently and we were able to process raw input text. The resulting parsed files allowed us to extract the base form of each inflected noun in addition to the parts of speech, dependencies, and grammatical case information. Of this we used the base form and grammatical case information to replace each inflected noun occurring in the test data with its base form, in addition to a place marker for cases deemed relevant. By this we mean that the nominative form, for example, does not result in inflectional variation, nor does it incorporate additional grammatical information, which would be of relevance in English. Often the inflections in Finnish become prepositions in English, so our hope was to retain this additional grammatical information and rely on the case placemarker being aligned to the relevant preposition in English. We decided not to include declensions where the declined form could be ambiguous, and left those unmodified.

We subsequently trained the alignments with our marked up test data. We used the base form and grammatical case information for each noun

[1] http://turkunlp.github.io/Finnish-dep-parser/

occurring in the training and test data and extracted lists of nouns where appropriate.

4.2 Issues encountered with stemming

Of course there is also inflectional variation within some cases, so a strict one-to-one mapping will not necessarily hold true. We did not substitute the base form for plural inflections, which did however result in losses, and which we would attempt to handle better in any future task. More problematic is the fact that a noun can decline in a similar manner for different cases - for example, the word 'kirjan' can be the base form of 'kirja', which means 'book', inflected in the genitive and accusative case - both have the same inflectional form. We dealt with this by only substituting the forms where there was no ambiguity. We determined that this was why we were not seeing improvements that were as significant as we had hoped. In addition, our attempts to rectify the issue were not sufficiently tuned.

Interestingly, we got good results when we only stemmed the nouns in the training set that also appeared in the dev and test sets (not submitted). This suggests that when we stemmed as many nouns as we could, it appeared to do as much harm as good and effectively cancelled itself out.

4.3 Filtering

We attempted an experiment with filtering, based on research proving that the translation direction of the training data makes a significant difference for both the translation model and the language model (Kurokawa et al., 2009; Lembersky et al., 2013; Lembersky et al., 2012). This research indicates a qualitative improvement with much less data. It would seem logical that training on translated data already incorporates some of the crosslingual transfer which is performed by a human translator, and therefore is valuable to capture.

To this end we constructed a directional corpus, filtering the whole of the Europarl for excerpts which were originally in the Finnish language. We did this by tracking the 'language' attribute in the markup to filter out any contributions which had originally been in Finnish. Once we had filtered these out we matched them with corresponding excerpts in the target language, in our case English. One major issue here was that due to the fact that there are only 26 Finnish members of the European Parliament out of a total number of 750, the amount of data that is in Finnish is relatively small. Our resulting filtered data corpus contained just 81,444 lines or sentences. This seemed to prove insufficient to influence the overall score. Unfortunately the DCEP data (Hajlaoui et al., 2014) has no way of determining what the original language was, and thus we had no additional sources for our filtered data.

4.4 True-casing (for BLEU-cased scores)

Due to an initial low BLEU-cased score it was decided that the true-casing had to be enhanced beyond simply capitalising the first letter of each sentence. In addition, time constraints and limited experience with available casing tools led to the creation of a relatively short script in order to improve the casing for the translated sentences. Two simple methods were implemented:

- Firstly, capitalisation statistics (ignoring first words) were taken from the unmodified Europarl corpus and applied to each individual word in the automated translation. For example, there would be instances in the corpus where 'The' appears with a capital 'T' as part of a name, and if this was applied directly then all occurrences of 'the' in the output translation would then be capitalised. Clearly this would not be acceptable and so a ratio of capitalised 'The' versus lower-case 'the' was recorded and if it was over a set limit then all occurrences of 'the' would be capitalised or else none would be. By itself this still has a number of limitations, but it was surprisingly accurate in this case, improving our original BLEU-cased score by nearly +2.0.
- Secondly, each sentence from our automated translation was then cross referenced with its respective sentence in the unmodified source text. Then, for each capitalised word in the source that also appeared in the output translation the capitalisation was carried over and applied. This was particularly effective for items such as place names and other named entities. This second option further enhanced the BLEU-cased score and bought the disparity levels (between cased and non-cased) largely in line with the other submissions (e.g. roughly -1.0).

It should be noted that this approach has its limitations and in the future it is anticipated that robust, tried and tested tools such as the Moses Truecaser/Recaser will be used to undertake any required casing tasks.

5 Alternative enhancements

5.1 Compound splitting

We also attempted to address the issue of compound splitting, given that Finnish is agglutinative in nature and so has many compound nouns which compact the grammatical inflections. The parsed files usefully gave us the compound forms of our nouns, however, due to lack of time we could not refine our implementation sufficiently.

5.2 Improved Language Model

The primary experimentation of using an enhanced language model that incorporated some of the Newscrawl data showed promising results. Ideally it would have been useful to spend time experimenting with various language models in order to gauge which aspects either positively or adversely affected the output translation. Clearly, for this task the Newscrawl data was largely in domain, and so the full set could have been an appropriate addition to be used in order to further enhance the language model and ultimately produce a more fluid output.

6 Results

Our primary results are displayed in Table 1.

System	BLEU	Cased	TER
Europarl only	12.9	12.3	0.791
Europarl+Newscrawl	13.4	12.5	0.792
Europarl+Stemming	13.4	12.4	0.792

Table 1: Showing the respective BLEU, BLEU-Cased, and Translation Error Rate scores of the three different systems.

Essentially the improvements over the baseline (Europarl only: 12.9) are fairly significant in both cases. This does appear to suggest that extending the language model and applying stemming (separately in this case) are both pertinent enhancements that can be used to improve the overall output translation. However, the fact that the system with fairly extensive stemming is comparable to a standard Europarl system with a slightly enhanced language model highlights a couple of points:

- Further extending the language model should carry significant gains and produce a smoother final translation.
- Stemming has potential, but our methods were a little too simplistic and some of the issues we encountered appeared to cause damage. This suggests using more robust and complex methods to handle the problems and ambiguity could produce much stronger improvements.
- There is potential to combine an extended language model and stemming information in the same system, which again should produce significant improvements.

7 Conclusions

In this paper we presented our submission, which was produced from a system built using the CDEC decoder. Our improvements included preprocessing to deal with morphological variation in Finnish, as the source language, and an attempt at directional filtering. It appeared that as this was our first submission, we were starting from scratch and had significant time consuming groundwork preparation to perform before any enhancements could me made. Ultimately, a number of improvements were made, but the results were not as strong as initially hoped, and we found that ambiguity and other issues encountered during the stemming introduced a degree of damage, which in turn seemed to put a glass ceiling on our BLEU scores. As such, these problems need to be dealt with in a more concrete and elegant manner.

Finally, using a lightly extended (in domain) language model produced a positive result and so there is scope to explore this avenue further. It is anticipated that experimenting with, and managing the language model could well produce significant gains.

References

Waleed Ammar, Victor Chahuneau, Michael Denkowski, Greg Hanneman, Wang Ling, Austin Matthews, Kenton Murray, Nicola Segall, Yulia Tsvetkov, Alon Lavie, and Chris Dyer. 2013. The CMU machine translation systems at WMT 2013: Syntax, synthetic translation options, and pseudo-references. In *Proceedings of the Eighth Workshop on Machine Translation*.

Victor Chahuneau, Eva Schlinger, Noah A. Smith, and Chris Dyer. 2013. Translating into morphologically rich languages with synthetic phrases. In *Proc. of EMNLP*.

Chris Dyer, Jonathan Weese, Hendra Setiawan, Adam Lopez, Ferhan Ture, Vladimir Eidelman, Juri Ganitkevitch, Phil Blunsom, and Philip Resnik. 2010. Cdec: A decoder, alignment, and learning framework for finite-state and context-free translation models. In *Proceedings of the ACL 2010 System Demonstrations*, ACLDemos '10, pages 7–12, Stroudsburg, PA, USA. Association for Computational Linguistics.

Najeh Hajlaoui, David Kolovratník, Jaakko Väyrynen, Ralf Steinberger, and Dániel Varga. 2014. DCEP -digital corpus of the european parliament. In *Proceedings of the Ninth International Conference on Language Resources and Evaluation (LREC-2014), Reykjavik, Iceland, May 26-31, 2014.*, pages 3164–3171.

Katri Haverinen, Jenna Nyblom, Timo Viljanen, Veronika Laippala, Samuel Kohonen, Anna Missil, Stina Ojala, Tapio Salakoski, and Filip Ginter. 2014. Building the essential resources for finnish: the turku dependency treebank. *Language Resources and Evaluation*, 48(3):493–531.

Philipp Koehn and Christof Monz. 2005. Shared task: Statistical machine translation between european languages. In *Proceedings of the ACL Workshop on Building and Using Parallel Texts*, pages 119–124. Association for Computational Linguistics.

David Kurokawa, Cyril Goutte, and Pierre Isabelle. 2009. Automatic detection of translated text and its impact on machine translation. In *In Proceedings of MT-Summit XII*, pages 81–88.

Gennadi Lembersky, Noam Ordan, and Shuly Wintner. 2012. Language models for machine translation: Original vs. translated texts. *Comput. Linguist.*, 38(4):799–825, December.

Gennadi Lembersky, Noam Ordan, and Shuly Wintner. 2013. Improving statistical machine translation by adapting translation models to translationese. *Comput. Linguist.*, 39(4):999–1023, December.

Minh-Thang Luong, Preslav Nakov, and Min-Yen Kan. 2010. A Hybrid Morpheme-Word Representation for Machine Translation of Morphologically Rich Languages. In *Proceedings of the 2010 Conference on Empirical Methods in Natural Language Processing*, pages 148–157, Cambridge, MA, October. Association for Computational Linguistics.

Morphological Segmentation and OPUS for Finnish-English Machine Translation

Jörg Tiedemann[1], **Filip Ginter**[2], **and Jenna Kanerva**[2,3]
[1] Department of Linguistics and Philology, Uppsala University, Sweden
[2] Department of IT, University of Turku, Finland
[3] University of Turku Graduate School (UTUGS), Finland
jorg.tiedemann@lingfil.uu.se, figint@utu.fi, jmnybl@utu.fi

Abstract

This paper describes baseline systems for Finnish-English and English-Finnish machine translation using standard phrase-based and factored models including morphological features. We experiment with compound splitting and morphological segmentation and study the effect of adding noisy out-of-domain data to the parallel and the monolingual training data. Our results stress the importance of training data and demonstrate the effectiveness of morphological pre-processing of Finnish.

1 Introduction

The basic goal of our submissions is to establish some straightforward baselines for the translation between Finnish and English using standard technology such as phrase-based and factored statistical machine translation, in preparation for a more focused future effort in combination with the state-of-the-art techniques in SMT for morphologically complex languages (see e.g. (Fraser et al., 2012)). The translation between Finnish and English (in both directions) is a new task in this year's workshop adding a new exciting challenge to the established setup. The main difficulty in this task is to manage the rich morphology of Finnish which has several implications on training and expected results with standard SMT models (see the illustration in Figure 1). Moreover, the monolingual and parallel training data is substantially smaller which makes the task even tougher compared with other languages pairs in the competition. In our contribution, we focus on Finnish-English emphasizing the need of additional training data and the necessity of morphological pre-processing. In particular, we explore the use of factored models with multiple translation paths and the use of morphological segmentation based on proper morphological annotation and simple rule-based heuristics.

Syksyllä taidemuseossa avataan uudet näyttelyt
Autumn+ADE art_museum+INE open+PASS new+PL exhibition+PL
In_autumn in_art_museum will_be_opened new exhibitions
New exhibitions will be opened in the art museum in autumn

Figure 1: A sentence illustrating the inflective and compounding nature of Finnish in contrast to English. (ADE, INE: adessive, inessive cases, PASS: passive, PL: plural)

We also add noisy out-of-domain data for better coverage and show the impact of that kind of data on translation performance. We also add a system for English-Finnish but without special treatment of Finnish morphology. In this translation direction we only consider the increase of training data which results in significant improvements without any language-specific optimization.

In the following, we will first present our systems and the results achieved with our models before discussing the translation produced in more detail. The latter analyses pinpoint issues and problems that provide valuable insights for future development.

2 Basic Setup and Data Sets

All our translation systems are based on Moses (Koehn et al., 2007) and standard components for training and tuning the models. We apply KenLM for language modeling (Heafield et al., 2013), fast_align for word alignment (Dyer et al., 2013) and MERT for parameter tuning (Och, 2003). All our models use lowercased training data and the results that we report refer to lowercased output of our models. All language models are of order five and use the standard modified Kneser-Ney smoothing implemented in KenLM. All phrase tables are pruned based on significance testing (Johnson et al., 2007) and reducing translation options to at most 30 per phrase type. The maximum phrase length is seven.

For processing Finnish, we use the Finnish dependency parser pipeline[1] developed at the University of Turku (Haverinen et al., 2014). This pipeline integrates all pre-processing steps that are necessary for data-driven dependency parsing including tokenization, morphological analyses and part-of-speech tagging, and produces dependency analyses in a minor variant of the Stanford Dependencies scheme (de Marneffe et al., 2014). Especially useful for our purposes is the morphological component which is based on OMorfi - an open-source finite-state toolkit with a large-coverage morphology for modern Finnish (Lindén et al., 2009). The parser has recently been evaluated to have LAS (labeled attachment score) of 80.1% and morphological tagging accuracy of 93.4% (Pyysalo et al., 2015).

The data sets we apply are on the one hand the official data sets provided by WMT and, on the other hand, additional parallel corpora from OPUS and large monolingual data sets for Finnish coming from various sources. OPUS includes a variety of parallel corpora coming from different domains and we include all sources that involve Finnish and English (Tiedemann, 2012). The most important corpora in terms of size are the collection of translated movie subtitles (OpenSubtitles) and EU publications (DGT, EUbookshop, EMEA). Some smaller corpora provide additional parallel data with varying quality. Table 1 lists some basic statistics of Finnish-English corpora included in OPUS. The final two rows in the table compare the overall size after cleaning the corpora with the pre-processing scripts provided by Moses with the training data provided by WMT for Finnish-English. We can see that OPUS adds a substantial amount of parallel training data, more than ten times as many sentence pairs with over six times more tokens. A clear drawback of the data sets in OPUS is that they come from distant domains such as movie subtitles and that their quality is not always very high. User contributed subtitle translations, for example, include many spelling errors and the alignment is also quite noisy. EUbookshop and EMEA documents are converted from PDF leading to various problems as well (Tiedemann, 2014; Skadiņš et al., 2014). Software localization data (GNOME, KDE4) contains variables and code snippets which are not appropriate for the WMT test domain. One of the main questions we wanted to answer with our experiments is whether this kind of data is useful at all despite the noise it adds.

corpus	sentences	en-words	fi-words
Books	3.6K	69.7K	54.5K
DGT	3.1M	61.8M	46.9M
ECB	157.6K	4.5M	3.4M
EMEA	1.1M	14.2M	11.9M
EUbookshop	2.0M	51.4M	37.6M
JRC-Acquis	19.7k	388.7k	273.6k
GNOME	62.2K	313.3K	254.6K
KDE4	108.1K	596.0K	578.6K
OpenSubtitles	110.1K	856.3K	604.7K
OpenSubtitles2012	12.9M	111.5M	74.4M
OpenSubtitles2013	9.8M	87.8M	55.7M
Tatoeba	12.2K	103.2K	77.0K
WMT-clean	2.1M	52.4M	37.6M
OPUS-clean	29.4M	328.1M	227.6M

Table 1: Finnish-English data in OPUS. WMT-clean and OPUS-clean refer to the entire parallel training data set from WMT and OPUS, respectively, after pre-processing with the standard Moses cleanup script.

Table 1 also illustrates the morphological differences between English and Finnish. Based on the token counts we can clearly see that word formation is quite different in both languages which has significant implications for word alignment and translation. Due to the rich morphology in Finnish we expect that adding more training data is even more crucial than for morphologically less complex languages. To verify this assumption we also include additional monolingual data for language modeling for the English-Finnish translation direction taken from the Finnish Internet Parsebank,[2] a 3.7B token corpus gathered from an Internet crawl and parsed with the abovementioned dependency parser pipeline (Kanerva et al., 2014). For English we include the fifth edition of the LDC Giga-Word corpus.

3 Factored Models for Finnish-to-English

Our baseline models apply a standard pipeline to extract phrase-based translation models from raw lowercased text. We use constrained settings with WMT data only and unconstrained settings with additional OPUS data. Our primary systems apply factored models that include three competing translation paths:

- Surface form translation

[1] `http://turkunlp.github.io/Finnish-dep-parser`

[2] `http://bionlp.utu.fi/finnish-internet-parsebank.html`

- Translation of lemmatized input
- Translation of lemmatized and morphosyntactically tagged input

The unconstrained system replaces the first translation path with a phrase table extracted from the entire corpus including all OPUS data. However, we did not parse the OPUS data and take the other two models from WMT data only. We tuned our systems with half of the provided development data (using every second sentence) and tested our models on the other half of the development data. Table 2 lists various models that we tested during development and the various components are explained in more detail in the sections below.

system	*BLEU*
constrained	
baseline	16.2
factored	17.8
factored+pseudo	18.2
unconstrained	
baseline+WordNetTrans	16.5
baseline+WordNetTrans&Syn	16.6
baseline+opus	19.0
baseline+opus+WordNetTrans	19.1
baseline+opus+WordNetTrans&Syn	19.1
factored+opus	19.2
factored+opus+pseudo	19.9
factored+opus+pseudo+word2vec	20.0
factored+opus+pseudo+WordNetSyn	20.1

Table 2: The performance of various Finnish-English translation models on development data. *Pseudo* indicates the use of inflection pseudo-tokens, *word2vec* refers to the use of word2vec synonyms and *WordNetSyn* refers to the inclusion of WordNet synonyms for out-of-vocabulary words. *WordNetTrans* refers to translations added from the bilingual Finnish-English WordNet for OOV words.

3.1 Inflection Pseudo-Tokens

Due to the highly inflective nature of the language, a Finnish morphological marker often corresponds to a separate English word. This is especially prominent for many Finnish cases which typically correspond to English prepositions. For example, the Finnish word *talossakin* has the English translation *also in a/the house* where the inessive case (*ssa* marker) corresponds to the English preposition *in* and the clitic *kin* corresponds to the English adverb *also*. To account for this phenomenon, we pre-process the Finnish data by inserting dummy tokens for certain morphological markers, allowing them to be aligned with the English words in system training phase. These dummy tokens are always inserted in front of the text span dominated by the word from which the token was generated in the dependency parse. Thus, for instance, the case marker of the head noun of a nominal phrase produces a dummy token in front of this phrase, where the corresponding English preposition would be expected. The pseudo-tokens are generated rather conservatively in these three situations:

- a case marker other than nominative, partitive, and genitive on a head of a nominal phrase (*nommod* and *nommod-own* dependency relations in the SD scheme version produced by the parser)
- a possessive marker (eng. *my, our, etc.*) in any context
- the clitic *kin/kaan* (eng. *also*) in any context

To shed some further light on the effectiveness of the pseudo-token generation, we carry out a focused manual evaluation on the test dataset. In randomly selected 100 sentences, we marked every nominal phrase head inflected in other than nominative, partitive, and genitive case and checked in the system output whether this exact phrase head was translated correctly (as judged by the annotator, not the reference translation), regardless of the correctness of the remainder of the sentence. We compare the final system with and without the dummy token generation component, in a randomized fashion such that it was not possible to distinguish during the annotation which of the two systems the translation originated from. In total, the 100 sentences contained 148 inflected phrase heads of interest. Of these, the system with pseudo-token generation translated correctly 100/148 (68%) and without pseudo-token generation 89/148 (60%). This difference is, however, not statistically significant at p=0.12 (two-tail McNemar's test). In addition to this manual evaluation, we have also observed a small advantage for the pseudo-token generation in terms of development set BLEU score. Somewhat surprisingly, we find that only 85/148 (57%) of these inflected heads were translated using a prepositional phrase in the reference translation, showing that the correspondence of Finnish cases with English prepositions is not as strong as might intuitively seem. Of those inflected heads which were translated as a prepositional phrase in the reference, 57/85 (67%) were correct for the system with pseudo-tokens and 49/85 (58%) for the system without, whereas for those that have not been translated as a prepositional phrase in the reference, the proportions are 43/63 (68%) and 40/63 (63%). Due to the small sample size, it is difficult to draw solid conclusions but the numbers at least hint at the intuitive expectation that the pseudo-token generation would give better results especially in cases where the translation corresponds to a prepositional phrase. The overall quality of translation of inflected nominal phrase heads however leaves much room for improvement.

3.2 Compounds

Finnish is a compounding language, once again leading to a situation whereby a single Finnish word corresponds to multiple English words. Further, compounding in Finnish is highly productive and reliable translations cannot be learned but for the most common compounds. In most cases, the compounds are correctly analyzed by the Finnish parsing pipeline, including the boundaries of the lemmas which form the compound. To assist the alignment as well as the translation process itself, we split the compound lemmas into the constituent parts as a pre-processing step in the Finnish-English direction. The following example illustrates this process ("EU support for enterprises") taken from the development data:

compound:	EU-yritystukien
segmented lemma:	EU|yritys|tuki
PoS:	N
morphology:	NUM_Pl|CASE_Gen
factored segments:	EU|EU|_|_ yritys|yritys|_|_ tukien|tuki|N|NUM_Pl+CASE_Gen

As shown above, PoS and morphology are only attached to the final component of the compound and string matching heuristics are used to split surface forms as well based on the segmentation of the lemma.

3.3 Synonyms and Lexical Resources

One of the major problems for statistical machine translation with limited resources is the treatment of out-of-vocabulary (OOV) words. This problem is even more severe with morphologically rich languages such as Finnish. Table 3 shows the OOV ratio in the development data that we used for testing our models. We can see that the factored models significantly reduce the amount of unknown word type and tokens.

In our final setup we tried to address the problem of remaining OOVs by expanding the input with synonyms from external resources. We looked at two possible sources: distributional models trained on large monolingual data sets and manually created lexico-semantic databases. For the former, we trained distributed continuous-vector space models using the popular word2vec toolkit[3] (Mikolov et al., 2013) on the 3.7B tokens of the Finnish Internet Parsebank data, using the default settings and the skip-gram model. We tested the use of the ten most similar words for each unknown word coming from our word2vec model (according to cosine similarity in their vector representations) to replace OOV words in the input. The second alternative uses the Finnish WordNet[4] (Niemi et al., 2012) to replace OOV words with synonyms that are provided by the database. We apply the HFST-based thesaurus for efficient WordNet lookup that enables the lookup and generation of inflected synonyms.[5] Table 4 shows the statistics of unknown words that can be expanded in the development test data. The table shows that word2vec expansion has a better coverage than WordNet but both resources propose a large number of synonyms that are not included the phrase table and, hence, cannot be used to improve the translations. However, both strategies produce a large number of spurious (context-independent) synonyms and discarding them due to the lack of phrase table coverage is not necessarily a bad thing. The results of applying our two OOV-handling strategies on the same data set are shown in Table 2.

FinnWordNet also includes a bilingual thesaurus based on the linked Finnish WordNet (Niemi and Lindén, 2012). The HFST tools provide a convenient interface for querying this resource with inflected word forms. We applied this external resources as yet another module for handling OOV words in the input. For this we used the XML

OOVs	types	tokens
constrained		
baseline	2,451 (28.7%)	2,869 (14.5%)
factored	847 (14.5%)	958 (6.7%)
unconstrained		
baseline	1,212 (14.2%)	1,414 (7.1%)
factored	386 (6.6%)	442 (3.1%)

Table 3: OOV ratios in the development test data (half of the WMT 2015 development data).

[3]http://code.google.com/p/word2vec/

[4]http://www.ling.helsinki.fi/en/lt/research/finnwordnet/

[5]http://www.ling.helsinki.fi/en/lt/research/finnwordnet/download.shtml#hfst

	OOVs	synonyms
constrained (factored)		
word2vec	626	6,260
- covered by phrase table	371	968
WordNetSyn	318	17,742
- covered by phrase table	262	1,380
unconstrained (factored)		
word2vec	210	2,100
- covered by phrase table	140	480
WordNetSyn	67	2,883
- covered by phrase table	66	361

Table 4: Synonyms extracted from WordNet and word2vec word embeddings for OOVs in the development test data.

markup functionality of Moses to provide translations along with the source language input. The lookup usually leads to several alternative translations including repeated entries (see Table 5 for some statistics). We use relative frequencies and an arbitrary chosen weight factor of 0.1 to determine the probability of the WordNet translation option given to the Moses decoder. The bilingual strategy can also be combined with the synonym approach described above. Here, we prefer translations from the bilingual WordNet and add synonyms if no translation can be found. The results on the development test set are shown in Table 2 as well. Note that we could not use XML markup in connection with factored input. There is, to our knowledge, no obvious way to combine non-factored XML markup with factored input.

WordNetTrans	OOVs	translations
constrained (factored)	336	3,622
unconstrained (factored)	78	532

Table 5: Translations extracted for OOVs in the development test data from the bilingual Finnish-English WordNet.

3.4 Untranslated Words

To evaluate the overall impact of our OOV approach, we inspect untranslated Finnish words in 200 random sentences in the Finnish-English test set output and assign these words into several categories. The corresponding counts are presented in Table 6. Inflected forms account for the vast majority of untranslated output, and of these, inflected proper names constitute more than half. Given that the inflection rules in Finnish are highly productive, a focused effort especially on resolving inflected proper names should be able to account for the majority of the remaining untranslated output. However, since only 52 of the 200 inspected sentences contained untranslated output, no major gains in translation quality can be expected.

category	count
Inflected proper name	35
Inflected non-compound form	13
Inflected compound	9
Other	5
Typo	3
Base form	3
Proper name base form	1

Table 6: Categorization of untranslated Finnish words in the Finnish-English system output.

3.5 Final Results

Our results on the 2015 newstest set are shown in Table 7. Our primary system is the unconstrained factored model with pseudo-tokens and WordNet synonyms. Contrastive runs include the phrase-based baselines and constrained settings in factored and non-factored variants. In the human evaluation, the primary system ranked first shared with five other systems, but this cluster of systems was outperformed by one of the online baselines.

system	$BLEU$	TER
unconstrained		
baseline	18.9	0.737
primary	19.3	0.728
constrained		
baseline	15.5	0.780
factored	17.9	0.749

Table 7: Our final systems tested with the newstest 2015 data set (lowercased BLEU).

4 English-to-Finnish with OPUS

The main purpose of running the other translation direction was to test the impact of additional training data on translation performance. Once again, we simply used the entire database of English-Finnish parallel data sets provided by WMT and OPUS and tested a straightforward phrase-based model without any special treatment and language-specific tools. Again, we relied on lowercased models and used standard procedures to train and tune model parameters. The results are shown in Table 8. In the human evaluation, the primary system ranked first, but was outperformed by both online baselines.

Similar to Finnish-English we can see a strong effect of additional training data. This is not surprising but re-assuring that even noisy data from distant

system	$BLEU_{dev}$	$BLEU$	TER
constrained	12.7	10.7	0.842
unconstrained	15.7	14.8	0.796

Table 8: English-Finnish translation with (*unconstrained*) or without (*constrained*) OPUS (lowercased BLEU and TER on newstest 2015; $BLEU_{dev}$ on development test data).

Feature	Reference	System	Difference
Case Nom	3701/10289	4739/9996	**+11.44pp**
Person Sg3	1620/3947	1991/3867	**+10.44pp**
Mood Ind	2216/3947	2461/3867	**+7.50pp**
Tense Prs	1259/3947	1470/3867	**+6.12pp**
Voice Act	3388/3947	3414/3867	**+2.45pp**
Punct	2874/19772	2283/20004	**+2.38pp**
Infinitive 1	274/3947	352/3867	**+2.16pp**
Unknown	1239/19772	1611/20004	**+1.79pp**
Tense Prt	957/3947	991/3867	**+1.38pp**
Pers pron	344/10289	453/9996	**+1.19pp**
Case Gen	2637/10289	2050/9996	**-5.12pp**
Pcp Prs	227/3947	87/3867	**-3.50pp**
Cmp Pos	1917/10289	1546/9996	**-3.17pp**
Pcp Prf	647/3947	515/3867	**-3.07pp**
Person Pl3	403/3947	277/3867	**-3.05pp**
Voice Pass	436/3947	317/3867	**-2.85pp**
Case Ela	517/10289	219/9996	**-2.83pp**
Uppercase	3126/19772	2624/20004	**-2.69pp**
Prop noun	1675/10289	1399/9996	**-2.28pp**
Case Ine	771/10289	530/9996	**-2.19pp**

Table 9: The ten most over- and under-represented morphological features in the system output as compared to the reference translation. The relative frequency of each feature is calculated with respect to the token count of the word category which exhibits it: nouns, adjectives, pronouns and numerals for case and number, verbs for features like person and tense, and all tokens for generic features like unknown and uppercase.

domains can contribute significantly when training statistical MT models with scarce in-domain training data. The overall quality, however, is still poor as our manual inspections reveal as well. The following section discusses some of the issues that may guide developments in the future.

4.1 Morphological Richness

To study how well the morphological variation is handled in the English-to-Finnish translation direction, we compare the morphological richness of the system output and reference translations. Most over- and under-represented morphological features are shown in Table 9.

For words inflecting in case and number, the nominative case is highly over-represented in the system output. As the nominative case corresponds to the basic form of a word (canonical form), presumably the translation system fails to produce correct inflections when translating from English to Finnish and uses the basic form too often. This naturally leads to the under-representation of other cases. From Table 9 we can see that, e.g., the genitive, elative and inessive cases are under-represented in the system output. Similar behavior can be seen with verb features as well. Frequent verb inflections are over-represented to the detriment of rarer variants. For example, third person singular and first infinitive (canonical form) are over-represented compared to other persons. Additionally, active forms dominate over passive, and present and past tenses over participial counterparts. Both of these word categories indicate that the morphological variation is weaker in the system output than in reference translations. This shows that the system is not fully able to account for the rich morphology of the Finnish language.

From Table 9 we can also notice several features not directly related to morphology. As expected, the proportion of words not recognized by the Finnish morphological analyzer (*Unknown* row) is higher in system output than in reference translations. This likely reflects words passed through the pipeline untranslated. Moreover, system output has more punctuation tokens and less uppercased words, which is due to the re-capitalization procedure we apply on the originally lowercased output of the decoder.

5 Conclusions

This paper presents baseline systems for the translation between Finnish and English in both directions. Our main effort refers to the inclusion of additional training data and morphological pre-processing for the translation from Finnish to English. We can show that additional noisy and unrelated training data has a significant impact on translation performance and that morphological analyses is essential in this task. Our models perform well relative to other systems submitted to WMT but still underperform in quality as manual inspections reveal. The challenge of translating from and to morphologically rich languages with scarce domain-specific resources is still far from being solved with currents standard technology in statistical machine translation and provides an exciting research field for future work.

References

Marie-Catherine de Marneffe, Timothy Dozat, Natalia Silveira, Katri Haverinen, Filip Ginter, Joakim Nivre, and Christopher D Manning. 2014. Universal Stanford Dependencies: A cross-linguistic typology. In *Proceedings of LREC*, pages 4585–4592.

Chris Dyer, Victor Chahuneau, and Noah A. Smith. 2013. A simple, fast, and effective reparameterization of IBM Model 2. In *Proceedings of NAACL*, pages 644–648.

Alexander Fraser, Marion Weller, Aoife Cahill, and Fabienne Cap. 2012. Modeling inflection and word-formation in SMT. In *Proceedings of the 13th Conference of the European Chapter of the Association for Computational Linguistics*, pages 664–674. Association for Computational Linguistics.

Katri Haverinen, Jenna Nyblom, Timo Viljanen, Veronika Laippala, Samuel Kohonen, Anna Missilä, Stina Ojala, Tapio Salakoski, and Filip Ginter. 2014. Building the essential resources for Finnish: the Turku Dependency Treebank. *Language Resources and Evaluation*, 48(3):493–531.

Kenneth Heafield, Ivan Pouzyrevsky, Jonathan H. Clark, and Philipp Koehn. 2013. Scalable Modified Kneser-Ney Language Model Estimation. In *Proceedings of ACL*, pages 690–696.

Howard Johnson, Joel Martin, George Foster, and Roland Kuhn. 2007. Improving translation quality by discarding most of the phrasetable. In *Proceedings of EMNLP-CoNLL*, pages 967–975.

Jenna Kanerva, Juhani Luotolahti, Veronika Laippala, and Filip Ginter. 2014. Syntactic n-gram collection from a large-scale corpus of Internet Finnish. In *Proceedings Baltic HLT*, pages 184–191.

Philipp Koehn, Hieu Hoang, Alexandra Birch, Chris Callison-Burch, Marcello Federico, Nicola Bertoldi, Brooke Cowan, Wade Shen, Christine Moran, Richard Zens, Christopher J. Dyer, Ondřej Bojar, Alexandra Constantin, and Evan Herbst. 2007. Moses: Open Source Toolkit for Statistical Machine Translation. In *Proceedings of ACL*, pages 177–180.

Krister Lindén, Miikka Silfverberg, and Tommi Pirinen. 2009. HFST tools for morphology — an efficient open-source package for construction of morphological analyzers. In *State of the Art in Computational Morphology*, volume 41 of *Communications in Computer and Information Science*, pages 28–47. Springer.

Tomas Mikolov, Kai Chen, Greg Corrado, and Jeffrey Dean. 2013. Efficient estimation of word representations in vector space. *CoRR*, abs/1301.3781.

Jyrki Niemi and Krister Lindén. 2012. Representing the translation relation in a bilingual WordNet. In *Proceedings of LREC*, pages 2439–2446.

Jyrki Niemi, Krister Lindén, and Mirka Hyvärinen. 2012. Using a bilingual resource to add synonyms to a wordnet: FinnWordNet and Wikipedia as an example. In *In Proceedings of the 6th International Global WordNet Conference (GWC 2012)*, pages 227–231, Matsue, Japan.

Franz Josef Och. 2003. Minimum Error Rate Training in Statistical Machine Translation. In *Proceedings of ACL*, pages 160–167.

Sampo Pyysalo, Jenna Kanerva, Anna Missilä, Veronika Laippala, and Filip Ginter. 2015. Universal dependencies for Finnish. In *Proceedings of NoDaLiDa 2015*, pages 163–172. NEALT.

Raivis Skadiņš, Jörg Tiedemann, Roberts Rozis, and Daiga Deksne. 2014. Billions of parallel words for free: Building and using the EU bookshop corpus. In *Proceedings of LREC*, pages 1850–1855.

Jörg Tiedemann. 2012. Parallel data, tools and interfaces in OPUS. In *Procedings of LREC*, pages 2214–2218.

Jörg Tiedemann. 2014. Improved text extraction from PDF documents for large-scale natural language processing. In Alexander Gelbukh, editor, *Computational Linguistics and Intelligent Text Processing*, volume 1 of *Lecture Notes in Computer Science LNCS 8403*, pages 102–112. Springer.

Abu-MaTran at WMT 2015 Translation Task: Morphological Segmentation and Web Crawling

Raphael Rubino[⋆], **Tommi Pirinen**[†], **Miquel Esplà-Gomis**[‡], **Nikola Ljubešić**[γ], **Sergio Ortiz-Rojas**[⋆], **Vassilis Papavassiliou**[♮], **Prokopis Prokopidis**[♮], **Antonio Toral**[†]

[⋆] Prompsit Language Engineering, S.L., Elche, Spain
{rrubino,sortiz}@prompsit.com
[†] NCLT, School of Computing, Dublin City University, Ireland
{atoral,tpirinen}@computing.dcu.ie
[‡] Dep. Llenguatges i Sistemes Informàtics, Universitat d'Alacant, Spain
mespla@dlsi.ua.es
[γ] Department of Information and Communication Sciences, University of Zagreb, Croatia
nljubesi@ffzg.hr
[♮] Institute for Language and Speech Processing, Athena Research and Innovation Center, Greece
{vpapa, prokopis}@ilsp.gr

Abstract

This paper presents the machine translation systems submitted by the Abu-MaTran project for the Finnish–English language pair at the WMT 2015 translation task. We tackle the lack of resources and complex morphology of the Finnish language by (i) crawling parallel and monolingual data from the Web and (ii) applying rule-based and unsupervised methods for morphological segmentation. Several statistical machine translation approaches are evaluated and then combined to obtain our final submissions, which are the top performing English-to-Finnish unconstrained (all automatic metrics) and constrained (BLEU), and Finnish-to-English constrained (TER) systems.

1 Introduction

This paper presents the statistical machine translation (SMT) systems submitted by the Abu-MaTran project for the WMT 2015 translation task. The language pair concerned is Finnish–English with a strong focus on the English-to-Finnish direction. The Finnish language is newly introduced this year as a particular translation challenge due to its rich morphology and to the lack of resources available, compared to e.g. English or French.

Morphologically rich languages, and especially Finnish, are known to be difficult to translate using phrase-based SMT systems mainly because of the large diversity of word forms leading to data scarcity (Koehn, 2005). We assume that data acquisition and morphological segmentation should contribute to decrease the out-of-vocabulary rate and thus improve the performance of SMT. To gather additional data, we decide to build on previous work conducted in the Abu-MaTran project and crawl the Web looking for monolingual and parallel corpora (Toral et al., 2014). In addition, morphological segmentation of Finnish is used in our systems as pre- and post-processing steps. Four segmentation methods are proposed in this paper, two unsupervised and two rule-based.

Both constrained and unconstrained translation systems are submitted for the shared task. The former ones are trained on the data provided by the shared task, while the latter ones benefit from crawled data. For both settings, we evaluate the impact of the different SMT approaches and morphological segmentation methods. Finally, the outputs of individually trained systems are combined to obtain our primary submissions for the translation tasks.

This paper is structured as follows: the methods for data acquisition from the Web are described in Section 2. Morphological segmentation is presented in Section 3. The data and tools used in our experiments are detailed in Section 4. Finally, the results of our experiments are shown in Section 5, followed by a conclusion in Section 6.

2 Web Crawling

In this section we describe the process we followed to collect monolingual and parallel data through Web crawling. Both types of corpora are gathered through one web crawl of the Finnish (*.fi*) top-level domain (TLD) with the SPIDERLING crawler[1] (Suchomel and Pomikálek, 2012). This crawler performs language identification during the crawling process and thus allows simultaneous multilingual crawling. The whole unconstrained dataset gathered from the Web is built in 40 days using 16 threads. Documents written in Finnish and English are collected during the crawl.

2.1 Monolingual Data

The Finnish and English data collected during the crawl amounts to $5.6M$ and $3.9M$ documents, containing $1.7B$ and $2.0B$ words for Finnish and English respectively (after processing, which includes removing near-duplicates). Interestingly, the amount of Finnish and English data on the Finnish TLD is quite similar. For comparison, on the Croatian domain only 10% of the data is written in English (Ljubešić and Klubička, 2014). While the Finnish data is used in further steps for building the target-language model, both datasets are used in the task of searching for parallel data described in the next subsection.

2.2 Parallel Data

In our experiments, we adapt the BITEXTOR[2] tool to detect parallel documents from a collection of downloaded and pre-processed websites. The pre-processing performed by SPIDERLING includes language detection, boilerplate removal, and HTML format cleaning. Therefore, the only modules of BITEXTOR used for this task are those performing document and segment alignment, relying on HUNALIGN[3] (Varga et al., 2005) and an English–Finnish bilingual lexicon.[4] Confidence scores for aligned segments are computed thanks to these two resources.

From a total of $12.2K$ web domains containing both Finnish and English documents, BITEXTOR is able to identify possible parallel data on $10.7k$ domains (87.5%). From these domains, $2.1M$ segment pairs are extracted without any additional restrictions, and $1.2M$ when additional restrictions on the document pairing are set. Namely, these restrictions discard (i) document pairs where less than 5 segments are aligned; and (ii) those with an alignment score lower than 0.2 according to HUNALIGN. The first collection can be considered recall-oriented and the second one precision-oriented.

In this first step, a large amount of potentially parallel data is obtained by post-processing data collected with a TLD crawl, which is not primarily aimed at finding parallel data. To make use of this resource in a more efficient way, we re-crawl some of the most promising web sites (we call them *multilingual hotspots*) with the ILSP-FC crawler specialised in locating parallel documents during crawling. According to Esplà-Gomis et al. (2014), BITEXTOR and ILSP-FC have shown to be complementary, and combining both tools leads to a larger amount of parallel data.

ILSP-FC (Papavassiliou et al., 2013) is a modular crawling system allowing to easily acquire domain-specific and generic corpora from the Web.[5] This crawler includes a de-duplicator which checks all documents in a pairwise manner to identify near-duplicates. This is achieved by comparing the quantised word frequencies and the paragraphs of each pair of candidate duplicate documents. A document-pair detector also examines each document in the same manner and identifies pairs of documents that could be considered parallel. The main methods used by the pair detector are URL similarity, co-occurrences of images with the same filename in two documents, and the documents' structural similarity.

In order to identify the *multilingual hotspots*, we process the output of the Finnish TLD and generate a list containing the websites which have already been crawled and the number of stored English and Finnish webpages for each website. Assuming that a website with comparable numbers of webpages for each language is likely to contain bitexts of good quality, we keep the websites with Finnish to English ratio over 0.9. Then, ILSP-FC processes the $1,000$ largest such websites, considered the most bitext-productive multilingual websites, in order to detect parallel documents. We identify a total of $58,839$ document pairs ($8,936$, $17,288$ and $32,615$ based on URL similarity, co-occurrences of images and structural similarity, respectively). Finally, HUNALIGN is applied on these document pairs, resulting in $1.2M$ segment pairs after duplicate removal. The parallel corpus used in our experiments is the union without duplicates of the largest

[1] http://nlp.fi.muni.cz/trac/spiderling

[2] http://sf.net/p/bitextor/

[3] http://mokk.bme.hu/resources/hunalign

[4] http://sf.net/p/bitextor/files/bitextor/bitextor-4.1/dictionaries/

[5] http://nlp.ilsp.gr/redmine/projects/ilsp-fc

corpora collected with BITEXTOR and ILSP-FC, leading to $2.8M$ segment pairs.

3 Morphological Segmentation

Morphological segmentation is a method of analysis of word-forms in order to reduce morphological complexity. There are few variations on how to define morphological segmentation, we use the most simple definition: a morphological segmentation of a word is defined by 0 or more segmentation points from where the word can be split into segments. The letter sequences between segmentation points are not modified, i.e. no lemmatisation or segment analysis is performed (or retained) in the actual SMT data. An example of a linguistically derived morphological segmentation of an English word-form *cats* would be `cat→ ←s`, where → ← denotes the segmentation point,[6] and `cat` and `s` are the segments.

We use four segmentation approaches that can be divided in two categories: (i) rule-based, based on morphological dictionaries and weighted finite-state technology HFST (Lindén et al., 2009)[7], further detailed in subsection 3.1, and (ii) statistical, based on unsupervised learning of morphologies, further detailed in subsection 3.2. All segments are used as described in subsection 3.3.

3.1 Rule-based Segmentation

Rule-based morphological segmentation is based on linguistically motivated computational descriptions of the morphology by dividing the word-forms into *morphs* (minimal segments carrying semantic or syntactic meaning). The rule-based approach to morphological segmentation uses a morphological dictionary of words and an implementation of the morphological grammar to analyse word-forms. In our case, we use OMORFI (Pirinen, 2015), an open-source implementation of the Finnish morphology.[8] OMORFI's segmentation produces named segment boundaries: stem, inflection, derivation, compound-word and other etymological. The two variants of rule-based segmentation we use are based on selection of the boundary points: *compound segmentation* uses compound segments and discards the rest (referred in tables and figures to as `HFST Comp`), and *morph segmentation* uses compound and inflectional morph segments (`HFST Morph` in tables and figures). In cases of ambiguous segments, the weighted finite-state automata 1-best search is used with default weights.[9] For example, the words *kuntaliitoksen selvittämisessä* ("examining annexation") is segmented by `hfst-comp` as 'kunta→←liitoksen selvittämisessä' and `hfst-morph` as 'kunta→←liitokse→←n selvittämise→←ssä'.

3.2 Unsupervised Segmentation

Unsupervised morphological segmentation is based on a statistical model trained by minimising the number of different character sequences observed in a training corpus. We use two different algorithms: MORFESSOR Baseline 2.0 (Virpioja et al., 2013) and FLATCAT (Grönroos et al., 2014). The segmentation models are trained using the Europarl v8 corpus. Both systems are used with default settings. However, with FLATCAT we discard the non-morph boundaries and we have not used semi-supervised features. For example, the phrase given in previous sub-section: `morfessor` produces 1-best segmentation: and 'Kun→←ta→←liito→←ksen selvittä→←misessä' and `flatcat` 'Kun→←tali→←itoksen selvittämis→←essä'

3.3 Segments in the SMT Pipeline

The segmented data is used exactly as the word-form-based data during training, tuning and testing of the SMT systems,[10] except during the pre-processing and post-processing steps. For pre-processing, the Finnish side is segmented prior to use. For the post-processing of segmented-Finnish-to-English, boundary markers are removed. For the other direction, two types of tokens with boundary markers are observed: *matching* arrows `a→ ←b` and *stray* arrows `a→ x` or `x ←b`. For *matching* arrows, an empty string is used to join the morphs, while the morphs with *stray* arrows are deleted.

4 Datasets and Tools

This section presents the tools, the monolingual and parallel data used to train our SMT systems. All the corpora are pre-processed prior to training the

[6]we follow this arrow notation throughout the paper as well as in the actual implementation

[7]`http://hfst.sf.net`

[8]`http://github.com/flammie/omorfi/`

[9]For details of implementation and reproducibility, the code is available in form of automake scriptlets at `http://github.com/flammie/autostuff-moses-smt/`.

[10]The parameters of the word alignment, phrase extraction and decoding algorithms have not been modified to take into account the nature of the segmented data.

language and translation models. We rely on the scripts included in the MOSES toolkit (Koehn et al., 2007) and perform the following operations: punctuation normalisation, tokenisation, true-casing and escaping of problematic characters. The truecaser is lexicon-based, trained on all the monolingual and parallel data. In addition, we remove sentence pairs from the parallel corpora where either side is longer than 80 tokens.

4.1 Translation Models

We empirically evaluate several types of SMT systems: phrase-based SMT (Och and Ney, 2004) trained on word forms or morphs as described in Section 3, Factored Models (Koehn and Hoang, 2007) including morphological and suffix information as provided by OMORFI,[11] in addition to surface forms, and finally hierarchical phrase-based SMT (Chiang, 2005) as an unsupervised tree-based model. All the systems are trained with MOSES, relying on MGIZA (Gao and Vogel, 2008) for word alignment and MIRA (Watanabe et al., 2007) for tuning. This tuning algorithm was shown to be faster and as efficient as MERT for model core features, as well as a better stability with larger numbers of features (Hasler et al., 2011).

In order to compare the individually trained SMT systems, we use the same parallel data for each model, as well as the provided development set to tune the systems. The phrase-based SMT system is augmented with additional features: an Operation Sequence Model (OSM) (Durrani et al., 2011) and a Bilingual Neural Language Model (BiNLM) (Devlin et al., 2014), both trained on the parallel data used to learn the phrase-table. All the translation systems also benefit from two additional reordering models, namely a phrase-based model with three different orientations (monotone, swap and discontinuous) and a hierarchical model with four orientations (non merged discontinuous left and right orientations), both trained in a bidirectional way (Koehn et al., 2005; Galley and Manning, 2008).

Our constrained systems are trained on the data available for the shared task, while unconstrained systems are trained with two additional sets of parallel data, the FIENWAC crawled dataset (cf. Section 2.2) and Open Subtitles, henceforth OSUBS.[12] The details about the corpora used to train the translation models are presented in Table 1. Figure 1 shows how different segmentation methods affect the vocabulary size; given that linguistic segmentation have larger vocabularies as statistical their contribution to translation models may be at least partially complementary.

[11] using the script `omorfi-factorise.py`

[12] `http://opus.lingfil.uu.se/`

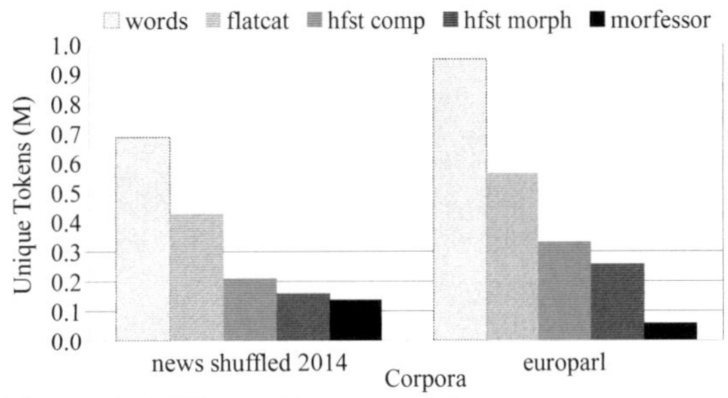

Figure 1: Effects of segmentation on unique token counts for Finnish.

Corpus	Sentences (k)	Words (M) Finnish	Words (M) English
	Constrained System		
Europarl v8	1,901.1	36.5	50.9
	Unconstrained System		
fienwac.in	640.1	9.2	13.6
fienwac.outt	838.9	12.5	18.1
fienwac.outb	838.9	13.9	18.1
osubs.in	492.2	3.6	5.6
osubs.outt	1,169.6	8.8	14.4
osubs.outb	1,169.6	7.8	13.0

Table 1: Parallel data used to train the translation models, after pre-processing.

The two unconstrained parallel datasets are split into three subsets: pseudo in-domain, pseudo out-of-domain top and pseudo out-of-domain bottom, henceforth `in`, `outt` and `outb`. We rank the sentence pairs according to bilingual cross-entropy difference on the devset (Axelrod et al., 2011) and calculate the perplexity on the devset of LMs trained on different portions of the top ranked sentences (the top 1/64, 1/32 and so on). The subset for which we obtain the lowest perplexities is kept as `in` (this was 1/4 for `fienwac` (403.89 and 3610.95 for English and Finnish, respectively), and 1/16 for `osubs` (702.45 and 7032.2). The remaining part of each dataset is split in two sequential parts in ranking order of same number of lines, which are kept as `outt` and `outb`.

The out-of-domain part of `osubs` is further processed with vocabulary saturation (Lewis and Eetemadi, 2013) in order to have a more efficient and compact system (Rubino et al., 2014). We traverse the sentence pairs in the order they are ranked

Corpus	Sentences (k)	Words (M)
Europarl v8	2,218.2	59.9
News Commentary v10	344.9	8.6
News Shuffled		
2007	3 782.5	90.2
2008	12 954.5	308.1
2009	14 680.0	347.0
2010	6 797.2	157.8
2011	15 437.7	358.1
2012	14 869.7	345.5
2013	21 688.4	495.2
2014	28 221.3	636.6
Gigaword 5th	28,178.1	4,831.5

Table 2: English monolingual data, after pre-processing, used to train the constrained language model.

and filter out those for which we have seen already each 1-gram at least 10 times. This results in a reduction of 3.2x on the number of sentence pairs (from $7.3M$ to $2.3M$) and 2.6x on the number of words (from $114M$ to $44M$).

The resulting parallel datasets (7 in total: Europarl and 3 sets for each `fienwac` and `osubs`) are used individually to train translation and reordering models before being combined by linear interpolation based on perplexity minimisation on the development set. (Sennrich, 2012)

4.2 Language Models

All the Language Models (LM) used in our experiments are 5-grams modified Kneser-Ney smoothed LMs trained using KenLM (Heafield et al., 2013). For the constrained setup, the Finnish and the English LMs are trained following two different approaches. The English LM is trained on the concatenation of all available corpora while the Finnish LM is obtained by linearly interpolating individually trained LMs based on each corpus. The weights given to each individual LM is calculated by minimising the perplexity obtained on the development set. For the unconstrained setup, the Finnish LM is trained on the concatenation of all constrained data plus the additional monolingual crawled corpora (noted *FiWaC*). The data used to train the English and Finnish LMs are presented in Table 2 and Table 3 respectively.

5 Results

We tackle the English-to-Finnish direction in the unconstrained task, while both directions are presented for the constrained task. Systems' outputs are combined using MEMT (Heafield and Lavie, 2010) using default settings, except for the beam size (set to $1,500$) and radius (5 for Finnish and 7 for English), following empirical results obtained on the development set.

Corpus	Sentences (k)	Words (M)
Constrained System		
News Shuffle 2014	1,378.8	16.5
Unconstrained System		
FiWaC	146,557.4	1,996.3

Table 3: Finnish monolingual data, after pre-processing, used to train the language models.

System	Dev BLEU	Dev TER	Test BLEU	Test TER
Phrase-Based	13.51	0.827	12.33	0.843
Factored Model	13.08	0.827	11.89	0.847
Hierarchical	13.05	0.822	12.11	0.830
HFST Comp	**13.57**	**0.814**	12.66	0.828
HFST Morph	13.19	0.818	**12.77**	**0.819**
Morfessor	12.21	0.860	11.58	0.864
Flatcat	12.67	0.844	12.05	0.849
Combination	14.61	0.786	13.54	0.801

Table 4: Results obtained on the development and test sets for the constrained English-to-Finnish translation task. Best individual system in bold.

5.1 Constrained Results

Individual systems trained on the provided data are evaluated before being combined. The results obtained for the English-to-Finnish direction are presented in Table 4.[13] The BLEU (Papineni et al., 2002) and TER (Snover et al., 2006) scores obtained by the system trained on compound-segmented data (*HFST Comp*) show a positive impact of this method on SMT according to the development set, compared to the other individual systems. The unsupervised segmentation methods do not improve over phrase-based SMT, while the hierarchical model shows an interesting reduction of the TER score compared to a classic phrase-based approach. On the test set, the use of inflectional morph segments as well as compounds (*HFST Morph*) leads to the best results for the individual systems on both evaluation metrics. The combination of these 7 systems improves substantially over the best individual system for the development and the test sets.

The results for the other translation direction (Finnish to English) are shown in Table 5 and

[13] We use NIST mteval v13 and TERp v0.1, both with default parameters.

System	Dev BLEU	Dev TER	Test BLEU	Test TER
Phrase-Based	17.19	0.762	16.90	0.759
Hierarchical	16.98	0.768	15.93	0.773
HFST Comp	17.87	0.748	16.68	0.753
HFST Morph	**18.64**	**0.735**	17.22	0.752
Morfessor	16.83	0.769	15.96	0.756
Flatcat	16.78	0.766	**17.33**	**0.741**
Combination	19.66	0.719	18.77	0.726

Table 5: Results obtained on the development and test sets for the constrained Finnish-to-English translation task. Best individual system in bold.

follow the same trend as observed with Finnish as target: the morphologically segmented data helps improving over classic SMT approaches. The two metrics indicate better performances of *HFST Morph* on the development set, while *Flatcat* reaches the best scores on the test set. The results obtained with the segmented data on the two translation directions and the different segmentation approaches are fluctuating and do not indicate which method is the best. Again, the combination of all the systems results in a substantial improvement over the best individual system across both evaluation metrics. The top 3 systems presented in Table 5, namely *Combination*, *HFST Morph* and *Phrase-Based* correlates with the results reported by the manual evaluation.[14]

5.2 Unconstrained Results

We present the results obtained on the unconstrained English-to-Finnish translation task in Table 6. Two individual systems are evaluated, using word-forms and compound-based data, and show that the segmented data leads to lower TER scores, while higher BLEU are reached by the word-based system. The combination of these two systems in addition to the constrained outputs of the remaining systems (hierarchical, factored model, HFST Morph, Morfessor and Flatcat) is evaluated in the last row of the table, and shows .3pt BLEU gain on the test set over the phrase-based approach using word forms.

The human evaluation conducted on the English–Finnish translation direction shows interesting results. While our unconstrained *Combination* system outperforms our other manually evaluated systems, the quality of the unconstrained *Phrase-Based* output is lower than the constrained *Combination* one. The opposite is observed on the automatic metrics, with a difference of 2.5pts BLEU and $.2pt$ TER.

[14]http://www.statmt.org/wmt15/results.html

System	Dev BLEU	Dev TER	Test BLEU	Test TER
Phrase-Based	**16.16**	0.804	**16.07**	0.801
HFST Comp	15.80	**0.796**	15.06	**0.800**
Combination	17.25	0.776	16.38	0.779

Table 6: Results obtained on the development and test sets for the unconstrained English-to-Finnish translation task. Best individual system in bold.

6 Conclusion

Our participation in WMT15's translation task focus on investigating the use of several morphological segmentation methods and Web data acquisition in order to handle the data scarcity and the rich morphology of Finnish. We evaluate several SMT approaches, showing the usefulness of morphological segmentation for Finnish SMT. In particular, the rule-based methods lead to the best results on the constrained English–Finnish task compared to our other individual systems.

In addition, the manual evaluation results indicate that combining diverse SMT systems' outputs, including morphologically segmented ones, can outperform a classic phrase-based approach trained on larger parallel and monolingual corpora. The combination of the different SMT systems leads to the best results for both translation directions, as shown by automatic metrics and manual evaluation. Finally, the acquisition of additional training data improves over the constrained systems and is a successful example of the Abu-MaTran crawling pipeline. However, the discrepancy observed on the results using the different segmentation methods requires a deeper analysis of the SMT output, which is planned as future work.

Acknowledgments

The research leading to these results has received funding from the European Union Seventh Framework Programme FP7/2007-2013 under grant agreement PIAP-GA-2012-324414 (Abu-MaTran). We would like to thank Kenneth Heafield for his help to our questions re MEMT.

References

Amittai Axelrod, Xiaodong He, and Jianfeng Gao. 2011. Domain adaptation via pseudo in-domain data selection. In *Proceedings of the Conference on Empirical Methods in Natural Language Processing*, pages 355–362. Association for Computational Linguistics.

David Chiang. 2005. A Hierarchical Phrase-based Model for Statistical Machine Translation. In *Proceedings of ACL*, pages 263–270.

Jacob Devlin, Rabih Zbib, Zhongqiang Huang, Thomas Lamar, Richard Schwartz, and John Makhoul. 2014. Fast and Robust Neural Network Joint Models for Statistical Machine Translation. In *Proceedings of ACL*, pages 1370–1380.

Nadir Durrani, Helmut Schmid, and Alexander Fraser. 2011. A Joint Sequence Translation Model with Integrated Reordering. In *Proceedings of ACL/HLT*, pages 1045–1054.

Miquel Esplà-Gomis, Filip Klubička, Nikola Ljubešić, Sergio Ortiz-Rojas, Vassilis Papavassiliou, and Prokopis Prokopidis. 2014. Comparing two acquisition systems for automatically building an english-croatian parallel corpus from multilingual websites. In *Proceedings of the 9th International Conference on Language Resources and Evaluation*, LREC'14, Reykjavik, Iceland.

Michel Galley and Christopher D Manning. 2008. A simple and effective hierarchical phrase reordering model. In *Proceedings of the Conference on Empirical Methods in Natural Language Processing*, pages 848–856. Association for Computational Linguistics.

Qin Gao and Stephan Vogel. 2008. Parallel Implementations of Word Alignment Tool. In *Software Engineering, Testing, and Quality Assurance for Natural Language Processing*, pages 49–57.

Stig-Arne Grönroos, Sami Virpioja, Peter Smit, and Mikko Kurimo. 2014. Morfessor flatcat: An hmm-based method for unsupervised and semi-supervised learning of morphology. In *Proceedings of COLING 2014, the 25th International Conference on Computational Linguistics*, pages 1177–1185.

Eva Hasler, Barry Haddow, and Philipp Koehn. 2011. Margin Infused Relaxed Algorithm for Moses. *The Prague Bulletin of Mathematical Linguistics*, 96:69–78.

Kenneth Heafield and Alon Lavie. 2010. Combining machine translation output with open source: The carnegie mellon multi-engine machine translation scheme. *The Prague Bulletin of Mathematical Linguistics*, 93:27–36.

Kenneth Heafield, Ivan Pouzyrevsky, Jonathan H. Clark, and Philipp Koehn. 2013. Scalable Modified Kneser-Ney Language Model Estimation. In *Proceedings of ACL*, pages 690–696.

Philipp Koehn and Hieu Hoang. 2007. Factored Translation Models. In *Proceedings of EMNLP-CoNLL*, pages 868–876.

Philipp Koehn, Amittai Axelrod, Alexandra Birch, Chris Callison-Burch, Miles Osborne, David Talbot, and Michael White. 2005. Edinburgh system description for the 2005 iwslt speech translation evaluation. In *IWSLT*, pages 68–75.

Philipp Koehn, Hieu Hoang, Alexandra Birch, Chris Callison-Burch, Marcello Federico, Nicola Bertoldi, Brooke Cowan, Wade Shen, Christine Moran, Richard Zens, et al. 2007. Moses: Open Source Toolkit for Statistical Machine Translation. In *Proceedings of ACL*, pages 177–180.

Philipp Koehn. 2005. Europarl: A Parallel Corpus for Statistical Machine Translation. In *MT summit*, volume 5, pages 79–86.

William D Lewis and Sauleh Eetemadi. 2013. Dramatically reducing training data size through vocabulary saturation. In *Proceedings of the Eighth Workshop on Statistical Machine Translation*, pages 281–291.

Krister Lindén, Miikka Silfverberg, and Tommi Pirinen. 2009. Hfst tools for morphology–an efficient open-source package for construction of morphological analyzers. In *State of the Art in Computational Morphology*, pages 28–47. Springer.

Nikola Ljubešić and Filip Klubička. 2014. {bs,hr,sr}WaC – web corpora of Bosnian, Croatian and Serbian. In *Proceedings of the 9th Web as Corpus Workshop (WaC-9)*, pages 29–35, Gothenburg, Sweden. Association for Computational Linguistics.

Franz Josef Och and Hermann Ney. 2004. The Alignment Template Approach to Statistical Machine Translation. *Computational linguistics*, 30(4):417–449.

Vassilis Papavassiliou, Prokopis Prokopidis, and Gregor Thurmair. 2013. A modular open-source focused crawler for mining monolingual and bilingual corpora from the web. In *Proceedings of the Sixth Workshop on Building and Using Comparable Corpora*, pages 43–51, Sofia, Bulgaria, August. Association for Computational Linguistics.

Kishore Papineni, Salim Roukos, Todd Ward, and Wei-Jing Zhu. 2002. BLEU: A Method for Automatic Evaluation of Machine Translation. In *Proceedings of ACL*, pages 311–318.

Tommi A Pirinen. 2015. Omorfi—free and open source morphological lexical database for Finnish. In *Nordic Conference of Computational Linguistics NODALIDA 2015*, pages 313–317.

Raphael Rubino, Antonio Toral, Víctor M. Sánchez-Cartagena, Jorge Ferrández-Tordera, Sergio Ortiz Rojas, Gema Ramírez-Sánchez, Felipe Sánchez-Martínez, and Andy Way. 2014. Abu-matran at wmt 2014 translation task: Two-step data selection and rbmt-style synthetic rules. In *Proceedings of the Ninth Workshop on Statistical Machine Translation*, pages 171–177, Baltimore, Maryland, USA, June. Association for Computational Linguistics.

Rico Sennrich. 2012. Perplexity minimization for translation model domain adaptation in statistical machine translation. In *Proceedings of the 13th Conference of the European Chapter of the Association for Computational Linguistics*, pages 539–549. Association for Computational Linguistics.

Matthew Snover, Bonnie Dorr, Richard Schwartz, Linnea Micciulla, and John Makhoul. 2006. A Study of Translation Edit Rate with Targeted Human Annotation. In *Proceedings of AMTA*, pages 223–231.

Vít Suchomel and Jan Pomikálek. 2012. Efficient web crawling for large text corpora. In *Proceedings of the 7th Web as Corpus Workshop*, WAC7, pages 39–43, Lyon, France.

Antonio Toral, Raphael Rubino, Miquel Esplà-Gomis, Tommi Pirinen, Andy Way, and Gema Ramirez-Sanchez. 2014. Extrinsic evaluation of web-crawlers in machine translation: a case study on croatian–english for the tourism domain. In *Proceedings of EAMT*, pages 221–224.

Dániel Varga, László Németh, Péter Halácsy, András Kornai, Viktor Trón, and Viktor Nagy. 2005. Parallel corpora for medium density languages. In *Recent Advances in Natural Language Processing*, pages 590–596, Borovets, Bulgaria.

Sami Virpioja, Peter Smit, Stig-Arne Grönroos, Mikko Kurimo, et al. 2013. Morfessor 2.0: Python implementation and extensions for morfessor baseline.

Taro Watanabe, Jun Suzuki, Hajime Tsukada, and Hideki Isozaki. 2007. Online large-margin training for statistical machine translation. In *Proceedings of the 2007 Joint Conference on Empirical Methods in Natural Language Processing and Computational Natural Language Learning (EMNLP-CoNLL)*, pages 764–773, Prague, Czech Republic, June. Association for Computational Linguistics.

The University of Illinois submission to the WMT 2015 Shared Translation Task

Lane Schwartz, Bill Bryce, Chase Geigle, Sean Massung, Yisi Liu, Haoruo Peng, Vignesh Raja, Subhro Roy and **Shyam Upadhyay**
University of Illinois at Urbana-Champaign
Urbana, IL 61801, USA
`lanes@illinois.edu`

Abstract

In this year's WMT translation task, Finnish-English was introduced as a language pair of competition for the first time. We present experiments examining several variations on a morphologically-aware statistical phrase-based machine translation system for translating Finnish into English. Our system variations attempt to mitigate the issue of rich agglutinative morphology when translating from Finnish into English. Our WMT submission for Finnish-English preprocesses Finnish data with omorfi (Pirinen, 2015), a Finnish morphological analyzer. We also present results for two other language pairs with morphologically interesting source languages, namely German-English and Czech-English.

1 Introduction

Students enrolled in the Spring 2015 graduate-level course in statistical machine translation (MT) at the University of Illinois were invited to develop MT systems within the context of the 2015 Workshop on Statistical Machine Translation (WMT) shared translation task. Each group of 2-3 students chose one language pair, developed a baseline MT system for that language pair using Moses (Koehn et al., 2007), and chose one specific linguistic dimension along which to experiment. In this work, we present the results of four groups of experiments — two Finnish-English (§3.1 and §3.2), and one each for Czech-English (§4) and German-English (§5).

The first author was the instructor, and the subsequent authors were students in the work described here.

2 Methodology

We use the current stable release (v3) of Moses, a state-of-the-art statistical phrase-based machine translation system.

We trained translation models using the Europarl corpus (Koehn, 2005), using the latest available versions (v7 for German-English and Czech-English, and v8 for Finnish-English), as well as the Common Crawl corpus and News Commentary (v10) corpus for German-English and Czech-English, and the Wiki Headlines corpus for Finnish-English.

We trained a back-off language model (LM) with modified Kneser-Ney smoothing (Katz, 1987; Kneser and Ney, 1995; Chen and Goodman, 1998) on the English Gigaword v5 corpus (Parker et al., 2011) using `lmplz` from KenLM (Heafield et al., 2013).

3 Finnish-English

We tried various morphological tokenization schemes on the *source* language (Finnish) in order to mitigate its strong agglutination. The *target* language (English) was tokenized with the default Moses tokenizer script.

3.1 Finnish tokenization using Morfessor and word-lattices

We begin by adapting the lattice technique of Dyer et al. (2009) to Finnish. We train a standard phrase-based machine translation model on a new corpus: on the source side we concatenate the original data with its one-best segmentation according to a Morfessor (Creutz and Lagus, 2007) model trained on the original data, and on the target side we simply concatenate it with itself. The result is a corpus that is twice as long as the original data, but that aligns both segmented and unsegmented Finnish sentences with their English counterparts. This ensures that we will have phrases in our phrase

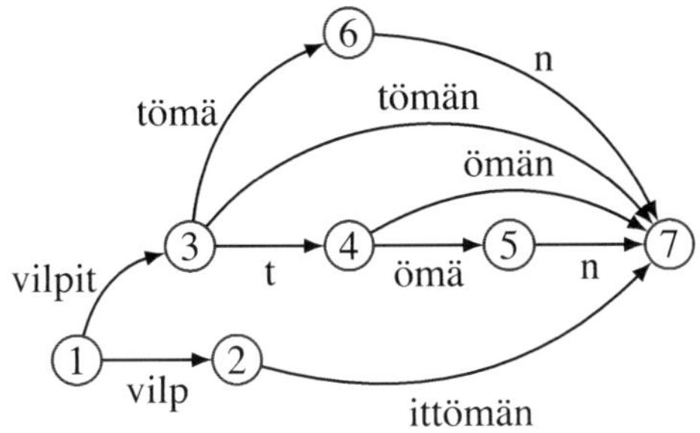

Figure 1: A word lattice that represents the top five segmentations for the Finnish word *vilpittömän*.

table that correspond with both the original unsegmented words as well as for individual morphemes.

At tuning and test time, we then decompose our input into a word lattice input that reflects the uncertainty of the decomposition of each word in the sentence (Dyer et al., 2008). We construct the lattice by considering the top five best segmentations for each word according to our Morfessor model. The start and end of each word in the original sentence is a node, and we place edges and nodes between the two such that the edge is labeled with a string output and its target is a node that represents the partial output of the word thus far. Each of the edges is also weighted with a certain probability, reflecting the likelihood of using that specific edge, given that we are at a specific node.

We calculate edge probabilities as follows. Let $p(v|u, \Theta)$ be the probability of going to node v given that we are at node u under the trained Morfessor model Θ (we only concern ourselves with the case where v is an adjacent to u). Let $\mathbf{s}$ be a segmentation for the current word, represented as a set of edges (n_1, n_2) through the graph. Then, we set

$$p(v \mid u, \Theta) = \frac{\sum_{\mathbf{s}:(u,v)\in\mathbf{s}} p(\mathbf{s} \mid \Theta)}{\sum_{\mathbf{s}':(u,v')\in\mathbf{s}'} p(\mathbf{s}' \mid \Theta)},$$

where the numerator is a summation of the Morfessor segmentation probabilities for segmentations that use the edge (u, v), and the denominator is a summation of the Morfessor segmentation probabilities for all segmentations that pass through node u.

However, Morfessor gives us log likelihood scores for its segmentations. Call these $\ell_{\mathbf{s}}$. We then compute the following, in order to avoid roundoff errors as much as possible:

System	LM	TM	BLEU	-cased
Baseline	5	5	**16.95**	**15.09**
Morfessor	5	8	15.67	14.88
Hiero	6	5	14.99	14.45
Lattice ($n = 2$)	6	8	14.67	14.00
Lattice ($n = 5$)	6	8	14.68	13.95

Table 1: Results for Finnish-English (§3.1).

$$p(v \mid u, \Theta) = \frac{\sum_{\mathbf{s}:(u,v)\in\mathbf{s}} 2^{\ell_{\mathbf{s}}-\ell_{max}}}{\sum_{\mathbf{s}':(u,v')\in\mathbf{s}'} 2^{\ell_{\mathbf{s}'}-\ell_{max}}},$$

where ℓ_{max} is the highest log likelihood segmentation for the current word. This can be seen as simply multiplying the numerator and denominator by the fixed constant $2^{-\ell_{max}}$. The code for performing this lattice generation is freely available online.[1] We use a Morfessor model trained on the Finnish side of the Europarl parallel training data with $\alpha = 0.5$.

Table 1 shows the output of our systems on the testing data from WMT 2015. We report the scores that were obtained from Moses evaluation scripts using multi-BLEU; the numbers in the shared task are slightly different as they use the NIST BLEU scripts. Our baseline is a phrase-based default Moses configuration with the 5-gram language model, and we found this outperformed a hierarchical phrase based configuration with the same maximum phrase length and a 6-gram language model. Among the segmentation methods, using a single one-best segmentation with Morfessor performed the best — the word lattice method had disappointing performance using either the top five or top two best segmentations for the lattice generation. We were unable to combine the word lattice and hierarchical phrase-based approaches together as Moses does not yet support these two features at the same time.

3.2 Finnish tokenization using omorfi

In addition to the experiments described above, we build three variations utilizing omorfi (Pirinen, 2015) to morphologically segment the Finnish data. We use omorfi to decompose each agglutinated Finnish word into its component morphemes and each morpheme to a default case or form. Inflectional morphemes which capture information

[1] https://github.com/smassung/uiuc-wmt15/tree/master/chase

```
Istuntokauden
Istuntokauden Istunto#kausi N Gen Sg
```

Figure 2: The first word of Finnish Europarl corpus, as processed by omorfi.

such as the person, number, tense, voice, and mood of verbs as well as the number and case of nouns is lost in the lemmatization, and therefore, when lemmatization has taken place, all of this information is lost to the system. Figure 2 illustrates this process; the token "Istuntokauden" is broken into two morpheme lemmas, separated by a "#" sign. We discard the inflectional information, which here denotes that the original token was a singular noun in genitive case.

As a baseline, we build a system using Moses and provided the data described above with none of the Finnish data having been processed by omorfi. Tuning was done using MERT (Och, 2003).

In the first variation (V1), all Finnish data is first segmented by omorfi. The intuition behind this technique is simply that there are more words in the target text than would align well with agglutinative words in the source text. By using the morphemes of the source language rather than the unsegmented words, the output source tokens might more easily align with the target tokens.

In the second variation (V2), the omorfi-segmented Finnish data from the first variation is concatenated with the unprocessed Finnish. Target language data is concatenated with itself in training to align each target sentence with both the unprocessed and morphologically-analyzed variations of its source sentence. The intuition here is that any Finnish tokens which are their own lemmas (i.e. do not inflect) will potentially align with the same target token twice, and will bear a stronger alignment probability than with other tokens in the translation model. Function words and adpositions would be among those which undergo such double alignment, and which may serve as anchors for the alignment of the entire sentence.

In the third variation (V3), the translation table created during the second variation is consulted during segmentation of the tuning and test data. If an original token could be found in the table before being broken into morphemes by omorfi, then that token is left unprocessed. If a token could not be found, then it was passed to omorfi and the morphemes returned replaced the token in the data.

System	LM	TM	BLEU	-cased
Baseline	5	5	16.14	15.25
V1-omorfi	5	5	14.79	14.00
V2-omorfi	5	5	15.14	14.32
V3-omorfi	5	5	**16.90**	**15.98**

Table 2: Results for Finnish-English (§3.2).

The resulting tuning and testing datasets are thus partially analyzed for morphemes. In this way, more common Finnish agglutinations are retained while less common ones are broken into potentially more common individual morphemes.

Results are shown in Table 2. Only V3 performed better than the baseline of using default Moses tokenization for Finnish. This variation comes closest to a balance between alignment with shorter target phrases — achieved by breaking down agglutinative words into morphemes — and retaining what inflectional information can be retained — since unprocessed and therefore unlemmatized words retain all grammatical inflection.

3.2.1 Variation 1: All data fully processed by omorfi

For the first variation on our system, we pass to omorfi all of the Finnish data described above used for training, tuning, and testing. Therefore, for each token in the text, either the lemma of the original token was returned by omorfi if the token was not found to be an agglutination of stem and morphemes, or, if the token was found to be an agglutination, a lemmatized token of each morpheme was returned, and these new tokens stood in place of the agglutinative token found in the original text.

The intuition behind this technique is simply that there are more words in the target text than would align well with agglutinative words in the source text. By creating more tokens out of the original source tokens, the smaller source tokens might more easily align with the target tokens. The new tokens returned by omorfi were always present in the source text in their non-lemma forms, but because the same morpheme could be added to different stems, the unique word formation may hide a relation between the appearance of that morpheme in a source sentence and a single word of English in the target sentence.

Using only source data which has been fully processed by omorfi in the training, tuning, and testing stages, BLEU scores were 14.00 (case-sensitive) and 14.79 (case-insensitive), that is 1.25 and 1.35

points below the baseline respectively.

3.2.2 Variation 2: Concatenated original source data and omorfi-processed data

For the second variation on our system, we used the same omorfi-processed Finnish data which was used for the first variation. This time, however, the omorfi-processed training, tuning, and testing data was concatenated with the original training, tuning, and testing data respectively. So for example, the data used for training was the original set of sentences from Europarl, followed by the same set of sentences but processed by omorfi as described above. Each of the training, tuning, and testing sets therefore contained exactly twice as many sentences as the original testing data. Likewise, the set of target sentences in each case was twice as many, but the target data was not processed for morphology, such that the second half of the target language training, tuning, and testing sets was exactly the same as the first half.

Designing the datasets in this way effected that, in the case of alignment for example, both the original Finnish sentence was aligned with the English as well as the omorfi-processed Finnish sentence. The intuition here is that Finnish tokens which are their own lemmas (i.e. do not inflect) will potentially align with the same target token twice, and will bear a stronger alignment proability than other tokens in the translation model. Function words and adpositions would be among those which undergo such double alignment, and which may serve as anchors for the alignment of the entire sentence.

For all other words — those for which omorfi returns morphologically analyzed output - two potentially useful alignments could be formed: First, there would be an alignment of the unprocessed source token with several target tokens, and so a phrasal alignment in which the English word aligns with the agglutinative word containing the proper morpheme. Second, there would be an alignment closer to one-to-one between the target word and the proper morpheme lemma returned by omorfi. Concatenating the unprocessed training, tuning, and testing sets in the source language with the omorfi-processed training, tuning, and testing sets respectively resulted in BLEU scores of 14.32 (case-sensitive) and 15.14 (case-insensitive), that is 0.93 and 1.00 points below the baseline respectively.

3.2.3 Variation 3: Consultation of the baseline translation table

For the third and final variation of our system, we preprocess the tuning and testing sets in the source language by consulting the translation table created for the second variation. For each token in the Finnish tuning and testing data, the translation table was consulted for the presence of that token as a unigram. If the token was found in the translation table, then it was rendered as is in the output of this step. If the token was not found in the translation table, then the token was passed to omorfi and the resulting morpheme lemmas were rendered as output. The resulting tuning and testing sets, therefore contained either an agglutinative form as found in the original Finnish or a processed string of morpheme lemmas (or perhaps simply the lemma) returned by omorfi from the original token, but not both.

The intuition here was to overcome the lemmatization process which occurs from passing all of the data through omorfi. It may be the case that different inflections of the same lemma tune better to different English words, but the lemmatization process effects that different English words tune to the same Finnish lemma, causing confusion. Leaving known inflected forms in the tuning and testing data gives this variation an advantage over the first variation. By tuning and testing on known tokens and morphologically analyzing unknown tokens in these datasets, the resulting BLEU scores were 15.98 (case-sensitive) and 16.90 (case-insensitive), 0.73 and 0.76 points above the baseline respectively.

4 Czech-English

For Czech-English, we train baseline phrase-based systems with no special handling of Czech morphology. We also consider experimental variants in which Czech words are morphologically segmented. We use Morphessor (Creutz and Lagus, 2007) for morphological segmentation.

Finally, we consider a re-ranking technique based on the degree of commonality between parts-of-speech (POS) in each source sentence and each respective translation of that source sentence. To this end, we use MorphoDiTa (Straková et al., 2014) and the Stanford CoreNLP toolkit (Manning et al., 2014) to POS tag the Czech and English sentences, respectively. We next construct a dictionary that maps POS tags from one language to tags in the other. After translating with Moses, each English translation in the n-best list is augmented with a POS intersection score, and rerank taking this new score into account. We define the POS intersection score as simply the number of identical POS tags between a Czech sentence and the hypothesized English translation.

System	BLEU	BLEU-c
Moses trained on Europarl	18.59	17.72
Moses trained on Europarl, Common Crawl and News Commentary	20.69	19.83
Stemming as pre-processing, Moses trained on Europarl	17.88	17.08
Morfessor trained on Europarl, Moses trained on Europarl	16.48	15.74
POS intersection, Moses trained on Europarl	15.68	13.46
Morfessor trained on Europarl, POS intersection, Moses trained on Europarl	13.43	13.74

Table 3: Results for Czech into English.

5 German-English and English-German

For German-English and English-German, we focus primarily on the effects of source clause reordering transformations. In this approach, we transform source language $\mathbf{s}$ into $\mathbf{s}'$, such that the clause structure of sentences in $\mathbf{s}'$ more closely follow the clause structure of target language $\mathbf{t}$.

5.1 English to German

With the goal of restructuring English source sentences to have more German-like structure, we define the following transformation rules:

1. Detect all clauses in a sentence which might require transformation. We selected spans of text, which were labeled as S or SBAR by the parser. We do not include clauses which begin with "to".

2. For each clause, we apply the following rules in order :

   (a) If there exists a verb phrase (detected by a shallow parser) with "to", we move the remaining portion of the verb phrase (starting with token "to") to the end of the clause.

   (b) If there exists a verb phrase (detected by a shallow parser) with a token with VBN part of speech tag, we move the remaining portion of the verb phrase (starting with VBN token) to the end of the clause.

   (c) If there exists a verb phrase (detected by a shallow parser) starting with a modal verb, we leave the modal verb but move the rest of the verb phrase to the end of the clause.

We used a state-of-the-art shallow parser (Punyakanok and Roth, 2001) in conjunction with a constituent parser (Socher et al., 2013) to implement the above transformation rules. For the purposes of the English-German language pair, we pre-process all English data into equivalent English′ data using the above transformation rules.

We train a German language model on the German side of the Europarl, Common Crawl, and News Commentary corpora, and a translation model on the English′-German Europarl corpus. Our development set for tuning was the WMT newstest data from 2008–2014. Results for the WMT newtest-2015 data set under the baseline (en-de) and restructured (en′-de) conditions are shown in Table 4.

System	BLEU	BLEU-cased	TER
en-de	16.6	16.3	0.933
en′-de	17.9	17.2	0.731

Table 4: Results for English and English′ translated into German.

5.2 German to English

Holmqvist et al. (2011) report improvements on German-English when modifying German text to be more like English. To this end, we utilize a subset of the clause restructuring rules (rules 4 & 6) from Collins et al. (2005):

- If a finite verb (VVFIN) and a particle (PTKVZ) are found in the same clause (subtree labeled as S), then move the particle to precede the verb.

- Before applying rule 6, we first remove all internal VP nodes, and replace them by their children in the tree. Then, for every clause which dominates a finite verb, infinitival verb and a negative particle (PTKNEG), then the negative particle is moved to directly follow the finite verb.

We used the Stanford Parser (Manning et al., 2014) for parsing German sentences and then applied the relevant rules. The reordered sentences were the yield of the transformed tree. The reordered sentences were then segmented using the jWordSplitter [2] for compound splitting.

We train an English 6-gram language model on the Gigaword corpus, and a translation model on the German′-English Europarl corpus. Our development set for tuning was the WMT newstest data from 2008–2014. Results for the WMT newtest-2015 data set under the baseline (de-en) and restructured (de′-en) conditions are shown in Table 5.

System	BLEU	BLEU-cased	TER
de-en	21.4	22.2	0.938
de′-en	24.9	23.8	0.641

Table 5: Results for German and German′ translated into English.

6 Discussion and Conclusion

Overall, tackling the rich morphology of Finnish proved to be effective in improving upon the baseline, but not by much, and only in the case where the translation model could be consulted as to whether source words in the tuning and testing data were known.

The variation of our Finnish-English system in §3.2.1 breaks down the Finnish data into those components which make up the agglutinated words, treating the morphemes, rather than the original tokens, as the words. In teasing out the morphemes from the original data, more individual word alignments can be created between source and target tokens, but inflectional data such as the case of nouns and the person and tense of verbs, is lost. In this case, different English tokens which may truthfully align to differently inflected forms of the same lemma may instead compete for alignment with the lemma in the translation table, thus creating confusion and resulting in evaluation below the baseline.

[2]http://sourceforge.net/projects/jwordsplitter/

The second variation (in §3.2.2) creates the potential for alignments between agglutinated Finnish words with groups of English words, but also between Finnish lemmas and single English words. While there is more potential for a correct alignments — still despite inflectional information being lost — the approach is still brute force, and there is still confusion created in the translation table since some of the probability given to the correct alignment, whatever that may be, is taken by the alignment of some English words with the agglutinated or non-agglutinated Finnish counterpart.

The third variation (in §3.2.3), while addressing the issue of over-lemmatization created in the first variation, does in fact improve on the baseline. In this final case, inflected forms found in the training data retain their inflection, and so the first person singular form of the verb "to be" in Finnish has greater chance of being translated into "am" rather than the lemmatized form being translated into the most prevalent form of "to be" in the target language training data — "is" for example.

Still the problem of Finnish morphology is very hard for a translation system into English. Our system has only addressed the derivational morphology of Finnish agglutination. We have not at all addressed the inflectional morphology of Finnish, and so much information about the role of certain tokens in the source sentence is lost. Some necessary English words, such as personal pronouns, may be lost on the system because the presence of an English pronoun such as "I" in the best English translation may only be encoded in the inflectional morphology of the Finnish.

In further research, we may try a factored model for our system which encodes not only the lemma or lemmas produced by omorfi, but also the grammatical information from the original inflectional morphology. Further still, our system has not addressed the potential problems of reordering between the source and target languages.

At the very least, a rule could be implemented which places Finnish postpositions in front of their objects as a preprocessing step. As Finnish is a head-final language like English, it is possible that no further rule-based reordering would have to be done, but more research is warranted to make this claim. With these complications yet to be addressed, there is certainly more that we may do in the future to improve evaluation.

References

Stanley F. Chen and Joshua Goodman. 1998. An empirical study of smoothing techniques for language modeling. Technical report, Harvard University.

Michael Collins, Philipp Koehn, and Ivona Kučerová. 2005. Clause restructuring for statistical machine translation. In *Proceedings of the 43rd Annual Meeting on Association for Computational Linguistics*, ACL '05, pages 531–540, Stroudsburg, PA, USA. Association for Computational Linguistics.

Mathias Creutz and Krista Lagus. 2007. Unsupervised Models for Morpheme Segmentation and Morphology Learning. *ACM Trans. Speech Lang. Process.*, 4(1):3:1–3:34, February.

Christopher Dyer, Smaranda Muresan, and Philip Resnik. 2008. Generalizing word lattice translation. In *Proceedings of ACL-08: HLT*, pages 1012–1020. Association for Computational Linguistics.

Chris Dyer, Hendra Setiawan, Yuval Marton, and Philip Resnik. 2009. The University of Maryland Statistical Machine Translation System for the Fourth Workshop on Machine Translation. In *Proceedings of the Fourth Workshop on Statistical Machine Translation*, StatMT '09, pages 145–149, Stroudsburg, PA, USA. Association for Computational Linguistics.

Kenneth Heafield, Ivan Pouzyrevsky, Jonathan H. Clark, and Philipp Koehn. 2013. Scalable modified kneser-ney language model estimation. In *Proceedings of the 51st Annual Meeting of the Association for Computational Linguistics (Volume 2: Short Papers)*, pages 690–696, Sofia, Bulgaria, August. Association for Computational Linguistics.

Maria Holmqvist, Sara Stymne, and Lars Ahrenberg. 2011. Experiments with word alignment, normalization and clause reordering for smt between english and german. In *Proceedings of the Sixth Workshop on Statistical Machine Translation*, pages 393–398, Edinburgh, Scotland, July. Association for Computational Linguistics.

Slava Katz. 1987. Estimation of probabilities from sparse data for the language model component of a speech recognizer. *IEEE Transactions on Acoustics, Speech and Signal Processing*, 35:400–401, March.

Reinhard Kneser and Hermann Ney. 1995. Improved backing-off for *m*-gram language modeling. In *Proceedings of the IEEE International Conference on Acoustics, Speech and Signal Processing (ICASSP'95)*, pages 181–184, Detroit, Michigan, USA, May. IEEE Computer Society.

Philipp Koehn, Hieu Hoang, Alexandra Birch, Chris Callison-Burch, Marcello Federico, Nicola Bertoldi, Brooke Cowan, Wade Shen, Christine Moran, Richard Zens, Chris Dyer, Ondrej Bojar, Alexandra Constantin, and Evan Herbst. 2007. Moses: Open source toolkit for statistical machine translation. In *Proceedings of the 45th Annual Meeting of the Association for Computational Linguistics Companion Volume Proceedings of the Demo and Poster Sessions*, pages 177–180, Prague, Czech Republic, June. Association for Computational Linguistics.

Philipp Koehn. 2005. Europarl: A parallel corpus for statistical machine translation. In *Proceedings of the 10th Machine Translation Summit (MT Summit X)*, pages 79–86, Phuket, Thailand, September.

Christopher Manning, Mihai Surdeanu, John Bauer, Jenny Finkel, Steven Bethard, and David McClosky. 2014. The stanford corenlp natural language processing toolkit. In *Proceedings of 52nd Annual Meeting of the Association for Computational Linguistics: System Demonstrations*, pages 55–60, Baltimore, Maryland, June. Association for Computational Linguistics.

Franz Josef Och. 2003. Minimum error rate training in statistical machine translation. In *Proceedings of the 41st Annual Meeting of the Association for Computational Linguistics*, pages 160–167, Sapporo, Japan, July. Association for Computational Linguistics.

Robert Parker, David Graff, Junbo Kong, Ke Chen, and Kazuaki Maeda. 2011. English Gigaword Fifth Edition LDC2011T07. Philadelphia, Pennsylvania, USA. Linguistic Data Consortium.

Tommi A. Pirinen. 2015. Omorfi — Free and open source morphological lexical database for Finnish. In *Proceedings of the 20th Nordic Conference of Computational Linguistics (NODALIDA '15)*, pages 313–315, Vilnius, Lithuania, May.

Vasin Punyakanok and Dan Roth. 2001. The use of classifiers in sequential inference. In *Advances in Neural Information Processing Systems 14 (NIPS '01)*, pages 995–1001. MIT Press.

Richard Socher, John Bauer, Christopher D. Manning, and Ng Andrew Y. 2013. Parsing with compositional vector grammars. In *Proceedings of the 51st Annual Meeting of the Association for Computational Linguistics (Volume 1: Long Papers)*, pages 455–465, Sofia, Bulgaria, August. Association for Computational Linguistics.

Jana Straková, Milan Straka, and Jan Hajič. 2014. Open-Source Tools for Morphology, Lemmatization, POS Tagging and Named Entity Recognition. In *Proceedings of 52nd Annual Meeting of the Association for Computational Linguistics: System Demonstrations*, pages 13–18, Baltimore, Maryland, June. Association for Computational Linguistics.

Edinburgh's Syntax-Based Systems at WMT 2015

Philip Williams[1], Rico Sennrich[1], Maria Nadejde[1], Matthias Huck[1], Philipp Koehn[1,2]
[1]School of Informatics, University of Edinburgh
[2]Center for Speech and Language Processing, The Johns Hopkins University

Abstract

This paper describes the syntax-based systems built at the University of Edinburgh for the WMT 2015 shared translation task. We developed systems for all language pairs except French-English. This year we focused on: translation out of English using tree-to-string models; continuing to improve our English-German system; and source-side morphological segmentation of Finnish using Morfessor.

1 Introduction

This year's WMT shared translation task featured five language pairs: English paired with Czech, Finnish, French, German, and Russian. We built syntax-based systems in both translation directions for all language pairs except English-French.

For English → German, we continued to develop our string-to-tree system, which has proven highly competitive in previous years. Additions this year included the use of a dependency language model, an alternative tuning metric, and soft source-syntactic constraints.

For translation from English into Czech, Finnish, and Russian, we built STSG-based tree-to-string systems. Support for this type of model is a recent addition to the Moses toolkit. In previous years, our systems have all used string-to-tree models and have only translated into English and German.

For Finnish → English, we experimented with unsupervised morphological segmentation using Morfessor 2.0 (Virpioja et al., 2013).

For the remaining systems (Czech → English, German → English, and Russian → English), our systems were essentially the same as last year's (Williams et al., 2014) except for the addition of this year's training data.

2 System Overview

2.1 Pre-processing

The training data was pre-processed using scripts from the Moses toolkit. We first normalized the data using the `normalize-punctuation.perl` script then performed tokenization, parsing, and truecasing. To parse the English data, we used the Berkeley parser (Petrov et al., 2006; Petrov and Klein, 2007). To parse the German data, we used the ParZu dependency parser (Sennrich et al., 2013).

2.2 Word Alignment

For word alignment we used either MGIZA++ (Gao and Vogel, 2008), a multi-threaded implementation of GIZA++ (Och and Ney, 2003), or `fast_align` (Dyer et al., 2013). In preliminary experiments, we found that the tree-to-string systems were particularly sensitive to the choice of word aligner, echoing a previous observation by Neubig and Duh (2014). See the individual tree-to-string system descriptions in Section 3.

2.3 Language Model

We used all available monolingual data to train one interpolated 5-gram language model for each system. Using either lmplz (Heafield et al., 2013) or the SRILM toolkit (Stolcke, 2002), we first trained an individual language model for each of the supplied monolingual training corpora. These models all used modified Kneser-Ney smoothing (Chen and Goodman, 1998). We then interpolated the individual models using SRILM, providing the target-side of the system's tuning set (Section 2.7) for perplexity-based weight optimization.

2.4 String-to-Tree Model

For English → German and the systems that translate into English, we used a string-to-tree model.

2.4.1 Grammar

The string-to-tree translation model is based on a synchronous context-free grammar (SCFG) with linguistically-motivated labels on the target side.

SCFG rules were extracted from the word-aligned parallel data using the Moses implementation (Williams and Koehn, 2012) of the GHKM algorithm (Galley et al., 2004; Galley et al., 2006).

Minimal GHKM rules were composed into larger rules subject to restrictions on the size of the resulting tree fragment. We used the settings shown in Table 1, which were chosen empirically during the development of 2013's systems (Nadejde et al., 2013).

Parameter	Unbinarized	Binarized
Rule depth	5	7
Node count	20	30
Rule size	5	7

Table 1: Parameter settings for rule composition. The parameters were relaxed for systems that used binarization to allow for the increase in tree node density.

Further to the restrictions on rule composition, fully non-lexical unary rules were eliminated using the method described in Chung et al. (2011) and rules with scope greater than 3 (Hopkins and Langmead, 2010) were pruned from the translation grammar. Scope pruning makes parsing tractable without the need for grammar binarization.

2.4.2 Feature Functions

Our core set of string-to-tree feature functions is unchanged from previous years. It includes the n-gram language model's log probability for the target string, the target word count, the rule count, and various pre-computed rule-specific scores. For a grammar rule r of the form

$$C \rightarrow \langle \alpha, \beta, \sim \rangle$$

where C is a target-side non-terminal label, α is a string of source terminals and non-terminals, β is a string of target terminals and non-terminals, and $\sim$ is a one-to-one correspondence between source and target non-terminals, we score the rule according to (logarithms of) the following functions:

- $p(C, \beta \mid \alpha, \sim)$ and $p(\alpha \mid C, \beta, \sim)$, the direct and indirect translation probabilities.
- $p_{lex}(\beta \mid \alpha)$ and $p_{lex}(\alpha \mid \beta)$, the direct and indirect lexical weights (Koehn et al., 2003).
- $p_{pcfg}(\pi)$, the monolingual PCFG probability of the tree fragment π from which the rule was extracted.
- $\exp(-1/count(r))$, a rule rareness penalty.

2.5 Tree-to-String Model

For English → Czech, English → Finnish, and English → Russian, we used a tree-to-string model.

2.5.1 Grammar

In the tree-to-string model, the translation grammar is a synchronous tree-substitution grammar (Eisner, 2003) with parse tree fragments on the source-side and strings of terminals and non-terminals on the target-side.

As with the string-to-tree models, the grammar was extracted from the word-aligned parallel data using the Moses implementation of the GHKM algorithm. Minimal GHKM rules were composed into larger rules subject to the same size restrictions (Table 1). Unlike string-to-tree rule extraction, fully non-lexical unary rules were included in the grammar and scope pruning was not used.

2.5.2 Feature Functions

The tree-to-string feature functions are similar to those of the string-to-tree model. For a grammar rule r of the form

$$\langle \pi, \beta, \sim \rangle$$

where π is a source-side tree fragment, β is a string of target terminals and non-terminals, and $\sim$ is a one-to-one correspondence between source and target non-terminals, we score the rule according to (logarithms of) the following functions:

- $p(\beta \mid \pi, \sim)$ and $p(\pi \mid \beta, \sim)$, the direct and indirect translation probabilities.
- $p_{lex}(\beta \mid \pi)$ and $p_{lex}(\pi \mid \beta)$, the direct and indirect lexical weights (Koehn et al., 2003).
- $\exp(-1/count(r))$, a rule rareness penalty.

2.6 Decoding

Decoding for the string-to-tree models is based on Sennrich's (2014) recursive variant of the CYK+ parsing algorithm combined with LM integration via cube pruning (Chiang, 2007). Decoding for the tree-to-string models is based on the rule matching algorithm by Zhang et al. (2009) combined with LM integration via cube pruning.

2.7 Tuning

The feature weights were tuned using the Moses implementation of MERT (Och, 2003) for all systems except English-to-German, for which we used k-best MIRA (Cherry and Foster, 2012) due to the use of sparse features.

For the tree-to-string systems, we used all of the previous years' test sets as tuning data (except newstest2014, which was used as the development test set). For the string-to-tree systems, we used subsets of the test data to speed up decoding.

3 Individual Systems

In this section we describe individual systems and present experimental results. In many cases, the only difference from the generic setup of the previous section is that we perform right binarization of the training and test parse trees.

We also built hierarchical phrase-based systems (Chiang, 2007), which we refer to in tables as 'Hiero.' These systems were built using the Moses toolkit, with standard settings. They were not used in the submission and are included for comparison only.

For each system, we present results for both the development test set (newstest2014 in most cases) and for the test set (newstest2015) for which reference translations were provided after the system submission deadline. We refer to these as 'devtest' and 'test', respectively.

3.1 English to Czech

For English → Czech we built a tree-to-string system. We used `fast_align` for word alignment due to the large training data size and on the strength of its performance for English → Finnish and English → Russian. We used all test sets from 2008 to 2013 as tuning data. Table 2 gives the mean BLEU scores, averaged over three MERT runs. Our submitted system was the right binarized system that, out of the three runs, scored highest on devtest.

system	devtest	test
Hiero	20.2	16.8
Tree-to-string	19.0	15.7
+ right binarization	19.5	16.1

Table 2: English to Czech translation results (BLEU) on devtest (newstest2014) and test (newstest2015) sets.

3.2 English to Finnish

In preliminary English → Finnish experiments, we compared the use of MGIZA++ and `fast_align`. Since there was only one test set provided, in these initial experiments we split newsdev2015 into two halves, using the first half for tuning and the second half for testing. Table 3 gives the mean BLEU scores, averaged over three MERT runs.

	MGIZA++	`fast_align`
Hiero	11.7	11.6
Tree-to-string	11.5	12.3
+ right binarization	11.9	12.8

Table 3: Comparison of word alignment tools for English to Finnish. BLEU on subset of newsdev2015.

For our final system, we used `fast_align` for word alignment and we used the full newsdev2015 test set as tuning data. Table 4 gives the mean BLEU scores for this setup. Our submitted system was the right binarized system that, out of the three MERT runs, scored highest on devtest.

system	dev	test
Hiero	11.4	11.5
Tree-to-string	11.9	11.8
+ right binarization	12.2	12.3

Table 4: Final English to Finnish translation results (BLEU) on dev (newsdev2015) and test (newstest2015) sets.

3.3 English to German

We experiment with the following additions to last year's submission system: a relational dependency language model (RDLM) (Sennrich, 2015); tuning on the syntactic metric HWCM (Liu and Gildea, 2005; Sennrich, 2015); soft source-syntactic constraints (Huck et al., 2014); a large-scale n-gram Neural Network language model (NPLM) (Vaswani et al., 2013); treebank binarization (Sennrich and Haddow, 2015); particle verb restructuring (Sennrich and Haddow, 2015). We do not include syntactic constraints in this year's baseline. Our string-to-tree baseline uses a dependency representation of compounds, as described in (Sennrich and Haddow, 2015).

RDLM is a relational dependency language model which predicts the dependency relations

system	BLEU	2+ SUBJ
original trees	20.1	0
+ RDLM	21.0	0
+ RDLM (bidir.)	21.2	0
right binarization	20.4	272
head binarization	20.5	152
+ RDLM	21.3	43
+ RDLM (bidir.)	21.5	32

Table 5: English to German translation results (on newstest2013) with different binarizations and language models. *2+ SUBJ*: number of finite clauses with more than one subject.

system	devtest	test
Hiero	19.2	21.0
String-to-tree baseline	19.8	21.4
+ $\frac{\text{HWCM+BLEU}}{2}$ tuning	20.1	21.6
+ head binarization	20.5	22.3
+ RDLM (bidirectional)	21.5	23.3
+ source-syntactic constraints	21.6	23.8
+ 5-gram NPLM	22.0	24.1
+ less pruning (**submission**)	22.0	24.0
+ particle verb restructuring	22.0	24.4

Table 6: English to German translation results (BLEU) on devtest (newstest2013) and test (newstest2015) sets.

and words in the translation hypotheses based on the dependency relations and words of the ancestor and sibling nodes in the dependency tree. Our model contains several extensions over the original paper (Sennrich, 2015). Like the original paper, we use an ancestor context size of 2, but we increase the sibling context size from 1 to 3, and allow bidirectional context, using the 3 closest siblings to both the left and right of the current node. The original model predicts a virtual stop node as the last child of each tree, which models the probability that a node has no more children. This is mirrored by a virtual start node in the bidirectional model.

We binarize the treebanks before rule extraction. We note that treebank binarization allows the extraction of rules that overgeneralize, e.g. allowing structures with zero, or multiple, preterminals per node, effectively allowing verb clauses without verb and similar. We use *head binarization* (Sennrich and Haddow, 2015), which ensures that each constituent contains exactly one head. During decoding, the generated target trees are unbinarized to allow scoring with RDLM. Table 5 shows that both right binarization and head binarization overgeneralize, exemplified by the fact that they allow finite clauses to have multiple subjects[1]. The RDLM reduces this problem, and the bidirectional RDLM slightly outperforms the unidirectional variant, both in terms of BLEU and the number of overgeneralizations.

For the soft source-syntactic constraints, we annotate the source text with the Stanford Neural Network dependency parser (Chen and Manning, 2014), along with heuristic projectivization (Nivre and Nilsson, 2005).

[1]Compound subjects are represented as a single node.

The NPLM is a 5-gram feed-forward neural language model, and for both RDLM and NPLM we use a single hidden layer of size 750, a 150-dimensional input embedding layer with a vocabulary size of 500000, noise-contrastive estimation with 100 noise samples, and 2 iterations over the monolingual training set. Estimating LM probabilities for OOV words is a well-known problem, and we avoid this by filtering the translation model according to the vocabulary of the neural models.

The impact of all experimental components is shown in Table 6. Each system in Tables 5 and 6 was tuned separately with MIRA. For our submission system, we increased the Moses parameters *cube-pruning-pop-limit* from 1000 to 4000, and *rule-limit* from 100 to 400, but this had little effect on devtest, and gave even slightly lower BLEU on test. Particle verb restructuring, which was done after the submission deadline, increases BLEU on test. In total, we observe substantial improvements over our baseline, which roughly corresponds to last year's submission systems: 2.2 BLEU on devtest, and 3.0 BLEU on test.

3.4 English to Russian

For English → Russian we built a tree-to-string system. During preliminary experiments we found that `fast_align` gave consistent gains over MGIZA++ (albeit smaller than Finnish → English at around 0.3 BLEU). In final experiments we used `fast_align` for word alignment and we used the 2012 and 2013 test sets as tuning data. Table 7 gives the mean BLEU scores, averaged over three MERT runs. Our submitted system was the right binarized system that, out of the three runs, scored highest on devtest.

system	devtest	test
Hiero	29.8	23.8
Tree-to-string	27.5	22.1
+ right binarization	28.3	23.0

Table 7: English to Russian translation results (BLEU) on devtest (newstest2014) and test (newstest2015) sets.

3.5 Czech to English

For Czech → English we built a string-to-tree system. We used all test sets from 2008 to 2013 as tuning data. Table 8 gives the mean BLEU scores, which are averaged over three MERT runs. Our submitted system was the right binarized system that, out of the three runs, scored highest on devtest.

system	devtest	test
Hiero	28.5	24.9
String-to-tree	27.8	24.4
+ right binarization	27.8	24.5

Table 8: Czech to English translation results (BLEU) on devtest (newstest2014) and test (newstest2015) sets.

3.6 Finnish to English

In preliminary Finnish → English experiments, we tried using Morfessor to segment Finnish words into morphemes. We used Morfessor 2.0 (with default settings) to learn an unsupervised segmentation model from all of the available Finnish data, which was then used to segment all words in the source-side training and test data. We compared systems with and without segmentation and using a system combination of the two — an approach that has been shown to improve translation quality for this language pair (de Gispert et al., 2009).

As with English → Finnish, we split newsdev2015 into two halves, using the first half for tuning and the second half for testing. Table 9 shows the results: the column headed 'word' gives BLEU scores for the unsegmented systems; the column headed 'morph' gives scores for systems trained on segmented data; and the column headed 'syscomb' gives results for a system combination using MEMT (Heafield and Lavie, 2010).

For our final system, we used morphological segmentation but not system combination. We used the full newsdev2015 test as tuning data. Table 10 gives mean BLEU scores for this setup, averaged over three MERT runs. Our submitted system was the right binarized system that, out of the three, scored highest on newsdev2015.

	word	morph	syscomb
Hiero	17.8	19.1	19.2
String-to-tree	17.6	18.5	18.7
+ right binarization	17.8	18.9	18.9

Table 9: Finnish to English experiments with morphological segmentation.

system	dev	test
Hiero	18.6	17.5
String-to-tree	18.3	17.2
+ right binarization	18.5	17.7

Table 10: Finnish to English translation results (BLEU) on dev (newsdev2015) and test (newstest2015) sets.

3.7 German to English

For German → English we built a tree-to-string system with similar setup as last year's (Williams et al., 2014). Our submitted system was right binarized with the following extraction parameters: *Rule Depth = 7, Node Count = 100, Rule Size = 7*. At decoding time we used the following non-default parameter value: *max-chart-span = 25*. This limits sub derivations to a maximum span of 25 source words. For the Hiero baseline system we used *max-chart-span = 15*. For tuning we used a random subset of 2000 sentences drawn from the full tuning set.

We performed some preliminary experiments with neural bilingual language models, our re-implementation of the "joint" model of (Devlin et al., 2014). The bilingual language models are trained with the NPLM toolkit (Vaswani et al., 2013). We used 250-dimensional input embedding and hidden layers, and input and output vocabulary sizes of 500000 and 250000 respectively. One bilingual language model was a 5-gram model with an additional context of 9 source words, the affiliated source word and a window of 4 words on either side. A second model was a 1-gram model with an additional context of 13 source words. The language models were trained on the available parallel corpora.

We also added a 7-gram class-based language model, with 50 word classes trained using `mkcls`

system	devtest	test
Hiero	27.7	28.0
String-to-tree	28.7	28.7
+ bilingual LMs	28.6	28.7
+ bilingual & class LMs	28.3	28.7

Table 11: German to English translation results (BLEU) on devtest (newstest2014) and test (newstest2015) sets.

(Och, 1999). The language model was trained on all available monolingual corpora, filtering out singletons.

Table 11 shows the results. As the preliminary results were not encouraging, we did not include the bilingual LMs and class LMs in our submitted system.

3.8 Russian to English

For Russian → English we built a string-to-tree system, using the 2012 and 2013 test sets as tuning data. Table 12 gives the mean BLEU scores, averaged over three MERT runs. Our submitted system was the right binarized system that, out of the three runs, scored highest on devtest.

system	devtest	test
Hiero	31.2	27.1
String-to-tree	30.5	25.9
+ right binarization	30.6	26.2

Table 12: Russian to English translation results (BLEU) on devtest (newstest2014) and test (newstest2015) sets.

4 Manual Error Analysis

Our syntax-based systems for the German–English language pairs have greatly improved over the last years and outperformed traditional phrase-based statistical machine translation systems. Translating between German and English is a challenge for those systems, since extensive long distance reordering and long distance agreement constraints do not fit that approach. Are our syntax-based systems tackling these problems better? And what are the main remaining problems?

For both German–English and English–German, we analyzed 100 sentences, we carried out an error analysis using linguistic error categories that roughly match other efforts in this area (Vilar et al., 2006; Toral et al., 2013; Herrmann et al., 2014; Lommel et al., 2014; Aranberri, 2015). We used the following error annotation protocol:

1. A bilingual speaker corrects the machine translation output with minimal necessary edits to render an acceptable translation. This is done in view of the human reference translation, but typically a much more literal translation was obtained.
2. Each edit is noted in a list in the form "old string → new string", where either old or new string may also be empty or discontinuous.
3. In a second pass, all edits are classified with error categories.

Such an error analysis is subjective. There are many ways to correct errors (step 1), many ways to split corrections into units (step 2), and many ways to classify the errors (step 3). Moreover, analyzing only 100 sentences does not lead to strong statistically significant findings. With this in mind, the following analysis is broadly indicative of the main error types in our syntax-based systems.

Occasionally, parts of a machine translation are just too muddled that a sequence of edits could be established. This happened in 8 German–English sentences, and 7 English–German sentences.

4.1 German–English

16 sentences have no error, while 18 sentences have only one error. These are of course typically the shorter ones. The longest sentence without error is:

- Source: *Der Oppositionspolitiker Imran Khan wirft Premier Sharif vor, bei der Parlamentswahl im Mai vergangenen Jahres betrogen zu haben.*
- MT: *The opposition politician Imran Khan accuses Premier Sharif of having cheated in the parliamentary election in May of last year.*

This is not a trivial sentence, since it requires the translation of the complex subclause construction *accuses ... of having cheated*, which is rendered quite differently in German as *wirft ... vor ... betrogen zu haben*.

An overview of the major error categories is shown is Figure 13. On average, 2.85 errors per sentence were identified. This gives us guidance on the major problems we should be working on in the future.

Count	Category	Count	Category
29	Wrong content word - noun	6	Wrong content word - phrasal verb
25	Wrong content word - verb	6	Added function word - determiner
22	Wrong function word - preposition	5	Unknown word - noun
21	Inflection - verb	5	Missing content word - adverb
14	Reordering: verb	5	Missing content word - noun
13	Reordering: adjunct	5	Inflection - noun
12	Missing function word - preposition	4	Reordering: NP
10	Missing content word - verb	3	Missing content word - adjective
9	Wrong function word - other	3	Inflection - wrong POS
9	Wrong content word - wrong POS	3	Casing
9	Added punctuation	2	Unknown word - verb
8	Muddle	2	Reordering: punctuation
8	Missing function word - connective	2	Reordering: noun
8	Added function word - preposition	2	Reordering: adverb
7	Missing punctuation	2	Missing function word - determiner
7	Wrong content word - adverb	2	Inflection - adverb

Table 13: Main error types in German–English system (count in 100 sentences).

Lexical choice The biggest group of error types concern translation of basic concepts. On average, such errors occur 0.76 times per sentence. Given the vast number of content words that need to be translated, the actual performance on the task of lexical translation is pretty high, but it is by no means solved.

Count	Category
29	Wrong content word - noun
25	Wrong content word - verb
9	Wrong content word - wrong POS
7	Wrong content word - adverb
6	Wrong content word - phrasal verb

Prepositions We were surprised by the large number of errors revolving prepositions. Prepositions are frequent, but not as frequent as content words, so the performance on the preposition translation task is not as good. Prepositions mostly mark relationships of adjuncts, which involve quite complex considerations — the adjunct, the modified verb or noun phrase, identifying the relationship between them in the source sentence, and the fuzzy meaning of prepositions.

Count	Category
22	Wrong function word - preposition
12	Missing function word - preposition
8	Added function word - preposition

Reordering We were also surprised by the low number of reordering errors. The different word order between German and English has hampered translation quality for this language pair historically. While we cannot declare complete success, our syntax-based systems constitute great progress in this area.

Count	Category
14	Reordering: verb
13	Reordering: adjunct
4	Reordering: NP
2	Reordering: noun
2	Reordering: adverb

Other issues with verbs Reordering errors involving verbs top the list in the previous group of error types, but there are also other problems with verbs: their inflection and the unacceptable frequency of dropping verbs. The latter has its roots in faulty word alignment which are based on IBM Models which often fail to align the out-of-English-order German verb, thus enabling the translation model to drop them, which the language model often prefers. Inflection is here to be understood broadly, including the need for the right function words to form a grammatical correct verb complex (e.g., *will have been resolved*).

Count	Category
21	Inflection - verb
10	Missing content word - verb

Overall, the main thrust of future research should be focused on lexical choice, selecting correct prepositions, and producing the correct verb.

Count	Category	Count	Category
41	Wrong content word - verb	9	Compound merging
37	Wrong content word - noun	8	Added function word - preposition
33	Reordering - verb	7	Punctuation - inserted
30	Inflection - verb	7	Muddle
22	Missing function word - preposition	7	Missing function word - clausal connective
17	Inflection - np	7	Added function word - determiner
14	Wrong function word - preposition	5	Punctuation - missing
12	Wrong content word - phrasal verb	5	Missing content word - verb
12	Wrong content word - wrong POS	4	Reordering - adverb
12	Wrong function word - clausal connective	4	Wrong content word - adverb
11	Reordering - pp	3	Missing content word - adjective
11	Inflection - noun	2	Reordering - pronoun
10	Wrong function word - pronoun	2	Wrong content word - name
10	Missing function word - pronoun	2	Missing content word - adverb
10	Missing function word - determiner	2	Wrong content word - adjective
9	Reordering - noun	2	Added function word - pronoun

Table 14: Main error types in English–German system (count in 100 sentences).

4.2 English–German

12 Sentences had no error, 13 sentences only one error. Less than German–English, which supports the general contention that translating into German is harder. On average, a total of 3.8 errors per sentence were marked, one error per sentence more than German–English. An overview of the major error categories is shown is Figure 14.

The longest sentence with no error is:

- Source: *Congressmen Keith Ellison and John Lewis have proposed legislation to protect union organizing as a civil right.*

- Target: *Die Kongressabgeordneten Keith Ellison und John Lewis haben Gesetze zum Schutz der gewerkschaftlichen Organisation als Bürgerrecht vorgeschlagen.*

In terms of word order, this is not a complicated sentence (besides the verb movement *proposed*→*vorgeschlagen*), but it does involve switching of part-of-speech for two content words: *protect*→*Schutz* (verb→noun), *union*→*gewerkschaftlichen* (noun→adjective).

Lexical choice As with German–English, this is biggest group of error types, with 1.08 errors per sentence. Verb sense errors tend to be more subtle, such that a media outlet does not *sagt* (*says*) but *berichtet* (*reports*) a news item. For nouns, there were several stark errors, such the mis-translation of *patient* as *Geduld* (*patience*) in a medical context. In general, there is no reason to believe that models that more strongly draw on a wider context could not resolve many of these cases.

Count	Category
41	Wrong content word - verb
37	Wrong content word - noun
12	Wrong content word - phrasal verb
12	Wrong content word - wrong POS
4	Wrong content word - adverb
2	Wrong content word - adjective

Role and order of adjuncts and arguments While the overall sentence structure is mostly correct, there are often problems with the handling of adjunct and argument phrases. Their role is identified in German by a preposition or the case of a noun phrase (the main cause of inflection errors). Their position in the sentence is less strict, but mistakes can be and are made.

Count	Category
22	Missing function word - preposition
17	Inflection - np
14	Wrong function word - preposition
11	Reordering - pp
11	Inflection - noun
8	Added function word - preposition

Verbs Reordering errors of verbs mainly occur in complex subclause constructions. German verbs are more strongly inflected for count and person, and often a few function words are needed in just the right order and placement for a correct verb complex.

33	Reordering - verb
30	Inflection - verb
5	Missing content word - verb

Pronouns Due to grammatical gender of nouns in German, translating *it* and *they* is a complex undertaking. German verbs also require more frequently reflexive pronouns.

Count	Category
10	Wrong function word - pronoun
10	Missing function word - pronoun
2	Added function word - pronoun

Clausal connectives A specific problem of English–German translations are clausal connectives. In English, the relationship of the sub clause is often not explicitly marked (e.g., *Police say the rider*), while German requires a function word.

Count	Category
12	Wrong function word - clausal connective
7	Missing function word - clausal connective

Overall, while there are more structural problems than for German–English, often the remaining challenge is the disambiguation of lexical choices and the correct labelling of syntactic relationships.

5 Conclusion

This year we submitted syntax-based systems for all language pairs except English-French. Our English $\rightarrow$ German system included significant improvements over last year's and we intend to continue developing this system. We presented the first results using Moses' STSG-based tree-to-string model.

Acknowledgements

This project has received funding from the European Union's Horizon 2020 research and innovation programme under grant agreements 645452 (QT21) and 644402 (HimL), and from the Swiss National Science Foundation under grant P2ZHP1_148717.

References

Nora Aranberri. 2015. Smt error analysis and mapping to syntactic, semantic and structural fixes. In *Proceedings of the Ninth Workshop on Syntax, Semantics and Structure in Statistical Translation*, pages 30–38, Denver, Colorado, USA, June. Association for Computational Linguistics.

Stanley F. Chen and Joshua Goodman. 1998. An empirical study of smoothing techniques for language modeling. Technical report, Harvard University.

Danqi Chen and Christopher Manning. 2014. A Fast and Accurate Dependency Parser using Neural Networks. In *Proceedings of the 2014 Conference on Empirical Methods in Natural Language Processing (EMNLP)*, pages 740–750, Doha, Qatar.

Colin Cherry and George Foster. 2012. Batch Tuning Strategies for Statistical Machine Translation. In *Proceedings of the 2012 Conference of the North American Chapter of the Association for Computational Linguistics: Human Language Technologies*, pages 427–436, Montréal, Canada, June.

David Chiang. 2007. Hierarchical phrase-based translation. *Comput. Linguist.*, 33(2):201–228.

Tagyoung Chung, Licheng Fang, and Daniel Gildea. 2011. Issues concerning decoding with synchronous context-free grammar. In *Proceedings of the 49th Annual Meeting of the Association for Computational Linguistics: Human Language Technologies*, pages 413–417, Portland, Oregon, USA, June.

Adrià de Gispert, Sami Virpioja, Mikko Kurimo, and William Byrne. 2009. Minimum bayes risk combination of translation hypotheses from alternative morphological decompositions. In *Proceedings of Human Language Technologies: The 2009 Annual Conference of the North American Chapter of the Association for Computational Linguistics, Companion Volume: Short Papers*, pages 73–76, Boulder, Colorado, June.

Jacob Devlin, Rabih Zbib, Zhongqiang Huang, Thomas Lamar, Richard Schwartz, and John Makhoul. 2014. Fast and Robust Neural Network Joint Models for Statistical Machine Translation. In *Proceedings of the 52nd Annual Meeting of the Association for Computational Linguistics (Volume 1: Long Papers)*, pages 1370–1380, Baltimore, MD, USA, June.

Chris Dyer, Victor Chahuneau, and Noah A. Smith. 2013. A Simple, Fast, and Effective Reparameterization of IBM Model 2. In *Proceedings of the 2013 Conference of the North American Chapter of the Association for Computational Linguistics: Human Language Technologies*, pages 644–648, Atlanta, GA, USA, June.

Jason Eisner. 2003. Learning non-isomorphic tree mappings for machine translation. In *The Companion Volume to the Proceedings of 41st Annual Meeting of the Association for Computational Linguistics*, pages 205–208, Sapporo, Japan, July. Association for Computational Linguistics.

Michel Galley, Mark Hopkins, Kevin Knight, and Daniel Marcu. 2004. What's in a Translation Rule? In *HLT-NAACL '04*.

Michel Galley, Jonathan Graehl, Kevin Knight, Daniel Marcu, Steve DeNeefe, Wei Wang, and Ignacio Thayer. 2006. Scalable inference and training of context-rich syntactic translation models. In *ACL-44: Proceedings of the 21st International Conference on Computational Linguistics and the 44th annual meeting of the Association for Computational Linguistics*, pages 961–968, Morristown, NJ, USA.

Qin Gao and Stephan Vogel. 2008. Parallel implementations of word alignment tool. In *Software Engineering, Testing, and Quality Assurance for Natural Language Processing*, SETQA-NLP '08, pages 49–57, Stroudsburg, PA, USA.

Kenneth Heafield and Alon Lavie. 2010. Combining Machine Translation Output with Open Source The Carnegie Mellon Multi-Engine Machine Translation Scheme. *The Prague Bulletin of Mathematical Linguistics*, 93:27–36.

Kenneth Heafield, Ivan Pouzyrevsky, Jonathan H. Clark, and Philipp Koehn. 2013. Scalable modified Kneser-Ney language model estimation. In *Proceedings of the 51st Annual Meeting of the Association for Computational Linguistics*, pages 690–696, Sofia, Bulgaria, August.

Teresa Herrmann, Jan Niehues, and Alex Waibel. 2014. Manual analysis of structurally informed reordering in german-english machine translation. In *Proceedings of the Ninth International Conference on Language Resources and Evaluation (LREC-2014)*. European Language Resources Association (ELRA).

Mark Hopkins and Greg Langmead. 2010. SCFG decoding without binarization. In *Proceedings of the 2010 Conference on Empirical Methods in Natural Language Processing*, pages 646–655, Cambridge, MA, October.

Matthias Huck, Hieu Hoang, and Philipp Koehn. 2014. Preference Grammars and Soft Syntactic Constraints for GHKM Syntax-based Statistical Machine Translation. In *Proceedings of SSST-8, Eighth Workshop on Syntax, Semantics and Structure in Statistical Translation*, pages 148–156, Doha, Qatar.

Philipp Koehn, Franz Josef Och, and Daniel Marcu. 2003. Statistical phrase-based translation. In *NAACL '03: Proceedings of the 2003 Conference of the North American Chapter of the Association for Computational Linguistics on Human Language Technology*, pages 48–54, Morristown, NJ, USA.

Ding Liu and Daniel Gildea. 2005. Syntactic Features for Evaluation of Machine Translation. In *Proceedings of the ACL Workshop on Intrinsic and Extrinsic Evaluation Measures for Machine Translation and/or Summarization*, pages 25–32, Ann Arbor, Michigan.

Arle Lommel, Aljoscha Burchardt, Maja Popović, Kim Harris, Eleftherios Avramidis, and Hans Uszkoreit. 2014. Using a new analytic measure for the annotation and analysis of mt errors on real data. In *Proceedings of 17th Annual conference of the European Association for Machine Translation*, pages 165–172.

Maria Nadejde, Philip Williams, and Philipp Koehn. 2013. Edinburgh's Syntax-Based Machine Translation Systems. In *Proceedings of the Eighth Workshop on Statistical Machine Translation*, pages 170–176, Sofia, Bulgaria, August.

Graham Neubig and Kevin Duh. 2014. On the elements of an accurate tree-to-string machine translation system. In *Proceedings of the 52nd Annual Meeting of the Association for Computational Linguistics (Volume 2: Short Papers)*, pages 143–149, Baltimore, Maryland, June.

Joakim Nivre and Jens Nilsson. 2005. Pseudo-Projective Dependency Parsing. In *Proceedings of the 43rd Annual Meeting of the Association for Computational Linguistics (ACL'05)*, pages 99–106, Ann Arbor, Michigan.

Franz Josef Och and Hermann Ney. 2003. A systematic comparison of various statistical alignment models. *Comput. Linguist.*, 29(1):19–51, March.

Franz Josef Och. 1999. An Efficient Method for Determining Bilingual Word Classes. In *Proceedings of the 9th Conference of the European Chapter of the Association for Computational Linguistics (EACL)*, pages 71–76.

Franz Josef Och. 2003. Minimum error rate training in statistical machine translation. In *Proceedings of the 41st Annual Meeting on Association for Computational Linguistics - Volume 1*, ACL '03, pages 160–167, Morristown, NJ, USA.

Slav Petrov and Dan Klein. 2007. Improved Inference for Unlexicalized Parsing. In *Human Language Technologies 2007: The Conference of the North American Chapter of the Association for Computational Linguistics; Proceedings of the Main Conference*, pages 404–411, Rochester, New York, April.

Slav Petrov, Leon Barrett, Romain Thibaux, and Dan Klein. 2006. Learning accurate, compact, and interpretable tree annotation. In *Proceedings of the 21st International Conference on Computational Linguistics and the 44th annual meeting of the Association for Computational Linguistics*, ACL-44, pages 433–440.

Rico Sennrich and Barry Haddow. 2015. A Joint Dependency Model of Morphological and Syntactic Structure for Statistical Machine Translation. In *Proceedings of the 2015 Conference on Empirical Methods in Natural Language Processing (EMNLP)*, Lisbon, Portugal. Association for Computational Linguistics.

Rico Sennrich, Martin Volk, and Gerold Schneider. 2013. Exploiting Synergies Between Open Resources for German Dependency Parsing, POS-tagging, and Morphological Analysis. In *Proceedings of the International Conference Recent Advances in Natural Language Processing 2013*, pages 601–609, Hissar, Bulgaria.

Rico Sennrich. 2014. A cyk+ variant for scfg decoding without a dot chart. In *Proceedings of SSST-8, Eighth Workshop on Syntax, Semantics and Structure in Statistical Translation*, pages 94–102, Doha, Qatar, October.

Rico Sennrich. 2015. Modelling and Optimizing on Syntactic N-Grams for Statistical Machine Translation. *Transactions of the Association for Computational Linguistics*, 3:169–182.

Andreas Stolcke. 2002. SRILM – an Extensible Language Modeling Toolkit. In *Proc. of the Int. Conf. on Spoken Language Processing (ICSLP)*, volume 3, Denver, CO, USA, September.

Antonio Toral, Sudip Kumar Naskar, Joris Vreeke, Federico Gaspari, and Declan Groves. 2013. A web application for the diagnostic evaluation of machine translation over specific linguistic phenomena. In *Proceedings of the 2013 NAACL HLT Demonstration Session*, pages 20–23, Atlanta, Georgia, June. Association for Computational Linguistics.

Ashish Vaswani, Yinggong Zhao, Victoria Fossum, and David Chiang. 2013. Decoding with Large-Scale Neural Language Models Improves Translation. In *Proceedings of the 2013 Conference on Empirical Methods in Natural Language Processing*, pages 1387–1392, Seattle, WA, USA.

David Vilar, Jia Xu, Luis Fernando D'Haro, and Hermann Ney. 2006. Error analysis of statistical machine translation output. In *Proceedings of the 5th International Conference on Language Resources and Evaluation (LREC 06)*, pages 697–702.

Sami Virpioja, Peter Smit, Stig-Arne Grönroos, and Mikko Kurimo. 2013. Morfessor 2.0: Python implementation and extensions for morfessor baseline. Technical report, Aalto University, Helsinki.

Philip Williams and Philipp Koehn. 2012. GHKM Rule Extraction and Scope-3 Parsing in Moses. In *Proceedings of the Seventh Workshop on Statistical Machine Translation*, pages 388–394, Montréal, Canada, June.

Philip Williams, Rico Sennrich, Maria Nadejde, Matthias Huck, Eva Hasler, and Philipp Koehn. 2014. Edinburgh's Syntax-Based Systems at WMT 2014. In *Proceedings of the Ninth Workshop on Statistical Machine Translation*, pages 207–214, Baltimore, Maryland, USA, June.

Hui Zhang, Min Zhang, Haizhou Li, and Chew Lim Tan. 2009. Fast translation rule matching for syntax-based statistical machine translation. In *Proceedings of the 2009 Conference on Empirical Methods in Natural Language Processing*, pages 1037–1045, Singapore, August.

The FBK Participation in the WMT15 Automatic Post-editing Shared Task

Rajen Chatterjee
Fondazione Bruno Kessler
chatterjee@fbk.eu

Marco Turchi
Fondazione Bruno Kessler
turchi@fbk.eu

Matteo Negri
Fondazione Bruno Kessler
negri@fbk.eu

Abstract

In this paper, we describe the "FBK English-Spanish Automatic Post-editing (APE)" systems submitted to the APE shared task at the WMT 2015. We explore the most widely used statistical APE technique (*monolingual*) and its most significant variant (*context-aware*). In this exploration, we introduce some novel task-specific dense features through which we observe improvements over the default setup of these approaches. We show these features are useful to prune the phrase table in order to remove unreliable rules and help the decoder to select useful translation options during decoding. Our primary APE system submitted at this shared task performs significantly better than the standard APE baseline.

1 Introduction

Over the last decade a lot of research has been carried out to mimic the human post-editing process in the field of ***Automatic Post-Editing (APE)***. The objective of APE is to learn how to correct machine translation (MT) errors leveraging the human post-editing feedback. The variety of data generated by human feedback, in terms of post editing, possess an unprecedented wealth of knowledge about the dynamics (practical and cognitive) of the translation process. APE leverages the potential of this knowledge to improve MT quality. The problem is appealing for several reasons. On one side, as shown by Parton et al. (2012), APE systems can improve MT output by exploiting information unavailable to the decoder, or by performing deeper text analysis that is too expensive at the decoding stage. On the other side, APE represents the only way to rectify errors present in the "black-box" scenario where the MT system is unknown or its internal decoding information is not available.

The goal of the APE task is to challenge the research groups to improve the MT output quality by the use of a dataset consisting of triplets of sentences (source, MT output, human post-edition). We are facing the "MT-as-Black-box" scenario, so neither we have access to the MT engine nor do we have any decoding trace. The data for this pilot task belongs to generic news domain which reflects data sparseness, and the post-edition of the MT output is obtained through crowdsourcing which makes it vulnerable to noise thus making this task even more challenging.

To begin with, §2 discusses the statistical APE methods used to implement the APE systems. §3 describes the data set available for this shared task, and provides detail of the experimental setup. §4 is our major contribution which discusses the FBK-APE pipeline and shows that incorporation of task-specific dense features can be useful to enhance APE systems. Our final submitted system is reported in §5 followed by conclusion in §6.

2 Statistical APE Methods

In this paper we examine the most widely used statistical phrase-based post-editing strategy proposed by Simard et al. (2007) and its most significant variant proposed by Béchara et al. (2011). We describe the two methods and there pros and cons in the following subsections.

2.1 *APE-1* (Simard et al., 2007)

In this approach APE systems are trained in the same way as the statistical machine translation (SMT) system. But, as contrast to SMT which makes use of the source and target language parallel corpus, APE uses the MT output and its corresponding human post-edited data in the form of parallel corpus. One of the most important missing concepts in this *"monolingual translation"* is the inclusion of source information, which has been incorporated in the next approach.

2.2 *APE-2* (Béchara et al., 2011)

This technique is the most significant variant of (Simard et al., 2007), where they come up with a new data representation to include the source information along with the MT output on the source side of the parallel corpus. For each MT word f', the corresponding source word (or phrase) e is identified through word alignment and used to obtain a joint representation $f'\#e$. This results in a new intermediate language $F'\#E$ that represents the new source side of the parallel data used to train the statistical APE system. This *"context-aware"* variant seems to be more precise but faces two potential problems. First, preserving the source context comes at the cost of a larger vocabulary size and, consequently, higher data sparseness that will eventually reduce the reliability of the translation rules being learned. Second, the joint representation $f'\#e$ may be infected by the word alignment errors which may mislead the learning of translation option.

Recently, Chatterjee et al. (2015) showed a fair systematic comparison of these two approaches over multiple language pairs and revealed that inclusion of source information in the form of *context-aware* variant is useful to improve translation quality over standard *monolingual translation* approach. They also showed that using *monolingual translation* alignment to build *context-aware* APE helps to mitigate the sparsity issue at the level of word alignment and for this reasons, we use this configuration to implement APE-2 method.

3 Data set and Experimental setup

Data: In this shared task we are provided with a tri-parallel corpus consisting of source (src), MT output (mt), and human post-edits (pe). While APE-1 uses only the last two elements of the triplet, all of them are used in the context-aware APE-2. To obtain joint representation ($f'\#e$) in APE-2, word alignment model is trained on *src-mt* parallel corpus of the training data. The training set consist of ~11K triplets, we divide the development set into dev and test set consisting of 500 triplets each. Our evaluation is based on the performance achieved on this test set. We tokenize the data set using the tokenizer available in the MOSES(Koehn et al., 2007) toolkit. Training and evaluation of our APE systems are performed on the true-case data.

Experiment Settings: To develop the APE systems we use the phrase-based statistical machine translation toolkit MOSES(Koehn et al., 2007). For all the experiments mentioned in this paper we use *"grow-diag-final-and"* as alignment heuristic and *"msd-bidirectional-fe"* heuristic for reordering model. MGIZA++ (Gao and Vogel, 2008) is used for word alignment. The APE systems are tuned to optimize TER(Snover et al., 2006) with MERT(Och, 2003).

We follow an incremental strategy to develop the APE systems, at each stage of the APE pipeline we find the best configuration of a component and then proceed to explore the next component. Our APE pipeline consist of various stages like language model selection, phrase table pruning, and feature designing as discussed in the following sections.

Evaluation Metric: We select TER (Snover et al., 2006) as our evaluation metric because it mimics the human post-editing effort by measuring the edit operation needed to translate the MT output into its human-revised version.

Apart from TER as an evaluation metric we also compute number of sentences being modified[1] in the test set and then compute the precision as follow:

$$\text{Precision} = \frac{NumberofSentencesImproved}{NumberofSentencesModified}$$

Baseline: Our baseline is the MT output *as-is*. To evaluate, we use the corresponding human post-edited corpus which gives us **23.10** TER score.

4 APE Pipeline

In this section we describe various components that we explore at each stage of the pipeline. At each stage, we study the effect of several configuration of each component on both the APE methods (*APE-1* and *APE-2*)

4.1 Language Model Selection (APE-LM)

We use various data set to train multiple language models to see which of them have high impact on the translation quality. All the LMs are trained us-

[1]For each sentence in the test set, if the TER score of APE system is different than the baseline then we consider it as a modified sentence

ing IRSTLM toolkit (Federico et al., 2008) having order of 5 gram with kneser-ney smoothing. The data set varies in quality and quantity as described below:

- **LM 1** contains only the training data(∼11K) provided in this shared task. Although the data set contains few sentences to train a language model compared to the data used in MT, it is quite reliable because it is sampled from the same distribution of the test set.
- **LM 2** consists of News Commentary having ∼200K sentences, downloaded from WMT 2013 translation task.[2] This corpus belongs to the same domain of the APE data, but it is created under different conditions (*i.e.* involving professional translators and translating from scratch the source sentence) making it significantly different from the data used to build LM1.
- **LM 3** (Big data) contains News Crawl data from 2007-2012 contributing to ∼13M sentences, downloaded from WMT 2013 translation task [2]. This data set has huge amount of news crawled from the Web and covering several topics.
- **LM1+LM2+LM3:** All the previous language models are simultaneously used by the APE systems. A log-linear weight is assigned to each language model during the tuning stage.

	APE-1	**APE-2**
LM1	**23.95**	**24.59**
LM2	23.96	24.62
LM3	24.06	24.66
LM1+LM2+LM3	24.05	24.69

Table 1: Performance (TER score) of the APE systems using various LMs

Results of both the APE systems are shown in Table 1. We notice that the performance of the APE systems do not show much variation for different LMs. This can come from the fact that the *news commentary* and *new crawl* data might not resemble well the shared task data. For this reason, the in-domain LM1 is selected and used in the next stages.

[2]http://www.statmt.org/wmt13/translation-task.html

4.2 Pruning Strategy (APE-LM1-Prun)

To remove unreliable translation rules generated from the data obtained through crowd-sourcing, pruning strategies are investigated. First, we test the classic pruning technique by Johnson et al. (2007) which is based on the significance testing of phrase pair co-occurrence in the parallel corpus. According to our experiments, this technique is too aggressive when applied on limited amounts of sparse data. Nearly 5% of the phrase table is retained after pruning with mostly self-rules (translation options that contain same source and target phrase).

For this reason we develop a novel feature for pruning which measures the usefulness of a translation option present in the phrase table. For each translation option in the phrase table, all the parallel sentences are retrieved from the training set such that the source phrase of the translation option is present in the source sentence of the parallel corpus. We then substitute the target phrase of the translation option in the source sentence of the parallel corpus and then compute the TER score wrt. the corresponding target sentence. If TER increases then we increment the *neg-count* by 1, and if TER decreases we increment the *pos-count* by 1. Finally, we compute the *neg-impact* and the *pos-impact* as follows:

$$\textit{neg-impact} = \frac{\textit{neg-count}}{NumberofRetrievedSentences}$$

$$\textit{pos-impact} = \frac{\textit{pos-count}}{NumberofRetrievedSentences}$$

Once these ratios are computed for all translation options, we filter the phrase table by thresholding on the *neg-impact* to remove rules which are not useful (higher the *neg-impact* less useful it is). All translation options greater than or equal to the threshold value are filtered out. We apply this pruning strategy for both the APE methods over various threshold values.

Table 2 and Table 3 show the performance after pruning the APE-1-LM1 and APE-2-LM1 systems respectively. In Table 2, we observe that TER score for various threshold values are very close to each other, so in order to select the best threshold value we base our decision on precision. So for APE-1, we select the threshold value of 0.4 which shows the highest precision, namely **APE-1-LM1-Prun0.4**. For APE-2, it is evident from the result in Table 3 that the threshold value of 0.2

Threshold	TER	Number of sentences modified	Precision
0.8	23.90	88	0.12
0.6	23.91	90	0.13
0.4	23.98	94	**0.15**
0.2	23.77	70	0.12

Table 2: Performance (TER score) of the APE-1-LM1 after pruning at various threshold values

Threshold	TER	Number of sentences modified	Precision
0.8	24.29	130	0.20
0.6	23.99	103	0.18
0.4	23.66	70	0.18
0.2	23.46	50	**0.22**

Table 3: Performance (TER score) of the APE-2-LM1 after pruning at various threshold values

proves to be the best in terms of TER score (reduction by 1.13 point) as well as in terms of precision (**APE-2-LM1-Prun0.2**). These results suggest that our pruning technique has a larger impact on the APE-2 method compared to APE-1. This is motivated by the fact that the context-aware approach is affected by the data sparseness problem resulting in a large number of unreliable translation options that can be removed from the phrase table.

4.3 New Dense Features Design

The final stage of our APE pipeline is the feature design. When a translation system is trained using Moses, it generates translation model consisting of default dense features like phrase translation probability (direct and indirect) and lexical translation probability (direct and indirect). In the task of Automatic Post-editing where we have the source and target phrases in the same language, we can leverage this information to provide the decoder with some useful insights. In the light of this direction we design four task-specific dense features to raise the "awareness" of the decoder.

- **Similarity** ($f1$):
  This feature ($f1$) is quite similar to the one proposed in (Grundkiewicz and Junczys-Dowmunt, 2014) which measures the similarity between the source and target phrase of the translation options. The score for $f1$ is computed as follows:
  $$f1_{score} = e^{1-ter(s,t)}$$
  where ter measures the number of edit operations required to translate the source phrase s to the target phrase t and it is computed using TER(Snover et al., 2006).

- **Reliability** ($f2.1$ **and** $f2.2$) **:**
  We allow the model to learn the reliability of the translation option by providing it with the statistics of the quality (in terms of HTER) of the parallel sentences used to learn that particular translation option. Better the quality, higher the likelihood to learn reliable rules. For each translation option in the phrase table, all the parallel sentence pairs from the training data containing the source phrase in the machine translated sentence of the pair and target phrase in the post-edited sentence are retrieved along with their HTER score. These scores are then used to compute the following two features:
  Median ($f2.1$)**:** The median of the HTER values of all the retrieved pairs.
  Standard Deviation ($f2.2$)**:** The standard deviation of the HTER values of all the retrieved pairs.

- **Usefulness** ($f3$) **:** As discussed in Section 4.2 we use *pos-impact* as a feature to measure the positive impact of a translation option over the training set. Higher the positive impact, higher is its usefulness.

We study the impact of individual features when applied one at a time and when used all together.

Features	TER	Number of sentences modified	Precision
$f1$	23.87	81	0.16
f2.1, f2.2	23.92	94	**0.19**
$f3$	23.88	82	0.14
$f1$, $f2.1$, $f2.2$, $f3$	23.97	85	0.12

Table 4: Performance (TER score) of the APE-1-LM1-Prun0.4 for different features

Table 4 and Table 5 show the performance of various features for APE-1-LM1-prun0.4 and

Features	TER	Number of sentences modified	Precision
f1	23.50	52	**0.27**
*f*2.1, *f*2.2	23.50	53	0.20
*f*3.1	23.52	59	0.22
*f*1, *f*2.1, *f*2.2, *f*3.1	23.52	54	0.19

Table 5: Performance (TER score) of the APE-2-LM1-Prun0.2 for different features

APE-2-LM1-Prun0.2 systems respectively. We observe, on this data set, that the use of these features retains the APE performance in terms of TER score but slight improvement is observed in terms of precision over both the APE systems, which indicate its contribution to improve the translation quality.

5 Final Submitted Systems

Our primary system is the best system in Table 5 i.e. APE-2-LM1-Prun0.2-f1 and contrastive system is the best system in Table 4 i.e. APE-1-LM1-Prun0.4-f2.1-f2.2. According to the shared task evaluation report the scores of our submitted systems are shown in Table 6

Systems	Case Sensitive	Case Insensitive
Baseline (MT)	22.91	22.22
APE Baseline (Simard et al., 2007)	23.83	23.13
Primary	23.22	22.55
Contrastive	23.64	22.94

Table 6: APE shared task evaluation score (TER)

Although we could not beat the Baseline (MT), but we see a clear improvement over APE baseline (Simard et al., 2007) by the inclusion of our novel features and the use of the pruning strategy.

6 Conclusion

The APE shared task was challenging in many terms (*black-box MT, generic news domain data, crowdsourced post-editions*). Though we were unable to beat the MT baseline but we gained some positive experience through this shared task. First, our primary APE system performed significantly better (0.61 TER reduction) over the standard APE baseline (Simard et al., 2007) as reported in Table 6. Second, our novel dense feature (*neg-impact*) used to prune phrase table shows significant improvement in the *context-aware* APE performance. Third, other task-specific dense features which measure similarity and reliability of the translation options help to improve the precision of our APE systems. To encourage the use of our features we have publicly released the scripts at `https://bitbucket.org/turchmo/apeatfbk/src/master/papers/WMT2015/APE_2015_System_Scripts.zip`.

Acknowledgements

This work has been partially supported by the EC-funded H2020 project QT21 (grant agreement no. 645452).

References

Hanna Béchara, Yanjun Ma, and Josef van Genabith. 2011. Statistical post-editing for a statistical mt system. In *MT Summit*, volume 13, pages 308–315.

Rajen Chatterjee, Marion Weller, Matteo Negri, and Marco Turchi. 2015. Exploring the Planet of the APEs: a Comparative Study of State-of-the-art Methods for MT Automatic Post-Editing. In *Proceedings of the 53rd Annual Meeting of the Association for Computational Linguistics)*, Beijing, China.

Marcello Federico, Nicola Bertoldi, and Mauro Cettolo. 2008. Irstlm: an open source toolkit for handling large scale language models. In *Interspeech*, pages 1618–1621.

Qin Gao and Stephan Vogel. 2008. Parallel implementations of word alignment tool. In *Software Engineering, Testing, and Quality Assurance for Natural Language Processing*, pages 49–57. Association for Computational Linguistics.

Roman Grundkiewicz and Marcin Junczys-Dowmunt. 2014. The amu system in the conll-2014 shared task: Grammatical error correction by data-intensive and feature-rich statistical machine translation. *CoNLL-2014*, page 25.

John Howard Johnson, Joel Martin, George Foster, and Roland Kuhn. 2007. Improving translation quality by discarding most of the phrasetable.

Philipp Koehn, Hieu Hoang, Alexandra Birch, Chris Callison-Burch, Marcello Federico, Nicola Bertoldi, Brooke Cowan, Wade Shen, Christine Moran, Richard Zens, et al. 2007. Moses: Open source toolkit for statistical machine translation. In *Proceedings of the 45th annual meeting of the ACL on interactive poster and demonstration sessions*, pages 177–180. Association for Computational Linguistics.

Franz Josef Och. 2003. Minimum error rate training in statistical machine translation. In *Proceedings of the 41st Annual Meeting on Association for Computational Linguistics-Volume 1*, pages 160–167. Association for Computational Linguistics.

Kristen Parton, Nizar Habash, Kathleen McKeown, Gonzalo Iglesias, and Adrià de Gispert. 2012. Can automatic post-editing make mt more meaningful. *Proceeding EAMT*, 12:111–118.

Michel Simard, Cyril Goutte, and Pierre Isabelle. 2007. Statistical Phrase-Based Post-Editing. In *Proceedings of the Annual Conference of the North American Chapter of the Association for Computational Linguistics (NAACL HLT)*, pages 508–515, Rochester, New York.

Matthew Snover, Bonnie Dorr, Richard Schwartz, Linnea Micciulla, and John Makhoul. 2006. A study of translation edit rate with targeted human annotation. In *Proceedings of association for machine translation in the Americas*, pages 223–231.

USAAR-SAPE: An English–Spanish Statistical Automatic Post-Editing System

Santanu Pal[1], Mihaela Vela[1], Sudip Kumar Naskar[2], Josef van Genabith[1]
[1]Saarland University, Saarbrücken, Germany
[2]Jadavpur University, Kolkata, India
{santanu.pal, josef.vangenabith}@uni-saarland.de
m.vela@mx.uni-saarland.de
sudip.naskar@cse.jdvu.ac.in

Abstract

We describe the USAAR-SAPE English–Spanish Automatic Post-Editing (APE) system submitted to the APE Task organized in the Workshop on Statistical Machine Translation (WMT) in 2015. Our system was able to improve upon the baseline MT system output by incorporating Phrase-Based Statistical MT (PBSMT) technique into the monolingual Statistical APE task (SAPE). The reported final submission crucially involves hybrid word alignment. The SAPE system takes raw Spanish Machine Translation (MT) output provided by the shared task organizers and produces post-edited Spanish text. The parallel data consist of English Text, raw machine translated Spanish output, and their corresponding manually post-edited versions. The major goal of the task is to reduce the post-editing effort by improving the quality of the MT output in terms of fluency and adequacy.

1 Introduction

In this paper, we present the submission of Saarland University (USAAR) to the WMT2015 APE task. The system combines a hybrid word alignment system implementation with a monolingual PBSMT for the language pair English-Spanish (EN-ES), translating from English into Spanish.

In order to achieve the desired translation quality, translations provided by MT systems need to be corrected by human translators. Automatic MT post-editing (APE) (Knight and Chander, 1994) is the method of improving raw MT output, before performing human post-editing on it. The objective is to decreases the amount of errors produced by the MT systems, achieving in the end a productivity increase in the translation process.

Usually APE tasks focus on fluency errors produced by the MT system. The most frequent ones are incorrect lexical choices, incorrect word ordering, the insertion of a word, the deletion of a word. For the WMT2015 APE task, we adapted our system in order to automatically post-edit lexical choice errors, word insertions and deletions. The method is also able to correct to some extent word ordering.

The remainder of the paper is organized as follows. Section 2 gives an overview of the related work, Section 3 describes the various components of our system, in particular the corpus preprocessing module, the hybrid word alignment module and the PBSMT model. In Section 4, we outline the complete experimental setup. Section 5 presents the results of the automatic and human evaluation, followed by conclusion in Section 6.

2 Related Work

In order to implement the correction of repetitive errors in the MT output, various automatic or semi-automatic post-processing or automatic PE techniques have been developed. Although MT output needs to be post-edited by humans to produce publishable quality translation (Roturier, 2009; TAUS/CNGL Report, 2010), it is faster and cheaper to post-edit MT output than to perform human translation from scratch. In some cases, recent studies have shown that the quality of MT output plus PE can exceed the quality of human translation (Fiederer and O'Brien, 2009; Koehn, 2009; De Palma and Kelly, 2009) as well as the productivity (Zampieri and Vela, 2014). Aimed at cost-effective and timesaving use of MT, the PE process needs to be further optimised (TAUS/CNGL Report, 2010). Post-editing can be also used as a MT evaluation method, implying at least source and target language skills, different from ranking, that does nor require specific skills, a homogeneous group of evaluators being enough to perform the task (Vela and van Genabith, 2015) .

The aim of automatic post-editing (APE) is to improve the output of MT by post-processing it. One of the first approaches was the one introduced by Chen and Chen (1997) who proposed a combination of rule-based MT (RBMT) and statistical MT (SMT) systems aiming at merging the positive properties of each system type for a better machine translation output.

Simard et al. (2007a) and Simard et al. (2007b) have shown how a PBSMT system can be used for automatic post-editing of an RBMT system for translations from English to French and French to English. Because RBMT systems tend to produce repetitive errors, they train a SMT system to correct errors, with the aim of reducing the post-editing effort. The SMT system trains on the output of the RBMT system as the source language and the reference human translations as the target language. The evaluation of their system shows that the post-edited output had a better quality than the output of the RBMT system as well as the output of the same SMT system used in standalone translation mode.

Lagarda et al. (2009) use an approach similar to Simard et al. (2007a) for translations from English to Spanish. The evaluation of the method was performed automatically and manually by comparing the APE output with the output from an RBMT system and a SMT system. The two corpora used in the evaluation were transcriptions of parliamentary speeches and medical protocols. The evaluation results have shown that on transcriptions of parliamentary speeches the method improves the RBMT system.

Rosa et al. (2012) and Mareček et al. (2011) applied APE on English-to-Czech MT outputs on morphological level. Based on word alignment, the method learns during the training phase 20 hand-written rules based on the most frequent errors encountered in translation. The method addresses fluency in translation and corrects morphosyntactic categories of a word such as number, gender, case, person and dependency label.

Parton et al. (2012) present an approach to APE consisting of three stages: detecting errors, suggesting and ranking corrections for the errors, and applying the developed suggestions. For the last stage of their method, applying the corrections, Parton et al. (2012) developed two different methodologies, a rule-abased APE and a feedback APE. The rule-based APE performs either insertions or replacement to address an identified error. The feedback APE, an approach similar to the one proposed by Parton and McKeown (2010), passes the possible correction to the MT system, letting the MT decoder decide whether the errors should be corrected and about the method of correcting it. Parton et al. (2012) evaluated their approach with human evaluators and found that the adequacy of post-edited MT output improved both for rule-based and feedback APE. In terms of fluency the human evaluation has shown that adequacy increase in feedback APE is related to fluency but not for rule-based APE.

Denkowski (2015) has developed a method for integrating in real time post-edited MT output into a translation model, by extracting for each input sentence a grammar. The method, based on Levenberg et al. (2010) and Lopez (2008), allows the indexing of the the source and post-edited MT output, as well as the union of the already existing sentence pairs with the new post-edited data. The system can also remember the rules that are consistent with the post-edited data. This way, rules learned from human corections can be preferred. The experiments Denkowski (2015) ran on from English into and out of Spanish and Arabic data show that the process of translating with an adaptive grammar improves performance on post-editing tasks.

3 System Description

Our system is designed with three basic components: corpus preprocessing, hybrid word alignment and a PBSMT system integrated with the hybrid word alignment. The hybrid word alignment consists of the combination of multiple word alignments into a single word alignment table which is later used in a phrase-based SMT (PBSMT) system. Our SMT based SAPE systems were trained on monolingual Spanish MT output and the manually post-edited output.

3.1 Corpus Preprocessing

For training our system we used the sentence aligned training data provided by the organizers of the WMT2015 APE task. The training data consist of 11,272 parallel segments of English to Spanish MT translations as well as the post-edited translations of the MT output. The English source text, the machine translated Spanish output and the corresponding post-edited version contain 238,335, 257,644 and 257,881 tokens respectively.

The preprocessing of the training corpus was carried out first by stemming the Spanish MT output and the PE data using Freeling (Padró and Stanilovsky, 2012).

3.2 Hybrid Word Alignment

3.2.1 Statistical Word Alignment

GIZA++ (Och and Ney, 2003) is a statistical word alignment tool which implements maximum likelihood estimators for all the IBM-1 to IBM-5 models, a HMM alignment model as well as the IBM-6 model covering many to many alignments. GIZA++ facilitates fast development of statistical machine translation (SMT) systems. Like GIZA++, the Berkley Aligner (Liang et al., 2006) is also used to align words across sentence pairs. The Berkeley word aligner uses an extension of Cross Expectation Maximization and is jointly trained with HMM models. We use a third statistical word aligner called SymGiza++ (Junczys-Dowmunt and Szał, 2012), which modifies the counting phase of each model of Giza++ allowing for updating the symmetrized models between the chosen iterations of the original training algorithms. It computes symmetric word alignment models with the capability of taking advantage of multi-processor systems.

3.2.2 Edit Distance-Based Word Alignment

We use two different kind of edit distance based word aligners, where alignment is based on TER (Translation Edit Rate) and the METEOR word aligner. TER (Snover et al., 2006) was developed for automatic evaluation of MT outputs. TER can align two strings such as the reference (in this case the PE translation) and the hypothesis (MT output). In the our work, the reference string has been chosen to be the confusion network skeleton, and the hypotheses are aligned independently using the skeleton. These pair-wise alignments may be consolidated to form a confusion network. TER measures the ratio between the number of edit operations that are required to turn a hypothesis *H* into the corresponding reference *R* to the total number of words in the *R*. The allowable edit types include insertion (Ins), substitution (Sub), deletion (Del) and phrase shifts (Shft). TER is computed as

$$TER(H,R) = \frac{(Ins + Del + Sub + Shft) * 100\%}{\textit{total number of words in R}} \quad (1)$$

METEOR Alignment (Lavie and Agarwal, 2007) is also an automatic MT evaluation metric which provides an alignment between hypothesis (here the MT output) and reference (here the PE translation). Given a pair of strings such as *H* and *R* to be compared, METEOR initially establishes a word alignment between them. The alignment is provided by a mapping method between the words in the hypothesis *H* an reference *R* transaltion, which is built incrementally by the following sequence of word-mapping modules:

- **Exact:** maps if they are exactly the same
- **Porter stem:** maps if they are the same after they are stemmed using the Porter stemmer
- **WN synonymy:** maps if they are considered synonyms in WordNet

If multiple alignments exist, METEOR selects the alignment for which the word order in the two strings is most similar (i.e. having fewest crossing alignment links). The final alignment is produced between *H* and *R* as the union of all stage alignments (e.g. exact, Porter stemming and WN synonymy).

3.2.3 Hybridization

The hybrid word alignment method combines two different kinds of word alignment: the statistical alignment tools such as GIZA++ word alignment with grow-diag-final-and (GDFA) heuristic (Koehn, 2010) and SymGiza++ (Junczys-Dowmunt and Szał, 2012) and the Berkeley aligner (Liang et al., 2006), as well as edit distance-based aligners (Snover et al., 2006; Lavie and Agarwal, 2007). In order to combine these different word alignment tables (Pal et al., 2013) we used a mathematical union method. For the union method, we hypothesise that all alignments are correct. Duplicate entries are removed.

3.3 Phrase-Based SMT

Translation is modelled in SMT as a decision process, in which the translation

$$e_1^L = e_1 ... e_i ... e_I \quad (2)$$

of a source sentence

$$f_1^J = f_1 ... f_j ... f_J \quad (3)$$

is chosen to maximize in equation (4):

$$argmax_{I,e_1^L} P(e_1^L | f_1^J) = argmax_{I,e_1^L} P(f_1^J | e_1^L) * P(e_1^L) \quad (4)$$

where $P(f_1^J|e_1^L)$ is the translation model and $P(e_1^L)$ the target language model. In log-linear phrase-based SMT, the posterior probability is directly modeled as a log-linear combination of features (Och and Ney, 2003), involving *M* translational features, and the language model, as in equation (5):

$$logP(e_1^L|f_1^J) = \sum_{m=0}^{M} \lambda_m h_m(f_1^J, e_1^L, s_1^k) + \lambda_{LM} logP(e_1^L) \quad (5)$$

where $s_1^k = s_1 \ldots s_k$ denotes a segmentation of the source and target sentences respectively into the sequences of phrases ($\hat{e}_1^k = \hat{e}_1 \ \ldots \ \hat{e}_k$) and ($\hat{f}_1^k = \hat{f}_1 \ \ldots \ \hat{f}_k$) such that (we set $i_0 = 0$) in equation (6):

$$\forall 1 \leq k \leq K, s_k = (i_k, b_k, j_k), \quad (6)$$
$$\hat{e}_k = e_{i_{k-1}+1} ... e_{i_k}, \hat{f}_k = f_{b_k} ... f_{j_k}$$

and each feature $\hat{h}_m$ in (5) can be rewritten as in (7):

$$h_m(f_1^J, e_1^L, s_1^k) = \sum_{k=1}^{K} \hat{h}_m(\hat{f}_k, \hat{e}_k, s_k) \quad (7)$$

where $\hat{h}_m$ is a feature that applies to a single phrase-pair. It thus follows (8):

$$\sum_{m=1}^{M} \lambda_m \sum_{k=1}^{K} \hat{h}_m(\hat{f}_k, \hat{e}_k, s_k) = \sum_{k=1}^{K} \hat{h}(\hat{f}_k, \hat{e}_k, s_k) \quad (8)$$

where $\hat{h} = \sum_{k=1}^{K} \lambda_m \hat{h}_m$.

4 Experiments

We performed experiments on the development set provided by the organizers of the APE task in the WMT2015.

4.1 Data

Table 1 presents the statistics of the training, development and test sets released for the English–Spanish SAPE Task organized in WMT'2015. These data sets did not require any preprocessing in terms of encoding or alignment.

	SEN	Tokens		
		EN	ES-MT	ES-PE
Train	11,272	238,335	257,644	257,881
Dev	1,000	21,617	23,213	23,098
Test	1,817	38,244	40,925	–

Table 1: Statistics. SEN: Sentences, EN: English and ES: Spanish

4.2 Experimental Settings

The effectiveness of the present work is demonstrated by using the standard log-linear PBSMT model. For building our SAPE system, we experimented with various maximum phrase lengths for the translation model and n–gram settings for the language model. We found that using a maximum phrase length of 7 for the translation model and a 5-gram language model produces the best results in terms of BLEU (Papineni et al., 2002) scores for our SAPE model.

The other experimental settings were concerned with hybrid word alignment training algorithms (described in Section 3) and the phrase-extraction (Koehn et al., 2003). The reordering model was trained with the hierarchical, monotone, swap, left to right bidirectional (hier-mslr-bidirectional) (Galley and Manning, 2008) method and conditioned on both source and target language. The 5-gram target language model was trained using KenLM (Heafield, 2011). Phrase pairs that occur only once in the training data are assigned an unduly high probability mass (i.e. 1). To alleviate this shortcoming, we performed smoothing of the phrase table using the Good-Turing smoothing technique (Foster et al., 2006). System tuning was carried out using Minimum Error Rate Training (MERT) (Och, 2003) optimised with k-best MIRA (Cherry and Foster, 2012) on a held out development set. After the parameters were tuned, decoding was carried out on the held out test set.

5 Evaluation

The evaluation of our SAPE system was performed on the 1817 Spanish sentences. The baseline consisted of two systems, an MT baseline system and the APE the system of (Simard et al., 2007a). The evaluation was carried out using HTER (TER with human targeted references) score. In this year's WMT seven groups made a submission to the APE task. From the seven systems, our system was ranked on the third place, achieving a HTER score of 23.426 for case sensitive evaluation and 22.710 for the case insensitive evaluation, outperforming the baseline APE system scoring 23.839 for the case sensitive evaluation and 23.130 for the case insensitive evaluation.

6 Conclusion

This paper presents our system submitted in the English–Spanish APE Task for WMT2015. The system demonstrates the crucial role hybrid word alignment can play in SAPE tasks. Edit-distance based monolingual aligner provides alignment for our SAPE system. Incorporating hybrid word alignment into the state-of-the-art PBSMT pipeline provides additional improvements over the baseline APE system.

Acknowledgments

The research leading to these results has received funding from the EU FP7 Project EXPERT - the People Programme (Marie Curie Actions), under REA grant agreement no. 317471.

References

Kuang-Hua Chen and Hsin-Hsi Chen. 1997. A Hybrid Approach to Machine Translation System Design. *Computational Linguistics and Language Processing*, 23:241–265.

Colin Cherry and George Foster. 2012. Batch Tuning Strategies for Statistical Machine Translation. In *In Proceedings of the North American Chapter of the Association for Computational Linguistics on Human Language Technologies (NAACL-HLT)*, pages 427–436.

Donald De Palma and Nataly Kelly. 2009. Project Management for Crowdsourced Translation: How User-Translated Content Projects Work in Real Life. *Translation and Localization Project Management: The Art of the Possible*, pages 379–408.

Michael Denkowski. 2015. *Machine Translation for Human Translators*. Ph.D. thesis, Carnegie Mellon University.

Rebecca Fiederer and Sharon O'Brien. 2009. Quality and Machine Translation: a Realistic Objective. *Journal of Specialised Translation*, 11:52–74.

George Foster, Roland Kuhn, and Howard Johnson. 2006. Phrasetable Smoothing for Statistical Machine Translation. In *Proceedings of the Conference on Empirical Methods in Natural Language Processing (EMNLP)*, pages 53–61.

Michel Galley and Christopher D. Manning. 2008. A Simple and Effective Hierarchical Phrase Reordering Model. In *Proceedings of the Conference on Empirical Methods in Natural Language Processing (EMNLP)*, pages 848–856.

Kenneth Heafield. 2011. KenLM: Faster and Smaller Language Model Queries. In *Proceedings of the 6th Workshop on Statistical Machine Translation (WMT)*, pages 187–197.

Marcin Junczys-Dowmunt and Arkadiusz Szał. 2012. SyMGiza++: Symmetrized Word Alignment Models for Statistical Machine Translation. In *Proceedings of the International Conference on Security and Intelligent Information Systems (SIIS)*, pages 379–390.

Kevin Knight and Ishwar Chander. 1994. Automated Post-Editing of Documents. In *Proceedings of the 12th National Conference on Artificial Intelligence*, pages 779–784.

Philipp Koehn, Franz Josef Och, and Daniel Marcu. 2003. Statistical Phrase-based Translation. In *Proceedings of the North American Chapter of the Association for Computational Linguistics on Human Language Technology (NAACL-HLT)*, pages 48–54, Stroudsburg, PA, USA.

Philipp Koehn. 2009. A Process Study of Computer Aided Translation. *Machine Translation*, 23(4):241–263.

Philipp Koehn. 2010. *Statistical Machine Translation*. Cambridge University Press, New York, NY, USA, 1st edition.

Antonio Lagarda, Vicent Alabau, Francisco Casacuberta, Roberto Silva, and Enrique Díaz-de Liaño. 2009. Statistical Post-Editing of a Rule-based Machine Translation System. In *Proceedings of the North American Chapter of the Association for Computational Linguistics on Human Language Technologies (NAACL-HLT)*, pages 217–220, Stroudsburg, PA, USA.

Alon Lavie and Abhaya Agarwal. 2007. METEOR: An Automatic Metric for MT Evaluation with High Levels of Correlation with Human Judgments. In *Proceedings of the 2nd Workshop on Statistical Machine Translation (WMT)*, pages 228–231.

Abby Levenberg, Chris Callison-Burch, and Miles Osborne. 2010. Stream-based Translation Models for Statistical Machine Translation. In *Proceedings of Human Language Technologies*, pages 394–402, Stroudsburg, PA, USA.

Percy Liang, Ben Taskar, and Dan Klein. 2006. Alignment by Agreement. In *Proceedings of the North American Chapter of the Association of Computational Linguistics on Human Language Technologies (NAACL-HLT)*, pages 104–111.

Adam David Lopez. 2008. *Machine Translation by Pattern Matching*. ProQuest.

David Mareček, Rudolf Rosa, Petra Galuščáková, and Ondřej Bojar. 2011. Two-step Translation with Grammatical Post-Processing. In *Proceedings of the 6th Workshop on Statistical Machine Translation (WMT)*, pages 426–432.

Franz Josef Och and Hermann Ney. 2003. A Systematic Comparison of Various Statistical Alignment Models. *Computational Linguistics*, 29(1):19–51.

Franz Josef Och. 2003. Minimum Error Rate Training in Statistical Machine Translation. In *Proceedings of the 41st Annual Meeting on Association for Computational Linguistics*, pages 160–167.

Lluís Padró and Evgeny Stanilovsky. 2012. FreeLing 3.0: Towards Wider Multilinguality. In *Proceedings of the Language Resources and Evaluation Conference (LREC 2012)*, Istanbul, Turkey. ELRA.

Santanu Pal, Sudip Kumar Naskar, and Sivaji Bandyopadhyay. 2013. A Hybrid Word Alignment Model for Phrase-Based Statistical Machine Translation. *ACL 2013*, page 94.

Kishore Papineni, Salim Roukos, Todd Ward, and Wei-Jing Zhu. 2002. BLEU: A Method for Automatic Evaluation of Machine Translation. In *Proceedings of the 40th Annual Meeting on Association for Computational Linguistics*, pages 311–318.

Kristen Parton and Kathleen McKeown. 2010. MT Error Detection for Cross-lingual Question Answering. In *Proceedings of the 23rd International Conference on Computational Linguistics*, pages 946–954, Stroudsburg, PA, USA.

Kristen Parton, Nizar Habash, Kathleen McKeown, Gonzalo Iglesias, and Adriá de Gispert. 2012. Can Automatic Post-Editing Make MT More Meaningful? In *Proceedings of the 16th Annual Conference of the European Association for Machine Translation (EAMT)*.

Rudolf Rosa, David Mareček, and Ondřej Dušek. 2012. DEPFIX: A System for Automatic Correction of Czech MT Outputs. In *Proceedings of the 7th Workshop on Statistical Machine Translation (WMT)*, Stroudsburg, PA, USA.

Johann Roturier. 2009. Deploying Novel MT Technology to Raise the Bar for Quality: A Review of Key Advantages and Challenges. In *Proceedings of the 12th Machine Translation Summit*.

Michel Simard, Cyril Goutte, and Pierre Isabelle. 2007a. Statistical Phrase-based Post-Editing. In *In Proceedings of the North American Chapter of the Association for Computational Linguistics on Human Language Technologies (NAACL-HLT)*.

Michel Simard, Nicola Ueffing, Pierre Isabelle, and Roland Kuhn. 2007b. Rule-Based Translation with Statistical Phrase-Based Post-Editing. In *Proceedings of the 2nd Workshop on Statistical Machine Translation (WMT)*, pages 203–206.

Matthew Snover, Bonnie Dorr, Richard Schwartz, Linnea Micciulla, and John Makhoul. 2006. A Study of Translation Edit Rate with Targeted Human Annotation. In *Proceedings of Association for Machine Translation in the Americas (AMTA)*, pages 223–231.

TAUS/CNGL Report. 2010. Maschine Translation Post-Editing Guidelines Published. Technical report, TAUS.

Mihaela Vela and Josef van Genabith. 2015. Reassessing the WMT2013 Human Evaluation with Professional Translators Trainees. In *Proceedings of the 18th Annual Conference of the European Association for Machine Translation (EAMT)*.

Marcos Zampieri and Mihaela Vela. 2014. Quantifying the Influence of MT Output in the Translators Performance: A Case Study in Technical Translation. In *Proceedings of the EACL Workshop on Humans and Computer-assisted Translation (HaCat)*, May.

Why Predicting Post-Edition is so Hard? Failure Analysis of LIMSI Submission to the APE Shared Task

Guillaume Wisniewski and **Nicolas Pécheux** and **François Yvon**
Université Paris Sud and LIMSI-CNRS
91 403 ORSAY CEDEX, France
{wisniews,pecheux,yvon}@limsi.fr

Abstract

This paper describes the two systems submitted by LIMSI to the WMT'15 Shared Task on Automatic Post-Editing. The first one relies on a reformulation of the APE task as a Machine Translation task; the second implements a simple rule-based approach. Neither of these two systems manage to improve the automatic translation. We show, by carefully analyzing the failure of our systems that this counter-performance mainly results from the inconsistency in the annotations.

1 Introduction

This paper describes LIMSI submission to the WMT'15 Shared Task on Automatic Post-Editing (APE). This task aims at automatically correcting errors produced by an unknown Machine Translation (MT) system by learning from human post-editions.

For the first edition of this Shared Task we have submitted two APE systems. The first one, described in Section 3, is based on the approach of Simard et al. (2007) and considers the APE task as the automatic translation between a translation hypothesis and its post-edition. This straightforward approach does not succeed in improving translation quality. To understand the reasons of this failure, we present, in Section 4 a detailed analysis of the training data that highlights some of the difficulties of training an APE system.

The second submitted system implements a series of sieves, applying, each, a simple post-editing rule. The definition of these rules is based on our analysis of the most frequent error corrections. Experiments with this approach (Section 5) show that this system also hurts translation quality. However, analyzing its failures allows us to show that the main difficulties in correcting MT errors result from the inconsistency between the different post-editions.

2 Data Preprocessing

The Shared Task organizers provide training and development data that consist of respectively 11,272 and 1,000 examples. Each example is made of an English source sentence, its automatic translation in Spanish by an unknown MT system and a human revision of this translation. All sentences are tokenized. There are, on average, 22.88 words in each post-edition, the longest post-edition having 199 words and the shortest 3.

In a first pre-processing step we have removed all examples for which the ratio between the length of the automatic translation and the length of the corresponding post-edition was higher than 1.2 or lower than 0.8. As shown in Table 1, these examples correspond mainly to errors in sentence boundaries or to 'over-translation' (e.g. when the post-editor added the translated title in the third example of Table 1), that could have a negative impact on the training of an APE system. At the end, the training set we used in all our experiments is made of 10,404 sentences.

The source sentences and the automatic translation of the training and development set have been aligned at the word level using FASTALIGN (Dyer et al., 2013) and the grow-diag-final symmetrization heuristic. To improve alignment quality, the sources and the translations have been first concatenated to the English-Spanish Europarl dataset and the resulting corpus has been aligned as a whole. Spanish MT outputs and post-editions have also been PoS-tagged using FREELING,[1] a state-of-the-art rule-based PoS tagger for Spanish. We used a CRF-based model trained on the Penn Treebank for the English source sentences. All PoS tags have been mapped to the universal PoS

[1] http://nlp.lsi.upc.edu/freeling/

src n°3334	Gomez Flies To Miami To Be With Bieber !
tgt n°3334	Gómez Vuela a Miami para estar con Bieber !
pe n°3334	Gómez Vuela hasta Miami para estar con Bieber ! AQUÍ estan las Pruebas ! Parece que estos dos tortolitos están juntos de nuevo y esta vez , podrian estar cantando .. La pelea de Twitter entre Demi Lovato y Kathy Griffin fue tan serio que hasta se involucro la policia y hubieron amenazas de muerte !
src n°517	that are sooooo good !
tgt n°517	que son taaaan bueno !
pe n°517	La favorita de Perezcious , Lissie , acaba de lanzar un nuevo EP de covers ... ¡ que están taaaan buenos !
src n°4444	MAJOR Amazing Spider-Man 2 Spoiler Alert !
tgt n°4444	MAJOR Amazing Spider-Man 2 Spoiler Alert !
pe n°4444	GRAN Alerta de Spoiler para The Amazing Spider-Man 2 (El maravilloso Hombre Araña 2) !

Table 1: Examples of automatic translations and their post-editions for which the ratio between their length is higher than 1.2.

tagset of Petrov et al. (2012) to make interpretation easier. Note that these two procedures are error-prone (especially as we have no information about the tokenization) and may introduce some noise in our analysis (cf. Section 4).

We have also computed an edit distance between the automatic translations and their post-editions using Python standard `difflib` module that allows us to define an 'alignment', at the phrase-level,[2] between these two sentences. The `difflib` module implements the Ratcliff-Obershelp algorithm (Ratcliff and Metzener, 1988) that finds a sequence of edits transforming a sentence into another. While this sequence is not necessarily of minimal length, it is faster to compute, easier to use and, above all, more interpretable than the one computed using the standard minimum edit distance algorithm. In particular, `difflib` is able to automatically find edits between 'phrases' rather than between single words.

3 Automatic Post-Editing as Machine Translation

The first system we have developed for the Shared Task is inspired by the approach of Simard et al. (2007) and reduces the Automatic Post-Edition task as a Machine Translation task. Ignoring the source sentence, we train a standard phrase-based machine translation system using the automatic translation as a source sentence and its post-edition as the target sentence.

The word alignment between the automatic translation and the post-edited sentence, used as input in our APE-MT pipeline, has been computed using Meteor (Denkowski and Lavie, 2014). The APE-MT system has then been trained following the usual steps.[3] In our experiments, we used our in-house MT system NCODE (Crego et al., 2011) that implements a n-gram based translation model. As main features we used a 3-gram bilingual language model on words, a 4-gram bilingual language model on PoS factors and a 4-gram target language model trained only on the post-editions sentences, along with the conventional features (4 lexical features, 6 lexicalized reordering, distortion model, word and phrase penalty). We did allow reorderings during decoding. The training data is used to extract and compute the different models while the development data is used to perform the tuning step.

The results, evaluated by the hTER score[4] between the predicted and the human post-editions, are summarized in Table 2. This straightforward approach actually hurts performance and the results show that we are not able to predict post-editions: the output of the MT system is closer to the post-edition than the prediction of our APE-

[2] As usual in MT, we use 'phrase' to denote a sequence of consecutive words.

[3] see, for instance, `https://ncode.limsi.fr`

[4] All reported hTER scores are case-sensitive and have been computed using the scripts provided by the Shared Task organizers.

	train	development	test
MT output	23.32	23.21	22.91
APE-MT output	21.64	23.95	23.57

Table 2: hTER score achieved by MT system train to predict the post-edition from the MT output.

MT system. This is true even for the development data on which our system was tuned.

4 Data Analysis

To understand the results of our first APE model, we analyzed thoughtfully the data provided by the shared task organizers.

The risk of over-correcting The first important observation is that the MT system used to translate the source sentences achieves an hTER score of 23.32 on the training data, meaning that, roughly, more than three words out of four are correct and must not be modified. As a consequence, predicting which words must be post-edited is an highly unbalanced problem. It is, therefore, very likely that any modifications of the MT output could hurt translation quality. Let n denote the number of word of in the dataset and a the percentage of words that are mistranslated. If we are able to detect mistranslated words with a precision p and a recall r and to correct them with precision c, the number of errors after the automatic post-editing equals to the sum of the number of errors that have not been corrected $(n \times a \times (1 - r))$, the number of errors the correction of which is erroneous $(n \times a \times r \times (1 - c))$ and of the number correct words that have been modified $(n \times a \times r \times (1 - p) \div p)$. For the shared task training data, $n = 238,332$, $a = 0.25$ and we assume that $c = 0.8$, which is an optimistic estimate. To avoid introducing new error, the F_1 score of the system detecting mistranslated word must be higher that 0.7, which is far better than the performance achieved by most state-of-the-art word-level confidence estimation system.

Uniqueness of edits To characterize annotators edits, we have computed the distribution of the three basic operations (Table 3) as well as the 20 most frequent 'lexicalized' edits (Table 4). Several observations, similar to the findings of our analysis of an English-French post-editions corpus (Wisniewski et al., 2013), can be made from

operation	*count*	%
deletion	4,795	15.56%
insertion	5,873	19.07%
substitution	20,129	65.37%
total	30,797	100%

Table 3: Distribution of the edit types in the training set.

edits	occurrences	edits	occurrences
+¡	286	+la	108
+,	267	-el	107
+de	247	+el	102
+que	231	-los	101
-,	202	+los	92
-que	164	-se	92
-la	164	+en	88
+a	156	+se	85
-de	146	su → tu	71
+'	117	+las	68

Table 4: Most frequent post-edits on the training set. Additions and deletion are denoted by '+' and '-'; substitutions by '→' .

these two tables. First, and most importantly, it appears that most edits are unique: even the most frequent edit (insertion of '¡') only accounts for a negligible part of all edits. Overall, 24.74% of all edits are unique. As a consequence, it is very unlikely that any approach, such as the one described in Section 3, that relies solely on word-level pattern recognition and transformation, will be able to generalize the observed corrections to new sentences. This explains why our APT-MT systems improves on the training data, on which transformation where learned, but fails to generalize (Table 2).

Importance of edits related to punctuation Second, it appears that the most frequent edits are mainly insertions or deletions of either a frequent word or a punctuation. Table 5 shows the distribution of edits that concern *only* punctuations. These edits account for an important part of all the modifications made by the post-editors: correcting them automatically would reduce the hTER score by more than 3 points. Some of these edits correspond to genuine translation errors that must be corrected for the output sentence to be gram-

edits	count	%
addition	581	1.88
deletion	394	1.27
substitution	85	0.27
Total	1,060	3.42

Table 5: Number of edits involving *only* punctuation.

Accesorios → accesorios	Guía → guía
Campo → campo	está loco → Está Loco
algas → alGAS	Inglés → inglés
legión → Legión	poderes → PODERES
thefamily → TheFamily	mucho → MUCHO

Table 6: Examples of substitutions that involve only changes in case.

substitution	count
VERB → VERB	2,372
NOUN → NOUN	1,243
ADP → ADP	605
ADJ → ADJ	571
PRON VERB → VERB	225
DET → DET	224
VERB → NOUN	178
NOUN → VERB	169
DET NOUN → DET NOUN	151
NOUN → ADJ	147
NOUN → DET NOUN	146
ADV → ADV	136
DET NOUN → NOUN	119
PRON → PRON	109
ADJ → NOUN	89
VERB ADP → VERB	76
total	6,560

Table 7: PoS of the words involved in a substitution.

matically correct. In particular, in Spanish, all interrogative and exclamatory sentences or clauses have to begin with an inverted question mark (¿) or exclamation mark (¡). These long-range dependencies are difficult to capture with a phrase-based system, which explains why inverted punctuation often have to be inserted by the post-editors. However, many other modifications (especially the insertion and deletion of comas) are more an improvement of style and their presence in a 'minimal' post-edition can be questioned.

We will now consider the most frequent types of edits and focus on three different kind of substitutions.

Importance of edits related to change in case We first looked at changes in case: it appears that 1.16% of all edits are solely a change in case. Table 6 gives some examples of such edits. The high proportion of edits related to case is not really surprising as it can be assumed that the MT system has been trained on lower-cased data and its output has been re-cased in a second, independent step, which is a difficult task. However, as for the punctuations, word case rarely affects the meaning of a sentence and its correction can be considered more as 'normalization' rather than 'mandatory' edits.

Correcting verb endings To better characterize the different kind of substitutions, we have represented, Table 7, the PoS of the words involved in a substitution. This table shows that many of the substitutions that occur during post-edition keep the grammatical structure of the sentence unchanged and only modify lexical choices: in 26.7% of the substitutions, the PoS of the words that are edited are kept unchanged. Interestingly, as for lexicalized edits presented in Table 4 most of the 'PoS substitutions' are unique. But, when looking at the tail of the distribution, it appears that many of these unique transformations are due to error in alignment (e.g. when a single word is replaced by 6 or 7 words) or to error in PoS prediction.

Looking more closely at verb modifications, it appears that, in 39.68% of them, the prefix[5] of the words is the same, suggesting that a lot of edits consist in changing the verb conjugation, which might be surprising as it could be expected that the language model would resolve such difficulties. Table 8 gives some examples of verb post-editings. Surprisingly, this observation is no longer true for modifications of nouns: in less than 10% of them, the prefix is the same before and after post-editing.

5 A Multi-Sieve Approach to Automatic Post-Editing

5.1 Main Principles

We consider a simple Automatic Post-Edition architecture based on a sieve that applies simple post-editing rules. Using such a simple rule-based approach has two main motivations. First, by focusing on very precise categories of errors, we expect to avoid 'over-correcting' the translation hypotheses as our APE-MT model; second, analyz-

[5]The prefix is defined as the first five letters of a word.

same prefix	different prefix
piensa → piense (thinks)	significa → representa (means)
escritos → escritas (NULL)	significa → representa (NULL)
guardar → guardan (save)	superar → batir beat
afeitado → afeitadas (shaven)	preocupa → ocupa preoccupies
visita → visitas (visit)	Ofender → ofendiendo Offending
tratando → tratar (trying)	metió → metí (NULL)
adecuado → adecuada (suited)	tengo → conseguí (I)
presentan → presente (come)	dejar → deje (quit)
pregunta → preguntaste (asking)	seguir → cumplir (keep)
enseñado → enseñó (taught)	invertido → investido (invested)

Table 8: Example of verb substitutions with the source word they are aligned with.

ing the errors of these simple rules will be much easier than analyzing the output of a complete MT system such as the one presented in Section 3 and we expect to gain some insights about the interplay between the different factors at stake.

In this work, we have considered three post-editing rules that correspond to the main categories of errors identified in Section 4. These rules aim at:

- predicting word case;
- predicting exclamation and interrogation marks;
- predicting verbal endings.

Prediction of word case We used a very naive approach to predict the case of a word by assuming that a translated word should have the same case as the source word it is aligned with. We therefore converted all words that were aligned with a lower-cased, upper-cased or title-cased word to their lower-cased, upper-cased or title-cased version, respectively. To account for missing alignment links, we also converted all target word in upper-case when all the words of the source sentence were upper-cased.

Prediction of exclamation and interrogation marks As explained in Section 4, in Spanish, interrogative and exclamatory sentences or clauses have to begin with an inverted question mark (¿) or exclamation mark (¡). We use the method described in Algorithm 1 to insert question marks[6] at the beginning and end of clauses. This method simply inserts the same punctuation mark as in the source sentence[7] at the end of the sentence and finds the beginning of the clause by looking for a set of specific characters to insert the inverted punctuation mark right after it. When the beginning of the clause can not be found, the inverted punctuation mark is inserted at the beginning of the sentence.

Algorithm 1: Insert question marks at end and beginning of clauses .

```
input: s = (s_i)_{i=1}^{|s|} a source sentence
remove '?' and '¿' from target sentence
if '?' ∉ s then
    return s
add '?' at end of target sentence
for i ∈ [[|s|, 0]] do
    if i = 0 or s_i ∈ '–:,"“-' then
        insert '¿' at the (i+1)^th position
        break
```

Correcting Verbs Ending We used a two-step models to correct verb endings. In a first step we generate, for each verb identified in the translation hypothesis, a list of candidates containing conjugation variants for this verb form. We then choose the verb form which maximizes the language model score of the modified sentence as the correction. To generate the list of candidates, we extracted automatically the conjugation tables of Spanish Wiktionary[8], building a list of 587,832 verb forms with their lemma. We used, as a scoring model, a 5-gram language model trained on the Spanish data of the WMT campaign.

This post-edition rule is more prone to errors than the previous two rules as it relies on a language model (that was trained on data with a different tokenization) and on an external resource to generate the candidates (that is neither complete nor completely accurate).

5.2 Experimental Results

Table 9 shows the result, evaluated on the Shared Task development set, of the multi-sieve approach described in the previous section. As for the MT model presented in Section 3, our model degrades translation quality, even if it makes only a small number of precise modifications, showing that there are more errors introduced by our multi-

[6]The same method was used to insert exclamation marks.

[7]Only inserting the inverted punctuation mark slightly hurts performance: it appears that not all interrogative sentence are translated into an interrogative sentence.

[8]es.wiktionary.org

	hTER
baseline	23.320
+case correction	23.396
+punctuation correction	23.708
+verb correction	24.217

Table 9: hTER score achieved by our multi-sieve approach on the development data.

sieve approach than there are errors that are corrected.

The analysis of our errors shows that the observed drop in performance can be explained by the inconsistencies in the post-editions. For instance, in the case of interrogative sentences, there are 558 translation hypotheses in the training set that end with an interrogative mark, 203 of which do not contain an inverted mark. Applying Algorithm 1, will correct all of them. However, it also appears that, in 108 of these 203 sentences (53%) no inverted interrogative marks were added by the post-editors — resulting in 'un-grammatical' sentences. At the end, even the correct introduction of inverted question marks would make translation hypotheses less similar to the human post-edition. A similar observation can be made for the exclamatory sentences.

Regarding the correction of case, the proposed post-edition rule achieves very good performance when its application is restricted to the word that have to be post-edited (i.e. when using the post-edition as an oracle to identify which words must be corrected): it is able to correctly predict the case of the word in almost 85% of the case. The erroneous corrections mainly result from alignment errors. However, when applied on the whole corpora it will also change the case of many words the post-editors have not modified. When we looked at these words we did not see any reasons why they should not have been modified.

6 Discussion and Conclusion

We described two different approaches to Automatic Post-Editing: the first one casts the problem as a monolingual MT task; the second one uses a series of simple, yet effective, post-edition sieves. Unfortunately, none of our systems was able to outperform the simplest do-nothing baseline. While better post-editions methods have yet to be found, we argue that this negative result is mainly explained by the difficulty of the task at hand and the small amount of available data. Indeed, none of the participants to this pilot Shared Task managed to outperform the baseline. This is confirmed by an in-depth analysis of the task which shows that: (a) most of the post-edition operations are nearly unique, which makes very difficult to generalize from a small amount of data; and (b) even when they are not, inconsistencies in the annotations between the different post-editions prevent from improving over the baseline.

Acknowledgments

This work was partly supported by the French "National Research Agency" (ANR) under project ANR-12-CORD-0015/Transread.

References

Josep Maria Crego, François Yvon, and José B. Mariño. 2011. N-code: an open-source Bilingual N-gram SMT Toolkit. *Prague Bulletin of Mathematical Linguistics*, 96:49–58.

Michael Denkowski and Alon Lavie. 2014. Meteor universal: Language specific translation evaluation for any target language. In *Proceedings of the EACL 2014 Workshop on Statistical Machine Translation*.

Chris Dyer, Victor Chahuneau, and Noah A. Smith. 2013. A simple, fast, and effective reparameterization of ibm model 2. In *NAACL*, pages 644–648, Atlanta, Georgia, June. Association for Computational Linguistics.

Slav Petrov, Dipanjan Das, and Ryan McDonald. 2012. A universal part-of-speech tagset. In *LREC*, Istanbul, Turkey, may.

John W. Ratcliff and D. E. Metzener. 1988. Pattern matching: The gestalt approach. *Dr. Dobb's Journal*.

Michel Simard, Cyril Goutte, and Pierre Isabelle. 2007. Statistical phrase-based post-editing. In *Human Language Technologies 2007: The Conference of the North American Chapter of the Association for Computational Linguistics; Proceedings of the Main Conference*, pages 508–515, Rochester, New York, April. Association for Computational Linguistics.

Guillaume Wisniewski, Anil Kumar Singh, Natalia Segal, and François Yvon. 2013. Design and analysis of a large corpus of post-edited translations: quality estimation, failure analysis and the variability of post-edition. *Machine Translation Summit*, 14:117–124.

Hierarchical Machine Translation With Discontinuous Phrases

Miriam Kaeshammer
University of Düsseldorf
Universitätsstraße 1
40225 Düsseldorf, Germany
kaeshammer@phil.uni-duesseldorf.de

Abstract

We present a hierarchical statistical machine translation system which supports discontinuous constituents. It is based on synchronous linear context-free rewriting systems (SLCFRS), an extension to synchronous context-free grammars in which synchronized non-terminals span $k \geq 1$ continuous blocks on either side of the bitext. This extension beyond context-freeness is motivated by certain complex alignment configurations that are beyond the alignment capacity of current translation models and their relatively frequent occurrence in hand-aligned data. Our experiments for translating from German to English demonstrate the feasibility of training and decoding with more expressive translation models such as SLCFRS and show a modest improvement over a context-free baseline.

1 Introduction

In statistical machine translation, phrase-based translation models with a beam search decoder (Koehn et al., 2003) and tree-based models with a CYK decoder represent two prominent types of approaches. The latter usually employ some form of synchronous context-free grammar (SCFG). They can be grouped into so-called hierarchical phrase-based models that are formally syntax-based, such as in Chiang (2007), and models where hierarchical units are somehow linguistically motivated, e.g. in Zollmann and Venugopal (2006) and Hoang and Koehn (2010).

The adequacy of all of these models has been questioned, as the space of alignments that they generate is limited. Inside-out alignments are beyond the alignment capacity of SCFG of rank 2 (henceforth 2-SCFG) and inversion transduction grammar (Wu, 1997), but they can be generated with phrase-based translation models thanks to the reordering component of standard decoders. Cross-serial discontinuous translation units (CDTU) (Søgaard and Kuhn, 2009) and bonbon configurations (Simard et al., 2005) in contrast can neither be generated by a phrase-based translation system nor by an SCFG-based one. It is thereby assumed that a translation unit, the transitive closure of a set of nodes of the bipartite alignment graph, represents minimal translational equivalence, and therefore that an adequate translation grammar formalism should be able to generate each translation unit separately.

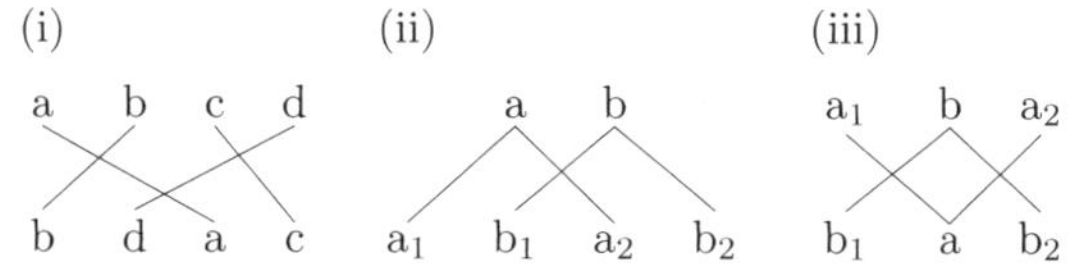

Figure 1: Complex alignment configurations: (i) inside-out alignment; (ii) CDTU; (iii) bonbon. The configurations can also occur upside down.

The aforementioned problematic alignment configurations are schematically depicted in Figure 1. Alignment (i) is an inside-out alignment; it is formed by four translation units (a, b, c and d). CDTUs (ii) and bonbons (iii) each consist of two intertwined discontinuous translation units.

Several studies have investigated the alignment capacity of SCFG-based and phrase-based translation models in different setups (Wellington et al., 2006; Søgaard and Kuhn, 2009; Søgaard and Wu, 2009; Søgaard, 2010; Kaeshammer, 2013). For example, Wellington et al. (2006) find that inside-out alignments occur in 5% of their manually aligned English-Chinese sentence pairs. In the study of Kaeshammer (2013), 9% of the sentence pairs in a Spanish-French data set and 5.5% of the sentence pairs in an English-German data set cannot be generated by a 2-SCFG. In addition, Kaeshammer and Westburg (2014) qualitatively investigate the instances of the complex alignment configurations in the same English-German data set and find that even though some of them are due to annotation errors, most of them are correctly annotated phenomena that one would like to be able to generate when translating.

To be able to induce the alignment configurations in question, more expressive translation models and corresponding decoding algorithms are necessary. For the phrase-based models, Galley and Manning (2010) propose a translation model that uses discontinuous phrases and a corresponding beam search decoder. For tree-based models, a grammar formalism beyond the power of context-free grammar is necessary. Søgaard (2008) proposes to apply range concatenation grammar; Kaeshammer (2013) puts forward the idea of using synchronous linear context-free rewriting systems (SLCFRS), a direct extension of SCFG to discontinous constituents. To the best of our knowledge, neither of the two proposals have resulted in an actual machine translation system.

With this work, we extend the line of research proposed in Kaeshammer (2013), and present the first full tree-based statistical machine translation system that allows for discontinuous constituents. It is thus able to produce the complex alignment configurations in Figure 1. As such, it combines the advantage of being able to learn and generate discontinuous phrases with the benefits of tree-based translation models.

Currently, our system is hierarchical phrase-based, i.e. it does not make use of linguistically motivated syntactic annotation. However, it will be straightforward to transfer methods to integrate linguistic constituency information from the SCFG-based machine translation literature (such as Zollmann and Venugopal (2006)) to our approach. This is particularly interesting, since, in the monolingual parsing community, approaches that are able to produce constituency trees with discontinuous constituents have become increasingly popular (Maier, 2010; van Cranenburgh and Bod, 2013; Kallmeyer and Maier, 2013). Recently, such parsers have reached a speed with which it would actually be feasible to parse the training set of a machine translation system (Versley, 2014; Maier, 2015; Fernández-González and Martins, 2015), which is necessary to train syntactically motivated translation grammars.

In this work, we define a translation model based on SLCFRS, explain the training of a corresponding hierarchical phrase-based grammar, provide details about a corresponding decoder and results of experiments for translating from German to English.

2 Model

Our translation model is a weighted synchronous LCFRS. Conceptually, this grammar formalism is very close to synchronous CFG, with the addition that non-terminals span tuples of strings (instead of just strings) on either side of the bitext. Just as SCFGs, an SLCFRS can be used for synchronous parsing of parallel sentences as well as for translating monolingual sentences. For the latter, the source side of the synchronous grammar is used to parse the input text, thereby generating target side derivations from which the translations can be read off.

2.1 Synchronous LCFRS

An LCFRS[1] (Vijay-Shanker et al., 1987; Weir, 1988) is a tuple $G = (N, T, V, P, S)$ where N is a finite set of non-terminals with a function dim: $N \rightarrow \mathbb{N}$ determining the *fan-out* of each $A \in N$; T and V are disjoint finite sets of terminals and variables; $S \in N$ is the start symbol with $dim(S) = 1$; and P is a finite set of rewriting rules

$$A(\alpha_1, \dots, \alpha_{dim(A)}) \rightarrow A_1(Y_1^{(1)}, \dots, Y_{dim(A_1)}^{(1)}) \cdots A_m(Y_1^{(m)}, \dots, Y_{dim(A_m)}^{(m)})$$

where $A, A_1, \dots, A_m \in N$, $Y_j^{(i)} \in V$ for $1 \leq i \leq m$, $1 \leq j \leq dim(A_i)$ and $\alpha_i \in (T \cup V)^*$ for $1 \leq i \leq dim(A)$, for a *rank* $m \geq 0$. For all $r \in P$, it holds that every variable Y in r occurs exactly once in the left-hand side (LHS) and exactly once in the right-hand side (RHS) of r.

A non-terminal is instantiated with respect to some input string w such that terminals and variables are consistently mapped to w. A rule r explains how an instantiated LHS non-terminal can be rewritten by its instantiated RHS non-terminals. A derivation starts with the start symbol S instantiated to the input string w. All strings that can

[1]We use the syntax of simple range concatenation grammars (Boullier, 1998), an equivalent formalism.

$$\begin{array}{ll}\langle A(a,c) \to \varepsilon & , C(a,c) \to \varepsilon\rangle \\ \langle B(b,d) \to \varepsilon & , D(bd) \to \varepsilon\rangle \\ \langle A(aX,cZ) \to A_{\boxed{1}}(X,Z) & , C(aX,Zc) \to C_{\boxed{1}}(X,Z)\rangle \\ \langle B(bY,dU) \to B_{\boxed{1}}(Y,U) & , D(bYd) \to D_{\boxed{1}}(Y)\rangle \\ \langle S(XYZU) \to A_{\boxed{1}}(X,Z)B_{\boxed{2}}(Y,U) , & \\ & S(XYZ) \to C_{\boxed{1}}(X,Z)D_{\boxed{2}}(Y)\rangle\end{array}$$

Figure 2: Rules of an SLCFRS for $L = \{\langle a^n b^m c^n d^m, a^n b^m d^m c^n\rangle \,|\, n,m > 0\}$, taken from Kaeshammer (2013).

$$\begin{array}{l}\langle S_{\boxed{1}}(aabccd), S_{\boxed{1}}(aabdcc)\rangle \\ \quad \Rightarrow \langle A_{\boxed{2}}(aa,cc)B_{\boxed{3}}(b,d), C_{\boxed{2}}(aa,cc)D_{\boxed{3}}(bd)\rangle \\ \quad \Rightarrow \langle A_{\boxed{2}}(aa,cc), C_{\boxed{2}}(aa,cc)\rangle \\ \quad \Rightarrow \langle A_{\boxed{4}}(a,c), C_{\boxed{4}}(a,c)\rangle \\ \quad \Rightarrow \varepsilon\end{array}$$

Figure 3: Derivation of $\langle aabccd, aabdcc\rangle$ using the rules in Figure 2.

be rewritten to ε are in the language of the grammar. For more formal definitions, see for example Kallmeyer (2010).

The *rank* of a grammar G is the maximal rank of any of its rules, and its *fan-out* is the maximal fan-out of any of its non-terminals. G is called a (u, v)-LCFRS if it has rank u and fan-out v. A CFG is the special case of an LCFRS with fan-out $v = 1$. An LCFRS is *monotone* if, for every rule and every RHS non-terminal, the order of the variables in the arguments of this non-terminal is the same as the order of these variables in the arguments of the LHS non-terminal of this rule. This means that the order of (instantiated) arguments of the LHS non-terminal of a rule always corresponds to their order in the input sentence. An LCFRS is called *ε-free* if all of its rules in P are ε-free, which means that none of their LHS arguments is the empty string ε.[2]

The definition of synchronous LCFRS (SLCFRS) follows the definition of synchronous CFG, as for example in Satta and Peserico (2005). An SLCFRS (Kaeshammer, 2013) is a tuple $G = (N_s, N_t, T_s, T_t, V_s, V_t, P, S_s, S_t)$ where N_s, T_s, V_s, S_s, resp. N_t, T_t, V_t, S_t are defined as for LCFRS. They denote the alphabets for the *source* and *target side* respectively. P is a finite set of synchronous rewriting rules $\langle r_s, r_t, \sim\rangle$ where r_s and r_t are LCFRS rewriting rules based on N_s, T_s, V_s and N_t, T_t, V_t respectively, and $\sim$ is a bijective mapping of the non-terminals in the RHS of r_s to the non-terminals in the RHS of r_t. This link relation is represented by co-indexation in the synchronous rules. During a derivation, the yields of two co-indexed non-terminals have to be explained from one synchronous rule. $\langle S_s, S_t\rangle$ is the start pair. In such a derivation, we call the yield of S_s the *source side yield* and the yield of S_t the *target side yield*. SLCFRS are equivalent to simple range concatenation transducers (Bertsch and Nederhof, 2001).

Figure 2 shows an example. The synchronous rules translate cross-serial dependencies into nested ones. A sample derivation is shown in Figure 3.

The tuple $(N_s, T_s, V_s, P_s, S_s)$ is called the *source side grammar* G_s and $(N_t, T_t, V_t, P_t, S_t)$ the *target side grammar* G_t, where P_s is the set of all r_s in P and P_t is the set of all r_t in P. The *rank* u of a SLCFRS G is the maximal rank of G_s and G_t, and the *fan-out* v of G is the sum of the fan-outs of G_s and G_t. One may write $v_{v_{G_s}|v_{G_t}}$ to make clear how the fan-out of G is distributed over the source and the target side. As in the monolingual case, a corresponding grammar G is called a (u, v)-SLCFRS. The rank of the corresponding grammar in Figure 2 is 2 and its fan-out $4_{2|2}$. We call an SLCFRS *monotone* if the source side grammar as well as the target side grammar is monotone. We call an SLCFRS *ε-free* if the source side grammar as well as the target side grammar is ε-free.

We further define some terms which will be used in the following sections. A *range* in a string w_1^n is a pair $\langle l, r\rangle$ with $0 \leq l \leq r \leq n$. Its *yield* $\langle l, r\rangle(w)$ is the string w_{l+1}^r. The yield of a vector of ranges $\boldsymbol{\rho}(w)$ is the vector of the yields of the single ranges.

2.2 Definition

Given a source sentence f and an SLCFRS, generally, many derivations will have f as the source side yield, leading to many (different) target side yields, i.e. possible translations e. As it is standard in statistical machine translation, we use a log-linear model over derivations D to weight those translation options. The definition closely follows the model definition for SCFG, see Chiang (2007)

[2]An LCFRS is also ε-free if it contains a rule $S(\varepsilon) \to \varepsilon$, but S does not appear in any RHS of the rules in P.

for example.

$$P(D) \propto \prod_i \phi_i(D)^{\lambda_i}$$
$$\propto P_{LM}(e)^{\lambda_{LM}} \cdot w(D)$$

where ϕ_i are features defined on the derivations, and λ_i are feature weights to be set during tuning. An n-gram language model provides a feature $P_{LM}(e)$ for the probability of seeing the target sentence e as derived by D. The other features $(i \neq LM)$ are defined on the rules of a weighted SLCFRS which are used in the derivation D.

A weighted SLCFRS is an SLCFRS that is additionally equipped with a weight function w which assigns a weight to each synchronous rule $r \in P$. To fit the log-linear model, we define w as

$$w(r) = \prod_{i \neq LM} \phi_i(r)^{\lambda_i}$$

The weight of a derivation D is then

$$w(D) = \prod_{r \in D} w(r)$$

2.3 Features

We use the following standard features $\phi_i(r)$:

- translation probabilities in both directions $P(r_s|r_t)$ and $P(r_t|r_s)$,
- lexical weights $lex(r_s|r_t)$ and $lex(r_t|r_s)$ (Koehn et al., 2003) that estimate how well the terminals in the rule translate to each other,
- a rule penalty $\exp(1)$,
- a word penalty $\exp(-|w_t|)$ where $|w_t|$ is the number of terminals that occur in r_t.

In addition, we devise features that characterize the amount of expressivity beyond context-freeness of the applied rules. The *source gap degree* of r is the fan-out of r_s minus 1, and the *target gap degree* of r is the fan-out of r_t minus 1. See Maier and Lichte (2011) for more details about gap degree. These features can be read off the rules r directly. They allow the model to learn a preference for or against using the more powerful rules.

We also use glue rules, as proposed by Chiang (2005), which allow for a monotone combination of synchronous constituents as in a phrase-based model. A glue rule feature of value $\exp(1)$ with its weight λ_{glue} controls their usage.

3 Training

The synchronous rules are extracted from a corpus of parallel sentences that have already been word-aligned. Following Och and Ney (2004) and Chiang (2005), we extract all rules that are consistent with the word alignment A of a sentence pair $\langle f, e \rangle$ in a two-step procedure. First, *initial phrase pairs* are extracted; they correspond to terminal rules. Second, hierarchical rules are created by replacing phrase pairs that are contained within other phrase pairs with non-terminals/variables.

The crucial difference to previous work on translation with SCFG is that initial phrases do not have to be continuous. Instead, a phrase is a set of word indices, as in Galley and Manning (2010). Given $\langle f, e \rangle$ and a corresponding word alignment A, a phrase pair $(\bar{s}, \bar{t})$ is consistent with A if the following holds:

$$\forall (i,j) \in A : i \in \bar{s} \leftrightarrow j \in \bar{t}$$
$$\wedge\ \exists i \in \bar{s}, j \in \bar{t} : (i,j) \in A$$

For each initial phrase pair $(\bar{s}, \bar{t})$, a terminal synchronous rule of the following form is created and added to P:

$$\langle X(\boldsymbol{\rho}_s(f)) \rightarrow \varepsilon, X(\boldsymbol{\rho}_t(e)) \rightarrow \varepsilon \rangle$$

$\boldsymbol{\rho}_s$ and $\boldsymbol{\rho}_t$ are range vectors, applied to the source sentence f and target sentence e respectively. $\boldsymbol{\rho}_s$ (respectively $\boldsymbol{\rho}_t$) is obtained by partitioning $\bar{s}$ (respectively $\bar{t}$) such that each subset contains all and only consecutive indices, designating a continuous block of the discontinuous phrase. Such a subset X is turned into a range $\langle l, r \rangle$ with $l = \min(X)$ and $r = \max(X)$. The ranges obtained from $\bar{s}$ (respectively $\bar{t}$), in ascending order, form $\boldsymbol{\rho}_s$ (respectively $\boldsymbol{\rho}_t$).

Furthermore, if P contains a rule $\langle X(\boldsymbol{\alpha}) \rightarrow \boldsymbol{\Psi}, X(\boldsymbol{\beta}) \rightarrow \boldsymbol{\Theta} \rangle$ that has been built from a phrase pair $(\bar{s}, \bar{t})$ and the set of phrase pairs contains a pair $(\bar{s}', \bar{t}')$ such that $\bar{s}' \subset \bar{s}$ and $\bar{t}' \subset \bar{t}$, we add the following new rule to P:

$$\langle X(\boldsymbol{\alpha}') \rightarrow \boldsymbol{\Psi} X_{\boxed{k}}(Y_1, \ldots, Y_{h_s}),$$
$$X(\boldsymbol{\beta}') \rightarrow \boldsymbol{\Theta} X_{\boxed{k}}(Z_1, \ldots, Z_{h_t}) \rangle$$

A new non-terminal X is added to the RHS of r_s and r_t. k is an index that is not yet used in the bijective mapping of non-terminals in $\boldsymbol{\Psi}$ and $\boldsymbol{\Theta}$. Range vectors $\boldsymbol{\rho}_{s'}$ and $\boldsymbol{\rho}_{t'}$ are deduced from $\bar{s}'$ and $\bar{t}'$ as described above. Each range in $\boldsymbol{\rho}_{s'}$ (respectively $\boldsymbol{\rho}_{t'}$) is associated with a variable Y_i for

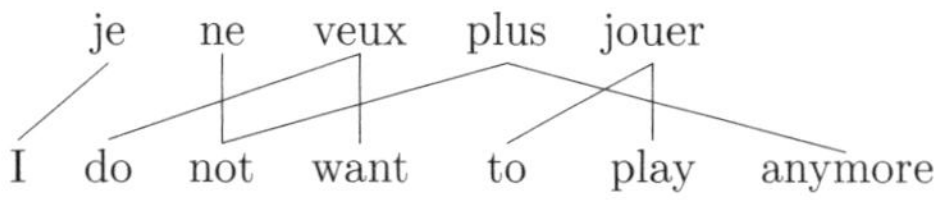

Initial phrase pairs:

1. jouer — to play
2. veux — do ... want
3. ne veux plus — do not want ... anymore
4. ne veux plus jouer — do not want to play anymore

...

Rules:

1. $\langle X(\text{jouer}) \rightarrow \varepsilon,\ X(\text{to play}) \rightarrow \varepsilon\rangle$
2. $\langle X(\text{veux}) \rightarrow \varepsilon,\ X(\text{do, want}) \rightarrow \varepsilon\rangle$
3. $\langle X(\text{ne veux plus}) \rightarrow \varepsilon,\ X(\text{do not want, anymore}) \rightarrow \varepsilon\rangle$
4. $\langle X(\text{ne veux plus jouer}) \rightarrow \varepsilon,$
   $X(\text{do not want to play anymore}) \rightarrow \varepsilon\rangle$
5. $\langle X(\text{ne } Y_1 \text{ plus}) \rightarrow X_{\boxed{1}}(Y_1),$
   $X(Z_1 \text{ not } Z_2, \text{anymore}) \rightarrow X_{\boxed{1}}(Z_1, Z_2)\rangle$
6. $\langle X(\text{ne veux plus } Y_1) \rightarrow X_{\boxed{1}}(Y_1),$
   $X(\text{do not want } Z_1 \text{ anymore}) \rightarrow X_{\boxed{1}}(Z_1)\rangle$
7. $\langle X(\text{ne } Y_1 \text{ plus } Y_2) \rightarrow X_{\boxed{1}}(Y_1)X_{\boxed{2}}(Y_2),$
   $X(Z_1 \text{ not } Z_2 Z_3 \text{ anymore}) \rightarrow X_{\boxed{1}}(Z_1, Z_2)X_{\boxed{2}}(Z_3)\rangle$

...

Figure 4: Sample rules that are extracted from the provided aligned sentence pair.

$1 \leq i \leq h_s$ (respectively Z_j for $1 \leq j \leq h_t$), where h_s (respectively h_t) is the length of $\boldsymbol{\rho}_{s'}$ (respectively $\boldsymbol{\rho}_{s'}$). They have to be variables that are not yet in use in $\boldsymbol{\alpha}$ (respectively $\boldsymbol{\beta}$). Those variables constitute the arguments of the new synchronous non-terminal X. Accordingly, h_s and h_t are the fan-outs of X on the source and the target side respectively. $\boldsymbol{\alpha}'$ (respectively $\boldsymbol{\beta}'$) is created from $\boldsymbol{\alpha}$ (respectively $\boldsymbol{\beta}$) by replacing the terminals that correspond to ranges in $\boldsymbol{\rho}_{s'}$ (respectively $\boldsymbol{\rho}_{t'}$) with the variable Y_i (respectively Z_j) that as been associated to the range. Note that this extraction yields only monotone and ε-free (S)LCFRS, which simplifies parsing.

The discontinuous rule extraction procedure is exemplified in Figure 4. Rule #5 for example was created from rule #3 by substituting phrase pair #2. Note that phrase pairs #1 and #4 are also extracted by a phrase-based system, and rules #1, #4 and #6 are also generated by a hierarchical phrase-based, i.e. SCFG-based, system. Rule #6 would usually be written down as

$$X \rightarrow \langle \text{ne veux plus } X_{\boxed{1}}, \text{do not want to } X_{\boxed{1}} \text{ anymore}\rangle$$

However, just as Galley and Manning (2010), we extract many more rules that also capture discontinuous translation units. In addition, we also extract rules which are discontinuous and hierarchical at the same time. They capture relationships between possibly discontinuous translation units.

Enumerating all discontinuous phrase pairs is exponential in the maximum phrase length. Therefore, in addition to the constraints that are generally set for SCFG extraction (e.g. phrase length, number of non-terminals, adjacent non-terminals on the source side, unaligned words at phrase edges, see Chiang (2007)), we also restrict the number of words that can be in a gap, we disallow unaligned blocks, and we restrict the number of continuous blocks in a phrase to 2. The latter is motivated by the results presented in Kaeshammer (2013) where a fan-out of $4_{2|2}$ is enough to derive the alignments in all data sets. We furthermore analyse the alignments of the training data before running the extraction and only allow discontinuous phrase pairs in synchronous spans which contain any of the alignment configurations that are beyond the power of SCFG.

As derivations are not observable in the training data, we use the method described in Chiang (2007) to hypothesize a distribution based on the counts of the extracted rules and then use relative-frequency estimation to obtain $P(r_s|r_t)$ and $P(r_t|r_s)$.

4 Decoder

Our decoder closely follows the methodology of current SCFG decoders, with the difference that it is able to handle source and target discontinuities in the form of SLCFRS rules. The goal is to find the target sequence e of the highest scoring derivation D according to the model defined in Section 2.2 that yields $\langle f, e\rangle$, where f is the given input sentence.

We parse the input sentence with a bottom-up CYK parser using the source side of the SLCFRS translation grammar. This corresponds to monolingual probabilistic LCFRS parsing, which has been described for example in Kallmeyer and Maier (2013). Using the rules, parse items are built. They are of the form $[A, \boldsymbol{\rho}]$, where A is a non-terminal label and $\boldsymbol{\rho}$ is a range vector indicating which part of the input is covered by this item. For the label, we use a combination of the source side label and the target side label in order to ensure valid target side derivations. Smaller items, i.e. items that cover less input words, are created before larger items. Equal items are combined, thereby retaining their origin via hyperedges.

When creating a new item using a specific rule, the variables and arguments in the rule have to be replaced consistently with ranges $\langle l, r \rangle$ of the input sentence. Roughly, this means that terminals and variables are instantiated with ranges such that for ranges that are adjacent in an argument of the LHS non-terminal, the concatenation of the two ranges has to be defined, i.e. $r_1 = l_2$ for $\langle l_1, r_1 \rangle$ and $\langle l_2, r_2 \rangle$. For example, given the input ${}_0il_1ne_2mange_3plus_4$, $X(\langle 1, 4 \rangle) \rightarrow X(\langle 2, 3 \rangle)$ is an instantiation of the source side of rule #5 from Figure 4. We can make further assumptions about rule instantiations, as our rules are all monotone, ε-free and we do not allow for empty gaps to avoid spurious ambiguity.

In the implementation, we first replace all terminals with all possible ranges with respect to the input sentence in an initialisation step; for instance $X(\langle 1, 2 \rangle\, Y_1\, \langle 3, 4 \rangle) \rightarrow X(Y_1)$ for the previous example. During the actual parsing, we are then only concerned with how variables are instantiated. We implement different pruning methods, such as limiting the number of target side rules for the same source side rule, and limiting the number of incoming hyperedges for one parse item.

Because of the specific form of the grammar that we have extracted (rank 2, fan-out $4_{2|2}$), we implement a specific parser for $(2, 2)$-LCFRS. Accordingly, the range vector $\boldsymbol{\rho}$ of an item has the form $\langle \langle i_1, j_1 \rangle, \langle i_2, j_2 \rangle \rangle$, where i_2 and j_2 are undefined if the yield of the item is continuous. Such range vectors can be stored and retrieved more efficiently than general range vectors, i.e. for full LCFRS (which are typically implemented as bit vectors of the size of the input sentence). Also parsing time complexity is directly dependent on the fan-out v_s of the monolingual grammar: $\mathcal{O}(|G_s| \cdot |f|^{v_s \cdot (u+1)})$ with rank $u = 2$ and fan-out $v_s = 2$ in our case.

Finally, the parse hypergraph that we obtain from parsing with the source side of the grammar is intersected with an n-gram language model to also integrate $P_{LM}(e)$. We use cube pruning for this step (Chiang, 2007; Huang and Chiang, 2007). The difference to SCFG-based implementations is that the target string of a hypothesis that is scored by the language model is not necessarily continuous, but consists of a tuple of continuous blocks of target words, e.g. $\langle$do not want, anymore$\rangle$ if we would like to score a hypothesis which has been built from rule #3 in Figure 4. Therefore, each continuous block is scored separately and contributes its score to the overall score of the hypothesis. Furthermore, we need to store one language model state (simply put remembering the first and last $n - 1$ words of the block) for each block. This means that a language model state in our implementation is a vector of conventional language model states of the length of the size of the target tuple of the hypothesis. Note that since our grammar has a target fan-out of 2, this vector has a maximal length of 2, but this is not a fixed limit in the implementation.

Since obtaining the k-best translations for a given input sentence is essential for tuning, we implement k-best extraction on the hypergraph that we obtain after cube pruning. We adopt the lazy strategy from Huang and Chiang (2005).

The decoder is implemented in C++, including code from KenLM[3] for language modelling.

5 Experiments

5.1 Setup

We run experiments for German-to-English, based on data that has been used in the WMT 2014 translation task[4]. For training of the translation models, we use the parallel sentences from Europarl and the News Commentary Corpus up to a length of 30 words (1.3M sentence pairs). For language modeling, we use the KenLM Language Model Toolkit[5]. We train a 3-gram language model on all available monolingual English data (Europarl, News Commentary, News Crawl, 92.7M sentences). From the available development data, we use `newstest2013` as the development test set (max. 25 words). From the rest, we randomly select 3000 sentence pairs of a maximal length of 25 words as development set. We further refine this set to sentences without out-of-vocabulary source words by decoding the development set once and selecting the corresponding sentences. We thus end up with 1694 sentence pairs for tuning. As our test set, we use the cleaned test set that has been made available (2280 sentence pairs with a maximal length of 30 words).

[3]`http://kheafield.com/code/kenlm/developers/`

[4]`http://www.statmt.org/wmt14/translation-task.html`

[5]`http://kheafield.com/code/kenlm/`

We normalize the punctuation, tokenize and truecase all our data using the scripts that are available in Moses[6] (Koehn et al., 2007). Furthermore, we perform compound splitting for German, also with the script provided in Moses.

The training data is word-aligned by running multi-threaded GIZA++ in both directions and then symmetrizing the alignments using the `grow-diag-final-and` heuristics as implemented in the Moses training script (step 1–4). Lexical translation probabilities are also emitted as part of this pipeline. For grammar extraction, we limit the length of initial phrases and the number of words in a gap to 10. We neither allow unaligned words at edges of initial phrases nor unaligned blocks.

Before decoding a data set with our decoder, we filter the large translation grammar with respect to the input data by extracting per-sentence-grammars. These only contain rules whose terminals match the words in the sentence to translate.

For the reported results, we set the buffer size for cube pruning to 400. We do not limit the number of words a non-terminal can span. We neither restrict the number of incoming hyperedges for the parse items nor the number of target side rules for the same source side rule.

Tuning the feature weights is done with minimum error rate training (Och, 2003), maximizing BLEU-4 (Papineni et al., 2002) and using the 200 best translations. For our own decoder, we use the very flexible implementation Z-MERT v1.50 (Zaidan, 2009). For Moses, we use the provided tuning script `mert-moses.pl`.

All reported BLEU scores have been calculated with the Moses script `multi-bleu.perl`, using the lowercase option `-lc`. Because of the variance that is introduced by tuning, we repeated each experiment four times and report the average of the final BLEU scores as well as the standard deviation.

5.2 Results

We compare different versions of our system against each other. The baseline is a system which uses only SCFG rules, i.e. a hierarchical phrase-based system. We refer to it as SYS(1,1), as it uses an SLCFRS of fan-out $2_{1|1}$. SYS(1,2) is a system which uses a grammar of fan-out $3_{1|2}$, i.e. it builds only continuous constituents on the source side, but allows for discontinuous constituents with two blocks on the target side. SYS(2,1) is the analogous system which restricts the target side to continuous constituents. Finally, SYS(2,2) uses an SLCFRS of fan-out $4_{2|2}$.

		devtest		test	
system	feat	BLEU	std	BLEU	std
SYS(1,1)	-	24.13	0.10	23.23	0.11
SYS(1,2)	-	23.39	0.32	23.24	0.09
SYS(2,1)	-	24.17	0.09	**23.41**	0.06
SYS(2,2)	-	23.90	0.13	22.90	0.03
SYS(2,2)	S	24.06	0.23	23.17	0.19
SYS(2,2)	T	**24.20**	0.15	23.35	0.04
SYS(2,2)	S+T	24.18	0.20	23.32	0.13
MOSES		24.33	0.08	23.34	0.20

Table 1: Averaged BLEU scores over four tuning runs; the feat column indicates whether additional source/target gap degree features have been used

Table 1 displays the main results. Allowing gaps on the source and the target side (SYS(2,2)) leads to a decline in BLEU score compared to the baseline. We hypothesize that this is due to weak probability estimates because of data sparseness and the additional ambiguity that is caused by the new rules with discontinuities. However, when adding the features about the gap degree of the rules used in the derivation, the model has an additional way of influencing which kind of rules are used. Especially controlling for the target gap degree turns out to be important and leads to a small improvement in BLEU score. Note, however, that rules with target gaps are not totally dismissed when this feature is switched on. Usage of rules with a target gap goes down from on average 734.5 rules in SYS(2,2) to on average 76.5 rules in SYS(2,2)-T in the test set. They are used less often, but, it seems, in a more controlled and sensible way.

This tendency is further confirmed with the experiments in which the discontinuous rules are only used on one side. While restricting the source side derivations to continuous yields does not improve the BLEU score (it rather severely degrades it in the case of the devtest set), restricting the target side derivations leads to a small improvement in BLEU score, and even to the best system for the test set. This is in particular interesting with respect to translation times since restricting the target side to continuous yields means removing the additional complexity that target gaps mean for the

[6] `http://www.statmt.org/moses/`

	SYS(1,1)	SYS(2,1)	=
e1	43	49	3
e2	46	47	2

Table 2: Result of the manual system comparison

		e2		
		SYS(1,1)	SYS(2,1)	=
	SYS(1,1)	**29**	13	1
e1	SYS(2,1)	15	**33**	1
	=	2	1	0

Table 3: Confusion matrix of the decisions of the manual evaluation

language model integration (see Section 4).

We also report results for the hierarchical phrase-based system in Moses trained on the same data as our systems. We tried to use the same settings as for our comparable system SYS(1,1). However, given the number of parameters during training and decoding, the various interpretations thereof and numerous implementation details to consider, it is not too surprising that the Moses system actually produces different translations than ours. The reported numbers merely serve as a point of reference, indicating that the translations produced by our system are not totally far off.

5.3 Manual Evaluation

We furthermore performed a manual evaluation in form of a system comparison using our own installation of the Appraise tool (Federmann, 2012). We compare the baseline SYS(1,1) against SYS(2,1), the best-performing setup on the test set. For each of them, we randomly selected one of the four configurations that lead to the reported averaged BLEU score. We then selected those translations of the test set where SYS(2,1) uses at least one SLCFRS rule with a discontinuity (95 sentences).

We asked two native speakers of English (e1, e2) with basic knowledge of German to evaluate our test sentences. They were shown the source sentence, a reference translation, the SYS(1,1) translation and the SYS(2,1) translation. The latter two were presented anonymized and in random order. The options for the evaluators were (a) translation A is better than B, (b) translation B is better than A, and (c) translations A and B are of equal quality. We specifically asked them to use option (c) as rarely as possible.

Table 2 shows the results. While our human evaluators do not demonstrate a clear preference for one of the systems, there is, however, a slight preference for the system that uses discontinuous rules (SYS(2,1)). In spite of the inter-annotator agreement being not very high (Cohen's $\kappa = 0.338$), the tendency for SYS(2,1) is also perceivable for the translations for which the evaluators agree in their decisions, see Table 3.

5.4 Translation Example

We finish this section with an actual translation example. It is picked because it makes crucial use of the discontinuous SLCFRS rules. It is taken from the test set.

In Figure 5, the following rule, which has a fan-out of 2 on the source side, leads to an overall grammatical sentence structure and a meaningful translation:

$$\langle\, X(\text{wäre}\ ,\, Y_1\ \text{gewesen}\ Y_2) \rightarrow X_{\boxed{1}}(Y_1)X_{\boxed{2}}(Y_2)\,,$$
$$X(\text{would have been}\ Y_1 Y_2) \rightarrow X_{\boxed{1}}(Y_1)X_{\boxed{2}}(Y_2)\,\rangle$$

The rule derives the synchronous constituent labelled $X_{\boxed{4}}$ in Figure 5. Besides providing a correct verbal translation in a specific tense, it also establishes a relationship to the adjective ($X_{\boxed{1}}$) and the infinitive subordinate clause ($X_{\boxed{2}}$), thereby still leaving room for the adverb in terms of the gap on the source side. The adverb is then introduced with the following rule, leading to the constituent labelled $X_{\boxed{5}}$ in Figure 5:

$$\langle\, X(Y_1\ \text{damit auch}\ Y_2) \rightarrow X_{\boxed{1}}(Y_1, Y_2)\,,$$
$$X(\text{also}\ Y_1) \rightarrow X_{\boxed{1}}(Y_1)\,\rangle$$

This rule can be seen as capturing the different placement of the adverb *auch/also* in German and English.

Note that the alignment that is induced by the SYS(2,1) derivation is also derivable with a $2_{1|1}$-SLCFRS. One general possibility is to allow rules of rank $u > 2$. Another possibility is to put the individual phrases together in a different order and hierarchy. For example, in an SCFG rule, the discontinuous verb phrase could be combined with the adjective and the adverb first, which leads to a continuous constituent. Then the subordinate clause would be added in a later derivation step. However, in the derivation for the best translation of SYS(1,1), this does not happen because a corresponding specific rule has not been learned. The translation produced by SYS(1,1) is not grammatical and misses important concepts, such as *geeignet* (*suitable*).

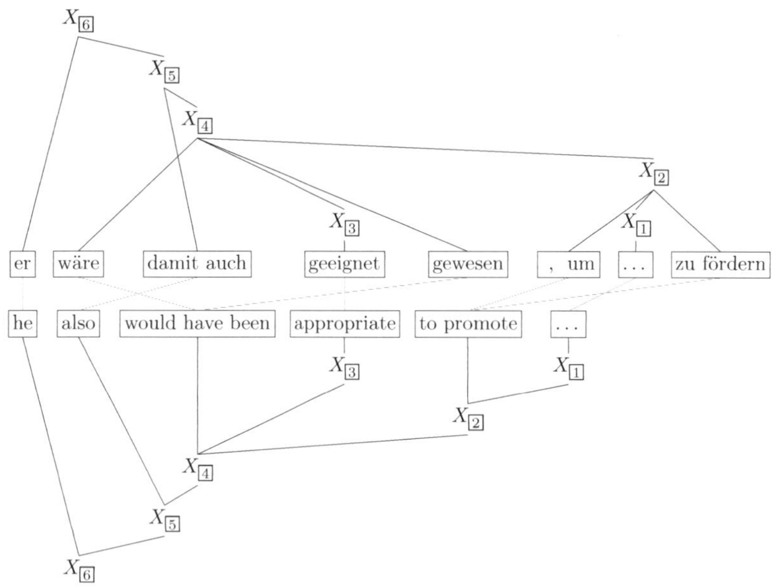

Source: er wäre damit auch geeignet gewesen , um die ... zu fördern

Reference: it would thus be suitable to assist ...

SYS(1,1): it would also have to be , in order to promote the ...

SYS(2,1): he also would have been appropriate to promote the ...

Figure 5: Test sentence with translations provided by the SCFG and the SLCFRS system, including the derivation of the SLCFRS system SYS(2,1).

6 Related Work

Several other translation models have been proposed which are expressive enough to generate the complex alignment configurations in Figure 1. Most notably, Galley and Manning (2010) propose a phrase-based translation system which allows for discontinuous phrase pairs, building upon the idea of a translation model proposed by Simard et al. (2005). They evaluate their system on a Chinese-to-English translation task and achieve some improvement in BLEU score over a phrase-based and a hierarchical phrase-based system. Unfortunately, we could not evaluate directly against their approach since the current documentation[7] of their system, Phrasal (Green et al., 2014), does not mention the discontinuous phrases anymore. We also could not obtain the data sets they used for their experiments.

In some sense, our work is the hierarchical, tree-based counterpart to the phrase-based approach of Galley and Manning (2010). This means that our translation grammar rules unify two types of "gaps" of previous approaches: (a) gaps in the sense of non-terminals that are inserted into longer phrases when hierarchical rules are created, as in Chiang (2007); their purpose is a better generalization of the translation rules, and (b) gaps in the sense of discontinuities in the yield of a translation rule, on the source side, on the target side or both, driven by the idea of allowing for more flexible phrases such that generated alignment structures are not restricted.

Besides the suggestion of Kaeshammer (2013) to use SLCFRS as the translation grammar formalism, which we have detailed and implemented in this work, Søgaard (2008) proposes to apply range concatenation grammar, an even more expressive formalism than LCFRS, and to use its ability to copy substrings during the derivation. This approach has downsides, such as no tight probabilities estimators, which are mentioned in Søgaard and Kuhn (2009).

An early advocate of translation modeling beyond context-free grammar formalisms is Melamed, who proposes to use Generalized Multitext Grammars, which are weakly equivalent to LCFRS (Melamed, 2004; Melamed et al., 2004). The incentive for this lies in linguistically motivated translation grammars and the general observation that discontinuous constituents are necessary for monolingual modelling of syntax.

7 Conclusions and Future Work

With this work, we extend the hierarchical phrase-based machine translation approach to discontinuous phrases, using SLCFRS as the translation grammar formalism. Since SLCFRS is a direct

[7] `http://www-nlp.stanford.edu/wiki/Software/Phrasal`, accessed on June 27, 2015

extension to SCFG, previous work on hierarchical phrase-based translation, in particular the model definition, training and decoding, can be extended to SLCFRS in a more or less direct manner. Evaluating our new system on a German-to-English translation task revealed a modest improvement in BLEU score over the SCFG baseline. Human evaluators showed a slight preference for translations produced by the SLCFRS system.

In the future, we will evaluate our approach on other language pairs, for example Chinese-English which has been used in related work. Furthermore, we would like to make use of recent advances in monolingual parsing of discontinuous constituents and use phrase-structure trees supporting discontinuous constituents for tree-based machine translation.

Acknowledgments

I would like to thank Laura Kallmeyer and Wolfgang Maier for discussions and comments and the reviewers for their suggestions. This research was funded by the German Research Foundation as part of the project *Grammar Formalisms beyond Context-Free Grammars and their use for Machine Learning Tasks*. Computational support and infrastructure was provided by the *Centre for Information and Media Technology* (ZIM) at the University of Düsseldorf (Germany).

References

Eberhard Bertsch and Mark-Jan Nederhof. 2001. On the complexity of some extensions of rcg parsing. In *IWPT*.

Pierre Boullier. 1998. Proposal for a Natural Language Processing syntactic backbone. Technical Report 3342, INRIA.

David Chiang. 2005. A hierarchical phrase-based model for statistical machine translation. In *Proceedings of the 43rd Annual Meeting on Association for Computational Linguistics*, pages 263–270.

David Chiang. 2007. Hierarchical phrase-based translation. *Computational Linguistics*, 33(2):201–228.

Christian Federmann. 2012. Appraise: An open-source toolkit for manual evaluation of machine translation output. *The Prague Bulletin of Mathematical Linguistics*, 98:25–35, September.

Daniel Fernández-González and André Martins. 2015. Parsing as reduction. *arXiv preprint arXiv:1503.00030*.

Michel Galley and Christopher D. Manning. 2010. Accurate non-hierarchical phrase-based translation. In *Human Language Technologies: The 2010 Annual Conference of the North American Chapter of the Association for Computational Linguistics*, pages 966–974.

Spence Green, Daniel Cer, and Christopher D. Manning. 2014. Phrasal: A toolkit for new directions in statistical machine translation. In *Proceedings of the Ninth Workshop on Statistical Machine Translation*, pages 114–121. Association for Computational Linguistics.

Hieu Hoang and Philipp Koehn. 2010. Improved translation with source syntax labels. In *Proceedings of the Joint Fifth Workshop on Statistical Machine Translation and MetricsMATR*, pages 409–417. Association for Computational Linguistics.

Liang Huang and David Chiang. 2005. Better k-best parsing. In *Proceedings of the Ninth International Workshop on Parsing Technology*, pages 53–64. Association for Computational Linguistics.

Liang Huang and David Chiang. 2007. Forest rescoring: Faster decoding with integrated language models. In *Annual Meeting-Association For Computational Linguistics*, volume 45, page 144.

Miriam Kaeshammer and Anika Westburg. 2014. On complex word alignment configurations. In *Proceedings of the Ninth International Conference on Language Resources and Evaluation (LREC'14)*, pages 1773–1780, Reykjavik, Iceland, May.

Miriam Kaeshammer. 2013. Synchronous linear context-free rewriting systems for machine translation. In *Proceedings of the Seventh Workshop on Syntax, Semantics and Structure in Statistical Translation*, pages 68–77. Association for Computational Linguistics.

Laura Kallmeyer and Wolfgang Maier. 2013. Data-driven parsing using Probabilistic Linear Context-Free Rewriting Systems. *Computational Linguistics*, 39(1).

Laura Kallmeyer. 2010. *Parsing beyond context-free grammars*. Springer Science & Business Media.

Philipp Koehn, Franz Josef Och, and Daniel Marcu. 2003. Statistical phrase-based translation. In *Proceedings of the 2003 Conference of the North American Chapter of the Association for Computational Linguistics on Human Language Technology*, pages 48–54. Association for Computational Linguistics.

Philipp Koehn, Hieu Hoang, Alexandra Birch, Chris Callison-Burch, Marcello Federico, Nicola Bertoldi, Brooke Cowan, Wade Shen, Christine Moran, Richard Zens, et al. 2007. Moses: Open source toolkit for statistical machine translation. In *Proceedings of the 45th annual meeting of the ACL on interactive poster and demonstration sessions*, pages 177–180. Association for Computational Linguistics.

Wolfgang Maier and Timm Lichte. 2011. Characterizing discontinuity in constituent treebanks. In *Formal Grammer 2009, Revised Selected Papers*, volume 5591 of *LNAI*. Springer.

Wolfgang Maier. 2010. Direct parsing of discontinuous constituents in German. In *Proceedings of the NAACL HLT 2010 First Workshop on Statistical Parsing of Morphologically-Rich Languages*.

Wolfgang Maier. 2015. Discontinuous incremental shift-reduce parsing. In *Proceedings of ACL-IJCNLP 2015*, Beijing, China.

I. Dan Melamed, Giorgio Satta, and Benjamin Wellington. 2004. Generalized multitext grammars. In *Proceedings of the 42nd Annual Conference of the Association for Computational Linguistics (ACL)*.

I. Dan Melamed. 2004. Statistical machine translation by parsing. In *Proceedings of the 42nd Annual Conference of the Association for Computational Linguistics (ACL)*.

Franz Josef Och and Hermann Ney. 2004. The alignment template approach to statistical machine translation. *Computational linguistics*, 30(4):417–449.

Franz Josef Och. 2003. Minimum error rate training in statistical machine translation. In *Proceedings of the 41st Annual Meeting on Association for Computational Linguistics-Volume 1*, pages 160–167. Association for Computational Linguistics.

Kishore Papineni, Salim Roukos, Todd Ward, and Wei-Jing Zhu. 2002. Bleu: a method for automatic evaluation of machine translation. In *Proceedings of the 40th annual meeting on association for computational linguistics*, pages 311–318. Association for Computational Linguistics.

Giorgio Satta and Enoch Peserico. 2005. Some computational complexity results for synchronous context-free grammars. In *Proceedings of Human Language Technology Conference and Conference on Empirical Methods in Natural Language Processing (HLT/EMNLP)*, pages 803–810.

Michel Simard, Nicola Cancedda, Bruno Cavestro, Marc Dymetman, Eric Gaussier, Cyril Goutte, Kenji Yamada, Philippe Langlais, and Arne Mauser. 2005. Translating with non-contiguous phrases. In *Proceedings of Human Language Technology Conference and Conference on Empirical Methods in Natural Language Processing (HLT/EMNLP)*, pages 755–762.

Anders Søgaard and Jonas Kuhn. 2009. Empirical lower bounds on alignment error rates in syntax-based machine translation. In *Proceedings of the Third Workshop on Syntax and Structure in Statistical Translation (SSST '09)*. Association for Computational Linguistics.

Anders Søgaard and Dekai Wu. 2009. Empirical lower bounds on translation unit error rate for the full class of inversion transduction grammars. In *Proceedings of the 11th International Conference on Parsing Technologies*, pages 33–36.

Anders Søgaard. 2008. Range concatenation grammars for translation. In *Proceedings of Coling 2008: Companion volume: Posters*.

Anders Søgaard. 2010. Can inversion transduction grammars generate hand alignments? In *Proceedings of the 14th Annual Conference of the European Association for Machine Translation (EAMT)*.

Andreas van Cranenburgh and Rens Bod. 2013. Discontinuous parsing with an efficient and accurate dop model. In *Proceedings of the International Conference on Parsing Technologies (IWPT 2013)*.

Yannick Versley. 2014. Experiments with easy-first nonprojective constituent parsing. In *Proceedings of the First Joint Workshop on Statistical Parsing of Morphologically Rich Languages and Syntactic Analysis of Non-Canonical Languages*, pages 39–53.

K. Vijay-Shanker, David Weir, and Aravind K. Joshi. 1987. Characterizing structural descriptions used by various formalisms. In *Proceedings of the 25th Annual Meeting of the Association for Computational Linguistics*.

David Weir. 1988. *Characterizing Mildly Context-Sensitive Grammar Formalisms*. Ph.D. thesis, University of Pennsylviania, Philadelphia, PA.

Benjamin Wellington, Sonjia Waxmonsky, and I. Dan Melamed. 2006. Empirical lower bounds on the complexity of translational equivalence. In *Proceedings of the 21st International Conference on Computational Linguistics and 44th Annual Meeting of the Association for Computational Linguistics*, pages 977–984.

Dekai Wu. 1997. Stochastic inversion transduction grammars and bilingual parsing of parallel corpora. *Computational linguistics*, 23(3):377–403.

Omar Zaidan. 2009. Z-mert: A fully configurable open source tool for minimum error rate training of machine translation systems. *The Prague Bulletin of Mathematical Linguistics*, 91:79–88.

Andreas Zollmann and Ashish Venugopal. 2006. Syntax augmented machine translation via chart parsing. In *Proceedings of the Workshop on Statistical Machine Translation, HLT/NAACL*.

Discontinuous Statistical Machine Translation with Target-Side Dependency Syntax

Nina Seemann and **Andreas Maletti**
Institute for Natural Language Processing, Universität Stuttgart
Pfaffenwaldring 5b, 70569 Stuttgart, Germany
{seemanna,maletti}@ims.uni-stuttgart.de

Abstract

For several languages only potentially non-projective dependency parses are readily available. Projectivizing the parses and utilizing them in syntax-based translation systems often yields particularly bad translation results indicating that those translation models cannot properly utilize such information. We demonstrate that our system based on multi bottom-up tree transducers, which can natively handle discontinuities, can avoid the large translation quality deterioration, achieve the best performance of all classical syntax-based translation systems, and close the gap to phrase-based and hierarchical systems that do not utilize syntax.

1 Introduction

Syntax-based machine translation, in which the transfer is achieved from and/or to the level of syntax, has become widely used in the statistical machine translation community (Bojar et al., 2014). Different grammar formalisms have been proposed and evaluated as translation models driving the translation systems. We use a variant of the local multi bottom-up tree transducer as proposed by Maletti (2011). More precisely, we use a *string-to-tree* variant of it, which offers two immediate advantages: (i) The source side of the rules is a simple string containing terminal symbols and the unique non-terminal X. Consequently, we do not need to match an input sentence parse, which allows additional flexibility. It has been demonstrated that this flexibility in the input often yields improved translation quality (Chiang, 2010). (ii) The target language side offers discontinuities because rules can contain a sequence of target tree fragments instead of a single tree fragment. These fragments are applied synchronously, which allows the model to synchronously develop discontinuous parts in the output (e.g., to realize agreement). Overall, this translation model already proved to be useful when translating from English into German, Chinese, and Arabic as demonstrated by Seemann et al. (2015). The goal of the current contribution is to adjust the approach and the system to Eastern European languages, for which we expect discontinuities to occur. The existing system (Seemann et al., 2015) cannot readily be applied since it requires constituent-like parses for the target side in our string-to-tree setting. However, for the target languages discussed here (Polish and Russian), only dependency parses are readily available. Those parses relate the lexical items of the sentence via edges that are labeled with the syntactic function between the head and its dependent. Overall, these structures also form trees, but they are often non-projective for our target languages. Such non-projective dependency trees do not admit a constituent-like tree representation, so we first need to convert them into projective dependency trees, which can be converted easily into a constituent-like tree representation. The conversion into projective dependency trees is known to preserve discontinuities, so we expect that out model is an ideally suited syntax-based translation model for those target languages.

We evaluate our approach in 2 standard translation tasks translating from English to both Polish and Russian. Those two target languages have rather free word order, so we expect discontinuities to occur frequently. For both languages, we use a (non-projective) dependency parser to obtain the required target trees, which we projectivize. Indeed, we confirm that non-projective parses are a frequent phenomenon in both languages. We then train our translation model on the constituent-like parse trees obtained from the projective dependency trees and evaluate the obtained machine translation systems. In both cases, our system significantly outperforms the string-to-tree syntax-based component (Hoang et al., 2009) of MOSES. To put our evaluation scores into perspective, we also report scores for a vanilla phrase-based system (Och and Ney, 2004), a GHKM-based system (Galley et al., 2004), and a hierarchical phrase-based system (Chiang, 2007). It shows that our system suffers much less from the syntactic discontinuities and is thus much better suited for syntax-based translation systems in such settings.

2 Related work

Modern statistical machine translation systems (Koehn, 2009) are build using various different translation models as their core. Syntax-based systems are widely used nowadays due to their innate ability to handle non-local reordering and other linguistic phenomena. For certain language pairs they even outperform phrase-based models (Och and Ney, 2004) and constitute the state-of-the-art (Bojar et al., 2014). Our MBOT is a variant of the shallow local multi bottom-up tree transducer presented by Braune et al. (2013). Alternative models include the synchronous tree substitution grammars of Eisner (2003), which use a single source and target tree fragment per rule. Our MBOT rules similarly contain a single source tree fragment, but a sequence of target tree fragments. The latter feature enables discontinuous translations. Another model that offers this feature for the source and the target language side is the non-contiguous synchronous tree-sequence substitution grammar of Sun et al. (2009), which offers sequences of tree fragments on both sides.

The idea of utilizing dependency trees in machine translation is not novel. Bojar and Hajič (2008) built a system based on synchronous tree substitution grammars for English-to-Czech that uses projective dependency trees. Xie et al. (2011) present a dependency-to-string model that extracts head-dependent rules with reordering information. Their model requires a custom decoder to deal with the dependency information in the input. Li et al. (2014) follow up on this work by transforming these dependency trees into (a kind of) constituency trees. In this approach, they are able to use the conventional syntax-based models of MOSES. In contrast to our work, these two models do not use the syntactic functions provided by the parser but rather extract head-dependent rules based on the lexical items. Sennrich et al. (2015) transformed (non-projective) dependency trees into constituency trees using the syntactic functions provided by the parser. They used the string-to-tree GHKM model (Williams and Koehn, 2012) of MOSES and evaluated their approach on an English-to-German translation task. It shows that the system utilizing the (transformed) dependency parses outperforms competing systems utilizing various variants of constituent parses for the German side. We follow up on their work for translation tasks, where constituent parses are not readily available, and achieve translation quality that is comparable to phrase-based systems for two language pairs (English-to-Polish and English-to-Russian).

3 Transformation of Dependency Trees into Constituency Trees

In this section, we present a short overview of dependency parsing and introduce the non-projective tree structures that occur as parses. We need to transform these structures into projective trees, which are then converted into the shape of classical constituency trees.

3.1 Description

The syntax of languages with relatively free word order, which includes Polish and Russian, is often difficult to express in terms of constituency structure (Kallestinova, 2007). Since the parts that need to (grammatically) agree can occur spread out over the whole sentence, constituents cannot be hierarchically organized as in a classical constituency parse tree. Dependency parses do not pre-suppose such a hierarchical structure and are thus often more suitable for languages with free word order.

In a dependency parse each occurrence of a lexical item (i.e., token) in the input sentence forms a node. The dependency parser constructs a tree structure over those nodes by relating them via edges pointing from a *head* node h to its *dependent* node d. Such an edge is denoted by $h \rightarrow d$. In addition, each edge is assigned a label indicating the type of the syntactic dependence. Often an artificial root node is added for convenience. An example parse for a Polish sentence is depicted in Figure 1.

Next, we distinguish between projective and

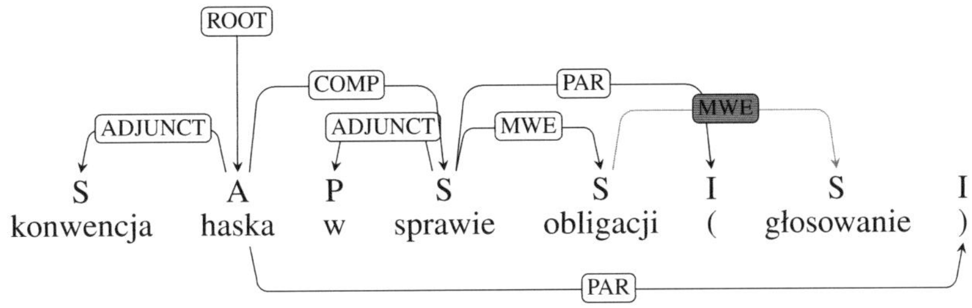

Figure 1: Non-projective Polish dependency tree [gloss: *hague convention on securities (vote)*].

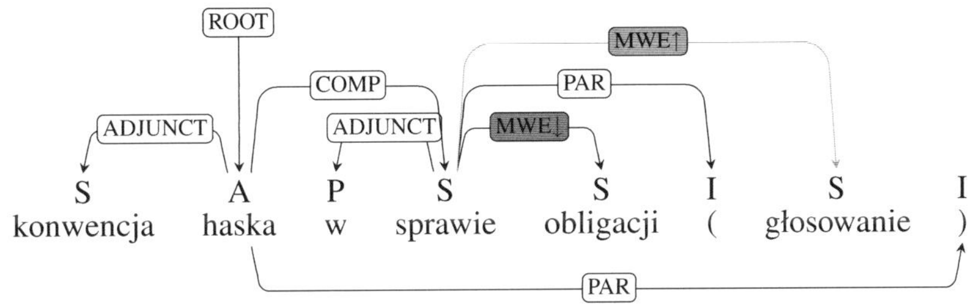

Figure 2: Projective dependency parse obtained by 'path'-lifting.

non-projective edges. The edge $h \rightarrow d$ is *projective* if and only if its head node h dominates[1] all nodes representing the tokens in the linear span between h and d. For example, the edge 'obligacji $\rightarrow$ głosowanie' is non-projective because 'obligacji' does not dominate '(', which occurs in the relevant linear span. A dependency parse is projective if and only if all its edges are projective. A non-projective dependency parse is easily recognized in graphical representations because it has a crossing edge provided that all the edges are drawn on one side of the sentence as in Figure 1.

Non-projective dependency structures cannot be directly used in the translation framework MOSES (Koehn et al., 2007), so we first have to turn them into projective trees. To this end, Kahane et al. (1998) came up with the idea of *lifting*. Given a non-projective edge $h \rightarrow d$ there exists (at least) one node n that occurs in the linear span between h and d such that n is not dominated by h. In the lifting process, the edge $h \rightarrow d$ is replaced by an edge $g \rightarrow d$, where g is the lowest node that dominates both h and n (i.e., the least common ancestor of h and n). Repeating this process for all non-projective edges eventually yields a projective tree. Nivre and Nilsson (2005) refined this approach and introduced three additional ways of lifting: 'head', 'head+path', and 'path', which perform the same replacement but annotate different information in the labels to document the lifting process. The annotation schemes 'head' and 'head+path' might increase the number of labels quadratically, whereas 'path' only introduces a linear number of new labels. Since we deal with millions of trees in our syntax-based machine translation experiments, we need to select a compromise between (i) inflating the number of labels and (ii) documenting the lifts. We decided to use the 'path' scheme to obtain projective parse trees for our experiments (see Section 5).

Let us explain the 'path' scheme. In the situation described earlier, in which the edge $h \rightarrow d$ was replaced by the edge $g \rightarrow d$, we set the label of $g \rightarrow d$ to the label of the original edge $h \rightarrow d$ annotated by ↑ to indicate that this edge was lifted. Additionally, all edges connecting the new head g and the syntactical head h are annotated with ↓ indicating where the syntactic head is found. Figure 2 shows the projective tree obtained from the non-projective parse of Figure 1. In it we have the new edge 'sprawie $\rightarrow$ głosowanie' with label 'MWE↑'. Moreover, the edge 'sprawie $\rightarrow$ obligacji' now has the label MWE↓ because it is the edge that connects the new head with the syntactical head of 'głosowanie'.

In principle, one can imagine other ways to projectivize a tree; e.g., we can just replace the head

[1] A node n *dominates* a node d iff n is an ancestor of d; i.e., there is a path from n to d.

of a non-projective edge by the root. From a linguistic point of view, it makes more sense to attach it (as described) to the least common ancestor, which in a sense is the minimal required change that leaves the remaining edges in place. Furthermore, the used implementation always lifts the most nested[2] non-projective edge until the tree is projective. In this way, the minimal number of lifts required to projectivize the tree is achieved as demonstrated by Buch-Kromann (2005).

3.2 Implementation

We aim to investigate string-to-tree machine translation systems, so we need syntactic annotations on the target side. First, the target-side sentences (in Polish and Russian) are annotated with part-of-speech tags with the help of TREETAGGER (Schmid, 1994). The TREETAGGER output is then converted into the (comma-separated) CONNL-X format[3], which lists each token of the sentence in one line with 10 attributes like word position, word form, lemma, and part-of-speech tag. A new sentence is started by an empty line. This representation is passed to the MALT parser (Nivre et al., 2006; Sharoff and Nivre, 2011), which fills the remaining attribute fields like position of the head and the label of dependency edges. The resulting output represents the (potentially) non-projective dependency parses of the target-side sentences.

In the next step, we apply the 'path'-lifting as described in Section 3.1. In total, we performed 500,507 lifts for Polish (corpus size: 14,147,378 tokens) and 137,893 lifts for Russian (corpus size: 30,808,946 tokens) to make the corresponding parses projective. As described in Section 3.1 we introduce at most 3 additional labels for each existing label. In Table 1 we report for each corpus the exact number of original parse labels and the number of labels newly introduced by the transformation into projective parses.

Finally, we transform the projective dependency parse trees directly into the standard representation of constituent parse trees in MOSES.[4] We use the part-of-speech tags as pre-terminal nodes. Additionally, we make the labels and part-of-speech tags more uniform as follows:

[2]deepest or most distant from the root

[3]documented on http://ilk.uvt.nl/conll/

[4]http://www.ims.uni-stuttgart.de/forschung/ressourcen/werkzeuge/mbotmoses.html

Corpus	Lang.	Number of labels original	new
EUROPARL	PL	25	67
YANDEX	RU	75	118
Commoncrawl	RU	71	84
News commentary	RU	71	84
Patronymic names	RU	13	0
Names	RU	31	0
WIKI headlines	RU	54	19

Table 1: Number of parse labels before and after the 'path'-lifting.

- All parentheses are labeled 'PAR'.
- All slashes, quotation marks, and dashes are labeled 'PUNCT' and their part-of-speech tag is 'INTJ'.
- All punctuation marks are labeled 'PUNC' and their part-of-speech tag is ','.
- If the tagger did not assign a part-of-speech tag, then we label it 'UNK'.

The final constituency tree representation obtained from the projective dependency tree of Figure 2 is shown in Figure 3.

4 Translation Model

We use the string-to-tree variant (Seemann et al., 2015) of the multi bottom-up tree transducer (Maletti, 2010) as translation model. For simplicity, we call the variant 'MBOT'. A more detailed discussion of the model can be found in (Seemann et al., 2015; Maletti, 2011). Let us attempt a high-level description. An MBOT is a synchronous grammar (Chiang, 2006) that is similar to a synchronous context-free grammar. Instead of a single source and target fragment in each rule, MBOT rules are of the form $s \longrightarrow (t_1, \ldots, t_n)$ containing a single *source string* s and potentially several *target tree fragments* $t_1, \ldots, t_n$. The source string is built from the lexical items and the special placeholder X, which can also occur several times. Each occurrence of X is linked to some non-lexical leaves in the target tree fragments. In contrast to most synchronous grammars, each placeholder occurrence can link to several leaves in the target tree fragments indicating that these parts are supposed to develop synchronously. However, each non-lexical leaf in the target tree fragments links to exactly one placeholder occurrence (see top rule in Figure 4). A finite set of such rules constitutes an MBOT. Several rules of an MBOT for trans-

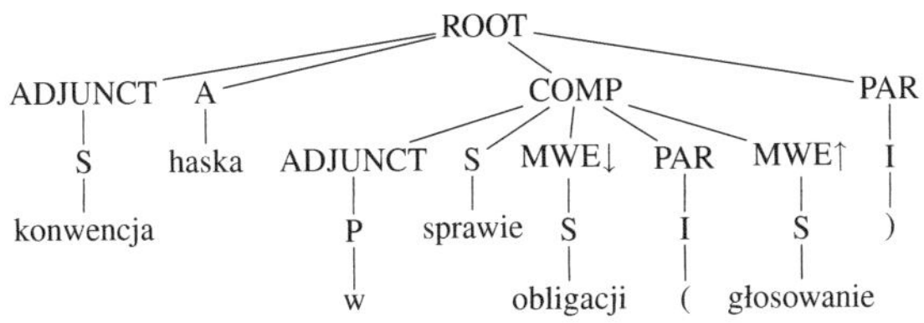

Figure 3: Final constituency representation for the parse of Figure 2.

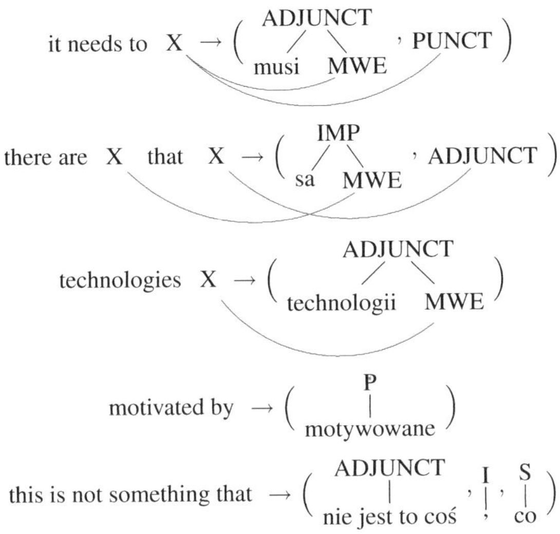

Figure 4: Several rules of an MBOT.

lating from English (source) to Polish (target) are shown in Figure 4. The bottom rule is both lexical and discontinuous. Note that it can be used in a continuous manner, but it is as well possible to plug additional material between the three target tree fragments.

The rules were extracted with the method described and the implementation provided by Seemann et al. (2015). The standard log-linear model (Koehn, 2009) is used with the following features:

(1) forward translation weight
(2) indirect translation weight
(3) forward lexical translation weight
(4) indirect lexical translation weight
(5) target-side language model
(6) word penalty
(7) rule penalty
(8) gap penalty 100^{1-c}, where c is the number of target tree fragments used in the derivation of the output tree.

All those features are standard except for the gap penalty, which is intended to discourage derivations that involve large numbers of target tree fragments, thus providing a feature to favor or disfavor continuous derivations. As usual, the (forward and indirect) translation weights are obtained as products of corresponding rule weights, which are obtained by maximum likelihood estimation. All rules that were extracted at most 10 times are smoothed using GOOD-TURING smoothing (Good, 1953). Both lexical translation weights are obtained from the co-occurrence statistics obtained during word alignment. The standard decoder of MBOT-MOSES by Braune et al. (2013) is used to generate translations using our model. As in the standard syntax-based component (Hoang et al., 2009), this decoder is a CYK+ chart parser based on standard X-style parse trees with integrated language model scoring that is accelerated by cube pruning (Chiang, 2007).

5 Experimental Results

We evaluate the MBOT-based system (see Section 4) on two translation tasks: English-to-Polish and English-to-Russian. For both target languages only (potentially) non-projective dependency parses are easily available. Our goal is to evaluate whether the discontinuity offered by the MBOT model helps in tasks involving such dependency parses. Consequently, the baseline system is the syntax-based component (Hoang et al., 2009) of the MOSES toolkit (Koehn et al., 2007), which uses a translation model that only permits continuous rules. Both systems are *string-to-tree* in the sense that the projectivized parses are only used on the target side. As mentioned in Section 3, the non-projective parses are obtained using the MALT parser and then converted to constituent-like trees. Glue-rules in both systems ensure that partial translation candidates can always be concatenated without any reordering.

5.1 Setup

We use standard and freely available resources to build our machine translation systems. In summary, for Russian we use the resources provided by the 2014 Workshop on Statistical Machine Translation (Bojar et al., 2014). The Polish data is taken from the EUROPARL corpus (Koehn, 2005).

Next, let us describe the preparation and evaluation for both tasks (English-to-Polish and English-to-Russian). An overview of the used resources is presented in Table 2. First, the training data was

	English to Polish	English to Russian
training data size	≈ 618K sentence pairs	≈ 1.7M sentence pairs
target-side parser	Malt parser (Nivre et al., 2006; Sharoff and Nivre, 2011)	
parser grammar	(Wróblewska and Przepiórkowski, 2012)	(Nivre et al., 2008)
language model (LM)	5-gram SRILM (Stolcke, 2002)	
additional LM data	Polish sentences in EuroParl	WMT 2014
LM data size	≈ 626K sentences	≈ 43M sentences
development test size	3,030 sentences	3,000 sentences
test size	3,029 sentences	3,003 sentences

Table 2: Summary of the experimental setup.

length-ratio filtered, tokenized, and lowercased. We used GIZA++ (Och, 2003) with the 'grow-diag-final-and' heuristic (Koehn et al., 2005) to automatically derive the word alignments. The feature weights of the log-linear models were trained with the help of minimum error rate training (Och and Ney, 2003) and optimized for 4-gram BLEU (Papineni et al., 2002) on the development test set (lowercased, tokenized). In the end, the systems were evaluated (also using 4-gram BLEU) on the test set. Significance judgments of the differences in the reported translation quality (as measured by BLEU) were computed with the pairwise bootstrap resampling technique of Koehn (2004) on 1,000 samples. Table 2 summarizes the setup information.

A particular detail is worth mentioning. The authors were unable to identify standard development and test sets for the English-to-Polish translation task. Consequently, we manually removed one session of the EUROPARL corpus. After removing duplicate sentences, we used the odd numbered sentences as development set and the even numbered sentences as test set.

5.2 Analysis

We present the quantitative evaluation for both experiments in Table 3. In both cases (English-to-Polish and English-to-Russian) the MBOT system significantly outperforms the baseline, which is the syntax-based component of MOSES. For Polish we obtain a BLEU score of 23.43 resulting in a gain of 2.14 points over the baseline. Similarly, for Russian we achieve a BLEU score of 26.13, which is an increase of 1.47 points over the baseline. To put our results in perspective, we also trained a GHKM system, a phrase-based system, and a hierarchical phrase-based system (Hiero) with standard settings for each translation task on the same resources as described in Table 2 and present their evaluation also in Table 3.

Translation task	System	BLEU
English-to-Polish	Baseline	21.29
	MBOT	**23.43**
	GHKM	23.31
	Phrase-based	24.35
	Hiero	24.56
English-to-Russian	Baseline	24.66
	MBOT	**26.13**
	GHKM	25.97
	Phrase-based	27.90
	Hiero	27.72

Table 3: Evaluation results incl. MOSES phrase-based system, GHKM-based system, and hierarchical system for reference. The bold MBOT results are statistically significant improvements over the baseline (at confidence $p < 1\%$).

Based on the observed BLEU scores, it seems likely that our MBOT-based approach can almost completely avoid the large quality drop observed between a (hierarchical) phrase-based system, which does not utilize the syntactic annotation, and a continuous string-to-tree syntax-based model. The availability of discontinuous tree fragments yields significant improvements in translation quality (as measured by BLEU) and an overall performance similar to (hierarchical) phrase-based systems. However, we also observe that outscoring a (hierarchical) phrase-based remains a challenge, so it remains to be seen whether syntactic information can actually help the translation quality in those translation tasks.

To quantitatively support our claim that the multiple target tree fragments (and the discontinuity) of an MBOT are useful, we provide statistics on the MBOT rules that were used to decode the test set. To this end, we distinguish several types of rules. A rule is *continuous* if it has only 1 target tree fragment, and all other rules are (potentially) *discontinuous*. Additionally, we distinguish *lexical* rules, which only contain lexical items as leaves, and *structural* rules, which contain at least one non-lexical leaf. In Table 4 we report how many rules of each type are used during decoding.[5]

For Polish, 41% of all used rules were discontinuous and only 4% were structural. Similarly, 35% of the used Russian rules were discontinuous and again only 4% were structural. The low proportion of structural rules is not very surprising since both languages are known to be morphologically rich and thus have large lexicons (167,657 lexical items in Polish and 911,397 lexical items in Russian). Another interesting point is the distribution of *discontinuous structural rules*. Polish and Russian use 83% and 62%, respectively, showing that the majority of the used structural rules is discontinuous in both tasks. Additionally using the data of Seemann et al. (2015), we can confirm that morphologically rich languages have a small minority of structural rules (4%, 4%, and 5% for Polish, Russian, and German, respectively), whereas Arabic and Chinese use a much larger proportion of structural rules (26% and 18%, respectively). In addition, we suspect that the additional non-projectivity of Polish makes discontinuous rules more useful (as an indicator for induced discontinuity). Whereas for Russian, German, Arabic and Chinese approx. 2 out of 3 used structural rules are discontinuous (62%, 64%, 67%, and 68%, respectively), more than 4 out of 5 (83%) used structural rules are discontinuous for Polish.

Finally, we present a fine-grained analysis based on the number of target tree fragments in Table 4. Useful Polish rules have at most 6 target tree fragments, whereas Russian rules with up to 9 target tree fragments have been used. Similar numbers have been reported in (Seemann et al., 2015). Using their data, we also note that Polish, Russian, and Chinese seem to use a larger percentage of discontinuous rules with 2 output tree fragments (80%–90%) compared to German and Arabic (50%–60%).

6 Conclusion

We presented an application of string-to-tree local multi bottom-up tree transducers as translation model of a syntax-based machine translation system. The obtained system uses rules with a string on the source language side and a sequence of target tree fragments on the target language side. The availability of several target tree fragments in a single rule enables the model to realize discontinuous translations. We expected that particularly translation into languages with discontinuous constituents would benefit from our model. However, such languages often have rather free word order and often only dependency parsers are available for them. The mentioned discontinuities often produce non-projective parses, which we need to transform into projective constituent-like parse trees before they can be utilized in MOSES. Hence, we (i) applied a lifting technique to projectivize the dependency trees, which stores information about the performed lift operations in the new labels, and (ii) transformed the obtained projective dependency trees into constituent-like trees.

Next, we demonstrated that the discontinuous string-to-tree system significantly outperforms the standard MOSES string-to-tree system on two different translation tasks (English-to-Polish and English-to-Russian) with large gains of 2.14 and 1.47 BLEU points, respectively. We also trained a vanilla phrase-based system, a GHKM-based system, and a hierarchical system for each translation task. In comparison to the string-to-string phrase-based system, the discontinuous string-to-tree system is only 0.92 BLEU points worse on English-to-Polish and 1.77 BLEU points worse for English-to-Russian. It thus remains to be seen whether machine translation systems can benefit from syntactic information in those translation tasks, but the proposed model at least avoids the large quality drop observed for the continuous string-to-tree system.

Finally, we analyzed the rules used by our system to decode the test sets. In summary, it shows that both our target languages (Polish and Russian) require a lot of lexical rules, which is most

[5] The provided analysis tools currently do not support an analysis whether a discontinuous rule was actually used in a discontinuous manner or whether the components were later combined in a continuous manner. The reported numbers thus represent potential discontinuity.

Translation task	Type	Lex	Struct	Total	Target tree fragments 2	3	4	5	≥ 6
English-to-Polish	cont.	25,327	307	25,634					
	discont.	16,312	1,595	17,907	15,805	1,818	254	27	3
English-to-Russian	cont.	24,100	664	24764					
	discont.	12,767	1,108	13,875	11,087	2,308	412	58	10

Table 4: Number of rules per type used when decoding test (Lex = lexical rules; Struct = structural rules; [dis]cont. = [dis]contiguous).

likely due to the morphological richness of the languages. Furthermore, they use a lot of discontinuous structural rules, which confirms our assumption that a system allowing discontinuous target tree fragments is the right choice for such languages.

Acknowledgment

The authors would like to express their gratitude to the reviewers for their helpful comments. Furthermore, we would like to thank ANDERS BJÖRKELUND and WOLFGANG SEEKER for their shared expertise on dependency parsing.

The authors were financially supported by the German Research Foundation (DFG) grant MA 4959 / 1-1, which we gratefully acknowledge.

References

Ondřej Bojar and Jan Hajič. 2008. Phrase-based and deep syntactic English-to-Czech statistical machine translation. In *Proc. 3rd WMT*, pages 143–146. Association for Computational Linguistics.

Ondřej Bojar, Christian Buck, Christian Federmann, Barry Haddow, Philipp Koehn, Johannes Leveling, Christof Monz, Pavel Pecina, Matt Post, Herve Saint-Amand, Radu Soricut, Lucia Specia, and Aleš Tamchyna. 2014. Findings of the 2014 workshop on statistical machine translation. In *Proc. 9th WMT*, pages 12–58. Association for Computational Linguistics.

Fabienne Braune, Nina Seemann, Daniel Quernheim, and Andreas Maletti. 2013. Shallow local multi bottom-up tree transducers in statistical machine translation. In *Proc. 51st ACL*, pages 811–821. Association for Computational Linguistics.

Matthias Buch-Kromann. 2005. *Discontinuous Grammar — A dependency-based model of human parsing and language learning*. Ph.D. thesis, Copenhagen Business School.

David Chiang. 2006. An introduction to synchronous grammars. In *Proc. 44th ACL*. Association for Computational Linguistics. Part of a tutorial given with Kevin Knight.

David Chiang. 2007. Hierarchical phrase-based translation. *Computational Linguistics*, 33(2):201–228.

David Chiang. 2010. Learning to translate with source and target syntax. In *Proc. 48th ACL*, pages 1443–1452. Association for Computational Linguistics.

Jason Eisner. 2003. Learning non-isomorphic tree mappings for machine translation. In *Proc. 41st ACL*, pages 205–208. Association for Computational Linguistics.

Michel Galley, Mark Hopkins, Kevin Knight, and Daniel Marcu. 2004. What's in a translation rule? In *Proc. NAACL*, pages 273–280. Association for Computational Linguistics.

Irving J. Good. 1953. The population frequencies of species and the estimation of population parameters. *Biometrika*, 40(3–4):237–264.

Hieu Hoang, Philipp Koehn, and Adam Lopez. 2009. A unified framework for phrase-based, hierarchical, and syntax-based statistical machine translation. In *Proc. 6th IWSLT*, pages 152–159. ISCA.

Sylvain Kahane, Alexis Nasr, and Owen Rambow. 1998. Pseudo-projectivity: A polynomially parsable non-projective dependency grammar. In *Proc. 36th ACL*, pages 646–652. Association for Computational Linguistics.

Elena Dmitrievna Kallestinova. 2007. *Aspects of Word Order in Russian*. Ph.D. thesis, University of Iowa, IA, USA.

Philipp Koehn, Amittai Axelrod, Alexandra Birch Mayne, Chris Callison-Burch, Miles Osborne, and David Talbot. 2005. Edinburgh system description for the 2005 IWSLT Speech Translation Evaluation. In *Proc. 2nd IWSLT*, pages 68–75. ISCA.

Philipp Koehn, Hieu Hoang, Alexandra Birch, Chris Callison-Burch, Marcello Federico, Nicola Bertoldi, Brooke Cowan, Wade Shen, Christine Moran,

Richard Zens, Chris Dyer, Ondřej Bojar, Alexandra Constantin, and Evan Herbst. 2007. Moses: Open source toolkit for statistical machine translation. In *Proc. 45th ACL*, pages 177–180. Association for Computational Linguistics.

Philipp Koehn. 2004. Statistical significance tests for machine translation evaluation. In *Proc. EMNLP*, pages 388–395. Association for Computational Linguistics.

Philipp Koehn. 2005. Europarl: A parallel corpus for statistical machine translation. In *Proc. 10th MT Summit*, pages 79–86. Association for Machine Translation in the Americas.

Philipp Koehn. 2009. *Statistical Machine Translation*. Cambridge University Press.

Liangyou Li, Jun Xie, Andy Way, and Qun Liu. 2014. Transformation and decomposition for efficiently implementing and improving dependency-to-string model in Moses. In *Proc. 8th SSST*, pages 122–131. Association for Computational Linguistics.

Andreas Maletti. 2010. Why synchronous tree substitution grammars? In *Proc. HLT-NAACL*, pages 876–884. Association for Computational Linguistics.

Andreas Maletti. 2011. How to train your multi bottom-up tree transducer. In *Proc. 49th ACL*, pages 825–834. Association for Computational Linguistics.

Joakim Nivre and Jens Nilsson. 2005. Pseudo-projective dependency parsing. In *Proc. 43rd ACL*, pages 99–106. Association for Computational Linguistics.

Joakim Nivre, Johan Hall, and Jens Nilsson. 2006. Maltparser: A data-driven parser-generator for dependency parsing. In *Proc. 5th LREC*, pages 2216–2219. European Language Resources Association.

Joakim Nivre, Igor M. Boguslavsky, and Leonid L. Iomdin. 2008. Parsing the SYNTAGRUS treebank of Russian. In *Proc. 22nd CoLing*, pages 641–648. Association for Computational Linguistics.

Franz J. Och and Hermann Ney. 2003. A systematic comparison of various statistical alignment models. *Computational Linguistics*, 29(1):19–51.

Franz J. Och and Hermann Ney. 2004. The alignment template approach to statistical machine translation. *Computational Linguistics*, 30(4):417–449.

Franz J. Och. 2003. Minimum error rate training in statistical machine translation. In *Proc. 41st ACL*, pages 160–167. Association for Computational Linguistics.

Kishore Papineni, Salim Roukos, Todd Ward, and Wei-jing Zhu. 2002. BLEU: a method for automatic evaluation of machine translation. In *Proc. 40th ACL*, pages 311–318. Association for Computational Linguistics.

Helmut Schmid. 1994. Probabilistic part-of-speech tagging using decision trees. In *Proc. Int. Conf. New Methods in Language Processing*, pages 44–49. University of Manchester, Institute of Science and Technology.

Nina Seemann, Fabienne Braune, and Andreas Maletti. 2015. String-to-tree multi bottom-up tree transducers. In *Proc. 53rd ACL*, pages 815–824. Association for Computational Linguistics.

Rico Sennrich, Philip Williams, and Matthias Huck. 2015. A tree does not make a well-formed sentence: Improving syntactic string-to-tree statistical machine translation with more linguistic knowledge. *Computer Speech & Language*, 32(1):27–45.

Serge Sharoff and Joakim Nivre. 2011. The proper place of men and machines in language technology processing Russian without any linguistic knowledge. In *Proc. Dialogue*, pages 657–670. Russian State University for the Humanities.

Andreas Stolcke. 2002. SRILM — an extensible language modeling toolkit. In *Proc. 7th INTERSPEECH*, pages 257–286. ISCA.

Jun Sun, Min Zhang, and Chew Lim Tan. 2009. A non-contiguous tree sequence alignment-based model for statistical machine translation. In *Proc. 47th ACL*, pages 914–922. Association for Computational Linguistics.

Philip Williams and Philipp Koehn. 2012. GHKM rule extraction and scope-3 parsing in Moses. In *Proc. 7th WMT*, pages 388–394. Association for Computational Linguistics.

Alina Wróblewska and Adam Przepiórkowski. 2012. Induction of dependency structures based on weighted projection. In *Proc. 4th ICCCI*, volume 7653 of LNAI, pages 364–374. Springer.

Jun Xie, Haitao Mi, and Qun Liu. 2011. A novel dependency-to-string model for statistical machine translation. In *Proc. EMNLP*, pages 216–226. Association for Computational Linguistics.

ListNet-based MT Rescoring

[†]Jan Niehues, [*]Quoc Khanh Do, [*]Alexandre Allauzen and [†]Alex Waibel
[†]Karlsruhe Institute of Technology, Karlsruhe, Germany
[*]LIMSI-CNRS, Orsay, France
[†]firstname.surname@kit.edu [*]surname@limsi.fr

Abstract

The log-linear combination of different features is an important component of SMT systems. It allows for the easy integartion of models into the system and is used during decoding as well as for n-best list rescoring. With the recent success of more complex models like neural network-based translation models, n-best list rescoring attracts again more attention. In this work, we present a new technique to train the log-linear model based on the ListNet algorithm. This technique scales to many features, considers the whole list and not single entries during learning and can also be applied to more complex models than a log-linear combination.

Using the new learning approach, we improve the translation quality of a large-scale system by 0.8 BLEU points during rescoring and generate translations which are up to 0.3 BLEU points better than other learning techniques such as MERT or MIRA.

1 Introduction

Nowadays, statistical machine translation is the most promising approach to translate from one natural language into another one, when sufficient training data is available. While there are several powerful approaches to model the translation process, nearly all of them rely on a log-linear combination of different models. This approach allows the system an easy integration of additional models into the translation process and therefore a great flexibility to address the various issues and the different language pairs.

The log-linear model is used during decoding and for n-best list rescoring. Recently, the success of rich but computationally complex models, such as neural network based translation models (Le et al., 2012), leads to an increased interest in rescoring. It was shown that the n-best list rescoring is an easy and efficient way to integrate complex models.

From a machine learning perspective the log-linear model is used to solve a ranking problem. Given a list of candidates associated with different features, we need to find the best ranking according to a reference ranking. In machine translation, this ranking is, for example, given by an automatic evaluation metric. One promising approach for this type of problems is the ListNet algorithm (Cao et al., 2007), which has already been applied successfully to the information retrieval task. Using this algorithm it is possible to train many features. In contrast to other algorithms, which work only on single pairs of entries, it considers the whole list during learning. Furthermore, in addition to train the weights of a linear combination, it can be used for more complex models such as neural networks.

In this paper, we present an adaptation of this algorithm to the task of machine translation. Therefore, we investigate different methods to normalize the features and adapt the algorithm to directly optimize a machine translation metric. We used the algorithm to train a rescoring model and compared it to several existing training algorithms.

In the following section, we first review the related work. Afterwards, we introduce the ListNet algorithm in Section 3. The adaptation to the problem of rescoring machine translation n-best lists will be described in the next section. Finally, we will present the results on different language pairs and domains.

2 Related Work

The first approach to train the parameters of the log-linear combination model in statistical machine translation was the minimum error rate training (MERT) (Och, 2003). Although new methods have been presented, this is still the standard method in many machine translation systems. One problem of this technique is that it does not scale well with many features. More recently, Watanabe et al. (2007) and Chiang et al. (2008) presented a learning algorithm using the MIRA technique. A different technique, PRO, was presented in (Hopkins and May, 2011). Additionally, several techniques to maximize the expected BLEU score (Rosti et al., 2011; He and Deng, 2012) have been proposed. The ListNet algorithm, in contrast, minimizes the difference between the model and the reference ranking. All techniques have the advantage that they can scale well to many features and an intensive comparison of these methods is reported in (Cherry and Foster, 2012).

The problem of ranking is well studied in the machine learning community (Chen et al., 2009). These methods can be grouped into pointwise, pairwise and listwise algorithms. The PRO algorithm is motivated by a pairwise technique, while the work presented in this paper is based on the listwise algorithm ListNet presented in (Cao et al., 2007). Other methods based on more complex models have also been presented, for example (Liu et al., 2013), which uses an additive neural network instead of linear models.

3 ListNet

The ListNet algorithm (Cao et al., 2007) is a listwise approach to the problem of ranking. Every list of candidates that need to be ranked is used as an instance during learning. The algorithm has already been successfully applied to the task of information retrieval.

In order to use the listwise approach for learning, we need to define a loss function that considers a whole list. The idea in the ListNet algorithm is to define two probability distributions respectively on the hypothesized and reference ranking. Then a metric that compares both distributions can define the loss function. In this case, we will learn a scoring function that defines a probability distribution over the possible permutations of the candidate list which is similar to the reference ranking.

For a given set of m candidate lists $l = \{l^{(1)}, \dots, l^{(m)}\}$, each list $l^{(i)}$ contains a set of $n^{(i)}$ features vectors $x^{(i)} = \{x_1^{(i)} \dots, x_{n^{(i)}}^{(i)}\}$ associated to a set of reference scores $y^{(i)} = \{y_1^{(i)} \dots, y_{n^{(i)}}^{(i)}\}$, where $n^{(i)}$ is the number of elements in the list $l^{(i)}$. The aim is then to find a function f_ω that assigns a score to every feature vector $x_j^{(i)}$. This function is fully defined by its set of parameters ω. Using the vector of scores $z^{(i)} = \{f_\omega(x_1^{(i)}) \dots, f_\omega(x_{n^{(i)}}^{(i)})\}$ and the reference scores $y^{(i)}$, a listwise loss function must be defined to learn the function f_ω.

Since the number of permutations is $n!$ hence prohibitive, Cao et al. (2007) suggests to replace the probability distribution over all the permutations by the probability that an object is ranked first. This can be defined as:

$$P_s(j) = \frac{\exp(s_j)}{\sum_{k=1}^{n} \exp(s_k)}, \tag{1}$$

where s_j is a score assigned to the j-th entry of the list, either $z_j^{(i)}$ or $y_j^{(i)}$. Then a loss function is defined by the cross entropy to compare the distribution of the reference ranking with the induced ranking:

$$L(y^{(i)}, z^{(i)}) = -\sum_{j=1}^{n} P_{y^{(i)}}(j) \log(P_{z^{(i)}}(j)) \tag{2}$$

The gradient of the loss function with respect to the parameters ω can be computed as follows:

$$\begin{aligned} \Delta\omega &= \frac{\delta L(y^{(i)}, z^{(i)})}{\delta\omega} = \\ &- \sum_{j=1}^{n^{(i)}} P_{y^{(i)}}(x_j^{(i)}) \frac{\delta f_\omega(x_j^{(i)})}{\delta\omega} \\ &+ \frac{1}{\sum_{j=1}^{n^{(i)}} \exp(f_\omega(x_j^{(i)}))} \\ &\sum_{j=1}^{n^{(i)}} \exp(f_\omega(x_j^{(i)})) \frac{\delta f_\omega(x_j^{(i)})}{\delta\omega} \end{aligned} \tag{3}$$

4 Rescoring

In this work, we used a log-linear model to rescore the hypothesis of the n-best lists. The log-linear model selects the hypothesis translations $\hat{e}_i$ of source sentence f_i according to Equation 4.

$$\hat{e}_i = \operatorname*{argmax}_{j \in \{1 \dots n^{(i)}\}} \sum_{k=1}^{K} \omega_k h_k(e_i^j, f_i) \tag{4}$$

K is the number of features, h_k are the different features and ω_k are the parameters of the model that need to be learned using the ListNet algorithm.

In this case, the sets of candidate lists l are the n-best lists generated for the development data. The scores $x_j^{(i)} = \{h_1(e_i^j, f_i) \ldots h_K(e_i^j, f_i)\}$ are the features of the translation hypothesis ranked in position j for the sentence i. The features include conventional scores calculated during decoding, as well as additional models such as neural network translation models.

4.1 Score normalization

The scores $(x_j^{(i)})_k$ are, for example, language model log-probabilities. Since the language model probabilities are calculated as the product of several n-gram probabilities, these values are typically very small. Therefore, the log-probabilities are negative numbers with a high absolute value. Furthermore, the range of feature values may greatly differ. This can lead to problems in the calculation of $\exp(f_\omega(x_j^{(i)}))$. Therefore, we investigated two techniques to normalize the scores, feature normalization and final score normalization

In the feature normalization, all values of scores observed on the development data are rescaled into the range of $[-1, 1]$ using a linear transformation. Let $m_k = \min_{i,j}\{(x_j^{(i)})_k\}$ denote the minimum value of the feature k observed on the development set and similarly M_k for the maximum. The original scores are replaced by their rescaled version $(\hat{x}_j^{(i)})_k$ as follows:

$$(\hat{x}_j^{(i)})_k = \frac{2 * (x_j^{(i)})_k - (M_k + m_k)}{M_k - m_k} \tag{5}$$

The same transformation based on the minimal and maximal feature values on the development data is applied to the test data.

When using the final score normalization, we normalize the resulting scores $f_\omega(x_j^{(i)})$. This is done separately for every n-best list. We calculate the highest absolute value M_i by:

$$M_i = \max_{j=1}^{n^{(i)}}(|f_\omega(x_j^{(i)})|) \tag{6}$$

Then we use the rescaled scores denoted $\overline{f}_\omega$ and defined as follows:

$$\overline{f}_\omega(x_j^{(i)}) = f_\omega(x_j^{(i)}) * \frac{r}{M_i}, \tag{7}$$

where r is the desired target range of possible scores.

Although both methods could be applied together, we did only use one of them, since both methods have similar effects.

If not stated differently, we use the feature normalization method in our experiments.

4.2 Metric

To estimate the weights, we need to define a probability distribution P_y associated to the reference ranking y following Euqation 1. In this work, we propose a distribution based on machine translation evaluation metrics.

The most widely used evaluation metric is BLEU (Papineni et al., 2002), which only produces a score at the corpus level. As proposed by Hopkins and May (2011), we will use a smoothed sentence-wise BLEU score to generate the reference ranking. In this work, we use the BLEU+1 score introduced by Liang et al. (2006). When using $s_j = \text{BLEU}(x_j^{(i)})$ in Equation 1, whe get the follwing defintion of the probability distribution P_y:

$$P_{y^{(i)}}(x_j^{(i)}) = \frac{\exp(\text{BLEU}(x_j^{(i)}))}{\sum_{j'=1}^{n^i} \exp(\text{BLEU}(x_{j'}^{(i)})} \tag{8}$$

However, the raw use of BLEU+1 may lead to a very flat probability distribution, since the difference in BLEU among translation candidates in the n-best list is in general relatively small. Motivated by initial experiments, we use instead the BLEU+1 percentage of each sentence.

4.3 Training

Since the loss function defined in Equation 2 is differentiable and convex *w.r.t* the parameters ω, the stochastic gradient descent can be applied for optimization purpose. The model is trained by randomly selecting sentences from the development set and by applying batch updates after rescoring ten source sentences. The training process ends after 100,000 batches and the final model is selected according to its performance on the development data. The learning rate was empirically selected using the development data. We investigated fixed learning rates around 1 as well as dynamically updating the learning rate.

5 Evaluation

The proposed approach is evaluated in two widely known translation tasks. The first is the large scale translation task of WMT 2015 for the German–English language pair in both directions. The second is the task of translating English TED lectures into German using the data from the IWSLT 2015 evaluation campaign (Cettolo et al., 2014). The systems using the ListNet-based rescoring were submitted to this evaluation campaigns and when evaluated using the BLEU score they were all ranking within the top 3. Before discussing the results, we summarize the translation systems used for experiments along with the additionnal features that rely on continuous space translation models.

5.1 Systems

The baseline system is an in-house implementation of the phrase-based approach. The system used to generate n-best lists for the news tasks is trained on all the available training corpora of the WMT 2015 Shared Translation task. The system uses a pre-reordering technique and facilitates several translation and language models. A full system description can be found in (Cho et al., 2015). The German to English baseline system uses 19 features and the English to German systems uses 22 features. Both systems are tuned on news-test2013 which also serves to train the rescoring step using ListNet. The news-test2014 is dedicated for evaluation purpose. On both sets, 300-best lists are generated.

In addition to baseline features, we also analyze the influence of features calculated on the n-best list after decoding. Since we only need to calculate the scores for the entries in the n-best lists and not for all partial derivations considered during decoding, we can use more complex models.

For the English to German translation task, we used neural network translation models as introduced in (Le et al., 2012). This model decomposes the sequence of phrase pairs proposed by the translation system in two sequences of source and target words respectively, synchronized by the segmentation into phrase pairs. This decomposition defines four different scores to evaluate a hypothesis. In such architecture, the size of the output vocabulary is a bottleneck when normalized distributions are needed. For efficient computation, these models rely on a tree-structured output layer called SOUL (Le et al., 2011). An effective alternative, which however only delivers unnormalized scores, is to train the network using the Noise Contrastive Estimation (Gutmann and Hyvärinen, 2010; Mnih and Teh, 2012) denoted by NCE in the rest of the paper. In this work, we used these both solutions as well as their combination.

For the German to English translation task, we added a source side discriminative word lexicon (Herrmann, 2015). This model used a multi-class maximum entropy classifier for every source word to predict the translation given the context of the word. In addition, we used a neural network translation model using the technique of RBM (Restricted Boltzman Machine)-based language models (Niehues and Waibel, 2012).

The baseline system for the TED translation task uses the IWSLT 2015 training data. The system was adapted to the domain by using language model and translation model adaptation techniques. A detailed description of all models used in this system can be found in (Slawik et al., 2014). Overall, the baseline system uses 23 different features. The system is tuned on test2011 and test2012 was used to evaluate the different approaches. In the additional experiments, n-best lists generated for dev2010 and test2010 are used as additional training data for the rescoring.

5.2 Other optimization techniques

For comparison, experimental results include performance obtained with the most widely used algorithms: MERT, KB-MIRA (Cherry and Foster, 2012) as implemented in Moses (Koehn et al., 2007), along with the PRO algorithm. For the latter, we used the MegaM[1] version (Daumé III, 2004). All the results correspond to three random restarts and the weights are chosen according to the best performance on the development data.

5.3 WMT – English to German

The results for the English to German news translation task are summarized in Table 1. The translations generated by the phrase-based decoder reach a BLEU score of 20.19. We compared the presented approach with MERT, KB-MIRA and PRO. KB-MIRA and MERT improve the performance by at most 0.3 BLEU points. In contrast, the PRO technique and the ListNet algorithm presented in this paper improve the translation quality by 0.8 BLEU points to 21 BLEU points.

Using the NCE-based or SOUL-based neural network translation models improve the perfor-

[1] http://www.umiacs.umd.edu/~hal/megam/

	Baseline		NCE		SOUL		SOUL+NCE	
System	Dev	Test	Dev	Test	Dev	Test	Dev	Test
Baseline		20.19						
MERT	20.63	20.52	21.24	20.92	21.36	20.84	21.36	20.94
KB-MIRA	20.64	20.38	21.51	20.96	21.65	20.83	21.71	21.06
PRO	20.17	**21.01**	21.04	21.25	21.18	21.31	21.14	21.34
ListNet	19.95	20.98	21.00	**21.51**	21.02	**21.54**	21.14	**21.63**

Table 1: WMT Results for English to German

	Baseline		SDWL		SDWL+RBMTM	
System	Dev	Test	Dev	Test	Dev	Test
Baseline		27.77				
MERT	28.18	27.80	28.24	27.65	28.23	27.64
KB-MIRA	28.23	**28.06**	28.18	28.00	28.00	27.88
PRO	27.38	28.01	27.56	28.14	28.68	28.04
ListNet	28.00	27.87	27.89	**28.18**	27.94	**28.28**

Table 2: WMT Results for German to English

mance up to 21.31 using one of the existing algorithms. Again, the best performance was reached using the PRO algorithm. If we use the ListNet algorithm, we can improve the translation score to 21.54 BLEU points. For this condition, this algorithm outperforms the other by 0.2 BLEU point. When using the two models, the ListNet algorithm achieves an additional gain of 0.1 BLEU point. Moreover, we can observe that MERT and KB-MIRA always yield the best results on the development set, whereas BLEU scores on the test set are lower. The opposite trend is observed with ListNet[2] showing a better generalization power.

In summary, in all conditions, the ListNet algorithm outperforms MERT and KB-MIRA. Only in one condition the PRO algorithm generates translations with a BLEU score as high as the ListNet algorithm. The ListNet algorithm outperforms to the best other algorithms by up to 0.3 BLEU points. The baseline translation is improved by 0.8 BLEU points with only conventional features, and by 1.4 BLEU points when using additional models. Furthermore, as shown by the lower scores on the development data, the ListNet algorithm seems to be less prone to overfitting.

5.4 WMT – German to English

The German to English news translation task results are shown in Table 2. The baseline system yields a BLEU score of 27.77 on the test set. This is slightly outperformed by the ListNet algorithm by 0.1 BLEU point. In this configuration, the KB-MIRA-based rescoring and the PRO algorithm slightly outperform the ListNet algorithm by 0.2 BLEU points. MERT generates a BLEU score worse than the ListNet algorithm. When adding the source discriminative word lexicon (SDWL) only or adding this model and the RBM-based translation model, the ListNet based algorithm outperforms again all other models. While the other algorithms could only gain slightly from these models, the ListNet-based optimization improves the BLEU score up to 28.28 points. This is the best performance reached on this task with a 0.1 BLEU point improvement over other optimization algorithms.

5.5 TED – English to German

In addition to the experiments on the news domain, we performed experiments on the task of translating English TED talks into German. The results of these experiments are summarized in Table 3.

In this task, the MERT algorithm performs better than the KB-MIRA and PRO algorithms and generates translations with a BLEU score of 23.46 points. By optimizing the weights of the log-linear model using the ListNet algorithm, we increased the BLEU score slightly to 23.51 points. But in this condition all optimization could not improve the system over the initial translation, which reaches a BLEU score of 23.67 points.

[2] and with PRO to a lesser extent

	Baseline		extra Dev Data	
System	Dev	Test	Dev	Test
Baseline		23.67		
MERT	27.69	23.46	25.63	23.36
KB-MIRA	27.47	23.19	25.65	23.76
PRO	26.67	23.10	25.00	23.65
ListNet	27.37	**23.51**	25.49	**24.08**

Table 3: TED Results for English to German

In addition to the integration of additional features, the rescoring technique also allows an easy facilitation of additional development data. For this task, additional development data is available. Therefore, we also trained all rescoring algorithms on the concatenation of the original development data and the additional two development sets.

The KB-MIRA and PRO algorithm can facilitate this data and generate translation with a higher BLEU score. In contrast, when using the MERT algorithm, the BLEU score is not improved by the additional data. Therefore, the KB-MIRA algorithm performs better than MERT and PRO and can improve the baseline system by 0.1 BLEU points. With the ListNet algorithm it is possible to select translations with a BLEU score that is 0.6 points better than system trained on the smaller development set. The ListNet rescoring improves the baseline system by 0.4 BLEU points and the best other learning algorithm, KB-MIRA, by 0.3 BLEU points.

5.6 Convergence of the ListNet algorithm

To assess the convergence speed of the ListNet algorithm, the Figure 1 plots the evolution of the BLEU+1 score measured on the development set for the English to German translation task. We can observe a fast convergence along with a satisfactory stability. This is an important characteristic of this algorithm in comparison with the randomness exhibited by some usual tuning algorithm such as MERT.

5.7 Score normalization

On the German to English translation task, we compared the normalization of the features used in the previous experiments with normalizing the final score as described in Section 4.1. We evaluated different target feature ranges between 0.5 and 100. The results for these experiments are summarized in Figure 2.

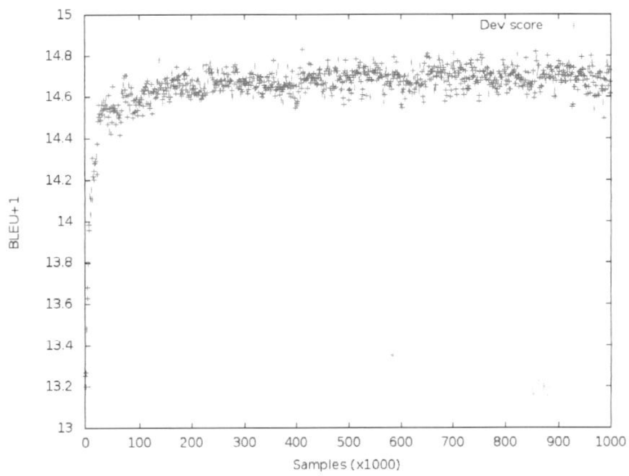

Figure 1: Evolution of the BLEU+1 score measured on the development set as a function of the number of training sentences.

As shown in the graph, if the range of possible scores is too low, no learning is possible. The best performance on the development is reached at a value of ten with 20.21 BLEU points on the development data and 20.64 on the test data. This is also nearly the best performance on the test data.

In comparison, the feature normalization achieves a BLEU score of 19.95 on the development data and 20.98 on the test data as shown in Table 1. Although the normalization of the final score can outperform the feature normalization on the development data, the feature normalization performs best on the test data in this task.

6 Conclusion

We presented in this paper a new way to train the log-linear model of a statistical machine translation system based on an adaptation of the ListNet algorithm to the task of ranking translation hypotheses. This algorithm can be applied to many features and considers the whole n-best list for training. The algorithm can also be applied for

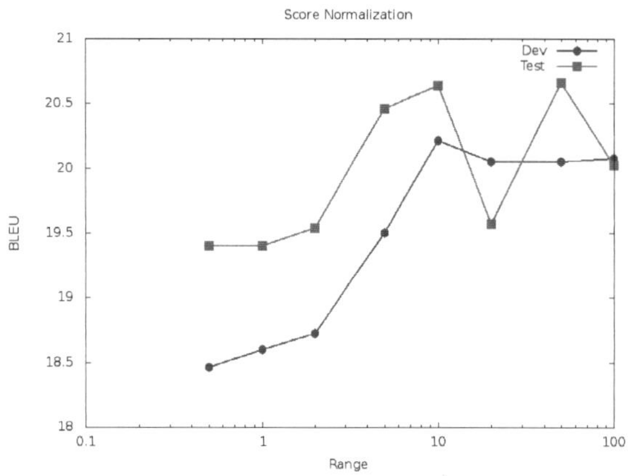

Figure 2: Score normalization

more complex models than the log-linear model used in most machine translation systems.

Using this technique translation quality is improved as measured in BLEU scores on large scale translation tasks. Without any additional feature, we improved the BLEU score by 0.8 points and 0.1 points compared to the initial translations. Further 0.6 BLEU points was gained by using additional models in the rescoring. The algorithm outperformed the MERT training in all configurations and other algorithms in most configurations. Moreover, experimental results show that our approach is less prone to overfitting which is an important issue of many optimization techniques.

Acknowledgments

The project leading to this application has received funding from the European Union's Horizon 2020 research and innovation programme under grant agreement n° 645452.

References

Z. Cao, T. Qin, T.-Y. Liu, M.-F. Tsai, and H. Li. 2007. Learning to rank: from pairwise approach to listwise approach. In *Proceedings of the 24th international conference on Machine learning*, ICML'07, pages 129–136, New York, NY, USA. ACM.

M. Cettolo, J. Niehues, S. Stker, L. Bentivogli, and M. Federico. 2014. Report on the 11th iwslt evaluation campaign. In *Proceedings of the 11th International Workshop on Spoken Language Translation (IWSLT 2014)*, Lake Tahoe, California, USA.

W. Chen, T. Liu, Y. Lan, Z. Ma, and H. Li. 2009. Ranking measures and loss functions in learning to rank. In *Advances in Neural Information Processing Systems 22*, pages 315–323.

Colin Cherry and George Foster. 2012. Batch tuning strategies for statistical machine translation. In *Proceedings of the North American Chapter of the Association for Computational Linguistics: Human Language Technologies (NAACL-HLT)*, pages 427–436, Montréal, Canada, June.

D. Chiang, Y. Marton, and P. Resnik. 2008. Online large-margin training of syntactic and structural translation features. In *Proceedings of the Conference on Empirical Methods in Natural Language Processing (EMNLP 2008)*, Honolulu, Hawaii, USA.

E. Cho, T. Ha, J. Niehues, T. Herrmann, M. Mediani, Y. Zhang, and A. Waibel. 2015. The karlsruhe institute of technology translation systems for the wmt 2015. In *Proceedings of the Tenth Workshop on Statistical Machine Translation (WMT 2015)*, Lisboa, Portugal.

H. Daumé III. 2004. Notes on CG and LM-BFGS optimization of logistic regression.

Michael Gutmann and Aapo Hyvärinen. 2010. Noise-contrastive estimation: A new estimation principle for unnormalized statistical models. In Yeh Whye Teh and Mike Titterington, editors, *Proceedings of th International Conference on Artificial Intelligence and Statistics (AISTATS)*, volume 9, pages 297–304.

X. He and L. Deng. 2012. Maximum expected bleu training of phrase and lexicon translation models. In *Proceedings of the 50th Annual Meeting of the Association for Computational Linguistics(ACL 2012)*, pages 292–301, Jeju, Korea.

Teresa Herrmann. 2015. *Linguistic Structure in Statistical Machine Translation*. Ph.D. thesis, Karlsruhe Institute of Technology.

M. Hopkins and J. May. 2011. Tuning as ranking. In *In Proceedings of the 2011 Conference on Empirical Methods in Natural Language Processing*.

P. Koehn, H. Hoang, A. Birch, C. Callison-Burch, M. Federico, N. Bertoldi, B. Cowan, W. Shen, C. Moran, R. Zens, C. Dyer, O. Bojar, A. Constantin, and E. Herbst. 2007. Moses: Open source toolkit for statistical machine translation. In *Proceedings of the 45th Annual Meeting of the Association for Computational Linguistics (ACL 2007)*, Prague, Czech Republic.

Hai-Son Le, Ilya Oparin, Alexandre Allauzen, Jean-Luc Gauvain, and François Yvon. 2011. Structured output layer neural network language model. In *Proceedings of the International Conference on Audio, Speech and Signal Processing*, pages 5524–5527.

Hai-Son Le, Alexandre Allauzen, and François Yvon. 2012. Continuous space translation models with neural networks. In *Proceedings of the North American Chapter of the Association for Computational Linguistics: Human Language Technologies (NAACL-HLT)*, pages 39–48, Montréal, Canada, June. Association for Computational Linguistics.

P. Liang, A. Bouchard-Côté, D. Klein, and B. Taskar. 2006. An end-to-end discriminative approach to machine translation. In *Proceedings of the 44th Annual Meeting of the Association for Computational Linguistics (ACL 2006)*, pages 761–768, Sydney, Australia.

L. Liu, T. Watanabe, E. Sumita, and T. Zhao. 2013. Additive neural networks for statistical machine translation. In *Proceedings of the 51st Annual Meeting of the Association for Computational Linguistics (ACL 2013)*, Sofia, Bulgaria, Bulgaria.

Andriy Mnih and Yeh Whye Teh. 2012. A fast and simple algorithm for training neural probabilistic language models. In *Proceedings of the International Conference of Machine Learning (ICML)*.

J. Niehues and A. Waibel. 2012. Continuous space language models using restricted boltzmann machines. In *Proceedings of the Ninth International Workshop on Spoken Language Translation (IWSLT 2012)*, Hong Kong.

F.J. Och. 2003. Minimum error rate training in statistical machine translation. In *Proceedings of the 41th Annual Meeting of the Association for Computational Linguistics (ACL 2003)*, Sapporo, Japan.

K. Papineni, S. Roukos, T. Ward, and W.-jing Zhu. 2002. Bleu: a method for automatic evaluation of machine translation. In *Proceedings of the 40th Annual Meeting of the Association for Computational Linguistics (ACL 2002)*, pages 311–318, Philadelphia, Pennsylvania.

A.-V.I. Rosti, B. Zhang, S. Matsoukas, and R. Schwartz. 2011. Expected bleu training for graphs: Bbn system description for wmt11 system combination task. In *Proceedings of the Sixth Workshop on Statistical Machine Translation (WMT 2011)*, pages 159–165, Edinburgh, UK.

I. Slawik, M. Mediani, J. Niehues, Y. Zhang, E. Cho, T. Herrmann, T. Ha, and A. Waibel. 2014. The kit translation systems for iwslt 2014. In *Proceedings of the 11th International Workshop on Spoken Language Translation (IWSLT 2014)*, Lake Tahoe, USA.

T. Watanabe, J. Suzuki, H. Tsukada, and H. Isozaki. 2007. Online large-margin training for statistical machine translation. In *Proceedings of the Conference on Empirical Methods in Natural Language Processing (EMNLP 2007)*, Prague, Czech Republic.

*** Formatting Issue - Best Available Paper/Graphic ***

Results of the WMT15 Metrics Shared Task

Miloš Stanojević and **Amir Kamran**
University of Amsterdam
ILLC
{m.stanojevic,a.kamran}@uva.nl

Philipp Koehn
Johns Hopkins University
DCS
phi@jhu.edu

Ondřej Bojar
Charles University in Prague
MFF ÚFAL
bojar@ufal.mff.cuni.cz

Abstract

This paper presents the results of the WMT15 Metrics Shared Task. We asked participants of this task to score the outputs of the MT systems involved in the WMT15 Shared Translation Task. We collected scores of 46 metrics from 11 research groups. In addition to that, we computed scores of 7 standard metrics (BLEU, SentBLEU, NIST, WER, PER, TER and CDER) as baselines. The collected scores were evaluated in terms of system level correlation (how well each metric's scores correlate with WMT15 official manual ranking of systems) and in terms of segment level correlation (how often a metric agrees with humans in comparing two translations of a particular sentence).

1 Introduction

Automatic machine translation metrics play a very important role in the development of MT systems and their evaluation. There are many different metrics of diverse nature and one would like to assess their quality. For this reason, the Metrics Shared Task is held annually at the Workshop of Statistical Machine Translation[1], starting with Koehn and Monz (2006) and following up to Macháček and Bojar (2014).

The systems' outputs, human judgements and evaluated metrics are described in Section 2. The quality of the metrics in terms of system level correlation is reported in Section 3. Section 4 is devoted to segment level correlation.

2 Data

We used the translations of MT systems involved in WMT15 Shared Translation Task (Bojar et al., 2015) together with reference translations as the test set for the Metrics Task. This dataset consists of 87 systems' outputs and 10 reference translations in 10 translation directions (English from and into Czech, Finnish, French, German and Russian). The number of sentences in system and reference translations varies among language pairs ranging from 1370 for Finnish-English to 2818 for Russian-English. For more details, please see the WMT15 overview paper (Bojar et al., 2015).

2.1 Manual MT Quality Judgements

During the WMT15 Translation Task, a large scale manual annotation was conducted to compare the translation quality of participating systems. We used these collected human judgements for the evaluation of the automatic metrics.

The participants in the manual annotation were asked to evaluate system outputs by ranking translated sentences relative to each other. For each source segment that was included in the procedure, the annotator was shown five different outputs to which he or she was supposed to assign ranks. Ties were allowed.

These collected rank labels for each five-tuple of outputs were then interpreted as pairwise comparisons of systems and used to assign each system a score that reflects how high that system was usually ranked by the annotators. Several methods have been tested in the past for the exact score calculation and WMT15 has adopted TrueSkill as the official one. Please see the WMT15 overview paper for details on how this score is computed.

For the metrics task in 2014, we were still using the "Pre-TrueSkill" method called "> Others", see Bojar et al. (2011). Since we are now moving to the golden truth calculated by TrueSkill, we report also the average "Pre-TrueSkill" score in the relevant tables for comparison.

[1] http://www.statmt.org/wmt15

*** Formatting Issue - Best Available Paper/Graphic ***

Metric	Participant
BEER, BEER_TREEPEL	ILLC – University of Amsterdam (Stanojević and Sima'an, 2015)
BS	University of Zurich (Mark Fishel; no corresponding paper)
CHRF, CHRF3	DFKI (Popović, 2015)
DPMF, DPMFCOMB	Chinese Academy of Sciences and Dublin City University (Yu et al., 2015)
DREEM	National Research Council Canada (Chen et al., 2015)
LEBLEU-DEFAULT, LEBLEU-OPTIMIZED	Lingsoft and Aalto University (Virpioja and Grönroos, 2015)
METEOR-WSD, RATATOUILLE	LIMSI-CNRS (Marie and Apidianaki, 2015)
UOW-LSTM	University of Wolverhampton (Gupta et al., 2015a)
UPF-COBALT	Universitat Pompeu Fabra (Fomicheva et al., 2015)
USAAR-ZWICKEL-*	Saarland University (Vela and Tan, 2015)
VERTA-W, VERTA-EQ, VERTA-70ADEQ30FLU	University of Barcelona (Comelles and Atserias, 2015)

Table 1: Participants of WMT15 Metrics Shared Task

2.2 Participants of the Metrics Shared Task

Table 1 lists the participants of the WMT15 Shared Metrics Task, along with their metrics. We have collected 46 metrics from a total of 11 research groups.

Here we give a short description of each metric that performed the best on at least one language pair.

2.2.1 BEER and BEER_TREEPEL

BEER is a trained metric, a linear model that combines features capturing character n-grams and permutation trees. BEER has participated last year in sentence-level evalution. The main additions this year are corpus-level aggregation of sentence-level scores and a syntactic version called BEER_TREEPEL. BEER_TREEPEL includes features checking the match of each type of arc in the dependency trees of the hypothesis and the reference.

BEER was the best for en-de and en-ru at the system level and en-fi and en-ru at the sentence level. BEER_TREEPEL was the best for system-level evaluation of ru-en.

2.2.2 BS

The metric BS has no corresponding paper, so we include a summary by Mark Fishel here: The BS metric was an attempt of moving in a different direction than most state-of-the-art metrics and reduce complexity and language resource dependence to the minimum. The score is obtained from the number and lengths of "bad segments": continuous subsequences of words that are present only in the hypothesis or the reference, but not both. To account for morphologically complex languages and smooth the score for sparse word forms poor man's lemmatization is added: the floor of one third of each word's characters are removed from the word's end. The final score is either the log-sum of the bad segment lengths (BS) or a simple sum (TOTAL-BS).

BS and DPMF were the best for system-level English-French evaluation.

2.2.3 CHRF3

CHRF3 calculates a simple F-score combination of the precision and recall of character n-grams of length 6. The F-score is calculated with $\beta = 3$, giving triple the weight to recall.

CHRF3 was the best for en-fi and en-cs at the system level and en-cs at the sentence level.

2.2.4 DPMF and DPMFCOMB

DPMF is a syntax-based metric but unlike many syntax-based metrics, it does not compute score on substructures of the tree returned by a syntactic parser. Instead, DPMF parses the reference translation with a standard parser and trains a new parser on the tree of the reference translation. This new parser is then used for scoring the hypothesis. Additionally, DPMF uses F-score of unigrams in combination with the syntactic score.

DPMFCOMB is a combination of DPMF with several other metrics available in the evaluation tool Asiya[2].

DPMF and BS were the best for system-level evaluation of English-French. DPMF also tied for the best place with UOW-LSTM for French-English. DPMFCOMB was the best for fi-en, de-en and cs-en at the sentence level.

2.2.5 DREEM

DREEM uses distributed word and sentence representations of three different kinds: one-hot representation, a distributed representation learned with a neural network and a distributed sentence

[2]http://asiya-faust.cs.upc.edu/

representation learned with a recursive autoencoder. The final score is the cosine similarity of the representation of the hypothesis and the reference, multiplied with a length penalty.

DREEM was the best for fi-en system-level evaluation.

2.2.6 LEBLEU-OPTIMIZED

LEBLEU is a relaxation of the strict word n-gram matching that is used in standard BLEU. Unlike other similar relaxations, LEBLEU uses fuzzy matching of longer chunks of text that allows, for example, to match two independent words with a compound. LEBLEU-OPTIMIZED applies fuzzy match threshold and n-gram length optimized for each language pair.

LEBLEU-OPTIMIZED was the best for en-de at the sentence level.

2.2.7 RATATOUILLE

RATATOUILLE is a metric combination of BLEU, BEER, Meteor and few more metrics out of which METEOR-WSD is a novel contribution. METEOR-WSD is an extension of Meteor that includes synonym mappings to languages other than English based on alignments and rewards semantically adequate translations in context.

RATATOUILLE was the best for sentence-level French-English evaluation in both directions.

2.2.8 UOW-LSTM

UOW-LSTM uses dependency-tree recursive neural network to represent both the hypothesis and the reference with a dense vector. The final score is obtained from a neural network trained on judgements from previous years converted to similarity scores, taking into account both the distance and angle of the two representations.

UOW-LSTM tied for the best place in fr-en system-level evaluation with DPMF.

2.2.9 UPF-COBALT

UPF-COBALT pays an increased attention to syntactic context (for example arguments, complements, modifiers etc.) both in aligning the words of the hypothesis and reference as well as in scoring of the matched words. It relies on additional resources including stemmers, WordNet synsets, paraphrase databases and distributed word representations. UPF-COBALT system-level score was calculated by taking the ratio of sentences in which each system from a set of competitors was assigned the highest sentence-level score.

UPF-COBALT was the best on system-level evaluation for de-en and, together with VERTA-70ADEQ30FLU, for cs-en.

2.2.10 VERTA-70ADEQ30FLU

VERTA-70ADEQ30FLU aims at the combination of adequacy and fluency features that use many sources of different linguistic information: synonyms, lemmas, PoS tags, dependency parses and language models. On previous works VERTA's linguistic features combination were set depending on whether adequacy or fluency was evaluated. VERTA-70ADEQ30FLU is a weighted combination of VERTA setups for adequacy (0.70) and fluency (0.30).

VERTA-70ADEQ30FLU was, together with UPF-COBALT, the best on cs-en on system level.

2.2.11 Baseline Metrics

In addition to the submitted metrics, we have computed the following two groups of standard metrics as baselines for the system level:

- **Mteval.** The metrics BLEU (Papineni et al., 2002) and NIST (Doddington, 2002) were computed using the script `mteval-v13a.pl`[3] which is used in the OpenMT Evaluation Campaign and includes its own tokenization. We run `mteval` with the flag `--international-tokenization` since it performs slightly better (Macháček and Bojar, 2013).

- **Moses Scorer.** The metrics TER (Snover et al., 2006), WER, PER and CDER (Leusch et al., 2006) were computed using the Moses scorer which is used in Moses model optimization. To tokenize the sentences, we used the standard tokenizer script as available in Moses toolkit.

For segment level baseline, we have used the following modified version of BLEU:

- **SentBLEU.** The metric SentBLEU is computed using the script sentence-bleu, part of the Moses toolkit. It is a smoothed version of BLEU that correlates better with human judgements for segment level.

[3] `http://www.itl.nist.gov/iad/mig/tools/`

*** Formatting Issue - Best Available Paper/Graphic ***

We have normalized all metrics' scores such that better translations get higher scores.

For computing the scores we used the same script from the last year metric task.

3 System-Level Results

Same as last year, we used Pearson correlation coefficient as the main measure for system level metrics correlation. We use the following formula to compute the Pearson's r for each metric and translation direction:

$$r = \frac{\sum_{i=1}^{n}(H_i - \bar{H})(M_i - \bar{M})}{\sqrt{\sum_{i=1}^{n}(H_i - \bar{H})^2}\sqrt{\sum_{i=1}^{n}(M_i - \bar{M})^2}} \quad (1)$$

where H is the vector of human scores of all systems translating in the given direction, M is the vector of the corresponding scores as predicted by the given metric. $\bar{H}$ and $\bar{M}$ are their means respectively.

Since we have normalized all metrics such that better translations get higher score, we consider metrics with values of Pearson's r closer to 1 as better.

You can find the system-level correlations for translations into English in Table 2 and for translations out of English in Table 3. Each row in the tables contains correlations of a metric in each of the examined translation directions. The upper part of each table lists metrics that participated in all language pairs and it is sorted by average Pearson correlation coefficient across translation directions. The lower part contains metrics limited to a subset of the language pairs, so the average correlation cannot be directly compared with other metrics any more. The best results in each direction are in bold. The reported empirical confidence intervals of system level correlations were obtained through bootstrap resampling of 1000 samples (confidence level of 95%).

The move to TrueSkill golden truth slightly increased the correlations and changed the ranking of the metrics a little, but the general patterns hold. (The correlation between "Average" and "Pre-TrueSkill Average" is .999 for both directions.)

Both tables also include the average Spearman's rank correlation, which used to be the evaluation measure in the past. Spearman's rank correlation considers only the ranking of the systems and not the distances between them. It is thus more susceptible to instability if several systems have similar scores.

3.1 System-Level Discussion

As in the previous years, many metrics outperform BLEU both into as well as out of English. Note that the original BLEU was designed to work with 4 references and WMT provides just one; see Bojar et al. (2013) for details on BLEU correlation with varying number of references, up to several thousands. This year, BLEU with one reference reaches the average correlation of .92 into English or .78 out of English. The best performing metrics get up to .98 into English and .92 out of English. CDER is the best of the baselines, reaching .94 into English and .81 out of English.

The winning metric for each language pair is different, with interesting outliers: DREEM performed best when evaluating English translations from Finnish but on average, 12 other metrics into English performed better and DREEM appears to be among the worst metrics out of English. RATATOUILLE is fifth to tenth when evaluated by average Pearson but wins in both directions in average Spearman's rank correlation.

Two metrics confirm the effectiveness of character-level measures, esp. the winners for out of English evaluation: CHRF3 and BEER. The metric CHRF3 is particularly interesting because it does not require any resources whatsoever. It is defined as a simple F-measure of character-level 6-grams (spaces are ignored), with recall weighted 3 times more than precision. The balance between the precision and recall seems important depending on morphological richness of the target language: for evaluations into English, CHRF (equal weights) performs better than CHRF3.

As we already observed in the past, the winning metrics are trained on previous years of WMT. This holds for DPMFCOMB, UOW-LSTM and BEER including BEER_TREEPEL. DPMF and UPF-COBALT are not combination or trained metrics of any kind, DPMF is based on dependency analysis of the candidate and reference sentences and UPF-COBALT uses contextual information of compared words in the candidate and the reference.

We see an interesting difference in the performance of UOW-LSTM. It is the second metric in system-level correlation but falls among the worst ones in segment-level correlations, see Table 4 below. Gupta et al. (2015b) suggest that the discrepancy in performance could be based by low inter-annotator agreement and Kendall's τ not reflecting the distances in translation quality between candidates, an issue similar to what we see with Pearson vs. Spearman's rank correlations.

Another dense-representation metric, DREEM, seems to suffer a similar discrepancy when evaluating into English. Out of English, DREEM did not perform very well.

An untested speculation is that the dense sentence-level representation present in some form in both UoW-LSTM as well as in DREEM confuses the metrics in their judgements of individual sentences.

3.2 Comparison with BLEU

In Appendix A, we provide two correlation plots for each language pair. The first plot visualizes the correlation of BLEU and manual judgements, the second plot shows the correlation for the best performing metric for that pair.

The BLEU plots include grey ellipses to indicate the confidence intervals of both BLEU as well as manual judgements. The ellipses are tilted only to indicate that BLEU and the manual score are dependent variables. Only the width and height of each ellipse represent a value, that is the confidence interval in each direction. The same vertical confidence intervals hold for plots in the right-hand column, but since we don't have any confidence estimates for the individual metrics, we omit them.

Czech-English plots indicate that UPF-COBALT was able to account for the very different behaviour of the transfer-based deep-syntactic system CU-TECTO. It was also able to appreciate the higher translation quality of montreal, UEDIN-* and online-b. The big cluster of systems labelled TT-* are submissions to the WMT15 Tuning Task (Stanojević et al., 2015).

For English-Czech, we see that UEDIN-JHU and MONTREAL are overfit for BLEU. In terms of BLEU, they are very close to the winning system CU-CHIMERA (a combination of CU-TECTO and phrase-based Moses, followed by automatic post-editing). CHRF3 is able to recognize the overfitting for MONTREAL, a neural-network based system, but not for UEDIN-JHU. CHRF3 also better recognizes the distance in quality between larger systems (from COMMERCIAL1 above) and the small-data tuning task systems.

For German-English, we see the same overfit of UEDIN-JHU towards BLEU. While neither UPF-COBALT nor CHRF3 could recognize this for translations involving Czech, the issue is spotted by UPF-COBALT for systems involving German. Syntax-based systems like UEDIN-SYNTAX for English-German and (presumably) ONLINE-B for German-English are among those where the correlation got most improved over BLEU.

The French dataset was in a different domain, which may explain why the best performing metric DPMF does actually not improve much above BLEU. DPMF uses a syntactic parser on the reference, and the performance of parsers on discussions is likely to be lower than the generally used news domain.

In Finnish results, we see again UEDIN-JHU and ABUMATRAN (Rubino et al., 2015) overvalued by BLEU. DREEM based on distributed representation of words and sentences is able to recognize this for translation into English but it falls among the worst metrics in the other direction. For translation into Finnish, character-based n-grams of CHRF3 are much more reliable. Variants of ABUMATRAN were again those most overvalued by BLEU. ABUMATRAN uses several types of morphological segmentation and reconstructs Finnish words from the segments by concatenation. ABUMATRAN is loaded with many other features, like web-crawled data and domain handling, and system combination of several approaches. The optimization towards BLEU (unreliable for Finnish, as we have learned in this task), could be among the main reasons behind the comparably lower manual scores.

For Russian, BEER is the best metric, in its syntax-aware variant BEER_TREEPEL for evaluating English. Compared to BLEU, the improvement in correlation is not that striking for Russian-English. (It would be interesting to know whether ONLINE-G is better than ONLINE-B because of English syntax or addressing source-side morphology better. BEER_TREEPEL captures both aspects.) In the other direction, targetting Russian, BLEU was effectively unable to rank the systems at all. It is probably the character-level features in BEER that allow it to reach a very good correlation, .97.

Correlation coefficient / Direction / Considered Systems	Pearson Correlation Coefficient fr-en 7	fi-en 14	de-en 13	cs-en 16	ru-en 13	Average	Pre-TrueSkill Average	Spearman's Average
DPMFCOMB	.995 ± .004	.958 ± .011	.973 ± .009	.991 ± .002	.974 ± .008	**.978** ± .007	.970 ± .012	.882 ± .041
UoW-LSTM	**.997** ± .003	.976 ± .008	.960 ± .010	.983 ± .003	.963 ± .009	.976 ± .007	≀ **.976** ± .011	≀ .916 ± .038
BEER_TREEPEL	.981 ± .008	.971 ± .010	.952 ± .012	.992 ± .002	**.981** ± .008	.975 ± .008	.962 ± .014	.861 ± .051
DPMF	**.997** ± .003	.951 ± .011	.960 ± .010	.984 ± .003	.973 ± .008	.973 ± .007	≀ .965 ± .012	≀ .893 ± .035
UPF-COBALT	.987 ± .006	.962 ± .010	**.981** ± .007	**.993** ± .002	.929 ± .014	.971 ± .008	≀ .970 ± .012	.888 ± .040
METEOR-WSD	.982 ± .007	.950 ± .012	.953 ± .011	.983 ± .003	.976 ± .008	.969 ± .008	.960 ± .014	.832 ± .051
BEER	.979 ± .008	.965 ± .010	.946 ± .012	.983 ± .003	.971 ± .009	.969 ± .009	.958 ± .015	≀ .838 ± .049
VERTA-70ADEQ30FLU	.982 ± .007	.949 ± .012	.934 ± .014	**.993** ± .002	.972 ± .010	.966 ± .009	.952 ± .015	≀ .883 ± .038
VERTA-W	.977 ± .008	.955 ± .011	.928 ± .015	.988 ± .003	.964 ± .011	.963 ± .010	.949 ± .016	.873 ± .042
CHRF	.993 ± .005	.947 ± .012	.934 ± .014	.981 ± .004	.938 ± .013	.959 ± .009	.944 ± .016	.871 ± .037
RATATOUILLE	.986 ± .006	.902 ± .016	.958 ± .011	.961 ± .005	.955 ± .011	.952 ± .010	≀ .956 ± .014	≀ **.919** ± .039
VERTA-EQ	.983 ± .007	.921 ± .015	.906 ± .017	.990 ± .003	.953 ± .012	.950 ± .011	.934 ± .017	.857 ± .041
DREEM	.950 ± .012	**.977** ± .008	.889 ± .018	.986 ± .003	.929 ± .015	.946 ± .011	.927 ± .018	.825 ± .053
CDER	.983 ± .007	.966 ± .009	.890 ± .018	.960 ± .005	.920 ± .016	.944 ± .011	.923 ± .018	.814 ± .046
CHRF3	.979 ± .008	.903 ± .016	.956 ± .011	.968 ± .004	.898 ± .016	.941 ± .011	≀ .944 ± .016	≀ .818 ± .047
NIST	.980 ± .008	.894 ± .016	.901 ± .017	.973 ± .004	.910 ± .017	.932 ± .013	.906 ± .020	≀ .828 ± .055
LEBLEU-DEFAULT	.955 ± .012	.900 ± .016	.916 ± .016	.947 ± .006	.908 ± .015	.925 ± .013	≀ .926 ± .019	.814 ± .049
LEBLEU-OPTIMIZED	.984 ± .007	.900 ± .016	.916 ± .016	.976 ± .004	.842 ± .020	.923 ± .013	≀ .928 ± .018	≀ .855 ± .042
BS	.986 ± .007	.925 ± .014	.872 ± .019	.976 ± .004	.847 ± .021	.921 ± .013	.891 ± .021	.793 ± .045
PER	.978 ± .008	.871 ± .019	.846 ± .021	.963 ± .005	.931 ± .015	.918 ± .014	≀ .898 ± .021	≀ .811 ± .050
BLEU	.975 ± .009	.929 ± .014	.865 ± .020	.957 ± .006	.851 ± .022	.915 ± .014	.889 ± .021	.796 ± .052
TER	.979 ± .008	.872 ± .019	.890 ± .018	.907 ± .008	.907 ± .017	.911 ± .014	.884 ± .022	.768 ± .054
WER	.977 ± .009	.853 ± .020	.884 ± .018	.888 ± .008	.895 ± .018	.899 ± .015	.871 ± .023	.747 ± .057
USAAR-ZWICKEL-METEOR-MEDIAN	n/a	.936 ± .013	.961 ± .010	.976 ± .004	.965 ± .010	.959 ± .009	.955 ± .014	.871 ± .034
USAAR-ZWICKEL-METEOR-HARMONIC	n/a	.509 ± .032	.565 ± .030	.690 ± .013	.309 ± .034	.518 ± .027	.545 ± .041	.768 ± .033
USAAR-ZWICKEL-COSINE2METEOR-MEDIAN	n/a	−.220 ± .037	−.098 ± .037	.500 ± .015	.042 ± .035	.056 ± .031	.086 ± .046	−.038 ± .071
USAAR-ZWICKEL-METEOR-MEAN	n/a	.952 ± .011	.957 ± .011	.985 ± .003	.976 ± .008	.968 ± .008	.957 ± .014	.854 ± .034
USAAR-ZWICKEL-METEOR-ARIGEO	n/a	.952 ± .011	.957 ± .011	.985 ± .003	.976 ± .008	.968 ± .008	.957 ± .014	.854 ± .034
USAAR-ZWICKEL-METEOR-RMS	n/a	.958 ± .011	.944 ± .013	.988 ± .003	.974 ± .009	.966 ± .009	.947 ± .015	.861 ± .032
USAAR-ZWICKEL-COMET-RMS	n/a	.873 ± .019	.898 ± .016	.877 ± .009	.846 ± .019	.874 ± .016	.842 ± .025	.705 ± .050
USAAR-ZWICKEL-COMET-ARIGEO	n/a	.836 ± .021	.844 ± .020	.844 ± .010	.825 ± .021	.837 ± .018	.819 ± .028	.718 ± .049
USAAR-ZWICKEL-COSINE2METEOR-RMS	n/a	−.088 ± .038	−.302 ± .035	.390 ± .016	.379 ± .035	.095 ± .031	.087 ± .045	.038 ± .076
USAAR-ZWICKEL-COSINE-MEDIAN	n/a	−.414 ± .035	−.514 ± .033	.816 ± .010	.440 ± .035	.082 ± .028	.047 ± .041	−.020 ± .070
USAAR-ZWICKEL-COMET-MEAN	n/a	.836 ± .021	.844 ± .020	.844 ± .010	.825 ± .021	.837 ± .018	.819 ± .028	.718 ± .049
USAAR-ZWICKEL-COMET-HARMONIC	n/a	.445 ± .034	.525 ± .031	.602 ± .015	.307 ± .034	.470 ± .028	.487 ± .043	.561 ± .053
USAAR-ZWICKEL-COMET-MEDIAN	n/a	−.108 ± .038	.135 ± .036	.638 ± .013	.167 ± .035	.208 ± .030	.235 ± .046	.146 ± .069
USAAR-ZWICKEL-COSINE2METEOR-MEAN	n/a	−.119 ± .037	−.389 ± .034	.441 ± .016	.371 ± .035	.076 ± .031	.087 ± .045	.038 ± .076
USAAR-ZWICKEL-COSINE2METEOR-ARIGEO	n/a	−.119 ± .037	−.389 ± .034	.441 ± .016	.371 ± .035	.076 ± .031	.087 ± .045	.038 ± .076
USAAR-ZWICKEL-COSINE2METEOR-HARMONIC	n/a	−.341 ± .035	−.178 ± .038	−.050 ± .017	.253 ± .034	−.079 ± .031	−.083 ± .046	.025 ± .073
USAAR-ZWICKEL-COSINE-MEAN	n/a	nan	.002 ± .038	.906 ± .007	nan	nan	nan	.133 ± .052
USAAR-ZWICKEL-COSINE-HARMONIC	n/a	nan	−.124 ± .038	.897 ± .007	nan	nan	nan	.038 ± .048
USAAR-ZWICKEL-COSINE-RMS	n/a	nan	.064 ± .038	.910 ± .007	nan	nan	nan	.146 ± .052

Table 2: System-level correlations of automatic evaluation metrics and the official WMT human scores when translating into English. The symbol "≀" indicates where the average is out of sequence compared to the main Pearson average.

*** Formatting Issue - Best Available Paper/Graphic ***

*** Formatting Issue - Best Available Paper/Graphic ***

Correlation coefficient Direction Considered Systems	en-fr 7	en-fi 10	en-de 16	en-cs 15	en-ru 10	Average	Pre-TrueSkill Average	Spearman's Average
	Pearson Correlation Coefficient							
CHRF3	.932 ± .018	**.878** ± .017	.848 ± .020	**.977** ± .003	.946 ± .008	**.916** ± .013	.899 ± .021	.835 ± .032
BEER	.961 ± .014	.808 ± .021	**.879** ± .018	.962 ± .003	**.970** ± .006	**.916** ± .012	≀ **.907** ± .018	≀ .891 ± .036
LEBLEU-DEFAULT	.933 ± .018	.835 ± .020	.850 ± .019	.953 ± .004	.896 ± .011	.893 ± .014	.875 ± .021	.846 ± .042
LEBLEU-OPTIMIZED	.933 ± .018	.803 ± .022	.868 ± .019	.952 ± .004	.908 ± .010	.893 ± .014	≀ .882 ± .021	.845 ± .043
RATATOUILLE	.957 ± .015	.763 ± .025	.862 ± .019	.965 ± .003	.913 ± .010	.892 ± .014	.868 ± .021	≀ **.915** ± .029
CHRF	.930 ± .018	.841 ± .021	.690 ± .027	.971 ± .003	.915 ± .010	.869 ± .016	.846 ± .023	.837 ± .027
METEOR-WSD	.959 ± .014	.760 ± .024	.650 ± .029	.953 ± .004	.892 ± .011	.843 ± .017	.816 ± .024	.837 ± .036
CDER	.953 ± .015	.640 ± .029	.660 ± .028	.929 ± .004	.863 ± .012	.809 ± .018	.777 ± .025	.704 ± .051
NIST	.949 ± .015	.692 ± .028	.502 ± .032	.958 ± .003	.893 ± .003	.799 ± .018	.771 ± .026	≀ .769 ± .047
TER	.948 ± .015	.614 ± .032	.564 ± .031	.917 ± .005	.883 ± .011	.785 ± .019	.755 ± .026	.724 ± .050
WER	.941 ± .016	.608 ± .032	.568 ± .030	.910 ± .005	.884 ± .011	.782 ± .019	.752 ± .027	.702 ± .051
BLEU	.948 ± .016	.602 ± .030	.573 ± .030	.936 ± .004	.841 ± .013	.780 ± .019	.751 ± .027	.691 ± .052
PER	.949 ± .016	.603 ± .031	.316 ± .035	.908 ± .004	.858 ± .013	.727 ± .020	.696 ± .028	.609 ± .030
BS	**.964** ± .013	−.336 ± .035	.714 ± .026	.953 ± .004	.852 ± .013	.629 ± .018	.625 ± .025	≀ .686 ± .049
DREEM	.871 ± .023	.385 ± .032	−.074 ± .039	.883 ± .006	.968 ± .006	.607 ± .021	.608 ± .031	.682 ± .039
DPMF	**.964** ± .014	n/a	.724 ± .026	n/a	n/a	.844 ± .020	.827 ± .027	.823 ± .048
USAAR-ZWICKEL-METEOR-MEDIAN	n/a	n/a	.741 ± .025	n/a	n/a	.741 ± .025	.685 ± .038	.750 ± .046
USAAR-ZWICKEL-METEOR-MEAN	n/a	n/a	.635 ± .029	n/a	n/a	.635 ± .029	.581 ± .041	.615 ± .041
USAAR-ZWICKEL-METEOR-RMS	n/a	n/a	.542 ± .033	n/a	n/a	.542 ± .033	.494 ± .044	.541 ± .041
USAAR-ZWICKEL-COMET-HARMONIC	n/a	n/a	.396 ± .033	n/a	n/a	.396 ± .033	.386 ± .045	.309 ± .057
USAAR-ZWICKEL-METEOR-HARMONIC	n/a	n/a	.357 ± .032	n/a	n/a	.357 ± .032	.330 ± .048	≀ .550 ± .053
USAAR-ZWICKEL-COSINE-MEDIAN	n/a	n/a	.310 ± .036	n/a	n/a	.310 ± .036	.330 ± .048	.291 ± .071
USAAR-ZWICKEL-COMET-ARIGEO	n/a	n/a	.310 ± .037	n/a	n/a	.310 ± .037	.304 ± .048	≀ .671 ± .050
USAAR-ZWICKEL-COSINE2METEOR-MEDIAN	n/a	n/a	.044 ± .037	n/a	n/a	.044 ± .037	.031 ± .051	−.047 ± .066
USAAR-ZWICKEL-COSINE2METEOR-HARMONIC	n/a	n/a	−.004 ± .038	n/a	n/a	−.004 ± .038	.059 ± .050	≀ .009 ± .044
USAAR-ZWICKEL-COMET-MEDIAN	n/a	n/a	−.048 ± .038	n/a	n/a	−.048 ± .038	−.061 ± .050	≀ .032 ± .057
USAAR-ZWICKEL-COMET-RMS	n/a	n/a	−.117 ± .039	n/a	n/a	−.117 ± .039	−.127 ± .050	≀ .415 ± .054
USAAR-ZWICKEL-COMET-MEAN	n/a	n/a	−.126 ± .039	n/a	n/a	−.126 ± .039	−.135 ± .051	.412 ± .050
USAAR-ZWICKEL-COSINE2METEOR-ARIGEO	n/a	n/a	−.155 ± .036	n/a	n/a	−.155 ± .036	−.156 ± .050	−.168 ± .065
USAAR-ZWICKEL-COSINE2METEOR-MEAN	n/a	n/a	−.155 ± .036	n/a	n/a	−.155 ± .036	−.156 ± .050	−.168 ± .065
USAAR-ZWICKEL-COSINE2METEOR-RMS	n/a	n/a	−.197 ± .035	n/a	n/a	−.197 ± .035	−.188 ± .050	≀ −.188 ± .063
USAAR-ZWICKEL-METEOR-ARIGEO	n/a	n/a	−.419 ± .034	n/a	n/a	−.419 ± .034	−.336 ± .050	−.162 ± .071

Table 3: System-level correlations of automatic evaluation metrics and the official WMT human scores when translating out of English. The symbol "≀" indicates where the average is out of sequence compared to the main Pearson average.

4 Segment-Level Results

We measure the quality of metrics' segment-level scores using Kendall's τ rank correlation coefficient. In this type of evaluation, a metric is expected to predict the result of the manual pairwise comparison of two systems. Note that the golden truth is obtained from a compact annotation of five systems at once, while an experiment with text-to-speech evaluation techniques by Vazquez-Alvarez and Huckvale (2002) suggest that a genuine pairwise comparison is likely to lead to more stable results.

The basic formula for Kendall's τ is:

$$\tau = \frac{|Concordant| - |Discordant|}{|Concordant| + |Discordant|} \quad (2)$$

where $Concordant$ is the set of all human comparisons for which a given metric suggests the same order and $Discordant$ is the set of all human comparisons for which a given metric disagrees. The formula is not specific with respect to ties, i.e. cases where the annotation says that the two outputs are equally good.

The way in which ties (both in human and metric judgment) were incorporated in computing Kendall τ changed each year of WMT metric tasks. Here we adopt the version from WMT14. For a detailed discussion on other options, see Macháček and Bojar (2014).

The method is formally described using the following matrix:

		Metric		
		$<$	$=$	$>$
Human	$<$	1	0	-1
	$=$	X	X	X
	$>$	-1	0	1

Given such a matrix $C_{h,m}$ where $h, m \in \{<, =, >\}$[4] and a metric, we compute the Kendall's τ for the metric the following way:

We insert each extracted human pairwise comparison into exactly one of the nine sets $S_{h,m}$ according to human and metric ranks. For example the set $S_{<,>}$ contains all comparisons where the left-hand system was ranked better than right-hand system by humans and it was ranked the other way round by the metric in question.

To compute the numerator of Kendall's τ, we take the coefficients from the matrix $C_{h,m}$, use them to multiply the sizes of the corresponding sets $S_{h,m}$ and then sum them up. We do not include sets for which the value of $C_{h,m}$ is X. To compute the denominator of Kendall's τ, we simply sum the sizes of all the sets $S_{h,m}$ except those where $C_{h,m} = \text{X}$. To define it formally:

$$\tau = \frac{\sum\limits_{\substack{h,m \in \{<,=,>\} \\ C_{h,m} \neq \text{X}}} C_{h,m} |S_{h,m}|}{\sum\limits_{\substack{h,m \in \{<,=,>\} \\ C_{h,m} \neq \text{X}}} |S_{h,m}|} \quad (3)$$

To summarize, the WMT14 matrix specifies to:

- exclude all human ties,
- count metric's ties only for the denominator of Kendall τ (thus giving no credit for giving a tie),
- all cases of disagreement between human and metric judgements are counted as $Discordant$,
- all cases of agreement between human and metric judgements are counted as $Concordant$.

You can find the system-level correlations for translations into English in Table 4 and for translations out of English in Table 5. Again, the upper part of each table contains metrics participating in all language pairs and it is sorted by average τ across translation directions. The lower part contains metrics limited to a subset of the language pairs, so the average cannot be directly compared with other metrics any more.

4.1 Segment-Level Discussion

As usual, segment-level correlations are significantly lower than system-level ones. The highest correlation is reached by DPMFcomb on Czech-to-English: .495 of Kendall's τ. The correlations reach on average .447 into English and .400 out of English.

DPMFcomb is the clear winner into English, followed by BEER_Treepel, both of which consider syntactic structure of the sentence, combined with several other independent features or metrics.

RATATOUILLE, also a combined metric, is the best option for evaluation to and from French.

Metrics considering character-level n-grams (BEER and chrF3) are particularly good for

[4] Here the relation $<$ always means "is better than" even for metrics where the better system receives a higher score.

*** Formatting Issue - Best Available Paper/Graphic ***

Direction Extracted-pairs	fr-en 29770	fi-en 31577	de-en 40535	cs-en 85877	ru-en 44539	Average
DPMFCOMB	.395 ± .012	**.445** ± .012	**.482** ± .009	**.495** ± .007	**.418** ± .013	**.447** ± .011
BEER_TREEPEL	.389 ± .014	.438 ± .010	.447 ± .008	.471 ± .007	.403 ± .014	.429 ± .011
RATATOUILLE	**.398** ± .010	.421 ± .011	.441 ± .010	.472 ± .007	.393 ± .013	.425 ± .010
UPF-COBALT	.386 ± .012	.437 ± .013	.427 ± .011	.457 ± .007	.402 ± .013	.422 ± .011
BEER	.393 ± .012	.422 ± .012	.438 ± .010	.457 ± .008	.396 ± .014	.421 ± .011
CHRF	.383 ± .011	.417 ± .012	.424 ± .010	.446 ± .008	.384 ± .014	.411 ± .011
CHRF3	.383 ± .013	.397 ± .011	.421 ± .010	.449 ± .008	.386 ± .013	.407 ± .011
METEOR-WSD	.375 ± .012	.406 ± .010	.420 ± .011	.438 ± .008	.387 ± .012	.405 ± .010
DPMF	.368 ± .012	.411 ± .011	.418 ± .011	.436 ± .008	.378 ± .011	.402 ± .011
LEBLEU-OPTIMIZED	.376 ± .013	.391 ± .010	.399 ± .010	.438 ± .008	.374 ± .012	.396 ± .011
LEBLEU-DEFAULT	.373 ± .013	.383 ± .011	.402 ± .009	.436 ± .007	.376 ± .011	.394 ± .010
VERTA-EQ	.388 ± .012	.369 ± .013	.410 ± .011	.447 ± .007	.346 ± .013	.392 ± .011
VERTA-70ADEQ30FLU	.374 ± .012	.365 ± .014	.418 ± .011	.438 ± .007	.344 ± .013	.388 ± .011
VERTA-W	.383 ± .010	.344 ± .014	.416 ± .010	.445 ± .007	.345 ± .013	.387 ± .011
DREEM	.362 ± .012	.340 ± .010	.368 ± .011	.423 ± .007	.348 ± .013	.368 ± .011
UOW-LSTM	.332 ± .011	.376 ± .012	.375 ± .011	.385 ± .008	.356 ± .010	.365 ± .011
SENTBLEU	.358 ± .013	.308 ± .012	.360 ± .011	.391 ± .006	.329 ± .011	.349 ± .011
TOTAL-BS	.332 ± .013	.319 ± .013	.333 ± .010	.381 ± .007	.321 ± .011	.337 ± .011
USAAR-ZWICKEL-METEOR	n/a	.406 ± .011	.422 ± .011	.439 ± .008	.386 ± .012	.413 ± .011
USAAR-ZWICKEL-COMET	n/a	.021 ± .013	.050 ± .010	.072 ± .009	.084 ± .010	.057 ± .011
USAAR-ZWICKEL-COSINE2METEOR	n/a	.001 ± .013	−.011 ± .010	.020 ± .009	.041 ± .010	.013 ± .011
USAAR-ZWICKEL-COSINE	n/a	−.035 ± .013	−.019 ± .010	.090 ± .008	.014 ± .013	.012 ± .011

Table 4: Segment-level Kendall's τ correlations of automatic evaluation metrics and the official WMT human judgements when translating into English.

Direction Extracted-pairs	en-fr 34512	en-fi 32694	en-de 54447	en-cs 136890	en-ru 49302	Average
BEER	.352 ± .010	**.380** ± .010	.393 ± .010	.435 ± .006	**.439** ± .010	**.400** ± .009
CHRF3	.335 ± .013	.373 ± .012	.398 ± .008	**.446** ± .005	.420 ± .010	.395 ± .010
RATATOUILLE	**.366** ± .013	.318 ± .011	.381 ± .008	.429 ± .006	.436 ± .010	.386 ± .010
LEBLEU-OPTIMIZED	.347 ± .009	.368 ± .010	**.399** ± .008	.410 ± .006	.404 ± .011	.386 ± .009
CHRF	.342 ± .012	.359 ± .010	.372 ± .010	.444 ± .005	.410 ± .011	.385 ± .010
LEBLEU-DEFAULT	.345 ± .010	.368 ± .010	.398 ± .009	.406 ± .006	.404 ± .012	.384 ± .009
METEOR-WSD	.342 ± .012	.286 ± .010	.344 ± .007	.390 ± .006	.399 ± .010	.352 ± .009
DREEM	.338 ± .012	.280 ± .011	.317 ± .010	.395 ± .006	.366 ± .010	.339 ± .010
SENTBLEU	.318 ± .011	.227 ± .011	.294 ± .009	.360 ± .005	.347 ± .010	.309 ± .009
TOTAL-BS	.297 ± .011	.223 ± .009	.278 ± .009	.345 ± .005	.356 ± .011	.300 ± .009
DPMF	.335 ± .012	n/a	.350 ± .009	n/a	n/a	.343 ± .010
USAAR-ZWICKEL-METEOR	n/a	n/a	.342 ± .008	n/a	n/a	.342 ± .008
USAAR-ZWICKEL-COMET	n/a	n/a	.056 ± .019	n/a	n/a	.056 ± .009
USAAR-ZWICKEL-COSINE	n/a	n/a	−.007 ± .010	n/a	n/a	−.007 ± .010
USAAR-ZWICKEL-COSINE2METEOR	n/a	n/a	−.027 ± .019	n/a	n/a	−.027 ± .009

Table 5: Segment-level Kendall's τ correlations of automatic evaluation metrics and the official WMT human judgements when translating out of English.

*** Formatting Issue - Best Available Paper/Graphic ***

		2014	2015	Delta
BEER	Average en→*	.319±.011	.401±.009	0.082
	en-cs	.344±.009	.435±.006	0.091
	en-de	.268±.009	.396±.008	0.128
	en-fr	.292±.012	.352±.010	0.060
	en-ru	.440±.013	.440±.012	0.000
	Average *→en	.362±.013	.423±.010	0.061
	cs-en	.284±.016	.457±.008	0.173
	de-en	.337±.014	.438±.010	0.101
	fr-en	.417±.013	.393±.012	-0.024
	ru-en	.333±.011	.406±.009	0.073
SENTBLEU	Average en→*	.269±.011	.310±.009	0.041
	en-cs	.290±.009	.360±.005	0.070
	en-de	.191±.009	.296±.010	0.105
	en-fr	.256±.012	.318±.011	0.062
	en-ru	.381±.013	.347±.010	-0.034
	Average *→en	.285±.013	.351±.011	0.066
	cs-en	.213±.016	.391±.006	0.178
	de-en	.271±.014	.360±.011	0.089
	fr-en	.378±.013	.358±.013	-0.020
	ru-en	.263±.011	.340±.012	0.077
Average				0.07±0.06

Table 6: Kendall's τ scores for two metrics across years.

evaluation out of English and their margin seems to the highest for English-to-Finnish, up to .06 points.

Only two segment-level metrics took part in 2014 and 2015, BEER in a slightly improved implementation (with some small effect on the scores) and SENTBLEU in exactly the same implementation. Table 6 documents that this year, the scores are on average slightly higher. The main reason lies probably in the test set, which may be somewhat easier this year. French is different, the correlations decreased somewhat this year, which can be easily explained by the domain change: news in 2014 and discussions in 2015. The increase should not be caused by the redundancy cleanup of WMT manual rankings, see Bojar et al. (2015), since the collapsed systems get a tie after expanding and our implementation ignores all tied manual comparisons.

5 Conclusion

In this paper, we summarized the results of the WMT15 Metrics Shared Task, which assesses the quality of various automatic machine translation metrics. As in previous years, human judgements collected in WMT15 serve as the golden truth and we check how well the metrics predict the judgements at the level of individual sentences as well as at the level of the whole test set (system-level).

Across the two types of evaluation and the 10 language pairs, we saw great performance of trained and combined metrics (DPMFCOMB, BEER, RATATOUILLE and others). Neural networks for continuous word and sentence representations have also shown their generalization power, with an interesting discrepancy in system- vs. segment-level performance of UOW-LSTM and to a smaller degree of DREEM.

We value high the metric CHRF or CHRF3 for its extreme simplicity and very good performance at both system and segment level and especially out of English. We are curious to see if CHRF3 has the potential of becoming "the BLEU for the next five years". It would be very interesting to test its usability in system tuning. It is known that in tuning, metrics putting too much attention to recall can be easily tricked, but perhaps a careful setting of CHRF's β will be sufficient.

The WMT Metrics Task again attracted a good number of participants and the majority of submitted metrics are actually new ones. This is good news, indicating that MT metrics are an active field of research. Most, if not all metrics come with the source code, so it should be relatively easy to use them in own experiments. Still, we would expect much wider adoption of the metrics, if they made it for example to the standard Moses scorer or at least to the Asyia toolkit.

Acknowledgments

This project has received funding from the European Union's Horizon 2020 research and innovation programme under grant agreements n° 645452 (QT21) and n° 644402 (HimL). The work on this project was also supported by the Dutch organisation for scientific research STW grant nr. 12271.

References

Ondřej Bojar, Miloš Ercegovčević, Martin Popel, and Omar Zaidan. 2011. A Grain of Salt for the WMT Manual Evaluation. In *Proceedings of the Sixth Workshop on Statistical Machine Translation*, pages 1–11, Edinburgh, Scotland, July. Association for Computational Linguistics.

Ondřej Bojar, Matouš Macháček, Aleš Tamchyna, and Daniel Zeman. 2013. Scratching the Surface of Possible Translations. In *Proc. of TSD 2013*, Lecture Notes in Artificial Intelligence, Berlin / Heidelberg. Západočeská univerzita v Plzni, Springer Verlag.

Ondřej Bojar, Rajen Chatterjee, Christian Federmann, Barry Haddow, Matthias Huck, Chris Hokamp,

*** Formatting Issue - Best Available Paper/Graphic ***

Philipp Koehn, Varvara Logacheva, Christof Monz, Matteo Negri, Matt Post, Carolina Scarton, Lucia Specia, and Marco Turchi. 2015. Findings of the 2015 Workshop on Statistical Machine Translation. In *Proceedings of the Tenth Workshop on Statistical Machine Translation*, Lisboa, Portugal, September. Association for Computational Linguistics.

Boxing Chen, Hongyu Guo, and Roland Kuhn. 2015. Multi-level Evaluation for Machine Translation. In *Proceedings of the Tenth Workshop on Statistical Machine Translation*, Lisboa, Portugal, September. Association for Computational Linguistics.

Elisabet Comelles and Jordi Atserias. 2015. VERTa: a Linguistically-motivated Metric at the WMT15 Metrics Task. In *Proceedings of the Tenth Workshop on Statistical Machine Translation*, Lisboa, Portugal, September. Association for Computational Linguistics.

George Doddington. 2002. Automatic evaluation of machine translation quality using n-gram co-occurrence statistics. In *Proceedings of the Second International Conference on Human Language Technology Research*, HLT '02, pages 138–145, San Francisco, CA, USA. Morgan Kaufmann Publishers Inc.

Marina Fomicheva, Núria Bel, Iria da Cunha, and Anton Malinovskiy. 2015. UPF-Cobalt Submission to WMT15 Metrics Task. In *Proceedings of the Tenth Workshop on Statistical Machine Translation*, Lisboa, Portugal, September. Association for Computational Linguistics.

Rohit Gupta, Constantin Orasan, and Josef van Genabith. 2015a. Machine Translation Evaluation using Recurrent Neural Networks. In *Proceedings of the Tenth Workshop on Statistical Machine Translation*, Lisboa, Portugal, September. Association for Computational Linguistics.

Rohit Gupta, Constantin Orasan, and Josef van Genabith. 2015b. ReVal: A Simple and Effective Machine Translation Evaluation Metric Based on Recurrent Neural Networks. In *Proceedings of the Conference on Empirical Methods in Natural Language Processing*, EMNLP '15, Lisbon, Portugal.

Philipp Koehn and Christof Monz. 2006. Manual and automatic evaluation of machine translation between european languages. In *Proceedings of the Workshop on Statistical Machine Translation*, StatMT '06, pages 102–121, Stroudsburg, PA, USA. Association for Computational Linguistics.

Gregor Leusch, Nicola Ueffing, and Hermann Ney. 2006. Cder: Efficient mt evaluation using block movements. In *In Proceedings of EACL*, pages 241–248.

Matouš Macháček and Ondřej Bojar. 2013. Results of the WMT13 Metrics Shared Task. In *Proceedings of the Eighth Workshop on Statistical Machine Translation*, pages 45–51, Sofia, Bulgaria, August. Association for Computational Linguistics.

Matouš Macháček and Ondřej Bojar. 2014. Results of the WMT14 Metrics Shared Task. In *Proceedings of the Ninth Workshop on Statistical Machine Translation*, pages 293–301, Baltimore, Maryland, USA, June. Association for Computational Linguistics.

Benjamin Marie and Marianna Apidianaki. 2015. Alignment-based sense selection in METEOR and the RATATOUILLE recipe. In *Proceedings of the Tenth Workshop on Statistical Machine Translation*, Lisboa, Portugal, September. Association for Computational Linguistics.

Kishore Papineni, Salim Roukos, Todd Ward, and Wei-Jing Zhu. 2002. Bleu: A method for automatic evaluation of machine translation. In *Proceedings of the 40th Annual Meeting on Association for Computational Linguistics*, ACL '02, pages 311–318, Stroudsburg, PA, USA. Association for Computational Linguistics.

Maja Popović. 2015. chrF: character n-gram F-score for automatic MT evaluation. In *Proceedings of the Tenth Workshop on Statistical Machine Translation*, Lisboa, Portugal, September. Association for Computational Linguistics.

Raphael Rubino, Tommi Pirinen, Miquel Esplà-Gomis, Nikola Ljubešić, Sergio Ortiz Rojas, Vassilis Papavassiliou, Prokopis Prokopidis, and Antonio Toral. 2015. Abu-MaTran at WMT 2015 Translation Task: Morphological Segmentation and Web Crawling. In *Proceedings of the Tenth Workshop on Statistical Machine Translation*, Lisboa, Portugal, September. Association for Computational Linguistics.

Matthew Snover, Bonnie Dorr, Richard Schwartz, Linnea Micciulla, and John Makhoul. 2006. A study of translation edit rate with targeted human annotation. In *In Proceedings of Association for Machine Translation in the Americas*, pages 223–231.

Miloš Stanojević and Khalil Sima'an. 2015. BEER 1.1: ILLC UvA submission to metrics and tuning task. In *Proceedings of the Tenth Workshop on Statistical Machine Translation*, Lisboa, Portugal, September. Association for Computational Linguistics.

Miloš Stanojević, Amir Kamran, and Ondřej Bojar. 2015. Results of the WMT15 Tuning Shared Task. In *Proceedings of the Tenth Workshop on Statistical Machine Translation*, Lisboa, Portugal, September. Association for Computational Linguistics.

Yolanda Vazquez-Alvarez and Mark Huckvale. 2002. The reliability of the ITU-t p.85 standard for the evaluation of text-to-speech systems. In *Proc. of ICSLP - INTERSPEECH*.

*** Formatting Issue - Best Available Paper/Graphic ***

Mihaela Vela and Liling Tan. 2015. Predicting Machine Translation Adequacy with Document Embeddings. In *Proceedings of the Tenth Workshop on Statistical Machine Translation*, Lisboa, Portugal, September. Association for Computational Linguistics.

Sami Virpioja and Stig-Arne Grönroos. 2015. LeBLEU: N-gram-based Translation Evaluation Score for Morphologically Complex Languages. In *Proceedings of the Tenth Workshop on Statistical Machine Translation*, Lisboa, Portugal, September. Association for Computational Linguistics.

Hui Yu, Qingsong Ma, Xiaofeng Wu, and Qun Liu. 2015. CASICT-DCU Participation in WMT2015 Metrics Task. In *Proceedings of the Tenth Workshop on Statistical Machine Translation*, Lisboa, Portugal, September. Association for Computational Linguistics.

*** Formatting Issue - Best Available Paper/Graphic ***

A System-Level Correlation Plots

The following figures plot the system-level results of BLEU (left-hand plots) and the best performing metric for the given language pair (right-hand plots) against manual score. See the discussion in Section 3.2.

Czech-English

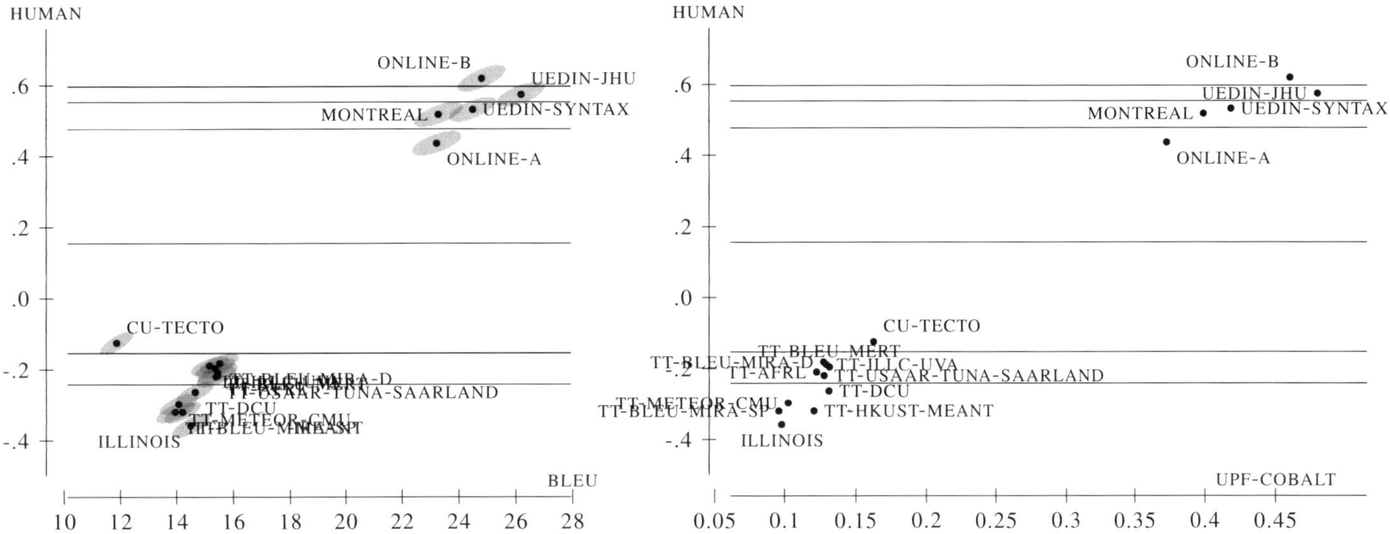

English-Czech

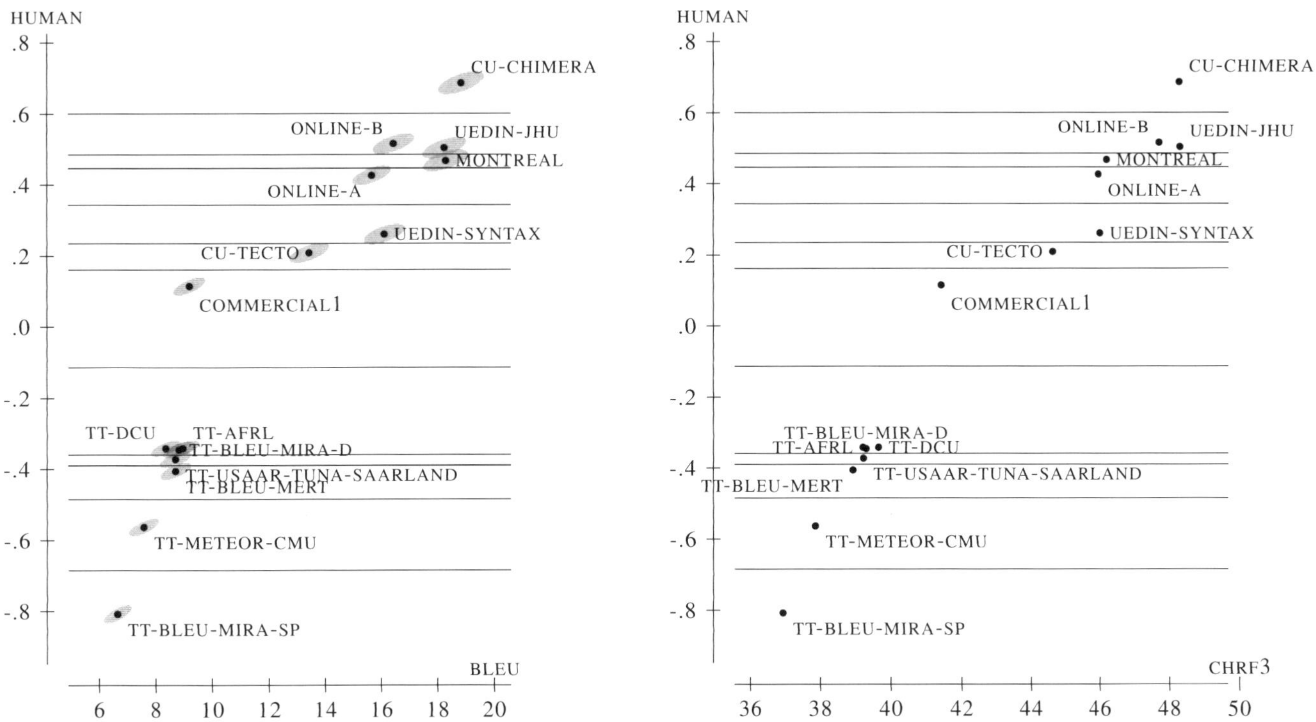

***** Formatting Issue - Best Available Paper/Graphic *****

German-English

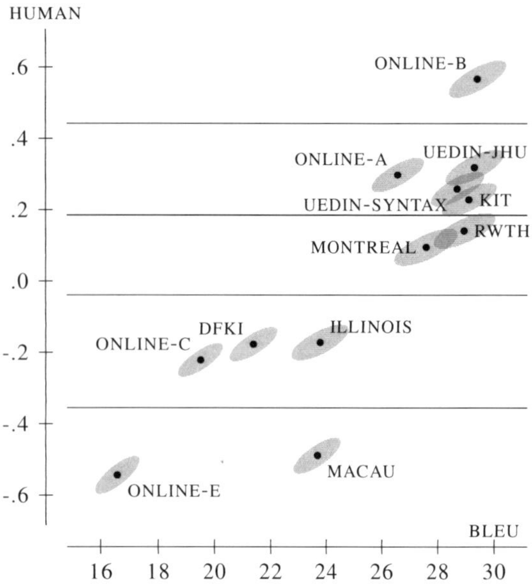

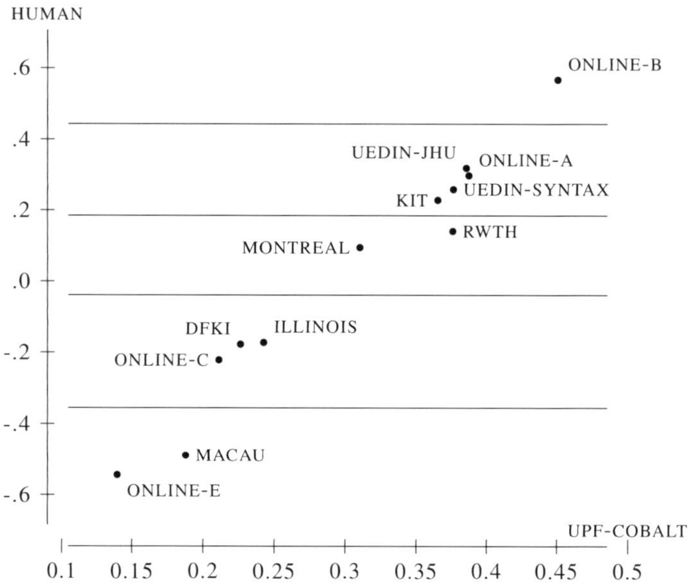

English-German

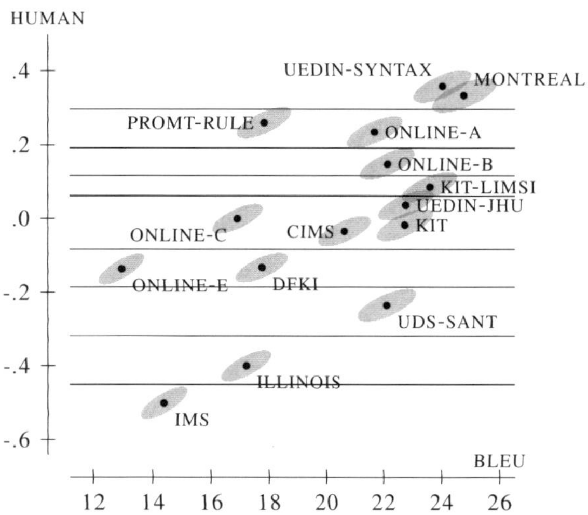

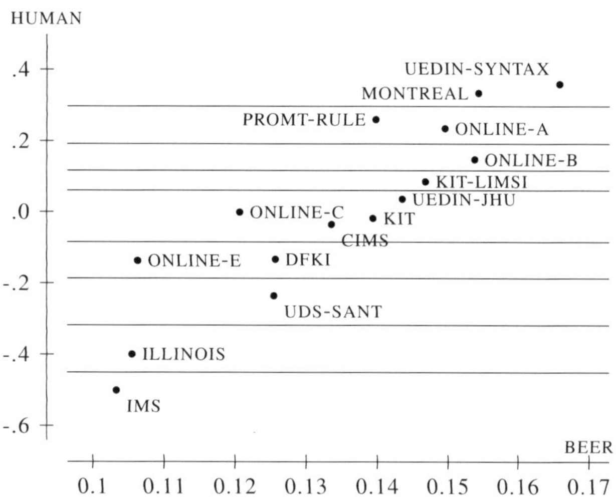

***** Formatting Issue - Best Available Paper/Graphic *****

French-English

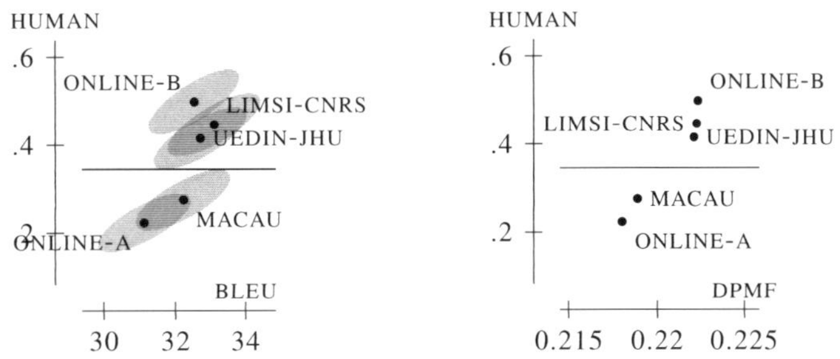

English-French

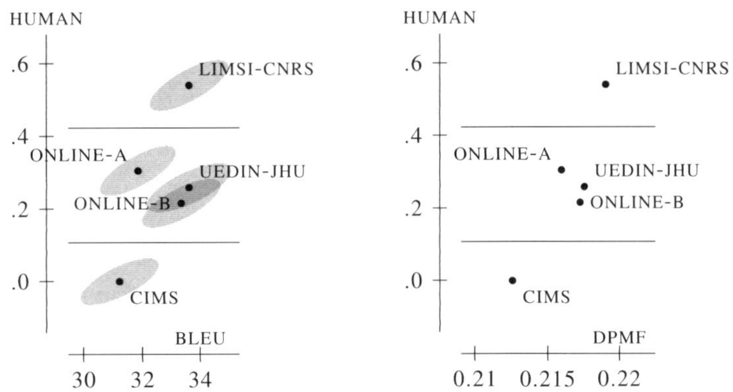

*** Formatting Issue - Best Available Paper/Graphic ***

Finnish-English

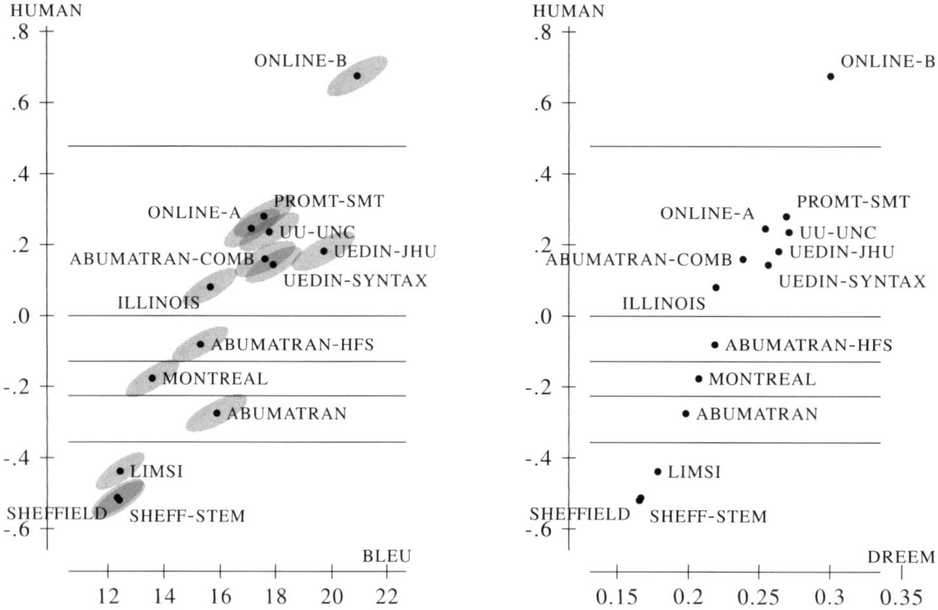

English-Finnish

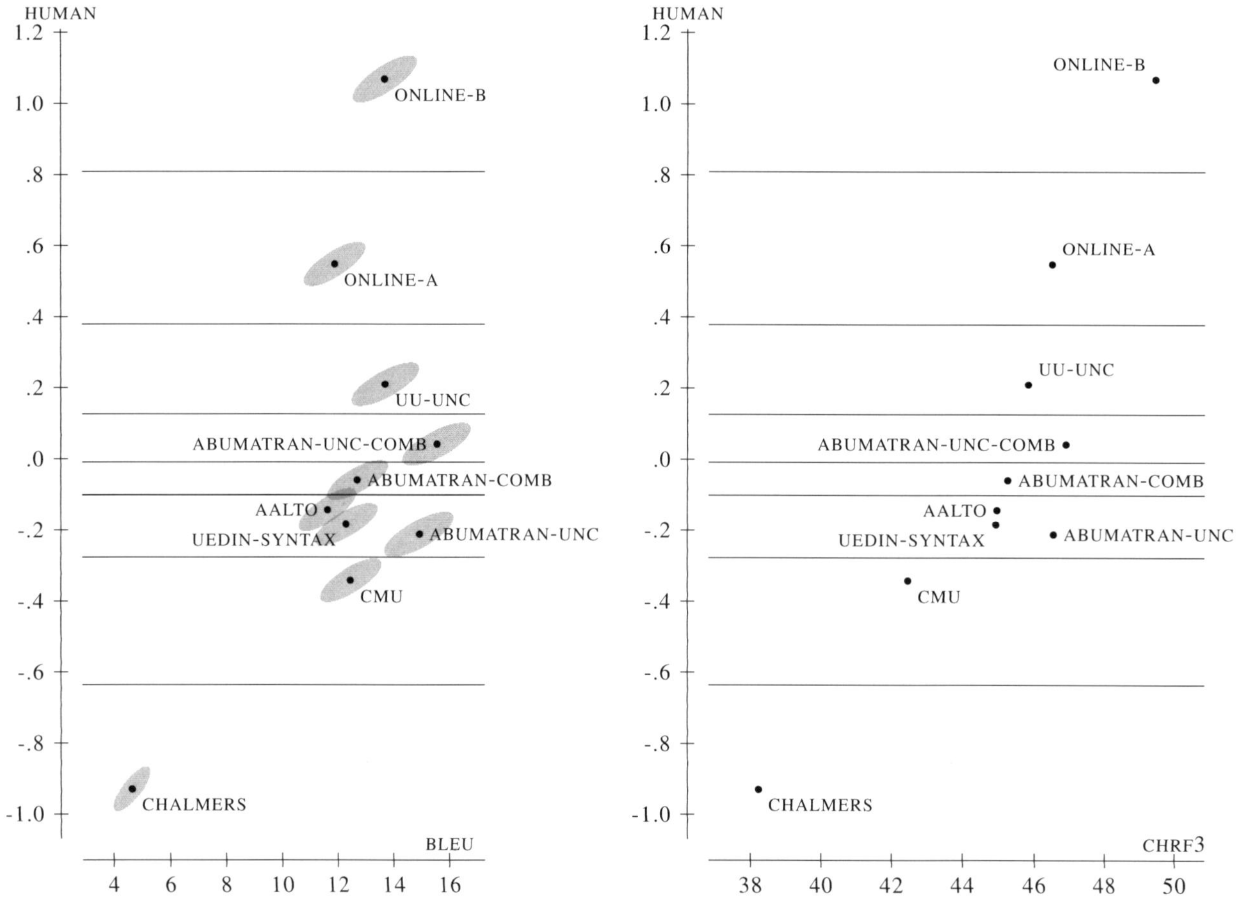

***** Formatting Issue - Best Available Paper/Graphic *****

Russian-English

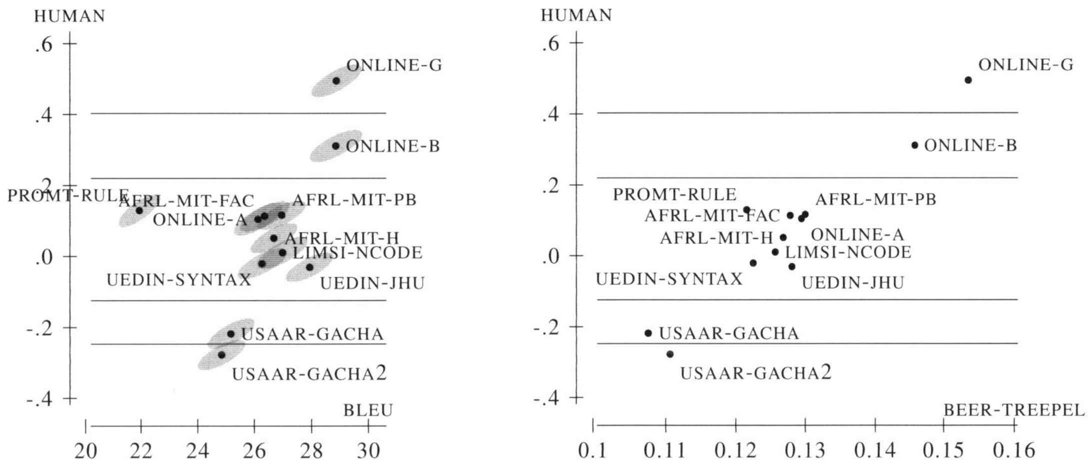

English-Russian

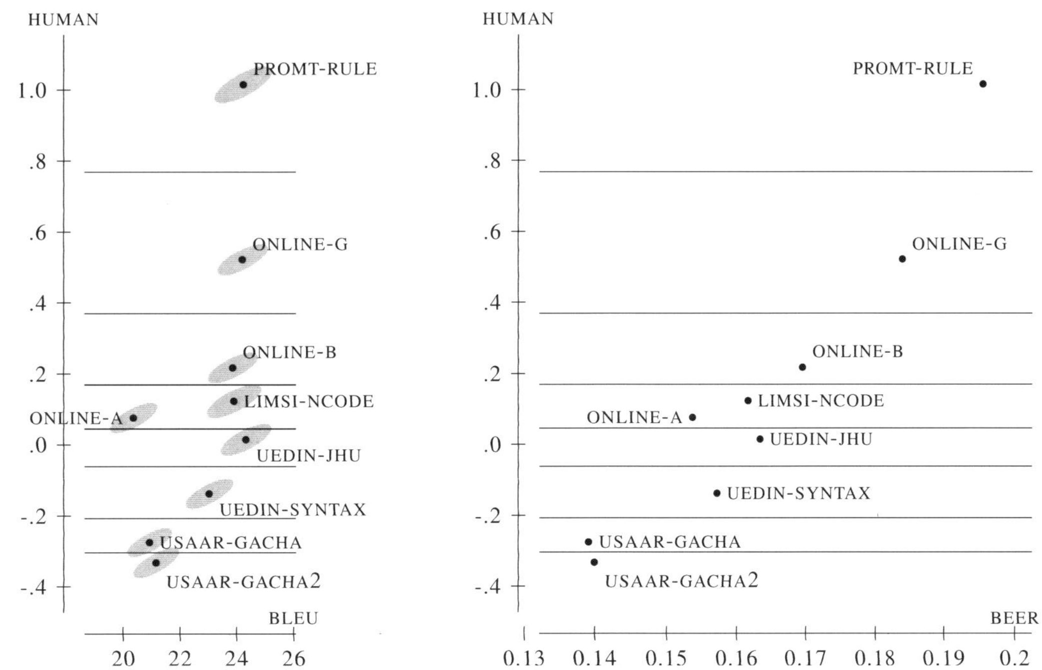

Results of the WMT15 Tuning Shared Task

Miloš Stanojević and **Amir Kamran**
University of Amsterdam
ILLC
{m.stanojevic,a.kamran}@uva.nl

Ondřej Bojar
Charles University in Prague
MFF ÚFAL
bojar@ufal.mff.cuni.cz

Abstract

This paper presents the results of the WMT15 Tuning Shared Task. We provided the participants of this task with a complete machine translation system and asked them to tune its internal parameters (feature weights). The tuned systems were used to translate the test set and the outputs were manually ranked for translation quality. We received 4 submissions in the English-Czech and 6 in the Czech-English translation direction. In addition, we ran 3 baseline setups, tuning the parameters with standard optimizers for BLEU score.

1 Introduction

Almost all modern statistical machine translation (SMT) systems internally consider translation candidates from several aspects. Some of these aspects can be very simple and one parameter is sufficient to capture them, such as the word penalty incurred for every word produced or the phrase penalty controlling whether the sentence should be translated in fewer or more independent phrases, leading to more or less word-for-word translation. Other aspects try to assess e.g. the fidelity of the translation, the fluency of the output or the amount of reordering. These are far more complex and formally captured in a model such as the translation model or language model.

Both the simple penalties as well as the scores from the more complex models are called *features* and need to be combined to a single score to allow for ranking of translation candidates. This is usually done using a linear combination of the scores:

$$\text{score}(e) = \sum_{m=1}^{M} \lambda_m h_m(e, f) \qquad (1)$$

where e and f are the candidate translation and the source, respectively, and $h_m(\cdot,\cdot)$ is one of the M penalties or models. The tuned parameters are $\lambda_m \in \mathbb{R}$, called *feature weights*.

Feature weights have a tremendous effect on the final translation quality. For instance the system can produce extremely long outputs, fabulating words just in order to satisfy a negatively-weighted word penalty, i.e. a bonus for each word produced. An inherent part of the preparation of MT systems is thus some optimization of the weight settings.

If we had to set the weights manually, we would have to try a few configurations and pick one that leads to reasonable outputs. The common practice is to use an optimization algorithm that examines many settings, evaluating the produced translations automatically against reference translations using some evaluation measure (traditionally called "metric" in the MT field). In short, the optimizer tunes model weights so that the final combined model score correlates with the metric score.

The metric score, in turn, is designed to correlate well with human judgements of translation quality, see Stanojević et al. (2015) and the previous papers summarizing WMT metrics tasks. However, a metric that correlates well with humans on final output quality may not be usable in weight optimization for various technical reasons. BLEU (Papineni et al., 2002) was shown to be very hard to surpass (Cer et al., 2010) and this is also confirmed by the results of the invitation-only WMT11 Tunable Metrics Task (Callison-Burch et al., 2010)[1]. Note however, that some metrics have been successfully used for system tuning (Liu et al., 2011; Beloucif et al., 2014).

The aim of the WMT15 Tuning Task[2] is to attract attention to the exploration of all the three

[1] http://www.statmt.org/wmt11/tunable-metrics-task.html

[2] http://www.statmt.org/wmt15/tuning-task/

	Source	Sentences cs	Sentences en	Tokens cs	Tokens en	Types cs	Types en
LM corpora	News Commentary v8	162309	247966	3.6M	6.2M	162K	81K
TM corpora	Europarl v7, CCrawl and News Comm. v9	911952		17.7M	20.8M	652K	361K
Dev set	newstest2014	3003		51K	60K	19K	13K
Test set	newstest2015	2656		39K	47K	16K	11K

Table 1: Data used in the WMT15 tuning task.

Direction	Dev Token	Dev Type	Test Token	Test Type
en-cs	2570	2032	2003	1655
cs-en	3891	3415	3381	3011

Table 2: Out of vocabulary word counts

aspects of model optimization: (1) the set of features in the model, (2) optimization algorithm, and (3) MT quality metric used in optimization.

For (1), we provide a fixed set of "dense" features and also allow participants to add additional "sparse" features. For (2), the optimization algorithm, task participants are free to use one of the available algorithms for direct loss optimization (Och, 2003; Zhao and Chen, 2009), which are usually capable of optimizing only a dozen of features, or one of the optimizers handling also very large sets of features (Cherry and Foster, 2012; Hopkins and May, 2011), or a custom algorithm. And finally for (3), participants can use any established evaluation metric or a custom one.

1.1 Tuning Task Assignment

Tuning task participants were given a complete model for the hierarchical variant of the machine translation system Moses (Hoang et al., 2009) and the development set (newstest2014), i.e. the source and reference translations. No "dev test" set was provided, since we expected that participants will internally evaluate various variants of their method by manually judging MT outputs. In fact, we offered to evaluate a certain number of translations into Czech for free to ease the participation for teams without any access to speakers of Czech; only one team used this service once.

A complete model consists of a rule table extracted from the parallel corpus, the default glue grammar and the language model extracted from the monolingual data. As such, this defines a fixed set of dense features. The participants were allowed to add any sparse features implemented in Moses Release 3.0 (corresponds to Github commit 5244a7b607) and/or to use any optimization algorithm and evaluation metric. Fully manual optimization was also not excluded but nobody seemed to take this approach.

Each submission in the tuning task consisted of the configuration of the MT system, i.e. the additional sparse features (if any) and the values of all the feature weights, λ_m.

2 Details of Systems Tuned

The systems that were distributed for tuning are based on Moses (Hoang et al., 2009) implementation of hierarchical phrase-based model (Chiang, 2005). The language models were 5-gram models with Kneser-Ney smoothing (Kneser and Ney, 1995) built using KenLM (Heafield et al., 2013). For word alignments, we used Mgiza++ (Gao and Vogel, 2008).

The parallel data used for training translation models consisted of the Europarl v7, News Commentary data (`parallel-nc-v9`) and CommonCrawl, as released for WMT14.[3] We excluded CzEng because we wanted to keep the task small and accessible to more groups.

Since the test set (newstest2015) and the development set (newstest2014) are in the news domain, we opted to exclude Europarl from the language model data. We did not add any monolingual news on top of News Commentary, which are quite close to the news domain. In retrospect, we should have added also some of the monolingual news data as released by WMT, esp. since we used a 5-gram LM.

Before any further processing, the data was tokenized (using Moses tokenizer) and lowercased. We also removed sentences longer than 60 words or shorter than 4 words. Table 1 summarizes the final dataset sizes and Table 2 provides details on out-of-vocabulary items.

Aside from the dev set provided, the participants were free to use any other data for tuning (making their submission "unconstrained"), but no participant decided to do that. All tuning task submissions are therefore also constraint in terms of

[3] `http://www.statmt.org/wmt14/translation-task.html`

System	Participant
BLEU-*	baselines
AFRL	United States Air Force Research Laboratory (Erdmann and Gwinnup, 2015)
DCU	Dublin City University (Li et al., 2015)
HKUST	Hong Kong University of Science and Technology (Lo et al., 2015)
ILLC-UvA	ILLC – University of Amsterdam (Stanojević and Sima'an, 2015)
METEOR-CMU	Carnegie Mellon University (Denkowski and Lavie, 2011)
USAAR-TUNA	Saarland University (Liling Tan and Mihaela Vela; no corresponding paper)

Table 3: Participants of WMT15 Tuning Shared Task

the WMT15 Translation Task (Bojar et al., 2015).

We leave all decoder settings (n-best list size, pruning limits etc.) at their default values. While the participants may have used different limits during tuning, the final test run was performed at our site with the default values. It is indeed only the feature weights that differ.

3 Tuning Task Participants

The list of participants and the names of the submitted systems are shown in Table 3, along with references to the details of each method.

USAAR-TUNA by Liling Tan and Mihaela Vela has no accompanying paper, so we sketch it here. The method sets each weight as the harmonic mean ($\frac{2xy}{x+y}$) of the weight proposed by batch MIRA and MERT. Batch MIRA and MERT are run side by side and the harmonic mean is taken and used in `moses.ini` at every iteration. The optimization stops when the averaged weights change only very little, which happened around iteration 17 or 18 in this case (Liling Tan, pc).

ILLC-UvA (Stanojević and Sima'an, 2015) was tuned using KBMIRA with modified version of BEER evaluation metric. The authors claim that standard trained evaluation metrics learn to give too much importance to recall and thus lead to overly long translations in tuning. For that reason they modify the training of BEER to value recall and precision equally. This modified version of BEER is used to train the MT system.

DCU (Li et al., 2015) is tuned with RED, an evaluation metric based on maching of dependency n-grams. Authors have tried tuning with both MERT and KBMIRA and found that KBMIRA gives better results so the submitted system uses KBMIRA.

HKUST (Lo et al., 2015) is with an improved version of MEANT. MEANT is an evaluation metric that pays more attention to semantic aspect of translation. Better correlation on the sentence level was achieved by integrating distributional semantics into MEANT and handling failures of the underlying semantic parser. The submission of HKUST contained a bug that was discovered after human evaluation period so the corrected submission HKUST-LATE is evaluated only with BLEU.

METEOR-CMU (Denkowski and Lavie, 2011) is a system tuned for an adapted version of Meteor. Meteor's parameters are set to give an equal importance to precision and recall.

AFRL (Erdmann and Gwinnup, 2015) is the only submission trained with a new tuning algorithm "Drem" instead of the standard MERT or KBMIRA. Drem uses scaled derivative-free trust-region optimization instead of line search or (sub)gradient approximations. For weight settings that were not tested in the decoder yet, it interpolates the decoder output using the information of which settings produced which translations. The optimized metric is a weighted combination of NIST, Meteor and Kendall's τ.

In addition to the systems submitted, we provided three baselines:

- BLEU-MERT-DENSE – MERT tuning with BLEU without additional features
- BLEU-MIRA-DENSE – KBMIRA tuning with BLEU without additional features
- BLEU-MIRA-SPARSE – KBMIRA tuning with BLEU with additional sparse features

Since all the submissions including the baselines were subject to manual evaluation, we did not run the MERT or MIRA optimizations more than once (as is the common practice for estimating variance due to optimizer instability). We simply used the default settings and stopping criteria and picked the weights that performed best on the dev set according to BLEU.

Of all the submissions, only the submission METEOR-CMU used sparse features. For a more interesting comparison, we set our baseline

(BLEU-MIRA-SPARSE) to use the very same set of sparse features. These features are automatically constructed using Moses' feature templates named PhraseLengthFeature0, SourceWordDeletionFeature0, TargetWordInsertionFeature0 and WordTranslationFeature0. They were made for the 50 most frequent words in the training data. For both language pairs these feature templates produce around 1000 features.

System Name	TrueSkill Score		BLEU
	Tuning-Only	All	
BLEU-MIRA-DENSE	0.153	-0.182	12.28
ILLC-UvA	0.108	-0.189	12.05
BLEU-MERT-DENSE	0.087	-0.196	12.11
AFRL	0.070	-0.210	12.20
USAAR-TUNA	0.011	-0.220	12.16
DCU	-0.027	-0.263	11.44
METEOR-CMU	-0.101	-0.297	10.88
BLEU-MIRA-SPARSE	-0.150	-0.320	10.84
HKUST	-0.150	-0.320	10.99
HKUST-LATE	—	—	12.20

Table 4: Results on Czech-English tuning

System Name	TrueSkill Score		BLEU
	Tuning-Only	All	
DCU	0.320	-0.342	4.96
BLEU-MIRA-DENSE	0.303	-0.346	5.31
AFRL	0.303	-0.342	5.34
USAAR-TUNA	0.214	-0.373	5.26
BLEU-MERT-DENSE	0.123	-0.406	5.24
METEOR-CMU	-0.271	-0.563	4.37
BLEU-MIRA-SPARSE	-0.992	-0.808	3.79
USAAR-BASELINE-MIRA	—	—	5.31
USAAR-BASELINE-MERT	—	—	5.25

Table 5: Results on English-Czech tuning

4 Results

We used the submitted `moses.ini` and (optionally) sparse `weights` files to translate the test set. The test set was not available to the participants at the time of their submission (not even the source side). We used the Moses recaser trained on the target side of the parallel corpus to recase the outputs of all the models.

Finally, the recased outputs were manually evaluated, jointly with regular translation task submissions of WMT (Bojar et al., 2015). This was not enough to reliably separate tuning systems in the Czech-to-English direction, so we asked task participants to provide some further rankings.

The resulting human rankings were used to compute the overall manual score using the TrueSkill method, same as for the main translation task (Bojar et al., 2015). We report two variants of the score: one is based on manual judgements related to tuning systems only and one is based on all judgements. Note that the actual ranking tasks shown to the annotators were identical, mixing tuning systems with regular submissions.

Tables 4 and 5 contain the results of the submitted systems sorted by their manual scores.

The horizonal lines represent separation between clusters of systems that perform similarly. Cluster boundaries are established by the same method as for the main translation task. Interestingly, cluster boundaries for Czech-to-English vary as we change the set of judgements.

Some systems do not have the TrueSkill score because they were either submitted after the deadline (HKUST-LATE) or served as additional baselines and performed similarly to our baselines (USAAR-BASELINE-MIRA and USAAR-BASELINE-MERT).

5 Discussion

There are a few interesting observations that can be made about the baseline results. Various details of the submissions including the exact weight settings are in Table 6.

5.1 Dense vs. Sparse Features

It is surprising how well the baseline based on KBMIRA and BLEU tuning (BLEU-MIRA-DENSE) performs on both language pairs. On Czech-English, it is better than all the other submitted systems while on English-Czech, only one system outperforms it (staying in the same performance cluster anyway).

Using BLEU-MIRA-DENSE for tuning dense features is becoming more common in the MT community, compared to the previous standard of using MERT. Our results confirm this practice. Preferring KBMIRA to MERT is often motivated by possibility to include sparse features, but we see that even for dense features only KBMIRA is better than MERT.

The sparse models, BLEU-MIRA-SPARSE and METEOR-CMU, however, perform rather poorly even though they were trained with KBMIRA. Both of the sparse submissions use the same set of features and the same tuning algorithm, although the optimization was run at different sites. The only difference is the metric they optimize. Tuning for Meteor (Denkowski and Lavie, 2011) gives better results than tuning for BLEU (Papineni et al., 2002). Unfortunately, we had no system with

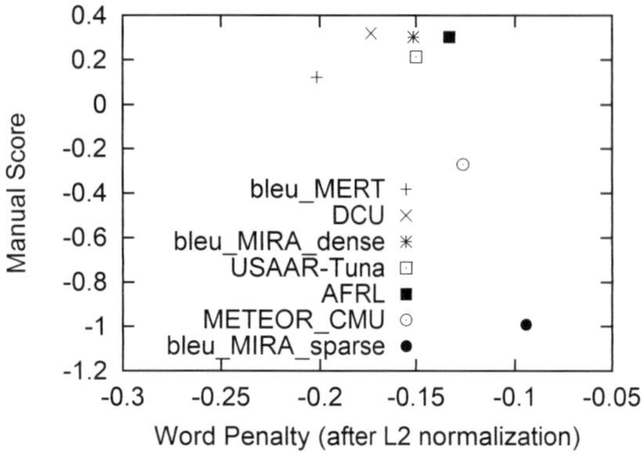

Figure 1: Relation between the word penalty and the final performance of systems translating from English to Czech.

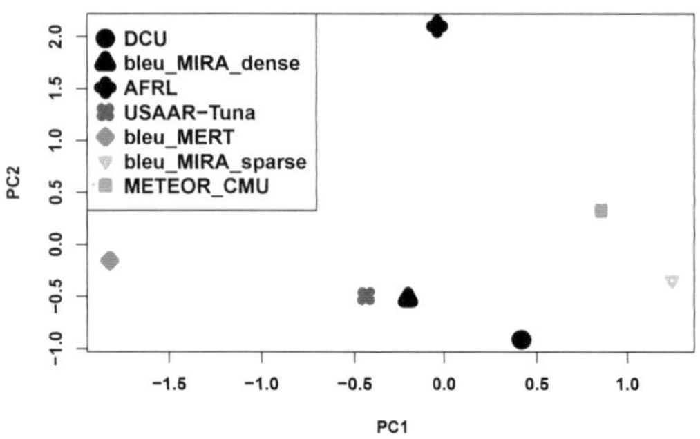

Figure 2: PCA for English-Czech. The darker the point, the higher the manual score.

dense features tuned for Meteor so we could not see if Meteor outperforms BLEU in the dense-only setting as well.

It is not clear why the sparse methods perform badly. One explanation could be the relatively small development set or some pruning settings. In any case, we find it unfortunate that sparse features in the hierarchical model harm performance in the default configuration[4].

5.2 Some Observations on Weight Settings

We tried to find some patterns in the weight settings and the performance of the system, but admittedly, it is difficult to make much sense of the few points in the 8-dimensional space.

For English-to-Czech, we can see a gist of a bell-like shape when normalizing the weights with L2 norm and plotting the word penalty and the

[4]MERT and two MIRA runs reached BLEU of not more than +0.02 points higher when the size of n-best list was increased from 100 to 200. So n-best list size does not seem to be the problem.

Czech-to-English	Type	Manual Score	Test BLEU	Dev BLEU	LM0	PhrPen	TM_0	TM_1	TM_2	TM_3	Glue	WrdPen
AFRL	dense	0.0700	12.20	14.83	0.1588	-0.3330	0.0545	0.0859	0.1958	0.1716	0.6309	-0.6227
bleu_MERT	dense	0.0870	12.11	14.64	0.0992	-0.0507	0.0688	0.0350	0.1296	0.0919	0.1820	-0.3428
bleu_MIRA_dense	dense	0.1530	12.28	14.85	0.0671	-0.1689	0.0363	0.0413	0.0747	0.0680	0.2982	-0.2454
bleu_MIRA_sparse	sparse	-0.1500	10.84	13.16	0.0906	-0.0568	0.0431	0.0556	0.0928	0.0933	0.3584	-0.2093
DCU	dense	-0.0270	11.44	13.58	0.0558	-0.1407	0.0360	0.0517	0.0856	0.0671	0.2481	-0.3150
HKUST_MEANT	dense	-0.1500	10.99	13.23	0.1333	0.0868	0.1318	0.0115	0.0534	0.1221	0.0500	-0.4110
HKUST_MEANT_LATE	dense	—	12.20	14.42	0.0638	-0.1696	0.0655	0.0217	0.0713	0.0677	0.3074	-0.2330
ILLC_UvA	dense	0.1080	12.05	14.57	0.0918	-0.1215	0.0452	0.0624	0.1103	0.0697	0.2295	-0.2696
METEOR_CMU	sparse	-0.1010	10.88	13.35	0.0936	-0.0103	0.0602	0.0509	0.1162	0.1187	0.2946	-0.2556
USAAR-Tuna	dense	0.0110	12.16	14.57	0.0789	-0.0715	0.0383	0.0575	0.1039	0.0744	0.1839	-0.2952

English-to-Czech	Type	Manual Score	Test BLEU	Dev BLEU	LM0	PhrPen	TM_0	TM_1	TM_2	TM_3	Glue	WrdPen
AFRL	dense	0.3030	5.34	6.96	0.0543	-0.4326	-0.0025	0.0382	0.2696	0.0788	0.8332	-0.1878
bleu_MERT	dense	0.1230	5.24	7.11	0.0510	-0.1353	0.0048	0.0169	0.1772	0.0408	0.3508	-0.2231
bleu_MIRA_dense	dense	0.3030	5.31	7.20	0.0380	-0.2046	-0.0004	0.0286	0.1338	0.0320	0.3936	-0.1689
bleu_MIRA_sparse	sparse	-0.9920	3.79	5.19	0.0364	-0.1232	-0.0053	0.0350	0.0905	0.0480	0.5524	-0.1093
DCU	dense	0.3200	4.96	6.87	0.0247	-0.1949	-0.0022	0.0367	0.1370	0.0345	0.3767	-0.1932
METEOR_CMU	sparse	-0.2710	4.37	5.86	0.0394	-0.0935	-0.0087	0.0331	0.1611	0.0673	0.4548	-0.1421
Saarland_baseline_mert	dense	—	5.25	7.16	0.0394	-0.1619	-0.0011	0.0218	0.1947	0.0211	0.3973	-0.1628
Saarland_baseline_mira	dense	—	5.31	7.11	0.0377	-0.2023	-0.0007	0.0293	0.1304	0.0344	0.3936	-0.1714
USAAR-Tuna	dense	0.2140	5.26	7.15	0.0386	-0.1799	-0.0008	0.0250	0.1562	0.0262	0.3954	-0.1670

Table 6: Detailed scores and weights of Czech-to-English (left) and English-to-Czech (right) systems.

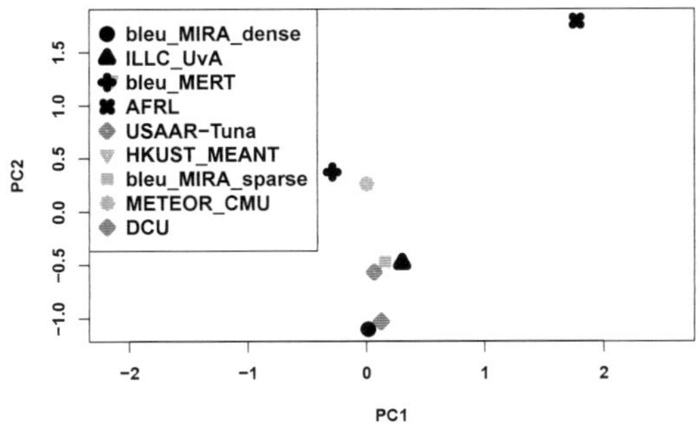

Figure 3: PCA for Czech-English. The darker the point, the higher the manual score.

	PC1	PC2
LM0	**-0.69**	0.44
PhrasePenalty0	0.15	**-0.63**
TranslationModel0_0	**-0.91**	-0.13
TranslationModel0_1	**0.91**	-0.03
TranslationModel0_2	-0.55	**0.72**
TranslationModel0_3	0.36	**0.75**
TranslationModel1	0.42	**0.84**
WordPenalty0	**0.84**	0.27

Table 7: Loadings (correlations) of each component with each feature function for English-Czech

manual score, see Figure 1. The middle values seemed to be a good setting. For the other translation direction or other weights, no such clear relation is apparent.

We tried to interpret the weight settings also using principal component analysis (PCA), despite the low number of observations. (Ideally, we would like to have at least 40–80 systems, we have 7 or 9). Before running PCA, we normalized the weights with L2 norm. After running Cattell Scree test, the results showed that two components would be appropriate to summarize the dataset. To make components more interpretable, we applied varimax rotation.

Figure 2 plots the two principal components of the set of systems for English-to-Czech. We see that the first component (PC1) explains the performance almost completely with middle values being the best. Looking at loadings (correlations of components with the original feature function dimensions) in Table 7, we learn, that PC1 primarily accounts for the first two weights of translation model (TM_0 and TM_1, which correspond to phrase and lexically-weighted inverse probabilities, resp.) and the word penalty (WrdPen) and language model weight (LM0). Knowing that in almost all systems the weight of word penalty is several times bigger than weights of TM_0, TM_1, and LM0, we conclude that tuning of word penalty (in balance with LM weight) was the most apparent decisive factor of English-Czech tuning task. The second component (PC2) primarily covers the weights of the remaining features, that is the direct translation probabilites and phrase penalty. Unfortunately, PC2 is not very informative about the final quality of the translation.

The Czech-to-English results in Figure 3 do not seem to lend themselves to any simple conclusion.

Based on closeness of systems in the PCA plots, we can say that for English-Czech, two out of three best systems (BLEU-MIRA-DENSE and DCU) found similar settings while AFRL stands out. Czech-English results show that systems of very similar weight settings give translations of very different quality. Again, AFRL stands out while leading to very good outputs.

6 Conclusion

This paper presented the WMT shared task in optimizing parameters of a given hierarchical phrase-based system (WMT Tuning Task) when translating from English to Czech and vice versa. The underlying system was intentionally restricted to small data setting and somewhat unusually, the data for the language model were smaller than for the translation model.

Overall, six teams took part in one or both directions, sticking to the constrained setting, with only METEOR-CMU and our baseline BLEU-MIRA-SPARSE using sparse features.

The submitted configurations were manually evaluated jointly with the systems of the main WMT translation task. Given the small data setting, we did not expect the tuning task systems to perform competitively to other submissions in the WMT translation task.

The results confirm that KBMIRA with the standard (dense) features optimized towards BLEU should be preferred over MERT. Two other systems (DCU and AFRL) performed equally well in English-to-Czech translation. The two systems using sparse features (METEOR-CMU and BLEU-MIRA-SPARSE) performed poorly, but the sample is too small to draw any conclusions from this. Overall, the variance in translation quality obtained using various weight settings is apparent and justifies the efforts put into optimization techniques.

Since the task attracted a good number of submissions and was generally considered interesting and useful by our colleagues, we plan to run the task again for WMT in 2016. The next year's underlying systems will use all data available in the WMT constraint setting, to test the tuning methods in the range where state-of-the-art systems operate.

Acknowledgments

We are grateful to Christian Federmann and Matt Post for all the processing of human evaluation and to the annotators who quickly helped us in getting additional judgements. Thanks also go to Matthias Huck for a thorough check of the paper, all outstanding errors are our own. This project has received funding from the European Union's Horizon 2020 research and innovation programme under grant agreements n° 645452 (QT21) and n° 644402 (HimL). The work on this project was also supported by the Dutch organisation for scientific research STW grant nr. 12271.

References

Meriem Beloucif, Chi-kiu Lo, and Dekai Wu. 2014. Improving MEANT Based Semantically Tuned SMT. In *Proc. of 11th International Workshop on Spoken Language Translation (IWSLT 2014)*, pages 34–41, Lake Tahoe, California.

Ondřej Bojar, Rajen Chatterjee, Christian Federmann, Barry Haddow, Matthias Huck, Chris Hokamp, Philipp Koehn, Varvara Logacheva, Christof Monz, Matteo Negri, Matt Post, Carolina Scarton, Lucia Specia, and Marco Turchi. 2015. Findings of the 2015 Workshop on Statistical Machine Translation. In *Proceedings of the Tenth Workshop on Statistical Machine Translation*, Lisboa, Portugal, September. Association for Computational Linguistics.

Chris Callison-Burch, Philipp Koehn, Christof Monz, Kay Peterson, Mark Przybocki, and Omar Zaidan. 2010. Findings of the 2010 Joint Workshop on Statistical Machine Translation and Metrics for Machine Translation. In *Proceedings of the Joint Fifth Workshop on Statistical Machine Translation and MetricsMATR*, pages 17–53, Uppsala, Sweden, July. Association for Computational Linguistics. Revised August 2010.

Daniel Cer, Christopher D. Manning, and Daniel Jurafsky. 2010. The best lexical metric for phrase-based statistical mt system optimization. In *Human Language Technologies: The 2010 Annual Conference of the North American Chapter of the Association for Computational Linguistics*, HLT '10, pages 555–563, Stroudsburg, PA, USA. Association for Computational Linguistics.

Colin Cherry and George Foster. 2012. Batch tuning strategies for statistical machine translation. In *Proceedings of the 2012 Conference of the North American Chapter of the Association for Computational Linguistics: Human Language Technologies*, NAACL HLT '12, pages 427–436, Stroudsburg, PA, USA. Association for Computational Linguistics.

David Chiang. 2005. A Hierarchical Phrase-Based Model for Statistical Machine Translation. In *Proceedings of the 43rd Annual Meeting of the Association for Computational Linguistics (ACL'05)*, pages 263–270, Ann Arbor, Michigan, June.

Michael Denkowski and Alon Lavie. 2011. Meteor 1.3: Automatic Metric for Reliable Optimization and Evaluation of Machine Translation Systems. In *Proceedings of the Sixth Workshop on Statistical Machine Translation*, pages 85–91, Edinburgh, Scotland, July. Association for Computational Linguistics.

Grant Erdmann and Jeremy Gwinnup. 2015. Drem: The AFRL Submission to the WMT15 Tuning Task. In *Proceedings of the Tenth Workshop on Statistical Machine Translation*, Lisboa, Portugal, September. Association for Computational Linguistics.

Qin Gao and Stephan Vogel. 2008. Parallel implementations of word alignment tool. In *In Proc. of the ACL 2008 Software Engineering, Testing, and Quality Assurance Workshop*.

Kenneth Heafield, Ivan Pouzyrevsky, Jonathan H. Clark, and Philipp Koehn. 2013. Scalable Modified Kneser-Ney Language Model Estimation. In *Proceedings of the 51st Annual Meeting of the Association for Computational Linguistics*, pages 690–696, Sofia, Bulgaria, August.

Hieu Hoang, Philipp Koehn, and Adam Lopez. 2009. A Unified Framework for Phrase-Based, Hierarchical, and Syntax-Based Statistical Machine Translation. In *Proceedings of IWSLT*, pages 152–159, Tokyo, Japan, December.

Mark Hopkins and Jonathan May. 2011. Tuning as ranking. In *Proceedings of the Conference on Empirical Methods in Natural Language Processing*, EMNLP '11, pages 1352–1362, Stroudsburg, PA, USA. Association for Computational Linguistics.

Reinhard Kneser and Hermann Ney. 1995. Improved backing-off for m-gram language modeling. In *IEEE International Conference on Acoustics, Speech, and Signal Processing (ICASSP),*, volume 1, pages 181–184. IEEE.

Liangyou Li, Hui Yu, and Qun Liu. 2015. MT Tuning on RED: A Dependency-Based Evaluation Metric. In *Proceedings of the Tenth Workshop on Statistical Machine Translation*, Lisboa, Portugal, September. Association for Computational Linguistics.

Chang Liu, Daniel Dahlmeier, and Hwee Tou Ng. 2011. Better Evaluation Metrics Lead to Better Machine Translation. In *Proceedings of the Conference on Empirical Methods in Natural Language Processing*, EMNLP '11, pages 375–384, Stroudsburg, PA, USA. Association for Computational Linguistics.

Chi-kiu Lo, Philipp Dowling, and Dekai Wu. 2015. Improving evaluation and optimization of MT systems against MEANT. In *Proceedings of the Tenth Workshop on Statistical Machine Translation*, Lisboa, Portugal, September. Association for Computational Linguistics.

Franz Josef Och. 2003. Minimum error rate training in statistical machine translation. In *Proceedings of the 41st Annual Meeting on Association for Computational Linguistics - Volume 1*, ACL '03, pages 160–167, Stroudsburg, PA, USA. Association for Computational Linguistics.

Kishore Papineni, Salim Roukos, Todd Ward, and Wei-Jing Zhu. 2002. BLEU: A Method for Automatic Evaluation of Machine Translation. In *Proceedings of the 40th Annual Meeting on Association for Computational Linguistics*, ACL '02, pages 311–318.

Miloš Stanojević and Khalil Sima'an. 2015. BEER 1.1: ILLC UvA submission to metrics and tuning task. In *Proceedings of the Tenth Workshop on Statistical Machine Translation*, Lisboa, Portugal, September. Association for Computational Linguistics.

Miloš Stanojević, Amir Kamran, Philipp Koehn, and Ondřej Bojar. 2015. Results of the WMT15 Metrics Shared Task. In *Proceedings of the Tenth Workshop on Statistical Machine Translation*, Lisboa, Portugal, September. Association for Computational Linguistics.

Bing Zhao and Shengyuan Chen. 2009. A simplex armijo downhill algorithm for optimizing statistical machine translation decoding parameters. In *HLT-NAACL (Short Papers)*, pages 21–24. The Association for Computational Linguistics.

Extended Translation Models in Phrase-based Decoding

Andreas Guta, Joern Wuebker, Miguel Graça, Yunsu Kim, Hermann Ney
Human Language Technology and Pattern Recognition Group
RWTH Aachen University
Aachen, Germany
`{surname}@cs.rwth-aachen.de`

Abstract

We propose a novel extended translation model (ETM) to counteract some problems in phrase-based translation: The lack of translation context when using single-word phrases and uncaptured dependencies beyond phrase boundaries. The ETM operates on word-level and augments the IBM models by an additional bilingual word pair and a reordering operation. Its implementation in a phrase-based decoder introduces translation and reordering dependencies for single-word phrases and dependencies across phrase boundaries. More, the model incorporates an explicit treatment of multiple and empty alignments. Its integration outperforms competitive systems that include lexical and phrase translation models as well as hierarchical reordering models on 4 language pairs significantly by +0.7% BLEU on average. Although simpler and using fewer dependencies, the ETM proves to be on par with 7-gram operation sequence models (Durrani et al., 2013b).

1 Introduction

The first successful steps in Statistical Machine Translation have been taken by applying word-based models in a source-channel approach (Brown et al., 1990; Brown et al., 1993). Within this framework, the language model (LM) is estimated on monolingual n-grams, whereas the translation models IBM-1 to IBM-5 are trained on bilingual data using word alignments. The disadvantage of word-to-word translation is overcome by phrase-based translation (PBT) (Och et al., 1999; Zens et al., 2002; Koehn et al., 2003) and log-linear model combination (Och and Ney, 2002).

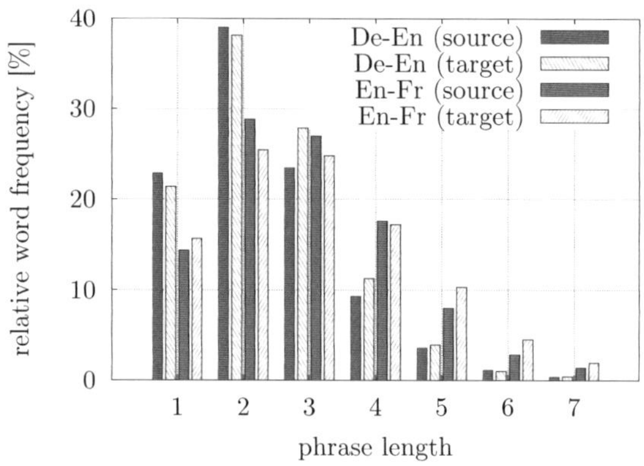

Figure 1: Relative frequency of words dependent on the length of the phrase they were decoded with for the IWSLT `dev2010` German→English and English→French corpora.

Nevertheless, phrase-based translation models have several drawbacks: (i) Single-word phrases are translated without any context. (ii) Dependencies beyond phrase boundaries are not modelled at all. (iii) Phrase-based translation models have difficulties modelling long-distance dependencies on source words with large gaps inbetween.

The open question is how much *actual* lexical context is included in decoding. Figure 1 depicts the relative word frequencies plotted against the length of the phrase they were translated with for the IWSLT 2014[1] German→English and English→French tasks. For English→French, more than 40% of the words are translated using single- or two-word phrases, i.e. with a lexical context of at most one word. For the German→English task, more reorderings occur and lead to less monotone alignments. Here, even 60% of all words are translated with a lexical context of at most one single word and over 20% are translated without any lexical context at all.

[1] `http://www.iwslt2014.org`

We address this problem by developing two variants of extended translation models (ETM), the *direct* (EdTM) for the Source→Target and the *inverse* (EiTM) for the Target→Source direction. They operate on word-level and augment the IBM models by an additional bilingual word pair and a reordering operation. We introduce them into the log-linear framework of a PBT system. Thus, the decoding of single-word phrases can benefit from lexical and reordering context. Moreover, the ETM allows to capture dependencies across phrase boundaries and long-range source dependencies. It incorporates reordering information for non-monotone and multiple alignments including unaligned words.

As a first step, we implement the ETM as a count model with interpolated Kneser-Ney smoothing (Chen and Goodman, 1998) using the Viterbi alignment and apply it in phrase-based decoding. Nevertheless, the long-term goal of this approach is to replace the phrases used in decoding by translation units that predict a single target word, but may depend on several source words, previously translated target words and the reordering context.

2 Previous Work

Various approaches have been taken to compensate the downside of the phrase translation model. Mariño et al. (2006) introduce a translation model based on n-grams of bilingual word pairs, i.e. a bilingual language model (BILM), with an n-gram decoder that requires monotone alignments. In (Niehues et al., 2011), this is further advanced by BILMs operating on non-monotone alignments within a PBT framework.

However, this differs from our approach: BILMs treat jointly aligned source words as atomic units, ignore source deletions and do not include reordering context.

The Operation Sequence Model (OSM) introduced in (Durrani et al., 2011; Durrani et al., 2013a) includes n-grams of both translation and reordering operations in a consistent framework. It utilizes minimal translation units (MTUs) and is applied in a corresponding OSM decoder. Experiments in (Durrani et al., 2013b) show that a slightly enhanced version of OSM performs best when integrated into the log-linear framework of a phrase-based decoder. Both the BILM (Stewart et al., 2014) and the OSM (Durrani et al., 2014) can be smoothed using word clusters.

In comparison, the ETM is much simpler: Since it predicts probabilities of single words, it has a lower vocabulary size. More, it does not make use of reordering gaps, i.e. it utilizes a simpler reordering approach. The OSM uses one joint model for reorderings and translations. In contrast, the ETM incorporates separate models to estimate the probability of words and the probability of reorderings. Furthermore, the OSM has the drawback that it extracts the MTUs sentence-wise, thus one word can appear in several MTUs extracted from different sentence pairs. Since an MTUs is treated as an atomic unit, this results in a distribution of probability mass on overlapping events. The ETM overcomes this drawback by operating on single words.

Guta et al. (2015) propose the conversion of bilingual sentence pairs and word alignments into joint translation and reordering (JTR) sequences. They investigate n-gram models with modified Kneser-Ney smoothing, feed-forward and recurrent neural networks trained on JTR sequences. In comparison to the OSM, JTR models have smaller vocabulary sizes, as they operate on words, and incorporate simpler reordering structures. Nevertheless, they are shown to perform slightly better than the OSM when included into the log-linear framework of a phrase-based decoder.

Although our approach is similar, there are the following significant differences: On the one hand, the ETM estimates the probability of single words conditioned on an extended lexical and reordering context, whereas the JTR n-gram model predicts the probability of bilingual word pairs. On the other hand, we do not assume linear sequences of dependencies, but propose and explicit treatment of multiply aligned words.

Deng and Byrne (2005) present an HMM approach for word-to-phrase alignments, which performs similar to IBM-4 on the task of bitext alignment and can also be applied for more powerful phrase induction. Feng et al. (2013) introduce an reordering model based on sequence labeling techniques by converting the reordering problem into a a tagging task. Zhang et al. (2013) explore different Markov chain orderings for an n-gram model on MTUs. These are not integrated into decoding, but used in N-best rescoring. Another generative, word-based Markov chain translation model is presented by Feng and Cohn (2013). It exploits a hierarchical Pitman-Yor process for smoothing, but is only applied to induce word alignments. Their follow-up work (Feng et al., 2014) introduces a Markov-model on MTUs, similar to the OSM described above.

Finally, there has been recent research on applying neural network models for extended context (Le et al., 2012; Auli et al., 2013; Hu et al., 2014; Devlin et al., 2014; Sundermeyer et al., 2014). All of these papers focus on lexical context and ignore the reordering aspect covered in our work.

3 Extended Translation Models

Given a source sentence f_1^J and its translation e_1^I, EiTM models the *inverse* probability $p(f_1^J|e_1^I)$ and EdTM the *direct* probability $p(e_1^I|f_1^J)$. We allow for source words to be translated to multiple target words and vice versa. The inverted alignment b_i denotes the sequence of source positions j aligned to target position i for $i = 1,\dots,I$. Its subsequence $b_i^{<j}$ includes all source positions in b_i preceding a given source position j:

$$b_i^{<j} = \left\{ \bar{j} \in b_i : \bar{j} < j \right\}.$$

Unaligned target words are aligned to the empty source word f_0, unaligned source words to the empty target word e_0. b_0 denotes the unaligned source positions. We introduce the fertility ϕ_i of a target word e_i. It determines the number of source words aligned to the target word e_i:

$$\phi_i = \begin{cases} 0, & b_i = \{0\} \\ |b_i|, & else \end{cases}$$

By analogy, we use $\phi_i^{<j}$ to denote the number of source positions in $b_i^{<j}$. Similar to the approach in (Feng and Cohn, 2013), we generalize reorderings to the following jump classes $\Delta_{j',j}^{\phi_i}$:

$$\Delta_{j',j}^{\phi_i} = \begin{cases} \downarrow \text{ ('insert')}, & \phi_i = 0 \\ \bullet \text{ ('stay')}, & \phi_i > 0, j = j' \\ \rightarrow \text{ ('forward')}, & \phi_i > 0, j = j'+1 \\ \curvearrowright \text{ ('jump forward')}, & \phi_i > 0, j > j'+1 \\ \leftarrow \text{ ('backward')}, & \phi_i > 0, j = j'-1 \\ \curvearrowleft \text{ ('jump backward')}, & \phi_i > 0, j < j'-1. \end{cases}$$

Figure 2 outlines the jump classes for subsequent target positions i' and i. As shown in Figure 3, for source positions $\bar{j} < j$ which are aligned to the

(a) forward (b) jump forward

Figure 3: Overview of the jump classes $\Delta_{\bar{j},j}$.

same target position i, there are two possible jump classes:

$$\Delta_{\bar{j},j} = \begin{cases} \rightarrow \text{ ('step forward')}, & j = \bar{j}+1 \\ \curvearrowright \text{ ('jump forward')}, & j > \bar{j}+1. \end{cases}$$

In the following, we depict the derivations of the EiTM and the EdTM. Although they operate in opposite translation directions, both models incorporate the inverted alignment b_1^I.

3.1 Extended Inverse Translation Model

In order to model the inverse probability $p(f_1^J|e_1^I)$, the unknown inverted alignment b_1^I is introduced as a hidden variable and approximated by the Viterbi alignment.

$$\begin{aligned} p(f_1^J|e_1^I) &= \sum_{b_1^I} p(f_1^J, b_1^I|e_1^I) \\ &\approx \max_{b_1^I} \left\{ p(f_{b_0}^{b_I}, b_1^I|e_1^I) \right\} \\ &= \max_{b_1^I} \left\{ p(f_{b_1}^{b_I}, b_1^I|e_1^I) \cdot \underbrace{p(f_{b_0}|f_{b_1}^{b_I}, b_1^I, e_1^I)}_{\text{deletion probability}} \right\} \end{aligned}$$

The inverse probability has been decomposed into the deletion probability $p(f_{b_0}|f_{b_1}^{b_I}, b_1^I, e_1^I)$ and the joint probability $p(f_{b_1}^{b_I}, b_1^I|e_1^I)$. The latter is reformulated using the Markov chain rule:

$$p(f_{b_1}^{b_I}, b_1^I|e_1^I) = \prod_{i=1}^{I} p(f_{b_i}, b_i|e_1^I, f_{b_1}^{b_{i-1}}, b_1^{i-1}).$$

In order to restrict the history, we assume the probability of (f_{b_i}, b_i) to be dependent only on the current target word e_i, its last *aligned* predecessor $e_{i'}$, the corresponding alignment $b_{i'}$ and the source words $f_{b_{i'}}$:

$$p(f_{b_1}^{b_I}, b_1^I|e_1^I) = \prod_{i=1}^{I} p(f_{b_i}, b_i|e_{i'}, e_i, f_{b_{i'}}, b_{i'}).$$

The conditional joint probability is factorized as

$$\begin{aligned} & p(f_{b_i}, b_i|e_{i'}, e_i, f_{b_{i'}}, b_{i'}) = \\ & \underbrace{p(f_{b_i}|e_{i'}, e_i, f_{b_{i'}}, b_{i'}, b_i)}_{\text{lexicon probability}} \cdot \underbrace{p(b_i|e_{i'}, e_i, f_{b_{i'}}, b_{i'})}_{\text{alignment probability}}, \end{aligned}$$

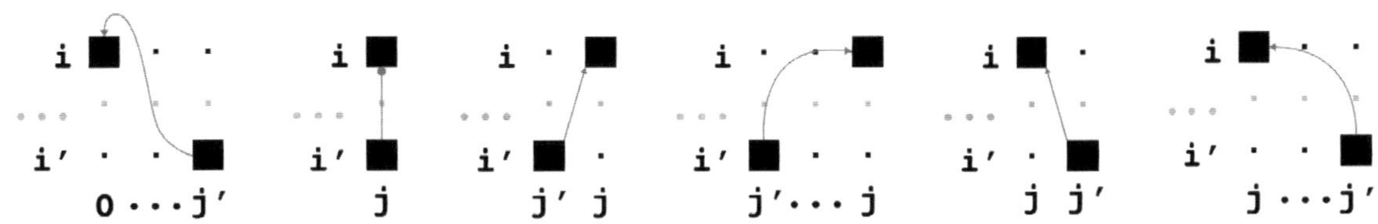

(a) insert (b) stay (c) forward (d) jump forward (e) backward (f) jump backward

Figure 2: Overview of the jump classes $\Delta^{\phi_i}_{j',j}$.

resulting in the lexicon probability of f_{b_i} and the alignment probability of b_i. In a nutshell, we have decomposed the inverse probability into the following three probabilities:

- deletion: $p(f_{b_0}|f_{b_1}^{b_I}, b_1^I, e_1^I)$
- lexicon: $\prod_{i=1}^{I} p(f_{b_i}|e_{i'}, e_i, f_{b_{i'}}, b_{i'}, b_i)$
- alignment: $\prod_{i=1}^{I} p(b_i|e_{i'}, e_i, f_{b_{i'}}, b_{i'})$

Below, we show how to estimate these probabilities using the EiTM deletion, lexicon and alignment models.

3.1.1 EiTM: Deletion Model

Due to its artificiality, e_0 has no preceding target word. We condition the deletion of f_{b_0} only on e_0 and assume conditional independence between the unaligned source words f_{b_0}:

$$p(f_{b_0}|f_{b_1}^{b_I}, b_1^I, e_1^I) = \prod_{j \in b_0} p(f_j|e_0).$$

3.1.2 EiTM: Lexicon Model

Firstly, we apply the Markov chain rule to obtain the factorized probabilities of single words f_j.

$$p(f_{b_i}|e_{i'}, e_i, f_{b_{i'}}, b_{i'}, b_i) = \prod_{j \in b_i} p(f_j|e_{i'}, e_i, f_{b_{i'}}, f_{b_i^{<j}}, b_{i'}, b_i)$$

Each source word f_j is dependent on all predecessors $f_{b_i^{<j}}$ aligned to the same target word e_i and all previously aligned source words $f_{b_{i'}}$. If we modelled the probability conditioned on the sets of source words $f_{b_{i'}}$ and $f_{b_i^{<j}}$, this would lead to sparsity problems due to the arbitrary number of source words contained in the sets.

In order to avoid this, we therefore condition the probability on the individual words contained in $f_{b_{i'}}, f_{b_i^{<j}}$. Without any additional information, we assume all words $f_{b_{i'}}, f_{b_i^{<j}}$ to be equally important for the prediction of f_j. Thus, we average over the probabilities conditioned on:

- all source words $f_{j'}$ aligned to the preceding target word $e_{i'}$,
- all preceding source words $f_{\bar{j}}$ aligned to the current target word e_i.

Moreover, we reduce the alignments $(b_{i'}, b_i)$ to their corresponding jump classes. As a final result we obtain:

$$p(f_j|e_{i'}, e_i, f_{b_{i'}}, f_{b_i^{<j}}, b_{i'}, b_i) = \frac{1}{\phi_{i'} + \phi_i^{<j}} \Big(\sum_{j' \in b_{i'}} p(f_j|e_i, f_{j'}, e_{i'}, \Delta^{\phi_i}_{j',j}) + \sum_{\bar{j} \in b_i^{<j}} p(f_j|e_i, f_{\bar{j}}, \Delta_{\bar{j},j}) \Big).$$

3.1.3 EiTM: Alignment Model

In principle, we follow the same derivation as for the lexicon model above. The probability of a source position $j \in b_i$ is computed as the average probability of a jump from a previously aligned source position, which either has to be aligned to the target predecessor i' or is a preceeding source position aligned to the same target word e_i.

$$p(b_i|e_{i'}, e_i, f_{b_{i'}}, b_{i'}) = \prod_{j \in b_i} \frac{1}{\phi_{i'} + \phi_i^{<j}} \Big(\sum_{j' \in b_{i'}} p(\Delta^{\phi_i}_{j',j}|e_i, f_{j'}, e_{i'}) + \sum_{\bar{j} \in b_i^{<j}} p(\Delta_{\bar{j},j}|e_i, f_{\bar{j}}) \Big).$$

To emphasize the core idea, Figure 4 demonstrates the application on a German→English translation example. Thin blue arcs denote the probabilities conditioned on distinct target words $e_{i'}$ and e_i, the thick red arc denotes the probabilities conditioned on a previous source word $f_{\bar{j}}$ aligned to the current target word. The shape of an arc symbolizes

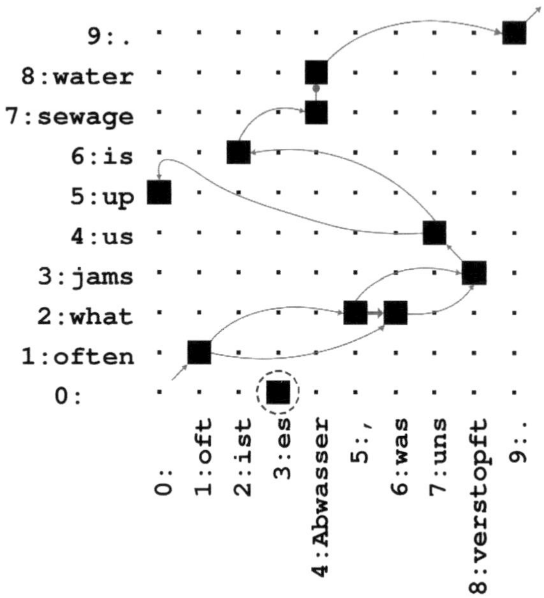

Figure 4: EiTM scoring for a sentence from the IWSLT German→English corpus including the word alignment.

the jump class, see Figures 2 and 3. The empty words are shown at positions $j, i = 0$. The deletion is indicated by a violet circle. The EiTM probability for the whole sentence pair is computed as follows:

$$p(f_1^9, b_1^9 | e_1^9) =$$

$$p(f_1 | e_1, \text{<s>}, \text{<s>}, \rightarrow) \cdot p(\rightarrow | e_1, \text{<s>}, \text{<s>})$$

$$\cdot\, p(f_5 | e_2, f_1, e_1, \curvearrowright) \cdot p(\curvearrowright | e_2, f_1, e_1) \tag{1}$$

$$\cdot\, \frac{p(f_6 | e_2, f_1, e_1, \curvearrowright) + p(f_6 | e_2, f_5, \rightarrow)}{2} \cdot \frac{p(\curvearrowright | e_2, f_1, e_1) + p(\rightarrow | e_2, f_5)}{2} \tag{2}$$

$$\cdot\, \frac{p(f_8 | e_3, f_5, e_2, \curvearrowright) + p(f_8 | e_3, f_6, e_2, \curvearrowright)}{2} \cdot \frac{p(\curvearrowright | e_3, f_5, e_2) + p(\curvearrowright | e_3, f_6, e_2)}{2} \tag{3}$$

$$\cdot\, p(f_7 | e_4, f_8, e_3, \leftarrow) \cdot p(\leftarrow | e_4, f_8, e_3)$$

$$\cdot\, p(f_0 | e_5, f_7, e_4, \downarrow) \cdot p(\downarrow | e_5, f_7, e_4) \tag{4}$$

$$\cdot\, p(f_2 | e_6, f_7, e_4, \curvearrowleft) \cdot p(\curvearrowleft | e_6, f_7, e_4) \tag{5}$$

$$\cdot\, p(f_4 | e_7, f_2, e_6, \curvearrowright) \cdot p(\curvearrowright | e_7, f_2, e_6)$$

$$\cdot\, p(f_4 | e_8, f_4, e_7, \bullet) \cdot p(\bullet | e_8, f_4, e_7) \tag{6}$$

$$\cdot\, p(f_9 | e_9, f_4, e_8, \curvearrowright) \cdot p(\curvearrowright | e_9, f_4, e_8) \tag{7}$$

$$\cdot\, p(\text{</s>} | \text{</s>}, f_9, e_9, \rightarrow) \cdot p(\rightarrow | \text{</s>}, f_9, e_9)$$

$$\cdot\, p(f_3 | e_0). \tag{8}$$

Lines (1), (2), (3) and (7) are dependencies included in the EiTM but not in phrase translation models due to the phrase extraction heuristics. The dependency on multiple preceding word pairs is exemplified in (2) and (3). (4) depicts the insertion of the target word $e_5 = \texttt{up}$ conditioned on the word pair $(e_4 = \texttt{us}, f_7 = \texttt{uns})$. Note that in (5) there is no dependency of $e_6 = \texttt{is}$ on its predecessor $e_5 = \texttt{up}$ and the empty word f_0, but on its *last aligned* predecessor $e_4 = \texttt{us}$ and the corresponding source word $f_7 = \texttt{uns}$. (6) shows an example of a source word aligned to multiple target words. The deletion probability of the source word $f_3 = \texttt{es}$ is presented in (8).

3.2 Extended Direct Translation Model

So far, we have introduced the EiTM, which models the *inverse* translation probability $p(f_1^J | e_1^I)$. Besides modelling $p(f_1^J | e_1^I)$ using extended translation models, our aim is to employ them to model the *direct* probability $p(e_1^I | f_1^J)$ as well.

For a start, the direct probability $p(e_1^I | f_1^J)$ can be modelled using the EiTM: Simply put, source and target corpora have to be swapped for the training of the EiTM. By doing so, the alignment has to be inverted as well, i.e. one has to use the direct alignment a_j which denotes the sequence of target positions i aligned to source position j. As a result, the EiTM models $p(e_{a_0}^{a_J}, a_1^J | f_1^J)$ when trained with inverted corpora and alignments.

During the decoding process, the partial hypotheses are generated successively. Thus, for each target word e_i that is hypothesized, all its predecessors have already been translated, i.e. its last aligned predecessor $e_{i'}$ and the corresponding alignment $b_{i'}$ and source words $f_{b_{i'}}$ are known.

Nevertheless, source words do not have to be translated in monotone order. In general, it cannot be guaranteed that the predecessor f_{j-1} of the first word f_j of a source phrase has been translated yet. Therefore, the last aligned predecessor of f_j and its aligned target words are generally unknown.

As a result, when applying the EiTM within phrase-based decoding for modelling the direct probability $p(e_1^I | f_1^J)$, dependencies beyond phrase boundaries cannot be captured.

Thus, we additionally develop the EdTM which models the direct translation probability $p(e_1^I | f_1^J)$. In comparison to the EiTM trained with swapped corpora and alignments, EdTM incorporates dependencies beyond phrase boundaries by keeping the *inverted* alignment b_1^I instead of using a_1^J. Analogue to the EiTM, the hidden alignment b_1^I is approximated by the Viterbi alignment.

$$p(e_1^I|f_1^J) \approxeq \max_{b_1^I}\Big\{ \underbrace{p(e_0|f_{b_0}^{b_I})}_{\text{deletion probability}} \cdot p(e_1^I, b_1^I|f_{b_0}^{b_I}, e_0)\Big\}$$

Applying the Markov chain rule and assuming (e_i, b_i) to be dependent only on the aligned source words f_{b_i}, the previously aligned target word $e_{i'}$ as well as the corresponding alignment $b_{i'}$ and the source words $f_{b_{i'}}$, we obtain:

$$p(e_1^I, b_1^I|f_{b_0}^{b_I}, e_0) = \prod_{i=1}^{I} p(e_i, b_i|f_{b_{i'}}, f_{b_i}, e_{i'}, b_{i'}).$$

We factorize the joint probability to obtain the lexicon probability of e_i and the alignment probability of b_i.

$$p(e_i, b_i|f_{b_{i'}}, f_{b_i}, e_{i'}, b_{i'}) = \underbrace{p(e_i|f_{b_{i'}}, f_{b_i}, e_{i'}, b_{i'}, b_i)}_{\text{lexicon probability}} \cdot \underbrace{p(b_i|f_{b_{i'}}, f_{b_i}, e_{i'}, b_{i'})}_{\text{alignment probability}}$$

The direct probability has been decomposed into the following three probabilities.

- deletion: $p(e_0|f_{b_0}^{b_I})$
- lexicon: $\prod_{i=1}^{I} p(e_i|f_{b_{i'}}, f_{b_i}, e_{i'}, b_{i'}, b_i)$
- alignment: $\prod_{i=1}^{I} p(b_i|f_{b_{i'}}, f_{b_i}, e_{i'}, b_{i'})$

Next, we introduce the corresponding EdTM deletion, lexicon and alignment models.

3.2.1 EdTM: Deletion Model

The EdTM deletion model approximates the probability of e_0 conditioned on all unaligned source words f_{b_0} and is obtained by averaging over all unaligned source words:

$$p(e_0|f_{b_0}^{b_I}) = \sum_{j \in b_0} \frac{p(e_0|f_j)}{\phi_0}.$$

3.2.2 EdTM: Lexicon Model

In contrast to the derivation of EiTM, the Markov chain rule cannot be applied at this point, since we do not model the probability of f_{b_i}, but the probability of e_i conditioned on f_{b_i}. Thus, we average over all aligned source words f_{b_i}, which results in:

$$p(e_i|f_{b_{i'}}, f_{b_i}, e_{i'}, b_{i'}, b_i) = \frac{1}{\phi_i} \sum_{j \in b_i} \frac{1}{\phi_{i'} + \phi_i^{<j}} \Big(\sum_{j' \in b_{i'}} p(e_i|f_j, e_{i'}, f_{j'}, \Delta_{j',j}^{\phi_i}) + \sum_{\bar{j} \in b_i^{<j}} p(e_i|f_j, f_{\bar{j}}, \Delta_{\bar{j},j}) \Big).$$

3.2.3 EdTM: Alignment Model

Applying the same assumptions as for the lexicon model, the EdTM alignment model results in:

$$p(b_i|f_{b_{i'}}, f_{b_i}, e_{i'}, b_{i'}) = \frac{1}{\phi_i} \sum_{j \in b_i} \frac{1}{\phi_{i'} + \phi_i^{<j}} \Big(\sum_{j' \in b_{i'}} p(\Delta_{j',j}^{\phi_i}|f_j, e_{i'}, f_{j'}) + \sum_{\bar{j} \in b_i^{<j}} p(\Delta_{\bar{j},j}|f_j, f_{\bar{j}}) \Big).$$

3.3 Count Models and Smoothing

So far, we have introduced the ETM and shown how to include unaligned words and multiple word dependencies. However, there are various possibilities to train the lexicon and alignment probabilities derived in Subsections 3.1 and 3.2.

As a starting point, we apply relative frequencies obtained from bilingual training data, where the Viterbi alignment is estimated using GIZA++ (Och and Ney, 2003). In order to address data sparseness, we apply interpolated Kneser-Ney smoothing as described in (Chen and Goodman, 1998). In comparison to monolingual n-grams used in LMs, we lack any clear order of e, f, e', f' and Δ, since they include bilingual and reordering information. Similar to the approach taken by Mariño et al. (2006), we model the probability of the bilingual word pair (e, f) given its predecessor (e', f', Δ) which also includes the jump class. The EdTM lexicon model for dependencies on previously aligned target words is computed as

$$p(e|f, e', f', \Delta) = \frac{p(e, f|e', f', \Delta)}{p(\cdot, f|e', f', \Delta)}, \tag{9}$$

where $p(e, f|e', f', \Delta)$ is the bigram distribution of (e, f) given its predecessor (e', f', Δ) with interpolated Kneser-Ney smoothing. The denominator $p(\cdot, f|e', f', \Delta)$ is obtained by marginalizing $p(e, f|e', f', \Delta)$ over all target words e. We follow the same approach for all other models in analogy.

	IWSLT		IWSLT		BOLT		BOLT	
	German	**English**	**English**	**French**	**Chinese**	**English**	**Arabic**	**English**
Sentences	4.32M		26.05M		4.08M		0.92M	
Run. Words	108M	109M	698M	810M	78M	86M	14M	16M
Vocabulary	836K	792K	2119K	2139K	384K	817K	285K	203K

Table 1: Statistics for the bilingual training data of the IWSLT 2014 German→English, English→French and the DARPA BOLT Chinese→English, Arabic→English translation tasks.

4 Integration into Phrase-based Decoding

In this work, we apply a standard phrase-based translation system (Koehn et al., 2003). The decoding process is implemented as a beam search for the best translation given a set of models $h_m(e_1^I, s_1^K, f_1^J)$. The goal of search is to maximize the log-linear feature score (Och and Ney, 2004):

$$\hat{e}_1^{\hat{I}} = \arg\max_{I, e_1^I, s_1^K} \left\{ \sum_{m=1}^{M} \lambda_m h_m(e_1^I, s_1^K, f_1^J) \right\}, \qquad (10)$$

where $s_1^K = s_1 \dots s_K$ is the hidden phrase alignment. The feature weights λ_m are tuned with minimum error rate training (MERT) (Och, 2003). The models h_m, that are part of all baselines presented in this work, are phrasal and lexical translation scores in both directions, an n-gram LM, a simple distance-based distortion model and word and phrase penalties. All phrase pairs that are licensed by the word alignment are extracted from the training corpus and their probabilities estimated as relative frequencies. Moreover, the word alignment each phrase pair has been extracted from is memorized in the phrase table.

Our extended translation models are integrated into this framework as additional features h_m. They are trained in both directions on a bilingual corpus and the Viterbi alignment, resulting in four additional features. When training in the Target→Source direction, the alignment direction is also swapped. Thus, EiTM and EdTM have the advantage of including context beyond phrase boundaries only when trained in the Source→Target direction.

To include the extended translation models into the phrasal decoder, the source position aligned to the last (not inserted) target word of the previously translated phrase has to be memorized in the search state of a partial hypothesis. Although this slightly affects hypothesis recombination and therefore leads to a larger search space, in practice it does not degrade the search accuracy, as experiments with relaxed pruning parameters have shown.

5 Evaluation

We perform experiments on the large-scale IWSLT 2014[2] (Cettolo et al., 2014) German→English, English→French and the large-scale DARPA BOLT Chinese→English, Arabic→English tasks. As mentioned in Section 4, all baseline systems include phrasal and lexical smoothing scores trained in both directions. Word alignments are trained with GIZA++, by sequentially running 5 iterations each for the IBM-1, HMM and IBM-4 alignment models.

The domain of IWSLT consists of lecture-type talks presented at TED conferences which are also available online[3]. The baseline systems are trained on all provided bilingual data. All systems are optimized on the `dev2010` and evaluated on the `test2010` corpus. The ETM is trained on the TED portions of the data: 138K sentences for German→English and 185K sentences for English→French.

For German→English, to estimate the 4-gram LM, we additionally make use of parts of the Shuffled News, LDC English Gigaword and 10^9-French-English corpora, selected by a cross-entropy difference criterion (Moore and Lewis, 2010). In total, 1.7 billion running words are taken for LM training. For English→French, we use a large general domain 5-gram LM and an in-domain 5-gram LM. Both are estimated with the KenLM toolkit (Heafield et al., 2013) using interpolated Kneser-Ney smoothing. For the general domain LM, we first select $\frac{1}{2}$ of the English Shuffled News, $\frac{1}{4}$ of the French Shuffled News as well as both the English and French Gigaword corpora

[2]`http://www.iwslt2014.org`
[3]`http://www.ted.com/`

by the same cross-entropy difference criterion. By concatenating this selection with all available remaining monolingual data, we build an unpruned LM.

The BOLT tasks are evaluated on the "discussion forum" domain. For Chinese→English, the baseline is trained on 4.08M general domain sentence pairs and the 5-gram LM on 2.9 billion running words in total. The ETM is trained on an in-domain subset of 67.8K sentences and the test set contains 1844 sentences. For the Arabic→English BOLT task, we use only the in-domain data for training the baseline and the ETM. The training and test sets contain text drawn from discussion forums in Egyptian Arabic. The evaluation set contains 1510 bilingual sentence pairs.

The baseline systems for all tasks - except the Arabic→English BOLT task, where preliminary experiments showed no improvement - contain a 7-gram word cluster language model (Wuebker et al., 2013) and for comparison, we also experiment with a hierarchical reordering model (HRM) (Galley and Manning, 2008). When integrated into a phrase-based decoder, Durrani et al. (2013b) have shown the OSM to outperform bilingual LMs on MTUs. Therefore, we directly compare ourselves with a 7-gram OSM implemented into our phrase-based decoder as an additional feature. The OSM is trained on the same data as the ETM for all tasks. Bilingual data statistics for all tasks are shown in Table 1. For each system setting we evaluate three MERT runs using `multeval` (Clark et al., 2011). Results are reported in BLEU (Papineni et al., 2001) and TER (Snover et al., 2006). The optimization criterion for all experiments is BLEU.

5.1 Model parameters

To measure the complexity of the extended translation models in comparison to the phrase-based translation model, we count the number of parameters to be trained for each.

Table 2 illustrates the phrase-table and ETM count table entries for the BOLT Arabic→English translation task, where both the phrase-based baseline and the ETM are trained on the same bilingual data consisting of 0.92M bilingual sentence pairs. Here, we only show the numbers for the Source→Target direction, as the numbers for the Target→Source direction are similar. The EdTM and EiTM each have roughly 35M parameters to be trained, i.e. there are approximately 70M parameters to be trained for the ETM in total. This is slightly more than the 57M parameters for the phrase translation model.

model	**# parameters**
phrase-based translation	57,155,149
EdTM	35,511,396
lexicon	19,899,812
alignment	15,276,718
deletion	334,866
EiTM	34,994,534
lexicon	20,153,114
alignment	14,791,722
deletion	49,698

Table 2: The number of model parameters for the BOLT Arabic→English bilingual training data after filtering.

		BLEU	TER
Baseline + HRM		30.7	49.3
+ EiTM	**+ EdTM**		
Ge↔En	*none*	31.4	48.3
none	Ge↔En	31.6	48.1
Ge→En	Ge→En	31.6	48.2
Ge↔En	Ge↔En	31.8	48.2

Table 3: Results for the German→English IWSLT data. The systems are optimized with MERT on the `dev2010` set. All results are statistically significant with ≥99% confidence.

5.2 Results

In order to compare the effect of the EiTM and EdTM used in a phrase-based decoder, we have trained the baseline including the HRM as described above on the full German→English bilingual data of the IWSLT task and the extended translation models on the TED data. The results evaluated on `test2010` are shown in Table 3.

Including the EiTM trained in both German→English and English→German directions into the phrasal decoder yields an absolute improvement of +0.7 BLEU and -1.0 TER, whereas including the EdTM yields +0.9 BLEU and -1.2 TER. This underlines that the EdTM is more suitable for translation than the EiTM because it predicts the direct probability

	Ge-En	En-Fr	Zh-En	Ar-En
Baseline	30.6	32.8	16.5	23.8
+ ETM	**31.4**	**33.8**	**16.8**	**24.1**
+ OSM	**31.6**	**34.1**	**17.3**	**24.1**
+ HRM	30.7	**33.1**	**17.0**	24.0
+ ETM	**31.8**	**33.9**	**17.5**	**24.4**
+ OSM	**31.8**	**34.5**	**17.6**	24.1

Table 4: Comparison of ETM to the HRM and OSM measured in BLEU. Statistically significant improvements with ≥99% confidence are printed in boldface.

of a target word, which corresponds to the actual translation direction. Note, that both EiTM and EdTM lose the advantage of modelling dependencies beyond phrase boundaries when trained in the inverse direction English→German. Therefore, we have evaluated their joint performance when trained only in German→English direction, which is similar to the performance of EdTM trained in both directions. This can be due to the fact that even though the EiTM trained in German→English direction incorporates dependencies beyond phrase boundaries, the EdTM trained in English→German direction profits from the better suited direct translation probability. The full ETM, i.e. EiTM and EdTM trained in both directions, yields the best overall performance gain of +1.1 BLEU and -1.1 TER over the baseline.

Moreover, we evaluate the performance of the (full) ETM compared to the HRM and a 7-gram OSM, which are all introduced as additional features into the log-linear framework of the baseline phrase-based decoder. The results are presented in Table 4. The ETM performs similarly to the HRM for the Chinese→English and Arabic→English tasks, resulting in +0.3 BLEU over the PBT baseline. For both IWSLT tasks, the ETM outperforms the HRM by +0.7 BLEU, gaining +0.8 BLEU for the German→English and +1.0 BLEU for the German→English task over the PBT baseline. The context captured by the ETM corresponds roughly to the context captured by a 3-gram OSM. Bearing this in mind, we compare the ETM to a 7-gram OSM, which yields +0.25 BLEU more than the ETM averaged over the four language pairs. Comparing the OSM vocabulary of 1.5M words for the Arabic→English task to the 285K words in the Arabic corpus, this results in an ETM vocabulary 5-times smaller than the OSM vocabulary.

We also compare the ETM to the OSM on top of a PBT system that also includes the HRM, which is shown in the last two lines of Table 4. The performance of the ETM benefits from the information introduced by the HRM, as the gain of using the ETM is further increased by +0.15 BLEU on average. Overall, the ETM gains consistent and statistically significant improvements of +0.7 BLEU on average for all four language pairs over a state-of-the-art phrase-based decoder including the HRM. On the other hand, OSM seems to have a higher overlap with HRM, as the gain of OSM compared to ETM is reduced to +0.1 BLEU on average. Thus, on top of the phrase-based system including the HRM, the ETM including a bilingual word pair and the corresponding reordering jump class proves to be competitive to a 7-gram OSM.

6 Discussion

We have integrated two variants of a novel extended translation model into a state-of-the-art phrase-based decoder. The ETM captures lexical and reordering context beyond phrase boundaries in both the Source→Target and Target→Source directions. Further, the model potentially captures long-range reorderings and utilizes multiple and empty alignments, allowing for target insertions and source deletions. As an initial step, we have implemented the ETM using relative frequencies with interpolated Kneser-Ney smoothing. Its consistent and statistically significant improvement of up to +1.1 BLEU and -1.1 TER respectively +0.7 BLEU on average has been shown for four large-scale translation tasks, outperforming competitive phrase-based systems that include lexical and phrase translation models and hierarchical reordering models.

Compared to a 7-gram OSM, the ETM is much simpler in design: It uses a smaller vocabulary size, estimates the probability of single words instead of bilingual MTUs, avoids the need of reordering gaps and includes less lexical and reordering context, thus being less sparse. For all that, it performs competitively to a 7-gram OSM on top of phrase-based systems including the HRM. This fact underlines the advantages introduced by the ETM: It operates on words rather than MTUs, explicitly models multiple alignments instead of incorporating linear dependencies and models reorderings in a less complex way.

So far we have used the ETM as an additional feature in a phrase-based decoder, but we believe that the usage of such a decoder is a limitation. First, the ETM is estimated on alignments, which themselves are optimized for the IBM models. Second, decoding is performed using phrases that are extracted from the alignments using heuristics. Therefore, the potential of a phrase-based decoder is also limited by these heuristics.

Based on these facts, we believe that the ETM will show its full potential when it is also integrated into the training of the alignment, leading not only to a higher alignment quality, but also to a joint optimization of the alignments and the ETM. Further, directly applying the ETM within a word-based decoder utilizing an extended translation and reordering context will redundantize phrases and thus any extraction heuristics. We believe that a consistent framework where the ETM is applied in both training the alignments and decoding will significantly advance machine translation.

For the short term, we will investigate better smoothing strategies and the possibilities of using neural networks instead of count models.

Acknowledgements

This work has received funding from the European Union's Horizon 2020 research and innovation programme under grant agreement n° 645452 (QT21). This material is partially based upon work supported by the DARPA BOLT project under Contract No. HR0011- 12-C-0015. Any opinions, findings and conclusions or recommendations expressed in this material are those of the authors and do not necessarily reflect the views of DARPA.

References

Michael Auli, Michel Galley, Chris Quirk, and Geoffrey Zweig. 2013. Joint Language and Translation Modeling with Recurrent Neural Networks. In *Conference on Empirical Methods in Natural Language Processing*, pages 1044–1054, Seattle, USA, October.

Peter F. Brown, John Cocke, Stephan A. Della Pietra, Vincent J. Della Pietra, Fredrick Jelinek, John D. Lafferty, Robert L. Mercer, and Paul S. Rossin. 1990. A Statistical Approach to Machine Translation. *Computational Linguistics*, 16(2):79–85, June.

Peter F. Brown, Stephan A. Della Pietra, Vincent J. Della Pietra, and Robert L. Mercer. 1993. The Mathematics of Statistical Machine Translation: Parameter Estimation. *Computational Linguistics*, 19(2):263–311, June.

Mauro Cettolo, Jan Niehues, Sebastian Stüker, Luisa Bentivogli, and Marcello Federico. 2014. Report on the 11th iwslt evaluation campaign, iwslt 2014. In *International Workshop on Spoken Language Translation*, pages 2–11, Lake Tahoe, CA, USA, December.

Stanley F. Chen and Joshuo Goodman. 1998. An Empirical Study of Smoothing Techniques for Language Modeling. Technical Report TR-10-98, Computer Science Group, Harvard University, Cambridge, MA, August.

Jonathan H. Clark, Chris Dyer, Alon Lavie, and Noah A. Smith. 2011. Better hypothesis testing for statistical machine translation: Controlling for optimizer instability. In *49th Annual Meeting of the Association for Computational Linguistics:shortpapers*, pages 176–181, Portland, Oregon, June.

Yonggang Deng and William Byrne. 2005. Hmm word and phrase alignment for statistical machine translation. In *Proceedings of Human Language Technology Conference and Conference on Empirical Methods in Natural Language Processing*, pages 169–176, Vancouver, British Columbia, Canada, October. Association for Computational Linguistics.

Jacob Devlin, Rabih Zbib, Zhongqiang Huang, Thomas Lamar, Richard Schwartz, and John Makhoul. 2014. Fast and Robust Neural Network Joint Models for Statistical Machine Translation. In *52nd Annual Meeting of the Association for Computational Linguistics*, pages 1370–1380, Baltimore, MD, USA, June.

Nadir Durrani, Helmut Schmid, and Alexander Fraser. 2011. A joint sequence translation model with integrated reordering. In *Proceedings of the 49th Annual Meeting of the Association for Computational Linguistics: Human Language Technologies*, pages 1045–1054, Portland, Oregon, USA, June. Association for Computational Linguistics.

Nadir Durrani, Alexander Fraser, and Helmut Schmid. 2013a. Model with minimal translation units, but decode with phrases. In *Proceedings of the 2013 Conference of the North American Chapter of the Association for Computational Linguistics: Human Language Technologies*, pages 1–11, Atlanta, Georgia, June. Association for Computational Linguistics.

Nadir Durrani, Alexander Fraser, Helmut Schmid, Hieu Hoang, and Philipp Koehn. 2013b. Can markov models over minimal translation units help phrase-based smt? In *Proceedings of the 51st Annual Meeting of the Association for Computational*

Linguistics (Volume 2: Short Papers), pages 399–405, Sofia, Bulgaria, August. Association for Computational Linguistics.

Nadir Durrani, Philipp Koehn, Helmut Schmid, and Alexander Fraser. 2014. Investigating the usefulness of generalized word representations in smt. In *COLING*, Dublin, Ireland, aug.

Yang Feng and Trevor Cohn. 2013. A markov model of machine translation using non-parametric bayesian inference. In *51st Annual Meeting of the Association for Computational Linguistics*, pages 333–342, Sofia, Bulgaria, August.

Minwei Feng, Jan-Thorsten Peter, and Hermann Ney. 2013. Advancements in reordering models for statistical machine translation. In *Annual Meeting of the Assoc. for Computational Linguistics*, pages 322–332, Sofia, Bulgaria, August.

Yang Feng, Trevor Cohn, and Xinkai Du. 2014. Factored markov translation with robust modeling. In *Proceedings of the Eighteenth Conference on Computational Natural Language Learning*, pages 151–159, Ann Arbor, Michigan, June. Association for Computational Linguistics.

Michel Galley and Christopher D. Manning. 2008. A simple and effective hierarchical phrase reordering model. In *Proceedings of the Conference on Empirical Methods in Natural Language Processing*, EMNLP '08, pages 848–856, Stroudsburg, PA, USA. Association for Computational Linguistics.

Andreas Guta, Tamer Alkhouli, Jan-Thorsten Peter, Joern Wuebker, and Hermann Ney. 2015. A comparison between count and neural network models based on joint translation and reordering sequences. In *Proceedings of the 2015 Conference on Empirical Methods in Natural Language Processing*, Lisboa, Portugal, September. Association for Computational Linguistics. to appear.

Kenneth Heafield, Ivan Pouzyrevsky, Jonathan H. Clark, and Philipp Koehn. 2013. Scalable modified Kneser-Ney language model estimation. In *Proceedings of the 51st Annual Meeting of the Association for Computational Linguistics*, pages 690–696, Sofia, Bulgaria, August.

Yuening Hu, Michael Auli, Qin Gao, and Jianfeng Gao. 2014. Minimum translation modeling with recurrent neural networks. In *Proceedings of the 14th Conference of the European Chapter of the Association for Computational Linguistics*, pages 20–29, Gothenburg, Sweden, April. Association for Computational Linguistics.

P. Koehn, F. J. Och, and D. Marcu. 2003. Statistical Phrase-Based Translation. In *Proceedings of the 2003 Meeting of the North American chapter of the Association for Computational Linguistics (NAACL-03)*, pages 127–133, Edmonton, Alberta.

Hai Son Le, Alexandre Allauzen, and François Yvon. 2012. Continuous Space Translation Models with Neural Networks. In *Conference of the North American Chapter of the Association for Computational Linguistics: Human Language Technologies*, pages 39–48, Montreal, Canada, June.

José B Mariño, Rafael E Banchs, Josep M Crego, Adrià de Gispert, Patrik Lambert, José A R Fonollosa, and Marta R Costa-jussà. 2006. N-gram-based Machine Translation. *Comput. Linguist.*, 32(4):527–549, December.

R.C. Moore and W. Lewis. 2010. Intelligent Selection of Language Model Training Data. In *ACL (Short Papers)*, pages 220–224, Uppsala, Sweden, July.

Jan Niehues, Teresa Herrmann, Stephan Vogel, and Alex Waibel, 2011. *Proceedings of the Sixth Workshop on Statistical Machine Translation*, chapter Wider Context by Using Bilingual Language Models in Machine Translation, pages 198–206. Association for Computational Linguistics.

Franz J. Och and Hermann Ney. 2002. Discriminative Training and Maximum Entropy Models for Statistical Machine Translation. In *Proc. of the 40th Annual Meeting of the Association for Computational Linguistics (ACL)*, pages 295–302, Philadelphia, PA, July.

Franz J. Och and Hermann Ney. 2003. A Systematic Comparison of Various Statistical Alignment Models. *Computational Linguistics*, 29(1):19–51, March.

Franz Josef Och and Hermann Ney. 2004. The Alignment Template Approach to Statistical Machine Translation. *Computational Linguistics*, 30(4):417–449, December.

Franz J. Och, Christoph Tillmann, and Hermann Ney. 1999. Improved Alignment Models for Statistical Machine Translation. In *Proc. Joint SIGDAT Conf. on Empirical Methods in Natural Language Processing and Very Large Corpora*, pages 20–28, University of Maryland, College Park, MD, June.

Franz Josef Och. 2003. Minimum Error Rate Training in Statistical Machine Translation. In *Proc. of the 41th Annual Meeting of the Association for Computational Linguistics (ACL)*, pages 160–167, Sapporo, Japan, July.

Kishore Papineni, Salim Roukos, Todd Ward, and Wei-Jing Zhu. 2001. Bleu: a Method for Automatic Evaluation of Machine Translation. IBM Research Report RC22176 (W0109-022), IBM Research Division, Thomas J. Watson Research Center, P.O. Box 218, Yorktown Heights, NY 10598, September.

Matthew Snover, Bonnie Dorr, Richard Schwartz, Linnea Micciulla, and John Makhoul. 2006. A Study of Translation Edit Rate with Targeted Human Annotation. In *Proceedings of the 7th Conference of the Association for Machine Translation in the Americas*, pages 223–231, Cambridge, Massachusetts, USA, August.

Darelene Stewart, Roland Kuhn, Eric Joanis, and George Foster. 2014. Coarse split and lump bilingual languagemodels for richer source information in smt. In *AMTA*, Vancouver, BC, Canada, oct.

Martin Sundermeyer, Tamer Alkhouli, Joern Wuebker, and Hermann Ney. 2014. Translation modeling with bidirectional recurrent neural networks. In *Conference on Empirical Methods in Natural Language Processing*, pages 14–25, Doha, Qatar, October.

Joern Wuebker, Stephan Peitz, Felix Rietig, and Hermann Ney. 2013. Improving statistical machine translation with word class models. In *Conference on Empirical Methods in Natural Language Processing*, pages 1377–1381, Seattle, USA, October.

Richard Zens, Franz Josef Och, and Hermann Ney. 2002. Phrase-Based Statistical Machine Translation. In *25th German Conf. on Artificial Intelligence (KI2002)*, pages 18–32, Aachen, Germany, September. Springer Verlag.

Hui Zhang, Kristina Toutanova, Chris Quirk, and Jianfeng Gao. 2013. Beyond left-to-right: Multiple decomposition structures for smt. In *Proceedings of the 2013 Conference of the North American Chapter of the Association for Computational Linguistics: Human Language Technologies*, pages 12–21, Atlanta, Georgia, June. Association for Computational Linguistics.

Investigations on Phrase-based Decoding with Recurrent Neural Network Language and Translation Models

Tamer Alkhouli, Felix Rietig, and Hermann Ney
Human Language Technology and Pattern Recognition Group
RWTH Aachen University, Aachen, Germany
{surname}@cs.rwth-aachen.de

Abstract

This work explores the application of recurrent neural network (RNN) language and translation models during phrase-based decoding. Due to their use of unbounded context, the decoder integration of RNNs is more challenging compared to the integration of feedforward neural models. In this paper, we apply approximations and use caching to enable RNN decoder integration, while requiring reasonable memory and time resources. We analyze the effect of caching on translation quality and speed, and use it to integrate RNN language and translation models into a phrase-based decoder. To the best of our knowledge, no previous work has discussed the integration of RNN translation models into phrase-based decoding. We also show that a special RNN can be integrated efficiently without the need for approximations. We compare decoding using RNNs to rescoring n-best lists on two tasks: IWSLT 2013 German→English, and BOLT Arabic→English. We demonstrate that the performance of decoding with RNNs is at least as good as using them in rescoring.

1 Introduction

Applying neural networks to statistical machine translation has been gaining increasing attention recently. Neural network language and translation models have been successfully applied to rescore the first-pass decoding output (Le et al., 2012; Sundermeyer et al., 2014; Hu et al., 2014; Guta et al., 2015). These models include feedforward and recurrent neural networks.

A more ambitious move is to apply neural networks directly during decoding, which in principle should give the models a better chance to influence translation in comparison to rescoring, as rescoring is limited to scoring and reranking fixed n-best lists. Recently, neural networks were used for standalone decoding using a simple beam-search word-based decoder (Sutskever et al., 2014; Bahdanau et al., 2015). Another approach is to apply neural models directly in a phrase-based decoder. We focus on this approach, which is challenging since phrase-based decoding typically involves generating tens or even hundreds of millions of partial hypotheses. Scoring such a number of hypotheses using neural models is expensive, mainly due to the usually large output layer. Nevertheless, decoder integration has been done in (Vaswani et al., 2013) for feedforward neural language models. Devlin et al. (2014) integrate feedforward translation models into phrase-based decoding reporting major improvements, which highlight the strength of the underlying models.

In related fields like e. g. language modeling, RNNs has been shown to perform considerably better than standard feedforward architectures (Mikolov et al., 2011; Arisoy et al., 2012; Sundermeyer et al., 2013; Liu et al., 2014). Sundermeyer et al. (2014) also show that RNN translation models outperform feedforward networks in rescoring. Given the success of feedforward translation models in phrase-based decoding, it is natural to ask how RNN translation models perform if they are integrated in decoding.

This paper investigates the performance of RNN language and translation models in phrase-based decoding. For RNNs that depend on an unbounded target context, their integration into a phrase-based decoder employing beam search requires relaxing the pruning parameters, which makes translation inefficient. Therefore, we apply approximations to integrate RNN translation models during phrase-based decoding. Auli and Gao (2014) use approximate scoring to integrate an RNN language model (LM), but to the best of our knowledge, no work yet has explored the integration of RNN translation models. In addition to approximate models, we integrate a special RNN model that only depends on the source context, allowing for exact, yet efficient integration into the decoder. We provide a detailed comparison between using the RNN models in decoding vs. rescoring on two tasks: IWSLT 2013 German→English and BOLT Arabic→English. In addition, we analyze the approximation effect on translation speed and quality.

Our integration follows (Huang et al., 2014), which uses caching strategies to apply an RNN LM in speech recognition. This can be viewed as a modification of the approximation introduced by Auli and Gao (2014), allowing for a flexible choice between translation quality and speed. We choose to integrate the word-based RNN translation models that were introduced in (Sundermeyer et al., 2014), due to their success in rescoring n-best lists.

The rest of this paper is structured as follows. In Section 2 we review the related work. The RNN LM integration and caching strategies are discussed in Section 3, while Section 4 discusses the integration of exact and approximate RNN translation models. We analyze the effect of approximation and caching on translation quality and speed in Section 5. The section also includes the translation experiments comparing decoding vs. rescoring. Finally we conclude with Section 6.

2 Related Work

Schwenk (2012) proposed a feedforward network that predicts phrases of a fixed maximum length, such that all phrase words are predicted at once. The prediction is conditioned on the source phrase. The model was used to compute additional phrase table scores, and the phrase table was used for decoding. No major difference was reported compared to rescoring using the model. Our work focuses on neural network scoring performed online during decoding, capturing dependencies that extend beyond phrase boundaries.

Online usage of neural networks during decoding requires tackling the costly output normalization step. Vaswani et al. (2013) avoid this step by training feedforward neural language models using *noise contrastive estimation*. Auli and Gao (2014) propose an expected BLEU criterion instead of the usual cross-entropy. They train recurrent neural LMs without the need to normalize the output layer, but training becomes computationally more expensive as each training example is an n-best list instead of a sentence. At decoding time, however, scoring with the neural network is faster since normalization is not needed. Furthermore, they integrate cross-entropy RNNs without affecting state recombination. They report results over a baseline having a LM trained on the target side of the parallel data. The results for the RNN LM trained with cross-entropy indicated that decoding improves over rescoring, with the difference ranging from 0.4% to 0.8% BLEU. In this work, we stick to RNNs trained using cross-entropy, with a class-factored output layer to reduce the normalization cost.

Devlin et al. (2014) augment the cross-entropy training objective function to produce approximately normalized scores directly. They also precompute the first hidden layer beforehand, resulting in large speedups. Major improvements over strong baselines were reported. While their work focuses on feedforward translation models, we investigate the decoder integration of RNN models instead, which poses additional challenges due to the unbounded history used by RNNs.

Huang et al. (2014) truncate the history and use it to cache the hidden RNN states, the normalization factors and the probability values. This is applied to an RNN LM in a speech recognition task. In this work, we apply these caching strategies to a recurrent LM for translation tasks. Furthermore, we analyze the degree of approximation and its influence on the search problem. We also extend caching and apply it to RNN translation models that are conditioned on source and target words.

Sundermeyer et al. (2014) proposed word- and phrase-based RNN translation models and applied them to rescore n-best lists, reporting major improvements. The RNN word-based models were shown to outperform a feedforward neural network. This work aims to enable the use of the word-based RNN models in phrase-based decoding, and to explore their effect on the search space during decoding.

3 RNN Language Model Integration

In this section we discuss the integration of the RNN LM using caching in details. These caching techniques will also be applied to the joint

RNN translation model in Section 4.2 with minor changes.

First, we will briefly introduce the RNN LM. The LM probability $p(e_i|e_1^{i-1})$ of the target word e_i at position i depends on the unbounded target history e_1^{i-1}. The probability can be computed using an RNN LM of a single hidden layer as follows:

$$y_{i-1} = A_1 \hat{e}_{i-1} \tag{1}$$

$$h(e_1^{i-1}) = \xi(y_{i-1}; A_2, h(e_1^{i-2})) \tag{2}$$

$$o(e_1^{i-1}) = A_3 h(e_1^{i-1}) \tag{3}$$

$$Z(e_1^{i-1}) = \sum_{w=1}^{|V|} e^{o_w(e_1^{i-1})} \tag{4}$$

$$p(e_i|e_1^{i-1}) = \frac{e^{o_{e_i}(e_1^{i-1})}}{Z(e_1^{i-1})} \tag{5}$$

where A_1, A_2 and A_3 denote the neural network weight matrices, $\hat{e}_{i-1}$ is the one-hot vector encoding the word e_{i-1}, and y_{i-1} is its word embedding vector. h is a vector of the hidden layer activations depending on the unbounded context, and it is computed recurrently using the function ξ, which we use to represent a generic recurrent layer. $o \in \mathbb{R}^{|V|}$ is a $|V|$-dimensional vector containing the raw unnormalized output layer values, where $|V|$ is the vocabulary size. The probability in Eq. 5 is computed using the softmax function, which requires the normalization factor Z. In this work, we use a class-factored output layer consisting of a class layer and a word layer (Goodman, 2001; Morin and Bengio, 2005). In this case, the LM probability is the product of the two:

$$p(e_i|e_1^{i-1}) = p(e_i|c(e_i), e_1^{i-1}) \cdot p(c(e_i)|e_1^{i-1})$$

where c denotes a word mapping from any target word to its unique class. Such factorization is used to reduce the normalization cost.

Phrase-based decoding involves the generation of a search graph consisting of nodes. Each node represents a search state uniquely identified by a triple $(C, \tilde{e}, j)$, where C denotes the coverage set, $\tilde{e}$ is the language model history, and j is the position of the last translated source word. During decoding, equivalent nodes are recombined. The degree of recombination is affected by the order of the LM history, where higher orders result in fewer recombinations. Our phrase-based decoder is based on beam search, where the search space is pruned and a limit is imposed on the number of hypotheses to explore. Since an RNN LM depends on the full target history e_1^{i-1}, a naïve integration of the RNN LM would define $\tilde{e} = e_1^{i-1}$, but this leads to an explosion in the number of nodes in the search graph, which in turn leads to reducing the variance between the hypotheses lying within the beam, and focusing the decoding effort on hypotheses that are similar to each other.

Since the RNN LM computes a hidden state $h(e_1^{i-1})$ encoding the sequence e_1^{i-1}, another way is to extend the search state of the node to $(C, \tilde{e}, j, h(e_1^{i-1}))$. However, such extension would pose the same problem for recombination as the one encountered if the full history sequence is stored. Therefore, we resort to approximate RNN LM evaluation in decoding. An approximation proposed in (Auli et al., 2013) is to extend the search node with the RNN hidden state, but to ignore the hidden state when deciding which nodes to recombine. That is, two search nodes are deemed equivalent if they share the same triple $(C, \tilde{e}, j)$, even if they have different RNN hidden states. Upon recombination, one of the two hidden states is kept and stored in the resulting recombined node.

3.1 Caching Strategies

In this work, we follow a modification of the approach by (Auli et al., 2013). Instead of storing the RNN hidden state in the search nodes, we truncate the RNN history to the most recent n words e_{i-n}^{i-1}, and store this word sequence in the node instead. As in (Auli et al., 2013), the added information is ignored when deciding on recombination. When the RNN hidden state is needed, it is retrieved from a cache using the truncated history as a key. The cache is shared between all nodes. While this might seem as an unnecessary complication, it introduces the flexibility of choosing the degree of approximation. The parameter n can be used to control the trade-off between accuracy and speed; more accurate RNN scores are obtained if n is set to a large value, or faster decoding is achieved if n is set to a small value. In principle, we can still simulate the case of storing the hidden RNN state directly in the search nodes by using large n values as we will see later. We will refer to n as the *caching order*.

During decoding, we use the cache C_{state} to store the hidden state $h(e_1^{i-1})$ using the key e_{i-n}^{i-1}.

The state $h(e_1^{i-1})$ is computed once, using the hidden state $h(e_1^{i-2})$ as given in Eq. 2, and the cached state is reused whenever it is needed. Note that the n-gram key is only used to look up the hidden state, which will have been computed recurrently encoding an unbounded history. This is different from a feedforward network which uses the n-gram as direct input to compute its output. We also introduce a cache C_{norm} to store the output layer's normalization factor $Z(e_1^{i-1})$ using the same key e_{i-n}^{i-1}, hence avoiding the sum of Eq. 4, which requires the expensive computation of the full raw output layer values $o(e_1^{i-1})$ using Eq. 3. If the normalization factor is found in the cache, computing Eq. 5 only requires the output value o_{e_i} corresponding to word e_i, which involves a dot product rather than a matrix-vector product. Since we use a class-factored output layer, we cache the normalization factor of the class layer. Finally, the cache C_{prob} is introduced to store the word probability using the caching key (e_i, e_{i-n}^{i-1}).

Fig. 1 shows the percentage of cache hits for different caching orders. We count a cache hit if a look up is performed on that cache and the entry is found, otherwise the look up counts as a cache miss. We observe high hit ratios even for high caching orders. This is due to the fact that most of the hits occur upon node expansion, where a node is extended by a new phrase, and where all candidates share the same history. We also observe that word probabilities are retrieved from the cache 70% of the time for high enough caching orders, which can be explained due to the similarities between the phrase candidates in their first word. Note also that the reported C_{norm} hit ratio is for the cases where the cache C_{prob} produces a cache miss. We report this hit ratio since the original C_{norm} hit ratio is equal to C_{state}'s hit ratio as they both use the same caching key.

We report the effect of caching on translation speed in Tab. 1, where we use a large caching order of 30 to simulate the search space covered when no caching is used. Using none of the caches and storing the hidden state in the search node instead has a speed of 0.03 words per second. This increases to 0.05 words per second when caching the hidden state. This is because caching computes each hidden state once, while storing the hidden state in the search node may lead to computing the same hidden state multiple times, as no global view of what has been computed is available. Caching the normalization constant yields a large speedup, due to the reduction of the number of times the full output layer is computed. Finally, caching word probabilities does not speed up translation further. This is due to the class-factored output layer we use, where computing the softmax for the word layer part (given a word class) uses a small matrix corresponding to the words that belong to the same class of the word in question. Overall, a speedup factor of 6 is achieved over the case where no caching is used. Achieving this speedup does not lead to a loss in translation quality, in fact, for all cases, the translation quality is the same due to the large caching order used.

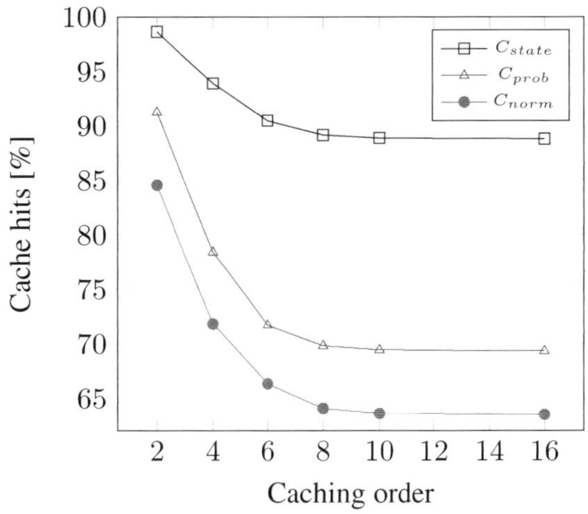

Figure 1: Cache hits for different caching orders when using an RNN LM in the decoder.

Cache	Speed [words/second]
none	0.03
C_{state}	0.05
$C_{state} + C_{norm}$	0.19
$C_{state} + C_{norm} + C_{prob}$	0.19

Table 1: The effect of using caching on translation speed. A large caching order of 30 is used to reduce the approximation effect of caching, leading to the same translation quality for all table entries.

4 RNN Translation Model Integration

One of the main contributions of this work is to integrate RNN translation models into phrase-based decoding. To the best of our knowledge, no such integration has been done before. We integrate two models that work on the word level. The models were proposed in (Sundermeyer et al., 2014). They assume a one-to-one alignment between the source sentence $f_1^I = f_1 \dots f_I$ and the target sentence $e_1^I = e_1 \dots e_I$. Such alignment is obtained using heuristics that make use of IBM 1 lexica. In the following, we discuss the integration of the bidirectional translation model (BTM), which can be done exactly and efficiently without resorting to approximations. In addition, we propose an approximate integration of the joint model (JM) which makes use of the same caching strategies discussed in Section 3.

4.1 Bidirectional Translation Model

The bidirectional translation model (BTM) is conditioned on the full source sentence, without dependence on previously predicted target words:

$$p(e_1^I|f_1^I) \approx \prod_{i=1}^{I} p(e_i|f_1^I). \tag{6}$$

This equation is realized by a network that uses forward and backward recurrent layers to capture the complete source sentence. The forward layer is a recurrent hidden layer that processes the source sequence from left to right, while a backward layer does the processing backwards, from right to left. The source sentence is basically split at a given position i, then past and future representations of the sentence are recursively computed by the forward and backward layers, respectively. Due to recurrency, the forward layer encodes f_1^i, and the backward layer encodes f_i^I, and together they encode the full source sentence f_1^I, which is used to score the output target word e_i.

Including the BTM in the decoder is efficient and scores can be computed exactly. This is because the model has no dependence on previous target words hypothesized during decoding. For a sentence of length I, and a target vocabulary size $|V|$, the number of distinct evaluations is at most $I \cdot |V|$. The term I corresponds to the number of possibilities where the source sentence may be split into past and future parts, and the term $|V|$ is the different possible target words that may be hypothesized. In phrase-based decoding, the number of distinct evaluations is in the order of thousands, as the number of target word candidates per sentence is limited by the phrase table. Since the input to the network is completely known at the beginning of decoding, it is enough that the full network is computed I times per source sentence, once per split position i for $1 \leq i \leq I$. Computing $p(e_i = e|f_1^I)$ amounts to looking up the normalized output layer value corresponding the word e from the network computed using the split position i.

4.2 Joint Model

The joint model (JM) conditions target word predictions on the hypothesized target history in addition to the source history and the current source word:[1]

$$p(e_1^I|f_1^I) = \prod_{i=1}^{I} p(e_i|e_1^{i-1}, f_1^i). \tag{7}$$

This equation can be modeled using a network similar to the RNN LM. While the RNN LM has the previous target word e_{i-1} as direct input to score the current target word e_i, the JM aggregates the word embeddings of the previous target word e_{i-1} and the current source word f_i. Due to recurrency, the hidden state will encode the sequence pair (e_1^{i-1}, f_1^i).

Since the JM is similar to the RNN LM in its dependence on the unbounded history, we apply caching strategies similar to those used with the RNN LM. JM computations are shared between instances that have a truncated source and target history in common. The cache key in this case is $(e_{i-n}^{i-1}, f_{i-n+1}^i)$ for the C_{state} and C_{norm} caches, and $(e_i, e_{i-n}^{i-1}, f_{i-n+1}^i)$ for the C_{prob} cache.

5 Experiments

5.1 Setup

We carry out experiments on the IWSLT 2013 German→English shared translation task.[2] The baseline system is trained on all available bilingual data, 4.3M sentence pairs in total, and uses a 4-gram LM with modified Kneser-Ney smoothing (Kneser and Ney, 1995; Chen and Goodman, 1998), trained with the SRILM toolkit (Stolcke, 2002). As additional data sources for the LM, we selected parts of the Shuffled News and LDC English Gigaword corpora based on the cross-entropy difference (Moore and Lewis, 2010), resulting in a total of 1.7 billion running words for

[1]We use a unidirectional rather than a bidirectional JM, dropping the future source information f_{i+1}^I. This is because the models we integrate reorder the source sentence following the target order, which can only be done for the past part of the source sentence at decoding time.

[2]http://www.iwslt2013.org

LM training. The state-of-the-art baseline is a standard phrase-based SMT system (Koehn et al., 2003) tuned with MERT (Och, 2003). It contains a hierarchical reordering model (Galley and Manning, 2008) and a 7-gram word cluster language model (Wuebker et al., 2013). All neural networks are trained on the TED portion of the data (138K segments). The experiments are run using an observation histogram size of 100, with a maximum of 16 lexical hypotheses per source coverage and a maximum of 32 reordering alternatives per source cardinality.

Additional experiments are performed on the Arabic→English task of the DARPA BOLT project. The system is a standard phrase-based decoder trained on 921K segments, amounting to 15.5M running words, and using 17 dense features. The neural network training is performed using the same data. We evaluate results on two data sets from the 'discussion forum' domain, `test1` and `test2`. The sizes of the data sets are: 1219 (`dev`), 1510 (`test1`), and 1137 (`test2`) segments. An additional development set containing 2715 segments is used during RNN training. The experiments are run using an observation histogram size of 100, with a maximum of 32 lexical hypotheses per source coverage and a maximum of 8 reordering alternatives per source cardinality.

The BTM consists of a linear projection layer, forward and backward long-short term memory (LSTM) layers and an additional LSTM to combine them. Each of the LM and JM has a projection layer and a single LSTM layer. All layers have 200 nodes, with 2000 classes used for the class-factored output layer.

All results are measured in case-insensitive BLEU [%] (Papineni et al., 2002) and TER [%] (Snover et al., 2006) on a single reference. The reported decoding results are averages of 3 MERT optimization runs. Rescoring experiments are performed using 1000-best lists (without duplicates), where an additional MERT iteration is performed. 20 such trials are carried out and the average results are reported. We used the multeval toolkit (Clark et al., 2011) for evaluation.

5.2 Approximation Analysis

First, we will analyze the caching impact on decoding. We compare RNN LM rescoring and decoding by marking a win for the method finding the better search score. Decoding with the RNN LM uses approximate scores while rescoring with same model uses the exact scores. Fig. 2 shows the percentage of improved hypotheses for RNN decoding (compared to RNN rescoring) and for RNN rescoring (compared to RNN decoding). The figure does not include tie cases, which occur when RNN LM decoding and rescoring yield the same hypothesis as their best finding. For the caching order $n = 8$, decoding finds a better search score for 33% of the sentences compared to rescoring, while rescoring has a better score in 17% of the cases compared to decoding. The remaining 50% cases (not shown in the figure) correspond to ties where both search methods select the same hypotheses. Increasing the caching order improves the decoding quality. For the caching order $n = 16$, rescoring outperforms decoding in 12% of the cases, i.e. for the remaining 88% cases, decoding is at least as good as rescoring.

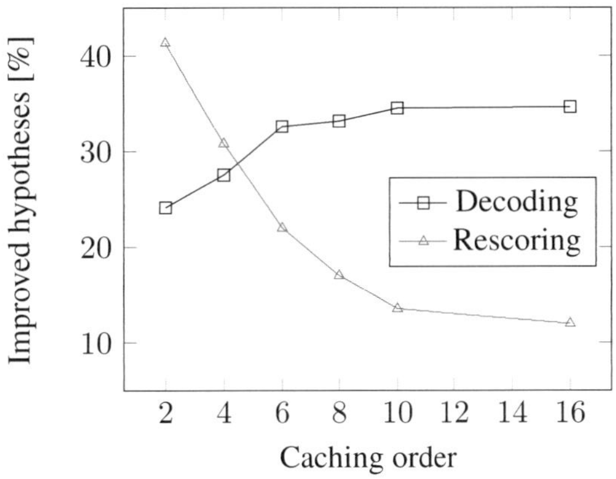

Figure 2: A comparison between applying the RNN LM in decoding using caching, and applying it exactly in rescoring.

Even for high caching orders, we observe that decoding does not completely beat rescoring. This can be attributed to the recombination approximation, as recombination disregards the RNN history. We performed another experiment to determine the effect of recombination on the RNN scores. In this experiment the RNN hidden state is stored in the search nodes, and no caching is used. This leaves recombination as the only source of approximation. We generated 1000-best lists using the approximate RNN LM scores during decoding. Afterwards, we computed the exact RNN scores of the 1000-best lists and compared them to the approximate scores. Fig. 3 shows the cumulative distribution of the absolute relative dif-

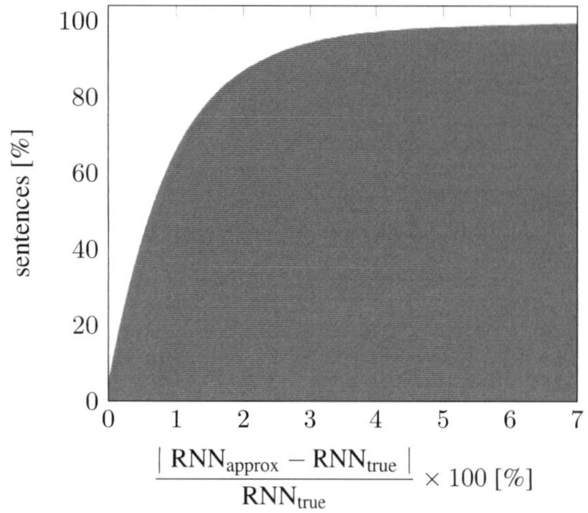

Figure 3: The cumulative distribution of the absolute relative difference between the approximate and true RNN score with respect to the true score. The distribution was generated using around 233k sentences, obtained from n-best lists generated by decoding the `dev` set of the IWSLT task.

ference between the approximate and true RNN scores with respect to the true scores. The figure suggests that recombining search nodes while ignoring the RNN hidden state leads to inexact RNN scores in most cases. For 66% of the cases the absolute relative error is at most 1%, and the error is at most 6% for 99% of the cases. As expected, ignoring the RNN during recombination leads to inexact RNN scores.

In Tab. 2, we compare between caching the RNN hidden state and the approach proposed in (Auli et al., 2013), which stores the RNN hidden state in the search node. The experiment aims to compare the two approaches in terms of translation quality. If the caching order is at least 6, no considerable difference is observed. This result is in favor of caching due to the speedup it achieves (cf. Tab. 1).

5.3 Translation Results

The IWSLT results are given in Tab. 3. We observe that decoding with RNNs improves the baseline by $1.0 - 1.7\%$ BLEU and $0.9 - 1.9\%$ TER on the `test` set. These improvements are at least as good as those of rescoring. This applies both for the exact BTM as well as the approximate LM and JM cases. In the case of BTM decoding, we observe an improvement of 0.1 BLEU and 0.5 TER compared to the corresponding rescoring experiment.

Caching Order	`dev`	`test`
2	33.1	30.8
4	33.4	31.2
6	33.9	31.6
8	33.9	31.5
16	34.0	31.5
30	33.9	31.5
-	33.9	31.5

Table 2: A comparison between storing the RNN state in the search nodes (last entry) or caching it using different caching orders (remaining entries). We report the BLEU [%] scores for the IWSLT 2013 German→English task.

	`dev`		`test`	
	BLEU	TER	BLEU	TER
baseline	33.4	46.1	30.6	49.2
LM Resc.	34.1	45.7	31.5	48.6
LM Dec.	33.9	45.7	31.6	48.3
+LM Resc.	34.1	45.8	31.9	48.4
BTM Resc.	34.4	45.3	32.2	47.8
BTM Dec.	34.4	44.9	**32.3**	**47.3**
JM Resc.	34.3	45.4	31.6	48.3
JM Dec.	34.4	45.6	31.6	48.2
+ JM Resc.	34.6	45.3	31.8	47.9

Table 3: IWSLT 2013 German→English results. Caching orders: $n = 8$ (LM), $n = 5$ (JM).

The decoding improvements in the LM and JM cases are minor compared to rescoring. We also experimented with rescoring the RNN decoding output, where rescoring was performed using the same RNN used in decoding to obtain exact scores. We took the best on `dev` among the 3 MERT runs and rescored it. This is indicated by the "+" sign. The results show that RNN LM rescoring can be improved if decoding is performed including the RNN LM. On `test` the gain is 0.4 BLEU and 0.2 TER, while the improvement is 0.2 BLEU and 0.4 TER in the JM case. This indicates that using the RNN model in decoding improves the n-best lists, allowing rescoring afterwards to choose better hypotheses. Overall, BTM decoding improves over the baseline by 1.7 BLEU and 1.9 TER.

	test1		test2	
	BLEU	TER	BLEU	TER
baseline	23.9	59.7	26.4	59.8
LM Resc.	24.3	59.3	26.9	59.3
LM Dec.	24.6	59.0	27.0	59.2
+LM Resc.	**25.0**	**58.8**	27.2	59.1
BTM Resc.	24.7	58.9	27.0	**58.9**
BTM Dec.	24.8	58.9	27.0	**58.9**
JM Resc.	24.4	59.0	27.2	59.0
JM Dec.	24.5	59.0	**27.3**	59.0
+ JM Rec.	24.5	59.0	**27.3**	59.0

Table 4: BOLT Arabic→English results. Caching orders: $n = 8$ (LM), $n = 10$ (JM).

Tab. 4 shows the results of the Arabic→English BOLT task. Again, the LM, JM and BTM models in decoding are at least as good as in rescoring. For the LM, we observe an improvement of 0.7 BLEU when LM rescoring is applied on the LM decoding output. The best result improves the baseline by 1.1 BLEU on test1 and 0.9 BLEU on test2.

In a final experiment to examine the power of the recurrent neural translation models, we performed phrase-based decoding without the conventional phrasal and lexical translation scores. Instead, we performed decoding with the BTM as described in Section 4.1, and augmented the phrase table with four additional features derived from the bidirectional translation model, the joint model, and the phrase-based translation and joint models described in (Sundermeyer et al., 2014). This was done by scoring each phrase pair in the phrase table as if it were a sentence pair. For this specific experiment, we trained the phrase-based models on phrase pairs obtained from forced-decoding the training data. That is, each training instance was a phrase pair instead of a sentence pair. For the sake of comparison, we trained the baseline translation model on the TED portion of the data; the same data used for neural training. The results are shown in Tab. 5. We observe a gap of only 1.2 BLEU on dev and 1.0 BLEU on test, with almost no difference in TER. We consider this an encouraging result, as it is possible that the word-based recurrent neural models used here are not capable of expressing their full potential due to their use in the phrase-based framework,

	dev		test	
	BLEU	TER	BLEU	TER
baseline	32.2	46.6	30.5	48.7
RNN	31.0	46.8	29.5	48.6

Table 5: The in-domain baseline has a translation model trained on the TED portion of the data only, while RNN denotes decoding with the BTM, in addition to 4 offline word- and phrase-based neural scores in the phrase table . The phrase-based models were trained on forced-aligned phrase-pairs rather than full sentences.

which only allows phrases given by the phrase table. Therefore, it would be interesting to examine the performance of the models outside the phrase-based framework.

5.4 Discussion

We observe that integrating RNN models into phrase-based decoding slightly outperforms applying them in a rescoring step. This is unlike the case of feedforward networks, which where integrated into phrase-based decoding in (Devlin et al., 2014), and resulted in large improvements compared to rescoring. Even when we use large caching orders, we observe no major improvements over rescoring. This can be attributed to the fact that deciding on recombining search nodes completely ignores the RNN hidden state, which could be a harsh approximation, given that the RNN hidden state encodes the complete history. We experimented with changing the LM order used to make recombination decisions, which we refer to as the recombination order. However, simply increasing the recombination order does not enhance the translation quality, and it starts to even have a negative impact. This can be explained due to the fact that our phrase-based decoder is based on beam search, which has fixed pruning parameters that allow a fixed number of hypotheses to be explored. Simply increasing the recombination order limits the variety in the beam. When the beam size is doubled,[3] both RNN decoding and rescoring improve, but the difference between them is still insignificant. To be able to benefit from the increase in recombination order, the beam size

[3]We doubled each of the observation histogram size, the number of lexical hypotheses per source coverage and the number of reordering alternatives per source cardinality.

should be appropriately increased. But using large beam sizes makes translation costly and infeasible. This calls for other more selective ways to make recombination decisions dependent on the RNN hidden state.

6 Conclusion

We investigated the integration of RNN language and translation models into a phrase-based decoder. We integrated exact RNN translation models that are conditioned on the source context only, and used caching to integrate approximate RNN translation models that are dependent on the target context. This is the first time RNN translation models are integrated into phrase-based decoding. We analyzed the effect of caching on translation quality and speed, and demonstrated that it achieves equivalent translation results compared to having the RNN hidden states stored in the decoder's search nodes, while being 6 times faster. Translation results indicated that applying the models in decoding is at least as good as applying them in rescoring n-best lists, but we observed no major advantage for RNN decoding. Future work will investigate approaches to make recombination dependent on the RNN hidden state in a feasible way, furthermore, we will explore how the RNN models perform in word-based decoding.

Acknowledgments

This material is partially based upon work supported by the DARPA BOLT project under Contract No. HR0011- 12-C-0015. Any opinions, findings and conclusions or recommendations expressed in this material are those of the authors and do not necessarily reflect the views of DARPA. The research leading to these results has also received funding from the European Union's Horizon 2020 research and innovation programme under grant agreement n° 645452 (QT21). We would like to thank Joern Wuebker for many insightful discussions.

References

Ebru Arisoy, Tara N. Sainath, Brian Kingsbury, and Bhuvana Ramabhadran. 2012. Deep neural network language models. In *Proceedings of the NAACL-HLT 2012 Workshop: Will We Ever Really Replace the N-gram Model? On the Future of Language Modeling for HLT*, pages 20–28, Montréal, Canada, June.

Michael Auli and Jianfeng Gao. 2014. Decoder Integration and Expected BLEU Training for Recurrent Neural Network Language Models. In *Annual Meeting of the Association for Computational Linguistics*, pages 136–142, Baltimore, MD, USA, June.

Michael Auli, Michel Galley, Chris Quirk, and Geoffrey Zweig. 2013. Joint Language and Translation Modeling with Recurrent Neural Networks. In *Conference on Empirical Methods in Natural Language Processing*, pages 1044–1054, Seattle, USA, October.

Dzmitry Bahdanau, Kyunghyun Cho, and Yoshua Bengio. 2015. Neural machine translation by jointly learning to align and translate. In *International Conference on Learning Representations*, San Diego, Calefornia, USA, May.

Stanley F. Chen and Joshua Goodman. 1998. An Empirical Study of Smoothing Techniques for Language Modeling. Technical Report TR-10-98, Computer Science Group, Harvard University, Cambridge, MA, August.

Jonathan H. Clark, Chris Dyer, Alon Lavie, and Noah A. Smith. 2011. Better hypothesis testing for statistical machine translation: Controlling for optimizer instability. In *49th Annual Meeting of the Association for Computational Linguistics*, pages 176–181, Portland, Oregon, June.

Jacob Devlin, Rabih Zbib, Zhongqiang Huang, Thomas Lamar, Richard Schwartz, and John Makhoul. 2014. Fast and Robust Neural Network Joint Models for Statistical Machine Translation. In *52nd Annual Meeting of the Association for Computational Linguistics*, pages 1370–1380, Baltimore, MD, USA, June.

Michel Galley and Christopher D. Manning. 2008. A simple and effective hierarchical phrase reordering model. In *Proceedings of the Conference on Empirical Methods in Natural Language Processing*, pages 848–856, Honolulu, Hawaii, USA, October.

Joshua Goodman. 2001. Classes for fast maximum entropy training. In *Acoustics, Speech, and Signal Processing, 2001. Proceedings.(ICASSP'01). 2001 IEEE International Conference on*, volume 1, pages 561–564. IEEE.

Andreas Guta, Tamer Alkhouli, Jan-Thorsten Peter, Joern Wuebker, and Hermann Ney. 2015. A Comparison between Count and Neural Network Models Based on Joint Translation and Reordering Sequences. In *Conference on Empirical Methods on Natural Language Processing*, page to appear, Lisbon, Portugal, September.

Yuening Hu, Michael Auli, Qin Gao, and Jianfeng Gao. 2014. Minimum translation modeling with recurrent neural networks. In *Proceedings of the 14th Conference of the European Chapter of the Association for Computational Linguistics*, pages 20–29, Gothenburg, Sweden, April.

Zhiheng Huang, Geoffrey Zweig, and Benoit Dumoulin. 2014. Cache based recurrent neural network language model inference for first pass speech recognition. In *Proceedings of the IEEE International Conference on Acoustics, Speech, and Signal Processing (ICASSP)*, pages 6404–6408, Florence, Italy, May.

Reinhard Kneser and Hermann Ney. 1995. Improved backing-off for M-gram language modeling. In *Proceedings of the International Conference on Acoustics, Speech, and Signal Processing*, volume 1, pages 181–184, May.

P. Koehn, F. J. Och, and D. Marcu. 2003. Statistical Phrase-Based Translation. In *Proceedings of the 2003 Meeting of the North American chapter of the Association for Computational Linguistics*, pages 127–133, Edmonton, Alberta, May/June.

Hai Son Le, Alexandre Allauzen, and François Yvon. 2012. Continuous Space Translation Models with Neural Networks. In *Conference of the North American Chapter of the Association for Computational Linguistics: Human Language Technologies*, pages 39–48, Montreal, Canada, June.

X. Liu, Y. Wang, X. Chen, M. J. F. Gales, and P. C. Woodland. 2014. Efficient lattice rescoring using recurrent neural network language models. In *Acoustics, Speech and Signal Processing (ICASSP), 2014 IEEE International Conference on*, pages 4941–4945, Florence, Italy, May.

Tomas Mikolov, Stefan Kombrink, Lukas Burget, JH Cernocky, and Sanjeev Khudanpur. 2011. Extensions of recurrent neural network language model. In *Acoustics, Speech and Signal Processing (ICASSP), 2011 IEEE International Conference on*, pages 5528–5531, Prague, Czech Republic, May.

R.C. Moore and W. Lewis. 2010. Intelligent Selection of Language Model Training Data. In *Proceedings of the 48th Annual Meeting of the Association for Computational Linguistics*, pages 220–224, Uppsala, Sweden, July.

Frederic Morin and Yoshua Bengio. 2005. Hierarchical probabilistic neural network language model. In *Proceedings of the international workshop on artificial intelligence and statistics*, pages 246–252, Barbados, January.

Franz Josef Och. 2003. Minimum Error Rate Training in Statistical Machine Translation. In *Proc. of the 41th Annual Meeting of the Association for Computational Linguistics (ACL)*, pages 160–167, Sapporo, Japan, July.

Kishore Papineni, Salim Roukos, Todd Ward, and Wei-Jing Zhu. 2002. Bleu: a Method for Automatic Evaluation of Machine Translation. In *Proceedings of the 41st Annual Meeting of the Association for Computational Linguistics*, pages 311–318, Philadelphia, Pennsylvania, USA, July.

Holger Schwenk. 2012. Continuous Space Translation Models for Phrase-Based Statistical Machine Translation. In *25th International Conference on Computational Linguistics (COLING)*, pages 1071–1080, Mumbai, India, December.

Matthew Snover, Bonnie Dorr, Richard Schwartz, Linnea Micciulla, and John Makhoul. 2006. A Study of Translation Edit Rate with Targeted Human Annotation. In *Proceedings of the 7th Conference of the Association for Machine Translation in the Americas*, pages 223–231, Cambridge, Massachusetts, USA, August.

Andreas Stolcke. 2002. SRILM – An Extensible Language Modeling Toolkit. In *Proc. of the Int. Conf. on Speech and Language Processing (ICSLP)*, volume 2, pages 901–904, Denver, CO, September.

Martin Sundermeyer, Ilya Oparin, Jean-Luc Gauvain, Ben Freiberg, Ralf Schlüter, and Hermann Ney. 2013. Comparison of feedforward and recurrent neural network language models. In *IEEE International Conference on Acoustics, Speech, and Signal Processing*, pages 8430–8434, Vancouver, Canada, May.

Martin Sundermeyer, Tamer Alkhouli, Joern Wuebker, and Hermann Ney. 2014. Translation Modeling with Bidirectional Recurrent Neural Networks. In *Conference on Empirical Methods on Natural Language Processing*, pages 14–25, Doha, Qatar, October.

Ilya Sutskever, Oriol Vinyals, and Quoc V. V Le. 2014. Sequence to sequence learning with neural networks. In *Advances in Neural Information Processing Systems 27*, pages 3104–3112, Montréal, Canada, December.

Ashish Vaswani, Yinggong Zhao, Victoria Fossum, and David Chiang. 2013. Decoding with large-scale neural language models improves translation. In *Proceedings of the 2013 Conference on Empirical Methods in Natural Language Processing*, pages 1387–1392, Seattle, Washington, USA, October.

Joern Wuebker, Stephan Peitz, Felix Rietig, and Hermann Ney. 2013. Improving statistical machine translation with word class models. In *Conference on Empirical Methods in Natural Language Processing*, pages 1377–1381, Seattle, USA, October.

Referential Translation Machines for Predicting Translation Quality and Related Statistics

Ergun Biçici
ADAPT Research Center
School of Computing
Dublin City University, Ireland
ergun.bicici@computing.dcu.ie

Qun Liu
ADAPT Research Center
School of Computing
Dublin City University, Ireland
qliu@computing.dcu.ie

Andy Way
ADAPT Research Center
School of Computing
Dublin City University, Ireland
away@computing.dcu.ie

Abstract

We use referential translation machines (RTMs) for predicting translation performance. RTMs pioneer a language independent approach to all similarity tasks and remove the need to access any task or domain specific information or resource. We improve our RTM models with the ParFDA instance selection model (Biçici et al., 2015), with additional features for predicting the translation performance, and with improved learning models. We develop RTM models for each WMT15 QET (QET15) subtask and obtain improvements over QET14 results. RTMs achieve top performance in QET15 ranking 1st in document- and sentence-level prediction tasks and 2nd in word-level prediction task.

1 Referential Translation Machine (RTM)

Referential translation machines are a computational model effectively judging monolingual and bilingual similarity while identifying translation acts between any two data sets with respect to interpretants. RTMs achieve top performance in automatic, accurate, and language independent prediction of machine translation performance and reduce our dependence on any task dependent resource. Prediction of translation performance can help in estimating the effort required for correcting the translations during post-editing by human translators. We improve our RTM models (Biçici and Way, 2014):

- by using improved ParFDA instance selection model (Biçici et al., 2015) allowing better language models (LM) in which similarity judgments are made to be built with improved optimization and selection of the LM data,
- by selecting TreeF features over source and translation data jointly instead of taking their intersection,
- with extended learning models including bayesian ridge regression (Tan et al., 2015), which did not obtain better performance than support vector regression in training results (Section 2.2).

We present top results with Referential Translation Machines (Biçici, 2015; Biçici and Way, 2014) at quality estimation task (QET15) in WMT15 (Bojar et al., 2015). RTMs pioneer a computational model for quality and semantic similarity judgments in monolingual and bilingual settings using retrieval of relevant training data (Biçici and Yuret, 2015) as interpretants for reaching shared semantics. RTMs use Machine Translation Performance Prediction (MTPP) System (Biçici et al., 2013; Biçici, 2015), which is a state-of-the-art performance predictor of translation even without using the translation by using only the source. We use ParFDA for selecting the interpretants (Biçici et al., 2015; Biçici and Yuret, 2015) and build an MTPP model. MTPP derives indicators of the closeness of test sentences to the available training data, the difficulty of translating the sentence, and the presence of acts of translation for data transformation. We view that acts of translation are ubiquitously used during communication:

Every act of communication is an act of translation (Bliss, 2012).

Figure 1 depicts RTM. Our encouraging results in QET provides a greater understanding of the acts of translation we ubiquitously use and how they can be used to predict the performance of translation. RTMs are powerful enough to be applicable in different domains and tasks while achieving top performance.

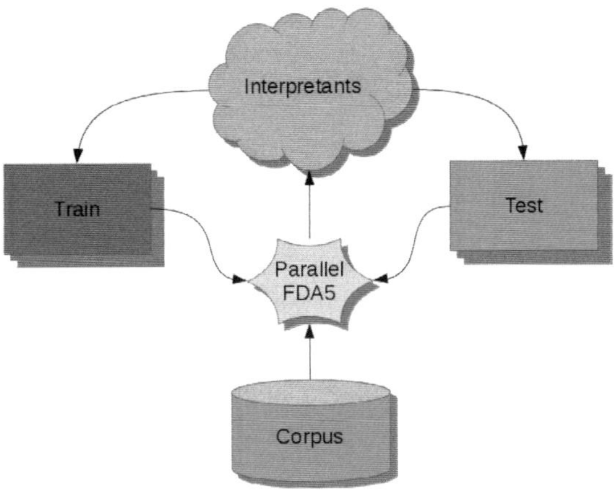

Figure 1: RTM depiction.

Task	Train	Test
Task 1 (en-es)	12271	1817
Task 2 (en-es)	12271	1817
Task 3 (en-de)	800	415
Task 3 (de-en)	800	415

Table 1: Number of sentences in different tasks.

2 RTM in the Quality Estimation Task

We participate in all of the three subtasks of the quality estimation task (QET) (Bojar et al., 2015), which include English to Spanish (en-es), English to German (en-de), and German to English (de-en) translation directions. There are three subtasks: sentence-level prediction (Task 1), word-level prediction (Task 2), and document-level prediction (Task 3). Task 1 is about predicting HTER (human-targeted translation edit rate) (Snover et al., 2006) scores of sentence translations, Task 2 is about binary classification of word-level quality, and Task 3 is about predicting METEOR (Lavie and Agarwal, 2007) scores of document translations.

Instance selection for the training set and the language model (LM) corpus is handled by ParFDA (Biçici et al., 2015), whose parameters are optimized for each translation task. LM are trained using SRILM (Stolcke, 2002). We tokenize and truecase all of the corpora using code released with Moses (Koehn et al., 2007) [1]. Table 1 lists the number of sentences in the training and test sets for each task.

[1] `mosesdecoder/scripts/`

2.1 RTM Prediction Models and Optimization

We present results using support vector regression (SVR) with RBF (radial basis functions) kernel (Smola and Schölkopf, 2004) for sentence and document translation prediction tasks and Global Linear Models (GLM) (Collins, 2002) with dynamic learning (GLMd) (Biçici, 2013; Biçici and Way, 2014) for word-level translation performance prediction. We also use these learning models after a feature subset selection (FS) with recursive feature elimination (RFE) (Guyon et al., 2002) or a dimensionality reduction and mapping step using partial least squares (PLS) (Specia et al., 2009), or PLS after FS (FS+PLS).

GLM relies on Viterbi decoding, perceptron learning, and flexible feature definitions. GLMd extends the GLM framework by parallel perceptron training (McDonald et al., 2010) and dynamic learning with adaptive weight updates in the perceptron learning algorithm:

$$\mathbf{w} = \mathbf{w} + \alpha \left(\Phi(\mathbf{x}_i, \mathbf{y}_i) - \Phi(\mathbf{x}_i, \hat{\mathbf{y}}) \right), \qquad (1)$$

where Φ returns a global representation for instance i and the weights are updated by α, which dynamically decays the amount of the change during weight updates at later stages and prevents large fluctuations with updates.

The learning rate updates the weight values with weights in the range $[a, b]$ using the following function taking error rate as the input:

$$f(x) = (\log_a b - 1)x^2 + 1 \qquad (2)$$

Learning rate curve for $a = 0.5$ and $b = 1.0$ is provided in Figure 2:

2.2 Training Results

We use mean absolute error (MAE), relative absolute error (RAE), root mean squared error (RMSE), and correlation (r) as well as relative MAE (MAER) and relative RAE (MRAER) to evaluate (Biçici, 2015; Biçici, 2013). MAER is mean absolute error relative to the magnitude of the target and MRAER is mean absolute error relative to the absolute error of a predictor always predicting the target mean assuming that target mean is known (Biçici, 2015). RTM test performance on various tasks sorted according to MRAER can help identify which tasks and subtasks may require more work. DeltaAvg (Callison-Burch et al.,

Task	Translation	Model	r	MAE	RAE	MAER	MRAER
Task1	en-es	FS SVR	0.355	0.1387	0.895	0.782	0.821
	en-es	FS+PLS SVR	0.362	0.1389	0.896	0.784	0.824
Task3	en-de	FS SVR	0.517	0.0737	0.734	0.289	0.678
	en-de	SVR	0.503	0.0765	0.761	0.307	0.737
	de-en	FS SVR	0.479	0.0473	0.738	0.267	0.665
	de-en	FS+PLS SVR	0.391	0.0515	0.804	0.288	0.81

Table 2: Training performance of the top 2 individual RTM models prepared for different tasks.

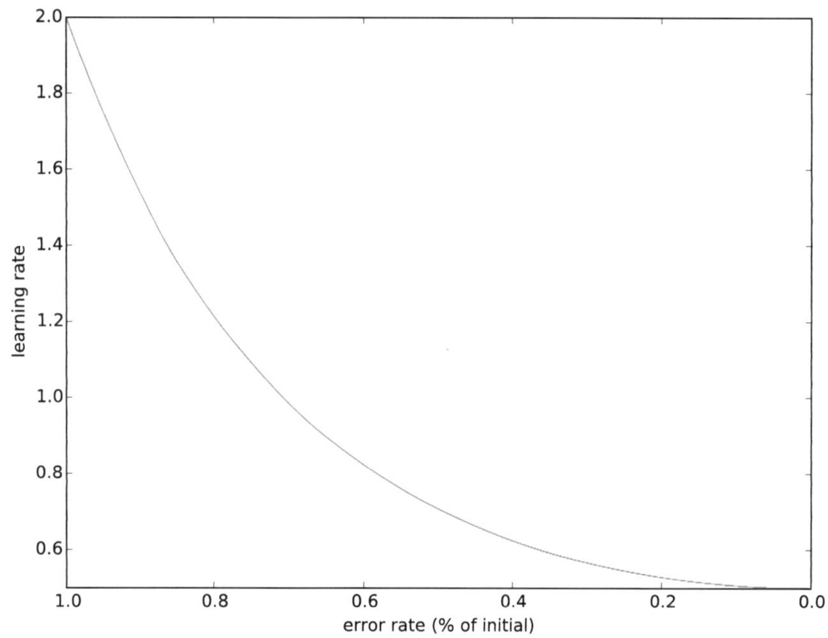

Figure 2: Learning rate curve.

Model	# splits	% error	weight range
GLMd	4	0.0227	$[0.5, 2]$
GLMd	5	0.0234	$[0.5, 2]$

Table 3: RTM-DCU Task 2 training results.

2012) calculates the average quality difference between the top $n-1$ quartiles and the overall quality for the test set.

Table 2 presents the training results for Task 1 and Task 3. Table 3 presents Task 2 training results. We refer to GLMd parallelized over 4 splits as GLMd s4 and GLMd with 5 splits as GLMd s5.

2.3 Test Results

Task 1: Predicting the HTER for Sentence Translations The results on the test set are given in Table 4. Rank lists the overall ranking in the task out of about 9 submissions. We obtain the rankings by sorting according to the predicted scores and randomly assigning ranks in case of ties. RTMs with FS followed by PLS and learning with SVR is able to achieve the top rank in this task.

Task 2: Prediction of Word-level Translation Quality Task 2 is about binary classification of word-level quality. We develop individual RTM models for each subtask and use GLMd model (Biçici, 2013; Biçici and Way, 2014), for predicting the quality at the word-level. The results on the test set are in Table 5 where the ranks are out of about 17 submissions. RTMs with GLMd becomes the second best system this task.

Task 3: Predicting METEOR of Document Translations Task 3 is about predicting METEOR (Lavie and Agarwal, 2007) and their ranking. The results on the test set are given in Table 4 where the ranks are out of about 6 submissions using $\mathrm{w}F_1$. RTMs achieve top rankings in this task.

Task	Translation	Model	DeltaAvg	r	MAE	RAE	MAER	MRAER	Rank
Task1	en-es	FS SVR	0.61	0.3665	0.1325	0.8963	0.8344	0.8488	3
	en-es	FS+PLS SVR	0.63	0.349	0.1335	0.903	0.8284	0.8353	1
Task3	en-de	FS SVR	0.65	0.6668	0.0728	0.7279	0.3249	0.6467	2
	en-de	SVR	0.76	0.6247	0.075	0.7499	0.3623	0.7245	1
	de-en	FS SVR	0.49	0.5521	0.0578	0.8763	0.395	0.9159	1
	de-en	FS+PLS SVR	0.42	0.6373	0.0494	0.7482	0.2996	0.68	2

Table 4: Test performance of the top 2 individual RTM models prepared for different tasks.

Model	wF_1	Rank	F_1 GOOD	F_1 BAD
GLMd s5	0.76	3	0.2391	0.8812
GLMd s4	0.7588	4	0.2269	0.8826

Table 5: RTM-DCU Task 2 results on the test set. wF_1 is the average weighted F_1 score.

2.4 RTMs Across Tasks and Years

We compare the difficulty of tasks according to MRAER levels achieved. In Table 6, we list the RTM test results for tasks and subtasks that predict HTER or METEOR from QET15, QET14 (Biçici and Way, 2014), and QET13 (Biçici, 2013). The best results when predicting HTER are obtained this year.

3 Conclusion

Referential translation machines achieve top performance in automatic, accurate, and language independent prediction of document-, sentence-, and word-level statistical machine translation (SMT) performance. RTMs remove the need to access any SMT system specific information or prior knowledge of the training data or models used when generating the translations. RTMs achieve top performance when predicting translation performance.

Acknowledgments

This work is supported in part by SFI as part of the ADAPT research center (`www.adaptcentre.ie`, 07/CE/I1142) at Dublin City University and in part by SFI for the project "Monolingual and Bilingual Text Quality Judgments with Translation Performance Prediction" (`computing.dcu.ie/~ebicici/Projects/TIDA_RTM.html`, 13/TIDA/I2740). We also thank the SFI/HEA Irish Centre for High-End Computing (ICHEC, `www.ichec.ie`) for the provision of computational facilities and support.

References

Ergun Biçici and Andy Way. 2014. Referential translation machines for predicting translation quality. In *Proc. of the Ninth Workshop on Statistical Machine Translation*, pages 313–321, Baltimore, Maryland, USA, June.

Ergun Biçici and Deniz Yuret. 2015. Optimizing instance selection for statistical machine translation with feature decay algorithms. *IEEE/ACM Transactions On Audio, Speech, and Language Processing (TASLP)*, 23:339–350.

Ergun Biçici, Declan Groves, and Josef van Genabith. 2013. Predicting sentence translation quality using extrinsic and language independent features. *Machine Translation*, 27:171–192, December.

Ergun Biçici, Qun Liu, and Andy Way. 2015. Parallel FDA5 for fast deployment of accurate statistical machine translation systems, benchmarks, and statistics. In *Proc. of the Tenth Workshop on Statistical Machine Translation*, Lisbon, Portugal, September. Association for Computational Linguistics.

Ergun Biçici. 2013. Referential translation machines for quality estimation. In *Proc. of the Eighth Workshop on Statistical Machine Translation*, pages 343–351, Sofia, Bulgaria, August.

Ergun Biçici. 2015. RTM-DCU: Predicting semantic similarity with referential translation machines. In *SemEval-2015: Semantic Evaluation Exercises - International Workshop on Semantic Evaluation*, Denver, Colorado, USA, 4-5 June.

Chris Bliss. 2012. Comedy is translation, February. http://www.ted.com/talks/chris_bliss_comedy_is_translation.html.

Ondrej Bojar, Rajan Chatterjee, Christian Federmann, Barry Haddow, Chris Hokamp, Matthias Huck, Pavel Pecina, Philipp Koehn, Christof Monz, Matteo Negri, Matt Post, Carolina Scarton, Lucia Specia, and Marco Turchi. 2015. Findings of the 2015 workshop on statistical machine translation. In *Proc. of the Tenth Workshop on Statistical Machine Translation*, Lisbon, Portugal, September.

Chris Callison-Burch, Philipp Koehn, Christof Monz, Matt Post, Radu Soricut, and Lucia Specia. 2012.

Task	Translation	Model	r	MAE	RAE	MAER	MRAER
QET15 Task1 HTER	en-es	FS SVR	0.3665	0.1325	0.8963	0.8344	0.8488
	en-es	FS+PLS SVR	0.349	0.1335	0.903	0.8284	0.8353
QET15 Task3 METEOR	en-de	FS SVR	0.6668	0.0728	0.7279	0.3249	0.6467
	en-de	SVR	0.6247	0.075	0.7499	0.3623	0.7245
	de-en	FS SVR	0.5521	0.0578	0.8763	0.395	0.9159
	de-en	FS+PLS SVR	0.6373	0.0494	0.7482	0.2996	0.68
QET14 Task1.2 HTER	en-es	SVR	0.5499	0.134	0.8532	0.7727	0.8758
QET13 Task1.1 HTER	en-es	PLS-SVR	0.5596	0.1326	0.8849	2.3738	1.6428

Table 6: Test performance of the top individual RTM results when predicting HTER or METEOR also including results from QET14 (Biçici and Way, 2014) and QET13 (Biçici, 2013).

Findings of the 2012 workshop on statistical machine translation. In *Proc. of the Seventh Workshop on Statistical Machine Translation*, pages 10–51, Montréal, Canada, June.

Michael Collins. 2002. Discriminative training methods for hidden markov models: theory and experiments with perceptron algorithms. In *Proc. of the ACL-02 conference on Empirical methods in natural language processing - Volume 10*, EMNLP '02, pages 1–8, Stroudsburg, PA, USA.

Isabelle Guyon, Jason Weston, Stephen Barnhill, and Vladimir Vapnik. 2002. Gene selection for cancer classification using support vector machines. *Machine Learning*, 46(1-3):389–422.

Philipp Koehn, Hieu Hoang, Alexandra Birch, Chris Callison-Burch, Marcello Federico, Nicola Bertoldi, Brooke Cowan, Wade Shen, Christine Moran, Richard Zens, Chris Dyer, Ondrej Bojar, Alexandra Constantin, and Evan Herbst. 2007. Moses: Open source toolkit for statistical machine translation. In *ACL*, pages 177–180, Prague, Czech Republic, June.

Alon Lavie and Abhaya Agarwal. 2007. METEOR: An automatic metric for MT evaluation with high levels of correlation with human judgments. In *Proc. of the Second Workshop on Statistical Machine Translation*, pages 228–231, Prague, Czech Republic, June.

Ryan McDonald, Keith Hall, and Gideon Mann. 2010. Distributed training strategies for the structured perceptron. In *Human Language Technologies: The 2010 Annual Conference of the North American Chapter of the Association for Computational Linguistics*, pages 456–464, Los Angeles, California, June.

Alex J. Smola and Bernhard Schölkopf. 2004. A tutorial on support vector regression. *Statistics and Computing*, 14(3):199–222, August.

Matthew Snover, Bonnie Dorr, Richard Schwartz, Linnea Micciulla, and John Makhoul. 2006. A Study of Translation Edit Rate with Targeted Human Annotation. In *Proc. of Association for Machine Translation in the Americas*,.

Lucia Specia, Nicola Cancedda, Marc Dymetman, Marco Turchi, and Nello Cristianini. 2009. Estimating the sentence-level quality of machine translation systems. In *Proc. of the 13th Annual Conference of the European Association for Machine Translation (EAMT)*, pages 28–35, Barcelona, Spain, May.

Andreas Stolcke. 2002. SRILM - an extensible language modeling toolkit. In *Proc. Intl. Conf. on Spoken Language Processing*, pages 901–904.

Liling Tan, Carolina Scarton, Lucia Specia, and Josef van Genabith. 2015. Usaar-sheffield: Semantic textual similarity with deep regression and machine translation evaluation metrics. In *Proc. of the 9th International Workshop on Semantic Evaluation (SemEval 2015)*, pages 85–89. Association for Computational Linguistics.

UAlacant word-level machine translation quality estimation system at WMT 2015

Miquel Esplà-Gomis **Felipe Sánchez-Martínez** **Mikel L. Forcada**
Departament de Llenguatges i Sistemes Informàtics
Universitat d'Alacant, E-03071 Alacant, Spain
{mespla,fsanchez,mlf}@dlsi.ua.es

Abstract

This paper describes the Universitat d'Alacant submissions (labelled as UAlacant) for the machine translation quality estimation (MTQE) shared task in WMT 2015, where we participated in the word-level MTQE sub-task. The method we used to produce our submissions uses external sources of bilingual information as a *black box* to spot sub-segment correspondences between a source segment S and the translation hypothesis T produced by a machine translation system. This is done by segmenting both S and T into overlapping sub-segments of variable length and translating them in both translation directions, using the available sources of bilingual information *on the fly*. For our submissions, two sources of bilingual information were used: machine translation (Apertium and Google Translate) and the bilingual concordancer Reverso Context. After obtaining the sub-segment correspondences, a collection of features is extracted from them, which are then used by a binary classifer to obtain the final "GOOD" or "BAD" word-level quality labels. We prepared two submissions for this year's edition of WMT 2015: one using the features produced by our system, and one combining them with the baseline features published by the organisers of the task, which were ranked third and first for the sub-task, respectively.

1 Introduction

Machine translation (MT) post-editing is nowadays an indispensable step that allows to use machine translation for dissemination. Consequently, MT quality estimation (MTQE) (Blatz et al., 2004; Specia et al., 2010; Specia and Soricut, 2013) has emerged as a mean to minimise the post-editing effort by developing techniques that allow to estimate the quality of the translation hypotheses produced by an MT system. In order to boost the scientific efforts on this problem, the WMT 2015 MTQE shared task proposes three tasks that allow to compare different approaches at three different levels: segment-level (sub-task 1), word-level (sub-task 2), and document-level (sub-task 3).

Our submissions tackle the word-level MTQE sub-task, which proposes a framework for evaluating and comparing different approaches. This year, the sub-task used a dataset obtained by translating segments in English into Spanish using MT. The task consists in identifying which words in the translation hypothesis had to be post-edited and which of them had to be kept unedited by applying the labels "BAD" and "GOOD", respectively. In this paper we describe the approach behind the two submissions of the Universitat d'Alacant team to this sub-task. For our submissions we applied the approach proposed by Esplà-Gomis et al. (2015b), who use black-box bilingual resources from the Internet for word-level MTQE. In particular, we combined two on-line MT systems, Apertium[1] and Google Translate,[2] and the bilingual concordancer Reverso Context[3] to spot sub-segment correspondences between a sentence S in the source language (SL) and a given translation hypothesis T in the target language (TL). To do so, both S and T are segmented into all possible overlapping sub-

[1] http://www.apertium.org
[2] http://translate.google.com
[3] http://context.reverso.net/translation/

segments up to a certain length and translated into the TL and the SL, respectively, by means of the sources of bilingual information mentioned above. These sub-segment correspondences are used to extract a collection of features that is then used by a binary classifier to determine the final word-level MTQE labels.

One of the novelties of the task this year is that the organisation provided a collection of baseline features for the dataset published. Therefore, we submitted two systems: one using only the features defined by Esplà-Gomis et al. (2015b), and another combining them with the baseline features published by the organisers of the shared task. The results obtained by our submissions were ranked third and first, respectively.

The rest of the paper is organised as follows. Section 2 describes the approach used to produce our submissions. Section 3 describes the experimental setting and the results obtained. The paper ends with some concluding remarks.

2 Sources of bilingual information for word-level MTQE

The approach proposed by Esplà-Gomis et al. (2015b), which is the one we have followed in our submissions for the MTQE shared task in WMT 2015, uses binary classification based on a collection of features computed for each word by using available sources of bilingual information. These sources of bilingual information are obtained from on-line tools and are used on-the-fly to detect relations between the original SL segment S and a given translation hypothesis T in the TL. This method has been previously used by the authors in other cross-lingual NLP tasks, such as word-keeping recommendation (Esplà-Gomis et al., 2015a) or cross-lingual textual entailment (Esplà-Gomis et al., 2012), and consists of the following steps: first, all the overlapping sub-segments σ of S up to given length L are obtained and translated into the TL using the sources of bilingual information available. The same process is carried out for all the overlapping sub-segments τ of T, which are translated into the SL. The resulting collections of sub-segment translations $M_{S\rightarrow T}$ and $M_{T\rightarrow S}$ are then used to spot sub-segment correspondences between T and S. In this section we describe a collection of features designed to identify these relations for their exploitation for word-level MTQE.

2.1 Positive features

Given a collection of sub-segment translations $M = \{\sigma, \tau\}$, such as the collections $M_{S\rightarrow T}$ and $M_{T\rightarrow S}$) described above, one of the most obvious features consists in computing the amount of sub-segment translations $(\sigma, \tau) \in M$ that confirm that word t_j in T should be kept in the translation of S. We consider that a sub-segment translation (σ, τ) confirms t_j if σ is a sub-segment of S, and τ is a sub-segment of T that covers position j. Based on this idea, we propose the collection of positive features Pos_n:

$$\mathrm{Pos}_n(j, S, T, M) = \frac{|\{\tau : (\sigma, \tau) \in \mathrm{conf}_n(j, S, T, M)\}|}{|\{\tau : \tau \in \mathrm{seg}_n(T) \land j \in \mathrm{span}(\tau, T)\}|}$$

where $\mathrm{seg}_n(X)$ represents the set of all possible n-word sub-segments of segment X and function $\mathrm{span}(\tau, T)$ returns the set of word positions spanned by the sub-segment τ in the segment T.[4] Function $\mathrm{conf}_n(j, S, T, M)$ returns the collection of sub-segment pairs (σ, τ) that confirm a given word t_j, and is defined as:

$$\mathrm{conf}_n(j, S, T, M) = \{(\sigma, \tau) \in M : \tau \in \mathrm{seg}_n(T) \land \sigma \in \mathrm{seg}_*(S) \land j \in \mathrm{span}(\tau, T)\}$$

where $\mathrm{seg}_*(X)$ is similar to $\mathrm{seg}_n(X)$ but without length constraints.[5]

We illustrate this collection of features with an example. Suppose the Catalan segment S ="Associació Europea per a la Traducció Automàtica", an English translation hypothesis T ="European Association for the Automatic Translation", and the most adequate (reference) translation T'="European Association for Machine Translation". According to the reference, the words *the* and *Automatic* in the translation hypothesis should be marked as BAD: *the* should be removed and *Automatic* should be replaced by *Machine*. Finally, suppose that the collection $M_{S\rightarrow T}$ of sub-segment pairs (σ, τ) is obtained by applying the available sources of bilingual information to translate into English the sub-segments in S up to length 3:[6]

[4] Note that a sub-segment τ may be found more than once in segment T: function $\mathrm{span}(\tau, T)$ returns all the possible positions spanned.

[5] Esplà-Gomis et al. (2015b) conclude that constraining only the length of τ leads to better results than constraining both σ and τ.

[6] The other translation direction is omitted for simplicity.

$M_{S\to T}$ ={**("Associació", "Association")**, **("Europea", "European")**, **("per", "for")**, ("a", "to"), **("la", "the")**, **("Traducció", "Translation")**, **("Automàtica", "Automatic")**, **("Associació Europea", "European Association")**, ("Europea per", "European for"), **("per a", "for")**, ("a la", "to the"), ("la Traducció", "the Translation"), ("Traducció Automàtica", "Machine Translation"), **("Associació Europea per", "European Association for")**, ("Europea per a", "European for the"), **("per a la", " for the")**, ("a la Traducció", "to the Translation"), ("la Traducció Automàtica", "the Machine Translation")}

Note that the sub-segment pairs (σ, τ) in bold are those confirming the translation hypothesis T, while the rest contradict some parts of the hypothesis. For the word *Machine* (which corresponds to word position 5), there is only one sub-segment pair confirming it *("Automàtica", "Automatic")* with length 1, and no one with lengths 2 and 3. Therefore, we have that:

$$\text{conf}_1(5, S, T, M) = \{(\text{"Automàtica"}, \text{"Automatic"})\}$$

$$\text{conf}_2(5, S, T, M) = \emptyset$$

$$\text{conf}_3(5, S, T, M) = \emptyset$$

In addition, we have that the sub-segments τ in $\text{seg}_*(T)$ covering the word *Automatic* for lengths in $[1, 3]$ are:

$$\{\tau : \tau \in \text{seg}_1(T) \wedge j \in \text{span}(\tau, T)\} = \{\text{"Automatic"}\}$$

$$\{\tau : \tau \in \text{seg}_2(T) \wedge j \in \text{span}(\tau, T)\} = \{\text{"the Automatic"}, \text{"Automatic Translation"}\}$$

$$\{\tau : \tau \in \text{seg}_3(T) \wedge j \in \text{span}(\tau, T)\} = \{\text{"for the Automatic"}, \text{"the Automatic Translation"}\}$$

Therefore, the resulting positive features for this word would be:

$$\text{Pos}_1(5, S, T, M) = \frac{\text{conf}_3(5, S, T, M)}{\{\tau : \tau \in \text{seg}_1(T) \wedge j \in \text{span}(\tau, T)\}} = \frac{1}{1}$$

$$\text{Pos}_2(5, S, T, M) = \frac{\text{conf}_2(5, S, T, M)}{\{\tau : \tau \in \text{seg}_2(T) \wedge j \in \text{span}(\tau, T)\}} = \frac{0}{2}$$

$$\text{Pos}_3(5, S, T, M) = \frac{\text{conf}_3(5, S, T, M)}{\{\tau : \tau \in \text{seg}_3(T) \wedge j \in \text{span}(\tau, T)\}} = \frac{0}{2}$$

A second collection of features, which use the information about the translation frequency between the pairs of sub-segments in M is also used. This information is not available for MT, but it is for the bilingual concordancer we have used (see Section 3). This frequency determines how often σ is translated as τ and, therefore, how reliable this translation is. We define $\text{Pos}_n^{\text{freq}}$ to obtain these features as:

$$\text{Pos}_n^{\text{freq}}(j, S, T, M) = \sum_{\forall(\sigma,\tau)\in\text{conf}_n(j,S,T,M)} \frac{\text{occ}(\sigma, \tau, M)}{\sum_{\forall(\sigma,\tau')\in M} \text{occ}(\sigma, \tau', M)}$$

where function $\text{occ}(\sigma, \tau, M)$ returns the number of occurrences in M of the sub-segment pair (σ, τ).

Following the running example, we may have an alternative and richer source of bilingual information, such as a sub-segmental translation memory, which contains 99 occurrences of word *Automàtica* translated as *Automatic*, as well as the following alternative translations: *Machine* (11 times), and *Mechanic* (10 times). Therefore, the positive feature using these frequencies for sub-segments of length 1 would be:

$$\text{Pos}_1^{\text{freq}}(5, S, T, M) = \frac{99}{99 + 11 + 10} = 0.825$$

Both positive features, $\text{Pos}(\cdot)$ and $\text{Pos}^{\text{freq}}(\cdot)$, are computed for t_j for all the values of sub-segment length $n \in [1, L]$. In addition, they can be computed for both $M_{S\to T}$ and $M_{T\to S}$; this yields $4L$ positive features in total for each word t_j.

2.2 Negative features

The negative features, i.e. those features that help to identify words that should be post-edited in the translation hypothesis T, are also based on sub-segment translations $(\sigma, \tau) \in M$, but they are used in a different way. Negative features use those sub-segments τ that fit two criteria: (a) they are the translation of a sub-segment σ from S but are not sub-segments of T; and (b) when they are aligned to T using the edit-distance algorithm (Wagner and Fischer, 1974), both their first word θ_1 and last word $\theta_{|\tau|}$ can be aligned, therefore delimiting a sub-segment τ' of T. Our hypothesis is that those words t_j in τ' which cannot be aligned to τ are likely to need postediting. We define our negative feature collection $\mathrm{Neg}_{mn'}$ as:

$$\mathrm{Neg}_{mn'}(j, S, T, M) = \sum_{\forall \tau \in \mathrm{NegEvidence}_{mn'}(j,S,T,M)} \frac{1}{\mathrm{alignmentsize}(\tau, T)}$$

where $\mathrm{alignmentsize}(\tau, T)$ returns the length of the sub-segment τ' delimited by τ in T. Function $\mathrm{NegEvidence}_{mn'}(\cdot)$ returns the set of sub-segments τ of T that are considered negative evidence and is defined as:

$$\mathrm{NegEvidence}_{mn'}(j, S, T, M) = \{\tau : (\sigma, \tau) \in M \\ \wedge \sigma \in \mathrm{seg}_m(S) \wedge |\tau'| = n' \wedge \\ \tau \notin \mathrm{seg}_*(T) \wedge \mathrm{IsNeg}(j, \tau, T)\}$$

In this function length constraints are set so that sub-segments σ take lengths $m \in [1, L]$. While for the positive features, only the length of τ was constrained, the experiments carried out by Esplà-Gomis et al. (2015b) indicate that for the negative features, it is better to constrain also the length of σ. On the other hand, the case of the sub-segments τ is slightly different: n' does not stand for the length of the sub-segments, but the number of words in τ which are aligned to T.[7] Function $\mathrm{IsNeg}(\cdot)$ defines the set of conditions required to consider a sub-segment τ a negative evidence for word t_j:

$$\mathrm{IsNeg}(j, \tau, T) = \exists j', j'' \in [1, |T|] : j' < j < j'' \\ \wedge \mathrm{aligned}(t_{j'}, \theta_1) \wedge \mathrm{aligned}(t_{j''}, \theta_{|\tau|}) \wedge \\ \nexists \theta_k \in \mathrm{seg}_1(\tau) : \mathrm{aligned}(t_j, \theta_k)$$

where $\mathrm{aligned}(X, Y)$ is a binary function that checks whether words X and Y are aligned or not.

For our running example, only two sub-segment pairs (σ, τ) fit the conditions set by function $\mathrm{IsNeg}(j, \tau, T)$ for the word *Automatic*: *("la Traducció", "the Translation")*, and *("la Traducció Automàtica", "the Machine Translation")*. As can be seen, for both (σ, τ) pairs, the words *the* and *Translation* in the sub-segments τ can be aligned to the words in positions 4 and 6 in T, respectively, which makes the number of words aligned $n' = 2$. In this way, we would have the evidences:

$$\mathrm{NegEvidence}_{2,2}(5, S, T, M) = \{\text{"the Translation"}\}$$

$$\mathrm{NegEvidence}_{3,2}(5, S, T, M) = \{\text{"the Machine Translation"}\}$$

As can be seen, in the case of sub-segment $\tau =$ *"the Translation"*, these alignments suggest that word *Automatic* should be removed, while for the sub-segment $\tau =$ *the Machine Translation"* they suggest that word *Automatic* should be replaced by word *Machine*. The resulting negative features are:

$$\mathrm{Neg}_{2,2}(5, S, T, M) = \tfrac{1}{3}$$

$$\mathrm{Neg}_{3,2}(5, S, T, M) = \tfrac{1}{3}$$

Negative features $\mathrm{Neg}_{mn'}(\cdot)$ are computed for t_j for all the values of SL sub-segment lengths $m \in [1, L]$ and the number of TL words $n' \in [2, L]$ which are aligned to words θ_k in sub-segment τ. Note that the number of aligned words between T and τ cannot be smaller than 2 given the constraints set by function $\mathrm{IsNeg}(j, \tau, T)$. This results in a collection of $L \times (L - 1)$ negative features. Obviously, for these features only $M_{S \to T}$ is used, since in $M_{T \to S}$ all the sub-segments τ can be found in T.

3 Experiments

This section describes the dataset provided for the word-level MTQE sub-task and the results obtained by our method on these datasest. This year, the task consisted in measuring the word-level MTQE on a collection of segments in Spanish that had been obtained through machine translation from English. The organisers provided a dataset consisting of:

- *training set*: a collection of 11,272 segments in English (S) and their corresponding machine translations in Spanish (T); for every word in T, a label was provided: BAD for the words to be post-edited, and GOOD for those to be kept unedited;
- *development set*: 1,000 pairs of segments (S, T) with the corresponding MTQE labels that can be used to optimise the binary classifier trained by using the training set;
- *test set*: 1,817 pairs of segments (S, T) for which the MTQE labels have to be estimated with the binary classifier trained on the training and the development sets.

[7] That is, the length of longest common sub-segment of τ and T.

3.1 Binary classifier

A *multilayer perceptron* (Duda et al., 2000, Section 6) was used for classification, as implemented in Weka 3.6 (Hall et al., 2009), following the approach by Esplà-Gomis et al. (2015b). A subset of 10% of the training examples was extracted from the training set before starting the training process and used as a validation set. The weights were iteratively updated on the basis of the error computed in the other 90%, but the decision to stop the training (usually referred as the convergence condition) was based on this validation set, in order to minimise the risk of overfitting. The error function used was based on the the optimisation of the metric used for ranking, i.e. the F_1^{BAD} metric.

Hyperparameter optimisation was carried out on the development set, by using a grid search (Bergstra et al., 2011) in order to choose the hyperparameters optimising the results for the metric to be used for comparison, F_1 for class *BAD*:

- *Number of nodes in the hidden layer*: Weka (Hall et al., 2009) makes it possible to choose from among a collection of predefined network designs; the design performing best in most cases happened to have a single hidden layer containing the same number of nodes in the hidden layer as the number of features.
- *Learning rate*: this parameter allows the dimension of the weight updates to be regulated by applying a factor to the error function after each iteration; the value that best performed for most of our training data sets was 0.1.
- *Momentum*: when updating the weights at the end of a training iteration, momentum smooths the training process for faster convergence by making it dependent on the previous weight value; in the case of our experiments, it was set to 0.03.

3.2 Evaluation

As already mentioned, two configurations of our system were submitted: one using only the features defined in Section 2, and one combining them with the baseline features. In order to obtain our features we used two sources of bilingual information, as already mentioned: MT and a bilingual concordancer. As explained above, for our experiments we used two MT systems which are freely available on the Internet: Apertium and Google Translate. The bilingual concordancer *Reverso Context* was also used for translating sub-segments. Actually, only the sub-sentential translation memory of this system was used, which provides the collection of TL translation alternatives for a given SL sub-segment, together with the number of occurrences of the sub-segments pair in the translation memory.

Four evaluation metrics were proposed for this task:

- The precision P^c, i.e. the fraction of instances correctly labelled among all the instances labelled as c, where c is the class assigned (either GOOD or BAD in our case);
- The recall R^c, i.e. the fraction of instances correctly labelled as c among all the instances that should be labelled as c in the test set;
- The F_1^c score, which is defined as

$$F_1^c = \frac{2 \times P^c \times R^c}{P^c + R^c};$$

  although the F_1^c score is computed both for GOOD and for BAD, it is worth noting that the F_1 score for the less frequent class in the data set (label BAD, in this case) is used as the main comparison metric;
- The F_1^w score, which is the version of F_1^c weighted by the proportion of instances of a given class c in the data set:

$$F_1^w = \frac{N^{\text{BAD}}}{N^{\text{TOTAL}}} F_1^{\text{BAD}} + \frac{N^{\text{GOOD}}}{N^{\text{TOTAL}}} F_1^{\text{GOOD}}$$

  where N^{BAD} is the number of instances of the class BAD, N^{GOOD} is the number of instances of the class GOOD, and N^{TOTAL} is the total number of instances in the test set.

3.3 Results

Table 1 shows the results obtained by our system, both on the development set during the training phase and on the test set. The table also includes the results for the baseline system as published by the organisers of the shared task, which uses the baseline features provided by them and a standard logistic regression binary classifier.

As can be seen in Table 1, the results obtained on the development set and the test set are quite similar and coherent, which highlights the robustness of the approach. The results obtained clearly outperform the baseline on the main evaluation metric (F_1^{BAD}). It is worth noting that, on this metric, the

Data set	System	P^{BAD}	R^{BAD}	F_1^{BAD}	P^{GOOD}	R^{GOOD}	F_1^{GOOD}	F_1^{w}
development set	SBI	31.2%	63.7%	41.9%	88.5%	66.7%	76.1%	69.5%
	SBI+baseline	33.4%	60.9%	43.1%	88.5%	71.1%	78.8%	72.0%
test set	baseline	—	—	16.8%	—	—	88.9%	75.3%
	SBI	30.8%	63.9%	41.5%	88.8%	66.5%	76.1%	69.5%
	SBI+baseline	32.6%	63.6%	43.1%	89.1%	69.5%	78.1%	71.5%

Table 1: Results of the two systems submitted to the WMT 2015 sub-task on word-level MTQE: the one using only sources of bilingual information (SBI) and the one combining these sources of information with the baseline features (SBI+baseline). The table also includes the results of the baseline system proposed by the organisation; in this case only the F_1 scores are provided because, at the time of writing this paper, the rest of metrics remain unpublished.

SBI and SBI+baseline submissions scored first and third among the 16 submissions to the shared task.[8] The submission scoring second obtained very similar results; for F_1^{BAD} it obtained 43.05%, while our submission obtained 43.12%. On the other hand, using the metric F_1^{w} for comparison, our submissions ranked 10 and 11 in the shared task, although it is worth noting that our system was optimised using only the F_1^{BAD} metric, which is the one chosen by the organisers for ranking submissions.

4 Concluding remarks

In this paper we described the submissions of the *UAlacant* team for the sub-task 2 in the MTQE shared task of the WMT 2015 (word-level MTQE). Our submissions, which were ranked first and third, used online available sources bilingual of information in order to extract relations between the words in the original SL segments and their TL machine translations. The approach employed is aimed at being system-independent, since it only uses resources produced by external systems. In addition, adding new sources of information is straightforward, which leaves considerable room for improvement. In general, the results obtained support the conclusions obtained by Esplà-Gomis et al. (2015b) regarding the feasibility of this approach and its performance.

Acknowledgements

Work partially funded by the Spanish Ministerio de Ciencia e Innovación through project TIN2012-32615 and by the European Commission through project PIAP-GA-2012-324414 (Abu-MaTran). We specially thank Reverso-Softissimo and Prompsit Language Engineering for providing the access to the Reverso Context concordancer, and to the University Research Program for Google Translate that granted us access to the Google Translate service.

[8] http://www.quest.dcs.shef.ac.uk/wmt15_files/results/task2.pdf

References

J.S. Bergstra, R. Bardenet, Y. Bengio, and B. Kégl. 2011. Algorithms for hyper-parameter optimization. In J. Shawe-Taylor, R.S. Zemel, P.L. Bartlett, F. Pereira, and K.Q. Weinberger, editors, *Advances in Neural Information Processing Systems 24*, pages 2546–2554.

J. Blatz, E. Fitzgerald, G. Foster, S. Gandrabur, C. Goutte, A. Kulesza, A. Sanchis, and N. Ueffing. 2004. Confidence estimation for machine translation. In *Proceedings of the 20th International Conference on Computational Linguistics*, COLING '04.

R. O. Duda, P. E. Hart, and D. G. Stork. 2000. *Pattern Classification*. John Wiley and Sons Inc., 2nd edition.

M. Esplà-Gomis, F. Sánchez-Martínez, and M.L. Forcada. 2012. UAlacant: Using online machine translation for cross-lingual textual entailment. In *Proceedings of the 6th International Workshop on Semantic Evaluation*, SemEval 2012), pages 472–476, Montreal, Canada.

M. Esplà-Gomis, F. Sánchez-Martínez, and M. L. Forcada. 2015a. Target-language edit hints in CAT tools based on TM by means of MT. *Journal of Artificial Intelligence Research*, 53:169–222.

M. Esplà-Gomis, F. Sánchez-Martínez, and M. L. Forcada. 2015b. Using on-line available sources of bilingual information for word-level machine translation quality estimation. In *Proceedings of the 18th Annual Conference of the European Associtation for Machine Translation*, pages 19–26, Antalya, Turkey.

M. Hall, E. Frank, G. Holmes, B. Pfahringer, P. Reutemann, and I.H. Witten. 2009. The WEKA Data Mining Software: an Update. *SIGKDD Explorations*, 11(1):10–18.

L. Specia and R. Soricut. 2013. Quality estimation for machine translation: preface. *Machine Translation*, 27(3-4):167–170.

L. Specia, D. Raj, and M. Turchi. 2010. Machine translation evaluation versus quality estimation. *Machine Translation*, 24(1):39–50.

R.A. Wagner and M.J. Fischer. 1974. The string-to-string correction problem. *Journal of the ACM*, 21(1):168–173.

QUality Estimation from ScraTCH (QUETCH): Deep Learning for Word-level Translation Quality Estimation

Julia Kreutzer and **Shigehiko Schamoni**
Computational Linguistics
Heidelberg University
69120 Heidelberg, Germany
{kreutzer,schamoni}@cl.uni-heidelberg.de

Stefan Riezler
Computational Linguistics & IWR
Heidelberg University
69120 Heidelberg, Germany
riezler@cl.uni-heidelberg.de

Abstract

This paper describes the system submitted by the University of Heidelberg to the Shared Task on Word-level Quality Estimation at the 2015 Workshop on Statistical Machine Translation. The submitted system combines a continuous space deep neural network, that learns a bilingual feature representation from scratch, with a linear combination of the manually defined baseline features provided by the task organizers. A combination of these orthogonal information sources shows significant improvements over the combined systems, and produces very competitive F_1-scores for predicting word-level translation quality.

1 Introduction

This paper describes the University of Heidelberg submission to the Shared Task on Word-level Quality Estimation (QE Task 2) at the 2015 Workshop on Statistical Machine Translation (WMT15). The task consists of predicting the word-level quality level ("OK"/"BAD") of English-to-Spanish machine translations, without the use of human references, and without insight into the translation derivations, that is, by treating the Machine Translation (MT) system that produced the translations as a black box.

The task organizers provided training and development data comprising tokenized MT outputs that were automatically annotated for errors as edit operations (replacements, insertions, or deletions) with respect to human post-edits (Snover et al., 2006). Furthermore, a set of 25 baseline features that operate on source and target translation, but do not use features of the SMT pipeline that produced the translations, was provided. Even though the distribution of binary labels is skewed towards "OK" labels, even more so than in the previous QE task at WMT14[1], the most common approach is to treat the problem as a supervised classification task. Furthermore, most approaches rely on manually designed features, including source and target contexts, alignments, and generalizations by linguistic categories (POS, syntactic dependency links, WordNet senses) as reported by Bojar et al. (2014), similar to the 25 feature templates provided by the organizers.

We apply the framework of Collobert et al. (2011) to learn bilingual correspondences "from scratch", i.e. from raw input words. To this aim, a continuous space deep neural network is pre-trained by initializing the lookup-table with distributed word representations (Mikolov et al., 2013b), and fine-tuned for the QE classification task by back-propagating word-level prediction errors using stochastic gradient descent (Rumelhart et al., 1986). Moreover, we train a linear combination of the manually defined baseline features provided by the task organizers. A combination of the orthogonal information based on the continuous space features and the manually chosen baseline features shows significant improvements over the combined systems, and produces very competitive F_1 scores for predicting word-level translation quality.

2 Deep Learning for Quality Estimation

Continuous space neural network models are credited with the advantage of superior modeling power by replacing discrete units such as words or n-grams by vectors in continuous space, allowing similar words to have similar representations, and avoiding data sparsity issues. These advantages have been demonstrated experimentally by showcasing meaningful structure in vector space

[1]A factor of 4.22 on WMT15 train, and 4.21 on WMT15 dev, as opposed to 1.84 for WMT14 train and 1.81 for WMT14 test for the same language pair.

representations (Mikolov et al. (2013c), Pennington et al. (2014) *inter alia*), or by producing state-of-the-art performance in applications such as language modeling (Bengio et al. (2003), Mikolov et al. (2010), *inter alia*) or statistical machine translation (Kalchbrenner and Blunsom (2013), Bahdanau et al. (2015), *inter alia*). The property that makes these models most attractive for various applications is the ability to learn continuous space representations "from scratch"(Collobert et al., 2011), and to infuse the representation with non-linearity. The deep layers of the neural network capture these representations – even a single hidden layer is sufficient (Hornik et al., 1989).

We present an approach to address the challenges of word-level translation quality estimation by learning these continuous space bilingual representations instead of relying on manual feature engineering. While the neural network architecture presented by Collobert et al. (2011) is limited to monolingual word-labeling tasks, we extend it to the bilingual context of QE. The multilayer feedforward neural network is pre-trained in an unsupervised fashion by initializing the lookup-table with `word2vec` representations (Mikolov et al., 2013b). This is not only an effective way of guiding the learning towards minima that still allow good generalization in non-convex optimization (Bengio, 2009; Erhan et al., 2010), but it also proves to yield considerably better results in our application. In addition, we train a linear combination of the manually defined baseline features provided by the task organizers. We combine these orthogonal information sources and find significant improvements over each individual system.

3 QUETCH

Our *QUality Estimation from scraTCH* (QUETCH) system is based on a neural network architecture built with `Theano` (Bergstra et al., 2010). We design a multilayer perceptron (MLP) architecture with one hidden layer, non-linear $\tanh$ activation functions and a lookup-table layer as proposed by Collobert et al. (2011). The lookup-table has the function of mapping word to continuous vectors and is updated during training. Figure 1 illustrates the connections between the input, hidden lookup-table and linear layer, and the output.

Training is done by optimizing the log-likelihood of the model given the training data via back-propagation and stochastic gradient descent (Rumelhart et al., 1986). Trainable parameters are the bias vectors ($\mathbf{b_1}$,$\mathbf{b_2}$) and weight matrices (W_1,W_2) of the linear layers and the matrix $M \in \mathbb{R}^{d_{wrd} \times |V|}$ that represents the lookup-table. Tunable hyper-parameters are the number of units of the hidden linear layer, the lookup-table dimensionality d_{wrd} and the learning rate. The number of output units is set to two, since the QE task 2 requires binary classification. The softmax over the activation of these output units is interpreted as score for the two classes.

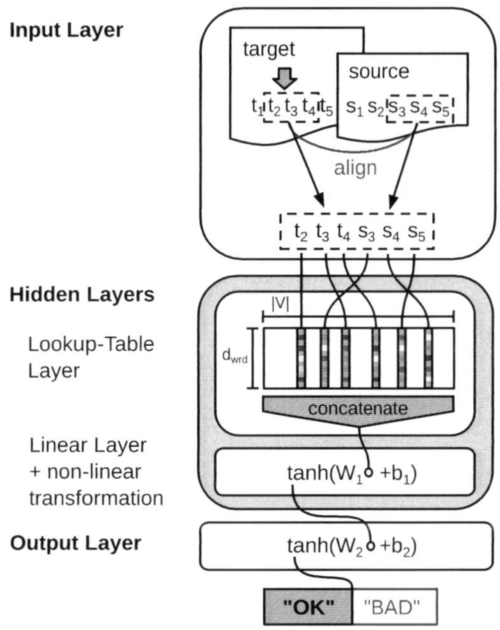

Figure 1: Neural network architecture for predicting word-level translation quality given aligned source and target sentences. The lookup-table matrix M contains d_{wrd}-dimensional vectors for each word in the vocabulary V. In this example, the context window sizes $|win_{src}|$ and $|win_{tgt}|$ are set to three and the target word t_3 is classified "OK".

3.1 Bilingual Representation Learning

Given a target word, we consider bilingual context information: From the target sentence we extract a fixed-size word window win_{tgt} centered at the target word. From the aligned source sentence we extract a fixed-size word window win_{src} centered at a position that is either estimated heuristically or via word alignments. Concatenating target and source windows, we obtain a bilingual context vector for a given target word. This context vector is the input for the lookup-table layer, which maps each context word to a d_{wrd}-dimensional vector[2]. All lookup-table output vectors are concatenated to form the input to the MLP hidden layer. Since the lookup-table representations of words are updated during training, QUETCH learns representations of words in bilingual contexts that are optimized for QE.

3.2 Unsupervised Pre-training

Usually, the parameters of a neural network are initialized with zeros or random numbers, i.e. no a-priori knowledge is captured in the network. However, the learning process can benefit from knowledge that is encoded into the architecture prior to training (Saxe et al., 2011). In case of QE, we want the model to know what well-written source and target sentences look like – before actually seeing translations. `word2vec` (Mikolov et al., 2013b; Mikolov et al., 2013a) offers efficient methods to pre-train word representations in an unsupervised fashion such that they reflect word similarities and relations. Initializing the lookup-table with pre-trained `word2vec` vectors allows us to incorporate prior linguistic knowledge about source and target language into QUETCH. During the learning process, these representations are further optimized for QE and the vocabulary encountered during training.

4 Baseline Features and System Combination

In contrast to word-based quality estimation tasks from previous years, this year's data additionally provides a number of baseline features. A straightforward approach would be to integrate the baseline features in the deep learning system on the same level as word-features and train lookup-tables for each feature class (Collobert et al., 2011). While this certainly works for word-similar features like POS-tags, this is not suitable for continuous numerical features. Preliminary tests of extending QUETCH with a lookup-table for POS-tags did not result in better F1 scores. Also, training took considerably longer, because of (1) the additional lookup-table to train and (2) the larger dimensionality of the vector representing a target word with its context. If we added all 25 features for each target word in the context window, the input to the first linear layer would grow by $25 * |win_{tgt}| * d_{wrd}$ dimensions.

For these reasons, we decided to design a system combination that treats the QUETCH system and the baseline features individually and independently. For many complex applications, system combination has proven to be effective strategy to boost performance. In machine translation tasks, Heafield and Lavie (2011) and Karakos et al. (2008), *inter alia*, increased overall performance by cleverly combining the outputs of several MT systems. In cross-lingual information retrieval, Schamoni and Riezler (2015) empirically showed that it is more beneficial to combine systems that are most dissimilar than those that have highest single scores.

Our approach is to train separate systems, one based on the deep learning approach described in Section 3, and one based solely on the baseline features provided for the shared task. In a final step, we combine both systems together with binarized versions of selected baseline features. From this modular combination of both systems, we can furthermore gain knowledge about their individual contribution to the combined system which will help to understand their usefulness for the QE task.

4.1 Baseline Features System

To obtain a system for baseline features that is most complementary to QUETCH, we used the Vowpal Wabbit (VW) toolkit (Goel et al., 2008) to train a linear classifier, i.e. a single-layer perceptron. We built new features by "pairing" baseline features, thus we quadratically expand the feature space and learn a weight for each possible pair.

Assuming two feature vectors $\mathbf{p} \in \{0,1\}^P$ and $\mathbf{q} \in \{0,1\}^Q$ of sizes P and Q where the nth dimension indicates the occurrence of the nth feature, we define our linear model as

$$f(\mathbf{p},\mathbf{q}) = \mathbf{p}^\top W \mathbf{q} = \sum_{i=1}^{P}\sum_{j=1}^{Q} p_i W_{ij} q_j,$$

where $W \in \mathbb{R}^{P\times Q}$ encodes a feature matrix (Bai et al., 2010; Schamoni et al., 2014). The value of $f(\cdot,\cdot)$ is the prediction of the classifier given a target vector $\mathbf{p}$ and a vector of related features $\mathbf{q}$.

To address the problem of data sparsity, we reduced the number of possible feature pairs by restricting the feature expansion to two groups: (1) *target words* are combined with *target context*

[2]All words are indexed within a vocabulary V. The vocabulary contains the entire training, development and test data of the QE task and is realized as a `gensim` dictionary (Řehůřek and Sojka, 2010).

words and *source aligned words*, and (2) *target POS tags* are combined with *source aligned POS tags*. In total, we observed 3.5M different features during training of the VW model.

4.2 System Combination

For the final system combination, we reused the VW toolkit. The combined systems comprises 82 features: the QUETCH-score, the VW-score, and the remaining 80 features are binary features derived from the baseline feature set. The QUETCH-score is the system's prediction combined with its likelihood, for VW we directly utilize the raw predictions with clipping at ± 1. Binarized features were inserted to enrich the classifier with additional non-linearity. They consist of (1) the binary features from the baseline feature set, and (2) binned versions of the numerical features from the same set. For small groups of discrete values we assigned a binary feature to each possible value, for larger groups and real-valued features we heuristically defined intervals ("bins") containing roughly the same number of instances. The integration of the single components for the system combination is illustrated in Figure 2.

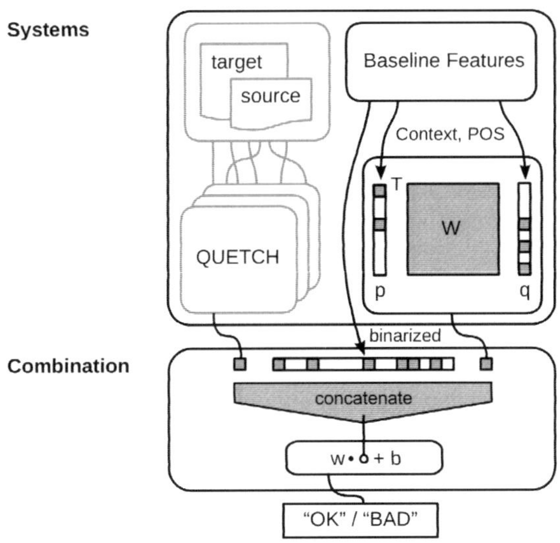

Figure 2: Architecture of the QUETCHPLUS system combination.

5 Experiments

5.1 WMT14

We first ran experiments on the WMT14 task 2 data to compare QUETCH's performance with the WMT14 submissions. With outlook to this year's task we considered only the binary classification task where words are labeled either "BAD" or "OK".

In contrast to the WMT15 data, the WMT14's data covers not only English to Spanish translations (en-es) but also German to English (de-en) and vice versa. Since the plain QUETCH system does not rely on language-specific features, we simply use the same deep learning architecture for all of these language pairs.

QUETCH is trained on the WMT14 training set, with a source and target window size of 3, a lookup-table dimensionality of 10, 300 hidden units, and a constant learning rate of 0.001. Test and training data were lowercased. The alignments used for positioning the target window as described in Section 3.1 were created with `fast_align` from the `cdec` toolkit (Dyer et al., 2010). The collection of corpora provided with WMT13's translation task[3] is utilized as source for unsupervised pre-training: Europarl v7 (Koehn, 2005), Common Crawl corpus, and News Commentary. Note that we did not use these corpora because of their parallel structure, but because they are large, multilingual, and are commonly used in WMT submissions.

Following the WMT14 evaluation (Bojar et al., 2014), we report on accuracy and BAD F_1-score, the latter being the task's primary evaluation metric. The WMT14 baselines trivially predict either only BAD or only OK labels. Table 1 presents the best F_1-scores during training and the according accuracies for QUETCH under different configurations.

The plain QUETCH system yields an acceptable accuracy, but the BAD F_1-scores are not competitive. Adding alignment information further improves the accuracy for all language pairs but de-en. It improves the F_1-score only for es-en and en-de, which indicates that the model is still prone to local optima. It is in fact pre-training that boosts the BAD F_1-score – this initial positioning in the parameter space appears to have a larger impact on the training outcome than the introduction

[3] `http://www.statmt.org/wmt13/translation-task.html`

	configuration	BAD F_1	Accuracy
en-es	(v)	0.4378	0.5087
	(a)	0.4164	0.5107
	(p)	0.5206	0.4026
	(a), (p)	**0.5228**	0.4196
es-en	(v)	0.2197	0.7604
	(a)	0.2470	0.7749
	(p)	0.3203	0.8051
	(a), (p)	**0.3396**	0.8076
en-de	(v)	0.3743	0.6090
	(a)	0.4197	0.6381
	(p)	0.4684	0.6060
	(a), (p)	**0.4863**	0.6271
de-en	(v)	0.2482	0.7001
	(a)	0.2426	0.6837
	(p)	0.3734	0.6657
	(a), (p)	**0.3791**	0.6792

Table 1: QUETCH results on WMT14 task 2 test data under different configurations: (v)anilla system, (p)retraining of word embeddings, (a)lignments from an SMT system.

of translation knowledge via alignments. However, we can achieve further improvement when combining both pre-training and alignments. As a result, QUETCH outperforms the official winning systems of the WMT14 QE task (see Table 2) and the trivial baselines for all language pairs. The fact that the overall tendencies are consistent across languages proves that QUETCH is capable of language-independent quality estimation.

	submission	BAD F_1	Acc.
en-es	FBK-UPV-UEDIN/RNN	0.4873	0.6162
es-en	RTM-DCU/RTU-GLMd	0.2914	0.8298
en-de	RTM-DCU/RTU-GLM	0.4530	0.7297
de-en	RTM-DCU/RTU-GLM	0.2613	0.7614

Table 2: Winning submissions of the WMT14 Quality Estimation Task 2 (Bojar et al., 2014).

5.2 WMT15

With the insights from the experiments on the WMT14 data we proceed to the experiments on the WMT15 en-es data. We introduce a weight w for BAD training samples, such that QUETCH is trained on each BAD sample w times. In this way, we easily counterbalance the skewed distribution of labels, without modifying the classifier's loss function. Also, we utilize the larger and non-parallel Wikicorpus (Reese et al., 2010) in English and Spanish for pre-training. As described in Section 1, 25 baseline features are supplied with training, development and test data. This allows us to evaluate the approach for system combination introduced in Section 4.

During training of the VW-system, we experimented with various loss functions (hinge, squared, logistic) and found the model trained on squared loss to return the highest accuracy. Unwanted collisions in VW's hashed weight vector were reduced by increasing the size of the hash to 28 bits. To prevent the model from degenerating towards OK-labels, we utilized VW's option to set the weight for each training instance individually and increased the weights of the BAD-labeled instances to 4.0.

The VW-system and the system combination were trained in a 10-fold manner, i.e. the VW-system was trained on 9 folds and the weights for system combination were tuned on the 10th fold of the training data. The final weights of the model for evaluation were averaged among all 10 folds.

Table 3 presents the results on the WMT15 data for both QUETCH, the baseline feature VW model, and the system combination referred to as QUETCH+. The QUETCH results were produced under the same parameter conditions as in the WMT14 experiments, and the newly introduced w is set to 2 for the submitted and the combined model, and 5 for another model that was explicitely designed for a high BAD F_1-score.

	configuration	BAD F_1	Accuracy
QUETCH	(v)	0.2535	0.7104
	(a)	0.2628	0.7099
	(p)	0.2535	0.7668
	(a), (p)	0.2793	0.7716
	†(a), (p), (w)	0.3527	0.7508
	(a), (p), (w)	0.3876	0.6031
	‡(a), (p), (w)	0.2985	0.7888
	‡VW	0.4084	0.7335
	†QUETCH+	**0.4305**	0.6977

Table 3: QUETCH results on en-es WMT15 task 2 test data under different configuration setting: (v)anilla model vs. models using (p)re-training, (a)lignments from an SMT-System, and (w)eighting of the BAD-instances. Submitted systems are preceded by †, components of the final QUETCH+ system are marked with ‡.

Although proceeding in the same manner as in the WMT14 experiments, we see slightly different tendencies here: Adding alignments has a positive effect on the BAD F_1-score, whereas pre-training improves mainly the accuracy. Still, the combination of both yields both a high BAD F_1-score and a high accuracy, which indicates that QUETCH succeeds in integrating both contributions in a complementary way. Adding BAD weights furthermore improves the BAD F_1-score, yet losing some accuracy. Further increasing the weight up to 5 strengthens this effect, such that we obtain a model with very high BAD F_1-score, but rather low accuracy.

The stand-alone VW model yields generally higher BAD F_1-score, but does not reach QUETCH's accuracy. To enhance the orthogonality of the two models for combination, we select a QUETCH model with extremely high accuracy for the system combination[4]. Interestingly, the system combination appears to profit from both models, resulting in the overall best BAD F_1-score. The resulting VW weights of 1.188 for QUETCH and 0.951 for VW underline each system's contribution. The next most important features for the combination were *pseudo_reference* and *is_proper_noun* with weights of 0.2208 and 0.1557, respectively.

system	BAD F_1	OK F_1	All F_1
baseline	0.1678	0.8893	0.7531
QUETCH	0.3527	0.8456	0.7526
QUETCH+	0.4305	0.7942	0.7256
UAlacant/OnLine-SBI-Baseline	0.4312	0.7807	0.7147

Table 4: Official test results on WMT15 task 2 for word level translation quality. The All F_1-score is the weighted average of BAD F_1 and OK F_1, where the weights are determined by the frequency of the classes in the test data. The UAlacant/OnLine-SBI-Baseline and the QUETCH+ predictions show no significant difference at p=0.05 and are both announced official winners.

Table 4 shows the final test results on the WMT15 task 2 for the main evaluation metric of F_1 for predicting BAD word level translation quality, the F_1 for predicting OK translations and their weighted average. Both submitted systems, QUETCH and QUETCH+, yield considerable improvements over the baseline. The QUETCH+ system that combines the neural network with the linearly weighted baseline features is nominally outperformed by one other system by 0.07% BAD F_1 points, but their difference is not significant at p=0.05.

[4]We observe that the training process first produces high BAD F_1-score models, then further improves the accuracy whilst slowly decreasing the BAD F_1-score. This is due to the fact that we do not optimize on the BAD F_1-score directly, but the log-likelihood of the data, which is skewed towards the OK label. This behavior allows us to select models with individual trade-offs between BAD F_1-score and accuracy at different stages of training.

6 Conclusion

We successfully applied a continuous space deep neural network to the task of quality estimation. With QUETCH we built a language-independent neural network architecture that learns representations for words in bilingual contexts from scratch. Furthermore we showed how this architecture benefits from unsupervised pre-training on large corpora. Winning the WMT15 QE task we found evidence that the combination of such a continuous space deep model with a discrete shallow model benefits from their orthogonality and produces very competitive F_1-scores for quality estimation. Further work will address the transfer to sentence-based predictions and the introduction of convolution and recurrence into the neural network architecture.

Acknowledgments.

This research was supported in part by DFG grant RI-2221/1-2 "Weakly Supervised Learning of Cross-Lingual Systems".

References

Dzmitry Bahdanau, Kyunghyun Cho, and Yoshua Bengio. 2015. Neural machine translation by jointly learning to align and translate. In *Proceedings of the International Conference on Learning Representations (ICLR)*, San Diego, CA.

Bing Bai, Jason Weston, David Grangier, Ronan Collobert, Kunihiko Sadamasa, Yanjun Qi, Olivier Chapelle, and Kilian Weinberger. 2010. Learning to rank with (a lot of) word features. *Information Retrieval Journal*, 13(3):291–314.

Yoshua Bengio, Rejean Ducharme, Pascal Vincent, and Christian Jauvin. 2003. A neural probabilistic language model. *Joural of Machine Learning Research*, 3:1137–1155.

Yoshua Bengio. 2009. Learning deep architectures for ai. *Foundations and trends® in Machine Learning*, 2(1):1–127.

James Bergstra, Olivier Breuleux, Frédéric Bastien, Pascal Lamblin, Razvan Pascanu, Guillaume Desjardins, Joseph Turian, David Warde-Farley, and Yoshua Bengio. 2010. Theano: a CPU and GPU math expression compiler. In *Proceedings of the Python for Scientific Computing Conference (SciPy)*, Austin, TX.

Ondrej Bojar, Christian Buck, Christian Federmann, Barry Haddow, Philipp Koehn, Johannes Leveling, Christof Monz, Pavel Pecina, Matt Post, Herve Saint-Amand, et al. 2014. Findings of the 2014 workshop on statistical machine translation. In *Proceedings of the Ninth Workshop on Statistical Machine Translation (WMT)*, Baltimore, MD.

Ronan Collobert, Jason Weston, Léon Bottou, Michael Karlen, Koray Kavukcuoglu, and Pavel Kuksa. 2011. Natural language processing (almost) from scratch. *The Journal of Machine Learning Research*, 12:2493–2537.

Chris Dyer, Adam Lopez, Juri Ganitkevitch, Jonathan Weese, Ferhan Ture, Phil Blunsom, Hendra Setiawan, Vladimir Eidelman, and Philip Resnik. 2010. cdec: A decoder, alignment, and learning framework for finite-state and context-free translation models. In *Proceedings of the ACL 2010 System Demonstrations*, Uppsala, Sweden.

Dumitru Erhan, Yoshua Bengio, Aaron Courville, Pierre-Antoine Manzagol, Pascal Vincent, and Samy Bengio. 2010. Why does unsupervised pre-training help deep learning? *The Journal of Machine Learning Research*, 11:625–660.

Sharad Goel, John Langford, and Alexander L. Strehl. 2008. Predictive indexing for fast search. In *Advances in Neural Information Processing Systems (NIPS)*, Vancouver, Canada.

Kenneth Heafield and Alon Lavie. 2011. CMU system combination in WMT 2011. In *Proceedings of the EMNLP 2011 Sixth Workshop on Statistical Machine Translation*, Edinburgh, Scotland, United Kingdom.

Kurt Hornik, Maxwell Stinchcombe, and Halber White. 1989. Multilayer feedforward networks are universal approximators. *Neural Networks*, 2:359–366.

Nal Kalchbrenner and Phil Blunsom. 2013. Recurrent continuous translation models. In *Proceedings of the 2013 Conference on Empirical Methods in Natural Language Processing (EMNLP)*, Seattle, WA.

Damianos Karakos, Jason Eisner, Sanjeev Khudanpur, and Markus Dreyer. 2008. Machine translation system combination using itg-based alignments. In *Proceedings of ACL-08: HLT, Short Papers*, Columbus, Ohio.

Philipp Koehn. 2005. Europarl: A parallel corpus for statistical machine translation. In *Proceedings of Machine Translation Summit X*, Phuket, Thailand.

Tomas Mikolov, Martin Karafiat, Lukas Burget, Jan Cernocky, and Sanjeev Khudanpur. 2010. Recurrent neural network based language model. In *Proceedings of Interspeech*, Makuhari, Chiba, Japan.

Tomas Mikolov, Kai Chen, Greg Corrado, and Jeffrey Dean. 2013a. Efficient estimation of word representations in vector space. In *Proceedings of Workshop at ICLR*, Scottsdale, AZ.

Tomas Mikolov, Ilya Sutskever, Kai Chen, Greg S Corrado, and Jeff Dean. 2013b. Distributed representations of words and phrases and their compositionality. In *Advances in neural information processing systems (NIPS)*, Lake Tahoe, CA.

Tomas Mikolov, Wen tau Yih, and Geoffrey Zweig. 2013c. Linguistic regularities in continuous space word representations. In *Proceedings of the Conference of the North American Chapter of the Association for Computational Linguistics: Human Language Technologies (NAACL-HLT)*, Atlanta, Georgia.

Jeffrey Pennington, Richard Socher, and Christopher Manning. 2014. Glove: Global vectors for word representation. In *Proceedings of the Conference on Empirical Methods in Natural Language Processing (EMNLP)*, Doha, Qatar.

Samuel Reese, Gemma Boleda, Montse Cuadros, Llus Padr, and German Rigau. 2010. Wikicorpus: A word-sense disambiguated multilingual wikipedia corpus. In *Proceedings of 7th Language Resources and Evaluation Conference (LREC)*, La Valleta, Malta.

Radim Řehůřek and Petr Sojka. 2010. Software Framework for Topic Modelling with Large Corpora. In *Proceedings of the LREC 2010 Workshop on New Challenges for NLP Frameworks*, Valletta, Malta.

David E. Rumelhart, Geoffrey E. Hinton, and Ronald J. Williams. 1986. Learning representations by back-propagating errors. *Nature*, 323.

Andrew Saxe, Pang W Koh, Zhenghao Chen, Maneesh Bhand, Bipin Suresh, and Andrew Y Ng. 2011. On random weights and unsupervised feature learning. In *Proceedings of the 28th International Conference on Machine Learning (ICML)*, Bellevue, WA.

Shigehiko Schamoni and Stefan Riezler. 2015. Combining Orthogonal Information in Large-Scale Cross-Language Information Retrieval. In *Proceedings of the 38th Annual ACM SIGIR Conference (SIGIR)*, Santiago, Chile.

Shigehiko Schamoni, Felix Hieber, Artem Sokolov, and Stefan Riezler. 2014. Learning translational and knowledge-based similarities from relevance rankings for cross-language retrieval. In *Proceedings of the Association of Computational Linguistics (ACL)*, Baltimore, MD.

Matthew Snover, Bonnie Dorr, Richard Schwartz, Linnea Micciulla, and John Makhoul. 2006. A study of translation edit rate with targeted human annotation. In *Proceedings of the 7th Conference of the Association for Machine Translation in the Americas (AMTA)*, Cambridge, MA.

LORIA System for the WMT15 Quality Estimation Shared Task

Langlois David
SMarT Group, LORIA
Inria, Villers-lès-Nancy, F-54600, France
Universit de Lorraine, LORIA, UMR 7503, Villers-lès-Nancy, F-54600, France
CNRS, LORIA, UMR 7503, Villers-lès-Nancy, F-54600, France
david.langlois@loria.fr

Abstract

We describe our system for WMT2015 Shared Task on Quality Estimation, task 1, sentence-level prediction of post-edition effort. We use baseline features, Latent Semantic Indexing based features and features based on pseudo-references. SVM algorithm allows to estimate the linear regression between the features vectors and the HTER score. We use a selection algorithm in order to put aside needless features. Our best system leads to a performance in terms of Mean Absolute Error equal to 13.34 on official test while the official baseline system leads to a performance equal to 14.82.

1 Introduction

This paper describes the LORIA submission to the WMT'15 Shared Task on Quality Estimation. We participated to the Task 1. This task consists in predicting the edition effort needed to correct a translated sentence. The organizers provide English sentences automatically translated into Spanish, and the corresponding post-edited sentences. The edition effort is measured by edit-distance rate (HTER (Snover et al., 2006)) between the translated sentence and its post-edited version.

Classically, our system extracts numerical features from sentences and applies a machine learning approach between numeric vectors and HTER scores.

As last year, no information is given about the Machine Translation (MT) system used to build data. Therefore, it is only possible to use blackbox features, or to use other MT systems whom output is compared to the evaluated target sentence.

Our submission deals with the both kinds of features. First, we use a Latent Semantic Analysis approach to measure the lexical similarity between a source and a target sentence. To our knowledge, this approach has never been used in the scope of Quality Estimation. Second, we use the output of 3 online MT systems, and we extract information about the intersection between the evaluated target sentence and the 3 translated sentences by online systems. This intersection is measured in terms of shared 1,2,3,4-grams.

The paper is structured as follows. Section 2 give details about experimental protocol and used data. We describe the features we use in Section 3. Then, we give results (Section 4) and we conclude.

2 Experimental protocol and used corpus

In this section, we describe how we obtain results starting from training, development and test corpus. The training and development corpus are composed of a set of triplets. Each triplet is made up of a source sentence, its automatic translation, and a score representing the translation quality.

For our experiments, we use the corpora the organizers provide. The source language is English, the target language is Spanish. For each source sentence s, a machine translation system (unknown to the participants) gives a translation t (we keep notations s and t throughout this article for source and target sentences from the evaluation campaign data). t is manually post-edited into pe. The score of (s, t) is the HTER score between t and pe (noted $hter$).

We use the official training corpus tr composed of 11272 triplets $(s, t, hter)$, and the official development corpus dev composed of 1000 triplets.

For each triplet $(s_i, t_i, hter_i)$ in tr, we extract the features vector from (s_i, t_i) (see Section 3 for the list of the features we use), this leads to $v_{(s_i,t_i)}$. Then, we use the SVM algorithm in order to estimate the regression between the $v_{(s_i,t_i)}$ (i from 1 to 11272) and the $hter_i$. For this estimation, we use the LibSVM tool (Chang and Lin, 2011), with a Radial Basis Function (with default parameters:

$C = 1, \lambda = \frac{1}{|v_{(s_i,t_i)}|}$).

Then, we use the obtained linear regression in order to predict the edit effort rate for each couple (s, t) from dev (or test corpus for final evaluation).

Filtering the features some features may not be useful because they provide more noise than information, or because training data is not sufficiently big to estimate the link between them and the scores. Therefore, it may be useful to apply an algorithm in order to select interesting features. For that, we use a backward algorithm (Guyon and Elisseeff, 2003) we yet described in (Langlois et al., 2012). This year, we did not use the initial step consisting in evaluating the correlations between features (see (Langlois et al., 2012)). The algorithm is applied on the dev corpus in order to minimise the MAE (Mean Absolute Error) score defined by $MAE(r, r') = \frac{\sum_{i=1}^{n} |r_i - r'_i|}{n}$ where r is the set of n predicted scores on dev, and r' is the set of HTER reference scores.

3 The features

We use three sources for our features. The first source is the baseline features. The second is based on information provided by Latent Semantic approach, and the third one is based on the information provided by 3 online MT systems.

3.1 The baseline features

These 17 features are provided by the organizers of the Quality Estimation Shared Task. They are extracted by the QuEst tool (Specia et al., 2013). We can find the list of these features in the QuEst website[1], (Specia et al., 2013) describe them precisely. Table 1 shows the list of these features. We can remark that no glassbox feature is used (no information about the translation process of the MT system is used). Moreover, there is not feature taking into account both the source and target sentences (basing on an external translation table for example). 13 features describe the source side, while only 4 describe the target side.

3.2 Latent Semantic Indexing Based Features

Latent Semantic Indexing (LSI) allows to measure the similarity between two documents. This measure is based on lexical contents of the both documents. To achieve this measure, the documents are projected into a Vector Space Model: one document is described by a numerical vector, two documents are compared by computing the distance between their corresponding vectors.

LSI has been applied to bilingual parallel corpora in the scope of Information Retrieval (Littman et al., 1998) and of measure of comparability of documents (Saad et al., 2014). Each document is composed of the pair $(source, target)$. The method describes the corpus by a $n \times m$ matrix M. n is the number of words in the union of source and target vocabularies. m is the number of parallel sentences (a 'document' can be simply a sentence). $M[i, j]$ is a numeric value representing the "presence" of word i in document j. This value can be the frequency of i in j, or the $tfidf$ value. This matrix is strongly sparse. Therefore, the LSI method applies a reduction of dimensions. Finally, it is possible to project a new document into the

id	S/T	description
1	S	number of tokens in s
2	T	number of tokens in t
3	S	average source token length
4	S	LM probability of source sentence
5	T	LM probability of target sentence
6	T	av. freq. of the target word in t
7	S	av. number of translations per word in s (as given by IBM 1 table thresholded such that $prob(t\|s) > 0.2$)
8	S	same as 7 but with $prob(t\|s) > 0.01$ and weighted by the inverse frequency of each word in the source corpus
9	S	$\%$ of unigrams in quartile 1 of frequency extracted from an external corpus
10	S	same as 9 for quartile 4
11	S	same as 9 for bigrams and quartile 1
12	S	same as 9 for bigrams and quartile 4
13	S	same as 9 for trigrams and quartile 1
14	S	same as 9 for trigrams and quartile 4
15	S	$\%$ of unigrams in s seen in an external corpus
16	S	number of punctuation marks in s
17	T	number of punctuation marks in t

Table 1: List of baseline features. id are given to refer later to a specific feature. S, T are for 'source' or 'target' feature.

[1] http://www.quest.dcs.shef.ac.uk/quest_files/features_blackbox_baseline_17

obtained low-dimension numeric space (called the LSI model).

The LSI method may be interesting for Quality Estimation because LSI allows to project a s sentence, and a t sentence into the same numeric space. In this space, each document is described by a numeric vector. We can compute the similarity between two vectors (two documents) by cosine distance. Two documents are similar if their lexical content is close. The interesting point for Quality Estimation is that similarity can model the 'proximity' between "dog" and "bark", "chien", "aboyer", (or "perro", "ladrar" in Spanish) for example because the input documents for building the LSI model are bilingual.

We propose to use this similarity as a feature for Quality Estimation. For that, we use a training set of $(source, target)$ sentences (actually, we use 2 different training corpus, see below). We build a corpus in which each document is made up of the concatenation of a $source$ sentence and its corresponding $target$ sentence. We build the matrix M of the $tfidf$ scores of the words in the $source$-$target$ sentences. This matrix has n lines (the number of different $source$ words + the number of different $target$ words occurring more than 1 in the training corpus) and m columns (the number of $source$-$target$ couples). Then, we have to choose the dimension of the reduced numeric space (this dimension is called the number of topics). We applied the LSI reduction to obtain a LSI model. In this LSI model, it is possible to project a $source$ sentence, or a $target$ sentence into the same numeric space. Then, the feature corresponding to a $(source, target)$ couple in development or test corpus is the cosine distance between the LSI vector corresponding to $source$, and the LSI vector corresponding to $target$.

We use two training corpus. the first one is tr the training corpus from the Quality Estimation Shared Task ($target$ is here pe because pe is a correct translation of s). This corpus is close to the experimental conditions, but it contains only 11272 sentences couples. This is quite low for the LSI approach. Therefore, we use also the English-Spanish part of the Europarl (Koehn, 2005) corpus composed of 2M sentences couples[2]. Each training corpus leads to one LSI model.

To synthesize, we extract a feature from a (s, t) couple in four steps:

1. **LSI** = buildLSI(training corpus,number of topics)
2. LSI_s = **LSI**(s)
3. LSI_t = **LSI**(t)
4. feature = cosine distance between LSI_s and LSI_t

LSI is a function which projects a sentence into the numeric LSI space. The number of topics is one crucial parameter of the LSI approach. In Section 4, we explore the performance of the LSI based features according to this parameter.

3.3 The Machine Translation systems based features

We propose here to use pseudo-references. The idea is to compare t with other translations of s, provided by other MT systems. We hypothesise that the more t and other target sentences from the same s share parts, the more correct t is.

Several online translation systems yet exist on the web, and a few of them provide API allowing to request translations. We used three online systems noted $\mathbb{A}$, $\mathbb{B}$ and $\mathbb{C}$[3]. We used each system $\mathbb{A}$, $\mathbb{B}$ and $\mathbb{C}$ to translate the sentences from tr and dev. Therefore, from each sentence s, we have four target sentences: t from the system we want to estimate the quality, $t_{\mathbb{A}}$ from system $\mathbb{A}$, $t_{\mathbb{B}}$ from system $\mathbb{B}$, and $t_{\mathbb{C}}$ from system $\mathbb{C}$.

For each online system, we define 9 features to describe how much t and t_X (X is $\mathbb{A}$, $\mathbb{B}$ or $\mathbb{C}$) share n-grams. Moreover, we define 4 features taking into account the three online systems together.

Pseudo-references has yet been used for Quality Estimation. (Luong et al., 2014) decide of the correctness of each word in t by checking its presence in two pseudo-references. The binary feature is based on the number of pseudo-references containing the evaluated word. (Wisniewski et al., 2014) define binary features for word-level Quality Estimation. These binary features indicate if the evaluated word occurs in a n-gram (n

[2]Release v7, http://www.statmt.org/europarl/

[3]We do not give the identity of these systems because one of them precises that its online service can not be used for evaluation purpose. Indeed, in the following experiments, we give results using or not each of the systems. These results do not allow to conclude that a system is better than another one (see Section 4), but a quick reading could lead to such a conclusion.

from 1 to 3) shared by t and the pseudo-reference sentence. (Wisniewski et al., 2014) do not precise the number of pseudo-references, but they use the lattice produced by their in-house system, this leads certainly to a high number of pseudo-references. (Luong et al., 2014; Wisniewski et al., 2014) works are applied to word-level Quality Estimation while we deal with sentence-level Quality Estimation. (Scarton and Specia, 2014) use features from pseudo-reference sentences for sentence-level quality estimation. The features they extract are classical measures of translation quality (BLEU, TER, METEOR, ROUGE) between t and pseudo-reference. (Scarton and Specia, 2014) cite different works (Soricut et al., 2012; Shah et al., 2013) using also these measures for Quality Estimation. Differently, in our work, we use n-grams statistics in order to measure the consensus between t and pseudo-references.

3.3.1 Amount of shared n-grams between t and t_X

We describe the intersection between t and each of $t_{\mathbb{A}}$, $t_{\mathbb{B}}$ and $t_{\mathbb{C}}$ by 9 features.

The first four ones are recall n-gram $R_{X,n}$:

$$R_{X,n}(t, t_X) = \frac{\sum_{ng \in t,\ |ng|=n} \delta(ng, t_X)}{|t_X|} \quad (1)$$

where X is $\mathbb{A}$, $\mathbb{B}$ or $\mathbb{C}$, ng is a n-gram of length n, $\delta(ng, t_X)$ is equal to 1 if ng is in t_X and equal to 0 otherwise, and $|t_X|$ is the number of n-gram in t_X. n takes its values between 1 and 4. Therefore, there are 4 features for each system.

The following four features are precision n-gram $P_{X,n}$, which are equivalent to $R_{X,n}(t, t_X)$, but the denominator is $|t|$. Here also, there are 4 features for each system.

For these 8 features, a n-gram in t_X is taken into account only one time. For example, if $t = a\ b\ a$, and $t_X = a\ b$, there is only one match for a when $n = 1$, even if there are two a in t.

The last feature is the maximum length words sequence from t that is also in t_X:

$$M(t, t_X) = \frac{\max[|ng|,\ s.t.\ ng \in t\ and\ ng \in t_X]}{|t|} \quad (2)$$

Each system leads to 9 features.

3.3.2 Taking into account the three online system together

We define 4 additional features which describe how many pseudo-references include a n-gram of t (n varies from 1 to 4). The idea is that if a n-gram from t occurs in 3 pseudo-references, it is likely a correct n-gram whereas if it occurs only in one pseudo-reference, it is more doubtful. These features are formalized by the following formula:

$$Inter(t, t_{\mathbb{A}}, t_{\mathbb{B}}, t_{\mathbb{C}}, n) = \frac{\sum_{i=1}^{i \le |t|-n+1} \sum_{X \in \{\mathbb{A},\mathbb{B},\mathbb{C}\}} \delta(t_i^{i+n-1}, t_X)}{3 \times (|t|-n+1)} \quad (3)$$

where t_a^b is the words sequence from t starting at position a and ending at position b, and other notations are defined as previously. n takes values from 1 to 4. Therefore, this leads to 4 additional features. In the following, we use the acronym $Inter$ to refer to these 4 features.

Overall, our system deals with 50 features: 17 from baseline, 2 from LSI approach, 9 for each of the three online systems, and 4 from the combination of these three systems.

4 Results

4.1 Baseline features

Table 2 shows the results in terms of MAE on development corpus of each baseline feature used alone (only one feature is used to predict the HTER score). The feature ids refer to the line number in Table 1. Source/Target information indicates if the feature is a 'source' one (S) or a 'target' one (T). The last line of Table 2 shows the MAE performance when all the 17 baseline features are used ('whole' line). The baseline system leads to a performance of 14.59. Interestingly, a feature alone leads to performance between 14.76 and 14.99. Thus, using only one feature allows to obtain good performance compared with using the whole set of features.

4.2 LSI based features

We use the *dev* corpus in order to estimate the number of topics for each LSI model leading to the best performance. For that, we test several values for the number of topics. We build one LSI model according to each of these values. Then,

S/T	id	MAE ($\times 100$)	S/T	id	MAE ($\times 100$)
S	9	14.99	T	17	14.95
T	6	14.99	S	16	14.94
T	2	14.98	S	15	14.94
S	7	14.98	S	13	14.93
T	5	14.97	S	3	14.91
S	1	14.97	S	12	14.82
S	4	14.96	S	8	14.80
S	10	14.96	S	14	14.76
S	11	14.95	whole		14.59

Table 2: MAE score on *dev* of each baseline feature, and of the whole 17 baseline features

we compute the LSI score of each (s, t) in tr. We add this score as a new feature to the 17 baseline. We apply the protocol of Section 2 in order to obtain the MAE score on the *dev* corpus. We show in Table 3 the results.

Nb Topics	LSI Training Corpus	
	tr	Europarl
10	14.55	14.54
20	14.55	14.54
30	14.52	14.57
40	14.52	14.59
50	14.51	14.58
60	14.50	14.58
70	14.49	14.57
80	**14.48**	14.56
90	14.49	14.55
100	14.49	14.56
150	14.50	14.53
200	14.50	14.50
250	14.51	14.50
300	14.51	14.50
350	14.50	14.49
400	14.52	14.49
500	14.52	**14.48**

Table 3: Performance in terms of MAE on *dev* of LSI feature according to the number of topics. The LSI feature is associated with the 17 baseline features.

The best performance are obtained for a number of topics equal to 80 for the tr corpus, and equal to 500 for the Europarl corpus. This is not surprising because Europarl corpus is strongly bigger than tr. Compared to baseline MAE (14.59), the LSI features leads to an improvement of 0.11 points.

4.3 Online systems based features

Table 4 shows the performance when online systems based features are used with the 17 baseline features. For each line, a 'X' indicates that the used features set includes the 9 features corresponding to the system of the column ($\mathbb{A}$, $\mathbb{B}$ or $\mathbb{C}$). The 'X' in column 'Inter' indicates that the features taking into account the three systems (formula 3) are used. The table shows that $\mathbb{B}$ is the most useful system, and that $\mathbb{C}$ is the less useful for prediction. Be careful that this does not give indication about the relative translation performance of online systems, but this indicates how the output quality of each system is correlated to the quality of the unknown system used by the organizers. The lack of usefulness of $\mathbb{C}$ for prediction is confirmed when the features from $\mathbb{A}$, $\mathbb{B}$ and $\mathbb{C}$ are combined. We obtain a better performance (13.93) when $\mathbb{C}$ is not used. Finally, adding the 'Inter' features does not lead to improvement. This may be because these features are correlated with '$\mathbb{A}$', '$\mathbb{B}$' and '$\mathbb{C}$': if a sentence is easy to translate, then, all systems should propose the same translation, this leads to high values for '$\mathbb{A}$', '$\mathbb{B}$' and '$\mathbb{C}$', and also for 'Inter'.

Baseline	$\mathbb{A}$	$\mathbb{B}$	$\mathbb{C}$	Inter	MAE ($\times 100$)
X			X		14.38
X	X				14.28
X		X			14.02
X	X	X	X		13.95
X	X	X	X	X	13.95
X	X	X			13.93

Table 4: MAE Score on *dev* corpus of online systems based features.

4.4 Whole set of features and filtering

In this section, we use the whole set of features: baseline, LSI based, and online system based. For the LSI features, we use the LSI models leading to best performance (see Section 4.2): with 80 topics for the tr corpus, with 500 topics for the Europarl corpus. Table 5 shows the performance in terms of MAE. In this table, we present results when filtering is applied, and when it is not applied. We present several combinations. If we do not use filtering we obtain best performance when we do not use '$\mathbb{C}$' features (13.87, line 6). But if we use fil-

Features set	Baseline	LSI		online system based features				MAE (×100)	
		tr 80	Europarl 500	$\mathbb{A}$	$\mathbb{B}$	$\mathbb{C}$	Inter	without filtering	with filtering
1	X		X	X	X	X		13.92	
2	X	X		X	X	X		13.91	
3	X	X	X	X	X	X		13.90	
4	X	X	X	X	X	X	X	13.90	13.70
5	X	X	X	X	X		X	13.88	
6	X	X	X	X	X			13.87	13.72

Table 5: Performance in terms of MAE on *dev* of the whole set of features

tering, it is is better to use the 50 features (13.90, line 4) and let the algorithm to automatically select the useful features: this leads to a performance of 13.70, better than 13.72 obtained by filtering the features set 6.

When we filter features set 4, we obtain 29 final features. 11 baseline features are kept (8 'S' and 3 'T'). Therefore, 'T' features are not numerous, but they are essential (3 are kept among 4). The LSI feature from *tr* is kept, but not the one from Europarl, maybe because the Europarl corpus is external to the Quality Estimation task. The selection of online systems based features confirms the relative usefulness of online systems $\mathbb{A}$, $\mathbb{B}$, and $\mathbb{C}$: only 2 '$\mathbb{C}$' features are kept, 4 '$\mathbb{A}$' features are kept, and 8 '$\mathbb{B}$' features are kept. Last, 3 'Inter' features among 4 are selected.

Finally, the baseline system (17 features) obtained a MAE score equal to 14.82 on the official test corpus. We submitted two systems, corresponding to line 4 in Table 5 (without and with filtering). The system without filtering led to a performance equal to 13.42 on the test corpus, and the same one after filtering led to a better performance equal to 13.34. Therefore, the results on the development corpus are confirmed by the test corpus.

5 Conclusion and perspectives

In this paper, we present our submission to the WMT2015 Quality Estimation Shared Task. Our system estimates quality at sentence level. In addition to the 17 baseline features, we use Latent Semantic Indexing based features which allow to measure the similarity between source and target sentences. Moreover we use pseudo-references from online machine translation systems, we extract n-gram statistics measuring the consensus between the target sentence and pseudo-references.

The features based on pseudo-references are more helpful for prediction than LSI based features. But there is a bias here, because we use only 2 LSI based features. We have now to extend the LSI approach. One first possibility is to use other ways to describe the latent semantic space, such as Latent Dirichlet Allocation (Blei et al., 2003). Second, the main drawback of LSI approach is that only lexical information is taken into account. One promising way is to include words sequence into the LSI model because Machine Translation is phrase based. We have yet tested this direction, but words sequences should be integrated carefully to obtain a tractable model.

References

D. M. Blei, A. Y. Ng, and M. I. Jordan. 2003. Latent dirichlet allocation. *the Journal of machine Learning research*, 3:993–1022.

C.-C. Chang and C.-J. Lin. 2011. LIBSVM: A library for support vector machines. *ACM Transactions on Intelligent Systems and Technology*, 2:27:1–27:27.

I. Guyon and A. Elisseeff. 2003. An introduction to variable and feature selection. *Journal of Machine Learning Research (Special Issue on Variable and Feature Selection)*, pages 1157–1182.

P. Koehn. 2005. Europarl: A parallel corpus for statistical machine translation. In *MT summit*, volume 5, pages 79–86.

D. Langlois, S. Raybaud, and Kamel Smaïli. 2012. Loria system for the WMT12 quality estimation shared task. In *Proceedings of the Seventh Workshop on Statistical Machine Translation*, pages 114–119.

M. L. Littman, S. T. Dumais, and T. K. Landauer. 1998. Automatic cross-language information retrieval using latent semantic indexing. In *Cross-language information retrieval*, pages 51–62. Springer.

N. Q. Luong, L. Besacier, and B. Lecouteux. 2014. Lig system for word level qe task at wmt14. In *Proceedings of the Ninth Workshop on Statistical Machine*

Translation, pages 335–341. Association for Computational Linguistics.

M. Saad, D. Langlois, and K. Smaïli. 2014. Cross-lingual semantic similarity measure for comparable articles. In *Advances in Natural Language Processing*, pages 105–115. Springer.

C. Scarton and L. Specia. 2014. Exploring consensus in machine translation for quality estimation. In *Proceedings of the Ninth Workshop on Statistical Machine Translation*, pages 342–347. Association for Computational Linguistics.

K. Shah, T. Cohn, and L. Specia. 2013. An investigation on the effectiveness of features for translation quality estimation. In *Proceedings of the Machine Translation Summit*, volume 14, pages 167–174.

M. Snover, B. Dorr, R. Schwartz, L. Micciulla, and J. Makhoul. 2006. A study of translation edit rate with targeted human annotation. In *Proceedings of association for machine translation in the Americas*, pages 223–231.

R. Soricut, N. Bach, and Z. Wang. 2012. The sdl language weaver systems in the wmt12 quality estimation shared task. In *Proceedings of the Seventh Workshop on Statistical Machine Translation*, pages 145–151. Association for Computational Linguistics.

L. Specia, K. Shah, J. GC De Souza, and T. Cohn. 2013. QuEst A translation quality estimation framework. In *ACL (Conference System Demonstrations)*, pages 79–84.

G. Wisniewski, N. Pécheux, A. Allauzen, and F. Yvon. 2014. Limsi submission for wmt'14 qe task. In *Proceedings of the Ninth Workshop on Statistical Machine Translation*, pages 348–354. Association for Computational Linguistics.

Data Enhancement and Selection Strategies for the Word-level Quality Estimation

Varvara Logacheva§, Chris Hokamp†, Lucia Specia§
§Department of Computer Science, University of Sheffield, UK
{v.logacheva,l.specia}@sheffield.ac.uk

†CNGL Centre for Global Intelligent Content
Dublin City University, Ireland
chokamp@computing.dcu.ie

Abstract

This paper describes the DCU-SHEFF word-level Quality Estimation (QE) system submitted to the QE shared task at WMT15. Starting from a baseline set of features and a CRF algorithm to learn a sequence tagging model, we propose improvements in two ways: (i) by filtering out the training sentences containing too few errors, and (ii) by adding incomplete sequences to the training data to enrich the model with new information. We also experiment with considering the task as a classification problem, and report results using a subset of the features with Random Forest classifiers.

1 Introduction

The WMT shared task on Quality estimation (QE) for Machine Translation (MT) has included the sub-task on the QE at the word level since the year 2013. The goal of this task is to assign a quality label to each word of an automatically translated sentence without using its reference translations. The set of possible output labels can vary. Labels can specify the edit action which should be performed on the word in order to improve the sentence (substitution, deletion, insertion) — these labels were used in the WMT13 QE task (Bojar et al., 2013). Labels can be further refined to specify the type of error: grammar error, wrong terminology, untranslated word, etc., motivated by the MQM error typology [1] — this tagging was used in last year's task (Bojar et al., 2014). In both cases, tags can be generalised to a binary label, "GOOD" or "BAD", indicating whether or not the word is correct.

This year, the word-level QE task (Task 2 in WMT15 QE shared task[2]) consists in assigning only a binary label ("GOOD" or "BAD") to every word in automatically translated sentences — that is, to identify if a word is suitable for this sentence or should be modified. The possible errors are substitution (word replacement) or insertion. This formulation of the task cannot detect deletions in the MT hypothesis, because there is a one-to-one correspondence between tokens in the hypothesis and output tags.

The data for the word-level QE task was produced for one translation direction, namely from English into Spanish. The training, development and test datasets have been translated automatically with an online statistical MT system, and then post-edited by human translators. Besides the datasets themselves, baseline feature sets were provided. The suggested baseline training model is conditional random fields (CRF) (Lafferty et al., 2001), which is one of the most widely used techniques for sequence labelling. The baseline tagging for this task was done with CRF model trained using CRF++ tool[3].

Our system uses the baseline features released for the task and the same tool which was used for baseline model generation. However, we performed data selection and bootstrapping techniques that led to significant improvement over the baseline.

2 Baseline setting

The goal of the system was to estimate the quality of machine-translated sentences at the word-level, i.e. to assign every word a label "GOOD" or "BAD" depending on its quality. Therefore, the training and test data contains the following information: the source sentences, their automatic

[1] http://www.qt21.eu/launchpad/content/multidimensional-quality-metrics

[2] http://www.statmt.org/wmt15/quality-estimation-task.html

[3] https://code.google.com/p/crfpp/

translations into the target language, the manual post-editions (corrections) of the automatic translations, and the word-level tags for the automatic translations.

The tags were acquired by aligning the machine translations with their post-editions using the TER tool (Snover et al., 2006). Unchanged words were assigned the label "GOOD", words which were substituted with another word or deleted by a post-editor were assigned the label "BAD". The "BAD" labels thus correspond to the "addition" and "substitution" edit operations in the word-level string alignment between the MT hypothesis and the post-edited segment.

The dataset contains automatic translations from English into Spanish. The training data consists of 11,271 sentences, the development and test sets have 1,000 and 1,817 sentences, respectively. The post-editions and tags for the test data were not made available until after the end of the evaluation period.

2.1 Features

We used a subset of features described by Luong et al. (2014), mainly the features that were listed as the most informative. This corresponds to the baseline feature set released for the shared task. The full list of features is the following:

- Word count features:
  - source and target token counts
  - source and target token count ratio
- Lexical features:
  - target token
  - target token's left and right contexts of 1 word
- Alignment features:
  - source word aligned to the target token
  - source word's left and right contexts of 1 word
- Boolean dictionary features:
  - target token is a stopword
  - target token is a punctuation mark
  - target token is a proper noun
  - target token is a number
- Target language model features:
  - order of the highest order ngram which ends with the target token
  - order of the highest order ngram which starts with the target token
  - backoff behaviour of the ngram (t_{i-2}, t_{i-1}, t_i), where t_i is the target token (backoff behaviour is computed as described in Raybaud et al. (2011))
  - backoff behavior of the ngram (t_{i-1}, t_i, t_{i+1})
  - backoff behavior of the ngram (t_i, t_{i+1}, t_{i+2})
- Source language model features:
  - order of the highest order ngram which ends with the source token
  - order of the highest order ngram which starts with the source token
- Boolean pseudo-reference feature: 1 if the token is contained in the pseudo-reference, 0 otherwise[4]
- Part-of-speech features[5]:
  - POS of the target token
  - POS of the source token
- WordNet features:
  - Number of senses for the target token
  - Number of senses for the source token

2.2 Alternative system

We performed additional experiments with a reduced feature set which does not contain lexical and alignment features. These features were excluded in order to enable the use of classifiers implemented in the `scikit-learn`[6] toolkit. The implementations in this toolkit can only deal with scalar features directly. Therefore, in order to use categorical features (e.g. strings), these need to be converted into one-hot vector representation.

The one-hot representation of a categorical feature is the representation of every possible feature

[4]The pseudo-reference used for this feature extraction is the automatic translation generated by an English-Spanish phrase-based statistical MT system trained on the Europarl corpus (Koehn, 2005) using Moses system with standard settings (http://www.statmt.org/moses/?n=Moses.Baseline).

[5]POS tagging was performed with TreeTagger tool http://www.cis.uni-muenchen.de/~schmid/tools/TreeTagger/

[6]http://scikit-learn.org/

value from a domain **D** as a vector of 0s and a single 1. The length of such vector is $|D|$ (length of the set of possible values of the feature), every position in the vector corresponds to a value from D. Each instance of this feature should correspond to a vector which has only one element with value 1 at the position of the categorical value taken by this instance of the feature. Since the categorical features used rely on a very large vocabulary, converting them into one-hot vectors would have increased the feature space significantly, resulting in very sparse feature vectors.

Systems using shorter feature sets (i.e. without lexical and alignment features) were trained with the Random Forest classifier in `scikit-learn` with default settings. This scenario considers each (feature vector, token, tag) tuple as a separate instance, so that we no longer explicitly model the dependencies in the sequence. However, contextual information about the token is still included in the feature set via several other features (see Section 2.1), so sequence information is not completely disregarded in this scenario.

2.3 Baseline results

The baseline results for our systems on the development set are outlined in Table 1. Since instances of the "GOOD" class are much more numerous than instances tagged as "BAD", the average F1-score is dominated by the F1-GOOD. However, the F1-GOOD is high for any system, as even a naive system tagging all words as "GOOD" would score high. This metric is thus uninformative. Therefore, the primary quality metric for this task is F1-BAD. The performance of the Random Forest classifier is significantly higher than that of CRF model, although it uses a smaller feature set and does not take the labelling context into account.

	F1-BAD	F1-GOOD	Weighted F1
Baseline (CRF)	0.18	0.88	0.75
Reduced (Random Forest)	0.24	0.86	0.78

Table 1: Baseline results.

The scores given here and further in the paper are for the development set, as this dataset was used for tuning the systems and choosing the settings to be submitted for the task. The scores for the test set on the official submissions are given in Section 5. These are a bit lower, but they maintain the relative trend (i.e. the systems that perform better on the development set perform better on the test set as well).

3 Generating Data by Bootstrapping New Examples

Although the size of training data is considerably larger than the size of datasets that have been used before, it may still be too sparse to perform QE at the word level. This is because not all tokens are shared between the training and test datasets. Instead of using a data selection method to choose training examples which correspond to the dev/test sets, we decided to enhance the training data with additional samples generated from the initial dataset. This corresponds more closely with a realistic deployment scenario for a word-level QE system, where the test set is unknown.

We tested two methods of additional data generation:

- In addition to every complete sentence from the training data we used sequences that consist of the first n words of this sentence, where $n \in [1, N]$ (N = number of words in the sentence). For example, for each sentence of 10 words we added nine new training examples: a sequence that consists of the first word only, a sequence that consists of the first two words, the first three words, etc. This strategy is further referred to as **1-to-N**.

- For every sentence from the training data we used all trigrams of this sentence as training examples. This strategy will be denoted as **ngram**.

Another idea is to perform bootstrapping not only to expand the training data, but also to break the test set into smaller chunks for tagging.

Bootstrapping for the test set is produced as follows. In order to tag a sequence $\mathbf{s} = s_1 s_2 \ldots s_n$ we convert it into a list of n sub-sequences $L_\mathbf{s} = [s_1;\ s_1 s_2;\ s_1 s_2 s_3;\ \ldots;\ s_1 s_2 \ldots s_n]$. Each sub-sequence from $L_\mathbf{s}$ is tagged by the system. The final tagging for every word $s_i \in \mathbf{s}$ is taken from a sub-sequence where s_i is the last symbol, so that we compose the final tagging for the sequence **s** from the tags for words s_i listed in bold: $[\mathbf{s_1};\ s_1\mathbf{s_2};\ s_1 s_2 \mathbf{s_3};\ \ldots;\ s_1 s_2 \ldots \mathbf{s_n}]$.

The described scenario refers to the **1-to-N** bootstrapping method for the test set. The **ngram** bootstrapping method for the test set can be used analogously.

The intuition behind this approach is the following. If we train a system on a set of incomplete sequences (1-to-N or ngrams), it might capture local dependencies which do not hold for complete sentences. Therefore, in order to improve the prediction accuracy we should test the system on incomplete sequences as well. There are many possibilities for combining the partial sequence predictions (e.g. averaging the scores of one word in different incomplete sequences or training a linear regression model to find a weight for every prediction), but in this experiment we tested only one strategy: taking the score of the i-th word from the i-th sequence.

	Training	plain	1-to-N	ngram
	Test ↓			
CRF	plain	0.170	0.238	0.213
	1-to-N	0.221	**0.251**	0.212
	ngram	0.170	0.238	0.226
Random Forest	plain	0.236		0.239
	1-to-N	**0.255**		0.237
	ngram	0.234		**0.255**

Table 2: Experiments with bootstrapped data (F1-score for "BAD" class). 'plain' setting means no bootstrapping (original data).

We tested all the training and test data bootstrapping techniques. The results are outlined in Table 2. We used three different training sets: the original dataset with no bootstrapping (denoted as 'plain' in the table), a dataset bootstrapped with the **1-to-N** strategy, and one bootstrapped with the **ngram** strategy, and three different test sets (analogously, plain, 1-to-N, and ngram). We trained two systems for every combination of datasets: one system performs sequence labelling with CRF, the other classifies words with a Random Forest classifier. That would give us $3 \times 3 \times 2 = 18$ systems. However, the experiments with training data enhanced with **1-to-N** strategy could not be performed for Random Forest classifier due to computational complexity, so we are effectively comparing 15 combinations of labelling strategies and bootstrapping techniques.

The CRF model benefits from both strategies: when bootstrapping only training data the F1-score increases from 0.17 to 0.21 (**ngram**) and 0.23 (**1-to-N**). Bootstrapping of test data brings an additional improvement: even when the training set is not changed, applying **1-to-N** strategy to the test increases the score from 0.17 to 0.22. However, **ngram** bootstrapping of the test proved ineffective unless it was applied to the training data as well.

We assume that bootstrapping the training data helps due to the fact that in the CRF model all instances within a sequence are influenced by each other: the choice of tag for a word is dependent on all other words, and not only the neighbours of the current word. Therefore, incomplete sentences create new dependencies that improve overall prediction accuracy.

As shown also in Table 2, we performed the same experiment with the Random Forest classifier in order to check if the incomplete data instances have a positive effect in the CRF model because of the properties of the algorithm or simply because of the increased dataset size. Our assumption was that since the Random Forest classifier output depends only on local context of a tagged word, it should not be influenced by the new training sequences. This hypothesis was corroborated by our experiment: the classifier trained on the extended dataset performed slightly better, but this difference is much smaller than the one observed for the CRF model with the additional data.

In order to check that the improvements are not only due to the increased dataset size, we performed the same experiments with duplicated training sentences. The output of this duplicated system is identical to the baseline system, showing the key component of the improvement are indeed the incomplete sentences. Our intuition is that since the new training sentences differ from the original ones, they provide new information to the sequence labelling model.

4 Data selection

An inspection of the training and development data showed that 15% of the sentences contain no errors and are thus less useful for model learning. In addition, the majority of the sentences have low edit distance (HTER) score, i.e. contain very few edits/errors. Figure 1 shows the HTER scores distribution for the training dataset: 50% of the sentences have HTER of 0.15 or lower (points below the bottom orange line in the figure), 75% of the sentences have HTER of 0.28 or lower (points below the middle green line). The distributions for the development and test sets are similar.

A large number of sentences with few or no ed-

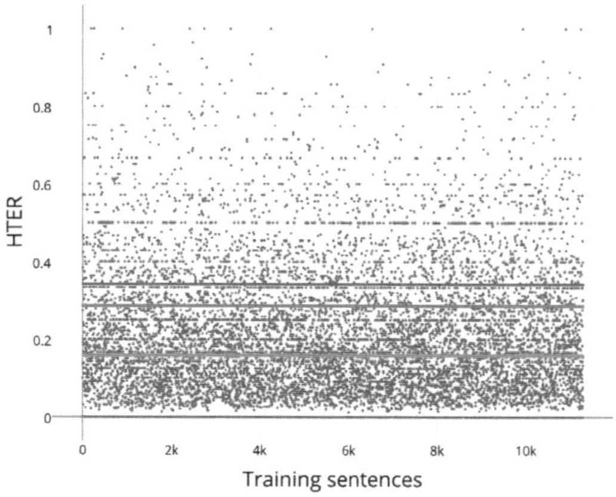

Figure 1: Distribution of HTER scores for the training data: each blue dot represents a training sentence. Dots below the orange line make 50% of the data, dots below the green line, 75% of data, dots above red line, the worst 2000 sentences (18% of the data).

its bias the models to tag more words as "GOOD", i.e. the tagging is too optimistic, which results in higher F1 score for the "GOOD" class and lower F1 score for the "BAD" class. Since our primary goal is improved F1 score for the "BAD" class, we modified the training set to increase the percentage of "BAD" labels.

In order to filter out sentences that have too few errors, we performed a simple training data selection strategy: we used only sentences with the highest amount of editing. To define the optimal number of sentences to select, we built models on different number of training sentences from 1,000 to 11,000 (the entire dataset). Figure 2 shows the learning curves for systems trained on increasing numbers of sentences. Note that the sentences we choose are sorted by their HTER score in decreasing order, i.e. the system trained on 1,000 sentences uses 1,000 sentences with the highest HTER scores (1,000 worst sentences).

Models built trained using only the 2,000 worst sentences have the best F1-BAD score using all learning algorithms. These 2,000 sentences represent 18% of the total available data (data points above the red line in Figure 1). This subset has sentences with HTER scores ranging from 0.34 to 1 and mean value of 0.49.

The highest score is achieved by the CRF model trained on **ngram**-bootstrapped data. However, the data selection strategy changes the effect of bootstrapping that we saw previously: the CRF

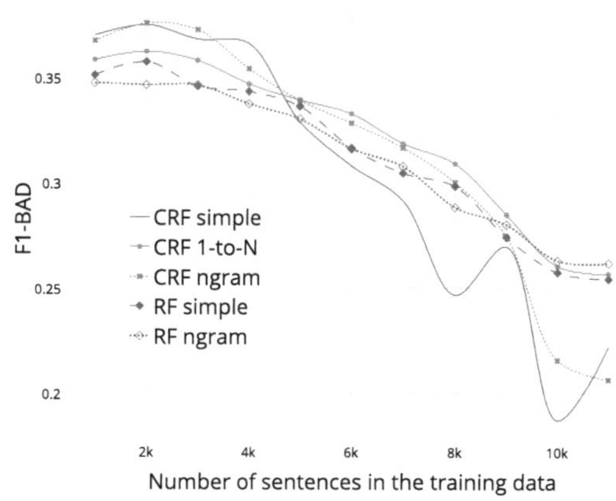

Figure 2: Performance of models trained on subsets of training data (F1 for the "BAD" class).

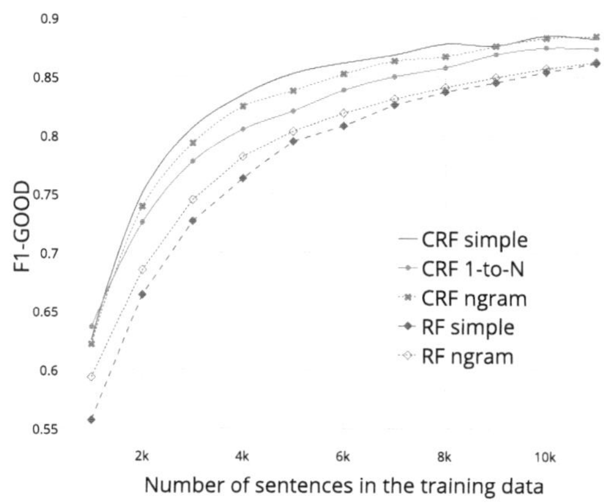

Figure 3: Performance of systems trained on subsets of training data (F1 for the "GOOD" class).

model without bootstrapping performs very similarly on small data subsets (up to 5,000 sentences), and even outperforms the CRF model with **1-to-N** bootstrapping. On the other hand, a CRF model without bootstrapping is less stable: its quality drops faster as new data is added. The Random Forest classifier has lower prediction accuracy than CRF models, but is more stable than the two models that have the highest scores on 2,000 sentences.

As shown in Figure 3, the learning curves in terms of the F1-score for the "GOOD" class are very different: the scores keeps increasing as we add more training instances. However, after adding 5,000 sentences the growth slows down. Note also that the models that have the least stable F1-BAD scores (CRF without bootstrapping and with **ngram** bootstrapping) show the highest F1-GOOD scores.

5 Official results of shared task

The experiments with data selection (Section 4) showed that all models achieve their highest scores when trained on a subset of 2,000 sentences of the training data with highest HTER. The CRF model with **ngram** bootstrapping yielded the highest F1-BAD of 0.375. We selected this setting as our first submission. Since we could not be sure that the distribution of classes is the same in the development and test sets, for the second submission we chose the same model trained on 5,000 sentences, to reach a balance between the F1-scores for the "BAD" and the "GOOD" classes.

Table 3 summarises the final results. The F1-BAD score of our first system for the test set is 0.366. This submission was ranked 4-th best out of 8. The second system performed worse at tagging the test set: the final F1-BAD score is 0.345, which places it in the 5-th position overall.

		F1-BAD	F1-GOOD	Weigted F1
CRF ngram	dev	0.375	0.738	0.669
2000 sent.	test	**0.366**	0.744	0.673
CRF ngram	dev	0.339	0.837	0.742
5000 sent.	test	**0.345**	0.845	0.75

Table 3: Final submission results. Scores in bold were used to compare systems submitted to the shared task.

6 Conclusions

We presented the systems submitted by the DCU-SHEFF team to the word-level QE task at WMT15. Our systems were trained on a set of baseline features released by the organisers of the shared task. We predicted the QE labels using a CRF model trained with CRF++ tool, which was also used to produce the baseline scores.

The main difference between the baseline and our models is that in our systems the training data is filtered prior to training. We use only a small subset of the training sentences which have the highest HTER scores (i.e. the highest percentage of words tagged with the "BAD" label). This led to an increase in the F1 score for the "BAD" class from 0.17 to 0.37.

We also suggested two bootstrapping strategies based on using sub-sequences from the training data as new training instances. These incomplete examples are particularly effective for training CRF models: we were able to improve the F1 score for the "BAD" class from 0.17 to 0.25. However, we were not able to achieve any improvement when the bootstrapping was performed on top of data filtering.

Acknowledgements

This work was supported by the People Programme (Marie Curie Actions) of the European Union's Framework Programme (FP7/2007-2013) under REA grant agreement n° 317471.

References

Ondřej Bojar, Christian Buck, Chris Callison-Burch, Christian Federmann, Barry Haddow, Philipp Koehn, Christof Monz, Matt Post, Radu Soricut, and Lucia Specia. 2013. Findings of the 2013 Workshop on Statistical Machine Translation. In *Proceedings of the Eighth Workshop on Statistical Machine Translation*, pages 1–44, Sofia, Bulgaria, August. Association for Computational Linguistics.

Ondrej Bojar, Christian Buck, Christian Federmann, Barry Haddow, Philipp Koehn, Johannes Leveling, Christof Monz, Pavel Pecina, Matt Post, Herve Saint-Amand, Radu Soricut, Lucia Specia, and Aleš Tamchyna. 2014. Findings of the 2014 workshop on statistical machine translation. In *Proceedings of the Ninth Workshop on Statistical Machine Translation*, pages 12–58, Baltimore, Maryland, USA, June. Association for Computational Linguistics.

Philipp Koehn. 2005. Europarl: A Parallel Corpus for Statistical Machine Translation. In *MT Summit X*.

John D. Lafferty, Andrew McCallum, and Fernando C. N. Pereira. 2001. Conditional random fields: Probabilistic models for segmenting and labeling sequence data. In *Proceedings of the Eighteenth International Conference on Machine Learning*, ICML '01, pages 282–289, San Francisco, CA, USA. Morgan Kaufmann Publishers Inc.

Ngoc Quang Luong, Laurent Besacier, and Benjamin Lecouteux. 2014. Lig system for word level qe task at wmt14. In *Proceedings of the Ninth Workshop on Statistical Machine Translation*, pages 335–341, Baltimore, Maryland, USA, June. Association for Computational Linguistics.

Sylvain Raybaud, David Langlois, and Kamel Smali. 2011. this sentence is wrong. detecting errors in machine-translated sentences. *Machine Translation*, 25(1):1–34.

Matthew Snover, Bonnie Dorr, Richard Schwartz, Linnea Micciulla, and John Makhoul. 2006. A study of translation edit rate with targeted human annotation. In *AMTA-2006: 7th Conference of the Association for Machine Translation in the Americas*, pages 223–231, Cambridge, Massachusetts, USA.

USHEF and USAAR-USHEF Participation in the WMT15 Quality Estimation Shared Task

Carolina Scarton[1], **Liling Tan**[2] and **Lucia Specia**[1]
[1]University of Sheffield, 211 Portobello Street, Sheffield, UK
[2]Saarland University, Campus A2.2, Saarbrücken, Germany
{c.scarton,l.specia}@sheffield.ac.uk
alvations@gmail.com

Abstract

We present the results of the USHEF and USAAR-USHEF submissions for the WMT15 shared task on document-level quality estimation. The USHEF submissions explored several document and discourse-aware features. The USAAR-USHEF submissions used an exhaustive search approach to select the best features from the official baseline. Results show slight improvements over the baseline with the use of discourse features. More interestingly, we found that a model of comparable performance can be built with only three features selected by the exhaustive search procedure.

1 Introduction

Evaluating the quality of Machine Translation (MT) systems outputs is a challenging topic. Several metrics have been proposed so far comparing the MT outputs to human translations (references) in terms of ngrams matches (such as BLEU (Papineni et al., 2002)) or error rates (such as TER (Snover et al., 2006)). However, in some scenarios, human references are not available. For example, the use of machine translation in a workflow where good enough translations are given to humans for post-editing. Another example is machine translation for *gisting* by users of online systems.

Quality Estimation (QE) approaches aim to predict the quality of MT outputs without relying on human references (Blatz et al., 2004; Specia et al., 2009). Features from source (original document) and target (MT outputs) and, when available, from the MT system are used to train supervised machine learning models (classifiers or regressors). A number of data points need to be annotated for quality (by humans or automatically) for training, using a given quality metric.

Most QE research is done at sentence level. This task has been a track at WMT shared task for the last four years (Callison-Burch et al., 2012; Bojar et al., 2013; Bojar et al., 2014). In addition to sentence level, the current edition offers for the first time a track on paragraph-level QE. Exploring quality beyond sentence level is interesting for completely automatic translation applications, i.e. without human review. For instance, consider a user looking for information on a product that has several reviews automatically translated into his/her language. This user have no knowledge about the source language. To ensure that the main message of the review is preserved, for this user the quality of each word or sentence individually is not as important as the quality of the review as a whole. Therefore, predicting the quality of the whole document (or paragraph, considering paragraph as short documents) becomes necessary.

This paper presents the University of Sheffield (USHEF) and University of Saarland (USAAR) submissions to the Task 3 of the WMT15 QE shared task: paragraph-level scoring and ranking. We submitted systems for both language pairs: English-German (EN-DE) and German-English (DE-EN).

Little previous research has been done to address document-level QE. Soricut and Echihabi (2010) proposed document-aware features in order to rank machine translated documents. Soricut and Narsale (2012) use sentence-level features and predictions to improve document-level QE. Finally, Scarton and Specia (2014) and Scarton (2015) introduced discourse-aware features, which are combined with baseline features adapted from sentence-level work, in order to predict the quality of full documents. Previous work led to some improvements over the baselines used. However, several problems remain to be addressed for improving document-level QE, such as the choice of quality label, as discussed by Scarton et al. (2015).

Our approach focuses on extracting various features and building models with different combination of these features. Two feature selection approaches are considered. The first one is based on Random Forests and backward feature selection. The second performs an exhaustive search on the entire feature space. Features are either based on previous work for sentence-level QE (e.g. number of tokens in the target document) or are discourse-aware (e.g. lexical repetition counts).

2 Document-level features

Along with the official baseline features, we use two different sets of features. The first set contains document-aware features, based on QuEst features for sentence-level QE (Specia et al., 2013; Specia et al., 2015). The second set are features that encompass discourse information, following previous work of Scarton and Specia (2014) and Scarton (2015).

2.1 Document-aware features

The 17 baseline features made available by the organisers are the same baseline features used for sentence-level QE, adapted for document-level.[1] However, as part of the QuEst framework, other sentence-level features can be easily adapted for document-level QE. Our complete set of document-aware features include:

- ratio of number of tokens in source and target (and in target and source)
- absolute difference between number tokens in source and target, normalised by source length
- language model (LM) perplexity of source/target document (with and without end of sentence marker)
- average number of translations per source word in the document (threshold: prob >0.01/0.05/0.1/0.2/0.5)
- average number of translations per source word in the document (threshold: prob >0.01/0.05/0.1/0.2/0.5) weighted by the frequency/inverse frequency of each word in the source corpus
- average unigram/bigram/trigram frequency in quartile 1/2/3/4 of frequency in the corpus of the source language
- percentage of distinct unigrams/bigrams/trigrams seen in a corpus of the source language (in all quartiles)
- average word frequency: on average, each type (unigram) in a source document appears n times in the corpus (in all quartiles)
- percentage of punctuation marks in source/target document
- percentage of content words in the source/target document
- ratio of percentage of content words in the source and target
- LM log probability of POS of the source/target document
- percentage of nouns in the source/target document
- percentage of verbs in the source/target document
- ratio of percentage of nouns in the source and target documents
- ratio of percentage of verbs in the source and target documents
- ratio of percentage of pronouns in the source and target documents
- number of dependencies with aligned constituents normalised by the total number of dependencies (maximum between source and target)
- number of sentences (source and target should be the same).

2.2 Discourse-aware features

Discourse is a linguistic phenomenon that happens document-wide and should be considered for document-level evaluation purposes. We considered the discourse-aware features presented in Scarton and Specia (2014), which are already implemented in the QuEst framework (called herein as discourse repetition features):

- word/lemma/noun repetition in the source/target document
- ratio of word/lemma/noun repetition between source and target documents.

Other discourse features were also explored (following the work of Scarton (2015)):

- number of pronouns in the source/target document
- number of discourse connectives in the source/target document
- number of pronouns of each type according to Pitler and Nenkova (2009)'s classification:

[1] http://www.quest.dcs.shef.ac.uk/quest_files/features_blackbox_baseline_17

Expansion, Temporal, Contingency, Comparison and *Non-discourse*
- number of EDU (elementary discourse units) breaks in the source (target) document
- number of RST (Rhetorical Structure Theory) *Nucleus* relations in the source/target document
- number of RST *Satellite* relations in the source/target document.

In order to extract the last set of features we use existing NLP tools: For identifying pronouns, we use the output of Charniak's parser (Charniak, 2000) (we count the PRP tags). Discourse connectives are automatically extracted by the parser of Pitler and Nenkova (2009). RST trees and EDUs are extracted by the discourse parser and discourse segmenter of Joty et al. (2013).

3 Experiments and results

Our systems use only the data provided by the task organisers. For features that require corpora or resources, only those provided by the organisers were used.

Tasks we participate in Task 3 (paragraph-level QE) in both subtasks, scoring and ranking. The evaluation for the scoring task was done using Mean Absolute Error (MAE) and the evaluation for the ranking task was done by DeltaAvg (official metrics of the competition).

Data the official data of Task 3 - WMT15 QE shared task consist of 1215 paragraphs for EN-DE and DE-EN, extracted from the corpora of WMT13 machine translation shared task (Bojar et al., 2013). For training, 800 paragraphs were used and, for test, 415 paragraphs were considered. METEOR (Banerjee and Lavie, 2005) was used as quality labels.

Feature combination we experimented with different feature sets:
- baseline (17 baseline features only)
- baseline + discourse repetition features[2]
- baseline + document-aware features
- baseline + discourse-aware features
- all features.

Backward feature selection[3] in order to perform feature selection, we used the Random Forest algorithm, as implemented in the scikit-learn toolkit (Pedregosa et al., 2011), to rank the features. Once this feature ranking is produced, we apply a backward feature selection approach. Starting with the features with lower posititition in the rank, the method consists in consistently eliminate features, aiming to obtain a feature set that better fit the predictions.

For both EN-DE and DE-EN, 38 features were selected. The set of features selected for both languages is:
- LM probability of source document
- LM perplexity of source document
- average trigram frequency in quartile 1/2/3/4 of frequency in a corpus of the source language
- percentage of distinct trigrams seen in a corpus of the source language (in all quartiles)
- ratio of percentage of pronouns in the source and target documents
- average number of translations per source word in the document (threshold: prob >0.1)
- average number of translations per source word in the document (threshold: prob >0.1) weighted by the frequency of each word in the source corpus
- noun/word/lemma repetition in the source document
- noun/lemma repetition in the target document
- ratio of noun/lemma/word repetition between source and target
- number of punctuation marks in the target document
- number of sentences in the source document
- number of connectives in the source document
- number of connectives in the *Expansion/Contingency/Comparison/Temporal/Non-discourse* class
- number of pronouns
- number of EDU breaks in the source document
- number of RST *Nucleus/Satellite* relations in the source document.

Features selected for EN-DE only:
- LM probability of target document
- LM perplexity of target document (with and without sentence markers)
- type/token ration
- average number of translations per source word in the document (threshold: prob $>0.2/0.5$)

[2]Official submission of USHEF team for EN-DE
[3]Official submission of USHEF team for DE-EN

- number of punctuation marks in the source document.

Features selected for DE-EN only:

- average source token length
- LM perplexity of source document (without sentence markers)
- average bigram frequency in quartile 1/2/3/4 of frequency in a corpus of the source language
- average number of translations per source word in the document (threshold: prob >0.01)
- average number of translations per source word in the document (threshold: prob >0.2) weighted by the inverse frequency of each word in the source corpus
- ratio of percentage of verbs in the source and target.

Exhaustive search[4] We investigate the efficacy of the baseline features by learning one Bayesian Ridge classifier for each feature and evaluating the classifiers based on MAE.

To examine the best set of features among the baseline features, we implemented an exhaustive feature selection search by enumerating all possible feature combinations. Given *n* number of features, *S*, there are 2^n-1 number of possible feature combinations since a *k*-combination of a set forms a subset of *k* distinct elements of *S*. The set of *n* elements, the number of *k*-combination is equal to the binomial coefficient:

$$(nk) = \frac{n(n-1) \quad ... \quad (n-k+1)}{k(k-1)...1} \tag{1}$$

And the sum of all possible *k*-combinations:

$$\sum_{0 \leq k \leq n} (nk) = \quad 2^n - 1 \tag{2}$$

We note that the exhaustive search for feature selection is only possible in low feature space but from the results above, it is possible to approximate the best feature combination by using the N-best performing features when the classifier is trained solely on each of the feature.

For both languages, the exhaustive search selected three features only. For EN-DE:

- average source token length
- percentage of unigrams in quartile 4 of frequency of source words in a corpus of the source language
- percentage of trigrams in quartile 4 of frequency of source words in a corpus of the source language.

For DE-EN:

- type/token ratio
- percentage of unigrams in quartile 1 of frequency of source words in a corpus of the source language
- percentage of trigrams in quartile 1 of frequency of source words in a corpus of the source language.

Machine learning algorithms for the feature combination experiments (with backward feature selection) we used the SVR implementation in the scikit-learn toolkit with parameters optimised via grid search.

3.1 Results

Table 1 shows the results of all experiments, for both language directions (EN-DE and DE-EN) and for scoring (MAE) and ranking (DeltaAvg) subtasks.[5]

For EN-DE, BFF showed the best result for scoring, and Baseline + discourse repetition showed the best result for ranking. For DE-EN, Backward feature selection showed the best results for both scoring and ranking (although BFF showed similar results for scoring).

However, no statistically significant difference was found between the systems. This means that the use of sophisticated discourse-aware features did not lead to improvements, with a simple combination of three features from the baseline set able to produce similar results. The reason for these results is most likely connected to the data. We expect the discourse-aware features to work better with documents, since they naturally contain discourse phenomena. However, the data of the shared task consists of short paragraphs, many with only one sentence only. In this case, discourse-aware features are less effective.

BFF systems investigate the efficacy of the baseline features by learning one Bayesian Ridge classifier for each feature and evaluating the classifiers based on the Mean Average Error (MAE).

[4]Official submission of USAAR-USHEF team for both language pairs - called BFF

[5]All experiments were applied to the official test set of Task 3. In order to improve readability, results for MAE and DeltaAvg were multiplied by 100.

	English-German		German-English	
Experiment	MAE ↓	DeltaAvg ↑	MAE ↓	DeltaAvg ↑
Baseline	10.05	1.6	7.35	0.59
Baseline + discourse repetition	9.55	**4.55**	6.60	1.02
Baseline + discourse-aware	9.67	4.38	7.06	1.31
Baseline + document-aware	9.57	4.55	7.68	0.37
All	9.58	4.47	6.63	0.91
Backward feature selection	10.00	3.40	**6.54**	**1.55**
BFF	**9.37**	3.98	6.56	0.4

Table 1: Results of all combinations of features

No.	Baseline Feature	MAE (DE-EN)	MAE (EN-DE)
1	number of tokens in the source document	7.21	11.69
2	number of tokens in the target document	7.31	10.81
3	average source token length	7.02	9.97
4	LM probability of source document	7.32	11.39
5	LM probability of target document	7.93	11.79
6	type/token ratio	**6.61**	9.95
7	average number of translations per source word in the document (threshold: prob >0.2)	7.49	10.70
8	average number of translations per source word in the document (threshold: prob >0.01) weighted by the inverse frequency of each word in the source corpus	6.67	**9.84**
9	percentage of unigrams in quartile 1 of frequency in a corpus of the source language	**6.61**	10.11
10	percentage of unigrams in quartile 4 of frequency in a corpus of the source language	6.72	**9.81**
11	percentage of bigrams in quartile 1 of frequency in a corpus of the source language	6.62	10.00
12	percentage of bigrams in quartile 4 of frequency in a corpus of the source language	6.64	10.05
13	percentage of trigrams in quartile 1 of frequency in a corpus of the source language	**6.59**	10.01
14	percentage of trigrams in quartile 4 of frequency in a corpus of the source language	6.62	9.97
15	percentage of unigrams in the source document seen in a corpus (SMT training corpus)	6.76	**9.75**
16	number of punctuation marks in source document	6.71	10.10
17	number of punctuation marks in target document	6.72	10.00

Table 2: MAE of classifiers trained with one baseline feature - the top three features are shown in bold

Table 2 shows the MAE of these classifiers.

We note that the exhaustive feature selection search is only possible in low feature spaces. However from the results above it is possible to approximate the best feature combination by using the N-best performing features when the classifier is trained solely on each of the feature. Unsurprisingly, the best feature set for DE-EN corresponds to the top three features that are most effective individually (when classifiers were built for these features individually). In the reverse direction (EN-DE), the best feature combination corresponds to the top 6 features that are most effective individually. The classifier trained on the top 3 features (8, 10, 15) for EN-DE yielded an MAE of 9.72.

MAE (DE-EN)	Feature Set	MAE (EN-DE)	Feature Set
6.56	(6, 9, 13)	**9.37**	(3, 10, 14)
6.57	(6, 13)	9.42	(3, 10, 13, 14)
6.59	(13)	9.43	(3, 8, 10, 11, 13, 14)
6.60	(9, 11, 13)	9.43	(3, 10, 11, 13, 14)
6.60	(9, 13, 17)	9.45	(3, 8, 10, 11, 13)

Table 3: Top five feature combinations with the lowest MAE

4 Conclusions

In this paper we presented the submissions from the USHEF and USAAR-USHEF teams for WMT15 QE shared task. We experimented with several feature combinations and used two types of feature selection methods: backward based on Random Forests and exhaustive search.

With the exhaustive search results, we showed that it is possible to build good quality regressors that outperform the baseline.

Acknowledgements

This work was supported by the People Programme (Marie Curie Actions) of the European Union's Framework Programme (FP7/2007-2013) under REA grant agreement n° 317471.

References

Satanjeev Banerjee and Alon Lavie. 2005. METEOR: An Automatic Metric for MT Evaluation with Improved Correlation with Human Judgments. In *ACL 2005 Workshop on Intrinsic and Extrinsic Evaluation Measures for MT and/or Summarization*.

John Blatz, Erin Fitzgerald, George Foster, Simona Gandrabur, Cyril Goutte, Alex Kulesza, Alberto Sanchis, and Nicola Ueffing. 2004. Confidence Estimation for Machine Translation. In *COLING 2014*, pages 315–321, Geneva, Switzerland.

Ondřej Bojar, Christian Buck, Chris Callison-Burch, Christian Federmann, Barry Haddow, Philipp Koehn, Christof Monz, Matt Post, Radu Soricut, and Lucia Specia. 2013. Findings of the 2013 Workshop on Statistical Machine Translation. In *WMT13*, pages 1–44, Sofia, Bulgaria.

Ondrej Bojar, Christian Buck, Christian Federman, Barry Haddow, Philipp Koehn, Johannes Leveling, Christof Monz, Pavel Pecina, Matt Post, Herve Saint-Amand, Radu Soricut, Lucia Specia, and Ales Tamchyna. 2014. Findings of the 2014 workshop on statistical machine translation. In *WMT14*, pages 12–58, Baltimore, MD.

Chris Callison-Burch, Philipp Koehn, Christof Monz, Matt Post, Radu Soricut, and Lucia Specia. 2012. Findings of the 2012 workshop on statistical machine translation. In *WMT12*, pages 10–51, Montréal, Canada.

Eugene Charniak. 2000. A maximum-entropy-inspired parser. In *NAACL 2000*, pages 132–139, Seattle, Washington.

Shafiq Joty, Giuseppe Carenini, Raymond T. Ng, and Yashar Mehdad. 2013. Combining intra- and multi-sentential rhetorical parsing for document-level discourse analysis. In *ACL 2013*, pages 486–496, Sofia, Bulgaria.

Kishore Papineni, Salim Roukos, Todd Ward, and Wei jing Zhu. 2002. BLEU: a Method for Automatic Evaluation of Machine Translation. In *ACL 2002*, pages 311–318, Philadelphia, PA.

Fabian Pedregosa, Gael Varoquaux, Alexander Gramfort, Vincent Michel, Bertrand Thirion, Olivier Grisel, Mathieu Blondel, Peter Prettenhofer, Ron Weiss, Vincent Dubourg, Jake Vanderplas, Alexandre Passos, David Cournapeau, Matthieu Brucher, Matthieu Perrot, and Édouard Duchesnay. 2011. Scikit-learn: Machine learning in Python. *Journal of Machine Learning Research*, 12:2825–2830.

Emily Pitler and Ani Nenkova. 2009. Using Syntax to Disambiguate Explicit Discourse Connectives in Text. In *ACL-IJCNLP 2009*, pages 13–16, Suntec, Singapore.

Carolina Scarton and Lucia Specia. 2014. Document-level translation quality estimation: exploring discourse and pseudo-references. In *EAMT 2014*, pages 101–108, Dubrovnik, Croatia.

Carolina Scarton, Marcos Zampieri, Mihaela Vela, Josef van Genabith, and Lucia Specia. 2015. Searching for Context: a Study on Document-Level Labels for Translation Quality Estimation. In *EAMT 2015*, pages 121–128, Antalya, Turkey.

Carolina Scarton. 2015. Discourse and document-level information for evaluating language output tasks. In *NAACL-SRW 2015*, pages 118–125, Denver, Colorado.

Matthew Snover, Bonnie Dorr, Richard Schwartz, Linnea Micciulla, and John Makhoul. 2006. A Study of Translation Edit Rate with Targeted Human Annotation. In *AMTA 2006*, pages 223–231, Cambridge, MA.

Radu Soricut and Abdessamad Echihabi. 2010. TrustRank: Inducing Trust in Automatic Translations via Ranking. In *ACL 2010*, pages 612–621, Uppsala, Sweden.

Radu Soricut and Sushant Narsale. 2012. Combining Quality Prediction and System Selection for Improved Automatic Translation Output. In *Proceedings of WMT 2012*, pages 163–170, Montréal, Canada.

Lucia Specia, Marco Turchi, Nicola Cancedda, Marc Dymetman, and Nello Cristianini. 2009. Estimating the Sentence-Level Quality of Machine Translation Systems. In *EACL 2009*, pages 28–37, Barcelona, Spain.

Lucia Specia, Kashif Shah, Jose G.C. de Souza, and Trevor Cohn. 2013. Quest - a translation quality estimation framework. In *ACL 2013*, pages 79–84, Sofia, Bulgaria.

Lucia Specia, Gustavo Paetzold, and Carolina Scarton. 2015. Multi-level Translation Quality Prediction with QuEst++. In *ACL 2015: System Demonstrations*, Beijing, China.

SHEF-NN: Translation Quality Estimation with Neural Networks

Kashif Shah§, Varvara Logacheva§, Gustavo Henrique Paetzold§, Frederic Blain§
Daniel Beck§, Fethi Bougares†, Lucia Specia§
§Department of Computer Science, University of Sheffield, UK
{kashif.shah,v.logacheva,ghpaetzold1,f.blain,debeck1,l.specia}
@sheffield.ac.uk

†LIUM, University of Le Mans, France
fethi.bougares@lium.univ-lemans.fr

Abstract

We describe our systems for Tasks 1 and 2 of the WMT15 Shared Task on Quality Estimation. Our submissions use (i) a continuous space language model to extract additional features for Task 1 (SHEF-GP, SHEF-SVM), (ii) a continuous bag-of-words model to produce word embeddings as features for Task 2 (SHEF-W2V) and (iii) a combination of features produced by QuEst++ and a feature produced with word embedding models (SHEF-QuEst++). Our systems outperform the baseline as well as many other submissions. The results are especially encouraging for Task 2, where our best performing system (SHEF-W2V) only uses features learned in an unsupervised fashion.

1 Introduction

Quality Estimation (QE) aims at measuring the quality of the Machine Translation (MT) output without reference translations. Generally, QE is addressed with various features indicating fluency, adequacy and complexity of the source-translation text pair. Such features are then used along with Machine Learning methods in order for models to be learned.

Features play a key role in QE. A wide range of features from the source segments and their translations, often processed using external resources and tools, have been proposed. These go from simple, language-independent features, to advanced, linguistically motivated features. They include features that rely on information from the MT system that generated the translations, and features that are oblivious to the way translations were produced. This leads to a potential bottleneck: feature engineering can be time consuming, particularly because the impact of features vary across datasets and language pairs. Also, most features in the literature are extracted from segment pairs in isolation, ignoring contextual clues from other segments in the text. The focus of our contributions this year is to introduce a new set of features which are language-independent, require minimal resources, and can be extracted in unsupervised ways with the use of neural networks.

Word embeddings have shown their potential in modelling long distance dependencies in data, including syntactic and semantic information. For instance, neural network language models (Bengio et al., 2003) have been successfully explored in many problems including Automatic Speech Recognition (Schwenk and Gauvain, 2005; Schwenk, 2007) and Machine Translation (Schwenk, 2012). While neural network language models predict the next word given a preceding context, (Mikolov et al., 2013b) proposed a neural network framework to predict the word given the left and right contexts, or to predict the word's left and right contexts in a given sentence. Recently, it has been shown that these distributed vector representations (or word embeddings) can be exploited across languages to predict translations (Mikolov et al., 2013a). The word representations are learned from large monolingual data independently for source and target languages. A small seed dictionary is used to learn mapping from the source into the target space. In this paper, we investigate the use of such resources in both sentence-level (Task 1) and word-level QE (Task 2). As we describe in what follows, we extract features from such resources and use them to learn prediction models.

2 Continuous Space Language Model Features for QE

Neural networks model non-linear relationships between the input features and target outputs.

They often outperform other techniques in complex machine learning tasks. The inputs to the neural network language model used here (called Continuous Space Language Model (CSLM)) are the h_j context words of the prediction: $h_j = w_{j-n+1}, ..., w_{j-2}, w_{j-1}$, and the outputs are the posterior probabilities of all words of the vocabulary: $P(w_j|h_j)\ \forall i \in [1, N]$ where N is the vocabulary size. CSLM encodes inputs using the so called one-hot coding, i.e., the ith word in the vocabulary is coded by setting all element to 0 except the ith element. Due to the large size of the output layer (vocabulary size), the computational complexity of a basic neural network language model is very high. Schwenk et al. (2012) proposed an implementation of the neural network with efficient algorithms to reduce the computational complexity and speed up the processing using a subset of the entire vocabulary called *short list*.

As compared to shallow neural networks, deep neural networks can use more hidden layers and have been shown to perform better. In all CSLM experiments described in this paper, we use deep neural networks with four hidden layers: a first layer for the word projection (320 units for each context word) and three hidden layers of 1024 units for the probability estimation. At the output layer, we use a $softmax$ activation function applied to a *short list* of the 32k most frequent words. The probabilities of the out of the *short list* words are obtained using a standard back-off n-gram language model. The training of the neural network is done by the standard back-propagation algorithm and outputs are the posterior probabilities. The parameters of the models are optimised on a held out development set.

Our CSLM models were trained with the CSLM toolkit [1]. We extracted the probabilities for Task 1's training, development and test sets for both source and its translation with their respective optimised models and used them as features along with other available features in a supervised learning algorithm. In Table 1, we report detailed statistics on the monolingual data used to train the back-off LM and CSLM. The training dataset consists of Europarl, News-commentary and News-crawl corpora with the Moore-Lewis data selection method (Moore and Lewis, 2010) to select the CSLM training data with respect to a Task's development set. The CSLM models are tuned using a concatenation of newstest2012 and newstest2013 of WMT's translation track.

Lang.	Train	Dev	LM px	CSLM px
en	4.3G	137.7k	164.63	116.58
es	21.2M	149.4k	145.49	87.14

Table 1: Training and dev datasets size (in number of tokens) and models perplexity (px).

3 Word Embedding Features for QE

The word embeddings used in our experiments are learned with the *word2vec* tool[2], introduced by (Mikolov et al., 2013b). The tool produces word embeddings using the Distributed Skip-Gram or Continuous Bag-of-Words (CBOW) models. The models are trained through the use of large amounts of monolingual data with a neural network architecture that aims at predicting the neighbours of a given word. Unlike standard neural network-based language models for predicting the next word given the context of preceding words, a CBOW model predicts the word in the middle given the representation of the surrounding words, while the Skip-Gram model learns word embedding representations that can be used to predict a word's context in the same sentence. As suggested by the authors, CBOW is faster and more adequate for larger datasets, so we used this model in our experiments.

We trained 500-dimensional representations with CBOW for all words in the vocabulary. We consider a 10-word context window to either side of the target word, sub-sampling option to 1e-05, and estimate the probability of a target word with the negative sampling method, drawing 10 samples from the noise distribution. The data used to train the models is the same as presented in Table 1. We then extracted word embeddings for all words in the Task 2 training, development and test sets from these models to be used as features. These distributed numerical representations of words as features aim at locating each word as a point in a 500-dimensional space.

Inspired by the work of (Mikolov et al., 2013a), we extracted another feature by mapping the source space onto a target space using a seed dictionary (trained with Europarl + News-commentary + News-crawl). A given word and

[1] `http://www-lium.univ-lemans.fr/cslm/`

[2] `https://code.google.com/p/word2vec/`

its continuous vector representation a could be mapped to the other language space by computing $z = Ma$, where M is a transformation matrix learned with stochastic gradient descent. The assumption is that the vector representations of similar words in different languages are related by a linear transformation because of similar geometric arrangements. The words whose representation are closest to a in the target language space, using cosine similarity, are considered as potential translations for a given word in the source language. Since the goal of QE is not to translate content, but to measure the quality of translations, we take the source-to-target similarity scores as a feature itself. To calculate it, we first learn word alignments (see Section 4.2.2), and then compute the similarity scores between target word and the source word aligned to it.

4 Experiments

We present experiments on the WMT15 QE Tasks 1 and 2, with CSLM features for Task 1, and word embedding features for Task 2.

4.1 Task 1

4.1.1 Dataset

Task 1's English-Spanish dataset consists respectively of a training set and development set with $11,271$ and $1,000$ source segments, their machine translations, the post-editions of the latter, and edit distance scores between between the MT and its post-edited version (HTER). The test set consists of $1,817$ English-Spanish source-MT pairs. Translations are produced by a single online statistical MT system. Each of the translations was post-edited by crowdsourced translators, and HTER labels were computed using the TER tool (settings: tokenised, case insensitive, exact matching only, with scores capped to 1).

4.1.2 Feature set

We extracted the following features:

- **AF**: 80 black-box features using the QuEst framework (Specia et al., 2013; Shah et al., 2013a) as described in Shah et al. (2013b).
- **CSLM**: A feature for each source and target sentence using CSLM as described in Section 2.
- **FS(AF)**: Top 20 features selected from the above 82 features with Gaussian Processes (GPs) by the procedure described in (Shah et al., 2013b).

4.1.3 Learning algorithms

We use the Support Vector Machines implementation in the `scikit-learn` toolkit (Pedregosa et al., 2011) to perform regression (SVR) on each feature set with either linear or RBF kernels and parameters optimised using grid search.

We also apply GPs with similar settings to those in our WMT13 submission (Beck et al., 2013) using `GPy` toolkit [3]. For models with feature selection, we train a GP, select the top 20 features according to the produced feature ranking, and then retrain a SparseGP on the full training set using these 20 features and 50 inducing points. To evaluate the prediction models we use Mean Absolute Error (MAE), its squared version – Root Mean Squared Error (RMSE), and Spearman's Correlation.

4.2 Task 2

4.2.1 Dataset

The data for this is the same as the one provided in Task 1. All segments have been automatically annotated for errors with binary word-level labels ("GOOD" and "BAD") by using the alignments provided by the TER tool (settings: tokenised, case insensitive, exact matching only, disabling shifts by using the '-d 0' option) between machine translations and their post-edited versions. The edit operations considered as errors ("BAD") are replacements and insertions.

4.2.2 Word alignment training

To extract word embedding features, as explained in Section 3, we need word-to-word alignments between source and target data. As word-level alignments between the source and target corpora were not made available by WMT, we first aligned the QE datasets with a bilingual word-level alignment model trained on the same data used for the *word2vec* modelling step, with the help of the GIZA++ toolkit (Och and Ney, 2003). Working on target side, we refined the resulting n-m target-to-source word alignments to a set of 1-m alignments by filtering potential spurious source-side candidates out. To do so, the decision was based on the lexical probabilities extracted from the previous alignment training step. Hence, each target-

[3] `http://sheffieldml.github.io/GPy/`

side token has been aligned to the source-side candidate with the highest lexical probability. To map our two monolingual vector spaces trained with word embedding models, we extracted a bilingual dictionary with the same settings used for word-alignment.

4.2.3 Data filtering

An inspection of the training and development data showed that 15% of the sentences contain no errors and are therefore less useful for model learning. In addition, most sentences have very low HTER score, showing that very few words are considered incorrect. Figure 1 shows the HTER scores distribution for the training dataset: 50% of the sentences have the HTER of 0.15 or lower (points below the bottom orange line on the Figure), 75% of the sentences have the score of 0.28 or lower (points below the middle green line). The distributions for the development and test sets are similar.

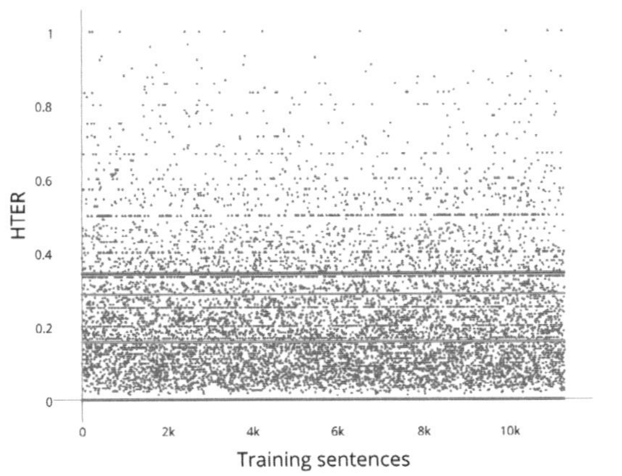

Figure 1: The distribution of HTER scores for the training data. Below orange line – 50% of the data, below green line – 75% of the data, above red line – worst 2000 sentences (18% of the data).

Sentences with few or no edits lead to models that tag more words as "GOOD", so the tagging is too optimistic, resulting in higher F1 score for the "GOOD" class but lower F1 score for the "BAD" class. This is an issue as obtaining a good F1 score for the "BAD" class is arguably the primary goal of a QE model (and also the main evaluation criterion for the task). Therefore, we decided to increase the percentage of "BAD" labels in the training data by filtering out sentences which have zero or too few errors. As a filtering strategy, we took only sentences with the highest proportions of editing.

We performed experiments with two subsets of the training sentences with the highest HTER score: $2,000$ samples (18% of the data, i.e., points above the top red line in Figure 1); and $5,000$ samples (44% of the data). Since the F1-score for the "BAD" class was higher on the dev set for the model built from the smaller subset, we chose it to perform the tagging for the official submission of the shared task. This subset contains sentences with HTER score from 0.34 to 1, an average score of 0.49, and variance of 0.018.

4.2.4 Learning algorithms

We learned binary tagging models for both SHEF-W2V and SHEF-QuEst++ using a Conditional Random Fields (CRF) algorithm (Lafferty et al., 2001). We used **pystruct** (Müller and Behnke, 2014) for SHEF-W2V, and **CRFSuite** (Okazaki, 2007) for SHEF-QuEst++. Both tools allow one to train a range of models. For pystruct we used the linear-chain CRF trained with a structured SVM solver, which is the default setting. For CRFSuite we used the Adaptive Regularization of Weight Vector (AROW) and Passive Aggressive (PA) algorithms, which have been shown to perform well in the task (Specia et al., 2015).

Systems are evaluated in terms of classification performance (Precision, Recall, F1) against the "GOOD" and "BAD" labels, and their weighted average of both F1 scores (W-F1). The main evaluation metric is the average F1 score for the "BAD" label.

4.3 Results

4.3.1 Task 1

We trained various models with different feature sets and algorithms and evaluated the performance of these models on the official development set. The results are shown in Table 2. Some interesting findings:

- SVM performed better than GP.
- SVM with linear kernel performed better than with RBF kernel.
- CSLM features alone performed better than the baseline features.
- CSLM features always bring improvements whenever added to either baseline or complete feature set.

System.	Kernel	Features	#. of Feats.	MAE	RMSE	Spear. Corr
Baseline (SVM)	RBF	BL	17	0.1479	0.1965	0.1651
SHEF-SVM	RBF	CSLM	2	0.1474	0.1959	0.1911
SHEF-SVM	RBF	BL+CSLM	19	0.1464	0.1950	0.1924
SHEF-SVM	RBF	AF	80	0.1497	0.1944	0.2259
SHEF-SVM	RBF	AF+CSLM	82	0.1452	0.1920	0.2325
SHEF-SVM	Linear	AF+CSLM	82	0.1422	0.1889	0.2736
SHEF-SVM	Linear	AF(FS)	20	0.1459	0.1896	0.2465
SHEF-GP	RBF	AF(FS)	20	0.1493	0.1917	0.2187

Table 2: Results on development set of Task 1.

System.	MAE	RMSE	DeltaAvg	Spear. Corr
Baseline	0.15	0.19	0.22	0.13
SHEF-SVM	0.14	0.18	0.51	0.28
SHEF-GP	0.15	0.19	0.31	0.28

Table 3: Official results on test set of Task 1.

- Linear SVM with selected features by GP achieves comparable results to linear SVM with the full feature set (82).
- Both CSLM features appear in the top 20 selected features by GP.

Based on these findings, as official submissions for Task 1, we put forward a system with linear SVM using 82 features, and another with GP on the selected feature set. The official results are shown in Table 3.

4.3.2 Task 2

For the SHEF-QuEst++ system, we combined all 40 features described in (Specia et al., 2015) with the source-to-target similarity feature described in Section 3. For the SHEF-W2V system, we tried several settings on the development data in order to define the best-performing set of features and dataset size. We used two feature sets:

- 500-dimensional word embedding vectors for the target word only.
- 500-dimensional word embedding vectors for the target word and the source word aligned to it.

In addition, both these feature sets included the source-to-target similarity feature. We performed the data filtering technique described in 4.2.3, and tested the systems using:

- The full dataset.
- 5K sentences with the highest HTER score.
- 2K sentences with the highest HTER score.

System	W-F1	F1 Bad	F1 Good
Baseline	75.48	17.07	89.07
MONO-ALL	72.31	0.35	89.39
MONO-5000	74.47	14.82	88.63
MONO-2000	65.83	35.38	73.06
MONO-2000-SIM	65.87	35.53	73.07
BI-ALL	72.23	0.0	89.38
BI-5000	75.37	22.77	87.86
BI-2000	64.78	38.64	70.99
BI-2000-SIM	64.56	38.45	70.76
QuEst++-AROW-SIM	68.58	38.54	75.72
QuEst++-PA-SIM	26.42	34.86	24.42

Table 4: Results on development set of Task 2.

Results on the development set are outlined in Table 4. The system names are formed as follows: "MONO" or "BI" indicate that the SHEF-W2V system was trained on the target or target+source word embeddings feature set. "ALL", "5000" and "2000" indicate that we used the entire training set, $5,000$ sentences or $2,000$ sentences, respectively. The prefix "SIM" means that the feature sets were enhanced with the vector similarity feature. Finally, "AROW" and "PA" correspond to the two learning algorithms used by SHEF-QuEst++.

Combining the target and source-side word embedding vectors was found to improve the performance of SHEF-W2V compared to using only target-side vectors. The impact of the similarity feature is less clear: it slightly improved the performance of the monolingual feature set, but decreased the scores for the bilingual feature set. We can also notice that the AROW algorithm is much more effective than the PA algorithm for SHEF-QuEst++.

Filtering out sentences that are mostly correct allowed to achieve much higher F1-scores for the "BAD" class. The best results were achieved with a relatively small subset of the data (18%). Therefore, as our official submissions, we chose the model using bilingual vectors trained on 2,000 sentences with the highest HTER score, and the same model extended with the similarity feature.

System.	W-F1	F1 Bad	F1 Good
Baseline	75.71	16.78	88.93
W2V-BI	65.73	38.43	71.63
W2V-Bi-SIM	65.27	38.40	71.52
QuEst++-AROW	64.69	37.69	71.11
QuEst++-AROW-SIM	62.07	38.36	67.58
QuEst++-PA	33.02	35.16	32.51
QuEst++-PA-SIM	26.25	34.30	24.38

Table 5: Official results on test set of Task 2.

The results on the test set are presented in Table 5, in which it is shown that the source-to-target similarity feature has gain 0.67% in F1 of "BAD" labels for SHEF-QuEst++ system with the AROW algorithm.

5 Conclusions

We have proposed several novel features for translation quality estimation, which are trained with the use of neural networks. When added to large standard feature sets for Task 1, the CSLM features led to improvements in prediction. Moreover, CSLM features alone performed better than baseline features on the development set. Combining the source-to-target similarity feature with the ones produced by QuEst++ improved its performance in terms of F1 for the "BAD" class. Finally, the results obtained by SHEF-W2V are quite promising: although it uses only features learned in an unsupervised fashion, it was able to outperform the baseline as well as many other systems.

Acknowledgements

This work was supported by the QT21 (H2020 No. 645452, Lucia Specia, Frederic Blain), Cracker (H2020 No. 645357, Kashif Shah) and EXPERT (EU FP7 Marie Curie ITN No. 317471, Varvara Logacheva) projects and funding from CNPq/Brazil (No. 237999/2012-9, Daniel Beck).

References

Daniel Beck, Kashif Shah, Trevor Cohn, and Lucia Specia. 2013. Shef-lite: When less is more for translation quality estimation. *Proceedings of WMT13.*

Yoshua Bengio, Réjean Ducharme, Pascal Vincent, and Christian Janvin. 2003. A neural probabilistic language model. *The Journal of Machine Learning Research.*

John D. Lafferty, Andrew McCallum, and Fernando C. N. Pereira. 2001. Conditional random fields: Probabilistic models for segmenting and labeling sequence data. In *Proceedings of the 18th ICML.*

Tomas Mikolov, Quoc V Le, and Ilya Sutskever. 2013a. Exploiting similarities among languages for machine translation.

Tomas Mikolov, Wen-tau Yih, and Geoffrey Zweig. 2013b. Linguistic regularities in continuous space word representations. In *Proceedings of NAACL 2013.*

Robert C Moore and William Lewis. 2010. Intelligent selection of language model training data. In *Proceedings of the 48th ACL.*

Andreas C. Müller and Sven Behnke. 2014. pystruct - learning structured prediction in python. *Journal of Machine Learning Research.*

Franz Josef Och and Hermann Ney. 2003. A systematic comparison of various statistical alignment models. *Computational Linguistics.*

Naoaki Okazaki. 2007. CRFsuite: a fast implementation of Conditional Random Fields. `http://www.chokkan.org/software/crfsuite/`.

F. Pedregosa, G. Varoquaux, A. Gramfort, V. Michel, B. Thirion, O. Grisel, M. Blondel, P. Prettenhofer, R. Weiss, V. Dubourg, J. Vanderplas, A. Passos, D. Cournapeau, M. Brucher, M. Perrot, and E. Duchesnay. 2011. Scikit-learn: Machine learning in Python. *Journal of Machine Learning Research.*

Holger Schwenk and Jean-Luc Gauvain. 2005. Training neural network language models on very large corpora. In *Proceedings of the Conference on Human Language Technology and Empirical Methods in Natural Language Processing.*

Holger Schwenk. 2007. Continuous space language models. *Computer Speech & Language.*

Holger Schwenk. 2012. Continuous space translation models for phrase-based statistical machine translation. In *Proceedings of COLING.*

Kashif Shah, Eleftherios Avramidis, Ergun Biçicic, and Lucia Specia. 2013a. Quest - design, implementation and extensions of a framework for machine translation quality estimation. *Prague Bull. Math. Linguistics.*

Kashif Shah, Trevor Cohn, and Lucia Specia. 2013b. An investigation on the effectiveness of features for translation quality estimation. In *Proceedings of the Machine Translation Summit.*

Lucia Specia, Kashif Shah, José G. C. de Souza, and Trevor Cohn. 2013. QuEst - A translation quality estimation framework. In *Proceedings of 51st ACL.*

Lucia Specia, Gustavo H. Paetzold, and Carolina Scarton. 2015. Multi-level translation quality prediction with quest++. In *Proceedings of The 53rd ACL.*

Strategy-Based Technology for Estimating MT Quality

Liugang Shang
Knowledge Engineering and Human-Computer Interaction center, Shenyang Aerospace University, Shenyang, China
1437260083@qq.com

Dongfeng Cai
Knowledge Engineering and Human-Computer Interaction center , Shenyang Aerospace University, Shenyang, China
caidf@vip.163.com

Duo Ji
Knowledge Engineering and Human-Computer Interaction center, Shenyang Aerospace University, Shenyang, China
jiduo_1@163.com

Abstract

This paper introduces our SAU-KERC system that achieved F1 score of 0.39 in the world-level quality estimation task in WMT2015. The goal is to assign each translated word a "OK" or "BAD" label indicating translation quality. We adopt the sequence labeling model, conditional random fields (CRF), to predict the labels. Since "BAD" labels are rare in the training and development sets, recognition rate of "BAD" is low. To solve this problem, we propose two strategies. One is to replace "OK" label with sub-labels to balance label distribution. The other is to reconstruct the training set to include more "BAD" words.

1 Introduction

QE task is proposed to estimate the quality of machine translation without relying on reference translations. It contains three levels -- word, sentence, and document and our work focuses on the word-level task. The word-level task was proposed in 2013 and was divided into binary classification and multi-class classification. This year only binary classification was considered in WMT2015.

OK/BAD: If a word need editing, then it is BAD. It is OK, otherwise.

As a confidence estimation problem, methods aim to confidence estimation before 2013. A lot of researchers started to investigate confidence measures for machine translation for nearly a decade (Gandrabur and Foster, 2003; Quirk, 2004; Ueffing et al., 2003). Many different confidence measures are investigated in(Blatz et al 2003). They are based on source and target language models features, n-best list, word-lattices, translation tables, and so on. The authors also present efficient ways of classifying words as "correct" or "incorrect" by using native Bayes, single- or multi-layer perceptron. (Blatz et al 2003) combines several features and use neural network and naïve Bayes learning algorithms to predict whether a word is ok or bad. (Xiong et al., 2010) combines syntax feature, vocabulary feature and word posterior probability feature, which are extracted based on LG parsing, and use the binary classifier based on Maximum Entropy Model to predict the label of each word in machine translation(ok or bad).

Some good ideas are proposed in word-level QE task of WMT. (Luong et al., 2013) use both internal and external features into a conditional random fields(CRF) model to predict the label for each word in the MT hypothesis. (Wisniewskiet al., 2014) rely on a random forest classifier and 16 features to predict the label of a word. (Souza et al., 2014) train two classifier models by using bidirectional long short-term memory recurrent neural networks and CRF to complete word level QE Task.

In WMT2015, the high ratio of OK labels in the training set and development set makes the task an unbalanced classification problem. Generally, it is hard to solve unbalanced classification problem effectively using common machine learning algorithms and features. To balance the label distribution, we propose two strategies: refining OK label(ROL) and changing training set structure(CTS). We augment the CRF model with these two strategies to improve the performance.

The rest of this paper is organized as follows. Section 2 gives the selected features. Section 3 introduces the learning algorithm and the strategies we used. Section 4 shows the structure of experimental data. Section 5 analyzes the experiment results. The last part is our summary of this task.

2 Feature

The features used in this paper were from portion of features provided by organizer and portion of (Luong et al., 2014) features.

2.1 Organizer's Feature

Target word: the combinations of target words in the window ±2(two before, two after of current word).
First aligned word: source word with maximum alignment probability with target word.
Is stop word: whether the target word is a stop word, punctuation symbol, proper name or number.
Back-off: a score assigned to the word according to how many times the target Language Model has to Back-off in order to assign a probability to the word sequence, as described in (Raybaud et al., 2011).
Target/source pos: the target word pos and the source word pos; the bigram and trigram sequences.
Polysemy count: the number of senses of each word.

2.2 LIG System Feature

Target pos /target LM: the longest target word n-gram length and the longest target pos n-gram length.
Is in google: taking google translation as a pseudo-reference translation, we check whether a target word appear in the sentence generated by Google.

2.3 Other Feature

Target word frequency: the number of times the word appears in the machine translation result.
The distance between source and target word: the distance between positions of a target word and its aligned word in the sentence; if a target has not aligned word, then the distance is maximum.

2.4 Feature selection

In the CRF feature template, we chose 85 combinations of features in total. In fact, there are thousands of combinations of features which can be extended by the ten basic features, but too many features combined together do not contributed to the MT estimation system, instead this will cause a negative impact. Another problem is that if too much features are combined together, the current data set will have a good effect, but if the data set will appear for a bad effect, which is characterized by over-fitting. Thus feature selection is very critical for each system, and it directly affects the classifier accuracy and generalization ability.

At present, (Yu S H et al. 2007) feature selection can be divided into three strategies according to the formation of features subsets, namely global optimization, random search and heuristic search. Global optimization strategy commonly uses branch and bound algorithm, which search space is O(2^n), random search strategy commonly use a genetic algorithm, which search space is smaller than O(2^n). Heuristic search strategy commonly uses algorithms which have separate feature combination, the sequence former selection method (SFS), the sequence behind selection algorithms (SBS). Its search space is O(N^2), although the heuristic search strategy has high efficiency, the result of heuristic search is not the global optimum(Yao Xu et al. 2012).

The selection method used in this paper is to add a feature to see if it has a contribution to the system. Eventually we keep 85 features, but it is not the optimal combination. We test data sets by using ten-fold cross-validation approach to prevent overfitting.

3 Labeling Method

Word level QE task of WMT2015 aims at marking each word in MT as OK or BAD. There must be some corresponding relationship among words in a MT output, so we also can regard word-level QE task as Sequence labeling task. We combine the ML method of CRF(using pocket CRF toolkit) with features describes in section 2 to train a sequence labeling model to predict word label.

The parameterization of CRF is shown as follows:

$$\mathrm{P(y|x)} = \frac{1}{Z(x)} exp\left(\sum_{i,k} \lambda_k t_k \left(y_{i-1}, y_i, x, i\right) + \sum_{i,l} \mu_l s_l \left(y_i, x, i\right)\right)$$

t_k is defined as characteristic function at the edge, called transfer features which depend on the current position and the previous one; s_l is defined as characteristic function at the node, called state characteristics which depend on the current position. The conditional probability of each tag sequence equals to the sum of state probability and transfer probability of input sequence.

In QE task, the ratio between OK and BAD roughly equals to 4:1, which is very unbalanced. So it leads to two phenomena as fellows: 1. the probability labeling OK is much larger than the probability labeling BAD. 2. The probability that transfer to OK is much larger than the probability that transfer to BAD in train corpus; which will result in model bias. So the performance of the model trained just by using CRF and features of section 2 is not satisfactory.

In order to solve the unbalanced problem of word label, we propose two strategies: 1. Refine OK label(ROL); 2. Change train set structure(CTS).

3.1 Refine OK Label

We divide OK into OK_B, OK_I, OK_E and OK. OK_B is the start of OK continuous sequence; OK_I is the middle section of OK continuous sequence; OK_E is the end of OK continuous sequence; OK indicates the discontinuous label of OK as shown in figure 1. ROL can reduce the probability that a word is marked as OK to a certain extent. When we regard each label of words as a state, we can draw that ROL can reduce the probability of transfer to OK and enhance the probability of transfer to BAD tags in each output.

Target:	Es	totalmente	gratuito	y	esas	cosas	!
Label:	OK	OK	OK	OK	BAD	BAD	OK
Refine label:	OK_B	OK_I	OK_I	OK_E	BAD	BAD	OK

Figure 1: Refine OK Label

3.2 Change Train Set Structure

Our first strategy smooths the ratio between labels by refining OK label. However, even with refining, the proportion of BAD is still much smaller than other labels. So the second strategy we proposed will raise the proportion of bad by changing the structure of train set.
Implementation of this strategy:

a. Calculated the proportion of bad in each MT sentence in train set
b. Delete MT sentence that has no BAD label in train set.
c. MT sentence that BAD ratio is greater than threshold K be added repeatedly into train set.

This strategy will reduce the number of OK and increase the number of BAD, consequently reducing the ratio between OK and BAD.

4 Experiment

4.1 Data

There is just one translation corpus from English to Spanish in word-level QE task of WMT2015. The detail information of corpus shows in table 1:

	EN-ES		
	Train	Dev	Test
Sentence	11271	1000	1817
Word	257548	23207	40899
OK : BAD	4.22 : 1	4.21 : 1	4.30 : 1

Table 1: Corpus structural information

As shown in table 1, the proportion of OK and BAD unbalanced, which will lead to an offset model. It needs strategies in section 3 to balance the ratio between OK and BAD. The train set after processing show in table 2:

Train set	**Pre-process**	**Post-process**
sentence	11271	14559
word	257548	311998
OK/BAD	4.22 : 1	1:6.9
OK_B/BAD	///	1:3.7
OK_I/BAD	///	1.3:1
OK_E/BAD	///	1:3.7
OK_ALL/BAD	**4.2:1**	**1.9:1**

Table 2: Training data information after change

4.2 Threshold K Determination

There is a threshold K in the strategy of changing training set structure. The size of threshold has influence on MT estimation performance, so we conducted a series of tests to analysis the size of K. Meaningful range of the threshold value of K should ensure reducing the proportion of OK and BAD. From table 1, the ratio between OK and BAD is 4.22/1, so we set threshold in range of [0.2,0.95] in experiment, its step size is 0.05. Experiments were carried out when OK label is not refined on the development set. The testing result is shown in table 3:

K value	F_BAD	F_OK	F_all
0.20	0.348	0.871	0.771
0.25	0.349	0.870	0.770
0.30	**0.350**	0.872	0.772
0.35	0.348	0.874	0.773
0.40	0.344	0.873	0.772
0.45	0.342	0.875	0.773
0.50	0.333	0.877	0.773
0.55	0.330	0.879	0.774
0.60	0.327	0.879	0.774
0.65	0.329	0.881	0.775
0.70	0.325	0.881	0.774
0.75	0.320	0.881	0.774
0.80	0.317	0.882	0.773
0.85	0.319	0.882	0.774
0.90	0.318	0.882	0.774
0.95	0.318	0.882	0.774

Table 3: Threshold experiment

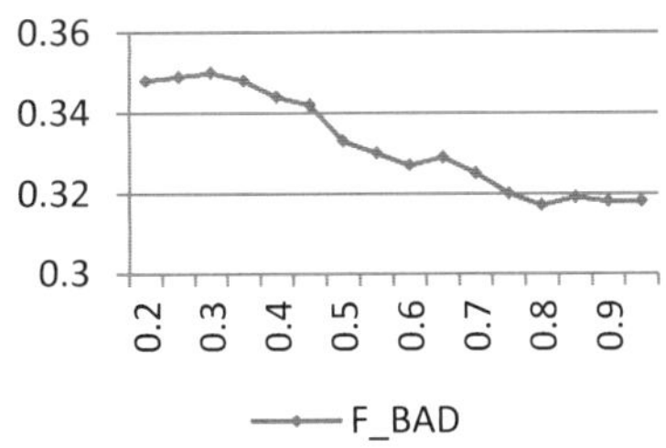

Figure 2: F score of BAD

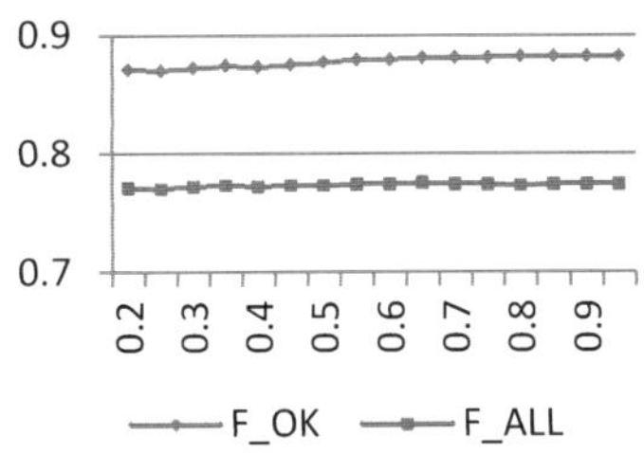

Figure 3: F score of OK

As shown in Figure2 and Figure3, changing in the threshold K have a certain effect on BAD label, but has little effect on the F1 score of OK and all labels. In Figure 1, the F1 score of BAD is highest when threshold K takes 0.3. However, we had set the value of K at 0.6 due to time reason during QE task. We believe that the score will be higher when K is equal to 0.3.

4.3 QE Experimental Analysis

There are four comparative experiments to prove the validity of the strategies proposed in this paper. Experiment names are as follows:

WY: do not change the structure of train set, not refine OK label.

WF: do not change the structure of train set, refine OK with OK_B, OK_I, OK_E, OK.

ZY: change the structure of train set, do not refine OK label.

ZF: change the structure of train set, refine OK label with OK_B, OK_I, OK_E, OK.

strategy	F_BAD	F_OK	F_AVG
WY	28.56	88.58	77.12
WF	34.53	87.63	77.44
ZY	32.71	88.16	77.52
ZF	38.34	86.84	77.53

Table 4: The results on development corpus

strategy	F_BAD	F_OK	F_AVG
WY	28.34	88.75	77.34
WF	34.28	87.97	77.83
ZY	32.69	88.3	77.80
ZF	39.11	86.36	77.44

Table 5: The results on test corpus

In QE task of WMT2015, Label distribution disequilibrium phenomenon can lead to Paranoid problem, which impacts the performance of QE system seriously. As shown in table 4 and table 5, the strategies that refine OK label and change structure of train set can solve label disequilibrium problem to a certain degree. The F_BAD is 34.28 when using the strategy of refining OK label alone, and the F_BAD is 32.69 when using the strategy of changing structure of training set. The strategy that refines OK label is more effective than the one that change the structure of the training set.

5 Conclusion

For the problem of Label distribution disequilibrium in word-level QE task of WMT2015, We proposed two strategies: one is refining OK label, the other one is changing structure of train set. Combined with the strategies, we use CRF and some grammar features to train a model which can enhance the correct number of BAD label, and the strategy of ROL is more effective. But, from Table 5, the F1 scores of the original method is that F_BAD is 28.34 and the F_OK is 88.75. When we add the two strategies, the F_BAD increases to 39.11 and the F_OK reduces to 86.36. In the future, we hope to overcome the shortcomings of the two strategies to improve both F1 scores of the two labels.

Reference

Blatz J, Fitzgerald E, Foster G, et al. Confidence estimation for machine translation[C]//Proceedings of the 20th international conference on Computational Linguistics. Association for Computational Linguistics, 2004: 315.

Quirk. 2004. Training a sentence-level machine translation confidence metric. In Proc. LREC, pages 825–828, Lisbon, Portugal, May.

Ueffing N, Macherey K, Ney H. Confidence measures for statistical machine translation[C]//In Proc. MT Summit IX. 2003.

John Blatz, Erin Fitzgerald, George Foster, Simona Gandrabur, Cyril Goutte, Alex Kulesza, Alberto Sanchis, and Nicola Ueffing. Confidence estimation for machine translation. Technical report, JHU/CLSP Summer Workshop, 2003.

Xiong D, Zhang M, Li H. 2010. Error Detection for Statistical Machine Translation Using Linguistic Features[J]. Acl Proceedings of Annual Meeting of the Association for Computational Linguistics, 604-611.

Luong N Q, Lecouteux B, Besacier L, et al. LIG system for WMT13 QE task: Investigating the usefulness of features in word confidence estimation for MT. Proceedings of The eighth Workshop on Statistical Machine Translation, 2013:384--389.

Guillaume Wisniewski, Nicolas P´echeux, et al. 2014. LIMSI Submission for WMT'14 QE Task. Proceedings of The ninth Workshop on Statistical Machine Translation, pages 348-354.

Jos´e G. C. de Souza, Jes ´us Gonz´alez-Rubio, Christian Buck. 2014. FBK-UPV-UEdin participation in the WMT14 Quality Estimation shared-task. Proceedings of The ninth Workshop on Statistical Machine Translation, pages 322-328

Ngoc-Quang Luong, Laurent Besacier, Benjamin Lecouteux. 2014. LIG System for Word Level QE task at WMT14. Proceedings of The ninth Workshop on Statistical Machine Translation,pages 335-341.

S. Raybaud, D. Langlois, and K. Smali. 2011. "this sentence is wrong." detecting errors in machine translated sentences. In Machine Translation,pages 1–34.

Yao Xu, Wang Xiaodan, Zhang Xi etc. Methods of feature selection [J]. Control and Decision, 2012,27(2);

Yu S H, Ma Z, Yang X H. 2007. Nonsmooth finite-time control ofuncertain second-order nonlinear systems[J]. J of Control Theory and Applications, 5(2): 171-176.

UGENT-LT3 SCATE System for Machine Translation Quality Estimation

Arda Tezcan **Veronique Hoste** **Bart Desmet** **Lieve Macken**
Department of Translation, Interpreting and Communication
Ghent University
Groot-Brittanniëlaan 45, 9000 Ghent, Belgium
{arda.tezcan, veronique.hoste, bart.desmet, lieve.macken}@ugent.be

Abstract

This paper describes the submission of the UGENT-LT3 SCATE system to the WMT15 Shared Task on Quality Estimation (QE), viz. English-Spanish word and sentence-level QE. We conceived QE as a supervised Machine Learning (ML) problem and designed additional features and combined these with the baseline feature set to estimate quality. The sentence-level QE system re-uses the word level predictions of the word-level QE system. We experimented with different learning methods and observe improvements over the baseline system for word-level QE with the use of the new features and by combining learning methods into ensembles. For sentence-level QE we show that using a single feature based on word-level predictions can perform better than the baseline system and using this in combination with additional features led to further improvements in performance.

1 Introduction

Machine Translation (MT) Quality Estimation (QE) is the task of providing a quality indicator for unseen automatically translated sentences without relying on reference translations (Gandrabur & Foster, 2003; Blatz et al., 2004). Predicting the quality of MT output has many applications in computer-aided translation workflows that utilize MT, including error analysis (Ueffing and Ney 2007), filtering translations for human post-editing (Specia et al., 2009) and comparing the quality of different MT systems (Rosti et al. 2007).

The most common approach is to treat the QE problem as a supervised Machine Learning (ML) task, using standard regression or classification algorithms. A considerable amount of related work on both word and sentence-level QE is described in the WMT shared tasks of previous years (Bojar et al., 2014; Bojar et al., 2013).

The WMT 2015 QE shared task proposes three evaluation tasks: (1) scoring and ranking sentences according to predicted post-editing effort given a source sentence and its translation; (2) predicting the individual words that require post-editing; and (3) predicting the quality at document level. In this paper, we describe the UGENT-LT3 SCATE submissions to task 1 (sentence-level QE) and task 2 (word-level QE).

Sentence-level and word-level QE are related tasks. Sentence-level QE assigns a global score to an automatically translated sentence whereas word-level QE is more fine-grained and tries to detect the problematic word sequences. Therefore we first developed a word-level QE system and incorporate the word-level predictions as additional features in the sentence-level QE system. The usefulness of including word-level predictions in sentence-level QE has already been demonstrated by de Souza et al. (2014)

For both tasks, we extracted additional features and combine these with the baseline feature set to estimate quality. The new features try to capture either *accuracy* or *fluency* errors, where *accuracy* is concerned with how much of the meaning expressed in the source is also expressed in the target text, and *fluency* is concerned with to what extent the translation is well-formed, regardless of sentence meaning. This distinction is well known in quality assessment schemes for MT (White, 1995; Secară, 2005; Lommel et al., 2014). Some of the additional features are based on ideas that were explored in previous work on QE, such as; context features for the target word and of POS tags, (Xiong et al., 2010), alignment context features (Bach et al., 2011) and adequacy and fluency indicators (Specia et al., 2013).

The rest of this paper is organized as follows. Section 2 and Section 3 give an overview of the shared task on word-level QE and sentence-level QE respectively and describe also the features we extracted, the learning methods and the additional language resources we used and the experiments we conducted. Finally, in Section 4, we discuss the results we obtained and the observations we made.

2 Word-level Quality Estimation

The word-level QE task is conceived as a binary classification task. The goal is to label translation errors at word level by marking words either as "GOOD" or "BAD". The WMT2015 QE task focuses on the F1 score for the "BAD" class as the main evaluation metric. For the word-level QE task, the organizers provided a data set of English-Spanish sentence pairs generated by a statistical MT system, which consists of a training set of 11,271 sentences, a development set of 1,000 sentences and a test set of 1,817 sentences. All the target sentences of the training and development data sets contain binary reference labels for each word, which were automatically derived by aligning the MT output and the post-edited translations using TERCOM (Snover et al., 2006). The distribution of the binary labels in the training and development sets is provided in Table 1.

	# Words	*% GOOD*	*% BAD*
training set	257548	80.85	19.15
dev. set	23207	80.82	19.18

Table 1: Distribution of the binary labels on the training and development set for word-level QE

2.1 Language Resources and Features

In our experiments, in addition to the provided 25 baseline features which were described in the WMT14 QE shared task (Bojar et al., 2014), we added 55 features to characterize each target word of the MT output. The new features were extracted from the provided training data and additional language resources we gathered. The new features try to model the two main MT error categories: *accuracy* and *fluency*. For *fluency*, we extracted surface-level features as well as more abstract PoS-based features and Named Entity (NE) information. For *accuracy*, we used bilingual information. In the following subsections, we describe the additional language resources and list out the additional features we used in the WMT 2015 word-level QE task. Necessary preprocessing operations are applied on the target sentences (depending on the feature type) prior to feature extraction.

2.1.1 Additional Resources

Since most of the new features rely on statistical information, we used two additional data resources. As monolingual data resource, we used a corpus of more than 13 million Spanish sentences collected from the News Crawl Corpus[1] (years 2007-2013) to build two types of language models: one based on surface forms and one based on PoS codes. The following preprocessing steps have been applied on the data before building the language models: normalizing punctuation and numbers, tokenization, named entity recognition using the Stanford NER tool (Finkel et al., 2005), lowercasing, and PoS-tagging using FreeLing (Padró and Stanilovsky, 2012). The surface form LM has been built using KenLM (Heafield 2011). For the PoS LM, we used IRSTLM with Witten-Bell smoothing (Federico et al., 2008) as the modified Kneser-Ney smoothing, which is used by KENLM, is not well defined when there are no singletons (Chen and Goodman 1999), which leads to modeling issues in the PoS corpus.

As bilingual data, we selected 6 million sentence pairs from OPUS (Tiedemann 2012) from various domains and used the Moses toolkit (Koehn et al. 2006) to obtain word and phrase alignments. Even though there are more bilingual sentences available, to avoid a bias to one specific domain, a similar number of sentences of different domains were selected. The following preprocessing steps have been applied on the data prior to training: normalization on punctuation and numbers, tokenization, NER (only the Spanish side) and lowercasing. The phrase table has been pruned to exclude alignments with a *direct alignment probability* $P(t|s) < 0.01$, where s denotes *source* and t denotes *target text*.

The resulting language models and phrase tables were stored in databases and indexed to speed up lookup.

2.1.2 Fluency Features

The fluency features try to capture whether the Spanish MT translations adhere to the norms of the Spanish language. Most of the fluency features are derived from the two language models

[1] http://www.statmt.org/wmt13/translation-task.html

described in section 2.1.1 and use the context around the focus word (w_i). To ensure computational feasibility, we limited the language models to 3-gram sequences. However, for each w_i, for which we extract a contextual feature, we generate three 3-gram features depending on the position of w_i using a sliding window approach:

- $w_{i-2}\, w_{i-1}\, w_i$
- $w_{i-1}\, w_i\, w_{i+1}$
- $w_i\, w_{i+1}\, w_{i+2}$

This sliding window approach (sw) is used for extracting all context features. In the table below, these features are indicated with "*sw*" together with the total number of features extracted by this approach.

The following fluency features were used:

- The LM score of $\boldsymbol{w_i}$ (one feature);
- (sw) The LM scores of the 3-gram context of $\boldsymbol{w_i}$ (three features);
- (sw) Binary features indicating whether a 3-gram context exists in the 3-gram database (three features);
- Separate features of the PoS codes of w_{i-1}, w_i, w_{i+1} (three features);
- Separate features of the simplified PoS codes (only main category) of w_{i-1}, w_i, w_{i+1} (three features);
- (sw) The PoS sequences of the 3-gram context of $\boldsymbol{w_i}$ (three features);
- (sw) The simplified PoS sequences of the 3-gram context of $\boldsymbol{w_i}$ (three features);
- The PoS LM score of PoS tag of $\boldsymbol{w_i}$ (one feature);
- (sw) The PoS LM scores of the 3-gram PoS context of $\boldsymbol{w_i}$ (three features);
- (sw) Binary features indicating whether a 3-gram PoS context exists in the 3-gram PoS database (three features);
- (sw) The Log-Likelihood Ratio (LLR)[2] of the 3-gram PoS context of $\boldsymbol{w_i}$ (three features);
- (sw) Binary features indicating whether the LLR of the 3-gram PoS context of the focus word is above the critical value 3.84 (95th percentile; significant al the level of $p < 0.05$) (three features);
- Binary features indicating whether $\boldsymbol{w_i}$ is the first word or the last word in a sentence (two features);
- Binary features indicating whether $\boldsymbol{w_{i-1}}, \boldsymbol{w_i}$ or $\boldsymbol{w_{i+1}}$ is a NE (three features);
- (sw) NE annotation of the 3-gram context of $\boldsymbol{w_i}$ (three features).

2.1.3 Accuracy Features

The accuracy features try to capture errors that can only be identified when comparing source and target sentences: wrong translations, additions and deletions. Some accuracy features are derived from the phrase table described in section 2.1.1. Other accuracy features make use of the alignment features that were given in de baseline feature set. The following accuracy features were used:

- (sw) Phrase table alignment scores of any possible alignment of words in the source sentence with words in the target sentence, containing $\boldsymbol{w_i}$, using *direct translation probability* (six features are defined for n-grams of size 1-3);
- (sw) Same phrase table as above with the additional condition that the source alignment for each $\boldsymbol{w_i}$ (which is provided as a baseline feature) is included in the alignments found (six features are defined similarly);
- Binary feature indicating whether $\boldsymbol{w_i}$ is identical to its source alignment, the alignment given as in the baseline features (one feature);
- Binary features indicating whether $\boldsymbol{w_i}$ and its source alignment are either both content words or both function words, based on the PoS codes of $\boldsymbol{w_i}$ and its source alignment, given as in the baseline features (two features).

2.2 Learning Methods

We use Conditional Random Fields (CRFs) (Lafferty et al., 2001) and Memory-Based Learning (MBL) (Daelemans and Van den Bosch, 2005) as ML methods for word-level QE. CRFs take an input sequence X with its associated features, and try to infer a hidden sequence Y, containing the class labels. They are as such comparable to Hidden Markov Models (HMMs) and Maximum Entropy Markov Models (MEMMs). However, CRFs, unlike HMMs, do not assume that all features are independent, and they can take future observations into account using a

[2] LLR compares frequencies weighted over two different corpora (in our case the Spanish MT output and the Spanish News Crawl Corpus) and assigns high LLR values to sequences in the Spanish MT output having much lower or higher frequencies than expected.

forward-backward algorithm, unlike MEMMs, thus avoiding two fundamental limitations of those models (Lafferty et al, 2001). We used the CRF++ toolkit, version 0.58 (Lafferty et al., 2001). In MBL, on the other hand, a so-called lazy learner, which stores all training instances in memory and at classification time, a new test instance X is compared to all instances Y in the memory. The similarity between the instances is computed using a distance metric $\Delta(X, Y)$. The extrapolation is done by assigning the most frequent category within the found set of most similar example(s) (the k-nearest neighbors) as the category of the new test example. We used TiMBL, version 6.4.2 (Daelemans et al., 2010) in our experiments. In addition, we used Gallop (Desmet et al, 2013), a genetic algorithm (GA) toolbox for optimizing the classifiers on two levels: feature selection and hyper-parameter optimization.

2.3 Experiments

We carried out experiments with the two ML methods and three different feature sets, namely the baseline features (b), the new features (n) we described in Section 2.2 and a merged feature set (m), which contain all features from the first two groups. We trained CRF models with basic unigram (uni) and bigram (bi) templates and the default settings for the regularization algorithm and the hyper-parameters. While unigram templates use each feature as it is, bigram templates automatically create additional features, combining the features for $\boldsymbol{w_{i-1}}$ and $\boldsymbol{w_{i}}$. TiMBL learning is performed with explicitly defined numerical features. For a first round of experiments, both learners were applied relying on their default parameter settings. Figure 1 summarizes the classification results of the first round of experiments, where evaluation metrics are defined as follows:

$$Accuracy = \frac{\text{tp} + \text{tn}}{\text{tp} + \text{tn} + \text{fp} + \text{fn}}$$

$$F1\,"BAD" = \frac{2 \cdot P_{BAD} \cdot R_{BAD}}{P_{BAD} + R_{BAD}}$$

where tp, tn, fp, fn denote *true positives*, *true negatives*, *false positives* and *false negatives* respectively, and P_{BAD} and R_{BAD} denote *precision* and *recall* for the "BAD" class. Figure 1 shows that merging the baseline features with the newly designed features improves the classification performance on the "BAD" class for both learning methods (systems "CRF m-uni", "CRF m-bi" and "TiMBL m"). For this experiment, the unigram CRF systems generally have a better performance than the bigram systems.

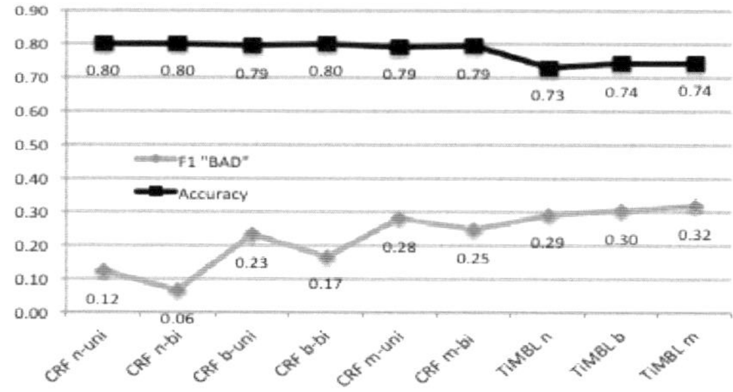

Figure 1: Classification performance of different feature groups and learning methods.

In order to gain more insight into which features are most informative for our task, we performed feature selection using a GA-based search. Given that it is by no means certain that the default parameters, in both learners, are also the optimal parameter settings for our classification task, we performed joint feature selection and parameter optimization. For this purpose, we used Gallop with 3-fold cross-validation, population size of 100 and a maximum of 50 generations.

Due to time limitations, we used a reduced training data set of 60,000 feature vectors for the Gallop experiments. Unfortunately, we were not able to improve the results of "*TiMBL m*" by using only the features or the hyper-parameters that are selected by Gallop. Some of the features that were consistently selected by Gallop in the 5-best scoring feature sequences, are the following: LM scores of 3-gram context, binary features indicating whether the 3-gram context appears in the LM or POS-LM, binary feature indicating whether the target word is identical to the source alignment, binary feature indicating whether the target word and the corresponding source alignment are both content or function words.

Based on the hypothesis that both learners use a different learning strategy and might thus make different types of errors, we performed a final experiment with classifier ensembles, using two simple methods. While the first method uses the TiMBL word-level predictions as an additional feature in CRF (hybrid-1), the second method combines the labels of the best CRF and TiMBL systems ("*CRF m-uni*" and "*TiMBL m*") by voting for the "BAD" label if (1) any of the systems labels the target word as "BAD" (hybrid-2A) or (2) both systems label the target word as "BAD" (hybrid-2B). The classification performance of the ensemble systems, together with the best TiMBL system, are provided in Table 2.

	Accuracy	*F1 "BAD"*
TiMBL-m	0,74	0.317
Hybrid 1	0,79	0.292
Hybrid 2A	**0,81**	0.161
Hybrid 2B	0,73	**0.375**

Table 2: Classification performance of the best TiMBL system, in comparison with the ensemble systems on the development set.

Based on all the results, we selected the following systems for the submission of this year's shared task on word-level QE:

- *SCATE-HYBRID*: Hybrid 2B
- *SCATE-MBL*: TiMBL-m

These two systems obtained comparable scores (F1 "BAD") on the test set of 0.367 and 0.305 respectively.

3 Sentence-level Quality Estimation

The sentence-level QE task aims at predicting Human mediated Translation Edit Rate (HTER) (Snover et al., 2006) between the raw MT output and its manually post-edited version. In addition to *scoring* the sentences for quality, a *ranking* variant of this task is defined as ranking all MT sentences, for all source sentences, from best to worst.

3.1 Features and Language Resources

In our experiments, in addition to 17 baseline features that were provided together with the data sets, we designed 17 additional features. In this section, we briefly list out the additional features we used in WMT 2015 sentence-level QE task. We used the same additional language resources as in the word-level QE task to extract additional features. As mentioned before, we include the word level predictions as features for sentence-level QE. The following additional features were used:

- The percentage of predicted "BAD" tokens in the target sentence (p_{BAD}).
- The percentage of PoS n-grams in the target sentence that appear in the PoS n-gram database more than once (p_{POS}). Five features are extracted for n-grams of size 2-6.
- The percentage of n-grams in the target sentence that appear in the n-gram database at least once (p_{tok}). Four features are extracted for n-grams of size 2-5.
- The percentage of n-grams in the target sentence that appear in the phrase table, being aligned to n-grams from the corresponding source sentence with *direct alignment probability (EN-to-ES)* $P(t|s) > 0.01$ (p_{pt}). Seven features are extracted for n-grams of size 1-7.

3.2 Learning Methods

We use LibSVM (Chang and Lin 2011) to train a regression model using Support Vector Machines (SVMs) with a Radial Basis Function (RBF) kernel.

3.3 Experiments

In a first set of experiments we compare the performance of a system using the baseline features with three systems using only a single feature (p_{BAD}), that is the percentage of predicted "BAD" tokens in the target sentence. We extract this feature from three different word-level QE systems "*TiMBL m*", "*CRF m-uni*" and "*HYBRID_2B*". The performance of these sentence-level QE systems are measured with Mean Squared Error (MSE), Squared Correlation Coefficient (r^2) and Mean Average Error (MAE), which are defined as follows:

$$\mathrm{MSE} = \frac{1}{n}\sum_{i=1}^{n}(f(x_i) - y_i)^2$$

$$r^2 = \frac{(n\sum_{i=1}^{n} f(x_i)y_i - \sum_{i=1}^{n} f(x_i)\sum_{i=1}^{n} y_i)^2}{(n\sum_{i=1}^{n} f(x_i)^2 - (\sum_{i=1}^{n} f(x_i))^2)\,(n\sum_{i=1}^{n} y_i^2 - (\sum_{i=1}^{n} y_i)^2)}$$

$$\mathrm{MAE} = \frac{1}{n}\sum_{i=1}^{n}|f(x_i) - y_i|$$

where $f(x_1), \ldots, f(x_n)$ are the decision values predicted by LibSVM and $y_1, \ldots, y_n$ are the true values. We train the systems with default values for hyper-parameters and perform evaluation on the development set provided for the sentence-level QE task. Figure 3 summarizes the performance of baseline features in comparison with P_{BAD}, which is obtained from different word-level QE systems. In addition to the systems above, we build a final system, which uses the given reference labels to extract P_{BAD} (P_{BAD} - ReferenceLabels). The purpose of building and evaluating this system is to show an upper boundary for the performance of P_{BAD}, as a single feature.

	MSE	r^2	MAE
baseline	0,039	0,03	0,147
P_{BAD} – Timbl m	0,038	0,06	0,145
P_{BAD} - CRF m-uni	0,037	0,08	0,145
P_{BAD} - HYBRID 2B	0,036	0,10	0,144
P_{BAD} - ReferenceLabels	**0,005**	**0,89**	**0,055**

Table 3: Sentence-level QE performance of SVM systems using baseline features vs. p_{BAD} extracted from three different systems.

As a second set of experiments we enrich the baseline feature set by combining it with the additional features that are described in Section 3.1. For the feature P_{BAD} we use the best output, coming from the system "HYBRID_2B". Table 4 shows the impact of the different feature sets on the overall performance.

	MSE	r^2	MAE
basel.	0,037	0,03	0,147
p_{BAD}	0,036	0,07	0,147
basel.+p_{POS}	0,037	0,04	0,147
basel.+p_{POS}+p_{pt}	0,036	0,06	0,145
basel.+p_{POS}+p_{pt}+p_{tok}	0,036	0,07	0,143
basel.+p_{POS}+p_{pt}+p_{tok}+p_{BAD}	0,035	0,10	0,142

Table 4: Performance of the SVM systems on sentence-level QE, using different feature sets

Based on the results, we selected the following two systems for the submission of this year's shared task on sentence-level QE:

- *SCATE-SVM-single*: SVM trained with the single feature p_{BAD}
- *SCATE-SVM*: SVM trained with baseline and new features (base.+p_{POS}+p_{pt}+p_{tok}+p_{BAD})

	MSE	r^2	MAE
p_{BAD}	0.035	0.07	0,146
basel.+pos+pt+tok+p_{BAD}	**0.034**	**0.10**	**0,142**

Table 5: Performance of the submitted sentence-level QE systems on development set, compared with the baseline system.

We apply grid search to optimize the γ, ε and C parameters using 5-fold cross validation prior to building SVM models to use for our submissions. We perform *sentence ranking* based on the predicted HTER scores for both systems. Table 5 gives an overview of the performance of the two optimized systems we submit on the development set. On the test set, the performance (MAE) of both of these systems was 0.14, based on the official results.

4 Results and Discussion

For the word-level QE task, we extracted additional features based on *accuracy* and *fluency* of translations, for labeling words for quality as a ML classification problem. The results showed that the additional features, as a whole, were found to be relevant for the two different learning methods. We obtained better results using both MBL and CRF when we used the additional features in combination with the baseline feature set. We also observe that MBL performs better than CRF when looking at the F1 scores on the "BAD" class for this task, even though it performs worse when overall classification accuracy is considered. One possible explanation for MBL obtaining a better performance could be the use of similarity-based reasoning as a smoothing method for estimating low-frequency events, considering the heterogeneous nature of the "BAD" class for this specific task and the suitability of MBL for handling exceptions (Daelemans and Van den Bosch, 2005).

Finally, a simple combination of the two classifiers into an ensemble system provides a better system for classifying the "BAD" class, which encourages us to carry out more experiments with ensemble systems for the word-level QE task.

For sentence-level QE, we trained regression models using additional features we extracted, in combination with the baseline feature set. We see in Table 4 that a single feature, which is based only on the predicted word labels, can lead to a sentence-level QE system with better performance than a system built with 17 baseline features. For demonstrating the potential of this single feature further, we built a system based on the given correct word labels, which defines a high upper bound for quality estimations, as expected. As a result we show that a word-level QE system that is accurate "enough" can lead to successful sentence-level QE. In the future, we would like to investigate more closely the relationship between word-level and sentence-level QE and examine the portability of the developed systems to English-Dutch.

Acknowledgements

This research has been carried out in the framework of the SCATE[3] project funded by the Flemish government agency IWT.

[3] http://www.ccl.kuleuven.be/scate

References

Nguyen Bach, Fei Huang, and Yaser Al-Onaizan. 2011. "Goodness: A method for measuring machine translation confidence." In *Proceedings of the 49th Annual Meeting of the Association for Computational Linguistics: Human Language Technologies-Volume 1*, pp. 211-219. Association for Computational Linguistics,

John Blatz, Erin Fitzgerald, George Forster, Simona Gandrabur, Cyril Goutte, Alberto Kulesza, AlexSanchis, and Nicola Ueffing. 2003. "Confidence Estimation for Machine Translation." In *Summer Workshop, Center for Language and Speech Processing*, 853–56. Genève.

Ondrej Bojar, Christian Buck, Christian Federmann, Barry Haddow, Philipp Koehn, Johannes Leveling, Christof Monz, Pavel Pecina, Matt Post, Herve Saint-Amand, Radu Soricut, Lucia Specia. 2014. "Findings of the 2014 Workshop on Statistical Machine Translation." *WMT* Ninth Work: 12–58.

Ondrej Bojar, Christian Buck, Chris Callison-Burch, Christian Federmann, Barry Haddow, Philipp Koehn, Christof Monz, Matt Post, Radu Soricut, and Lucia Specia. 2013. Findings of the 2013 Workshop on Statistical Machine Translation. In *Eighth Workshop on Statistical Machine Translation*, pp. 1–44, WMT, Sofia, Bulgaria.

Chih-Chung Chang and Chih-Jen Lin. 2011. "LIBSVM: A library for support vector machines." *ACM Transactions on Intelligent Systems and Technology (TIST)* 2.3 (2011): 27.

Stanley Chen and Joshua Goodman. 1998. An empirical study of smoothing techniques for language modeling. *Technical Report TR-10-98*, Harvard University, August

Lluís Padró Cirera and Evgeny Stanilovsky. 2012. "FreeLing 3.0: Towards Wider Multilinguality." *International Conference on Language Resources and Evaluation*, 2473–79.

Walter Daelemans, Jakub Zavrel, Ko van der Sloot (2010). *TiMBL: Tilburg Memory Based Learner, version 6.3.* reference guide. Technical Report 10-01, ILK.

Walter Daelemans and Antal van den Bosch. 2005. *Memory-Based Language Processing.* Cambridge University Press.

Bart Desmet, Veronique Hoste, David Verstraeten, Jan Verhasselt. 2013. Gallop Documentation. Tech. Rep. LT3 13-03

Marcello Federico, Nicola Bertoldi and Mauro Cettolo. 2008. "IRSTLM: An Open Source Toolkit for Handling Large Scale Language Models." In *Proceedings of the Annual Conference of the International Speech Communication Association, INTERSPEECH*, 1618–21.

Jenny Rose Finkel, Trond Grenager and Christopher Manning. 1997. "Incorporating Non-Local Information into Information Extraction Systems by Gibbs Sampling." In *Proceedings of the 43rd Annual Meeting on Association for Computational Linguistics*, 363–70.

Simona Gandrabur and George Foster. 2003. "Confidence Estimation for Text Prediction." In *Proc.~Conf.~on Natural Language Learning (CoNLL)*, 95–102. Edmonton.

Kenneth Heafield. 2011. "KenLM : Faster and Smaller Language Model Queries." In *Proceedings of the Sixth Workshop on Statistical Machine Translation*, 187–97.

Philipp Koehn, Wade Shen, Marcello Federico, Nicola Bertoldi, Chris Callison-Burch, Brooke Cowan, Chris Dyer, et al. 2006. "Open Source Toolkit for Statistical Machine Translation." In *Proceedings of the 45th Annual Meeting of the ACL on Interactive Poster and Demonstration Sessions*, 177–80.

John Lafferty, Andrew Mccallum and Fernando Pereira. 2001. "Conditional Random Fields: Probabilistic Models for Segmenting and Labeling Sequence Data. In Proceedings of 18th." *International Conference on Machine Learning* pages: 282–89.

Arle Richard Lommel, Aljoscha Burchardt, Maja Popovic, Kim Harris, Eleftherios Avramidis, Hans Uszkoreit. 2014. Using a new analytic measure for the annotation and analysis of MT errors on real data. *Proceedings of the 17th Annual Conference of the European Association for Machine Translation, Pages 165-172, Dubrovnik, Croatia, European Association for Machine Translation, Croatian Language Technologies Society.*

Antti-Veikko I Rosti, Bing Xiang, Spyros Matsoukas, Richard Schwartz, Necip Fazil Ayan and Bonnie J Dorr. 2007. "Combining Output from Multiple Machine Translation Systems." In

Human Language Technologies 2007: The Conference of the North American Chapter of the Association for Computational Linguistics; Proceedings of the Main Conference, 228–35.

Alina Secară. 2005. "Translation Evaluation - a State of the Art Survey." In *Proceedings of the eCoLoRe/MeLLANGE Workshop, Leeds*, 39–44.

Matthew Snover, Bonnie Dorr, Richard Schwartz, Linnea Micciulla and John Makhoul. 2006. "A Study of Translation Edit Rate with Targeted Human Annotation." In *Proceedings of Association for Machine Translation in the Americas*, 223–31.

José GC De Souza, Jesús González-Rubio, Christian Buck, Marco Turchi, and Matteo Negri. 2014. "FBK-UPV-UEdin Participation in the WMT14 Quality Estimation Shared-Task." In *Acl 2014*, 322–28.

Lucia Specia, Marco Turchi, Nicola Cancedda, Marc Dymetman and Nello Cristianini. 2009. "Estimating the Sentence-Level Quality of Machine Translation Systems." In *13th Conference of the European Association for Machine Translation*, 28–37.

Lucia Specia, Kashif Shah, José GC De Souza, and Trevor Cohn. 2013. "QuEst-A translation quality estimation framework." In *ACL (Conference System Demonstrations)*, pp. 79-84.

Jörg Tiedemann. 2012. "Parallel Data, Tools and Interfaces in OPUS." In *Lrec*, 2214–18.

Nicola Ueffing and Hermann Ney. 2007. "Word-Level Confidence Estimation for Machine Translation." *Computational Linguistics* 33 (1). MIT Press: 9–40.

S. John White. 1995. "Approaches to Black Box MT Evaluation." In *MT Summit V Proceedings*, 10.

Deyi Xiong, Min Zhang, and Haizhou Li. 2010. "Error detection for statistical machine translation using linguistic features." In *Proceedings of the 48th Annual Meeting of the Association for Computational Linguistics*, pp. 604-611. Association for Computational Linguistics,

Multi-level Evaluation for Machine Translation

Boxing Chen, Hongyu Guo and Roland Kuhn
National Research Council Canada
first.last@nrc-cnrc.gc.ca

Abstract

Translations generated by current statistical systems often have a large variance, in terms of their quality against human references. To cope with such variation, we propose to evaluate translations using a multi-level framework. The method varies the evaluation criteria based on the clusters to which a translation belongs. Our experiments on the WMT metric task data show that the multi-level framework consistently improves the performance of two benchmarking metrics, resulting in better correlation with human judgment.

1 Introduction

The aims of automatic Machine Translation (MT) evaluation metrics, which measure the quality of translations against human references, are twofold. Firstly, they enable rapid comparisons between different statistical machine translation (SMT) systems. Secondly, they are necessary to the tuning of parameter values during system trainings.

To attain these goals, many machine translation metrics have been introduced in recent years. For example, metrics such as BLEU (Papineni et al., 2002), NIST (Doddington, 2002), and TER (Snover et al., 2006) rely on word n-gram surface matching. Also, metrics that make use of linguistic resources such as synonym dictionaries, part-of-speech tagging, or paraphrasing tables, have been proposed, including Meteor (Banerjee and Lavie, 2005) and its extensions, TER-Plus (Snover et al., 2009), and TESLA (Liu et al., 2011). In addition, attempts to deploy syntactic features or semantic information for evaluation have also been made, giving rise to the STM and DSTM (Liu and Gildea, 2005), DEPREF (Wu et al., 2013) and MEANT family (Lo and Wu, 2011) metrics.

All these evaluation metrics deploy a single evaluation criterion or use the same source of information to evaluate translations. Nevertheless, translations generated by current statistical systems often have widely varying scores, in terms

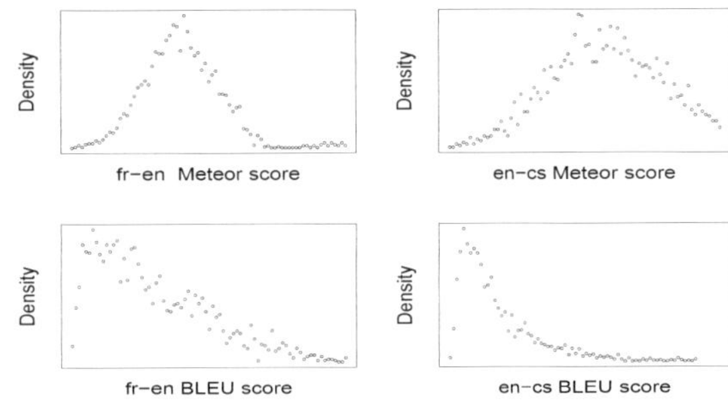

Figure 1: Distributions of translation quality. X-axis is in the range of [0,1].

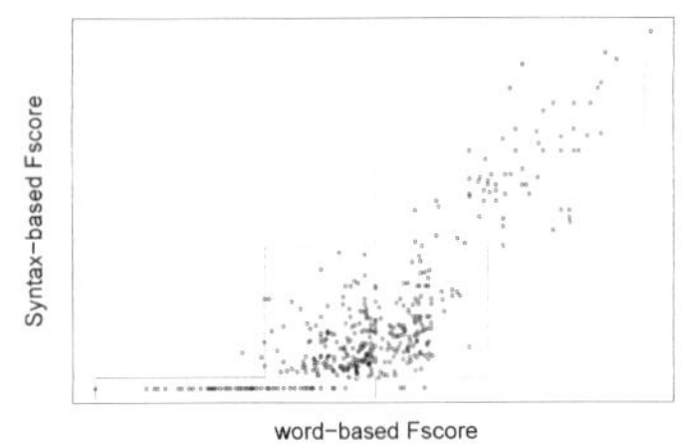

Figure 2: Clusters of translations based on quality. Both X-axis and Y-axis are in the range of [0,1].

of their quality against human references. As a result, current metrics often perform better for a portion of translations but worse against the others. Consider, for example, two widely used metrics, namely the sentence-level Meteor and BLUE. Figure 1 depicts the distributions of the two metrics' evaluation scores, computed on system outputs for two WMT test sets, i.e., the *newstest2013.fr-en* and *newstest2012.en-cs*. As shown in Figures 1, the variances of the created evaluation scores are large across evaluation metrics as well as test sets.

Such widely varying evaluation quality, however, may be clustered into multiple sub-regions, as illustrated in Figure 2. Here, we sample 300 sentences from the system output of the *newstest2013.fr-en* test set; we depict the F-measure based on dependency triplet (dependency type, governor word, and dependent word) on the Y-axis against the word-based F-measure on the X-axis. We observe a straight line at the bottom left corner (blue box) of the graph representing sentences which all have dependency triplet F-score of zero; if we want to distinguish between them in terms of their quality score, we must rely on word matching rather than on syntax. The situation in the upper right corner (green box) of the graph is quite different. Here, the word-based F-measure and dependency-based F-measure have a roughly linear correlation, suggesting that a combination of word-based and syntactic information might be a better measure of quality than either alone. These observations imply that a metric may benefit from applying different sources of information at different quality levels.

In this paper, we propose a multi-level automatic evaluation framework for MT. Our strategy first roughly classifies the translations into different quality levels. Next, it rates the translations by exploiting several different information sources, with the weight on each source depending on its quality level. We apply our method to two metrics: the Meteor and a new metric, DREEM, which is based on distributed representations. Our experiments on the WMT metric task data show that the multi-level framework consistently improves the performance of these two metrics.

2 Multi-level Evaluation

The multi-level evaluation framework works on the sentence level. Specifically, we first assign each test sentence to one of the three categories: low-, medium-, or high-quality translations. Next, we evaluate the translations within each category with a tailored set of weights of the metric on the information sources.

To this end, we deploy a simple strategy for the category clustering. Note that more sophisticate strategies could be deployed; we leave this to our future work. Here, we first use a scoring function to compute a score between the translation and its reference. Next, the category assignment of the translation is then determined by a pre-defined score threshold.

In detail, suppose we have a translation (t) and its reference (r). The multi-level metric scores the translation pair as follows.

$$\text{Score(t,r)} = \begin{cases} M(t,r,w_l) & \text{if } (F(t,r) \leq \theta_1) \\ M(t,r,w_m) & \text{if } (\theta_1 < F(t,r) \leq \theta_2) \\ M(t,r,w_h) & \text{otherwise} \end{cases}$$

where $M(t,r,w)$ is a metric, w is the weight, $F(t,r)$ is the simple classification scoring function. Also, θ is a threshold, and its value is automatically tuned on development data set.

For the classification function, we employ a formula which combines word-based F-measure (denoted as $F_W(t,r)$) and a F-measure (denoted as $F_D(t,r)$) based on dependency triplet (dependency type, governor word, dependent word), as follows:

$$F(t,r) = \lambda \cdot F_W(t,r) + (1-\lambda) \cdot F_D(t,r) \quad (1)$$

where the free parameter λ is tuned on development data.

It is worth noting that, for languages which dependency parser is not available, we only use the word-based F-measure as the classification function. Specifically, we use Equation 1 for Into-English task, and the word-based F-measure for Out-of-English task in this paper.

In a scenario where there are multiple references, we compute the score with each reference, then choose the highest one. In addition, we treat the document-level score as the weighted average of sentence-level scores, with the weights being the reference lengths, as follows.

$$\text{Score}_d = \frac{\sum_{i=1}^{D} \text{len}(r_i)\text{Score}_i}{\sum_{i=1}^{D} \text{len}(r_i)} \quad (2)$$

where Score_i is the score of sentence i, and D is the number of sentences in the document.

3 Evaluation metrics

We apply our multi-level approach to two metrics. The first one is Meteor (Banerjee and Lavie, 2005), which has been widely used for machine translation evaluations. The second one is DREEM, a new metric based on distributed representations generated by deep neural networks.

3.1 Metric Meteor

We use the latest version of Meteor, i.e. Meteor Universal (Denkowski and Lavie, 2014) in this paper. Meteor computes a one-to-one alignment between matching words in a translation and a reference. The space of possible alignments is constructed by exhaustively identifying all possible matches of the following types: exact word matches, word stem matches, synonym word matches, and matches between phrases listed as paraphrases. Alignment is then conducted as a beam search.

From the final alignment, the translation's Meteor score is calculated as follows. First, content and function words are identified in the hypothesis and reference according to a function word list. Next, the weighted precision and recall using match weights (w_i ...w_n) and content-function word weight (δ) are computed, as follows:

$$P = \frac{\sum_i w_i \cdot (\delta \cdot m_i(t_c) + (1-\delta) \cdot m_i(t_f))}{\delta \cdot |t_c| + (1-\delta) \cdot |t_f|} \quad (3)$$

$$R = \frac{\sum_i w_i \cdot (\delta \cdot m_i(r_c) + (1-\delta) \cdot m_i(r_f))}{\delta \cdot |r_c| + (1-\delta) \cdot |r_f|} \quad (4)$$

These two are then combined into a weighted harmonic mean, where a large α means recall is weighted more heavily.

$$\text{Fmean} = \frac{P \cdot R}{\alpha \cdot P + (1-\alpha) \cdot R} \quad (5)$$

To penalize reorderings, this value is then scaled by a fragmentation penalty based on the number of chunks and number of matched words.

$$\text{Meteor}(t, r) = (1 - \gamma \cdot (\frac{\#\text{chunk}}{\#\text{match}})^\beta) \cdot \text{Fmean} \quad (6)$$

In our studies, we fine-tune all the parameters for both multi-level and non-multi-level scoring frameworks.

3.2 Representation based metric

Distributed representations for words and sentences have been shown to significantly boost the performance of a NLP system (Turian et al., 2010). A representation-based translation evaluation metric, DREEM, is introduced in (Anonymous, 2015). The metric has shown to be able to achieve state-of-the-art performance, compared to popular metrics such as BLEU and Meteor. Therefore, in this paper, we also adapt this metric for our experiments.

In a nutshell, the DREEM metric evaluates translations by employing three different types of word and sentence representations: one-hot representations, distributed word representations learned from a neural network model, and distributed sentence representations computed with a recursive autoencoder (RAE). Two different RAE-based representations are used in this metric: one is based on a greedy unsupervised RAE, while the other is based on a syntactic parse tree. To combine the advantages of these four different representations, the authors concatenate them to form one vector representation for each sentence.

In detail, suppose that we have the sentence representations for the translations (t) and references (r). The translation quality is measured by DREEM with a similarity score computed with the Cosine function and a length penalty. Let the size of the vector be N. The quality score is calculated as follows.

$$\text{Score}(t, r) = \text{Cos}^\alpha(t, r) \times P_{len} \quad (7)$$

$$\text{Cos}(t, r) = \frac{\sum_{i=1}^{i=N} v_i(t) \cdot v_i(r)}{\sqrt{\sum_{i=1}^{i=N} v_i^2(t)} \sqrt{\sum_{i=1}^{i=N} v_i^2(r)}} \quad (8)$$

$$P_{len} = \begin{cases} exp(1 - l_r/l_t) & \text{if } (l_t < l_r) \\ exp(1 - l_t/l_r) & \text{if } (l_t \geq l_r) \end{cases} \quad (9)$$

where α is a free parameter, $v_i(.)$ is the value of the vector element, P_{len} is the length penalty, and l_r, l_t are lengths of the translation and reference, respectively.

To use this metric in the multi-level framework, we keep the parameter α consistent for all levels, but use different weights to combine the representations. That is, we construct the representation vector as follows:

$$V = < w_1 \cdot V_{oh}, w_2 \cdot V_{wd}, w_3 \cdot V_{gRAE}, w_4 \cdot V_{tRAE} > \quad (10)$$

where V_{oh} is the one-hot representation, V_{wd} denotes the word representations, and V_{gRAE} and V_{tRAE} are representations learned with greedy RAE and tree-based RAE, respectively. The weights w_1 ... w_4 are tuned on development data.

4 Experiments

4.1 Settings

We conducted experiments on the WMT metric task data. Development sets include WMT 2012 all-to-English, and English-to-all submissions. Test sets contain WMT 2013, and WMT 2014 all-to-English, plus 2013, 2014 English-to-all submissions. The languages "all" include French, Spanish, German, Czech and Russian. For training the word embedding and recursive auto-encoder model, we used WMT 2014 training data [1]. We used the English, French, German and Czech sentences in "Europarl v7" and "News Commentary" for our experiments. To train the representations for Russian, we used the "Yandex 1M corpus".

4.2 Results

Following WMT 2014's metric task (Machacek and Bojar, 2014), to measure the correlation with

[1] http://www.statmt.org/wmt14/translation-task.html

	Into-English	
metric	seg τ	sys γ
Original BLEU	–	0.821
Sentence BLEU	0.259	0.841
Original Meteor	0.279	0.849
Sentence Meteor	0.279	0.863
$Multi-level_w$ Meteor	0.285	0.871
$Multi-level_{wd}$ Meteor	0.294*	0.885*
DREEM	0.287	0.875
$Multi-level_w$ DREEM	0.293	0.880
$Multi-level_{wd}$ DREEM	0.303*	0.892*

Table 1: Correlations with human judgment on the WMT data for the Into-English task. Results are averaged on all into-English test sets. $Multi-level_w$ stands for only using word-based F-measure as the classification function, while $Multi-level_{wd}$ denotes the use of a combination of word-based F-measure and dependency triplet based F-measure. * indicates the improvement over the non-multi-level metric is statistically significant, with a significance level of 0.05.

human judgment, we employed Kendall's rank correlation coefficient τ for the segment level, and used Pearson's correlation coefficient (γ in the below tables) for the system-level. We tested the significance through bootstrap resampling (confidence level of 95%).

We tuned the weights for the Into-English and Out-of-English tasks separately. According to the tuned thresholds, about 25% of the translations are classified to low-quality translations, around 20% belong to high-quality translations, and the rest fall in the medium-quality category.

Experimental results conducted on the Into-English and Out-of-English tasks are reported in Tables 1 and 2. We also compared to the standard de facto metric BLEU (Papineni et al., 2002).

Results, as shown in Tables 1 and 2, indicate that the representation-based metric DREEM obtained better performance than BLEU and Meteor on both tasks at both segment and system levels. The multi-level versions of these metrics consistently improved the performance over the non-multi-level ones on both segment and system levels.

4.3 Further Analysis

In addition to showing the superior performance of the multi-level framework, our experiments also indicate the following observations.

Firstly, for BLEU and Meteor, document-level score computed by weighted averaging sentence-level scores can get better system-level correlation with human judgment, compared to that of the original document-level score which is computed from aggregate statistics accumulated over the entire document.

	Out-of-English	
metric	seg τ	sys γ
Original BLEU	–	0.843
Sentence BLEU	0.221	0.846
Original Meteor	0.228	0.845
Sentence Meteor	0.228	0.853
$Multi-level_w$ Meteor	0.234	0.861
DREEM	0.236	0.904#
$Multi-level_w$ DREEM	0.241	0.922*#

Table 2: Correlations with human judgment on the WMT data for Out-of-English task. Results are averaged over all out-of-English test sets. # indicates DREEM is significantly better than its corresponding version of Meteor, with a significance level of 0.05. * indicates the improvement over the non-multi-level metric is statistically significant.

task	low	medium	high
Into-En	0.93	0.81	0.75
Out-of-En	0.99	0.90	0.81

Table 3: The value of parameter α in multi-level Meteor.

Secondly, for Meteor, recall received a larger weight for low-quality translations than for high-quality translations. For instance, as depicted in Table 3, the parameter α in Meteor is higher for low-quality translations.

Finally, the syntax feature received higher weight for high-quality translations than for low-quality translations. In contrast, as shown in Table 4, the surface n-gram feature was assigned larger weight for low-quality translations .

task	low	medium	high
one-hot	0.23	0.11	0.05
word vec	0.42	0.42	0.40
greedy RAE	0.18	0.20	0.20
tree RAE	0.17	0.27	0.35

Table 4: The weights of each representation in the multi-level DREEM tuned for Into-English task. The syntax-based tree RAE representation received higher weight for high-quality translations, while one-hot representation received higher weight for low-quality translations.

5 Conclusions

Translations generated by statistical systems typically have a large variance in terms of their scores against human references. Motivated by such observation, we propose a multi-level framework. It enables a metric to deploy different criteria for various quality levels of translations. Our experiments on the WMT metric task data show that the multi-level strategy consistently improves the performance of two benchmarking metrics on both segment and system levels.

References

Anonymous. 2015. Representation based translation evaluation metrics. In *Proceedings of the Association for Computational Linguistics (ACL)*, Beijing, China, July.

Satanjeev Banerjee and Alon Lavie. 2005. METEOR: An automatic metric for MT evaluation with improved correlation with human judgments. In *Proceedings of the ACL Workshop on Intrinsic and Extrinsic Evaluation Measures for Machine Translation and/or Summarization*, pages 65–72, Ann Arbor, Michigan, June. Association for Computational Linguistics.

Michael Denkowski and Alon Lavie. 2014. Meteor universal: Language specific translation evaluation for any target language. In *Proceedings of the Ninth Workshop on Statistical Machine Translation*, pages 376–380, Baltimore, Maryland, USA, June. Association for Computational Linguistics.

George Doddington. 2002. Authomatic evaluation of machine translation quality using n-gram cooccurrence statistics. In *Proceedings of the Human Language Technology Conference*, page 128132, San Diego, CA.

Ding Liu and Daniel Gildea. 2005. Syntactic features for evaluation of machine translation. In *ACL 2005 Workshop on Intrinsic and Extrinsic Evaluation Measures for Machine Translation and/or Summarization*, pages 25–32, Ann Arbor, MI.

Chang Liu, Daniel Dahlmeier, and Hwee Tou Ng. 2011. Better evaluation metrics lead to better machine translation. In *Proceedings of the 2011 Conference on Empirical Methods in Natural Language Processing*, pages 375–384, Edinburgh, Scotland, UK., July. Association for Computational Linguistics.

Chi-kiu Lo and Dekai Wu. 2011. Meant: An inexpensive, high-accuracy, semi-automatic metric for evaluating translation utility based on semantic roles. In *Proceedings of the 49th Annual Meeting of the Association for Computational Linguistics: Human Language Technologies*, pages 220–229, Portland, Oregon, USA, June. Association for Computational Linguistics.

Matous Machacek and Ondrej Bojar. 2014. Results of the wmt14 metrics shared task. In *Proceedings of the Ninth Workshop on Statistical Machine Translation*, pages 293–301, Baltimore, Maryland, USA, June. Association for Computational Linguistics.

Kishore Papineni, Salim Roukos, Todd Ward, and Wei-Jing Zhu. 2002. BLEU: A method for automatic evaluation of Machine Translation. In *Proceedings of the 40th Annual Meeting of the Association for Computational Linguistics (ACL)*, pages 311–318, Philadelphia, July. ACL.

Matthew Snover, Bonnie Dorr, Richard Schwartz, Linnea Micciulla, and John Makhoul. 2006. A study of translation edit rate with targeted human annotation. In *Proceedings of Association for Machine Translation in the Americas*.

Matthew G. Snover, Nitin Madnani, Bonnie Dorr, and Richard Schwartz. 2009. Ter-plus: Paraphrase, semantic, and alignment enhancements to translation edit rate. In *Machine Translation*, volume 23, pages 117–127.

Joseph Turian, Lev Ratinov, and Yoshua Bengio. 2010. Word representations: A simple and general method for semi-supervised learning. In *ACL*, pages 384–394.

Xiaofeng Wu, Hui Yu, and Qun Liu. 2013. DCU participation in WMT2013 metrics task. In *Proceedings of the Eighth Workshop on Statistical Machine Translation*, pages 435–439, Sofia, Bulgaria, August. Association for Computational Linguistics.

VERTa: a Linguistically-motivated Metric at the WMT15 Metrics Task

Elisabet Comelles
GRIAL
Universitat de Barcelona (UB)
Barcelona
Spain
elicomelles@ub.edu

Jordi Atserias
IXA Group
University of the Basque Country
(UPV/EHU)
Spain
jordi_atserias001@ehu.eus

Abstract

This paper describes VERTa's submission to the 2015 EMNLP Workshop on Statistical Machine Translation. VERTa is a linguistically-motivated metric that combines linguistic features at different levels. In this paper, VERTa is described briefly, as well as the three versions submitted to the workshop: VERTa-70Adeq30Flu, VERTa-EQ and VERTa-W. Finally, the experiments conducted with the WMT14 data are reported and some conclusions are drawn.

1 Introduction

In the last decade Automatic Machine Translation (MT) Evaluation has become a key field in Natural Language Processing due to the amount of texts that are translated over the world and the need for a quick, reliable and inexpensive way to evaluate the quality of the output text. Therefore, a large number of metrics have been developed, which range from very simple metrics to more complex ones. Within simple metrics there are those that do not use any type of linguistic information, such as BLEU (Papineni et al., 2002) which is one of the most well-known and widely used, since it is fast and easy to use. Other metrics though, rely on linguistic information used at lexical level such as METEOR (Denkowski and Lavie, 2014); at syntactic level, using either constituent analysis (Liu and Hildea, 2005) or dependency analysis (Owczarzack et al., 2007a and 2007b; He et al., 2010); while others use more complex information such as semantic roles (Giménez and Márquez, 2007 and 2008; Lo et al., 2012). However, all these metrics focus on partial aspects of language which might lead to a biased evaluation. As a consequence, in the last years researchers have been exploring different ways to combine a wide variety of linguistic features, either using machine-learning techniques (Leusch and Ney, 2009; Albrecht and Hwa, 2007a and 2007b; Gautam and Bhattacharyya, 2014; Joty et al., 2014) or in a more simple and straightforward way (Giménez, 2008; Giménez and Márquez, 2010; Specia and Giménez, 2010, González et al., 2014). Nevertheless, little research has been carried out in order to explore the suitability of the linguistic features used and how they should be combined, from a linguistic point of view. Therefore, this paper proposes a new version of VERTa, a linguistically-motivated metric (Comelles and Atserias, 2014) which uses a wide variety of linguistic features at different levels and which aims at moving away from a biased evaluation and providing a more holistic approach to MT evaluation. Last year VERTa participated in the WMT15 and achieved promising results at system level, this year we would like to improve the metric's performance at segment level. To this aim, a Language Model Module has been added, as well as a NERC component.

In this paper we provide a brief description of the different modules in VERTa and how they are combined, section 3 present the three versions submitted to the WMT15 and reports the experiments performed with WMT14 data into English, and finally in section 4 some conclusions are drawn.

2 VERTa: A Linguistically-motivated Metric

VERTa claims to be a linguistically-motivated metric because before its development a thorough analysis was carried out in order to identify those linguistic phenomena that an MT evaluation metric should take into account when evaluating MT output by means of reference translations. With the results of this analysis (Comelles, 2015) we decided on the linguistic features that would be more appropriate and on how they should be combined depending on whether Adequacy or Fluency was evaluated. Therefore, VERTa consists of six modules which can work independently or in combination: *Lexical Similarity Module (L)*, *Morphological Similarity Module (M)*, *N-gram Similarity Module (N)*, *Dependency Similarity Module (D)*, *Semantic Similarity Module (S)* and *Language Model (LM) Module*.

All metrics use a weighted precision and recall over the number of matches of the particular element of each level (words, dependency triples, n-grams, etc) as shown below.

$$P = \frac{\sum_{\partial \in D} W_\partial * nmatch_\partial(\nabla(h))}{|\nabla(h)|}$$

$$R = \frac{\sum_{\partial \in D} W_\partial * nmatch_\partial(\nabla(r))}{|\nabla(r)|}$$

Where r is the reference, h is the hypothesis and ∇ is a function that given a segment will return the elements of each level (e.g. words at lexical level and triples at dependency level). D is the set of different functions to project the level element into the features associated to each level, such as word-form, lemma or partial-lemma at lexical level. $nmatch_\partial()$ is a function that returns the number of matches according to the feature ∂ (i.e. the number of lexical matches at the lexical level or the number of dependency triples that match at the dependency level). Finally, W is the set of weights [0 1] associated to each of the different features in a particular level in order to combine the different kinds of matches considered in that level.

Next, all modules forming VERTa are described.

2.1 Lexical Similarity Module

The Lexical Module matches lexical items in the hypothesis and reference sentences. This module does not only use superficial information such as the wordform, but it also takes into account lemmatization and lexical semantics. Hence, different types of matches are allowed and applied in the order established in Table 1. In addition, different weights can be assigned depending on their importance as regard semantics.

	Match	Examples	
		HYP	**REF**
1	Word-form	*east*	*east*
2	Synonym[1]	*believed*	*considered*
3	Hypernym	*barrel*	*keg*
4	Hyponym	*keg*	*barrel*
5	Lemma	*is_BE*	*are_BE*
6	Part-lemma[2]	*danger*	*dangerous*

Table 1. Lexical matches and examples

2.2 Morphological Similarity Module

This module uses the information provided by the Lexical Module in combination with Part-of-Speech (PoS) tags[3].

Similar to the Lexical Similarity Module, this module matches items in the hypothesis and reference segments and a set of weights can be assigned to each type of match (see Table 2).

	Match	Examples	
		HYP	**REF**
1	(Word-form, PoS)	(he, PRP)	(he, PRP)
2	(Synonym, PoS)	(VIEW, NNS)	(OPINON, NNS)
3	(Hypern., PoS)	(PUBLICA-TION, NN)	(MAGA-ZINE, NN)
4	(Hypon., PoS)	(MAGA-ZINE, NN)	(PUBLICA-TION, NN)
5	(LEMMA, PoS)	can_(CAN, MD)	Could_(CAN, MD)

Table 2. Morphological module matches

This module aims at making up for the broader coverage of the Lexical Module, thus preventing matches such as *invites* and *invite*, which although similar in meaning do not share the same morphosyntactic features.

2.3 Dependency Similarity Module

The Dependency Module makes it possible to capture similarities beyond the external structure of a sentence and uses dependency structures to link syntax and semantics. Thus, this module allows for identifying sentences with the same meaning but different syntactic constructions

[1] Information on synonyms, lemmas, hypernyms and hyponyms is obtained from WordNet 3.0.

[2] Lemmas that share the first four letters.

[3] The corpus has been PoS tagged using the Stanford Parser (de Marneffe et al. 2006).

(e.g. active – passive alternations), as well as changes in word order.

This module works at sentence level and follows the approach used by (Owczarzack et al., 2007a and 2007b) and (He et al., 2010) with some linguistic additions in order to adapt it to our metric combination. Similar to the Morphological Module, the Dependency Similarity metric also relies first on those matches established at lexical level – word-form, synonymy, hypernymy, hyponymy and lemma – in order to capture lexical variation across dependencies and avoid relying only on surface word-form. Then, by means of flat triples with the form Label(Head, Mod) obtained from the parser[4], four different types of dependency matches have been designed (see Table 3) and weights can be assigned to each type of match.

	Match Type	Match Descr.
1	Complete	Label1=Label2 Head1=Head2 Mod1=Mod2
2	Partial_no_label	Label1≠Label2 Head1=Head2 Mod1=Mod2
3	Partial_no_mod	Label1=Label2 Head1=Head2 Mod1≠Mod2
4	Partial_no_head	Label1=Label2 Head1≠Head2 Mod1=Mod2

Table 3. Dependency matches

In addition, VERTa also enables the user to assign different weights to the dependency categories according to the type of evaluation performed.

Finally, a set of language-dependent rules has been implemented in order to a) widen the range of syntactically-different but semantically-equivalent expressions, and b) restrict certain dependency relations (e.g. subject, object).

2.4 N-gram Similarity Module

This module matches chunks in the hypothesis and reference segments. N-grams can be calculated over lexical items (considering the information provided by the Lexical Module), over PoS and over the combination of lexical items and PoS. The n-gram length can go from bigrams to sentence-length grams. This module is particularly useful when evaluating Fluency because it deals with word order.

2.5 Semantic Similarity Module

The Semantic Similarity Module covers different features: Named Entities (NEs), Time Expression (TIMEX) and sentence polarity.

As regards NEs, the module uses Named Entity Recognition and classification (NERC[5]) and Named Entity Linking (NEL[6]). By means of NERC NEs of the same type are identified and matched, whereas NEL helps in matching NEs referring to the same entity regardless of their external form.

Regarding Time Expressions, the Stanford Temporal Tagger (Chang and Manning, 2012) is used to identify and match syntactically-different time expressions with the same referent.

Finally, following Wetzel and Bond (2012), who reported that negation might pose a problem to SMT systems, the metric checks and compares the polarity of the hypothesis and reference segments using the dictionary strategy described in Atserias et al. (2012).

It must be noticed, though, that in the different versions of VERTa submitted to the WMT15 only NERC is used since the rest of features did not prove to be very effective.

2.6 Language Model Module

This is a new module in VERTa, which dramatically differs from the rest of modules because the Language Model (LM) is only applied to the hypothesis sentence. By using a language model we aim at accounting for those segments that, even being syntactically different from their corresponding reference translations, are still fluent; in other words, we will be able to check the correct construction and plausibility of the hypothesis, even if it is very different or not included in any of the reference segments.

In this module we use the berkeleylm[7] implementation (Pauls and Klein, 2011), which allows for uploading LMs in different formats (e.g. arpa LM, google LM). In the experiments presented in section 3, the LM used is the NewsLM[8] re-

[4] Both hypothesis and reference strings are annotated with dependency relations by means of the Stanford parser (de Marneffe et al. 2006).

[5] In order to identify NEs we use the Supersense Tagger (Ciaramita and Altun, 2006).

[6] The NEL Module uses a graph-based NEL tool (Hachey, Radford and Curran, 2010) which links NEs in a text with those in Wikipedia pages.

[7] https://code.google.com/p/berkeleylm/

[8] http://www.quest.dcs.shef.ac.uk/quest_files/de-en/news.3gram.en.lm

leased in the WMT13 Quality Estimation Task as a baseline feature.

3 Experiments

The experiments reported in this section were carried out on the data released in WMT14, all languages into English. Language "all" includes Czech (cs), French (fr), German (de), Hindi (hi) and Russian (ru). All experiments were carried out at segment level and the evaluation sets provided by WMT organizers were used to calculate segment-level correlations.

Our goal in these experiments was two-fold: first, we wanted to test if the combination of Adequacy and Fluency features reported in Comelles (2015) was suitable for the ranking of sentences; and second, we wanted to study if the best weights for each module varied depending on the language pair.

3.1 Adequacy & Fluency Combination

This combination derives from the experiments reported in Comelles (2015), where VERTa was used to find the best combination of linguistic features in order to evaluate Adequacy and Fluency separately.

In those experiments we found out that in order to evaluate Adequacy the most effective modules were the Lexical Module, the Dependency Module, the N-gram Module and the Semantic Module (see Table 4). The strongest influence of the Lexical and the Dependency Modules is not surprising since the former accounts for lexical semantics and the latter links syntax and semantics. It must be highlighted that in the Dependency Module all types of matches were used in order to allow for matching different syntactic structures conveying the same meaning. As for the N-gram Module, n-grams were calculated over lexical items and the n-gram length was restricted to bigrams. Both N-gram and Semantic Modules showed a minor influence since the N-gram Module is more fluency-oriented and the Semantic Module focuses on very partial aspects of the evaluation.

As for the evaluation of Fluency, the ideal combination was achieved when the Dependency Module, the Language Model Module, the N-gram Module and the Morphological Module were combined (see Table 4). Some adjustments had to be performed in the Dependency and N-gram Modules. In the former only the Exact match was used so as to prevent matching constructions conveying similar meaning but which might not be completely grammatical. In the latter, n-grams were calculated over PoS and the n-grams length ranged from bigrams to sentence-length grams. The highest influence of the Dependency, N-gram and LM Modules is clear since they account for syntactic structures, morphosyntax and word order. On the other hand, the low impact of the Morphological Module is due to the fact that English does not show a rich inflectional morphology and SMT systems do not seem to have problem when dealing with it.

Module	Adequacy Weight	Fluency Weight
Lexical	0.47	--
Morphological	--	0.04
Dependency	0.43	0.37
N-gram	0.05	0.29
Semantic	0.05	--
LM	--	0.30

Table 4. Modules combination for Adequacy and Fluency

Since our aim was finding the best way to combine Adequacy and Fluency, we performed several experiments until we found that the best correlation was obtained when the combination was Adequacy (0.70) and Fluency (0.30) (see Table 5). This indicates that semantics has a stronger influence than syntax even when dealing with ranking of segments.

Language Pair	Correlation Coef.
fr-en	0.406
de-en	0.323
hi-en	0.387
cz-en	0.268
ru-en	0.312
Average	0.339

Table 5. Kendall's Correlation for the Adequacy-Fluency Combination

After analyzing these results we decided to submit VERTa-70Adeq30Flu, which combined Adequacy and Fluency features with the weight combination reported above: Adequacy (0.70) and Fluency (0.30).

3.2 Language-dependent Weights

A second experiment was performed in order to study if the best weights of the modules varied depending on the language pair. To this aim, we tried all modules in VERTa with different weight combinations (see Table 6). Last year's data was used to estimate the best weights for VERTa's modules by systematically testing all the different weight combinations (all integer weight combinations totaling 100 using a step of 5).

According to the results obtained, the module that influences the most in almost all language pairs (i.e. de-en, cz-en and ru-en) is the Dependency Module. This might be due to the fact that the dependency relations are a halfway stage between syntax and semantics. They help to link the surface structure of a sentence with its deep structure, closer to semantics. In addition, the Dependency Module relies on information provided by the Lexical Module which is related to lexical semantics, again escaping the word-form and moving towards meaning. The exceptions to the remarkable influence of the Dependency Module are the fr-en pair, where the LM Module shows a stronger influence than the rest of modules, and the hi-en pair, where the Lexical Module is assigned the highest weight. As for the Lexical Module, its influence is rather low for most of the languages – with the exception of the hi-en pair – however, it shows a good performance when the average correlation is calculated. Regarding the N-gram Module, its influence is similar in most language pairs (i.e. hi-en, cz-en and ru-en), as well as the average score, which might be explained by the importance of word order. The Morphological Module does not seem to be very suitable because it only proves efficient for the de-en pair, and up to a certain point for the cz-en pair. Finally, the Semantic Module does not show any impact, which might be due to the fact that only NEs were used and, as already mentioned, they only account for a very partial aspect of the translation.

Lang.	**Weight Combination**[9]						**Corr.**
	L	*M*	*D*	*N*	*S*	*LM*	
fr-en	0	10	10	10	0	70	0.427
de-en	10	20	50	10	0	10	0.323
hi-en	40	0	20	20	0	20	0.390
cz-en	10	10	50	20	10	0	0.269
ru-en	20	0	30	30	0	20	0.318
Aver.	30	0	40	20	0	10	0.339

Table 6. Kendall's Correlation for language-dependent weight combinations

[9] Weights corresponding to: Lexical Module (L), Morphological Module (M), Dependency Module (D), N-gram Module (N), Semantic Module (S) and LM Module (LM).

Given the results obtained, we decided to submit two more versions of VERTa:

- VERTa-W. This version uses the following settings, except for the fr-en pair: Lexical Module (0.30), Dependency Module (0.40), N-gram Module (0.20) and Language Model Module (0.10). The reason why these modules and weights are chosen is that they were the settings that obtained the best average correlation at segment level (see Table 6). As regards the fr-en language pair, since it showed a completely different behaviour to the rest of language pairs, different modules and weights were used. Hence the settings used for the fr-en pair are those reported in Table 6, which involve a really strong influence of the Language Model Module. Using these settings to evaluate the rest of language pairs drops the average correlation of all languages significantly, from 0.339 to 0.310.

- VERTa-EQ. In line with last year's submission, this submission combines all modules in VERTa with equal weights assigned to each module, thus combining linguistic features in a more simple and straightforward way.

3.3 Comparing Different Versions of VERTa

In this section the different versions of VERTa submitted to the WMT15 are compared to those submitted to the WMT14 (see Table 7). In addition, the best and worst systems of the 2014 edition are also included for the sake of comparison.

WMT15 results show that both VERTa-W and VERTa-70Adeq30Flu achieve similar results in the average correlation and for the hi-en language pair. However, VERTa-W performs better for the fr-en and, especially, for the ru-en pair. The reason why VERTa-W performs better for the fr-en pair is that, as explained in section 3.2, the settings used differ completely from those used for the rest of language pairs, since experiments showed that a higher influence of the LM Modules was advisable. As for the ru-en pair, the more efficient performance might be due to the fact that in VERTa-W the Morphological Module and the Semantic Module are disregarded, which coincides with the best setting for ru-en shown in Table 6.

On the other hand, VERTa-70Adeq30Flu performs better for the de-en and cz-en pairs. In both cases this is due to the fact that both

Metric		fr-en	de-en	hi-en	cz-en	ru-en	Average
WMT14	**VERTa-W**	0.399	0.321	0.386	0.263	0.315	0.337
	VERTa-EQ	0.407	0.315	0.384	0.263	0.312	0.336
	Best-WMT14	0.433	0.380	0.434	0.328	0.355	0.386
	Worst-WMT14	0.005	0.001	0.000	0.002	0.001	0.002
WMT15	**VERTa-W**	**0.408**	0.321	**0.387**	0.262	**0.316**	**0.339**
	VERTa-EQ	0.393	0.313	0.370	0.260	0.292	0.325
	VERTa-70Adeq30Flu	0.406	**0.323**	**0.387**	**0.268**	0.312	**0.339**

Table 7. Comparison between VERTa's submission to WMT14 and WMT15

Morphological and Semantic Modules are used in this version which, according to the weight combination in Table 6, allows for a better performance of the metric when evaluating those two language pairs.

As for VERTa-EQ, the last version submitted to WMT15, its performance is the lowest of the three submissions. This is a direct consequence of assigning the same weights to all modules, when experiments have clearly shown that there are some modules more effective than others.

As regards the difference between WMT14 and WMT15 submissions, unfortunately our results have not improved as much as we expected. Nevertheless, both VERTa-W and VERTa-70Adeq30Flu improve their average score in 0.002, from 0.337 to 0.339. As for the scores obtained for each language pair, the cz-en pair undergoes the most remarkable improvement, moving from 0.263 up to 0.268.

4 Conclusions and Future Work

In this paper we have described VERTa, a linguistically-motivated MT metric and the three versions submitted to the WMT15: VERTa-70Adeq30Flu, VERTa-W and VERTa-EQ. VERTa-70Adeq30Flu combines Adequacy features and Fluency features to rank MT segments; VERTa-W uses some of the modules in VERTa with different weights assigned to each module; and finally, VERTa-EQ uses all modules in VERTa with equal weights assigned.

Two first versions of VERTa were submitted last year; however, our current submissions to WMT15 include two more modules: the first new module uses a NERC component whereas the second uses a Language Model.

By means of our experiments we have been able to study two key areas in automatic MT evaluation: a) how Adequacy and Fluency features can be used and adapted to ranking-based evaluation; and b) how VERTa behaves when different pairs of languages are considered.

Our experiments have shown that VERTa shows a stable performance for almost all language pairs evaluated, with the exception of the fr-en pair, for which the LM Module seemed to be the most effective one. Such high influence might indicate that when translating from French into English word order plays an important role and MT evaluation metrics should handle it effectively.

Finally, we have compared our new versions to the versions submitted last year, and although results are not outstanding, VERTa's performance at segment level has improved slightly, especially in the case of VERTa-70Adeq30Flu and VERTa-W.

In the future we would like to apply machine-learning techniques to the combination of modules since we think our metric could greatly benefit from this approach. In addition, since our metric uses a wide range of NLP tools, we would like to explore how NLP tool errors influence the performance of the metric.

References

J. S. Albrecth and R. Hwa. 2007. A Re-examination of Machine Learning Approaches for Sentence-Level MT Evaluation. In *The Proceedings of the 45th Annual Meeting of the ACL*, Prague, Czech Republic.

J. S. Albrecth and R. Hwa. 2007. Regression for Sentence-Level MT Evaluation with Pseudo References. In *The Proceedings of the 45th Annual Meeting of the ACL*, Prague, Czech Republic.

J. Atserias, R. Blanco, J. M. Chenlo and C. Rodriquez. 2012. FBM-Yahoo at RepLab 2012, *CLEF (Online Working Notes/Labs/Workshop) 2012*, September 20, 2012.

A. X. Chang and Ch. D. Manning. 2012. SUTIME: A Library for Recognizing and Normalizing Time Expressions. *8th International Conference on Language Resources and Evaluation (LREC 2012)*.

M. Ciaramita and Y. Altun. 2006. Broad-coverage sense disambiguation and information extraction with a supersense sequence tagger. Empirical Methods in *Natural Language Processing (EMNLP)*.

E. Comelles. 2015. *Automatic Machine Translation Evaluation: A Qualitative Approach*. Doctoral Dissertation. University of Barcelona.

E. Comelles and J. Atserias. 2014. VERTa participation in the WMT14 Metrics Task in *Proceedings of the Ninth Workshop on Statistical Machine Translation (ACL-2014)*. Baltimore, Maryland, USA.

M.C. de Marneffe, B. MacCartney and Ch. D. Manning. 2006. Generating Typed Dependency Parses from Phrase Structure Parses in *Proceedings of the 5th Edition of the International Conference on Language Resources and Evaluation (LREC-2006)*. Genoa, Italy.

M. J. Denkowski and A. Lavie. 2014. Meteor Universal: Language Specific Translation Evaluation for Any Target Language in *Proceedings of the Ninth Workshop on Statistical Machine Translation (ACL-2014)*. Baltimore, Maryland, USA.

S. Gautam, and P. 2014. LAYERED: Metric for Machine Translation Evaluation in *Proceedings of the Ninth Workshop on Statistical Machine Translation (ACL-2014)*. Baltimore, Maryland, USA.

J. Giménez and Ll. Màrquez. 2007. Linguistic features for automatic evaluation of heterogeneous MT systems in *Proceedings of the 2nd Workshop on Statistical Machine Translation (ACL),* Prague, Czech Repubilc.

J. Giménez and Ll. Màrquez. 2008. A smorgasbord of features for automatic MT evaluation in *Proceedings of the 3rd Workshop on Statistical Machine Translation (ACL)*. Columbus. OH.

J. Gimenez. 2008. *Empirical Machine Translation and its Evaluation*. Doctoral Dissertation. UPC.

J. Giménez and Ll. Márquez. 2010. Linguistic Measures for Automatic Machine Translation Evaluation. *Machine Translation*, 24(3–4),77–86. Springer.

M. González, A. Barrón-Cedeño and Ll. Márquez. 2014. IPA and STOUT: Leveraging Linguistic and Source-based Features for Machine Translation Evaluation in *Proceedings of the Ninth Workshop on Statistical Machine Translation (ACL-2014)*. Baltimore, Maryland, USA.

B. Hachey, W. Radford and J. R. Curran. 2011. Graph-based named entity linking with Wikipedia in *Proceedings of the 12th International conference on Web information system engineering*, pages 213-226, Springer-Verlag, Berlin, Heidelberg.

Y. He, J. Du, A. Way and J. van Genabith. 2010. The DCU Dependency-based Metric in WMT-Metrics MATR 2010. *In Proceedings of the Joint Fifth Workshop on Statistical Machine Translation and Metrics MATR (WMT 2010)*, Uppsala, Sweden.

S. Joty, F. Guzmán, Ll. Márquez and P. Nakov. 2014. DiscoTK: Using Discourse Structure for Machine Translation Evaluation in *Proceedings of the Ninth Workshop on Statistical Machine Translation (ACL-2014)*. Baltimore, Maryland, USA.

G. Leusch and H. Ney. 2008. BLEUSP, INVWER, CDER: Three improved MT evaluation measures. In *NIST Metrics for Machine Translation 2008 Evaluation (MericsMATR08)*, Waikiki, Honolulu, Hawaii, October 2008.

D. Liu and D. Hildea. 2005. Syntactic Features for Evaluation of Machine Translation in *Proceedings of the ACL Workshop on Intrinsic and Extrinsic Evaluation Measures for Machine Translation and/or Summarization*, Ann Arbor

Ch. Lo, A. K. Tumurulu and D. Wu. 2012. Fully Automatic Semantic MT Evaluation. *Proceedings of the 7th Wrokshop on Statistical Machine Translation*, Montréal, Canada, June 7-8.

K. Owczarzak, J. van Genabith and A. Way. 2007. Dependency-Based Automatic Evaluation for Machine Translation in *Proceedings of SSST, NAACL-HLT/AMTA Workshop on Syntax and Structure I Statistical Translation,* Rochester, New York.

K. Owczarzak, J. van Genabith and A. Way. 2007. Labelled Dependencies in Machine Translation Evaluation in *Proceedings of the ACL Workshop on Statistical Machine Translation,* Prague, Czech Republic.

K. Papineni, S. Roukos, T. Ward and W. Zhu. 2002. BLEU: A Method for Automatic Evaluation of Machine Translation. In *Proceedings of the 40th Annual Meeting of the Association for Computational Linguistics* (ACL02). Philadelphia. PA.

A. Pauls and D. Klein. 2011. Faster and smaller *N*-gram language models in *Proceedings of the 49th Annual Meeting of the Association for Computational Linguistics: Human Language Technologies - Volume 1* (HLT '11), Vol. 1. Association for Computational Linguistics, Stroudsburg, PA, USA.

L. Specia and J. Giménez. 2010. Combining Confidence Estimation and Reference-based Metrics for Segment-level MT Evaluation. *The Ninth Conference of the Association for Machine Translation in the Americas* (AMTA 2010), Denver, Colorado.

D. Wetzel and F. Bond. 2012. Enriching Parallel Corpora for Statistical Machine Translation with Semantic Negation Rephrasing. *Proceedings of SSST-6, Sixth Workshop on Syntax, Semantics and Structure in Statistical Translation*, Jeju, Republic of Korea.

UPF-Cobalt Submission to WMT15 Metrics Task

Marina Fomicheva **Núria Bel** **Iria da Cunha**
IULA, Universitat Pompeu Fabra
{marina.fomicheva,nuria.bel,iria.dacunha}@upf.edu

Anton Malinovskiy
Nuroa Internet S. L.
amalinovskiy@gmail.com

Abstract

An important limitation of automatic evaluation metrics is that, when comparing Machine Translation (MT) to a human reference, they are often unable to discriminate between acceptable variation and the differences that are indicative of MT errors. In this paper we present UPF-Cobalt evaluation system that addresses this issue by penalizing the differences in the syntactic contexts of aligned candidate and reference words. We evaluate our metric using the data from WMT workshops of the recent years and show that it performs competitively both at segment and at system levels.

1 Introduction

Current automatic MT evaluation methods are grounded on the following key idea: the closer an MT is to a professional Human Translation (HT), the higher its quality. Thus, metrics typically calculate evaluation scores based on some sort of similarity between machine and human translations. The performance of evaluation systems is in its turn evaluated by calculating the correlation with human judgments. Manual quality assessment can be conducted in various ways: adequacy and fluency scoring, calculating post-editing cost or post-editing time, error analysis, ranking, etc. In the latter case, humans are asked to compare the outputs of different MT systems and rank them in terms of quality. Ranking-based evaluation has gained a lot of attention in the recent years and is used in important evaluation campaigns such as the Metrics task at the Workshop on Machine Translation (WMT). This setting is preferred, since it has been shown to yield higher inter-annotator agreement than absolute quality assessment (Callison-Burch et al., 2007).

In our opinion, one of the main reasons why the correlation between automatic evaluation and human rankings is still not satisfactory is that metrics' scores are not discriminative enough to approximate human comparisons. Given various candidate translations of the same source sentence, all of them different from the reference, evaluation systems are often unable to determine which translation is better as they cannot tell apart candidate-reference differences related to acceptable linguistic variation and the differences induced by MT errors. Furthermore, if all candidate translations contain a number of translation errors, metrics fail to predict the human ranking because they make no estimation of the relative importance of different types of MT errors for the overall translation quality.

We suggest that the aforementioned limitations can be addressed by means of enhancing word comparison with contextual information. Variation between two translation options is acceptable if semantically similar words in the corresponding sentences occur in equivalent contexts. In case of translation errors either the lexical choice is inappropriate or the syntactic contexts of the words are different (incorrect choice of function words, word order errors, etc.).

Our evaluation metric, UPF-Cobalt[1] exploits contextual information by means of weighting the contribution of each pair of lexically similar words in candidate and reference translations depending on whether they occur in similar syntactic environments. Syntactic functions of the words in context are taken into consideration. In this way, more

This work was supported by IULA (UPF) and the FI-DGR grant program of the Generalitat de Catalunya.

[1]The metric is freely available for download at https://github.com/amalinovskiy/upf-cobalt.

fine-grained distinctions can be made regarding the relative importance of mistranslated material.

In this paper we present UPF-Cobalt submission to the WMT15 Metrics task. Experiments show that UPF-Cobalt achieves competitive results, both at segment and at system levels. On WMT14 data, our metric would have been ranked as second-best performing metric at segment level, and tied with the first best-performing metric at system level.

The rest of this paper is organized as follows. Section 2 describes UPF-Cobalt. In Section 3 we present the experiments and analyze the results. Section 4 examines relevant pieces of related work. Finally, in Section 5 we give the conclusions and suggest directions for future work.

2 Metric Description

Following MacCartney et al. (2006), we argue that for measuring sentence similarity and related tasks, identifying similar words and deciding on the relation between the two sentences should be kept separate. This is especially relevant for MT evaluation where system output may share a high number of similar words with the reference and still be grammatically ill-formed and totally unacceptable. Thus, not only the number but also the characteristics of the correspondences between candidate and reference words must be taken into consideration. Therefore, we follow a two-stage approach to evaluation. First, MT is aligned to the reference. Next, the candidate translation is scored taking into account both the number of aligned words and their roles in the corresponding sentences.

2.1 Monolingual Word Aligner

We assume that using better candidate-reference alignment results in better MT evaluation. Research in the area of monolingual alignment demonstrates that exploiting syntactic context to discriminate between candidate pairs for alignment significantly improves the results (MacCartney et al., 2008; Thadani et al., 2012; Yao et al, 2013; Sultan et al., 2014). The alignment module of UPF-Cobalt builds on an existing system Monolingual Word Aligner (MWA)[2] which takes context information into account and has been shown to significantly improve on state-of-the-art results (Sultan et al., 2014).

MWA exploits lexical similarity and contextual evidence to make alignment decisions. Lexical similarity component identifies possible candidates for alignment. In addition to exact and lemma match, Paraphrase Database (Ganitkevitch et al., 2013) of lexical and phrasal paraphrases is employed to recognize semantically similar words.[3]

We enhance MWA with additional lexical similarity resources to maximize the coverage of the alignment. In addition to the paraphrase database, UPF-Cobalt employs WordNet synsets (Miller and Fellbaum, 2007) and distributional similarity (Turney and Pantel, 2010). WordNet is commonly used in MT evaluation and related fields for dealing with lexical variation. By contrast, to the best of our knowledge, distributional similarity has not yet been exploited for the evaluation task.

We use publically available distributional similarity resource (Levy and Goldberg, 2014), which contains dependency-based word embeddings. To minimize the noise, we establish the following restrictions. To be considered candidates for alignment the words must have the cosine similarity higher than a threshold (based on data observation, we currently define it as 0.25). Also, they must have at least one pair of exact matching content words in their contexts.

Contextual evidence is used to choose the best alignment candidates and is defined as the number of similar words in the contexts of the words to be aligned. At syntactic level, the context is constituted by the head and dependent nodes in a dependency graph.[4] Context words are considered as evidence for alignment if they are lexically similar and have the same or equivalent syntactic relations with the words to be aligned.

Sultan et al. (2014) have developed a list of mappings between different syntactic functions that instantiate the same semantic relation. Thus, for example, the dependency relation between subject and predicate in an active clause and by-agent and predicate in a passive clause are defined to be equivalent. We consider that this functionality is helpful for addressing syntactic variation in reference-based MT evaluation and reuse it for

[2] `https://github.com/ma-sultan/monolingual-word-aligner`.

[3] MWA does not support phrase-level alignments, but the framework is flexible enough to integrate them in the future.

[4] The dependencies are extracted with Stanford dependency parser (de Marneffe et al., 2006).

scoring.

2.2 Scoring Method

Given a candidate-reference alignment, we further need to know if the correspondences identified at the alignment stage are actually indicative of MT quality. UPF-Cobalt computes a score for each pair of aligned words as a combination of their lexical similarity and the differences of the syntactic contexts in which the words occur.

Lexical Similarity. The weights for different types of lexical similarity are established heuristically, depending on the accuracy of the lexical resource that was used for aligning them:[5]

- Word form: 1.0
- Lemma or stem: 0.9
- WordNet synsets: 0.8
- Paraphrase database: 0.6
- Distributional similarity: 0.5

Context Penalty. Context penalty is applied in cases where aligned words play different roles in the corresponding sentences. For each pair of aligned nodes (*h*) in the candidate translation and (*r*) in the reference translation context penalty is calculated as follows:

$$CP(h,r) = \frac{\sum_{1..i} w(c_i)}{count(c)} \times ln(count(c)+1)$$
$$w(c_i) = \begin{cases} 0, & \text{if } c_i \in |A| \\ w(dep(c_i)), & \text{otherwise} \end{cases} \quad (1)$$

Where (*c*) refers to the words that belong to the syntactic context of the reference word (*r*) (immediate neighbors in the dependency graph).[6] If the context word is found in the set of aligned word pairs $|A|$ and its counterpart in the candidate translation has the same or equivalent syntactic relation with the word (*h*), the weight $w(c_i)$ equals to 0. Otherwise, the weight is defined according to the relative importance of the dependency function of the context word. Intuitively, mistranslating or omitting words with syntactic functions that correspond to arguments alters the context to a greater extent than dropping a determiner or an adjunct. We define three groups of syntactic functions accordingly and establish the corresponding weights as follows:

- Arguments and complements: 1.0
- Modifiers and adjuncts: 0.8
- Specifiers and auxiliaries: 0.2

The natural logarithm of $count(c)$ in Formula (1) gives a higher value to the contextual difference when the number of context words is high, while limiting the increase if the number of context words continues to grow. The final value of context penalty is normalized from 0 to 1 using logarithmic function:

$$Pen(h,r) = 2 \times \frac{1}{1+e^{-CP(h,r)}} \quad (2)$$

Given the values of lexical similarity and context penalty, the score for each pair of aligned word is defined as follows:

$$a(h,r) = LexSim(h,r) - Pen(h,r) \quad (3)$$

Sentence-level score is then calculated as a weighted combination of precision and recall over the sum of the scores for aligned candidate and reference words. To obtain system-level scores, we computed the ratio of sentences in which each system was assigned the highest sentence-level score by our metric.

3 Experiments

We conduct experiments with the data from WMT13 and WMT14 Metrics tasks (Macháček and Bojar, 2013; Macháček and Bojar, 2014). To evaluate our metric's performance at segment level, we use Kendall's Tau correlation (τ) with human rankings, as defined in (Macháček and Bojar, 2014). At system level, we use Pearson correlation coefficient (r). Table 1 presents the results averaged over all into-English translation directions. For the sake of comparison, we provide the results for the best performing metrics that participated in WMT13 and WMT14 Metrics tasks, as well as baseline metrics BLEU (Papineni et al., 2002) and Meteor (Denkowski and Lavie, 2014).

As shown in Table 1, our approach is competitive (UPF-Cobalt would have been ranked as the best performing metric on WMT13 data and as the second best on WMT14 data) and generalizes well

[5] We experimented with optimizing the weights for different types of lexical similarity, as well as for the classes of dependency functions discussed below. However, the optimization gave approximately the same values, showing that our intuition was essentially correct.

[6] Context penalty is calculated both on reference and on candidate sides and the resulting values are averaged.

	Segment-level		System-level	
Metric	WMT13	WMT14	WMT13	WMT14
DiscoTK-Party-Tuned (Guzman et al., 2014)	-	0.386	-	0.944
BEER (Stanojević and Sima'an, 2014)	-	0.362	-	-
REDCombSent (Wu and Yu, 2014)	-	0.356	-	-
SimpBLEU-Recall (Song et al., 2013)	0.215	-	0.923	-
Depref-Align (Wu et al., 2013)	0.238	-	0.926	-
BLEU (Papineni et al., 2002)	0.197	0.285	0.854	0.888
Meteor (Denkowski and Lavie, 2014)	0.264	0.354	0.950	0.829
UPF-Cobalt	0.273	0.367	0.956	0.944

Table 1: Evaluation results on WMT13 and WMT14 datasets at segment and system levels

across different datasets with no need for parameter optimization.

In addition to the overall evaluation, we performed a series of ablation tests in order to assess the impact of the individual features of UPF-Cobalt. Each row in Table 2 below shows a feature excluded from the metric and the averaged Kendall's tau segment-level correlation for WMT14 dataset.

	Kendall's (τ)
UPF-Cobalt	0.367
(-) context penalty	0.319
(-) distrib. similarity	0.357
(-) weights on dep. functions	0.360
(-) equiv. dep. types	0.363

Table 2: Ablation test results

Context penalty. To estimate the benefit of using our context penalty we substituted it with fragmentation penalty from Meteor, which explicitly penalizes differences in sequential word order. As expected, this results in a significant drop in the correlation. Thus, this new component is indeed crucial for our metric's performance.

MWA has been shown to outperform Meteor in the alignment task. However, contrary to our expectations, simply using a more accurate aligner does not suffice to improve the correlation (Meteor achieves 0.354 correlation on this dataset). Manual inspection of the results shows that this is primarily due to the fact that MWA does not support phrase-level alignments. This functionality is highly relevant for the evaluation task as it allows covering acceptable variation that involves multiword expressions. We plan to integrate phrasal alignments in the metric in the future.

Distributional similarity. Removing this component implies a considerable decrease in the correlation. Qualitative analysis of the results shows that its main contribution concerns cases of quasi-synonyms, i.e. words that can be considered synonymous only given the similarity of their contexts. The noise introduced by the component is neutralized by context penalty. If unrelated words are aligned, their context penalty will be high and aligning them won't increase sentence-level evaluation score. Also, in the ranking formulation of the evaluation task, distributional similarity helps to discriminate between low-quality translations. That is to say, it allows distinguishing sentences where words are at least minimally related from sentences, in which, for instance, source-language words are simply left untranslated.

Dependency weights. To test if giving different weights to contextual differences according to the dependency functions of the words involved, we put the values of all the weights to 1. This negatively affects the results, confirming that some differences are stronger indicators of MT errors than others. Thus, using the proposed weighting scheme the metric is capable of discriminating more or less serious MT errors based on the relative importance of mistranslated material.

Equivalence of syntactic constructions. Eliminating this functionality produces a smaller decrease in the correlation. Representing syntactic context as immediate neighbors of the word in a dependency graph allows covering a limited set of equivalent constructions, which are not frequent enough to have a significant impact on the results. The framework is flexible and more complex context equivalence definitions can be integrated in the future.

To appreciate the advantages of the metric, Table 3 provides a qualitative comparison of UPF-Cobalt's performance with strong baseline metric Meteor.[7] In this example, Meteor assigns low

[7]Stanford typed dependencies from Marneffe and Manning, (2008) are used for the description of syntactic relations.

	Equivalent dep. types	Scores	
Ref: An Obama voter 's cry of despair.		UPF-Cobalt	Meteor
Cand1: The cry of despair of a voter for Obama.	*prep_of* ≈ *poss* *prep_for* ≈ *nn*	0.804	0.389
Cand2: The cry of despair of a voter Obama.	*prep_of* ≈ *poss* *appos* ≠ *nn*	0.646	0.393

Table 3: Example of candidate and reference translations with the corresponding Meteor and UPF-Cobalt scores

scores to both candidate translations, due to the differences in word order and the presence of function words absent in the reference. However, it is clear that Candidate 1 is perfectly acceptable, whereas Candidate 2 contains an error concerning the relation between the words "voter" and "Obama". UPF-Cobalt correctly assigns a higher score to Candidate 1. Here all the content words are aligned and no context penalty is applied, since the syntactic contexts in which the words occur are equal or equivalent. Thus, *prep_for* relation in the candidate translation is equivalent to noun compound modifier relation *nn* in the reference and *prep_of* label in the candidate corresponds to possession modifier *poss* in the reference. UPF-Cobalt assigns a lower score to Candidate 2 due to the differences in the syntactic contexts of the words "voter" (context penalty – 0.426) and "Obama" (context penalty – 0.286), which constitute a translation error. Thus, context penalty values calculated for each pair of aligned words can be used for spotting and locating translation errors.

Qualitative analysis of the results also shows an interesting pattern in cases where UPF-Cobalt is outperformed by other metrics. This pattern is particularly relevant in the ranking evaluation setting. Consider the following example.

Ref: *Nevada has already completed a pilot.*
Cand1: *Nevada already has completed the pilot project.*
Cand2: *Nevada has already completed the pilot project.*

When ranking translations humans intend to avoid ties whenever possible. Both Candidate 1 and Candidate 2 are essentially correct, but the second translation is more adequate with regards to the norms and conventions of target language use. UPF-Cobalt assigns equal scores to both MTs. Thus, it successfully avoids penalizing acceptable differences in word order (the differences that do not affect the output of the dependency parser). However, it is not able to make more fine-grained distinctions regarding the fluency of MT. This issue can be addressed by integrating target language model features in the metric.

4 Related Work

Metrics based on string-level comparison take context into account in a simplistic manner. For instance, BLEU (Papineni et al., 2002) uses n-grams with length (1-4) and Meteor (Denkowski and Lavie, 2014) addresses the differences in sequential word order by means of fragmentation penalty, based on the number of adjacent aligned words. This often leads to penalizing acceptable differences induced by the use of semantically equivalent expressions. At the same time, spurious matches of the words that coincide in their surface form but play totally different roles in the corresponding sentences can incorrectly increase evaluation score.

To address these limitations a series of linguistically informed approaches have been proposed. Amigó et al. (2006) measure the degree of overlap between the dependency trees of candidate and reference translations. Giménez and Màrquez (2010) propose a combination of specialized similarity measures operating at different linguistic levels (lexical, syntactic and semantic). Guzman et al. (2014) further enrich this metric set with discourse level information. Padó et al. (2009) measure MT quality based on a rich set of features motivated by textual entailment.

Our work follows this line of research and exploits syntactic context to characterize the correspondences between the words in candidate and reference translations. In addition, we address the problem of syntactic variation that has rarely been dealt with in linguistically-informed MT evaluation. As shown in Fomicheva et al. (2015), this kind of variation is a regular source of differences between human reference and MT. Structural shifts (Ahrenberg and Merkel, 2000) are common practice in HT. Translators often introduce optional changes to the original sentence in order to adhere to specific principles of target language use, including stylistic issues and discourse processing conditions. MT may not contain such shifts but still be grammatically well-formed and perfectly deliver the contents of the source sentence. By taking into consideration the equivalence of syntactic constructions it is possible to avoid penalizing MT in these cases.

5 Conclusions and Future Work

We have shown that using contextual information helps to distinguish candidate translations that are different from the reference and still essentially correct from those that share high number of words with HT but fail to preserve the meaning of the source sentence due to translation errors.

Also, we enhanced existing methods for addressing meaning-preserving variation by exploiting distributional similarity at lexical level and classes of equivalent dependency types at syntactic level. The results demonstrate that the metric achieves competitive performance on WMT13 and WMT14 data.

As future work, we consider improving the metric by extending the alignment component to phrase-level and refining the equivalent dependency types to increase the coverage of linguistic variation at syntactic level. Another interesting direction would be to integrate target-language features and take into consideration the properties of non-aligned material. Finally, we plan to test if the metric can be successfully used for error detection and classification.

References

Lars Ahrenberg and Magnus Merkel. 2000. Correspondence Measures for MT Evaluation. In *Proceedings of the Second International Conference on Linguistic Resources and Evaluation*, 1255–1261. Athens, Greece.

Chris Callison-Burch, Cameron Fordyce, Philipp Koehn, Chrstof Monz, and Josh Schroeder. 2007. (Meta-)Evaluation of machine translation. In *Proceedings of the Second Workshop on Statistical Machine Translation*, 136–158. Prague, Czech Republic. Association for Computational Linguistics (ACL).

Michael Denkowski and Alon Lavie. 2014. Meteor Universal: Language Specific Translation Evaluation for Any Target Language. In *Proceedings of the Ninth Workshop on Statistical Machine Translation*. Baltimore, USA. ACL.

Marina Fomicheva, Núria Bel, and Iria da Cunha. 2015. Neutralizing the Effect of Translation Shifts on Automatic Machine Translation Evaluation. In *Gelbukh, Alexander (ed.) Computational Linguistics and Intelligent Text Processing: 16th International Conference, CICLing 2015: Proceedings 1*, 596–607.

Juri Ganitkevitch, Benjamin Van Durme, and Chris Callison-Burch. 2013. PPDB: The Paraphrase Database. In *Proceedings of the 2013 Conference of the North American Chapter of the Association for Computational Linguistics (NAACL)*, 758–764. ACL.

Jesus Giménez and Lluís Màrquez. 2010. Linguistic Measures for Automatic Machine Translation Evaluation. *Machine Translation*, 24(3-4):77–86.

Francisco Guzman, Shafiq Joty, Lluís Màrquez, Alessandro Moschitti, Preslav Nakov, and Massimo Nicosia. 2014. Learning to Differentiate Better from Worse Translations. In *Proceedings of the 2014 Conference on Empirical Methods in Natural Language Processing (EMNLP)*, 214–220. Doha, Qatar. ACL.

Omer Levy and Yoav Goldberg. 2014. Dependency-based word embeddings. In *Proceedings of the 52nd Annual Meeting of the ACL (Volume 2: Short Papers)*. Baltimore, USA. ACL.

Bill MacCartney, Michel Galley, and Christopher D. Manning. 2008. A Phrase-Based Alignment Model for Natural Language Inference. In *Proceedings of the 2008 EMNLP Conference*, 214–220. Honolulu, USA. ACL.

Bill MacCartney, Trond Grenager, Marie de Marneffe, Daniel Cer, and Christopher D. Manning. 2006. Learning to recognize features of valid textual entailments. In *Proceedings of the NAACL – Human Language Technologies*.

Matouš Macháček and Ondřej Bojar. 2014. Results of the WMT14 metrics shared task. In *Proceedings of the Ninth Workshop on Statistical Machine Translation*. Baltimore, USA. ACL.

Matouš Macháček and Ondřej Bojar. 2013. Results of the WMT13 metrics shared task. In *Proceedings of the Eighth Workshop on Statistical Machine Translation*, 45–51. Sofia, Bulgaria. ACL.

Marie-Catherine de Marneffe and Christopher D. Manning. 2008. Stanford typed dependencies manual. Technical Report, Stanford University.

Marie-Catherine de Marneffe, Bill MacCartney, and Christopher D. Manning. 2006. Generating Typed Dependency Parses from Phrase Structure Parses. In *Proceedings of the International Conference on Language Resources and Evaluation*, 449–454.

George Miller and Christiane Fellbaum. 2007. WordNet. `http://wordnet.princeton.edu`.

Sebastian Padó, Daniel Cer, Michel Galley, Dan Jurafsky, and Christopher D. Manning. 2009. Measuring machine translation quality as semantic equivalence: A metric based on entailment features. *Machine Translation*, 23:181–193.

Kishore Papineni, Salim Roukos, Todd Ward, and WeiJing Zhu. 2002. BLEU: a method for automatic evaluation of machine translation. In *Proceedings of 40th Annual Meeting of the ACL*, 311–318. Philadelphia, USA.

Xingyi Song, Trevor Cohn, and Lucia Specia. 2013. BLEU deconstructed: Designing a better MT Evaluation Metric. In *Proceedings of the 14th International Conference on Intelligent Text Processing and Computational Linguistics*.

Miloš Stanojević and Khalil Sima'an. 2014. BEER: A Smooth Sentence Level Evaluation Metric with Rich Ingredients. In *Proceedings of the Ninth Workshop on Statistical Machine Translation*. Baltimore, USA. ACL.

Arafat Md Sultan, Steven Bethard, and Tamara Summer. 2014. Back to Basics for Monolingual Alignment: Exploiting Word Similarity and Contextual Evidence. *Transactions of the Association of Computational Linguistics*, volume 2(1):219–230.

Kapil Thadani, Scott Martin, and Michael White. 2012. A Joint Phrasal and Dependency Model for Paraphrase Alignment. In *Proceedings of 24th International Conference on Computational Linguistics, COLING 2012*, 1229–1238. Bombay, India.

Peter D. Turney and Patrick Pantel. 2010. From Frequency to Meaning: Vector Space Models of Semantics. *Journal of Artificial Intelligence Research*, 37:141–188.

Xiaofeng Wu, Hui Yu, and Qun Liu. 2014. RED: DCU-CASICT Participation in WMT2014 Metrics Task. In *Proceedings of the Ninth Workshop on Statistical Machine Translation*. Baltimore, USA. ACL.

Xiaofeng Wu, Hui Yu, and Qun Liu. 2013. DCU Participation in WMT2013 Metrics Task. In *Proceedings of the Eighth Workshop on Statistical Machine Translation*. Sofia, Bulgaria. ACL.

Xuchen Yao, Benjamin Van Durme, Chris Callison-Burch, and Peter Clark. 2013. Semi-Markov Phrase-based Monolingual Alignment. In *Proceedings of the 2013 EMNLP Conference*, 590–600. ACL.

Machine Translation Evaluation using Recurrent Neural Networks

Rohit Gupta[1], **Constantin Orăsan**[1], **Josef van Genabith**[2]
[1]Research Group in Computational Linguistics, University of Wolverhampton, UK
[2]Saarland University and German Research Center for Artificial Intelligence (DFKI), Germany
{r.gupta, c.orasan}@wlv.ac.uk
josef.van_genabith@dfki.de

Abstract

This paper presents our metric (UoW-LSTM) submitted in the WMT-15 metrics task. Many state-of-the-art Machine Translation (MT) evaluation metrics are complex, involve extensive external resources (e.g. for paraphrasing) and require tuning to achieve the best results. We use a metric based on dense vector spaces and Long Short Term Memory (LSTM) networks, which are types of Recurrent Neural Networks (RNNs). For WMT-15 our new metric is the best performing metric overall according to Spearman and Pearson (Pre-TrueSkill) and second best according to Pearson (TrueSkill) system level correlation.

1 Introduction

Deep learning approaches have turned out to be successful in many NLP applications such as paraphrasing (Mikolov et al., 2013b; Socher et al., 2011), sentiment analysis (Socher et al., 2013b), parsing (Socher et al., 2013a) and machine translation (Mikolov et al., 2013a). While dense vector space representations such as those obtained through Deep Neural Networks (DNNs) or Recurrent Neural Networks (RNNs) are able to capture semantic similarity for words (Mikolov et al., 2013b), segments (Socher et al., 2011) and documents (Le and Mikolov, 2014) naturally, traditional measures can only achieve this using resources like WordNet and paraphrase databases.

This paper presents a novel, efficient and compact MT evaluation measure based on RNNs. Our metric (Gupta et al., 2015) is simple in the sense that it does not require much machinery and resources apart from the dense word vectors. This cannot be said of most of the state-of-the-art MT evaluation metrics, which tend to be complex and require extensive feature engineering. Our metric is based on RNNs and particularly on Tree Long Short Term Memory (Tree-LSTM) networks (Tai et al., 2015). LSTM is a sequence learning technique which uses a memory cell to preserve a state over a long period of time. This enables distributed representations of sentences using distributed representations of words. Tree-LSTM (Tai et al., 2015) is a recent approach, which is an extension of the simple LSTM framework (Hochreiter and Schmidhuber, 1997; Zaremba and Sutskever, 2014).

2 Related Work

Many metrics have been proposed for MT evaluation. Earlier popular metrics are based on n-gram counts (e.g. BLEU (Papineni et al., 2002) and NIST (Doddington, 2002)) or word error rate. Other popular metrics like METEOR (Denkowski and Lavie, 2014) and TERp (Snover et al., 2008) also use external resources like WordNet and paraphrase databases. However, system-level correlation with human judgements for these metrics remains below 0.90 Pearson correlation coefficient (as per WMT-14 results, BLEU-0.888, NIST-0.867, METEOR-0.829, TER-0.826, WER-0.821).

Recent best performing metrics in the WMT-14 metric shared task (Machácek and Bojar, 2014) used a combination of different metrics. The top performing system DiskoTK-Party-Tuned (Joty et al., 2014) in the WMT-14 task uses five different discourse metrics and twelve different metrics from the ASIYA MT evaluation toolkit (Giménez and Màrquez, 2010). The metric computes the number of common sub-trees between a reference and a translation using a convolution tree kernel (Collins and Duffy, 2001). The basic version of the metric does not perform well but in combination with the other 12 metrics from the ASIYA toolkit obtained the best results for the WMT-14 metric shared task. Another top performing metric LAYERED (Gautam and Bhattacharyya, 2014), uses linear interpolation of different metrics. LAYERED uses BLEU and TER to capture lexical similarity, Hamming score and Kendall Tau Distance (Birch and Osborne, 2011) to identify syntactic similarity, and dependency parsing (De Marneffe et al., 2006) and the Universal Networking Language[1] for semantic similarity.

For our participation in the WMT-15 task, we used our metric ReVal (Gupta et al., 2015). ReVal metric is based on dense vector spaces and Tree Long Short Term Memory networks. This metric achieved state of the art results for the WMT-14 dataset. The metric including training data is available at https://github.com/rohitguptacs/ReVal.

3 LSTMs and Tree-LSTMs

Recurrent Neural Networks allow processing of arbitrary length sequences, but early RNNs had the problem of vanishing and exploding gradients (Bengio et al., 1994). RNNs with LSTM (Hochreiter and Schmidhuber, 1997) tackle this problem by introducing a memory cell composed of a unit called constant error carousel (CEC) with multiplicative input and output gate units. Input gates protect against irrelevant inputs and output gates against current irrelevant memory contents. This architecture is capable of capturing important pieces of information seen in a bigger context. Tree-LSTM is an extension of simple LSTM. A typical LSTM processes the information sequentially whereas Tree-LSTM architectures enable sentence representation through a syntactic structure. Equation (1) represents the composition of a hidden state vector for an LSTM architecture. For a simple LSTM, c_t represents the memory cell and o_t the output gate at time step t in a sequence. For Tree-LSTM, c_t represents the memory cell and o_t represents the output gate corresponding to node t in a tree. The structural processing of Tree-LSTM makes it more favourable for representing sentences. For example, dependency tree structure captures syntactic features and model parameters capture the importance of words (content vs. function words).

$$h_t = o_t \odot \tanh c_t \tag{1}$$

[1] http://www.undl.org/unlsys/unl/unl2005/UW.htm

Figure 1 shows simple LSTM and Tree-LSTM architectures.

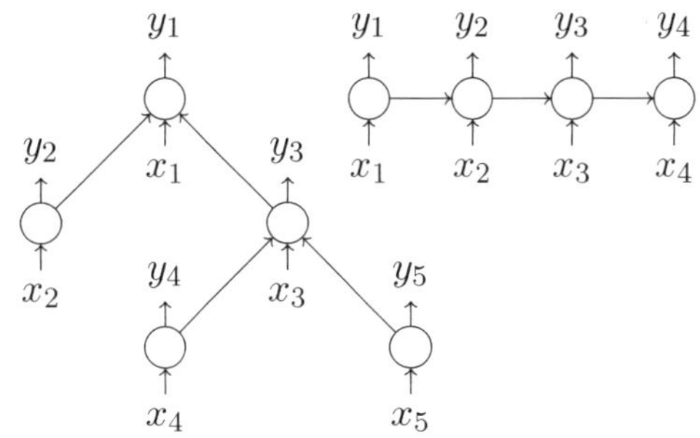

Figure 1: Tree-LSTM (left) and simple LSTM (right)

4 Evaluation Metric

We used the ReVal (Gupta et al., 2015) metric for this task. This metric represents both the reference (h_{ref}) and the translation (h_{tra}) using a dependency Tree-LSTM (Tai et al., 2015) and predicts the similarity score $\hat{y}$ based on a neural network which considers both distance and angle between h_{ref} and h_{tra}:

$$\begin{aligned} h_\times &= h_{ref} \odot h_{tra} \\ h_+ &= |h_{ref} - h_{tra}| \\ h_s &= \sigma\left(W^{(\times)}h_\times + W^{(+)}h_+ + b^{(h)}\right) \\ \hat{p}_\theta &= \text{softmax}\left(W^{(p)}h_s + b^{(p)}\right) \\ \hat{y} &= r^T\hat{p}_\theta \end{aligned} \tag{2}$$

where, σ is a sigmoid function, $\hat{p}_\theta$ is the estimated probability distribution vector and $r^T = [1\ 2 ... K]$. The cost function $J(\theta)$ is defined over probability distributions p and $\hat{p}_\theta$ using regularised Kullback-Leibler (KL) divergence.

$$J(\theta) = \frac{1}{n}\sum_{i=1}^{n} \text{KL}\left(p^{(i)}||\hat{p}_\theta^{(i)}\right) + \frac{\lambda}{2}||\theta||_2^2 \tag{3}$$

In Equation 3, i represents the index of each training pair, n is the number of training pairs and p is the sparse target distribution such that $y = r^T p$ is defined as follows:

$$p_j = \begin{cases} y - \lfloor y \rfloor, & j = \lfloor y \rfloor + 1 \\ \lfloor y \rfloor - y + 1, & j = \lfloor y \rfloor \\ 0 & \text{otherwise} \end{cases}$$

Metric	fr-en	fi-en	de-en	cs-en	ru-en	PAvg	Pre-TrueSkills Avg	SAvg
UoW-LSTM	**.997** ± .003	**.976** ± .008	.960 ± .010	.983 ± .003	.963 ± .009	.976 ± .007	**.976** ± .011	**.916** ± .038
DPMFCOMB	.995 ± .004	.958 ± .011	.973 ± .009	.991 ± .002	.974 ± .008	**.978** ± .007	.970 ± .012	.882 ± .041
BEER_TREEPEL	.981 ± .008	.971 ± .010	.952 ± .012	.992 ± .002	**.981** ± .008	.975 ± .008	.962 ± .014	.861 ± .051
DPMF	**.997** ± .003	.951 ± .011	.960 ± .010	.984 ± .003	.973 ± .008	.973 ± .007	.965 ± .012	.893 ± .035
UPF-COBALT	.987 ± .006	.962 ± .010	**.981** ± .007	**.993** ± .002	.929 ± .014	.971 ± .008	.970 ± .012	.888 ± .040
BLEU	.975 ± .009	.929 ± .014	.865 ± .020	.957 ± .006	.851 ± .022	.915 ± .014	.889 ± .021	.796 ± .052
TER	.979 ± .008	.872 ± .019	.890 ± .018	.907 ± .008	.907 ± .017	.911 ± .014	.884 ± .022	.768 ± .054
WER	.977 ± .009	.853 ± .020	.884 ± .018	.888 ± .018	.895 ± .018	.899 ± .015	.871 ± .023	.747 ± .057

Table 1: Results WMT-15 Evaluation: System-Level Correlations

Test	fr-en	fi-en	de-en	cs-en	ru-en	Average
UoW-LSTM	.332 ± .011	.376 ± .012	.375 ± .011	.385 ± .008	.356 ± .010	.365 ± .011
DPMFCOMB	.395 ± .012	**.445** ± .012	**.482** ± .009	**.495** ± .007	**.418** ± .013	**.447** ± .011
BEER_TREEPEL	.389 ± .014	.438 ± .010	.447 ± .008	.471 ± .007	.403 ± .014	.429 ± .011
RATATOUILLE	**.398** ± .010	.421 ± .011	.441 ± .010	.472 ± .007	.393 ± .013	.425 ± .010
UPF-COBALT	.386 ± .012	.437 ± .013	.427 ± .011	.457 ± .007	.402 ± .013	.422 ± .011
SENTBLEU	.358 ± .013	.308 ± .012	.360 ± .011	.391 ± .006	.329 ± .011	.349 ± .011

Table 2: Results WMT-15 Evaluation: Segment-Level Correlations

for $1 \leq j \leq K$. Where, $y \in [1, K]$ is the similarity score of a training pair. For example, for $y = 2.7$, $p^T = [0\ 0.3\ 0.7\ 0\ 0]$. In our case, the similarity score y is a value between 1 and 5.

To compute our training data we automatically convert the human rankings of the WMT-13 evaluation data into similarity scores between the reference and the translation. These translation-reference pairs labelled with similarity scores are used for training. We also augment the WMT-13 data with 4500 pairs from the SICK training set (Marelli et al., 2014), resulting in a training dataset of 14059 pairs in total.

The metric uses *Glove* word vectors (Pennington et al., 2014) and the simple LSTM, the dependency Tree-LSTM and neural network implementations by Tai et al. (2015). Training is performed using a mini batch size of 25 with learning rate 0.05 and regularization strength 0.0001. The memory dimension is 300, hidden dimension is 100 and compositional parameters are 541,800. Training is performed for 10 epochs. System level scores are computed by aggregating and normalising the segment level scores. Full details can be found in (Gupta et al., 2015).[2]

5 Results

The results for WMT-15 are presented in Table 1 and Table 2.

Table 1 shows system-level Pearson correlation (TrueSkill) (see (Bojar et al., 2013) for difference between TrueSkill and Pre-TrueSkill system-ranking approaches) obtained on different language pairs as well as average (PAvg) over all language pairs. The second last column shows average Pearson correlation (Pre-TrueSkill). The last column shows average Spearman correlation (SAvg). The 95% confidence level scores are obtained using bootstrap resampling as used in the WMT-2015 metric task evaluation. Table 2 shows results on segment-wise Kendall tau correlation.

The first section of Table 1 and Table 2 shows the results of our ReVal metric as UoW-LSTM, the second section shows the other four top performing metrics and the third section shows baseline metrics (BLEU, TER and WER for system-level and SENTBLEU for segment level).

Table 1 shows that our metric obtains the best results overall for both Pearson (Pre-TrueSkill) and Spearman system-level correlation and second best overall using Pearson (TrueSkill) correlation. Table 2 shows that while improving over SENTBLEU our metric does not obtain high segment level scores.

6 Conclusion and Future Work

Our dense-vector-space-based ReVal metric is simple, elegant and fully competitive with the best of the current complex alternative approaches that involve system combination, extensive external resources, feature engineering and tuning. In future work we will investigate the difference between system and segment level evaluation scores.

Acknowledgement

The research leading to these results has received funding from the People Programme (Marie Curie Actions) of the European Unions Seventh Framework Programme FP7/2007-2013/ under REA grant agreement no. 317471 and the EC- funded project QT21 under Horizon 2020, ICT 17, grant agreement no. 645452.

References

Yoshua Bengio, Patrice Simard, and Paolo Frasconi. 1994. Learning long-term dependencies with gradient descent is difficult. *IEEE Transactions on Neural Networks*, 5(2):157–166.

Alexandra Birch and Miles Osborne. 2011. Reordering metrics for MT. In *Proceedings of the 49th Annual Meeting of the Association for Computational Linguistics: Human Language Technologies-Volume 1*, pages 1027–1035. Association for Computational Linguistics.

Ondřej Bojar, Rajen Chatterjee, Barry Haddow, Matthias Huck, Philipp Koehn, Matteo Negri, and Lucia Specia. 2013. Findings of the 2013 Workshop on Statistical Machine Translation. In *Proceedings of the Eighth Workshop on Statistical Machine Translation*, pages 1–44, Sofia, Bulgaria, August. Association for Computational Linguistics.

Michael Collins and Nigel Duffy. 2001. Convolution kernels for natural language. In *Advances in Neural Information Processing Systems*, pages 625–632.

Marie-Catherine De Marneffe, Bill MacCartney, Christopher D Manning, et al. 2006. Generating typed dependency parses from phrase structure parses. In *Proceedings of LREC*, volume 6, pages 449–454.

Michael Denkowski and Alon Lavie. 2014. Meteor universal: Language specific translation evaluation

[2]Please refer to L+Sick(100, 300) in (Gupta et al., 2015) for more details and results on the WMT-14 settings.

for any target language. In *Proceedings of the EACL 2014 Workshop on Statistical Machine Translation*.

George Doddington. 2002. Automatic evaluation of machine translation quality using n-gram co-occurrence statistics. In *Proceedings of the second international conference on Human Language Technology Research*, pages 138–145. Morgan Kaufmann Publishers Inc.

Shubham Gautam and Pushpak Bhattacharyya. 2014. Layered: Metric for machine translation evaluation. In *Proceedings of the Ninth Workshop on Statistical Machine Translation*.

Jesús Giménez and Lluís Màrquez. 2010. Linguistic measures for automatic machine translation evaluation. *Machine Translation*, 24(3-4):209–240.

Rohit Gupta, Constantin Orăsan, and Josef van Genabith. 2015. Reval: A simple and effective machine translation evaluation metric based on recurrent neural networks. In *Proceedings of the 2015 Conference on Empirical Methods in Natural Language Processing (EMNLP)*, Lisbon, Portugal.

Sepp Hochreiter and Jürgen Schmidhuber. 1997. Long short-term memory. *Neural computation*, 9(8):1735–1780.

Shafiq Joty, Francisco Guzmán, Lluís Màrquez, and Preslav Nakov. 2014. DiscoTK: Using Discourse Structure for Machine Translation Evaluation. In *Proceedings of the Ninth Workshop on Statistical Machine Translation*.

Quoc Le and Tomas Mikolov. 2014. Distributed representations of sentences and documents. In *Proceedings of The 31st International Conference on Machine Learning*, pages 1188–1196.

Matouš Machácek and Ondrej Bojar. 2014. Results of the WMT-14 metrics shared task. In *Proceedings of the Ninth Workshop on Statistical Machine Translation*.

Marco Marelli, Stefano Menini, Marco Baroni, Luisa Bentivogli, Raffaella Bernardi, and Roberto Zamparelli. 2014. A sick cure for the evaluation of compositional distributional semantic models. In *Proceedings of LREC 2014*.

Tomas Mikolov, Quoc V Le, and Ilya Sutskever. 2013a. Exploiting Similarities among Languages for Machine Translation. *CoRR*, pages 1–10.

Tomas Mikolov, Ilya Sutskever, Kai Chen, Greg S Corrado, and Jeff Dean. 2013b. Distributed representations of words and phrases and their compositionality. In *Advances in Neural Information Processing Systems*, pages 3111–3119.

Kishore Papineni, Salim Roukos, Todd Ward, and Wei-Jing Zhu. 2002. BLEU: a method for automatic evaluation of machine translation. In *Proceedings of the ACL*, pages 311–318.

Jeffrey Pennington, Richard Socher, and Christopher D Manning. 2014. Glove: Global vectors for word representation. In *Proceedings of the Empiricial Methods in Natural Language Processing (EMNLP 2014)*, pages 1532–1543.

Matthew Snover, Nitin Madnani, Bonnie Dorr, and Richard Schwartz. 2008. TERp system description. In *MetricsMATR workshop at AMTA*. Citeseer.

Richard Socher, Eh Huang, and Jeffrey Pennington. 2011. Dynamic Pooling and Unfolding Recursive Autoencoders for Paraphrase Detection. In *Advances in Neural Information Processing Systems*, pages 801–809.

Richard Socher, John Bauer, Christopher D. Manning, and Andrew Y. Ng. 2013a. Parsing With Compositional Vector Grammars. *In Proceedings of the ACL*, pages 455–465.

Richard Socher, Alex Perelygin, and Jy Wu. 2013b. Recursive deep models for semantic compositionality over a sentiment treebank. In *Proceedings of EMNLP*, pages 1631–1642.

Kai Sheng Tai, Richard Socher, and Christopher D. Manning. 2015. Improved semantic representations from tree-structured long short-term memory networks. In *Proceedings of the 53rd Annual Meeting of the Association for Computational Linguistics and the 7th International Joint Conference on Natural Language Processing (Volume 1: Long Papers)*, pages 1556–1566, Beijing, China. Association for Computational Linguistics.

Wojciech Zaremba and Ilya Sutskever. 2014. Learning to execute. *arXiv preprint arXiv:1410.4615*.

Alignment-based sense selection in METEOR and the RATATOUILLE recipe

Benjamin Marie
LIMSI-CNRS, Orsay, France
Lingua et Machina, Le Chesnay, France
benjamin.marie@limsi.fr

Marianna Apidianaki
LIMSI-CNRS, Orsay, France
marianna@limsi.fr

Abstract

This paper describes Meteor-WSD and RATATOUILLE, the LIMSI submissions to the WMT15 metrics shared task. Meteor-WSD extends synonym mapping to languages other than English based on alignments and gives credit to semantically adequate translations in context. We show that context-sensitive synonym selection increases the correlation of the Meteor metric with human judgments of translation quality on the WMT14 data. RATATOUILLE combines Meteor-WSD with nine other metrics for evaluation and outperforms the best metric (BEER) involved in its computation.

1 Introduction

The Meteor metric evaluates translation hypotheses by aligning them to reference translations and calculating sentence-level similarity scores (Banerjee and Lavie, 2005; Denkowski and Lavie, 2010). The space of possible alignments for a hypothesis-reference pair is constructed by identifying all possible matches between the sentences according to different matchers mapping words with identical surface forms or having the same stem, WordNet synonyms and paraphrases. These modules add flexibility to the metric and improve its correlation with human judgments of translation quality but they fail to account for important semantics-related aspects. For example, Meteor and Meteor-NEXT treat all the variants available for a particular text fragment in WordNet (Fellbaum, 1998) or a pivot paraphrase database (Bannard and Callison-Burch, 2005) as semantically equivalent. Consequently, erroneous matches can be made by mapping synonyms found in different WordNet synsets and describing different senses. Similarly, pivot paraphrase sets merge sense boundaries in cases of polysemous words (Apidianaki et al., 2014), which means that paraphrases of different senses are considered as equivalent and can be mapped during evaluation. To avoid erroneous matches between text segments, it is thus important to restrict the available word and phrase variants to the ones that are correct in a specific context.

Context-based synonym selection is the main idea behind the Meteor-WSD metric submitted to the WMT15 Metrics Shared Task. The mechanism used for sense selection is described in detail in the next section where we also present the results obtained by the Meteor-WSD metric on the WMT14 evaluation dataset. Section 3 presents the RATATOUILLE metric which integrates Meteor-WSD together with nine other evaluation metrics. We report results in all language pairs and directions of the WMT14 dataset, except for hi-en.

2 Meteor-WSD

2.1 Context-dependent sense selection

A first attempt to integrate context-based sense selection in Meteor is described in Apidianaki and Marie (2015). Word sense disambiguation (WSD) was performed using the Babelfy tool (Moro et al., 2014) which relies on the multilingual resource BabelNet (Navigli and Ponzetto, 2012). BabelNet is a wide coverage semantic network where senses are described by synsets (synonym and paraphrase sets) containing lexicographic and encyclopedic knowledge extracted from various sources in many languages and are linked between them by different types of relations. Depending on the language, the lexical and phrase variants available in the synsets come from different sources such as WordNet, Wikipedia, Wiktionary, OmegaWiki as well as Machine Translation output. The Babelfy tool jointly performs WSD and Entity Linking by exploiting BabelNet's graph structure and selects multilingual BabelNet synsets that correctly describe the semantics of words in context.[1] In Apidianaki and Marie (2015), Babelfy assigned BabelNet synsets to words in the English references of the WMT14 dataset. The WordNet literals found in the synset selected for an English word served to filter the WordNet synonym set used by the basic Meteor configuration in order to keep only variants that were good in this specific context and discard the ones corresponding to other senses. The reported MT evaluation results showed the beneficial impact of disambiguation which improved the correlation of the metric to human judgments from almost all languages involved in the WMT14 evaluation into English (except for Czech-English). Naturally, performance strongly depends on the quality of the WSD annotations.

In this work, we use a recent version of the alignment-based WSD method proposed by Apidianaki and Gong (2015) which gives better disambiguation results than Babelfy on the WMT14 data. Disambiguation is now applied to references of all languages in the data, not only in English. The WSD method used in our experiments still relies on alignments but implements a mechanism that improves WSD in languages other than English compared to the previous version. More precisely, Apidianaki and Gong (2015) showed that the problematic sorting performed by the default BabelNet sense ranking mechanism in languages other than English has a strong negative impact on WSD. [2] In our experiments, we implement an alternative solution that eliminates the need for sense ranking. Furthermore, the currently used version integrates a multiword expression (MWE) identification step prior to disambiguation.

2.2 Data preparation

The WMT14 shared task involved five language pairs: English-French / German / Czech / Russian / Hindi. We provide results for all languages except for Hindi, and for both translation directions. Source and reference texts are lemmatised and part-of-speech tagged using the TreeTagger (Schmid, 1994), except for Czech where the MorphoDiTa tool (Straková et al., 2014) is used. The texts are then aligned at the lemma level using GIZA++ (Och and Ney, 2003).

2.3 Alignment-based MWE extraction

We identify candidate multiword expressions in the reference texts prior to disambiguation using word alignments and filter them using information in the BabelNet resource (version 2.5).[3] We consider as a candidate MWE a sequence of words in one language that is aligned to a single word in the other language (a $n:1$ alignment).[4] For example, *téléphone portable* is considered as a candidate French MWE because both its parts are aligned to *cellphone*. We validate a candidate MWE if it constitutes a separate entry in the BabelNet resource either in its lemmatised or in its unlemmatised form (retrieved from the text), otherwise we discard it. This procedure eliminates many noisy MWEs but some good ones are also left out because they are not present in the resource.

If a BabelNet entry is found for the MWE, the variants provided in the corresponding synset are extracted. For instance, we extract *téléphone mobile*, *téléphone cellulaire*, and *GSM* as variants of *téléphone portable*. The variants retrieved from BabelNet are used to annotate the instances of the MWEs in the reference texts. A validated MWE is thus considered as a unit and is excluded from disambiguation. The WSD step, that follows, assigns a sense to all content words (nouns, verbs, adjectives and adverbs) in the reference text that were not identified as part of a MWE.

2.4 Alignment-based disambiguation

The procedure for selecting the most adequate BabelNet synset for an occurrence of a word (w) in context is described in Figure 1. First, we find the synsets of w (S_w) in BabelNet 2.5 and filter them to keep only synsets that contain both w and its aligned translation t in this context ($S_w^t \subseteq S_w$). If only one synset is retained, we keep the variants (synonyms and paraphrases) of the same language as w provided in this synset. If several

[1]The Babelfy API can be downloaded from `http://babelfy.org`

[2]The BabelNet API sorts English senses according to their frequencies in WordNet, which are calculated from the sense annotated English corpus SemCor. As frequency information is not available for languages other than English, the BabelNet API sorts senses in lexicographic order, a criterion that fails to reflect their importance.

[3]The resource can be found at `http://babelnet.org` together with detailed statistics regarding the number of lemmas, senses and named entities provided, and the knowledge sources that were exploited for each language. Note that BabelNet's coverage varies a lot across languages.

[4]In future work, we intend to extend this heuristic to $n:m$ alignments linking sequences of two or more words in the two languages as in de Caseli et al. (2010).

Notation:
S_w: the set of BabelSynsets for w
t: a translation of w in context
S_w^t: the set of synsets in which t appears
V_w: the set of synonyms/paraphrases of w
l: language

The Sense Selection Algorithm:
$S_w^t \leftarrow \emptyset$
$S_w \leftarrow$ `getBabelSynsets`(w)
for each BabelSynset $s \in S_w$ **do**
  if $t \in s$ **then**
    add s to S_w^t
if $|S_w^t| \geq 1$ **then**
  for each BabelSynset $s \in S_w^t$ **do**
    $V_w \leftarrow$ `getVariants`(s, l)
  return (V_w)
else
  if l = English **then**
    $V_w \leftarrow$ `getVariants(getBFS(`S_w, l`),`l`)`
  else
    for each BabelSynset $s \in S_w$ **do**
      $V_w \leftarrow$ `getVariants`(s, l)
    return (V_w)

Figure 1: The `getBabelSynsets` function retrieves the synsets available for w in BabelNet. The `getVariants` function returns the variants of w in the same language found in the synsets. If no synset is retained through alignment, the system falls back to the BFS baseline. The `getBFS` function ranks English synsets according to importance and returns the most frequent one (BabelNet First Sense).

synsets are retained, we keep the variants found in all synsets. Given the fine granularity of BabelNet senses (similar to WordNet), the intuition behind this merge is that different synsets containing the word and its translation describe closely-related senses.[5] Grouping the synsets that contain the aligned translation eliminates the need for sense sorting which is problematic in languages other than English, as explained in Section 2.1.

The system falls back to the most frequent sense provided by the default sense comparator of the BabelNet 2.5 API (`BabelSynsetComparator`) for unaligned English words or when the aligned translation is not found in any synset. To avoid applying the sense sorting procedure to languages other than English, we keep all available synsets for unaligned words in these languages or for words whose alignment is not found in any synset. In these cases, variants from all synsets are grouped together and no disambiguation is performed.

Disambiguation is applied to all content words in the texts (nouns, verbs, adjectives and adverbs). We impose no constraints on the part-of-speech category of the synsets where the word and its translation need to be found. If, for example, *world* and its French translation *monde* are found in both nominal and adjectival synsets, we extract all variants available in the synsets. This adds flexibility to the matching given that a word of a certain grammatical category might be translated by a word of a different category in another language.

The WSD method enriches each reference sentence with semantic variants valid in this precise context. For example, variants provided for the sentence: *Only healthcare workers allowed in*, include {exclusively, solely, alone, ...}, {health care practitioner, healthcare provider, health care professionals, ...}, {let, permit}. The disambiguation might fail, especially in cases where alignment information is not available or cannot be used because of the limited coverage of the BabelNet resource in languages other than English. When the annotations are correct, they help the Meteor metric reward translations in the hypothesis that are different from the ones in the reference but still semantically correct.

2.5 Results

Our results are reported using Kendall's τ for segment-level evaluation and Pearson's correlation coefficient for system-level evaluation, all computed with the official scripts and human judgments provided by the WMT14 shared metrics task organizers. The *xx* column in the results tables shows the average of all the language pairs involved. [6]

The results of Meteor-WSD at the segment-level are reported in Table 1. Meteor-WSD correlates slightly better with human judgments than standard Meteor when English is the target language, with an average improvement of .001. The results are also better than the results obtained by our previous version of Meteor-WSD (Apidianaki and Marie, 2015), especially for the cs-en language pair where correlation goes from .278 to .282. The differences between Meteor and

[5]The merge would lead to errors only in cases of parallel ambiguities where the word and its translation carry the same distant senses. Using translations in multiple languages could improve accuracy in these cases.

[6]This means that the score given for xx-en is the average of the scores of all language pairs with English as a target language. For xx-xx, the score is the average of all scores for all language pairs.

Metric	fr-en	de-en	cs-en	ru-en	xx-en	en-fr	en-de	en-cs	en-ru	en-xx	xx-xx
Meteor-1.5	.406	.334	.282	.329	.338	.280	.238	.318	.427	.316	.327
Meteor-WSD	.410	.332	.282	.332	.339	.280	.240	.321	.437	.320	.330

Table 1: Segment-level Kendall's τ correlations of Meteor-WSD and the official WMT14 human judgments.

Metric	fr-en	de-en	cs-en	ru-en	xx-en	en-fr	en-de	en-cs	en-ru	en-xx	xx-xx
Meteor-1.5	.975	.927	.980	.805	.922	.941	.263	.976	.923	.776	.849
Meteor-WSD	.975	.927	.979	.828	.927	.946	.258	.981	.929	.779	.852

Table 2: System-level Pearson's coefficient correlations of Meteor-WSD and the official WMT14 human judgments.

Meteor-WSD scores are much larger when English is the source language, probably due to the fact that we activate the synonymy module[7] and perform disambiguation in the other languages using the semantic information provided in BabelNet while Meteor uses synonyms only for English. This means that the synonyms left after disambiguation in languages other than English are useful and help to improve the correlation with human judgments. Table 2 presents our results at the system-level. As for the segment-level task, Meteor-WSD performs better than Meteor for almost all language pairs, with a significant improvement of .023 for the ru-en language pair.

3 A Metric Combination: RATATOUILLE

3.1 The Metrics

RATATOUILLE is a metric combination involving ten metrics mainly dedicated to segment-level evaluation: PER, WER, CDER (Leusch et al., 2006), TER (Snover et al., 2006), GTM 1.3 (Melamed et al., 2003), sentence-level BLEU, Meteor 1.5, Meteor-WSD, RIBES 1.03.1 (Echizen'ya et al., 2013) and BEER 1.0 (Stanojević and Sima'an, 2014). For the metrics PER, WER, CDER, TER and sentence-level BLEU we used the implementations available in MOSES (Koehn et al., 2007). For the metrics RIBES[8] and BEER[9] we used the implementations published by their authors, and the implementation available in the Asiya toolkit[10] (Giménez and Màrquez, 2010) for the GTM metric.

3.2 Tuning

Each metric of the combination gives a score for the evaluated segment. The score computed by RATATOUILLE is the result of the log-linear combination of each metric's score. The weight for each metric score is tuned using a similar approach to PRO (Hopkins and May, 2011), already used by Guzmán et al. (2014) in the context of metric combination evaluation. In this pairwise approach, candidate translation pairs are classified into two categories: correctly or incorrectly ordered, reducing the tuning to a binary classification problem. We studied two configurations, retaining all possible translation pairs or only pairs including translations separated by at least three ranks in the human judgments. We follow PRO which uses only pairs of translations of significant different quality and does not learn to tease apart translations of similar quality. Translation pairs used to tune the metric for a given language pair include translations in the same target language independently of the source language. If no human judgments are available for a given language pair, we use all the translation pairs independently of the target and source languages to tune the metric.[11] The classifier used is a MaxEnt from the scikit-learn python library (Pedregosa et al., 2011).

[7]As the synonymy module has no pre-defined weight for such translation directions, we tuned its weight on the WMT13 human judgments for each translation direction, searching empirically for the best weight between 0 and 1 with a 0.2 step size.

[8]http://www.kecl.ntt.co.jp/icl/lirg/ribes/index.html

[9]https://github.com/stanojevic/beer/

[10]http://nlp.lsi.upc.edu/asiya/

[11]For the fi-en language pair in the WMT15 metrics task, we used translation pairs from xx-en to tune the metric for fi-en and from en-xx to tune the metric for en-fi.

RATATOUILLE tuning set	fr-en	de-en	cs-en	ru-en	xx-en	en-fr	en-de	en-cs	en-ru	en-xx	xx-xx
`all`	.426	.336	.294	.337	.348	.292	.286	.352	.459	.347	.348
`>=3`	.425	.342	.297	.340	.351	.293	.292	.345	.456	.347	.349

Table 3: Segment-level Kendall's τ correlations of RATATOUILLE and the official WMT14 human judgments using all WMT13 human judgments (`all`) or only all the translation pairs containing translations separated by at least 3 ranks (`>=3`).

Metric	fr-en	de-en	cs-en	ru-en	xx-en	en-fr	en-de	en-cs	en-ru	en-xx	xx-xx
BEER	.417	.337	.284	.333	.343	.292	.268	.344	.440	.336	.340
RATATOUILLE w/o Meteor-WSD	.423	.343	.296	.338	.350	.293	.291	.344	.454	.346	.348
RATATOUILLE w/o Meteor-1.5	.425	.341	.297	.339	.351	.293	.292	.345	.458	.347	.349
RATATOUILLE	.425	.342	.297	.340	.351	.293	.292	.345	.456	.347	.349

Table 4: Segment-level Kendall's τ correlations of RATATOUILLE and the official WMT14 human judgments.

Metric	fr-en	de-en	cs-en	ru-en	xx-en	en-fr	en-de	en-cs	en-ru	en-xx	xx-xx
Meteor 1.5	.975	.927	.980	.805	.922	.941	.263	.976	.923	.776	.849
RATATOUILLE w/o Meteor-WSD	.974	.900	.994	.804	.918	.955	.403	.979	.946	.821	.869
RATATOUILLE w/o Meteor-1.5	.974	.899	.993	.804	.918	.958	.408	.979	.945	.823	.870
RATATOUILLE	.974	.901	.993	.804	.918	.959	.408	.979	.944	.823	.870

Table 5: System-level Pearson's coefficient correlations of RATATOUILLE and the official WMT14 human judgments.

3.3 Results

To tune RATATOUILLE, we used only the human judgments provided at WMT13.[12] As shown by Joty et al. (2014), using more data brings no improvements when tuning metric combinations. For system-level scores, the RATATOUILLE score for each sentence is first passed through a sigmoid function[13] and the final system score is the average of all sentence scores.

In the first experiments with RATATOUILLE, we tried to find a better subset of tuning examples among all the WMT13 translation pairs. We present in Table 3 our results when tuning on all translation pairs or on a subset including only translation pairs separated by at least three ranks in the human judgments. In spite of an important reduction in the number of translation pairs used to tune, we observed slight improvements in the average for xx-en, from .348 to .351, while the average for en-xx remains the same. We assume that this is probably due to the small number of translation pairs remaining for tuning after filtering; these are far less numerous for language pairs with English as source language than for language pairs with English as target language. Since on average the translation pair filtering gives better results, we report results for our experiments where we used the `>=3` subsets to tune RATATOUILLE.

The results obtained for RATATOUILLE at the segment-level are presented in Table 4 along with the results of BEER, the best metric among the metrics that participated in the WMT14 metrics task for all language pairs. RATATOUILLE gives significantly better results than BEER – as expected, since BEER is used by RATATOUILLE – with an average improvement of .009. The largest improvements are observed for en-de (+.024) and en-ru (+.016). For en-fr and en-cs, RATATOUILLE results are only slightly better than BEER results (+.001), meaning probably that BEER is not assisted by the other metrics in RATATOUILLE to improve correlation with human judgments.

BEER did not participate in the WMT14 system-level evaluation. Meteor participated in this evaluation for all language pairs, so in Table 5 we present the RATATOUILLE results along with the results for Meteor. At this level, RATATOUILLE performs better than Meteor but

[12] `http://www.statmt.org/wmt13/results.html`

[13] We found out that not converting the scores with a sigmoid function leads to a slightly lower correlation. Indeed without this conversion scores are not bounded and can be very different between sentences especially for long sentences for which scores are very high, giving them more weight when computing the average for the system-level score.

not for all language pairs. We observe, for instance, a loss of .026 for de-en while we notice a strong improvement of .145 for en-de. This confirms the difficulty to have consistent results across language pairs at the system level as shown in the official results of the WMT14 metrics task where only one metric (PER) performed best on more than one translation directions, en-cs and en-ru, while different metrics perfomed best for each of the remaining en-xx translation directions.

For both segment and system levels, we also observed that withdrawing Meteor-1.5 from RATATOUILLE does not change the results on average, while withdrawing Meteor-WSD slightly decreases RATATOUILLE performance. This means that Meteor-WSD can successfully replace Meteor-1.5 in RATATOUILLE giving slightly better results.

4 Conclusion

We have shown the positive impact brought by introducing a word sense disambiguation step in an MT evaluation metric. Although lexical variation was addressed in previous metrics such as Meteor and Meteor-NEXT, synonyms and paraphrases were considered without taking the actual context into account. The improved correlation of the Meteor-WSD metric to human judgments of translation quality confirms the important role of the context in sense and synonym selection. The performance of the disambiguation method remains a crucial factor determining the performance of the MT evaluation metric. In future work, we intend to experiment with ways of improving disambiguation quality and increasing its coverage. Moreover, we intend to integrate context-based filtering of paraphrases to help the Meteor-WSD metric establish better matches between the compared translations. Last but not least, as BEER uses Meteor to align hypotheses and reference translations, we plan to replace Meteor by Meteor-WSD in BEER to improve this alignment and produce a better correlation with human judgments than the original BEER metric.

5 Acknowledgements

We would like to thank the anonymous reviewers for their helpful comments and suggestions. This work was partly supported by ANR project Transread (ANR-12-CORD-0015).

References

Marianna Apidianaki and Li Gong. 2015. LIMSI: Translations as Source of Indirect Supervision for Multilingual All-Words Sense Disambiguation and Entity Linking. In *Proceedings of the 9th International Workshop on Semantic Evaluation (SemEval-2015)*, Denver, Colorado, USA.

Marianna Apidianaki and Benjamin Marie. 2015. METEOR-WSD: Improved Sense Matching in MT Evaluation. In *Proceedings of the Ninth Workshop on Syntax, Semantics and Structure in Statistical Translation*, pages 49–51, Denver, Colorado, USA, June.

Marianna Apidianaki, Emilia Verzeni, and Diana Mccarthy. 2014. Semantic Clustering of Pivot Paraphrases. In *Proceedings of the Ninth International Conference on Language Resources and Evaluation (LREC'14)*, Reykjavik, Iceland.

Satanjeev Banerjee and Alon Lavie. 2005. METEOR: An Automatic Metric for MT Evaluation with Improved Correlation with Human Judgments. In *Proceedings of the ACL Workshop on Intrinsic and Extrinsic Evaluation Measures for Machine Translation and/or Summarization*, pages 65–72, Ann Arbor, Michigan, USA.

Colin Bannard and Chris Callison-Burch. 2005. Paraphrasing with Bilingual Parallel Corpora. In *Proceedings of the 43rd Annual Meeting of the Association for Computational Linguistics (ACL'05)*, pages 597–604, Ann Arbor, Michigan, June.

Helena Medeiros de Caseli, Carlos Ramisch, Maria das Graças Volpe Nunes, and Aline Villavicencio. 2010. Alignment-based extraction of multiword expressions. *Language Resources and Evaluation*, 44(1-2):59–77.

Michael Denkowski and Alon Lavie. 2010. Extending the METEOR Machine Translation Evaluation Metric to the Phrase Level. In *Human Language Technologies: The 2010 Annual Conference of the North American Chapter of the Association for Computational Linguistics*, pages 250–253, Los Angeles, California, USA.

Hiroshi Echizen'ya, Kenji Araki, and Eduard Hovy. 2013. Automatic evaluation metric for machine translation that is independent of sentence length. In *Proceedings of the International Conference Recent Advances in Natural Language Processing RANLP 2013*, pages 230–236, Hissar, Bulgaria, September. INCOMA Ltd. Shoumen, BULGARIA.

Christiane Fellbaum, editor. 1998. *WordNet: an electronic lexical database*. MIT Press.

Jesús Giménez and Lluís Màrquez. 2010. Asiya: An Open Toolkit for Automatic Machine Translation (Meta-)Evaluation. *The Prague Bulletin of Mathematical Linguistics*.

Francisco Guzmán, Shafiq Joty, Lluís Màrquez, and Preslav Nakov. 2014. Using discourse structure improves machine translation evaluation. In *Proceedings of the 52nd Annual Meeting of the Association for Computational Linguistics (ACL'14)*, pages 687–698, Baltimore, Maryland, USA, June.

Mark Hopkins and Jonathan May. 2011. Tuning as ranking. In *Proceedings of the Conference on Empirical Methods in Natural Language Processing*, EMNLP '11, pages 1352–1362, Stroudsburg, PA, USA.

Shafiq Joty, Francisco Guzmán, Lluís Màrquez, and Preslav Nakov. 2014. Discotk: Using discourse structure for machine translation evaluation. In *Proceedings of the Ninth Workshop on Statistical Machine Translation (WMT'14)*, pages 402–408, Baltimore, Maryland, USA, June.

Philipp Koehn, Hieu Hoang, Alexandra Birch, Chris Callison-Burch, Marcello Federico, Nicola Bertoldi, Brooke Cowan, Wade Shen, Christine Moran, Richard Zens, Chris Dyer, Ondrej Bojar, Alexandra Constantin, and Evan Herbst. 2007. Moses: Open Source Toolkit for Statistical Machine Translation. In *Proceedings of ACL, demo session*, Prague, Czech Republic.

Gregor Leusch, Nicola Ueffing, and Hermann Ney. 2006. Cder: Efficient mt evaluation using block movements. In *In Proceedings of the 13th Conference of the European Chapter of the Association for Computational Linguistics (EACL-06)*.

Dan I. Melamed, Ryan Green, and Joseph P. Turian. 2003. Precision and recall of machine translation. In *Proceedings of the 2003 Conference of the North American Chapter of the Association for Computational Linguistics on Human Language Technology: Companion Volume of the Proceedings of HLT-NAACL 2003–short Papers - Volume 2*, NAACL-Short '03, pages 61–63, Stroudsburg, PA, USA.

Andrea Moro, Alessandro Raganato, and Roberto Navigli. 2014. Entity Linking meets Word Sense Disambiguation: a Unified Approach. *Transactions of the Association for Computational Linguistics (TACL)*, 2:231–244.

Roberto Navigli and Simone Paolo Ponzetto. 2012. BabelNet: The Automatic Construction, Evaluation and Application of a Wide-Coverage Multilingual Semantic Network. *Artificial Intelligence*, 193:217–250.

Franz Josef Och and Hermann Ney. 2003. A Systematic Comparison of Various Statistical Alignment Models. *Computational Linguistics*, 29:19–51.

F. Pedregosa, G. Varoquaux, A. Gramfort, V. Michel, B. Thirion, O. Grisel, M. Blondel, P. Prettenhofer, R. Weiss, V. Dubourg, J. Vanderplas, A. Passos, D. Cournapeau, M. Brucher, M. Perrot, and E. Duchesnay. 2011. Scikit-learn: Machine Learning in Python. In *Journal of Machine Learning Research*, volume 12, pages 2825–2830.

Helmut Schmid. 1994. Probabilistic Part-of-Speech Tagging Using Decision Trees. In *Proceedings of the International Conference on New Methods in Language Processing*, pages 44–49, Manchester, UK.

Matthew Snover, Bonnie Dorr, Richard Schwartz, Linnea Micciulla, and John Makhoul. 2006. A Study of Translation Edit Rate with Targeted Human Annotation. In *Proceedings of AMTA*, Cambridge, USA.

Miloš Stanojević and Khalil Sima'an. 2014. BEER: BEtter Evaluation as Ranking. In *Proceedings of the Ninth Workshop on Statistical Machine Translation*, pages 414–419, Baltimore, Maryland, USA, June.

Jana Straková, Milan Straka, and Jan Hajič. 2014. Open-Source Tools for Morphology, Lemmatization, POS Tagging and Named Entity Recognition. In *Proceedings of 52nd Annual Meeting of the Association for Computational Linguistics: System Demonstrations*, pages 13–18, Baltimore, Maryland, June. Association for Computational Linguistics.

CHRF: character n-gram F-score for automatic MT evaluation

Maja Popović
Humboldt University of Berlin
Germany
maja.popovic@hu-berlin.de

Abstract

We propose the use of character n-gram F-score for automatic evaluation of machine translation output. Character n-grams have already been used as a part of more complex metrics, but their individual potential has not been investigated yet. We report system-level correlations with human rankings for 6-gram F1-score (CHRF) on the WMT12, WMT13 and WMT14 data as well as segment-level correlation for 6-gram F1 (CHRF) and F3-scores (CHRF3) on WMT14 data for all available target languages. The results are very promising, especially for the CHRF3 score – for translation from English, this variant showed the highest segment-level correlations outperforming even the best metrics on the WMT14 shared evaluation task.

1 Introduction

Recent investigations have shown that character level n-grams play an important role for automatic evaluation as a part of more complex metrics such as MTERATER (Parton et al., 2011) and BEER (Stanojević and Sima'an, 2014a; Stanojević and Sima'an, 2014b). However, they have not been investigated as an individual metric so far. On the other hand, the n-gram based F-scores, especially the linguistically motivated ones based on Part-of-Speech tags and morphemes (Popović, 2011), are shown to correlate very well with human judgments clearly outperforming the widely used metrics such as BLEU and TER.

In this work, we propose the use of the F-score based on character n-grams, i.e. the CHRF score. We believe that this score has a potential as a stand-alone metric because it is shown to be an important part of the previously mentioned complex measures, and because, similarly to the morpheme-based F-score, it takes into account some morpho-syntactic phenomena. Apart from that, in contrast to the related metrics, it is simple, it does not require any additional tools and/or knowledge sources, it is absolutely language independent and also tokenisation independent.

The CHRF scores were calculated for all available translation outputs from the WMT12 (Callison-Burch et al., 2012), WMT13 (Bojar et al., 2013) and WMT14 (Bojar et al., 2014) shared tasks, and then compared with human rankings. System-level correlation coefficients are calculated for all data, segment-level correlations only for WMT14 data. The scores were calculated for all available target languages, namely English, Spanish, French, German, Czech, Russian and Hindi.

2 CHRF score

The general formula for the CHRF score is:

$$\text{CHRF}\beta = (1 + \beta^2)\frac{\text{CHRP} \cdot \text{CHRR}}{\beta^2 \cdot \text{CHRP} + \text{CHRR}} \quad (1)$$

where CHRP and CHRR stand for character n-gram precision and recall arithmetically averaged over all n-grams:

- CHRP
  percentage of n-grams in the hypothesis which have a counterpart in the reference;

- CHRR
  percentage of character n-grams in the reference which are also present in the hypothesis.

and β is a parameter which assigns β times more importance to recall than to precision – if $\beta = 1$, they have the same importance.

3 Experiments on WMT12, WMT13 and WMT14 test data

3.1 Experiments

As a first step, we carried out several experiments regarding n-gram length. Since the optimal n for word-based measures is shown to be $n = 4$, MTERATER used up to 10-gram and BEER up to 6-gram, we investigated those three variants. In addition, we investigated a dynamic n calculated for each sentence as the average word length. The best correlations are obtained for 6-gram, therefore we carried out further experiments only on them.

Apart from the n-gram length, we investigated the influence of the space treating it as an additional character. However, taking space into account did not yield any improvement regarding the correlations and therefore has been abandoned.

words	This is an example.
characters	T h i s i s a n e x a m p l e .
+space	T h i s _ i s _ a n _ e x a m p l e .

Table 1: Example of an English sentence with its corresponding character sequences without and with taking the space into account.

In the last stage of our current experiments, we have compared two β values on the WMT14 data: the standard CHRF with $\beta = 1$ i.e. the harmonic mean of precision and recall, as well as CHRF3 where $\beta = 3$, i.e. the recall has three times more weight. The number 3 has been taken arbitraly as a preliminary value, and the CHRF3 is tested only on WMT14 data – more systematic experiments in this direction should be carried out in the future work.

3.2 Correlations with human rankings

System-level correlations

The evaluation metrics were compared with human rankings on the system-level by means of Spearman's correlation coefficients ρ for the WMT12 and WMT13 data and Pearson's correlation coefficients r for the WMT14 data. Spearman's rank correlation coefficient is equivalent to Pearson correlation on ranks, and it makes fewer assumptions about the data.

Average system-level correlations for CHRF score(s) together with the word n-gram F-score WORDF and the three mostly used metrics BLEU (Papineni et al., 2002), TER (Snover et al., 2006) and METEOR (Banerjee and Lavie, 2005) are shown in Table 2. It can be seen that the CHRF score is comparable or better than the other metrics, especially the CHRF3 score.

Table 3 presents the percentage of translation outputs where the particular F-score metric (WORDF, CHRF and CHRF3) has higher correlation (no ties) than the particular standard metric (BLEU, TER and METEOR). It can be seen that the WORDF score outperforms BLEU and TER for about 60% of documents, however METEOR only in less than 40%. Standard CHRF is better than METEOR for half of the documents, and better than BLEU and TER for 68% of the documents thus being definitely more promising than the word-based metrics. Finally, CHRF3 score outperforms all standard metric for about 70-80% of texts, thus being the most promising variant.

Segment-level correlations

The segment-level quality of metrics is measured using Kendall's τ rank correlation coefficient. It measures the metric's ability to predict the results of the manual pairwise comparison of two systems. The τ coefficients were calulated only on the WMT14 data using the official WMT14 script, and the obtained WMT14 variant is reported for the WORDF score, both CHRF scores, as well as for the best ranked metrics in the shared evaluation task.

Table 4 shows the τ coefficients for translation into English (above) and for translation from English (below). For translation into English, it can be seen that the CHRF3 score is again the most promising F-score. Furthermore, it can be seen that the correlations for both CHRF scores are close to the two best ranked metrics (DISCOTKPARTY and BEER) and the METEOR metrics, which is very well ranked too. For translation from English, the CHRF3 score yields the highest average correlation, and the CHRF score is comparable with the best ranked BEER metric.

4 Conclusions

The results presented in this paper show that the character n-gram F-score CHRF represents a promising metric for automatic evaluation of machine translation output for several reasons: it is language-independent, tokenisation-independent and it shows good correlations with human judgments both on the system- as well as

year	WORDF	CHRF	CHRF3	BLEU	TER	METEOR
2014 (r)	0.810	0.805	0.857	0.845	0.814	0.822
2013 (ρ)	0.874	0.873	/	0.835	0.791	0.876
2012 (ρ)	0.659	0.696	/	0.671	0.682	0.690

Table 2: Average system-level correlations on WMT14 (Pearson's r), WMT13 and WMT12 data (Spearman's ρ) for word 4-gram F1 score, character 6-gram F1 score and character 6-gram F3 score together with the three mostly used metrics BLEU, TER and METEOR.

rank>	WORDF	CHRF	CHRF3
BLEU	64.3	67.9	80.0
TER	60.7	67.9	70.0
METEOR	39.3	50.0	70.0

Table 3: *rank>* for three F-scores (WORDF, CHRF and CHRF3) in comparison with three standard metrics (BLEU, TER and METEOR) – percentage of translation outputs where the given F-score metrics has higher correlation than the given standard metric.

Kendall's τ	fr-en	de-en	hi-en	cs-en	ru-en	avg.
WORDF	0.356	0.258	0.276	0.200	0.262	0.270
CHRF	0.402	0.318	0.395	0.253	0.320	0.338
CHRF3	0.391	0.332	0.394	0.278	0.322	0.343
DISCOTKPARTY	0.433	0.380	0.434	0.328	0.355	0.386
BEER	0.417	0.337	0.438	0.284	0.333	0.362
METEOR	0.406	0.334	0.420	0.282	0.329	0.354

Kendall's τ	en-fr	en-de	en-hi	en-cs	en-ru	avg.
WORDF	0.251	0.205	0.202	0.281	0.381	0.264
CHRF	0.296	0.247	0.253	0.331	0.443	0.314
CHRF3	0.304	0.269	0.294	0.331	0.457	0.331
BEER	0.292	0.268	0.250	0.344	0.440	0.319
METEOR	0.280	0.238	0.264	0.318	0.427	0.306

Table 4: Segment-level Kendall's τ correlations on WMT 14 data for WORDF, CHRF and CHRF3 score together with the best performing metrics on the shared evaluation task.

on the segment-level, especially the CHRF3 variant. Therefore both of the CHRF scores were submitted to the WMT15 shared metrics task. In future work, different β values should be investigated, as well as different weights for particular n-grams. Apart from this, CHRF is so far tested on only one non-European language (Hindi) – application on more languages using different writing systems such as Arabic, Chinese, etc. has to be explored systematically.

Acknowledgments

This publication has emanated from research supported by QTLEAP project (Quality Translation by Deep Language Engineering Approach) – ECs FP7 (FP7/2007-2013) under grant agreement number 610516, QT21 project funded by the European Union's Horizon 2020 research and innovation programme under grant number 645452, and TRAMOOC project (Translation for Massive Open Online Courses) partially funded by the European Commission under H2020-ICT-2014/H2020-ICT-2014-1 under grant agreement number 644333. Special thanks to Miloš Stanojević for suggesting experiments with the β parameter.

References

Satanjeev Banerjee and Alon Lavie. 2005. METEOR: An Automatic Metric for MT Evaluation with Improved Correlation with Human Judgements. In *Proceedings of the ACL 05 Workshop on Intrinsic and Extrinsic Evaluation Measures for MT and/or Summarization*, pages 65–72, Ann Arbor, MI, June.

Ondřej Bojar, Christian Buck, Chris Callison-Burch, Christian Federmann, Barry Haddow, Philipp Koehn, Christof Monz, Matt Post, Radu Soricut, and Lucia Specia. 2013. Findings of the 2013 Workshop on Statistical Machine Translation. In *Proceedings of the Eighth Workshop on Statistical Machine Translation (WMT-13)*, pages 1–44, Sofia, Bulgaria, August.

Ondřej Bojar, Christian Buck, Christian Federmann, Barry Haddow, Philipp Koehn, Johannes Leveling, Christof Monz, Pavel Pecina, Matt Post, Herve Saint-Amand, Radu Soricut, Lucia Specia, and Aleš Tamchyna. 2014. Findings of the 2014 Workshop on Statistical Machine Translation. In *Proceedings of the Ninth Workshop on Statistical Machine Translation (WMT-14)*, page 1258, Baltimore, Maryland, USA, June.

Chris Callison-Burch, Philipp Koehn, Christof Monz, Matt Post, Radu Soricut, and Lucia Specia. 2012. Findings of the 2012 Workshop on Statistical Machine Translation. In *Proceedings of the Seventh Workshop on Statistical Machine Translation (WMT-12)*, page 1051, Montral, Canada, June. Association for Computational Linguistics.

Kishore Papineni, Salim Roukos, Todd Ward, and Wei-Jing Zhu. 2002. BLEU: a Method for Automatic Evaluation of Machine Translation. In *Proceedings of the 40th Annual Meeting of the Association for Computational Linguistics (ACL 02)*, pages 311–318, Philadelphia, PA, July.

Kristen Parton, Joel Tetreault, Nitin Madnani, and Martin Chodorow. 2011. E-Rating Machine Translation. In *Proceedings of the Sixth Workshop on Statistical Machine Translation (WMT-11)*, pages 108–115, Edinburgh, Scotland.

Maja Popović. 2011. Morphemes and POS tags for n-gram based evaluation metrics. In *Proceedings of the Sixth Workshop on Statistical Machine Translation (WMT-11)*, pages 104–107, Edinburgh, Scotland, July.

Matthew Snover, Bonnie Dorr, Richard Schwartz, Linnea Micciulla, and John Makhoul. 2006. A Study of Translation Error Rate with Targeted Human Annotation. In *Proceedings of the 7th Conference of the Association for Machine Translation in the Americas (AMTA 06)*, pages 223–231, Boston, MA, August.

Miloš Stanojević and Khalil Sima'an. 2014a. BEER: BEtter Evaluation as Ranking. In *Proceedings of the Ninth Workshop on Statistical Machine Translation (WMT-14)*, pages 414–419, Baltimore, Maryland, June.

Miloš Stanojević and Khalil Sima'an. 2014b. Fitting Sentence Level Translation Evaluation with Many Dense Features. In *Proceedings of the 2014 Conference on Empirical Methods in Natural Language Processing (EMNLP-14)*, pages 202–206, Doha, Qatar, October. Association for Computational Linguistics.

BEER 1.1: ILLC UvA submission to metrics and tuning task

Miloš Stanojević
ILLC
University of Amsterdam
m.stanojevic@uva.nl

Khalil Sima'an
ILLC
University of Amsterdam
k.simaan@uva.nl

Abstract

We describe the submissions of ILLC UvA to the metrics and tuning tasks on WMT15. Both submissions are based on the BEER evaluation metric originally presented on WMT14 (Stanojević and Sima'an, 2014a). The main changes introduced this year are: (i) extending the learning-to-rank trained sentence level metric to the corpus level (but still decomposable to sentence level), (ii) incorporating syntactic ingredients based on dependency trees, and (iii) a technique for finding parameters of BEER that avoid "gaming of the metric" during tuning.

1 Introduction

In the 2014 WMT metrics task, BEER turned up as the best sentence level evaluation metric on average over 10 language pairs (Machacek and Bojar, 2014). We believe that this was due to:

1. *learning-to-rank* - type of training that allows a large number of features and also training on the same objective on which the model is going to be evaluated : ranking of translations
2. *dense features* - character n-grams and skip-bigrams that are less sparse on the sentence level than word n-grams
3. *permutation trees* - hierarchical decomposition of word order based on (Zhang and Gildea, 2007)

A deeper analysis of (2) is presented in (Stanojević and Sima'an, 2014c) and of (3) in (Stanojević and Sima'an, 2014b).

Here we modify BEER by

1. incorporating a better scoring function that give scores that are better scaled
2. including syntactic features and
3. removing the recall bias from BEER .

In Section 2 we give a short introduction to BEER after which we move to the innovations for this year in Sections 3, 4 and 5. We show the results from the metric and tuning tasks in Section 6, and conclude in Section 7.

2 BEER basics

The model underying the BEER metric is flexible for the integration of an arbitrary number of new features and has a training method that is targeted for producing good rankings among systems. Two other characteristic properties of BEER are its hierarchical reordering component and character n-grams lexical matching component.

2.1 Old BEER scoring

BEER is essentially a linear model with which the score can be computed in the following way:

$$score(h, r) = \sum_i w_i \times \phi_i(h, r) = \vec{w} \cdot \vec{\phi}$$

where $\vec{w}$ is a weight vector and $\vec{\phi}$ is a feature vector.

2.2 Learning-to-rank

Since the task on which our model is going to be evaluated is ranking translations it comes natural to train the model using *learning-to-rank* techniques.

Our training data consists of pairs of "good" and "bad" translations. By using a feature vector $\vec{\phi}_{good}$ for a good translation and a feature vector $\vec{\phi}_{bad}$ for a bad translation then using the following equations we can transform the ranking problem into a binary classification problem (Herbrich et al., 1999):

$$
\begin{aligned}
score(h_{good}, r) > score(h_{bad}, r) &\Leftrightarrow \\
\vec{w} \cdot \vec{\phi}_{good} > \vec{w} \cdot \vec{\phi}_{bad} &\Leftrightarrow \\
\vec{w} \cdot \vec{\phi}_{good} - \vec{w} \cdot \vec{\phi}_{bad} > 0 &\Leftrightarrow \\
\vec{w} \cdot (\vec{\phi}_{good} - \vec{\phi}_{bad}) > 0 & \\
\vec{w} \cdot (\vec{\phi}_{bad} - \vec{\phi}_{good}) < 0 &
\end{aligned}
$$

If we look at $\vec{\phi}_{good} - \vec{\phi}_{bad}$ as a positive training instance and at $\vec{\phi}_{bad} - \vec{\phi}_{good}$ as a negative training instance, we can train any linear classifier to find weight the weight vector $\vec{w}$ that minimizes mistakes in ranking on the training set.

2.3 Lexical component based on character n-grams

Lexical scoring of BEER relies heavily on character n-grams. Precision, Recall and F1-score are used with character n-gram orders from 1 until 6. These scores are more smooth on the sentence level than word n-gram matching that is present in other metrics like BLEU (Papineni et al., 2002) or METEOR (Michael Denkowski and Alon Lavie, 2014).

BEER also uses precision, recall and F1-score on word level (but not with word n-grams). Matching of words is computed over METEOR alignments that use WordNet, paraphrasing and stemming to have more accurate alignment.

We also make distinction between function and content words. The more precise description of used features and their effectiveness is presented in (Stanojević and Sima'an, 2014c).

2.4 Reordering component based on PETs

The word alignments between system and reference translation can be simplified and considered as permutation of words from the reference translation in the system translation. Previous work by (Isozaki et al., 2010) and (Birch and Osborne, 2010) used this permutation view of word order and applied Kendall τ for evaluating its distance from ideal (monotone) word order.

BEER goes beyond this *skip-gram* based evaluation and decomposes permutation into a hierarchical structure which shows how subparts of permutation form small groups that can be reordered all together. Figure 1a shows PET for permutation $\langle 2, 5, 6, 4, 1, 3 \rangle$. Ideally the permutation tree will be filled with nodes $\langle 1, 2 \rangle$ which would say that there is no need to do any reordering (everything is in the right place). BEER has features that compute the number of different node types and for each different type it assigns a different weight. Sometimes there are more than one PET for the same permutation. Consider Figure 1b and 1c which are just 2 out of 3 possible PETs for permutation $\langle 4, 3, 2, 1 \rangle$. Counting the number of trees that could be built is also a good indicator of the permutation quality. See (Stanojević and Sima'an, 2014b) for details on using PETs for evaluating word order.

3 Corpus level BEER

Our goal here is to create corpus level extension of BEER that decomposes trivially at the sentence level. More concretely we wanted to have a corpus level BEER that would be the average of the sentence level BEER of all sentences in the corpus:

$$
BEER_{corpus}(c) = \frac{\sum_{s_i \in c} BEER_{sent}(s_i)}{|c|} \quad (1)
$$

In order to do so it is not suitable to to use previous scoring function of BEER . The previous scoring function (and training method) take care only that the better translation gets a higher score than the worse translation (on the sentence level). For this kind of corpus level computations we have an additional requirement that our sentence level scores need to be scaled proportional to the translation quality.

3.1 New BEER scoring function

To make the scores on the sentence level better scaled we transform our linear model into a probabilistic linear model – logistic regression with the following scoring function:

$$
score(h, r) = \frac{1}{1 + e^{-\sum_i w_i \times \phi_i(h,r)}}
$$

There is still a problem with this formulation. During training, the model is trained on the difference between two feature vectors $\vec{\phi}_{good} - \vec{\phi}_{bad}$, while during testing it is applied only to one feature vector $\vec{\phi}_{test}$. $\vec{\phi}_{good} - \vec{\phi}_{bad}$ is usually very close to the separating hyperplane, whereas $\vec{\phi}_{test}$ is usually very far from it. This is not a problem for ranking but it presents a problem if we want well scaled scores. Being extremely far from the

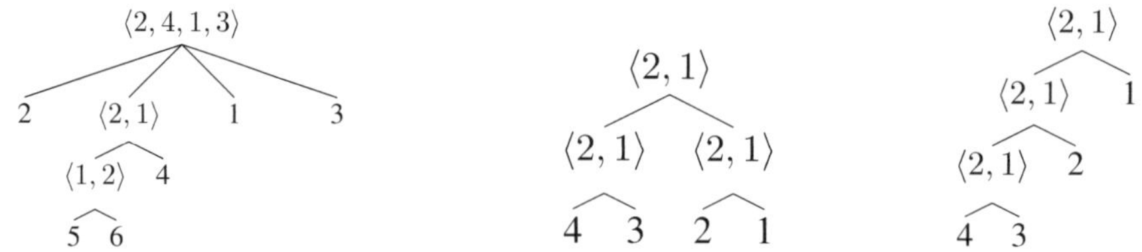

(a) Complex PET (b) Fully inverted PET 1 (c) Fully inverted PET 2

Figure 1: Examples of PETs

separated hyperplane gives extreme scores such as 0.9999999999912 and 0.00000000000000213 as a result which are obviously not well scaled.

Our model was trained to give a probability of the "good" translation being better than the "bad" translation so we should also use it in that way – to estimate the probability of one translation being better than the other. But which translation? We are given only one translation and we need to compute its score. To avoid this problem we pretend that we are computing a probability of the test sentence being a better translation than the reference for the given reference. In the ideal case the system translation and the reference translation will have the same features which will make logistic regression output probability 0.5 (it is uncertain about which translation is the better one). To make the scores between 0 and 1 we multiply this result with 2. The final scoring formula is the following:

$$score(h, r) = \frac{2}{1 + e^{-\sum_i w_i \times (\phi_i(h,r) - \phi_i(r,r))}}$$

4 BEER + Syntax = BEER_Treepel

The standard version of BEER does not use any syntactic knowledge. Since the training method of BEER allows the usage of a large number of features, it is trivial to integrate new features that would measure the matching between some syntax attributes of system and reference translations.

The syntactic representation we exploit is a dependency tree. The reason for that is that we can easily connect the structure with the lexical content and it is fast to compute which can often be very important for evaluation metrics when they need to evaluate on large data. We used Stanford's dependency parser (Chen and Manning, 2014) because it gives high accuracy parses in a very short time.

The features we compute on the dependency trees of the system and its reference translation are:

1. POS bigrams matching
2. dependency words bigram matching
3. arc type matching
4. valency matching

For each of these we compute precision, recall and F1-score.

It has been shown by other researchers (Popović and Ney, 2009) that POS tags are useful for abstracting away from concrete words and measure the grammatical aspect of translation (for example it can captures agreement).

Dependency word bigrams (bigrams connected by a dependency arc) are also useful for capturing long distance dependencies.

Most of the previous metrics that work with dependency trees usually ignore the type of the dependency that is (un)matched and treat all types equally (Yu et al., 2014). This is clearly not the case. Surely subject and complement arcs are more important than modifier arc. To capture this we created individual features for precision, recall and F1-score matching of each arc type so our system could learn on which arc type to put more weight.

All words take some number of arguments (valency), and not matching that number of arguments is a sign of a, potentially, bad translation. With this feature we hope to capture the aspect of not producing the right number of arguments for all words (and especially verbs) in the sentence.

This model BEER_Treepel contains in total 177 features out of which 45 are from original BEER .

5 BEER for tuning

The metrics that perform well on metrics task are very often not good for tuning. This is because recall has much more importance for human judgment than precision. The metrics that put more weight on recall than precision will be better with

tuning metric	BLEU	MTR	BEER	Length
BEER	16.4	**28.4**	**10.2**	115.7
BLEU	**18.2**	28.1	10.1	103.0
BEER_no_bias	18.0	27.7	9.8	**99.7**

Table 1: Tuning results with BEER without bias on WMT14 as tuning and WMT13 as test set

correlation with human judgment, but when used for tuning they will create overly long translations.

This bias for long translation is often resolved by manually setting the weights of recall and precision to be equal (Denkowski and Lavie, 2011; He and Way, 2009).

This problem is even bigger with metrics with many features. When we have metric like BEER_Treepel which has 117 features it is not clear how to set weights for each feature manually. Also some features might not have easy interpretation as precision or recall of something. Our method for automatic removing of this recall bias, which is presented in (Stanojević, 2015), gives very good results that can be seen in Table 1.

Before the automatic adaptation of weights for tuning, tuning with standard BEER produces translations that are 15% longer than the reference translations. This behavior is rewarded by metrics that are recall-heavy like METEOR and BEER and punished by precision heavy metrics like BLEU. After automatic adaptation of weights, tuning with BEER matches the length of reference translation even better than BLEU and achieves the BLEU score that is very close to tuning with BLEU. This kind of model is disliked by METEOR and BEER but by just looking at the length of the produced translations it is clear which approach is preferred.

6 Metric and Tuning task results

The results of WMT15 metric task of best performing metrics is shown in Tables 2 and 3 for the system level and Tables 4 and 5 for segment level.

On the sentence level for out of English language pairs on average BEER was the best metric (same as the last year). Into English it got 2nd place with its syntactic version and 4th place as the original BEER .

On the corpus level BEER is on average second for out of English language pairs and 6th for into English. BEER and BEER_Treepel are the best for en-ru and fi-en.

System Name	**TrueSkill Score** Tuning-Only	All	**BLEU**
BLEU-MIRA-DENSE	0.153	-0.177	12.28
ILLC-UvA	0.108	-0.188	12.05
BLEU-MERT-DENSE	0.087	-0.200	12.11
AFRL	0.070	-0.205	12.20
USAAR-TUNA	0.011	-0.220	12.16
DCU	-0.027	-0.256	11.44
METEOR-CMU	-0.101	-0.286	10.88
BLEU-MIRA-SPARSE	-0.150	-0.331	10.84
HKUST	-0.150	-0.331	10.99
HKUST-LATE	—	—	12.20

Table 6: Results on Czech-English tuning

The difference between BEER and BEER_Treepel are relatively big for de-en, cs-en and ru-en while for fr-en and fi-en the difference does not seem to be big.

The results of WMT15 tuning task is shown in Table 6. The system tuned with BEER without recall bias was the best submitted system for Czech-English and only the strong baseline outperformed it.

7 Conclusion

We have presented ILLC UvA submission to the shared metric and tuning task. All submissions are centered around BEER evaluation metric. On the metrics task we kept the good results we had on sentence level and extended our metric to corpus level with high correlation with high human judgment without losing the decomposability of the metric to the sentence level. Integration of syntactic features gave a bit of improvement on some language pairs. The removal of recall bias allowed us to go from overly long translations produced in tuning to translations that match reference relatively close by length and won the 3rd place in the tuning task. BEER is available at `https://github.com/stanojevic/beer`.

Acknowledgments

This work is supported by STW grant nr. 12271 and NWO VICI grant nr. 277-89-002. QT21 project support to the second author is also acknowledged (European Unions Horizon 2020 grant agreement no. 64545). We are thankful to Christos Louizos for help with incorporating a dependency parser to BEER Treepel.

Correlation coefficient	Pearson Correlation Coefficient					
Direction	fr-en	fi-en	de-en	cs-en	ru-en	Average
DPMFCOMB	.995 ± .006	.951 ± .013	**.949** ± .016	**.992** ± .004	.871 ± .025	**.952** ± .013
RATATOUILLE	.989 ± .010	.899 ± .019	.942 ± .018	.963 ± .008	**.941** ± .018	.947 ± .014
DPMF	**.997** ± .005	.939 ± .015	.929 ± .019	.986 ± .005	.868 ± .026	.944 ± .014
METEOR-WSD	.982 ± .011	.944 ± .014	.914 ± .021	.981 ± .006	.857 ± .026	.936 ± .016
CHRF3	.979 ± .012	.893 ± .020	.921 ± .020	.969 ± .007	.915 ± .023	.935 ± .016
BEER_TREEPEL	.981 ± .011	**.957** ± .013	.905 ± .021	.985 ± .005	.846 ± .027	.935 ± .016
BEER	.979 ± .012	.952 ± .013	.903 ± .022	.975 ± .006	.848 ± .027	.931 ± .016
CHRF	.997 ± .005	.942 ± .015	.884 ± .024	.982 ± .006	.830 ± .029	.927 ± .016
LEBLEU-OPTIMIZED	.989 ± .009	.895 ± .020	.856 ± .025	.970 ± .007	.918 ± .023	.925 ± .017
LEBLEU-DEFAULT	.960 ± .015	.895 ± .020	.856 ± .025	.946 ± .010	.912 ± .022	.914 ± .018

Table 2: System-level correlations of automatic evaluation metrics and the official WMT human scores when translating into English.

Correlation coefficient	Pearson Correlation Coefficient					
Metric	en-fr	en-fi	en-de	en-cs	en-ru	Average
CHRF3	.949 ± .021	**.813** ± .025	.784 ± .028	**.976** ± .004	.913 ± .011	**.887** ± .018
BEER	.970 ± .016	.729 ± .030	.811 ± .026	.951 ± .005	**.942** ± .009	.880 ± .017
LEBLEU-OPTIMIZED	.949 ± .020	.727 ± .030	**.896** ± .020	.944 ± .005	.867 ± .013	.877 ± .018
LEBLEU-DEFAULT	.949 ± .020	.760 ± .028	.827 ± .025	.946 ± .005	.849 ± .014	.866 ± .018
RATATOUILLE	.962 ± .017	.675 ± .031	.777 ± .028	.953 ± .005	.869 ± .013	.847 ± .019
CHRF	.949 ± .021	.771 ± .027	.572 ± .037	.968 ± .004	.871 ± .013	.826 ± .020
METEOR-WSD	.961 ± .018	.663 ± .032	.495 ± .039	.941 ± .005	.839 ± .014	.780 ± .022
BS	−.977 ± .014	.334 ± .039	−.615 ± .036	−.947 ± .005	−.791 ± .016	−.600 ± .022
DPMF	**.973** ± .015	n/a	.584 ± .037	n/a	n/a	.778 ± .026

Table 3: System-level correlations of automatic evaluation metrics and the official WMT human scores when translating out of English.

Direction	fr-en	fi-en	de-en	cs-en	ru-en	Average
DPMFCOMB	.367 ± .015	**.406** ± .015	**.424** ± .015	**.465** ± .012	**.358** ± .014	**.404** ± .014
BEER_TREEPEL	.358 ± .015	.399 ± .015	.386 ± .016	.435 ± .013	.352 ± .013	.386 ± .014
RATATOUILLE	**.367** ± .015	.384 ± .015	.380 ± .015	.442 ± .013	.336 ± .014	.382 ± .014
BEER	.359 ± .015	.392 ± .015	.376 ± .015	.417 ± .013	.336 ± .013	.376 ± .014
METEOR-WSD	.347 ± .015	.376 ± .015	.360 ± .015	.416 ± .013	.331 ± .014	.366 ± .014
CHRF	.350 ± .015	.378 ± .015	.366 ± .016	.407 ± .013	.322 ± .014	.365 ± .014
DPMF	.344 ± .014	.368 ± .015	.363 ± .015	.413 ± .013	.320 ± .014	.362 ± .014
CHRF3	.345 ± .014	.361 ± .016	.360 ± .015	.409 ± .012	.317 ± .014	.359 ± .014
LEBLEU-OPTIMIZED	.349 ± .015	.346 ± .015	.346 ± .014	.400 ± .013	.316 ± .015	.351 ± .014
LEBLEU-DEFAULT	.343 ± .015	.342 ± .015	.341 ± .014	.394 ± .013	.317 ± .014	.347 ± .014
TOTAL-BS	−.305 ± .013	−.277 ± .015	−.287 ± .014	−.357 ± .013	−.263 ± .014	−.298 ± .014

Table 4: Segment-level Kendall's τ correlations of automatic evaluation metrics and the official WMT human judgments when translating into English. The last three columns contain average Kendall's τ computed by other variants.

Direction	en-fr	en-fi	en-de	en-cs	en-ru	Average
BEER	.323 ± .013	**.361** ± .013	**.355** ± .011	**.410** ± .008	**.415** ± .012	**.373** ± .011
CHRF3	.309 ± .013	.357 ± .013	.345 ± .011	.408 ± .008	.398 ± .012	.363 ± .012
RATATOUILLE	**.340** ± .013	.300 ± .014	.337 ± .011	.406 ± .008	.408 ± .012	.358 ± .012
LEBLEU-DEFAULT	.321 ± .013	.354 ± .013	.345 ± .011	.385 ± .008	.386 ± .012	.358 ± .011
LEBLEU-OPTIMIZED	.325 ± .013	.344 ± .012	.345 ± .012	.383 ± .008	.385 ± .012	.356 ± .011
CHRF	.317 ± .013	.346 ± .012	.315 ± .013	.407 ± .008	.387 ± .012	.355 ± .012
METEOR-WSD	.316 ± .013	.270 ± .013	.287 ± .012	.363 ± .008	.373 ± .012	.322 ± .012
TOTAL-BS	−.269 ± .013	−.205 ± .012	−.231 ± .011	−.324 ± .008	−.332 ± .012	−.273 ± .011
DPMF	.308 ± .013	n/a	.289 ± .012	n/a	n/a	.298 ± .013
PARMESAN	n/a	n/a	n/a	.089 ± .006	n/a	.089 ± .006

Table 5: Segment-level Kendall's τ correlations of automatic evaluation metrics and the official WMT human judgments when translating out of English. The last three columns contain average Kendall's τ computed by other variants.

References

Alexandra Birch and Miles Osborne. 2010. LRscore for Evaluating Lexical and Reordering Quality in MT. In *Proceedings of the Joint Fifth Workshop on Statistical Machine Translation and MetricsMATR*, pages 327–332, Uppsala, Sweden, July. Association for Computational Linguistics.

Danqi Chen and Christopher D Manning. 2014. A fast and accurate dependency parser using neural networks. In *Empirical Methods in Natural Language Processing (EMNLP)*.

Michael Denkowski and Alon Lavie. 2011. Meteor 1.3: Automatic metric for reliable optimization and evaluation of machine translation systems. In *Proceedings of the Sixth Workshop on Statistical Machine Translation*, WMT '11, pages 85–91, Stroudsburg, PA, USA. Association for Computational Linguistics.

Y. He and A. Way. 2009. Improving the objective function in minimum error rate training. *Proceedings of the Twelfth Machine Translation Summit*, pages 238–245.

Ralf Herbrich, Thore Graepel, and Klaus Obermayer. 1999. Support Vector Learning for Ordinal Regression. In *In International Conference on Artificial Neural Networks*, pages 97–102.

Hideki Isozaki, Tsutomu Hirao, Kevin Duh, Katsuhito Sudoh, and Hajime Tsukada. 2010. Automatic Evaluation of Translation Quality for Distant Language Pairs. In *Proceedings of the 2010 Conference on Empirical Methods in Natural Language Processing*, EMNLP '10, pages 944–952, Stroudsburg, PA, USA. Association for Computational Linguistics.

Matous Machacek and Ondrej Bojar. 2014. Results of the wmt14 metrics shared task. In *Proceedings of the Ninth Workshop on Statistical Machine Translation*, pages 293–301, Baltimore, Maryland, USA, June. Association for Computational Linguistics.

Michael Denkowski and Alon Lavie. 2014. Meteor Universal: Language Specific Translation Evaluation for Any Target Language. In *Proceedings of the ACL 2014 Workshop on Statistical Machine Translation*.

Kishore Papineni, Salim Roukos, Todd Ward, and Wei-Jing Zhu. 2002. Bleu: A method for automatic evaluation of machine translation. In *Proceedings of the 40th Annual Meeting on Association for Computational Linguistics*, ACL '02, pages 311–318, Stroudsburg, PA, USA. Association for Computational Linguistics.

Maja Popović and Hermann Ney. 2009. Syntax-oriented evaluation measures for machine translation output. In *Proceedings of the Fourth Workshop on Statistical Machine Translation*, StatMT '09, pages 29–32, Stroudsburg, PA, USA. Association for Computational Linguistics.

Miloš Stanojević and Khalil Sima'an. 2014a. BEER: BEtter Evaluation as Ranking. In *Proceedings of the Ninth Workshop on Statistical Machine Translation*, pages 414–419, Baltimore, Maryland, USA, June. Association for Computational Linguistics.

Miloš Stanojević and Khalil Sima'an. 2014b. Evaluating Word Order Recursively over Permutation-Forests. In *Proceedings of SSST-8, Eighth Workshop on Syntax, Semantics and Structure in Statistical Translation*, pages 138–147, Doha, Qatar, October. Association for Computational Linguistics.

Miloš Stanojević and Khalil Sima'an. 2014c. Fitting Sentence Level Translation Evaluation with Many Dense Features. In *Proceedings of the 2014 Conference on Empirical Methods in Natural Language Processing (EMNLP)*, pages 202–206, Doha, Qatar, October. Association for Computational Linguistics.

Miloš Stanojević. 2015. Removing Biases from Trainable MT Metrics by Using Self-Training. *arXiv preprint arXiv:1508.02445*.

Hui Yu, Xiaofeng Wu, Jun Xie, Wenbin Jiang, Qun Liu, and Shouxun Lin. 2014. Red: A reference dependency based mt evaluation metric. In *COLING'14*, pages 2042–2051.

Hao Zhang and Daniel Gildea. 2007. Factorization of synchronous context-free grammars in linear time. In *In NAACL Workshop on Syntax and Structure in Statistical Translation (SSST*.

Predicting Machine Translation Adequacy with Document Embeddings

Mihaela Vela
Saarland University
Saarbrücken, Germany
m.vela@mx.uni-saarland.de

Liling Tan
Saarland University
Saarbrücken, Germany
liling.tan@uni-saarland.de

Abstract

This paper describes USAAR's submission to the the *metrics shared task* of the Workshop on Statistical Machine Translation (WMT) in 2015. The goal of our submission is to take advantage of the semantic overlap between hypothesis and reference translation for predicting MT output adequacy using language independent document embeddings. The approach presented here is learning a Bayesian Ridge Regressor using document skip-gram embeddings in order to automatically evaluate Machine Translation (MT) output by predicting semantic adequacy scores. The evaluation of our submission – measured by the correlation with human judgements – shows promising results on system-level scores.

1 Introduction

Translation is becoming an utility in everyday life. The increased availability of real-time machine translation services relying on Statistical Machine Translation (SMT) allows users who do not understand the language of the source text to quickly gist the text and understand its general meaning. For these users, accurate meaning of translated words is more important than the fluency of the translated sentence.

However, SMT suffers from poor lexical choices. Fluent but inadequate translations are commonly produced due to the strong bias towards the language model component that prefers consecutive words based on the data that the system is trained on.

Current state of art MT evaluation metrics are generally able to identify problems with grammaticality of the translation but less evidently accuracy of translated semantics, e.g. incorrect translation of ambiguous words or wrong assignment of semantic roles. In the example below, the ideal Machine Translation (MT) evaluation metric should appropriately penalise poor lexical choice, such as *braked*, and reward or at least allow leeway for semantically similar translations, such as *external trade*.

Source (DE):
Auch der Auenhandel bremste die Konjunktur.

Phrase-based MT:
The foreign trade braked the economy.

Neural MT:
External trade also slowed the economy.

Reference (EN):
Foreign goods trade had slowed, too.

The German word *bremste* is commonly used as *braked* in the context of driving, but the appropriate translation should have been *slowed* in the example mentioned above. Although the phrase *external trade* differs from *foreign goods trade* in the reference sentence, it should be considered as an acceptable translation.

We propose a semantically grounded, language independent approach using Semantic Textual Similarity (STS) to evaluate the adequacy of the machine translation outputs with respect to their reference translations.

The remainder of this paper is structured as follows. Section 2 gives an overview of the related work in the field of MT evaluation. Section 3 presents the approach behind the USAAR submission to the metrics shared task. In Section 4 we present the data and experiments for this submission. Section 5 covers the evaluation of our metric by the WMT2015 metrics task organisers and in Section 6 we conclude on our WMT2015 metrics task submission.

2 Related Work

Researchers in the field of MT evaluation have proposed a large variety of methods for assessing the quality of automatically produced translations. Approaches range from fully automatic quality scoring to efforts aimed at the development of "human" evaluation scores that try to exploit the (often tacit) linguistic knowledge of human evaluators.

2.1 Automatic Evaluation of MT

MT output is usually evaluated by automatic language-independent metrics that can be applied to MT output, independent of the target language. Automatic metrics typically compute the closeness (adequacy) of a hypothesis to a reference translation and differ from each other by how this closeness is measured. The most popular MT evaluation metrics are IBM BLEU (Papineni et al., 2002) and NIST (Doddington, 2002), used not only for tuning MT systems, but also as evaluation metrics for translation shared tasks, such as the Workshop on Statistical Machine Translation (WMT).

IBM BLEU uses n-gram precision by matching machine translation output against one or more reference translations. It accounts for adequacy and fluency by calculating word precision, i.e. the n-gram precision.

$$BLEU = BP \cdot \exp\left(\sum_{n=1}^{N} w_n \log p_n\right) \quad (1)$$

$$BP = \begin{cases} 1 & \text{if } c > r \\ -e^{(1-r/c)} & \text{if } c \leq r \end{cases} \quad (2)$$

In order to deal with the over generation of common words, precision counts are clipped, meaning that a reference word is exhausted after it is matched against the same word in the hypothesis. This is then called the modified n-gram precision. For BLEU, the modified n-gram precision is calculated with N=4, the results being combined by using the geometric mean. Instead of recall, BLEU computes the Brevity Penalty (BP) (see formula in 2), thus penalising candidate translations which are shorter than the reference translations.

The NIST metric is derived from IBM BLEU. The NIST score is the arithmetic mean of modified n-gram precision for N=5 scaled by the BP. Additionally, NIST also considers the information gain of each n-gram, giving more weight to more informative (less frequent) n-grams and less weight to less informative (more frequent) n-grams.

Another often used machine translation evaluation metric is METEOR (Denkowski and Lavie, 2014). Unlike IBM BLEU and NIST, METEOR evaluates a candidate translation by calculating precision and recall on the unigram level and combining them into a parametrised harmonic mean. The result from the harmonic mean is then scaled by a fragmentation penalty which penalizes gaps and differences in word order. METEOR is described in detail in Section 3.1.

Besides these evaluation metrics, several other metrics are used for the evaluation of MT output. Some of these are the WER (word error-rate) metric based on the Levensthein distance (Levenshtein, 1966), the position-independent error rate metric PER (Tillmann et al., 1997) and the translation edit rate metric TER (Snover et al., 2006) with its newer version TERp (Snover et al., 2009).

The semantics of both hypotheses and reference translations is considered by MEANT (Lo et al., 2012). MEANT, based on HMEANT (Lo and Wu, 2011a; Lo and Wu, 2011b; Lo and Wu, 2011c), is a fully automatic semantic MT evaluation metric, measuring semantic fidelity by determining the degree of parallelism of verb frames and semantic roles between hypothesis and reference translations. Some approaches aim at combining several linguistic and semantic aspects. Gonzàlez et al. (2014) as well as Comelles and Atserias (2014) introduce their fully automatic approaches to machine translation evaluation using lexical, syntactic and semantic information when comparing the machine translation output with reference translations.

2.2 Human Evaluation of MT

Human MT evaluation approaches employ the knowledge of human annotators to assess the quality of automatically produced translations along the two axes of target language correctness and semantic fidelity. The Linguistics Data Consortium (LDC) introduced a MT evaluation task that elicits quality judgement of MT output from human annotators using a numerical scale (Linguistics Data Consortium, 2005). These judgements were split into two categories: adequacy, the degree of meaning preservation, and fluency, target language correctness.

Adequacy judgements require annotators to rate the amount of meaning expressed in the reference translation that is also present in the translation hypothesis. Fluency judgements require annotators to rate how well the translation hypothesis in the target language is formed, disregarding the sentence meaning. Although evaluators are asked to assess the fluency and adequacy of a hypothesis translation on a Likert scale separately, Callison-Burch et al. (2007) reported high correlation between annotators' adequacy and fluency scores.

MT output is also evaluated by measuring human post-editing time for productivity (Guerberof, 2009; Zampieri and Vela, 2014), or by asking evaluators to rank MT system outputs (by ordering a set of translation hypotheses according to their quality). Vela and van Genabith (2015) show that this task is very easy to accomplish for evaluators, since it does not imply specific skills, a homogeneous group being enough to perform this task. This is also the method applied during the last years WMTs, where humans are asked to rank machine translation output by using APPRAISE (Federmann, 2012), a software tool that integrates facilities for such a ranking task.

An indirect human evaluation method, that is also employed for error analysis, are reading comprehension tests (e.g. Maney et al. (2012), Weiss and Ahrenberg (2012)). Other evaluation metrics try to measure the effort that is necessary for "repairing" MT output, that is, for transforming it into a linguistically correct and faithful translation. One such metric is HTER (Snover et al., 2006), which uses human annotators to generate targeted reference translations by means of post-editing, the rationale being that by this the shortest path between a hypothesis and its correct version can be found.

2.3 Semantic Textual Similarity

Given two snippets of text, the Semantic Textual Similarity (STS) task attempts to measure their semantic equivalence on a scale of 1 to 5 (Agirre et al., 2014). The STS task is organized annually during the SemEval workshop and systems are evaluated based on their Pearson correlation coefficient with the human annotations.

The STS is similar to the task of determining the adequacy of a translation hypothesis with respect to a reference translation. The STS task is usually treated as a regression task where systems are trained using features such as:

(i) linguistics annotation overlaps between the two text snippets, e.g. syntactic dependency, lexical paraphrases, part of speech (Šarić et al., 2012; Han et al., 2012; Pilehvar et al., 2013)

(ii) machine translation metrics as features in training a supervised regressor (Rios et al., 2012; Barrón-Cedeño et al., 2013; Huang and Chang, 2014; Tan et al., 2015b)

(iii) word/document embeddings similarity (Sultan et al., 2015; Arora et al., 2015).

Linguistic annotations are restricted by the availability of the annotation tools, that are often language dependent. Machine translation evaluation metrics generally provide a shallow comparison between hypotheses and reference translations focusing on capturing the grammatical similarities between the texts, whereas the use of document embeddings focuses on capturing the semantic similarity between texts. Word embeddings dates back to the traditional Latent Semantic Analysis (LSA) vector spaces used for information retrieval (Landauer and Dutnais, 1997) to the current trend of using neural nets for NLP/MT tasks (Bordes et al., 2011; Huang et al., 2012; Bordes et al., 2012; Chen and Manning, 2014; Bowman et al., 2015).

3 Our Approach

Although consensus exists that lexical-based metrics cannot cover the entire range of linguistic phenomena (Vela et al., 2014a; Vela et al., 2014b), the goal in the MT community remains to have a language independent metric that takes into account for lexical, syntactic and semantic information when mapping the MT output against the reference translation. The questions that have to be accounted for in such a language-independent metric are:

(i) Is there a lexical overlap between reference and hypothesis translation?

(ii) Is there a syntactic overlap between reference and hypothesis translation?

(iii) Is there a semantic overlap between reference and hypothesis translation?

In the ideal situation one would also take into account lexical, syntactic and semantic information from the source text. Specific information (on lexical, syntactic, semantic level) from the source text could help improving not only the translation process, but also the evaluation.

As pointed out in Section 2, there are several approaches which tend to cover the entire range of linguistic phenomena in the evaluation process. The approach presented in this paper is leaned on the STS approach, mentioned in Section 2.3, aiming to provide a language independent adequacy score using document embedding similarity as opposed to the traditional synonyms and paraphrase overlap approach used in METEOR. The matching of synonyms in METEOR relies on WordNet (Miller, 1995), which is a limited resource, making it impossible to use the synonymy module from METEOR for other languages than English. The provided or self-extracted paraphrase tables for METEOR are available only for languages for which big corpora are available, making it difficult to provide paraphrases for under-resourced languages. Since METEOR relies on the WordNet synonymy and language dependent paraphrase tables for its semantic component, our goal is to substitute this components with a language independent component.

Different from the STS task, the WMT metrics task provides the ranks of the systems' hypotheses instead of absolute human evaluation scores of the translation hypotheses. To generate the absolute scores, we use the METEOR scores between the translation hypotheses and the reference translations.

To induce the word embeddings, we trained a skip-gram model phrasal word2vec neural net (Mikolov et al., 2013) using `gensim` (Řehůřek and Sojka, 2010). The neural nets were trained to produce 400 dense features for 100 epochs with a window size of 5 for all words from the WMT metrics task data.

$$v(doc) = \frac{\sum_i^n v(w_i)}{n} \qquad (3)$$
$$doc = \{w_1, ..., w_n\}$$

To generate the document embeddings, *v(doc)*, we sum the word embeddings from the document and normalised it by the number of words. The setup for the skip-gram model and the document vector is similar the techniques uses in STS tasks (Sultan et al., 2015; Tan et al., 2015a).

$$sim(hyp, ref) = v(hyp) \cdot v(ref) \qquad (4)$$

The document embedding similarity is achieved by the dot product between the translation hypothesis (*hyp*) and the reference translation (*ref*). Geometrically, the dot product between the hypothesis and the reference translation yields the cosine similarity between two vectors. Alternatively, one could also calculate the cosine similarity by summing the square of the word vector of the intersecting word embeddings and normalise the document by the root of the sum square for all words in the documents (Tan, 2013)[1].

Using the similarity scores between the hypothesis and reference embeddings, we train a Bayesian Ridge Regressor targeting the METEOR scores as the desired output.

3.1 METEOR

METEOR (Metric for Evaluation of Translation with Explicit ORdering) (Denkowski and Lavie, 2014) is an MT evaluation metric which tries to consider both grammatical and semantic knowledge. The metric is based on the alignment between a hypothesis translation and a reference translation containing four modules. The number of modules to be used depends on the availability of resources for a specific language. The first module generates the alignments based on the surface forms of the words in the hypothesis and reference translation. The next module performs the alignment on word stems, followed by the alignment of words listed as synonyms in WordNet (Miller, 1995). The last module is responsible for the paraphrase matching between the hypothesis and reference translation, based on the provided or the self-extracted paraphrase tables. For the final score calculation all matches are generalised to phrase/chunk matches with a start position and phrase length in each sentence.

Different from other evaluation metrics, METEOR makes the distinction between content words and function words in the hypothesis (h_c, h_f) and reference (r_c, r_f) translation. This distinction is made by a provided function words list.

[1]An implementation of the alternative cosine can be fount at `http://tinyurl.com/pywsd-cosine`. The original implementation is reported in (Tan and Bond, 2013)

From the final alignment between hypothesis and reference translation, precision (P) and recall (R) is calculated by weighting content words and function words differently. This is described by Denkowski and Lavie (2014) as follows. For each of the matchers (m_i) count the number of content and function words covered by matches of this type in the hypothesis ($m_i(h_c), m_i(h_r)$) and reference ($m_i(r_c), m_i(r_r)$) translation. The weighted precision (P) and recall (R) is computed by using the matcher weights $w_i...w_n$ and the function word weight γ as shown in 5 and 6.

$$P = \frac{\sum_i w_i \cdot (\delta \cdot m_i(h_c) + (1-\delta) \cdot m_i(h_c))}{\gamma \cdot \mid h_c \mid + (1-\gamma) \cdot \mid h_f \mid} \tag{5}$$

$$R = \frac{\sum_i w_i \cdot (\delta \cdot m_i(r_c) + (1-\delta) \cdot m_i(r_c))}{\gamma \cdot \mid r_c \mid + (1-\gamma) \cdot \mid r_f \mid} \tag{6}$$

The harmonic mean is calculated by the formula in equation 7.

$$F_{mean} = \frac{P \cdot R}{\alpha \cdot P + (1-\alpha) \cdot P} \tag{7}$$

METEOR also accounts for word order differences and gaps by scaling F_{mean} by the fragmentation penalty (Pen). The fragmentation penalty (Pen) in equation 8 is computed by using the total number of matched words (m) and the number of chunks (ch).

$$Pen = \gamma \cdot \left(\frac{ch}{m}\right)^{\beta} \tag{8}$$

The final score is then:

$$Score = (1 - Pen) \cdot F_{mean} \tag{9}$$

The parameters α, β, γ, δ and $w_i...w_n$ are parameters that can be used for tuning METEOR for a given task.

3.2 Cosine Similarity

Cosine similarity is a similarity measure that can handle the fact that very similar documents (in our case sentences) may have different lengths. The cosine similarity of two documents is calculated by deriving a vector ($\vec{V}$) for each sentence or document d, denoted as $\vec{V}(d)$[2]. The set of documents in a collection is viewed as a set of vectors in a vector space, each term (meaning a word) having its own axis. By this kind of representation the initial ordering of terms in the document is lost, since cosine similarity does not incorporate context.

The cosine of two vectors can be derived by using the Euclidean dot product formula:

$$a \cdot b = \mid a \mid\mid b \mid \cos\theta \tag{10}$$

Derived from the formula in (10) the similarity between two documents d_1 and d_2 can be computed by the cosine similarity of their vector representations $\vec{V}(d_1)$ and $\vec{V}(d_2)$.

$$\cos(\theta) = \frac{\vec{V}(d_1) \cdot \vec{V}(d_2)}{\mid \vec{V}(d_1) \mid\mid \vec{V}(d_2) \mid} \tag{11}$$

The numerator in (11) represents the dot product of the vectors $\vec{V}(d_1)$ and $\vec{V}(d_2)$ and is defined as shown in equation (12).

$$\vec{V}(d_1) \cdot \vec{V}(d_2) = \sum_{i=1}^{n} \vec{V_i}(d_1) \times \vec{V_i}(d_2) \tag{12}$$

The denominator corresponds to the product of the Euclidean length of the vectors $\vec{V_i}(d_1)$ and $\vec{V_i}(d_1)$.

$$\mid \vec{V}(d_1) \mid = \sqrt{\sum_{i=1}^{n} \vec{V_i}(d_1)} \tag{13}$$

The vectors are length normalised by the formulas in (13) and (14).

$$\mid \vec{V}(d_2) \mid = \sqrt{\sum_{i=1}^{n} \vec{V_i}(d_2)} \tag{14}$$

3.3 ZWICKEL: A Regression-based Metric

Similar to the Semantic Textual Similarity (STS) and MT Quality Estimation approaches (Scarton et al., 2015), we treat the MT metric task as a regression task with the aim of learning a Bayesian Ridge function that maps the cosine similarity feature to the target METEOR score.

A Bayesian Regressor finds a maximum a posteriori solution under a Gaussian prior N over the parameters w with the precision of λ^{-1}. The α and λ parameters are treated as random variables estimated from the data.

$$p(y|X, w, \alpha) == N(y|X, w, \alpha) \tag{15}$$

[2] The normalization of the terms in the vector is computed by using using $TF * IDF$

The Bayesian Ridge estimates a probabilistic regression model with a zero-mean prior for the parameter w, given by a spherical Gaussian:

$$p(w|\lambda) = N(w|0, \lambda^{-1}I_p) \qquad (16)$$

Without the caveats of mathematical argot, we refer to the cosine similarities as X, and to the METEOR scores as Y. We aim to learn a regressor that outputs the paraphrase and synonym METEOR scores using the cosine similarities, without the paraphrase/synonym tables. Essentially, this leads to a language independent METEOR measure based on cosine similarity between translation and reference vectors.

3.4 COMET: A Combination of METEOR and ZWICKEL

We noticed that the outputs of the basic `ZWICKEL` score is conservative and does not allow an extreme 0.0 or 1.0 score unlike the METEOR score. Thus, we created a *"switch-like metric"*, `COMET`, that treat the METEOR scores as oracle when METEOR reports 0.0 or 1.0 scores, otherwise it falls back to `ZWICKEL`.

4 Experiments

This year's USAAR submission to the WMT metrics shared task concentrated on evaluating translations into German and into English, assigning a score both at sentence and system level.

4.1 Training Data

For training our system we used the available data from the previous WMT shared tasks by conflating them into a single data set[3]. The into German set consisted of 359545 sentence pairs and the into English set consisted of 1194017 sentence pairs.

4.2 Test Data

The test data for our evaluation metrics consist of all system outputs from this year's translation task performed on the newstest2015 data set. Depending on the source language the data sets consist of a different number of sentences. Into English we evaluated MT systems having the following source languages:

- Czech with 10 system submissions and 2655 translated sentences per system
- German with 13 system submissions and 2168 translated sentences per system
- Finnish with 14 system submissions and 1369 translated sentences per system
- Russian with 13 system submissions and 2817 translated sentences per system

Into German we evaluated 16 systems with 2168 translated sentences per system.

Based on the sentence scores we provided also a system score for each language pair. The system score was calculated by using different means (median, arithmetic mean, arithmetic geometric mean, harmonic mean and root squared mean) for each proposed metric.

4.3 USAAR's Submission to the WMT2015 Metrics Shared Task

In order to evaluate the efficacy of our method we contributed with three systems to the metrics task:

- `COSINE`: the raw document embedding similarity, i.e. *sim(hyp, ref)*
- `ZWICKEL`: the cosine-based metric outputs from the regressor described above
- `COMET`: the combination of `ZWICKEL` outputs from the regressor and METEOR

5 Evaluation

All submissions to the metrics task were evaluated[4] at system level by computing their Pearson correlation coefficient with human judgements. For the evaluation of translations into English our best submission is `COMET`, achieving on average a correlation coefficient of 0.788 ± 0.026. For the evaluation of translations from English into German, `COMET` is again our best submission with a correlation coefficient of 0.448 ± 0.40.

Table 5 shows the system-level Pearson correlation coefficient for `COSINE`, `ZWICKEL` and `COMET`[5] for each language pair into English and for the language pair English-German.

Spearman's correlation coefficient was also computed, but just the average over all language

[3]We have compiled the WMT08-15 metrics task data sets into a single python-readable library that is easily accessible at `https://github.com/alvations/warmth`.

[4]The numbers reported in this section are provided by the organisers of the WMT2015 metrics shared task

[5]For the translations into English the system-level score is the root mean square of the sentence-level scores. For the translations from English into German the best system-level scores are achieved by the arithmetic geometric mean of the sentence-level scores.

	Pearson Correlation Coefficient		
Language pair	COSINE	ZWICKEL	COMET
Finnish-English	NaN	-0.093±0.043	0.834±0.023
German-English	0.008±0.052	0.286±0.052	0.847±0.027
Czech-English	0.912±0.013	0.406±0.031	0.896±0.014
Russian-English	NaN	0.264±0.052	0.603±0.041
English-German	NaN	-0.232±0.044	0.448±0.040

Table 1: Pearson correlation coefficient for COSINE, ZWICKEL and COMET.

	Spearman's Correlation Coefficient		
Average	COSINE	ZWICKEL	COMET
into English	0.122±0.079	0.066±0.087	0.665±0.069
into German	0.084±0.084	-0.235±0.069	0.588±0.072

Table 2: System-level Spearman's correlation coefficient for COSINE, ZWICKEL and COMET.

pairs into English and into German. From the results in Table 5 we notice that COMET was the metric performing best for both translations into English and German, achieving a coefficient of 0.665±0.069 for translations into English and 0.588±0.072 for translations from German into English.

6 Conclusion

This paper presents USAAR's submission to the WMT2015 metrics shared task. Our aim of our submission was a language independent method for predicting MT adequacy based on the semantic similarity between hypothesis and reference translation by using document embeddings. We contributed with three evaluation metrics, COMET, a combination of a cosine-based metric and METEOR, being the one correlating best with the human evaluators.

Previous studies have shown that METEOR systematically underestimate the quality of the translations (Vela et al., 2014b). Future work on our approach using document embeddings and cosine similarities could be used to also predict different scores (i.e. other than METEOR). Additionally, further experiments on document/word embeddings would be beneficial to find the best-fit solution for the cosine similarity calculation between a machine translation and its reference translation.

Acknowledgements

The research leading to these results has received funding from the People Programme (Marie Curie Actions) of the European Union's Seventh Framework Programme FP7/2007-2013/ under REA grant agreement no. 317471.

References

Eneko Agirre, Carmen Banea, Claire Cardie, Daniel Cer, Mona Diab, Aitor Gonzalez-Agirre, Weiwei Guo, Rada Mihalcea, German Rigau, and Janyce Wiebe. 2014. SemEval-2014 Task 10: Multilingual Semantic Textual Similarity. In *Proceedings of the 8th International Workshop on Semantic Evaluation (SemEval 2014)*, Dublin, Ireland, August.

Piyush Arora, Chris Hokamp, Jennifer Foster, and Gareth Jones. 2015. DCU: Using Distributional Semantics and Domain Adaptation for the Semantic Textual Similarity SemEval-2015 Task 2. In *Proceedings of the 9th International Workshop on Semantic Evaluation (SemEval 2015)*, pages 143–147, Denver, Colorado, June.

Alberto Barrón-Cedeño, Lluís Màrquez, Maria Fuentes, Horacio Rodriguez, and Jordi Turmo. 2013. UPC-CORE: What Can Machine Translation Evaluation Metrics and Wikipedia Do for Estimating Semantic Textual Similarity? In *2nd Joint Conference on Lexical and Computational Semantics (SEM)*, pages 143–147, Atlanta, Georgia, USA, June.

Antoine Bordes, Jason Weston, Ronan Collobert, and Yoshua Bengio. 2011. Learning Structured Embeddings of Knowledge Bases. In *Proceedings of the Association for the Advancement of Artificial Intelligence (AAAI)*.

Antoine Bordes, Xavier Glorot, Jason Weston, and Yoshua Bengio. 2012. Joint learning of words and meaning representations for open-text semantic parsing. In *Proceedings of the 18th International Conference on Artificial Intelligence and Statistics*, pages 127–135, La Palma, Canary Islands, April.

Samuel R. Bowman, Christopher Potts, and Christopher D. Manning. 2015. Learning Distributed Word Representations for Natural Logic Reasoning. In *Proceedings of the Association for the Advancement of Artificial Intelligence Spring Symposium (AAAI)*, pages 10–13, March.

Chris Callison-Burch, Cameron Fordyce, Philipp Koehn, Christof Monz, and Josh Schroeder. 2007. (Meta-) Evaluation of Machine Translation. In *Proceedings of the 2nd Workshop on Statistical Machine Translation (WMT)*, pages 136–158.

Danqi Chen and Christopher Manning. 2014. A Fast and Accurate Dependency Parser using Neural Networks. In *Proceedings of the Conference on Empirical Methods in Natural Language Processing (EMNLP)*, pages 740–750, Doha, Qatar, October.

Elisabet Comelles and Jordi Atserias. 2014. VERTa Participation in the WMT14 Metrics Task. In *Proceedings of the 9th Workshop on Statistical Machine Translation (WMT)*, pages 368–375, Baltimore, Maryland, USA, June. Association for Computational Linguistics.

Michael Denkowski and Alon Lavie. 2014. Meteor Universal: Language Specific Translation Evaluation for Any Target Language. In *Proceedings of the Workshop on Statistical Machine Translation (WMT)*.

George Doddington. 2002. Automatic Evaluation of Machine Translation Quality Using N-gram Co-Occurrence Statistics. In *Proceedings of the 2nd International Conference on Human Language Technologies (HLT)*, pages 138–145.

Christian Federmann. 2012. Appraise: An Open-Source Toolkit for Manual Evaluation of Machine Translation Output. *PBML*, 98:25–35, 9.

Meritxell Gonzàlez, Alberto Barrón-Cedeño, and Lluís Màrquez. 2014. IPA and STOUT: Leveraging Linguistic and Source-based Features for Machine Translation Evaluation. In *Proceedings of the 9th Workshop on Statistical Machine Translation (WMT)*, pages 394–401, Baltimore, Maryland, USA, June. Association for Computational Linguistics.

Ana Guerberof. 2009. Productivity and Quality in the Post-editing of Outputs from Translation Memories and Machine Translation. *International Journal of Localization*, 7(1).

Aaron L. F. Han, Derek F. Wong, and Lidia S. Chao. 2012. LEPOR: A Robust Evaluation Metric for Machine Translation with Augmented Factors. In *Proceedings of COLING 2012: Posters*, pages 441–450, Mumbai, India, December.

Pingping Huang and Baobao Chang. 2014. SSMT:A Machine Translation Evaluation View To Paragraph-to-Sentence Semantic Similarity. In *Proceedings of the 8th International Workshop on Semantic Evaluation (SemEval 2014)*, pages 585–589, Dublin, Ireland, August.

Eric H. Huang, Richard Socher, Christopher D. Manning, and Andrew Y. Ng. 2012. Improving word representations via global context and multiple word prototypes. In *Proceedings of the 50th Annual Meeting of the Association for Computational Linguistics (ACL)*, pages 873–882.

Thomas K. Landauer and Susan T. Dutnais. 1997. A Solution to Platos Problem: The Latent Semantic Analysis Theory of Acquisition, Induction, and Representation of Knowledge. *PSYCHOLOGICAL REVIEW*, 104(2):211–240.

Vladimir Iosifovich Levenshtein. 1966. Binary Codes Capable of Correcting Deletions, Insertions and Reversals. *Soviet Physics Doklady*, 10(8):707–710.

Linguistics Data Consortium. 2005. Linguistic Data Annotation Specification: Assessment of Fluency and Adequacy in Translations.

Chi-Kiu Lo and Dekai Wu. 2011a. MEANT: An Inexpensive, High-accuracy, Semi-automatic Metric for Evaluating Translation Utility Based on Semantic Roles. In *Proceedings of the 49th Annual Meeting of the Association of Computational Linguistics: Human Language Technologies (ACL-HLT)*, pages 220–229.

Chi-Kiu Lo and Dekai Wu. 2011b. SMT vs. AI redux: How Semantic Frames Evaluate MT More Accurately. In *Proceedings of the 22nd International Joint Conference on Artificial Intelligence (IJCAI)*.

Chi-Kiu Lo and Dekai Wu. 2011c. Structured vs. Flat Semantic Role Representations for Machine Translation Evaluation. In *Proceedings of the 5th Workshop on Syntax and Structure in Statistical Translation (SSST)*.

Chi-kiu Lo, Anand Karthik Tumuluru, and Dekai Wu. 2012. Fully Automatic Semantic MT Evaluation. In *Proceedings of the 7th Workshop on Statistical Machine Translation (WMT)*, pages 243–252, Montréal, Canada, June. Association for Computational Linguistics.

Tucker Maney, Linda Sibert, Dennis Perzanowski, Kalyan Gupta, and Astrid Schmidt-Nielsen. 2012. Toward Determining the Comprehensibility of Machine Translations. In *Proceedings of the 1st PITR*, pages 1–7.

Tomas Mikolov, Kai Chen, Greg Corrado, and Jeffrey Dean. 2013. Efficient Estimation of Word Representations in Vector Space. *arXiv*, 1301.3781.

George A. Miller. 1995. WordNet: A Lexical Database for English. *Communications of the ACM*, 38(11):39–41, November.

Kishore Papineni, Salim Roukos, Todd Ward, and Wei-Jing Zhu. 2002. BLEU: A Method for Automatic Evaluation of Machine Translation. In *Proceedings of the 40th Annual Meeting of the Association for Computational Linguistics (ACL)*, pages 311–318.

Mohammad Taher Pilehvar, David Jurgens, and Roberto Navigli. 2013. Align, Disambiguate and Walk: A Unified Approach for Measuring Semantic Similarity. In *Proceedings of the 51st Annual Meeting of the Association for Computational Linguistics*, pages 1341–1351, Sofia, Bulgaria, August.

Miguel Rios, Wilker Aziz, and Lucia Specia. 2012. UOW: Semantically Informed Text Similarity. In *The 1st Joint Conference on Lexical and Computational Semantics (SEM)*, pages 673–678, Montréal, Canada, June.

Carolina Scarton, Marcos Zampieri, Mihaela Vela, Josef van Genabith, and Lucia Specia. 2015. Searching for Context: a Study on Document-Level Labels for Translation Quality Estimation. In *Proceedings of the 18th Annual Conference of the European Association for Machine Translation (EAMT)*, pages 121–128, Antalya, Turkey, May.

Matthew Snover, Bonnie Dorr, Richard Schwartz, Linnea Micciulla, and John Makhoul. 2006. A Study of Translation Edit Rate with Targeted Human Annotation. In *Proceedings of the Association for Machine Translation in the Americas (AMTA)*, pages 223–231.

Matthew Snover, Nitin Madnani, Bonnie Dorr, and Richard Schwartz. 2009. Fluency, Adequacy, or HTER? Exploring Different Human Judgments with a Tunable MT Metric. In *Proceedings of the 4th Workshop on Statistical Machine Translation (WMT)*, pages 259–268.

Md Arafat Sultan, Steven Bethard, and Tamara Sumner. 2015. DLS@CU: Sentence Similarity from Word Alignment and Semantic Vector Composition. In *Proceedings of the 9th International Workshop on Semantic Evaluation (SemEval 2015)*, pages 148–153, Denver, Colorado, June.

Liling Tan and Francis Bond. 2013. Xling: Matching query sentences to a parallel corpus using topic models for wsd. In *Proceedings of the 7th International Workshop on Semantic Evaluation (SemEval 2013)*, pages 167–170, Atlanta, Georgia, USA, June.

Liling Tan, Rohit Gupta, and Josef van Genabith. 2015a. Usaar-wlv: Hypernym generation with deep neural nets. In *Proceedings of the 9th International Workshop on Semantic Evaluation (SemEval 2015)*, pages 932–937.

Liling Tan, Carolina Scarton, Lucia Specia, and Josef van Genabith. 2015b. USAAR-SHEFFIELD: Semantic Textual Similarity with Deep Regression and Machine Translation Evaluation Metrics. In *Proceedings of the 9th International Workshop on Semantic Evaluation (SemEval 2015)*, pages 85–89, Denver, Colorado, June.

Liling Tan. 2013. Examining Crosslingual Word Sense Disambiguation. Master's thesis, Nanyang Technological University.

Christoph Tillmann, Stephan Vogel, Hermann Ney, Alexander Zubiaga, and Hassan Sawaf. 1997. Accelerated DP Based Search For Statistical Translation. In *Proceedings of the EUROSPEECH*, pages 2667–2670.

Mihaela Vela and Josef van Genabith. 2015. Reassessing the WMT2013 Human Evaluation with Professional Translators Trainees. In *Proceedings of the 18th Annual Conference of the European Association for Machine Translation (EAMT)*, pages 161–168, May.

Mihaela Vela, Anne-Kathrin Schumann, and Andrea Wurm. 2014a. Beyond Linguistic Equivalence. An Empirical Study of Translation Evaluation in a Translation Learner Corpus. In *Proceedings of the EACL Workshop on Humans and Computer-assisted Translation (HaCat)*, pages 47–56, April.

Mihaela Vela, Anne-Kathrin Schumann, and Andrea Wurm. 2014b. Human Translation Evaluation and its Coverage by Automatic Scores. In *Proceedings of the Language Resources and Evaluation Conference Workshop on Automatic and Manual Metrics for Operational Translation Evaluation (MTE)*, pages 20–30, May.

Radim Řehůřek and Petr Sojka. 2010. Software framework for topic modelling with large corpora. In *Proceedings of Language Resources and Evaluation Conference*, pages 46–50, Valletta, Malta.

Frane Šarić, Goran Glavaš, Mladen Karan, Jan Šnajder, and Bojana Dalbelo Bašić. 2012. TAKELAP: Systems for Measuring Semantic Text Similarity. In *Proceedings of the 1st Joint Conference on Lexical and Computational Semantics (SEM)*, pages 441–448.

Sandra Weiss and Lars Ahrenberg. 2012. Error Profiling for Evaluation of Machine-translated Text: a Polish-English Case Study. In *Proceedings of the 8th Language Resources and Evaluation Conference (LREC)*, pages 1764–1770.

Marcos Zampieri and Mihaela Vela. 2014. Quantifying the Influence of MT Output in the Translators Performance: A Case Study in Technical Translation. In *Proceedings of the EACL Workshop on Humans and Computer-assisted Translation (HaCat)*, pages 93–98, April.

LeBLEU: N-gram-based Translation Evaluation Score for Morphologically Complex Languages

Sami Virpioja
Lingsoft, Inc.
Helsinki, Finland
sami.virpioja@lingsoft.fi

Stig-Arne Grönroos
Aalto University
Dept. of Signal Processing and Acoustics
stig-arne.gronroos@aalto.fi

Abstract

This paper describes the LeBLEU evaluation score for machine translation, submitted to WMT15 Metrics Shared Task. LeBLEU extends the popular BLEU score to consider fuzzy matches between word n-grams. While there are several variants of BLEU that allow to non-exact matches between words either by character-based distance measures or morphological preprocessing, none of them use fuzzy comparison between longer chunks of text. The results on WMT data sets show that fuzzy n-gram matching improves correlations to human evaluation especially for highly compounding languages.

1 Introduction

The quality of machine translation has improved to the level that the translation hypotheses are useful starting points for human translators for almost any language pair. In the post-editing task, the ultimate way to evaluate the machine translation quality is to measure the editing time. Editing times are naturally related to the number and types of the edits—and thus the number of keystrokes (Frederking and Nirenburg, 1994)—the post-editor needs to get the final translation from the hypothesis. If we compare the raw translation hypothesis and its post-edited version, an appropriate edit distance measure should correlate to the edit time. However, implementing such a measure is far from trivial.

In automatic speech recognition, common evaluation measures are Word Error Rate (WER) and Letter Error Rate (LER) that are based on the Levenshtein edit distance (Levenshtein, 1966). LER is more reasonable measure than WER for morphologically complex languages, in which the same word can occur in many inflected and derived forms (Creutz et al., 2007). However, both give too high penalty for the variations in word ordering, which are frequent in translations. Even in English, there are often at least two grammatically correct orders for a complex sentence. For languages in which the grammatical roles are marked by morphology and not the word order, there may be many more options.

An edit distance measure suitable for machine translation would require move operations. However, such measures are computationally very expensive: finding the minimum edit distance with moves is NP-hard (Shapira and Storer, 2002), making it cumbersome for evaluation and unsuitable for automatic tuning of the translation models. Possible solutions include limiting the move operations or searching only for an approximate solution. For example, Translation Edit Rate (TER) by Snover et al. (2006) uses a shift operation that moves a contiguous sequence of words to another location, as well as a greedy search algorithm to find the minimum distance. Stanford Probabilistic Edit Distance Evaluation (SPEDE) by Wang and Manning (2012) applies a probabilistic push-down automaton that captures non-nested, limited distance word swapping.

A different approach to avoid the requirement of exactly same word order in the hypothesis and reference translations is to concentrate on comparing only small parts of the full texts. For example, the popular BLEU metric by Papineni et al. (2002) considers only local ordering of words. To be precise, it calculates the geometric mean precision of the n-grams of length between one and four. As high precision is easy to obtain by providing a very short hypothesis translation, hypotheses that are shorter than the reference are penalized by a brevity penalty.

BLEU, TER and many other word-based methods assume that a single word (or n-gram) is either correct or incorrect, nothing in between. This is problematic for inflected or derived words (e.g. "translate" and "translated" are considered two different words) as well as compound words (e.g. "salt-and-pepper" vs. "salt and pepper"). This is a minor issue for English, but it makes the evaluation unreliable for many other languages. For example, in English–German translation, producing "Arbeits Geberverband" from "employers' organization" would give no hits if the reference had the compound "Arbeitgeberverband".

A common approach to the problem of inflected word forms—as well as to the simpler issues of uppercase letters and punctuation characters—is preprocessing. For example, METEOR (Banerjee and Lavie, 2005; Denkowski and Lavie, 2011) uses a stemmer. Popović (2011) applies and combines BLEU-style scores based on part-of-speech (POS) tags as well as morphemes induced by the unsupervised method by Creutz and Lagus (2005). Also the AMBER score by Chen and Kuhn (2011) combines many BLEU variants, and in some variants, the words are heuristically segmented.

Our approach is to extend the BLEU metric to work better on morphologically complex languages without using any language-specific resources. Instead of giving one point for exactly same n-gram or zero points for any difference, we include "soft" or "fuzzy" hits for word n-grams based on letter edit distance. We call the score LeBLEU; this name can be interpreted either as "Letter-edit-BLEU" or "Levenshtein-BLEU". LeBLEU has two main parameters, n-gram length and fuzzy match threshold, that are easy to tune for different types of languages.[1]

There are at least three previous approaches that resemble LeBLEU in that they try not to over-penalize different word orderings and word forms, but do not require any preprocessing tools or resources. Denoual and Lepage (2005) simply use the standard BLEU score on the level of characters, treating word delimiters as any other characters. In order to capture long enough sequences of text, they increase the maximum n-gram length to 18. Compared to word-based BLEU, their method does not increase the correlations to human evaluation in English.

Homola et al. (2009) propose a score that is a weighted combination of two measures: an alignment score that applies letter edit distances between the word forms and a structural score that measures the differences in word order. In contrast to LeBLEU, it still strongly penalizes errors in compounding, as the alignment is word-to-word and fuzzy matches are accepted only if the LER between a pair of words is lower than 15%.

More recently, Libovický and Pecina (2014) have proposed "tolerant BLEU", a variant of BLEU that similarly to LeBLEU finds fuzzy matches between hypothesis and reference words. Instead of Levenshtein edit distance, they apply a specific affix distance measure that requires an exact match in the middle of the words. Moreover, they apply a more complex procedure, in which the words between the hypothesis and reference are first aligned using the Munkres algorithm. Then the hypothesis words are replaced by the matched reference words while applying a penalty based on the affix distance, and finally standard BLEU calculations are performed on the modified hypothesis. Similarly to the method by Homola et al. (2009), there is no matching between word n-grams of different lengths.

2 Method

LeBLEU differs from the standard BLEU (Papineni et al., 2002) in the following aspects (in the order of decreasing importance):

First, the matching of word n-grams is fuzzy: for a close match, the hits are increased according to a similarity score. The similarity score is one minus letter edit distance normalized by the length of the longer n-gram in characters. Even though we use the term "letter edit", the calculations are based on all characters, including the spaces between the words. If the similarity score is lower than the selected threshold parameter δ, the fuzzy match is ignored.

In contrast to standard BLEU, there is no need for lowercasing or even tokenization. For example, a punctuation character following a word is included in the n-gram as a part of the word. Thus, with a reasonably low threshold parameter, missing the punctuation character will result only in a relative small decrease in the score.

Second, to facilitate the matching of compound words, the hypothesis n-grams are not matched only to reference n-grams of the same order, but n-grams of any order between one and $2n$, where n is highest order of hypothesis n-gram considered.

Third, the brevity penalty is not based on the

[1] In contrast, for example the AMBER score by Chen and Kuhn (2011) includes nearly 20 weight parameters.

number of word tokens but the number of characters in the data. By this, we try to avoid giving too much penalty for mistakes in compound words. Character-based penalty is also one of the penalty variants in AMBER (Chen and Kuhn, 2011).

Fourth, when calculating mean over the different n-gram orders, arithmetic mean is taken instead of geometric mean. That the arithmetic mean is often a better choice than the geometric mean has been noted also by Song et al. (2013).

2.1 Algorithm

Our algorithm for calculating the LeBLEU score consists of four phases: First, the hypothesis n-grams and their frequencies are collected. Second, hypothesis n-grams are matched to the reference n-grams, collecting the normalized letter-edit scores. Third, the scores are summed up for each n-gram order and normalized by the total number of hypothesis n-grams. Finally, average precision over n-gram orders is calculated and multiplied by the brevity penalty.

Only the second phase differs significantly from calculating the standard BLEU score. It is also the most time-consuming part of the algorithm, so we will describe the implemented optimizations in more detail. We also discuss how further speed-up can be obtained by sampling the hypothesis n-grams in the first phase.

2.1.1 Calculating distances between n-grams

As we need to compare all hypothesis n-grams (up to n) to all reference n-grams (up to $2n$), the worst-case complexity for the number of Levenshtein calculations is $O(n^2HR)$ for hypothesis sentence of H words, reference sentence of R words and maximum n-gram order n. We use several strategies to optimize this task without changing the resulting scores.

To calculate the Levenshtein distances, we use a modified version of python-Levenshtein, a Python extension module written in C.[2] The number of function calls from Python to C is minimized by passing in two lists of strings to compare: all extracted n-grams from the hypothesis and reference. This strategy results in a large number of comparisons, making it attractive to prune comparisons that will not affect the final score due to the threshold parameter δ.

[2] Our fork is available from `https://github.com/Waino/python-Levenshtein`.

Two lower bounds for Levenshtein distance were used for pruning. The first lower bound is given by the difference in lengths of the two strings: the number of letter edits is at least the absolute difference of the lengths. The second lower bound is the bag distance (Bartolini et al., 2002), which uses the difference between character histograms calculated from the compared strings. In addition to the lower bounds, we use early stopping of the dynamic programming algorithm for Levenshtein distance, if all possible paths have grown past the pruning threshold.

For each hypothesis n-gram, the pruning threshold is initially set to δ. As we are looking only for the m-best matches (where m is the number of times the hypothesis n-gram occurred in the sentence), we can constraint the threshold whenever better matches to the reference n-grams are found. For example, if the two best matches are required, a third score that is worse than the current second-best cannot affect the score. Keeping track of the desired number of best matches can be accomplished using for example a heap data structure. However, most of the n-grams occur only once, in which case the heap degenerates into a single item. To simplify the implementation, we adjust the threshold only in this case.

2.1.2 Sampling of n-grams

Regardless of the optimizations above, the evaluation speed may get impractically slow for very long sentences. In such cases, a suitable approximation is to estimate the precision for only a subset of the hypothesis n-grams. If the sample size is limited to L n-grams, the time complexity becomes $O(LnR)$. A sensible scheme is to select n-grams evenly from the hypothesis sentence. In practice, we exclude or include n-grams starting from every kth word for a suitable value of k.[3] If the gaps are never longer than $n-1$ words, all words in the hypothesis will influence the result. We set the maximum n-gram sample size L to 2000. If $n=4$, this means that we use all n-grams if the number of words in the hypothesis $H \leq 500$. Some words in the hypothesis would be completely discarded only if $H > 2000$.

[3] If $L/H < 0.5$, we set $k = \lfloor H/L \rfloor$ and include every kth word. Otherwise we set $k = \lfloor H/(H-L) \rfloor$ and exclude every kth word.

3 Experiments

We study the proposed evaluation score using the data sets from the shared tasks of the Workshops on Statistical Machine Translation (WMT). The data sets contain human evaluations for different machine translation systems and system combination outputs. The translation hypotheses are ranked both in the level of segments (individual sentences) and systems. The translation hypotheses and references were used as inputs to the LeBLEU score as such: no preprocessing was performed on the texts.

3.1 Parameter tuning

We tuned the two parameters of the evaluation score on the data sets published from the WMT 2013 and 2014 shared tasks (Macháček and Bojar, 2013; Macháček and Bojar, 2014). We ran a grid search on the parameters for each language and level. We tested four values of the maximum n-gram length n (from 1 to 4) and six values of the fuzzy match threshold δ (from 0.2 to 0.8 using step size 0.1).

Our WMT 2015 submission includes two versions regarding the method parameters: "default" and "optimized". For the default submission, we selected the parameters based on the smallest rank sum over all languages, data sets (2013/2014) and levels of evaluation (system/segment). These parameters, which we set as the default parameters for our implementation, are $n = 4$ and $\delta = 0.4$.

For the optimized submission, we took the parameters with the best average correlation over WMT 2013 and 2014 data sets for each language pair and level of evaluation. The results are shown in Table 1. For the Finnish language that was not present in the 2013 and 2014 shared tasks, we took the best parameters for German, another language with complex morphology and long compound words.

		segment		system	
Source	Target	n	δ	n	δ
English	French	4	0.7	4	0.4
English	German	3	0.2	4	0.2
English	Czech	2	0.3	4	0.3
English	Russian	2	0.3	2	0.2
French	English	3	0.6	4	0.6
German	English	4	0.5	4	0.4
Czech	English	4	0.5	4	0.7
Russian	English	4	0.5	4	0.3

Table 1: Results of parameter optimization for each language pair and level of evaluation (segment or system).

3.2 Results for the WMT shared tasks

Table 2 shows the results from the WMT 2013, WMT 2014, and WMT 2015. Topline for system-level data of WMT 2013 is not included due to the use of Spearman's rank correlation instead of Pearson's product-moment correlation. Segment-level results of WMT 2013 are dominated by single submission, SIMPBLEU-RECALL by Song et al. (2013). Considering morphologically complex languages, LeBLEU would have ranked first in English–German and second in English–Czech and English–Russian. For translations to English, LeBLEU would have ranked in the top five among the 10 methods.

For WMT 2014 segment-level data, optimized LeBLEU provides the highest correlations for all language pairs from English. It also outperforms all the included methods for English–German and English–Russian system-level data. For system-level English–French, it would have ranked 5th. For system-level English–Czech, the optimized parameters yielded lower correlation than the default ones, and neither come close to the topline. Somewhat surprisingly, LeBLEU provides the top correlation for system-level German–English and third best for system-level Czech–English translations. For other system-level pairs to English, and all segment-level pairs to English, the correlations are reasonably high but quite far from the respective toplines. We can also compare LeBLEU to two related methods, standard BLEU and AMBER (Chen and Kuhn, 2011). LeBLEU outperforms both in almost all tasks already with the default parameters. The only exception is the system-level English–Czech task, in which BLEU provided a slightly higher correlation.

In the WMT 2015 evaluation, LeBLEU provides quite stable correlations across the different language pairs: Segment-level correlations are between 0.345–0.436 with default parameters and 0.347–0.438 with optimized parameters. System-level correlations are between 0.850–0.955 with default parameters and 0.842–0.984 with optimized parameters, except for English–Finnish, which gets 0.835 with the default parameters and

			WMT 2013			WMT 2014					WMT 2015		
Source	Target	Level	def.	opt.	top	def.	opt.	ref-B	ref-A	top	def.	opt.	top
English	French	segment	.231	.234	**.261**	.292	**.296**	.256	.264	.293	.345	.347	**.366**
English	Finnish	segment	–	–	–	–	–	–	–	–	.368	.368	**.380**
English	German	segment	.247	**.260**	.254	**.273**	**.273**	.191	.227	.268	.398	**.399**	.398
English	Czech	segment	.167	.168	**.192**	.342	**.349**	.290	.302	.344	.406	.410	**.446**
English	Russian	segment	.230	.233	**.245**	.446	**.449**	.381	.397	.440	.404	.404	**.439**
French	English	segment	.255	.259	**.303**	.380	.395	.378	.367	**.433**	.373	.376	**.398**
Finnish	English	segment	–	–	–	–	–	–	–	–	.383	.391	**.445**
German	English	segment	.256	.262	**.318**	.324	.320	.271	.313	**.380**	.402	.399	**.482**
Czech	English	segment	.225	.227	**.388**	.278	.282	.213	.246	**.328**	.436	.438	**.495**
Russian	English	segment	.229	.230	**.234**	.302	.309	.263	.294	**.355**	.376	.374	**.418**
English	French	system	.971	.971	–	.947	.947	.937	.928	**.960**	.933	.933	**.964**
English	Finnish	system	–	–	–	–	–	–	–	–	.835	.803	**.878**
English	German	system	.947	.919	–	.451	**.531**	.216	.241	.357	.850	.868	**.879**
English	Czech	system	.842	.857	–	.973	.964	.976	.972	**.988**	.953	.952	**.977**
English	Russian	system	.787	.870	–	.926	**.941**	.915	.926	**.941**	.896	.908	**.970**
French	English	system	.948	.956	–	.964	.964	.952	.948	**.981**	.955	.984	**.997**
Finnish	English	system	–	–	–	–	–	–	–	–	.900	.900	**.977**
German	English	system	.933	.933	–	**.963**	**.963**	.832	.910	.943	.916	.916	**.981**
Czech	English	system	.960	.946	–	.918	.988	.909	.744	**.993**	.947	.976	**.993**
Russian	English	system	.836	.855	–	.805	.799	.789	.797	**.870**	.908	.842	**.981**

Table 2: Performance of LeBLEU in recent WMT metrics shared tasks. Pearson's correlation coefficients (system-level data) and average Kendall's tau correlation coefficients (segment-level data) for LeBLEU with default parameters (def.), LeBLEU with optimized parameters (opt.), and topline method for the shared task (top). For WMT 2014 data, also two reference methods are included: BLEU (ref-B) and AMBER (ref-A).

only 0.803 with the German-optimized parameters. The choice of German-based parameters was clearly unsuccessful, and the effect of optimization for evaluation in Finnish remains to be seen. On average, optimization based on WMT 2013 and 2014 data sets improved the performance.

Compared to other methods submitted to WMT 2015, LeBLEU outperformed others in segment-level English–German translation. It also ranked second in system-level English–German and third in segment-level English–French. Moreover, even though unoptimized for the task, it ranked third in segment-level and fourth in system-level English–Finnish evaluations.

4 Conclusions

We have described the LeBLEU evaluation score for machine translation. It is an extension of the popular BLEU evaluation metric, but much more suitable for evaluating machine translation to morphologically complex languages. The extension is conceptually simple and does not require any language-specific resources. Instead, morphological variants and mistakes in compound words are accepted by using fuzzy matching between the word n-grams in the hypothesis and reference translations.

In the WMT15 shared task, LeBLEU provided high correlations to the human evaluations especially when translating from English to a morphologically more complex language. In particular, it outperformed other methods in the segment-level evaluation of English–German translation. The performance is equally good for WMT 2013 and 2014 data sets. This is remarkable especially as the method uses neither rule-based nor data-driven tools for morphological processing. As German is a highly compounding language, this indicates that the mistakes in compound words are frequently over-penalized by the current evaluation methods.

Implementation for the LeBLEU evaluation score is available from `https://github.com/Waino/LeBLEU`.

Acknowledgments

We thank Vesa Siivola for his help on the initial implementation of the method and useful comments on the manuscript.

References

Satanjeev Banerjee and Alon Lavie. 2005. METEOR: An automatic metric for MT evaluation with improved correlation with human judgments. In *Proceedings of the ACL Workshop on Intrinsic and Extrinsic Evaluation Measures for Machine Translation and/or Summarization*, pages 65–72, Ann Arbor, Michigan, June. Association for Computational Linguistics.

Ilaria Bartolini, Paolo Ciaccia, and Marco Patella. 2002. String matching with metric trees using an approximate distance. In *String processing and information retrieval*, pages 271–283. Springer.

Boxing Chen and Roland Kuhn. 2011. AMBER: A modified BLEU, enhanced ranking metric. In *Proceedings of the Sixth Workshop on Statistical Machine Translation*, pages 71–77, Edinburgh, Scotland, July. Association for Computational Linguistics.

Mathias Creutz and Krista Lagus. 2005. Unsupervised morpheme segmentation and morphology induction from text corpora using Morfessor 1.0. Technical Report A81, Publications in Computer and Information Science, Helsinki University of Technology.

Mathias Creutz, Teemu Hirsimäki, Mikko Kurimo, Antti Puurula, Janne Pylkkönen, Vesa Siivola, Matti Varjokallio, Ebru Arisoy, Murat Saraçlar, and Andreas Stolcke. 2007. Morph-based speech recognition and modeling of out-of-vocabulary words across languages. *ACM Transactions on Speech and Language Processing*, 5(1):3:1–3:29, December.

Michael Denkowski and Alon Lavie. 2011. Meteor 1.3: Automatic metric for reliable optimization and evaluation of machine translation systems. In *Proceedings of the Sixth Workshop on Statistical Machine Translation*, pages 85–91, Edinburgh, Scotland, July. Association for Computational Linguistics.

Etienne Denoual and Yves Lepage. 2005. BLEU in characters: towards automatic MT evaluation in languages without word delimiters. In *Companion Volume to the Proceedings of the Second International Joint Conference on Natural Language Processing*, pages 81–86.

Robert Frederking and Sergei Nirenburg. 1994. Three heads are better than one. In *Proceedings of the Fourth Conference on Applied Natural Language Processing*, pages 95–100, Stuttgart, Germany, October. Association for Computational Linguistics.

Petr Homola, Vladislav Kuboň, and Pavel Pecina. 2009. A simple automatic MT evaluation metric. In *Proceedings of the Fourth Workshop on Statistical Machine Translation*, pages 33–36, Athens, Greece, March. Association for Computational Linguistics.

Vladimir I. Levenshtein. 1966. Binary codes capable of correcting deletions, insertions and reversals. *Soviet Physics Doklady*, 10(8):707–710.

Jindřich Libovický and Pavel Pecina. 2014. Tolerant BLEU: a submission to the WMT14 metrics task. In *Proceedings of the Ninth Workshop on Statistical Machine Translation*, pages 409–413, Baltimore, Maryland, USA, June. Association for Computational Linguistics.

Matouš Macháček and Ondřej Bojar. 2013. Results of the WMT13 metrics shared task. In *Proceedings of the Eighth Workshop on Statistical Machine Translation*, pages 45–51, Sofia, Bulgaria, August. Association for Computational Linguistics.

Matouš Macháček and Ondřej Bojar. 2014. Results of the WMT14 metrics shared task. In *Proceedings of the Ninth Workshop on Statistical Machine Translation*, pages 293–301, Baltimore, Maryland, USA, June. Association for Computational Linguistics.

Kishore Papineni, Salim Roukos, Todd Ward, and Wei-Jing Zhu. 2002. BLEU: a method for automatic evaluation of machine translation. In *Proceedings of 40th Annual Meeting of the Association for Computational Linguistics*, pages 311–318, Philadelphia, PA, USA, July. Association for Computational Linguistics.

Maja Popović. 2011. Morphemes and POS tags for n-gram based evaluation metrics. In *Proceedings of the Sixth Workshop on Statistical Machine Translation*, pages 104–107, Edinburgh, Scotland, July. Association for Computational Linguistics.

Dana Shapira and James A. Storer. 2002. Edit distance with move operations. In *Proceedings of the 13th Annual Symposium on Computational Pattern Matching*, pages 85–98.

Matthew Snover, Bonnie Dorr, Richard Schwartz, Linnea Micciulla, and John Makhoul. 2006. A study of translation edit rate with targeted human annotation. In *Proceedings of Association for Machine Translation in the Americas*, pages 223–231.

Xingyi Song, Trevor Cohn, and Lucia Specia. 2013. BLEU deconstructed: Designing a better MT evaluation metric, March. On-line: `http://staffwww.dcs.shef.ac.uk/people/X.Song/song13deconstructed.pdf`. Accessed Oct 2013.

Mengqiu Wang and Christopher Manning. 2012. SPEDE: Probabilistic edit distance metrics for MT evaluation. In *Proceedings of the Seventh Workshop on Statistical Machine Translation*, pages 76–83, Montréal, Canada, June. Association for Computational Linguistics.

CASICT-DCU Participation in WMT2015 Metrics Task

Hui Yu[†] **Qingsong Ma**[†] **Xiaofeng Wu**[‡] **Qun Liu**[‡†]
[†]Key Laboratory of Intelligent Information Processing
Institute of Computing Technology, Chinese Academy of Sciences
[‡]ADAPT Centre, School of Computing, Dublin City University
{yuhui,maqingsong}@ict.ac.cn
{xiaofengwu}@computing.dcu.ie
{liuqun}@ict.ac.cn

Abstract

Human-designed sub-structures are required by most of the syntax-based machine translation evaluation metrics. In this paper, we propose a novel evaluation metric based on dependency parsing model, which does not need this human involvement. Experimental results show that the new single metric gets better correlation than METEOR on system level and is comparable with it on sentence level. To introduce more information, we combine the new metric with many other metrics. The combined metric obtains state-of-the-art performance on both system level evaluation and sentence level evaluation on WMT 2014.

1 Introduction

Automatic evaluation metrics play an important role in machine translation research. At present, most of the automatic evaluation metrics evaluate the translation quality by comparing the similarity between the hypothesis and the reference.

The lexicon-based metrics can only use lexical information, such as BLEU (Papineni et al., 2002), NIST(Doddington, 2002) and METEOR (Lavie and Agarwal, 2007). To evaluate the hypothesis on syntactic level, some researchers proposed the syntax-based metrics. Liu and Gildea (2005) proposed a constituent-tree-based metric STM and a dependency-tree-based metric HWCM. The syntax-based metric proposed by Owczarzak et al (2007) uses the Lexical-Functional Grammar (LFG) dependency tree. Some metrics introduce the syntactic information on the basis of lexical information, such as MAXSIM (Chan and Ng, 2008) and the metric proposed by Zhu et al. (2010). These metrics evaluate the syntactic similarity by comparing the sub-structures extracted from the trees of hypothesis and reference. To avoid parsing the hypothesis in order to prevent translation error propagation, some researchers propose a kind of syntax-based evaluation metric which only uses the tree of reference, such as BLEUÂTRE (Mehay and Brew, 2007) and RED (Yu et al., 2014).

The syntax-based metrics either use the sub-structures of both the reference and the hypothesis tree, or only use that on the reference side. Therefore, for these metrics, sub-structures designed by human are required. In this paper, we propose a novel dependency-parsing-model-based metric in the view of dependency tree generation, which completely avoids this human involvement. A dependency parsing model is trained by the reference dependency tree, through which we can obtain the dependency tree of the hypothesis and the corresponding score. The syntactic similarity between the hypothesis and the reference can be evaluated by this score. In order to obtain the lexicon similarity, we also introduce the unigram F-score to the new metric. The experimental results show that the new metric gets the state-of-the-art performance in the single metrics on system level evaluation, and gets the comparable correlation with METEOR on sentence level evaluation. We also propose a combined metric[1] which combines the new metric with many other metrics together. The combined metric obtains state-of-the-art performance on both system level and sentence level.

The remainder of this paper is organized as follows: Section 2 describes the dependency-parsing-model-based metric; Section 3 presents the combined metric; Section 4 gives the experiment results; Conclusions are discussed in Section 5.

[1]Combined metrics directly use the scores of many kinds of metrics, such as BLEU, TER, METEOR and some syntax-based metrics. For the metrics using different kinds of information types (lexicon, syntax and semantic information) as features, we still think they are single metrics, because they don't use the score of other metrics.

2 DPMF: Evaluation Metric Based on Dependency Parsing Model

We evaluate the syntactic similarity via the **D**ependency **P**aring **M**odel score of hypothesis and evaluate the lexical similarity via the unigram **F**-score. So we name the new metric as DPMF.

There are four steps to obtain the dependency parsing model score of the hypothesis. 1) Obtain the reference dependency tree which can be generated by the automatic parsing tools or labeled by human. 2) Train a dependency parsing model using the reference dependency tree. 3) Parse the hypothesis using the dependency parsing model and get the probability of the hypothesis dependency tree. 4) Normalize the probability of the hypothesis dependency tree. We define the normalized probability of the hypothesis dependency tree as the dependency parsing model score. After obtaining the dependency parsing model score of a hypothesis, we multiply this score by unigram F-score to get the final score of DPMF. The detailed description of our metric will be found in paper Yu et al. (2015a). We only give the experiment results in this paper.

3 DPMF$_{comb}$: A Combined Evaluation Metric

From the published results of WMT 2014, we can see that the combined metrics such as DISCOTK-PARTY (Joty et al., 2014) and UPC-STOUT (Gonzàlez et al., 2014) obtained great success which can make use of many single metrics. In most of the cases, combined metrics can obtain good correlations, so we also propose a combined metric which combines DPMF with some other single metrics. The combined metric is named as DPMF$_{comb}$ and it involves DPMF, REDp, ENTFp[2] and some metrics included in the open source toolkit Asiya[3].

We introduce REDp, ENTFp and Asiya briefly in the rest of this section.

3.1 REDp

RED (Yu et al., 2014) employs the reference dependency tree which contains both the lexical and syntactic information, leaving the hypothesis side unparsed to avoid error propagation. The score of RED is obtained using F-score. The precision and recall are calculated using the dependency tree of the reference and the string of the hypothesis. To extend the limited reference, they introduce some linguistic resources into RED and propose a new version REDp, which is employed in our combined metric. We merge the extended version REDp into our combined metric.

3.2 ENTFp

The widely-used lexicon-based evaluation metrics cannot adequately reflect the fluency of the translations. The n-gram-based metrics, like BLEU, limit the maximum length of matched fragments to N and cannot catch the matched fragments longer than N, so they can only reflect the fluency indirectly. METEOR, which is not limited by n-gram, uses the number of matched chunks but it does not consider the length of each chunk. To avoid this defect, we propose an entropy-based method ENTF, which is a metric by introducing unigram F-score on the base of ENT (Yu et al., 2015b). ENT aims at reflecting the fluency of translations through the distribution of matched words, while the unigram F-score can evaluate the accuracy. We introduce stem, synonym and paraphrase into ENTF to extend the limited number of reference and name it as ENTFp.

3.3 Asiya

We use Asiya MT evaluation toolkit (Giménez and Màrquez, 2010) to produce the score of many metrics, which can be used in DPMF$_{comb}$. Asiya provides a rich set of specialized similarity metrics that use different level of linguistic information, namely lexical, syntactic and semantic.

In our experiment, we calculate scores of the default metric set provided by Asiya. For the into-English language pairs, the default metric set contains 55 metrics, including lexicon-based metrics, syntax-based metrics and semantic-based metrics. The weights of all these 55 scores together with the scores of DPMF, REDp and ENTFp are trained with SVM-rank[4].

4 Experiments

To evaluate the performance of DPMF and DPMF$_{comb}$, we carry out the experiments on both system level evaluation and sentence level evaluation. In this section, we first describe the data sets

[2]The source code of DPMF, REDp and ENTFp can be found in http://github.com/YuHui0117/AMTE

[3]http://asiya-faust.cs.upc.edu/

[4]http://www.cs.cornell.edu/People/tj/svm_light/svm_rank.html

and the baseline metrics in the experiments, and then give and analyse the experimental results.

4.1 Data

We use the data from the WMT 2014 evaluation campaign as test data. The language pairs are Czech-to-English, German-to-English, French-to-English and Russian-English. The number of translation systems for each language pair are shown in Table 1.

data	cs-en	de-en	fr-en	ru-en
WMT2014	5	13	8	13

Table 1: The number of translation systems for each language pair on WMT 2014. cs-en means Czech-to-English. de-en means German-to-English. fr-en means French-to-English. ru-en means Russian-to-English.

DPMF_{comb} is a combined metric which includes 58 single metrics. The training data used to train the weight of each single metric are the English-targeted language pairs in WMT 2012 and WMT 2013.

4.2 Baseline

The baselines are the widely-used lexicon-based metrics, such as BLEU[5], TER[6] and METEOR[7]. In addition, according to the published results of WMT 2014, we also give the correlation of the metric with the best performance on average, DISCOTK-PARTY-TUNED (Joty et al., 2014), which is a combined metric including many kinds of other metrics. For fairness, we also give the result of the metric with the best performance on average in the single metrics, VERTA-W(Comelles and Atserias, 2014) on system level and BEER (Stanojevic and Sima'an, 2014) on sentence level respectively. For our combined metric, to evaluate the effect of adding DPMF, REDp and ENTFp, we also give the correlation of the metric only combining the single metrics in Asiya.

4.3 System Level Correlation

To verify the effectiveness of DPMF, we carry out the system level experiments on WMT 2014. To evaluate the correlation with human judges, Spearman's rank correlation coefficient ρ is used. ρ is calculated using Formula (1).

$$\rho = 1 - \frac{6\sum d_i^2}{n(n^2-1)} \qquad (1)$$

d_i is the difference between the human rank and metrics rank for system i. n is the number of systems.

We give the system level correlations for every metric in Table 2. From Table 2, we can see that DPMF is better than BLEU and TER on all the language pairs. The correlation of DPMF is also better than METEOR and the best single metric VERTA-W on average. But DPMF is lower than the combined metrics DISCOTK-PARTY-TUNED and Asiya. After combining DPMF with other metrics, DPMF_{comb} obtains better correlations than DISCOTK-PARTY-TUNED and Asiya on average. We can see that DPMF_{comb} obtains state-of-the-art performance on system level. From the comparison between DPMF_{comb} and Asiya, we can see that adding DPMF, REDp and ENTFp into the combined metric is useful on system level.

4.4 Sentence Level Correlation

To further evaluate the performance of DPMF and DPMF_{comb}, we carry out the experiments on sentence level. On sentence level, Kendall's τ correlation coefficient is used. τ is calculated using the following equation.

$$\tau = \frac{\text{num\_con\_pairs} - \text{num\_dis\_pairs}}{\text{num\_con\_pairs} + \text{num\_dis\_pairs}}$$

num_con_pairs is the number of concordant pairs and num_dis_pairs is the number of disconcordant pairs.

Table 3 gives the correlations of all the metrics. We can see that DPMF is better than BLEU on each language pair and it is comparable with METEOR on average. The stat-of-the-art performance on sentence level is obtained after combining DPMF with other metrics, namely, DPMF_{comb}, which outperforms the combined metrics DISCO-PARTY-TUNED and Asiya. From the comparison between DPMF_{comb} and Asiya, we can see that adding DPMF, REDp and ENTFp into the combined metric is useful on sentence level.

[5]ftp://jaguar.ncsl.nist.gov/mt/resources/mteval-v13a.pl
[6]http://www.cs.umd.edu/~snover/tercom
[7]http://www.cs.cmu.edu/~alavie/METEOR/download/meteor-1.4.tgz

metrics	cs-en	de-en	fr-en	ru-en	average
TER	.976	.775	.952	.809	.878
BLEU	.909	.832	.952	.789	.871
METEOR	.980	.927	.975	.805	.922
DISCOTK-PARTY-TUNED	.975	.943	.977	.870	.941
VERTA-W	.934	.867	.959	.848	.902
Asiya	.954	.936	**.978**	.871	.935
DPMF	**.999**	.920	.967	.832	.930
DPMF_{comb}	.974	**.950**	**.978**	**.872**	**.944**

Table 2: System level correlations on WMT 2014. Asiya represents the combined metric only using the metrics in Asiya. The value in bold is the best result in each column. *average* stands for the average result of all the language pairs for each metric on WMT 2014.

metrics	cs-en	de-en	fr-en	ru-en	average
BLEU	.216	.259	.367	.256	.275
METEOR	.282	.334	.406	.329	.338
BEER	.284	.337	.417	.333	.343
DISCOTK-PARTY-TUNED	.328	.380	.433	.355	.374
Asiya	**.333**	.388	.437	.355	.378
DPMF	.283	.332	.404	.324	.336
DPMF_{comb}	.332	**.398**	**.443**	**.364**	**.384**

Table 3: Sentence level correlations on WMT 2014. Asiya represents the combined metric only using the metrics in Asiya. The value in bold is the best result in each column. *average* stands for the average result of all the language pairs for each metric on WMT 2014.

5 Conclusion

In this paper, we propose a new dependency-parsing-model-based metric DPMF and a combined metric DPMF_{comb}. DPMF evaluates the syntactic similarity through the dependency parsing model and evaluates the lexical similarity by unigram F-score. Experimental results show that the correlation of DPMF is better than BLEU, TER, METEOR and VERTA-w on system level. On sentence level, DPMF is better than BLEU, and comparable with METEOR. After combining DPMF with other metrics, DPMF_{comb} obtains the state-of-the-art performance on both system level and sentence level on WMT 2014.

Acknowledgments

This research is supported by China's NSFC grant 61379086 and the European Union Horizon 2020 Programme (H2020) under grant agreement no. 645452 (QT21). The ADAPT Centre for Digital Content Technology is funded under the SFI Research Centres Programme (Grant 13/RC/2106) and is co-funded under the European Regional Development Fund.

References

Yee Seng Chan and Hwee Tou Ng. 2008. Maxsim: A maximum similarity metric for machine translation evaluation. In *Proceedings of ACL-08: HLT*, pages 55–62.

Elisabet Comelles and Jordi Atserias. 2014. Verta participation in the wmt14 metrics task. In *Proceedings of the Ninth Workshop on Statistical Machine Translation*, pages 368–375, Baltimore, Maryland, USA, June. Association for Computational Linguistics.

George Doddington. 2002. Automatic evaluation of machine translation quality using n-gram co-occurrence statistics. In *Proceedings of the Second International Conference on Human Language Technology Research*, HLT '02, pages 138–145, San Francisco, CA, USA. Morgan Kaufmann Publishers Inc.

Jesús Giménez and Lluís Màrquez. 2010. Asiya: An Open Toolkit for Automatic Machine Translation (Meta-)Evaluation. *The Prague Bulletin of Mathematical Linguistics*, (94):77–86.

Meritxell Gonzàlez, Alberto Barrón-Cedeño, and Lluís Màrquez. 2014. Ipa and stout: Leveraging linguistic and source-based features for machine translation evaluation. In *Proceedings of the Ninth Workshop on Statistical Machine Translation*, pages 394–401, Baltimore, Maryland, USA, June. Association for Computational Linguistics.

Shafiq Joty, Francisco Guzmán, Lluís Màrquez, and Preslav Nakov. 2014. Discotk: Using discourse structure for machine translation evaluation. In *Proceedings of the Ninth Workshop on Statistical Machine Translation*, pages 402–408, Baltimore, Maryland, USA, June. Association for Computational Linguistics.

Alon Lavie and Abhaya Agarwal. 2007. Meteor: an automatic metric for mt evaluation with high levels of correlation with human judgments. In *Proceedings of the Second Workshop on Statistical Machine Translation*, StatMT '07, pages 228–231, Stroudsburg, PA, USA. Association for Computational Linguistics.

Ding Liu and Daniel Gildea. 2005. Syntactic features for evaluation of machine translation.

Dennis Mehay and Chris Brew. 2007. BLEUÂTRE: Flattening Syntactic Dependencies for MT Evaluation. In *Proceedings of the 11th Conference on Theoretical and Methodological Issues in Machine Translation (TMI)*.

Karolina Owczarzak, Josef van Genabith, and Andy Way. 2007. Evaluating machine translation with lfg dependencies. *Machine Translation*, 21(2):95–119, June.

K. Papineni, S. Roukos, T. Ward, and W.J. Zhu. 2002. BLEU: a method for automatic evaluation of machine translation. In *Proceedings of the 40th annual meeting on association for computational linguistics*, pages 311–318. Association for Computational Linguistics.

Milos Stanojevic and Khalil Sima'an. 2014. Beer: Better evaluation as ranking. In *Proceedings of the Ninth Workshop on Statistical Machine Translation*, pages 414–419, Baltimore, Maryland, USA, June. Association for Computational Linguistics.

Hui Yu, Xiaofeng Wu, Jun Xie, Wenbin Jiang, Qun Liu, and Shouxun Lin. 2014. Red: A reference dependency based mt evaluation metric. In *Proceedings of COLING 2014, the 25th International Conference on Computational Linguistics: Technical Papers*, pages 2042–2051, Dublin, Ireland, August. Dublin City University and Association for Computational Linguistics.

Hui Yu, Xiaofeng Wu, Wenbin Jiang, Qun Liu, and Shouxun Lin. 2015a. An Automatic Machine Translation Evaluation Metric Based on Dependency Parsing Model. *ArXiv e-prints*, August.

Hui Yu, Xiaofeng Wu, Wenbin Jiang, Qun Liu, and Shouxun Lin. 2015b. Improve the Evaluation of Translation Fluency by Using Entropy of Matched Sub-segments. *ArXiv e-prints*, August.

Junguo Zhu, Muyun Yang, Bo Wang, Sheng Li, and Tiejun Zhao. 2010. All in strings: a powerful string-based automatic mt evaluation metric with multiple granularities. In *Proceedings of the 23rd International Conference on Computational Linguistics: Posters*, COLING '10, pages 1533–1540, Stroudsburg, PA, USA. Association for Computational Linguistics.

Drem: The AFRL Submission to the WMT15 Tuning Task

Grant Erdmann
Air Force Research Laboratory
grant.erdmann@us.af.mil

Jeremy Gwinnup
SRA International[†]
jeremy.gwinnup.ctr@us.af.mil

Abstract

We define a new algorithm, named "Drem", for tuning the weighted linear model in a statistical machine translation system. Drem has two major innovations. First, it uses scaled derivative-free trust-region optimization rather than other methods' line search or (sub)gradient approximations. Second, it interpolates the decoder output, using information about which decodes produced which translations.

1 Introduction

While searching for the best translation of a text, statistical machine translation systems generate several different quantitative descriptors of the translation, called "features". These features are combined into a single score, by weighting and summing them. A tuning algorithm chooses the weights used in this combination.

MERT (Och, 2003) is the standard tuning algorithm. Many different varieties of error rate training exist, with various techniques, including expectation, line-search, Nelder–Mead simplex (Zhao and Chen, 2009), particle swarm optimization (Suzuki et al., 2011), and stabilization (Foster and Kuhn, 2009). It has been experienced that MERT fails to perform well in larger feature spaces, but recently there has been evidence of a regularized MERT succeeding in high dimensions (Galley et al., 2013).

Other methods have been designed as wholesale replacements for MERT, including MIRA (Chiang et al., 2008), k-best MIRA (Cherry and Foster, 2012), PRO (Hopkins and May, 2011), and Rampion (Gimpel and Smith, 2012).

[†]This work is sponsored by the Air Force Research Laboratory under Air Force contract FA-8650-09-D-6939-029.

MERT's continued use indicates an improved dense-feature optimizer for weighted linear models would be welcome. It is in this context that we introduce our tuning algorithm, named "Drem". In contrast to known varieties of MERT, Drem is not a line-search, simplex, or particle swarm optimization method. It is a derivative-free trust-region method, with several advancements to cater to the particular nature of MT system optimization.

2 Background and definitions

A feature vector $\boldsymbol{f} \in \mathbb{R}^k$ has the relative importance of its components determined by a weight vector $\boldsymbol{w} \in \mathbb{R}^k$. For a weighted linear model, the score used by the decoder to choose the best translation is the scalar product,

$$s(\boldsymbol{w}, \boldsymbol{f}) = \boldsymbol{w}^T \boldsymbol{f} \tag{1}$$

which we call the decoder score. The output of the decoder run on a corpus $\mathcal{C}$ at a weight $\boldsymbol{w}$ is an n-best list $\mathcal{N}(\boldsymbol{w}, \mathcal{C})$. The n-best list can be thought of as a collection of elements of the form $(j, t, \boldsymbol{f})$, where $j \in \mathcal{J}$ is the segment (typically sentence) index within $\mathcal{C}$, t is the text of the translation, and $\boldsymbol{f}$ is the feature vector. The objective of tuning is to choose the weights $\boldsymbol{w}$ such that the translation with the highest decoder score (i.e., the "1-best") will be the segment's best translation. For the test error a human performs an evaluation.

In order to produce the best results on the test set, it is important to optimize some measure of error on a given bilingual development set, $\mathcal{C}_{\text{dev}}$. In tuning we will use the common practice of iteratively decoding and optimizing, and we define $\boldsymbol{w}^{(m)}$ to be the weight used in the m-th decode. During optimization, the development error metric at a weight $\boldsymbol{w}$ (where no decode has been performed) is approximated using only results from prior decodings. At this un-decoded weight we must perform a "pseudo-decoding" to approximate the result of decoding at it.

In Drem we define a pseudo-decoder scoring function s_{dev}, changed from the standard decoder score (1) to incorporate a "fear" of including a translation that was produced by decoding a weight far from the weight under consideration. Several different methods, including MIRA (Chiang et al., 2008), k-best MIRA (Cherry and Foster, 2012), Rampion (Gimpel and Smith, 2012), and Ultraconservative Updating (Liu et al., 2012), and stabilization methods of Foster and Kuhn (2009), include this fear by adding a distance penalty to the error function being optimized. We believe that changing the pseudo-decoder score, rather than the error minimized, is a novel technique and qualitatively different from other treatments.

Our optimization technique is novel in that it is not a line search method like MERT, nor a (sub)gradient approximation method, nor a simplex method. Rather, it is a regression-based derivative-free trust-region method. Use of regression on scaled weights allows us to take smooth approximations of the error function, which should aid the method's robustness. Trust-region optimization supports the multiresolution placement of regression points, providing a thorough search.

3 Tuner description

We divide the tuner description into three sections. In §3.1 we describe optimization techniques used to optimize efficiently, avoiding local optima. In §3.2 we describe techniques used to make the translations in optimization similar to the output of the decoder. In §3.3 we give techniques used to make the result of tuning robust to human evaluation of test sets.

3.1 Optimization

3.1.1 Scaling

The scalar product (1) used in the determination of the 1-best translation means that the decoder output is scale-invariant. However, many tuning algorithms (excluding MERT and Drem, but including MIRA (Chiang et al., 2008), Ultraconservative Updating (Liu et al., 2012), and others) are impacted by the magnitude of the weight vectors. In this section we show how we rescale all weights and features to change to an intrinsic unit scaling.

Our first step in defining the coordinate system is whitening the feature space, which is transforming the features to be uncorrelated and have equal variance. Whitening the features removes the complications of features with dramatically different scales and features that tend to move nearly in lock-step with each other.

We perform the whitening of the feature space by performing principal component analysis of the matrix M, which we define to be the mean covariance matrix. That is, M is the average of the sample covariance matrices for the different segments, where we consider data from "relatively good" decodes[1].

Principal component analysis of M provides the scaling matrix A, which is used to produce the whitened features $\boldsymbol{\varphi}$:

$$\boldsymbol{\varphi} = A\boldsymbol{f}$$

In order to maintain ordering of the product $\boldsymbol{w}^T\boldsymbol{f}$ under the new scaling of the features, we also rescale the weights via

$$\boldsymbol{\lambda} = \frac{A^{-1}\boldsymbol{w}}{\|A^{-1}\boldsymbol{w}\|}$$

We will use the notational convenience of the implicit transformation between the unscaled variables $\boldsymbol{w}$ and $\boldsymbol{f}$ and the scaled variables $\boldsymbol{\lambda}$ and $\boldsymbol{\varphi}$. The scaling matrix A is constant throughout a Drem run, so this should produce no ambiguity.

With these scaled weights on the unit $(k-1)$-sphere, we can use a standard cosine difference between different weights:

$$\text{dist}(\boldsymbol{\lambda}_1, \boldsymbol{\lambda}_2) = \text{acos}(\boldsymbol{\lambda}_1^T\boldsymbol{\lambda}_2) \tag{2}$$

which implies that all distances between vectors will be between zero and π. This distance function is appealing as a geometrically natural measure of distance between direction vectors.

3.1.2 Derivative-free trust-region optimization

Our tuning process can be summarized as performing the development error minimization

$$\boldsymbol{w}^* = \arg\min_{\boldsymbol{w}} \mathcal{E}_{\text{dev}}(\boldsymbol{w}, \mathcal{C}_{\text{dev}}) \tag{3}$$

We choose to perform this optimization using a trust-region method (Conn et al., 2000). We repeatedly solve a problem of the form

$$\boldsymbol{\lambda}^* = \arg\min_{\boldsymbol{\lambda}:\text{dist}(\boldsymbol{\lambda},\boldsymbol{\lambda}_0)<\delta} m_\delta(\boldsymbol{\lambda}, \boldsymbol{\lambda}_0) \tag{4}$$

[1]Defined by the user, and precise definition has little impact. We use metrics scaled like BLEU, and weights are "relatively good" if they give an error within 0.0025 of the best decode's.

where δ is the so-called "trust-region radius", and m_δ (to be defined in §3.1.3) is a simple model approximately equal to $\mathcal{E}_{\text{dev}}$.

When an improvement to $\mathcal{E}_{\text{dev}}$ (or $\mathcal{E}_{\text{dev,robust}}$ in §4) is found via (4), a step is taken in that direction. The trust-region radius is enlarged if the improvement is significant, and maintained or decreased otherwise.

Problem (4) is optimized repeatedly, with different central weights $\boldsymbol{\lambda}_0$ and different trust-region radii δ. Convergence is declared if the trust-region radius becomes small enough or the maximum number of iterations is reached[2].

A new, optimal weight $\boldsymbol{w}$ is the output of each Drem run. It will be used to decode the development corpus, and then Drem will be re-run. Overall convergence is achieved if the Drem output weights converge.

This trust-region method is in stark contrast to MERT's line search methodology on a piecewise continuous error. MERT relies heavily on searching along a line, keeping track of where the one-best translations (and therefore the error) change on that line. MERT's method is designed for a piecewise constant error and would be inapplicable for (4). Both our pseudo-decoder score and development error metrics are continuous.

3.1.3 Error surface modeling via sampling

We choose to evaluate the error function at a few sampled points around the current best weight and fit a quadratic or linear model m_δ to it (Conn et al., 2009).

For a linear model, we choose the evaluation set at the scale δ to be the $2(k-1)+1$ points consisting of the central point $\boldsymbol{\lambda}_0$ of the trust-region and the $2(k-1)$ points found by taking steps of $\pm\delta$ in each of the $k-1$ coordinate directions.

The model of the error is defined as the model $m_\delta(\boldsymbol{\lambda}, \boldsymbol{\lambda}_0)$ that minimizes the squared error between the error evaluations and the model.

Using least-squares regularization to model the error surface completely avoids the issue of needing to approximate a gradient or subgradient of the error function. This is by design and avoids the tendency of local behavior to dominate global behavior, in both computational effort and final result (Conn et al., 2009).

[2]Precise definitions of the many optimization parameters have little impact. Our threshold for the minimum trust-region radius is 0.001, and we allow up to 30 iterations of solving (4) per Drem run.

The local coordinate basis on the unit sphere is arbitrary in the definition of $m_\delta(\boldsymbol{\lambda}, \boldsymbol{\lambda}_0)$. We will use this feature to our advantage, choosing a different random basis every time we perform an optimization iteration. This gives the benefit of function evaluation in many random directions at each step, with negligible cost.

3.2 Pseudo-decoder improvement

We now turn to how we will use the information available to Drem to simulate decoding at a new weight.

3.2.1 Decode score interpolation

For development error, we include a penalty so that a translation will get a lower score ("fade away") as one moves farther from the decode weights that produced that translation. Our pseudo-decoder score is an adjusted version of (1),

$$s_{\text{dev}}(j, t, \boldsymbol{\varphi}, \boldsymbol{\lambda}) = s(\boldsymbol{w}, \boldsymbol{f}) + p(j, t, \boldsymbol{\varphi}, \boldsymbol{\lambda}) \quad (5)$$

where p is the penalty for considering a translation at a weight which is distant from the weights which produced it.

We have freedom in choosing the distance penalty function p. Many optimizers, such as MERT, have no such penalty function, so we can replicate their pseudo-decoders by setting p identically equal to zero. We choose to interpolate instead. That is, the decoder and the pseudo-decoder will produce the same n-best list and scores at that weight (modulo inclusion of translations with infinitely bad scores). In equations, this is

$$p(j, t, \boldsymbol{\varphi}, \boldsymbol{\lambda}^{(m)}) = \begin{cases} 0, & (j, t, \boldsymbol{f}) \in \mathcal{N}(\boldsymbol{w}^{(m)}, \mathcal{C}_{\text{dev}}) \\ -\infty, & \text{otherwise} \end{cases}$$

We give our standard choice for p here. Let $d_{\text{min}}(\boldsymbol{\lambda})$ be the distance of a weight $\boldsymbol{\lambda}$ from the nearest weight where the current segment was decoded:

$$d_{\text{min}}(\boldsymbol{\lambda}) = \min_m \operatorname{dist}(\boldsymbol{\lambda}, \boldsymbol{\lambda}^{(m)})$$

and let $d(j, t, \boldsymbol{\varphi}, \boldsymbol{\lambda})$ be the distance to the nearest weight that produced the given translation $(j, t, \boldsymbol{\varphi})$. We define the maximum distance that can produce a finite score to be a multiple of this minimum distance, $d_{\text{max}} = 1000 d_{\text{min}}$. Then we define the penalty function to be

$$p(j, t, \boldsymbol{\varphi}, \boldsymbol{\lambda}) = \begin{cases} 0, & d = d_{\text{min}} \\ \frac{d_{\text{min}} - d}{d_{\text{max}} - d}, & d_{\text{min}} < d < d_{\text{max}} \\ -\infty, & \text{otherwise} \end{cases}$$

We find Drem's decode score interpolation to be extraordinarily beneficial when n-best list reranking is part of the system. If the ranking from the initial decoder differs substantially from that of the rescorer, we have seen other tuners have difficulty producing translations which are both produced by the first decoder and scored highly by the rescorer.

3.2.2 Tabu search

We, like Foster and Kuhn (2009), feel that early tuning iterations should focus on exploring the space. This helps to develop the psuedo-decoder's knowledge of the decoder's output at various weights. To this end, we have the option of constraining the output of a tuning iteration to be a certain distance from all previous decodes. As in Foster and Kuhn (2009), we reduce the effect in later iterations, to allow convergence. We set this distance to 0.25 for the first twenty iterations of Drem, and zero for the final three iterations.

3.2.3 Historical restarts

We, like Foster and Kuhn (2009), have observed that random restarts are often not valuable for tuning. In Drem this may be due in part to the repeatedly randomized coordinate systems. However, historical restarts can sometimes help recover from an early misstep. The set of starting points will then consist of the given weight and the three prior decode weights with the best development error metric values. If enough distinct historical restarts are not available, random restarts will be added until four distinct starting points are found.

3.2.4 Merging replicates

Our final option in this section is related to the standard practice of running several replicates of the tuning process and choosing to use the weights output by just one of them. Instead of choosing a single replicate's result, we allow the user to merge the n-best lists of all the replicates at some mid-way point of Drem. This improves the knowledge of the pseudo-decoder, allowing Drem to use this information to select its final answer.

We allow ten replicates to proceed for twenty iterations of Drem, then merge their n-best lists and optimize for three further iterations.

3.3 Generalization to test data

We find that the weights found by Drem (and other tuners) do not always generalize well to test data. The proper choices here depend strongly on how the development corpus and evaluation metric differ from the test corpus and evaluation metric.

3.3.1 Error function smoothing

To generalize from a development corpus to an unseen test corpus, we choose to smooth the metric function optimized. We do this by using expected metric scores, as in Smith and Eisner (2006), Och (2003), Cherry and Foster (2012), and Liu et al. (2012). We average the sufficient statistics of the available translations, taking the weight of a translation as $\exp(\alpha s_{\text{dev}}(j,t,\boldsymbol{\varphi},\boldsymbol{\lambda}))/Z_j$. Here Z_j normalizes the probability of the translations of segment j. The smoothing parameter α can vary, with examples in the literature including $\alpha = 1$ (Cherry and Foster, 2012), $\alpha = 3$ (Liu et al., 2012), and $\alpha = \infty$ (i.e., the standard 1-best score, which would be used if the test set was identical to the dev set). We choose our standard setting of $\alpha = 1$.

3.3.2 Metric choice

The most difficult part of this tuning task may well be choosing a development error to optimize that will give a final result that will match well to human judgment. We choose to maximize a combination of NIST score (NIST Report, 2002), Meteor 1.5 score (Denkowski and Lavie, 2014), and Kendall's τ score (Birch and Osborne, 2011)[3]:

$$0.045 \cdot \text{NIST} + 0.45 \cdot \text{Meteor} + 0.1 \cdot \text{Kendall's } \tau$$

where the weights are chosen based on experience, and we smooth all metrics with $\alpha = 1$. The combined score aims to avoid pitfalls of any individual metric. This metric was developed by performing our own human evaluation of the Czech–English direction and requesting human evaluation from the task organizers for the English–Czech direction.

4 Unused options

Drem has several options that were not necessary for this task, and we give a few of them here.

A quadratic model could be chosen in §3.1.3, where we add the cross-terms to get an evaluation set of $2(k-1)^2+1$ points. For the tuning task, tests showed no improvement in the final result with the quadratic model.

In addition to smoothing in the "depth" of the n-best list, we can also smooth the error spatially.

[3]dev set alignments were created by GIZA++, trained on the supplied training and dev corpora

In §3.1.2, we would replace $\mathcal{E}_{\text{dev}}$ with $\mathcal{E}_{\text{dev,robust}}$, where $\mathcal{E}_{\text{dev,robust}}$ is the average taken over a set of nearby weights. For the tuning task, tests showed no improvement in the final result with this spatial smoothing.

We tested the ability of Drem to handle sparse features, adding a total of 58 nontrivial `TargetWordInsertion` and `SourceWordDeletion` features. Drem ran successfully on this larger feature space, to apparent convergence. However, the resulting translations of the dev set were not qualitatively better, despite the increased risk of overfitting to the dev set.

5 Implementation

The Drem algorithm was programmed and run in GNU Octave 3.6.4 in Scientific Linux. It is designed to be called from the command prompt as a drop-in replacement for the MERT executable that is provided with Moses (Koehn et al., 2007). Additional arguments, such as metric choice, expectation parameter α, quadratic or linear error surface model, etc., can be added to the command line.

Tuning proceeded as described above. For this task the test data are unavailable, so we do not know how the test set differs from the development set. We choose parameters for smoothing and robustification that have generalized well in the past, keeping in mind that we could make better choices (such as paring down the dev set) if we knew how the source text of the test differed from the development text.

Convergence appeared to be achieved in both translation directions.

It is noteworthy that for English–Czech the weight for the feature `TranslationModel0` was tuned to near zero. We restarted the tuning process with it fixed at zero and achieved very similar results.

A comparison of results of the Tuning Task can be found in (WMT, 2015).

6 Discussion

In this paper we have introduced a new method for tuning the weighted linear model which arises in finding a statistical machine translation system. We have created a new, lower-dimensional search space in which all features are uncorrelated and have approximately equal variation. We have created a new method for extrapolating known n-best lists to a new point, effectively reordering its simulated n-best list by penalizing the pseudo-decoder score of less trustworthy translations. Finally, we have employed a new, multi-scale optimization method which avoids approximating derivatives and for robustness smooths the error function and its local approximations.

Several different implementations fit within Drem's framework. This paper presents a batch implementation of Drem. The algorithm requires minor modifications if partial decodes are performed, and this has promise for tuning more efficiently.

References

Alexandra Birch and Miles Osborne. 2011. Reordering metrics for mt. In *Proceedings of the 49th Annual Meeting of the Association for Computational Linguistics: Human Language Technologies*, pages 1027–1035, Portland, Oregon, USA, June. Association for Computational Linguistics.

Colin Cherry and George Foster. 2012. Batch tuning strategies for statistical machine translation. In *Proceedings of the 2012 Conference of the North American Chapter of the Association for Computational Linguistics: Human Language Technologies*, pages 427–436, Montréal, Canada, June. Association for Computational Linguistics.

David Chiang, Yuval Marton, and Philip Resnik. 2008. Online large-margin training of syntactic and structural translation features. In *Proceedings of the 2008 Conference on Empirical Methods in Natural Language Processing*, pages 224–233, Honolulu, Hawaii, October. Association for Computational Linguistics.

Andrew R. Conn, Nicholas I. M. Gould, and Philippe L. Toint. 2000. *Trust-Region Methods*. Society for Industrial and Applied Mathematics.

Andrew R. Conn, Katya Scheinberg, and Luis N. Vicent. 2009. *Introduction to Derivative-Free Optimization*. Society for Industrial and Applied Mathematics.

Michael Denkowski and Alon Lavie. 2014. Meteor universal: Language specific translation evaluation for any target language. In *Proceedings of the Ninth Workshop on Statistical Machine Translation*, pages 376–380, Baltimore, Maryland, USA, June. Association for Computational Linguistics.

Opinions, interpretations, conclusions and recommendations are those of the authors and are not necessarily endorsed by the United States Government. Cleared for public release on 02 Jun 2015. Originator reference number RH-15-114114. Case number 88ABW-2015-2731.

George Foster and Roland Kuhn. 2009. Stabilizing minimum error rate training. In *Proceedings of the Fourth Workshop on Statistical Machine Translation*, pages 242–249, Athens, Greece, March. Association for Computational Linguistics.

Michel Galley, Chris Quirk, Colin Cherry, and Kristina Toutanova. 2013. Regularized minimum error rate training. In *Proceedings of the 2013 Conference on Empirical Methods in Natural Language Processing*, pages 1948–1959, Seattle, Washington, USA, October. Association for Computational Linguistics.

Kevin Gimpel and Noah A. Smith. 2012. Structured ramp loss minimization for machine translation. In *Proceedings of the 2012 Conference of the North American Chapter of the Association for Computational Linguistics: Human Language Technologies*, pages 221–231, Montréal, Canada, June. Association for Computational Linguistics.

Mark Hopkins and Jonathan May. 2011. Tuning as ranking. In *Proceedings of the 2011 Conference on Empirical Methods in Natural Language Processing*, pages 1352–1362, Edinburgh, Scotland, UK., July. Association for Computational Linguistics.

Philipp Koehn, Hieu Hoang, Alexandra Birch, Chris Callison-Burch, Marcello Federico, Nicola Bertoldi, Brooke Cowan, Wade Shen, Christine Moran, Richard Zens, Chris Dyer, Ondrej Bojar, Alexandra Constantin, and Evan Herbst. 2007. Moses: Open source toolkit for statistical machine translation. In *Proceedings of the 45th Annual Meeting of the Association for Computational Linguistics Companion Volume Proceedings of the Demo and Poster Sessions*, pages 177–180, Prague, Czech Republic, June. Association for Computational Linguistics.

Lemao Liu, Tiejun Zhao, Taro Watanabe, Hailong Cao, and Conghui Zhu. 2012. Expected error minimization with ultraconservative update for SMT. In *Proceedings of COLING 2012: Posters*, pages 723–732, Mumbai, India, December. The COLING 2012 Organizing Committee.

NIST Report. 2002. Automatic evaluation of machine translation quality using n-gram co-occurrence statistics. Technical report, National Institute of Standards and Technology.

Franz Josef Och. 2003. Minimum error rate training in statistical machine translation. In *Proceedings of the 41st Annual Meeting of the Association for Computational Linguistics*, Sapporo, Japan, July.

David A. Smith and Jason Eisner. 2006. Minimum risk annealing for training log-linear models. In *Proceedings of the COLING/ACL 2006 Main Conference Poster Sessions*, pages 787–794, Sydney, Australia, July. Association for Computational Linguistics.

Jun Suzuki, Kevin Duh, and Masaaki Nagata. 2011. Distributed minimum error rate training of smt using particle swarm optimization. In *Proceedings of 5th International Joint Conference on Natural Language Processing*, pages 649–657, Chiang Mai, Thailand, November. Asian Federation of Natural Language Processing.

WMT. 2015. Findings of the 2015 workshop on statistical machine translation. In *Proceedings of the Tenth Workshop on Statistical Machine Translation (WMT '15)*, Lisbon, Portugal, September. Association for Computational Linguistics.

Bing Zhao and Shengyuan Chen. 2009. A simplex Armijo downhill algorithm for optimizing statistical machine translation decoding parameters. In *Proceedings of Human Language Technologies: The 2009 Annual Conference of the North American Chapter of the Association for Computational Linguistics, Companion Volume: Short Papers*, pages 21–24, Boulder, Colorado, June. Association for Computational Linguistics.

MT Tuning on RED: A Dependency-Based Evaluation Metric

Liangyou Li* **Hui Yu†** **Qun Liu*†**
* ADAPT Centre, School of Computing
Dublin City University, Ireland
† Key Laboratory of Intelligent Information Processing
Institute of Computing Technology
Chinese Academy of Sciences, China
{liangyouli,qliu}@computing.dcu.ie
yuhui@ict.ac.cn

Abstract

In this paper, we describe our submission to WMT 2015 Tuning Task. We integrate a dependency-based MT evaluation metric, RED, to Moses and compare it with BLEU and METEOR in conjunction with two tuning methods: MERT and MIRA. Experiments are conducted using hierarchical phrase-based models on Czech–English and English–Czech tasks. Our results show that MIRA performs better than MERT in most cases. Using RED performs similarly to METEOR when tuning is performed using MIRA. We submit our system tuned by MIRA towards RED to WMT 2015. In human evaluations, we achieve the 1st rank in all 7 systems on the English–Czech task and 6/9 on the Czech–English task.

1 Introduction

Statistical Machine Translation (SMT) is modeled as a weighted combination of several features. Tuning in SMT refers to learning a set of optimized weights, which minimize a defined translation error on a tuning set. Typically, the error is measured by an automatic evaluation metric. Thanks to its simplicity and language independence, BLEU (Papineni et al., 2002) has served as the optimization objective since the 2000s. Although various lexical metrics, such as TER (Snover et al., 2006) and METEOR (Lavie and Denkowski, 2009) etc., have been proposed, none of them can truly replace BLEU in a phrase-based system (Cer et al., 2010).

However, BLEU has no proficiency to deal with synonyms, paraphrases, and syntactic equivalent etc. (Callison-Burch et al., 2006). In addition, as a lexical and n-gram-based metric, BLEU may be not suitable for optimization in a syntax-based model.

In this paper, we integrate a reference dependency-based MT evaluation metric, RED[1] (Yu et al., 2014), into the hierarchical phrase-based model (Chiang, 2005) in Moses (Koehn et al., 2007). In doing so, we explore whether a syntax-based translation system will perform better when it is optimized towards a syntax-based evaluation criteria. We compare RED with two other evaluation metrics, BLEU and METEOR (Section 2). Two tuning algorithms are used (Section 3). They are MERT (Och, 2003), MIRA (Cherry and Foster, 2012). Experiments are conducted on Czech–English and English–Czech translation (Section 4).

2 Evaluation Metrics

An evaluation metric, which has a higher correlation with human judgments, may be used to train a better system. In this paper, we compare three metrics: BLEU, METEOR, and RED.

2.1 BLEU

BLEU is the most widely used metric in SMT. It is lexical-based and language-independent. BLEU scores a hypothesis by combining n-gram precisions over reference translations with a length penalty.

A n-gram precision p_n is calculated separately for different n-gram lengths. BLEU combines these precisions using a geometric mean. The resulting score is subsequently scaled by a length penalty, which penalizes a hypothesis if it is shorter than references. Equation (1) shows a formula for calculating BLEU scores:

$$BLEU = BP \cdot \left(\prod_{n=1}^{N} p_n^{w_n} \right), \qquad (1)$$

where,

$$BP = \min\{1.0, \exp(1 - |r|/|h|)\},$$

[1] REference Dependency

r and h are a reference and a hypothesis, respectively. In this paper, we use $N = 4$ and uniform weights $w_n = \frac{1}{N}$.

Even though widely used in SMT, BLEU has some pitfalls. Because of strictly relying on lexical sequences, BLEU cannot correctly score meaning equivalents, such as synonyms and paraphrases. It does not distinguish between content words and functional words as well. In addition, the penalty is not sufficient to be an equivalent replacement of n-gram recall.

2.2 METEOR

METEOR relies on unigrams but considers both precision and recall. It evaluates a hypothesis by aligning it to a reference. METEOR identifies all possible matches between a hypothesis-reference pair with the following matchers:

- **Exact**: match words that have the same word form.
- **Stem**: match words whose stems are identical.
- **Synonym**: match words when they are defined as synonyms in the WordNet database[2].
- **Paraphrase**: match a phrase pair when they are listed as paraphrases in a paraphrase table.

Typically, there is more than one possible alignment. In METEOR, a final alignment is obtained by beam search in the entire alignment space. Given the final alignment, METEOR calculates a unigram precision P and a unigram recall R by assigning different weights to function words and content words to distinguish them, as in Equation (2) and Equation (3).

$$P = \frac{\sum_i w_i \cdot (\delta \cdot m_i(h_c) + (1-\delta) \cdot m_i(h_f))}{\delta \cdot |h_c| + (1-\delta) \cdot |h_f|} \quad (2)$$

$$R = \frac{\sum_i w_i \cdot (\delta \cdot m_i(r_c) + (1-\delta) \cdot m_i(r_f))}{\delta \cdot |r_c| + (1-\delta) \cdot |r_f|} \quad (3)$$

where m_i is the ith matcher, h_c and r_c are content words in a hypothesis and a reference, h_f and r_f are functions words in a hypothesis and a reference, respectively. Then the precision and recall are combined as in Equation (4).

[2] https://wordnet.princeton.edu/

$$Fmean = \frac{P \cdot R}{\alpha \cdot P + (1-\alpha) \cdot R} \quad (4)$$

To consider differences in word order, a penalty is calculated on the basis of the total number (m) of matched words and the number (ch) of chunks. A chunk is defined as a sequence of matches, which are contiguous and have identical word order. The penalty is formulated as in Equation (5):

$$Pen = \gamma \cdot \left(\frac{ch}{m}\right)^{\beta}. \quad (5)$$

The final METEOR score is calculated as follows:

$$Score = (1 - Pen) \cdot Fmean. \quad (6)$$

α, β, γ, δ and w_i are constants, which can be optimized to maximize the correlation with human judgments.

By considering synonym, paraphrases, METEOR has shown to be highly correlated with human judgments. However, these resources are language-dependent. Besides, METEOR is unigram-based and thus has a lack of incorporating syntactic structures.

2.3 RED

Instead of collecting n-grams from word sequences as in BLEU, RED extracts n-grams according to a dependency structure of a reference, called *dep-ngrams*, which have two types: headword chain (Liu and Gildea, 2005) and fixed/floating structures (Shen et al., 2010). A headword chain is a sequence of words which corresponds to a path in a dependency tree, while a fixed/floating structure covers a sequence of contiguous words. Figure 1 shows an example of different types of dep-$n$grams.

A $Fmean$ score is separately calculated for each different dep-$n$gram lengths. Then, they are linearly combined as follows:

$$RED = \sum_{n=1}^{N} w_n \cdot Fmean_n \quad (7)$$

Inspired by other metrics, such as TERp (Snover et al., 2009) and METEOR, RED integrates some resources as follows:

- Stem and synonym: used to align words. This increases the possibility of matching a dep-$n$gram. Different matchers are assigned

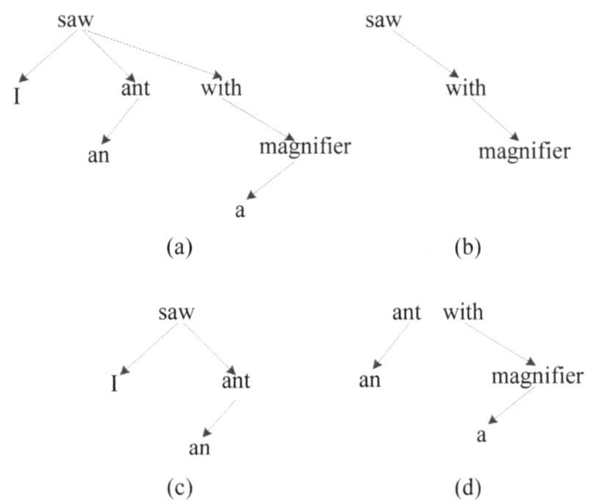

Figure 1: An illustration of dep-$n$grams. (a) is a dependency tree, (b) is a headword chain, (c) is a fixed structure and (d) is a floating structure.

different weights, this results in a scale factor for a dep-$n$gram as in Equation (8).

$$s_m = \frac{\sum_{i=1}^{n} w_{m_i}}{n} \tag{8}$$

- Paraphrase: used for extracting *paraphrase-$n$grams*. In this case, RED ignores the dependency structure of a reference. A paraphrase-$n$gram has a weight w_{par}.

- Function Word: used to distinguish content words from function words. The function word score of a dep-$n$gram or a paraphrase-$n$gram can be calculated as follows:

$$s_f = \frac{cnt_f \cdot w_f + cnt_c \cdot (1 - w_f)}{cnt_f + cnt_c}, \tag{9}$$

where cnt_f and cnt_c are the number of function words and the number of content words.

Ideally, both a precision score P and a recall score R are based on the total number of dep-$n$grams in a hypothesis and a reference, respectively. However, in RED only dependency structures on the reference are available. Therefore, it uses the length of the hypothesis to approximate the number of the dep-$n$grams in the hypothesis to calculate P. Formulas for P and R are as follows:

$$P = \frac{score_{par} + score_{dep}}{|c|}, \tag{10}$$

$$R = \frac{score_{par} + score_{dep}}{Count_n(r) + Count_n(par)}, \tag{11}$$

where

$$score_{par} = \sum_{par \in P_n} w_{par} \cdot s_f, \tag{12}$$

$$score_{dep} = \sum_{d \in D_n} p(d, c) \cdot s_m \cdot s_f, \tag{13}$$

r and c are the reference and the hypothesis, P_n is the set of paraphrase-$n$grams, D_n is the set of dep-$n$grams. $p(d, c)$ is a match score which is 0 if no match is found; otherwise, it is a value between 0 and 1[3].

3 Tuning Algorithms

Tuning algorithms in SMT are designed to optimize decoding weights so that a defined translation error, typically measured by an automatic metric, is minimal on a development set. In this paper, we compare two algorithms: MERT and MIRA.

First, we introduce some notations. Let $\langle x, y\rangle \in D$ be a tuning set, where x and y are a source and a target, respectively. Let $\delta_y(d_x)$ be an error made by a derivation d on the source x given y as a reference. Let $\ell_m(D, \mathbf{w})$ be the total error measured by a metric m on the tuning set D with parameters $\mathbf{w}$.

3.1 MERT

MERT learns weights to rank candidate translations of each source sentence so that the final document-level score measured by a specific metric on the one-best translations is the highest. Formally, it tries to minimize the document-level error on the translations produced by the highest scoring translation derivation for each source sentence, as in Equation 14.

$$\ell_{MERT}(D, \mathbf{w}) = \oplus_{\langle x,y\rangle \in D} \delta_y(d_x^*), \tag{14}$$

where

$$d_x^* = \operatorname*{argmax}_{d_x} \mathbf{w} \cdot \Phi(d_x), \tag{15}$$

Φ are feature functions of the decoding model, $\mathbf{w} \cdot \Phi(d_x)$ is a score assigned to a deviation d_x

[3]If a headword chain $n$gram d in a reference r has a match in a hypothesis c, $p(d, c) = exp\{-\frac{\sum_{i=1}^{n-1} dist_{r_i} - dist_{c_i}}{n-1}\}$, where $dist_{r_i}$ and $dist_{c_i}$ are relative distances between ith word and $(i+1)$th word in the reference and hypothesis, respectively. If a fixed/floating structure is matched, $p(d, c) = 1$.

by the decoding model, $\oplus$ represents the accumulation of potentially non-decomposable sentential errors, which then produces a document-level evaluation score.

3.2 MIRA

MIRA is an online large margin learning algorithm (Crammer and Singer, 2003). Its application to MT decoding model tuning was firstly explored by Watanabe et al. (2007) and then refined by Chiang et al. (2008) and Cherry and Foster (2012). The MIRA we use tries to separate a "fear" derivation $d^-(x, y)$ from a "hope" one $d^+(x, y)$ by a margin propositional to their metric difference (Chiang et al., 2008). The two derivations are defined as follows:

$$d^+(x, y) = \underset{d}{\operatorname{argmax}}\, \mathbf{w} \cdot \Phi(d) - \delta_y(d) \quad (16)$$

$$d^-(x, y) = \underset{d}{\operatorname{argmax}}\, \mathbf{w} \cdot \Phi(d) + \delta_y(d) \quad (17)$$

Their model-score difference and metric-score difference are defined in Equation (18) and Equation (19), respectively.

$$\Delta s(x, y) = \delta_y(d^+(x, y)) - \delta_y(d^-(x, y)) \quad (18)$$

$$\Delta m(x, y) = \mathbf{w} \cdot (\Phi(d^+(x, y)) - \Phi(d^-(x, y))\} \quad (19)$$

Cherry and Foster (2012) adapt a batch strategy in MIRA. The error, that batch MIRA tries to minimize is defined as below:

$$\ell_{MIRA}(D, \mathbf{w}) = \frac{1}{2C}||\mathbf{w} - \mathbf{w}_0|| + \sum_{\langle x,y\rangle \in D} L(x, y) \quad (20)$$

where C is a constant and $L(x, y)$ is a loss over a source x and a reference y, which is defined in Equation (21).

$$L(x, y) = \max\{0, \Delta s(x, y) - \Delta m(x, y)\} \quad (21)$$

4 Experiments

We conduct experiments on Czech–English and English–Czech hierarchical phrase-based translation systems built using Moses with default configurations and default feature functions.

We use WMT newstest2014 as our development data, while our test data consists of the concatenation of newstest2012 and newstest2013, which includes 6,003 sentence pairs in total[4]. English sentences are parsed into dependency structures by Stanford parser (Marneffe et al., 2006). Czech sentences are parsed by a Perl implementation[5] of the MST parser (McDonald et al., 2005).

Train \ Eval.		BLEU	METEOR	RED
MERT	BLEU	18.90	28.38	19.91
	METEOR	18.68	28.64	20.02
	RED	18.07	28.17	19.97
MIRA	BLEU	19.12	28.54	20.02
	METEOR	19.10	28.56	20.05
	RED	17.74	28.82	20.02

Table 1: Czech–English evaluation performance. In each column, the intensity of shades indicates the rank of values.

4.1 Metrics Setting

As described in Section 2.1, we use the standard BLEU parameters[6]. We use METEOR 1.4[7] in our experiments with default optimized parameters. Specifically, for Czech to English translation, we adopt all four lexical matching strategies with parameter values: $\alpha = 0.85$, $\beta = 0.2$, $\gamma = 0.6$, $\delta = 0.75$ and $w_i = 1.0, 0.6, 0.8, 0.6$. For English to Czech translation, we use two lexical matching strategies, including *exact* and *paraphrase*, with parameter values: $\alpha = 0.95$, $\beta = 0.2$, $\gamma = 0.6$, $\delta = 0.8$ and $w_i = 1.0, 0.4$.

In RED, we use all four matchers in the Czech–English task while we do not use *stem* and *synonym* in the English–Czech task. The same parameter values are used in both tasks. We set $N = 3$, the corresponding $w_i = 0.6, 0.5, 0.1$. We set $w_{m_i} = 0.9, 0.6, 0.6$ for three matchers including exact, stem and synonym and $w_{par} = 0.6$ for the paraphrase matcher. We set $w_f = 0.2$ for function words and $\alpha = 0.9$ for combining P and R in $Fmean$.

4.2 Results

Table 1 and Table 2 show our experimental results on two tasks, respectively. We have several findings as below:

- In both tasks best scores are achieved when

[4] http://statmt.org/wmt14/translation-task.html

[5] http://search.cpan.org/~rur/Treex-Parser-MSTperl

[6] i.e., up to 4-gram matching with uniform weighting of n-gram precisions.

[7] http://www.cs.cmu.edu/~alavie/METEOR/

Train \ Eval.		BLEU	METEOR	RED
MERT	BLEU	11.25	17.36	14.95
	METEOR	10.44	17.00	14.86
	RED	9.51	16.81	14.58
MIRA	BLEU	11.52	17.54	15.14
	METEOR	11.43	17.56	15.26
	RED	11.29	17.67	15.25

Table 2: English–Czech evaluation performance. In each column, the intensity of shades indicates the rank of values.

MIRA is used rather than MERT. In most cases, MIRA is better than MERT.

- When RED is used in MERT, we obtain a worse performance than that of BLEU and METEOR in almost all cases, especially in the English–Czech task.
- When BLEU is used as the evaluation metric, the best score is obtained by using BLEU as the optimization objective in tuning as well. This follows the findings in Cer et al. (2010).
- The best METEOR score is achieved when RED is used to tune our system while the best RED score is obtained when METEOR is used to tune. Taking that the same resources are used in the two metrics into consideration, this may indicate that the two metrics are correlated.

5 Submission

We submit our system tuned by MIRA towards RED. In human evaluations, we get 6th out of 9 systems on the Czech–English task and the 1st rank in all 7 systems on the English–Czech task.

Such human judgments suggest that RED performs better on Czech than English. We guess this is because dependency n-grams have better capability of handling free word order in Czech sentences. This hypothesis can be an avenue for future work.

6 Conclusion

In this paper, we describe our submissions to WMT 2015 tuning task on Czech–English and English–Czech tasks. They are hierarchical phrase-based models both tuned by MIRA towards a dependency-based metric, RED. In human evaluations, our system gets the 1st rank in the English–Czech task.

Acknowledgements

This research has received funding from the People Programme (Marie Curie Actions) of the European Union's Seventh Framework Programme FP7/2007-2013/ under REA grant agreement no. 317471. The ADAPT Centre for Digital Content Technology is funded under the SFI Research Centres Programme (Grant 13/RC/2106) and is co-funded under the European Regional Development Fund.

We thank Xiaofeng Wu for his discussion and anonymous reviewers for their insightful comments. In particular, we thank reviewer #2 for providing detailed suggestions.

References

Chris Callison-Burch, Miles Osborne, and Philipp Koehn. 2006. Re-evaluating the Role of BLEU in Machine Translation Research. In *Proceedings of the 11th Conference of the European Chapter of the Association for Computational Linguistics*, pages 249–256.

Daniel Cer, Christopher D. Manning, and Daniel Jurafsky. 2010. The Best Lexical Metric for Phrase-based Statistical MT System Optimization. In *Human Language Technologies: The 2010 Annual Conference of the North American Chapter of the Association for Computational Linguistics*, pages 555–563, Los Angeles, California.

Colin Cherry and George Foster. 2012. Batch Tuning Strategies for Statistical Machine Translation. In *Proceedings of the 2012 Conference of the North American Chapter of the Association for Computational Linguistics: Human Language Technologies*, NAACL HLT '12, pages 427–436, Montreal, Canada.

David Chiang, Yuval Marton, and Philip Resnik. 2008. Online Large-margin Training of Syntactic and Structural Translation Features. In *Proceedings of the Conference on Empirical Methods in Natural Language Processing*, pages 224–233, Honolulu, Hawaii.

David Chiang. 2005. A Hierarchical Phrase-based Model for Statistical Machine Translation. In *Proceedings of the 43rd Annual Meeting on Association for Computational Linguistics*, pages 263–270, Ann Arbor, Michigan.

Koby Crammer and Yoram Singer. 2003. Ultraconservative online algorithms for multiclass problems. *Journal of Machine Learning Research*, 3:951–991, March.

Philipp Koehn, Hieu Hoang, Alexandra Birch, Chris Callison-Burch, Marcello Federico, Nicola Bertoldi,

Brooke Cowan, Wade Shen, Christine Moran, Richard Zens, Chris Dyer, Ondej Bojar, Alexandra Constantin, and Evan Herbst. 2007. Moses: Open Source Toolkit for Statistical Machine Translation. In *Proceedings of the 45th Annual Meeting of the ACL on Interactive Poster and Demonstration Sessions*, ACL '07, pages 177–180, Prague, Czech Republic.

Alon Lavie and Michael J. Denkowski. 2009. The Meteor Metric for Automatic Evaluation of Machine Translation. *Machine Translation*, 23(2-3):105–115, September.

Ding Liu and Daniel Gildea. 2005. Syntactic Features for Evaluation of Machine Translation. In *Proceedings of the ACL Workshop on Intrinsic and Extrinsic Evaluation Measures for Machine Translation and/or Summarization*, pages 25–32.

Marie-Catherine de Marneffe, Bill MacCartney, and Christopher D. Manning. 2006. Generating Typed Dependency Parses from Phrase Structure Parses. In *Language Resources and Evaluation*.

Ryan McDonald, Koby Crammer, and Fernando Pereira. 2005. Online large-margin training of dependency parsers. In *Proceedings of the 43rd Annual Meeting on Association for Computational Linguistics*, pages 91–98, Ann Arbor, Michigan.

Franz Josef Och. 2003. Minimum Error Rate Training in Statistical Machine Translation. In *Proceedings of the 41st Annual Meeting on Association for Computational Linguistics - Volume 1*, pages 160–167, Stroudsburg, PA, USA. Association for Computational Linguistics.

Kishore Papineni, Salim Roukos, Todd Ward, and Wei-Jing Zhu. 2002. BLEU: A Method for Automatic Evaluation of Machine Translation. In *Proceedings of the 40th Annual Meeting on Association for Computational Linguistics*, ACL '02, pages 311–318, Philadelphia, Pennsylvania.

Libin Shen, Jinxi Xu, and Ralph Weischedel. 2010. String-to-dependency Statistical Machine Translation. *Computational Linguistics*, 36(4):649–671, December.

M. Snover, B. Dorr, R. Schwartz, L. Micciulla, and J. Makhoul. 2006. A Study of Translation Edit Rate with Targeted Human Annotation. In *Proceedings of Association for Machine Translation in the Americas*, pages 223–231, Cambridge, Massachusetts, USA, August.

Matthew Snover, Nitin Madnani, Bonnie J. Dorr, and Richard Schwartz. 2009. Fluency, Adequacy, or HTER?: Exploring Different Human Judgments with a Tunable MT Metric. In *Proceedings of the Fourth Workshop on Statistical Machine Translation*, pages 259–268, Athens, Greece.

Taro Watanabe, Jun Suzuki, Hajime Tsukada, and Hideki Isozaki. 2007. Online Large-Margin Training for Statistical Machine Translation. In *Proceedings of the 2007 Joint Conference on Empirical Methods in Natural Language Processing and Computational Natural Language Learning*, pages 764–773, Prague, June.

Hui Yu, Xiaofeng Wu, Jun Xie, Wenbin Jiang, Qun Liu, and Shouxun Lin. 2014. RED: A Reference Dependency Based MT Evaluation Metric. In *Proceedings of COLING 2014, the 25th International Conference on Computational Linguistics: Technical Papers*, pages 2042–2051, Dublin, Ireland, August. Dublin City University and Association for Computational Linguistics.

Improving evaluation and optimization of MT systems against MEANT

Chi-kiu Lo[*]
NRC-CNRC
Multilingual Text Processing
National Research Council Canada
1200 Montreal Road, Ottawa,
Ontario K1A 0R6, Canada
ChiKiu.Lo@nrc-cnrc.gc.ca

Philipp C. Dowling[*]
TUM
Fakultät für Informatik
Technische Universität München
Boltzmannstraße 3,
85748 Garching bei München, Germany
dowling@cs.tum.edu

Dekai Wu
HKUST
Human Language Technology Center
HK University of Science and Technology
Clear Water Bay
Kowloon, Hong Kong
dekai@cs.ust.hk

Abstract

We show that, consistent with MEANT-tuned systems that translate into Chinese, MEANT-tuned MT systems that translate into English also outperforms BLEU-tuned systems across commonly used MT evaluation metrics, even in BLEU. The result is achieved by significantly improving MEANT's sentence-level ranking correlation with human preferences through incorporating a more accurate distributional semantic model for lexical similarity and a novel backoff algorithm for evaluating MT output which automatic semantic parser fails to parse. The surprising result of MEANT-tuned systems having a higher BLEU score than BLEU-tuned systems suggests that MEANT is a more accurate objective function guiding the development of MT systems towards producing more adequate translation.

1 Introduction

Lo and Wu (2013) showed that MEANT-tuned system for translating into Chinese outperforms BLEU-tuned system across commonly used MT evaluation metrics, even in BLEU. However, such phenomena are not observed in MEANT-tuned system for translating into English. In this paper, for the first time, we present MT systems for translating into English, which is tuned to a improved version of MEANT, also outperforms BLEU-tuned system across commonly used MT evaluation metrics, even in BLEU. The improvements in MEANT include incorporating more accurate distributional semantic model for lexical similarity and a novel backoff algorithm for evaluating MT output which the automatic semantic parser failed to parse. Empirical results show that the new version of MEANT is significantly improved in terms of sentence-level ranking correlation with human preferences.

The accuracy of MEANT relies heavily on the accuracy of the model that determines the lexical similarities of the semantic role fillers. However, the discrete context vector model based on the raw co-occurrence counts used in the original proposal of MEANT does not work well in predicting the similarity of the lexicons used in the reference and machine translations. Recent work by Baroni *et al.* (2014) shows that word embeddings trained by predict models outperforms the count based models in various lexical semantic tasks. Baroni *et al.* (2014) argues that *predict* models such as word2vec (Mikolov *et al.*, 2013) outperform count based models on a wide range of lexical semantic tasks. It is also common knowledge that raw co-occurrence counts do not work very well and performance can be improved when transformed by reweighing the counts for context informativeness and dimensionality reduction. In contrast to conventional word vector models, prediction based word vector models estimate the vectors directly as a supervised task, where the weights in a word vector are set to maximize the probability of the contexts in which the word is observed in the corpus (Bengio *et al.*, 2006; Collobert and Weston, 2008; Collobert *et al.*, 2011; Huang *et al.*, 2012; Mikolov *et al.*, 2013; Turian *et al.*, 2010).

In this paper, we show that MEANT's correlation with human adequacy judgments can be further improved by incorporating the word embeddings trained by the predict models. Subsequently, tuning MT system against the improved version of MEANT produce more adequate translations than tuning against BLEU.

2 The family of MEANT

MEANT and its variants (Lo *et al.*, 2012) measure weighted f-scores over corresponding seman-

[*]This work was completed at HKUST.

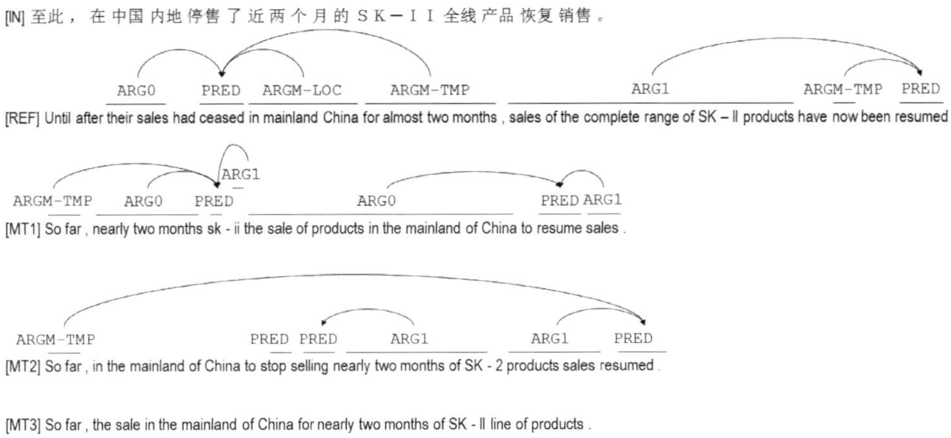

Figure 1: Examples of automatic shallow semantic parses. Both the reference and machine translations are parsed using automatic English SRL. There are no semantic frames for MT3 since there is no predicate in the MT output.

tic frames and role fillers in the reference and machine translations. MEANT typically outperforms BLEU, NIST, METEOR, WER, CDER and TER in correlation with human adequacy judgment, and is relatively easy to port to other languages, requiring only an automatic semantic parser and a monolingual corpus of the output language, which is used to train the discrete context vector model for computing the lexical similarity between the semantic role fillers of the reference and translation. Lo *et al.* (2014) describe a cross-lingual quality estimation variant, XMEANT, capable of evaluating translation quality without the need for expensive human reference translations, by utilizing semantic parses of the original foreign input sentence instead of a reference translation. MEANT is generally computed as follows:

1. Apply an automatic shallow semantic parser to both the reference and machine translations. (Figure 1 shows examples of automatic shallow semantic parses on both reference and MT.)

2. Apply the maximum weighted bipartite matching algorithm to align the semantic frames between the reference and machine translations according to the lexical similarities of the predicates.

3. For each pair of the aligned frames, apply the maximum weighted bipartite matching algorithm to align the arguments between the reference and MT output according to the lexical similarity of role fillers.

4. Compute the weighted f-score over the matching role labels of these aligned predicates and role fillers according to the following definitions:

$$
\begin{aligned}
q^0_{i,j} &\equiv \text{ARG } j \text{ of aligned frame } i \text{ in MT} \\
q^1_{i,j} &\equiv \text{ARG } j \text{ of aligned frame } i \text{ in REF} \\
w^0_i &\equiv \frac{\text{\#tokens filled in aligned frame } i \text{ of MT}}{\text{total \#tokens in MT}} \\
w^1_i &\equiv \frac{\text{\#tokens filled in aligned frame } i \text{ of REF}}{\text{total \#tokens in REF}} \\
w_{\text{pred}} &\equiv \text{weight of similarity of predicates} \\
w_j &\equiv \text{weight of similarity of ARG } j \\
\mathbf{e}_{i,\text{pred}} &\equiv \text{the pred string of the aligned frame } i \text{ of MT} \\
\mathbf{f}_{i,\text{pred}} &\equiv \text{the pred string of the aligned frame } i \text{ of REF} \\
\mathbf{e}_{i,j} &\equiv \text{role fillers of ARG } j \text{ of the aligned frame } i \text{ of MT} \\
\mathbf{f}_{i,j} &\equiv \text{role fillers of ARG } j \text{ of the aligned frame } i \text{ of REF} \\
s(e,f) &= \text{lexical similarity of token } e \text{ and } f \\
\text{prec}_{\mathbf{e},\mathbf{f}} &= \frac{\sum_{e\in\mathbf{e}} \max_{f\in\mathbf{f}} s(e,f)}{|\,\mathbf{e}\,|} \\
\text{rec}_{\mathbf{e},\mathbf{f}} &= \frac{\sum_{f\in\mathbf{f}} \max_{e\in\mathbf{e}} s(e,f)}{|\,\mathbf{f}\,|} \\
s_{i,\text{pred}} &= \frac{2\cdot \text{prec}_{\mathbf{e}_{i,\text{pred}},\mathbf{f}_{i,\text{pred}}}\cdot \text{rec}_{\mathbf{e}_{i,\text{pred}},\mathbf{f}_{i,\text{pred}}}}{\text{prec}_{\mathbf{e}_{i,\text{pred}},\mathbf{f}_{i,\text{pred}}}+\text{rec}_{\mathbf{e}_{i,\text{pred}},\mathbf{f}_{i,\text{pred}}}} \\
s_{i,j} &= \frac{2\cdot \text{prec}_{\mathbf{e}_{i,j},\mathbf{f}_{i,j}}\cdot \text{rec}_{\mathbf{e}_{i,j},\mathbf{f}_{i,j}}}{\text{prec}_{\mathbf{e}_{i,j},\mathbf{f}_{i,j}}+\text{rec}_{\mathbf{e}_{i,j},\mathbf{f}_{i,j}}}
\end{aligned}
$$

$$
\text{precision} = \frac{\sum_i w^0_i \frac{w_{\text{pred}} s_{i,\text{pred}} + \sum_j w_j s_{i,j}}{w_{\text{pred}} + \sum_j w_j |q^0_{i,j}|}}{\sum_i w^0_i} \quad (1)
$$

$$
\text{recall} = \frac{\sum_i w^1_i \frac{w_{\text{pred}} s_{i,\text{pred}} + \sum_j w_j s_{i,j}}{w_{\text{pred}} + \sum_j w_j |q^1_{i,j}|}}{\sum_i w^1_i} \quad (2)
$$

$$
\text{MEANT} = \frac{2\cdot \text{precision}\cdot \text{recall}}{\text{precision}+\text{recall}} \quad (3)
$$

where w_{pred} and w_j are the weights of the lexical similarities of the predicates and role fillers of the arguments of type j of all frame between the reference translations and the MT output. There is a total of 12 weights for the set of semantic role labels in MEANT as defined in Lo and Wu (2011b). The value of these weights are determined in supervised manner using a simple grid search to optimize the correlation with human adequacy judgments (Lo and Wu, 2011a) for MEANT and in unsupervised manner using relative frequency of each semantic role label in the references for UMEANT (Lo and Wu, 2012). Thus UMEANT is useful when human judgments on adequacy of the development set are unavailable. $s_{i,\text{pred}}$ and $s_{i,j}$ are the phrasal similarities of the predicates and role fillers of the arguments of type j between the reference translations and the MT output. Lo *et al.* (2012) and Tumuluru *et al.* (2012) described how the lexical similarities, $s(e, f)$, are computed using a discrete context vector model and how the phrasal similarities are computed by aggregating the lexical similarities via various heuristics. In the latest version of MEANT (Lo *et al.*, 2014), as shown in above, it uses f-score to aggregate individual token similarities into the phrasal similarities of semantic role fillers. Another MEANT's variant, IMEANT (Wu *et al.*, 2014), which uses ITG to constrain the token alignments between the semantic role fillers of the reference and the machine translations and is shown outperforming MEANT (Lo *et al.*, 2014).

3 Improvements to MEANT

We improve the performance of MEANT by incorporating a word embedding model for more accurate evaluation of the semantic role filler similarity and a novel backoff algorithm for evaluating translations when the automatic semantic parser fails to reconstruct the semantic structure of the translations. Our evaluation results show that the new version of MEANT is significantly improved in correlating with human ranking preferences at both the sentence-level and the document-level.

3.1 Discrete context vectors vs. word embeddings

MEANT's discrete context vector model is very sparse because of the extremely high dimension of the discrete context vector model. The number of dimensions of a vector in the discrete context vector model is the total number of token types in the training corpus. The vector sparsity issue makes the lexical similarity highly sensitive of exact token matching and thus hurts the accuracy of MEANT. We aim at tackling the sparse vector issue by replacing the discrete context vector model with the continuous word embeddings in order to further improve the accuracy of MEANT.

We first train the word embeddings on the same monolingual corpus as the discrete context vector model, i.e. Gigaword, for a fair comparison. However, since the memory consumption of the word embeddings is significantly reduced when comparing with the discrete context vector model due to the reduced dimension in the vectors, it is now possible to increase the size of the training corpus of the word embeddings so as to improve the token coverage of the lexical similarity model. We compare the in-house Gigaword word embeddings which covers 1.2 million words and phrases with the Google pretrained word embeddings (Mikolov *et al.*, 2013) that is trained on a 100 billion tokens news dataset and covers 3 million words and phrases. We show that the high portability of MEANT is preserved when replacing the discrete context vector model with word embeddings as the size of the monolingual training data for the word embeddings does not significantly affect the correlation of MEANT with human adequacy judgments.

Another interesting property of the word embeddings is the compositionality of words vectors into phrases. As described in Mikolov *et al.* (2013), for example, the result of linear vector calculation vec("Madrid")-vec("Spain")+vec("France") is closer to vec("Paris") than to any other vectors. It seems to be natural that phrasal similarity of the semantic role fillers could be more accurately computed using the composite phrase vector than using the align-and-aggregate approach because the vector composition approach is not affected by the errors of token misalignment. However, we show that surprisingly, the align-and-aggregate approach outperforms the naive linear word vector composition in computing the phrasal similarities of the semantic role fillers.

3.2 Backoff algorithm for evaluating translations without semantic parse

MEANT fails to evaluate the quality of the translations if the automatic semantic parser fails to reconstruct the semantic structure of the translations. According to the error analysis in Lo and Wu (2013) , the two main reasons for the automatic shallow semantic parser failing to identify the semantic frames are the failure to identify the semantic frames for copula or existential senses of "be" in a perfectly grammatical sentence and the absence of any predicate verb at all in the sentence. They showed that manually reconstructing the "be" semantic frames for MEANT yields significantly higher correlation with human adequacy judgment. Thus, we present a novel backoff algorithm for MEANT to reconstruct the "be" semantic frame and evaluate the whole sentence using the lexical similarity function and weigh it according to the ratio of unlabeled tokens in the MT/REF.

The reconstruction of the "be" semantic frame is triggered when the automatic shallow semantic parser fails to find a semantic frame in the sentence. It utilizes the syntactic parse of the sentence and labels the verb-to-be as the predicate. Then, it labels the constituent of the NP subtree sibling immediate left to the predicate as the "who" role, the constituent of the NP subtree sibling immediate right to the predicate as the "what" role and any constituent of other subtree siblings of the predicate as "other" role. The reconstructed "be" frame is then evaluated the same way as other semantic frames using MEANT.

When there is no predicate verb in the whole sentence, we evaluate the whole sentence using the lexical similarity function and weighted according to the amount of unlabeled tokens in the MT/REF. Thus, equation (1), (2) and (3) are replaced by equation (4), (5) and (6).

$$
\begin{aligned}
w^0_{\text{nf}} &\equiv \frac{\text{\#tokens that are not fillers of any role in MT}}{\text{total \#tokens in MT}} \\
w^1_{\text{nf}} &\equiv \frac{\text{\#tokens that are not fillers of any role in REF}}{\text{total \#tokens in REF}} \\
\mathbf{e}_{\text{sent}} &\equiv \text{the whole sentence string of MT} \\
\mathbf{f}_{\text{sent}} &\equiv \text{the whole sentence string of REF} \\
s_{\text{sent}} &= \frac{2 \cdot \text{prec}_{\mathbf{e}_{\text{sent}},\mathbf{f}_{\text{sent}}} \cdot \text{rec}_{\mathbf{e}_{\text{sent}},\mathbf{f}_{\text{sent}}}}{\text{prec}_{\mathbf{e}_{\text{sent}},\mathbf{f}_{\text{sent}}} + \text{rec}_{\mathbf{e}_{\text{sent}},\mathbf{f}_{\text{sent}}}}
\end{aligned}
$$

$$
\text{precision} = \frac{\sum_i w^0_i \frac{w_{\text{pred}} s_{i,\text{pred}} + \sum_j w_j s_{i,j}}{w_{\text{pred}} + \sum_j w_j |q^0_{i,j}|} + w^0_{\text{nf}} s_{\text{sent}}}{\sum_i w^0_i + w^0_{\text{nf}}} \tag{4}
$$

$$
\text{recall} = \frac{\sum_i w^1_i \frac{w_{\text{pred}} s_{i,\text{pred}} + \sum_j w_j s_{i,j}}{w_{\text{pred}} + \sum_j w_j |q^1_{i,j}|} + w^1_{\text{nf}} s_{\text{sent}}}{\sum_i w^1_i + w^1_{\text{nf}}} \tag{5}
$$

$$
\text{MEANT} = \frac{\text{precision} \cdot \text{recall}}{\alpha \cdot \text{precision} + (1-\alpha) \cdot \text{recall}} \tag{6}
$$

Note that we have also introduced the weight α for the precision and recall. Later, we show that optimal value of α for MT evaluation is different from that for MT optimization.

3.3 Results

Table 1 shows the document-level Pearson's score correlation and table 2 shows the sentence-level Kendall's rank correlation with human preferences of the improved version of MEANT with the previous version of MEANT (Lo *et al.*, 2014) on WMT2014 metrics task test set (Macháček and Bojar, 2014). For the sake of stable performance across all the tested language pairs, the weights of the semantic role labels are estimated in unsupervised manner.

First and the most importantly, the document-level score correlation with human preferences of all versions of MEANT consistently outperforms all the submitted metrics in Macháček and Bojar (2014). While the variations on document-level correlation with human preferences of different versions of MEANT are not significant, we focus on discussing about the sentence-level results.

On sentence-level ranking, MEANT with Gigaword word embeddings correlates significantly better with human preference than MEANT with Gigaword discrete context vectors. Although the Google pretrained word embeddings covers more than twice as many token types as the Gigaword word embeddings, our results show that MEANT incorporated with the Google pretrained word embeddings only marginally better that incorporated with the Gigaword word embeddings. Our results show that MEANT's portability to languages with lower resources is preserved as MEANT with Gigaword word embeddings achieves comparable accuracy without using huge amount of resources.

While the linear vector composition property of word embeddings receive a lot of attention recently, our results show that, surprisingly, MEANT with word embeddings using the align-and-aggregate approach in computing the phrasal similarities significantly outperforms that using the simple linear vector composition across all language pairs in the test set. Our results suggest that more investigation on using word embeddings is necessary for it to be useful for efficient evaluation of phrasal similarities.

Our results also show that MEANT with an α value of 1, i.e. recall only, significantly outperforms that with balanced precision and recall weighting, in correlation with human preferences. This could be due to the fact that MT sys-

Table 1: System-level Pearson's score correlation with human preferences of MEANT on WMT2014 metrics track test set

metric	cs-en	de-en	fr-en	hi-en	ru-en	ave.
MEANT (Lo *et al.*, 2014) (i.e. α=0.5)						
+ Gigaword discrete context vectors & fillers alignment	0.975	0.973	0.972	0.957	0.877	0.951
+ Gigaword word embeddings & fillers alignment	0.939	0.967	0.979	0.948	0.912	0.949
+ Google pretrained word embeddings & vector composition	0.919	0.955	0.981	0.941	0.940	0.947
+ Google pretrained word embeddings & fillers alignment	0.948	0.970	0.979	0.950	0.922	0.954
MEANT (α=1)						
+ Google pretrained word embeddings & fillers alignment	0.990	0.965	0.977	0.921	0.909	0.952
+backoff	0.986	0.970	0.981	0.947	0.915	0.960

Table 2: Sentence-level Kendall's rank correlation with human preferences of MEANT on WMT2014 metrics track test set

metric	cs-en	de-en	fr-en	hi-en	ru-en	ave.
MEANT (Lo *et al.*, 2014) (i.e. α=0.5)						
+ Gigaword discrete context vectors & fillers alignment	0.188	0.209	0.235	0.229	0.193	0.211
+ Gigaword word embeddings & fillers alignment	0.192	0.235	0.252	0.230	0.206	0.223
+ Google pretrained word embeddings & vector composition	0.195	0.222	0.242	0.231	0.201	0.218
+ Google pretrained word embeddings & fillers alignment	0.206	0.229	0.253	0.236	0.214	0.228
MEANT (α=1)						
+ Google pretrained word embeddings & fillers alignment	0.229	0.257	0.285	0.243	0.239	0.251
+ backoff	0.267	0.301	0.336	0.324	0.266	0.299

tems tend to under-generate (i.e. missing meaning in the translation output) rather than over-generate. This also explains why the precision-oriented metrics, such as BLEU, usually correlate poorly with human adequacy judgments.

Lastly, our results show that the novel backoff algorithm significantly improves MEANT's correlation with human preferences.

4 Tuning against the new MEANT

Lo *et al.* (2013b) show that for MT system translating into Chinese, tuning against MEANT outperforms the common practice of tuning against BLEU or TER across commonly used MT evaluation metrics, i.e. beating BLEU-tuned systems in BLEU and TER-tuned systems in TER. However, for MT system translating into English, previous work (Lo *et al.*, 2013a; Lo and Wu, 2013) show that tuning against MEANT only achieves balanced performance in both n-gram based metrics and edit distance based metrics, without overfitting to either type of metrics. We argue with the significant improvement in sentence-level correlation with human preferences in evaluating translations in English, the performance of MT system tuned against the newly improved MEANT would also improved.

For WMT2015 tuning task, we tuned the basic Czech-English baseline system against the newly improved MEANT using the official development set and k-best MERT (with 100-best hypothesis list). Unfortunately, there is a bug in the integration of MEANT and Moses k-best MERT in the submitted system. Table 3 and 4 shows the results of both the submitted buggy system and the debugged version of the experiments on the official dev and test test.

In the previous section, MEANT with an α value of 1, i.e. 100% recall, has the highest correlation with human preferences on the test set. However, surprisingly, our tuning experiment results show that tuning against a balanced precision-recall version of MEANT yields better scores across the commonly used MT evaluation metrics. This is because the optimization algorithm needs the guidance from precision to avoid blindly generating too many words which would achieve high recall.

More importantly, our results show that MT system tuning against the improved MEANT beats the BLEU-tuned system across the commonly used MT evaluation metrics, even in BLEU.

5 Related Work

Most of the common used MT evaluation metrics like BLEU (Papineni *et al.*, 2002), NIST (Doddington, 2002), CDER (Leusch *et al.*, 2006), WER (Nießen *et al.*, 2000), and TER (Snover *et al.*, 2006) rely heavily on the exact match of the surface form of the tokens in the reference and the MT output. Thus, they do not only fail to capture the

Table 3: Translation quality of MT system tuned against MEANT and BLEU on WMT15 tuning task dev set. MEANT reported here is the version using Google pretrained word embeddings with α=1 and backoff algorithm.

system	BLEU	NIST	WER	PER	CDER	TER	MEANT
BLEU-tuned	19.38	6.48	67.63	50.48	58.17	63.57	42.77
MEANT-tuned (official submitted buggy system)	18.20	6.27	70.09	51.84	59.93	65.53	42.23
MEANT-tuned (α=1)	18.96	6.44	68.41	50.77	58.74	64.30	43.43
MEANT-tuned (α=0.5)	**19.74**	**6.62**	**66.31**	**49.22**	**57.20**	**62.28**	**43.62**

Table 4: Translation quality of MT system tuned against MEANT and BLEU on WMT15 tuning task test set. MEANT reported here is the version using Google pretrained word embeddings with α=1 and backoff algorithm.

system	BLEU	NIST	WER	PER	CDER	TER	MEANT
BLEU-tuned	17.06	5.99	69.67	52.86	59.85	65.71	40.10
MEANT-tuned (official submitted buggy system)	15.89	5.80	71.82	53.93	61.43	67.59	39.34
MEANT-tuned (α=1)	16.75	5.95	70.19	53.05	60.29	66.25	40.12
MEANT-tuned (α=0.5)	**17.15**	**6.08**	**68.53**	**52.03**	**59.07**	**64.65**	**40.23**

meaning similarities of lexicons that do not share the same surface form, but also ignore the meaning structures of the translations.

METEOR (Banerjee and Lavie, 2005; Denkowski and Lavie, 2014) evaluates lexical similarities beyond surface-form by incorporating a large collection of linguistic resources, like synonym table from hand-crafted WordNet and paraphrase table learned from large parallel corpus. Another trend of improving MT evaluation metrics is incorporating the evaluation of meaning structure of the translations. Owczarzak *et al.* (2007a,b) improved the correlation with human *fluency* judgments by using LFG to extend the approach of evaluating syntactic dependency structure similarity in Liu and Gildea (2005), but did not improve the correlation with human *adequacy* judgments when comparing to METEOR. Similarly, TINE, an automatic recall-oriented basic meaning event structured based evaluation metric (Rios *et al.*, 2011) correlated with human adequacy judgment comparable to that of BLEU but not as high as that of METEOR. ULC (Giménez and Màrquez, 2007, 2008) incorporates several semantic similarity features and shows improved correlation with human judgement of translation quality (Callison-Burch *et al.*, 2007; Giménez and Màrquez, 2007; Callison-Burch *et al.*, 2008; Giménez and Màrquez, 2008) but no work has been done towards tuning an MT system using a pure form of ULC perhaps due to its expensive run time.

By incorporating word embeddings into MEANT, translations are evaluated via both the structural and lexical semantics accurately and thus, MT system tuned against the improved MEANT beats BLEU-tuned system across commonly used metrics, even in BLEU.

6 Conclusion

In this paper we presented the first results of using word embeddings to improve the correlation with human adequacy judgments of MEANT, the state-of-the-art semantic MT evaluation metric. We also showed that using a smaller and easy-to-obtain monolingual corpus (e.g., Gigaword, Wikipedia) for training the word embeddings does not significantly affect the accuracy of MEANT. We showed that the align-and-aggregate approach outperforms the naive linear word vector composition, although the compositional property is highly advertised as the advantage of using word embeddings. We also described a novel backoff algorithm in MEANT for evaluating the meaning accuracy of the MT output when automatic shallow semantic parser fails to parse the sentence. In this tuning shared task, we successfully integrate MEANT with the Moses framework. This enable further investigation into tuning MT system against MEANT using newer tuning techniques and features. Most importantly, we show that tuning MT system against the improved version of MEANT outperforms BLEU-tuned system across all commonly used MT evaluation metrics, even in BLEU.

Acknowledgements

This material is based upon work supported in part by the Defense Advanced Research Projects Agency (DARPA) under BOLT contract nos. HR0011-12-C-0014 and HR0011-12-C-0016, and GALE contract nos. HR0011-06-C-0022 and HR0011-06-C-0023; by the European Union under the FP7 grant agreement no. 287658; and by the Hong Kong Research Grants Council (RGC) research grants GRF620811, GRF621008, and GRF612806. Any opinions, findings and conclusions or recommendations expressed in this material are those of the authors and do not necessarily reflect the views of DARPA, the EU, or RGC.

References

Satanjeev Banerjee and Alon Lavie. METEOR: An automatic metric for MT evaluation with improved correlation with human judgments. In *Workshop on Intrinsic and Extrinsic Evaluation Measures for Machine Translation and/or Summarization*, Ann Arbor, Michigan, June 2005.

Marco Baroni, Georgiana Dinu, and Germán Kruszewski. Don摲 count, predict! a systematic comparison of context-counting vs. context-predicting semantic vectors. In *Proceedings of the 52nd Annual Meeting of the Association for Computational Linguistics*, volume 1, 2014.

Yoshua Bengio, Holger Schwenk, Jean-Sébastien Senécal, Fréderic Morin, and Jean-Luc Gauvain. Neural probabilistic language models. In *Innovations in Machine Learning*, pages 137–186. Springer, 2006.

Chris Callison-Burch, Cameron Fordyce, Philipp Koehn, Christof Monz, and Josh Schroeder. (meta-) evaluation of machine translation. In *Second Workshop on Statistical Machine Translation (WMT-07)*, 2007.

Chris Callison-Burch, Cameron Fordyce, Philipp Koehn, Christof Monz, and Josh Schroeder. Further meta-evaluation of machine translation. In *Third Workshop on Statistical Machine Translation (WMT-08)*, 2008.

Ronan Collobert and Jason Weston. A unified architecture for natural language processing: Deep neural networks with multitask learning. In *Proceedings of the 25th international conference on Machine learning*, pages 160–167. ACM, 2008.

Ronan Collobert, Jason Weston, Léon Bottou, Michael Karlen, Koray Kavukcuoglu, and Pavel Kuksa. Natural language processing (almost) from scratch. *The Journal of Machine Learning Research*, 12:2493–2537, 2011.

Michael Denkowski and Alon Lavie. METEOR universal: Language specific translation evaluation for any target language. In *9th Workshop on Statistical Machine Translation (WMT 2014)*, 2014.

George Doddington. Automatic evaluation of machine translation quality using n-gram co-occurrence statistics. In *The second international conference on Human Language Technology Research (HLT '02)*, San Diego, California, 2002.

Jesús Giménez and Lluís Màrquez. Linguistic features for automatic evaluation of heterogenous MT systems. In *Second Workshop on Statistical Machine Translation (WMT-07)*, pages 256–264, Prague, Czech Republic, June 2007.

Jesús Giménez and Lluís Màrquez. A smorgasbord of features for automatic MT evaluation. In *Third Workshop on Statistical Machine Translation (WMT-08)*, Columbus, Ohio, June 2008.

Eric H Huang, Richard Socher, Christopher D Manning, and Andrew Y Ng. Improving word representations via global context and multiple word prototypes. In *Proceedings of the 50th Annual Meeting of the Association for Computational Linguistics: Long Papers-Volume 1*, pages 873–882. Association for Computational Linguistics, 2012.

Gregor Leusch, Nicola Ueffing, and Hermann Ney. CDer: Efficient MT evaluation using block movements. In *11th Conference of the European Chapter of the Association for Computational Linguistics (EACL-2006)*, 2006.

Ding Liu and Daniel Gildea. Syntactic features for evaluation of machine translation. In *Workshop on Intrinsic and Extrinsic Evaluation Measures for Machine Translation and/or Summarization*, Ann Arbor, Michigan, June 2005.

Chi-kiu Lo and Dekai Wu. MEANT: An inexpensive, high-accuracy, semi-automatic metric for evaluating translation utility based on semantic roles. In *49th Annual Meeting of the Association for Computational Linguistics: Human Language Technologies (ACL HLT 2011)*, 2011.

Chi-kiu Lo and Dekai Wu. SMT vs. AI redux: How semantic frames evaluate MT more accurately. In *Twenty-second International Joint Conference on Artificial Intelligence (IJCAI-11)*, 2011.

Chi-kiu Lo and Dekai Wu. Unsupervised vs. supervised weight estimation for semantic MT evaluation metrics. In *Sixth Workshop on Syntax, Semantics and Structure in Statistical Translation (SSST-6)*, 2012.

Chi-kiu Lo and Dekai Wu. Can informal genres be better translated by tuning on automatic semantic metrics? In *14th Machine Translation Summit (MT Summit XIV)*, 2013.

Chi-kiu Lo, Anand Karthik Tumuluru, and Dekai Wu. Fully automatic semantic MT evaluation. In *7th Workshop on Statistical Machine Translation (WMT 2012)*, 2012.

Chi-kiu Lo, Karteek Addanki, Markus Saers, and Dekai Wu. Improving machine translation by training against an automatic semantic frame based evaluation metric. In *51st Annual Meeting of the Association for Computational Linguistics (ACL 2013)*, 2013.

Chi-kiu Lo, Meriem Beloucif, and Dekai Wu. Improving machine translation into Chinese by tuning against Chinese MEANT. In *International Workshop on Spoken Language Translation (IWSLT 2013)*, 2013.

Chi-kiu Lo, Meriem Beloucif, Markus Saers, and Dekai Wu. XMEANT: Better semantic MT evaluation without reference translations. In *52nd Annual Meeting of the Association for Computational Linguistics (ACL 2014)*, 2014.

Matouš Macháček and Ondřej Bojar. Results of the WMT14 metrics shared task. In *Ninth Workshop on Statistical Machine Translation (WMT 2014)*, Baltimore, Maryland USA, June 2014.

Tomas Mikolov, Kai Chen, Greg Corrado, and Jeffrey Dean. Efficient estimation of word representations in vector space. *arXiv preprint arXiv:1301.3781*, 2013.

Sonja Nießen, Franz Josef Och, Gregor Leusch, and Hermann Ney. A evaluation tool for machine translation: Fast evaluation for MT research. In *The Second International Conference on Language Resources and Evaluation (LREC 2000)*, 2000.

Karolina Owczarzak, Josef van Genabith, and Andy Way. Dependency-based automatic evaluation for machine translation. In *Syntax and Structure in Statistical Translation (SSST)*, 2007.

Karolina Owczarzak, Josef van Genabith, and Andy Way. Evaluating machine translation with LFG dependencies. *Machine Translation*, 21:95–119, 2007.

Kishore Papineni, Salim Roukos, Todd Ward, and Wei-Jing Zhu. BLEU: a method for automatic evaluation of machine translation. In *40th Annual Meeting of the Association for Computational Linguistics (ACL-02)*, pages 311–318, Philadelphia, Pennsylvania, July 2002.

Miguel Rios, Wilker Aziz, and Lucia Specia. TINE: A metric to assess MT adequacy. In *Sixth Workshop on Statistical Machine Translation (WMT 2011)*, 2011.

Matthew Snover, Bonnie Dorr, Richard Schwartz, Linnea Micciulla, and John Makhoul. A study of translation edit rate with targeted human annotation. In *7th Biennial Conference Association for Machine Translation in the Americas (AMTA 2006)*, pages 223–231, Cambridge, Massachusetts, August 2006.

Anand Karthik Tumuluru, Chi-kiu Lo, and Dekai Wu. Accuracy and robustness in measuring the lexical similarity of semantic role fillers for automatic semantic MT evaluation. In *26th Pacific Asia Conference on Language, Information, and Computation (PACLIC 26)*, 2012.

Joseph Turian, Lev Ratinov, and Yoshua Bengio. Word representations: a simple and general method for semi-supervised learning. In *Proceedings of the 48th Annual Meeting of the Association for Computational Linguistics*, pages 384–394. Association for Computational Linguistics, 2010.

Dekai Wu, Chi-kiu Lo, Meriem Beloucif, and Markus Saers. Better semantic frame based mt evaluation via inversion transduction grammars. 2014. SSST.

An Investigation of Machine Translation Evaluation Metrics in Cross-lingual Question Answering

Kyoshiro Sugiyama, Masahiro Mizukami, Graham Neubig, Koichiro Yoshino, Sakriani Sakti, Tomoki Toda, Satoshi Nakamura
Graduate School of Information Science
Nara Institute of Science and Technology
Takayamacho 8916-5, Ikoma, Nara
{sugiyama.kyoshiro.sc7, neubig}@is.naist.jp

Abstract

Through using knowledge bases, question answering (QA) systems have come to be able to answer questions accurately over a variety of topics. However, knowledge bases are limited to only a few major languages, and thus it is often necessary to build QA systems that answer questions in one language based on an information source in another (cross-lingual QA: CLQA). Machine translation (MT) is one tool to achieve CLQA, and it is intuitively clear that a better MT system improves QA accuracy. However, it is not clear whether an MT system that is better for human consumption is also better for CLQA. In this paper, we investigate the relationship between manual and automatic translation evaluation metrics and CLQA accuracy by creating a data set using both manual and machine translations and perform CLQA using this created data set.[1] As a result, we find that QA accuracy is closely related with a metric that considers frequency of words, and as a result of manual analysis, we identify 3 factors of translation results that affect CLQA accuracy.

1 Introduction

Question answering (QA) is the task of searching for an answer to question sentences using some variety of information resource. Generally, documents, web pages, or knowledge bases are used as these information resources. When the language of the question differs from the language of the information resource, the task is called cross-lingual question answering (CLQA) (Magnini et al., 2004; Sasaki et al., 2007). Machine translation (MT) is one of the most widely used tools to achieve CLQA (Mori and Kawagishi, 2005; Fujii et al., 2009; Kettunen, 2009).[2]

In the realm of monolingual question answering, recent years have seen a large increase in the use of structured knowledge bases such as Freebase (Bollacker et al., 2008), as they allow for accurate answering of questions over a variety of topics (Frank et al., 2007; Cai and Yates, 2013). However, knowledge bases are limited to only a few major languages. Thus, CLQA is particularly important for QA using knowledge bases.

In contrast to the CLQA situation, where an MT system is performing translation for a downstream system to consume, in standard translation tasks the consumer of results is a human (Matsuzaki et al., 2015). In this case, it is important to define an evaluation measure which has high correlation with human evaluation, and the field of MT metrics has widely studied which features of MT results are correlated with human evaluation, and how to reflect these features in automatic evaluation (Machácek and Bojar, 2014).

However, translations which are good for humans may not be suitable for question answering. For example, according to the work of Hyodo and Akiba (2009), a translation model trained using a parallel corpus without function words achieved higher accuracy than a model trained using full sentences on CLQA using documents or web pages, although it is not clear whether these results will apply to more structured QA using knowledge bases. There is also work on optimizing translation to improve CLQA accuracy (Riezler et al., 2014; Haas and Riezler, 2015), but these methods require a large set of translated question-answer pairs, which may not be available in many

[1] All data used in the experiments will be released upon publishing of the paper.

[2] MT is also used in mono-lingual QA tasks when question sentences are translated into the formal language used to query the information resource (Andreas et al., 2013).

languages. Correspondingly, it is of interest to investigate which factors of translation output affect CLQA accuracy, which is the first step towards designing MT systems that achieve better accuracy on the task.

In this paper, to investigate the influence of translation on CLQA using knowledge bases, we create a QA data set in which each question has been translated both manually and by a number of MT systems. We then perform CLQA using this data set and investigate the relationship between translation evaluation metrics and QA accuracy. As a result, we find that QA accuracy is closely related to NIST score, a metric that considers the frequency of words, indicating that proper translation of infrequent words has an important role in CLQA tasks using knowledge bases. In addition, as a result of fine-grained manual analysis, we identify a number of factors of translation results that affect CLQA.

2 Data sets

To create data that allows us to investigate the influence of translation on QA, we started with a standard QA data set, and created automatic and manual translations. In this section, we describe the data construction in detail.

As our seed data, we used a data set called Free917 (Cai and Yates, 2013). Free917 is a question set made for QA using the large-scale knowledge base "Freebase," and is widely used in QA research (Cai and Yates, 2013; Berant et al., 2013). It consists of 917 pairs of question sentences and "logical forms" which are computer-processable expressions of the meaning of the question that can be fired against the Freebase database to return the correct answer. Following Cai and Yates (2013), we divide this data into a training set (512 pairs), dev set (129 pairs) and test set (276 pairs). In the remainder of the paper, we refer to the questions in the test set before translation as the original (OR) set.

Next, to investigate the influence of translation quality on the accuracy of QA, we created a question set with five different varieties of translation results. First we translated the question sentences included in the OR set into Japanese manually (the JA set). Then, we created translations of the JA set into English by five different methods:

Manual translation We asked a professional translation company to manually translate the questions from Japanese to English (the HT set).

GT and YT The questions are translated using Google Translate[3] (GT) and Yahoo Translate[4] (YT) systems, these commercial systems can be used via web pages. While the details of these systems are not open to the public, it is likely that Google takes a largely statistical MT approach, while the Yahoo engine is rule-based.

Moses The questions are translated using a phrase-based system built using Moses (Koehn et al., 2007) (the Mo set). A total of 277 million sentences from various genres are used in training.

Travatar The questions are translated using Travatar (Neubig, 2013) (the Tra set), a tool for forest-to-string MT that has achieved competitive results on the Japanese-English language pair. The training data is the same as Moses.

Table 1: A sample of translations and logical forms in the test set

Set	Question	Logical form
OR	what is europe 's area	(location.location.area en.europe)
JA	ヨーロッパの面積は	
HT	what is the area of europe	
GT	the area of europe	
YT	the area of europe	
Mo	the area of europe	
Tra	what is the area of europe	

3 QA system

To perform QA, we used the framework of Berant et al. (2013), as implemented in SEMPRE. [5] SEMPRE is a QA system that has the ability to use large-scale knowledge bases, such as Freebase.

In this section, we describe the framework briefly and consider how translation may affect each element of it. We show an example of how this system works in Figure 1.

Alignment A lexicon, which is a mapping from natural language phrases to logical predicates, is constructed using a large text

[3]https://translate.google.co.jp/
[4]http://honyaku.yahoo.co.jp/
[5]http://nlp.stanford.edu/software/sempre/

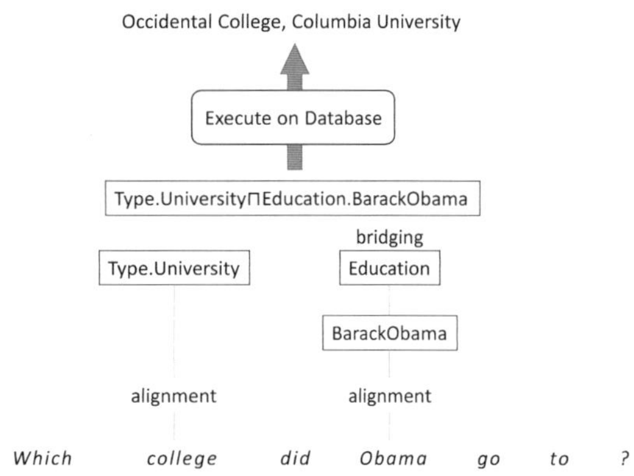

Figure 1: Framework of the SEMPRE semantic parsing system used to perform QA

corpus, which is linked to the knowledge base through the use of named entity prediction. By default, SEMPRE uses ClueWeb09[6] (Callan et al., 2009) as the large text corpus and Freebase as the knowledge base. During the QA process itself, this lexicon is used to convert entities into logical forms through a process called alignment.

Translation has the potential to affect this part by changing the words in the translation. Because the strings in the sentence are used to look up which logical form to use, a mistranslated word may result in a failure in lookup.

Bridging To create the query for the knowledge base, SEMPRE merges neighboring logical forms in a binary tree structure. Bridging is an operation that generates predicates compatible with neighboring predicates.

Translation has the potential to affect this operation by changing the word order in the translation. Because adjacent logical forms are combined in the bridging process, the different word order may cause changes in the combination of logical forms.

Scoring and learning The previous two steps are not deterministic, and thus the system must select the best of many candidates. Scoring evaluates candidates according to a scoring function, and learning is optimization of the weights used in the scoring function.

It is possible that translation also affects this process, with a different set of weights being ideal for CLQA than monolingual QA. On the other hand, to train these weights it is necessary to have a translated version of the QA training set, which represents a significant investment, and thus we do not examine this within the scope of this paper.

[6]http://www.lemurproject.org/clueweb09.php/

4 Experiments

In our experiments, we examine the effect of various features of translation quality on CLQA. To do so, we use the data sets described in Section 2, and we performed QA with the system described in Section 3. In the experiments, we suppose a situation in which Japanese question sentences are translated into English and inputted into an English-language QA system.

4.1 Result 1: Evaluation of translation quality

First, we evaluate translation quality of each system using 4 automatic evaluation measures BLEU+1 (Lin and Och, 2004), WER (Leusch et al., 2003), NIST (Doddington, 2002) and RIBES (Isozaki et al., 2010) and manual evaluation of acceptability (Goto et al., 2013).

BLEU+1 BLEU (Papineni et al., 2002) is the most popular automatic evaluation metric of machine translation quality, and BLEU+1 is a smoothed version that can be used with single sentences. It is based on n-gram precision, and the score is from 0 to 1, where 0 is the worst and 1 is the best.

WER Word error rate (WER) is the edit distance between the translation and reference normalized by the sentence length. The formula of WER is as follows:

$WER = \frac{S+D+I}{N}$

where

- S is the number of substitutions.
- D is the number of deletions.
- I is the number of insertions.
- N is the number of word in the reference.

The score is a real number more than 0, and can be over 1 when the length of the output is larger than the reference. Like BLEU, WER focuses on matches between words, but is less lenient with regards to word ordering, having a strong performance for linear matches between the two sentences. WER is an error rate, thus lower WER is better. To adjust direction of axis to match the other measures, we use the value of $1 - WER$.

RIBES RIBES is a metric based on rank correlation coefficient of word order in the translation and reference, and thus focuses on whether the MT system was able to achieve the correct ordering. It has been shown effective for the evaluation of language pairs with greatly different structure such as Japanese and English. The score is from 0 to 1, where 0 is the worst and 1 is the best.

NIST NIST is a metric based on n-gram precision and each n-gram's weight. Rarer n-grams have a higher weight. Therefore, less frequent words such as content words are given more importance than function words such as "of," "in," and others. The score is a real number more than 0.

Acceptability Acceptability is a 5-grade manual evaluation metric. It combines aspects of both fluency and adequacy, with levels 1-3 evaluating semantic content, and 3-5 evaluating syntactic correctness.

Figure 2 shows the result of the evaluation for each system. Note that NIST and Acceptability have been normalized between 0 and 1 by dividing by the highest possible achievable value.

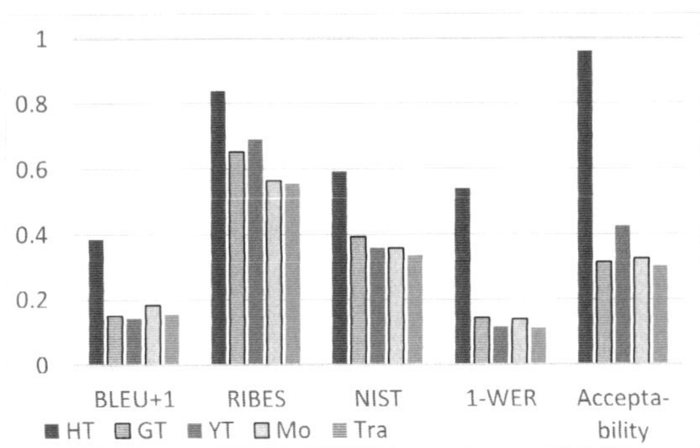

Figure 2: Evaluation scores (mean)

From this, we can see that HT has the best score on all metrics. Indicating that human translation is still more accurate than machines in this language pair and task. Next comes commercial systems, with GT being the 2nd best on BLEU and NIST, while YT is higher than GT on RIBES and manual evaluation. This confirms previous reports (Isozaki et al., 2010) that RIBES is well correlated with human judgments of acceptability for Japanese-English translation tasks. In the next section, we examine whether this observation also holds when it is not a human but a computer doing the language understanding.

4.2 Result 2: QA accuracy

Next, we performed QA using the created data sets. We found that for 12 questions in the test set even the correct logical form did not return any answer, so we eliminate these questions and analyze the remaining 264 questions.

Figure 3 shows QA accuracy of each data set.

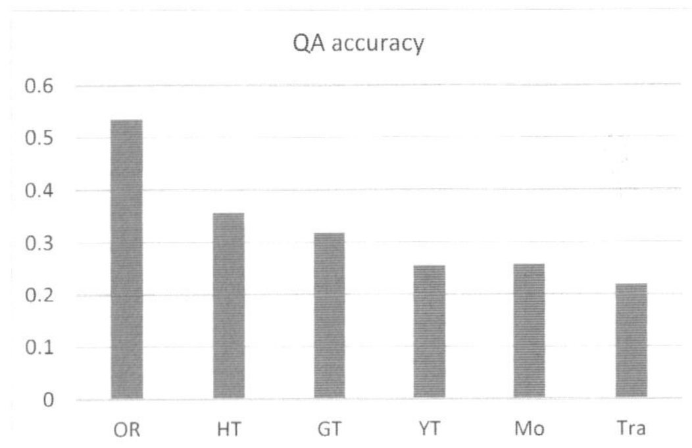

Figure 3: QA accuracy of each data set

Here, we can see that accuracy of the OR set is about 53%. Accuracy of the HT set is the highest of the translated data sets. However, although HT has high translation quality, its accuracy is significantly ($p < 0.01$ according to the Student's t-test) lower than OR. YT is the second for acceptability but its accuracy is lower than GT and Mo. This indicates that there is, in fact, a significant difference between translations that are good for humans, and those that are good for QA systems.

In the next section, we analyze these phenomena in detail.

5 Discussion

5.1 Correlation between translation quality and QA accuracy

First, we analyze the sentence-level correlation between evaluation scores and QA accuracy to attempt to gain more insights about the features of translation results that affect QA accuracy, and potential implications for evaluation. One thing to

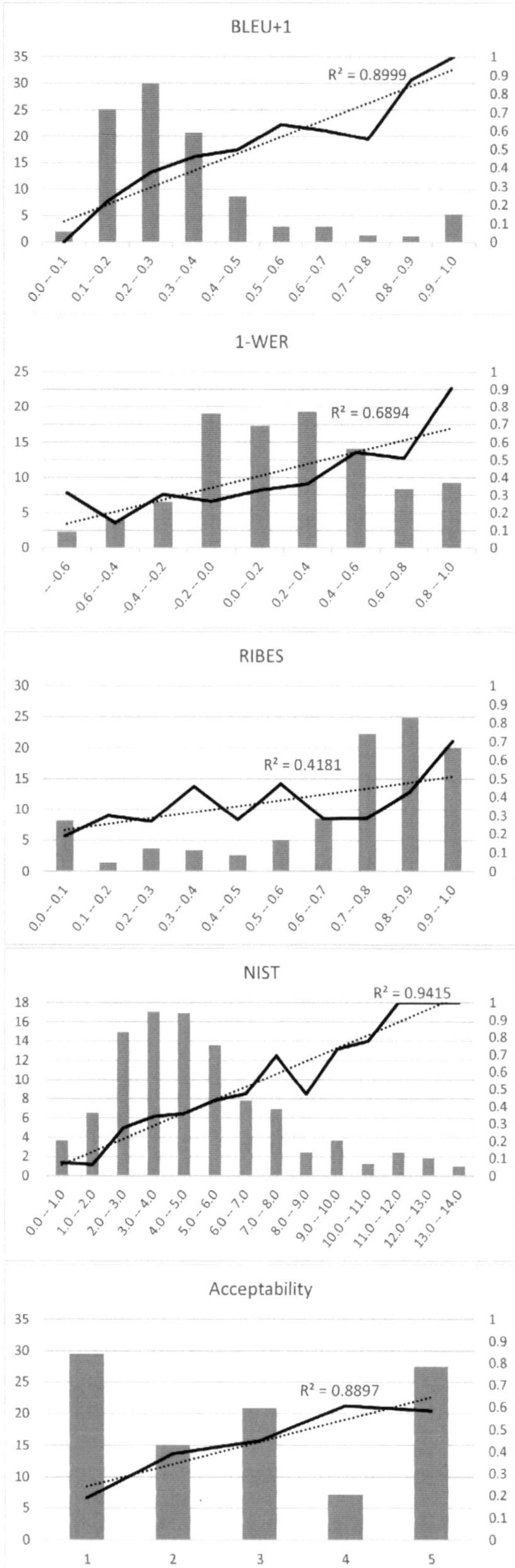

Figure 4: Correlation between QA accuracy and evaluation score (correct group)
Horizontal axis: Range of evaluation score
Bar (left axis): Percentage of # questions
Line (right axis): Rate of QA accuracy (average in the range)

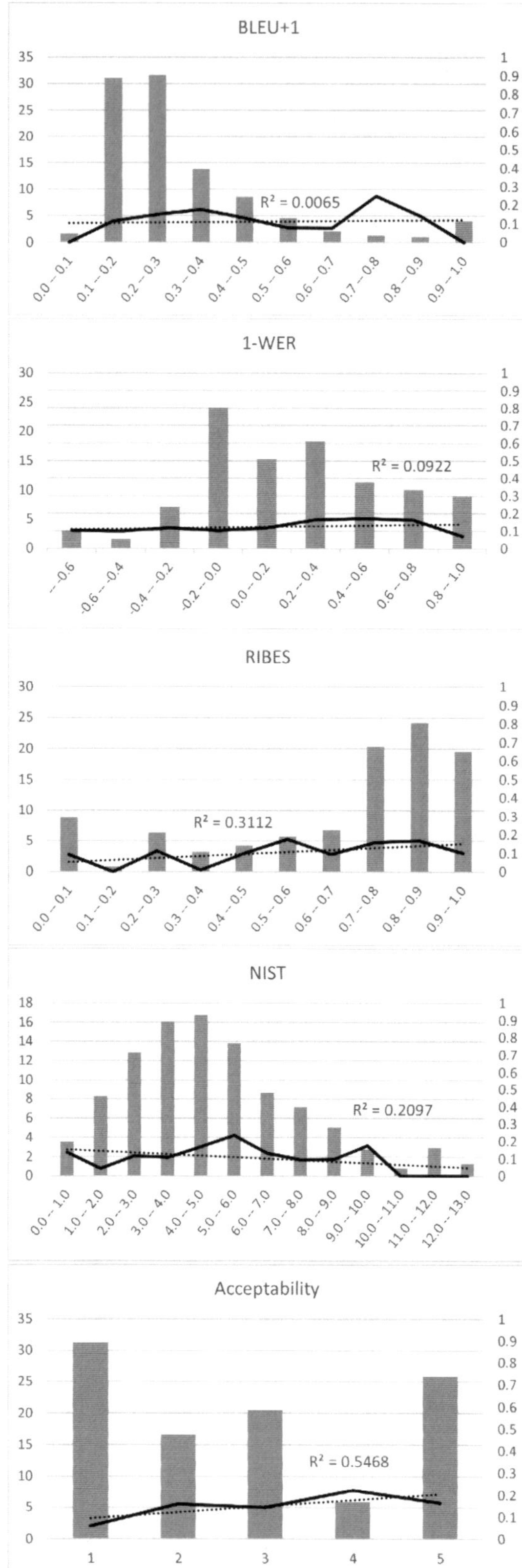

Figure 5: Correlation between QA accuracy and evaluation score (incorrect group)
Horizontal axis: Range of evaluation score
Bar (left axis): Percentage of # questions
Line (right axis): Rate of QA accuracy (average in e range)

be noted first is that even with the original set OR, only approximately half of the questions were answered correctly, and thus in some cases the question might be difficult to answer even with the correct translation result. To take this effect into account, we divide the questions in two groups. The "correct" group consists of $141 * 5 = 705$ translated questions of the 141 question answered correctly in OR and the "incorrect" group consists of $123 * 5 = 615$ translated questions of the remaining 123 questions.

Figure 4 shows correlation between QA accuracy and evaluation score of the correct group. The bar graphs indicate the percentage of the number of the questions in each range of evaluation scores. From these figures, we can first note that there is some correlation between all investigated evaluation metrics and QA accuracy, demonstrating that translation accuracy is, in fact, important for CLQA. We can also see that QA accuracy is most closely related to NIST score. Recall that NIST is a metric that considers the frequency of each word, resulting in content words being treated as more important than function words. According to this result, it seems that content words are important for translation in CLQA tasks, which is natural given the importance of matching entities in the alignment step of Section 3. It is also encouraging that NIST score also seems to be effective at assessing this automatically.

On the other hand, RIBES, which has higher correlation with human evaluation as shown in Section 4, has the lowest correlation with CLQA accuracy. Thus, we can see that the overall order of words might not be as important in translation for CLQA. In other words, looking back at the QA framework in Section 3, this means that the "alignment" process is likely more sensitive to errors than the "bridging" process, which may not be affected as heavily by word order.

Figure 5 shows correlation between QA accuracy and evaluation score of the incorrect group. In contrast to the correct group, in the incorrect group, QA accuracy has very little correlation with all of the scores. Even the manually evaluated adequacy score has only moderate correlation. These results show that if the reference sentences cannot be answered correctly, the sentences are not suitable, even for negative examples. Thus, when evaluating MT systems for CLQA, we may benefit from creating a set of references that are answered correctly by the system before performing evaluation.[7]

5.2 Case studies

In this section, we show some examples of QA results that changed as a result of translation. In addition, we consider what causes the change and implications for evaluation.

Table 2: Examples of changes in content words

○	OR	when was interstate 579 formed
-	JA	州間高速道路 579 号が作られたのはいつですか
×	HT	when was interstate highway 579 made
×	GT	when is the interstate highway no. 579 has been made
×	YT	when is it that expressway 579 between states was made
×	Mo	interstate highway 579) was made when
○	Tra	when interstate 579) was built
○	OR	who was the librettist for the magic flute
-	JA	魔笛の台本を作成したのは誰ですか
×	HT	who wrote the libretto to the magic flute
×	GT	who was it that created the script of the magic flute
×	YT	who is it to have made a script of the the magic flute
×	Mo	the magic flute scripts who prepared
×	Tra	who made of magic script
○	-	who librettist magic flute

Table 2 shows the examples of change of content words. In the first example, the phrase "interstate 579" has been translated in various ways (e.g. "interstate highway 579," "expressway 579," ...). Only OR and Tra have the phrase "interstate 579" and have been answered correctly. The output logical forms of other translations lack the entity of the highway "interstate 579," mistaking it for another entity. For example, the phrase "interstate highway 579" is instead aligned to the entity of the music album "interstate highway." Similarly, in the second example, the translations that don't have "librettist" were answered incorrectly. Here, we created a new sentence, "who librettist magic flute," which was answered correctly.

These observations show that the change of content words to the point that they do not match entities in the entity lexicon is a very important problem. To ameliorate this problem, it may be possible to modify the translation system to consider the named entity lexicon as a feature in the translation process.

Next, we show examples of another common cause of mis-answered questions in Table 3. In the

[7]It should be noted that the shapes of the translation accuracy distributions of two groups are similar, therefore, it is difficult for MT evaluation metrics to help to choose better datasets.

Table 3: Examples of mis-translated question words

○	OR	how many religions use the bible
-	JA	聖書を使う宗教はいくつありますか
×	HT	how many religions use sacred scriptures
○	GT	how many religions that use the bible
○	YT	how many religion to use the bible are there
○	Mo	how many pieces of religion, but used the bible
×	Tra	use the bible religions do you have
○	OR	how many tv programs did danny devito produce
-	JA	ダニー・デヴィートは何件のテレビ番組をプロデュースしましたか
○	HT	how many television programs has danny devito produced
×	GT	danny devito or has produced what review television program
×	YT	did danni devito produce several tv programs
×	Mo	what kind of tv programs are produced by danny devito
×	Tra	danny devito has produced many tv programs

first example, the sentence of Tra has all the content words of OR, but was answered incorrectly. Likewise, in the second example, "tv (television) programs," "danny devito," and "produce(d)" have appeared in all translations. However, these translations have been answered incorrectly, other than HT. It can be seen that to answer these questions correctly, the sentence must include a phrase such as "how many," which indicates the question type. This demonstrates that correct translation of question words is also important. It should be noted that these words are frequent, and thus even NIST score will not be able to perform adequate evaluation, indicating that other measures may be necessary.

Table 4: Examples of translations with mistaken syntax

○	OR	what library system is the sunset branch library in
-	JA	サンセット・ブランチ図書館はどの図書館システムに所属しますか
○	HT	to what library system does sunset branch library belong
○	GT	sunset branch library do you belong to any library system
○	YT	which library system does the sunset branch library belong to
○	Mo	sunset branch library, which belongs to the library system
○	Tra	sunset branch library, belongs to the library system?
×	OR	what teams did babe ruth play for
-	JA	ベイブ・ルースはどのチームの選手でしたか
×	HT	what team did babe ruth play for
○	GT	did the players of any team babe ruth
○	YT	was babe ruth a player of which team
○	Mo	how did babe ruth team
○	Tra	babe ruth was a team player

Table 4 shows examples regarding syntax. In the first example, all of the sentences were answered correctly, while GT, Mo, and Tra are grammatically incorrect. On the other hand, in the second example, the sentences of OR and HT are grammatically correct, but were answered incorrectly. The OR and HT translations resulted in the QA system outputting Babe Ruth's batting statistics, probably because "babe ruth" and "play" are adjacent in sentences. These cases indicate that, at least for the relatively simple questions in Free917, achieving correct word ordering plays only a secondary role in achieving high QA accuracy.

6 Conclusion

To investigate the influence of translation quality on QA using knowledge bases, we created question data sets using several varieties of translation and compared them with regards to QA accuracy. We found that QA accuracy has high correlation with NIST score, which is sensitive to the change of content words, although these results only hold when evaluating with references that actually result in correct answers. In addition, by analysis of examples, we found 3 factors which cause changes of QA results: content words, question types, and syntax. Based on these results, we can make at least two recommendations for the evaluation of MT systems constructed with cross-lingual QA tasks in mind: 1) NIST score, or another metric putting a weight an content words should be used. 2) References that are actually answerable by the QA system should be used.

We should qualify this result, however, noting the fact that the results are based on the use solely of the SEMPRE parsing system. While SEMPRE has shown highly competitive results on standard QA tasks, we also plan to examine other methods such as Berant and Liang (2014)'s semantic parsing through paraphrasing, which may be less sensitive to superficial differences in surface forms of the translation results. We also plan to to optimize machine translation systems using this analysis, possibly through incorporation into the response-based learning framework of Riezler et al. (2014).

Acknowledgment

Part of this work was supported by the NAIST Big Data Project and by the Commissioned Research of National Institute of Information and Communications Technology (NICT), Japan.

References

Jacob Andreas, Andreas Vlachos, and Stephen Clark. 2013. Semantic parsing as machine translation. In *Proc. of ACL*, pages 47–52.

Jonathan Berant and Percy Liang. 2014. Semantic parsing via paraphrasing. In *Proc. of ACL*, volume 7, pages 1415–1425.

Jonathan Berant, Andrew Chou, Roy Frostig, and Percy Liang. 2013. Semantic parsing on Freebase from question-answer pairs. In *Proc. of EMNLP*, pages 1533–1544.

Kurt Bollacker, Colin Evans, Praveen Paritosh, Tim Sturge, and Jamie Taylor. 2008. Freebase: a collaboratively created graph database for structuring human knowledge. In *Proc. of SIGMOD*, pages 1247–1250.

Qingqing Cai and Alexander Yates. 2013. Large-scale semantic parsing via schema matching and lexicon extension. In *Proc. of ACL*, pages 423–433.

Jamie Callan, Mark Hoy, Changkuk Yoo, and Le Zhao. 2009. Clueweb09 data set.

George Doddington. 2002. Automatic evaluation of machine translation quality using n-gram co-occurrence statistics. In *Proc. of HLT*, pages 138–145.

Anette Frank, Hans-Ulrich Krieger, Feiyu Xu, Hans Uszkoreit, Berthold Crysmann, Brigitte Jörg, and Ulrich Schäfer. 2007. Question answering from structured knowledge sources. *Journal of Applied Logic*, 5(1):20–48.

Atsushi Fujii, Masao Utiyama, Mikio Yamamoto, and Takehito Utsuro. 2009. Evaluating effects of machine translation accuracy on cross-lingual patent retrieval. In *Proc. of SIGIR*, pages 674–675.

Isao Goto, Ka Po Chow, Bin Lu, Eiichiro Sumita, and Benjamin K Tsou. 2013. Overview of the patent machine translation task at the NTCIR-10 workshop. In *Proc. of NTCIR-10*, pages 260–286.

Carolin Haas and Stefan Riezler. 2015. Response-based learning for machine translation of open-domain database queries. In *Proc. of NAACL HLT*, pages 1339–1344.

Tatsuhiro Hyodo and Tomoyosi Akiba. 2009. Improving translation model for smt-based cross language question answering. In *Proc. of FIT*, volume 8, pages 289–292.

Hideki Isozaki, Tsutomu Hirao, Kevin Duh, Katsuhito Sudoh, and Hajime Tsukada. 2010. Automatic evaluation of translation quality for distant language pairs. In *Proc. of EMNLP*, pages 944–952.

Kimmo Kettunen. 2009. Choosing the best mt programs for clir purposes–can mt metrics be helpful? In *Proc. of ECIR*, pages 706–712.

Philipp Koehn, Hieu Hoang, Alexandra Birch, Chris Callison-Burch, Marcello Federico, Nicola Bertoldi, Brooke Cowan, Wade Shen, Christine Moran, Richard Zens, et al. 2007. Moses: Open source toolkit for statistical machine translation. In *Proc. of ACL*, pages 177–180.

Gregor Leusch, Nicola Ueffing, and Hermann Ney. 2003. A novel string-to-string distance measure with applications to machine translation evaluation. In *Proc. of MT Summit IX*, pages 240–247.

Chin-Yew Lin and Franz Josef Och. 2004. Orange: A method for evaluating automatic evaluation metrics for machine translation. In *Proc. of COLING*, pages 501–507.

Matouš Machácek and Ondrej Bojar. 2014. Results of the WMT14 metrics shared task. *WMT 2014*, pages 293–301.

Bernardo Magnini, Simone Romagnoli, Alessandro Vallin, Jesús Herrera, Anselmo Penas, Víctor Peinado, Felisa Verdejo, and Maarten de Rijke. 2004. The multiple language question answering track at CLEF 2003. In *Comparative Evaluation of Multilingual Information Access Systems*, pages 471–486. Springer.

Takuya Matsuzaki, Akira Fujita, Naoya Todo, and Noriko H Arai. 2015. Evaluating machine translation systems with second language proficiency tests. In *Proc. of ACL*, pages 145–149.

Tatsunori Mori and Masami Kawagishi. 2005. A method of cross language question-answering based on machine translation and transliteration. In *Proc. of NTCIR-5*.

Graham Neubig. 2013. Travatar: A forest-to-string machine translation engine based on tree transducers. In *Proc. of ACL*, pages 91–96.

Kishore Papineni, Salim Roukos, Todd Ward, and Wei-Jing Zhu. 2002. Bleu: a method for automatic evaluation of machine translation. In *Proc. of ACL*, pages 311–318.

Stefan Riezler, Patrick Simianer, and Carolin Haas. 2014. Response-based learning for grounded machine translation. In *Proc. of ACL*.

Yutaka Sasaki, Chuan-Jie Lin, Kuang-hua Chen, and Hsin-Hsi Chen. 2007. Overview of the NTCIR-6 cross-lingual question answering (CLQA) task. In *Proc. of NTCIR-6*, volume 6.

Dependency Analysis of Scrambled References for Better Evaluation of Japanese Translations

Hideki Isozaki and Natsume Kouchi*
Okayama Prefectural University
111 Kuboki, Soja-shi, Okayama, 719-1197, Japan
isozaki@cse.oka-pu.ac.jp

Abstract

In English-to-Japanese translation, BLEU (Papineni et al., 2002), the de facto standard evaluation metric for machine translation (MT), has very weak correlation with human judgments (Goto et al., 2011; Goto et al., 2013). Therefore, RIBES (Isozaki et al., 2010; Hirao et al., 2014) was proposed. RIBES measures similarity of the word order of a machine-translated sentence and that of a corresponding human-translated reference sentence.

RIBES has much stronger correlation than BLEU but most Japanese sentences have alternative word orders (scrambling), and one reference sentence is not sufficient for fair evaluation. Isozaki et al. (2014) proposed a solution to this problem. This solution generates semantically equivalent word orders of reference sentences. Automatically generated word orders are sometimes incomprehensible or misleading, and they introduced a heuristic rule that filters out such bad sentences. However, their rule is too conservative and generated alternative word orders for only 30% of reference sentences.

In this paper, we present a rule-free method that uses a dependency parser to check scrambled sentences and generated alternatives for 80% of sentences. The experimental results show that our method improves *sentence-level* correlation with human judgments. In addition, strong *system-level* correlation of single reference RIBES is not damaged very much.

We expect this method can be applied to other languages such as German, Korean, Turkish, Hindi, etc.

*This work was done while the second author was a graduate student of Okayama Prefectural University.

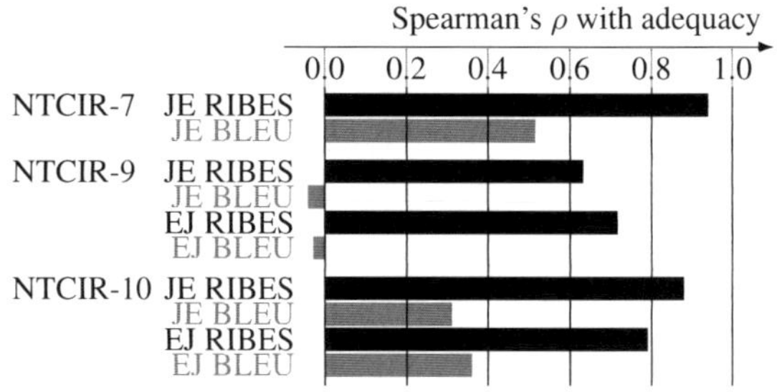

Figure 1: RIBES has better correlation with adequacy than BLEU (**system-level** correlation)

1 Introduction

For translation among European languages, BLEU (Papineni et al., 2002) has strong correlation with human judgments and almost all MT papers use BLEU for evaluation of translation quality. However, BLEU has very weak correlation with human judgments in English-to-Japanese/Japanese-to-English translation, and a new metric RIBES (Isozaki et al., 2010; Hirao et al., 2014) has strong correlation with human judgments. RIBES measures similarity of the word order of a machine translated sentence and that of a human-translated reference sentence. Figure 1 compares RIBES and BLEU in terms of Spearman's ρ with human judgments of adequacy based on NTCIR-7/9/10 data (Isozaki et al., 2010; Goto et al., 2011; Goto et al., 2013).

Japanese and English have completely different word order, and phrase-based SMT systems tend to output bad word orders. RIBES correctly points out their word order problems.

In this paper, we propose a method to improve "**sentence-level** correlation", which is useful for MT developers to find problems of their MT systems. If the sentence-level correlation is strong, low RIBES scores indicate bad translations, and we will find typical failure patterns from them.

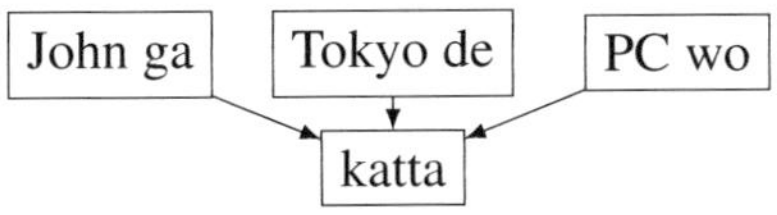

(a) "John ga Tokyo de PC wo katta"

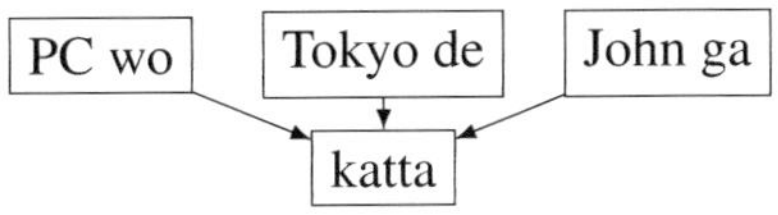

(b) "PC wo Tokyo de John ga katta"

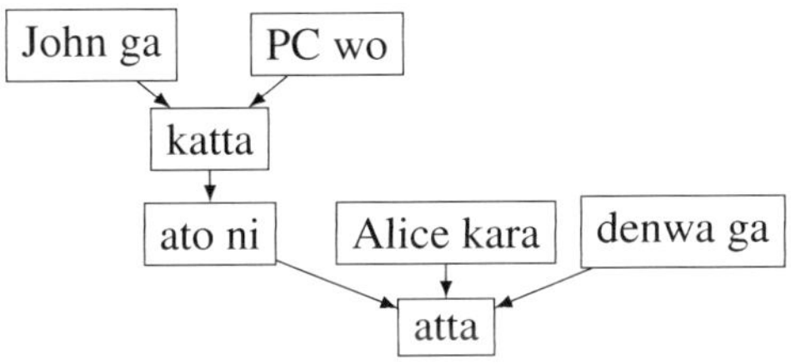

(c) "John ga PC wo katta ato ni Alice kara denwa ga atta"

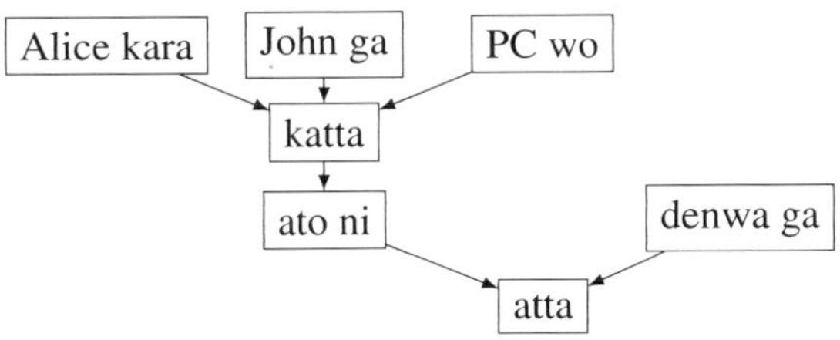

(d) "Alice kara John ga PC wo katta ato ni denwa ga atta"

Figure 2: Dependency trees

However, improvement of **sentence-level** correlation is more difficult than **system-level** correlation and current automatic evaluation metrics do not have strong correlation. (Leusch et al., 2003; Stanojević and Sima'an, 2014; Echizen-ya and Araki, 2010; Callison-Burch et al., 2012)

1.1 Scrambling

As for Japanese translation, however, we should consider "scrambling" or acceptable reordering of phrases. For example, "John ga Tokyo de PC wo katta" (John bought a PC in Tokyo) consists of the main verb "katta" (bought) and its modifiers. "Ga", "de", and "wo" are case markers.

- "Ga" is a nominative case marker.
- "De" is a locative case marker.
- "Wo" is an accusative case marker.

This sentence can be reordered as follows.

1. John ga Tokyo de PC wo katta . (1.00)
2. John ga PC wo Tokyo de katta . (0.86)
3. Tokyo de John ga PC wo katta . (0.86)
4. Tokyo de PC wo John ga katta . (0.71)
5. PC wo John ga Tokyo de katta . (0.71)
6. PC wo Tokyo de John ga katta . (0.57)

All of the above sentences are acceptable and have the same meaning, and this is called "*scrambling*". However, RIBES outputs different scores for these sentences. When we use the first one as the reference sentence, RIBES output scores in the parentheses. Human judges will give almost equal scores to all of them, and we should improve these RIBES scores for better evaluation.

Scrambling is also observed in other languages such as German (Maier et al., 2014), Korean (Chun, 2013), Turkish (ldız et al., 2014), Hindi (Sharma and Paul, 2014), etc.

Figure 2 (a) shows the dependency tree of "John ga Tokyo de PC wo katta". Each box indicates a *bunsetsu* (chunk). Arrows indicate modification relations. The source node of an arrow modifies the target node of the arrow. The root "katta" has three modifiers (children), "John ga", "Tokyo de", and "PC wo". We can generate $3! = 6$ word orders by post-order traversal of this tree because the order of siblings does not matter. Figure 2 (b) shows a permutation and its dependency tree. In this case, all permutations are acceptable.

However, more complex dependency trees tend to generate misleading/incomprehensible sentences. Figure 2 (c) shows such a sentence: "John ga PC wo katta ato ni Alice kara denwa ga atta". (After John bought a PC, there was a phone call from Alice). "X ato ni Y" means "After X, Y". "Denwa" means "a phone call". "Atta" means "there was".

This tree has $2! \times 3! = 12$ post-order permutations. Some of them are misleading. For example, "Alice kara John ga PC wo katta ato ni denwa ga atta" sounds like "After John bought a PC from Alice, there was a phone call" because "Alice kara" (from Alice) precedes "katta" (bought). This sentence will have a dependency tree in Figure 2 (d).

1.2 Rule-based filtering of bad sentences

Isozaki et al. (2014) tried to solve the above problem by automatic generation of reordered sentences and use of a heuristic rule (constraint) to filter out bad sentences.

- Use a Japanese dependency parser to get dependency trees of reference sentences.
- Check the dependency trees and manually correct wrong ones because sentence-level accuracy of dependency analyzers are still

low.

- In order to get Japanese-like head final sentences, output words in the corrected dependency tree in post-order. That is, recursively output all child nodes before a mother node. They called this method "postOrder".
- The above "postOrder" generates misleading/incomprehensible sentences. In order to inhibit them, they introduced the following rule called "Simple Case Marker Constraint":

  > If a reordered sentence has a case marker phrase of a verb that precedes another verb before the verb, the sentence is rejected. "wo" case markers can precede adjectives before the verb.

  Here, we call this "rule2014".

This "rule2014" improved **sentence-level** correlation of NTCIR-7 EJ data. However, rule2014 is so conservative that only 30% of reference sentences obtained alternative word orders. In the next section, we present a method that covers more reference sentences.

2 Methodology

2.1 Our idea

We do not want to introduce more rules to cover more sentences. Instead we present a rule-free method. Our idea is simple: if a reordered sentence is misleading or incomprehensible, a dependency parser will output a dependency tree different from the original dependency tree. That is, use a dependency parser for detecting misleading sentences.

We apply a dependency parser to the reordered reference sentences. If the dependency parser outputs the same dependency tree with the original reference sentence except sibling orders, accept the word order as a new reference. Otherwise, it is a misleading word order and reject it. (We do not parse MT output because it is often broken and dependency analysis will fail.)

For example, "PC wo Tokyo de John ga katta" has the dependency tree in Figure 2 (b). This tree is the same as (a) except the order of three siblings. We don't care about the order of siblings, and accept this as a new reference sentence. On the other hand, the parser shows that "Alice kara John ga PC wo katta ato ni denwa ga atta" has the dependency tree in (d), which is different from (c) and we reject this sentence. We call this method "**compDep**" because it compares dependency trees of reordered reference sentences with the original dependency tree.

Each MT output sentence is evaluated by the best of RIBES scores for remaining reordered reference sentences. This is a sentence-level score. A system's score (system-level score) is the average of sentence-level scores of all test sentences.

2.2 Data and tools

We use NTCIR-7 PatentMT EJ data (Fujii et al., 2008) and NTCIR-9 PatentMT EJ data (Goto et al., 2011).[1] NTCIR-7 EJ human judgment data consists of 100 sentences × five MT systems. NTCIR-9 EJ human judgment data consists of 300 sentences × 17 MT systems. NTCIR provided **only one reference sentence** for each sentence. When we use only the provided reference sentences, we call it "single ref".

We apply a popular Japanese dependency parser CaboCha[2] to the reference sentences, and manually corrected its output just like Isozaki et al. (2014). 40% of NTCIR-7 dependency trees and 50% of NTCIR-9 dependency trees were corrected.

Based on the corrected dependency trees, we generate all post-order permutations. Then we apply CaboCha to these reordered sentences. We compare the dependency tree of the original reference sentence with that of a reordered reference sentence.

We accept a reordered reference sentence only when its tree is the same as that of the original reference sentence except the sibling order.

This tree comparison is implemented by removing word IDs and chunk IDs from the trees keeping their dependency structures and sorting children of each node by their surface strings. These *sorted* dependency trees are compared recursively from their roots.

3 Experimental Results

Table 1 shows that our compDep method succeeded in generating more reordered sentences (permutations) than rule2014. The column with #perms = 1 indicates failure of generation of reordered sentences. As for NTCIR-7, rule2014 failed for 70%

[1]NTCIR-8 did not provide human judgments. NTCIR-10 submission data was not publicly available yet at the time of writing this paper.

[2]http://code.google.com/p/cabocha/

NTCIR-7 EJ

#perms	1	2–10	11–100	101–1000	>1000	total
single ref	100	0	0	0	0	100
rule2014	70	30	0	0	0	100
compDep	**20**	61	15	4	0	100
postOrder	1	41	41	13	4	100

NTCIR-9 EJ

#perms	1	2–10	11–100	101–1000	>1000	total
single ref	300	0	0	0	0	300
rule2014	267	25	7	1	0	300
compDep	**41**	189	63	5	2	300
postOrder	0	100	124	58	18	300

Table 1: Distribution of the number of generated permutations (#perms=1 indicates the number of sentences for which the method didn't generate alternative word orders)

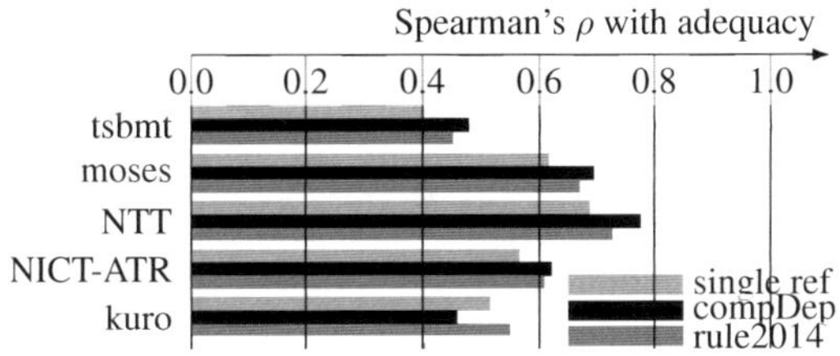

Figure 3: Improvement of **sentence-level** correlation with adequacy (NTCIR-7 EJ)

of reference sentences while compDep failed for only 20%. As for NTCIR-9, rule2014 failed for 89% (267/300) while compDep failed for only 14% (41/300).

From the viewpoint of the number of such failures, postOrder (§1.2) is the best method, but postOrder does not filter out bad sentences, and it leads to the loss of **system-level** correlation with adequacy (See §3.2).

3.1 Sentence-level correlation

Here, we focus on adequacy because it is easy to generate fluent sentences if we disregard adequacy. Figure 3 shows NTCIR-7 EJ results. our compDep succeeded in improving **sentence-level** correlation with adequacy for four MT systems among five. The average of ρ was improved from single ref's 0.558 to 0.606.

Figure 4 shows NTCIR-9 EJ results. our compDep succeeded in improving **sentence-level** correlation of all 17 MT systems. The average of ρ was improved from single ref's 0.385 and rule2014's 0.396 to compDep's 0.420. The improvement from single ref to compDep is statistically significant with $p = 0.000015$ (two-sided sign test) for NTCIR-9 data. The improvement from rule2014 to compDep is also statistically significant with $p = 0.01273$.

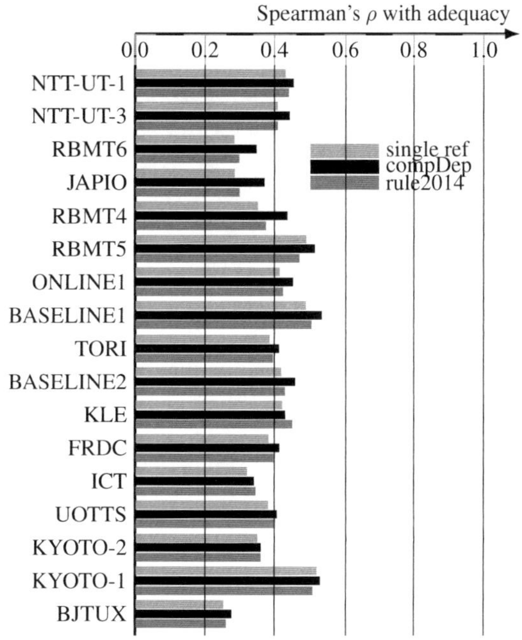

Figure 4: Improvement of **sentence-level** correlation with adequacy (NTCIR-9 EJ)

3.2 System-level correlation

Isozaki et al. (2014) pointed out that postOrder loses system-level correlation with adequacy because it also generates bad word orders.

Figure 5 shows that **system-level** correlation of compDep is comparable to that of single ref and rule2014. Spearman's ρ of compDep in NTCIR-7 (0.90) looks slightly worse than single ref and rule2014 (1.00). However, this is not a big problem because the NTCIR-7 correlation is based on only five systems as described in §2.2, and the NTCIR-9 correlation based on 17 systems did not degrade very much (compDep: 0.690, single ref: 0.695, rule2014: 0.668).

Table 2 shows details of **system-level** correlation of NTCIR-7 EJ. Single reference RIBES and rule2014 completely follows the order of adequacy. On the other hand, compDep slightly violates this order at the bottom of the table. NICT-ATR and kuro is swapped.

The "single ref" and "rule2014" scores of this table are slightly different from that of Table 5 of Isozaki et al. (2014). This difference is caused by the difference of normalization of punctuation symbols and full-width/half-width alphanumeric letters.

Figure 6 shows that the effects of manual correction of dependency trees. The average of sin-

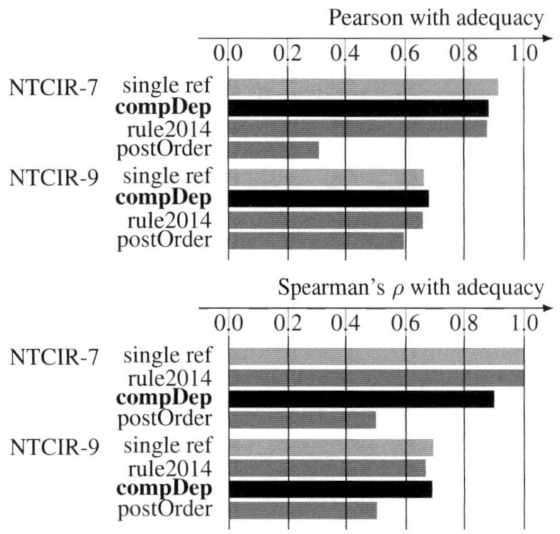

Figure 5: **System-level** correlation with adequacy

	Adequacy	Averaged RIBES		
		single ref	rule2014	compDep
tsbmt	3.527	0.722	0.726	0.750
Moses	2.897	0.707	0.720	0.745
NTT	2.740	0.670	0.682	0.722
NICT-ATR	2.587	0.658	0.667	0.706
kuro	2.420	0.633	0.643	0.711

Table 2: Details of **system-level** RIBES scores (NTCIR-7 EJ)

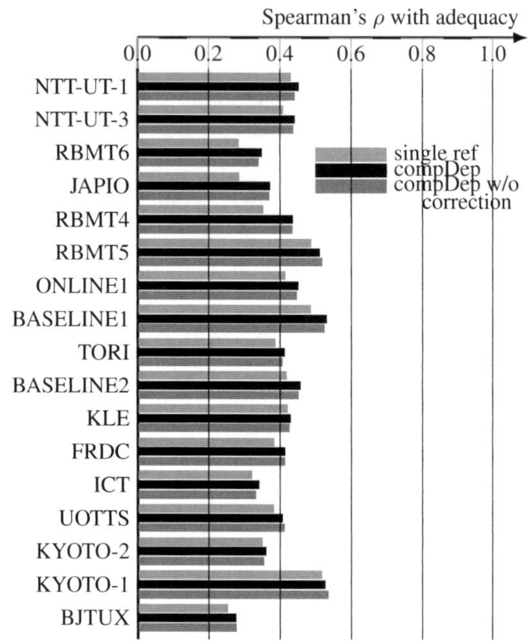

Figure 6: Effects of manual correction on compDep's correlation with adequacy (NTCIR-9 EJ)

gle ref, compDep, and compDep without correction are 0.388, 0.422, and 0.420, respectively. Thus, the difference between compDep (with correction) and compDep without correction is very small and we can skip the manual correction step.

We used dependency analysis twice in the above method. First, we used it for generation of reordered reference sentences. Second, we used it for detecting misleading word orders.

In the first usage, we manually corrected dependency trees of the *given* reference sentences. In the second usage, however, we did not correct dependency trees of *reordered* reference sentences because some sentences have thousands of permutations (Table 1) and it is time-consuming to correct all of them manually. Moreover, some reordered sentences are meaningless or incomprehensible, and we cannot make their correct dependency trees. Therefore, we did not correct them. Our experimental results have shown that we can omit correction in the first step.

4 Related Work

Our method uses syntactic information. Use of syntactic information in MT evaluation is not a new idea.

Liu and Gildea (2005) compared parse trees of reference sentences and MT output sentences. They proposed four methods: STM, TKM, HWCM, DSTM, and DTKM. STM measures similarity by the number of matching subtrees. TKM uses Tree Kernel for the measurement. HWCM uses n-gram matches in dependency trees. DSTM and DTKM are dependency tree versions of STM and TKM respectively.

Owczarzak et al. (2007) used LFG-based typed dependency trees. They also introduced processing of paraphrases.

Chan and Ng (2008) proposed MAXSIM that is based on a bipartite graph matching algorithm and assigns different weights to matches. Dependency relation are used as a factor in this framework.

Zhu et al. (2010) proposed an SVM-based MT metric that uses different features in different granularities. Dependency relations are used as a feature in this framework.

We designed our method not to parse MT outputs because some MT outputs are broken and it is difficult to parse them. Our method does not parse MT outputs and we expect our method is more robust than these methods.

Recently, Yu et al. (2014) proposed RED, an evaluation metric based on reference dependency trees. They also avoided parsing of "results of noisy machine translations" and used only dependency trees of reference sentences. However, their research motivation is completely different from ours. They did not mention *scrambling* at all, and they did not try to generate reordered reference sentences, but it is closely related to our method. It might be possible to make a better evaluation method by combining our method and their method.

Some readers might think that adequacy is not very reliable. WMT-2008 (Callison-Burch et al., 2008) gave up using adequacy as a human judgement score because of unreliability. NTCIR organizers used relative comparison to improve reliability of adequacy. The details are described in Appendix A of Goto et al. (2011).

5 Conclusions

RIBES (Isozaki et al., 2010) is a new evaluation metric of translation quality for distant language pairs. It compares the word order of an MT output sentence with that of a corresponding reference sentence. However, most Japanese sentences can be reordered and a single reference sentence is not sufficient for fair evaluation. Isozaki et al. (2014) proposed a rule-based method for this problem but it succeeded in generating alternative word orders for only 11–30% of reference sentences.

In this paper, we proposed a method that uses a dependency parser to detect misleading reordered sentences. Only when a reordered sentence has the same dependency tree with its original reference sentence except the order of siblings, we accept the reordered sentence as a new reference sentence. This method succeeded in generating alternative word orders for 80–89% and improved **sentence-level** correlation of RIBES with adequacy and its **system-level** correlation is comparable to the single reference RIBES.

In conventional MT evaluations, we have to prepare multiple references for better evaluation. This paper showed that we can automatically generate multiple references without much effort.

Future work includes use of the generated reference sentences in other metrics such as BLUE. We expect that this method is applicable to other languages such as German, Korean, Turkish, Hindi, etc. because they have scrambling.

References

Chris Callison-Burch, Cameron Fordyce, Philipp Koehn, Christof Monz, and Josh Schroeder. 2008. Futther meta-evaluation of machine translation. In *Proc. of the Workshop on Statistical Machine Translation*, pages 70–106.

Chris Callison-Burch, Philipp Koehn, Christof Monz, Matt Post, Radu Soricut, and Lucia Specia. 2012. Findings of the 2012 workshop on statistical machine translation. In *Proc. of the Workshop on Statistical Machine Translation*, pages 10–51.

Yee Seng Chan and Hwee Tou Ng. 2008. MAXSIM: A maximum similarity metric for machine translation evaluation. In *Proc. of the Annual Meeting of the Association of Computational Linguistics (ACL)*, pages 55–62.

Jihye Chun. 2013. Verb Cluster, Non-Projectivity, and Syntax-Topology Interface in Korean. In *Proc. of the Second International Conference on Dependency Linguistics*, pages 51–59.

Hiroshi Echizen-ya and Kenji Araki. 2010. Automatic evaluation method for machine translation using noun-phrase chunking. In *Proc. of the Annual Meeting of the Association of Computational Linguistics (ACL)*, pages 108–117.

Atsushi Fujii, Masao Utiyama, Mikio Yamamoto, and Takehito Utsuro. 2008. Overview of the patent translation task at the NTCIR-7 workshop. In *Working Notes of the NTCIR Workshop Meeting (NTCIR)*, pages 389–400.

Isao Goto, Bin Lu, Ka Po Chow, Eiichiro Sumita, and Benjamin K. Tsou. 2011. Overview of the patent machine translation task at the NTCIR-9 workshop. In *Working Notes of the NTCIR Workshop Meeting (NTCIR)*.

Isao Goto, Ka Po Chow, Bin Lu, Eiichiro Sumita, and Benjamin K. Tsou. 2013. Overview of the patent machine translation task at the NTCIR-10 workshop. In *Working Notes of the NTCIR Workshop Meeting (NTCIR)*.

Tsutomu Hirao, Hideki Isozaki, Katsuhito Sudoh, Kevin Duh, Hajime Tsukada, and Masaaki Nagata. 2014. Evaluating translation quality with word order correlations (in Japanese). *Journal of Natural Language Processing*, 21(3):421–444.

Hideki Isozaki, Tsutomu Hirao, Kevin Duh, Katsuhito Sudoh, and Hajime Tsukada. 2010. Automatic evaluation of translation quality for distant language pairs. In *Proc. of the Conference on Empirical Methods in Natural Language Processing (EMNLP)*, pages 944–952.

Hideki Isozaki, Natsume Kouchi, and Tsutomu Hirao. 2014. Dependency-based automatic enumeration of semantically equivalent word orders for evaluating Japanese translations. In *Proc. of the Workshop on Statistical Machine Translation*, pages 287–292.

Olcay Taner Yıldız, Ercan Solak, Onur Görğ , and Razieh Ehsani. 2014. Constructing a Turkish-English Parallel TreeBank. In *Proc. of the Annual Meeting of the Association of Computational Linguistics (ACL)*, pages 112–117.

Gregor Leusch, Nicola Ueffing, and Hermann Ney. 2003. A novel string-to-string distance measure with applications to machine translation evaluation. In *Machine Translation Summit*, pages 240–247.

Ding Liu and Daniel Gildea. 2005. Syntactic features for evaluation of machine translation. In *Proceedings of the ACL Workshop on Intrinsic and Extrinsic Evaluation Measures for Machine Translation*, pages 25–32.

Wolfgang Maier, Miriam Kaeshammer, Peter Baumann, and Sandra Kubler. 2014. Discosuite - A parser test suite for German discontinuous structures. In *Proc. of the Language Resources and Evaluation Conference (LREC)*, pages 2905–2912.

Karolina Owczarzak, Josef van Genabith, and Andy Way. 2007. Dependency-based automatic evaluation for machine translation. In *Proceedings of SSST, NAACL-HLT 2007 / AMTA Workshop on Syntax and Structure in Statistical Translation,*, pages 80–87.

Kishore Papineni, Salim Roukos, Todd Ward, and Wei-Jing Zhu. 2002. BLEU: a method for automatic evaluation of machine translation. In *Proc. of the Annual Meeting of the Association of Computational Linguistics (ACL)*, pages 311–318.

Rahul Sharma and Soma Paul. 2014. A hybrid approach for automatic clause boundary identification in hindi. In *Proc. of the 5th Workshop on South and Southeast Asian NLP*, pages 43–49.

Miloš Stanojević and Khalil Sima'an. 2014. Fitting sentence level translation evaluation with many dense features. In *Proc. of the Conference on Empirical Methods in Natural Language Processing (EMNLP)*, pages 202–206.

Hui Yu, Xiaofeng Wu, Jun Xie Wenbin Jiang, Qun Liu, and Shouxun Lin. 2014. RED: A Reference Dependency Based MT Evaluation Metric. In *Proc. of the International Conference on Computational Linguistics (COLING)*, pages 2042–2051.

Junguo Zhu, Muyun Yang, Bo Wang, Sheng Li, and Tiejun Zhao. 2010. All in Strings: a Powerful String-based Automatic MT Evaluation Metric with Multiple Granularities. In *Proc. of the International Conference on Computational Linguistics (COLING)*, pages 1533–1540.

How do Humans Evaluate Machine Translation

Francisco Guzmán Ahmed Abdelali Irina Temnikova Hassan Sajjad and **Stephan Vogel**
ALT Research Group
Qatar Computing Research Institute, HBKU
{fguzman,aabdelali,itemnikova,hsajjad,svogel}@qf.org.qa

Abstract

In this paper, we take a closer look at the MT evaluation process from a *glass-box* perspective using eye-tracking. We analyze two aspects of the evaluation task – the background of evaluators (*monolingual or bilingual*) and the sources of information available, and we evaluate them using time and consistency as criteria. Our findings show that *monolinguals* are slower but more consistent than *bilinguals*, especially when only target language information is available. When exposed to various sources of information, evaluators in general take more time and in the case of *monolinguals*, there is a drop in consistency. Our findings suggest that to have consistent and cost effective MT evaluations, it is better to use *monolinguals* with only target language information.

1 Introduction

Each year thousands of human judgments are used to evaluate the quality of Machine Translation (MT) systems to determine which algorithms and techniques are to be considered the new state-of-the-art. In a typical scenario human judges evaluate a system's output (or *hypothesis*) by comparing it to a source sentence and/or to a reference translation. Then, they score the hypothesis according to a set of defined criteria such as *fluency* and *adequacy* (White et al., 1994); or rank a set of hypotheses in order of preference (Vilar et al., 2007; Callison-Burch et al., 2007).

Evaluating MT output can be a challenging task for a number of reasons: it is tedious and therefore evaluators can lose interest quickly; it is complex, especially if the guidelines are not well defined; and evaluators can have difficulty distinguishing between different aspects of the translations (Callison-Burch et al., 2007). As a result, evaluations suffer from low inter- and intra-annotator agreements (Turian et al., 2003; Snover et al., 2006). Yet, as Sanders et al. (2011) argue, using human judgments is essential to the progress of MT because: (*i*) automatic translations are produced for a human audience; and (*ii*) human understanding of the *real* world allows to assess the importance of the errors made by MT systems.

Most of the research in human evaluation has focused on analyzing the criteria to use for evaluation, and has regarded the evaluation process as a *black-box*, where the inputs are different sources of information (i.e source text, reference translation, and translation hypotheses), and the output is a score (or preference ranking).

In this paper, we focus on analyzing evaluation from a different perspective. First, we regard the process as a *glass-box* and use eye-tracking to monitor the times evaluators spend digesting different sources of information (*scenarios*) before making a judgment. Secondly, we contrast how the availability of such sources can affect the outcome of the evaluation. Finally, we analyze how the background of the evaluators (in this case whether they are *monolingual* or *bilingual*) has an effect on the consistency and speed in which translations are evaluated. Our main research questions are:

- Given different *scenarios*, what source of information do evaluators use to evaluate a translation? Do they use the source text, the target text, or both? Does the availability of specific information changes the consistency of the evaluation?

- Are there differences of behavior between *bilinguals* (i.e. evaluators fluent in both source and target languages) and *monolinguals* (i.e. evaluators fluent only in the target language)? Which group is more consistent?

Our goal is to provide actionable insights that can help to improve the process of evaluation, especially in large-scale shared-tasks such as WMT. In the next sections we summarize related work, provide details of our experimental setup, and analyze and discuss the results of our experiment.

2 Related Work

Previous work on human evaluation has focused on various aspects of the evaluation process ranging from categorization of the possible scenarios (Sanders et al., 2011) to the effectiveness of the evaluation criteria (Callison-Burch et al., 2007). Callison-Burch et al. (2007) define several criteria to evaluate the effectiveness of a MT evaluation task: (*i*) The *ease* with which humans are able to perform the task; (*ii*) the *agreement* with respect to other annotators; and (*iii*) the *speed* with which annotations can be collected.

Based on those criteria they recommended that evaluations should be done in the form of ranking translations against each other instead of assigning absolute scores to individual translation because ranking is easier to perform, can be done faster, and produces evaluations with higher levels of inter-annotator agreement. As a result, recent WMT evaluations have adopted this evaluation-by-ranking approach and instructions are *kept minimal* by only asking the evaluator to rank hypotheses from worst to best (Bojar et al., 2011).

In this work, we consider the three criteria proposed by Callison-Burch et al. (2007): *ease*, *agreement* and *speed*; but with a few differences. Regarding *ease*, instructions are kept minimal, and the evaluation criteria is left to the evaluator to decide (or discover). Furthermore, by framing the evaluation as a game we aim to keep participants engaged, and make the evaluation task easier. With respect to the other two criteria, we use them to analyze two different aspects of the evaluation process: the sources of information available to the evaluator, and the background of the evaluator.

Eye-tracking has been previously used in MT evaluation research for different purposes. Doherty et al. (2010) used eye-tracking to evaluate the comprehensibility of machine translation output in French, by asking native speakers to read MT output. They found that eye-tracking data had a slight correlation with HTER scores.

Stymne et al. (2012) applied eye-tracking to machine translation error analysis. They found that longer gaze time and and a higher number of fixations correlate with high number of errors in the MT output. Doherty and O'Brien (2014) used eye-tracking to evaluate the quality of raw machine translation output in terms of its *usability* by an end user. They concluded that eye-tracking correlates well with the other measures which they used for their study. In this work, we use eye-tracking to observe which sources of information evaluators use while performing an MT evaluation task and how this impacts the task completion time and the consistency in their judgements.

3 Method

In order to understand how humans evaluate MT, we ran an evaluation experiment using eye-tracking, involving 20 human participants, half of them *monolingual* in English and the other half *bilingual* in Spanish-English. We chose the Spanish-English language pair because of the large amount of freely available data (e.g. WMT) and the sizable pool of available participants in our environment. In our setup, we contrasted the evaluation procedure under alternative *scenarios* in which different sources of information (e.g. source sentence, reference translation) are available. To keep things simple, we only asked participants to evaluate one translation at a time and provide a single score representing the translation quality. To prevent biasing the behavior of the participants, and to encourage them to evaluate translations *naturally*, participants were not given any precise instructions regarding the requirements of a *good* translation. To increase engagement, we formulated the evaluation experiment as a game, where participants are provided feedback after each evaluation according to how close their own score was to a precomputed quality score. Below, we further describe the data used, the different *scenarios*, the background of the participants, and other details of our experiment.

3.1 Data

In our experiments we used the WMT12 (Callison-Burch et al., 2012) human evaluation data for Spanish-English systems. The data consists of 1141 ranking annotations, in which each evaluator ranked five out of the 12 participating systems.

The annotation effort generated a total of 5705 labels with an inter-annotator agreement of $\kappa = 0.222$. Unfortunately, many of the translations have rankings coming from a single evaluator only.In practical terms, this means that at least two evaluators had to evaluate the translations of the same source sentence, and at least two systems were ranked by both of those evaluators. In the WMT12 data, a total of 923 different source sentences were evaluated. From these, we kept only the 155 that complied with our requirement.

To control for length (i.e number of words), we divided the sentences into three equally sized groups based on the sentence length of their reference translations. Discarding the five longest ones the resulting sets *long*, *medium*, and *short* averaged 30.88, 18.18, and 10.18 words.

To have diversity in the quality of the translations, we collected two translations per source sentence, one of superior quality (*best*), and another one of inferior quality (*worst*). We measured quality according to the *expected wins* (Callison-Burch et al., 2012). In total, we used 300 different translations.[1]

3.2 Sources of Information

Our evaluation setup is based on a typical Appraise configuration (Federmann, 2012), where evaluators are provided with different sources of information in different areas of the screen: (*i*) the hypothesis to be evaluated; (*ii*) the source sentence; (*iii*) the context of the source sentence (previous and next sentences in the same source document); (*iv*) the reference translation for the source sentence; and (*v*) the context of the reference translation (previous and next sentences in the same reference document). Figure 1 presents a snapshot of our experimental setup, along with the labels for the corresponding areas of the screen.

To *ease* the scoring procedure, instead of providing a set of predefined levels of quality (e.g. 1 to 5), we used a continuous range (a slider from 0 to 100), and let the evaluator freely set the level of translation quality.

To contrast the effect that different sources of information have on the evaluation procedure, we explored three different evaluation *scenarios*:

- **Scenario 1** (*source-only*) shows participants the translated sentence (in English) along with the source text of the translation (in Spanish), including the context of the source sentence (one sentence before and one sentence after the translated sentence).
- **Scenario 2** (*source+target*) shows participants the translated sentence (in English), along with the source text of the translation (in Spanish), and a reference translation done by a human (also in English), plus context for both source and reference.
- **Scenario 3** (*target-only*) shows the translated sentence (in English) only with a reference translation including its context (in English).

3.3 Feedback

To keep participants engaged, they were given feedback according to a previously computed quality score for each translation. This score was calculated using a linear interpolation of the *expected wins* score obtained from the ranking evaluations (normalized to the range [0, 100]) and DISCOTK$_{party}$ (Joty et al., 2014), a high-performing automatic MT metric based on discourse (Guzmán et al., 2014), which won the WMT 2014 metrics task. This was done because expected wins only provide relative scores (i.e. which of two translations is ranked better given the same source sentence), while the participants were evaluating *absolute* scores. To keep things simple, we provided feedback based on the difference between the evaluator's score and the computed quality scores. Participants were given a five scale feedback depending on the magnitude of these differences (5: [0–10], 4: [11–20], 3: [21–30], 2: [31–40], 1: [>40]). In Section 5.2 we analyze the impact of feedback on the evaluator behavior.

3.4 Participants

In our experiment we had 20 participants 27 to 45 years old. Seven of the participants were female, and 13 were male. Seventeen of our participants were computer scientists; ten had experience with manually translating documents; and four had experience with machine translation evaluation.

All the recruited participants were proficient in English. However, half of the participants were recruited taking into account their mastery of the Spanish Language. For the analysis, participants were divided into two groups of ten people each:

[1]For reproducibility, the full data matrix can be obtained at https://github.com/Qatar-Computing-Research-Institute/wmt15eyetracking

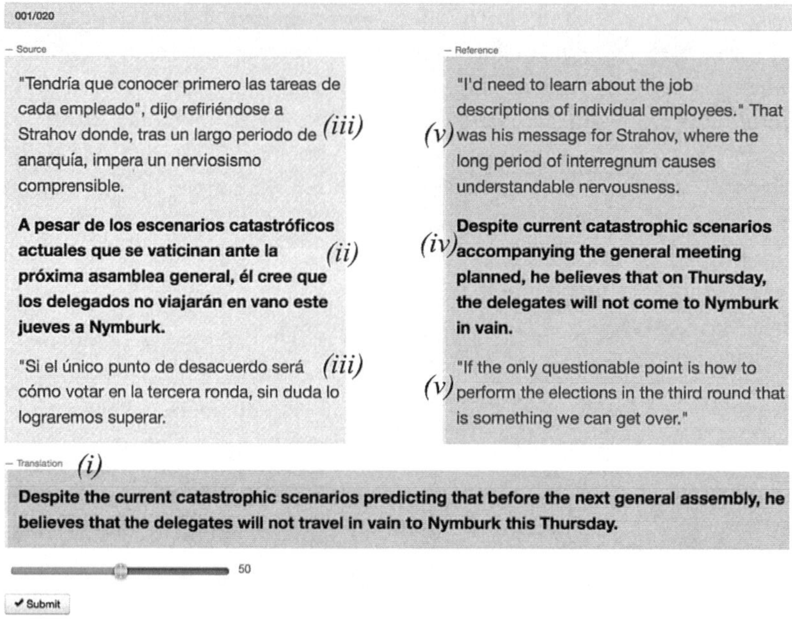

Figure 1: Our modified evaluation layout showing: the translation (*i*) ; the source (*ii*) , (*iii*) ; the reference (*iv*) , (*v*) ; and the scoring *slider*.

- **Bilingual** participants did speak the source language (Spanish) at a native or advance level of comprehension.
- **Monolingual** participants did not speak the source language. Note that this group included some speakers of other Romance languages. However, the participants insisted that their understanding of Spanish was not enough to correctly comprehend the source text.

3.5 Experimental Design

We planned our experiment to collect 1200 evaluations, 60 from each of the 20 participants. To do so, we designed an experimental matrix in which we considered the following variables: (*i*) evaluator type: *monolingual*, *bilingual*; (*ii*) length of reference: *short*, *medium*, *long*; (*iii*) *scenario*: *source-only*, *source+target*, *target-only*; and (*iv*) type of translation: *worst*, *best*.

In our experimental matrix, each participant evaluated 60 translations evenly divided into: 20 translations in each of the *scenario*; 20 translations from each length type; 30 translations of each quality type. On the other hand, each translation was evaluated by four different participants, two *bilingual* and two *monolingual*. To avoid any bias, we made sure that each evaluator saw each source sentence only once.

3.6 Eye-tracking Setup

We used the EyeTribe eye-tracker [2] to collect *gaze* information from the participants. The information was sent in messages to a modified version of Appraise[3] at a rate of 60Hz (a packet in every 16ms).

Each message contained the gaze position in the screen of both eyes, a flag indicating if the point represented a *fixation*, a time stamp, and other device-related information. To ensure optimal readings, participants were asked to calibrate the eye-tracking device before starting the experiments, and a warning message was displayed whenever the eye-tracker lost track of the participant's gaze.

3.7 Instructions and Exit Survey

Participants were asked to move as little as possible to not interrupt the readings of the eye-tracker, and to not interrupt their work while working through the translations belonging to one *scenario*, as the time for executing all sentences in one scenario was measured. Before conducting the evaluation, participants were shown two tutorials, one showing how to calibrate the eye-tracker and one showing how to conduct the experiment.

[2]http://dev.theeyetribe.com/api/

[3]Available at: https://github.com/Qatar-Computing-Research-Institute/iAppraise

After the tutorials they were asked to perform a warm-up exercise consisting of two sentences per *scenario*. Then, the participants proceeded to evaluate the 20 translations in each of the *scenarios* in the following order *source-only*, *source+target* and *target-only*[4].

After the experiment, the participants were asked to fill in an on-line exit survey, which collected their impressions about the experiment and their physiological status during the experiment.

From the survey we learned about the physiological state of the participants: 55% of them were in a normal state, 15% were slightly tired or sleepy, 25% were tired, and 10% were sleep-deprived or sick. Yet, all these reports were evenly distributed among *bilinguals* and *monolinguals*.

There were only few complaints about the setup, and they were related to: (*i*) the lack of precise instructions of what constitutes a *good* translation, (*ii*) the large range of the evaluation score (0-100), (*iii*) the difficulty to understand the context of the translations, and (*iv*) the cognitive overhead needed to evaluate *long* translations, especially in the *source+target scenario*. As expected, some of the *monolingual* participants noted that in the *source-only scenario* they mostly evaluated the readability of the translation, as they had no knowledge of the source language.

4 Results

In this section we analyze the process that participants use to evaluate translation. We focus on three different aspects. First, we use eye-tracking data to observe in which areas do participants spend most of their time. Next, we analyze the time that participants take to complete the evaluation. Finally, we analyze the scores given by the participants, and their consistency.

4.1 How Long Does it Take?

One important aspect to take into account is the time at which annotations can be collected (Callison-Burch et al., 2007). To discount the time a participant spends idle (be either by fatigue, distraction, etc.), here we analyze only the *focused* time, i.e. the amount of time a participant gaze is focused in *areas of interest*.

[4]In hindsight, randomizing the order in which the *scenarios* were performed would have allowed to answer an additional set of questions.

In our experiments, we observed that on average annotations take 26.06 seconds to be collected, which is in line with the measurements reported by Callison-Burch et al. (2007). In Table 1, we further break down the task durations by: (*i*) type of evaluator (i.e. *monolingual* and *bilingual*), (*ii*) *scenario* (i.e. *source-only*, *source+target*, and *target-only*); and (*iii*) the length of the source sentence (i.e. *short*, *medium*, *long*).

	scnr.	usr_type	*long*	*med*	*short*	avg
1	src	biling	36.89	24.54	17.92	26.46
2	src	mono	44.11	28.58	19.17	30.55
3	src+tgt	biling	40.16	23.99	15.46	26.59
4	src+tgt	mono	46.76	29.69	21.63	32.71
5	tgt	biling	26.41	15.03	10.54	**17.28**
6	tgt	mono	35.90	19.41	12.69	22.77

Table 1: Average task duration time (in seconds) according to type of setup, type of evaluator and source sentence length.

The first observation to make is that *bilingual* evaluators are consistently faster than *monolingual* evaluators in evaluation. This is true even in the *target-only* condition, where both evaluators can leverage the same amount of information (i.e. both are fluent in English). This can have two possible explanations: (*i*) *bilingual* evaluators develop *internal* rules that allow them to perform the task faster, and (*ii*) since the order of the conditions was fixed (i.e evaluators performed first the *source-only* tasks, then the *source+target* tasks and lastly the *target-only* tasks), this could mean that the *bilingual* evaluators got *more efficient* sooner, just because the *source-only* task wasn't noise to them. However, we show later that (*i*) is more plausible.

The second observation to make is that evaluators tend to take longer to evaluate scenarios with more sources of information available. This is true for *monolingual* if we analyze the results either by *scenario* or by source length[5]. Surprisingly, *monolingual* participants in the *source-only* condition perform the task 7% faster than in the *source+target* condition, which leads to hypothesize that the more information is in the screen, the longer the task will take, even if the information is not particularly useful for the task completion. On the other hand *bilingual* take the least time when evaluating *target-only* scenario.

[5]Longer source sentences have more words.

To measure the significance of our observations, we fitted a random intercepts model and analyzed the relationship between task duration time, length of the sentences, type of evaluator and type of scenario while taking into account the variability between evaluators. Therefore, as fixed effects, we had the length of the sentences, the type of evaluator (*bilingual* and *monolingual*) and the *scenario* into the model. We also included the interaction between the type of evaluator and the length of the sentences. As random effects, we had intercepts for each of the 20 evaluators. P-values were obtained by likelihood ratio tests of the full model with the effect in question against the model without the effect in question.

In general, the effect of *scenario* is highly significant ($\chi^2_2 = 121.71$, $p = 2.2e^{-16}$), and for long sentences the *target-only* scenario is 8.52 and 9.6 seconds faster than the *source-only* and *source+target* scenarios, respectively. The effect of the type of evaluator is also significant ($\chi^2_3 = 7.45$, $p = 0.05$), and on average *bilingual* are faster than *monolingual* by 7.76 seconds for long sentences. These results were obtained using R (R Core Team, 2015) and lme4 (Bates et al., 2015), following Winter (2013).

4.2 Where Do Evaluators Look?

The eye-tracking data allowed us to analyze the behavior of the evaluators across different conditions. In particular, we focused in the *dwell* time, i.e. the amount of time an evaluator is looking at a particular *area of interest* in the screen. In Table 2, we present the proportional *dwell* time (out of the *focused* time) that the evaluators spent in the different areas of the screen: (*i*) translation, (*ii*) source (with previous and next context), (*iii*) reference (with previous and next context), (*iv*) and the sum of the source and reference times.

From the table, the main observation is that evaluators spend most of their time looking at regions other than the translation (src+ref). This supports the hypothesis that evaluators try to understand the source and reference before making a judgment about the translation. However, there are some peculiarities worth noting. First, *bilingual* participants spend less time reading the translation than their *monolingual* counterparts.

	scnr.	usr_type	tra	ref	src	src+ref
1	src	mono	0.18	-	0.82	0.82
2	src	biling	0.12	-	0.88	0.88
3	src+tgt	mono	0.13	0.24	0.63	0.87
4	src+tgt	biling	0.07	0.16	0.78	0.93
5	tgt	mono	0.26	0.74	-	0.74
6	tgt	biling	0.19	0.81	-	0.81

Table 2: Proportional time spent by evaluators while focusing in different regions of the screen: translation (trans), reference and its context (ref), source and its context (src), and the aggregate of src and ref.

For example, this means that on average, in the *target-only* condition, a *bilingual* evaluator would spend 5 ($0.19 * 26.41$) seconds[6] focused on a *long* translation while a *monolingual* evaluator would spend 9.3 ($0.26 * 35.9$) seconds, that is almost double the time. In contrast, the difference times both *bilingual* and *monolingual* evaluators would spend reading the reference is only a factor of 1.2 (21.3 and 26.6 seconds, respectively). This tells that *bilingual* are faster (mostly) because they spend *less* time reading the translation.

Another interesting observation is that *monolingual* spend a sizable proportion of their time reading the source (which they supposedly *do not* understand), even in the *source+target* scenario. This suggests that *monolingual* evaluators develop *rules-of-thumb* to analyze the source, even if it is a foreign language (e.g. translation of named entities, numbers, dates). This can be an artifact of the relatedness between English and Spanish, or an priming effect induced by the order in which the tasks were done (i.e by asking *monolingual* evaluators to score *source-only* tasks first, we forced them into developing this behavior). The analysis of such phenomena, while interesting, is beyond the scope of this paper.

Finally, if we look across conditions, we observe that evaluators spend a larger proportion of their time evaluating the translation in the *target-only* condition than in the *source-only* and *source+target* conditions. Yet, when we calculate the expected focused time in the translation region for each condition (across different lengths and evaluator types), we obtain 4.48, 4.35 and 2.85 seconds for each condition, respectively.

[6]This time does not need to be continuously spent on the same region. For example, a evaluator might analyze a first portion of a translation, then move back to the reference, and then return to the translation.

This tells us that having more information on the screen (the case of *source+target*) decreases the total amount of time spent reading the translation. In other words, if a evaluator has more sources of information to evaluate a translation, s/he'll spend more time performing the task, but less time evaluating the translation itself.

4.3 Score Consistency

Another important aspect to take into account is how consistent are the scores provided by different evaluators, and how this consistency varies depending on the type of evaluator, and the *scenario* that is used. Unlike other studies where categorical and ordinal scores are produced, here each annotation generates a score in a continuous scale[7]. Thus, using the standard inter-annotator agreement is impractical. Instead, we evaluate *consistency* as the standard deviation of scores for each translation with respect to a class or group average (i.e. *monolingual* or *bilingual*). This quantity gives us an idea of how much variation there is in the score for a specific translation across different groups of evaluators. To be able to compare across evaluators, we normalized their individual scores to a 0-1 range using *minmax*. Then, computed the consistency as follows:

$$\sigma_c^2 = \frac{1}{N_c} \sum_{i \in T} \sum_{j \in C} (\tilde{x}_{ij} - \bar{\tilde{x}}_{ic})^2 \quad (1)$$

where $\tilde{x}_{ij}$ is the *normalized* score of translation i by an evaluator j who belongs to class c (e.g. *monolingual*), and $\bar{\tilde{x}}_{ic}$ is the average score given to translation i by evaluators in class c, and N_c is the total number of translations scored by evaluators in class c.

In Table 3 we present the consistency measurements for *monolingual* and *bilingual* evaluators across the different conditions.

First note that *monolingual* evaluators are more consistent within their group (σ_c) than the *bilingual* evaluators. This observation holds true across all the different scenarios. Note also that *monolingual* evaluators are the *most* consistent in the *target-only* condition. We hypothesize that this is due to the longer times spent analyzing the translation in comparison to *bilingual* evaluators.

[7]Actually it is an ordinal scale from 0-100, but for practical purposes we treat it as continuous

	scnr.	usr_type	σ_c
1	src	mono	15.14
2	src	biling	16.17
3	src+tgt	mono	14.88
4	src+tgt	biling	15.96
5	tgt	mono	**14.13**
6	tgt	biling	16.81

Table 3: Consistency scores: standard deviation with respect to the class average (σ_c) for the scores produced by different types of evaluators across different conditions. Lower scores means higher consistency. Each measure is calculated over $N = 200$ points.

But also, we think this is related to the simplicity of the task. There is less information to analyze. On the other hand *bilingual*, have a larger variation, which can be attributed to the heterogeneity of *rules of thumb* that the evaluators develop from looking at the source. Finally, note how *bilingual* have a problem of consistency with the *target-only* task. Without more fine-grained information, we can only hypothesize that this is due to the lack of familiarity with the scenario. Before performing tasks in the *target-only* scenario, they were relying primarily on the source to evaluate.

4.4 Summary of Observations

We have observed that there are differences in how translations are evaluated according to the type of evaluator, and the scenario. In summary, the observations are:

- The *bilingual* evaluators perform the tasks faster than the *monolingual*. They also spend less time evaluating the translation.

- The *monolingual* evaluators are slower, but more consistent in the scores they provide.

- The more information is displayed in the screen, it will take to longer to complete the evaluation, even though, less time will be spent actually evaluating the translation. Displaying more information also correlates with lower consistency between evaluators.

5 Discussion

Using eye-tracking allowed us to dive into the process of evaluation and explore new aspects regarding the behavior of evaluators. However, there were a few additional questions that might arise from our setup and experimental results. In this section we address some of them.

5.1 Is Bilingual Adequacy Necessary?

Bilingual evaluators are considered to be the *gold standard* for the evaluation of machine translation (Dorr et al., 2011). However, the use of monolingual evaluators has been previously advocated, since the end-users of MT are in fact monolingual (Sanders et al., 2011). The results obtained in this paper lead us to challenge the inclusion of *bilingual* evaluators for MT evaluation. As seen in the results, *monolingual* evaluators were slower than *bilinguals*, but they were more consistent in their evaluations. Given the open-ended nature of *bilingual* evaluation (e.g. given a source text, they can formulate their own set of plausible translations), we believe that the evaluations of *bilinguals* can be more subjective and prone to influence by the evaluator's background and knowledge of a specific subject. Moreover, recruiting *bilingual* evaluators can be harder and more expensive. We consider that consistency should be a primary goal of any evaluation task. Therefore, it seems more practical to rely only on *monolinguals* for the evaluation of machine translation. Our findings are in line with the observations in the post-editing community where *monolinguals* were more apt for the task and improved the fluency and comprehensibility of translations (Mitchell et al., 2013). Our findings are also in partial agreement with White et al. (1993) (which is not directly comparable to our work, as it does not compare monolinguals and bilinguals performing the same task), who state that less time is spent in evaluation techniques that use only target side information.

5.2 Can Feedback Bias the Evaluation?

The process of evaluation can be cumbersome, especially if the evaluation sessions last for long; hence we used feedback to boost the engagement of participants throughout the evaluation process. This is a double-edged sword, as the feedback has the potential to bias the evaluators and influence their decision.

To rule-out any potential bias from the feedback, we investigated the effects that the progression in which the tasks were performed might have on the differences between the evaluator scores and the feedback scores.

If the evaluators *learned* to reproduce the feedback scores, we would expect that the feedback error (τ_c) would decrease as a function of time. We calculated the feedback error as follows:

$$\tau_c^2 = \frac{1}{N_c} \sum_{i \in T} \sum_{j \in C} (\tilde{x}_{ij} - f_i)^2 \qquad (2)$$

where f_i is the feedback score for translation i, and other variables are the same as in eq. 1.

We fitted a linear model to the data, using the *scenario*, the evaluator type and the progression (time) as predictors; and the feedback error as a response. We did not find that the progression had any significant effect ($p = 0.2856$) on the feedback error. This means that the feedback did not bias the scoring behavior of the evaluators.

5.3 Can We do More with Eye-tracking?

Eye-tracking technology has proven useful in different scenarios related to translation. Yet, here we have only used the eye-tracking device to measure the *dwell* time an evaluator spends reading a specific portion of the screen. Nonetheless, one can think of more refined uses for this technology.

Potentially, using eye-tracking can give us a fine-grained insight on how evaluators differentiate *good* from *bad* translations, making it easier to *learn* the intrinsic rules of thumb that they use during the evaluation process. The applications for this are manifold. For example, by learning which type of errors (e.g. morphological, syntactic, semantic) can make a stronger impact on the reading behavior while evaluating, we could help to develop *better* automatic MT evaluation metrics. Additionally, we can use gaze-data to model the evaluation score (or rank) given by an evaluator, and thus reduce the subjective score bias. This can help to alleviate the high variance found in evaluation.

However, there are several challenges that need to be solved before moving forward in this nascent area. The most important is related to the accuracy of the eye-tracking devices, which is a requirement to track which specific words are looked-at in the screen.

Eye-tracking errors can be divided into two categories: variable (device-related precision) and systematic. Fortunately, the former has improved over the past years, and high-precision devices can be now acquired for only a few hundred dollars. The latter, however is more complex. Often, a loss in accuracy known as *drift* is observed as time progresses, requiring frequent re-calibrations of the eye-tracking device.
This can be due to evaluator movements, and other environmental factors. Reducing and eliminating drift is imperative to make progress in this area. Up to now, only heuristic approaches have been proposed (Mishra et al., 2012), leaving plenty of room for improvement.

6 Conclusion

In this paper, we analyzed the process of MT evaluation from a *glass-box* perspective, using eye-tracking data. We contrasted two main aspects of the evaluation tasks: the background of the evaluators, and the sources of information available to them during the evaluation task. We used time and consistency as our main criteria for comparison. Our results show that: (*i*) *monolingual* evaluators take relatively longer to evaluate translations (except when only the target language information is available, then they complete the tasks in less time), yet they are more consistent in their judgements. (*ii*) The amount of information provided to evaluators can affect their performance. We observed that when more information is available, the tasks take longer to complete, and yield less consistent results.

Therefore, based on our empirical results, we suggest that future evaluation campaigns be done with *monolingual* evaluators in a *target-only scenario*. We argue that this setting can increase the consistency of results while reducing the potential costs of recruiting *bilinguals*.

In future studies we would like to extend our explorations into using eye-tracking to model the behavior of evaluators and to help predict reliable and unreliable translations. In particular, we would like to explore the application of eye-tracking in ranking scenarios. We believe that given the popularity and availability of *low-cost* devices, eye-tracking can position itself as a useful aid to reduce subjectivity in evaluation.

References

Douglas Bates, Martin Maechler, Benjamin M. Bolker, and Steven Walker. 2015. Fitting linear mixed-effects models using lme4. *Journal of Statistical Software*, arXiv:1406.5823.

Ondrej Bojar, Miloš Ercegovčević, Martin Popel, and Omar Zaidan. 2011. A grain of salt for the wmt manual evaluation. In *Proceedings of the Sixth Workshop on Statistical Machine Translation*, Edinburgh, Scotland.

Chris Callison-Burch, Cameron Fordyce, Philipp Koehn, Christof Monz, and Josh Schroeder. 2007. (Meta-) Evaluation of Machine Translation. In *Proceedings of the Second Workshop on Statistical Machine Translation*, Prague, Czech Republic.

Chris Callison-Burch, Philipp Koehn, Christof Monz, Matt Post, Radu Soricut, and Lucia Specia. 2012. Findings of the 2012 Workshop on Statistical Machine Translation. In *Proceedings of the Seventh Workshop on Statistical Machine Translation*, pages 10–51, Montréal, Canada, June. Association for Computational Linguistics.

Stephen Doherty and Sharon O'Brien. 2014. Assessing the Usability of Raw Machine Translated Output: A User-Centered Study Using Eye Tracking. *International Journal of Human-Computer Interaction*, 30(1):40–51.

Stephen Doherty, Sharon O'Brien, and Michael Carl. 2010. Eye Tracking as an MT Evaluation Technique. *Machine translation*, 24(1):1–13.

Bonnie Dorr, Matthew Snover, and Nitin Madnani. 2011. Introduction. In Joseph Olive, Caitlin Christianson, and John McCary, editors, *Handbook of Natural Language Processing and Machine Translation*, pages 745–758. Springer.

Christian Federmann. 2012. Appraise: An Open-source Toolkit for Manual Evaluation of MT Output. *The Prague Bulletin of Mathematical Linguistics*, 98:25–35.

Francisco Guzmán, Shafiq Joty, Lluís Màrquez, and Preslav Nakov. 2014. Using discourse structure improves machine translation evaluation. In *Proceedings of 52nd Annual Meeting of the Association for Computational Linguistics*, Baltimore, Maryland, USA.

Shafiq Joty, Francisco Guzmán, Lluís Màrquez, and Preslav Nakov. 2014. DiscoTK: Using discourse structure for machine translation evaluation. In *Proceedings of the Ninth Workshop on Statistical Machine Translation*, Baltimore, Maryland, USA.

Abhijit Mishra, Michael Carl, and Pushpak Bhattacharyya. 2012. A Heuristic-Based Approach for Systematic Error Correction of Gaze Data for Reading. In *Proceedings of the First Workshop on Eye-tracking and Natural Language Processing*, Mumbai, India.

Linda Mitchell, Johann Roturier, and Sharon O'Brien. 2013. Community-based Post-editing of Machine-translated Content: Monolingual vs. Bilingual. In *Proceedings of the Machine Translation Summit XIV*, Nice, France.

R Core Team, 2015. *R: A Language and Environment for Statistical Computing*. R Foundation for Statistical Computing, Vienna, Austria.

Gregory Sanders, Mark Przybocki, Nitin Madnani, and Matthew Snover. 2011. Human Subjective Judgments. In Joseph Olive, Caitlin Christianson, and John McCary, editors, *Handbook of Natural Language Processing and Machine Translation*, pages 750–759. Springer.

Matthew Snover, Bonnie Dorr, Richard Schwartz, Linnea Micciulla, and John Makhoul. 2006. A Study of Translation Edit Rate with Targeted Human Annotation. In *Proceedings of the 7th Biennial Conference of the Association for Machine Translation in the Americas*, Cambridge, Massachusetts, USA.

Sara Stymne, Henrik Danielsson, Sofia Bremin, Hongzhan Hu, Johanna Karlsson, Anna Prytz Lillkull, and Martin Wester. 2012. Eye Tracking as a Tool for Machine Translation Error Analysis. In *Proceedings of the International Conference on Language Resources and Evaluation*, Istanbul, Turkey.

Joseph Turian, Luke Shen, and I. Dan Melamed. 2003. Evaluation of Machine Translation and its Evaluation. In *Proceedings of Machine Translation Summit IX*, New Orleans, LA, USA.

David Vilar, Gregor Leusch, Hermann Ney, and Rafael E. Banchs. 2007. Human Evaluation of Machine Translation Through Binary System Comparisons. In *Proceedings of the Second Workshop on Statistical Machine Translation*, Prague, Czech Republic.

John S White, Theresa A O'Connell, and Lynn M Carlson. 1993. Evaluation of machine translation. In *Proceedings of the workshop on Human Language Technology*, Stroudsburg, PA, USA.

John White, Theresa O'Connell, and Francis O'Mara. 1994. The ARPA MT Evaluation Methodologies: Evolution, Lessons, and Future Approaches. In *Proceedings of the Association for Machine Translation in the Americas Conference*, Columbia, Maryland, USA.

Bodo Winter. 2013. Linear models and linear mixed effects models in R with linguistic applications. arXiv:1308.5499.

Local System Voting Feature for Machine Translation System Combination

Markus Freitag, Jan-Thorsten Peter, Stephan Peitz, Minwei Feng and Hermann Ney
Human Language Technology and Pattern Recognition Group
Computer Science Department
RWTH Aachen University
D-52056 Aachen, Germany
<surname>@cs.rwth-aachen.de

Abstract

In this paper, we enhance the traditional confusion network system combination approach with an additional model trained by a neural network. This work is motivated by the fact that the commonly used binary system voting models only assign each input system a global weight which is responsible for the global impact of each input system on all translations. This prevents individual systems with low system weights from having influence on the system combination output, although in some situations this could be helpful. Further, words which have only been seen by one or few systems rarely have a chance of being present in the combined output. We train a local system voting model by a neural network which is based on the words themselves and the combinatorial occurrences of the different system outputs. This gives system combination the option to prefer other systems at different word positions even for the same sentence.

1 Introduction

Adding more linguistic informed models (e.g. language model or translation model) additionally to the standard models into system combination seems to yield no or only small improvements. The reason is that all these models should have already been applied during the decoding process of the individual systems (which serve as input hypotheses for system combination) and hence already fired before system combination. To improve system combination with additional models, we need to define a model which can not be applied by an individual system.

In state-of-the-art confusion network system combination the following models are usually applied:

System voting (globalVote) models For each word the voting model for system i ($1 \leq i \leq I$) is 1 iff the word is from system i, otherwise 0.

Binary primary system model (primary) A model that marks the primary hypothesis.

Language model 3-gram language model (LM) trained on the input hypotheses.

Word penalty Counts the number of words.

To gain improvements with additional models, it is better to define models which are not used by an individual system. A simple model which can not be applied by any individual system is the binary system voting model (globalVote). This model is the most important one during system combination decoding as it determines the impact of each individual system. Each system i is assigned one globalVote model which fires if the word is generated by system i. Nevertheless, this simple model is independent of the actual words and the score is only based on the global preferences of the individual systems. This disadvantage prevents system combination from producing words which have only been seen by systems with low system weights (low globalVote model weights). To give systems and words with low weights a chance to affect the final output, we define a new local system voting model (localVote) which makes decisions based on the current word options and not only on a general weight. The local system voting model allows system combination to prefer different system outputs at different word positions even for the same sentence.

Motivated by the success of neural networks in language modelling (Bengio et al., 2006, Schwenk and Gauvain, 2002) and translation modelling (Son et al., 2012), we choose feedforward neural networks to train the novel model. Instead of calculating the probabilities in a discrete space, the neural network projects the words into a continuous space. This projection gives us the option to assign probability also to input sequences which were not observed in the training data. In system combination each training sentence has to be translated by all individual system engines which is time consuming. Due to this we have a small amount of training data and thus it is very likely that many input sequences of a test set have not be seen during training.

The remainder of this paper is structured as follows: in Section 2, we discuss some related work. In Section 3, the novel local system voting model is described. In Section 4, experimental results are presented which are analyzed in Section 5. The paper is concluded in Section 6.

2 Related Work

In confusion network decoding, pairwise alignments between all system outputs are generated. From the calculated alignment information, a confusion network is built from which the system combination output is determined using majority voting and additional models. The hypothesis alignment algorithm is a crucial part of building the confusion network and many alternatives have been proposed in the literature:

(Bangalore et al., 2001) use a multiple string alignment (MSA) algorithm to identify the unit of consensus and applied a posterior language model to extract the consensus translations. In contrast to the following approaches, MSA is unable to capture word reorderings.

(Matusov et al., 2006) produce pairwise word alignments with the statistical alignment algorithm toolkit GIZA++ that explicitly models word reordering. The context of a whole document of translations rather than a single sentence is taken into account to produce the alignments.

(Sim et al., 2007) construct a consensus network by using TER (Snover et al., 2006) alignments. Minimum bayes risk decoding is applied to obtain a primary hypothesis to which all other hypotheses are aligned.

(Rosti et al., 2007) extend the TER alignment approach and introduce an incremental TER alignment which aligns one system at a time to all previously aligned hypotheses.

(Karakos et al., 2008) use the inversion transduction grammar (ITG) formalism (Wu, 1997) and treat the alignment problem as a problem of bilingual parsing to generate the pairwise alignments.

(He et al., 2008) propose an indirect hidden markov model (IHMM) alignment approach to address the synonym matching and word ordering issues in hypothesis alignment.

(Heafield and Lavie, 2010) use the METEOR toolkit to calculate pairwise alignments between the hypotheses.

All confusion network system combination approaches only use the global system voting models. Regarding to this chapter, there has been similar effort in the area of speech recognition:

(Hillard et al., 2007) Similar work has been presented for system combination of speech recognitions systems: the authors train a classifier to learn which system should be selected for each output word. The learning target for each slot is the set of systems which match the reference word, or the null class if no systems match the reference word. Their novel approach outperforms the ROVER baseline by up to 14.5% relatively on an evaluation set.

3 Novel Local System Voting Model

In the following subsections we introduce a novel local system voting model (localVote) trained by a neural network. The purpose of this model is to prefer one particular path in the confusion network and therefore all local word decisions between two nodes leading to this particular path. More precisely, we want the neural network to learn an oracle path extracted from the confusion network graph which leads to the lowest error score. In Subsection 3.1, we describe a polynomial approximation algorithm to extract the best sentence level BLEU (sBLEU) path in a confusion network. Taking this path as reference path, we define the model in Subsection 3.2 followed by its integration in the linear model combination in Subsection 3.3.

3.1 Finding sBLEU-optimal Hypotheses

In this section, we describe a polynomial approximation algorithm to extract the best sBLEU hypothesis from a confusion network. (Leusch et al., 2008) showed that this problem is generally NP-hard for the popular BLEU (Papineni et al., 2002) metric. Nevertheless, we need some paths which serve as “reference paths“.

Using BLEU as metric to extract the best possible path is problematic as in the original BLEU definition there is no smoothing for the geometric mean. This has the disadvantage that the BLEU score becomes zero already if the four-gram precision is zero, which can happen obviously very often with short or difficult translations. To allow for sentence-wise evaluation, we use the sBLEU metric (Lin and Och, 2004), which is basically BLEU where all n-gram counts are initialized with 1 instead of 0. The brevity penalty is calculated only on the current hypothesis and reference sentence.

We use the advantage that confusion networks can be sorted topologically. We walk the confusion network from the start node to the end node, keeping track of all n-grams seen so far. At each node we keep a k-best list containing the partial hypotheses with the most n-gram matches leading to this node and recombine only partial hypotheses containing the same translation. As the search space can become exponentially large, we only keep k possible options at each node. This pruning can lead to search errors and hence yield non-optimal results. If needed for hypotheses with the same n-gram counts, we prefer hypotheses with a higher translation score based on the original models. For the final node we add the brevity penalty to all possible translations.

As we are only interested in arc decisions which match a reference word, we simplify the confusion network before applying the algorithm. If all arcs between two adjacent nodes are not present in the reference, we remove all of them and add a single arc labeled with "UNK". This reduces the vocabulary size and still gives us the same best sBLEU scores as before. In Figure 1, a confusion network of four input hypotheses is given. As the words *black*, *red*, *orange*, and *green* are all not present in the reference, all of them are mapped to one single "UNK" arc (cf. Figure 2). The best sBLEU path is *the UNK car*.

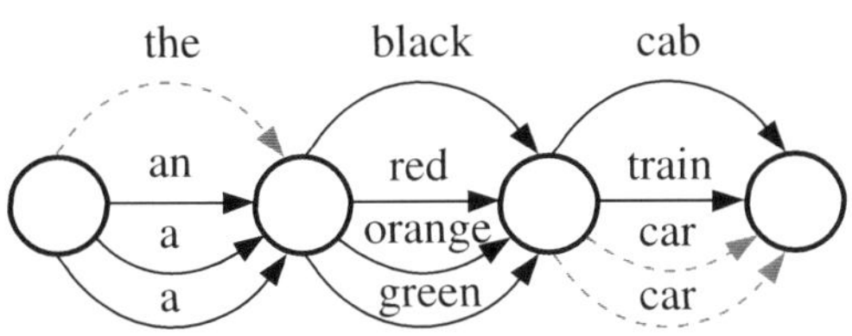

Figure 1: System A: *the black cab* ; System B: *an red train* ; System C: *a orange car* ; System D: *a green car* ; Reference: *the blue car* .

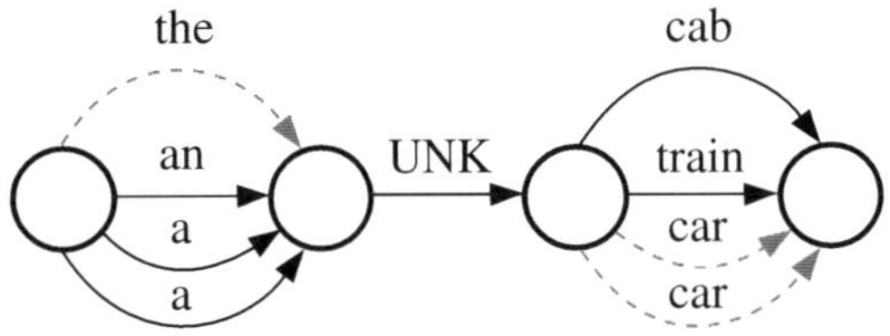

Figure 2: As the words *black*, *red*, *orange*, and *green* in Figure 1 are all not present in the reference (*the blue car*), they are mapped to one single "UNK" arc.

3.2 localVote Model Training

The purpose of the new localVote model is to prefer the best sBLEU path and therefore to learn the word decisions between all adjacent nodes which lead to this particular path. During the extraction of the best sBLEU hypotheses from the confusion network, we keep track of all arc decisions. This gives us the possibility to generate local training examples based only on the I arcs between two nodes. For the confusion network illustrated in Figure 2, we generate two training examples for the neural network training. Based on the arcs *the*, *an*, *a* and *a* we learn the output *the*. Based on the arcs *cab*, *train*, *car* and *car* we learn the output *car*.

In all upcoming system setups, we use the open source toolkit NPLM (Vaswani et al., 2013) for training and testing the neural network models. We use the standard setup as described in the paper and use the neural network with one projection layer and one hidden layer. For more details we refer the reader to the original paper of the NPLM toolkit. The inputs to the neural network are the I words produced by the I different individual systems. The outputs are the posterior probabilities of all words of the vocabulary. The input uses the so-called 1-of-n coding, i.e. the i-th word of the vocabulary is coded by setting the i-th element of the vector to 1 and all the other elements to 0.

For a system combination of I individual systems, a training example consists of $I+1$ words. The first I words (input of the neural network) are representing the words of the individual systems, the last position (output of the neural network) serves as slot for the decision we want to learn (extracted from the best sBLEU path). We do not add the "UNK" arcs to the neural network training as they do not help to increase the sBLEU score. Figure 3 shows the neural network training example for the last words of Figure 2. The output of each

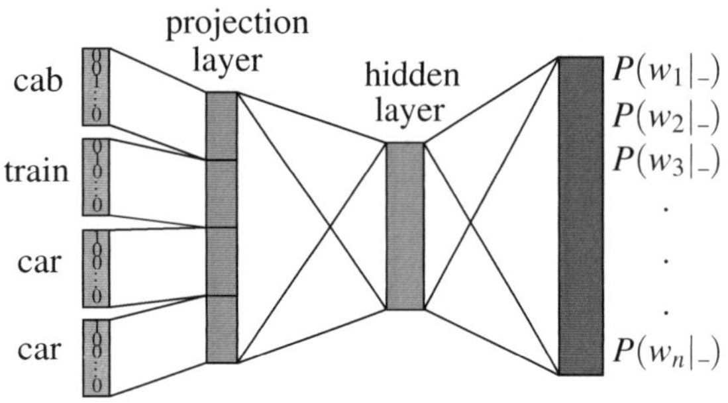

Figure 3: Unigram neural network training example: System *A* produces *cab*, System *B train*, System *C car*, System *D car*, reference is *car*. 1-of-*n* encoding was applied to map words to a suitable neural network input.

Table 1: Training examples from Figure 2.

input layer				
Sys A	Sys B	Sys C	Sys D	ref
the	an	a	a	the
cab	train	car	car	car

individual system provides one input word. In Table 1 the two training examples for Figure 2 are illustrated.

As a neural network training example only consists of the I words between two adjacent nodes, we are able to produce several training examples for each sentences. For a system combination of I systems and a development set of S sentences with an average sentence length of L, we can generate up to $I * S * L$ neural network training examples.

Further, we can expand the model to use arbitrary history size, if we take the predecessor words into account. Instead of just using the local word decision of a system, we add additionally the predecessors of the individual systems into the training data. In Figure 4, we e.g. use the bigram *red train* instead of the unigram *train* for system *B* into the training data. In Table 2 all bigram training examples of Figure 2 can be seen.

3.3 localVote model Integration

Having a trained localVote model, we then add it as an additional model into the confusion network. We calculate for each arc the probability of the word in the trained neural network. E.g. for Figure 1, we extract the probabilities for all arcs by the strings illustrated in Table 3. Finally, we add the scores as a new model and assign it a weight which is trained additionally to the standard model

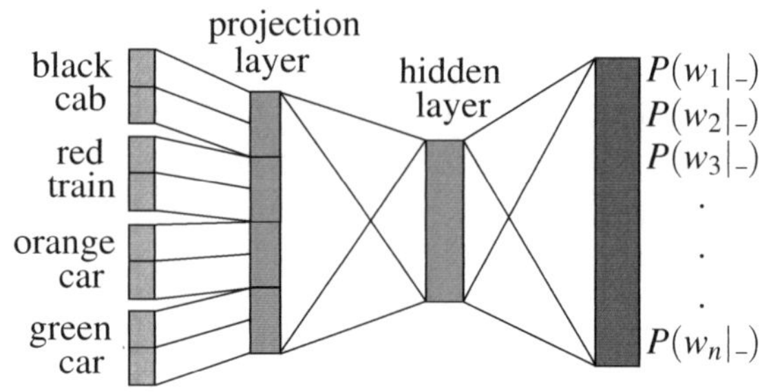

Figure 4: Bigram neural network training example: System *A* produces *black cab*, System *B red train*, System *C orange car*, System D *green car*, reference is *car*.

Table 2: Training examples (bigram) from Fig. 2.

input layer				
Sys *A*	Sys *B*	Sys *C*	Sys *D*	ref
<s>the	<s>an	<s>a	<s>a	the
black cab	red train	orange car	green car	car

weights with MERT.

Table 3: Calculating the probability for all possible output words from Figure 1. The output layer is the current generated word.

input layer				
Sys A	Sys B	Sys C	Sys D	arc word
the	an	a	a	the
the	an	a	a	an
the	an	a	a	a
black	red	orange	green	black
black	red	orange	green	red
black	red	orange	green	orange
black	red	orange	green	green
cab	train	car	car	cab
cab	train	car	car	train
cab	train	car	car	car

3.4 Word Classes

The neural network training sets are relatively small as all sentences have to be translated by all individual system engines. This results in many unseen words in the test sets. To overcome this problem, we use word classes (Och, 1999) instead of words which were trained (10 iterations) on the target part of the bilingual training corpus in some experiments. We use the trained word classes on both input layer and output layer.

4 Experiments

All experiments have been conducted with the open source system combination toolkit Jane (Freitag et al., 2014). For training and scoring neural networks, we use the open source toolkit NPLM (Vaswani et al., 2013). NPLM is a toolkit for training and using feedforward neural language models. Variations in neural network architecture have been tested. We tried various hidden layer sizes as well as projection layer sizes. We achieved similar results for all setups and decided to stick to 1 hidden layer whose size is 200, a learning rate of 0.08 and let the training run 20 epochs in all experiments.

Translation quality is measured in lowercase with BLEU (Papineni et al., 2002) and TER (Snover et al., 2006) whereas the performance of each setup is the best score on the tune set across five different MERT runs. The system combination weights of the linear model are optimized with MERT on 200-best lists with (TER-BLEU)/2 as optimization criterion. For all language pairs we use three different test sets. In the following the test set for extracting the training examples for the neural network training is labeled as *tune (NN)*. The test set *tune (MERT)* indicates the tune set for MERT and *test* indicates the blind test set.

The individual systems are different extensions of phrase-based or hierarchical phrase-based systems. The systems are built on the same amount of preprocessed training data and differ mostly in the models which are used to score the translation options. Further, some systems are syntactical augmented based on syntax trees on either source or target side.

4.1 BOLT Chinese→English

For Chinese→English, we use the current BOLT data set (corpus statistics are given in Table 4). The test sets consist of text drawn from "discussion forums" in Mandarin Chinese. We use nine individual systems to perform the system combination experiments. The lambda weights are optimized on a tune set of 985 sentences (tune (MERT)). We train the proposed localVote model on 15,323,897 training examples extracted from the 1844 sentences tune (NN) set.

As a first step we have to determine the k-best pruning threshold for extracting the SBLEU optimal path from the current confusion networks (cf. Section 3.1). In Figure 5 the (TER-BLEU)/2 results of the SBLEU optimal hypotheses extracted with different k-best sizes are given. Although, the BLEU score improves by setting k to a higher value, the computational time increases. To find a tradeoff between running time and performance, we set the k-best size to 1200 in the following experiments.

Table 4: Corpus statistics Chinese→English.

	Chinese	English
Sentences	13M	
Running words	255M	279M
Vocabulary	370K	833K
Tune sentences	1844 (NN), 985 (MERT)	
Test sentences	1124	

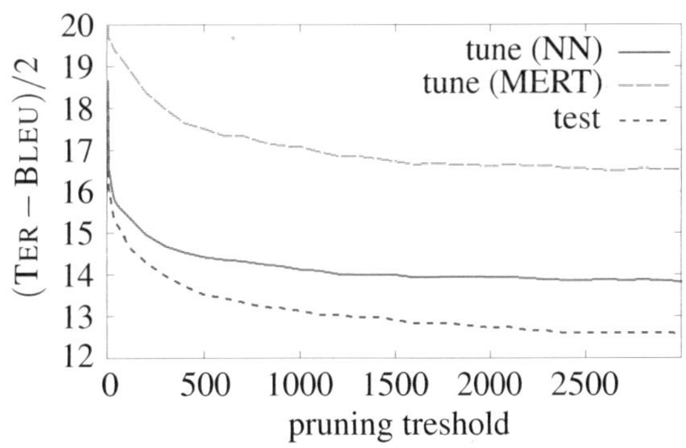

Figure 5: (TER − BLEU)/2 scores for different k-best pruning thresholds on the BOLT Chinese→English data set.

Experimental results are given in Table 5. The *baseline* is a system combination run without any localVote model of nine individual systems using the standard models as described in (Freitag et al., 2014). The *oracle* score is calculated on the hypothesis of the SBLEU best path extracted with $k = 1200$. We train the neural network on 15,323,897 training examples generated from the 1844 tune (NN) sentences. By training a neural network based on unigram decisions (*unigram NN*), we gain small improvements of -0.6 points in TER. As we have only few sentences of training data, many words have not been seen during neural network training. To overcome this problem, we train 1500 word classes on the target part of the bilingual data. Learning the localVote model on word classes (*unigram wcNN*) gain improvement of +0.7 points in BLEU and -0.6 points in

Table 5: Results for the BOLT Chinese→English translation task. The localVote models of the systems *+unigram NN* and *+unigram wcNN* are trained based on one word per system. The localVote models of the systems *+bigram NN* and *+bigram wcNN* are trained based on two words per system. For systems labeled with *wcNN*, the neural network is trained on word classes. Significance is marked with † for 95% confidence and ‡ for 99% confidence, and is measured with the bootstrap resampling method as described in (Koehn, 2004).

system	tune		test	
	BLEU	TER	BLEU	TER
baseline	17.9	61.5	18.3	60.9
+unigram NN	18.1	61.2	18.3	60.3†
+unigram wcNN	18.4	61.5	19.0‡	60.3†
+bigram NN	18.1	61.3	18.6†	60.3†
+bigram wcNN	18.1	61.2	18.7†	59.9‡
oracle	28.6	62.3	31.1	57.2

TER. By taking a bigram history into the training of the neural network, we reach only small further improvement. Compared to the *baseline*, the system combination *+bigram NN* outperforms the *baseline* by +0.3 points in BLEU and -0.6 points in TER. By using word classes (*+bigram wcNN*) we gain improvement of +0.4 points in BLEU and -1.0 points in TER.

All results are reached with a word class size of 1500. In Figure 6 the $(\text{TER} - \text{BLEU})/2$ scores on tune(MERT) of system combinations including one unigram localVote model trained with different word class sizes are illustrated. Independent of the word class size, system combination including a localVote model always performs better compared to the baseline. The best performance is reached by a word class size of 1500. One reason for the loss of performance when using no word classes is the size of the neural network tune set. Within a size of 1844 sentences, many words of the test set have never been seen during neural network training. The test set has a vocabulary size of 6106 within 2487 words (40.73%) are not present in the training set (tune (NN)) of the neural network. For the MERT tune set 2556 words (40.91%) are not present in the neural network training set. Word classes tackle this problem and it is much more likely that each word class has been seen during the training procedure of the neural network.

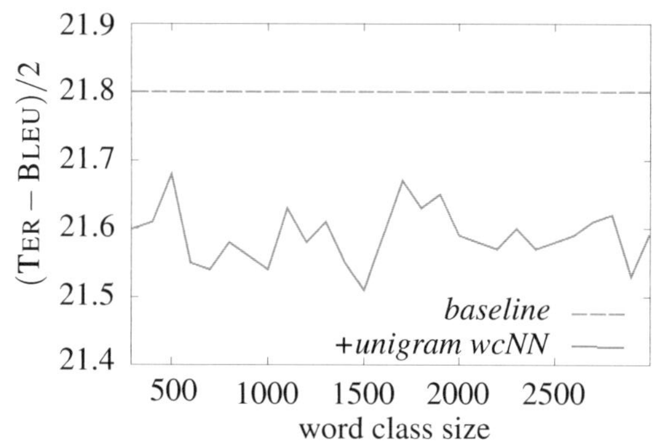

Figure 6: $(\text{TER} - \text{BLEU})/2$ scores for different word class sizes on the BOLT Chinese→English tune (MERT) set.

4.2 BOLT Arabic→English

For Arabic→English, we use the current BOLT data set (corpus statistics are given in Table 6). The test sets consist of text drawn from "discussion forums" in Egyptian Arabic. We train the neural network on 6,591,158 training examples extracted from the 1510 sentences tune (NN) dev set. The model weights are optimized on a 1080 sentences tune set. All results are system combinations of five individual systems. The test set has a vocabulary size of 3491 within 1510 words (43.25%) are not present in the training set (tune (NN)) of the neural network. For the MERT tune set 1549 words (43.24%) are not part of the neural network training set.

We run the same experiment pipeline as for Chinese→English and first determine the k-best threshold for getting the oracle paths in the confusion networks. As the Arabic→English system combination is only based on 5 individual systems, the confusion networks are much smaller. We set the pruning threshold to 1000 ($k = 1000$) which is a good tradeoff between running time and performance. Figure 7 shows the $(\text{TER} - \text{BLEU})/2$ scores for different k-best pruning thresholds. Increasing k to a higher value then 1000 improves the $(\text{TER} - \text{BLEU})/2$ only slightly.

Experimental results are given in Table 7. The *baseline* is a system combination run without any localVote model of five individual systems using the standard models as described in (Freitag et al., 2014). The *oracle* score represents the score

Table 6: Corpus statistics BOLT Arabic→English.

	Arabic	English
Sentences	8M	
Running words	189M	186M
Vocabulary	608K	519K
Tune sentences	1510 (NN), 1080 (MERT)	
Test sentences	1137	

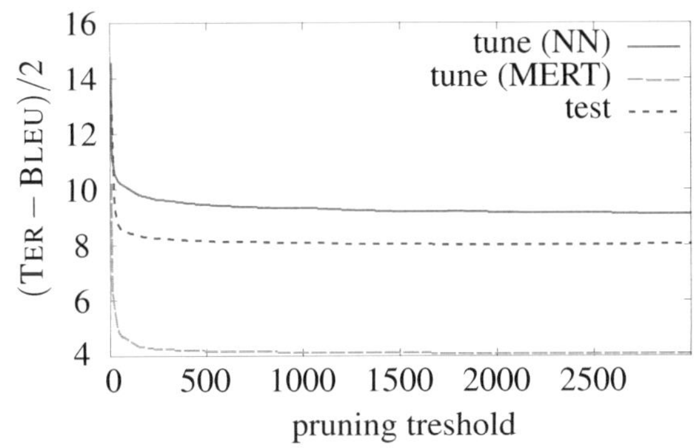

Figure 7: (TER − BLEU)/2 scores for different k-best pruning thresholds on the BOLT Arabic→English tune (MERT) set.

of the sBLEU best path extracted with $k = 1000$. Training a localVote model based on the best sBLEU path (*+unigram NN*) gives us improvement of +0.9 points in BLEU compared to the *baseline*. Adding bigram context to the neural network training (*+bigram NN*) yields improvement of +0.8 points in BLEU compared to the *baseline* system combination. By training word classes on the bilingual part of the training data, we gain additional improvements. When using word classes and a history size of two, *+bigram wcNN* yields the best performance with +1.1 points in BLEU compared to the *baseline*.

All results are conducted with a word class size of 1000. The tune set performance of different unigram localVote models trained on different word class sizes are illustrated in Figure 8. The results are fluctuating and we set the word class size to 1000 in all Arabic→English experiments.

5 Analysis

In this section we compare the final translations of the Chinese→English system combination *+bigram wcNN* with the *baseline*. The word occurrence distributions for both setups are illustrated in Table 8. This table shows how many input systems produce a certain word and finally if it is part

Table 7: Results for the BOLT Arabic→English translation task. The localVote models of the systems *+unigram NN* and *+unigram wcNN* are trained by a neural network based on one word per system. The localVote models of the systems *+bigram NN* and *+bigram wcNN* are trained by a neural network based on two words per system. For systems labeled with *wcNN*, the neural network is trained on word classes for both input and output layer. Significance is marked with ‡ for 99% confidence and is measured with the bootstrap resampling method as described in (Koehn, 2004).

system	**tune**		**test**	
	BLEU	TER	BLEU	TER
baseline	30.1	51.2	27.6	55.8
+unigram NN	31.4	51.2	28.5‡	56.0
+unigram wcNN	31.1	51.1	28.3‡	55.7
+bigram NN	31.3	51.1	28.4‡	55.8
+bigram wcNN	31.4	51.2	28.7‡	56.0
oracle	38.1	46.3	34.8	50.9

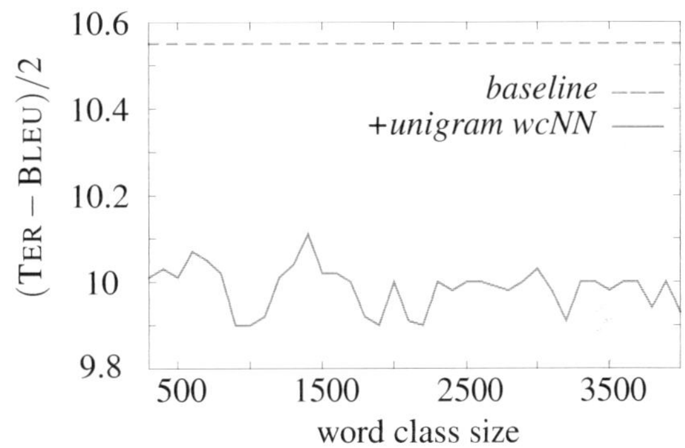

Figure 8: (TER − BLEU)/2 tune set scores for different word class sizes on the BOLT Arabic→English task.

of the system combination output. As the original idea of system combination is based on majority voting, it should be more likely that a word which is produced by more input systems is in the final system combination output than a word which is only produced by few input systems. E.g. 11008 words have been produced by all 9 individual systems from which all of them are in both the system combination *baseline* and the advanced system *+bigram wcNN*. If a word is only produced by 8 individual systems, a ninth system does not produce this word. 98,9% of the words produced by only 8 different individual systems are in the final

Table 8: Word occurrence distribution for the Chinese→English setup. First column indicates in how many systems a word appears. E.g. 120/14072 (0.9%) indicates that 14072 words only appear in one individual input system from which 120 (0.9%) are present in the baseline system combination hypothesis.

#	*baseline*	*+bigram wcNN*
1	120/14072 (0.9%)	214/14072 (1.5%)
2	592/ 6129 (9.7%)	764/ 6129 (12.5%)
3	1141/ 4159 (27.4%)	1319/ 4159 (31.7%)
4	1573/ 3241 (48.5%)	1669/ 3241 (51.5%)
5	2051/ 2881 (71.2%)	1993/ 2881 (69.2%)
6	2381/ 2744 (86.8%)	2332/ 2744 (85.0%)
7	2817/ 2965 (95.0%)	2820/ 2965 (95.1%)
8	3818/ 3860 (98.9%)	3815/ 3860 (98.8%)
9	11008/11008(100.0%)	11008/11008(100.0%)

baseline system combination output. The missing words result mostly from alignment errors produced by the pairwise alignment algorithm when aligning the single systems together.

We observe the problem that the globalVote models prevent words, which have only been produced by few systems, to be present in the system combination output. In Table 8, you can see that words which are only produced by 1-4 individual systems are more likely to be present in the final output when including the novel localVote model. As e.g. in the baseline 592 of the 6129 words which have only been produced by two individual system are in the output, the advanced *+bigram wcNN* setup contains additional 172 words. These statistics demonstrate the functionality of the novel localVote model which does not only improve the translation quality in terms of BLEU, but also tackles the problem of the dominating globalVote models.

The Arabic→English word occurrence distribution is illustrated in Table 9. A similar scenario as for the Chinese→English translation task can be observed. The words which only occur in few individual systems have a much higher chance to be in the final output when using the novel local voting system model. It is also visible that the neural network model prevents some words of being in the combined output even if the word have been produced by 4 of 5 systems. The novel local system voting model gives system combination the option to select words which have only be generated by few individual systems.

Table 9: Word occurrence distribution for the Arabic→English setup. First column indicates in how many systems a word appears. E.g. 214/5791 (3.7%) indicates that 5791 words only appear in one individual input system from which 214 (3.7%) are present in the baseline system combination hypothesis.

#	*baseline*	*+bigram wcNN*
1	214/ 5791 (3.7%)	285/ 5791 (4.9%)
2	1225/ 3200 (38.3%)	1243/ 3200 (38.8%)
3	2162/ 2719 (79.5%)	2297/ 2719 (84.5%)
4	3148/ 3207 (98.2%)	3119/ 3207 (97.3%)
5	14602/14602(100.0%)	14602/14602(100.0%)

6 Conclusion

In this work we proposed a novel local system voting model (localVote) which has been trained by a feedforward neural network. In contrast to the traditional globalVote model, the presented localVote model takes the word contents and their combinatorial occurrences into account and does not only promote global preferences for some individual systems. This advantage gives confusion network decoding the option to prefer other systems at different positions even in the same sentence. As all words are projected to a continuous space, the neural network gives also unseen word sequences a useful probability. Due to the relatively small neural network training set, we used word classes in some experiments to tackle the data sparsity problem.

Experiments have been conducted with high quality input systems for the BOLT Chinese→English and Arabic→English translation tasks. Training an additional model by a neural network with word classes yields translation improvement from up to +0.9 points in BLEU and -0.5 points in TER. We also took word context into account and added the predecessors of the individual systems to the neural network training which yield additional small improvement. We analyzed the translation results and the functionality of the localVote model. The occurrence distribution shows that words which have been produced by only few input systems are more likely to be part of the system combination output when using the proposed model.

Acknowledgement

This material is partially based upon work supported by the DARPA BOLT project under Contract No. HR0011-12-C-0015. Any opinions, findings and conclusions or recommendations expressed in this material are those of the authors and do not necessarily reflect the views of DARPA. Further, this paper has received funding from the European Union's Horizon 2020 research and innovation programme under grant agreement n° 645452 (QT21).

References

Srinivas Bangalore, German Bordel, and Giuseppe Riccardi. 2001. Computing consensus translation from multiple machine translation systems. In *IEEE Workshop on Automatic Speech Recognition and Understanding (ASRU)*, pages 351–354, Madonna di Campiglio, Italy, December.

Yoshua Bengio, Holger Schwenk, Jean-Sébastien Senécal, Fréderic Morin, and Jean-Luc Gauvain. 2006. Neural probabilistic language models. In *Innovations in Machine Learning*, pages 137–186. Springer.

Markus Freitag, Matthias Huck, and Hermann Ney. 2014. Jane: Open source machine translation system combination. In *Conference of the European Chapter of the Association for Computational Linguistics (EACL)*, pages 29–32, Gothenburg, Sweden, April. Association for Computational Linguistics.

Xiaodong He, Mei Yang, Jianfeng Gao, Patrick Nguyen, and Robert Moore. 2008. Indirect-HMM-based Hypothesis Alignment for Combining Outputs from Machine Translation Systems. In *Conference on Empirical Methods in Natural Language Processing (EMNLP)*, pages 98–107, Honolulu, HI, USA, October.

Kenneth Heafield and Alon Lavie. 2010. Combining Machine Translation Output with Open Source: The Carnegie Mellon Multi-Engine Machine Translation Scheme. *The Prague Bulletin of Mathematical Linguistics*, 93:27–36.

Dustin Hillard, Björn Hoffmeister, Mari Ostendorf, Ralf Schlüter, and Hermann Ney. 2007. i rover: improving system combination with classification. In *Conference of the North American Chapter of the Association for Computational Linguistics (NAACL)*, pages 65–68, Rochester, NY, USA, April. Association for Computational Linguistics.

Damianos Karakos, Jason Eisner, Sanjeev Khudanpur, and Markus Dreyer. 2008. Machine translation system combination using ITG-based alignments. In *46th Annual Meeting of the Association for Computational Linguistics on Human Language Technologies (ACL): Short Papers*, pages 81–84, Columbus, OH, USA, June.

Philipp Koehn. 2004. Statistical significance tests for machine translation evaluation. In *Conference on Empirical Methods in Natural Language Processing (EMNLP)*, pages 388–395, Barcelona, Spain, July.

Gregor Leusch, Evgeny Matusov, and Hermann Ney. 2008. Complexity of finding the bleu-optimal hypothesis in a confusion network. In *Conference on Empirical Methods in Natural Language Processing (EMNLP)*, pages 839–847, Honolulu, HI, USA, October.

Chin-Yew Lin and Franz Josef Och. 2004. Automatic evaluation of machine translation quality using longest common subsequence and skip-bigram statistics. In *The 42nd Annual Meeting on Association for Computational Linguistics (ACL)*, page 605, Barcelona, Spain, July.

Evgeny Matusov, Nicola Ueffing, and Hermann Ney. 2006. Computing Consensus Translation from Multiple Machine Translation Systems Using Enhanced Hypotheses Alignment. In *Conference of the European Chapter of the Association for Computational Linguistics (EACL)*, pages 33–40, Trento, Italy, April.

Franz Josef Och. 1999. An Efficient Method for Determining Bilingual Word Classes. In *Ninth Conference on European Chapter of the Association for Computational Linguistics (EACL)*, pages 71–76, Bergen, Norway, June.

Kishore Papineni, Salim Roukos, Todd Ward, and Wei-Jing Zhu. 2002. Bleu: a method for automatic evaluation of machine translation. In *40th Annual Meeting on Association for Computational Linguistics (ACL)*, pages 311–318, Philadelphia, PA, USA, July.

Antti-Veikko Rosti, Necip Fazil Ayan, Bing Xiang, Spyridon Matsoukas, Richard Schwartz, and Bonnie Dorr. 2007. Combining outputs from multiple machine translation systems. In *The Annual Conference of the North American Chapter of the Association for Computational Linguistics (NAACL-HLT)*, pages 228–235, Rochester, NY, USA, April.

Holger Schwenk and Jean-Luc Gauvain. 2002. Connectionist language modeling for large vocabulary continuous speech recognition. In *IEEE International Conference on Acoustics, Speech, and Signal Processing (ICASSP)*, volume 1, pages I–765, Orlando, FL, USA, May.

Khe Chai Sim, William J. Byrne, Mark J.F. Gales, Hichem Sahbi, and Phil C. Woodland. 2007. Consensus Network Decoding for Statistical Machine

Translation System Combination. In *IEEE International Conference on Acoustics, Speech and Signal Processing (ICASSP)*, pages 105–108, Honolulu, HI, USA, April.

Matthew Snover, Bonnie Dorr, Richard Schwartz, Linnea Micciula, and John Makhoul. 2006. A Study of Translation Edit Rate with Targeted Human Annotation. In *Association for Machine Translation in the Americas (AMTA)*, pages 223–231, Cambridge, MA, USA, August.

Le Hai Son, Alexandre Allauzen, and François Yvon. 2012. Continuous space translation models with neural networks. In *The 2012 Conference of the North American Chapter of the Association for Computational Linguistics: Human Language Technologies (NAACL HLT)*, pages 39–48, Montreal, Canada, June.

Ashish Vaswani, Yinggong Zhao, Victoria Fossum, and David Chiang. 2013. Decoding with large-scale neural language models improves translation. In *Conference on Empirical Methods in Natural Language Processing (EMNLP)*, pages 1387–1392, Seattle, WA, USA, October.

Dekai Wu. 1997. Stochastic inversion transduction grammars and bilingual parsing of parallel corpora. *Computational linguistics*, 23(3):377–403.

Author Index

Association for Computational Linguistics
209 N. Eighth Street
Stroudsburg, Pennsylvania 18360

ISBN 978-1-5108-1188-1

CURRAN ASSOCIATES INC.
proceedings.com